READING, WRITING, AND THE HUMANITIES

READING, WRITING, AND THE HUMANITIES

JO RAY McCUEN
Glendale Community College

ANTHONY C. WINKLER

HARCOURT BRACE JOVANOVICH, PUBLISHERS
San Diego   New York   Chicago   Austin   Washington, D.C.
London   Sydney   Tokyo   Toronto

PREFACE

The humanities, as we conceive of them for the sake of this book, consist of subjects whose primary emphasis is centered on human beings and their preoccupations. This meaning of humanities has come down to us from the Renaissance, a period that occurred in western civilization from the fourteenth through the midseventeenth centuries and was accompanied by a virtual explosion of human vitality and art. Biography emerged as a respected literary form. Painting abandoned the rigid stylizations of medievalism and began to individualize the human figure. History discovered anew the teachings and thought of classical antiquity, and the philosophers of Greece and Rome were read and studied with an evangelical interest formerly reserved only for the writings of prophets. It was as if humans stirred, awoke, looked upon their earthly garden with the eyes of the newborn, and rejoiced.

In selecting philosophy, history, and literature as our primary categories for grouping the readings, we have retained this early meaning of humanities as consisting of subjects whose emphasis is mainly human-centered. It is in philosophy that thinkers will be found gazing at the heavens and speculating about human nature. History tells us where the human family has been and where it is likely to go. Literature infuses human emotion into events that may themselves be philosophical or historical. Finally, we end each chapter with two paintings, to give us a glimpse of how humans have interpreted on canvas the world around them.

Our chapter titles are variations on some profound and timeless questions that writers and thinkers in the humanities have grappled with for centuries, while the subtitles declare the underlying issue that is the featured theme. These titles and subtitles are listed below:

Chapter 1: Where Do We Come From? Origins
Chapter 2: What Do We Know? Illusion and Reality
Chapter 3: When Are We Free? Freedom
Chapter 4: Why Do We Love? Love
Chapter 5: Why Do We Fight? War
Chapter 6: Why Do We Suffer? Good and Evil
Chapter 7: What Divides Us? Class and Caste
Chapter 8: What End Awaits? Death and Immortality

Our apparatus is extensive. We open with two original essays, one instructing the student in the techniques of critical reading, the other briefly explaining the principles of the writing process. Each chapter is prefaced by an original essay that discusses its theme and contents. Each anthologized piece is introduced by a biography of the author and a headnote entitled "Advice for Reading," which helps the student derive meaning from the selection. We then follow the selection with "Questions for Critical Thinking" and a writing assignment that is thoroughly explained in a note entitled "Writing Advice." For those teachers who opt not to use the featured writing assignment, we provide at least one, and sometimes two, alternate topics for writing.

A unique feature of this book is its use of art to visually echo and underscore the theme of the individual chapters. Each chapter ends with two paintings that amplify the ideas and themes implicit in the writings and afford both teacher and student a unique opportunity for spirited discussion. The Instructor's Manual contains some explicatory material on the paintings, as well as suggestions for using them in the classroom. Also contained in the manual are answers to the questions for critical thinking.

Many people have contributed helpful suggestions and advice for improving this book, notable among them Hazel McCuen, whose help and research saved us hours of work. Thanks also to our reviewers, Paula Gillespie, Marquette University; Irwin Weiser, Purdue University; and Allan Crawley, Boston College. At Harcourt Brace Jovanovich we would also like to thank Marlane Miriello and Karen Allanson, acquisition editors; Julia Ross, manuscript editor; Kay Faust, designer; Diane Southworth, production manager; Cindy Robinson, art editor; and Eleanor Garner, permissions editor.

Anthony C. Winkler and Jo Ray McCuen

CONTENTS

READING, WRITING, AND THE HUMANITIES

INTRODUCTION

HOW TO READ CRITICALLY

What Is Critical Reading?

Critical reading is the concentrated, thoughtful interpretation of writing. It is the opposite of skimming, scanning, or browsing and requires you to set aside your immediate reaction to a work and dig below the surface for meaning. As you read, you make a conscious effort to analyze, deduce, find connections, detect bias, and imagine an opposition to arguments. This is not the kind of reading you would use on the sports page, a detective story, or a popular magazine. But it is exactly the kind of reading necessary for a college education. Here are seven suggestions to help you read critically.

1. *Understand what you are reading.*

Misreading a writer is a common fault of casual reading. For example, it is not unusual for students to completely misread Swift's ironic sarcasm and consequently react with horror to the writer's "modest proposal." But Swift was trying to rouse the Irish out of their indolence and get them to correct the political and economic abuses savaging the people and country. His proposal to kill and cannibalize infants is ironic and sarcastic, not serious.

Skipping difficult passages is another fairly common fault of uncritical reading. But doing so is a mistake and likely to cause you to miss a significant point. If you do not understand a passage, you should reread it—again and again if necessary—no matter how tortuous and abstract it might be. Some works simply cannot be grasped on a first pass and must be reread.

2. *If you are dealing with new or unfamiliar material, do the background research into its history and culture.*

Because every written work is the product of a specific person writing in a particular place and time, the critical reader often needs to enquire about the writer as well as the writer's history and culture. For example, only a superficial reading of Dante's *Inferno* (Chapter 8) is possible without a knowledge of the tumultuous history and culture in which the poet lived and which profoundly affected his work. Dante wrote the poem during his exile from Florence after the defeat of his political faction, a circumstance that accounts for his bitterness towards his enemies, many of whom he portrayed as suffering the torments of hell. His adoration of Beatrice is based on the medieval exaltation of women, which is partly traceable to the attitude of the Catholic church of his day towards the Virgin Mary. To clarify this background, much of which would have been obvious to a medieval reader, we urge you to read the explicating endnotes provided by the translator, John Ciardi, and reprinted with this excerpt from *The Inferno*. But the overall point exemplified by this discussion of Dante is that cultural and historical background is often indispensable to understanding the particular attitude or views of an author.

Another example can be found in Chapter 7 of this book, *The Communist Manifesto*, a document in which Karl Marx urges workers of the world to unite and eradicate the wealth of private property. If you know nothing about the conditions and circumstances that inspired Marx to pen his famous manifesto, you should at least scan an encyclopedia for the necessary background. Or, if you are reading an essay on early California history and do not understand a reference to "coolie labor," you should do the little research necessary to find out what that term means. You will discover that "coolie labor" referred to unskilled contract laborers imported from China to work on the first United States continental railroad. These workers were so harshly treated that their importation was outlawed by the Chinese Exclusion Act of 1888. In sum, critical reading requires a knowledge not only of the author's biography but also of the author's historical and cultural background.

3. *Look for biases and hidden assumptions.*

The personal beliefs and preconceived biases of a writer will frequently creep into the work. For instance, in the selection "Two Germans" (in Chapter 6), the Nazi officer in charge of the Duesseldorf concentration camp during World War II claims that he was only doing his duty. Obeying his superiors and maintaining order were, to his mind, paramount, regardless of the costs in innocent lives. A critical reader would naturally challenge that bias, but first it must be detected. In another selection, "Barn Burning," by William Faulkner, a poor crop farmer torches the barn of a southern aristocrat, rationalizes his arson as an act of class retribution, and even tries to convince his own son of this viewpoint. Again, the critical reader will draw a different moral conclusion. To uncover the hidden biases or assumptions in a work, you should check an author's age, sex, education, ethnic background, philosophical stance, and other biographical facts. To this end, we have provided biographical headnotes for all of the selections in this book.

Note also whether or not the narrator of the piece is the author or simply a *persona*. The term "persona," which means "mask," originated from Greek drama when the actors used to wear a mask on the stage to disguise their real appearance. The persona of a literary work may or may not represent the personal views of the author. Many arguments have raged about when a character may be said to speak for the author or simply as a self-contained character. Nor are there any snap formulas for telling the difference, other than what can be deduced by common sense and from obvious contextual and biographical clues. For example, *All Quiet on the Western Front*, reproduced in Chapter 5, is generally taken to reflect the trench warfare experiences and antimilitaristic views of its writer, with some critics even condemning it as "romanticized journalism" as a result. Remarque fought in the trenches and wrote his story partly from imagination and partly from memory. But it was his known World War I background that led critics to deduce that the narrator was really speaking for the author. On the other hand, we have no evidence—either biographical or contextual—that the "I" character who narrates "At Daybreak" is Calvino himself. Instead, this "I" is simply a persona constructed for telling the story.

Mistaking the persona's views for the author's is common. When the persona in Jonathan Swift's "A Modest Proposal" suggests that children of the Irish poor be fattened and eaten, he is neither speaking literally for Swift nor expressing the author's advocacy of cannibalism. Quite the contrary, he is reflecting the wrath and outrage Swift feels at the brutalizing treatment of the Irish young at the hands of cruel English landlords. Such harsh treatment, charges Swift, is equivalent to cannibalism; but he is not seriously suggesting that children be eaten.

4. *Imagine an opposition for all opinions presented.*

If an author insists that cats and dogs are just as important as people and therefore should never be used in scientific research, imagine what would happen to medical research if this premise became law. Imagine, for example, the consequences on human diabetics if Banting had been barred from experimenting with dogs in his successful quest for insulin (*see* "Banting: Who Found Insulin," Chapter 2). Or, if a writer argues that the Arabic punishment of cutting off a thief's hand is fairer than our own system of incarceration, simply reverse the argument and see what support you can find for the superiority of imprisonment over dismemberment. In brief, always be on the lookout for ideas and facts that support the other side. Doing so leads to objectivity and fairmindedness.

5. *Separate emotion from truth.*

A writer's emotional stake in an issue can trigger a misrepresented, exaggerated, or distorted treatment of it. The victim of a rape, for example, is unlikely to take a dispassionate view on the topic of how rapists should be punished. That same person, however, is likely to have rare insight for writing on the psychological trauma of rape. In some polarizing topics, abortion for example, emotionalism will invariably be present. Some writers will passionately argue that abortion is murder, while others will just as hotly contend that the fetus is only a microscopic clump of cells. To separate emotion from fact in such a debate is virtually impossible. Reading critically, however, requires you to be alert to sloganeering, lurid depictions, and tearjerking appeals.

6. *Evaluate the evidence.*

Numerous magazines—even scientific journals—are regularly glutted with unsubstantiated claims. One author claims to have discovered a hormone that will prevent obesity; another, that the existence of extraterrestrial life is a mathematical necessity; a third, that efforts to eradicate the medfly are also killing humans. Whom shall you believe? What sources provide trustworthy evidence? Some sources of evidence are indeed practical, scholarly, and accurate; but others are merely speculative, outdated, misleading, and even outright wrong. Errors, half truths, or irrelevant facts litter nearly every subject, discipline, and area of knowledge. Here are some common-sense guidelines for evaluating sources of evidence:

* *Choose the simplest among competing theories.* This rule is referred to as "Occam's Razor." It advises you to shun bizarre or exotic interpretations if a simpler explanation that accounts for the evidence is available. For example, if a mountain hiker finds what looks like a huge footprint, you should not immediately assume that it was left by a monster. A hoax, a practical joke, or even a big-footed hiker can just as easily explain that evidence. The same caution applies to the precipitous belief in ghosts, UFOs, and miracle cures.

* *Note the date of evidence.* What was true in 1950 is often untrue today. For instance, in 1950 American car manufacturers dominated the world market. Today the Japanese do. In the early part of our century sociologists had difficulties charting homosexual practices, since gays kept their lives private; today more information is available because gays are much more open. In writing about any topic, you should attach greater importance to the more recent data.

* *Verify one source against another.* Reading in a subject will quickly acquaint you with any consensus of opinion among the experts that will help in verifying sources. For instance, no self-respecting anthropologist today believes that fossil evidence establishes "Piltdown Man" as the missing link between humans and apes, although many books written in the early fifties and still on the library shelves continue to make that claim. Piltdown Man was exposed as a forgery in 1953 when his remains were shown to be composed of the cranium of a man and the mandible of an ape.

* *Check your critical judgments against those of experts.* For instance, *The Book Review Digest* is a good source of critical opinions to help you rate the works of a certain fiction writer. When evaluating contemporary movies, music, painting, or sculpture, check the columns of key reviews in well-established newspapers. These opinions do not always stand the test of time, but at least they are made by experienced and respected critics who are less likely to make preposterous claims. *Contemporary*

Authors, the *Directory of American Scholars,* or *American Men and Women of Science*, are useful sources for checking an author's credentials.

* *Beware of statistics.* Figures can be misleading even when they sound convincing. For example, the advertising claim that three out of four doctors use Bayer aspirin is silly. How many doctors were in the sample—four? What kinds of doctors took part in the poll and why? Were they paid participants? Without answers to these questions—which no advertiser will ever provide—the claim is unverifiable and cannot be judged as more than copywriting glibness. On the other hand, a statistic claiming that the revenue from the Hudson River Toll Bridge was $3,700,000 in 1933 as compared with $9,675,000 in 1960 can presumably be verified by the proper government agency.

Of course, we cannot take time to check every single statistic and must frequently use common sense to assess its probable truthfulness. For instance, the claim by a respected historian that there were 10,000 television sets in the United States at the time of World War II, 10 million at the time of the Korean War, and 100 million at the time of the Vietnamese War, sounds reasonable enough to be accepted at face value, given a source of impeccable credentials. But you should always question the credibility of sources that use exaggerated figures, such as, "All the gas stations in California are owned by Arabs," or "Most Colombians believe in taking cocaine as a social drug."

Some statistics are used figuratively, such as the claim, "Thousands upon thousands of children go to bed hungry in the United States every night." This might be distressingly true, but without the possibility of verification, it might also be hyperbole. In sum, the idea is to use statistical data with a sense of ethics and care.

7. *Check both sides of an issue.*

In judging whether or not an author's treatment is balanced, especially on a controversial subject, check to see whether both sides of the issue are discussed fairly. For instance, an essay on the effectiveness of the presidency of Richard Nixon must cite opinions from both his admirers and detractors or be lopsided. Likewise, an essay on the United States' nuclear deterrence should take into account not only the opinions and views of military generals but also those of pacifists.

WRITING EXPOSITORY PROSE

Expository prose is prose written for the practical purpose of detailing and explaining— a broad heading under which will fall most of the essay assignments students must typically do. Examples of expository prose include this article, the diary entry, the engineering report, and the business memo—all of which share a similar practical purpose of transmitting factual details, suggestions, and information.

Writing expository prose or, for that matter, writing anything at all, involves a process. By *process* we mean a sequence of coordinated steps and acts deliberately taken to achieve a desired result or end. In the case of expository prose, the end is the organized essay, the clear memo, the practical report. When you pick up your pen to write, or even when you start thinking about what to say and how to express your thoughts on paper, you have begun the writing process, which is divisible into three stages: invention, composition, and revision. Experience and research reveal that while many writers will flit back and forth between these stages as they write, and while some will even scramble the sequence, most will nevertheless do some inventing, composing, and revising before the work is finished.

We will briefly examine each of these three stages and advise on what to expect as you work through them in your own efforts at writing. We will then discuss how *audience* should enter into your writing strategies. Finally, we will review the essential characteristics universally present in any competent work of expository prose.

Invention

In its common usage, the word "invention" suggests something newly made or patented, some breakthrough in science or the practical arts. In the world of writing, invention means dreaming up ideas and notions to write about. To invent in the literary sense is to see your subject in a "writeable" way, to come up with ideas and things to say about it. Most of the time, but not always, writers acquire the basic material for invention by researching the subject. You read long and hard about it, gathering information, facts, opinions, and accepted wisdom. You distill all this material, using it to shape and form your own opinion, which you express in your own particular way.

But that is not always how invention works. Many writers, indeed, do not know what they intend to say before they have said it. Many begin writing with one particular viewpoint in mind and find themselves expressing quite another, one perhaps they did not even suspect they held. "How do I know what I think until I see what I say?" asked the English novelist and critic E. M. Forster. In fact, seldom do you know what you think and what you intend to say until you have said it. And then once you have said it, very likely it will surprise you. For the beginner who wails, "I don't know what to say!" the practical reply is, "You can't know what to say until you have said it." Writers generally find what they want to say only by trying to say it.

Make notes. Make a rough outline of your ideas. Put something, anything, down on paper. Jot down a list of the points you think you might like to include and then take a stab at incorporating them into a draft. Read what you have written and see whether you agree with it. Tinker, alter, edit, and change until the writing strikes the note you particularly like. None of this is necessarily easy or automatic, and you are almost certain to find yourself disliking what you have initially written. But that is, in fact, a good sign, for if you dislike what you have said, you have a better idea of what you do not want to say, and therefore, of what you do want to say.

Books and libraries are, as we have said, a common source of material for invention. But so are your thoughts, haphazard though they may be. And so are your memories and even your personal experience. Experts in the field or subject about which you are writing constitute another useful source of material. Virtually every campus is a cornucopia of experts you can seek out and question. For that matter, ask yourself questions about your subject. Do this on paper in written self-dialogue, and you will be astonished at the fertility of your own imagination.

Composition

This stage is, for most writers, the very nub of the writing process. It is here that you put down on paper exactly what you want to say, proceeding as the crow flies in a straight line from opening paragraph to climactic conclusion. Or so the composition process was once pictured in the textbooks.

But that conception of composing is mainly fiction. It is emphatically true that most writers do not write in a straight line. Certainly, we do not. We scribble, backtrack, advance a few hesitant steps, retreat, scratch out, write over, insert, crumple pages, and begin anew. Sometimes we hit a blank part of the page and lurch to a dead stop. But always, when we do, we never merely stare into space or bite our fingernails. What we do is read what we have written so far, tinkering with it as we read. We read until we are back to where we became stuck and usually then are ready to advance another tentative sentence or two. Sometimes our reading shows us a misstep or wrong turn and we have to backtrack and pick up our composing from that point.

Of course, there are a few writers who sit down and simply work from start to finish and very rarely miss a step. But these are truly a gifted few. Most work much as we have described, taking small stumbling steps towards their conclusions. It is, in fact, a rather ordinary occurrence for writers to discover halfway through the work that all the research they have done is either inadequate or irrelevant. Then they must be off to the library again, or off to the writing corner to scribble and invent and think anew on paper. Writing often results in exactly this kind of discovery, with the writer finding the point he or she had been meaning to make.

The best advice we can give you about composing is this: write down what you think you think; read over again and again what you have written, changing it as much as you like until you find what you really do think. Writing is never a static process. It almost always involves a creative and dynamic process of discovery.

Revision

Virtually all writers rewrite. Some rewrite incessantly, backtracking constantly over what they have written to make changes. That, in fact, is how we work. Others rewrite in one sitting. "Writing *is* rewriting," insists Donald Murray, the English teacher and critic. Endless studies of writers' manuscripts, including classic works, reveal that even the lavishly gifted reworked their pages, paragraphs, and sentences. The list of hardcore revisers range from the English poet John Keats, to Mark Twain, to Ernest Hemingway. Revising is, in fact, a healthy and normal way of discovering exactly what you want to say.

Every writer eventually evolves a personal method and technique for rewriting. But, generally, rewriting occurs in three parts: revising, editing, and proofreading— more or less in that sequence.

Revising means making wholesale changes in the manuscript, transposing entire paragraphs, excising whole pages, changing long passages. It is the heaviest and earliest of the three stages of rewriting and is usually done during the composition process.

Editing occurs later, when we have down on paper what we want to say, but are not entirely satisfied with it. So we reread the manuscript, making little changes here and there. Sometimes, if we still are not happy with what we have done, we may even nag ourselves into wholesale revising.

Proofreading is the final clean-up. We have put into final form what we want to say, and we go through it one last time, scrubbing any venial errors such as grammatical lapses or misspellings.

It cannot be emphasized enough that the key to rewriting is rereading. During the composition process, we repeatedly reread what we have written. Studies show that most professional writers do likewise. If you find yourself stuck in the middle and unable to budge, reread from the beginning what you have on the page. As you read, little changes for bettering the text will occur to you. And by the time you have come to the part where you became stuck, you will probably have a good feel for what you need to do or say to become unstuck.

Audience

An essential element affecting the writing and rewriting strategies of most writers is audience. No competent writer would write a children's book in the style of a doctoral dissertation. Nor would any writer who hopes to earn bread by the pen write an obituary notice in flippant style unless, of course, farcical humor was the underlying purpose. But since student writers seldom write children's books or obituaries, neither of these farfetched scenarios apply.

But the fact is, nonetheless, that students are not exempt from considerations about audience. Indeed, student writers are probably asked to address their work to a wider variety of audiences than are most working writers. You write for your history class, for your sociology class, for your English teacher. You may even have to write for your biology and psychology classes. Each class will constitute a different audience, with vastly different expectations about the style and purpose of your prose. Each, in fact, consists of a *community*—a set of like-minded readers who exert specific demands and expectations on their writers. The scientific disciplines, for example, generally do not allow the use of "I" in their papers—although this taboo is waning among some specialties—generally lean towards passive constructions, and almost always have specific requirements for the inclusion of data. As a writer, you therefore need to be acutely aware of the requirements and demands of the community for which you are penning your essays. And the best way to find out—it may be the only way—is to read its literature extensively.

If you have to write essays for sociology, find a few sociology papers and read them. Pay attention to the acceptable mannerisms of phrasing and style. Attend to how data is incorporated into the papers, and to whether footnotes, endnotes, or parenthetical citations are used. Note the level of formality or informality that is acceptable. And when you do write papers for a particular discipline, be sure to use the format and style it endorses.

Characteristics of Expository Prose

Competent expository prose meets three minimum requirements: (1) it makes a point; (2) it supports its point; (3) it is clearly organized. Unfailingly build these three characteristics into every essay you write and, assuming you write grammatically and with some measure of style, your work will automatically profit.

1. Make a point.

In the most pedantic sense of the word, the point of an essay is its major theme or focus. It is what you, as a writer, are trying to get across when you sit down to write. As you read the essays in this book, you will discover that every one of them advocates a strong, even an occasionally passionate, viewpoint. Sometimes this point is expressed in a capsule sentence called a thesis, which summarizes the writer's opinion or viewpoint. "We hold these truths to be self-evident, that all men are created equal, that they are endowed by their Creator with certain unalienable Rights, and that among these are Life, Liberty, and the pursuit of Happiness," declares Jefferson in the Declaration of Independence. And then he summarizes the actions of the king that have conspired to usurp these unalienable rights. In other essays this main point is implicitly present, but not explicitly summarized in a thesis. Fay Cooper-Cole, for example, in "A Witness at the Scopes Trial" is obviously reminiscing throughout his essay, even though he does not specifically characterize this purpose in a thesis.

You may not know at the outset exactly what point you intend to advocate, argue, or prove in the essay. That is what you will find out as you write. However, experience teaches that the thesis worded to have an argumentative edge has more built-in momentum and drive for virtually any writer. It would be harder for most of us to write a cold-blooded description of the abortion procedure than to argue that a woman has the right, or doesn't have the right, to abort. If you possibly can, word your thesis or main point to reflect an argumentative stand you fervently believe in.

Especially tedious and tiresome to write about are bland subjects that tempt us to platitudes. "How I Spent My Summer Vacation," "Christmas Is Overly Commercialized," "College Football Is Bad for Players," are examples of overused topics about which it is nearly impossible to pen anything fresh or original. Better to take a less-conventional approach—to argue that summer vacations should be abolished, that commercialization is a wonderful thing at Christmas, that college football makes boys into hunks—than to try to squeeze the last drop of originality out of hackneyed topics. Challenging stuffy old ideas generally adds spark, energy, and drama to an essay.

2. Support your point.

All the essays included in this book back their points with *supporting details*. These details are narrowly focused, concrete rather than abstract, vivid rather than vague. For example, in his "Allegory of the Cave" Plato treats a highly philosophical subject, the difference between illusion and reality. Yet in support of his implicit thesis—that pure truth must always be sought, no matter what the risk—he gives us a starkly vivid picture of prisoners chained in a cave who mistake shadows on a wall for reality. Consider, as another example, Jonathan Schell's "Effects of Nuclear War," which regales us with an unnerving parade of facts and examples of the devastation we can expect from a nuclear holocaust. We are treated to grim details of the nuclear fireball whose blinding energy would vaporize and incinerate the whole environment. These horrifying details serve to convince us that the unthinkable calamity of nuclear war must be avoided.

The kinds of details writers usually cite in support of their points are facts, reasoning, experience, and authority.

Facts A fact is information that accurately represents reality. Facts are subjected to but unchanged by interpretation. For instance, in 1848 the Women's Suffrage Movement held its first convention in Seneca Falls, New York, and passed a declaration that said, "We hold these truths to be self-evident: that all men and women are created equal." The historical fact of this meeting can neither be changed nor denied, although interpretations of its meaning will naturally differ. That Joseph Stalin massacred five million Kulak peasants between 1919 and 1933 in his campaign to force collectivism on farmers is a grisly fact. Some Communist nations regarded the slaughter as necessarily brutal, but other world powers saw it as unbridled and murderous barbarism.

In citing facts remember these admonitions:

1. Facts should be accompanied by a traceable source. If you do not explicitly state where you got the cited fact from, your context should at least make clear where it can likely be found. Readers must have the opportunity to investigate a suspect source.

2. Facts must be relevant to your point. If, for instance, you are writing a paper arguing for the preservation of baby seals, you might legitimately cite facts about the decline of the population, but you should definitely spare the reader a recital of incidental facts about the digestive system of seals.

3. Facts must be valid. If you are quoting statistics about the number of blacks that are unemployed in California or New York, make sure that your source is current and reliable. Do not quote some old study or discredited belief or opinion. Use, instead, the latest statistics from the appropriate state agency dealing with human resources.

Reasoning Next to raw facts, reasoning probably represents the strongest support a writer can cite to back up a point. By reasoning we mean the weight of logical argument that can be marshalled in support of a point. This logic is not necessarily a collection of facts and data. More likely than not, it will simply consist of reasoned explanation, causal analysis, argument, and rebuttal. Here is an example of a writer's use of reasoning to support a point. It is taken from Isaac Asimov's article "Armies of the Night":

> *Creationists frequently stress the fact that evolution is "only a theory," giving the impression that a theory is an idle guess. A scientist, one gathers, arising one morning with nothing particular to do, decides that perhaps the moon is made of Roquefort cheese and instantly advances the Roquefort-cheese theory.*
>
> *A theory (as the word is used by scientists) is a detailed description of some facet of the universe's workings that is based on long observations and experiments and has survived the critical study of scientists generally.*
>
> *For example, we have the description of the cellular nature of living organisms (the "cell theory"); of objects attracting each other according to a fixed rule (the "theory of gravitation"); of energy behaving in discrete bits (the "quantum theory"); of light traveling through a vacuum at a fixed measurable velocity (the "theory of relativity"), and so on.*
>
> *All are theories; all are firmly founded; all are accepted as valid descriptions of this or that aspect of the universe. They are neither guesses nor speculations. And no theory is better founded, more closely examined, more critically argued and more thoroughly accepted, than the theory of evolution. If it is "only" a theory, that is all it has to be.*

Most of us respect and admire logic and like to think that we are reasonable and consistent in our beliefs and thinking. The last thing we want is to be accused of holding illogical positions or clinging to irrational ways. Using reasoning to support your views, and assail your opponent's, is consequently an effective ploy of argument.

Experience Experience, either your own or that of another person, can be excellent material for supporting a point. You can appeal to experience when a contention cannot be settled by facts and statistics but must be decided by common sense. Consider, for example, Victor Frankl's essay about his experience in a German concentration camp. He supports his point—that love is the salvation of man—by relating how the memory of his beloved wife helped him endure the brutality of a Nazi concentration camp during World War II. On the other hand, in the essay "In the Beginning," Robert Jastrow cites the irritation of astronomers over the "Big Bang" theory to show that even the scientific mind can become testy when evidence conflicts with cherished beliefs.

Authority   One way to strengthen your point is to quote an authority whose opinion agrees with yours or who can shed light on your position. Bear in mind, however, that no authority wields omniscient influence and that prestige in one field does not naturally confer believability in another. For instance, Woody Allen is a world-famous movie producer and director, but he would not be considered an authority on black holes, quarks, quantum mechanics, or any other topic of physics. Better to cite Albert Einstein, Stephen Hawking, Albert Michelson, or someone similar as your physics authority. Always mention the credentials of your authority as a preamble to your quotation. Here are two examples:

> *As Stephen Hawking, Professor of Mathematics at Cambridge University and widely regarded as the most brilliant theoretical physicist since Einstein, has remarked. . . .*
>
> *Margaret Mead, famous anthropologist specializing in primitive Polynesian societies, suggests that. . . .*

An authority may also be anonymous as, for example, the opinions of reputable dictionaries and encyclopedias. For instance, the following appeal to anonymous authority is effective: "According to the current edition of the *New Columbia Encyclopedia,* the first labor laws to protect mine workers were enacted in 1842 by the British Parliament."

Tracking down the credentials of an authority may require you to play the detective. Remember that merely publishing a book or attracting public attention does not automatically make someone an authority. Peer recognition is the best criterion of someone's standing in a field or subject. And an excellent reference source for checking authorities is the *Who's Who* series, which list noted specialists in a variety of subjects.

3. *Make your point clear.*

Having a point and knowing exactly how to express it is no guarantee of clarity. That comes with additional effort and labor. To begin with, you should regard the paragraph as the primary rhetorical unit of your expository essay. And you should try to express your ideas in paragraphs that are organized, relevant, and smooth. Here are three suggestions for writing clear paragraphs:

Organize your writing   Clarity in writing requires the exercise of common sense and logic. Think about the ideas you wish to present and arrange them in a sensible order. Work them out on paper as you write. Typically, a paragraph will open with a general statement followed by specific information and details. Kushner does exactly this in paragraph 42 of his essay "The Story of a Man Named Job." He begins by suggesting the attitude we should adopt when bad things happen to good people:

> We can maintain our own self-respect and sense of goodness without having to feel that God has judged us and condemned us. We can be angry at what has happened to us, without feeling that we are angry at God. More than that, we can recognize our anger at life's unfairness, our instinctive compassion at seeing people suffer, as coming from God who teaches us to be angry at injustice and to feel compassion for the afflicted. Instead of feeling that we are opposed to God, we can feel that our indignation is God's anger at unfairness working through us, that when we cry out, we are still on God's side, and He is still on ours.

A simple organizing scheme is to enumerate successive points—first, second, third, and so on. Naturally, you cannot do this over and over again without seeming repetitious and tedious. Another way to proceed is to adopt a spatial orientation, useful especially in physical descriptions, where you systematically move from up to down or from right to left. But the point is to try to devise a shape or structure to the paragraph for enclosing and ordering your ideas.

Stick to what's relevant to your point Digressing, wandering from the primary point into secondary issues, is the error most responsible for ruining otherwise healthy paragraphs. Sometimes the writer thinks a minor point so fascinating that it simply cannot be left out. It can be. Sometimes the writer is beguiled by information and details laboriously collected during research and thinks they cannot be omitted. They can be omitted. If a fact or anecdote has nothing to do with the primary purpose of your paragraph, shelve it. Editorial judgment must be exercised on what to leave out of, as well as on what to put in, an essay. Stick unwaveringly to the point and do not stray from it. Notice how this paragraph unrelentingly focuses on answering its opening question:

> What did tonnage mean in 1492? Not weight or displacement of the vessel, or her deadweight capacity; tonnage simply meant her cubic capacity in terms of wine tuns. The Castilian tonelada, or the Portuguese tonel (both of which I translate "ton"), was really a tun of wine, a large cask equivalent in volume to two pipas or pipes, the long, tapering hogsheads in which port wine is still sold. As wine was a common cargo, and both pipe and tun of standard dimensions, a vessel's carrying capacity below decks in terms of toneladas became a rough-and-ready index of her size; and so a ship's tonnage in 1492 meant the number of tuns or twice the number of pipes of wine she could stow. The tun, tonelada or ton being roughly (very roughly) equivalent to 40 cubic feet, this last figure became in the course of time the unit of burthen (or tonnage or capacity) for English vessels, and was so used in America until the Civil War. From the seventeenth century on, it became customary in every country to fix a vessel's official tonnage by a formula composed of her length, breadth and depth, which gave a rough measure of her capacity. But in 1492 tonnage meant simply the number of tuns of wine that the ship could stow, as estimated by the owner or verified by common report. It was not a constant but a variable.

> **Samuel Eliot Morrison, Admiral of the Ocean Sea**

The author never once strays from his purpose and point, and for his pains achieves a tight and compressive focus.

Show relationships between sentences Sentences are not automatically joined in overall meaning and sense simply because they follow one another on the page. It is necessary, instead, for the writer to build into sentences a continuity of meaning and sense. Writers do this through the use of transitions and parallel phrasing between sentences, and through the repetition of key words in a paragraph. Common transition words include *but, however, moreover, nevertheless, therefore, indeed, for example*, and *of course*. Here is an example, from Ortega y Gasset's "The Crowd Phenomenon." The transitions are in roman type:

> *The members of the ubiquitous* mass *have not come from out of the blue. The* number *of people was constant for a good while;* moreover, *after any war one would expect* the *number* to decrease. But *here we come up against the first important modern fac-*tor. *The individuals who make up the present* mass *already existed before*—but *not as a* mass, *not as "masses." Scattered about the world in small* groups, *or even alone, they lived in diverse ways, dissociated and distant from one another. Each* group, *even each individual, occupied a* space, *each his own* space *so to say, in the fields, in a village, a town, or even in some quarter of a big city.*

The author uses such transitional words as *but* and *moreover*; he repeats several key words such as *number, mass, group*; and he uses parallel construction such as in the. . . , in a. . . , in some. . . .

Particularly useful as an introduction to supporting details is the handy phrase *for example*, as in this paragraph written by one of our students:

> *In America the car has taken on some distinctly religious overtones. For example, the van is a type of chapel where the family can commune with nature and each other; the weekly car wash is a baptismal ritual; and the periodic trade-in for a better model is a pilgrimage to find renewal. Bumper stickers proclaim the gospel in terse summaries such as "Honk if you Love Jesus," "Guess who's coming again," or "Smile, for God loves you."*

Of course, all these examples show what certain professional writers have already done and are intended only to suggest a model for your own efforts. But the result you eventually achieve in your own writing will be found inevitably to vary with the effort you exert. That is the nature of writing. It is seldom easy. And usually when the writing has been easy its effect is, as the English playwright Richard Brinsley Sheridan (1751–1816) put it, "vile" and "hard" on the reader.

CHAPTER ONE

Where Do We Come From?
ORIGINS

All life has a beginning, but only human life—so far as we can tell—has the desire and capacity to ponder its own origins. We know when we each began individually and celebrate the occasion as a birthday. We know when life ends for others and mourn the passing of friends and loved ones. Between this beginning and ending lie mystery, doubt, angst, and speculation. We wonder where we came from. We occasionally worry about what will happen to us after life ends. In this fitful musing it is inevitable that we should drift to those writers and subjects where such speculations find natural expression— the humanities. Unlike science, which deliberately separates fact from feeling in its searching, the humanities are peopled by writers and thinkers who scan the whole heavens and undivided earth for answers while speculating not only with their minds but also with their hearts.

For a book in the humanities such as this one, then, there is no better place to start than at the beginning—of time, of space, and of us. "Where do we come from?" we ask as we gaze at the limitless sky speckled with stars and planets adrift in the unimaginable inkiness of infinity. It is the purpose of this book to encourage such self-exploration, to urge you to ask, "Who am I? How did I come to be here?" These are not questions to be afraid of or to quail from. Our humanity, our sense of self and personal wholeness, demand that we unflinchingly look at and question the dark and underlying mystery of our beginning.

Two traditional adversaries in human thought—religion and science—are the most common sources for answers to these questions, and until the twentieth century, religion was definitely the more dominant. Through the Judeo-Christian Bible it told us—people of the Western world—that in a moment of loneliness God created the heavens, the earth, and us, molding life and spirit out of the dust and dirt to which we must all eventually return. That an infinitely wise and benevolent being loved, valued, and cared about us was comforting, and for centuries our forebears found solace and hope in this belief.

But under the sway of religion the world of human thought was neither Edenic nor peaceful. With the certitude of religious dogmas came dissension, sectarian wars, and inquisitions. Cruelties and barbarisms were inflicted by believers upon those who clung to different creeds. Some doubters found that the religious worldview demeaned the dignity of humans and stifled the desire to speculate and think. Slowly, with the accumulating evidence from science, the tide began to turn against the dominance of religion on human thought.

The decisive shift began in the middle of the nineteenth century when British naturalist Charles Darwin proposed that all animals had evolved and were evolving still according to a system of natural selection. In place of a benign and loving God raising humans out of dust, Darwin's theory offered a mechanistic explanation for being. We do not walk erect and on two feet because God created us in his image, the theory said in effect, but because this posture left our arms and hands free to wield stones and clubs. Slowly, Darwin's theory gained acceptance among scientists, in spite of intermittent challenges by religious factions. In 1925, for example, a young teacher named John Scopes was forced to stand trial in Dayton, Tennessee, to defend his right to teach scientific evolution as a theory of the origins of life. Lately, the so-called "scientific creationists" have joined the fray as they clamor for the biblical account to be given equal time in public school textbooks.

With that backdrop, this opening chapter presents a sampling of diverse opinions you should read critically to form your own views. It begins with Genesis 1–3, the Biblical account of how the universe was created that is still believed by millions all over the world, especially Christians. In this account, an awesome divinity creates the world and all species out of nothing with humans as his culminating masterpiece. The painting *The Creation of Adam* (at the end of this chapter) by Michelangelo portrays this creative act as an event of stupendous power and rare beauty. Its counterpoint, *The Birth of a Tear*, by Edgar Ende, parodies this view as pompous and high-flown while suggesting that all creation ends in sorrow.

A variety of other opinions compete for your attention. Supporting the hard-and-fast scientific position is Isaac Asimov, who attempts to refute the arguments by believers of the biblical account. Robert Jastrow takes the middle ground. As a scientist, he examines evidence for the Big Bang as a historical truth, but is at a loss to explain why such a cataclysmic explosion should ever have happened.

Annie Dillard and Loren Eiseley are astounded observers who can only stand and wonder amid the endless parade of mysteries. Dillard describes three scenes of nature—a frog being killed by a giant water bug, a bird diving gracefully through the air to land on the ground, and sharks in a feeding frenzy—and puzzles over their meaning. Eiseley muses in poetic prose about how dead fossils could ever have lived and marvels over the mysterious force that could have pumped life into otherwise inert chemicals.

The chapter also includes a delightful piece of science fiction by Italo Calvino and a mythological story about the Star of Bethlehem by Arthur C. Clarke. The literature section ends with two poems, one by the Romantic poet William Blake, the other by a modern science-fiction writer. Blake is puzzled that the same creator who made the terrifying tiger could also have made the gentle lamb, while Aldiss wonders what will happen when human beings ultimately use their knowledge about genetics to create a perfect race.

The paradox of both religion and science, as you will glean from reading the material of this chapter, is that although adversarial opposites, both rest on the acceptance of underlying axioms that can neither be proved nor disproved and draw on a common prop for their arguments. Religion freely admits to this prop, even boasts of it. Science will either flatly deny it or admit to it only grudgingly, depending on which scientist you ask. The common prop is faith. The present and troubling answer is—we still do not know where we came from. But the least we can do is wonder.

PHILOSOPHY

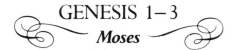

GENESIS 1–3
Moses

Authorship of Genesis is usually ascribed to Moses, although scholars differ on the strength of this claim. Moses, Hebrew lawgiver, was probably born in Egypt in the thirteenth century B.C. The Bible, which is the source of information about his life, relates that Moses led his people out of Egyptian bondage to the edge of Canaan (ancient Palestine in the Middle East). From the beginning of his life, he was under divine protection, and as a young man, he received a message from God through a burning bush. Through Moses, the Hebrews received the Ten Commandments, the criminal code and the liturgical law that formed the moral and ethical basis of their society. Moses died at an ancient age after viewing the Promised Land from Mt. Pisgah. He was buried at Moab. Information about the life of Moses is contained in the books of Exodus, Leviticus, Numbers, and Deuteronomy, which, along with Genesis, are collectively known as The Pentateuch.

Reading Advice

The Book of Genesis attempts to explain the beginning of the world, the creation of man, and the fall of humankind from Edenic grace into a sorry world of sinfulness and death, doing so in a style that is simple, direct, repetitious, and elegantly oral. The translation from Hebrew used here is from the "Authorized" or King James Version (1611) of the Bible, the most widely read English Bible, and the one that exerted considerable influence upon the subsequent style of English language and literature.

Genesis uses a distinctive, even abrupt, storytelling style for which we have to make allowances as we read. The effect of this abrupt style is a starkly told tale with a narrow focus on a strictly sequential plot. The writer's implicit purpose is to transcribe and record sacred myth for the faithful. He is not arguing or defending the faith but simply stating what he believes. Thousands of years later, you must be willing to concede him this context of devoutness and belief as you read his version of how the heavens and earth, and humans, began.

CHAPTER 1

*I*n the beginning God created the heaven and the earth.

2 And the earth was without form, and void; and darkness was upon the face of the deep. And the Spirit of God moved upon the face of the waters.

3 And God said, Let there be light: and there was light.

4 And God saw the light, that it was good: and God divided the light from the darkness.

5 And God called the light Day, and the darkness he called Night. And the evening and the morning were the first day.

6 ¶ And God said, Let there be a firmament in the midst of the waters, and let it divide the waters from the waters.

7 And God made the firmament, and divided the waters which were under the firmament from the waters which were above the firmament: and it was so.

8 And God called the firmament Heaven. And the evening and the morning were the second day.

9 ¶ And God said, Let the waters under the heaven be gathered together unto one place, and let the dry land appear: and it was so.

10 And God called the dry land Earth; and the gathering together of the waters called he Seas: and God saw that it was good.

11 And God said, Let the earth bring forth grass, the herb yielding seed, and the fruit tree yielding fruit after his kind, whose seed is in itself, upon the earth: and it was so.

12 And the earth brought forth grass, and herb yielding seed after his kind, and the tree yielding fruit, whose seed was in itself, after his kind: and God saw that it was good.

13 And the evening and the morning were the third day.

14 ¶ And God said, Let there be lights in the firmament of the heaven to divide the day from the night; and let them be for signs, and for seasons, and for days, and years:

15 And let them be for lights in the firmament of the heaven to give light upon the earth: and it was so.

16 And God made two great lights; the greater light to rule the day, and the lesser light to rule the night: he made the stars also.

17 And God set them in the firmament of the heaven to give light upon the earth,

18 And to rule over the day and over the night, and to divide the light from the darkness: and God saw that it was good.

19 And the evening and the morning were the fourth day.

20 And God said, Let the waters bring forth abundantly the moving creature that hath life, and fowl that may fly above the earth in the open firmament of heaven.

21 And God created great whales, and every living creature that moveth, which the waters brought forth abundantly, after their kind, and every winged fowl after his kind: and God saw that it was good.

22 And God blessed them, saying, Be fruitful,

and multiply, and fill the waters in the seas, and let fowl multiply in the earth.

23 And the evening and the morning were the fifth day.

24 ¶ And God said, Let the earth bring forth the living creature after his kind, cattle, and creeping thing, and beast of the earth after his kind: and it was so.

25 And God made the beast of the earth after his kind, and cattle after their kind, and every thing that creepeth upon the earth after his kind: and God saw that it was good.

26 ¶ And God said, Let us make man in our image, after our likeness; and let them have dominion over the fish of the sea, and over the fowl of the air, and over the cattle, and over all the earth, and over every creeping thing that creepeth upon the earth.

27 So God created man in his own image, in the image of God created he him; male and female created he them.

28 And God blessed them, and God said unto them, Be fruitful, and multiply, and replenish the earth, and subdue it: and have dominion over the fish of the sea, and over the fowl of the air, and over every living thing that moveth upon the earth.

29 ¶ And God said, Behold, I have given you every herb bearing seed, which is upon the face of all the earth, and every tree, in the which is the fruit of a tree yielding seed; to you it shall be for meat.

30 And to every beast of the earth, and to every fowl of the air, and to every thing that creepeth upon the earth, wherein there is life, I have given every green herb for meat: and it was so.

31 And God saw every thing that he had made, and, behold, it was very good. And the evening and the morning were the sixth day.

CHAPTER 2

1 Thus the heavens and the earth were finished, and all the host of them.

2 And on the seventh day God ended his work which he had made: and he rested on the seventh day from all his work which he had made.

3 And God blessed the seventh day, and sanctified it: because that in it he had rested from all his work which God created and made.

4 ¶ These are the generations of the heavens and of the earth when they were created, in the day that the LORD God made the earth and the heavens,

5 And every plant of the field before it was in the earth, and every herb of the field before it grew: for the LORD God had not caused it to rain upon the earth, and there was not a man to till the ground.

6 But there went up a mist from the earth, and watered the whole face of the ground.

7 And the LORD God formed man of the dust of the ground, and breathed into his nostrils the breath of life; and man became a living soul.

8 ¶ And the LORD God planted a garden eastward in Eden; and there he put the man whom he had formed.

9 And out of the ground made the LORD God to grow every tree that is pleasant to the sight, and good for food; the tree of life also in the midst of the garden, and the tree of knowledge of good and evil.

10 And a river went out of Eden to water the garden; and from thence it was parted, and became into four heads.

11 The name of the first is Pison: that is it which compasseth the whole land of Havilah, where there is gold;

12 And the gold of that land is good: there is bdellium and the onyx stone.

13 And the name of the second river is Gihon: the same is it that compasseth the whole land of Ethiopia.

14 And the name of the third river is Hiddekel: that is it which goeth toward the east of Assyria. And the fourth river is Euphrates.

15 And the LORD God took the man, and put him into the garden of Eden to dress it and to keep it.

16 And the LORD God commanded the man, saying, Of every tree of the garden thou mayest freely eat:

17 But of the tree of the knowledge of good and evil, thou shalt not eat of it: for in the day that thou eatest thereof thou shalt surely die.

18 ¶ And the LORD God said, It is not good that the man should be alone; I will make him

an help meet for him.

19 And out of the ground the LORD God formed every beast of the field, and every fowl of the air; and brought them unto Adam to see what he would call them; and whatsoever Adam called every living creature, that was the name thereof.

20 And Adam gave names to all cattle, and to the fowl of the air, and to every beast of the field; but for Adam there was not found an help meet for him.

21 And the LORD God caused a deep sleep to fall upon Adam, and he slept: and he took one of his ribs, and closed up the flesh instead thereof;

22 And the rib, which the LORD God had taken from man, made he a woman, and brought her unto the man.

23 And Adam said, This is now bone of my bones, and flesh of my flesh: she shall be called Woman, because she was taken out of Man.

24 Therefore shall a man leave his father and his mother, and shall cleave unto his wife: and they shall be one flesh.

25 And they were both naked, the man and his wife, and were not ashamed.

CHAPTER 3

1 Now the serpent was more subtil than any beast of the field which the LORD God had made. And he said unto the woman, Yea, hath God said, Ye shall not eat of every tree of the garden?

2 And the woman said unto the serpent, We may eat of the fruit of the trees of the garden:

3 But of the fruit of the tree which is in the midst of the garden, God hath said, Ye shall not eat of it, neither shall ye touch it, lest ye die.

4 And the serpent said unto the woman, Ye shall not surely die:

5 For God doth know that in the day ye eat thereof, then your eyes shall be opened, and ye shall be as gods, knowing good and evil.

6 And when the woman saw that the tree was good for food, and that it was pleasant to the eyes, and a tree to be desired to make one wise, she took of the fruit thereof, and did eat, and gave also unto her husband with her; and he did eat.

7 And the eyes of them both were opened, and they knew that they were naked; and they sewed fig leaves together, and made themselves aprons.

8 And they heard the voice of the LORD God walking in the garden in the cool of the day: and Adam and his wife hid themselves from the presence of the LORD God amongst the trees of the garden.

9 And the LORD God called unto Adam, and said unto him, Where art thou?

10 And he said, I heard thy voice in the garden, and I was afraid, because I was naked; and I hid myself.

11 And he said, Who told thee that thou wast naked? Hast thou eaten of the tree, whereof I commanded thee that thou shouldest not eat?

12 And the man said, The woman whom thou gavest to be with me, she gave me of the tree, and I did eat.

13 And the LORD God said unto the woman, What is this that thou hast done? And the woman said, The serpent beguiled me, and I did eat.

14 And the LORD God said unto the serpent, Because thou hast done this, thou art cursed above all cattle, and above every beast of the field; upon thy belly shalt thou go, and dust shalt thou eat all the days of thy life:

15 And I will put enmity between thee and the woman, and between thy seed and her seed; it shall bruise thy head, and thou shalt bruise his heel.

16 Unto the woman be said, I will greatly multiply thy sorrow and thy conception; in sorrow thou shalt bring forth children; and thy desire shall be to thy husband, and he shall rule over thee.

17 And unto Adam he said, Because thou hast hearkened unto the voice of thy wife, and hast eaten of the tree, of which I commanded thee, saying, Thou shalt not eat of it: cursed is the ground for thy sake; in sorrow shalt thou eat of it all the days of thy life;

18 Thorns also and thistles shall it bring forth to thee; and thou shalt eat the herb of the field;

19 In the sweat of thy face shalt thou eat bread, till thou return unto the ground; for out of it wast thou taken: for dust thou art, and unto dust shalt thou return.

20 And Adam called his wife's name Eve; because she was the mother of all living.

21 Unto Adam also and to his wife did the LORD God make coats of skins, and clothed them.

22 ¶ And the LORD God said, Behold, the man is become as one of us, to know good and evil: and now, lest he put forth his hand, and take also of the tree of life, and eat, and live for ever:

23 Therefore the LORD God sent him forth from the garden of Eden, to till the ground from whence he was taken.

24 So he drove out the man; and he placed at the east of the garden of Eden Cherubims, and a flaming sword which turned every way, to keep the way of the tree of life.

Questions for Critical Thinking

1. According to Genesis, what is the source of human misery?

2. Based on the three punishments exacted on Eve for having eaten from the Tree of Knowledge (3:16), what inferences can be drawn about the nature of woman before the Fall?

3. What does the Genesis story imply about the pre-Fall relationship that existed between Adam and Eve? How was the relationship between man and woman subsequently changed by the Fall?

4. What is your opinion of the Genesis story? Do you regard it as myth, legend, or literal truth? Give reasons for your answer.

5. What do you think the serpent looked like before it was cursed by the wrath of God to crawl on its stomach?

6. What objection do you think a modern nondoctrinal reader might raise against the story in Genesis that depicted Adam naming the birds and the beasts of the field? How might a fundamentalist answer this objection?

7. Read Genesis 2:24. What might a critical reader find oddly inconsistent and inexplicable about this verse?

Writing Assignment

1. Write an essay describing the personality of God as inferred from the portrayal of him in Genesis. Support your impressions with specific references to the text.

Writing Advice

The assignment requires you to carefully read Genesis and draw conclusions from it about the writer's portrayal of God's personality. This is not as mystifying a task as it might first sound. Ordinarily, we judge personality by looks, speech, and actions, and the same criteria would apply to drawing inferences about the personality of God. Since the writer does not describe God, we can draw no conclusions from his looks. But we do know what God says; and we know what he does. Here are some steps you might take in putting together your essay:

1. Look carefully at what God says and does. How does God react to his act of creation? While the writer tells us nothing about God's motive in creating the earth, he does describe what God judges "good," giving the discerning reader a glimpse of the divinity's tastes.

2. Ask yourself how God reacts to his human creations. What is his attitude towards them—is it paternalistic, possessive, jealous, indifferent, strict, or indulgent? What restrictions does he fetter his human creations with and do they strike you as reasonable or unreasonable? Does God resemble a caring mother or a stern father?

3. Examine God's reactions to the breaking of his law and draw conclusions about him from the punishment he metes out to Adam and Eve. Does the punishment strike you as fair, just, or harsh? What does it tell you about God?

4. Once you have drawn some conclusions about the portrayal of God in Genesis, formulate your overall impressions of God's personality in a summary sentence that might work as a thesis and begin to write. Note, however, that you should not simply put down your impressions without any textual support of them. For example, if you allege that God is portrayed as a lover of light and of nature, you should cite specific passages in the text that support this impression.

Alternate Writing Assignment

Infer from the Genesis story what the relationship between Adam and Eve must have been like before the Fall. In an essay, reconstruct this relationship, using the text as a source of inferential evidence.

PHILOSOPHY

ARMIES OF THE NIGHT
Issac Asimov

Isaac Asimov (b. 1920), American scientist and prolific author, was born in the USSR and brought to the United States at the age of three. In 1955 he became professor of biochemistry at Boston University, where he earned a reputation as a serious scientist and researcher. It is as a writer, however, that Asimov is most widely known, and his works of science fiction such as *I, Robot* (1950), *The Caves of Steel* (1954), and *The Gods*

Themselves (1973) have won him a large and loyal following of readers. Asimov has written over 340 books and counting, on subjects ranging from science fiction, to biblical criticism, to Shakespeare. His forte as a writer is lucid explanation, and he is widely admired for his ability to present scientific ideas and concepts in plain language easily grasped by the layman.

Reading Advice

Asimov is taking issue with the march of creationism and its insistence that schools give equal time to biblical accounts of how the universe began. His forum is a New York magazine, and his ample skills as a lucid explainer are dazzlingly displayed. He chooses as his primary tactic to list and discuss, one by one, the major premises and arguments of the creationists, and then systematically answer and refute them. In support of his arguments Asimov draws from his comprehensive grasp of scientific details and historical events while using a writing style that presents his ideas, work-manlike, in a minimum of words.

As befitting his magazine audience, Asimov writes mainly in journalistic paragraphs, which make their points with economy, logic, and a modicum of evidence. The journalistic paragraph does not amass substantial detail behind every point nor does it attempt to weigh in with a scholarly array of facts and data.

The numerous headings above the paragraphs are designed to highlight upcoming arguments and primary points, and is a reader aid regularly featured in magazines and textbooks. Paying attention to these headings will alert you to the next point in the discussion and so help you follow Asimov's argument.

Scientists thought it was settled.   1

The universe, they had decided, is about 20 billion years old, and Earth itself   2
is 4.5 billion years old. Simple forms of life came into being more than three
billion years ago, having formed spontaneously from nonliving matter. They
grew more complex through slow evolutionary processes and the first hominid
ancestors of humanity appeared more than four million years ago. *Homo sapiens*
itself—the present human species, people like you and me—has walked the
earth for at least 50,000 years.

But apparently it isn't settled. There are Americans who believe that the   3
earth is only about 6,000 years old; that human beings and all other species
were brought into existence by a divine Creator as eternally separate varieties
of beings, and that there has been no evolutionary process.

They are creationists—they call themselves "scientific" creationists—and   4
they are a growing power in the land, demanding that schools be forced to
teach their views. State legislatures, mindful of votes, are beginning to succumb
to the pressure. In perhaps 15 states, bills have been introduced, putting forth
the creationist point of view, and in others, strong movements are gaining
momentum. In Arkansas, a law requiring that the teaching of creationism
receive equal time was passed this spring and is scheduled to go into effect in

September 1982, though the American Civil Liberties Union has filed suit on behalf of a group of clergymen, teachers and parents to overturn it. And a California father named Kelly Segraves, the director of the Creation-Science Research Center, sued to have public-school science classes taught that there are other theories of creation besides evolution, and that one of them was the Biblical version. The suit came to trial in March, and the judge ruled that educators must distribute a policy statement to schools and textbook publishers explaining that the theory of evolution should not be seen as "the ultimate cause of origins." Even in New York, the Board of Education has delayed since January in making a final decision, expected this month, on whether schools will be required to include the teaching of creationism in their curriculums.

The Rev. Jerry Falwell, the head of the Moral Majority, who supports the   5
creationist view from his television pulpit, claims that he has 17 million to 25 million viewers (though Arbitron places the figure at a much more modest 1.6 million). But there are 66 electronic ministries which have a total audience of about 20 million. And in parts of the country where the Fundamentalists predominate—the so-called Bible Belt—creationists are in the majority.

They make up a fervid and dedicated group, convinced beyond argument of   6
both their rightness and righteousness. Faced with an apathetic and falsely secure majority, smaller groups have used intense pressure and forceful campaigning—as the creationists do—and have succeeded in disrupting and taking over whole societies.

Yet, though creationists seem to accept the literal truth of the Biblical story   7
of creation, this does not mean that all religious people are creationists. There are millions of Catholics, Protestants and Jews who think of the Bible as a source of spiritual truth and accept much of it as symbolically rather than literally true. They do not consider the Bible to be a textbook of science, even in intent, and have no problem teaching evolution in the secular institutions.

To those who are trained in science, creationism seems like a bad dream, a   8
sudden reliving of a nightmare, a renewed march of an army of the night risen to challenge free thought and enlightenment.

The scientific evidence for the age of the earth and for the evolutionary   9
development of life seems overwhelming to scientists. How can anyone question it? What are the arguments the creationists use? What is the "science" that makes their views "scientific"? Here are some of them:

The Argument from Analogy

A watch implies a watchmaker, say the creationists. If you were to find a   10
beautifully intricate watch in the desert, far from habitation, you would be sure that it had been fashioned by human hands and somehow left there. It would pass the bounds of credibility that it had simply formed, spontaneously, from the sands of the desert.

By analogy, then, if you consider humanity, life, earth and the universe, all   11
infinitely more intricate than a watch, you can believe far less easily that it "just
happened." It, too, like the watch, must have been fashioned, but by more-
than-human hands—in short by a divine Creator.

This argument seems unanswerable, and it has been used (even though not   12
often explicitly expressed) ever since the dawn of consciousness. To have explained
to prescientific human beings that the wind and the rain and the sun follow
the laws of nature and do so blindly and without a guiding hand would have
been utterly unconvincing to them. In fact, it might well have gotten you stoned
to death as a blasphemer.

There are many aspects of the universe that still cannot be explained sat-   13
isfactorily by science; but ignorance implies only ignorance that may someday
be conquered. To surrender to ignorance and call it God has always been
premature, and it remains premature today.

In short, the complexity of the universe—and one's inability to explain it   14
in full—is not in itself an argument for a Creator.

The Argument from General Consent

Some creationists point out that belief in a Creator is general among all peoples   15
and all cultures. Surely this unanimous craving hints at a great truth. There
would be no unanimous belief in a lie.

General belief, however, is not really surprising. Nearly every people on   16
earth that considers the existence of the world assumes it to have been created
by a god or gods. And each group invents full details for the story. No two
creation tales are alike. The Greeks, the Norsemen, the Japanese, the Hindus,
the American Indians and so on and so on all have their own creation myths,
and all of these are recognized by Americans of Judeo-Christian heritage as
"just myths."

The ancient Hebrews also had a creation tale—two of them, in fact. There   17
is a primitive Adam-and-Eve-in-Paradise story, with man created first, then
animals, then woman. There is also a poetic tale of God fashioning the universe
in six days, with animals preceding man, and man and woman created together.

These Hebrew myths are not inherently more credible than any of the others,   18
but they are our myths. General consent, of course, proves nothing: There can
be a unanimous belief in something that isn't so. The universal opinion over
thousands of years that the earth was flat never flattened its spherical shape
by one inch.

The Argument by Belittlement

Creationists frequently stress the fact that evolution is "only a theory," giving   19
the impression that a theory is an idle guess. A scientist, one gathers, arising

one morning with nothing particular to do, decides that perhaps the moon is made of Roquefort cheese and instantly advances the Roquefort-cheese theory.

A theory (as the word is used by scientists) is a detailed description of some   20
facet of the universe's workings that is based on long observation and, where possible, experiment. It is the result of careful reasoning from those observations and experiments and has survived the critical study of scientists generally.

For example, we have the description of the cellular nature of living organ-   21
isms (the "cell theory"); of objects attracting each other according to a fixed rule (the "theory of gravitation"); of energy behaving in discrete bits (the "quantum theory"); of light traveling through a vacuum at a fixed measurable velocity (the "theory of relativity"), and so on.

All are theories; all are firmly founded; all are accepted as valid descriptions   22
of this or that aspect of the universe. They are neither guesses nor speculations. And no theory is better founded, more closely examined, more critically argued and more thoroughly accepted, than the theory of evolution. If it is "only" a theory, that is all it has to be.

Creationism, on the other hand, is not a theory. There is no evidence, in   23
the scientific sense, that supports it. Creationism, or at least the particular variety accepted by many Americans, is an expression of early Middle Eastern legend. It is fairly described as "only a myth."

The Argument from Imperfection

Creationists, in recent years, have stressed the "scientific" background of their   24
beliefs. They point out that there are scientists who base their creationists beliefs on a careful study of geology, paleontology and biology and produce "textbooks" that embody those beliefs.

Virtually the whole scientific corpus of creationism, however, consists of the   25
pointing out of imperfections in the evolutionary view. The creationists insist, for example, that evolutionists cannot show true transition states between species in the fossil evidence; that age determinations through radioactive breakdown are uncertain; that alternate interpretations of this or that piece of evidence are possible, and so on.

Because the evolutionary view is not perfect and is not agreed upon in every   26
detail by all scientists, creationists argue that evolution is false and that scientists, in supporting evolution, are basing their views on blind faith and dogmatism.

To an extent, the creationists are right here. The details of evolution are not   27
perfectly known. Scientists have been adjusting and modifying Charles Darwin's suggestions since he advanced this theory of the origin of species through natural selection back in 1859. After all, much has been learned about the fossil record and about physiology, microbiology, biochemistry, ethology and various other branches in life science in the last 125 years, and it is to be expected that we can improve on Darwin. In fact, we have improved on him.

Nor is the process finished. It can never be, as long as human beings continue   28
to question and to strive for better answers.

The details of evolutionary theory are in dispute precisely because scientists   29
are not devotees of blind faith and dogmatism. They do not accept even as
great a thinker as Darwin without question, nor do they accept any idea, new
or old, without thorough argument. Even after accepting an idea, they stand
ready to overrule it, if appropriate new evidence arrives. If, however, we grant
that a theory is imperfect and that details remain in dispute, does that disprove
the theory as a whole?

Consider, I drive a car, and you drive a car. I do not know exactly how an   30
engine works. Perhaps you do not either. And it may be that our hazy and
approximate ideas of the workings of an automobile are in conflict. Must we
then conclude from this disagreement that an automobile does not run, or that
it does not exist? Or, if our senses force us to conclude that an automobile does
exist and run, does that mean it is pulled by an invisible horse, since our engine
theory is imperfect?

However much scientists argue their differing beliefs in details of evolution-   31
ary theory, or in the interpretation of the necessarily imperfect fossil record,
they firmly accept the evolutionary process itself.

The Argument from Distorted Science

Creationists have learned enough scientific terminology to use it in their attempts   32
to disprove evolution. They do this in numerous ways, but the most common
example, at least in the mail I receive, is the repeated assertion that the second
law of thermodynamics demonstrates the evolutionary process to be impossible.

In kindergarten terms, the second law of thermodynamics says that all   33
spontaneous change is in the direction of increasing disorder—that is, in a
"downhill" direction. There can be no spontaneous buildup of the complex
from the simple, therefore, because that would be moving "uphill." According
to the creationist argument, since, by the evolutionary process, complex forms
of life evolve from simple forms, that process defies the second law, so creationism must be true.

Such an argument implies that this clearly visible fallacy is somehow invisible   34
to scientists, who must therefore be flying in the face of the second law through
sheer perversity.

Scientists, however, do know about the second law and they are not blind.   35
It's just that an argument based on kindergarten terms is suitable only for
kindergartens.

To lift the argument a notch above the kindergarten level, the second law   36
of thermodynamics applies to a "closed system"—that is, to a system that does
not gain energy from without, or lose energy to the outside. The only truly
closed system we know of is the universe as a whole.

Within a closed system, there are subsystems that can gain complexity   37
spontaneously, provided there is a greater loss of complexity in another interlocking subsystem. The overall change then is a complexity loss in line with
the dictates of the second law.

Evolution can proceed and build up the complex from the simple, thus   38
moving uphill, without violating the second law, as long as another interlocking
part of the system—the sun, which delivers energy to the earth continually—
moves downhill (as it does) at a much faster rate than evolution moves uphill.

If the sun were to cease shining, evolution would stop and so, eventually,   39
would life.

Unfortunately, the second law is a subtle concept which most people are   40
not accustomed to dealing with, and it is not easy to see the fallacy in the
creationist distortion.

There are many other "scientific" arguments used by creationists, some   41
taking quite clever advantage of present areas of dispute in evolutionary theory,
but every one of them is as disingenuous as the second-law argument.

The "scientific" arguments are organized into special creationist textbooks,   42
which have all the surface appearance of the real thing, and which school
systems are being heavily pressured to accept. They are written by people who
have not made any mark as scientists, and, while they discuss geology, paleontology and biology with correct scientific terminology, they are devoted almost
entirely to raising doubts over the legitimacy of the evidence and reasoning
underlying evolutionary thinking on the assumption that this leaves creationism
as the only possible alternative.

Evidence actually in favor of creationism is not presented, of course, because   43
none exists other than the word of the Bible, which it is current creationist
strategy not to use.

The Argument from Irrelevance

Some creationists pull all matters of scientific evidence to one side and consider   44
all such things irrelevant. The Creator, they say, brought life and the earth and
the entire universe into being 6,000 years ago or so, complete with all the
evidence for an eons-long evolutionary development. The fossil record, the
decaying radioactivity, the receding galaxies were all created as they are, and
the evidence they present is an illusion.

Of course, this argument is itself irrelevant, for it can neither be proved nor   45
disproved. It is not an argument, actually, but a statement. I can say that the
entire universe was created two minutes ago, complete with all its history books
describing a nonexistent past in detail, and with every living person equipped
with a full memory; you, for instance, in the process of reading this article in
midstream with a memory of what you had read in the beginning—which you
had not really read.

What kind of a Creator would produce a universe containing so intricate   46
an illusion? It would mean that the Creator formed a universe that contained
human beings whom He had endowed with the faculty of curiosity and the
ability to reason. He supplied those human beings with an enormous amount
of subtle and cleverly consistent evidence designed to mislead them and cause
them to be convinced that the universe was created 20 billion years ago and
developed by evolutionary processes that included the creation and development of life on Earth.

Why?   47

Does the Creator take pleasure in fooling us? Does it amuse Him to watch   48
us go wrong? Is it part of a test to see if human beings will deny their senses
and their reason in order to cling to myth? Can it be that the Creator is a cruel
and malicious prankster, with a vicious and adolescent sense of humor?

The Argument from Authority

The Bible says that God created the world in six days, and the Bible is the   49
inspired word of God. To the average creationist this is all that counts. All
other arguments are merely a tedious way of countering the propaganda of all
those wicked humanists, agnostics and atheists who are not satisfied with the
clear word of the Lord.

The creationist leaders do not actually use that argument because that would   50
make their argument a religious one, and they would not be able to use it in
fighting a secular school system. They have to borrow the clothing of science,
no matter how badly it fits and call themselves "scientific" creationists. They
also speak only of the "Creator," and never mention that this Creator is the
God of the Bible.

We cannot, however, take this sheep's clothing seriously. However much the   51
creationist leaders might hammer away at their "scientific" and "philosophical"
points, they would be helpless and a laughing stock if that were all they had.

It is religion that recruits their squadrons. Tens of millions of Americans,   52
who neither know or understand the actual arguments for—or even against—
evolution, march in the army of the night with their Bibles held high. And
they are a strong and frightening force, impervious to, and immunized against,
the feeble lance of mere reason.

Even if I am right and the evolutionists' case is very strong, have not   53
creationists, whatever the emptiness of their case, a right to be heard?

If their case is empty, isn't it perfectly safe to discuss it since the emptiness   54
would then be apparent?

Why, then, are evolutionists so reluctant to have creationism taught in the   55
public schools on an equal basis with evolutionary theory? Can it be that the
evolutionists are not as confident of their case as they pretend. Are they afraid
to allow youngsters a clear choice?

First, the creationists are somewhat less than honest in their demand for   56
equal time. It is not their views that are repressed: Schools are by no means
the only place in which the dispute between creationism and evolutionary
theory is played out.

There are the churches, for instance, which are a much more serious influ-   57
ence on most Americans than the schools are. To be sure, many churches are
quite liberal, have made their peace with science and find it easy to live with
scientific advance—even with evolution. But many of the less modish and
citified churches are bastions of creationism.

The influence of the church is naturally felt in the home, in the newspapers   58
and in all of surrounding society. It makes itself felt in the nation as a whole,
even religiously liberal areas, in thousands of subtle ways; in the nature of
holiday observance, in expressions of patriotic fervor, even in total irrelevancies.
In 1968, for example, a team of astronauts circling the moon were instructed
to read the first few verses of Genesis as though NASA felt it had to placate
the public lest they rage against the violation of the firmament. At the present
time, even the current President of the United States has expressed his creationist sympathies.

It is only in school that American youngsters in general are ever likely to   59
hear any reasoned exposition of the evolutionary viewpoint. They might find
such a viewpoint in books, magazines, newspapers or even, on occasion, on
television. But church and family can easily censor printed matter or television.
Only the school is beyond their control.

But only just barely beyond. Even though schools are now allowed to teach   60
evolution, teachers are beginning to be apologetic about it, knowing full well
their jobs are at the mercy of school boards upon which creationists are a
stronger and stronger influence.

Then, too, in schools, students are not required to believe what they learn   61
about evolution—merely to parrot it back on tests. If they fail to do so, their
punishment is nothing more than the loss of a few points on a test or two.

In the creationist churches, however, the congregation is required to believe.   62
Impressionable youngsters, taught that they will go to hell if they listen to the
evolutionary doctrine, are not likely to listen in comfort or to believe if they
do.

Therefore, creationists, who control the church and the society they live in   63
and who face the public school as the only place where evolution is even briefly
mentioned in a possibly favorable way, find they cannot stand even so minuscule
a competition and demand "equal time."

Do you suppose their devotion to "fairness" is such that they will give equal   64
time to evolution in their churches?

Second, the real danger is the manner in which creationists want their "equal   65
time."

In the scientific world, there is free and open competition of ideas, and even   66
a scientist whose suggestions are not accepted is nevertheless free to continue
to argue his case.

In this free and open competition of ideas, creationism has clearly lost. It   67
has been losing in fact, since the time of Copernicus four and a half centuries
ago. But creationists, placing myth above reason, refuse to accept the decision
and are now calling on the Government to force their views on the schools in
lieu of the free expression of ideas. Teachers must be forced to present creationism as though it has equal intellectual respectability with evolutionary
doctrine.

What a precedent this sets.   68

If the Government can mobilize its policemen and its prisons to make certain   69
that teachers give creationism equal time, they can next use force to make sure
that teachers declare creationism the victor so that evolution will be evicted
from the classroom altogether.

We will have established the full groundwork, in other words, for legally   70
enforced ignorance and for totalitarian thought control.

And what if the creationists win? They might, you know, for there are millions   71
who, faced with the choice between science and their interpretation of the
Bible, will choose the Bible and reject science, regardless of the evidence.

This is not entirely because of a traditional and unthinking reverence for   72
the literal words of the Bible; there is also a pervasive uneasiness—even an
actual fear—of science that will drive even those who care little for Funda-
mentalism into the arms of the creationists. For one thing, science is uncertain.
Theories are subject to revision; observations are open to a variety of interpretations, and scientists quarrel among themselves. This is disillusioning for
those untrained in the scientific method, who thus turn to the rigid certainty
of the Bible instead. There is something comfortable about a view that allows
for no deviation and that spares you the painful necessity of having to think.

Second, science is complex and chilling. The mathematical language of sci-   73
ence is understood by very few. The vistas it presents are scary—an enormous
universe ruled by chance and impersonal rules, empty and uncaring, ungrasp-
able and vertiginous. How comfortable to turn instead to a small world, only
a few thousand years old, and under God's personal and immediate care; a
world in which you are His peculiar concern and where He will not consign
you to hell if you are careful to follow every word of the Bible as interpreted
for you by your television preacher.

Third, science is dangerous. There is no question but that poison gas, genetic   74
engineering and nuclear weapons and power stations are terrifying. It may be
that civilization is falling apart and the world we know is coming to an end.
In that case, why not turn to religion and look forward to the Day of Judgment,
in which you and your fellow believers will be lifted into external bliss and

have the added joy of watching the scoffers and disbelievers writhe forever in torment.

So why might they not win?   75

There are numerous cases of societies in which the armies of the night have   76
ridden triumphantly over minorities in order to establish a powerful orthodoxy
which dictates official thought. Invariably, the ride is toward long-range disaster.

Spain dominated Europe and the world in the 16th century, but in Spain   77
orthodoxy came first, and all divergence of opinion was ruthlessly suppressed.
The result was that Spain settled back into blankness and did not share in the
scientific, technological and commercial ferment that bubbled up in other
nations of Western Europe. Spain remained an intellectual backwater for centuries.

In the late 17th century, France in the name of orthodoxy revoked the Edict   78
of Nantes and drove out many thousands of Huguenots, who added their
intellectual vigor to lands of refuge such as Great Britain, the Netherlands and
Prussia, while France was permanently weakened.

In the more recent times, Germany hounded out the Jewish scientists of   79
Europe. They arrived in the United States and contributed immeasurably to
scientific advancement here, while Germany lost so heavily that there is no
telling how long it will take to regain its former scientific eminence. The Soviet
Union, in its fascination with Lysenko, destroyed its geneticists, and set back
its biological sciences for decades. China, during the Cultural Revolution, turned
against Western science and is still laboring to overcome the devastation that
resulted.

Are we now, with all these examples before us, to ride backward into the   80
past under the same tattered banner of orthodoxy? With creationism in the
saddle, American science will wither. We will raise a generation of ignoramuses
ill-equipped to run the industry of tomorrow, much less to generate the new
advances of the days after tomorrow.

We will inevitably recede into the backwater of civilization and those nations   81
that retain open scientific thought will take over the leadership of the world
and the cutting edge of human advancement.

I don't suppose that the creationists really plan the decline of the United   82
States, but their loudly expressed patriotism is as simple-minded as their "science." If they succeed, they will, in their folly, achieve the opposite of what
they say they wish.

Questions for Critical Thinking

1. With what element of religious belief does the theory of evolution seem to be in
    irreconcilable conflict? Can you conceive of any reconciliation between the com-
    peting claims of evolution and religion, or does the belief in evolution automatically
    mean the rejection of religion?

2. What other beliefs, commonly held in the past, can you cite that have since been discredited by later evidence and experience? What does this tell us about human beings and their society?

3. In paragraph 30, Asimov supports the theory of evolution with an extended analogy. How appropriate, or inappropriate, is this analogy to his defense of evolution?

4. In paragraphs 56 through 64, Asimov answers his own question, "Why are evolutionists so reluctant to have creationism taught in the public schools on an equal basis with evolutionary theory?" What, essentially, is he accusing creationists of in these paragraphs?

5. In his discussion of "The Argument from Irrelevance," what tactic does Asimov use to refute the claims of the creationists? How persuasive do you find his argument here?

6. Asimov's tactic is to list the arguments of the opposition and then answer them. What advantages does this tactic afford a writer?

7. Asimov says in paragraph 73 that science presents a vista of "an enormous universe ruled by chance and impersonal rules, empty and uncaring, graspable and vertiginous." How does this picture agree or disagree with your view of the universe as depicted by science?

8. In what way has evolution affected your personal religious beliefs?

Writing Assignment

1. What impact do you think the findings and discoveries of science should have on the religious and moral views of a fair-minded and reasonable person? Write an essay that explores this subject, citing the effects of science on your own moral and religious opinions.

Writing Advice

This particular assignment does not call solely for an objective discussion, but partly for personal opinion. Your aim should be to discuss not only the obligations you think a reasonable person should have towards science but also the effects science has had on your own religious beliefs. You should avoid the stuffy objective style that might be appropriate for a research paper and aim, instead, for the informal tone and style of a respectful personal letter. You may freely call yourself "I" in the essay and mention personal experiences. Pay particular attention to the following points as you begin to write:

1. Try to formulate what you think should be the attitude of the intelligent amateur towards the constant revelations of science. Do you think, for example, that moral and ethical beliefs should change with scientific thinking or be founded on

unchangeable principles and values? If so, what should be the basis for holding these principles and values?

2. What implications for belief or disbelief in God do you think science has? Can you think of an example in your own life where some revelation or discovery of science has caused you to alter a fundamental religious belief? If you can, cite the experience as a personal example.

3. There is no right or wrong answer to this assignment, the question being designed mainly to get you to think. Be sure, however, to support your opinions with either personal experience or with the cited views, testimonials, or experiences of others. When an essay written on such an abstract subject fails, it typically does so not for lack of the writer's opinion, but for lack of support.

Alternate Writing Assignments

1. Asimov admits that the case for evolution is incomplete, with parts of it still unproven. After doing a close reading of his article, write an essay in which you sketch the obvious elements of belief present in his argument for evolution.

2. If you agree with the creationist's view, write an essay rebutting Asimov's argument.

PHILOSOPHY

WHO IS MAN?
Loren Eiseley

Loren Eiseley (1907–1977), American anthropologist, science historian, poet and naturalist, was for many years a professor of anthropology at the University of Pennsylvania. Much admired during his life for his rich, poetic writings, Eiseley led anthropological expeditions and conducted exploratory digs for universities and for the Smithsonian Institution. Among his many books are *The Immense Journey* (1957), *The Unexpected Universe* (1969), *The Invisible Pyramid* (1970), and *The Night Country* (1971), from which this selection comes.

Reading Advice

Poets rarely write with conviction about science, and scientists rarely venture to write poetically. The happy exception to this observation is Loren Eiseley, a first-rate scientist who also wrote about nature and life in a wonderfully simple and poetic style. His use of imagery and language is so compressed, deft, and sure, that he is able to sum up in a sentence an idea that scientific writers, practicing the drier style of their disciplines, must labor over.

Not for the speed reader, however, is this sort of writing, nor for any who would grapple with the page as though it were a corn to be husked. The reader must approach Eiseley's work with the attitude of the weekend sailor, who knows that pleasure lies in the journey, not the arrival. For Eiseley is not attempting to transmit bits of data or kernels of factual truth. Rather, he is describing a timeless feeling, a sentiment we all occasionally share, some of us fearfully. But it is also a feeling that must be voiced if we are even briefly to escape the loneliness of solitary confinement in our individual selves.

As an evolutionist I never cease to be 1 astounded by the past. It is replete with more features than one world can realize. Perhaps it was this that led the philosopher George Santayana to speak of men's true natures as not adequately manifested in their condition at any given moment, or even in their usual habits. "Their real nature," he contended, "is what they would discover themselves to be if they possessed self-knowledge, or as the Indian scripture has it, if they became what they are." I should like to approach this mystery of the self, which so intrigued the great philosopher, from a mundane path strewn with the sticks and stones through which the archaeologist must pick his way.

Let me use as illustration a very heavy and peculiar stone which I keep upon 2 my desk. It has been split across and, carbon black, imprinted in the gray shale, is the outline of a fish. The chemicals that composed the fish—most of them at least—are still there in the stone. They are, in a sense, imperishable. They may come and go, pass in and out of living things, trickle away in the long erosion of time. They are inanimate, yet at one time they constituted a living creature.

Often at my desk, now, I sit contemplating the fish. Nor does it have to be 3 a fish. It could be the long-horned Alaskan bison on my wall. For the point is, you see, that the fish is extinct and gone, just as those great heavy-headed beasts are gone, just as our massive-faced and shambling forebears of the Ice Age have vanished. The chemicals still about me here took a shape that will never be seen again so long as grass grows or the sun shines. Just once out of all time there was a pattern that we call *Bison regius,* a fish called *Diplomystus humilis,* and, at this present moment, a primate who knows, or thinks he knows, the entire score.

In the past there has been armor, there have been bellowings out of throats 4 like iron furnaces, there have been phantom lights in the dark forest and toothed reptiles winging through the air. It has all been carbon and its compounds, the black stain running perpetually across the stone.

"I Am Dead"

But though the elements are known, nothing in all those shapes is now return-able. No living chemist can shape a dinosaur; no living hand can start the dreaming tentacular extensions that characterize the life of the simplest ameboid cell. Finally, as the greatest mystery of all, I who write these words on paper, cannot establish my own reality. I am, by any reasonable and considered logic, dead. This may be a matter of concern, or even a secret, but if it is any consolation, I can assure you that all men are as dead as I. For on my office desk, to prove my words, is the fossil out of the stone, and there is the carbon of life stained black on the ancient rock.

There is no life in the fossil. There is no life in the carbon in my body. As the idea strikes me, and it comes as a profound shock, I run down the list of elements. There is no life in the iron, there is no life in the phosphorus, the nitrogen does not contain me, the water that soaks my tissues is not I. What am I then? I pinch my body in a kind of sudden desperation. My heart knocks, my fingers close around the pen. There is, it seems, a semblance of life here.

But the minute I start breaking this strange body down into its constituents, it is dead. It does not know me. Carbon does not speak, calcium does not remember, iron does not weep. Even if I hastily reconstitute their combinations in my mind, rebuild my arteries, and let oxygen in the grip of hemoglobin go hurrying through a thousand conduits, I have a kind of machine, but where in all this array of pipes and hurried flotsam is the dweller?

From whence, out of what steaming pools or boiling cloudbursts, did he first arise? What forces can we find which brought him up the shore, scaled his body into an antique, reptilian shape and then cracked it like an egg to let a soft-furred animal with a warmer heart emerge? And we? Would it not be a good thing if man were tapped gently like a fertile egg to see what might creep out? I sometimes think of this as I handle the thick-walled skulls of the animal men who preceded us or ponder over those remote splay-footed creatures whose bones lie deep in the world's wastelands at the very bottom of time.

With the glooms and night terrors of those vast cemeteries I have been long familiar. A precisely similar gloom enwraps the individual life of each of us. There are moments, in my bed at midnight, or watching the play of moonlight on the ceiling, when this ghostliness of myself comes home to me with appalling force, when I lie tense, listening as if removed, far off, to the footfalls of my own heart, or seeing my own head on the pillow turning restlessly with the round staring eyes of a gigantic owl. I whisper "Who?" to no one but myself in the silent, sleeping house—the living house gone back to sleep with the sleeping stones, the eternally sleeping chair, the picture that sleeps forever on the bureau, the dead, also sleeping, though they walk in my dreams. In the midst of all this dark, this void, this emptiness, I, more ghostly than a ghost, cry "Who? Who?" to no answer, aware only of other smaller ghosts like the bat sweeping by the window or the dog who, in repeating a bit of his own lost history, turns restlessly among nonexistent grasses before he subsides again upon the floor.

Questions for Critical Thinking

1. What about human nature is likely to contribute to our lack of self-knowledge of which George Santayana speaks? (*See* paragraph 1.)

2. Eiseley was an eminent anthropologist with impeccable scientific credentials. What rhetorical advantage do you think his scientific background added to this article?

3. What era of prehistory, and what creatures, is Eiseley poetically describing in paragraph 4?

4. Eiseley says that he is dead and so are all men. In what way does he implicitly regard you as dead? Do you agree with him and how do you cope, if so, with being dead in the way he means?

5. What theory of life does Eiseley poetically sketch in paragraph 8?

6. What presumed difference exists between the dog's grasp of its "lost history" and the human's? Whose view do you think is more likely to lead to self-contentment?

Writing Assignment

Each of us has a singular conception of who we are and what lies ahead for us. This frequently unexpressed sense of definition and purpose is at the very basis of our self-concept. Write an essay in which you answer Eiseley's question, "Who is man?" by saying who you are.

Writing Advice

The assignment calls for philosophical speculation, not for a hard and fast definition. You cannot prove that your self-concept is absolutely and finally right, nor should you even try. Basically, you should aim for formulating and expressing the principal beliefs behind your own self-identity and self-definition. Consider the following as you plan your essay:

1. The question is not asking for a factual definition. Answering it properly involves giving more than your name, age, address, gender, and citizenship. These facts about you are demographically more meaningful to a college administration than to a privately held sense of self-identity.

2. Do you think, for instance, that you are a soulless creation of chemicals and atoms and that upon your eventual death you pass away into the constituent elements of which you are composed? Or do you believe that you possess an elemental spark of life that will survive your physical death? How important to your self-definition is this basic belief? If you believe only in the materialist explanation of being, your essay might begin, "I am a complex combination of chemical elements, nothing more." If you subscribe to the view that humans are both physical and spiritual, you could lead-off your essay with this opinion, "I am the sum total of personality traits that have been infused in me by the divine spirit."

3. What goals and ambitions do you have that characterize you as a distinct individual? Where do you hope to be fifty years from now, and what do you hope to have accomplished?

4. What are your family antecedents, upbringing, and background, and how important in defining your sense of self are these historical facts? Do you have a strong sense of nationalistic pride that helps shape your self-identity? Do you think of yourself, for example, as inseparably American, French, Mexican, or Jamaican?

   Note that the specific details you will use to give backing to your generalizations about yourself will most likely be autobiographical. You should also try to say not only what you think about yourself but why, and what experiences and insights led you to arrive at your conclusions.

Alternate Writing Assignment

In his philosophical speculation, Eiseley is really writing about the mysteries and pangs of self-knowledge caused by self-consciousness. Define self-consciousness in an essay and say whether it applies only to humans or to what extent also to animals.

HISTORY

A WITNESS AT THE SCOPES TRIAL
Fay-Cooper Cole

Fay-Cooper Cole (1881–1961) was a professor of anthropology at the University of Chicago who did archaeological work in the United States and abroad. His books include *Kincaid—A Prehistoric Illinois Metropolis* (1951), *The Bukidnon of Mindanao* (1956), and *The Peoples of Malaysia* (1968). In 1925 Cole volunteered to testify as an expert witness for the defense when a young high-school science teacher, John Thomas Scopes, was charged with violating the laws of Tennessee against teaching the theory of evolution. The following is Cole's account of what he witnessed at that famous Scopes trial.

Reading Advice

This article bears a cool and professional journalist's touch. It begins with a quotation lead—an appeal from Clarence Darrow for help—and proceeds swiftly to a crisp summation of background, and then to a spare but effective recounting of highlights in the Scopes trial. Its narrator is content to remain modestly in the background and act as an observant reporter of the events unfolding around him.

What will challenge a modern reader's patience, however, is the roster of repetitive but unfamiliar names, many of whom were crucial players in the drama. In some instances, you may need to look up the names of occasional bit players who put in brief but significant appearances. For example, the author briefly mentions that H. L. Mencken proved such an agitator that the defense team finally asked him to leave. But if you did not know that Mencken was possibly the most famous essayist and editor of his day, you would entirely miss the full import of this incident.

*T*his is Clarence Darrow," said the   1
voice at the other end of the wire, "I suppose you have been reading the papers, so you know Bryan and his outfit are prosecuting that young fellow Scopes. Well, Malone, Colby and I have put ourselves in a mess by offering to defend. We don't know much about evolution. We don't know whom to call as witnesses. But we do know we are fighting your battle for academic freedom. We need the help of you fellows at the University, so I am asking three of you to come to my office to help lay plans."

That afternoon in Darrow's office three of us from the University of Chi-   2
cago—Horatio Hackett Newman, professor of biology; Shailer Mathews, dean of the Divinity School; and I—met to outline the strategy for what turned out to be one of the most publicized trials of the century. The Scopes trial proved also to be a historic occasion in the cause of popular understanding of science. A century ago the educated world was shaken by the discoveries of Charles Darwin and Alfred Russel Wallace, and the evidence they presented for the evolution of life on this planet. In 1959, as we celebrate the centenary of the *Origin of Species,* few informed persons, if any, question the theory of evolution. However, the century has witnessed several attempts to stifle investigation and outlaw the teaching of the theory. The best known of these was the Scopes trial, held in Dayton, Tenn., in 1925. The trial resulted in an immense revival of public interest in Darwin and in evolution; there has been no comparable

effort since then to suppress this advance in man's understanding of himself and the world he lives in.

To understand the trial and what lay back of it, one must recall the climate   3
of the 1920s. It was a time of uncertainty, unrest and repression. We had just emerged from a world war. Old standards were badly shaken; the young were labeled "the lost generation"; intolerance was rampant. The Ku Klux Klan was on the march, not only in the South but in the North as well. In many towns in Illinois, Indiana and other parts of the Midwest, staid business men—even members of the clergy—put on "white nighties" and burned fiery crosses to put the Negro, the Jew, the Catholic and the immigrant "in their places." The Fundamentalists, under the leadership of William Jennings Bryan, had organized in some 20 states and were putting pressure on all institutions of learning to curb the teaching of science, particularly evolution, which they considered in contradiction to the Bible. Prohibitive bills had been passed in Tennessee and Mississippi and were pending in six other states.

Then came the great opportunity. In the little town of Dayton the high-   4
school science teacher and football coach, 24-year-old John Thomas Scopes, found himself engaged in a discussion of the new law with George W. Rappelyca, a young mining engineer and superintendent of the local coal mines. Scopes expressed bewilderment that the state should supply him with a textbook that presented the theory of evolution, yet make him a lawbreaker if he taught the theory. Rappelyca agreed that it was a crazy law and clearly unconstitutional. Then suddenly he asked: "Why don't I have you arrested for teaching evolution from that text and bring the whole thing to an end?" Scopes replied: "Fair enough."

Scopes was duly arrested. But neither of the principals had any idea of what   5
they were starting. Within a few hours the Chattanooga papers carried the story. Soon it was spread across the nation. The Fundamentalists were quick to realize the opportunity to dramatize their battle against evolution. Bryan and his associates offered their services to the Prosecution. They were accepted. Here was big news.

At this point, it happened, three lawyers met in New York City for a con-   6
ference on some business matters. They were Clarence Darrow, controversialist and defender of unpopular causes; Bainbridge Colby, an eminent corporation lawyer and, like Bryan, a former Secretary of State; and Dudley Field Malone, a leading Catholic layman and a fashionable barrister. Their conversation turned to the Tennessee situation. One said: "It is a shame. That poor teacher, who probably doesn't know what it is all about, is to be sacrificed by the Funda-mentalists." Another said: "Someone ought to do something about it." The third replied: "Why don't we?" Through the American Civil Liberties Union they offered to defend young Scopes. Their offer was accepted.

This was real news! Bryan, three times candidate for the presidency of the   7
U.S., the great Fundamentalist leader and orator, on one side. On the other,

three of the nation's most famous lawyers, including Darrow, master jury-pleader. The papers were full of the story.

This was the background of Darrow's call to me and of our meeting at his   8
office in Chicago early in the summer of 1925. By telephone, wire and letter
we proceeded to assemble a panel of expert witnesses: scientists to testify on
the theory of evolution and theologians to give evidence on the history and
interpretation of the Bible. In addition to Newman, Mathews and myself, our
panel finally included Kirtley Mather, professor of geology at Harvard; Jacob
G. Lipman, director of the New Jersey Agricultural Experiment Station at
Rutgers University; W. C. Curtis, professor of zoology at the University of
Missouri; Wilbur Nelson, state geologist of Tennessee; Maynard Metcalf, professor of zoology at Johns Hopkins University; Charles Judd, head of the University of Chicago School of Education; and Rabbi Herman Rosenwasser of San
Francisco, a noted Hebrew scholar. All of us, along with our counsel, undertook
to go to Dayton at our own expense and to serve without fee.

The trial was scheduled for Friday, July 10. But long before that date the   9
town was crowded with newspapermen, Fundamentalist supporters and others
who were just curious. No one was willing to house "the heretics," that is, the
scientific witnesses and defense attorneys. So an old "haunted house" on a hill
overlooking the town was fitted out as a dormitory.

When I reached town, I took care not to associate myself at once with the   10
Defense group, and was able to wander about for a time listening to the talk
of the local people. For the most part they were extremely partisan to the
Fundamentalist cause. But they were apprehensive of the famous Darrow, and
they were not yet aware of his plan to present expert testimony on evolution
and the scriptures.

That evening I joined the group at the "haunted house" and there met young   11
Scopes for the first time. He was a fine, clean-cut young man, a little shy and
apparently overwhelmed by the controversy he had stirred up. He expressed
amazement that famous lawyers like Darrow, Colby, Malone and Arthur Garfield
Hays (counsel to the American Civil Liberties Union) should come to his
defense, and that a group of well-known scientists should join them.

Little happened on the first day of the trial beyond the selection of the jury.   12
A panel was offered, and Darrow accepted it without change after a casual
examination. But he did bring out the fact that 11 jurors were Fundamentalist
church members. All admitted that they knew little about science or evolution.
One said that the only Darwin he had ever heard about ran a local notion
store. One could not read or write.

The events of Sunday provided us with an interesting insight into the local   13
climate of opinion. Charles Francis Potter, a liberal Unitarian minister and
writer who had been invited to conduct services at the Methodist-Episcopal
church, was barred from the pulpit by the parishioners. Meanwhile Bryan
addressed an overflow house at the Southern Methodist church. That afternoon,

in an open courtyard in the center of town, Bryan talked to an immense audience. He said he welcomed the opportunity to bring "this slimy thing, evolution, out of the darkness. . . . Now the facts of religion and evolution would meet at last in a duel to the death." It was a fine example of Bryan's oratory, and it swept the crowd.

The court opened on Monday with a prayer in which a local clergyman   14
urged God to preserve his sacred word against attack. It was a scarcely veiled plea to the jury.

The Defense filed a motion to quash the indictment on the ground that the   15
act violated the Constitution of the State of Tennessee and Section 1 of the Fourteenth Amendment of the Constitution of the United States, which extends the Bill of Rights to limit action by the governments of the states. The Defense argued further that the indictment was contrary to a U.S. Supreme Court decision which says: "The law knows no heresy, and is committed to the support of no dogma, nor to the establishment of any sect." In support of this attack on the indictment, the Defense declared that it wished to offer the testimony of scientists and biblical scholars. These expert witnesses, the Defense contended, would show that there was no necessary conflict between evolution and Christianity.

Though the Defense asked that judgment on its motion to dismiss should   16
be reserved until its witnesses had been heard, Judge John T. Raulston ordered the argument to proceed. On motion of the Prosecution, he sent the jury from the courtroom. Apparently the introduction of scientific witnesses had taken Bryan and his associates by surprise. Their ultimate response to our efforts to argue the underlying issues of the case was to lose them the trial in the minds of the American people.

That afternoon Darrow pressed for dismissal with an eloquent attack on   17
ignorance and bigotry. Coatless in the sweltering courtroom, tugging at his suspenders, he paced up and down, firing shot after shot at the Prosecution. He stressed the danger to freedom of press, church and school if men like Bryan could impose their opinions and interpretations on the law of the land. "The fires of bigotry and hate are being lighted," he said. "This is as bold an attempt to destroy learning as was ever made in the Middle Ages. . . . The statute says you cannot teach anything in conflict with the Bible." He argued that in the U.S. there are over 500 churches and sects which differ over certain passages in the Bible. If the law were to prevail, Scopes would have to be familiar with the whole Bible and all its interpretations; among all the warring sects, he would have to know which one was right in order not to commit a crime.

Darrow said: "Your Honor, my client is here because ignorance and bigotry   18
are rampant, and that is a mighty strong combination. . . . If today you can make teaching of evolution in the public schools a crime, tomorrow you can make it a crime to teach it in the private schools. At the next session of the

Legislature you can ban books and newspapers. You can set Catholic against Protestant, and Protestant against Protestant, when you try to foist your own religion upon the minds of men. If you can do the one, you can do the other. After a while, Your Honor, we will find ourselves marching backward to the glorious days of the 16th century when bigots lighted the fagots to burn men who dared to bring any intelligence and enlightenment to the human mind."

The speech made a profound impression. Townspeople agreed that anything 19 might happen with that man Darrow around. Judge Raulston adjourned court until Wednesday in order that he might consider the motion to quash.

That night, as we gathered in our haunted house for a conference, a terrific 20 storm swept the town. When a brilliant flash of lightning struck nearby, Darrow said: "Boys, if lightning strikes this house tonight . . . !"

Tuesday was a quiet day. At Rappelyca's office, where he had been invited 21 to take advantage of the secretarial facilities, Potter found that the stenographer would not take dictation from any Unitarian minister. Rappelyca himself was arrested three times for speeding in the course of his service to us as guide and chauffeur. We were besieged by Holy Rollers, who came in from the hills to convert us. We also had to protect ourselves from a supporter. H. L. Mencken had come to town. His vitriolic articles so antagonized the people we wanted most to reach that we had to persuade him to leave the scene.

After the jury was sworn in on Wednesday, the Court ruled against the 22 Defense motion to quash the indictment. The law, said Judge Raulston, did not deprive anyone of speech, thought or opinion, for no one need accept employment in Tennessee. He ruled the law constitutional, saying that the public has the right to say, by legislative act or referendum, whether Latin, chemistry or astronomy might be taught in its schools.

The Prosecution then called the county superintendent of schools, the heads 23 of the school board and seven students. All testified to what Scopes had taught. Darrow limited his cross-examination to establishing simply that the State had furnished the textbook. After offering the King James version of the Bible as an exhibit, the Prosecution rested.

The first witness for the Defense was Maynard Metcalf. A recognized sci- 24 entist, he was also an eminent Congregational layman and teacher of one of the largest Bible classes in the country. Darrow established his competence as a witness, then asked a question on evolution. The Prosecution at once challenged the testimony as irrelevant; according to them the only question was: Did Scopes violate the law?

The judge agreed to hear arguments on this point the next day. Meanwhile 25 he excused the jury, with instructions not to enter the courtroom or to remain within hearing of the loudspeakers. A lot of angry jurors filed out. They had not only lost their reserved seats, but also were barred from the proceedings entirely.

The trial reached its high point on Thursday. After an impassioned plea by   26
the State's Attorney against the admission of expert testimony, Bryan took over
for the Prosecution. Instead of making good on his challenge of "a duel to the
death," he argued against the presentation of scientific evidence. He said that
the jury did not need the help of scientists or Bible experts to decide the facts
and to interpret the law: "The law is what the people decided." He then
presented an enlargement of the picture of the evolutionary tree from the
textbook Scopes had used; it showed man in a circle with other mammals.
Bryan shouted: "Talk about putting Daniel in the lions' den. How dare these
scientists put man in a little ring with lions and tigers and everything that
smells of the jungle. . . . One does not need to be an expert to know what the
Bible says. . . . Expert testimony is not needed!"

With that speech Bryan lost the argument with the press and with the radio   27
audience. When Malone had finished his reply, Bryan had also lost the argument,
for a time, with most of his Dayton followers.

Malone was a Patrick Henry that day. He asked whether our children are   28
to know nothing of science beyond that permitted by certain sects. "I have
never seen greater need for learning," he declared, "than is exhibited by the
Prosecution, which refuses information offered by expert witnesses. . . . Why
this fear of meeting the issue? Mr. Bryan has said this is to be a duel to the
death. I know little about dueling, Your Honor, but does it mean that our only
weapon, the witnesses, is to be taken away while the Prosecution alone carries
the sword? This is not my idea of a duel. . . . We do not fear all the truth they
can present as facts. We are ready. We stand with progress. We stand with
science. We stand with intelligence. We feel that we stand with the fundamental
freedoms in America. We are not afraid. Where is the fear? We defy it." Then,
turning toward Bryan and pointing his finger, he cried: "There is the fear!"

The crowd went out of control—cheering, stamping, pounding on desks—   29
until it was necessary to adjourn court for 15 minutes to restore order.

I was sitting next to the aisle. Beside me was a Chattanooga policeman, one   30
of the squad brought in to protect us from the Ku Klux Klan. As Malone
finished, my guard beat the desk in front of me so hard with his club that a
corner of the desk broke off. His chief came up and asked: "Why didn't you
cheer when Malone made that speech?" My guard replied: "Hell. What did
you think I was doing? Rapping for order?"

We had won for the day. Even the hostile crowd was with us.   31

That night Darrow said: "Today we have won, but by tomorrow the judge   32
will have recovered and will rule against us. I want each one of you to go to
the stenographer's room the first thing in the morning and prepare a statement
for the press, saying what you would have said if allowed to testify in court."

As we were preparing our statements next morning, Judge Raulston looked   33
in. I was nearest to the door. He asked what we were doing. When I told him,
he asked the others in turn. Then he went to Darrow and told him he must

not release the testimony: "It might reach the jury." Darrow replied: "Your Honor, you can do what you please with that jury. You can lock it up, but you cannot lock up the American people. The testimony will be released."

When court resumed, the judge ruled against us on all points. Rising and   34
pushing his long hair from his forehead, Darrow spoke slowly and clearly. "The outcome is plain. We expect to protect our rights in some other court. Is that plain?" The judge replied: "I hope, Colonel Darrow, you don't attempt to reflect upon the Court." To which Darrow drawled: "Your Honor has the right to hope." The insult was deliberate. For an instant there was complete silence; then the judge mumbled that he had the right to do something else. A moment later he adjourned court until Monday.

Public reaction to the ruling was emphatic, and Bryan's prestige was shaken.   35
Townspeople admitted to me, one of the "heretics," that they could not understand why Bryan had backed down. They asked: "What can you do now, if you can't talk?"

On Monday Darrow apologized to the Court, momentarily relieving the   36
tension. Then, in order to secure the foundation for appeal, Hays read into the record the prepared statements of the scientific and other scholarly witnesses, and concluded by placing in evidence three versions of the Bible that differed from one another and from the King James version submitted by the Prosecution. Suddenly Hays electrified the crowd with the announcement that the Defense wished to call Bryan to the stand "as a biblical witness."

Darrow submitted Bryan to grueling examination. In reply to Darrow's   37
questions Bryan stated that he accepted the Bible literally as God's revealed word. What he didn't understand he accepted on simple faith. He believed that Eve was the first woman, created from Adam's rib; that God had sent childbirth pains to all women because of her transgression; that the snake must crawl on its belly because it tempted Eve; that everything outside the Ark, except fish, perished in the flood; that all existing animals had descended from the pairs saved by Noah; that all men spoke one language until the Tower of Babel; and that present languages had developed since then. Only once did he falter, when he admitted that the seven days of creation might mean seven epochs. He conceded that he was not familiar with the work of archaeologists, who had uncovered civilizations more than 5,000 years old, but he declared that he had never had much interest in those scientists who disputed the Bible. Repeatedly the State's Attorney tried to stop the questioning, but always Bryan replied: "No. Let it go on. I am not afraid to defend my religion."

Finally Malone intervened, saying he would have asked the same questions,   38
but only to challenge Bryan's literal interpretation of the King James version. As a churchman and a Christian, however, he objected to any effort by counsel for the State to pin Darrow's views of religion on the defense. "I don't want this case to be changed by Mr. Darrow's agnosticism or Mr. Bryan's brand of

religion." Malone further observed that this was supposed to be a trial by jury, yet the jury had not been permitted in the court for more than 15 minutes since being sworn in.

On Tuesday Judge Raulston struck the examination of Bryan from the record. The only question remaining, he said, was: What did Scopes teach? To this ruling Darrow replied: "Your Honor, we are wasting time. You should call the jury and instruct it to bring in a verdict of guilty." The Court did so, and Scopes was fined $100.   39

Scopes had come on to graduate study in geology at the University of Chicago when the Tennessee Supreme Court heard Darrow's appeal and at last handed down its decision in January, 1927. The court narrowly affirmed the anti-evolution statute, but threw out the $100 fine on a technicality. It brought an end to the formal proceedings by advising the State to desist from further prosecution: "We see nothing to be gained by prolonging the life of this bizarre case."   40

The Defense was also content to accept the Court's advice. No attempt at repression has ever backfired so impressively. Where one person had been interested in evolution before the trial, scores were reading and inquiring at its close. Within a year the prohibitive bills which had been pending in other states were dropped or killed. Tennessee had been made to appear so ridiculous in the eyes of the nation that other states did not care to follow its lead.   41

At the University of Chicago I had been teaching modest-sized classes. When the University resumed in the autumn my lecture hall was filled. Students were standing along the walls and sitting in the windows. I thought I was in the wrong room. When I asked a boy at the door what class was meeting, he replied: "Anthropology. The prof who teaches it defended that fellow Scopes." From that time on Introductory Anthropology had to be limited to lecture-hall capacity. My mail, mostly hostile, increased until the University gave up trying to put it in my box, but tied it in bundles and sent it to my office.   42

Some time after the trial I was summoned to the office of Frederick Wood-ward, acting president of the University. He handed me a long document, a series of resolutions from a Southern Baptist conference. They took the University to task for the part members of its faculty had taken in the trial, taking note of the University's strong Baptist origins. They voiced objections to Professors Judd, Newman and Mathews, but reserved the real condemnation for me—the witness on human evolution. I was "a snake in the grass corrupting the youth of a nation," and so on, concluding with "and we have been investigating Professor Cole still further, and we find that he is not even a Baptist."   43

I began to laugh, but the president said: "This is no laughing matter. You are a rather new man here, but already we have more demands for your removal than any other man who has been on our faculty. These resolutions are typical and were considered of such importance that they were read yesterday at the   44 meeting of the Board of Trustees." "Yes," I replied. "And what did they do?" He reached across his desk and handed me a piece of paper. They had raised my salary.

Questions for Critical Thinking

1. The author writes, "In 1959, as we celebrate the centenary of the *Origin of the Species*, few informed persons, if any, question the theory of evolution." How accurately does this statement reflect the reality today?

2. How would you characterize the tone of this article? What is a reader likely to infer about the author from its tone and style?

3. The author describes the composition of the jury in paragraph 12 but fails to share with us his personal impressions of them. Why do you think he did this, and how effective do you judge this tactic to be?

4. The defense at the Scopes trial claimed, and offered expert witnesses to testify to the effect, that no necessary conflict existed between evolution and Christianity. What is your opinion of this claim?

5. Bryan claimed in his prosecution of the case that the law against teaching evolution was justified because it is "what the people decided." What risk does this viewpoint pose to a democracy?

6. If the people of Tennessee or any other state democratically vote to restrict the teaching of evolution to their children, what right does the Federal government or any other outside jurisdiction have to intervene?

7. Darrow voiced this opinion in one of his arguments: "If today you can make teaching of evolution in the public schools a crime, tomorrow you can make it a crime to teach it in the private schools. At the next session of the Legislature you can ban books and newspapers. You can set Catholic against Protestant, and Protestant against Protestant. . . . Your honor, we will find ourselves marching backward to the glorious days of the 16th century when bigots lighted faggots to burn men who dared to bring any intelligence and enlightenment to the human mind." What is the popular name given to this chained-calamities reasoning? How realistic do you judge this scenario to be?

Writing Assignment

Argue the point pro or con in an essay that locals have the right to democratically decide the contents of textbooks taught to their children in public schools.

Writing Advice

First, decide where you stand on this particular issue and why. Do you think that local school districts should have the right to decide the contents of texts used solely by their own children, especially if the choice of texts has widespread public support from the community? Second, decide what grounds you have to support your views. Bear in mind particularly the following:

1. Give your reasoning. Merely to assert a belief without specifying your reasons for holding it is wholly unconvincing. Perhaps you think people have a constitutional right to choose what to teach their children. Or you may feel that the federal government has no business telling a community what to include in their textbooks. In any event, state not only what you think but why.

2. Find support for your views. Look for testimonials from experts and authorities that back up your views. Cite the credentials of these experts and show how their opinions coincide with yours.

3. Anticipate the opposition. Try to decide what the opposing argument is likely to be to your position and then refute it. For example, if you claim that people do not have the right to ignorance, an opponent might reply that no universal definition of "ignorance" exists. You can counter by showing how your meaning of "ignorance" is commonsensical enough to be broadly accepted by most reasonable people.

4. Show the consequences of your view and your opponent's. For example, assuming you take the con position, you could argue that giving local school boards the right to decide on textbook contents could result in the imposition of the sectarian beliefs of the majority on the minority. You could then demonstrate how this imposition would be contrary to guarantees under the Constitution.

Alternate Writing Assignment

Research the facts of, and write a brief biographical sketch about, the life of John Scopes, the principal behind the famous trial.

HISTORY

IN THE BEGINNING
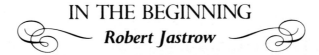 *Robert Jastrow*

Robert Jastrow (b. 1925), American astronomer, is the founder and director of NASA's Goddard Institute for Space Studies, Professor of Astronomy and Geology at Columbia, and Professor of Earth Sciences at Dartmouth College. Born in New York and educated at Columbia University, Jastrow, in addition to serving as a popular television commentator on space science, is also the best-selling author of several books, among them *Until the Sun Dies* (1971), *Red Giants and White Dwarfs* (1979), and *The Enchanted Loom: The Mind of the Universe* (1981).

Reading Advice

Astronomers do not usually pen speculations about God, except when provoked by religious fundamentalists, and their replies on such occasions are likely to be disagreeable and unfriendly. The selection that follows, however, is a refreshing departure from this general rule. In it a well-known astronomer explains the so-called "Big Bang" beginning of the universe—which theorizes that our universe emerged out of an enormous cosmic explosion—and wryly notes its apparent and embarrassing validation of the Genesis myth.

Jastrow's explanations are crisp and nontechnical; his rhetorical framework is narrational. His guiding purpose is partly to inform and argue his premise; but it is also to entertain. He tells of the best minds of several generations scratching for understanding with tools of scientific observation, mathematics, and logic, and finding—to their consternation—that an ancient and primitive people, writing in the darkness of antiquity, may have been right all along in their description of the suddenness with which the universe actually began.

*W*hen an astronomer writes about God, his colleagues assume he is either over the hill or going bonkers. In my case it should be understood from the start that I am an agnostic in religious matters. However, I am fascinated by some strange developments going on in astronomy—partly because of their religious implications and partly because of the peculiar reactions of my colleagues.   1

The essence of the strange developments is that the Universe had, in some sense, a beginning—that it began at a certain moment in time, and under circumstances that seem to make it impossible—not just now, but *ever*—to find out what force or forces brought the world into being at that moment. Was it, as the Bible says, that   2

> "Thou, Lord, in the beginning hast laid the
> foundations of the earth, and the
> heavens are the work of thine hands?"

No scientist can answer that question; we can never tell whether the Prime Mover willed the world into being, or the creative agent was one of the familiar forces of physics; for the astronomical evidence proves that the Universe was created twenty billion years ago in a fiery explosion, and in the searing heat of that first moment, all the evidence needed for a scientific study of the cause of the great explosion was melted down and destroyed.

This is the crux of the new story of Genesis. It has been familiar for years   3
as the "Big Bang" theory, and has shared the limelight with other theories,
especially the Steady State cosmology; but adverse evidence has led to the
abandonment of the Steady State theory by nearly everyone, leaving the Big
Bang theory exposed as the only adequate explanation of the facts.

The general scientific picture that leads to the Big Bang theory is well known.   4
We have been aware for fifty years that we live in an expanding Universe, in
which all the galaxies around us are moving apart from us and one another at
enormous speeds. The Universe is blowing up before our eyes, as if we are
witnessing the aftermath of a gigantic explosion. If we retrace the motions of
the outward-moving galaxies backward in time, we find that they all come
together, so to speak, fifteen or twenty billion years ago.[1]

At that time all the matter in the Universe was packed into a dense mass,   5
at temperatures of many trillions of degrees. The dazzling brilliance of the
radiation in this dense, hot Universe must have been beyond description. The
picture suggests the explosion of a cosmic hydrogen bomb. The instant in which
the cosmic bomb exploded marked the birth of the Universe.

Now we see how the astronomical evidence leads to a biblical view of the   6
origin of the world. The details differ, but the essential elements in the astronomical and biblical accounts of Genesis are the same: the chain of events
leading to man commenced suddenly and sharply at a definite moment in time,
in a flash of light and energy.

Some scientists are unhappy with the idea that the world began in this way.   7
Until recently many of my colleagues preferred the Steady State theory, which
holds that the Universe had no beginning and is eternal. But the latest evidence
makes it almost certain that the Big Bang really did occur many millions of
years ago. In 1965 Arno Penzias and Robert Wilson of the Bell Laboratories
discovered that the earth is bathed in a faint glow of radiation coming from
every direction in the heavens. The measurements showed that the earth itself
could not be the origin of this radiation, nor could the radiation come from
the direction of the moon, the sun, or any other particular object in the sky.
The entire Universe seemed to be the source.

The two physicists were puzzled by their discovery. They were not thinking   8
about the origin of the Universe, and they did not realize that they had stumbled
upon the answer to one of the cosmic mysteries. Scientists who believed in the
theory of the Big Bang had long asserted that the Universe must have resembled
a white-hot fireball in the very first moments after the Big Bang occurred.
Gradually, as the Universe expanded and cooled, the fireball would have become

---

1. The exact moment in which this happened is uncertain by several billion years. Because of this
uncertainty, I have picked twenty billion years, a round number, as *the* age of the Universe. The important
point is not precisely when the cosmic explosion occurred, but that it occurred at a sharply defined
instant some billions of years ago.

less brilliant, but its radiation would have never disappeared entirely. It was the diffuse glow of this ancient radiation, dating back to the birth of the Universe, that Penzias and Wilson apparently discovered.[2]

No explanation other than the Big Bang has been found for the fireball   9
radiation. The clincher, which has convinced almost the last doubting Thomas, is that the radiation discovered by Penzias and Wilson has exactly the pattern of wavelengths expected for the light and heat produced in a great explosion. Supporters of the Steady State theory have tried desperately to find an alternative explanation, but they have failed. At the present time, the Big Bang theory has no competitors.

Theologians generally are delighted with the proof that the Universe had a   10
beginning, but astronomers are curiously upset. Their reactions provide an interesting demonstration of the response of the scientific mind—supposedly a very objective mind—when evidence uncovered by science itself leads to a conflict with the articles of faith in our profession. It turns out that the scientist behaves the way the rest of us do when our beliefs are in conflict with the evidence. We become irritated, we pretend the conflict does not exist, or we paper it over with meaningless phrases.

The First Billion Years

Why did the universe begin in an explosion? What were conditions like before   11
the explosion? Did the Universe even exist prior to that moment? Most astronomers decline to consider these questions. Milne[3] wrote, "We can make no propositions about the state of affairs [in the beginning]; in the Divine act of creation God is unobserved and unwitnessed." More recently, James Peebles, of Princeton University, who has made important contributions to the theory of the expanding Universe, said, "What the Universe was like at day minus one, before the big bang, one has no idea. The equations refuse to tell us, I refuse to speculate."

But assuming that some unknown force brought the Universe into being in   12
a hot and highly compressed state, physicists can predict with confidence what happened thereafter. Because of complications introduced by the branch of physics called quantum mechanics, their predictions do not start in the very instant of the explosion—at which time the density was infinite—but only 10^{-43} seconds after that moment, when the density was a finite, but staggering, 10^{90} tons per cubic inch.[4] At this stage all of the Universe that we can see

---

2. Ralph Alpher and Robert Herman predicted the fireball radiation in 1948 but no one paid attention to their prediction. They were ahead of their time.

3. Edward Milne (1896–1950) British mathematician and astrophysicist.

4. There are no names for numbers this large. Written out, it would fill two lines of the page with zeroes.

today was packed into the space of an atomic nucleus. The pressure and temperature were also extremely high, and the Universe was a fiery sea of radiation, from which particles emerged only to fall back, disappearing and reappearing ceaselessly.

The Universe expanded rapidly, and when it was one second old, the density   13
had fallen to the density of water and the temperature had decreased a billion degrees. At this time the fundamental building blocks of matter—electrons, protons, neutrons, and their antimatter counterparts, as well as the ghostlike particles called neutrinos—condensed out of the sea of hot radiation like droplets of molten steel condensing out of the metallic vapor in a furnace.

The Universe continued to expand, and the temperature dropped further.   14
When it fell to around 10 million degrees, protons and neutrons stuck together in groups of four to form helium nuclei. This happened when the Universe was about three minutes old. Calculations indicate that roughly 30 percent of the hydrogen in the Universe was transformed into helium in this way, in the first three minutes of the Universe's existence.

It might be expected that after helium was formed, other substances would   15
be built up in more complicated nuclear reactions, until all the remaining chemical elements existed. However, the calculations indicate that this does not occur. The reason is that a wide gap exists between helium and the next stable nucleus. By the time helium had been formed, and the next step was about to commence, the temperature and density in the Universe had fallen so low that the gap could not be crossed.

Thus, the theory of the expanding Universe accounts for the presence of an   16
abundance of hydrogen and helium in the Universe, but it fails to explain the existence of carbon, oxygen, iron, gold and all the other chemical elements. Only the story of stellar births and deaths can explain the presence of these substances in the world today.

After the first three minutes, nothing much happened for the next million   17
years. A glow of radiation, left over from the cosmic fireball, pervaded the Universe, obscuring visibility like a thick fog. Particles moved erratically through the fog, colliding with other particles and sometimes with packets of radiant energy.

When the Universe was about one million years old, atoms appeared for   18
the first time. An atom consists of an electron circling in orbit around a nucleus. When the Universe was younger and hotter, any electron captured into an orbit around a nucleus to form an atom was knocked out of its orbit almost immediately, under the smashing impact of the violent collisions that occur at very high temperatures. But by now the temperature had fallen sufficiently so that most electrons could remain in orbit after they were captured. From this moment on, much of the matter in the Universe consisted of atoms.

At the same time the obscuring fog of radiation cleared up, and the Universe   19
suddenly became transparent. The reason for this change was that light, which
is a form of radiation, cannot pass through electrically charged particles, such
as electrons and protons; however, atoms, which are electrically neutral, do not
block radiation appreciably. As soon as the electrons in the Universe had
combined with protons or other nuclei to form atoms, rays of light were able
to travel great distances unhindered, and it became possible to see from one
end of the Universe to the other.[5]

The void of space has remained transparent down to the present day. This   20
fact has enabled astronomers to see far out into the Universe, and far back into
time. In recent years they have photographed quasars—galaxy-like objects of
exceptional brilliance—at distances of 15 billion light years. When we see these
quasars, we observe the Universe as it was 15 billion years ago, only a few
billion years after the beginning cosmic explosion. One might hope that with
an even larger telescope the astronomer could look back to the earliest moments
in the life of the Universe. But now we know that because of the obscuring
fog of radiation, we will never be able to see anything that happened in the
first million years, let alone the first few minutes.

Returning to the main story, with the further passage of time the materials   21
of the expanding Universe cooled and condensed into galaxies, and, within the
galaxies, into stars. The galaxies began to form when the Universe was roughly
one billion years old. The formation of stars probably began shortly after the
formation of the first galaxies. After nearly 20 billion years of continuing
expansion, the Universe reached the state in which it exists today.

Questions for Critical Thinking

1. The author begins by telling us that he is an agnostic in religious matters. What
   is an agnostic, where did the word come from, and why was it necessary for the
   author to disclose this about himself?

2. If science could perform an experiment to categorically prove once and for all
   whether God exists, should it? Why or why not?

3. What do you think would be the effect upon the world's behavior if it could be
   scientifically demonstrated beyond a doubt that God did exist?

4. What do you think would be the effect upon the world's behavior if it could be
   scientifically demonstrated beyond a doubt that God did *not* exist?

---

5. Of course, no eye was present to perceive the Universe. Neither galaxies, stars, planets nor life existed
at that time.

5. Read the selection from Genesis at the beginning of this chapter. In what way does its account of creation tally with the picture of our origins emerging from the scientific evidence? How does it differ?

6. Jastrow accuses scientists of being "curiously upset" by the correspondence between the findings of astronomy and the creation account in Genesis. Why should any scientist be upset at this correspondence?

7. Can you envision any discovery from science that might justify the teaching of creationism in the public schools?

8. According to Carl Sagan, the noted astronomer, saying that God created the universe raises as many questions as it answers. What sort of questions does this assertion raise in your mind?

Writing Assignment

A great scientific discovery has been made proving incontrovertibly that God exists. Write an essay speculating on the effects on human behavior, institutions, and learning such a discovery would likely have.

Writing Advice

Begin by asking yourself what effects on you such a discovery would likely have. Then ask yourself how your family and friends would be affected. Make notes and add whatever sidelights and details you can think of to support your claimed effects.

1. In this assignment, your main point will not be dictated by evidence, facts, opinions, or the findings of experts. Since the premise of the essay is inventive, you alone must decide how you would be affected and changed by any incontrovertible proof of the existence of God. Would you change your personal behavior? Would you alter your career plans? How would your family and friends likely be affected?

2. The supporting details for this essay must come from your own inventiveness and will naturally vary with the kinds of effects you think the discovery likely to exert. For example, if you think that science and scientists as a whole are likely to change, you should say how and give specific supporting examples.

3. The essay should be neither strictly objective or wholly personal, but something in-between. You should naturally use "I" to refer to yourself when you describe how your personal behavior would probably change in the light of this discovery, but you should not deal exclusively with its effects on you. Imagine the consequences on the world as a whole, state them, and supply specific details in support of your speculations.

Alternate Writing Assignments

1. A great scientific discovery has been made proving incontrovertibly that God does *not* exist. Write an essay speculating on the effects on human behavior, institutions, and learning such a discovery would likely have.

2. Do you agree with Jastrow that the latest astronomical thinking closely agrees with the biblical account of creation? Write an essay comparing and contrasting the accounts in Genesis and in Jastrow, showing where they agree and where they differ.

LITERATURE

HEAVEN AND EARTH IN JEST
Annie Dillard

Annie Dillard (b. 1945 in Pittsburgh, Pa.), is an American writer much beloved for her essays and poems about God and nature. Educated at the Ellis School and Hollins College in Virginia, her works include *Tickets for a Prayer Wheel* (poems, 1974); *Pilgrim at Tinker Creek* (essays, 1974), for which she won a Pulitzer Prize; and *Teaching a Stone to Talk* (essays, 1982).

Reading Advice

If this article seems utterly anecdotal and imagistic, it is because the author is trying to convey to us perceptions that are essentially personal, intimate, and philosophical. That there is beauty in the universe is a proposition with which few would take issue. That the beauty has some meaning beyond its effects on our senses, is another issue entirely and one likely to stir argument. Like many nature writers, Dillard is aiming to make her prose photographic. She is depicting vivid scenes that she herself has witnessed in her tramping around Tinker Creek, and she is drawing, or trying to draw, morals and lessons from them.

To read this article, you should begin by shedding any utilitarian expectations you might have about it. Dillard is not trying to teach a skill, sketch a theory, or impart a series of facts. Like a poet, she is partly trying to express the inexpressible, and partly journalizing about her own world and private thoughts. Her organization is primarily episodic, and her examples linked by a thematic thread apparent only in the last

Excerpts from *Pilgrim at Tinker Creek* by Annie Dillard. Copyright © 1974 by Annie Dillard. Reprinted by permission of Harper & Row, Publishers, Inc.

paragraph. But the reward for the persistent reader is a dazzling array of images and descriptions that evoke the variety, wonder, and exquisite beauty of nature.

I used to have a cat, an old fighting tom,   1
who would jump through the open window by my bed in the middle of the night and land on my chest. I'd half-awaken. He'd stick his skull under my nose and purr, stinking of urine and blood. Some nights he kneaded my bare chest with his front paws, powerfully, arching his back, as if sharpening his claws, or pummeling a mother for milk. And some mornings I'd wake in daylight to find my body covered with paw prints in blood; I looked as though I'd been painted with roses.

It was hot, so hot the mirror felt warm. I washed before the mirror in a   2 daze, my twisted summer sleep still hung about me like sea kelp. What blood was this, and what roses? It could have been the rose of union, the blood of murder, or the rose of beauty bare and the blood of some unspeakable sacrifice or birth. The sign on my body could have been an emblem or a stain, the keys to the kingdom or the mark of Cain. I never knew. I never knew as I washed, and the blood streaked, faded, and finally disappeared, whether I'd purified myself or ruined the blood sign of the passover. We wake, if we ever wake at all, to mystery, rumors of death, beauty, violence. . . . "Seem like we're just set down here," a woman said to me recently, "and don't nobody know why."

These are morning matters, pictures you dream as the final wave heaves you   3 up on the sand to the bright light and drying air. You remember pressure, and a curved sleep you rested against, soft, like a scallop in its shell. But the air hardens your skin; you stand; you leave the lighted shore to explore some dim headland, and soon you're lost in the leafy interior, intent, remembering nothing.

I still think of that old tomcat, mornings, when I wake. Things are tamer   4 now; I sleep with the window shut. The cat and our rites are gone and my life is changed, but the memory remains of something powerful playing over me. I wake expectant, hoping to see a new thing. If I'm lucky I might be jogged awake by a strange birdcall. I dress in a hurry, imagining the yard flapping with auks, or flamingos. This morning it was a wood duck, down at the creek. It flew away.

I live by a creek, Tinker Creek, in a valley in Virginia's Blue Ridge. An   5 anchorite's hermitage is called an anchor-hold; some anchor-holds were simple sheds clamped to the side of a church like a barnacle to a rock. I think of this house clamped to the side of Tinker Creek as an anchor-hold. It holds me at anchor to the rock bottom of the creek itself and it keeps me steadied in the current, as a sea anchor does, facing the stream of light pouring down. It's a good place to live; there's a lot to think about. The creeks—Tinker and Carvin's—are an active mystery, fresh every minute. Theirs is the mystery of the continuous creation and all that providence implies: the uncertainty of vision, the horror of the fixed, the dissolution of the present, the intricacy of beauty, the pressure of fecundity, the elusiveness of the free, and the flawed nature of perfection. The mountains—Tinker and Brushy, McAfee's Knob and Dead Man—are a passive mystery, the oldest of all. Theirs is the one simple mystery of creation from nothing, of matter itself, anything at all, the given. Mountains are giant, restful, absorbent. You can heave your spirit into a mountain and the mountain will keep it, folded, and not throw it back as some creeks will. The creeks are the world with all its stimulus and beauty; I live there. But the mountains are home.

The wood duck flew away. I caught only a glimpse of something like a bright   6
torpedo that blasted the leaves where it flew. Back at the house I ate a bowl of oatmeal; much later in the day came the long slant of light that means good walking.

If the day is fine, any walk will do; it all looks good. Water in particular   7
looks its best, reflecting blue sky in the flat, and chopping it into graveled shallows and white chute and foam in the riffles. On a dark day, or a hazy one, everything's washed-out and lack-luster but the water. It carries its own lights. I set out for the railroad tracks, for the hill the flocks fly over, for the woods where the white mare lives. But I go to the water.

Today is one of those excellent January partly cloudies in which light chooses   8
an unexpected part of the landscape to trick out in gilt, and then shadow sweeps it away. You know you're alive. You take huge steps, trying to feel the planet's roundness arc between your feet. Kazantzakis says that when he was young he had a canary and a globe. When he freed the canary, it would perch on the globe and sing. All his life, wandering the earth, he felt as though he had a canary on top of his mind, singing.

West of the house, Tinker Creek makes a sharp loop, so that the creek is   9
both in back of the house, south of me, and also on the other side of the road, north of me. I like to go north. There the afternoon sun hits the creek just right, deepening the reflected blue and lighting the sides of trees on the banks. Steers from the pasture across the creek come down to drink; I always flush a rabbit or two there; I sit on a fallen trunk in the shade and watch the squirrels in the sun. There are two separated wooden fences suspended from cables that cross the creek just upstream from my tree-trunk bench. They keep the steers from escaping up or down the creek when they come to drink. Squirrels, the neighborhood children, and I use the downstream fence as a swaying bridge across the creek. But the steers are there today.

I sit on the downed tree and watch the black steers slip on the creek bottom. 10
They are all bred beef: beef heart, beef hide, beef hocks. They're a human
product like rayon. They're like a field of shoes. They have cast-iron shanks and
tongues like foam insoles. You can't see through to their brains as you can with
other animals; they have beef fat behind their eyes, beef stew.

I cross the fence six feet above the water, walking my hands down the rusty 11
cable and tightroping my feet along the narrow edge of the planks. When I hit
the other bank and terra firma,[1] some steers are bunched in a knot between
me and the barbed-wire fence I want to cross. So I suddenly rush at them in
an enthusiastic sprint, flailing my arms and hollering, "Lightning! Copperhead!
Swedish meatballs!" They flee, still in a knot, stumbling across the flat pasture.
I stand with the wind on my face.

When I slide under a barbed-wire fence, cross a field, and run over a 12
sycamore trunk felled across the water, I'm on a little island shaped like a tear
in the middle of Tinker Creek. On one side of the creek is a steep forested
bank; the water is swift and deep on that side of the island. On the other side
is the level field I walked through next to the steers' pasture; the water between
the field and the island is shallow and sluggish. In summer's low water, flags
and bulrushes grow along a series of shallow pools cooled by the lazy current.
Water striders patrol the surface film, crayfish hump along the silt bottom
eating filth, frogs shout and glare, and shiners and small bream hide among
roots from the sulky green heron's eye. I come to this island every month of
the year. I walk around it, stopping and staring, or I straddle the sycamore log
over the creek, curling my legs out of the water in winter, trying to read. Today
I sit on dry grass at the end of the island by the slower side of the creek. I'm
drawn to this spot. I come to it as to an oracle; I return to it as a man years
later will seek out the battlefield where he lost a leg or an arm.

A couple of summers ago I was walking along the edge of the island to see 13
what I could see in the water, and mainly to scare frogs. Frogs have an inelegant
way of taking off from invisible positions on the bank just ahead of your feet,
in dire panic, emitting a froggy "Yike!" and splashing into the water. Incredibly,
this amused me, and, incredibly, it amuses me still. As I walked along the grassy
edge of the island, I got better and better at seeing frogs both in and out of
the water. I learned to recognize, slowing down, the difference in texture of
the light reflected from mudbank, water, grass, or frog. Frogs were flying all
around me. At the end of the island I noticed a small green frog. He was exactly
half in and half out of the water, looking like a schematic diagram of an
amphibian, and he didn't jump.

He didn't jump; I crept closer. At last I knelt on the island's winter-killed 14
grass, lost, dumbstruck, staring at the frog in the creek just four feet away. He

---

1. From Latin for "firm earth."

was a very small frog with wide, dull eyes. And just as I looked at him, he slowly crumpled and began to sag. The spirit vanished from his eyes as if snuffed. His skin emptied and drooped; his very skull seemed to collapse and settle like a kicked tent. He was shrinking before my eyes like a deflating football. I watched the taut, glistening skin on his shoulders ruck, and rumple, and fall. Soon, part of his skin, formless as a pricked balloon, lay in floating folds like bright scum on the top of the water: it was a monstrous and terrifying thing. I gaped bewildered, appalled. An oval shadow hung in the water behind the drained frog; then the shadow glided away. The frog skin bag started to sink.

I had read about the giant water bug, but never seen one. "Giant water bug"   15 is really the name of the creature, which is an enormous, heavy-bodied, brown insect. It eats other insects, tadpoles, fish, and frogs. Its grasping forelegs are mighty and hooked inward. It seizes a victim with these legs, hugs it tight, and paralyzes it with enzymes injected during a vicious bite. That one bite is the only bite it ever takes. Through the puncture shoot the poisons that dissolve the victim's muscles and bones and organs—all but the skin—and through it the giant water bug sucks out the victim's body, reduced to a juice. This event is quite common in warm fresh water. The frog I saw was being sucked by a giant water bug. I had been kneeling on the island grass; when the unrecognizable flap of frog skin settled on the creek bottom, swaying, I stood up and brushed the knees of my pants. I couldn't catch my breath.

Of course, many carnivorous animals devour their prey alive. The usual   16 method seems to be to subdue the victim by downing or grasping it so it can't flee, then eating it whole or in a series of bloody bites. Frogs eat everything whole, stuffing prey into their mouths with their thumbs. People have seen frogs with their wide jaws so full of live dragonflies they couldn't close them. Ants don't even have to catch their prey; in the spring they swarm over newly hatched, featherless birds in the nest and eat them tiny bite by bite.

That it's rough out there and chancy is no surprise. Every live thing is a   17 survivor on a kind of extended emergency bivouac. But at the same time we are also created. In the Koran, Allah asks, "The heaven and the earth and all in between, thinkest thou I made them *in jest?*" It's a good question. What do we think of the created universe, spanning an unthinkable void with an unthinkable profusion of forms? Or what do we think of nothingness, those sickening reaches of time in either direction? If the giant water bug was not made in jest, was it then made in earnest? Pascal[2] uses a nice term to describe the notion of the creator's, once having called forth the universe, turning his back to it: *Deus Absconditus.*[3] Is this what we think happened? Was the sense of it there, and God absconded with it, ate it, like a wolf who disappears round the edge of the house with the Thanksgiving turkey? "God is subtle," Einstein said, "but

2. Blaise Pascal (1623–1662) French philosopher and mathematician.
3. From Latin for "the vanished God."

not malicious." Again, Einstein said that "nature conceals her mystery by means of her essential grandeur, not by her cunning." It could be that God has not absconded but spread, as our vision and understanding of the universe have spread, to a fabric of spirit and sense so grand and subtle, so powerful in a new way, that we can only feel blindly of its hem. In making the thick darkness a swaddling band for the sea, God "set bars and doors" and said, "Hitherto shalt thou come, but no further." But have we come even that far? Have we rowed out to the thick darkness, or are we all playing pinochle in the bottom of the boat?

Cruelty is a mystery, and the waste of pain. But if we describe a world to compass these things, a world that is a long, brute game, then we bump against another mystery: the inrush of power and light, the canary that sings on the skull. Unless all ages and races of men have been deluded by the same mass hypnotist (who?), there seems to be such a thing as beauty, a grace wholly gratuitous. About five years ago I saw a mockingbird make a straight vertical descent from the roof gutter of a four-story building. It was an act as careless and spontaneous as the curl of a stem or the kindling of a star.   18

The mockingbird took a single step into the air and dropped. His wings were still folded against his sides as though he were singing from a limb and not falling, accelerating thirty-two feet per second per second, through empty air. Just a breath before he would have been dashed to the ground, he unfurled his wings with exact, deliberate care, revealing the broad bars of white, spread his elegant, white-banded tail, and so floated onto the grass. I had just rounded a corner when his insouciant step caught my eye; there was no one else in sight. The fact of his free fall was like the old philosophical conundrum about the tree that falls in the forest. The answer must be, I think, that beauty and grace are performed whether or not we will or sense them. The least we can do is try to be there.   19

Another time I saw another wonder: sharks off the Atlantic coast of Florida. There is a way a wave rises above the ocean horizon, a triangular wedge against the sky. If you stand where the ocean breaks on a shallow beach, you see the raised water in a wave is translucent, shot with lights. One late afternoon at low tide a hundred big sharks passed the beach near the mouth of a tidal river in a feeding frenzy. As each green wave rose from the churning water, it illuminated within itself the six- or eight-foot-long bodies of twisting sharks. The sharks disappeared as each wave rolled toward me; then a new wave would swell above the horizon, containing in it, like scorpions in amber, sharks that roiled and heaved. The sight held awesome wonders: power and beauty, grace tangled in a rapture with violence.   20

We don't know what's going on here. If these tremendous events are random combinations of matter run amok, the yield of millions of monkeys at millions of typewriters, then what is it in us, hammered out of those same typewriters,   21 that they ignite? We don't know. Our life is a faint tracing on the surface of mystery, like the idle, curved tunnels of leaf miners on the face of a leaf. We must somehow take a wider view, look at the whole landscape, really see it, and describe what's going on here. Then we can at least wail the right question into the swaddling band of darkness, or, if it comes to that, choir the proper praise.

Questions for Critical Thinking

1. The author opens with an anecdote about her old tomcat. What information can you infer about her from this anecdote?

2. The author ends her second paragraph by quoting an unidentified woman. What is the purpose of this quotation?

3. How do you think a hard-headed realist would likely reply to the author's claim that beauty is a mystery?

4. Do you agree with the author that beauty and grace are performed whether or not anyone is there to witness them? Why or why not?

5. What does the author mean by saying that we "can at least wail the right question into the swaddling band of darkness, or, if it comes to that, choir the proper praise." Who is likely to "wail" a question? Who, to "choir the proper praise"? To which group do you belong?

6. If you number yourself among the wailers, what question would you likely wail at the "swaddling band of darkness"?

7. What personally satisfying answer can you give to the author's rhetorical question: "If these tremendous events are random combinations of matter run amok, the yield of millions of monkeys at millions of typewriters, then what is it in us, hammered out of these same typewriters, that they ignite?"

Writing Assignment

Following Dillard's example, write an essay describing your favorite nature haunt.

Writing Advice

Good description is based on a dominant impression, selective observations, and the use of vivid imagery. By "dominant impression" we mean the primary characteristic of the subject you are describing. You should express this dominant impression as accurately as possible in a single sentence or a few sentences, which will serve as your theme. Dillard, for example, sees Tinker Creek as a place where the mystery and vagaries of creation are everywhere, and once she has enunciated that major impression, she selects appropriate details and examples that support it.

To capture the intensity of a dominant impression, the descriptive writer often sacrifices fidelity to absolute fact. Dillard's Tinker Creek, for example, cannot be perpetually bursting with mystery and beauty. If it is like any ordinary creek, it surely must occasionally seem boring, dirty, drab, humdrum, and common. However, the descriptive writer is not trying to capture what is commonplace but only what has made an indelible impression on his or her senses. That impression will be the major point or thesis of the descriptive essay.

If the factual essay supports opinion with data and facts, the descriptive essay supports a dominant impression with images, adjectives, and descriptive details. These images can include outright comparisons—"summer sleep still hung around me like sea kelp"—called similes, or the implied comparison of a metaphor—"water . . . chopping blue sky into graveled shadows."

Straight off we can tell you that the only certain route to vivid imagery is the hard labor of incessant rewriting. Again and again have descriptive writers testified to this fact. The apt word, adjective, image, simile or metaphor only rarely springs from the writer's pen in one spontaneous leap. More often than not, the writer has had to sit, hunched over paper and desk for minutes and hours, scratching and groping for just the right descriptive phrase. When it comes, however, it seems so natural and right that a reader is likely to think its discovery effortless. It rarely is.

Remember that your aim is not to "write pretty" but to write vividly and that it is therefore wiser to be spare and accurate in your imagery than overripe and lush. The effect of an inept adjective or, even worse, a forced image, is one of a lingering bad aftertaste. Sometimes the apt image is more striking when set off by itself in the paragraph than when diminished by the presence of drabber cousins.

Don't overlook the powerful effect that can come from the simple enumeration of what you see. Every visual does not have to be prettied with an image or metaphor. Here, for example, is Dillard telling us plainly and in almost a cataloging fashion what lies about her: "West of the house, Tinker Creek makes a sharp loop, so that the creek is both in the back of the house, south of me, and also on the other side of the road, north of me. There the afternoon sun hits the creek just right, deepening the reflected blue and lighting the sides of the trees on the banks. Steers from the pasture across the creek come down to drink; I always flush a rabbit or two there; I sit on a fallen trunk in the shade and watch the squirrels in the sun." This gives us a very clear idea of what Tinker Creek looks like and does so in plain language.

Alternate Writing Assignment

Dillard is justly celebrated for her colorful, descriptive prose. Write an essay analyzing her use of language and imagery in her descriptions. Pay close attention to her construction of metaphors and similes.

LITERATURE

AT DAYBREAK
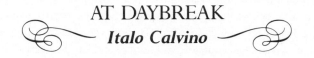
Italo Calvino

Italo Calvino (b. 1923 in San Remo, Italy) is one of Italy's foremost writers. An essayist, writer and journalist, Calvino joined the partisans and fought against the Germans during World War II. Later, his stories about these experiences won him worldwide acclaim. Many of his numerous books have been translated into English, among them *The Path to the Nest of Spiders* (1947, winner of the Premio Riccione prize in Italy) and *Cosmicomics* (1968).

Reading Advice

It is the dawn of the universe, when the blackness of the immensities is little more than a chilly soup of nebulae, star dust, and whirling galactic debris. Living on a condensing nebula is a family composed of typical and distinctly recognizable character types. An elderly gentleman, with an unpronounceable name, is recollecting what life was like back then during his childhood when the seeping pseudopods of the nebula began to harden and take on a lumpy solidity.

This is the farfetched premise of "At Daybreak" and one that may require the reader to exercise what the English critic Samuel Taylor Coleridge (1772–1834) called a "suspension of disbelief," meaning a willingness to temporarily suspend strict acceptance of reality and enter into the imaginative world of the literary work. Calvino's story not only amuses us with its outlandish humor but also faithfully and imaginatively sketches what the universe must have looked like then, had there been a human eye to gaze upon the coiling and spinning brew.

*T*he planets of the solar system, G. P. Kuiper explains, began to solidify in the darkness, through the condensation of a fluid, shapeless nebula. All was cold and dark. Later the Sun began to become more concentrated until it was reduced almost to its present dimensions, and in this process the temperature rose and rose, to thousands of degrees, and the Sun started emitting radiations in space.

Pitch-dark it was,—*old Qfwfq confirmed,*—I was only a child, I can barely remember it. We were there, as usual, with Father and Mother, Granny Bb'b, some uncles and aunts who were visiting, Mr. Hnw, the one who later became a horse, and us little ones. I think I've told you before the way we lived on the nebulae: it was like lying down, we were flat and very still, turning as they turned. Not that we were lying outside, you understand, on the nebula's surface; no, it was too cold out there. We were underneath, as if we had been tucked in under a layer of fluid, grainy matter. There was no way of telling time; whenever we started counting the nebula's turns there were disagreements, because we didn't have any reference points in the darkness, and we ended up arguing. So we preferred to let the centuries flow by as if they were minutes; there was nothing to do but wait, keep covered as best we could, doze, speak out now and then to make sure we were all still there; and, naturally, scratch ourselves; because—they can say what they like—all those particles spinning around had only one effect, a troublesome itching.

What we were waiting for, nobody could have said; to be sure, Granny Bb'b remembered back to the times when matter was uniformly scattered in space, and there was heat and light; even allowing for all the exaggerations there must have been in those old folks' tales, those times had surely been better in some ways, or at least different; but as far as we were concerned, we just had to get through that enormous night.

My sister G'd(w)^n fared the best, thanks to her introverted nature: she was a shy girl and she loved the dark. For herself, G'd(w)^n always chose to stay in places that were a bit removed, at the edge of the nebula, and she would contemplate the blackness, and toy with the little grains of dust in tiny cascades, and talk to herself, with faint bursts of laughter that were like tiny cascades of dust, and—waking or sleeping—she abandoned herself to dreams. They weren't dreams like ours (in the midst of the darkness, we dreamed of more darkness, because nothing else came into our minds); no, she dreamed—from what we could understand of her ravings—of a darkness a hundred times deeper and more various and velvety.

My father was the first to notice something was changing. I had dozed off, when his shout wakened me: "Watch out! We're hitting something!"

Beneath us, the nebula's matter, instead of fluid as it had always been, was beginning to condense.

To tell the truth, my mother had been tossing and turning for several hours, saying; "Uff, I just can't seem to make myself comfortable here!" In other words, according to her, she had become aware of a change in the place where she was lying: the dust wasn't the same as it had been before, soft, elastic, uniform, so you could wallow in it as much as you liked without leaving any print; instead, a kind of rut or furrow was being formed, especially where she was accustomed to resting all her weight. And she thought she could feel underneath her something like granules or blobs or bumps; which perhaps, after all, were buried hundreds of miles farther down and were pressing through all those layers of soft dust. Not that we generally paid much attention to these premonitions of my mother's: poor thing, for a hypersensitive creature like herself, and already well along in years, our way of life then was hardly ideal for the nerves.

And then it was my brother Rwzfs, an infant at the time; at a certain point   7
I felt him—who knows?—slamming or digging or writhing in some way, and I asked: "What are you doing?" And he said: "I'm playing."

"Playing? With what?"   8

"With a thing," he said.   9

You understand? It was the first time. There had never been things to play   10
with before. And how could we have played? With that pap of gaseous matter? Some fun: that sort of stuff was all right perhaps for my sister G'd(w)^n. If Rwzfs was playing, it meant he had found something new: in fact, afterwards, exaggerating as usual, they said he had found a pebble. It wasn't a pebble, but it was surely a collection of more solid matter or—let's say—something less gaseous. He was never very clear on this point; that is, he told stories, as they occurred to him, and when the period came when nickel was formed and nobody talked of anything but nickel, he said: "That's it: it was nickel. I was playing with some nickel!" So afterwards he was always called "Nickel Rwzfs." (It wasn't, as some say now, that he had turned into nickel, unable—retarded as he was—to go beyond the mineral phase; it was a different thing altogether, and I only mention this out of love for truth, not because he was my brother: he had always been a bit backward, true enough, but not of the metallic type, if anything a bit colloidal; in fact, when he was still very young, he married an alga, one of the first, and we never heard from him again.)

In short, it seemed everyone had felt something: except me. Maybe it's   11
because I'm absent-minded. I heard—I don't know whether awake or asleep— our father's cry: "We're hitting something!," a meaningless expression (since before then nothing had ever hit anything, you can be sure), but one that took on meaning at the very moment it was uttered, that is, it meant the sensation we were beginning to experience, slightly nauseating, like a slab of mud passing under us, something flat, on which we felt we were bouncing. And I said, in a reproachful tone: "Oh, Granny!"

Afterwards I often asked myself why my first reaction was to become angry   12
with our grandmother. Granny Bb'b, who clung to her habits of the old days, often did embarrassing things: she continued to believe that matter was in uniform expansion and, for example, that it was enough to throw refuse anywhere and it would rarefy and disappear into the distance. The fact that the

process of condensation had begun some while ago, that is, that dirt thickened on particles so we weren't able to get rid of it—she couldn't get this into her head. So in some obscure way I connected this new fact of "hitting" with some mistake my grandmother might have made and I let out that cry.

Then Granny Bb'b answered: "What is it? Have you found my cushion?"   13

This cushion was a little ellipsoid of galactic matter Granny had found   14 somewhere or other during the first cataclysms of the universe; and she always carried it around with her, to sit on. At a certain point, during the great night, it had been lost, and she accused me of having hidden it from her. Now, it was true I had always hated that cushion, it seemed so vulgar and out of place on our nebula, but the most Granny could blame me for was not having guarded it always as she had wanted me to.

Even my father, who was always very respectful toward her, couldn't help   15 remarking: "Oh see here, Mamma, something is happening—we don't know what—and you go on about that cushion!"

"Ah, I told you I couldn't get to sleep!" my mother said: another remark   16 hardly appropriate to the situation.

At that point we heard a great "Pwack! Wack Sgrr!" and we realized that   17 something must have happened to Mr. Hnw: he was hawking and spitting for all he was worth.

"Mr. Hnw! Mr. Hnw! Get hold of yourself! Where's he got to now?" my   18 father started saying, and in that darkness, still without a ray of light, we managed to grope until we found him and could hoist him onto the surface of the nebula, where he caught his breath again. We laid him out on that external layer which was then taking on a clotted, slippery consistency.

"Wrrak! This stuff closes on you!" Mr. Hnw tried to say, though he didn't   19 have a great gift for self-expression. "You go down and down, and you swallow! Skrrrack!" He spat.

There was another novelty: if you weren't careful, you could now sink on   20 the nebula. My mother, with a mother's instinct, was the first to realize it. And she cried: "Children: are you all there? Where are you?"

The truth was that we were a bit confused, and whereas before, when   21 everything had been lying regularly for centuries, we were always careful not to scatter, now we had forgotten all about it.

"Keep calm. Nobody must stray," my father said.   22

"G'd(w)^n! Where are you? And the twins? Has anybody seen the twins?   23 Speak up!"

Nobody answered. "Oh, my goodness, they're lost!" Mother shouted. My   24 little brothers weren't yet old enough to know how to transmit any message: so they got lost easily and had to be watched over constantly. "I'll go look for them!" I said.

"Good for you, Qfwfq, yes, go!" Father and Mother said, then, immediately   25
repentant: "But if you do go, you'll be lost, too! No, stay here. Oh, all right,
go, but let us know where you are: whistle!"

I began to walk in the darkness, in the marshy condensation of that nebula,   26
emitting a constant whistle. I say "walk"; I mean a way of moving over the
surface, inconceivable until a few minutes earlier, and it was already an achievement to attempt it now, because the matter offered such little resistance that,
if you weren't careful, instead of proceeding on the surface you sank sideways
or even vertically and were buried. But in whatever direction I went and at
whatever level, the chances of finding the twins remained the same: who could
guess where the two of them had got to?

All of a sudden I sprawled; as if they had—we would say today—tripped   27
me up. It was the first time I had fallen, I didn't know what "to fall" was, but
we were still on the softness and I didn't hurt myself. "Don't trample here," a
voice said, "I don't want you to, Qfwfq." It was the voice of my sister G'd(w)^n.

"Why? What's there?"   28

"I made some things with things . . ." she said. It took me a while to realize,   29
groping, that my sister, messing about with that sort of mud, had built up a
little hill, all full of pinnacles, spires, and battlements.

"What have you done there?"   30

G'd(w)^n never gave you a straight answer. "An outside with an inside in it."   31

I continued my walk, falling every now and then. I also stumbled over the   32
inevitable Mr. Hnw, who was stuck in the condensing matter again, head-first.
"Come, Mr. Hnw. Mr. Hnw! Can't you possibly stay erect?" and I had to help
him pull himself out once more, this time pushing him from below, because I
was also completely immersed.

Mr. Hnw, coughing and puffing and sneezing (it had never been so icy cold   33
before), popped up on the surface at the very spot where Granny Bb'b was
sitting. Granny flew into the air, immediately overcome with emotion: "My
grandchildren! My grandchildren are back!"

"No, no, Mamma. Look, it's Mr. Hnw!" Everything was confused.   34

"But the grandchildren?"   35

"They're here!" I shouted, "and the cushion is here, too!"   36

The twins must long before have made a secret hiding place for themselves   37
in the thickness of the nebula, and they had hidden the cushion there, to play
with. As long as matter had been fluid, they could float in there and do
somersaults through the round cushion, but now they were imprisoned in a
kind of spongy cream: the cushion's central hole was clogged up, and they felt
crushed on all sides.

"Hang on to the cushion," I tried to make them understand. "I'll pull you   38
out, you little fools!" I pulled and pulled and, at a certain point, before they

knew what was happening, they were already rolling about on the surface, now covered with a scabby film like the white of an egg. The cushion, instead, dissolved as soon as it emerged. There was no use trying to understand the phenomena that took place in those days; and there was no use trying to explain to Granny Bb'b.

Just then, as if they couldn't have chosen a better moment, our visiting relatives got up slowly and said: "Well, it's getting late; I wonder what our children are up to. We're a little worried about them. It's been nice seeing all of you again, but we'd better be getting along."   39

Nobody could say they were wrong; in fact, they should have taken fright and run off long since; but this couple, perhaps because of the out-of-the-way place where they lived, were a bit gauche. Perhaps they had been on pins and needles all this time and hadn't dared say so.   40

My father said: "Well, if you want to go, I won't try to keep you. But think it over: maybe it would be wiser to stay until the situation's cleared up a bit, because as things stand now, you don't know what sort of risk you might be running." Good common sense, in short.   41

But they insisted: "No, no, thanks all the same. It's been a real nice get-together, but we won't intrude on you any longer," and more nonsense of the sort. In other words, we may not have understood very much of the situation, but they had no notion of it at all.   42

There were three of them: an aunt and two uncles, all three very tall and practically identical; we never really understood which uncle was the husband and which the brother, or exactly how they were related to us: in those days there were many things that were left vague.   43

They began to go off, one at a time, each in a different direction, toward the black sky, and every now and then, as if to maintain contact, they cried: "Oh! Oh!" They always acted like this: they weren't capable of behaving with any sort of system.   44

They had hardly left when their cries of "Oh! Oh!" could be heard from very distant points, though they ought to have been still only a few paces away. And we could also hear some exclamations of theirs, whose meaning we couldn't understand: "Why, it's hollow here!" "You can't get past this spot!" "Then why don't you come here?" "Where are you?" "Jump!" "Fine! And what do I jump over?" "Oh, but now we're heading back again!" In other words, everything was incomprehensible, except the fact that some enormous distances were stretching out between us and those relatives.   45

It was our aunt, the last to leave, whose yells made the most sense: "Here I am, all alone, stuck on top of a piece of this stuff that's come loose . . ."   46

And the voices of the two uncles, weak now in the distance, repeated: "Fool . . . Fool . . . Fool . . ."   47

We were peering into this darkness, crisscrossed with voices, when the   48
change took place: the only real, great change I've ever happened to witness,
and compared to it the rest is nothing. I mean this thing that began at the
horizon, this vibration which didn't resemble those we then called sounds, or
those now called the "hitting" vibrations, or any others; a kind of eruption,
distant surely, and yet, at the same time, it made what was close come closer;
in other words, all the darkness was suddenly dark in contrast with something
else that wasn't darkness, namely light. As soon as we could make a more careful
analysis of the situation, it turned out that: first, the sky was dark as before
but was beginning to be not so dark; second, the surface where we were was
all bumpy and crusty, an ice so dirty it was revolting, which was rapidly
dissolving because the temperature was rising at full speed; and, third, there
was what we would later have called a source of light, that is, a mass that was
becoming incandescent, separated from us by an enormous empty space, and
it seemed to be trying out all the colors one by one, in iridescent fits and starts.
And there was more: in the midst of the sky, between us and that incandescent
mass, a couple of islands, brightly lighted and vague, which whirled in the void
with our uncles on them and other people, reduced to distant shadows, letting
out a kind of chirping noise.

So the better part was done: the heart of the nebula, contracting, had   49
developed warmth and light, and now there was the Sun. All the rest went on
revolving nearby, divided and clotted into various pieces, Mercury, Venus, the
Earth, and others farther on, and whoever was on them, stayed where he was.
And, above all, it was deathly hot.

We stood there, open-mouthed, erect, except for Mr. Hnw who was on all   50
fours, to be on the safe side. And my grandmother! How she laughed! As I said
before, Granny Bb'b dated from the age of diffused luminosity, and all through
this dark time she had kept saying that any minute things would go back the
way they had been in the old days. Now her moment seemed to have come;
for a while she tried to act casual, the sort of person who accepts anything
that happens as perfectly natural; then, seeing we paid her no attention, she
started laughing and calling us: "Bunch of ignorant louts . . . Knownothings
. . ."

She wasn't speaking quite in good faith, however; unless her memory by   51
then had begun to fail her. My father, understanding what little he did, said to
her, prudently as always: "Mamma, I know what you mean, but really, this
seems quite a different phenomenon . . ." And he pointed to the terrain: "Look
down!" he exclaimed.

We lowered our eyes. The Earth which supported us was still a gelatinous,   52
diaphanous mass, growing more and more firm and opaque, beginning from
the center where a kind of yolk was thickening; but still our eyes managed to

penetrate through it, illuminated as it was by that first Sun. And in the midst of this kind of transparent bubble we saw a shadow moving, as if swimming and flying. And our mother said: "Daughter!"

We all recognized $G'd(w)^n$: frightened perhaps by the Sun's catching fire, 53 following a reaction of her shy spirit, she had sunk into the condensing matter of the Earth, and now she was trying to clear a path for herself in the depths of the planet, and she looked like a gold and silver butterfly as she passed into a zone that was still illuminated and diaphanous or vanished into the sphere of shadow that was growing wider and wider.

"$G'd(w)^n$! $G'd(w)^n$!" we shouted and flung ourselves on the ground, also 54 trying to clear a way, to reach her. But the Earth's surface now was coagulating more and more into a porous husk, and my brother Rwzfs, who had managed to stick his head into a fissure, was almost strangled.

Then she was seen no more: the solid zone now occupied the whole central 55 part of the planet. My sister had remained in there, and I never found out whether she had stayed buried in those depths or whether she had reached safety on the other side until I met her, much later, at Canberra in 1912, married to a certain Sullivan, a retired railroad man, so changed I hardly recognized her.

We got up. Mr. Hnw and Granny were in front of us, crying, surrounded 56 by pale blue-and-gold flames.

"Rwzfs! Why have you set fire to Granny?" Father began to scold, but, 57 turning toward my brother, he saw that Rwzfs was also enveloped in flames. And so was my father, and my mother, too, and I—we were all burning in the fire. Or rather: we weren't burning, we were immersed in it as in a dazzling forest; the flames shot high over the whole surface of the planet, a fiery air in which we could run and float and fly, and we were gripped by a kind of new joy.

The Sun's radiations were burning the envelopes of the planets, made of 58 helium and hydrogen: in the sky, where our uncles and aunt were, fiery globes spun, dragging after them long beards of gold and turquoise, as a comet drags its tail.

The darkness came back. By now we were sure that everything that could 59 possibly happen had happened, and "yes, this is the end," Grandmother said, "mind what us old folks say . . ." Instead, the Earth had merely made one of its turns. It was night. Everything was just beginning.

Questions for Critical Thinking

1. What point do the prefacing remarks by G. P. Kuiper serve?
2. What primary technique does the author use to engage our interest in a story whose premise is preposterous?

3. Why does the author give his characters such odd and unpronounceable names?

4. Anticlimax is the use of lesser or more trivial details when the reader expects something greater or more serious. Point to at least one successful use of anticlimax in this narrative.

5. What recognizable character types does the author depict as family members in this story? How many of these stereotypical family types can you recognize?

6. The author writes: "G'd(w)n never gave you a straight answer. 'An outside with an inside in it.' " What does he seem to be making fun of here?

7. Which of the two pieces, Jastrow's or Calvino's, gives the more vivid depiction of possible conditions at the dawn of the universe?

8. How would you characterize the author's tone? How does the tone contribute to the sense of believability in this story?

Writing Assignment

Calvino's fictional family is composed of some distinctly recognizable character types. Write an essay discussing these types and describing the traits that make them so highly recognizable.

Writing Advice

This assignment calls for you to closely read the text and identify the character types the author uses in telling his story. Identifying and describing these types will constitute your main point. Your supporting details will be drawn from the text itself and consist of dialogue, action, and traits that confirm your interpretations. In delineating your character types, you may draw comparisons between them and similar ones that have appeared in popular literature and television sitcoms.

A finite number of ways exist for an author to depict a character. We know about a character from what the author personally tells us, what the character does or says, and what other characters tell us. For example, the character of Granny Bb'b is depicted partly by the narrator's memory of her—he tells us that she had a favorite gaseous cushion and was always talking about the old days that she felt certain would soon return. We learn from him that she frequently embarrassed the family and that she was hard-headed in her beliefs. Granny's dialogue is scanty, and what little she does say confirms the narrator's impression of her as a slightly fuddled but basically good-hearted grandmother. She is, in short, little different from umpteen other grandmotherly types common in sitcoms and pulp magazines.

To do this assignment, first make a list of the major characters in the story and then try to find the traits that stereotype them. For example, what "maternal" traits does the author attribute to the mother? What "paternal" traits to the father? What type of character is the sister? How is the little brother described? What does he do or say to make him instantly identifiable as the typical little brother of family dramas?

In writing your essay, you should not merely sketch the character types without backing up your descriptions of them with specific references to the text. For example, if you depict the sister, G'd(w)^n, as a dreamy teenager, you should cite passages from the text that support this interpretation. The aim of this exercise is to teach you not only to draw broad inferences from a text but also to support them with specifics.

Alternate Writing Assignment

Following Calvino's lead, recollect and tell the story of the temptation of Adam and Eve and their expulsion from Eden as if you had personally witnessed it.

LITERATURE

THE STAR

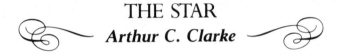

Arthur C. Clarke

Arthur C. Clarke (b. 1917, Somerset, England) writer and physicist, is the author of hundreds of science-fiction short stories, several nonfiction books, many noteworthy novels, and the screenplay, regarded as a classic, of the movie *2001: A Space Odyssey*. A graduate of King's College, University of London, Clarke was briefly the editor of *Science Abstracts* before launching his career as a speculative science-fiction writer. His nonfiction books include *Interplanetary Flight* (1950), and *The Making of a Moon* (1957). Numbered among his novels are *The Sounds of Mars* (1951) and *Rendezvous with Rama* (1974). His hundreds of stories have been collected in various volumes, including *The Other Side of the Story* (1958), and *The Nine Billion Names of God* (1955).

Reading advice

Science fiction differs from ordinary fiction not so much in character or action as in time and place. Nearly always it takes place in a future time and place where extraordinary inventions and devices exist and where astounding feats and events are possible. The skilled "sci-fi" writer will begin by immediately "roping off" the arena of the story and hinting at what is possible in this imaginary landscape, exactly what Clarke does in his opening paragraph. To read and relish such a story, we must accept the technology of this fictional time and place as a given and concede to the author that his characters possess powers and skills beyond our own. In short, we must employ the same suspension of disbelief we advocated for reading "At Daybreak" by Italo Calvino.

When it is written to be argumentative, as this one surely is, the sci-fi short story can be a powerful piece of imaginative logic. Arthur C. Clarke is a master of constructing fictional scenarios that pose provocative questions about the nature of man, life, and God. With deft and sure exposition, Clarke takes us aboard a space ship sailing for earth, and into the thoughts and feelings of a Jesuit astronomer who has just made a discovery so stupendous that he fears it threatens the very existence of his order. We do not learn until the very end what momentous truth he has unearthed: and when we do find out, we are left—as much of Clarke's fiction often leaves us—with some troubling questions.

*I*t is three thousand light-years to the   1
Vatican. Once, I believed that space could have no power over faith, just as I believed that the heavens declared the glory of God's handiwork. Now I have seen that handiwork, and my faith is sorely troubled. I stare at the crucifix that hangs on the cabin wall above the Mark VI Computer, and for the first time in my life I wonder if it is no more than an empty symbol.

I have told no one yet, but the truth cannot be concealed. The facts are   2
there for all to read, recorded on the countless miles of magnetic tape and the thousands of photographs we are carrying back to Earth. Other scientists can interpret them as easily as I can, and I am not one who would condone that tampering with the truth which often gave my order a bad name in the olden days.

The crew were already sufficiently depressed: I wonder how they will take   3
this ultimate irony. Few of them have any religious faith, yet they will not relish using this final weapon in their campaign against me—that private, good-natured, but fundamentally serious war which lasted all the way from Earth. It amused them to have a Jesuit as chief astrophysicist: Dr. Chandler, for instance, could never get over it. (Why are medical men such notorious atheists?) Sometimes he would meet me on the observation deck, where the lights are always low so that the stars shine with undiminished glory. He would come up to me in the gloom and stand staring out of the great oval port, while the heavens crawled slowly around us as the ship turned end over end with the residual spin we had never bothered to correct.

"Well, Father," he would say at last, "it goes on forever and forever, and   4
perhaps *Something* made it. But how you can believe that Something has a special interest in us and our miserable little world—that just beats me." Then the

argument would start, while the stars and nebulae would swing around us in silent, endless arcs beyond the flawlessly clear plastic of the observation port.

It was, I think, the apparent incongruity of my position that caused most   5 amusement to the crew. In vain I would point to my three papers in the *Astrophysical Journal,* my five in the *Monthly Notices of the Royal Astronomical Society.* I would remind them that my order has long been famous for its scientific works. We may be few now, but ever since the eighteenth century we have made contributions to astronomy and geophysics out of all proportion to our numbers. Will my report on the Phoenix Nebula end our thousand years of history? It will end, I fear, much more than that.

I do not know who gave the nebula its name, which seems to me a very   6 bad one. If it contains a prophecy, it is one that cannot be verified for several billion years. Even the word "nebula" is misleading: this is a far smaller object than those stupendous clouds of mist—the stuff of unborn stars—that are scattered throughout the length of the Milky Way. On the cosmic scale, indeed, the Phoenix Nebula is a tiny thing—a tenuous shell of gas surrounding a single star.

Or what is left of a star . . .   7

The Rubens engraving of Loyola[1] seems to mock me as it hangs there above   8 the spectrophotometer tracings. What would *you,* Father, have made of this knowledge that has come into my keeping, so far from the little world that was all the Universe you knew? Would your faith have risen to the challenge, as mine has failed to do?

You gaze into the distance, Father, but I have traveled a distance beyond any   9 that you could have imagined when you founded our order a thousand years ago. No other survey ship has been so far from Earth: we are at the very frontiers of the explored Universe. We set out to reach the Phoenix Nebula, we succeeded, and we are homeward bound with our burden of knowledge. I wish I could lift that burden from my shoulders, but I call to you in vain across the centuries and the light-years that lie between us.

On the book you are holding the words are plain to read. AD MAIOREM DEI   10 GLORIAM[2], the message runs, but it is a message I can no longer believe. Would you still believe it, if you could see what we have found?

We knew, of course, what the Phoenix Nebula was. Every year, in our Galaxy   11 alone, more than a hundred stars explode, blazing for a few hours or days with thousands of times their normal brilliance before they sink back into death and obscurity. Such are the ordinary novae—the commonplace disasters of the Universe. I have recorded the spectrograms and light curves of dozens since I started working at the Lunar Observatory.

---

1. Saint Ignatius of Loyola (1491–1556), founder of the Jesuits in 1540.
2. Latin. "For the greater glory of God."

But three or four times in every thousand years occurs something beside   12
which even a nova pales into total insignificance.

When a star becomes a *supernova,* it may for a little while outshine all the   13
massed suns of the Galaxy. The Chinese astronomers watched this happen in
A.D. 1054, not knowing what it was they saw. Five centuries later, in 1572, a
supernova blazed in Cassiopeia so brilliantly that it was visible in the daylight
sky. There have been three more in the thousand years that have passed since
then.

Our mission was to visit the remnants of such a catastrophe, to reconstruct   14
the events that led up to it, and, if possible, to learn its cause. We came slowly
in through the concentric shells of gas that had been blasted out six thousand
years before, yet were expanding still. They were immensely hot, radiating even
now with a fierce violet light, but were far too tenuous to do us any damage.
When the star had exploded, its outer layers had been driven upward with
such speed that they had escaped completely from its gravitational field. Now
they formed a hollow shell large enough to engulf a thousand solar systems,
and at its center burned the tiny, fantastic object which the star had now
become—a White Dwarf, smaller than the Earth, yet weighing a million times
as much.

The glowing gas shells were all around us, banishing the normal night of   15
interstellar space. We were flying into the center of the cosmic bomb that had
detonated millennia ago and whose incandescent fragments were still hurtling
apart. The immense scale of the explosion, and the fact that the debris already
covered a volume of space many billions of miles across, robbed the scene of
any visible movement. It would take decades before the unaided eye could
detect any motion in these tortured wisps and eddies of gas, yet the sense of
turbulent expansion was overwhelming.

We had checked our primary drive hours before, and were drifting slowly   16
toward the fierce little star ahead. Once it had been a sun like our own, but it
had squandered in a few hours the energy that should have kept it shining for
a million years. Now it was a shrunken miser, hoarding its resources as if trying
to make amends for its prodigal youth.

No one seriously expected to find planets. If there had been any before the   17
explosion, they would have been boiled into puffs of vapor, and their substance
lost in the greater wreckage of the star itself. But we made the automatic search,
as we always do when approaching an unknown sun, and presently we found
a single small world circling the star at an immense distance. It must have been
the Pluto of this vanished Solar System, orbiting on the frontiers of the night.
Too far from the central sun ever to have known life, its remoteness had saved
it from the fate of all its lost companions.

The passing fires had seared its rocks and burned away the mantle of frozen   18
gas that must have covered it in the days before the disaster. We landed, and
we found the Vault.

Its builders had made sure that we should. The monolithic marker that stood   19
above the entrance was now a fused stump, but even the first long-range
photographs told us that here was the work of intelligence. A little later we
detected the continent-wide pattern of radioactivity that had been buried in
the rock. Even if the pylon above the vault had been destroyed, this would
have remained, an immovable and all but eternal beacon calling to the stars.
Our ship fell toward this gigantic bull's-eye like an arrow into its target.

The pylon must have been a mile high when it was built, but now it looked   20
like a candle that had melted down into a puddle of wax. It took us a week to
drill through the fused rock, since we did not have the proper tools for a task
like this. We were astronomers, not archaeologists, but we could improvise.
Our original purpose was forgotten: this lonely monument, reared with such
labor at the greatest possible distance from the doomed sun, could have only
one meaning. A civilization that knew it was about to die had made its last bid
for immortality.

It will take us generations to examine all the treasures that were placed in   21
the Vault. They had plenty of time to prepare, for their sun must have given
its first warnings many years before the final detonation. Everything that they
wished to preserve, all the fruit of their genius, they brought here to this distant
world in the days before the end, hoping that some other race would find it
and that they would not be utterly forgotten. Would we have done as well, or
would we have been too lost in our own misery to give thought to a future
we could never see or share?

If only they had had a little more time! They could travel freely enough   22
between the planets of their own sun, but they had not yet learned to cross
the interstellar gulfs, and the nearest Solar System was a hundred light-years
away. Yet even had they possessed the secret of the Transfinite Drive, no more
than a few million could have been saved. Perhaps it was better thus.

Even if they had not been so disturbingly human as their sculpture shows,   23
we could not have helped admiring them and grieving for their fate. They left
thousands of visual records and the machines for projecting them, together
with elaborate pictorial instructions from which it will not be difficult to learn
their written language. We have examined many of these records, and brought
to life for the first time in six thousand years the warmth and beauty of a
civilization that in many ways must have been superior to our own. Perhaps
they only showed us the best, and one can hardly blame them. But their worlds
were very lovely, and their cities were built with a grace that matches anything
of man's. We have watched them at work and play, and listened to their musical
speech sounding across the centuries. One scene is still before my eyes—a
group of children on a beach of strange blue sand, playing in the waves as
children play on Earth. Curious whiplike trees line the shore, and some very
large animal is wading in the shallows yet attracting no attention at all.

And sinking into the sea, still warm and friendly and life-giving, is the sun   24
that will soon turn traitor and obliterate all this innocent happiness.

Perhaps if we had not been so far from home and so vulnerable to loneliness,   25
we should not have been so deeply moved. Many of us had seen the ruins of
ancient civilizations on other worlds, but they had never affected us so profoundly. This tragedy was unique. It is one thing for a race to fail and die, as
nations and cultures have done on Earth. But to be destroyed so completely in
the full flower of its achievement, leaving no survivors—how could that be
reconciled with the mercy of God?

My colleagues have asked me that, and I have given what answers I can.   26
Perhaps you could have done better, Father Loyola, but I have found nothing
in the *Exercitia Spiritualia*[3] that helps me here. They were not an evil people: I
do not know what gods they worshiped, if indeed they worshiped any. But I
have looked back at them across the centuries, and have watched while the
loveliness they used their last strength to preserve was brought forth again into
the light of their shrunken sun. They could have taught us much: why were
they destroyed?

I know the answers that my colleagues will give when they get back to   27
Earth. They will say that the Universe has no purpose and no plan, that since
a hundred suns explode every year in our Galaxy, at this very moment some
race is dying in the depths of space. Whether that race has done good or evil
during its lifetime will make no difference in the end: there is no divine justice,
for there is no God.

Yet, of course, what we have seen proves nothing of the sort. Anyone who   28
argues thus is being swayed by emotion, not logic. God has no need to justify
His actions to man. He who built the Universe can destroy it when He chooses.
It is arrogance—it is perilously near blasphemy—for us to say what He may
or may not do.

This I could have accepted, hard though it is to look upon whole worlds   29
and peoples thrown into the furnace. But there comes a point when even the
deepest faith must falter, and now, as I look at the calculations lying before me,
I know I have reached that point at last.

We could not tell, before we reached the nebula, how long ago the explosion   30
took place. Now, from the astronomical evidence and the record in the rocks
of that one surviving planet, I have been able to date it very exactly. I know
in what year the light of this colossal conflagration reached our Earth. I know
how brilliantly the supernova whose corpse now dwindles behind our speeding
ship once shone in terrestrial skies. I know how it must have blazed low in the
east before sunrise, like a beacon in that oriental dawn.

---

3. *Spiritual Exercises,* a book written by Saint Loyola showing how to attain spiritual union with God.

There can be no reasonable doubt: the ancient mystery is solved at last. Yet,   31
oh God, there were so many stars you could have used. What was the need to
give these people to the fire, that the symbol of their passing might shine above
Bethlehem?

Questions for Critical Thinking

1. Assume that the narrator's deductions are correct, and that he has lately visited
   the burned-out shell of the Star of Bethlehem. Why should that make the narrator
   question his faith and become so depressed?

2. Taking the premise of the story for granted, what justification can you give for
   God's action?

3. What can be inferred about the narrator from the brief but data-packed first
   paragraph?

4. "Why are medical men such notorious atheists?" the narrator asks in paragraph
   3. Answer this question if you agree with its premise. If you disagree, say why
   you do.

5. In what year does this story take place?

6. What is ironic about the name, the Phoenix Nebula, given the context and events
   of this story?

7. Loren Eiseley asked, "Who is man?" in his article. What answer do you think the
   narrator of "The Star" would most likely give?

8. Which would you prefer: no God at all, or a God capricious and cruel enough
   to obliterate an entire civilization just to shine a star above his son's birthplace?

Writing Assignment

The writer of science-fiction, in addition to treating character and plot like any
storyteller, also constructs an imaginary future world which must seem internally
coherent, consistent, and above all else, plausible. In an essay, describe the world
inhabited by the narrator of "The Star," saying how it is similar to ours, and how it
is different.

Writing Advice

Skillful science-fiction writers seldom interrupt their narratives with long descriptions
of the futuristic worlds inhabited by their characters. Usually, it is both more evocative

and effective for the writer to drop hints about the world, its people, and technology. That sort of hinting is exactly what Clarke does unobtrusively; to write an essay about the world of "The Star," will consequently try your powers of observation and deduction. Ask yourself, how is the world depicted in "The Star" different from our own? In what way do the people seem like us, and unlike us? How is their technology superior to our own?

One way to write this essay is to divide the world of "The Star" into a social as well as a technological component and write separately about each. For example, if you were looking for clues to the society inhabited by the characters of the story, you should pay attention to their dialogue, to the narrator's descriptions of his shipmates and their beliefs, and to the narrator himself as a man of his time. Ask yourself what the narrator's dual occupation says about the imagined evolution of priests and their duties. Notice how his shipmates react to the presence of a priest aboard a scientific expedition. What does their reaction indirectly say about the society he lives in? What else about the religious beliefs of his time can you deduce from the narrator's interactions with the other characters around him?

If you were to conclude that the narrator's society is less religious than our own and its people more worldly in their thinking, you could sum up this observation in a sentence such as, " 'The Star' portrays the world of the future as significantly more secular than our own, simmering with widespread hostility to religion." Then you would cite the evidence you have for this observation: the ribbing the narrator suffers at the hands of the crew, the argument he has with the doctor, the narrator's obser-vation that few of the crew members "have any religious faith." But then you would have to ask yourself whether the narrator, placed among a crew of technicians and scientists of today, wouldn't encounter a similar degree of irreligiousness.

Technologically, the society of "The Star" is plainly superior to our own. That the spaceship is three thousand light years away from the Vatican is implicit proof that his era is able to travel significantly faster than the speed of light. Notice also some of the technological "givens" assumed by the story: the pinpoint navigation, for example, that enables the crew to hone in on a target billions of miles distant from the earth; the shielding material encasing their spaceship that allows it to withstand the radiation of the supernova with no ill-effects.

To write this essay requires you to do more than to make assertions about the society and technology hinted at in "The Star." You must also back up your inferences with citations from the text and show how you arrived at your conclusions.

Alternate Writing Assignment

Imagining that you are the narrator of "The Star," write a report saying what you found in your investigation of the Phoenix Nebula.

LITERATURE

THE TYGER
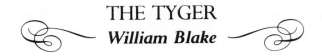
William Blake

William Blake (1757–1827), English poet, artist, engraver, and visionary, was born in London and educated briefly at the Royal Academy of Art. Blake was considered an eccentric mystic during his lifetime and, aside from *Poetical Sketches* (1783), self-published all his books. In 1782 he married Catherine Boucher, whom he educated, and who became his lifelong companion and assistant. Among Blake's many other works, which are now widely appreciated and studied, are *Songs of Innocence* (1789), and *Songs of Experience* (1794), both of which Blake published using a process which he invented that allowed text and illustrations to be engraved on the same plate.

Reading Advice

One of the simple keys to reading and grasping at least the surface meaning of a poem is to remember that poems are written in sentences and that sentences arranged in verse form still follow the rules of syntax. So, for example, this verse, "Tyger! Tyger! burning bright in the forests of the night, what immortal hand or eye could frame thy fearful symmetry?" is still a single sentence although it is laid out on the page as a stanza. (A sentence that winds through several poetic lines as this one does is said to be "enjambed"; a poetic line made up of a complete sentence is said to be "end-stopped.") Experience shows that beginning readers have a tendency to read enjambed lines as if they should be end-stopped, that is, to confuse the line with the sentence. Unless it is end-stopped, the line is generally not a coherent unit of meaning. The sentence is.

That it is the nature and power of poetry to condense profound and mystical questions in a quick imagistic turn of phrase is demonstrated once again in this poem, "The Tyger." Blake muses over the same wonders and riddles of life and creation as do Wald, Eiseley, Dillard, and Clarke, but does so in the darting language of poetry, where one apt image does the work of ten paragraphs.

> *Tyger! Tyger! burning bright*
> *In the forests of the night,*
> *What immortal hand or eye*
> *Could frame thy fearful symmetry?*

In what distant deeps or skies
Burnt the fire of thine eyes?
On what wings dare he aspire?
What the hand dare seize the fire?

And what shoulder, and what art,
Could twist the sinews of thy heart?
And, when thy heart began to beat,
What dread hand? and what dread feet?

What the hammer? what the chain?
In what furnace was thy brain?
What the anvil? what dread grasp
Dare its deadly terrors clasp?

When the stars threw down their spears,
And watered heaven with their tears,
Did he smile his work to see?
Did he who made the lamb make thee?

Tyger! Tyger! burning bright
In the forests of the night,
What immortal hand or eye,
Dare frame thy fearful symmetry?

Questions for Critical Thinking

1. What thematic similarities can you detect between "The Tyger" and Annie Dillard's "Heaven and Earth in Jest"?

2. From what viewpoint does this poem seem to be written? What does the use of this viewpoint add to the poem?

3. What does the tiger symbolize in this poem? What characteristic of the real-life tiger has earned it this symbolism?

4. With what animal is the tiger contrasted in this poem? What contrasting quality does that other animal usually symbolize?

5. On what extended metaphor is stanza 4 based? What is the implication of this stanza?

6. What imagistic rationale exists behind the line, "Tyger! Tyger! Burning bright"?

Writing Assignment

Write an essay that defines the term "symbol" and interprets the symbolic meaning of Blake's tiger.

Writing Advice

The essay should consist of two parts: the first should define "symbol"; the second should say what you think Blake's tiger symbolizes.

Definition is such an important component in expository prose that some English classes teach it as a strategy for writing essays. Consulting a dictionary or an encyclopedia is a good first step to take in writing a definition. But it is a modest first step, since dictionaries generally provide only the skeletal meaning of a word and cannot accurately cover the nuances found in contextual meaning. Only an extended definition can do that—one which elaborates on the proposed meaning with examples and further details. So, for example, after you've said what a "symbol" is, you should then add to your definition by showing how symbols acquire and radiate meaning. You might even explain why any man would prefer to be called a "tiger" rather than a "sheep," even though no man can literally be either one. You could also demonstrate when a word is not functioning as a symbol but merely as a literal referent, as "tiger" does in this sentence: "A man-eating tiger is a tiger that has been compelled, through stress of circumstances beyond its control, to adopt a diet alien to it." It is plain to anyone who reads English that here the author means "tiger" literally and little else. But how do we know that?

The second part of the essay should sum up your interpretation of the symbolic meaning of Blake's tiger. Exactly what meaning an author intends for a symbol is an arguable subject, with any given interpretation just as likely to evoke disagreement as assent. But to decipher the meaning of a symbol, including Blake's tiger, requires you to pay attention to its context. Blake's tiger is contextually framed with words such as "fearful," "burning bright," "dread," "deadly," which assure us that the intended meaning is certainly not one of benignity and gentleness.

Note that you should prove whatever meaning you attribute to Blake's symbolic tiger with quotations from the work itself. Like algebra problems, literary analyses require not only the solution but also the calculations that led to it. If you say that Blake's tiger is a symbol of the ruthlessness and cruelty of nature, you must then ground this interpretation in the poem by citing specific words and phrases that support this reading.

Alternate Writing Assignment

One of the striking features about Blake's "The Tyger" is that it resembles a child's nursery rhyme in its prosody and simplicity of language. Write an essay analyzing what effect this has on the overall impact of the work.

LITERATURE

PROGRESSION OF THE SPECIES

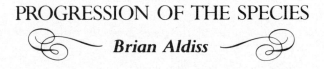

Brian Aldiss

Brian Aldiss (b. 1925) is an English writer, editor, and bookseller. A prolific writer, mainly of science fiction works, Aldiss was educated at Framlingham College, England, and is the winner of numerous awards for his science fiction books and stories. Among his many published works are *The Brightfount Diaries* (1955), *Report on Probability* (1968), *Brothers of the Head* (1977), and *An Island Called Moreau* (1981).

Reading Advice

The poem "Progression of the Species" is likely to challenge any who rely heavily on punctuation to aid meaning. For example, this sentence, "Let's face it though / We hate change," as it is presently punctuated could mean, "Let's face it, though, we hate change," or "Though we hate change, let's face it." Context advises us that the second meaning is probably meant, but the poem could withstand being read either way. We point out this example to you as a warning of why it will be necessary to read this poem more than once.

The scenario described in this modern poem is not as farfetched or unlikely as we might think. Mapping of the human chromosomes is already underway, and in the not-too-distant future, scientists believe that genetic intervention may be technically possible. But interfering in the processes of life itself is not a morally simple decision. Although Aldiss speaks of engineering out the Neanderthal, no one knows where such a step might eventually lead, what kind of creature it might inadvertently produce, or what correcting steps nature could take if our experiments should accidentally unleash a monster worse than the one we have carried within us since the darkness of ancient time.

Long before a woman knows she's pregnant
And greets the news with fear or smiles
The news had head and heart and heart beats.
It's then no bigger than a tadpole.
The cells are working on that.
Although I never understood how
A radio set works, this cellular multiplicity
Comes within the realm of graspable ideas

For "Progression of the Species," by Brian Aldiss, from *Fine Frenzy,* eds. Robert Baylor, Brenda Stokes. New York: McGraw-Hill, 1972. Reprinted by permission of the author.

And proves itself pure madness.
Those cells are programmed with the stuttering messages   10
Called life. Our generation's cracked
The code of life—we know about
The information in the genes inside the chromosomes.

Soon they'll have it all pegged,
Know which nucleic acid brings us curly hair
Which schizophrenic tendencies
Which gift of gab
Which stronger eyesight
Which sweet temper.
Because people are never content with being   20
Clever, they have to get cleverer.
They'll find the way, a century from now,
To make a synthetic gene, a splendid little thing,
To insert it—hypodermic gliding through the testicles—
Into the proto-embryo.

It'll be the end of us and the beginning
Of perfect people
Sweet temper artificially disseminated
A DNA utopia with never an angry word or
Cruel deed. Let's face it though   30
We hate change. The thought of perfection
Scares us the moment we
Have head and heart and heart beats.

You know why, Mischief's our common lot—
Original sin is not half as original
As perfection. Those better people
Would look back on us with a loving sorrow
As the Neanderthals of the pre-DNA Age.
In them, the gaudy inferno of the undermined
Would droop and die and disappear
Unregretted—as with us, each generation   40
The Neanderthal dies from us
Our head and heart and heart beats.

This is the progression of the species
We can manage it for ourselves, thanks
From now on.

Questions for Critical Thinking

1. If geneticists do indeed determine exactly which genes are responsible for every human trait, what effect would that discovery have on the creation/evolution debate?

2. If we could deliberately choose specific traits for our offspring by genetic engineering, should we? Why or why not?

3. If you had the choice, what specific traits would you choose to genetically engineer into your children?

4. What does the author mean by "programmed with the stuttering messages / Called life." Why are the messages "stuttering"?

5. What allusion is implicitly contained in the line, "Mischief's our common lot." Do you agree with this sentiment? Why or why not?

6. What, according to the author, is already happening to the Neanderthal within, even without genetic engineering? Do you agree or disagree? Why?

7. What is the Neanderthal within us like? What value, if any, does this creature have for humans?

Writing Assignment

Write an essay arguing for or against the genetic engineering of humans.

Writing Advice

Before you can write this essay, you must ask yourself where you stand on the topic and why. And you must not only be able to give reasons for your belief, you must also be able to show where and why your stand is correct and any other completely wrong. For the argumentative essay is not purely a forum for the unbridled expression of personal opinion, although personal opinion will certainly form the backbone of any argument. Not self-expression, but persuasion, is its primary aim. You must show not what you think but why it is right and logical to think as you do. Doing so will require you to find logical reasons for your opinions and perhaps to cite any facts and experts you can find to support your case.

Begin by asking yourself where you stand on this topic. Do you think genetic engineering must never be allowed under any circumstances? Do you think genetic engineering should be a private decision taken between a patient and doctor without meddling by the state? Or do you think it all right to genetically engineer only to overcome defective traits, but never for the purpose of producing a superior human being? First, list your stand. Then, list your reasons behind it. If you take a con position, ask yourself what ill-effects you foresee from unrestrained genetic engineering. Write them down and work them into your argument. Do the same if you take the pro position. Next, visit the library and look for ammunition to back your case. See what the experts have to say. Read what fears they have about genetic engineering, or what hopes they hold for its future. Note that it is not entirely a bad thing if you change your mind and your position as you read. Unprejudiced people are always prepared to change their opinions in the face of contrary evidence.

The specific details you will need to support your case should include your own reasoned opinion together with the testimony of experts, as well as any facts and data about genetic engineering you can uncover. Don't forget to also list and rebut the opposition's argument somewhere in the paper. If you are for genetic engineering, imagine what arguments the opposition would marshall against your stand and then rebut them. Anticipating the opposition is usually an effective technique of argument and one likely to add punch to any paper.

Alternate Writing Assignment

Imagine that genetic engineering on a vast scale is now available and that everyone is free to use it without limitations. What would you do? Would you use the technology to engineer your child? Write an essay describing the traits you would engineer into your son or daughter and saying why (or why you would not).

A R T

THE CREATION OF ADAM
Michelangelo Buonarroti

About the Artist

Michelangelo Buonarroti (1475–1564), Italian sculptor, painter, architect, and poet, is revered as perhaps the most outstanding artistic figure of the Renaissance. His work consists of some of the most renowned masterpieces of painting, sculpture, and architecture that influenced generations of subsequent artists. In 1489 he entered the art school held in the gardens of the Medicis, the most influential family of that period in Florence, where he attracted the attention of Lorenzo de'Medici with whom Michelangelo lived between 1490 and 1492. Between 1496 and 1501, Michelangelo lived and worked in Rome, producing the marble statue of *Bacchus* and his famous *Pietà* (St. Peter's, Rome).

Returning to Florence in 1501, he executed the magnificent *David* for the Piazza della Signoria. In 1505 he went to Rome at the command of Pope Julius II, for whom he painted the ceiling of the Sistine Chapel between 1508 and 1512. It is ranked among the world's greatest masterpieces. Although he regarded himself first as a sculptor, Michelangelo's genius for architecture is evident from the great dome of St. Peter's

Cathedral, Rome, primarily his design, and his reorganization of the Capitoline Hill in Rome, which he undertook in 1537.

Living in an age that made artists dependent on the sponsorship of rich patrons, Michelangelo was frustrated much of his life by this dependence and by the jealousy of other artists. A great collection of his drawings and paintings are housed in the Louvre, Paris; the Uffizi and Casa Buonarroti, Florence; and in the British Museum, London.

About the Art

The Creation of Adam, one of the central panels on the ceiling of the Sistine Chapel, is regarded as a bold departure from the traditional representation of this primal event of religious myth. God and Adam are pictured as two complementary figures whose bodies are infused with arcs, curves, and a dynamic sense of motion. Between the outstretched fingers of God and Adam is a small gap between which the spark of life leaps. Angels and a cautiously staring figure under the arm of God, currently identified as the Virgin Mary, peer out in witness to the momentous moment. The figure of God is pagan in its human form and suspended in billowy drapery, while Adam is earthbound and material. Characteristics of Michelangelo's style are implicit in both figures: the heavy musculature, for example, of both Adam and God, and the twisting counterpoise between the two figures. *The Creation of Adam* is often cited as an example of how Renaissance artists incorporated human and pagan forms in their depiction of Christian spiritual figures and events.

ART

THE BIRTH OF A TEAR
Edgar Carl Alfons Ende

About the Artist

Edgar Carl Alfons Ende (1901–1965) was a German painter best known for his symbolic interpretations. His early training came as a result of being apprenticed to a scene painter. After brief formal studies at the Kunstgewerbeschule in Altona, he moved to Munich, where the Nazi government forbade him to exhibit his work. In 1947 he cofounded the Neue Gruppe München. During his mature years Ende's work was exhibited in major museums internationally.

About the Art

Painted in 1947, *The Birth of a Tear* is a sardonic evocation of Michelangelo's *Creation of Adam*. But unlike Michelangelo's representation of God, Ende's creative figure is androgynous, uniting a delicate, ethereal female head with a huge, muscular male body—suggesting perhaps a composite human agency, rather than the biblical male divinity. Whereas Michelangelo's God creates life with a touch, Ende's figure goes through extensive ritual conjurations to coalesce the tear. Once engendered, the tear seems to have the capacity to dissolve gloom and offer relief from suffering, as seen in the luminescent blue aura emanating from the primordial tear. The message of the painting seems to be that once human beings lost their innocence, sorrow intruded, necessitating the healing balm of tears.

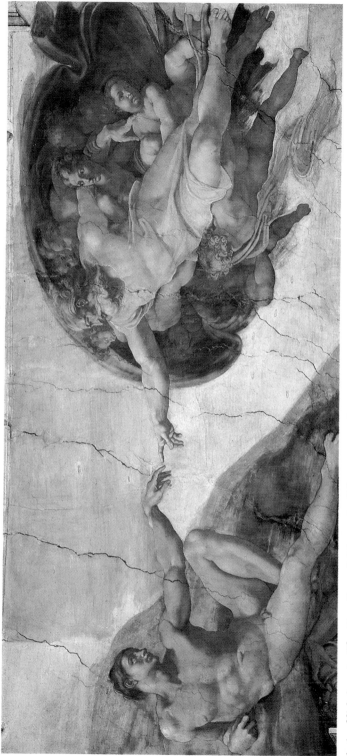

1–1 *Michelangelo*, **The Creation of Adam**, *detail from ceiling of Sistine Chapel, 1508–1512, The Vatican, Rome. Scala/Art Resource, N.Y.*

1–2   Edgar Ende, **The Birth of a Tear,** *1947, 50 × 68 cm. Staatsgalerie moderner Kunst Munchen.*

CHAPTER WRITING ASSIGNMENTS

After reading the assigned selections and studying the paintings of the chapter, write an essay that answers one of the following questions:

(a) What reconciliation, if any, is possible between religious and scientific accounts of our origins? Why is such reconciliation possible or impossible?

(b) What obstacles to religious belief are intrinsically present in nature?

(c) What is the nature of religious faith, and how does it differ from scientific faith?

(d) What consolations can the nonbeliever deduce from the picture of the world and the universe painted by science?

(e) What do you regard as the more likely basis for thought: brain chemistry or philosophical outlook? Why?

(f) Given our lengthy and tumultuous evolution past, what effects caused by the "Neanderthal" within do you think still linger with us?

(g) What do you regard as the ultimate underlying mystery of life and nature? Why?

Make specific references to the selections you have read in this chapter, cite passages from the authors and, if necessary, supplement your answer with material uncovered on your own in the library.

CHAPTER TWO

What Do We Know?
ILLUSION AND REALITY

The philosophical debate over illusion versus reality is an ancient argument between those who believe in the perceptions of the senses and those who do not. On a superficial level, the world around us is a solid and substantial presence, manifesting from day to day a burgherlike stability and sameness. If we are to believe our senses, it is a wonder of certainty, even of cloddish predictability. But that is only the superficial view. Science has peered into the heart of the world's substantiality and found it composed of shifting, whirling atoms. Should the spinning atoms properly align for a millisecond, physics tells us that an elephant could stroll untouched through the stone walls of a cathedral.

We do not know whether the world is real or an illusion. We cannot trust our senses. Philosophy cannot prove that we exist. It is our hard fate to be submerged forever in the depths of selfhood, from which we squint myopically at the world through separate periscopes. Using the language of mathematics and the rigid protocols of experimental methodology, science has struggled to overcome this limitation of individual human perception, with some practical success. But no one has ever devised an irrefutable answer to the philosophers' theory that the entire spectacle of the world may be nothing more than an illusion coded in the perceptions of often sputtering, misfiring neurons. The German philosopher Arthur Schopenhauer (1788–1860), before descending into final madness, declared the world just such a dream of conspiring souls. Jorge Luis Borges, the Argentine poet, depicts in a poem, "Daybreak," the terror behind this appalling belief. He pictures an anxious man tromping the streets of a city just before dawn, desperately afraid to sleep lest his beloved Buenos Aires dissolve into nothingness as its last wakeful dreamer succumbs.

The materialists, on the other hand, counter with pragmatic assertions of belief in a world that is real and substantial. Pressed by his friend and biographer James Boswell (1740–1795) to answer the Scottish philosopher David Hume (1711–1776), who argued that causation was nothing more than successive perception inside our heads, Samuel Johnson (1709–1784) gruffly replied, "I refute him thus," and kicked a stone. The stone went flying and materialism seemed triumphant. But the unknowing stone would have gone flying just as impartially in a dream.

Who are we? Where do we come from? Do we have souls in our bodies? If we have no souls, then we are entirely made of matter, says Pascal, and nothing is more inconceivable than that "matter knows itself." Yet what is a soul, and where in the human body does it exist? Is it hard-wired to the brain, or adrift in the tributaries and underground streams of plasma that pulse and trickle through our organs and limbs? And why is it that when a certain part of the brain is touched by a probe, molten memories and dreams mysteriously bubble to the surface of consciousness?

Over the centuries many thinkers have grappled with the problem of what is real and what illusory, and a few of the best disputants are represented in this chapter. We begin with Plato, who argues in his famous "Allegory of the Cave" that we are like beings chained in a dark cave and forced to gape at shadows reflected on the wall, which we mistake for truth. Centuries later, Blaise Pascal pictures us as groping vainly between the infinitesimal and the infinite. Stephen Hawking surveys what we think we know about our world, and points out the paradox of trying to formulate a unified theory of the universe. Paul De Kruif weighs in with a stirring tale of how a medical researcher, through laborious experiments, discovered insulin and saved millions of lives. Tom Bethell acquaints us with a quiet revolution that has occurred in Darwinism, overturning yet another "truth." In the literature section, Franz Kafka's mild-mannered salesman in "The Metamorphosis" wakes up and finds himself transformed into a grotesque dung beetle; in Guy de Maupassant's "False Gems" a seemingly virtuous wife is shown to be untrue; and in Alfred, Lord Tennyson's "The Lady of Shalott" an artist defies an ancient curse, gazes at reality and is struck dead by what she sees. Two paintings complete the chapter—James Ensor's *L'Intrigue*, about the masks people wear, and *Visit to the Plastic Surgeon,* by Remedios Varo, which depicts a woman's delusion about how to stay young.

It was left to American practicality as evidenced in the pragmatic school of philosophy founded by Charles Sanders Peirce (1839–1914) to cut through, if not settle, the debate that is the theme of this chapter and one which lingers still, long after many of its most vociferous contenders are dead and either aglow in the light of posthumous revelation or swaddled in the eternal darkness of the grave. "The bottom of being is opaque to us," declared William James (1842–1910) before abandoning philosophy for experimental psychology where empirical truth, or the semblance of consistency that passes for truth, can be coaxed out in milligrams through laboratory experiments. There was wisdom in his position. The world may be real or it may be an illusion. That it behaves uncannily alike in either case offers a smidgen of comfort.

PHILOSOPHY

ALLEGORY OF THE CAVE
Plato

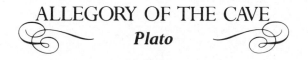

Ranked among the foremost thinkers of the Western world, Plato (427?– 347 B.C.) was
a Greek philosopher who lived for a time with Dionysius the Elder, tyrant of Syracuse.
After being educated according to the most enlightened principles of his age, he became
a student of Socrates in 407 B.C. and eventually established a school in Athens, the
Academy, which taught mathematics and philosophy.

Plato's central philosophy posits the existence of ideal and unchangeable forms,
which are the pure models of every idea or object to be found in the world, their
counterparts on the earthly plane being merely impure imitations. The search for truth
is a search for these archetypes in their ideal and pure state and for the Good, which
in Plato's cosmos was universal and constant for every thinker. Philosophy taught
humans to avoid the deception and seduction of earthly imitations and to strive for
perception of the underlying ideal form of the idea or object.

Rival thinkers in Plato's own day found his concept of ideal forms mystifying, and
the more empirical Aristotle (384 – 322 B.C.) often wondered where such forms were
actually to be found and observed. A visionary and idealistic thinker, Plato has had a
profound impact on all Western thought, with his influence reaching into virtually
every avenue of religion, art, and literature.

Reading Advice

Plato's writings fall into two characteristic groups, epistles and dialogues, with the
dialogues being the primary vehicle for conveying his philosophical thought. His dialogues contain the teachings of Socrates (469 – 399 B.C.), who left behind no writings
of his own. Typically, a dialogue consists of a lengthy exchange between Socrates and
a well-meaning but erring student, who is gradually led by a series of questions (to
which the student has the annoying habit of giving just the right wrong answers) to a
discovery of truth. What is especially astonishing about Plato is the directness and
simplicity of his writing style, which is entirely free of the roundaboutness and abstruse-
ness found in the works of later philosophers. Simplicity of style, however, does not
necessarily mean simple ideas, as this excerpt amply proves.

Nowhere is Plato's directness better displayed than in the "Allegory of the Cave."
An allegory is an extended metaphor with meanings that radiate beyond the immediate
narrative context. And the core of this excerpt is the extended allegory in which the
dilemma all thinkers face is suggested by an elaborate description of prisoners in a cave
who are deceived by shadows. Having drawn the picture of the befuddled cave thinkers,

From *The Republic*. Translated by Benjamin Jowett.

Socrates then proposes an interpretation of what his own allegory means. The "Allegory of the Cave" is so aptly and cleverly constructed that it is widely regarded as among the best allegorical arguments ever.

*A*nd now, I said, let me show in a 1
figure how far our nature is enlightened or unenlightened:—Behold! human beings living in an underground den, which has a mouth open towards the light and reaching all along the den; here they have been from their childhood, and have their legs and necks chained so that they cannot move, and can only see before them, being prevented by the chains from turning round their heads. Above and behind them a fire is blazing at a distance, and between the fire and the prisoners there is a raised way; and you will see, if you look, a low wall built along the way, like the screen which marionette players have in front of them, over which they show the puppets.

I see. 2

And do you see, I said, men passing along the wall carrying all sorts of 3
vessels, and statues and figures of animals made of wood and stone and various materials, which appear over the wall? Some of them are talking, others silent.

You have shown me a strange image, and they are strange prisoners. 4

Like ourselves, I replied; and they see only their own shadows, or the 5
shadows of one another, which the fire throws on the opposite wall of the cave?

True, he said; how could they see anything but the shadows if they were 6
never allowed to move their heads?

And of the objects which are being carried in like manner they would only 7
see the shadows?

Yes, he said. 8

And if they were able to converse with one another, would they not suppose 9
that they were naming what was actually before them?

Very true. 10

And suppose further that the prison had an echo which came from the 11
other side, would they not be sure to fancy when one of the passers-by spoke that the voice which they heard came from the passing shadow?

No question, he replied. 12

To them, I said, the truth would be literally nothing but the shadows of the 13
images.

That is certain. 14

And now look again, and see what will naturally follow if the prisoners are 15
released and disabused of their error. At first, when any of them is liberated and compelled suddenly to stand up and turn his neck round and walk and look towards the light, he will suffer sharp pains; the glare will distress him,

and he will be unable to see the realities of which in his former state he had
seen the shadows; and then conceive some one saying to him, that what he
saw before was an illusion, but that now, when he is approaching nearer to
being and his eye is turned towards more real existence, he has a clearer vision—
what will be his reply? And you may further imagine that his instructor is
pointing to the objects as they pass and requiring him to name them,—will
he not be perplexed? Will he not fancy that the shadows which he formerly
saw are truer than the objects which are now shown to him?

Far truer.   16

And if he is compelled to look straight at the light, will he not have a pain   17
in his eyes which will make him turn away to take refuge in the objects of
vision which he can see, and which he will conceive to be in reality clearer
than the things which are now being shown to him?

True, he said.   18

And suppose once more, that he is reluctantly dragged up a steep and rugged   19
ascent, and held fast until he is forced into the presence of the sun himself, is
he not likely to be pained and irritated? When he approaches the light his eyes
will be dazzled, and he will not be able to see anything at all of what are now
called realities.

Not all in a moment, he said.   20

He will require to grow accustomed to the sight of the upper world. And   21
first he will see the shadows best, next the reflections of men and other objects
in the water, and then the objects themselves; then he will gaze upon the light
of the moon and the stars and the spangled heaven; and he will see the sky
and the stars by night better than the sun or the light of the sun by day?

Certainly.   22

Last of all he will be able to see the sun, and not mere reflections of him   23
in the water, but he will see him in his own proper place, and not in another;
and he will contemplate him as he is.

Certainly.   24

He will then proceed to argue that this is he who gives the season and the   25
years, and is the guardian of all that is in the visible world, and in a certain
way the cause of all things which he and his fellows have been accustomed to
behold?

Clearly, he said, he would first see the sun and then reason about him.   26

And when he remembered his old habitation, and the wisdom of the den   27
and his fellow prisoners, do you not suppose that he would felicitate himself
on the change, and pity them?

Certainly, he would.   28

And if they were in the habit of conferring honors among themselves on   29
those who were quickest to observe the passing shadows and to remark which
of them went before, and which followed after, and which were together; and
who were therefore best able to draw conclusions as to the future, do you

think that he would care for such honors and glories, or envy the possessors of them? Would he not say with Homer,

> Better to be the poor servant of a poor master,

and to endure anything, rather than think as they do and live after their manner?

Yes, he said, I think that he would rather suffer anything than entertain these false notions and live in this miserable manner.   30

Imagine once more, I said, such as one coming suddenly out of the sun to   31
be replaced in his old situation; would he not be certain to have his eyes full of darkness?

To be sure, he said.   32

And if there were a contest, and he had to compete in measuring the shadows 33
with the prisoners who had never moved out of the den, while his sight was still weak, and before his eyes had become steady (and the time which would be needed to acquire this new habit of sight might be very considerable), would he not be ridiculous? Men would say of him that up he went and down he came without his eyes; and that it was better not even to think of ascending; and if any one tried to loose another and lead him up to the light, let them only catch the offender, and they would put him to death.

No question, he said.   34

This entire allegory, I said, you may now append, dear Glaucon, to the   35
previous argument; the prison house is the world of sight, the light of the fire is the sun, and you will not misapprehend me if you interpret the journey upwards to be the ascent of the soul into the intellectual world according to my poor belief, which, at your desire, I have expressed—whether rightly or wrongly God knows. But, whether true or false, my opinion is that in the world of knowledge the idea of good appears last of all, and is seen only with an effort; and, when seen, is also inferred to be the universal author of all things beautiful and right, parent of light and of the lord of light in this visible world, and the immediate source of reason and truth in the intellectual; and that this is the power upon which he who would act rationally either in public or private life must have his eye fixed.

I agree, he said, as far as I am able to understand you.   36

Moreover, I said, you must not wonder that those who attain to this beatific 37
vision are unwilling to descend to human affairs; for their souls are ever has-tening into the upper world where they desire to dwell; which desire of theirs is very natural, if our allegory may be trusted.

Yes, very natural.   38

And is there anything surprising in one who passes from divine contempla-   39
tions to the evil state of man, misbehaving himself in a ridiculous manner; if, while his eyes are blinking and before he has become accustomed to the sur-rounding darkness, he is compelled to fight in courts of law, or in other places, about the images or the shadows of images of justice, and is endeavoring to

meet the conceptions of those who have never yet seen absolute justice?

Anything but surprising, he replied.   40

Anyone who has common sense will remember that the bewilderments of   41
the eyes are of two kinds, and arise from two causes, either from coming out
of the light or from going into the light, which is true of the mind's eye, quite
as much as of the bodily eye; and he who remembers this when he sees anyone
whose vision is perplexed and weak, will not be too ready to laugh; he will
first ask whether that soul of man has come out of the brighter life, and is
unable to see because unaccustomed to the dark, or having turned from darkness
to the day is dazzled by excess of light. And he will count the one happy in his
condition and state of being, and he will pity the other; or, if he have a mind
to laugh at the soul which comes from below into the light, there will be more
reason in this than in the laugh which greets him who returns from above out
of the light into the den.

That, he said, is a very just distinction.   42

But then, if I am right, certain professors of education must be wrong when   43
they say that they can put a knowledge into the soul which was not there
before, like sight into blind eyes.

They undoubtedly say this, he replied.   44

Whereas, our argument shows that the power and capacity of learning exists   45
in the soul already; and that just as the eye was unable to turn from darkness
to light without the whole body, so too the instrument of knowledge can only
by the movement of the whole soul be turned from the world of becoming
into that of being, and learn by degrees to endure the sight of being, and of
the brightest and best of being, or in other words, of the good.

Very true.   46

And must there not be some art which will effect conversion in the easiest   47
and quickest manner; not implanting the faculty of sight, for that exists already,
but that knowledge which we have already shown to be the greatest of all—
they must continue to ascend until they arrive at the good; but when they have
ascended and seen enough we must not allow them to do as they do now.

What do you mean?   56

I mean that they remain in the upper world: but this must not be allowed;   57
they must be made to descend again among the prisoners in the den, and
partake of their labors and honors, whether they are worth having or not.

But is not this unjust? he said; ought we to give them a worse life, when   58
they might have a better?

You have again forgotten, my friend, I said, the intention of the legislator,   59
who did not aim at making any one class in the State happy above the rest;
the happiness was to be in the whole State, and he held the citizens together
by persuasion and necessity, making them benefactors of the State, and therefore
benefactors of one another; to this end he created them, not to please themselves, but to be his instruments in binding up the State.

True, he said, I had forgotten.   60

Observe, Glaucon, that there will be no injustice in compelling our philos-   61
ophers to have a care and providence of others; we shall explain to them that
in other States, men of their class are not obliged to share in the toils of politics:
and this is reasonable, for they grow up at their own sweet will, and the
government would rather not have them. Being self-taught, they cannot be
expected to show any gratitude for a culture which they have never received.
But we have brought you into the world to be rulers of the hive, kings of
yourselves and of the other citizens, and have educated you far better and more
perfectly than they have been educated, and you are better able to share in the
double duty. Wherefore each of you, when his turn comes, must go down to
the general underground abode, and get the habit of seeing in the dark. When
you have acquired the habit, you will see ten thousand times better than the
inhabitants of the den, and you will know what the several images are, and
what they represent, because you have seen the beautiful and just and good in
their truth. And thus our State, which is also yours, will be a reality, and not
a dream only, and will be administered in a spirit unlike that of other States,
in which men fight with one another about shadows only and are distracted
in the struggle for power, which in their eyes is a great good. Whereas the
truth is that the State in which the rulers are most reluctant to govern is always
the best and most quietly governed, and the State in which they are most eager,
the worst.

Quite true, he replied.   62

And will our pupils, when they hear this, refuse to take their turn at the   63
toils of State, when they are allowed to spend the greater part of their time
with one another in the heavenly light?

Impossible, he answered; for they are just men, and the commands which   64
we impose upon them are just; there can be no doubt that every one of them
will take office as a stern necessity, and not after the fashion of our present
rulers of State.

Yes, my friend, I said; and there lies the point. You must contrive for your   65
future rulers another and a better life than that of a ruler, and then you may
have a well-ordered State; for only in the State which offers this, will they rule
who are truly rich, not in silver and gold, but in virtue and wisdom, which are
the true blessings of life. Whereas if they go to the administration of public
affairs, poor and hungering after their own private advantage, thinking that
hence they are to snatch the chief good, order there can never be; for they will
be fighting about office, and the civil and domestic broils which thus arise will
be the ruin of the rulers themselves and of the whole State.

Most true, he replied.   66

And the only life which looks down upon the life of political ambition is   67
that of true philosophy. Do you know of any other?

Indeed, I do not, he said.   68

Questions for Critical Thinking

1. What is Plato's attitude, deduced from this allegory, towards the so-called common man?

2. How does the composition and rule of the United States live up to, or refute, the concept of political leadership implied in this allegory?

3. What does this allegory imply about the nature of truth? Do you agree with this view?

4. The dialogue is between Socrates and Glaucon. What is the role of Glaucon in this piece? How would you characterize his part in this dialogue?

5. In his description of the returnee to the cave whose eyes are made dim and weak by the unaccustomed shadows, what popular stereotype of the thinker does Plato depict? What is your view of this stereotype?

6. Do you agree with Plato that the intellectual is doomed always to be at odds with popular belief and thinking? If so, why? If not, why not?

7. Plato writes that if an observer should "laugh at the soul which comes from below into the light, there will be more reason in this than the laugh which greets him who returns from above out of the light into the den." What differences can you perceive in the laughter?

Writing Assignment

Write an essay that proposes and explains your definition of truth and contrasts it with Plato's.

Writing Advice

This assignment asks you to do two things: first, to define your conception of truth; second, to contrast your definition of truth with Plato's in the "Allegory of the Cave." Cave." Ask yourself whether or not you subscribe to Plato's vision of truth as "good" that is "the universal author of all things beautiful and right, parent of light and of the lord of light in this visible world, and the immediate source of reason and truth in the intellectual. . . ."

In explaining how you think Plato sees "truth" you should support your deductions with frequent references to the text. So, for example, if you argue that Plato sees truth as a single and unwavering entity that is the same for all observers, you should cite passages for the text in support of this interpretation.

Note also that the question asks for your definition of truth, implying that truth in our age may have more than one definition (it does). What exactly do you mean by truth? How is your truth arrived at and verified? Is verification the ultimate test of truth as you define it, or do you use some other measure to decide what is true and what untrue? Can your truth be bad, evil, and ugly—unlike Plato's—or is truth as you conceive of it always good? If so, explain and give examples.

Once you have covered Plato's idea of truth as well as your own, you should then explain how your respective concepts agree or differ. Be specific. If you say that Plato's concept of truth is absolute regardless of the observer while yours is not, give examples that clarify the differences. If your idea of truth agrees with Plato's, be sure to detail the exact correspondences.

This essay is bound to have at least two or more distinct parts that will require skillful transitions between them. Certainly one part will be devoted to inferring and defining Plato's idea of truth; another will be given over to a similar explanation of your own; while a third might deal with the comparisons or contrasts between the two views. Consider using a transition paragraph to bridge the gap as you move between topics. For example, as you shift the discussion from the two definitions of truth—yours and Plato's—to the contrast or comparison between them, you could write a transition paragraph in this vein:

> *Plato's concept of truth is an absolute one, regardless of the observer. Mine, on the other hand, stresses the role of the observer. But there are other significant differences between our views.*
> *To begin with, no modern concept of truth would be complete without. . . .*

And then you proceed to compare and contrast the differences.

Alternate Writing Assignment

Write an essay that applies the lessons of Plato's "Allegory of the Cave" to a discussion of prejudice.

PHILOSOPHY

PENSÉES
Blaise Pascal

A child prodigy in mathematics, Blaise Pascal (1623–62), French scientist and religious philosopher, was hailed at 16 for the originality of a mathematical paper on conic sections, and credited at 19 with the invention of a calculating machine. His contributions to science are memorialized today in Pascal's Law of the equilibrium of fluids, which led to practical applications in modern hydraulic systems. *Pensées*, Pascal's philosophical speculations about God and faith, was published posthumously and quickly became a classic of religious thought.

Reading Advice

Reading this selection calls for attentiveness and concentration. This is no fluffy magazine piece that can be breezed through while commuting on a train or munching a hamburger in a noisy cafeteria. Pascal is best confronted in a quiet nook of the library with no surrounding distractions. To savor his wisdom requires an exercise in active reading. Make marginal notes about issues and ideas he raises. Underline important concepts. Try to rephrase key statements in your own words.

In this particular selection from *Pensées*, Pascal is musing about the paradox of being, about the mysteries we are daily and mostly perfunctorily immersed in. Although science and knowledge have come far since Pascal's day, little distance has been gained on the ultimate issues. So, while we may catch Pascal in an occasional error of his times—for example, medicine tells us that belief in the existence of "humors" in the blood is nonsense (paragraph 3)—still, some three hundred years later, we can do little more than gape and wonder along with him at the puzzling mind–body duality that is unique to the human creature.

*L*et man contemplate the whole of   1
nature in her full and grand majesty, and turn his vision from the low objects which surround him. Let him gaze on that brilliant light, set like an eternal lamp to illuminate the universe; let the earth appear to him a point in comparison with the vast circle described by the sun; and let him wonder at the fact that this vast circle is itself but a very fine point in comparison with that described by the stars in their revolution round the firmament. But if our view be arrested there, let our imagination pass beyond; it will sooner exhaust the power of conception than nature that of supplying material for conception. The whole visible world is only an imperceptible atom in the ample bosom of nature. No idea approaches it. We may enlarge our conceptions beyond all imaginable space; we only produce atoms in comparison with the reality of things. It is an infinite sphere, the centre of which is everywhere, the circumference nowhere. In short it is the greatest sensible mark of the almighty power of God, that imagination loses itself in that thought.

Returning to himself, let man consider what he is in comparison with all   2
existence; let him regard himself as lost in this remote corner of nature; and from the little cell in which he finds himself lodged, I mean the universe, let him estimate at their true value the earth, kingdoms, cities, and himself. What is a man in the Infinite?

But to show him another prodigy equally astonishing, let him examine the   3
most delicate things he knows. Let a mite be given him, with its minute body

and parts incomparably more minute, limbs with their joints, veins in the limbs, blood in the veins, humours in the blood, drops in the humours, vapours in the drops. Dividing these last things again, let him exhaust his powers of conception, and let the last object at which he can arrive be now that of our discourse. Perhaps he will think that here is the smallest point in nature. I will let him see therein a new abyss. I will paint for him not only the visible universe, but all that he can conceive of nature's immensity in the womb of this abridged atom. Let him see therein an infinity of universes, each of which has its firmament, its planets, its earth, in the same proportion as in the visible world; in each earth animals, and in the last mites, in which he will find again all that the first had, finding still in these others the same thing without end and without cessation. Let him lose himself in wonders as amazing in their littleness as the others in their vastness. For who will not be astounded at the fact that our body, which a little while ago was imperceptible in the universe, itself imperceptible in the bosom of the whole, is now a colossus, a world, or rather a whole, in respect to the nothingness which we cannot reach? He who regards himself in this light will be afraid of himself, and observing himself sustained in the body given him by nature between those two abysses of the Infinite and Nothing, will tremble at the sight of these marvels; and I think that, as his curiosity changes into admiration, he will be more disposed to contemplate them in silence than to examine them with presumption.

For in fact what is man in nature? A Nothing in comparison with the Infinite, an All in comparison with the Nothing, a mean between nothing and everything. Since he is infinitely removed from comprehending the extremes, the end of things and their beginning are hopelessly hidden from him in an impenetrable secret; he is equally incapable of seeing the Nothing from which he was made, and the Infinite in which he is swallowed up. 4

What will he do then, but perceive the appearance of the middle of things, in an eternal despair of knowing either their beginning or their end. All things proceed from the Nothing, and are borne towards the Infinite. Who will follow these marvellous processes? The Author of these wonders understands them. None other can do so. 5

Through failure to contemplate these Infinities, men have rashly rushed into the examination of nature, as though they bore some proportion to her. It is strange that they have wished to understand the beginnings of things, and thence to arrive at the knowledge of the whole, with a presumption as infinite as their object. For surely this design cannot be formed without presumption or without a capacity infinite like nature. 6

If we are well informed, we understand that, as nature has graven her image and that of her Author on all things, they almost all partake of her double infinity. Thus we see that all the sciences are infinite in the extent of their researches. For who doubts that geometry, for instance, has an infinite infinity 7 of problems to solve? They are also infinite in the multitude and fineness of their promises; for it is clear that those which are put forward as ultimate are not self-supporting, but are based on others which, again having others for their support, do not permit of finality. But we represent some as ultimate for reason, in the same way as in regard to material objects we call that an indivisible point beyond which our senses can no longer perceive anything, although by its nature it is infinitely divisible.

Of these two Infinities of science, that of greatness is the most palpable, and hence a few persons have pretended to know all things. "I will speak of the whole," said Democritus.[1]

But the infinitely little is the least obvious. Philosophers have much oftener claimed to have reached it, and it is here they have all stumbled. This has given rise to such common titles as *First Principles, Principles of Philosophy,* and the like, as ostentatious in fact, though not in appearance, as that one which blinds us, *De omni scibili.*[2]

We naturally believe ourselves far more capable of reaching the centre of things than of embracing their circumference. The visible extent of the world visibly exceeds us; but as we exceed little things, we think ourselves more capable of knowing them. And yet we need no less capacity for attaining the Nothing than the All. Infinite capacity is required for both, and it seems to me that whoever shall have understood the ultimate principles of being might also attain to the knowledge of the Infinite. The one depends on the other, and one leads to the other. These extremes meet and reunite by force of distance, and find each other in God, and in God alone.

Let us then take our compass; we are something, and we are not everything. The nature of our existence hides from us the knowledge of first beginnings which are born of the Nothing; and the littleness of our being conceals from us the sight of the Infinite.

Our intellect holds the same position in the world of thought as our body occupies in the expanse of nature.

Limited as we are in every way, this state which holds the mean between two extremes is present in all our impotence. Our senses perceive no extreme. Too much sound deafens us; too much light dazzles us; too great distance or proximity hinders our view. Too great length and too great brevity of discourse tend to obscurity; too much truth is paralysing (I know some who cannot understand that to take four from nothing leaves nothing). First principles are too self-evident for us; too much pleasure disagrees with us. Too many concords are annoying in music; too many benefits irritate us; we wish to have the wherewithal to over-pay our debts. We feel neither extreme heat nor extreme

8

9

10

11

12

13

---

1. Democritus (460–370) Greek philosopher, who held that all things were made up of atoms.
2. Concerning everything knowable.

cold. Excessive qualities are prejudicial to us and not perceptible by the senses; we do not feel but suffer them. Extreme youth and extreme age hinder the mind, as also too much and too little education. In short, extremes are for us as though they were not, and we are not within their notice. They escape us, or we them.

This is our true state; this is what makes us incapable of certain knowledge and of absolute ignorance. We sail within a vast sphere, ever drifting in uncertainty, driven from end to end. When we think to attach ourselves to any point and to fasten to it, it wavers and leaves us; and if we follow it, it eludes our grasp, slips past us, and vanishes for ever. Nothing stays for us. This is our natural condition, and yet most contrary to our inclination; we burn with desire to find solid ground and an ultimate sure foundation whereon to build a tower reaching to the Infinite. But our whole groundwork cracks, and the earth opens to abysses. 14

Let us therefore not look for certainty and stability. Our reason is always deceived by fickle shadows; nothing can fix the finite between the two Infinites, which both enclose and fly from it. 15

If this be well understood, I think that we shall remain at rest, each in the state wherein nature has placed him. As this sphere which has fallen to us as our lot is always distant from either extreme, what matters is that man should have a little more knowledge of the universe? If he has it, he but gets a little higher. Is he not always infinitely removed from the end, and is not the duration of our life equally removed from eternity, even if it lasts ten years longer? 16

In comparison with these Infinities all finites are equal, and I see no reason for fixing our imagination on one more than on another. The only comparison which we make of ourselves to the finite is painful to us. 17

If man made himself the first object of study, he would see how incapable he is of going further. How can a part know the whole? But he may perhaps aspire to know at least the parts to which he bears some proportion. But the parts of the world are all so related and linked to one another, that I believe it impossible to know one without the other and without the whole. 18

Man, for instance, is related to all he knows. He needs a place wherein to abide, time through which to live, motion in order to live, elements to compose him, warmth and food to nourish him, air to breathe. He sees light; he feels bodies; in short, he is in a dependent alliance with everything. To know man, then, it is necessary to know how it happens that he needs air to live, and, to know the air, we must know how it is thus related to the life of man, etc. Flame cannot exist without air; therefore to understand the one, we must understand the other. 19

Since everything then is cause and effect, dependent and supporting, mediate and immediate, and all is held together by a natural though imperceptible chain, which binds together things most distant and most different, I hold it equally 20 impossible to know the parts without knowing the whole, and to know the whole without knowing the parts in detail.

[The eternity of things in itself or in God must also astonish our brief 21 duration. The fixed and constant immobility of nature, in comparison with the continual change which goes on within us, must have the same effect.]

And what completes our incapability of knowing things, is the fact that they 22 are simple, and that we are composed of two opposite natures, different in kind, soul and body. For it is impossible that our rational part should be other than spiritual; and if any one maintain that we are simply corporeal, this would far more exclude us from the knowledge of things, there being nothing so inconceivable as to say that matter knows itself. It is impossible to imagine how it should know itself.

So if we are simply material, we can know nothing at all; and if we are 23 composed of mind and matter, we cannot know perfectly things which are simple, whether spiritual or corporeal. Hence it comes that almost all philosophers have confused ideas of things, and speak of material things in spiritual terms, and of spiritual things in material terms. For they say boldly that bodies have a tendency to fall, that they seek after their centre, that they fly from destruction, that they fear the void, that they have inclinations, sympathies, antipathies, all of which attributes pertain only to mind. And in speaking of minds, they consider them as in a place, and attribute to them movement from one place to another; and these are qualities which belong only to bodies.

Instead of receiving the ideas of these things in their purity, we colour them 24 with our own qualities, and stamp with our composite being all the simple things which we contemplate.

Who would not think, seeing us compose all things of mind and body, but 25 that this mixture would be quite intelligible to us? Yet it is the very thing we least understand. Man is to himself the most wonderful object in nature; for he cannot conceive what the body is, still less what the mind is, and least of all how a body should be united to a mind. This is the consummation of his difficulties, and yet it is his very being.

Questions for Critical Thinking

1. In the main, how does Pascal's conception of the universe as outlined in this selection differ radically from Plato's in the "Allegory of the Cave"?

2. Do you agree with Pascal that the wish "to understand the beginnings of things, and thence to arrive at a knowledge of the whole" is an effort of infinite presumption? Why or why not?

3. In what way can too much education hinder the mind, as Pascal alleges in paragraph 13?

4. What similarities can you find between Pascal's and Plato's philosophical views?

5. Whose viewpoint, Pascal's or Plato's, is likely to be more sympathetic to the attitudes and quests of modern science? Why?

6. "What matters it that man should have a little more knowledge of the world?" asks Pascal. What answer can you give him?

7. Why is it impossible, as Pascal states in paragraph 22, for matter to know itself? What is your opinion of this view?

8. To whose views are you more sympathetic—Plato's or Pascal's? Why?

Writing Assignment

Write an essay contrasting the effects of too much with too little education.

Writing Advice

One way to write this essay is to begin by asking yourself what effects, good or bad, can occur from too much or too little education. Create a chart with two columns. Head one column "Too Much Education," and the other "Too Little Education," or some such title. In the left margin of the columns indicate the particular basis you are using for your contrast. For example, you may wish to contrast the effects of too much and too little education on one's personality, career choices, and general health. This is what the skeleton of your chart might look like:

	Too Much	_Too Little_
Personality		
Career		
Health		

To complete your list of main points, you merely need to fill in the blanks. For example, you might note that too little education restricts one's career choices to menial work or manual labor, while too much automatically overqualifies an applicant and severely narrows job options. Other effects will no doubt occur to you; we are merely giving an example.

Once you have filled in this chart, you will have the material and details for writing a point-by-point contrast. The next step is to incorporate your points into appropriate paragraphs. Basically, you have two options. First, you may draw an intraparagraph contrast—alternately discussing within a single paragraph the effects of too much and, of too little, education. Or, you may devote an entire paragraph first to one half of the contrast, and then another complete paragraph to the other. Using one method or the other is a matter of a writer's preference.

Of course, none of this systematic listing and planning may suit your particular composing style. You may be the sort who doodles and thinks and then writes and rewrites in one sitting. Or you may wish to read about the topic before you commit pen to paper. The only caution we would urge is that you be fair to both parts of your topic. Do not, for example, write three paragraphs on the effects of too much education on personality and only two sentences on the effects of too little. Lopsidedness is a frequent error of contrasts, and it is common for a writer to get lost in the material and give short shrift to one side while heavily favoring the other. Listing your main points of contrast in a chart is an efficient way to safeguard against this error.

Alternate Writing Assignment

Write an essay discussing Pascal's opinion that "extreme youth and extreme age hinder the mind."

PHILOSOPHY

OUR PICTURE OF THE UNIVERSE
Stephen Hawking

Stephen Hawking (b. 1942), Lucasian professor of mathematics at Cambridge University, is an English mathematician and physicist who is widely regarded as the most brilliant theoretical physicist since Einstein. Afflicted with crippling Lou Gehrig's disease since 1963, Hawking is confined to a wheelchair, cannot read without the help of an automatic page-turner, and can write only by dictating to a secretary. His work on black holes and the theory of "supergravity" is considered ground-breaking and brilliantly intuitive. He is the author of several books, including *The Large Scale Structure of Space-Time* (with G. R. R. Ellis, 1973), and *A Brief History of Time* (1988).

Reading Advice

"Our Picture of the Universe" is the first chapter of the bestselling *A Brief History of Time*, and though it bears signs of gearing-up for a bigger argument, it still presents a fascinating glimpse into what we do know and do not know about time, the universe, and our origin. Hawking is not a journalist but a world-class mathematician and astronomer, and the concepts he struggles to put into print are more crisply communicated by the symbols of mathematics than by words. Yet he admits he tried hard not to use mathematics in his work, having heeded the advice of a friend who warned him that every equation put into the book would halve its sales.

Nevertheless, this is not the sort of work suitable for light bedtime reading. The author's topic is the universe, time, and our origins, and he does not shirk from attempting to survey past theories and from sharing with us his own original thoughts. His compensating virtues are a good style and an eye for the necessary explanatory asides that help make matters clearer. To the reader with absolutely no background in astronomy, we suggest keeping a brief encyclopedia handy and consulting it whenever an unfamiliar name or theory is mentioned.

A well-known scientist (some say it   1
was Bertrand Russell) once gave a public lecture on astronomy. He described how the earth orbits around the sun and how the sun, in turn, orbits around the center of a vast collection of stars called our galaxy. At the end of the lecture, a little old lady at the back of the room got up and said: "What you have told us is rubbish. The world is really a flat plate supported on the back of a giant tortoise." The scientist gave a superior smile before replying, "What is the tortoise standing on?" "You're very clever, young man, very clever," said the old lady. "But it's turtles all the way down!"

Most people would find the picture of our universe as an infinite tower of   2
tortoises rather ridiculous, but why do we think we know better? What do we know about the universe, and how do we know it? Where did the universe come from, and where is it going? Did the universe have a beginning, and if so, what happened *before* then? What is the nature of time? Will it ever come to an end? Recent breakthroughs in physics, made possible in part by fantastic new technologies, suggest answers to some of these longstanding questions. Someday these answers may seem as obvious to us as the earth orbiting the sun—or perhaps as ridiculous as a tower of tortoises. Only time (whatever that may be) will tell.

As long ago as 340 B.C. the Greek philosopher Aristotle, in his book *On the*   3
Heavens, was able to put forward two good arguments for believing that the earth was a round sphere rather than a flat plate. First, he realized that eclipses of the moon were caused by the earth coming between the sun and the moon. The earth's shadow on the moon was always round, which would be true only if the earth was spherical. If the earth had been a flat disk, the shadow would have been elongated and elliptical, unless the eclipse always occurred at a time when the sun was directly under the center of the disk. Second, the Greeks knew from their travels that the North Star appeared lower in the sky when viewed in the south than it did in more northerly regions. (Since the North Star lies over the North Pole, it appears to be directly above an observer at the North Pole, but to someone looking from the equator, it appears to lie just

at the horizon.) From the difference in the apparent position of the North Star in Egypt and Greece, Aristotle even quoted an estimate that the distance around the earth was 400,000 stadia. It is not known exactly what length a stadium was, but it may have been about 200 yards, which would make Aristotle's estimate about twice the currently accepted figure. The Greeks even had a third argument that the earth must be round, for why else does one first see the sails of a ship coming over the horizon, and only later see the hull?

Aristotle thought that the earth was stationary and that the sun, the moon,   4 the planets, and the stars moved in circular orbits about the earth. He believed this because he felt, for mystical reasons, that the earth was the center of the universe, and that circular motion was the most perfect. This idea was elaborated by Ptolemy in the second century A.D. into a complete cosmological model. The earth stood at the center, surrounded by eight spheres that carried the moon, the sun, the stars, and the five planets known at the time, Mercury, Venus, Mars, Jupiter, and Saturn. The planets themselves moved on smaller circles attached to their respective spheres in order to account for their rather complicated observed paths in the sky. The outermost sphere carried the so-called fixed stars, which always stay in the same positions relative to each other but which rotate together across the sky. What lay beyond the last sphere was never made very clear, but it certainly was not part of mankind's observable universe.

Ptolemy's model provided a reasonably accurate system for predicting the   5 positions of heavenly bodies in the sky. But in order to predict these positions correctly, Ptolemy had to make an assumption that the moon followed a path that sometimes brought it twice as close to the earth as at other times. And that meant that the moon ought sometimes to appear twice as big as at other times! Ptolemy recognized this flaw, but nevertheless his model was generally, although not universally, accepted. It was adopted by the Christian church as the picture of the universe that was in accordance with Scripture, for it had the great advantage that it left lots of room outside the sphere of fixed stars for heaven and hell.

A simpler model, however, was proposed in 1514 by a Polish priest, Nicholas   6 Copernicus. (At first, perhaps for fear of being branded a heretic by his church, Copernicus circulated his model anonymously.) His idea was that the sun was stationary at the center and that the earth and the planets moved in circular orbits around the sun. Nearly a century passed before this idea was taken seriously. Then two astronomers—the German, Johannes Kepler, and the Italian, Galileo Galilei—started publicly to support the Copernican theory, despite the fact that the orbits it predicted did not quite match the ones observed. The death blow to the Aristotelian/Ptolemaic theory came in 1609. In that year, Galileo started observing the night sky with a telescope, which had just been invented. When he looked at the planet Jupiter, Galileo found that it was accompanied by several small satellites or moons that orbited around it. This implied that everything did *not* have to orbit directly around the earth, as Aristotle and Ptolemy had thought. (It was, of course, still possible to believe that the earth was stationary at the center of the universe and that the moons of Jupiter moved on extremely complicated paths around the earth, giving the *appearance* that they orbited Jupiter. However, Copernicus's theory was much simpler.) At the same time, Johannes Kepler had modified Copernicus's theory, suggesting that the planets moved not in circles but in ellipses (an ellipse is an elongated circle). The predictions now finally matched the observations.

As far as Kepler was concerned, elliptical orbits were merely an ad hoc   7
hypothesis, and a rather repugnant one at that, because ellipses were clearly less perfect than circles. Having discovered almost by accident that elliptical orbits fit the observations well, he could not reconcile them with his idea that the planets were made to orbit the sun by magnetic forces. An explanation was provided only much later, in 1687, when Sir Isaac Newton published his *Philosophiae Naturalis Principia Mathematica,* probably the most important single work ever published in the physical sciences. In it Newton not only put forward a theory of how bodies move in space and time, but he also developed the complicated mathematics needed to analyze those motions. In addition, Newton postulated a law of universal gravitation according to which each body in the universe was attracted toward every other body by a force that was stronger the more massive the bodies and the closer they were to each other. It was this same force that caused objects to fall to the ground. (The story that Newton was inspired by an apple hitting his head is almost certainly apocryphal. All Newton himself ever said was that the idea of gravity came to him as he sat "in a contemplative mood" and "was occasioned by the fall of an apple.") Newton went on to show that, according to his law, gravity causes the moon to move in an elliptical orbit around the earth and causes the earth and the planets to follow elliptical paths around the sun.

The Copernican model got rid of Ptolemy's celestial spheres, and with them,   8
the idea that the universe had a natural boundary. Since "fixed stars" did not appear to change their positions apart from a rotation across the sky caused by the earth spinning on its axis, it became natural to suppose that the fixed stars were objects like our sun but very much farther away.

Newton realized that, according to his theory of gravity, the stars should   9
attract each other, so it seemed they could not remain essentially motionless. Would they not all fall together at some point? In a letter in 1691 to Richard Bentley, another leading thinker of his day, Newton argued that this would indeed happen if there were only a finite number of stars distributed over a finite region of space. But he reasoned that if, on the other hand, there were an infinite number of stars, distributed more or less uniformly over infinite space, this would not happen, because there would not be any central point for them to fall to.

This argument is an instance of the pitfalls that you can encounter in talking   10
about infinity. In an infinite universe, every point can be regarded as the center,
because every point has an infinite number of stars on each side of it. The
correct approach, it was realized only much later, is to consider the finite
situation, in which the stars all fall in on each other, and then to ask how things
change if one adds more stars roughly uniformly distributed outside this region.
According to Newton's law, the extra stars would make no difference at all to
the original ones on average, so the stars would fall in just as fast. We can add
as many stars as we like, but they will still always collapse in on themselves.
We now know it is impossible to have an infinite static model of the universe
in which gravity is always attractive.

It is an interesting reflection on the general climate of thought before the   11
twentieth century that no one had suggested that the universe was expanding
or contracting. It was generally accepted that either the universe had existed
forever in an unchanging state, or that it had been created at a finite time in
the past more or less as we observe it today. In part this may have been due
to people's tendency to believe in eternal truths, as well as the comfort they
found in the thought that even though they may grow old and die, the universe
is eternal and unchanging.

Even those who realized that Newton's theory of gravity showed that the   12
universe could not be static did not think to suggest that it might be expanding.
Instead, they attempted to modify the theory by making the gravitational force
repulsive at very large distances. This did not significantly affect their predictions of the motions of the planets, but it allowed an infinite distribution of
stars to remain in equilibrium—with the attractive forces between nearby stars
balanced by the repulsive forces from those that were farther away. However,
we now believe such an equilibrium would be unstable: if the stars in some
region got only slightly nearer each other, the attractive forces between them
would become stronger and dominate over the repulsive forces so that the stars
would continue to fall toward each other. On the other hand, if the stars got
a bit farther away from each other, the repulsive forces would dominate and
drive them farther apart.

Another objection to an infinite static universe is normally ascribed to the   13
German philosopher Heinrich Olbers, who wrote about this theory in 1823.
In fact, various contemporaries of Newton had raised the problem, and the
Olbers article was not even the first to contain plausible arguments against it.
It was, however, the first to be widely noted. The difficulty is that in an infinite
static universe nearly every line of sight would end on the surface of a star.
Thus one would expect that the whole sky would be as bright as the sun, even
at night. Olbers's counterargument was that the light from distant stars would
be dimmed by absorption by intervening matter. However, if that happened
the intervening matter would eventually heat up until it glowed as brightly as
the stars. The only way of avoiding the conclusion that the whole of the night

sky should be as bright as the surface of the sun would be to assume that the stars had not been shining forever but had turned on at some finite time in the past. In that case the absorbing matter might not have heated up yet or the light from distant stars might not yet have reached us. And that brings us to the question of what could have caused the stars to have turned on in the first place.

The beginning of the universe had, of course, been discussed long before this. According to a number of early cosmologies and the Jewish/Christian/ Muslim tradition, the universe started at a finite, and not very distant, time in the past. One argument for such a beginning was the feeling that it was necessary to have "First Cause" to explain the existence of the universe. (Within the universe, you always explained one event as being caused by some earlier event, but the existence of the universe itself could be explained in this way only if it had some beginning.) Another argument was put forward by St. Augustine in his book *The City of God.* He pointed out that civilization is progressing and we remember who performed this deed or developed that technique. Thus man, and so also perhaps the universe, could not have been around all that long. St. Augustine accepted a date of about 5000 B.C. for the Creation of the universe according to the book of Genesis. (It is interesting that this is not so far from the end of the last Ice Age, about 10,000 B.C., which is when archaeologists tell us that civilization really began.)   14

Aristotle, and most of the other Greek philosophers, on the other hand, did not like the idea of a creation because it smacked too much of divine intervention. They believed, therefore, that the human race and the world around it had existed, and would exist, forever. The ancients had already considered the argument about progress described above, and answered it by saying that there had been periodic floods or other disasters that repeatedly set the human race right back to the beginning of civilization.   15

The questions of whether the universe had a beginning in time and whether it is limited in space were later extensively examined by the philosopher Immanuel Kant in his monumental (and very obscure) work, *Critique of Pure Reason,* published in 1781. He called these questions antinomies (that is, contradictions) of pure reason because he felt that there were equally compelling arguments for believing the thesis, that the universe had a beginning, and the antithesis, that it had existed forever. His argument for the thesis was that if the universe did not have a beginning, there would be an infinite period of time before any event, which he considered absurd. The argument for the antithesis was that if the universe had a beginning, there would be an infinite period of time before it, so why should the universe begin at any one particular time? In fact, his cases for both the thesis and the antithesis are really the same argument. They are both based on his unspoken assumption that time continues back forever, whether or not the universe had existed forever. As we shall see, the concept   16 of time has no meaning before the beginning of the universe. This was first pointed out by St. Augustine. When asked: What did God do before he created the universe? Augustine didn't reply: He was preparing Hell for people who asked such questions. Instead, he said that time was a property of the universe that God created, and that time did not exist before the beginning of the universe.

When most people believed in an essentially static and unchanging universe, the question of whether or not it had a beginning was really one of metaphysics or theology. One could account for what was observed equally well on the theory that the universe had existed forever or on the theory that it was set in motion at some finite time in such a manner as to look as though it had existed forever. But in 1929, Edwin Hubble made the landmark observation that wherever you look, distant galaxies are moving rapidly away from us. In other words, the universe is expanding. This means that at earlier times objects would have been closer together. In fact, it seemed that there was a time, about ten or twenty thousand million years ago, when they were all at exactly the same place and when, therefore, the density of the universe was infinite. This discovery finally brought the question of the beginning of the universe into the realm of science.   17

Hubble's observations suggested that there was a time, called the big bang, when the universe was infinitesimally small and infinitely dense. Under such conditions all the laws of science, and therefore all ability to predict the future, would break down. If there were events earlier than this time, then they could not affect what happens at the present time. Their existence can be ignored because it would have no observational consequences. One may say that time had a beginning at the big bang, in the sense that earlier times simply would not be defined. It should be emphasized that this beginning in time is very different from those that had been considered previously. In an unchanging universe a beginning in time is something that has to be imposed by some being outside the universe; there is no physical necessity for a beginning. One can imagine that God created the universe at literally any time in the past. On the other hand, if the universe is expanding, there may be physical reasons why there had to be a beginning. One could still imagine that God created the universe at the instant of the big bang, or even afterwards in just such a way as to make it look as though there had been a big bang, but it would be meaningless to suppose that it was created *before* the big bang. An expanding universe does not preclude a creator, but it does place limits on when he might have carried out his job!   18

In order to talk about the nature of the universe and to discuss questions such as whether it has a beginning or an end, you have to be clear about what a scientific theory is. I shall take the simple-minded view that a theory is just a model of the universe, or a restricted part of it, and a set of rules that relate   19 quantities in the model to observations that we make. It exists only in our minds and does not have any other reality (whatever that might mean). A theory is a good theory if it satisfies two requirements: It must accurately describe a large class of observations on the basis of a model that contains only a few arbitrary elements, and it must make definite predictions about the results of future observations. For example, Aristotle's theory that everything was made out of four elements, earth, air, fire, and water, was simple enough to qualify, but it did not make any definite predictions. On the other hand, Newton's theory of gravity was based on an even simpler model, in which bodies attracted each other with a force that was proportional to a quantity called their mass and inversely proportional to the square of the distance between them. Yet it predicts the motions of the sun, the moon, and the planets to a high degree of accuracy.

Any physical theory is always provisional, in the sense that it is only a   20
hypothesis: you can never prove it. No matter how many times the results of experiments agree with some theory, you can never be sure that the next time the result will not contradict the theory. On the other hand, you can disprove a theory by finding even a single observation that disagrees with the predictions of the theory. As philosopher of science Karl Popper has emphasized, a good theory is characterized by the fact that it makes a number of predictions that could in principle be disproved or falsified by observation. Each time new experiments are observed to agree with the predictions the theory survives, and our confidence in it is increased; but if ever a new observation is found to disagree, we have to abandon or modify the theory. At least that is what is supposed to happen, but you can always question the competence of the person who carried out the observation.

In practice, what often happens is that a new theory is devised that is really   21
an extension of the previous theory. For example, very accurate observations of the planet Mercury revealed a small difference between its motion and the predictions of Newton's theory of gravity. Einstein's general theory of relativity predicted a slightly different motion from Newton's theory. The fact that Einstein's predictions matched what was seen, while Newton's did not, was one of the crucial confirmations of the new theory. However, we still use Newton's theory for all practical purposes because the difference between its predictions and those of general relativity is very small in the situations that we normally deal with. (Newton's theory also has the great advantage that it is much simpler to work with than Einstein's!)

The eventual goal of science is to provide a single theory that describes the   22
whole universe. However, the approach most scientists actually follow is to separate the problem into two parts. First, there are the laws that tell us how the universe changes with time. (If we know what the universe is like at any one time, these physical laws tell us how it will look at any later time.) Second, there is the question of the initial state of the universe. Some people feel that

science should be concerned with only the first part; they regard the question of the initial situation as a matter for metaphysics or religion. They would say that God, being omnipotent, could have started the universe off any way he wanted. That may be so, but in that case he also could have made it develop in a completely arbitrary way. Yet it appears that he chose to make it evolve in a very regular way according to certain laws. It therefore seems equally reasonable to suppose that there are also laws governing the initial state.

It turns out to be very difficult to devise a theory to describe the universe all in one go. Instead, we break the problem up into bits and invent a number of partial theories. Each of these partial theories describes and predicts a certain limited class of observations, neglecting the effects of other quantities, or representing them by simple sets of numbers. It may be that this approach is completely wrong. If everything in the universe depends on everything else in a fundamental way, it might be impossible to get close to a full solution by investigating parts of the problem in isolation. Nevertheless, it is certainly the way that we have made progress in the past. The classic example again is the Newtonian theory of gravity, which tells us that the gravitational force between two bodies depends only on one number associated with each body, its mass, but is otherwise independent of what the bodies are made of. Thus one does not need to have a theory of the structure and constitution of the sun and the planets in order to calculate their orbits.

Today scientists describe the universe in terms of two basic partial theories— the general theory of relativity and quantum mechanics. They are the great intellectual achievements of the first half of this century. The general theory of relativity describes the force of gravity and the large-scale structure of the universe, that is, the structure on scales from only a few miles to as large as a million million million million (1 with twenty-four zeros after it) miles, the size of the observable universe. Quantum mechanics, on the other hand, deals with phenomena on extremely small scales, such as a millionth of a millionth of an inch. Unfortunately, however, these two theories are known to be inconsistent with each other—they cannot both be correct. One of the major endeavors in physics today, and the major theme of this book, is the search for a new theory that will incorporate them both—a quantum theory of gravity. We do not yet have such a theory, and we may still be a long way from having one, but we do already know many of the properties that it must have. And we shall see, in later chapters, that we already know a fair amount about the predictions a quantum theory of gravity must make.

Now, if you believe that the universe is not arbitrary, but is governed by definite laws, you ultimately have to combine the partial theories into a complete unified theory that will describe everything in the universe. But there is a fundamental paradox in the search for such a complete unified theory. The ideas about scientific theories outlined above assume we are rational beings who are free to observe the universe as we want and to draw logical deductions from what we see. In such a scheme it is reasonable to suppose that we might progress ever closer toward the laws that govern our universe. Yet if there really is a complete unified theory, it would also presumably determine our actions. And so the theory itself would determine the outcome of our search for it! And why should it determine that we come to the right conclusions from the evidence? Might it not equally well determine that we draw the wrong conclusion? Or no conclusion at all?

The only answer that I can give to this problem is based on Darwin's principle   26
of natural selection. The idea is that in any population of self-reproducing organisms, there will be variations in the genetic material and upbringing that different individuals have. These differences will mean that some individuals are better able than others to draw the right conclusions about the world around them and to act accordingly. These individuals will be more likely to survive and reproduce and so their pattern of behavior and thought will come to dominate. It has certainly been true in the past that what we call intelligence and scientific discovery has conveyed a survival advantage. It is not so clear that this is still the case: our scientific discoveries may well destroy us all, and even if they don't, a complete unified theory may not make much difference to our chances of survival. However, provided the universe has evolved in a regular way, we might expect that the reasoning abilities that natural selection has given us would be valid also in our search for a complete unified theory, and so would not lead us to the wrong conclusions.

Because the partial theories that we already have are sufficient to make   27
accurate predictions in all but the most extreme situations, the search for the ultimate theory of the universe seems difficult to justify on practical grounds. (It is worth noting, though, that similar arguments could have been used against both relativity and quantum mechanics, and these theories have given us both nuclear energy and the microelectronics revolution!) The discovery of a complete unified theory, therefore, may not aid the survival of our species. It may not even affect our life-style. But ever since the dawn of civilization, people have not been content to see events as unconnected and inexplicable. They have craved an understanding of the underlying order in the world. Today we still yearn to know why we are here and where we came from. Humanity's deepest desire for knowledge is justification enough for our continuing quest. And our goal is nothing less than a complete description of the universe we live in.

Questions for Critical Thinking

1. What is the state of our present knowledge of the universe, its origins, and operating laws?

2. How is your life affected by the knowledge that some astronomers predict the eventual disintegration of our universe by natural causes?

3. What effect upon our view of ourselves as a species do you think an earth-centered theory of the universe, such as Ptolemy's, would have if it were still applicable today?

4. How do astronomical findings affect your personal religious beliefs? If they do not affect your religious beliefs, explain why.

5. What comfort, if any, can humans find in the thought that even though they must grow old and die, the universe remains static and unchanging?

6. What is your opinion of those who contend that science should not be concerned about the origin of the universe? What justification can you give for the intense concern of science about a theory of origins?

7. Would a unified theory of the universe, including a theory that succeeded in completely explaining its origin, necessarily affect your belief in God? Why or why not?

8. In his approach to speculating about the universe and its origin, how does Hawking differ from Pascal?

Writing Assignment

Hawking writes: "In order to talk about the nature of the universe and to discuss questions such as whether it has a beginning or an end, you have to be clear about what a scientific theory is." Write an essay defining and explaining the meaning of "theory."

Writing Advice

The assignment calls for an extended definition of the word and concept "theory." To write an extended definition, you must do more than simply say what a word or concept is; you must also say what it is not, what experts and specialists have had to say about it, and what practical effect it exerts. It also helps to support your definition with examples, since your ultimate aim is to make the meaning of the word or concept absolutely clear.

1. You might begin with a lexical definition, meaning the sort of word-for-word definition found in a dictionary. It is sometimes helpful, depending on the word or concept you are defining, to open with an etymological discussion of the root meaning of the word. The etymology found in any good dictionary can provide a useful starting point for your discussion.

2. After you say what the word means, it often helps to say what it does not mean. For example, you might contrast "theory" with "prejudice" or "bias," and show how they differ. Or you might say how a theory is unlike a fact or an idea. Discussing what a word does *not* mean can substantially add to an understanding of its real meaning.

3. Consult and cite the opinions of experts and specialists, who have written or expressed their views on your defined term. Including the occasional pithy remark or comment of an acknowledged expert can add color and liveliness to your essay.

4. Give examples. Mention some well-known and accepted theories. Cite those theories whose validity is under attack—the theory of evolution, for example. Show how a theory acquires acceptability or how it falls into disrepute.

5. Explain the practical use and effect of a theory. How do scientists actually employ theories? What significance to working scientists do theories possess? How would science proceed if the concept of theory had not been devised?

Remember that the aim of your essay is to clarify the meaning of "theory." Your task is to add whatever amplification you must to the dictionary meaning until you have made "theory" unmistakably clear.

Alternate Writing Assignments

1. In an essay explain how and why astronomical theories and explanations about the universe affect or do not affect your religious beliefs.

2. There are people alive and functioning well in society today who still persist in the belief that the earth is flat. What practical effect does belief in current and accurate astronomical principles have on any life? In an essay, explore this question.

HISTORY

BANTING: WHO FOUND INSULIN
Paul De Kruif

Paul De Kruif (1890–1971) was born in Zeeland, Michigan, and educated at the University of Michigan, Ann Arbor, where he was briefly an assistant professor of bacteriology. During his long life he served as a researcher at the Pasteur Institute and the Rockefeller Institute for Medical Research. After his stint in the laboratory, he worked as a freelance writer and popularizer of medical science for nearly 50 years. His works include *Our Medicine Men* (1922), *Microbe Hunters* (1926), *Men Against Death* (1932), and *The Sweeping Wind, a Memoir* (1962).

Reading Advice

The following selection should be read with a proverbial grain of salt. De Kruif is taking poetic license and following the "you-are-there" style of history writing first practiced by the Victorian biography Lytton Strachey (1880–1932). But De Kruif was not there; he is merely assuming the literary perspective of the observer peering over Banting's shoulder, a view that adds narrative momentum and drive to the story. But he cannot know what Banting, as he toiled away in his laboratory, was thinking. And, though the author does not say so, many of the thoughts and sentiments he attributes to Banting must have been derived from inference and secondhand accounts.

Nevertheless, De Kruif's poetic liberties are amply repaid by the results—a stirring story of want and struggle followed by hard-earned discovery, vindication, and success. The reader gets a rare glimpse of Banting and his assistant George Best in their laboratory; the author paints an entirely convincing picture of the daily grit, grime, and boredom of medical research. And we come away with a better understanding of what medical truth is and the effort often expended in finding it. Banting bequeathed to the world a precious gift of understanding that helped prolong and save lives. The world rewarded Banting in 1923 with the Nobel Prize for Medicine and Physiology, an honor he shared with his sponsor, J. J. R. Macleod, who gave him the dogs and the assistant he begged for to do his priceless work.

*M*y father died of diabetes in 1917, a 1
starved shadow of the husky man he'd been in his prime. That was only four years before Banting began saving the lives of his diabetic dogs in the low-ceilinged room up under the roof of Toronto University Medical Building in the memorably hot summer of 1921. The sugar sickness struck my father in 1907 and it was terrible the way it suddenly changed him. I can see him now, as clearly as if it were yesterday, on the day I first realized something awful had got hold of him. It was a raw day in February with the sidewalks slippery. I met him shuffling down the middle of our village street. His face was gray and there was a droop to his shoulders that had always been so straight.

He tried everything. But those were the hopeless days when medical sci- 2
entists were proving no such thing as insulin was possible. The highest authorities would have given you a laugh if you'd predicted that such a recently graduated plow-boy as Banting would right soon be finding something that would help to stretch out diabetics' lives by decades.

My father was only a small-town business man but he had respect for science. 3
In those years while he was slowly dying, and I'd become a medical student, he was always asking me what researchers were discovering about this hole in him. So he described it. Dr. Foster at the University Hospital at Ann Arbor was giving him the very best modern diet treatment and that used to fix him up for a bit but then that acetone odor would come into his breath again. In

his blue spells he seemed to hold it against me that all the best scientists could offer him was a slow starvation almost as cruel as death. . . .

All over were thousands like him, living by starving. In 1917 I watched my father die, at sixty. It seems weird now to think that, since that lovely June day only fourteen years ago, two discoveries have been made, both to be told of in this book of men against death, and both would have helped to make my father's life much longer. If it had then existed, Banting's insulin would have controlled my father's diabetes. But his diabetes, unchecked, sapped his power to fight invading microbes. So finally hemolytic streptococcus got into his throat and its then unknown poison finished him off by wrecking his kidneys. How he might have dodged that, you'll read at the end of the story of these death-fighters.

For many days before he died my father's sunken cheeks made him look, once more, like the faded daguerreotypes taken of him when he was a boy. He was out of his head most of the time those spring days. Once he looked at me, suddenly clear-eyed, asking, "Paul, what's death . . . ?"

If it had only been a few years later, I might have come to him long before he'd got to this sad extremity, telling him: "Dad, I've got great news for you. . . ."

This has made me hungry to dig to the bottom of those events that took place on certain hot nights in 1921 in Toronto. Who was Banting that he could work this magic?

Of course Banting had no business to discover insulin, let alone try it. Diabetes is a medical sickness and Banting never presumed to be anything but a surgeon in those hard-time days of his just after the war. An enormous amount of exact, complicated, big-worded knowledge had been piled up by physiologists and bio-chemists telling how the sugar sickness kills its victims. Of this knowledge Banting was innocent and it had never been his ambition to be a diabetes specialist. He wasn't brilliant—just stubborn. He'd come back from war with a very deep, very ugly scar on one of his forearms. "I'm going to keep that arm," Banting told the surgeons who'd said he'd die if they didn't amputate.

He served a term as resident at the Hospital for Sick Children in Toronto. Then he hung up his shingle to be a small-town surgeon in London, Ontario. After waiting for twenty-eight days in a row till his first patient came and having four dollars on his books at the end of his first month's practice, he landed a job as a part-time demonstrator in the Western Ontario Medical School, not because he was scientifically ambitious but to help himself eat.

He was conscientious at that teaching job and had plenty of time to be, and night after night he sat in his threadbare quarters plugging up the lecture he had to give the medical students next day. Till that strange night of October 30, 1920 . . .

That night in his farmerish, peculiarly stubborn way he was getting it soaked into his head how, if we didn't have pancreases, we'd all die of diabetes. Of

4
5
6
7
8
9
10
11

course long before, in medical school, he'd learned how important this pancreas was for the digestion of food, how it's really a terrific and versatile little ferment factory, pouring through its duct leading to the small intestine a mysterious juice that chews up sugars, splits up fats, tears apart proteins for us to absorb and to use them.

Now Banting with his longish sort of inquisitive nose sat alone there this night hunched over his books, getting it through his head how Minkowski, the German, had cut the pancreas slick and clean out of a dog, sewed him up with every surgical precaution, then watched this poor beast—incredibly swiftly—get thin, get thirsty, get ravenously hungry, then lie down with just pep enough to raise his head to drink water that turned into urine loaded with sugar. . . . In less than ten days that dog died—of diabetes. 12

That ought to interest his students. Banting waded through a jungle of pancreas science to find out how the learned German, Langerhans, had spotted peculiar little islands in this remarkable gland—little bunches of cells strangely different from the ferment cells that made the digestive juices. These islands of Langerhans had never a duct leading from them. What could they be good for? 13

Banting got it down cold to tell his students that it was these insignificant Langerhans cells that really guarded us from diabetes. You could tie off the duct leading from a dog's pancreas so not a drop of digestive juice could flow out. That dog didn't get the sugar sickness. But just cut out the whole pancreas . . . ! 14

Ho-hum, this particular night's drudgery was mighty near finished. But he'd tell them this, finally, next morning: The American searcher, Opie, had probed into the pancreases of folks dead of the sugar sickness, and found how those Langerhans island cells looked shot, looked sick . . . 15

Did they make a hormone, maybe? When they're healthy, don't these island cells pour into our blood an internal secretion, a mysterious something, some "X" that helps all the cells of our bodies burn the sugar they need for energy? Well—nobody'd ever found such a life-saving "X". . . . 16

Here's Banting this night in October, 1920, finding out how dozens of searchers had spent years looking for this mysterious "X"—all failing. Here's Banting at the end of another day. His lecture's ready. All over Europe and America are millions of folks with diabetes, thousands dying. Here are children suddenly struck with it, wasting away into emaciated dwarfs, always dying. Here are young men and women in their prime, thirsty, drinking and still always thirsty, and hungry, eating, yet hungry, going down hill more slowly than the children, but watching their bodies run away in dreadful rivers of sugar, and dying. 17

What could any of them hope from Banting? He himself would have laughed if you'd told him that within an hour . . . 18

He has it thoroughly through his head for his students that it's the island 19 cells of the pancreases of all these doomed people that go mysteriously bad . . . but who can fix them? You can string out the lives of those poor kids for days, of the young grown-ups for months, by the Guelpa-Allen undernutrition treatment that's a polite term for slow starvation. That's that.

It's past bedtime. Idly he slits open a copy of the medical journal *Surgery,*   20
Gynecology, and Obstetrics that's arrived today. He begins to wool-gather through it. Ho-hum. . . . Wait . . . here's a new report on the pancreas and diabetes. A funny coincidence, this. . . . By Moses Baron . . . and who is this Moses? But wait . . .

Banting bends over the pages and now the drab lesson for those students   21
and his feeble, slowly growing surgical practice are as if they never existed. This Baron—here's something that's something! When people have gallstones that block off their pancreatic duct, and they die, when you take out their pancreas post mortem, you find the digestive-juice-making cells have shriveled, degenerated, died. *But the Langerhans island cells have stayed perfectly healthy!*

Banting's lost in this dull scientific report now. By George! Such people   22
don't have a sign of diabetes. And wait. It's the same with dogs, so writes Baron. Tie off their pancreas duct. Then operate. They live all right. Then operate again. The digestive-juice-making cells of their pancreas are degenerated. *But those island cells are okay*—like those gallstone people. And the dogs don't get diabetes. . . .

Banting's no longer a struggling doctor nor a miserably paid half-time lec-   23
turer. He goes to bed but his brain's in a buzz. He lies there . . . his brain is trying . . . that's the word for it. His brain aches from what he later quaintly called "trying to bridge a wide spark gap between two remote ideas." He can't sleep. His brain is strained the way it strains trying to recall a name on the verge of your memory or trying to get back an old tune you're on the edge of remembering.

Here's what gnawed him: Wasn't there some way to use those healthy island   24
cells from the degenerated pancreas of a dog with a tied-off duct to help keep alive a dying diabetic dog who'd had his pancreas cut out entirely?

At two that morning his hunch hit him. He got up, blinked at the light,   25
scrawled three sentences in his notebook:

"Tie off pancreatic duct of dogs. Wait 6 to 8 weeks for degeneration. Remove   26
residue and extract."

He went to sleep. Next morning he knew he wasn't made for a surgeon.   27

Now Banting's in the office of the famous Professor Macleod in the Depart-   28
ment of Physiology in the Medical School of the University of Toronto. He fishes for words. He's *got* to impress the Professor. But all he has is those three short sentences in his notebook, a fierce hunch, a plan of action, but words? Not Banting.

It's a contrast. Banting the farmerish up-country surgeon: Macleod as great   29
as there is in all North America on the science of how our bodies burn sugar
for energy. It's faintly ridiculous. Banting's like an inventor pleading his cause
without even a model.

Macleod was a distinguished man and a busy one. What, exactly, was Dr.   30
Banting driving at? What was his plan?

Banting fished for scientific expressions. . . . You see, if you tie off a dog's   31
pancreatic duct, the digestive juice cells will go to pieces. . . . The island cells
will stay healthy, and then . . .

Professor Macleod wanted to know had this degeneration after duct-tying   32
been completely proved, confirmed, scientifically? Wouldn't it take Banting—
after all he wasn't a scientist!—years to learn pancreas-anatomy, physiology,
and did he know the chemistry of the blood sugar? And clinical diabetes?

Banting was now the way he'd been with the surgeons when he wouldn't   33
let them amputate his mangled arm and . . . well, didn't Professor Macleod see?
You take out such a duct-tied, degenerated pancreas. Its digestive juice is gone.
There you've got the island cells—undigested, undamaged. *There'll be no juice
to ruin them.* There you'll have your hormone, your "X"! There'll be the internal
secretion needed for burning sugar. And then . . .

But how did Dr. Banting know there was an internal secretion in the   34
pancreas, ever? Mightn't a healthy pancreas prevent diabetes some other way?
Mightn't the pancreas change the blood running through it, remove poisons
from the blood that prevented the body using sugar? There wouldn't have to
be an "X" . . . Not necessarily!

Professor Macleod had gone on record suggesting this explanation in a   35
learned treatise only a little while before and that reduced Banting's fine hunch—
to nonsense.

Professor Macleod was a busy man but Banting fumbled and bent forward   36
and stuttered but stuck to it.

But how did Banting know the digestive juices of the pancreas were bad for   37
the island cells? If they weren't, then what good tying off the dog's ducts?

Banting felt it must be so. He repeated, he *felt* it.   38

Surely Professor Macleod deserves much for his patience in listening to this   39
fanatical scientific tyro. But at last Macleod asked Banting a question that was
absolutely unanswerable. . . .

How could *Banting* hope to accomplish what the highest trained physiologists   40
in the world had not succeeded in establishing or proving?

Well, Banting felt . . .   41

Well, what *did* Banting want, really?   42

"I would like ten dogs and an assistant for eight weeks," Banting said.   43

Professor Macleod will forever be famous for giving Banting exactly what   44
he asked for, no less, no more.

Banting wanted to drop his practice, his teaching, burn all bridges behind   45
him, so he told his old teacher, the great surgeon Starr. But Starr and his
friends Gallie and Robertson and the generous, dark-eyed Professor V. E. Henderson all thought he was, to say the least, a mild lunatic for giving up his
surgical career before barely starting it. They thought his wild idea would cool
off if he went back and finished his year out at London, Ontario, and they all
counseled him to go back. "Consequently I returned to London," Banting said.

But his idea instead of cooling, got hotter, burned in him all through that   46
winter, heated him from the top of his sandy hair to his toes. He was utterly
without animals, test-tubes, even any kind of a laboratory, so he read and read
and read about diabetes and the pancreas and the utter failure of all distinguished searchers to do any good whatever to dying diabetics by feeding them
pancreas or injecting them with it, and yet his hunch kept heating him. He
cared nothing about building a practice and when his eyes got tired from reading
he took up painting pictures, knowing absolutely nothing about it and with no
one to tell him. He painted in oils with water-color brushes because he didn't
know any better . . . but he painted.

May 16, 1921, and here he was at last, a scientist. Here he stood in a   47
miserable, grimy little cubby-hole of a room in the Medical Building in Toronto,
a self-appointed researcher, untitled, absolutely unpaid. He'd sold his office
furniture and instruments. Oh, that would keep him alive, till . . .

It was comical. He stood before a bench never having made an experiment   48
and insanely convinced that under his thatch he had the answer to the deep
horrible riddle of the sugar disease. That bench was all his laboratory because
the rest of this dreadful little room was used for routine chemistry by other
workers. Here was Banting with everything Macleod had promised him, ten
dogs, and eight weeks ahead of him in which to solve a most tangled medical
mystery. And an assistant, too, not a doctor, mind you, but only a medical
student, a boy just twenty-one. . . .

This assistant, Mr. Charles H. Best, was supposed to be skilled in the exact   49
chemical determination of the amounts of sugar in the urine and the blood of
his dogs who should become diabetic. Best did know more than Banting about
blood and urine chemistry because Banting knew next to nothing about it. Best
had blond hair and very wide-open blue eyes that were set in a pleasant face
of high complexion—not a grim face like Banting's. Probably the best qualification of Best was that he understood, almost as little as Banting, the folly of
this forlorn enterprise of eight weeks and ten dogs.

They began by failing.   50

Right off the bat they got busy to tie off the pancreas ducts of sundry of   51
the ten dogs Macleod had allowed Banting. Here was Banting's first good break:
he was a deft surgeon with four years of experience under the famous C. L.

Starr and the very ticklish operations were apparently great successes and the dogs recovered beautifully and here it was the 6th of July, beastly hot, and seven of the eight weeks were gone. . . .

Now the pancreases of these dogs should be degenerated. The pancreatic juice-producing cells should be dead. The island of Langerhans cells should be healthy, and now to inject them into pancreasless dogs dying with diabetes. Such doomed beasts were ready. . . .   52

Alas! Here were two dogs they'd just chloroformed, and both of them with perfectly full-sized pancreases. A miserable fizzle! And one week left. . . .   53

It was when the going got tough that Banting got good. Now the flash of his knife in his nimble hands, with him peering, head bent over the opened bodies of those dogs, eyes close to the slash, slash, slash of his knife delicately cutting all around those ducts he thought he'd tied off so tightly . . .   54

Blockhead he'd been. He'd tied them *too tight*! Then gangrene. Then oozing of serum. Then nature growing a new duct round the wall of the old one. . . . And only one week left . . .   55

Up and up the stairs from their work-bench went Banting and Best, round and round a narrow long winding stairs to a tiny room where they operated their dogs. It had no windows. Its grimy skylight let through more heat rays than light rays. Here in the strong smell of ether with the sweat running down their faces they operated the rest of their dogs all over again—   56

Here was good news: in some of these beasts with bellies slit open, the pancreas was mighty hard to find—was really degenerated. Now to make double sure, triple sure, Banting tied off even these ducts in two and three places, with different tightnesses of his ligatures. Then they sewed those dogs up again. Then they waited again in the heat.   57

Now at last the chance to test the hunch. Ten in the morning of July 27 and of course the eight-week limit Banting had asked for long since past. No money to pay Charlie Best for his time now, so Best borrowed money from Banting. A giant tractor couldn't have pulled Banting away from his little black bench now. Weeks ago, when work had just started, Macleod had left for Europe. It's again to the credit of Professor Macleod that he didn't write to stop Banting now that the eight weeks were up, and that he let Banting struggle on, but how he went on God knows.   58

This steamy hot day a poor dog, miserably thin, lies on their table. Nine days before Banting had slit out his pancreas and with the dog going down hill like a shot, day after day, Banting had drawn samples of dark blood from the beast's veins with a syringe while Best sat before his colorimeter, watching the sugar in the dog's blood go higher, higher. It got harder for the dog to stand up. He could hardly wag his tail when they came for him. He was horribly   59 thirsty and hungry as a wolf and it was precisely like a bad case of human diabetes. Pancreasless, this beast's body simply couldn't burn sugar.

The day before they'd given him sugar-water but not a bit of this glucose   60
stayed in him to help his starving tissues but all kept running out of him in rivers of urine.

This morning of July 27 he was dying. His eyes were glazed over as he lay   61
there hardly able to lift his head and right here by him was another dog, frisky, healthy. Weeks before, this one had recovered from Banting's operation to tie off his pancreas duct, and now . . .

The sickening smell of chloroform and swiftly Banting is into the belly of   62
this healthy animal, finding, exposing, neatly slitting out what's left of the pancreas. Yes!

Okay . . . degenerated, hardly the size of your thumb. Now all you hear is   63
the sick dog's breathing and Banting and Best growling monosyllables and the click of steel on steel and now here lies that shriveled morsel of what used to be pancreas in a mortar, chilled, ice-cold.

Best cuts it, mashes it, with a little cold salt water makes a brew of it, filters   64
this soup through paper, warms it gently to body heat, sucks it into a syringe. Now . . .

There's a quick gleam of metal and glass with Banting bending over the neck   65
of the doomed diabetic creature and now the soup made of the degenerated remains of the pancreas from the dog with the tied-off duct has gone into his dying diabetic brother's jugular vein. . . .

An hour goes by as if it were a minute. Best straightens up from his hunch-   66
backed squinting into the colorimeter where he's measuring the dying dog's blood sugar. "Fred," Best says, "his sugar's down! Way down to zero-point-one." That was hardly more than the sugar in the blood of a perfectly healthy animal. . . .

Upstairs there in the dog room Fred Banting didn't need Best's blood sugar   67
tests to tell him the fantastic thing that now was happening. This dog who hasn't even been able to lift his head for water to wet his poor parched mouth, raises his head now. He looks at Banting. Banting stares at him as he sits up. In an hour he's standing up and that hour's a blank, is no time at all to Banting who stands there in a daze of wild happiness. The dog looks at Banting and wags his tail when he should by rights be dead, but here he is, walking around, wobbly, but walking. . . .

Up and down and up and down that narrow spiral staircase, never realizing   68
how he's sweating, runs Best carrying urine from this miraculous dog down to his chemical bench. The day before their doses of sugar-water had run right through him. Now his body can use sugar again. It's unbelievable. In the next five hours his urine's sugar free, nearly . . . with seventy-five times less sugar than it held in the same five hours the day before. Upstairs alone in the heat,

Banting watches that dog who with bright eyes looks back at Banting and wags his tail for a thank-you.

The next day the dog is dead.   69

How could they have expected this miracle to have lasted? What they'd shot   70
into this pancreasless doomed creature was only a wee bit of borrowed pancreas, slit out of that dog whose duct had been tied. Well? Banting looked across at Best, hating to say it. But how many dogs would they have to sacrifice to keep one diabetic dog living, for a little? It was utterly impracticable!

Anyway, hadn't this first marvelous recovery been, maybe, accidental? Was   71
it true? Banting looked at Best, and back they went in the heat up those spiral stairs—visionaries, crazy pioneers. Nothing could stop them. No, it wasn't an accident, and here it was the 4th of August and here was another absolutely doomed diabetic dog raised from the dead, like Lazarus, no less. But alas . . .

Here was the deuce of it, the hopelessness of it, the sheer lunacy of going   72
on with it. First: the magic didn't last. When you brought your dying dogs back to life it was only a ghastly foolery, a matter of hours. Again: you'd have to keep on injecting pancreas soup made of other dogs' degenerated pancreases, and here was the impossibility of it . . .

To keep this second dog alive for just three days they'd had to kill two   73
healthy dogs, use all the degenerated pancreas from both of them. It was nonsense.

Those three terrible days Banting hadn't slept. He'd tried everything, inject-   74
ing liver prepared exactly like pancreas. Then he'd tried spleen and it had done no more good than liver which had done nothing whatever. No, it was beautiful how Banting's hunch that October night, 1920, had turned out to be absolutely right. Now all these three days it had been an outlandish see-saw of hope and despair for the dying diabetic creature. The second day, with their little supply of miraculous pancreas extract dwindling, Banting and Best had run from their black bench to that hellish attic and back to their bench again till midnight, when the dog was sinking. Then they really began working. It was marvelous. At midnight, at one, at two, at three, they shot dose after dose into the dying dog's jugular vein. He got stronger and stronger. At four in the morning at dawn as the robins were waking they gave him his last five ounces—all they had left. Seven in the morning, Best and Banting looked through red-rimmed eyes at Best's chemical test showing their good beast was excreting not a trace of sugar in his urine . . .

Noon the next day the dog was dead.   75

Long ago they'd run out of the ten dogs Banting thought he'd need to prove   76
his hunch was true. Macleod was away in Europe without the faintest notion of what Banting was up to. He never dreamed that right now, in his own department, there was boiling one of the most exciting adventures in the whole

record of science, with an ex-farmer boy-ex-surgeon, and a fourth year medical student the pioneers in it. Banting couldn't ask Macleod for dogs. "But we got plenty of dogs, all right," Banting said.

Three in the morning of August 19, and Banting sits alone in that attic. "I was sitting watching the terminal symptoms of Dog 92," Banting said. Dog 92 was their pet, had the run of the laboratory, and now she was dying. Pancreasless, for eight days they'd kept her alive, healthy, her blood sugar low, hardly any sugar in her urine, with her frolicking as if no sure doom hung over her. Now she was dying.   77

"I loved that dog," Banting said.   78

It had taken the degenerated pancreases of no less than five dogs to keep her alive eight days ... five they'd had to kill to keep this one living. What could be more senseless, even ghoulish? But she'd been a wonderful help to them. She'd hop up onto the table and lie quiet on her side while Banting drew blood from her for Best's blood sugar tests. Risking her life proved for them it was no use injecting pancreas that wasn't degenerated. Coming back from the grave she'd shown them that their pancreas extracts were much more life-saving, sugar-burning, when you extracted with acid than with alkali.   79

With one foot in the grave she'd come back miraculously so many times in succession after those doses of degenerated pancreas extract, that Banting was absolutely sure now he'd found his life-saving "X." He was so sure that he gave this mysterious stuff from the Langerhans islands of those degenerated pancreases a name ... "isletin."   80

That's the name it should have kept, but didn't.   81

But now Dog 92 was dying, with not a drop of this extract left. He sat there mulling it, bitterly. Why fight this cruel game longer? Isletin existed, was no longer his crazy fantasy. It did make diabetic doomed animals burn sugar, and live. But it was a nearly unattainable jewel, rarer than any precious stone, and in the world there were millions of sick diabetic folks needing it, hundreds of thousands dying for lack of it ...   82

"Suddenly it occurred to me ..." Banting said.   83

So, next morning, here was Best putting a perfectly normal dog whose pancreas duct had never been tied, under ether. Swift slashing by Banting. Brewing of extract from this dog's small intestine by Best. They were looking for *secretin*—which is made in animals' intestinal membranes, which is then absorbed and, going through the blood to the pancreas, sets it to secreting its digestive juice. One way or another Banting must get rid of this digestive juice that knocked out the life-saving isletin. So, for four whole hours that morning this dog breathed gently under the anaesthetic while Banting bent over her injecting her own secretin back into her. .... Till Best finds there's not a drop more of digestive juice leaking from the duct of that dog's exhausted pancreas. Then quick they take the pancreas out, chilling it, mincing it ...   84

Up above in the attic Dog 92 lies in her cage, just breathing . . .   85

Now it's seven in the evening. It's a go again. Her glazed eyes are clearing,   86
and now, when Banting opens the door of her cage, she jumps out, frisks
around, puts her paws against this grim kind master who's so often doomed
her, then saved her.

"I'll never forget my joy as I opened the door of her cage . . ." Banting said.   87

But again . . . idiotic, impractical. You couldn't go on exhausting the pan-   88
creases of living dogs, or cattle, or pigs, by this delicate operation to provide
isletin for millions of sick folks all over whose lives were running away in rivers
of sugar. It was only . . . scientific, beautiful, but useless. Banting slogged ahead,
hoping.

And why not? It was lovely the way Dog 92 was living. It was a record!   89
Twenty days she'd lived now without any pancreas in her. Then she died finally,
with Banting furious about it. There was absolutely nothing of your piddling
purely academic scientist about him. Not with his brain alone but with all of
his body he invented, cooked up idiotic schemes, devised impossible experiments to keep this beast's life spark glowing. Every now and again as now at
three that morning, a sudden "here's-the-way-to-get-around-*this*-corner" would
come to him. Then he'd tear into it as if God's hand had given him a great
push from behind. Who could stop him?

November now . . . and at last Banting had it. The leaves were gone from   90
all except the white oaks and the beech trees and it was bleak Ontario winter
not yet lovely with its blanket of snow and now never a doubt of it Banting
and Best had the trick to get unlimited supplies of their life-saving pancreas
extract—isletin.

Macleod had come back from Europe but Macleod was busy with his own   91
experiments on anoxaemia which had nothing to do with diabetes. Banting was
broke and so was Best and now they were at the end of their tether with the
goal almost touched but with it looking as if everything they'd sweat for had
gone for nothing. Till Professor V. E. Henderson came to their rescue, gave
Banting a job in his own Department of Pharmacology as lecturer, only Banting
didn't have to lecture at all, but did have money to eat to keep him alive to
experiment. . . .

How complicated, how silly their last summer's experiments looked now in   92
November! Now they were keeping profoundly diabetic, pancreasless dogs alive,
beautifully healthy, indefinitely, with pancreas from unborn calves.

It turned out to be so simple—why hadn't Banting thought of it in the first   93
place? One night, with things at low ebb, he'd thumbed through an old scientific
work by the searcher, Laguesse, on the pancreases of newborn babies. Those
pancreases are rich in islet cells of Langerhans, but with digestive juice cells
feebly developed.

Banting the nighthawk alone that night mulled over it; for Banting there   94
was something mystically good about notions you doped out alone in the night.
Sure . . .

If that's so for newborn babies, it's true for newborn animals; if it's true for   95
newborn animals, it's more true for embryo animals long before they're born
. . . their pancreases should be almost pure islet tissue! Banting went to Professor
Henderson next morning with this new hunch. "But how're you going to get
unborn puppies, Banting?" Henderson asked. It was impractical again. They'd
have to breed dogs, and wait.

No, not this time. Banting'd been a farm boy, knew cattle. Banting knew   96
cows are often bred to fatten them prior to slaughtering. . . . By noon next day
Banting and Best were back from the slaughter house with the pancreases of
nine calves—three to four months embryo. It was superb, precisely as he'd
hunched it. This stuff sent the poisonously high blood sugar of the very first
diabetic dog they tried it on, down like a shot. Now their worries seemed over.
Now it was as if he'd stumbled on a gold-mine of life-saving isletin and ideas
swarmed in his head.

Now they didn't have to depend on embryo calf pancreas any longer, finding   97
they could get big pancreas out of just slaughtered full-grown cattle and from
it extract this precious isletin if only they used the little simple trick of extracting
with acidified alcohol instead of salt water! Acidified alcohol checked the action
of the digestive juice that ruined the isletin and dissolved out, ready for use,
the magic isletin. It was too simple! Why do searchers seem always to have to
go into the jungle of the unknown, blindfolded, and backwards? But as Boss
Kettering says: "All problems are simple . . . after they're solved."

Here it was January, 1922, and the female, black-and-white, somewhat collie   98
dog, No. 33, had lived seventy days though her pancreas had been cut clean
out of her. . . . Sixty days ago she should have been dead. . . .

Why hadn't Banting thought in the very first place of the obvious trick of   99
holding the digestive-juice cells of the pancreas in check with acidified alcohol?
Again as Boss Kettering says: "Nothing is so obscure as the obvious."

Here it was January. That somewhat collie female dog, *completely diabetic,* had   100
lived seven times as long as she had any scientific right to.

Joe Gilchrist had graduated in the same class with Banting in medical school,   101
and even before that, when they were kids in knee-pants in Northern Ontario,
the Bantings and the Gilchrists used to have dinner together on Canadian
Thanksgiving Day. Joe had crocked up suddenly with the sugar sickness during
the war. For five years, now, he'd been getting thinner and thinner, with sugar
almost constantly showing in his urine, with the dreaded acetone odor stronger
and stronger on his breath. . . .

Gilchrist the doctor knew what it meant to have diabetes at his time of life.   102
He'd had a sunny disposition but now the acid-poisoning was driving him into

morose hopelessness. He dragged himself about on the rounds of his little medical practice in Toronto trying to support his mother. He dragged himself out on shuffling walks trying to make his sick body burn sugar and so keep down the acid poisons. He stuck to the terrible starvation diet of Dr. Allen that was the one slim, almost hopeless hope for young diabetics. It was hardly food enough for a baby. It kept him alive but didn't let him live. Then that fall of 1921 he bumped into Banting.

"Maybe I'll have something for you pretty soon, Joe," Banting said.   103

Then came October, and the flu got Gilchrist, one of those infections that's   104 the dread of every diabetic. It wrecked him so he couldn't eat three ounces of carbohydrate a day without showing sugar and he was hanging on by his eyebrows and couldn't work any more and knew that if he let down for just one meal, maybe, or at most two meals, the coma would get him. If he would just satisfy the hunger that gnawed and gnawed him, just that little bit, the coma would get him and almost surely finish him. . . .

Wouldn't it be better so? Wasn't it easier just to pass out—unconscious,   105 never knowing it at the end?

Gilchrist hung on, though you couldn't have blamed him if he'd let go.   106 Who'd have blamed him for not pinning too much hope on Fred Banting? He knew Banting for the stubborn plodder that he was, never brilliant. And, for Gilchrist, who was Banting? Only his friend since their marbles and football days. You see Gilchrist was too close to him. . . .

Already Banting had taken his jump from dogs to humans, had first of all   107 shot himself with this isletin, then shot his pal, Charlie Best, to prove that this stuff so life-saving to dogs, wouldn't harm humans. Then, too, there were a few very bad diabetics who'd been shot with the new "X" at the Toronto General Hospital and there were fantastic rumors. Then again Banting had gone to New Haven, Connecticut, and read a paper about this strange stuff and the wonderful things it would do for diabetic dogs, before a learned medical Congress at Yale University. It was said he'd stuttered, that they'd let him have not too much time to tell of it—what with all the important scientific papers to be read that day—but rumors were certainly floating around throughout the medical profession and even among plain folks. . . .

Finally here it's February 11, 1922, with Gilchrist in the laboratory with   108 Fred Banting and Charlie Best. He's their experimental animal now, very little better off than one of their dogs they'd made pancreasless. Will this new isletin make Joe's body burn sugar? They feed him an ounce of pure glucose. They make him breathe as deep a breath as his feeble life spark will let him breathe, into the Douglas bag. . . .

Will his body burn any of the sugar they've just fed him? Instead of devouring   109 itself, burning its own fat and protein?

"Nothing doing," Best says, taking the reading.   110

"R.Q. . . . zero point seven," Best tells Banting.   111

Gilchrist has this on the dogs: he knows what those grim figures mean as   112
well as Banting and Best. . . .

Now they shoot in the isletin with a quick jab of the syringe needle. . . .   113

They all sat there waiting. Now and again Gilchrist blew into the Douglas   114
bag for Best to test the amount of carbon dioxide he breathed out compared
to the amount of oxygen he breathed in. . . . An hour, two hours, and nothing
doing. The carbon dioxide proportion climbed no higher: Joe's body wasn't
burning the glucose they'd fed him. . . .

Banting was down in the dumps about it. Hardly daring to look at Joe,   115
Banting left to catch a train to go north to his folks. It was a washout. It was
the old grim story: what worked for dogs might do nothing for humans. . . .

Banting left just too soon. Best urged Joe to stay. "Let's have another go at   116
it, Joe," Best said. Now when Joe breathed into the Douglas bag, it was funny,
but he found he could breathe much better. He felt as if he had lungs again
and he wanted to breathe harder like a fellow testing his lungs on one of those
machines you blow up at a fair. Then he said: "Charlie, what's your shot done
to me?"

Suddenly for the first time in months his head felt clear as a bell again and   117
his legs lost their infernal heaviness. He hurried home, called Banting's folks
long distance to tell them to tell Banting what had happened, the moment he
got in from the train. He ate supper, for the first time in years, a real supper.
After supper he took two little cousins of his out for a walk. "And I'll never
forget it," Gilchrist said, "never . . .

"Everybody stared at me. There I was walking along grinning from ear to   118
ear. I walked along dragging my cousins after me and grinning," Joe said.

"Everybody we passed turned round staring at me. It was as if I was walking   119
on air. I hadn't felt like this in five years," Gilchrist said.

Next morning his legs began dragging again. Never mind, he'd go back, get   120
another shot of isletin—

He couldn't get another. Banting and Best had no more of it.   121

Those were tough days for Banting, though you'd think by now things would   122
have begun breaking right for him. By now Professor Macleod realized that his
young man with his hare-brained scheme had pulled off what the greatest
physiologists had failed at, utterly. Of course Macleod was proud that he'd
given Banting those first ten dogs and the assistant for eight weeks. Now
Macleod dropped his own work on anoxaemia. Together with all his assistants
Macleod went to work on this life-saving isletin of Banting and Best, and first
of all Macleod insisted its name be changed to *insulin*—that was maybe better
Latin, or something, I don't know. Macleod and his assistants set to work with
terrific energy, now, dotting i's and crossing the t's of the discovery that Banting

and Best had roughed out in its simple outlines. Macleod began making real *science* of it—

But Banting was through with such details. What bothered him now was   123
trying to save desperately sick folks now pouring into Toronto, on stretchers, *in extremis,* begging for his isletin. Starting from his stammering little speech in New Haven before the highbrows, rumors now brought them flocking. It was tough to have to tell a mother begging, pointing to her emaciated, languid, dry-skinned, thin-haired little girl . . . "We're sorry, but . . ."

It was a hurly-burly now. Everybody wanted to work on insulin. Dr. Collip,   124
on leave of absence from Alberta University, had come and Banting had shown him how they were getting their life-saving stuff out of pancreases with weak alcohol, then purifying it with alcohol very concentrated. Collip shut himself up privately and thought he'd got a way to get insulin so pure it wouldn't be dangerous to humans. Lord knows they needed plenty of it now, with all these dying folks coming, hoping, then finding they were only grabbing at another straw. . . .

Macleod put Collip to work to make insulin on a large scale. Banting and   125
Best were at this moment sort of lost in the shuffle. Alas for Collip—what worked well in his test-tubes failed in commercial manufacture. As for Banting, these were not nice days for him. He had no job. He was broke and owed money. Sick folks were leaving Toronto bowed down in the bitterest of all disappointments. Poor Joe Gilchrist was hanging to life by less than his eyebrows. . . .

Professor Macleod now appeared before the Association of American Phy-   126
sicians, the most scientific body of American physicians—so scientific that, without irreverence, it may be called somewhat snooty. Professor Macleod gave them great news. It was what sports would call a natural.

"I move that the Association tender to Dr. Macleod *and his associates*[1] a rising   127
vote expressing its appreciation of his achievement," said Woodyatt of Chicago.

"We are all agreed in congratulating Dr. Macleod *and his collaborators*[1] on   128
their miraculous achievement," said Allen, most famous of diabetes experts. It was Allen who'd perfected Dr. Guelpa's starvation treatment. . . .

Allen at the Rockefeller Institute, on dogs, had proved scientifically that   129
Guelpa was right. With unlimited dogs in the world's finest laboratory where it doesn't matter much if you break as much glassware in a week as Banting and Best had used for their whole discovery, Allen had proved starvation keeps diabetics alive a little longer. . . .

It was manly of Allen to congratulate Macleod. Allen himself had lowered   130
blood sugar in diabetes with pancreas extracts. "But the obvious reason why such experiments proved nothing, is found in the great toxicity of such extracts, so that the animals receiving them were injured instead of benefited," Allen admitted. . . .

---

1. These italics are, in both cases, this writer's.

"I wish to thank the Association very much in the name of my associates   131
and myself," Macleod answered.

Meanwhile Banting and Best were at their wits' end for insulin. Joe Gilchrist   132
didn't know how much longer his eyebrows would hold him. Suffering folks
were dragging themselves back home to die. It was now that Best showed
Banting the true helper he was. Authorities at Connaught Laboratories gave
Banting and Best money for dogs, rabbits, chemicals to buy unlimited pancreas.
Back they went with their old-time fury, to start where Collip had run on the
rocks—

"I was Fred and Charlie's human rabbit; I was the chief rabbit," Joe Gilchrist   133
said. Now every single batch of insulin, slowly getting less poisonous, stronger,
was tried out first on Joe. Best at the Connaught Laboratories was getting the
hang of it. . . .

It was ticklish business. In January Collip had found how insulin was a two-   134
edged sword and he'd invented a quick clever way to measure its dangerous
power. He shot it into healthy rabbits and it was remarkable how it burned
the sugar out of these beasts' blood. And when their blood sugar got down
just so low, they'd go into a coma, throw terrific convulsions, then die. There
was an exact arithmetic to it, and this test turned out to be the standard way
to find out the strength of any batch of insulin. Gilchrist was the human rabbit
for such tests. . . .

Now Banting and Gilchrist at the Christie Street Hospital for Returned   135
Soldiers in Toronto showed the real miracle of insulin. They gave it to none
but most desperately sick diabetic Canadian veterans and these boys now fought
a desperate battle with death hanging over them and they called Joe Gilchrist
not Doctor, but Captain.

One day, after a shot into himself of a new batch, Joe began sweating though   136
the room was cool. His knees wobbled. He couldn't remember what he was
doing. His brain couldn't find the words he hunted for. He was scared. He said
he felt like one of those poor rabbits with an overdose who go dashing round
frightened, insanely bumping into benches and tables. . . .

Joe saved his own life, thanks to Professor Henderson's simple trick of taking   137
a quick dose of glucose. Henderson had taught Banting that a little shot of
sugar raises the too low blood sugar of rabbits, literally bringing them back
from the grave.

Joe and his boys were a grand bunch of rabbits, all of them, those first days   138
in May and June, 1922, when insulin was still crude and dangerous. From
abscesses from its injection their arms, their legs, their thighs got crosshatched
with scars so you'd swear there was no place left to inject them. But they lived.
They weren't starving any longer. Strength flowed back into these boys who'd
become miserable objects of Government charity. . . .

"We're feeling great this morning, Captain," they'd tell Joe.   139

Jobs, the chance to earn their own livings, to be men again—this was   140
possible now. And they only laughed and never minded the terrible burning
and pain of those early shots of insulin, while Best fixed and fixed at making
it painless and safer.

"We weren't martyrs or heroes, absolutely not," Gilchrist said. "We all knew   141
we were dying. When you're that way you'll try—anything."

Of that scarred crew of human rabbits of the year 1922 at the Christie   142
Street Hospital in Toronto, to this day—though a few have passed on from
other causes—*not a single one has died of diabetes.*

It was weird for me not long ago when I sat, late at night, talking to healthy   143
Joe Gilchrist. Nine years ago in Banting's tough summer of 1921, Joe was a bag
of bones, starving. 1922—and he should have been dead. Now here he sat, an
energetic medical consultant, successful, laughing, sure he has as good a chance
for long life as the next man . . . all from two tiny shots of Banting's "X" that
go into him every day. . . . It was like talking to a man come back from the
grave.

May, 1922, and hardly a year had passed since those first fumbling experi-   144
ments of Banting and Best on their black bench and in their little hot attic.
Now Banting, Gilchrist, Campbell, Fletcher, and other Toronto doctors began
almost resurrecting folks with powerful insulin that Charlie Best slaved day and
night to make for them. Up till now, better than sixty diabetics out of every
hundred had died from coma. Practically all diabetic children perished from
this unconsciousness, stealing over them from the accumulation in their blood
of acid-poison from the faulty burning of fat lacking the good fire of carbohydrate to burn it.

Now with such children it was the way it had been with that famous Dog   145
92—unbelievable. . . .

Folks came who were losing two thousand calories or more in their urine   146
as sugar and acid. They came hungry for air, grasping. Hungry for food, when
they ate, they could only vomit. Thirsty, they couldn't retain even the liquid
that was given them. They were cold. Their wrecked pancreases could no longer
change their food into glycogen, the animal starch, for their liver and muscles
to then turn into sugar their bodies could burn—for energy. Failing so, the
bodies of these poor people turned on their own tissues in a horrible auto-
cannibalism. Their eyes became soft as jelly-fish. Their skin was parchment dry.
Their muscles seemed to melt away. Now at last coma—the merciful end for
them. From this coma, up till these May days of 1922, almost no diabetic had
ever returned to tell the story. . . .

Till insulin, with Banting and his helpers bending over these dying ones.   147

Now a flutter of the eyelids, a muttered "Where-am-I. . . ." Banting and his helpers returned eight of their first twelve cases of coma, not only to life but to strong life and health again.

What remedy in all death-fighting history could be as fantastic as this one, that made the last desperate end of a sickness almost as easy to treat as its very beginning?   148

Today there's absolutely no need for any diabetic dying in coma. In 1927 Dr. Joslin of Boston had 1,241 diabetics and 43 of them died, but not one of coma.   149

In another way Banting's insulin has turned the cruel course of the sugar sickness topsy-turvy. In the old days before Banting, children were the doomed ones. The older the diabetic the better his chances. Now this law is reversed to the natural law of life. Now there's no limit—within the limits of human life—to the years a diabetic child may live, Joslin says.   150

All over our country diabetics do die in coma but that's not the fault of Fred Banting. It's the fault of incompetent doctors. "I believe more deaths are chargeable to this deficiency than to any other single factor," Joslin says.   151

With good doctors people don't die of diabetes any longer at all. It's the enemy of old people, arteriosclerosis, that kills them. Joslin believes that diabetes—through Banting—has been actually turned into a good sickness that may help to clear up this mystery of the hardening of arteries in all people.   152

With an excess of fat diabetes begins, and from an excess of fat diabetics may die—because too much fat taken in food piles up in the blood and gets into the arteries. That's Joslin's hunch about it.   153

If Joslin can prevent his diabetics dying from hardening of their arteries by diets with not too much fat, then what will be the lesson for those of us, not sufferers from the sugar disease, but faced with this greatest of all threats of old age?   154

That's what those forlorn experiments of Fred Banting may finally lead to. Diabetics, kept healthy by insulin *and just the right diet,* may teach us all another way to stretch out our lives. Banting would certainly have smiled his slow farmerish smile in those tough days if he'd been told that this "X" he was chasing would bring the average age at death of Joslin's patients to ten years above the average age at death of all citizens of Massachusetts. . . .   155

Of course insulin isn't a cure, because bad diabetics have to go on taking it, balancing it against the right amount of food. But many have to take less and less of it and it looks as if, taking the load off the sick pancreas, that organ actually gradually may repair itself. . . .   156

"Injections of insulin annoy a baby less than the average child, and the average child less than the adult," Joslin says. You should see the smile on the face of one of Joslin's ten-year-old girl patients as she slips the syringe needle under her own skin. . . .   157

Memories carry me back to my father in his last days, dying while the   158
ovenbirds sang their cheerful "teacher!—teacher!—teacher!" just as they're
doing this May morning as I write. He would never have minded two daily
shots of insulin. . . .

So I sit, before this honest, simple Fred Banting, who looks much more like   159
a farmer than a highbrow scientist. As Joslin puts it, Banting has answered the
terrible question of the Lord to Ezekiel . . .

"Thus saith the Lord God unto these bones; Behold I will cause breath to   160
enter into you, and ye shall live:

"And I will lay sinews upon you, and will bring up flesh upon you, and cover   161
you with skin, and bring breath into you, and ye shall live;

". . . and breath came into them, and they lived, and stood upon their feet,   162
an exceeding great army."

The hundreds of thousands Fred Banting has saved ease my heartache that   163
comes from his being born a little too late to bring back breath and life to my
father.

A little while ago it was my honor to sit one evening in the company of a   164
gathering of extremely scientific searchers, who were relaxed and gossiping
scientifically.

Two of them smiled just a wee bit sniffishly at the mention of Fred Banting   165
. . . full of his discovery I'd maybe bubbled over a little about him.

They said it hadn't been Banting particularly, and when giving them the facts   166
I pushed them back to the wall, they said well, if it *had* been Banting he'd been
lucky and would never make another discovery like it.

But who will?   167

Questions for Critical Thinking

1. What is your opinion of the morality and ethics behind the kind of animal experimentation Banting performed in discovering insulin?

2. If the inferiority of animal species is your justification for animal experimentation, would a superior alien creature be justified in experimenting on humans? Why or why not?

3. The author manages to tell the story of Banting's quest dramatically, as if he had been there personally. What are some of the writing techniques he uses to make this narrative so lively?

4. Proposals have occasionally been made for medical experimentation on prisoners, especially the condemned. What is your opinion of the morality of such proposals?

5. Researchers are now experimenting with transplanting Isles of Langerhans cells from embryos into diabetes patients. What ethical implications does the use of such tissue from aborted embryos hold?

6. For the discovery of insulin, Macleod shared with Banting the Nobel Prize in Physiology and medicine in 1923. Given what the author tells us, how do you explain that Macleod received equal credit for Banting's discovery?

7. How might Plato's allegory of the cave be applied to Banting's quest for insulin?

8. What technique does the author use to tie together the beginning and end of his article?

Writing Assignment

Using this article as one source of supporting details, write an essay arguing for or against medical experimentation on animals.

Writing Advice

The argumentative essay is definitely the most contentious and therefore the most complex. Part of the complexity of this essay comes from the variety of appeals writers have traditionally employed in argument. One is not likely to find an emotional, heartfelt plea in an essay defining "theory." But such an appeal, among others, is the stuff of which arguments are commonly made.

Begin by deciding where you stand on the topic. If you do not know, then go to the library and read about it. Try formulating your opinion with some preliminary scribbling. Indeed, this is just the kind of explosive issue writers usually have to work out on paper to discover how they truly feel. You may start out holding one position and end up arguing the opposite, such a reversal being a sure sign of having achieved mastery enough over your material to generate a personal opinion.

What kind of evidence and appeals can you use to support your case?

First and most obvious, you can cite facts and statistics. You can do research into the incidence of animal experimentation, the costs in animal lives, and the benefits in new drugs and improved medical procedures. You can weigh the alternative experimental methods suggested by animal rights activists and evaluate what medical experts have to say about their effectiveness. Is it true that computer modeling can replace animal experiments? Can tissue culture really be used as an animal substitute to test the effectiveness of a new drug? Sifting through the thicket of conflicting views will school you in how to distinguish inflamed emotion from reasoned opinion.

Second and less obvious, you can use reason and logic to bolster your case. Accusing an opponent of inconsistency is often an effective logical ploy. Look for loopholes and inconsistent practices in your opponent's arguments. Is it, for example, logically consistent to picket a furrier while wearing leather shoes? Is the life of a cow less valuable than the life of a mink? On the other hand, is it logical and humane for five hundred cats to be blinded just so a new brand of mascara can win governmental approval? Of course, this kind of argument is essentially an attack on one's values. And although values are often founded on transcendental belief rather than on sheer logic, most of us still like to think that ours are grounded in reason.

Many effective arguments have even used occasional emotional appeals. It is, of course, shabby and ineffective to base one's entire argument on emotion. But the judicious use of emotion can add dramatic impact to an otherwise logical argument. The following is an example. The author began her article by writing about a professor's affection for Sabrina, his little dog, who unfailingly greets him at his doorstep when he returns from a hard day at the laboratory. She then shows the professor, the next day, as he enters his workplace:

> *The professor looked over the animals that would be used that day by his surgery students. He came across a female dog that had just been delivered by the dealer. Badly frightened, she whined and wagged her tail ingratiatingly as he paused in front of her cage. The professor felt a stab. The small dog bore an amazing resemblance to Sabrina. Quickly he walked away. Nevertheless, he made a note to remind himself to give orders for her vocal cords to be destroyed and for her to be conditioned for experimental surgery.*
>
> **Patricia Curtis, "The Argument against Animal Experimentation."**

This touching picture, interspersed in a logical argument, constitutes a moving appeal. Its counterpart on the other side of the question is the scenario of a five-year-old child dying of some horrible disease because researchers have been barred from the animal experimentation necessary to find a cure.

Finally, be sure to take into account, and rebut, the opposition's arguments. On an issue as controversial as this one, arguments tend to solidify into well-known and entrenched propositions. It is always an effective ploy to steal an opponent's thunder by anticipating and replying to what the opponent is certain to allege and argue.

Alternate Writing Assignment

After doing the appropriate research in the library, write an essay on the present state of knowledge about diabetes, assessing the accuracy of the author's optimistic forecast for the disease.

HISTORY

DARWIN'S MISTAKE
Tom Bethell

Tom Bethell (b. 1940) is a London-born naturalized United States citizen and magazine writer. Bethel was educated at the Royal Naval College and at Oxford University (M.A.,

1962). He has done jazz research in New Orleans and worked with New Orleans district attorney Jim Garrison on investigating the assassination of John F. Kennedy. A frequent contributor to *Harper's* magazine, Bethell is the author of *George Lewis: A Jazzman from New Orleans* (1977).

Reading Advice

This is a subtle article, focusing as it does on an alleged logical lapse that the author says Darwin committed in formulating his theory of evolution. Most of us think that Darwin discovered the theory of evolution as explained in his famous book, *The Origin of the Species* (1859). But the idea of evolution did not originate with Darwin; his especial contribution, instead, was to establish natural selection as the principle behind the gradual evolution and transformation of animal species. As Bethell tells us, natural selection became such a truism of scientific thinking that belief in it took on the fervor of orthodoxy.

Such was the state of affairs when this article opens, and the author begins by sharing with us some dogmatic and bullying pronouncements of belief in natural selection that, out of the mouths of any but scientists, would seem like downright opinionatedness. From there he leads us through successive bouts of questioning, dissent, argument, and refutation that have dogged the debate about natural selection, ending with the startling conclusion that Darwin's most hallowed principle has been, in many quarters, quietly discarded. Bethell is especially good at using rhetorical questions to further his discussion, and he has a keen eye for just the right quotation to help make his points in this article. Before you begin reading it, you would be well advised to become familiar with the principle behind the logical error known as a "tautology."

*H*ow do we come to have horses and   1
tigers and things? There are at least a million species in existence today, according to the paleontologist George Gaylord Simpson, and for every one extant, perhaps 100 are extinct. Such profusion! Such variety! How did it come about? The old answer was that they are created by God. But with the increasingly scientific temper of the eighteenth and nineteenth centuries, this explanation began to look insufficient. God was invisible, and so could not be part of any scientific explanation.

So an alternative explanation was proposed by a number of savants, among   2
them Jean Baptiste Lamarck[1] and Erasmus Darwin:[2] the various forms of life did not just appear (as at the tip of a magician's wand), but evolved by a process of gradual transformation. Horses came from something slightly less horselike,

---

1. Jean Baptiste Lamarck (1744–1829) was a French naturalist noted for his study and classification of invertebrates.
2. Erasmus Darwin (1731–1802) was an English physician and poet.

tigers from something slightly less tigerlike, and so on back, until finally, if you went back far enough in time, you would come to a primitive blob of life which itself got started (perhaps) by lightning striking the primeval soup.

"Either each species of crocodile has been specially created," said Thomas Henry Huxley,[3] "or it has arisen out of some pre-existing form by the operation of natural causes. Choose your hypothesis; I have chosen mine."

That's all very well, replied more conservative thinkers. If all of this life got here by evolution from more primitive life, then how did evolution occur? No answer was immediately forthcoming. Genesis prevailed. Then Charles Darwin (grandson of Erasmus) furnished what looked like the solution. He proposed the machinery of evolution, and claimed that it existed in nature. Natural selection, he called it.

His idea was accepted with great rapidity. Once stated it seemed only too obvious. The survival of the fittest—of course! Some types are fitter than others, and given the competition—the "struggle for existence"—the fitter ones will survive to propagate their kind. And so animals, plants, all life in fact, will tend to get better and better. They would have to, with the fitter ones inevitably replacing those that are less fit. Nature itself, then, had evolving machinery built into it. "How extremely stupid not to have thought of that!" Huxley commented, after reading the *Origin of Species*. Huxley had coined the term *agnostic*, and he remained one. Meanwhile, the Genesis version didn't entirely fade away, but it inevitably took on a slightly superfluous air.

The Evolution Debate

That was a little over 100 years ago. By the time of the Darwin Centennial Celebrations at the University of Chicago in 1959, Darwinism was triumphant. At a panel discussion Sir Julian Huxley[4] (grandson of Thomas Henry) affirmed that "the evolution of life is no longer a theory; it is a fact." He added sternly: "We do not intend to get bogged down in semantics and definitions." At about the same time, Sir Gavin de Beer of the British Museum remarked that if a layman sought to "impugn" Darwin's conclusions, it must be the result of "ignorance or effrontery." Garrett Hardin of the California Institute of Technology asserted that anyone who did not honor Darwin "inevitably attracts the speculative psychiatric eye to himself." Sir Julian Huxley saw the need for "true belief."

So that was it, then. The whole matter was settled—as I assumed, and as I imagined most people must. Darwin had won. No doubt there were backward

3
4
5
6
7

---

3. Thomas Henry Huxley (1825–1895) was an English biologist and educator. Huxley coined the word "agnostic" and became the Victorian era's most dogmatic exponent of Darwinism.
4. Julian Huxley (1887–   ) is an English biologist and writer.

folk tucked away in the remoter valleys of Appalachia who still clung to their comforting beliefs, but they, of course, lacked education. Not everyone was enlightened—goodness knows the Scopes trial's[5] had proved that, if nothing else. And some of them still wouldn't let up, apparently—they were trying to change the textbooks and get the Bible back into biology. Well, there are always diehards.

So it was only casually, about a year ago, that I picked up a copy of *Darwin*   8
Retried, a slim volume by one Norman Macbeth, a Harvard-trained lawyer. An odd field for a lawyer, certainly. But an endorsement on the cover by Karl Popper caught my eye. "I regard the book as . . . a really important contribution to the debate," Popper had written.

The debate? What debate? This interested me. I had studied philosophy, and   9
in my undergraduate days Popper was regarded as one of the top philosophers— especially important for having set forth "rules" for discriminating between genuine and pseudo science. And Popper evidently thought there had been a "debate" worth mentioning. In his bibliography Macbeth listed a few articles that had appeared in academic philosophy journals in recent years and evidently were a part of this debate.

That was, as I say, a year ago, and by now I have read these articles and a   10
good many others. In fact, I have spent a good portion of the last year fami- liarizing myself with this debate. It is surprising that so little word of it has leaked out, because it seems to have been one of the most important academic debates of the 1960s, and as I see it the conclusion is pretty staggering: Darwin's theory, I believe, is on the verge of collapse. In his famous book, *On the Origin of Species by Means of Natural Selection, or The Preservation of Favored Races in the Struggle for Life,* Darwin made a mistake sufficiently serious to undermine his theory. And that mistake has only recently been recognized as such. The machin- ery of evolution that he supposedly discovered has been challenged, and it is beginning to look as though what he really discovered was nothing more than the Victorian propensity to believe in progress. At one point in his argument, Darwin was misled. I shall try to elucidate here precisely where Darwin went wrong.

What was it, then, that Darwin discovered? What was this mechanism of   11
natural selection? Here it comes as a slight shock to learn that Darwin really didn't "discover" anything at all, certainly not in the same way that Kepler,[6] for example, discovered the laws of planetary motion. The *Origin of Species* was not a demonstration but an argument—"one long argument," Darwin himself

---

5. *See* "A Witness at the Scopes Trial," Fay-Cooper Cole, Chap. 1.
6. Johannes Kepler (1571–1630), German astronomer, formulated three mathematical statements that predicted planetary revolutions around the sun.

said at the end of the book—and natural selection was an idea, not a discovery. It was an idea that occurred to him in London in the late 1830s which he then pondered in the Home Counties over the next twenty years. As we now know, several other thinkers came up with the same or a very similar idea at about the same time. The most famous of these was Alfred Russel Wallace,[7] but there were several others.

The British philosopher Herbert Spencer[8] was one who came within a hair's   12
breadth of the idea of natural selection, in an essay called "The Theory of Population" published in the *Westminster Review* seven years before the *Origin of Species* came out. In this article Spencer used the phrase "the survival of the fittest" for the first time. Darwin then appropriated the phrase in the fifth edition of the *Origin of Species,* considering it an admirable summation of his argument. This argument was in fact an analogy, as follows:

While in his country retreat Darwin spent a good deal of time with pigeon   13
fanciers and animal breeders. He even bred pigeons himself. Of particular relevance to him was that breeders bred for certain characteristics (length of feather, length of wool, coloring), and that the offspring of the selected mates often tended to have the desired characteristic more abundantly, or more noticeably, than its parents. Thus, it could perhaps be said, a small amount of "evolution" had occurred between one generation and the next.

By analogy, then, the same process occurred in nature, Darwin thought. As   14
he wrote in the *Origin of Species:* "How fleeting are the wishes of man! how short his time! and consequently how poor will his productions be, compared with those accumulated by nature during whole geological periods. Can we wonder, then, that nature's productions should be far 'truer' in character than man's productions?"

Just as the breeders selected those individuals best suited to the breeders'   15
needs to be the parents of the next generation, so, Darwin argued, nature selected those organisms that were best fitted to survive the struggle for exis-tence. In that way evolution would inevitably occur. And so there it was: a sort of improving machine inevitably at work in nature, "daily and hourly scruti-nizing," Darwin wrote, "silently and insensibly working . . . at the improvement of each organic being." In this way, Darwin thought, one type of organism could be transformed into another—for instance, he suggested, bears into whales. So that was how we came to have horses and tigers and things—by natural selection.

---

7. Alfred Russel Wallace (1823–1913) was an English naturalist who evolved a concept similar to Darwin's.
8. Herbert Spencer (1820–1903) was an English philosopher who saw all phenomena as developing according to evolutionary principles.

The Great Tautology

For quite some time Darwin's mechanism was not seriously examined, until   16
the renowned geneticist T. H. Morgan, winner of the Nobel Prize for his work
in mapping the chromosomes of fruit flies, suggested that the whole thing
looked suspiciously like a tautology. "For, it may appear little more than a
truism," he wrote, "to state that the individuals that are the best adapted to
survive have a better chance of surviving than those not so well adapted to
survive."

The philosophical debate of the past ten to fifteen years has focused on   17
precisely this point. The survival of the fittest? Any way of identifying the fittest
other than by looking at the survivors? The preservation of "favored" races?
Any way of identifying them other than by looking at the preserved ones? If
not, then Darwin's theory is reduced from the status of scientific theory to
that of tautology.

Philosophers have ranged on both sides of this critical question: are there   18
criteria of fitness that are independent of survival? In one corner we have
Darwin himself, who assumed that the answer was yes, and his supporters,
prominent among them David Hull of the University of Wisconsin. In the other
corner are those who say no, among whom may be listed A. G. N. Flew, A. R.
Manser, and A. D. Barker. In a nutshell here is how the debate has gone:

Darwin, as I say, just assumed that there really were independent criteria of   19
fitness. For instance, it seemed obvious to him that extra speed would be useful
for a wolf in an environment where prey was scarce, and only those wolves
first on the scene of a kill would get enough to eat and, therefore, survive.
David Hull has supported this line of reasoning, giving the analogous example
of a creature that was better able than its mates to withstand desiccation in an
arid environment.

The riposte has been as follows: a mutation that enables a wolf to run faster   20
than the pack only enables the wolf to survive better if it does, in fact, survive
better. But such a mutation could also result in the wolf outrunning the pack
a couple of times and getting first crack at the food, and then abruptly dropping
dead of a heart attack, because the extra power in its legs placed an extra strain
on its heart. Fitness must be identified with survival, because it is the overall
animal that survives, or does not survive, not individual parts of it.

However, we don't have to worry too much about umpiring this dispute,   21
because a look at the biology books shows us that the evolutionary biologists
themselves, perhaps in anticipation of this criticism, retreated to a fortified
position some time ago, and conceded that "the survival of the fittest" was in
truth a tautology. Here is C. H. Waddington, a prominent geneticist, speaking
at the aforementioned Darwin Centennial in Chicago:

"Natural selection, which was at first considered as though it were a hypoth-   22 esis that was in need of experimental or observational confirmation turns out on closer inspection to be a tautology, a statement of an inevitable although previously unrecognized relation. It states that the fittest individuals in a population (defined as those which leave most offspring) will leave most offspring."

The admission that Darwin's theory of natural selection was tautological did   23
not greatly bother the evolutionary theorists, however, because they had already taken the precaution of redefining natural selection to mean something quite different from what Darwin had in mind. Like the philosophical debate of the past decade, this remarkable development went largely unnoticed. In its new form, natural selection meant nothing more than that some organisms have more offspring than others: in the argot, differential reproduction. This indeed was an empirical fact about the world, not just something true by definition, as was the case with the claim that the fittest survive.

The bold act of redefining selection was made by the British statistician and   24
geneticist R. A. Fisher in a widely heralded book called *The Genetical Theory of Natural Selection*. Moreover, by making certain assumptions about birth and death rates, and combining them with Mendelian genetics, Fisher was able to qualify the resulting rates at which population ratios changed. This was called population genetics, and it brought great happiness to the hearts of many biologists, because the mathematical formulae looked so deliciously scientific and seemed to enhance the status of biology, making it more like physics. But here is what Waddington recently said about *this* development:

"The theory of neo-Darwinism is a theory of the evolution of the population   25
in respect to leaving offspring and not in respect to anything else. . . . Everybody has it in the back of his mind that the animals that leave the largest number of offspring are going to be those best adapted also for eating peculiar vegetation, or something of this sort, but this is not explicit in the theory. . . . There you do come to what is, in effect, a vacuous statement: Natural selection is that some things leave more offspring than others; and, you ask, which leave more offspring than others; and it is those that leave more offspring, and there is nothing more to it than that. *The whole real guts of evolution—which is how do you come to have horses and tigers and things—is outside the mathematical theory* [my italics]."

Here, then, was the problem. Darwin's theory was supposed to have answered   26
this question about horses and tigers. They had gradually developed, bit by bit, as it were, over the eons, through the good offices of an agency called natural selection. But now, in its new incarnation, natural selection was only able to explain how horses and tigers became more (or less) numerous—that is, by "differential reproduction." This failed to solve the question of how they came into existence in the first place.

This was no good at all. As T. H. Morgan had remarked, with great clarity: 27
"Selection, then, has not produced anything new, but only more of certain

kinds of individuals. Evolution, however, means producing new things, not more of what already exists."

One more quotation should be enough to convince most people that Dar- 28
win's idea of natural selection was quietly abandoned, even by his most ardent supporters, some years ago. The following comment, by the geneticist H. J. Muller, another Nobel Prize winner, appeared in the Proceedings of the American Philosophical Society in 1949. It represents a direct admission by one of Darwin's greatest admirers that, however we come to have horses and tigers and things, it is not by natural selection. "We have just seen," Muller wrote, "that if selection could be somehow dispensed with, so that all variants survived and multiplied, the higher forms would nevertheless have arisen."

I think it should now be abundantly clear that Darwin made a mistake in 29
proposing his natural-selection theory, and it is fairly easy to detect the mistake. We have seen that what the theory so grievously lacks is a criterion of fitness that is independent of survival. If only there were some way of identifying the fittest beforehand, without always having to wait and see which ones survive, Darwin's theory would be testable rather than tautological.

But as almost everyone now seems to agree, fittest inevitably means "those 30
that survive best." Why, then, did Darwin assume that there were independent criteria? And the answer is, because in the case of artificial selection, from which he worked by analogy, *there really are independent criteria.* Darwin went wrong in thinking that this aspect of his analogy was valid. In our sheep example, remember, long wool was the "desirable" feature—the independent criterion. The lambs of woolly parental sheep may possess this feature even more than their parents, and so be "more evolved"—more in the desired direction.

In nature, on the other hand, the offspring may differ from their parents in 31
any direction whatsoever and be considered "more evolved" than their parents, provided only that they survive and leave offspring themselves. There is, then, no "selection" by nature at all. Nor does nature "act," as it is so often said to do in biology books. One organism may indeed be "fitter" than another from an evolutionary point of view, but the only event that determines this fitness is death (or infertility). This, of course, is not something which helps *create* the organism, but is something that terminates it. It occurs at the end, not the beginning of life.

Onward and Upward

Darwin seems to have made the mistake of just assuming that there were 32
independent criteria of fitness because he lived in a society in which change was nearly always perceived as being for the good. R. C. Lewontin, Agassiz' Professor of Zoology at Harvard, has written on this point: "The bourgeois revolution not only established change as the characteristic element of the

cosmos, but added direction and progress as well. A world in which a man could rise from humble origins must have seemed, to him at least, a good world. Change per se was a moral quality. In this light, Spencer's assertion that change *is* progress is not surprising." One may note also James D. Watson's remark in *The Double Helix* that "cultural traditions play major roles" in the development of science.

Lewontin goes on to point out that "the bourgeois revolution gave way to a period of consolidation, a period in which we find ourselves now." Perhaps that is why only relatively recently has the concept of natural selection come under strong attack.   33

There is, in a way, a remarkable conclusion to this brief history of natural selection. The idea started out as a way of explaining how one type of animal gradually changed into another, but then it was redefined to be an explanation of how a given type of animal became more numerous. But wasn't natural selection supposed to have a *creative* role? the evolutionary theorists were asked. Darwin had thought so, after all. Now watch how they responded to this: 34

The geneticist Theodosius Dobzhansky compared natural selection to "a human activity such as performing or composing music." Sir Gavin de Beer described it as a "master of ceremonies." George Gaylord Simpson at one point likened selection to a poet, at another to a builder. Ernst Mayr, Lewontin's predecessor at Harvard, compared selection to a sculptor. Sir Julian Huxley topped them all, however, by comparing natural selection to William Shakespeare.   35

Life on Earth, initially thought to constitute a sort of prima facie case for a creator, was, as a result of Darwin's idea, envisioned merely as being the outcome of a process and a process that was, according to Dobzhansky, "blind, mechanical, automatic, impersonal," and, according to de Beer, was "wasteful, blind, and blundering." But as soon as these criticisms were leveled at natural selection, the "blind process" itself was compared to a poet, a composer, a sculptor, Shakespeare—to the very notion of creativity that the idea of natural selection had originally replaced. It is clear, I think, that there was something very, very wrong with such an idea.   36

I have not been surprised to read, therefore, in Lewontin's recent book, *The Genetic Basis of Evolutionary Change* (1974), that in some of the latest evolutionary theories "natural selection plays no role at all." Darwin, I suggest, is in the process of being discarded, but perhaps in deference to the venerable old gentleman, resting comfortably in Westminster Abbey next to Sir Isaac Newton, it is being done as discreetly and gently as possible, with a minimum of publicity.   37

Questions for Critical Thinking

1. What is tautological about the assertion that the fittest members of a species leave more offspring?

2. The author admits to being surprised that so little about the Darwinism debate has leaked out. How do you explain this lack of publicity?

3. What effect do you think the invalidation of natural selection is likely to have on the theory of evolution itself?

4. Does the uncertainty over natural selection lend weight to the argument that creationism should be taught in the schools? Why or why not?

5. If "cultural traditions play major roles" in the development of science, how can scientific truth be attained free from the taint of culture?

6. What is wrong with attributing creativity to natural selection, as the author accuses scientists of doing in paragraph 36?

7. The author says that eventually "differential reproduction," or having many offspring, became an empirical definition of natural selection. What implications does this idea have in its application to human population growth?

Writing Assignments

Write a brief essay on tautology.

Writing Advice

This is an open assignment, one you are free to structure any way you like. Basically, however, the most obvious approach would be to write a definition of tautology. Take a look at the writing advice under Plato's "Allegory of the Cave" for specific instructions in how to do a definition. Then, as you begin the research, focus on finding material that answers these questions:

What is a tautology? Where does the word come from?
What is the practical effect of the tautology on logical arguments?
What are some examples of tautology? What famous arguments have been overturned as tautologies?
Which philosophers and thinkers have done work on tautology?
How can an argument be tested for tautology?
What historical role has the tautology played in some famous arguments?

An obvious example of tautology to use would be the one given by Bethell in this essay. But this is not the only one you should use. Many arguments have been challenged as tautologies, and a little spade work in the library should uncover some representative examples.

Alternate Writing Assignments

1. Write an essay arguing that the uncertainty surrounding the principle of natural selection is *not* reason enough to include creationism in the public school curriculum.

2. Write an essay arguing that the uncertainty surrounding the principle of natural selection *is* reason enough to include creationism in the public school curriculum.

LITERATURE

THE METAMORPHOSIS

Franz Kafka

Franz Kafka (1883–1924), born in Prague, Czechoslovakia, was a slow and meticulous German writer whose work was mainly published posthumously. Kafka studied law and worked for the workmen's compensation division of the Austrian government. His quixotic and allegorical vision of the stolid, humorless world of the German bourgeois was portrayed in cryptic stories, many of which are riveting in their fantastic depictions. His symbolic novels include *The Castle* (1930), and *The Trial* (1937). His stories include such acclaimed tales as "A Hunger Artist" (1938) and "The Judgment" (1945).

Reading Advice

This is another story based on a fantastic premise that requires of the reader suspension of disbelief (*see* the headnote to "At Daybreak" by Italo Calvino, Chapter 1). In both length and internal complexity, it is, in fact, more a novelette than a story. As you read, you may be tempted to fix your attention on the physical changes that have overcome Gregor, but if you do, you are likely to miss the rich interior transformation of the protagonist and his family. Ask yourself whether the people around Gregor react to his predicament in the way you would if some similar affliction should seize your brother one morning before breakfast.

In a nutshell, the situation is this: a traveling salesman wakes up one morning inexplicably transmogrified into an enormous bug. What can this alteration mean? It is exactly this sort of question, and story, that makes Kafka the *wunderkind* of dissertation writers. Here is detail so rich, robust, and meticulously laid down as to inspire reams of interpretation and earn a bushel of Ph.d.'s. Freudian underpinnings are everywhere evident; allegorical meanings flit dimly throughout the plot. Yet everywhere we gaze about in this demented and fantastic world, we glimpse a semblance of overlaid normalcy, as if everything—even the unbelievable and the astounding—were perfectly commonplace and routine.

*A*s Gregor Samsa awoke one morning   1
from uneasy dreams he found himself transformed in his bed into a gigantic insect. He was lying on his hard, as it were armor-plated, back and when he lifted his head a little he could see his dome-like brown belly divided into stiff

arched segments on top of which the bed quilt could hardly keep in position and was about to slide off completely. His numerous legs, which were pitifully thin compared to the rest of his bulk, waved helplessly before his eyes.

What has happened to me? he thought. It was no dream. His room, a regular human bedroom, only rather too small, lay quiet between the four familiar walls. Above the table on which a collection of cloth samples was unpacked and spread out—Samsa was a commercial traveler—hung the picture which he had recently cut out of an illustrated magazine and put into a pretty gilt frame. It showed a lady, with a fur cap on and a fur stole, sitting upright and holding out to the spectator a huge fur muff into which the whole of her forearm had vanished!   2

Gregor's eyes turned next to the window, and the overcast sky—one could hear rain drops beating on the window gutter—made him quite melancholy. What about sleeping a little longer and forgetting all this nonsense, he thought, but it could not be done, for he was accustomed to sleep on his right side and in his present condition he could not turn himself over. However violently he forced himself towards his right side he always rolled on to his back again. He tried it at least a hundred times, shutting his eyes to keep from seeing his struggling legs, and only desisted when he began to feel in his side a faint dull ache he had never experienced before.   3

Oh God, he thought, what an exhausting job I've picked on! Traveling about day in, day out. It's much more irritating work than doing the actual business in the office, and on top of that there's the trouble of constant traveling, of worrying about train connections, the bed and irregular meals, casual acquaintances that are always new and never become intimate friends. The devil take it all! He felt a slight itching up on his belly; slowly pushed himself on his back nearer to the top of the bed so that he could lift his head more easily; identified the itching place which was surrounded by many small white spots the nature of which he could not understand and made to touch it with a leg, but drew the leg back immediately, for the contact made a cold shiver run through him.   4

He slid down again into his former position. This getting up early, he thought, makes one quite stupid. A man needs his sleep. Other commercials live like harem women. For instance, when I come back to the hotel of a morning to write up the orders I've got, these others are only sitting down to breakfast. Let me just try that with my chief; I'd be sacked on the spot. Anyhow, that might be quite a good thing for me, who can tell? If I didn't have to hold my hand because of my parents I'd have given notice long ago, I'd have gone to the chief and told him exactly what I think of him. That would knock him endways from his desk! It's a queer way of doing, too, this sitting on high at a desk and talking down to employees, especially when they have to come quite near because the chief is hard of hearing. Well, there's still hope; once I've saved enough money to pay back my parents' debts to him—that should take   5 another five or six years—I'll do it without fail. I'll cut myself completely loose then. For the moment, though, I'd better get up, since my train goes at five.

He looked at the alarm clock ticking on the chest. Heavenly Father! he   6
thought. It was half-past six o'clock and the hands were quietly moving on, it was even past the half-hour, it was getting on toward a quarter to seven. Had the alarm clock not gone off? From the bed one could see that it had been properly set for four o'clock; of course it must have gone off. Yes, but was it possible to sleep quietly through that ear-splitting noise? Well, he had not slept quietly, yet apparently all the more soundly for that. But what was he to do now? The next train went at seven o'clock; to catch that he would need to hurry like mad and his samples weren't even packed up, and he himself wasn't feeling particularly fresh and active. And even if he did catch the train he wouldn't avoid a row with the chief, since the firm's porter would have been waiting for the five o'clock train and would have long since reported his failure to turn up. The porter was a creature of the chief's, spineless and stupid. Well, supposing he were to say he was sick? But that would be most unpleasant and would look suspicious, since during his five years' employment he had not been ill once. The chief himself would be sure to come with the sick-insurance doctor, would reproach his parents with their son's laziness and would cut all excuses short by referring to the insurance doctor, who of course regarded all mankind as perfectly healthy malingerers. And would he be so far wrong on this occasion? Gregor really felt quite well, apart from a drowsiness that was utterly superfluous after such a long sleep, and he was even unusually hungry.

As all this was running through his mind at top speed without his being   7
able to decide to leave his bed—the alarm clock had just struck a quarter to seven—there came a cautious tap at the door behind the head of his bed. "Gregor," said a voice—it was his mother's—"it's a quarter to seven. Hadn't you a train to catch?" That gentle voice! Gregor had a shock as he heard his own voice answering hers, unmistakably his own voice, it was true, but with a persistent horrible twittering squeak behind it like an undertone, that left the words in their clear shape only for the first moment and then rose up reverberating round them to destroy their sense, so that one could not be sure one had heard them rightly. Gregor wanted to answer at length and explain everything, but in the circumstances he confined himself to saying: "Yes, yes, thank you, Mother, I'm getting up now." The wooden door between them must have kept the change in his voice from being noticeable outside, for his mother contented herself with this statement and shuffled away. Yet this brief exchange of words had made the other members of the family aware that Gregor was still in the house, as they had not expected, and at one of the side doors his father was already knocking, gently, yet with his fist. "Gregor, Gregor," he called, "what's the matter with you?" And after a little while he called again in a deeper voice: "Gregor! Gregor!" At the other side door his sister was saying

in a low, plaintive tone: "Gregor? Aren't you well? Are you needing anything?" He answered them both at once: "I'm just ready," and did his best to make his voice sound as normal as possible by enunciating the words very clearly and leaving long pauses between them. So his father went back to his breakfast, but his sister whispered: "Gregor, open the door, do." However, he was not thinking of opening the door, and felt thankful for the prudent habit he had acquired in traveling of locking all doors during the night, even at home.

His immediate intention was to get up quietly without being disturbed, to put on his clothes and above all eat his breakfast, and only then to consider what else was to be done, since in bed, he was well aware, his mediations would come to no sensible conclusion. He remembered that often enough in bed he had felt small aches and pains, probably caused by awkward postures, which had proved purely imaginary once he got up, and he looked forward eagerly to seeing this morning's delusions gradually fall away. That the change in his voice was nothing but the precursor of a severe chill, a standing ailment of commercial travelers, he had not the least possible doubt. 8

To get rid of the quilt was quite easy; he had only to inflate himself a little and it fell off by itself. But the next move was difficult, especially because he was so uncommonly broad. He would have needed arms and hands to hoist himself up; instead he had only the numerous little legs which never stopped waving in all directions and which he could not control in the least. When he tried to bend one of them it was the first to stretch itself straight; and did he succeed at last in making it do what he wanted, all the other legs meanwhile waved the more wildly in a high degree of unpleasant agitation. "But what's the use of lying idle in bed," said Gregor to himself. 9

He thought that he might get out of bed with the lower part of his body first, but this lower part, which he had not yet seen and of which he could form no clear conception, proved too difficult to move; it shifted so slowly; and when finally, almost wild with annoyance, he gathered his forces together and thrust out recklessly, he had miscalculated the direction and bumped heavily against the lower end of the bed, and the stinging pain he felt informed him that precisely this lower part of his body was at the moment probably the most sensitive. 10

So he tried to get the top part of himself out first, and cautiously moved his head towards the edge of the bed. That proved easy enough, and despite its breadth and mass the bulk of his body at last slowly followed the movement of his head. Still, when he finally got his head free over the edge of the bed he felt too scared to go on advancing, for after all if he let himself fall in this way it would take a miracle to keep his head from being injured. And at all costs he must not lose consciousness now, precisely now; he would rather stay in bed. 11

But when after a repetition of the same efforts he lay in his former position   12
again, sighing, and watched his little legs struggling against each other more
wildly than ever, if that were possible, and saw no way of bringing any order
into this arbitrary confusion, he told himself again that it was impossible to
stay in bed and that the most sensible course was to risk everything for the
smallest hope of getting away from it. At the same time he did not forget
meanwhile to remind himself that cool reflection, the coolest possible, was
much better than desperate resolves. In such moments he focused his eyes as
sharply as possible on the window, but, unfortunately, the prospect of the
morning fog, which muffled even the other side of the narrow street, brought
him little encouragement and comfort. "Seven o'clock already," he said to
himself when the alarm clock chimed again, "seven o'clock already and still
such a thick fog." And for a little while he lay quiet, breathing lightly, as if
perhaps expecting such complete repose to restore all things to their real and
normal condition.

But then he said to himself: "Before it strikes a quarter past seven I must   13
be quite out of this bed, without fail. Anyhow, by that time someone will have
come from the office to ask for me, since it opens before seven." And he set
himself to rocking his whole body at once in a regular rhythm, with the idea
of swinging it out of the bed. If he tipped himself out in that way he could
keep his head from injury by lifting it at an acute angle when he fell. His back
seemed to be hard and was not likely to suffer from a fall on the carpet. His
biggest worry was the loud crash he would not be able to help making, which
would probably cause anxiety, if not terror, behind all the doors. Still, he must
take the risk.

When he was already half out of the bed—the new method was more a   14
game than an effort, for he needed only to hitch himself across by rocking to
and fro—it struck him how simple it would be if he could get help. Two
strong people—he thought of his father and the servant girl—would be amply
sufficient; they would only have to thrust their arms under his convex back,
lever him out of the bed, bend down with their burden and then be patient
enough to let him turn himself right over on to the floor, where it was to be
hoped his legs would then find their proper function. Well, ignoring the fact
that the doors were all locked, ought he really to call for help? In spite of his
misery he could not suppress a smile at the very idea of it.

He had got so far that he could barely keep his equilibrium when he rocked   15
himself strongly, and he would have to nerve himself very soon for the final
decision since in five minutes' time it would be a quarter past seven—when
the front doorbell rang. "That's someone from the office," he said to himself,
and grew almost rigid, while his little legs only jigged about all the faster. For
a moment everything stayed quiet. "They're not going to open the door," said

Gregor to himself, catching at some kind of irrational hope. But then of course the servant girl went as usual to the door with her heavy tread and opened it. Gregor needed only to hear the first good morning of the visitor to know immediately who it was—the chief clerk himself. What a fate, to be condemned to work for a firm where the smallest omission at once gave rise to the gravest suspicion! Were all employees in a body nothing but scoundrels, was there not among them one single loyal devoted man who, had he wasted only an hour or so of the firm's time in a morning, was so tormented by conscience as to be driven out of his mind and actually incapable of leaving his bed? Wouldn't it really have been sufficient to send an apprentice to inquire—if any inquiry were necessary at all—did the chief clerk himself have to come and thus indicate to the entire family, an innocent family, that this suspicious circumstance could be investigated by no one less versed in affairs than himself? And more through the agitation caused by these reflections than through any act of will Gregor swung himself out of bed with all his strength. There was a loud thump, but it was not really a crash. His fall was broken to some extent by the carpet, his back, too, was less stiff than he thought, and so there was merely a dull thud, not so very startling. Only he had not lifted his head carefully enough and had hit it; he turned it and rubbed it on the carpet in pain and irritation.

"That was something falling down in there," said the chief clerk in the next room to the left. Gregor tried to suppose to himself that something like what had happened to him today might some day happen to the chief clerk; one really could not deny that it was possible. But as if in brusque reply to this supposition the chief clerk took a couple of firm steps in the next-door room and his patent leather boots creaked. From the right-hand room his sister was whispering to inform him of the situation: "Gregor, the chief clerk's here." "I know," muttered Gregor to himself; but he didn't dare to make his voice loud enough for his sister to hear it. 16

"Gregor," said his father now from the left-hand room, "the chief clerk has come and wants to know why you didn't catch the early train. We don't know what to say to him. Besides, he wants to talk to you in person. So open the door, please. He will be good enough to excuse the untidiness of your room." "Good morning, Mr. Samsa," the chief clerk was calling amiably meanwhile. "He's not well," said his mother to the visitor, while his father was still speaking through the door, "he's not well, sir, believe me. What else would make him miss a train! The boy thinks about nothing but his work. It makes me almost cross the way he never goes out in the evenings; he's been here the last eight days and has stayed at home every single evening. He just sits there quietly at the table reading a newspaper or looking through railway timetables. The only amusement he gets is doing fretwork. For instance, he spent two or three evenings cutting out a little picture frame; you would be surprised to see how 17 pretty it is; it's hanging in his room; you'll see it in a minute when Gregor opens the door. I must say I'm glad you've come, sir; we should never have got him to unlock the door by ourselves; he's so obstinate; and I'm sure he's unwell, though he wouldn't have it to be so this morning." "I'm just coming," said Gregor slowly and carefully, not moving an inch for fear of losing one word of the conversation. "I can't think of any other explanation, madam," said the chief clerk, "I hope it's nothing serious. Although on the other hand I must say that we men of business—fortunately or unfortunately—very often simply have to ignore any slight indisposition, since business must be attended to." "Well, can the chief clerk come in now?" asked Gregor's father impatiently, again knocking on the door. "No," said Gregor. In the left-hand room a painful silence followed this refusal, in the right-hand room his sister began to sob.

Why didn't his sister join the others? She was probably newly out of bed   18
and hadn't even begun to put on her clothes yet. Well, why was she crying? Because he wouldn't get up and let the chief clerk in, because he was in danger of losing his job, and because the chief would begin dunning his parents again for the old debts? Surely these were things one didn't need to worry about for the present. Gregor was still at home and not in the least thinking of deserting the family. At the moment, true, he was lying on the carpet and no one who knew the condition he was in could seriously expect him to admit the chief clerk. But for such a small discourtesy, which could plausibly be explained away somehow later on, Gregor could hardly be dismissed on the spot. And it seemed to Gregor that it would be much more sensible to leave him in peace for the present than to trouble him with tears and entreaties. Still, of course, their uncertainty bewildered them all and excused their behavior.

"Mr. Samsa," the chief clerk called now in a louder voice, "what's the matter   19
with you? Here you are, barricading yourself in your room, giving only 'yes' and 'no' for answers, causing your parents a lot of unnecessary trouble and neglecting—I mention this only in passing—neglecting your business duties in an incredible fashion. I am speaking here in the name of your parents and of your chief, and I beg you quite seriously to give me an immediate and precise explanation. You amaze me, you amaze me. I thought you were a quiet, dependable person, and now all at once you seem bent on making a disgraceful exhibition of yourself. The chief did hint to me early this morning a possible explanation for your disappearance—with reference to the cash payments that were entrusted to you recently—but I almost pledged my solemn word of honor that this could not be so. But now that I see how incredibly obstinate you are, I no longer have the slightest desire to take your part at all. And your position in the firm is not so unassailable. I came with the intention of telling you all this in private, but since you are wasting my time no needlessly I don't see why your parents shouldn't hear it too. For some time past your work has

been most unsatisfactory; this is not the season of the year for a business boom, of course, we admit that, but a season of the year for doing no business at all, that does not exist, Mr. Samsa, must not exist."

"But, sir," cried Gregor, beside himself and in his agitation forgetting every- 20 thing else, "I'm just going to open the door this very minute. A slight illness, an attack of giddiness, has kept me from getting up. I'm still lying in bed. But I feel all right again. I'm getting out of bed now. Just give me a moment or two longer! I'm not quite so well as I thought. But I'm all right, really. How a thing like that can suddenly strike one down! Only last night I was quite well, my parents can tell you, or rather I did have a slight presentiment. I must have showed some sign of it. Why didn't I report it at the office! But one always thinks that an indisposition can be got over without staying in the house. Oh sir, do spare my parents! All that you're reproaching me with now has no foundation; no one has ever said a word to me about it. Perhaps you haven't looked at the last orders I sent in. Anyhow, I can still catch the eight o'clock train, I'm much the better for my few hours' rest. Don't let me detain you here, sir; I'll be attending to business very soon, and do be good enough to tell the chief so and to make my excuses to him!"

And while all this was tumbling out pell-mell and Gregor hardly knew what 21 he was saying, he had reached the chest quite easily, perhaps because of the practice he had had in bed, and was now trying to lever himself upright by means of it. He meant actually to open the door, actually to show himself and speak to the chief clerk; he was eager to find out what the others, after all their insistence, would say at the sight of him. If they were horrified then the responsibility was no longer his and he could stay quiet. But if they took it calmly, then he had no reason either to be upset, and could really get to the station for the eight o'clock train if he hurried. At first he slipped down a few times from the polished surface of the chest, but at length with a last heave he stood upright; he paid no more attention to the pains in the lower part of his body, however they smarted. Then he let himself fall against the back of a nearby chair, and clung with his little legs to the edges of it. That brought him into control of himself again and he stopped speaking, for now he could listen to what the chief clerk was saying.

"Did you understand a word of it?" the chief clerk was asking; "surely he 22 can't be trying to make fools of us?" "Oh dear," cried his mother, in tears, "perhaps he's terribly ill and we're tormenting him. Grete! Grete!" she called out then. "Yes Mother?" called his sister from the other side. They were calling to each other across Gregor's room. "You must go this minute for the doctor. Gregor is ill. Go for the doctor, quick. Did you hear how he was speaking?" "That was no human voice," said the chief clerk in a voice noticeably low beside the shrillness of the mother's. "Anna! Anna!" his father was calling through the hall to the kitchen, clapping his hands, "get a locksmith at once!" And the two girls were already running through the hall with a swish of skirts—how could his sister have got dressed so quickly?—and were tearing the front door open. There was no sound of its closing again; they had evidently left it open, as one does in houses where some great misfortune has happened.

But Gregor was now much calmer. The words he uttered were no longer understandable, apparently, although they seemed clear enough to him, even clearer than before, perhaps because his ear had grown accustomed to the sound of them. Yet at any rate people now believed that something was wrong with him, and were ready to help him. The positive certainty with which these first measures had been taken comforted him. He felt himself drawn once more into the human circle and hoped for great and remarkable results from both the doctor and the locksmith, without really distinguishing precisely between them. To make his voice as clear as possible for the decisive conversation that was now imminent he coughed a little, as quietly as he could, of course, since this noise too might not sound like a human cough for all he was able to judge. In the next room meanwhile there was complete silence. Perhaps his parents were sitting at the table with the chief clerk, whispering, perhaps they were all leaning against the door and listening.

Slowly Gregor pushed the chair towards the door, then let go of it, caught hold of the door for support—the soles at the end of his little legs were somewhat sticky—and rested against it for a moment after his efforts. Then he set himself to turning the key in the lock with his mouth. It seemed, unhappily, that he hadn't really any teeth—what could he grip the key with?— but on the other hand his jaws were certainly very strong; with their help he did manage to set the key in motion, heedless of the fact that he was undoubt- edly damaging them somewhere, since a brown fluid issued from his mouth, flowed over the key and dripped on the floor. "Just listen to that," said the chief clerk next door; "he's turning the key." That was a great encouragement to Gregor; but they should all have shouted encouragement to him, his father and mother too: "Go on, Gregor," they should have called out, "keep going, hold on to that key!" And in the belief that they were all following his efforts intently, he clenched his jaws recklessly on the key with all the force at his command. As the turning of the key progressed he circled round the lock, holding on now only with his mouth, pushing on the key, as required, or pulling it down again with all the weight of his body. The louder click of the finally yielding lock literally quickened Gregor. With a deep breath of relief he said to himself: "So I didn't need the locksmith," and laid his head on the handle to open the door wide.

Since he had to pull the door towards him, he was still invisible when it was really wide open. He had to edge himself very slowly round the near half of the double door, and to do it very carefully if he was not to fall plump upon his back just on the threshold. He was still carrying out this difficult manoeuvre, with no time to observe anything else, when he heard the chief clerk utter a loud "Oh!"—it sounded like a gust of wind—and now he could see the man, standing as he was nearest to the door, clapping one hand before his open mouth and slowly backing away as if driven by some invisible steady pressure. His mother—in spite of the chief clerk's being there her hair was still undone and sticking up in all directions—first clasped her hands and looked at his father, then took two steps towards Gregor and fell on the floor among her outspread skirts, her face quite hidden on her breast. His father knotted his fist with a fierce expression on his face as if he meant to knock Gregor back into his room, then looked uncertainly round the living room, covered his eyes with his hands and wept till his great chest heaved.

Gregor did not go now into the living room, but leaned against the inside of the firmly shut wing of the door, so that only half his body was visible and his head above it bending sideways to look at the others. The light had meanwhile strengthened; on the other side of the street one could see clearly a section of the endlessly long, dark gray building opposite—it was a hospital—abruptly punctuated by its row of regular windows; the rain was still falling, but only in large singly discernible and literally singly splashing drops. The breakfast dishes were set out on the table lavishly, for breakfast was the most important meal of the day to Gregor's father, who lingered it out for hours over various newspapers. Right opposite Gregor on the wall hung a photograph of himself on military service, as a lieutenant, hand on sword, a carefree smile on his face, inviting one to respect his uniform and military bearing. The door leading to the hall was open, and one could see that the front door stood open too, showing the landing beyond and the beginning of the stairs going down.

"Well," said Gregor, knowing perfectly that he was the only one who had retained any composure, "I'll put my clothes on at once, pack up my samples and start off. Will you only let me go? You see, sir, I'm not obstinate, and I'm willing to work; traveling is a hard life, but I couldn't live without it. Where are you going, sir? To the office? Yes? Will you give a true account of all this? One can be temporarily incapacitated, but that's just the moment for remembering former services and bearing in mind that later on, when the incapacity has been got over, one will certainly work with all the more industry and concentration. I'm loyally bound to serve the chief, you know that very well. Besides, I have to provide for my parents and my sister. I'm in great difficulties, but I'll get out of them again. Don't make things any worse for me than they are. Stand up for me in the firm. Travelers are not popular there, I know. People think they earn sacks of money and just have a good time. A prejudice there's no particular reason for revising. But you, sir, have a more comprehensive view of affairs than the rest of the staff, yes, let me tell you in confidence, a more comprehensive view than the chief himself, who, being the owner, lets his judgment easily be swayed against one of his employees. And you know

26

27

very well that the traveler, who is never seen in the office almost the whole
year round, can so easily fall a victim to gossip and ill luck and unfounded
complaints, which he mostly knows nothing about, except when he comes back
exhausted from his rounds, and only then suffers in person from their evil
consequences, which he can no longer trace back to the original causes. Sir,
sir, don't go away without a word to me to show that you think me in the right
at least to some extent!"

But at Gregor's very first words the chief clerk had already backed away   28
and only stared at him with parted lips over one twitching shoulder. And while
Gregor was speaking he did not stand still one moment but stole away towards
the door, without taking his eyes off Gregor, yet only an inch at a time, as if
obeying some secret injunction to leave the room. He was already at the hall,
and the suddenness with which he took his last step out of the living room
would have made one believe he had burned the sole of his foot. Once in the
hall he stretched his right arm before him towards the staircase, as if some
supernatural power were waiting there to deliver him.

Gregor perceived that the chief clerk must on no account be allowed to go   29
away in this frame of mind if his position in the firm were not to be endangered
to the utmost. His parents did not understand this so well; they had convinced
themselves in the course of years that Gregor was settled for life in this firm,
and besides they were so occupied with their immediate troubles that all
foresight had forsaken them. Yet Gregor had this foresight. The chief clerk must
be detained, soothed, persuaded and finally won over; the whole future of
Gregor and his family depended on it! If only his sister had been there! She
was intelligent; she had begun to cry while Gregor was still lying quietly on his
back. And no doubt the chief clerk, so partial to ladies, would have been guided
by her; she would have shut the door of the flat and in the hall talked him out
of his horror. But she was not there, and Gregor would have to handle the
situation himself. And without remembering that he was still unaware what
powers of movement he possessed, without even remembering that his words
in all possibility, indeed in all likelihood, would again be unintelligible, he let
go the wing of the door, pushed himself through the opening, started to walk
towards the chief clerk, who was already ridiculously clinging with both hands
to the railing on the landing; but immediately, as he was feeling for a support,
he fell down with a little cry upon all his numerous legs. Hardly was he down
when he experienced for the first time this morning a sense of physical comfort;
his legs had firm ground under them; they were completely obedient, as he
noted with joy; they even strove to carry him forward in whatever direction
he chose; and he was inclined to believe that a final relief from all his sufferings
was at hand. But in the same moment as he found himself on the floor, rocking
with suppressed eagerness to move, not far from his mother, indeed just in
front of her, she, who had seemed to completely crushed, sprang all at once

to her feet, her arms and fingers outspread, cried: "Help, for God's sake, help!" bent her head down as if to see Gregor better, yet on the contrary kept backing senselessly away; had quite forgotten that the laden table stood behind her; sat upon it hastily, as if in absence of mind, when she bumped into it; and seemed altogether unaware that the big coffee pot beside her was upset and pouring coffee in a flood over the carpet.

"Mother, Mother," said Gregor in a low voice, and looked up at her. The 30 chief clerk, for the moment, had quite slipped from his mind; instead he could not resist snapping his jaws together at the sight of the steaming coffee. That made his mother scream again, she fled from the table and fell into the arms of his father, who hastened to catch her. But Gregor had now no time to spare for his parents; the chief clerk was already on the stairs; with his chin on the banisters he was taking one last backward look. Gregor made a spring, to be as sure as possible of overtaking him; the chief clerk must have divined his intention, for he leaped down several steps and vanished; he was still yelling "Ugh!" and it echoed through the whole staircase.

Unfortunately, the flight of the chief clerk seemed completely to upset 31 Gregor's father, who had remained relatively calm until now, for instead of running after the man himself, or at least not hindering Gregor in his pursuit, he seized in his right hand the walking stick which the chief clerk had left behind on a chair, together with a hat and greatcoat, snatched in his left hand a large newspaper from the table and began stamping his feet and flourishing the stick and the newspaper to drive Gregor back into his room. No entreaty of Gregor's availed, indeed no entreaty was even understood; however humbly he bent his head his father only stamped on the floor the more loudly. Behind his father his mother had torn open a window, despite the cold weather, and was leaning far out of it with her face in her hands. A strong draught set in from the street to the staircase, the window curtain blew in, the newspapers on the table fluttered, stray pages whisked over the floor. Pitilessly Gregor's father drove him back, hissing and crying "Shoo!" like a savage. But Gregor was quite unpracticed in walking backwards, it really was a slow business. If he only had a chance to turn round he could get back to his room at once, but he was afraid of exasperating his father by the slowness of such a rotation and at any moment the stick in his father's hand might hit him a fatal blow on the back or on the head. In the end, however, nothing else was left for him to do since to his horror he observed that in moving backwards he could not even control the direction he took; and so, keeping an anxious eye on his father all the time over his shoulder, he began to turn round as quickly as he could, which was in reality very slowly. Perhaps his father noted his good intentions, for he did not interfere except every now and then to help him in the manoeuvre from a distance with the point of the stick. If only he would have stopped making that unbearable hissing noise! It made Gregor quite lose his head. He had turned almost completely round when the hissing noise so distracted him that he even turned a little the wrong way again. But when at last his head was fortunately right in front of the doorway, it appeared that his body was too broad simply to get through the opening. His father, of course, in his present mood was far from thinking of such a thing as opening the other half of the door, to let Gregor have enough space. He had merely the fixed idea of driving Gregor back into his room as quickly as possible. He would have never suffered Gregor to make the circumstantial preparations for standing up on end and perhaps slipping his way through the door. Maybe he was now making more noise than ever to urge Gregor forward, as if no obstacle impeded him; to Gregor, anyhow, the noise in his rear sounded no longer like the voice of one single father; this was really no joke, and Gregor thrust himself—come what might—into the doorway. One side of his body rose up, he was tilted at an angle in the doorway, his flank was quite bruised, horrid blotches stained the white door, soon he was stuck fast and, left to himself, could not have moved at all, his legs on one side fluttered trembling in the air, those on the other were crushed painfully to the floor—when from behind his father gave him a strong push which was literally a deliverance and he flew far into the room, bleeding freely. The door was slammed behind him with the stick, and then at last there was silence.

Not until it was twilight did Gregor awake out of a deep sleep, more like a   32
swoon than a sleep. He would certainly have waked up of his own accord not much later, for he felt himself sufficiently rested and well-slept, but it seemed to him as if a fleeting step and a cautious shutting of the door leading into the hall had aroused him. The electric lights in the street cast a pale sheen here and there on the ceiling and the upper surfaces of the furniture, but down below, where he lay, it was dark. Slowly, awkwardly trying out his feelers, which he now first learned to appreciate, he pushed his way to the door to see what had been happening there. His left side felt like one single long, unpleasantly tense scar, and he had actually to limp on his two rows of legs. One little leg, moreover, had been severely damaged in the course of that morning's events—it was almost a miracle that only one had been damaged—and trailed uselessly behind him.

He had reached the door before he discovered what had really drawn him   33
to it: the smell of food. For there stood a basin filled with fresh milk in which floated little sops of white bread. He could almost have laughed with joy, since he was now still hungrier than in the morning, and dipped his head almost over the eyes straight into the milk. But soon in disappointment he withdrew it again; not only did he find it difficult to feed because of his tender left side—

and he could only feed with the palpitating collaboration of his whole body—
he did not like the milk either, although milk had been his favorite drink and
that was certainly why his sister had set it there for him, indeed it was almost
with repulsion that he turned away from the basin and crawled back to the
middle of the room.

He could see through the crack of the door that the gas was turned on in   34
the living room, but while usually at this time his father made a habit of reading
the afternoon newspaper in a loud voice to his mother and occasionally to his
sister as well, not a sound was now to be heard. Well, perhaps his father had
recently given up this habit of reading aloud, which his sister had mentioned
so often in conversation and in her letters. But there was the same silence all
around, although the flat was certainly not empty of occupants. "What a quiet
life our family has been leading," said Gregor to himself, and as he sat there
motionless staring into the darkness he felt great pride in the fact that he had
been able to provide such a life for his parents and sister in such a fine flat.
But what if all the quiet, the comfort, the contentment were now to end in
horror? To keep himself from being lost in such thoughts Gregor took refuge
in movement and crawled up and down the room.

Once during the long evening one of the side doors was opened a little and   35
quickly shut again, later the other side door too; someone had apparently
wanted to come in and then thought better of it. Gregor now stationed himself
immediately before the living-room door, determined to persuade any hesitating
visitor to come in or at least to discover who it might be; but the door was
not opened again and he waited in vain. In the early morning, when the doors
were locked, they had all wanted to come in, now that he had opened one
door and the other had apparently been opened during the day, no one came
in and even the keys were on the other side of the doors.

It was late at night before the gas went out in the living room, and Gregor   36
could easily tell that his parents and his sister had all stayed awake until then,
for he could clearly hear the three of them stealing away on tiptoe. No one
was likely to visit him, not until the morning, that was certain; so he had plenty
of time to meditate at his leisure on how he was to arrange his life afresh. But
the lofty, empty room in which he had to lie flat on the floor filled him with
an apprehension he could not account for, since it had been his very own room
for the past five years—and with a half-unconscious action, not without a
slight feeling of shame, he scuttled under the sofa, where he felt comfortable
at once, although his back was a little cramped and he could not lift his head
up, and his only regret was that his body was too broad to get the whole of it
under the sofa.

He stayed there all night, spending the time partly in a light slumber, from   37
which his hunger kept waking him up with a start, and partly in worrying and
sketching vague hopes, which all led to the same conclusion, that he must lie

low for the present and, by exercising patience and the utmost consideration, help the family to bear the inconvenience he was bound to cause them in his present condition.

Very early in the morning, it was still almost night, Gregor had the chance to test the strength of his new resolutions, for his sister, nearly fully dressed, opened the door from the hall and peered in. She did not see him at once, yet when she caught sight of him under the sofa—well, he had to be somewhere, he couldn't have flown away, could he?—she was so startled that without being able to help it she slammed the door shut again. But as if regretting her behavior she opened the door again immediately and came in on tiptoe, as if she were visiting an invalid or even a stranger. Gregor had pushed his head forward to the very edge of the sofa and watched her. Would she notice that he had left the milk standing, and not for lack of hunger, and would she bring in some other kind of food more to his taste? If she did not do it of her own accord, he would rather starve than draw her attention to the fact, although he felt a wild impulse to dart out from under the sofa, throw himself at her feet and beg her for something to eat. But his sister at once noticed, with surprise, that the basin was still full, except for a little milk that had been spilt all around it, she lifted it immediately, not with her bare hands, true, but with a cloth and carried it away. Gregor was wildly curious to know what she would bring instead, and made various speculations about it. Yet what she actually did next, in the goodness of her heart, he could never have guessed at. To find out what he liked she brought him a whole selection of food, all set out on an old newspaper. There were old, half-decayed vegetables, bones from last night's supper covered with a white sauce that had thickened; some raisins and almonds; a piece of cheese that Gregor would have called uneatable two days ago; a dry roll of bread, a buttered roll, and a roll both buttered and salted. Besides all that, she set down again the same basin, into which she had poured some water, and which was apparently to be reserved for his exclusive use. And with fine tact, knowing that Gregor would not eat in her presence, she withdrew quickly and even turned the key, to let him understand that he could take his ease as much as he liked. Gregor's legs all whizzed towards the food. His wounds must have healed completely, moreover, for he felt no disability, which amazed him and made him reflect how more than a month ago he had cut one finger a little with a knife and had still suffered pain from the wound only the day before yesterday. Am I less sensitive now? he thought, and sucked greedily at the cheese, which above all the other edibles attracted him at once and strongly. One after another and with tears of satisfaction in his eyes he quickly devoured the cheese, the vegetables and the sauce; the fresh food, on the other hand, had no charms for him, he could not even stand the smell of it and actually dragged away to some little distance the things he could eat. He had long finished his meal and was only lying lazily on the same spot when his sister

38

turned the key slowly as a sign for him to retreat. That roused him at once, although he was nearly asleep, and he hurried under the sofa again. But it took considerable self-control for him to stay under the sofa, even for the short time his sister was in the room, since the large meal had swollen his body somewhat and he was so cramped he could hardly breathe. Slight attacks of breathlessness afflicted him and his eyes were starting a little out of his head as he watched his unsuspecting sister sweeping together with a broom not only the remains of what he had eaten but even the things he had not touched, as if these were now of no use to anyone, and hastily shoveling it all into a bucket, which she covered with a wooden lid and carried away. Hardly had she turned her back when Gregor came from under the sofa and stretched and puffed himself out.

In this manner Gregor was fed, once in the early morning while his parents   39
and the servant girl were still asleep, and a second time after they had all had their midday dinner, for then his parents took a short nap and the servant girl could be sent out on some errand or other by his sister. Not that they would have wanted him to starve, of course, but perhaps they could not have borne to know more about his feeding than from hearsay, perhaps too his sister wanted to spare them such little anxieties wherever possible, since they had quite enough to bear as it was.

Under what pretext the doctor and the locksmith had been got rid of on   40
that first morning Gregor could not discover, for since what he said was not understood by the others it never struck any of them, not even his sister, that he could understand what they said, and so whenever his sister came into his room he had to content himself with hearing her utter only a sigh now and then and an occasional appeal to the saints. Later on, when she had got a little used to the situation—of course she could never get completely used to it— she sometimes threw out a remark which was kindly meant or could be so interpreted. "Well, he liked his dinner today," she would say when Gregor had made a good clearance of his food; and when he had not eaten, which gradually happened more and more often, she would say almost sadly: "Everything's been left standing again."

But although Gregor could get no news directly, he overheard a lot from   41
the neighboring rooms, and as soon as voices were audible, he would run to the door of the room concerned and press his whole body against it. In the first few days especially there was no conversation that did not refer to him somehow, even if only indirectly. For two whole days there were family con-sultations at every mealtime about what should be done; but also between meals the same subject was discussed, for there were always at least two members of the family at home, since no one wanted to be alone in the flat and to leave it quite empty was unthinkable. And on the very first of these days the household cook—it was not quite clear what and how much she knew of the situation—

went down on her knees to his mother and begged leave to go, and when she departed, a quarter of an hour later, gave thanks for her dismissal with tears in her eyes as if for the greatest benefit that could have been conferred on her, and without any prompting swore a solemn oath that she would never say a single word to anyone about what had happened.

Now Gregor's sister had to cook too, helping her mother; true, the cooking   42
did not amount to much, for they ate scarcely anything. Gregor was always hearing one of the family vainly urging another to eat and getting no answer but: "Thanks, I've had all I want," or something similar. Perhaps they drank nothing either. Time and again his sister kept asking his father if he wouldn't like some beer and offered kindly to go and fetch it herself, and when he made no answer suggested that she could ask the concierge to fetch it, so that he need feel no sense of obligation, but then a round "No" came from his father and no more was said about it.

In the course of that very first day Gregor's father explained the family's   43
financial position and prospects to both his mother and his sister. Now and then he rose from the table to get some voucher or memorandum out of the small safe he had rescued from the collapse of his business five years earlier. One could hear him opening the complicated lock and rustling papers out and shutting it again. This statement made by his father was the first cheerful information Gregor had heard since his imprisonment. He had been of the opinion that nothing at all was left over from his father's business, at least his father had never said anything to the contrary, and of course he had not asked him directly. At that time Gregor's sole desire was to do his utmost to help the family to forget as soon as possible the catastrophe which had overwhelmed the business and thrown them all into a state of complete despair. And so he had set to work with unusual ardor and almost overnight had become a commercial traveler instead of a little clerk, with of course much greater chances of earning money, and his success was immediately translated into good round coin which he could lay on the table for his amazed and happy family. These had been fine times, and they had never recurred, at least not with the same sense of glory, although later on Gregor had earned so much money that he was able to meet the expenses of the whole household and did so. They had simply got used to it, both the family and Gregor; the money was gratefully accepted and gladly given, but there was no special uprush of warm feeling. With his sister alone had he remained intimate, and it was a secret plan of his that she, who loved music, unlike himself, and could play movingly on the violin, should be sent next year to study at the Conservatorium, despite the great expense that would entail, which must be made up in some other way. During his brief visits home the Conservatorium was often mentioned in the talks he had with his sister, but always merely as a beautiful dream which could

never come true, and his parents discouraged even these innocent references to it; yet Gregor had made up his mind firmly about it and meant to announce the fact with due solemnity on Christmas Day.

Such were the thoughts, completely futile in his present condition, that went 44 through his head as he stood clinging upright to the door and listening. Sometimes out of sheer weariness he had to give up listening and let his head fall negligently against the door, but he always had to pull himself together again at once, for even the slight sound his head made was audible next door and brought all conversation to a stop. "What can he be doing now?" his father would say after a while, obviously turning towards the door, and only then would the interrupted conversation gradually be set going again.

Gregor now was informed as amply as he could wish—for his father tended 45 to repeat himself in his explanations, partly because it was a long time since he had handled such matters and partly because his mother could not always grasp things at once—that a certain amount of investments, a very small amount it was true, had survived the wreck of their fortunes and had even increased a little because the dividends had not been touched meanwhile. And besides that, the money Gregor brought home every month—he had kept only a few dollars for himself—had never been quite used up and now amounted to a small capital sum. Behind the door Gregor nodded his head eagerly, rejoiced at this evidence of unexpected thrift and foresight. True, he could really have paid off some more of his father's debts to the chief with his extra money, and so brought much nearer the day on which he could quit his job, but doubtless it was better the way his father had arranged it.

Yet this capital was by no means sufficient to let the family live on the 46 interest of it; for one year, perhaps, or at the most two, they could live on the principal, that was all. It was simply a sum that ought not to be touched and should be kept for a rainy day; money for living expenses would have to be earned. Now his father was still hale enough but an old man, and he had done no work for the past five years and could not be expected to do much; during these five years, the first years of leisure in his laborious though unsuccessful life, he had grown rather fat and become sluggish. And Gregor's old mother, how was she to earn a living with her asthma, which troubled her even when she walked through the flat, and kept her lying on a sofa every other day panting for breath beside an open window? And was is sister to earn her bread, she who was still a child of seventeen and whose life hitherto had been so pleasant consisting as it did in dressing herself nicely, sleeping long, helping in the housekeeping, going out to a few modest entertainments and above all playing the violin? At first whenever the need for earning money was mentioned Gregor let go his hold on the door and threw himself down on the cool leather sofa beside it, he felt so hot with shame and grief.

Often he just lay there the long nights through without sleeping at all,   47
scrabbling for hours on the leather. Or he nerved himself to the great effort
of pushing an armchair to the window, then crawled up over the window sill
and, braced against the chair, leaned against the window panes, obviously in
some recollection of the sense of freedom that looking out of a window always
used to give him. For in reality day by day things that were even a little way
off were growing dimmer to his sight; the hospital across the street, which he
used to execrate for being all too often before his eyes, was not quite beyond
his range of vision, and if he had not known that he lived in Charlotte Street,
a quiet street but still a city street, he might have believed that his window
gave on a desert waste where gray sky and gray land blended indistinguishably
into each other. His quick-witted sister only needed to observe twice that the
armchair stood by the window; after that whenever she had tidied the room
she always pushed the chair back to the same place at the window and even
left the inner casements open.

If he could have spoken to her and thanked her for all she had to do for   48
him, he could have borne her ministrations better; as it was, they oppressed
him. She certainly tried to make as light as possible of whatever was disagreeable
in her task, and as time went on she succeeded, of course, more and more, but
time brought more enlightenment to Gregor too. The very way she came in
distressed him. Hardly was she in the room when she rushed to the window,
without even taking time to shut the door, careful as she was usually to shield
the sight of Gregor's room from the others, and as if she were almost suffocating
tore the casements open with hasty fingers, standing then in the open draught
for a while even in the bitterest cold and drawing deep breaths. This noisy
scurry of hers upset Gregor twice a day; he would crouch trembling under the
sofa all the time, knowing quite well that she would certainly have spared him
such a disturbance had she found it at all possible to stay in his presence
without opening the window.

On one occasion, about a month after Gregor's metamorphosis, when there   49
was surely no reason for her to be still startled at his appearance, she came a
little earlier than usual and found him gazing out of the window, quite motionless, and thus well placed to look like a bogey. Gregor would not have been
surprised had she not come in at all, for she could not immediately open the
window while he was there, but not only did she retreat, she jumped back as
if in alarm and banged the door shut; a stranger might well have thought that
he had been lying in wait for her there meaning to bite her. Of course he hid
himself under the sofa at once, but he had to wait until midday before she
came again, and she seemed more ill at ease than usual. This made him realize
how repulsive the sight of him still was to her, and that it was bound to go on
being repulsive, and what an effort it must cost her not to run away even from

the sight of the small portion of his body that stuck out from under the sofa. In order to spare her that, therefore, one day he carried a sheet on his back to the sofa—it cost him four hours' labor—and arranged it there in such a way as to hide him completely, so that even if she were to bend down she could not see him. Had she considered the sheet unnecessary, she would certainly have stripped it off the sofa again, for it was clear enough that this curtaining and confining of himself was not likely to conduce Gregor's comfort, but she left it where it was, and Gregor even fancied that he caught a thankful glance from her eye when he lifted the sheet carefully a very little with his head to see how she was taking the new arrangement.

For the first fortnight his parents could not bring themselves to the point   50
of entering his room, and he often heard them expressing their appreciation of his sister's activities, whereas formerly they had frequently scolded her for being as they thought a somewhat useless daughter. But now, both of them often waited outside the door, his father and his mother, while his sister tidied his room, and as soon as she came out she had to tell them exactly how things were in the room, what Gregor had eaten, how he had conducted himself this time and whether there was not perhaps some slight improvement in his condition. His mother, moreover, began relatively soon to want to visit him, but his father and sister dissuaded her at first with arguments which Gregor listened to very attentively and altogether approved. Later, however, she had to be held back by main force, and when she cried out: "Do let me in to Gregor, he is my unfortunate son! Can't you understand that I must go to him?" Gregor thought that it might be well to have her come in, not every day, of course, but perhaps once a week; she understood things, after all, much better than his sister, who was only a child despite the efforts she was making and had perhaps taken on so difficult a task merely out of childish thoughtlessness.

Gregor's desire to see his mother was soon fulfilled. During the daytime he   51
did not want to show himself at the window, out of consideration for his parent, but he could not crawl very far around the few square yards of floor space he had, nor could he bear lying quietly at rest all during the night, while he was fast losing any interest he had ever taken in food, so that for mere recreation he had formed the habit of crawling crisscross over the walls and ceiling. He especially enjoyed hanging suspended from the ceiling; it was much better than lying on the floor. One could breathe more freely; one's body swung and rocked lightly; and in the almost blissful absorption induced by this suspension it could happen to his own surprise that he let go and fell plump on the floor. Yet he now had his body much better under control than formerly, and even such a big fall did him no harm. His sister at once remarked the new distraction Gregor had found for himself—he left traces behind him of the sticky stuff on his soles wherever he crawled—and she got the idea in her head of giving him as wide a field as possible to crawl in and of removing the pieces of furniture

that hindered him, above all the chest of drawers and the writing desk. But that was more than she could manage all by herself; she did not dare ask her father to help her; and as for the servant girl, a young creature of sixteen who had had the courage to stay on after the cook's departure, she could not be asked to help, for she had begged as an especial favor that she might keep the kitchen door locked and open it only on a definite summons; so there was nothing left but to apply to her mother at an hour when her father was out. And the old lady did come, with exclamations of joyful eagerness, which, however, died away at the door of Gregor's room. Gregor's sister, of course, went in first, to see that everything was in order before letting his mother enter. In great haste Gregor pulled the sheet lower and tucked it more in folds so that it really looked as if it had been thrown accidentally over the sofa. And this time he did not peer out from under it; he renounced the pleasure of seeing his mother on this occasion and was only glad that she had come at all. "Come in, he's out of sight," said his sister, obviously leading her mother by the hand. Gregor could now hear the two women struggling to shift the heavy old chest from its place, and his sister claiming the greater part of the labor for herself, without listening to the admonitions of her mother who feared she might overstrain herself. It took a long time. After at least a quarter of an hour's tugging his mother objected that the chest had better be left where it was, for in the first place it was too heavy and could never be got out before his father came home, and standing in the middle of the room like that it would only hamper Gregor's movements, while in the second place it was not at all certain that removing the furniture would be doing a service to Gregor. She was inclined to think to the contrary; the sight of the naked walls made her own heart heavy, and why shouldn't Gregor have the same feeling, considering that he had been used to his furniture for so long and might feel forlorn without it. "And doesn't it look," she concluded in a low voice—in fact she had been almost whispering all the time as if to avoid letting Gregor, whose exact where-abouts she did not know, hear even the tones of her voice, for she was convinced that he could not understand her words—"doesn't it look as if we were showing him, by taking away his furniture, that we have given up hope of his ever getting better and are just leaving him coldly to himself? I think it would be best to keep his room exactly as it has always been, so that when he comes back to us he will find everything unchanged and be able all the more easily to forget what has happened in between."

On hearing these words from his mother Gregor realized that the lack of all direct human speech for the past two months together with the monotony of family life must have confused his mind, otherwise he could not account for the fact that he had quite earnestly looked forward to having his room emptied of furnishing. Did he really want his warm room, so comfortably fitted with old family furniture, to be turned into a naked den in which he would certainly

52

be able to crawl unhampered in all directions but at the price of shedding simultaneously all recollection of his human background? He had indeed been so near the brink of forgetfulness that only the voice of his mother, which he had not heard for so long, had drawn him back from it. Nothing should be taken out of his room; everything must stay as it was; he could not dispense with the good influence of the furniture on his state of mind; and even if the furniture did hamper him in his senseless crawling round and round, that was no drawback but a great advantage.

Unfortunately his sister was of the contrary opinion; she had grown accus-   53
tomed, and not without reason, to consider herself an expert in Gregor's affairs as against her parents, and so her mother's advice was now enough to make her determined on the removal not only of the chest and the writing desk, which had been her first intention, but of all the furniture except the indispensable sofa. This determination was not, of course, merely the outcome of childish recalcitrance and of the self-confidence she had recently developed so unexpectedly and at such cost; she had in fact perceived that Gregor needed a lot of space to crawl about in, while on the other hand he never used the furniture at all, so far as could be seen. Another factor might have been also the enthusiastic temperament of an adolescent girl, which seeks to indulge itself on every opportunity and which now tempted Grete to exaggerate the horror of her brother's circumstances in order that she might do all the more for him. In a room where Gregor lorded it all alone over empty walls no one save herself was likely ever to set foot.

And so she was not to be moved from her resolve by her mother who   54
seemed moreover to be ill at ease in Gregor's room and therefore unsure of herself, was soon reduced to silence and helped her daughter as best she could to push the chest outside. Now, Gregor could do without the chest, if need be, but the writing desk he must retain. As soon as the two women had got the chest out of his room, groaning as they pushed it, Gregor stuck his head out from under the sofa to see how he might intervene as kindly and cautiously as possible. But as bad luck would have it, his mother was the first to return, leaving Grete clasping the chest in the room next door where she was trying to shift it all by herself, without of course moving it from the spot. His mother however was not accustomed to the sight of him, it might sicken her and so in alarm Gregor backed quickly to the other side of the sofa, yet could not prevent the sheet from swaying a little in front. That was enough to put her on the alert. She paused, stood still for a moment and then went back to Grete.

Although Gregor kept reassuring himself that nothing out of the way was   55
happening, but only a few bits of furniture were being changed round, he soon had to admit that all this trotting to and fro of the two women, their little ejaculations and the scraping of furniture along the floor affected him like a vast disturbance coming from all sides at once, and however much he tucked

in his head and legs and cowered to the very floor he was bound to confess that he would not be able to stand it for long. They were clearing his room out; taking away everything he loved; the chest in which he kept his fret saw and other tools was already dragged off; they were now loosening the writing desk which had almost sunk into the floor, the desk at which he had done all his homework when he was at the commercial academy, at the grammar school before that, and yes, even at the primary school—he had no more time to waste in weighing the good intentions of the two women, whose existence he had by now almost forgotten, for they were so exhausted that they were laboring in silence and nothing could be heard but the heavy scuffling of their feet.

And so he rushed out—the women were just leaning against the writing desk in the next room to give themselves a breather—and four times changed his direction, since he really did not know what to rescue first, then on the wall opposite, which was already otherwise cleared, he was struck by the picture of the lady muffled in so much fur and quickly crawled up to it and pressed himself to the glass, which was a good surface to hold on to and comforted his hot belly. This picture at least, which was entirely hidden beneath him, was going to be removed by nobody. He turned his head towards the door of the living room so as to observe the women when they came back. 56

They had not allowed themselves much of a rest and were already coming; Grete had twined her arm round her mother and was almost supporting her. "Well, what shall we take now?" said Grete, looking round. Her eyes met Gregor's from the wall. She kept her composure, presumably because of her mother, bent her head down to her mother, to keep her from looking up, and said, although in a fluttering, unpremeditated voice: "Come, hadn't we better go back to the living room for a moment?" Her intentions were clear enough to Gregor, she wanted to bestow her mother in safety and then chase him down from the wall. Well, just let her try it! He clung to his picture and would not give it up. He would rather fly in Grete's face. 57

But Grete's words had succeeded in disquieting her mother, who took a step to one side, caught sight of the huge brown mass on the flowered wallpaper, and before she was really conscious that what she saw was Gregor screamed in a loud, hoarse voice: "Oh God, oh God!" fell with outspread arms over the sofa as if giving up and did not move. "Gregor!" cried his sister, shaking her fist and glaring at him. This was the first time she had directly addressed him since his metamorphosis. She ran into the next room for some aromatic essence with which to rouse her mother from her fainting fit. Gregor wanted to help too—there was still time to rescue the picture—but he was stuck fast to the glass and had to tear himself loose; he then ran after his sister into the next room as if he could advise her, as he used to do; but then had to stand helplessly behind her; she meanwhile searched among various small bottles and when she turned round started in alarm at the sight of him; one bottle fell on the floor 58 and broke; a splinter of glass cut Gregor's face and some kind of corrosive medicine splashed him; without pausing a moment longer Grete gathered up all the bottles she could carry and ran to her mother with them; she banged the door shut with her foot. Gregor was now cut off from his mother, who was perhaps nearly dying because of him; he dared not open the door for fear of frightening away his sister, who had to stay with her mother; there was nothing he could do but wait; and harassed by self-reproach and worry he began now to crawl to and fro, over everything, walls, furniture and ceiling, and finally in his despair, when the whole room seemed to be reeling round him, fell down on to the middle of the big table.

A little while elapsed, Gregor was still lying there feebly and all around was   59 quiet, perhaps that was a good omen. Then the doorbell rang. The servant girl was of course locked in her kitchen, and Grete would have to open the door. It was his father. "What's been happening?" were his first words; Grete's face must have told him everything. Grete answered in a muffled voice, apparently hiding her head on his breast: "Mother has been fainting, but she's better now. Gregor's broken loose." "Just what I expected," said his father, "just what I've been telling you, but you women would never listen." It was clear to Gregor that his father had taken the worst interpretation of Grete's all too brief statement and was assuming that Gregor had been guilty of some violent act. Therefore Gregor must now try to propitiate his father, since he had neither time nor means for an explanation. And so he fled to the door of his own room and crouched against it, to let his father see as soon as he came in from the hall that his son had the good intention of getting back into his room immediately and that it was not necessary to drive him there, but that if only the door were opened he would disappear at once.

Yet his father was not in the mood to perceive such fine distinctions. "Ah!"   60 he cried as soon as he appeared, in a tone which sounded at once angry and exultant. Gregor drew his head back from the door and lifted it to look at his father. Truly, this was not the father he had imagined to himself; admittedly he had been too absorbed of late in his new recreation of crawling over the ceiling to take the same interest as before in what was happening elsewhere in the flat, and he ought really to be prepared for some changes. And yet, and yet, could that be his father? The man who used to lie wearily sunk in bed whenever Gregor set out on a business journey; who welcomed him back of an evening lying in a long chair in a dressing gown; who could not really rise to his feet but only lifted his arms in greeting, and on the rare occasions when he did go out with his family, on one or two Sundays a year and on high holidays, walked between Gregor and his mother, who were slow walkers anyhow, even more slowly than they did, muffled in his old greatcoat, shuffling laboriously forward with the help of his crook-handled stick which he set down most cautiously at every step and, whenever he wanted to say anything, nearly always came to a full stop and gathered his escort around him? Now he was standing there in fine shape; dressed in a smart blue uniform with gold buttons, such as bank messengers wear; his strong double chin bulged over and the stiff high collar of his jacket; from under his bushy eyebrows his black eyes darted fresh and penetrating glances; his one-time tangled white hair had been combed flat on either side of a shining and carefully exact parting. He pitched his cap, which bore a gold monogram, probably the badge of some bank, in a wide sweep across the whole room on to a sofa and with the tail-ends of his jacket thrown back, his hands in his trouser pockets, advanced with a grim visage towards Gregor. Likely enough he did not himself know what he meant to do; at any rate he lifted his feet uncommonly high, and Gregor was dumbfounded at the enormous size of his shoe soles. But Gregor could not risk standing up to him, aware as he had been from the very first day of his new life that his father believed only the severest measures suitable for dealing with him. And so he ran before his father, stopping when he stopped and scuttling forward again when his father made any kind of move. In this way they circled the room several times without anything decisive happening, indeed the whole operation did not even look like a pursuit because it was carried out so slowly. And so Gregor did not leave the floor, for he feared that his father might take as a piece of peculiar wickedness any excursion of his over the walls or the ceiling. All the same, he could not stay this course much longer, for while his father took one step he had to carry out a whole series of movements. He was already beginning to feel breathless, just as in his former life his lungs had not been very dependable. As he was staggering along, trying to concentrate his energy on running, hardly keeping his eyes open; in his dazed state never even thinking of any other escape than simply going forward; and having almost forgotten that the walls were free to him, which in this room were well provided with finely carved pieces of furniture full of knobs and crevices—suddenly something lightly flung landed close behind him and rolled before him. It was an apple; a second apple followed immediately; Gregor came to a stop in alarm; there was no point in running on, for his father was determined to bombard him. He had filled his pockets with fruit from the dish on the sideboard and was now shying apple after apple, without taking particularly good aim for the moment. The small red apples rolled about the floor as if magnetized and cannoned into each other. An apple thrown without much force grazed Gregor's back and glanced off harmlessly. But another following immediately landed right on his back and sank in; Gregor wanted to drag himself forward, as if this startling, incredible pain could be left behind him; but he felt as if nailed to the spot and flattened himself out in a complete derangement of all his senses. With his last conscious look he saw the door of his room being torn open and his mother rushing out ahead of his screaming sister, in her under-bodice, for her daughter had loosened her clothing to let her breathe more freely and recover from her swoon, he saw his mother rushing towards his father, leaving one after another behind her on the floor her loosened petticoats, stumbling over her petticoats straight to his father and embracing him, in complete union with him—but here Gregor's sight began to fail—with her hands clasped round his father's neck as she begged for her son's life.

The serious injury done to Gregor, which disabled him for more than a month—the apple went on sticking in his body as a visible reminder, since no one ventured to remove it—seemed to have made even his father recollect that Gregor was a member of the family, despite his present unfortunate and repulsive shape, and ought not to be treated as an enemy, that, on the contrary, family duty required the suppression of disgust and the exercise of patience, nothing but patience. 61

And although his injury had impaired, probably for ever, his power of movement, and for the time being it took him long, long minutes to creep across his room like an old invalid—there was no question now of crawling up the wall—yet in his own opinion he was sufficiently compensated for this worsening of his condition by the fact that towards evening the living-room door, which he used to watch intently for an hour or two beforehand, was always thrown open, so that lying in the darkness of his room, invisible to the family, he could see them all at the lamp-lit table and listen to their talk, by general consent as it were, very different from his earlier eavesdropping. 62

True, their intercourse lacked the lively character of former times, which he had always called to mind with a certain wistfulness in the small hotel bedrooms where he had been wont to throw himself down, tired out, on damp bedding. They were now mostly very silent. Soon after supper his father would fall asleep in his armchair; his mother and sister would admonish each other to be silent; his mother, bending low over the lamp, stitched at fine sewing for an underwear firm; his sister, who had taken a job as a salesgirl, was learning shorthand and French in the evenings on the chance of bettering herself. Sometimes his father woke up, and as if quite unaware that he had been sleeping said to his mother: "What a lot of sewing you're doing today!" and at once fell asleep again, while the two women exchanged a tired smile. 63

With a kind of mulishness his father persisted in keeping his uniform on even in the house; his dressing gown hung uselessly on its peg and he slept fully dressed where he sat, as if he were ready for service at any moment and even here only at the beck and call of his superior. As a result, his uniform, which was not brand-new to start with, began to look dirty, despite all the loving care of the mother and sister to keep it clean, and Gregor often spent whole evenings gazing at the many greasy spots on the garment, gleaming with gold buttons always in a high state of polish, in which the old man sat sleeping in extreme discomfort and yet quite peacefully. 64

As soon as the clock struck ten his mother tried to rouse his father with   65
gentle words and to persuade him after that to get into bed, for sitting there
he could not have a proper sleep and that was what he needed most, since he
had to go to duty at six. But with the mulishness that had obsessed him since
he became a bank messenger he always insisted on staying longer at the table,
although he regularly fell asleep again and in the end only with the greatest
trouble could be got out of his armchair and into his bed. However insistently
Gregor's mother and sister kept urging him with gentle reminders, he would
go on slowly shaking his head for a quarter of an hour, keeping his eyes shut,
and refuse to get to his feet. The mother plucked at his sleeve, whispering
endearments in his ear, the sister left her lessons to come to her mother's help,
but Gregor's father was not to be caught. He would only sink down deeper in
his chair. Not until the two women hoisted him up by the armpits did he open
his eyes and look at them both, one after the other, usually with the remark:
"This is a life. This is the peace and quiet of my old age." And leaning on the
two of them he would heave himself up, with difficulty, as if he were a great
burden to himself, suffer them to lead him as far as the door and then wave
them off and go on alone, while the mother abandoned her needlework and
the sister her pen in order to run after him and help him farther.

Who could find time, in this overworked and tired-out family, to bother   66
about Gregor more than was absolutely needful? The household was reduced
more and more; the servant girl was turned off; a gigantic bony charwoman
with white hair flying round her head came in morning and evening to do the
rough work; everything else was done by Gregor's mother, as well as great piles
of sewing. Even various family ornaments, which his mother and sister used to
wear with pride at parties and celebrations, had to be sold, as Gregor discovered
of an evening from hearing them all discuss the prices obtained. But what they
lamented most was the fact that they could not leave the flat which was much
too big for their present circumstances, because they could not think of any
way to shift Gregor. Yet Gregor saw well enough that consideration for him
was not the main difficulty preventing the removal, for they could have easily
shifted him in some suitable box with a few air holes in it; what really kept
them from moving into another flat was rather their own complete hopelessness
and the belief that they had been singled out for a misfortune such as had
never happened to any of their relations or acquaintances. They fulfilled to the
uttermost all that the world demands of poor people, the father fetched breakfast for the small clerks in the bank, the mother devoted her energy to making
underwear for strangers, the sister trotted to and fro behind the counter at the
behest of customers, but more than this they had not the strength to do. And
the wound in Gregor's back began to nag at him afresh when his mother and
sister, after getting his father into bed, came back again, left their work lying,
drew close to each other and sat cheek by cheek; when his mother, pointing

towards his room said: "Shut that door now, Grete," and he was left again in darkness, while next door the women mingled their tears or perhaps sat dry-eyed staring at the table.

Gregor hardly slept at all by night or by day. He was often haunted by the idea that next time the door opened he would take the family's affairs in hand again just as he used to do; once more, after this long interval, there appeared in his thoughts the figures of the chief and the chief clerk, the commercial travelers and the apprentices, the porter who was so dull-witted, two or three friends in other firms, a chambermaid in one of the rural hotels, a sweet and fleeting memory, a cashier in a milliner's shop, whom he had wooed earnestly but too slowly—they all appeared, together with strangers or people he had quite forgotten, but instead of helping him and his family they were one and all unapproachable and he was glad when they vanished. At other times he would not be in the mood to bother about his family, he was only filled with rage at the way they were neglecting him, and although he had no clear idea of what he might care to eat he would make plans for getting into the larder to take food that was after all his due, even if he were not hungry. His sister no longer took thought to bring him what might especially please him, but in the morning and at noon before she went to business hurriedly pushed into his room with her foot any food that was available, and in the evening cleared it out again with one sweep of the broom, heedless of whether it had been merely tasted, or—as most frequently happened—left untouched. The cleaning of his room, which she now did always in the evenings, could not have been more hastily done. Streaks of dirt stretched along the walls, here and there lay balls of dust and filth. At first Gregor used to station himself in some particularly filthy corner when his sister arrived, in order to reproach her with it, so to speak. But he could have sat there for weeks without getting her to make any improvements; she could see the dirt as well as he did, but she had simply made up her mind to leave it alone. And yet, with a touchiness that was new to her, which seemed anyhow to have infected the whole family, she jealously guarded her claim to be the sole caretaker of Gregor's room. His mother once subjected his room to a thorough cleaning, which was achieved only by means of several buckets of water—all this dampness of course upset Gregor too and he lay widespread, sulky and motionless on the sofa—but she was well punished for it. Hardly had his sister noticed the changed aspect of his room that evening than she rushed in high dudgeon into the living room and, despite the imploringly raised hands of her mother, burst into a storm of weeping, while her parents—her father had of course been startled out of his chair—looked on at first in helpless amazement; then they too began to go into action; the father reproached the mother on his right for not having left the cleaning of Gregor's room to his sister; shrieked at the sister on his left that never again was she to be allowed to clean Gregor's room; while the mother tried to pull the father into his bedroom, since he was beyond himself with agitation; the sister, shaken with sobs, then beat upon the table with her small fists; and Gregor hissed loudly with rage because not one of them thought of shutting the door to spare him such a spectacle and so much noise.

Still, even if the sister, exhausted by her daily work, had grown tired of 68 looking after Gregor as she did formerly, there was no need for his mother's intervention or for Gregor's being neglected at all. The charwoman was there. This old widow, whose strong bony frame had enabled her to survive the worst a long life could offer, by no means recoiled from Gregor. Without being in the least curious she had once by chance opened the door of his room and at the sight of Gregor, who, taken by surprise, began to rush to and fro although no one was chasing him, merely stood there with her arms folded. From that time she never failed to open his door a little for a moment, morning and evening, to have a look at him. At first she even used to call him to her, with words which apparently she took to be friendly; such as "Come along, then, you old dung beetle!" or "Look at the old dung beetle, then!" To such allocutions Gregor made no answer, but stayed motionless where he was, as if the door had never been opened. Instead of being allowed to disturb him so senselessly whenever the whim took her, she should rather have been ordered to clean out his room daily, that charwoman! Once, early in the morning—heavy rain was lashing on the windowpanes, perhaps a sign that spring was on the way— Gregor was so exasperated when she began addressing him again that he ran for her, as if to attack her, although slowly and feebly enough. But the char- woman instead of showing fright merely lifted high a chair that happened to be beside the door, and as she stood there with her mouth wide open it was clear that she meant to shut it only when she brought the chair down on Gregor's back. "So you're not coming any nearer?" she asked, as Gregor turned away again, and quietly put the chair back into the corner.

Gregor was now eating hardly anything. Only when he happened to pass 69 the food laid out for him did he take a bit of something in his mouth as a pastime, kept it there for an hour at a time and usually spat it out again. At first he thought it was chagrin over the state of his room that prevented him from eating, yet he soon got used to the various changes in his room. It had become a habit in the family to push into his room things there was no room for elsewhere, and there were plenty of these now, since one of the rooms had been let to three lodgers. These serious gentlemen—all three of them with full beards, as Gregor once observed through a crack in the door—had a passion for order, not only in their own room but, since they were now members of the household, in all its arrangements, especially in the kitchen. Superfluous, not to say dirty, objects they could not bear. Besides, they had brought with them most of the furnishings they needed. For this reason many things could be dispensed with that it was no use trying to sell but that should not be thrown away either. All of them found their way into Gregor's room. The ash can likewise and the kitchen garbage can. Anything that was not needed for the moment was simply flung into Gregor's room by the charwoman, who did everything in a hurry; fortunately Gregor usually saw only the object, whatever it was, and the hand that held it. Perhaps she intended to take the things away again as time and opportunity offered, or to collect them until she could throw them all out in a heap, but in fact they just lay wherever she happened to throw them, except when Gregor pushed his way through the junk heap and shifted it somewhat, at first out of necessity, because he had not room enough to crawl, but later with increasing enjoyment, although after such excursions, being sad and weary to death, he would lie motionless for hours. And since the lodgers often ate their supper at home in the common living room, the living-room door stayed shut many an evening, yet Gregor reconciled himself quite easily to the shutting of the door, for often enough on evenings when it was opened he had disregarded it entirely and lain in the darkest corner of his room, quite unnoticed by the family. But on one occasion the charwoman left the door open a little and it stayed ajar even when the lodgers came in for supper and the lamp was lit. They sat themselves at the top end of the table where formerly Gregor and his father and mother had eaten their meals, unfolded their napkins and took knife and fork in hand. At once his mother appeared in the doorway with a dish of meat and close behind her his sister with a dish of potatoes piled high. The food steamed with a thick vapor. The lodgers bent over the food set before them as if to scrutinize it before eating, in fact the man in the middle, who seemed to pass for an authority with the other two, cut a piece of meat as it lay on the dish, obviously to discover if it were tender or should be sent back to the kitchen. He showed satisfaction, and Gregor's mother and sister, who had been watching anxiously, breathed freely and began to smile.

The family itself took its meals in the kitchen. None the less, Gregor's father   70
came into the living room before going into the kitchen and with one prolonged bow, cap in hand, made a round of the table. The lodgers all stood up and murmured something in their beards. When they were alone again they ate their food in almost complete silence. It seemed remarkable to Gregor that among the various noises coming from the table he could always distinguish the sound of their masticating teeth, as if this were a sign to Gregor that one needed teeth in order to eat, and that with toothless jaws even of the finest make one could do nothing. "I'm hungry enough," said Gregor sadly to himself, "but not for that kind of food. How these lodgers are stuffing themselves, and here am I dying of starvation!"

On that very evening—during the whole of his time there Gregor could   71
not remember ever having heard the violin—the sound of violin-playing came

from the kitchen. The lodgers had already finished their supper, the one in the middle had brought out a newspaper and given the other two a page apiece, and now they were leaning back at ease reading and smoking. When the violin began to play they pricked up their ears, got to their feet, and went on tiptoe to the hall door where they stood huddled together. Their movements must have been heard in the kitchen, for Gregor's father called out: "Is the violin-playing disturbing you gentlemen? It can be stopped at once." "On the contrary," said the middle lodger, "could not Fräulein Samsa come and play in this room, beside us, where it is much more convenient and comfortable?" "Oh certainly," cried Gregor's father, as if he were the violin-player. The lodgers came back into the living room and waited. Presently Gregor's father arrived with the music stand, his mother carrying the music and his sister with the violin. His sister quietly made everything ready to start playing; his parents, who had never let rooms before and so had an exaggerated idea of the courtesy due to lodgers, did not venture to sit down on their own chairs; his father leaned against the door, the right hand thrust between two buttons of his livery coat, which was formally buttoned up; but his mother was offered a chair by one of the lodgers and, since she left the chair just where he had happened to put it, sat down in a corner to one side.

Gregor's sister began to play; the father and mother, from either side, intently watched the movements of her hands. Gregor, attracted by the playing, ventured to move forward a little until his head was actually inside the living room. He felt hardly any surprise at his growing lack of consideration for the others; there had been a time when he prided himself on being considerate. And yet just on this occasion he had more reason than ever to hide himself, since owing to the amount of dust which lay thick in his room and rose into the air at the slightest movement, he too was covered with dust; fluff and hair and remnants of food trailed with him, caught on his back and along his sides; his indifference to everything was much too great for him to turn on his back and scrape himself clean on the carpet, as once he had done several times a day. And in spite of his condition, no shame deterred him from advancing a little over the spotless floor of the living room. 72

To be sure, no one was aware of him. The family was entirely absorbed in the violin-playing; the lodgers, however, who first of all had stationed themselves, hands in pockets, much too close behind the music stand so that they could all have read the music, which must have bothered his sister, had soon retreated to the window, half-whispering with downbent heads, and stayed there while his father turned an anxious eye on them. Indeed, they were making it more than obvious that they had been disappointed in their expectation of hearing good or enjoyable violin-playing, that they had had more than enough of the performance and only out of courtesy suffered a continued disturbance 73 of their peace. From the way they all kept blowing the smoke of their cigars high in the air through nose and mouth one could divine their irritation. And yet Gregor's sister was playing so beautifully. Her face leaned sideways, intently and sadly her eyes followed the notes of music. Gregor crawled a little farther forward and lowered his head to the ground so that it might be possible for his eyes to meet hers. Was he an animal, that music had such an effect upon him? He felt as if the way were opening before him to the unknown nourishment he craved. He was determined to push forward till he reached his sister, to pull at her skirt and so let her know that she was to come into his room with her violin, for no one here appreciated her playing as he would appreciate it. He would never let her out of his room, at least, not so long as he lived; his frightful appearance would become, for the first time, useful to him; he would watch all the doors of his room at once and spit at intruders; but his sister should need no constraint, she should stay with him of her own free will; she should sit beside him on the sofa, bend down her ear to him and hear him confide that he had had the firm intention of sending her to the Conservatorium, and that, but for his mishap, last Christmas—surely Christmas was long past?—he would have announced it to everybody without allowing a single objection. After this confession his sister would be so touched that she would burst into tears, and Gregor would then raise himself to her shoulder and kiss her on the neck, which, now that she went to business, she kept free of any ribbon or collar.

"Mr. Samsa!" cried the middle lodger, to Gregor's father, and pointed, without wasting any more words, at Gregor, now working himself slowly forwards. The violin fell silent, for middle lodger first smiled to his friends with a shake of the head and then looked at Gregor again. Instead of driving Gregor out, his father seemed to think it more needful to begin by soothing down the lodgers, although they were not at all agitated and apparently found Gregor more entertaining than the violin-playing. He hurried towards them and, spreading out his arms, tried to urge them back into their own room and at the same time to block their view of Gregor. They now began to be really a little angry, one could not tell whether because of the old man's behavior or because it just dawned on them that all unwittingly they had such a neighbor as Gregor next door. They demanded explanations of his father, they waved their arms like him, tugged uneasily at their beards, and only with reluctance backed towards their room. Meanwhile Gregor's sister, who stood there as if lost when her playing was so abruptly broken off, came to life again, pulled herself together all at once after standing for a while holding violin and bow in nervelessly hanging hands and staring at her music, pushed her violin into the lap of her mother, who was still sitting in her chair fighting asthmatically for breath, and ran into the lodgers' room to which they were now being shepherded by her father rather more quickly than before. One could see the pillows and blankets on the beds flying under her accustomed fingers and being laid in order. Before the lodgers had actually reached their room she had finished making the beds and slipped out.

The old man seemed once more to be so possessed by his mulish self-assertiveness that he was forgetting all the respect he should show to his lodgers. He kept driving them on and driving them on until in the very door of the bedroom the middle lodger stamped his foot loudly on the floor and so brought him to a halt. "I beg to announce," said the lodger, lifting one hand and looking also at Gregor's mother and sister, "that because of the disgusting conditions prevailing in this household and family"—here he spat on the floor with emphatic brevity—"I give you notice on the spot. Naturally I won't pay you a penny for the days I have lived here, on the contrary I shall consider bringing an action for damages against you, based on claims—believe me—that will be easily susceptible of proof." He ceased and stared straight in front of him, as if he expected something. In fact his two friends at once rushed into the breach with these words: "And we too give notice on the spot." On that he seized the door-handle and shut the door with a slam.

Gregor's father, groping with his hands, staggered forward and fell into his chair; it looked as if he were stretching himself there for his ordinary evening nap, but the marked jerkings of his head, which was as if uncontrollable, showed that he was far from asleep. Gregor had simply stayed quietly all the time on the spot where the lodgers had espied him. Disappointment at the failure of his plan, perhaps also the weakness arising from extreme hunger, made it impossible for him to move. He feared, with a fair degree of certainty, that at any moment the general tension would discharge itself in a combined attack upon him, and he lay waiting. He did not react even to the noise made by the violin as it fell off his mother's lap from under her trembling fingers and gave out a resonant note.

"My dear parents," said his sister, slapping her hand on the table by way of introduction, "things can't go on like this. Perhaps you don't realize that, but I do. I won't utter my brother's name in the presence of this creature, and so all I say is: we must try to get rid of it. We've tried to look after it and to put up with it as far as is humanly possible, and I don't think anyone could reproach us in the slightest."

"She is more than right," said Gregor's father to himself. His mother, who was still choking for lack of breath, began to cough hollowly into her hand with a wild look in her eyes.

His sister rushed over to her and held her forehead. His father's thoughts seemed to have lost their vagueness at Grete's words, he sat more upright, fingering his service cap that lay among the plates still lying on the table from the lodgers' supper, and from time to time looked at the still form of Gregor.

"We must try to get rid of it," his sister now said explicitly to her father, since her mother was coughing too much to hear a word, "it will be the death of both of you, I can see that coming. When one has to work as hard as we do, all of us, one can't stand this continual torment at home on top of it. At least I can't stand it any longer." And she burst into such a passion of sobbing that her tears dropped on her mother's face, where she wiped them off mechanically.

"My dear," said the old man sympathetically, and with evident understanding, "but what can we do?" 81

Gregor's sister merely shrugged her shoulders to indicate the feeling of helplessness that had now overmastered her during her weeping fit, in contrast to her former confidence. 82

"If he could understand us," said her father, half questioningly; Grete, still sobbing, vehemently waved a hand to show how unthinkable that was. 83

"If he could understand us," repeated the old man, shutting his eyes to consider his daughter's conviction that understanding was impossible, "then perhaps we might come to some agreement with him. But as it is—" 84

"He must go," cried Gregor's sister, "that's the only solution, Father. You must just try to get rid of the idea that this is Gregor. The fact that we've believed it for so long is the root of all our trouble. But how can it be Gregor? If this were Gregor, he would have realized long ago that human beings can't live with such a creature, and he'd have gone away on his own accord. Then we wouldn't have any brother, but we'd be able to go on living and keep his memory in honor. As it is, this creature persecutes us, drives away our lodgers, obviously wants the whole apartment to himself and would have us all sleep in the gutter. Just look, Father," she shrieked all at once, "he's at it again!" And in an access of panic that was quite incomprehensible to Gregor she even quitted her mother, literally thrusting the chair from her as if she would rather sacrifice her mother than stay so near to Gregor, and rushed behind her father, who also rose up, being simply upset by her agitation, and half-spread his arms out as if to protect her. 85

Yet Gregor had not the slightest intention of frightening anyone, far less his sister. He had only begun to turn round in order to crawl back to his room, but it was certainly a startling operation to watch, since because of his disabled condition he could not execute the difficult turning movements except by lifting his head and then bracing it against the floor over and over again. He paused and looked round. His good intentions seemed to have been recognized; the alarm had only been momentary. Now they were all watching him in melancholy silence. His mother lay in her chair, her legs stiffly outstretched and pressed together, her eyes almost closing for sheer weariness; his father and his sister were sitting beside each other, his sister's arm around the old man's neck. 86

Perhaps I can go on turning round now, thought Gregor, and began his   87
labors again. He could not stop himself from panting with the effort, and had
to pause now and then to take breath. Nor did anyone harass him, he was left
entirely to himself. When he had completed the turn-round he began at once
to crawl straight back. He was amazed at the distance separating him from his
room and could not understand how in his weak state he had managed to
accomplish the same journey so recently, almost without remarking it. Intent
on crawling as fast as possible, he barely noticed that not a single word, not
an ejaculation from his family, interfered with his progress. Only when he was
already in the doorway did he turn his head round, not completely, for his
neck muscles were getting stiff, but enough to see that nothing had changed
behind him except that his sister had risen to her feet. His last glance fell on
his mother, who was not quite overcome by sleep.

Hardly was he well inside his room when the door was hastily pushed shut,   88
bolted and locked. The sudden noise in his rear startled him so much that his
little legs gave beneath him. It was his sister who had shown such haste. She
had been standing ready waiting and had made a light spring forward. Gregor
had not even heard her coming, and she cried "At last!" to her parents as she
turned the key in the lock.

"And what now?" said Gregor to himself, looking round in the darkness.   89
Soon he made the discovery that he was now unable to stir a limb. This did
not surprise him, rather it seemed unnatural that he should ever actually have
been able to move on these feeble little legs. Otherwise he felt relatively
comfortable. True, his whole body was aching, but it seemed that the pain was
gradually growing less and would finally pass away. The rotting apple in his
back and the inflamed area around it, all covered with soft dust, already hardly
troubled him. He thought of his family with tenderness and love. The decision
that he must disappear was one that he held to even more strongly than his
sister, if that were possible. In this state of vacant and peaceful meditation he
remained until the tower clock struck three in the morning. The first broad-
ening of light in the world outside the window entered his consciousness once
more. Then his head sank to the floor of its own accord and from his nostrils
came the last faint flicker of his breath.

When the charwoman arrived early in the morning—what between her   90
strength and her impatience she slammed all the doors so loudly, never mind
how often she had been begged not to do so, that no one in the whole apartment
could enjoy any quiet sleep after her arrival—she noticed nothing unusual as
she took her customary peep into Gregor's room. She thought he was lying
motionless on purpose, pretending to be in the sulks; she credited him with
every kind of intelligence. Since she happened to have the long-handled broom
in her hand she tried to tickle him up with it from the doorway. When that

too produced no reaction she felt provoked and poked at him a little harder, and only when she had pushed him along the floor without meeting any resistance was her attention aroused. It did not take her long to establish the truth of the matter, and her eyes widened, she let out a whistle, yet did not waste much time over it but tore open the door of the Samsas' bedroom and yelled into the darkness at the top of her voice: "Just look at this, it's dead; it's lying here dead and done for!"

Mr. and Mrs. Samsa started up in their double bed and before they realized   91
the nature of the charwoman's announcement had some difficulty in overcoming the shock of it. But then they got out of bed quickly, one on either side, Mr. Samsa throwing a blanket over his shoulders, Mrs. Samsa in nothing but her nightgown; in this array they entered Gregor's room. Meanwhile the door of the living room opened, too, where Grete had been sleeping since the advent of the lodgers; she was completely dressed as if she had not been to bed, which seemed to be confirmed also by the paleness of her face. "Dead?" said Mrs. Samsa, looking questioningly at the charwoman, although she could have investigated for herself, and the fact was obvious enough without investigation. "I should say so," said the charwoman, proving her words by pushing Gregor's corpse a long way to one side with her broomstick. Mrs. Samsa made a movement as if to stop her, but checked it. "Well," said Mr. Samsa, "now thanks be to God." He crossed himself, and the three women followed his example. Grete, whose eyes never left the corpse, said: "Just see how thin he was. It's such a long time since he's eaten anything. The food came out again just as it went in." Indeed, Gregor's body was completely flat and dry, as could only now be seen when it was no longer supported by the legs and nothing prevented one from looking closely at it.

"Come in beside us, Grete, for a little while," said Mrs. Samsa with a   92
tremulous smile, and Grete, not without looking back at the corpse, followed her parents into their bedroom. The charwoman shut the door and opened the window wide. Although it was so early in the morning a certain softness was perceptible in the fresh air. After all, it was already the end of March.

The three lodgers emerged from their room and were surprised to see no   93
breakfast; they had been forgotten. "Where's our breakfast?" said the middle lodger peevishly to the charwoman. But she put her finger to her lips and hastily, without a word, indicated by gestures that they should go into Gregor's room. They did so and stood, their hands in the pockets of their somewhat shabby coats, around Gregor's corpse in the room where it was now fully light.

At that the door of the Samsas' bedroom opened and Mr. Samsa appeared   94
in his uniform, his wife on one arm, his daughter on the other. They all looked a little as if they had been crying; from time to time Grete hid her face on her father's arm.

"Leave my house at once!" said Mr. Samsa, and pointed to the door without   95 disengaging himself from the women. "What do you mean by that?" said the middle lodger, taken somewhat aback, with a feeble smile. The two others put their hands behind them and kept rubbing them together, as if in gleeful expectation of a fine set-to in which they were bound to come off the winners. "I mean just what I say," answered Mr. Samsa, and advanced in a straight line with his two companions towards the lodger. He stood his ground at first quietly, looking at the floor as if his thoughts were taking a new pattern in his head. "Then let us go, by all means," he said and looked up at Mr. Samsa as if in a sudden access of humility he were expecting some renewed sanction for this decision. Mr. Samsa merely nodded briefly once or twice with meaning eyes. Upon that the lodger really did go with long strides into the hall, his two friends had been listening and had quite stopped rubbing their hands for some moments and now went scuttling after him as if afraid that Mr. Samsa might get into the hall before them and cut them off from their leader. In the hall they all three took their hats from the rack, their sticks from the umbrella stand, bowed in silence and quitted the apartment. With a suspiciousness which proved quite unfounded Mr. Samsa and the two women followed them out to the landing; leaning over the banister they watched the three figures slowly but surely going down the long stairs, vanishing from sight at a certain turn of the staircase on every floor and coming into view again after a moment or so; the more they dwindled, the more the Samsa family's interest in them dwindled, and when a butcher's boy met them and passed them on the stairs coming up proudly with a tray on his head, Mr. Samsa and the two women soon left the landing and as if a burden had been lifted from them went back into their apartment.

They decided to spend this day in resting and going for a stroll; they had 96 not only deserved such a respite from work, but absolutely needed it. And so they sat down at the table and wrote three notes of excuse, Mr. Samsa to his board of management, Mrs. Samsa to her employer and Grete to the head of her firm. While they were writing, the charwoman came in to say that she was going now, since her morning's work was finished. At first they only nodded without looking up, but as she kept hovering there they eyed her irritably. "Well?" said Mr. Samsa. The charwoman stood grinning in the doorway as if she had good news to impart to the family but meant not to say a word unless properly questioned. The small ostrich feather standing upright on her hat, which had annoyed Mr. Samsa ever since she was engaged, was waving gaily in all directions. "Well, what is it then?" asked Mrs. Samsa, who obtained more respect from the charwoman than the others. "Oh," said the charwoman, giggling so amiably that she could not at once continue, "just this, you don't need to bother about how to get rid of the thing next door. It's been seen to already." Mrs. Samsa and Grete bent over their letters again, as if preoccupied; Mr. Samsa, who perceived that she was eager to begin describing it all in detail, stopped her with a decisive hand. But since she was not allowed to tell her story, she remembered the great hurry she was in, being obviously deeply huffed: "Bye, everybody," she said, whirling off violently, and departed with a frightful slamming of doors.

"She'll be given notice tonight," said Mr. Samsa, but neither from his wife   97
nor his daughter did he get any answer, for the charwoman seemed to have shattered again the composure they had barely achieved. They rose, went to the window and stayed there, clasping each other tight. Mr. Samsa turned in his chair to look at them and quietly observed them for a little. Then he called out: "Come along, now, do. Let bygones be bygones. And you might have some consideration for me." The two of them complied at once, hastened to him, caressed him and quickly finished their letters.

Then they all three left the apartment together, which was more than they   98
had done for months, and went by tram into the open country outside the town. The tram, in which they were the only passengers, was filled with warm sunshine. Leaning comfortably back in their seats they canvassed their prospects for the future, and it appeared on closer inspection that these were not at all bad, for the jobs they had got, which so far they had never really discussed with each other, were all three admirable and likely to lead to better things later on. The greatest immediate improvement in their condition would of course arise from moving to another house; they wanted to take a smaller and cheaper but also better situated and more easily run apartment than the one they had, which Gregor had selected. While they were thus conversing, it struck both Mr. and Mrs. Samsa, almost at the same moment, as they became aware of their daughter's increasing vivacity, that in spite of all the sorrow of recent times, which had made her cheeks pale, she had bloomed into a pretty girl with a good figure. They grew quieter and half unconsciously exchanged glances of complete agreement, having come to the conclusion that it would soon be time to find a good husband for her. And it was like a confirmation of their new dreams and excellent intentions that at the end of their journey their daughter sprang to her feet first and stretched her young body.

Questions for Critical Thinking

1. How does Kafka manage to sustain our interest in a story that is based on a preposterous premise?

2. In what way is Gregor changed by his metamorphosis? In what way is he not changed? What is significant about the way he is changed and unchanged?

3. How would you characterize the reactions of Gregor's family to his abrupt metamorphosis? How would your reactions differ should a member of your own family wake up one morning transmogrified into a dung beetle?

4. Whom or what is this story really about? What do you think is the focus of this story?

5. How would you characterize the relationship between Gregor and his father? How is the father changed by Gregor's metamorphosis?

6. How do you think the family would likely have reacted if Gregor had metamorphosed into some alluring and beautiful creature, say a glowingly beautiful angel? Why?

7. After Gregor dies, Mr. Samsa immediately evicts the lodgers from his household. Why? What significance does that action hold for the story?

8. What ironic contrast is drawn between Gregor and the lodgers during the violin recital? What nourishment did Gregor crave that, in the end, seems to have contributed to his death?

Writing Assignment

Write an essay analyzing the meaning or theme of "The Metamorphosis."

Writing Advice

That one interpretation of literature is just as good as another is a widespread but entirely untrue belief. True, critics and readers are apt to offer wildly differing interpretations of the same work. True, some schools of literary criticism encourage interpretations of ancient works that are vastly different from what an intelligent guess tells us was the writer's intent. But it is not true that because works are interpreted differently by different readers, every interpretation is therefore just as good and valid as another.

In writing this essay, then, you should not assume that there can be no right or wrong interpretation. Nor should you undertake an interpretation that you cannot justify with references and citations from the text itself. In fact, in a literary paper of this kind, the primary source of specific details will be quotations from the work. If, for example, you allege that the theme of the metamorphosis is the guilt suffered by the son for attempting to usurp his father's place in the household, you must support this reading with quotations from the story. Show the passages in the work that led you to this meaning. Cite incidents and dialogue that support it. If you cannot find support for an interpretation in the text itself, try a different tack. Literary meaning is not an absolute but will vary between readers. The allowable range of variation, however, is always restricted by what the author actually wrote.

Alternate Writing Assignment

In an interpretative essay apply the theme of "illusion and reality" to a reading of this story.

LITERATURE

FALSE GEMS
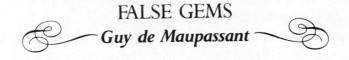
Guy de Maupassant

Guy de Maupassant (1850–1893), French novelist and short story writer, descended from an ancient Norman family and initially worked in a government office in Paris before his work became known and celebrated. Maupassant was heralded for his spare and unembellished style of writing and is considered a master of the realistic short story. In 1891, following an attack of syphilis, he went mad, dying two years later in a sanitarium. His best novels include *Une Vie* (1893) and *Pierre and Jean* (1888). But it is for his short stories, which number 300 in all, that Maupassant is justly celebrated, and his influence on the development of the genre both in Europe and the United States is nearly immeasurable.

Reading Advice

Generally, any difficulty a reader has with understanding the meaning of a short story can be traced to a headlong speed-reading plunge through its brevity. Yet the short story, in the hands of a master like Maupassant, can be as subtle and compressed as a poem and require of the reader a similar attentiveness. So although "False Gems" is deceptively easy reading, it is still packed with subtly revealing details.

Take, for example, the character of Madam Lantin, who occurs only in the first third of this brief tale. We see her coyly teasing her husband with her string of pearls, glimpse her exercising frugal management over their household, and then she is gone. But she lingers with us long after her brief incarnation. It takes Maupassant barely two hundred words to show us where Madame Lantin came from and what she was made of, to likewise evoke the plodding character of her husband, and to establish a fictional context for the lovers. His last cryptic paragraph is a master stroke of ironic summary, exactly the kind of deft compression that is easily overlooked by the racing reader.

$M.$ Lantin had met the young woman at a soirée, at the home of the assistant chief of his bureau, and at first sight had fallen madly in love with her. 1

She was the daughter of a country physician who had died some months previously. She had come to live in Paris, with her mother, who visited much 2 among her acquaintances, in the hope of making a favorable marriage for her daughter. They were poor and honest, quiet and unaffected.

The young girl was a perfect type of the virtuous woman whom every sensible young man dreams of one day winning for life. Her simple beauty had the charm of angelic modesty, and the imperceptible smile which constantly hovered about her lips seemed to be the reflection of a pure and lovely soul. Her praises resounded on every side. People never tired of saying: "Happy the man who wins her love! He could not find a better wife."   3

Now M. Lantin enjoyed a snug little income of 700 a year, and thinking he could safely assume the responsibilities of matrimony, proposed to this model young girl and was accepted.   4

He was unspeakably happy with her; she governed his household so cleverly and economically that they seemed to live in luxury. She lavished the most delicate attentions on her husband, coaxed and fondled him, and the charm of her presence was so great that six years after their marriage M. Lantin discovered that he loved his wife even more than during the first days of their honeymoon.   5

He only felt inclined to blame her for two things: her love of the theater, and a taste for false jewelry. Her friends (she was acquainted with some officers' wives) frequently procured for her a box at the the theater, often for the first representations of the new plays; and her husband was obliged to accompany her, whether he willed or not, to these amusements, though they bored him excessively after a day's labor at the office.   6

After a time, M. Lantin begged his wife to get some lady of her acquaintance to accompany her. She was at first opposed to such an arrangement; but, after much persuasion on his part, she finally consented—to the infinite delight of her husband.   7

Now, with her love for the theater came also the desire to adorn her person. True, her costumes remained as before, simple, and in the most correct taste; but she soon began to ornament her ears with huge rhinestones which glittered and sparkled like real diamonds. Around her neck she wore strings of false pearls, and on her arms bracelets of imitation gold. Her husband frequently remonstrated with her, saying: 8

"My dear, as you cannot afford to buy real diamonds, you ought to appear adorned with your beauty and modesty alone, which are the rarest ornaments of your sex."   9

But she would smile sweetly, and say: 10

"What can I do? I am so fond of jewelry. It is my only weakness. We cannot change our natures."   11

Then she would roll the pearl necklaces around her fingers, and hold up the bright gems for her husband's admiration, gently coaxing him: 12

"Look! are they not lovely? One would swear they were real."   13

M. Lantin would then answer, smilingly: 14

"You have Bohemian tastes, my dear."   15

Often of an evening, when they were enjoying a tête-à-tête by the fireside,   16
she would place on the tea table the leather box containing the "trash," as M.
Lantin called it. She would examine the false gems with a passionate attention
as though they were in some way connected with a deep and secret joy; and
she often insisted on passing a necklace around her husband's neck, and laughing
heartily would exclaim: "How droll you look!" Then she would throw herself
into his arms and kiss him affectionately.

One evening in winter she attended the opera, and on her return was chilled   17
through and through. The next morning she coughed, and eight days later she
died of inflammation of the lungs.

M. Lantin's despair was so great that his hair became white in one month.   18
He wept unceasingly; his heart was torn with grief, and his mind was haunted
by the remembrance, the smile, the voice—by every charm of his beautiful,
dead wife.

Time, the healer, did not assuage his grief. Often during office hours, while   19
his colleagues were discussing the topics of the day, his eyes would suddenly
fill with tears, and he would give vent to his grief in heartrending sobs. Everything in his wife's room remained as before her decease; and here he was wont
to seclude himself daily and think of her who had been his treasure—the joy
of his existence.

But life soon became a struggle. His income, which in the hands of his wife   20
had covered all household expenses, was now no longer sufficient for his own
immediate wants; and he wondered how she could have managed to buy such
excellent wines, and such rare delicacies, things which he could no longer
procure with his modest resources.

He incurred some debts and was soon reduced to absolute poverty. One   21
morning, finding himself with a cent in his pocket, he resolved to sell something,
and, immediately, the thought occurred to him of disposing of his wife's paste
jewels. He cherished in his heart a sort of rancor against the false gems. They
had always irritated him in the past, and the very sight of them spoiled somewhat the memory of his lost darling.

To the last days of her life, she had continued to make purchases; bringing   22
home new gems almost every evening. He decided to sell the heavy necklace
which she seemed to prefer, and which, he thought, ought to be worth about
six or seven francs; for although paste it was, nevertheless, of very fine
workmanship.

He put it in his pocket and started out in search of a jeweler's shop. He   23
entered the first one he saw; feeling a little ashamed to expose his misery, and
also to offer such a worthless article for sale.

"Sir," said he to the merchant, "I would like to know what this is worth."   24

The man took the necklace, examined it, called his clerk and made some   25
remarks in an undertone; then he put the ornament back on the counter, and
looked at it from a distance to judge of the effect.

M. Lantin was annoyed by all this detail and was on the point of saying: 26
"Oh! I know well enough it is not worth anything," when the jeweler said: "Sir,
that necklace is worth from twelve to fifteen thousand francs; but I could not
buy it unless you tell me now whence it comes."

The widower opened his eyes wide and remained gaping, not comprehending   27
the merchant's meaning. Finally he stammered: "You say—are you sure?" The
other replied dryly: "You can search elsewhere and see if anyone will offer you
more. I consider it worth fifteen thousand at the most. Come back here if you
cannot do better."

M. Lantin, beside himself with astonishment, took up the necklace and left   28
the store. He wished time for reflection.

Once outside, he felt inclined to laugh, and said to himself: "The fool! Had   29
I only taken him at his word! That jeweler cannot distinguish real diamonds
from paste."

A few minutes after, he entered another store in the Rue de la Paix. As soon   30
as the proprietor glanced at the necklace, he cried out:

"Ah, *parbleu*! I know it well; it was bought here."   31

M. Lantin was disturbed, and asked: 32

"How much is it worth?"   33

"Well, I sold it for twenty thousand francs. I am willing to take it back for   34
eighteen thousand when you inform me, according to our legal formality, how
it comes to be in your possession."

This time M. Lantin was dumbfounded. He replied: 35

"But—but—examine it well. Until this moment I was under the impression   36
that it was paste."

Said the jeweler: 37

"What is your name, sir?"   38

"Lantin—I am in the employ of the Minister of the Interior. I live at No.   39
16 Rue des Martyrs."

The merchant looked through his books, found the entry, and said: "That   40
necklace was sent to Mme. Lantin's address, 16 Rue des Martyrs, July 20, 1876."

The two men looked into each other's eyes—the widower speechless with   41
astonishment, the jeweler scenting a thief. The latter broke the silence by saying:

"Will you leave this necklace here for twenty-four hours? I will give you a   42
receipt."

"Certainly," answered M. Lantin, hastily. Then, putting the ticket in his   43
pocket, he left the store.

He wandered aimlessly through the streets, his mind in a state of dreadful   44 confusion. He tried to reason, to understand. His wife could not afford to purchase such a costly ornament. Certainly not. But, then, it must have been a present!—a present!—a present from whom? Why was it given her?

He stopped and remained standing in the middle of the street. A horrible   45
doubt entered his mind—she? Then all the other gems must have been presents, too! The earth seemed to tremble beneath him—the tree before him was falling—throwing up his arms, he fell to the ground, unconscious. He recovered his senses in a pharmacy into which the passers-by had taken him, and was then taken to his home. When he arrived he shut himself up in his room and wept until nightfall. Finally, overcome with fatigue, he threw himself on the bed, where he passed an uneasy, restless night.

The following morning he arose and prepared to go to the office. It was   46
hard to work after such a shock. He sent a letter to his employer requesting to be excused. Then he remembered that he had to return to the jeweler's. He did not like the idea; but he could not leave the necklace with that man. He dressed and went out.

It was a lovely day; a clear blue sky smiled on the busy city below, and men   47
of leisure were strolling about with their hands in their pockets.

Observing them, M. Lantin said to himself: "The rich, indeed, are happy.   48
With money it is possible to forget even the deepest sorrow. One can go where one pleases, and in travel find that distraction which is the surest cure for grief. Oh! if I were only rich!"

He began to feel hungry, but his pocket was empty. He again remembered   49
the necklace. Eighteen thousand francs! Eighteen thousand francs! What a sum!

He soon arrived in the Rue de la Paix, opposite the jeweler's. Eighteen   50
thousand francs! Twenty times he resolved to go in, but shame kept him back. He was hungry, however—very hungry, and had not a cent in his pocket. He decided quickly, ran across the street in order not to have time for reflection, and entered the store.

The proprietor immediately came forward, and politely offered him a chair;   51
the clerks glanced at him knowingly.

"I have made inquiries, M. Lantin," said the jeweler, "and if you are still   52
resolved to dispose of the gems, I am ready to pay you the price I offered."

"Certainly, sir," stammered M. Lantin.   53

Whereupon the proprietor took from the drawer eighteen large bills, counted   54
and handed them to M. Lantin, who signed a receipt and with a trembling hand put the money into his pocket.

As he was about to leave the store, he turned toward the merchant, who   55
still wore the same knowing smile, and lowering his eyes, said:

"I have—I have other gems which I have received from the same source.   56
Will you buy them also?"

The merchant bowed: "Certainly, sir."   57

M. Lantin said gravely: "I will bring them to you." An hour later he returned   58
with the gems.

The large diamond earrings were worth twenty thousand francs; the brace-   59
lets, thirty-five thousand; the rings, sixteen thousand; a set of emeralds and
sapphires, fourteen thousand; a gold chain with solitaire pendant, forty thousand—making the sum of one hundred and forty-three thousand francs.

The jeweler remarked, jokingly: 60

"There was a person who invested all her earnings in precious stones."   61

M. Lantin replied, seriously: 62

"It is only another way of investing one's money."   63

That day he lunched at Voisin's and drank wine worth twenty francs a bottle.   64
Then he hired a carriage and made a tour of the Bois, and as he scanned the
various turn-outs with a contemptuous air he could hardly refrain from crying
out to the occupants:

"I, too, am rich!—I am worth two hundred thousand francs."   65

Suddenly he thought of his employer. He drove up to the office, and entered   66
gaily, saying:

"Sir, I have come to resign my position. I have just inherited three hundred   67
thousand francs."

He shook hands with his former colleagues and confided to them some of   68
his projects for the future; then he went off to dine at the Café Anglais.

He seated himself beside a gentleman of aristocratic bearing, and during the   69
meal informed the latter confidentially that he had just inherited a fortune of
four hundred thousand francs.

For the first time in his life he was not bored at the theater, and spent the   70
remainder of the night in a gay frolic.

Six months afterward he married again. His second wife was a very virtuous   71
woman, with a violent temper. She caused him much sorrow.

Questions for Critical Thinking

1. From whose viewpoint is this story written? What makes the use of this point of
   view so effective?

2. What intimations are we given that M. Lantin's wife might possibly be false? Why
   were these hints and clues necessary?

3. What kind of spouse would you rather have—one who is loving and supportive
   but who secretly cheats, or one who is virtuous and true but who openly
   nags? Why?

4. What is ironic about the title?

5. Paragraph 70 says about M. Lantin that "For the first time in his life he was not bored at the theater, and spent the remainder of the night in a gay frolic." How do you account for this change in him?

6. What effect did newly found wealth have on M. Lantin? How would you compare its effect on him with the effect wealth also seemed to have had on his wife?

7. Had Madame Lantin not died prematurely, how do you suppose the relationship between her and her husband would have developed as they grew older?

8. What do you think M. Lantin would have done had he discovered his wife's unfaithfulness before her death? What would you have done in his place?

Writing Assignment

Madam Lantin recovers from her illness and does not die. But during her lengthy convalescence, M. Lantin tries to sell some of her fake jewels to cover her medical bills and discovers her unfaithfulness. Write an essay explaining what you think happened next and why.

Writing Advice

To write this essay, you need to draw some inferences about M. Lantin's personality and character from the story. What kind of man do you take M. Lantin to be? What do you think would be his likely reaction upon discovering his living wife's infidelity? Would he try his best to suppress the scandal and resolve the matter quietly within his own household? Or would he demand the vindication and revenge of a public divorce? What proof do you have from the story to support your inferences? Pay particular attention not only to what the author says about M. Lantin but also to what M. Lantin himself does and says. How does he react to the posthumous discovery of his wife's love affairs? What does he do with her jewelry? How does his sudden wealth affect him?

Note that this is the sort of assignment for which there is no clear-cut right or wrong answer. One writer, for example, could make a case that M. Lantin, with his bourgeois love for propriety and rectitude, would have upbraided his wife venomously and filed divorce charges against her. Another may take just the opposite tack—that he would most likely have hushed up the whole business, for fear of a scandal, and continued as before. In either case, you must prove your scenario by references to the text and by the strength of argument. You might even take a creative approach and write an alternative fictional ending for the story, based on the premise of the assignment—that Madam Lantin recovered and M. Lantin soon afterwards discovered her unfaithfulness.

Alternate Writing Assignments

1. Write an essay discussing the use of irony in this story.

2. Write an essay exploring whether it is better to have an unfaithful spouse who makes you happy than a faithful spouse who makes you miserable.

LITERATURE

THE LADY OF SHALOTT
Alfred, Lord Tennyson

Alfred, Lord Tennyson (1809–1892), was possibly the most famous poet of the Victorian age whose work was much beloved then and now. The son of a clergyman, Tennyson was educated at Cambridge, where he penned a prize-winning poem, "Timbuctoo" (1829), and began his friendship with Arthur Hallam whose sudden death in 1833 plunged the poet into prolonged despondency. Publication in 1842 of *Poems*, which included such classic poems as "The Lotus-Eaters," and "The Lady of Shalott," confirmed Tennyson as one of England's premier poets and won him a government pension. His masterful *In Memoriam* (1850), an elegiac sequence chronicling his despair at Hallam's death and ending with a ringing belief in immortality, was published the same year that Tennyson became poet laureate of England. In 1883 he was made a peer and given a seat in the House of Lords.

Reading Advice

Anyone who tries to read poetry as if it were reformatted prose is in for a difficult time. For there are some well-known devices of poetry that can make the form seem cryptic, even obscure to the prose reader. The main one is *compression* of language and incident. For example, in nine brief lines the opening stanza of this poem sketches a scene complete with a river, fields of barley and rye flowing to the skyline, the towers of fabulous Camelot, and an island in the middle of the river where the Lady of Shalott lives. But the description is so intense and compressed that the reader used to the more leisurely unfolding pace of prose is likely to miss it completely or find it confusing. A similar example of this compression occurs in stanza 8 when the Lady of Shalott renounces her former lifestyle with a single line, "I am half sick of shadows." Bear in mind this compression as you read and you will find the going easier.

"The Lady of Shalott" is as much read and taught today for its hypnotic rhythms and sustained and complex rhymes as it is for its ethereal vision of the artist, which is one interpretation commonly applied to this poem. Tennyson may have drawn his story from Sir Thomas Malory's *Morte d'Arthur*, but the outcome in his poem is strikingly different. Here, his lady is doomed to weave her looms from reflections in a mirror and cannot gaze upon reality itself without bringing down upon her head a fatal curse.

PART I

On either side the river lie
Long fields of barley and of rye,
That clothe the wold and meet the sky;
And thro' the field the road runs by
  To many-tower'd Camelot;
And up and down the people go,
Gazing where the lilies blow
Round an island there below,
  The island of Shalott.

Willows whiten, aspens quiver,   10
Little breezes dusk and shiver
Thro' the wave that runs for ever
By the island in the river
  Flowing down to Camelot.
Four gray walls, and four gray towers,
Overlook a space of flowers,
And the silent isle imbowers
  The Lady of Shalott.

By the margin, willow-veil'd,
Slide the heavy barges trail'd   20
By slow horses; and unhail'd
The shallop flitteth silken-sail'd
  Skimming down to Camelot:
But who hath seen her wave her hand?
Or at the casement seen her stand?
Or is she known in all the land,
  The Lady of Shalott?

Only reapers, reaping early
In among the bearded barley,

Hear a song that echoes cheerly   30
From the river winding clearly,
 Down to tower'd Camelot;
And by the moon the reaper weary,
Piling sheaves in uplands airy,
Listening, whispers " 'Tis the fairy
 Lady of Shalott."

PART II

There she weaves by night and day
A magic web with colors gay.
She had heard a whisper say,
A curse is on her if she stay   40
 To look down to Camelot.
She knows not what the curse may be,
And so she weaveth steadily,
And little other care hath she,
 The Lady of Shalott.

And moving thro' a mirror clear
That hangs before her all the year,
Shadows of the world appear.
There she sees the highway near
 Winding down to Camelot;   50
There the river eddy whirls,
And there the surly village-churls,
And the red cloaks of market girls,
 Pass onward from Shalott.

Sometimes a troop of damsels glad,
An abbot on an ambling pad,
Sometimes a curly shepherd-lad,
Or long-hair'd page in crimson clad,
 Goes by to tower'd Camelot;
And sometimes thro' the mirror blue   60
The knights come riding two and two:
She hath no loyal knight and true,
 The Lady of Shalott.

But in her web she still delights
To weave the mirror's magic sights,
For often thro' the silent nights

A funeral, with plumes and lights
 And music, went to Camelot;
Or when the moon was overhead,
Came two young lovers lately wed: 70
"I am half sick of shadows," said
 The Lady of Shalott.

PART III

A bow-shot from her bower-eaves,
He rode between the barley-sheaves,
The sun came dazzling thro' the leaves,
And flamed upon the brazen greaves
 Of bold Sir Lancelot.
A red-cross knight for ever kneel'd
To a lady in his shield,
That sparkled on the yellow field,   80
 Beside remote Shalott.

The gemmy bridle glitter'd free,
Like to some branch of stars we see
Hung in the golden Galaxy.
The bridle bells rang merrily
 As he rode down to Camelot;
And from his blazon'd baldric slung
A mighty silver bugle hung,
And as he rode his armor rung,
 Beside remote Shalott.   90

All in the blue unclouded weather
Thick-jewel'd shone the saddle-leather,
The helmet and the helmet-feather
Burn'd like one burning flame together,
 As he rode down to Camelot;
As often thro' the purple night,
Below the starry clusters bright,
Some bearded meteor, trailing light,
 Moves over still Shalott.

His broad clear brow in sunlight glow'd;   100
On burnish'd hooves his war-horse trode;
From underneath his helmet flow'd
His coal-black curls as on he rode,

As he rode down to Camelot.
From the bank and from the river
He flash'd into the crystal mirror,
"Tirra lirra," by the river
    Sang Sir Lancelot.

She left the web, she left the loom,
She made three paces thro' the room,   110
She saw the water-lily bloom,
She saw the helmet and the plume,
    She look'd down to Camelot.
Out flew the web and floated wide;
The mirror crack'd from side to side;
"The curse is come upon me," cried
    The Lady of Shalott.

PART IV

In the stormy east-wind straining,
The pale yellow woods were waning,
The broad stream in his banks complaining,   120
Heavily the low sky raining
    Over tower'd Camelot;
Down she came and found a boat
Beneath a willow left afloat,
And roundabout the prow she wrote
    The Lady of Shalott.

And down the river's dim expanse
Like some bold seër in a trance,
Seeing all his own mischance—
With a glassy countenance   130
    Did she look to Camelot.
And at the closing of the day
She loosed the chain, and down she lay,
The broad stream bore her far away,
    The Lady of Shalott.

Lying, robed in snowy white
That loosely flew to left and right—
The leaves upon her falling light—
Thro' the noises of the night
    She floated down to Camelot;   140

And as the boat-head wound along
The willowy hills and fields among,
They heard her singing her last song,
 The Lady of Shalott.

Heard a carol, mournful, holy,
Chanted loudly, chanted lowly,
Till her blood was frozen slowly,
And her eyes were darken'd wholly,
 Turn'd to tower'd Camelot.
For ere she reach'd upon the tide   150
The first house by the water-side,
Singing in her song she died,
 The Lady of Shalott.

Under tower and balcony,
By garden-wall and gallery,
A gleaming shape she floated by,
Dead-pale between the houses high,
 Silent into Camelot.
Out upon the wharfs they came,
Knight and burgher, lord and dame,   160
And round the prow they read her name,
 The Lady of Shalott.

Who is this? and what is here?
And in the lighted palace near
Died the sound of royal cheer;
And they cross'd themselves for fear,
 All the knights at Camelot:
But Lancelot mused a little space;
He said, "She has a lovely face;
God in his mercy lend her grace,   170
 The Lady of Shalott."
1832, 1842

Questions for Critical Thinking

1. How would you summarize, in your own words, the allegory behind this poem?

2. How might the meaning of this poem be contrasted with the message implicit in Plato's "Allegory of the Cave"?

3. In what way is the maxim, "The truth shall make you free," refuted by the allegorical meaning of this poem?

4. How would this poem, and its implications, be changed if instead of the "Lady of Shalott" it had been written about the "Lord of Shalott"?

5. Which of all the artists is stereotypically regarded as being the most likely to be wounded by reality? Why?

6. Why does the Lady of Shalott, in spite of the rumored curse, leave her mirror to gaze directly down at the passing Lancelot?

7. What part do weather and climatic changes play in this poem?

Writing Assignment

Write an essay analyzing the stereotype of the artist presented in this poem. Say whether or not you agree with this stereotype and to which artists you think it particularly applies.

Writing Advice

A stereotype is a conventional notion or idea held about a person or a group. It is probably not grounded in fact or reality but is widely enough believed to constitute a myth or half-truth. For example, one popular stereotype of the intellectual is as a bumbling and ineffectual person who is incapable of focusing on practical and worldly matters. This comical picture of the intellectual is the one usually shown on television sitcoms.

To do this writing assignment, begin by asking yourself what widespread stereotype of the artist is present in the poem's depiction of the Lady of Shalott. Ask yourself if we usually think of the artist as a person riveted on the practicalities of everyday affairs or as an otherworldly dreamer who cannot bear to face the truths of daily living. The Lady of Shallot is depicted in the poem as gazing at objects reflected in her mirror and as being under a curse not to look directly at Camelot. What does her mirror represent? What does Camelot stand for? What symbolic meaning can you infer from the fact that she sees everything obliquely, through the mirror's reflections?

Draw specific details to support your inferences from the poem itself, citing passages and incidents that confirm the stereotype of the artist you think is implied in the portrait of the lady. Various interpretations of the lady are possible since several stereotypes of the artist exist. Your job is to show which particular stereotype is implicitly contained in this portrait of the lady, to say what you think of the stereotype, and to conclude by saying to which artist you think it commonly applies.

Alternate Writing Assignments

1. Write an essay analyzing the allegorical implications of "The Lady of Shalott."

2. Write an essay exploring the part truth should play in the work of an artist, writer, or poet.

ART

VISIT TO THE PLASTIC SURGEON
Remedios Varo

About the Artist

Remedios Varo (1913–1963) was a Spanish painter of intense personal magnetism and powerful imagination. Brought up in a strict Spanish family and rigorously trained in academic art, Varo eventually escaped her routine environment by joining Barcelona's bohemian avant-garde, forming several romantic liaisons with local artists. But in 1937 the Spanish Civil War caused her to flee to Paris with the poet Benjamin Peret, who later became her husband. In Paris, because of Peret's fame as a poet, she was quickly accepted into the inner circle of surrealists. Forced again to flee from the Nazis in 1941, she and Peret secured a passage to Mexico, where they found a welcome refuge in Mexico City, which soon became Varo's inspiration for many paintings that were greatly admired by the Mexican public. Varo remained in Mexico city until her death. The daughter of a hydraulic engineer, Varo often used imagery related to her father's work—fantastic pulleys, paddles, wheels, and locomotives. Deeply superstitious and strongly in tune with nature, she painted her own inner visions—a world where gravity had no meaning and where strange figures could float on water in extra-worldly navigational crafts. Yet, the details of her phantasms are strangely convincing because of the accurate and recognizable details used by the artist. Varo's retrospectives have just recently begun to take on significance in the United States.

About the Art

The young Remedios Varo carefully observed all of the sights as she traveled with her parents throughout Spain and North Africa. One of the images that fascinated her and appears in many of her paintings is the veiled female figure of North African women wearing their traditional Muslim dress that revealed only their eyes. In *Visit to the Plastic Surgeon* the veil is turned to a humorous purpose, serving as a diaphanous shield for the huge nose of a woman on her way to the plastic surgeon to have her nose remodeled. As if to inspire confidence in the surgeon's ability, the office window displays a woman who has received two extra sets of breasts. The office building itself is in the architectural style of a religious shrine, where one might normally worship the Virgin Mary and pray for a miracle. Dr. Jaime Asche, a Mexican plastic surgeon for whom this parody was painted, remembers endless discussions in which Varo worried about the length of her own nose and the possible benefits of cosmetic surgery.

ART

L'INTRIGUE
James Sidney Ensor

About the Artist

James Sidney Ensor (1860–1949) was a Belgian painter credited with helping to give momentum to the German expressionism movement. However, his artistic roots go back to the much earlier works of Hieronymus Bosch (15th century) and Peter Bruegel (16th century), who influenced him to paint bizarre canvases that became the forerunners of the surrealistic movement. Ensor was a native of Ostend, a seaport resort crowded each summer with tourists whose bourgeois habits Ensor despised for their hypocritical pretense. Ensor shunned the human models used by contemporaries such as Toulouse-Lautrec, preferring to paint a spectral and macabre world in which grotesque masked skeletons and hanged men populate sideshows, carnivals, and city streets. His best-known work, severely criticized at the time for being blasphemous, is the *Entry of Christ into Brussels*. Here the artist portrays a crowded parade of masked creatures, who have no identity beyond being ugly and noisy—totally unworthy of Christ's mission. Ensor's colors are raw, hard, and strident, to match the repulsive crowds he depicts.

About the Art

The prevailing sense of doubt and isolation preceding World War I in Europe is clearly reflected in *L'Intrigue*, a painting with a carnival atmosphere in which all of the characters wear hideous masks to hide their real identities or to represent their sick fantasies in a world devoid of purpose or meaning. The faces are grinning, but the fun is merely an illusion; in reality these men and women are lonely and unconnected, despite the fact that they stand close to each other, forming a dense group. As we scrutinize the masks, we realize that they are the mummers' true faces, exposing the inner depravity people ordinarily hide. The central characters are elegantly attired with top hats and flowery evening apparel, but their faces are unmistakably demonic. In this scene, the artist has depicted fantasy and reality converging in a nightmarish existence.

2–1   Remedios Varo, Visit to the Plastic Surgeon, *1960. Private collection. Photo courtesy of Walter Gruen.*

2–2 *James Ensor, L'Intrigue, 1890, 90 × 150 cm. Koninklijk Museum voor Schone Kunsten, Antwerpen, België.*

Chapter Writing Assignments

After reading the assigned selections and studying the paintings of the chapter, write an essay that answers one of the following questions:

(a) What difference, if any, exists between scientific and artistic truth?

(b) How does illusion differ from reality?

(c) What are the consolations, if any, of illusion? What, of truth?

(d) What defense can you offer for a life based on illusion?

(e) Is truth always and necessarily better as a basis for living than illusion? Why or why not?

(f) Is it possible for humans to ever completely know the truth, or is some illusion always a necessary accompaniment to human existence?

Make specific references to the selections you have read in this chapter, cite passages from the authors and, if necessary, supplement your answer with material uncovered on your own in the library.

CHAPTER THREE

When Are We Free?
FREEDOM

As with many ideas, the idea of freedom is one that exists in both a practical and a theoretical realm. In the practical realm, freedom seems fairly straightforward, simple, and easy to define. Most people would say that they are free if permitted to exercise personal choice when confronted with alternatives in daily life. We would say that we are free if we can choose brand "x" over brand "y" when we buy toothpaste; that we are free if we can vote for one candidate over another in an election; that we are free if we can take this job over that. Deprived of this sort of practical daily choice, most of us would assert that we are decidedly unfree.

All this appears very straightforward and plain and the occasion for little argument. But freedom is not so simple in the theoretical realm. Indeed, the concept of freedom and free will is one over which philosophy has wrestled and puzzled for centuries but never has been able to satisfactorily define. Some philosophers, known as determinists, even insist that the whole idea of free will is nothing more than an illusion. Their argument can be illustrated with a simple and commonplace example.

A woman walker comes to a fork in a road. She hesitates briefly, then turns left and continues on her way. Just then, an armed soldier emerges from behind a tree and orders her to retreat. She returns to the fork, takes the right turn, and disappears from view.

To a rational observer, the woman was not free to exercise choice, since she had first chosen to go one way before being compelled by the soldier to go another. That, some would say, is a concrete and real illustration of the difference between being free and unfree.

Now consider this variation. The same woman approaches the same fork the next day, briefly mulls over her choices, and then takes the left turn. This time no soldier intervenes and she eventually disappears from view. Has she made a free choice? Now we say yes, for we believe it theoretically possible for her to have gone to the right.

But could she have really gone to the right? We do not know, say the determinists. Nor can we ever truly know. That she exercised free choice is an assumption we make because we believe in the existence of an interior self that can choose at will among internalized intentions. The woman herself might have said, "I intended to go to the right, but instead I went to the left." In actuality, however, she took only one turn. The other turn existed, if it existed at all, only as an intention, a phantom, an internalized vapor of individual neurology. She took only one turn—to the left. And that she *could* have taken another is only a theory.

Compounding this philosophical difficulty with freedom is the belief, held by some religions, in an omniscient and infallible God. If a timeless and eternal God does in fact infallibly know all, how can free will and choice be possible? That Judas would be born to betray Jesus must have been infallibly known to God millions of years before the event. Judas had no real choice in the matter, for he could not have chosen any other option than the infallible god had foreseen, since an infallible god cannot be wrong. That Hitler would rise up and torch the civilized world with his nationalistic madness must have also been plain to the infallible God hundreds of generations before the tyrant's birth. Hilter, again, would have had no choice. James Boswell (1740–1795), the Scottish biographer, mulled over this mystery for many years, wrote about it at length in his diaries, and took the perplexity of this paradox to his deathbed. It is one of the insoluble dilemmas that the philosopher confronts when thinking of freedom.

It is also a cliché, and sometimes a rueful one, that freedom burdens all humans with a harrowing responsibility for choice. Even the simplest and most innocently exercised choice can result in disease or death. We eat from the wrong dish in a restaurant and end up bedridden for months with hepatitis; we make love to the wrong stranger and die of AIDS; we choose one airline over another and are blown to bits in a fiery crash. Worse even than this perilously unpredictable freedom is our capacity for ruefully grasping afterwards where we made the fateful blunder. Animals do not share this burden, so far as we know, but freely walk the earth with an aboriginal and childlike innocence. Whether the bear leads its cubs down a path to a grazing pasture or straight into the guns of lurking hunters may be occasion for passing sorrow in the bear but never, so far as we can tell, for rueful second-guessing. Only humans peer backwards at yesterday's wrong turns with bitter longing.

Yet, for all the philosophical muddle surrounding the idea of freedom, the fact remains that throughout history humans have shown a willingness to die for political and economic freedom. Chief among our examples of this willingness is the United States, which fought a revolutionary war to rid itself of the rule of Great Britain because the colonists felt themselves tyrannically under the heel of George III. In

1990 events in Eastern Europe again confirmed this hunger for freedom when traditional Iron Curtain countries such as East Germany, Czechoslovakia, Poland, Hungary, Bulgaria and Romania threw over the shackles of Soviet domination and opted for independence. On May 20, 1989, Chinese troops stormed students protesting in Tienanmen Square for greater democracy, leaving the world breathless with the spectacle of a single student who defied a column of tanks with his defenseless body. If freedom is only an illusion, it is a powerful illusion to which millions have been martyred.

These are some of the issues with which the articles comprising this chapter grapple, either directly or obliquely.

We begin with Camus's famous "Myth of Sisyphus," in which he portrays humans as creatures scrabbling in an absurd and futile universe. Thoreau proposes his own anarchistic brand of freedom which urges everyone to hold nothing more sacred than personal conscience. William James explains to us the differences between the determinists, who think life offers no choice, and the indeterminists, who think life random and chaotic, while Thomas Jefferson thunders defiance in his famous Declaration of Independence against a tyrannical English king. In "The Leopold and Loeb Case," Clarence Darrow makes a heartrending plea for mercy to a jury, arguing that his clients were foredoomed to commit a brutal crime. Bert Beach then takes us on a historical journey to the background of the Magna Carta, which some consider the primal document of independence movements.

In the literature section, we are treated first to the existentialist's view of the world in "The Wall," by Nobel-prize winner Jean-Paul Sartre, and then to the sweeping historical vision of Carl Sandburg, who gives us a pithy lesson on the sacred words over which generations have fought wars. The final piece is Auden's ironic "The Unknown Citizen," a poetic epitaph for the modern conformist.

The focus of the two paintings is on the most practical side of freedom—politics. In Delacroix's *Liberty Leading the People* we see a romanticized view of war and revolution, while Jacob Lawrence's *Forward* gives us a glimpse into the struggle of black generations to overthrow the shackles of slavery.

Perhaps the nub of the argument about freedom is that whether we really are cosmically free or unfree is irrelevant; whether we sin because we must or because we will makes no practical difference. What really matters is whether we feel free or unfree. The philosophical debate notwithstanding, all of us know, or think we know, that an ordinary American citizen is freer than a prisoner, for we believe that the bars and walls enclosing the prisoner constitute a real impediment. And while deterministic philosophers might reply that it is as necessary for the prisoner to be in jail as for the citizen to roam the streets at will, few of them would willing swap the freedom of the street for the confinement of the prison. Given the choice, any of us would prefer to be theoretically unfree in the determinist's sense of the term than pragmatically unfree as defined by a prison warden.

PHILOSOPHY

THE MYTH OF SISYPHUS

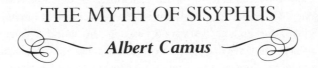
Albert Camus

Albert Camus (1913–1960), a French writer and philosopher born in Algiers, is considered one of the most important thinkers of the existential movement, although he vigorously denied allegiance with that school of thought, preferring not to be identified with any particular philosophical ideology. Noted for a concise and lucid writing style, Camus fought in the French Resistance during the German occupation of France and edited an underground paper, *Combat*. His most famous works are *The Stranger* (1946), *The Rebel* (1954), and *The Myth of Sisyphus* (1955). Awarded the Nobel Prize for Literature in 1957, Camus was killed in a car accident three years later.

Reading Advice

In Greek mythology, Sisyphus was the son of Aeolus—the Greek God of the winds who lived in a cave on the island of Aeolia—and was also the founding king of Corinth. He was said to have been extraordinarily clever and to have even outwitted Zeus, the chief god in the Greek pantheon. For his disrespect, Sisyphus was condemned by Zeus to the eternal monotony of ceaselessly rolling a heavy rock up a hill in Tartarus, the lowest region of the Greek underworld. Once atop the hill, the rock would promptly tumble back down, and Sisyphus would have to roll it up once again.

This is the famous but grim analogy to the human condition painted by Camus in his essay. Camus argues, however, that there are consolations available to Sisyphus, who finds fleeting happiness as he trundles down the hill to brace his back once again on yet another futile effort to roll a boulder up to the crest. Sisyphus has his rock as we do ours, declares Camus, and both can find occasional glory in its possession. Humanity is free, declares this viewpoint, but the freedom is one of stark and unceasing labor tinged by utter futility and meaninglessness. Since railing against the godless universe will accomplish nothing, one might as well bear the futile burden with dignity and grit. This particular essay is thought by many to summarize the pith of the existential point of view.

*T*he gods had condemned Sisyphus to   1 ceaselessly rolling a rock to the top of a mountain, whence the stone would fall back of its own weight. They had thought with some reason that there is no more dreadful punishment than futile and hopeless labor.

If one believes Homer, Sisyphus was the wisest and most prudent of mortals. 2
According to another tradition, however, he was disposed to practice the profession of highwayman. I see no contradiction in this. Opinions differ as to the
reasons why he became the futile laborer of the underworld. To begin with,
he is accused of a certain levity in regard to the gods. He stole their secrets.
Ægina, the daughter of Æsopus, was carried off by Jupiter. The father was
shocked by that disappearance and complained to Sisyphus. He, who knew of
the abduction, offered to tell about it on condition that Æsopus would give
water to the citadel of Corinth. To the celestial thunderbolts he preferred the
benediction of water. He was punished for this in the underworld. Homer tells
us also that that Sisyphus had put Death in chains. Pluto could not endure the
sight of his deserted, silent empire. He dispatched the god of war, who liberated
Death from the hands of her conqueror.

It is said also that Sisyphus, being near to death, rashly wanted to test his 3
wife's love. He ordered her to cast his unburied body into the middle of the
public square. Sisyphus woke up in the underworld. And there, annoyed by an
obedience so contrary to human love, he obtained from Pluto permission to
return to earth in order to chastise his wife. But when he had seen again the
face of this world, enjoyed water and sun, warm stones and the sea, he no
longer wanted to go back to the infernal darkness. Recalls, signs of anger,
warnings were of no avail. Many years more he lived facing the curve of the
gulf, the sparkling sea, and the smiles of earth. A decree of the gods was
necessary. Mercury came and seized the impudent man by the collar and,
snatching him from his joys, led him forcibly back to the underworld, where
his rock was ready for him.

You have already grasped that Sisyphus is the absurd hero. He *is,* as much 4
through his passions as through his torture. His scorn of the gods, his hatred
of death, and his passion for life won him that unspeakable penalty in which
the whole being is exerted toward accomplishing nothing. This is the price that
must be paid for the passions of this earth. Nothing is told us about Sisyphus
in the underworld. Myths are made for the imagination to breathe life into
them. As for this myth, one sees merely the whole effort of a body straining
to raise the huge stone, to roll it and push it up a slope a hundred times over;
one sees the face screwed up, the cheek tight against the stone, the shoulder
bracing the clay-covered mass, the foot wedging it, the fresh start with arms
outstretched, the wholly human security of two earth-clotted hands. At the
very end of his long effort measured by skyless space and time without depth,
the purpose is achieved. Then Sisyphus watches the stone rush down in a few
moments toward that lower world whence he will have to push it up again
toward the summit. He goes back down to the plain.

It is during that return, that pause, that Sisyphus interests me. A face that 5
toils so close to stones is already stone itself! I see that man going back down

with a heavy yet measured step toward the torment of which he will never know the end. That hour like a breathing-space which returns as surely as his suffering, that is the hour of consciousness. At each of those moments when he leaves the heights and gradually sinks toward the lairs of the gods, he is superior to his fate. He is stronger than his rock.

If this myth is tragic, that is because its hero is conscious. Where would his   6
torture be, indeed, if at every step the hope of succeeding upheld him? The workman of today works every day in his life at the same tasks, and this fate is no less absurd. But it is tragic only at the rare moments when it becomes conscious. Sisyphus, proletarian of the gods, powerless and rebellious, knows the whole extent of his wretched condition: it is what he thinks of during his descent. The lucidity that was to constitute his torture at the same time crowns his victory. There is no fate that cannot be surmounted by scorn.

If the descent is thus sometimes performed in sorrow, it can also take place   7
in joy. This word is not too much. Again I fancy Sisyphus returning toward his rock, and the sorrow was in the beginning. When the images of earth cling too tightly to memory, when the call of happiness becomes too insistent, it happens that melancholy rises in man's heart: this is the rock's victory, this is the rock itself. The boundless grief is too heavy to bear. These are our nights of Gethsemane. But crushing truths perish from being acknowledged. Thus, Œdipus at the outset obeys fate without knowing it. But from the moment he knows, his tragedy begins. Yet at the same moment, blind and desperate, he realizes that the only bond linking him to the world is the cool hand of a girl. Then a tremendous remark rings out: "Despite so many ordeals, my advanced age and the nobility of my soul make me conclude that all is well." Sophocles' Œdipus, like Dostoevsky's Kirilov, thus gives the recipe for the absurd victory. Ancient wisdom confirms modern heroism.

One does not discover the absurd without being tempted to write a manual   8
of happiness. "What! by such narrow ways——?" There is but one world, how-ever. Happiness and the absurd are two sons of the same earth. They are inseparable. It would be a mistake to say that happiness necessarily springs from the absurd discovery. It happens as well that the feeling of the absurd springs from happiness. "I conclude that all is well," says Œdipus, and that remark is sacred. It echoes in the wild and limited universe of man. It teaches that all is not, has not been, exhausted. It drives out of this world a god who had come into it with dissatisfaction and a preference for futile sufferings. It makes of fate a human matter, which must be settled among men.

All Sisyphus' silent joy is contained therein. His fate belongs to him. His   9
rock is his thing. Likewise, the absurd man, when he contemplates his torment, silences all the idols. In the universe suddenly restored to its silence, the myriad wondering little voices of the earth rise up. Unconscious, secret calls, invitations from all the faces, they are the necessary reverse and price of victory. There is

no sun without shadow, and it is essential to know the night. The absurd man says yes and his effort will henceforth be unceasing. If there is a personal fate, there is no higher destiny, or at least there is but one which he concludes is inevitable and despicable. For the rest, he knows himself to be the master of his days. At that subtle moment when man glances backward over his life, Sisyphus returning toward his rock, in that slight pivoting he contemplates that series of unrelated actions which becomes his fate, created by him, combined under his memory's eye and soon sealed by his death. Thus, convinced of the wholly human origin of all that is human, a blind man eager to see who knows that the night has no end, he is still on the go. The rock is still rolling.

I leave Sisyphus at the foot of the mountain! One always finds one's burden   10
again. But Sisyphus teaches the higher fidelity that negates the gods and raises rocks. He too concludes that all is well. This universe henceforth without a master seems to him neither sterile nor futile. Each atom of that stone, each mineral flake of that night-filled mountain, in itself forms a world. The struggle itself toward the heights is enough to fill a man's heart. One must imagine Sisyphus happy.

Questions for Critical Thinking

1. What freedom do humans have in a universe devoid of gods that they cannot have in a universe with gods?

2. Camus likens the human condition to that of Sisyphus, whom the gods have punished by forcing to perform absurd labor for eternity. What essential distinction, if any, exists between humans and Sisyphus that belies the analogy?

3. What consolations can be derived from acknowledging and accepting one's fate? Do you agree with Camus that Sisyphus is happy because "his fate belongs to him," or do you think this romantic twaddle?

4. Why can the suffering of animals never be "tragic" in the sense that Camus uses the word?

5. Given a choice between suffering without knowing why, or suffering and knowing not only the cause but the certain outcome, which would you opt for and why?

6. Do you agree with Camus that Sisyphus is happy? Why or why not?

7. How would the myth of Sisyphus differ if Sisyphus had been a woman?

8. What inferences about the meanings of "the tragic" and "tragedy" can you draw from this piece?

Writing Assignment

Camus intended *The Myth of Sisyphus* to be an extended analogy of the human condition. Write an essay analyzing the applicability of this analogy to your own personal worldview. State what analogy, in contrast, more aptly fits your particular outlook.

Writing Advice

Although this is a personal writing assignment, it is also a complicated one. First, you must describe your personal credo of philosophical beliefs. Then you must say whether your outlook agrees with Camus's depiction of the human condition in *Sisyphus*. If so, you simply show how and why you agree with him, using anecdote and personal experience to explain the philosophical similarities that exist between you. If not, then you must say where you disagree and why and then formulate an analogy of your own to dramatize your beliefs about your personal life and the human condition. This particular step will require inventiveness and creativity. There is no right or wrong answer.

The specific details you will draw on in writing this assignment will come almost entirely from personal experience and moral belief. You may cite instances and events that influenced your religious or irreligious outlook, and you may also include episodes and experiences that have helped shape the way you think. A major transition in this essay will occur as you move from an explanation of what Camus believes to a comparison or contrast of his ideas with yours. Another transition should link this discussion to the analogy explaining your own philosophical outlook, assuming that it differs from Camus's.

Alternate Writing Assignment

In an essay, compare and contrast suffering in a human with suffering in an animal.

PHILOSOPHY

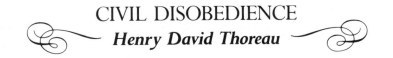

CIVIL DISOBEDIENCE
Henry David Thoreau

Henry David Thoreau (1817–1862), author and naturalist, is ranked among the most influential American writers and thinkers. Born in Concord, Mass., and educated at Harvard, Thoreau was a staunch individualist who believed that the individual was obliged to exercise the principles of his conscience against the will of the state. His essay, "Civil Disobedience," probably his best known and most influential work, grew out of his imprisonment for refusing to pay the poll tax that supported the Mexican-American War. In 1845, Thoreau built a small shack on the edge of Walden pond,

Civil Disobedience. Adapted by editor from *Walden and Other Writings* by Henry David Thoreau (New York: Bantam, 1981), 85–88, 90–97, 99–101, 103–104.

where he lived in solitude for the next two years. Out of this experiment came *Walden* (1854), his lengthy journals (published in 1906), and *A Week on the Concord and Merrimack Rivers* (1849).

Reading Advice

Probably no more committed egotist ever lived than Thoreau, who once confided in his journals, "I do not judge men by anything they can do. Their greatest deed is the impression they make on me." Here, in his most famous essay, he advocates this same intense and principled perversity, where men (Thoreau was too much a creature of his times to include women) are urged to oppose the will of the state in matters of conscience.

The influence on political thought and deed of this modestly long essay has been, to the chagrin of authorities over the world, nearly incalculable. Gandhi lived and waged his revolution in India by the creed of Thoreau. So did Martin Luther King, Jr., in his fight against racial injustice. During the 1960s and early 1970s, Thoreau was the champion and idol of the antiwar movement. Few people can live up to the impossible standards of principled conduct advocated by Thoreau, and it is even doubtful whether a modern and complex society such as ours could effectively function if everyone were to overnight adopt and follow this kind of dogmatic idealism. Yet in times of public dissent, Thoreau is always cast in the same role—as the foremost spokesman for the disaffected and aggrieved.

I heartily accept the motto,—"That 1
government is best which governs least;" and I should like to see it acted up to more rapidly and systematically. Carried out, it finally amounts to this, which also I believe—"That government is best which governs not at all;" and when men are prepared for it, that will be the kind of government which they will have. Government is at best but an expedient; but most governments are usually, and all governments are sometimes, inexpedient. The objections which have been brought against a standing army, and they are many and weighty, and deserve to prevail, may also at last be brought against a standing government. The standing army is only an arm of the standing government. The government itself, which is only the mode which the people have chosen to execute their will, is equally liable to be abused and perverted before the people can act through it. Witness the present Mexican war,[1] the work of comparatively few individuals using the standing government as their tool; for, in the outset, the people would not have consented to this measure.

This American government—what is it but a tradition, though a recent 2
one, endeavoring to transmit itself unimpaired to posterity, but each instant losing some of its integrity? It has not the vitality and force of a single living

---

1. The Mexican-American War (1846–1848).

man; for a single man can bend it to his will. It is a sort of wooden gun to the people themselves. But it is not the less necessary for this; for the people must have some complicated machinery or other, and hear its din, to satisfy that idea of government which they have. Governments show thus how successfully men can be imposed on, even impose on themselves, for their own advantage. It is excellent, we must all allow. Yet this government never of itself furthered any enterprise, but by the alacrity with which it got out of its way. *It* does not keep the country free. *It* does not settle the West. *It* does not educate. The character inherent in the American people has done all that has been accomplished; and it would have done somewhat more, if the government had not sometimes got in its way. For government is an expedient by which men would fain succeed in letting one another alone; and, as has been said, when it is most expedient, the governed are most let alone by it. Trade and commerce, if they were not made of India-rubber, would never manage to bounce over the obstacles which legislators are continually putting in their way; and, if one were to judge these men wholly by the effects of their actions and not partly by their intentions, they would deserve to be classed and punished with those mischievous persons who put obstructions on the railroads.

But, to speak practically and as a citizen, unlike those who call themselves 3
no-government men, I ask for, not at once no government, but *at once* a better government. Let every man make known what kind of government would command his respect, and that will be one step toward obtaining it.

After all, the practical reason why, when the power is once in the hands of 4
the people, a majority are permitted, and for a long period continue, to rule is not because they are most likely to be in the right, nor because this seems fairest to the minority, but because they are physically the strongest. But a government in which the majority rule in all cases cannot be based on justice, even as far as men understand it. Can there not be a government in which majorities do not virtually decide right and wrong, but conscience?—in which majorities decide only those questions to which the rule of expediency is applicable? Must the citizen ever for a moment, or in the least degree, resign his conscience to the legislator? Why has every man a conscience, then? I think that we should be men first, and subjects afterwards. It is not desirable to cultivate a respect for the law, so much as for the right. The only obligation which I have a right to assume is to do at any time what I think right. It is truly enough said, that a corporation has no conscience; but a corporation of conscientious men is a corporation *with* a conscience. Law never made men a whit more just; and, by means of their respect for it, even the well-disposed are daily made the agents of injustice. A common and natural result of an undue respect for law is, that you may see a file of soldiers, colonel, captain, corporal, privates, powder-monkeys, and all, marching in admirable order over hill and dale to the wars, against their wills, indeed, against their common sense

and consciences, which makes it very steep marching indeed, and produces a palpitation of the heart. They have no doubt that it is a damnable business in which they are concerned; they are all peaceably inclined. Now, what are they? Men at all? or small movable forts and magazines, at the service of some unscrupulous man in power? Visit the Navy Yard, and behold a marine, such a man as an American government can make, or such as it can make a man with its black arts—a mere shadow and reminiscence of humanity, a man laid out alive and standing, and already, as one may say, buried under arms. . . .

The mass of men serve the state thus, not as men mainly, but as machines, 5 with their bodies. They are the standing army, and the militia, jailors, constables, and so on. In most cases there is no free exercise whatever of the judgment or of the moral sense; but they put themselves on a level with wood and earth and stones; and wooden men can perhaps be manufactured that will serve the purpose as well. Such command no more respect than men of straw or a lump of dirt. They have the same sort of worth only as horses and dogs. Yet such as these even are commonly esteemed good citizens. Others—as most legislators, politicians, lawyers, ministers, and office-holders—serve the state chiefly with their heads; and, as they rarely make any moral distinctions, they are as likely to serve the Devil, without *intending* it, as God. A very few, as heroes, patriots, martyrs, reformers in the great sense, and *men,* serve the state with their consciences also, and so necessarily resist it for the most part; and they are commonly treated as enemies by it. A wise man will only be useful as a man, and will not submit to be "clay," and "stop a hole to keep the wind away" . . . :

> *"I am too high-born to be propertied,*
> *To be a secondary at control,*
> *Or useful serving-man and instrument*
> *To any sovereign state throughout the world."*

He who gives himself entirely to his fellow men appears to them useless 6 and selfish; but he who gives himself partially to them is pronounced a bene-factor and philanthropist.

How does it become a man to behave toward this American government 7 today? I answer, that he cannot without disgrace be associated with it. I cannot for an instant recognize the political organization as *my* government which is the *slave's* government also.[2]

All men recognize the right of revolution; that is, the right to refuse allegiance 8 to, and to resist, the government, when its tyranny or its inefficiency are great and unendurable. But almost all say that such is not the case now. But such was the case, they think, in the Revolution of 1775. If one were to tell me that this was a bad government because it taxed certain foreign commodities brought

---

2. Slavery was still legally in force in the southern United States at this time.

to its ports, it is most probable that I should not make an ado about it, for I can do without them. All machines have their friction; and possibly this does enough good to counterbalance the evil. At any rate, it is a great evil to make a stir about it. But when the friction comes to have its machine, and oppression and robbery are organized, I say, let us not have such a machine any longer. In other words, when a sixth of the population of a nation which has undertaken to be the refuge of liberty are slaves, and a whole country is unjustly overrun and conquered by a foreign army, and subjected to military law, I think that it is not too soon for honest men to rebel and revolutionize. What makes this duty the more urgent is the fact that the country so overrun is not our own, but ours is the invading army.[3]

Paley,[4] a common authority with many on moral questions in his chapter on the "Duty of Submission to Civil Government," resolves all civil obligation into expediency; and he proceeds to say, "that so long as the interest of the whole society requires it, that is, so long as the established government cannot be resisted or changed without public inconveniency, it is the will of God that the established government be obeyed, and no longer. . . . This principle being admitted, the justice of every particular case of resistance is reduced to a computation of the quantity of the danger and grievance on the one side, and of the probability and expense of redressing it on the other." Of this, he says, every man shall judge for himself. But Paley appears never to have contemplated those cases to which the rule of expediency does not apply, in which a people, as well as an individual, must do justice, cost what it may. If I have unjustly wrested a plank from a drowning man, I must restore it to him though I drown myself. This, according to Paley, would be inconvenient. But he that would save his life, in such a case, shall lose it. This people must cease to hold slaves, and to make war on Mexico, though it cost them their existence as a people. . . .

It is not a man's duty, as a matter of course, to devote himself to the eradication of any, even the most enormous wrong; he may still properly have other concerns to engage him; but it is his duty, at least, to wash his hands of it, and, if he gives it thought no longer, not to give it practically his support. If I devote myself to other pursuits and contemplations, I must first see, at least, that I do not pursue them sitting upon another man's shoulders. I must get off him first, that he may pursue his contemplations too. See what gross inconsistency is tolerated. I have heard some of my townsmen say, "I should like to have them order me out to help put down in insurrection of the slaves, or to march to Mexico;—see if I would go;" and yet these very men have each, directly by their allegiance, and so indirectly, at least, by their money, furnished a substitute.[5] The soldier is applauded who refuses to serve in an unjust war

9

10

---

3. Thoreau is referring here to the U.S. invasion of Mexico (1846–47).
4. William Paley (1743–1805), English theologian and moral philosopher.
5. Paying for a substitute soldier was a common method of avoiding military service at that time.

by those who do not refuse to support the unjust government which makes the war; he is applauded by those whose own act and authority he disregards and sets at naught. . . . Thus, under the name of Order and Civil Government, we are all made at last to pay homage to and support our own meanness. After the first blush of sin comes its indifference; and from immoral it becomes, as it were, *un*moral, and not quite unnecessary to that life which we have made. . . .

How can a man be satisfied to entertain an opinion merely, and enjoy *it?* Is   11
there any enjoyment in it, if his opinion is that he is aggrieved? If you are cheated out of a single dollar by your neighbor, you do not rest satisfied with knowing that you are cheated, or with saying that you are cheated, or even with petitioning him to pay you your due; but you take effectual steps at once to obtain the full amount, and see that you are never cheated again. Action from principle, the perception and the performance of right, changes things and relations; it is essentially revolutionary. . . . It not only divides states and churches, it divides families; yes, it divides the *individual,* separating the diabolical in him from the divine.

Unjust laws exist: shall we be content to obey them, or shall we endeavor   12
to amend them, and obey them until we have succeeded, or shall we transgress them at once? Men generally, under such a government as this, think that they ought to wait until they have persuaded the majority to alter them. They think that, if they should resist, the remedy would be worse than the evil. But it is the fault of the government itself that the remedy *is* worse than the evil. *It* makes it worse. Why is it not more apt to anticipate and provide for reform? Why does it not cherish its wise minority? Why does it cry and resist before it is hurt? Why does it not encourage its citizens to be on the alert to point out its faults, and *do* better than it would have them? Why does it always crucify Christ, and excommunicate Copernicus[6] and Luther,[7] and pronounce Washington and Franklin rebels? . . .

If the injustice is part of the necessary friction of the machine of government,   13
let it go, let it go: perchance it will wear smooth—certainly the machine will wear out. If the injustice has a spring, or a pulley, or a rope, or a crank, exclusively for itself, then perhaps you may consider whether the remedy will not be worse than the evil; but if it is of such a nature that it requires you to be the agent of injustice to another, then, I say, break the law. Let your life be a counter friction to stop the machine. What I have to do is to see, at any rate, that I do not lend myself to the wrong which I condemn.

As for adopting the ways which the state has provided for remedying the   14
evil, I know not of such ways. They take too much time, and a man's life will be gone. I have other affairs to attend to. I came into this world, not chiefly to make this a good place to live in, but to live in it, be it good or bad. A man

6. Nicolaus Copernicus (1473–1543), Polish-Prussian astronomer.
7. Martin Luther (1483–1546), German Protestant reformer.

has not everything to do, but something; and because he cannot do *everything*, it is not necessary that he should do *something* wrong. It is not my business to be petitioning the Governor or the Legislature any more than it is theirs to petition me; and if they should not hear my petition, what should I do then? But in this case the state has provided no way: its very Constitution is the evil. This may seem to be harsh and stubborn and unconciliatory; but it is to treat with the utmost kindness and consideration the only spirit that can appreciate or deserves it. So is all change for the better, like birth and death, which convulse the body.

I do not hesitate to say, that those who call themselves Abolitionists should   15
at once withdraw their support, both in person and property, from the government of Massachusetts and not wait till they constitute a majority of one. . . . I think that it is enough if they have God on their side, without waiting for that other one. Moreover, any man more right than his neighbors constitutes a majority of one already.

I meet this American government, or its representative, the state govern-   16
ment, directly, and face to face, once a year—no more—in the person of its tax-gatherer. This is the only way in which a man situated as I am necessarily meets it; and it then says distinctly, Recognize me; and the simplest and most effective, and, in the present posture of affairs, the most indispensable way of treating it is to deny it then. My civil neighbor, the tax-gatherer, is the very man I have to deal with—for it is, after all, with men and not with parchment that I quarrel—and he has voluntarily chosen to be an agent of the government. How shall he ever know well what he is and does as an officer of the government, or as a man, until he is obliged to consider whether he shall treat me, his neighbor, for whom he has respect, as a neighbor and well-disposed man, or as a maniac and disturber of the peace. . . . I know this well, that if one thousand, if one hundred, if ten men whom I could name—if ten *honest* men only—yes, if *one* HONEST man, in this State of Massachusetts, *ceasing to hold slaves,* were actually to withdraw from this copartnership, and be locked up in the county jail therefor, it would be the abolition of slavery in America. For it matters not how small the beginning may seem to be: what is once well done is done forever. . . .

Under a government which imprisons any unjustly, the true place for a just   17
man is also a prison. The proper place today, the only place which Massachusetts has provided for her freer and less desponding spirits, is in her prisons, to be put out and locked out of the State by her own act, as they have already put themselves out by their principles. It is there that the fugitive slave, and the Mexican prisoner on parole, and the Indian come to plead the wrongs of his race should find them; on that separate, but more free and honorable ground, where the State places those who are not *with* her, but *against* her—the only house in a slave State in which a free man can live with honor. If any think

that their influence would be lost there, and their voices no longer afflict the ear of the State, that they would not be as an enemy within its walls, they do not know by how much truth is stronger than error, nor how much more eloquently and effectively he can combat injustice who has experienced a little in his own person. Cast your whole vote, not a strip of paper merely, but your whole influence. A minority is powerless while it conforms to the majority; it is not even a minority then; but it is irresistible when it clogs by its whole weight. If the alternative is to keep all just men in prison, or give up war and slavery, the State will not hesitate which to choose. If a thousand men were not to pay their tax-bills this year, that would not be a violent and bloody measure, as it would be to pay them, and enable the State to commit violence and shed innocent blood. This is, in fact, the definition of a peaceable revolution, if any such is possible. If the tax-gatherer, or any other public officer, asks me, as one has done, "But what shall I do?" my answer is, "If you really wish to do anything, resign your office." When the subject has refused allegiance, and the officer has resigned his office, then the revolution is accomplished. But even suppose blood should flow. Is there not a sort of blood shed when the conscience is wounded? Through this wound a man's real manhood and immortality flow out, and he bleeds to an everlasting death. I see this blood flowing now. . . .

When I converse with the freest of my neighbors, I perceive that whatever they may say about the magnitude and seriousness of the question, and their regard for the public tranquillity, the long and the short of the matter is, that they cannot spare the protection of the existing government, and they dread the consequences to their property and families of disobedience to it. For my own part, I should not like to think that I ever rely on the protection of the State. But, if I deny the authority of the State when it presents its tax-bill, it will soon take and waste all my property, and so harass me and my children without end. This is hard. This makes it impossible for a man to live honestly, and at the same time comfortably, in outward respects. It will not be worth the while to accumulate property; that would be sure to go again. You must hire or squat somewhere, and raise but a small crop, and eat that soon. You must live within yourself, and depend upon yourself always tucked up and ready for a start, and not have many interests. A man may grow rich in Turkey even, if he will be in all respects a good subject of the Turkish government. Confucius[8] said: "If a state is governed by the principles of reason, poverty and misery are subjects of shame; if a state is not governed by the principles of reason, riches and honors are the subjects of shame." No: until I want the protection of Massachusetts to be extended to me in some distant Southern port, where my liberty is endangered, or until I am bent solely on building up an estate at home by peaceful enterprise, I can afford to refuse allegiance to Massachusetts,

18

---

8. Confucius (551–479 B.C.), Chinese philosopher.

and her right to my property and life. It costs me less in every sense to incur the penalty of disobedience to the State than it would to obey. I should feel as if I were worth less in that case. . . .

I have paid no poll-tax[9] for six years. I was put into a jail once on this   19
account, for one night; and, as I stood considering the walls of solid stone, two or three feet thick, the door of wood and iron, a foot thick, and the iron grating which strained the light, I could not help being struck with the foolishness of that institution which treated me as if I were mere flesh and blood and bones, to be locked up. I wondered that it should have concluded at length that this was the best use it could put me to, and had never thought to avail itself of my services in some way. I saw that, if there was a wall of stone between me and my townsmen, there was a still more difficult one to climb or break through before they could get to be as free as I was. I did not for a moment feel confined, and the walls seemed a great waste of stone and mortar. I felt as if I alone of all my townsmen had paid my tax. They plainly did not know how to treat me, but behaved like persons who are underbred. In every threat and in every compliment there was a blunder; for they thought that my chief desire was to stand the other side of that stone wall. I could not but smile to see how industriously they locked the door on my thoughts, which followed them out again without hindrance, and *they* were really all that was dangerous. As they could not reach me, they had resolved to punish my body; just as boys, if they cannot come at some person against whom they have a spite, will abuse his dog. I saw that the State was half-witted, that it was timid as a lone woman with her silver spoons, and that it did not know its friends from its foes, and I lost all my remaining respect for it, and pitied it.

Thus the State never intentionally confronts a man's sense, intellectual or   20
moral, but only his body, his senses. It is not armed with superior wit or honesty, but with superior physical strength. I was not born to be forced. I will breathe after my own fashion. Let us see who is the strongest. What force has a multitude? They only can force me who obey a higher law than I. . . .

When I came out of prison—for some one interfered, and paid that tax—   21
I did not see that great changes had taken place in the town such as observed by one who went in a youth and emerged a tottering and gray-headed man; and yet a change had to my eyes come over the scene—the town, and State, and country—greater than any that mere time could bring about. I saw yet more distinctly the State in which I lived. I saw to what extent the people among whom I lived could be trusted as good neighbors and friends; that their friendship was for summer weather only; that they did not greatly propose to do right; that they were a distinct race from me by their prejudices and superstitions; . . . that in their sacrifices to humanity they ran no risks, not

---

9. A tax required for the right to vote (now prohibited by a Constitutional amendment).

even to their property. . . . This may be to judge my neighbors harshly; for I believe that many of them are not aware that they have such an institution as the jail in their village. . . .

I have never declined paying the highway tax, because I am as desirous of   22 being a good neighbor as I am of being a bad subject; and as for supporting schools, I am doing my part to educate my fellow-countrymen now. It is for no particular item in the tax-bill that I refuse to pay it. I simply wish to refuse allegiance to the State, to withdraw and stand aloof from it effectively. I do not care to trace the course of my dollar, if I could, till it buys a man or a musket to shoot with—the dollar is innocent—but I am concerned to trace the effects of my allegiance. In fact, I quietly declare war on the State, after my fashion, though I will still make what use and get what advantage of her I can, as is usual in such cases.

If others pay the tax which is demanded of me, from a sympathy with the   23 State, they do but what they have already done in their own case, or rather they abet injustice to a greater extent than the State requires. If they pay the tax from a mistaken interest in the individual taxed, to save his property, or prevent his going to jail, it is because they have not considered wisely how far they let their private feelings interfere with the public good.

This, then, is my position at present. But one cannot be too much on his   24 guard in such a case, lest his action be biased by obstinacy or an undue regard for the opinions of men. Let him see that he does only what belongs to himself and to the hour.

I think sometimes, Why, this people mean well, they are only ignorant; they   25 would do better if they knew how: why give your neighbors this pain to treat you as they are not inclined to? But I think again, This is no reason why I should do as they do, or permit others to suffer much greater pain of a different kind. Again, I sometimes say to myself, When many millions of men, without heat, without ill will, without personal feeling of any kind, demand of you a few shillings only, without the possibility, such is their constitution, of retracting or altering their present demand, and without the possibility, on your side, of appeal to any other millions, why expose yourself to this overwhelming brute force? You do not resist cold and hunger, the winds and the waves, thus obstinately; you quietly submit to a thousand similar necessities. You do not put your head into the fire. But just in proportion as I regard this as not wholly a brute force, but partly a human force, and consider that I have relations to those millions as to so many millions of men, and not of mere brute or inanimate things, I see that appeal is possible, first and instantaneously, from them to the Maker of them, and, secondly, from them to themselves. But if I put my head deliberately into the fire, there is no appeal to fire or to the Maker of fire, and I have only myself to blame. If I could convince myself that I have any right to be satisfied with men as they are, and to treat them accordingly, and not according, in some respects, to my requisitions and expectations of what they and I ought to be, then, like a . . . fatalist, I should endeavor to be satisfied with things as they are, and say it is the will of God. And, above all, there is this difference between resisting this and a purely brute or natural force, that I can resist this with some effect; but I cannot expect, like Orpheus,[10] to change the nature of the rocks and trees and beasts.

I do not wish to quarrel with any man or nation. I do not wish to split   26 hairs, to make fine distinctions, or set myself up as better than my neighbors. I seek rather, I may say, even an excuse for conforming to the laws of the land. I am but too ready to conform to them. Indeed, I have reason to suspect myself on this head; and each year, as the tax-gatherer comes round, I find myself disposed to review the acts and position of the general and State governments, and the spirit of the people, to discover a pretext for conformity. . . .

No man with a genius for legislation has appeared in America. They are rare   27 in the history of the world. There are orators, politicians, and eloquent men, by the thousand; but the speaker has not yet opened his mouth to speak who is capable of settling the much-vexed questions of the day. We love eloquence for its own sake, and not for any truth which it may utter, or any heroism it may inspire. Our legislators have not yet learned the comparative value of free-trade and of freedom, of union, and of rectitude, to a nation. They have no genius or talent for comparatively humble questions of taxation and finance, commerce and manufactures, and agriculture. If we were left solely to the wordy wit of legislators in Congress for our guidance, uncorrected by the seasonable experience and the effective complaints of the people, America would not long retain her rank among the nations. For eighteen hundred years, though perchance I have no right to say it, the New Testament has been written; yet where is the legislator who has wisdom and practical talent enough to avail himself of the light which it sheds on the science of legislation?

The authority of government, even such as I am willing to submit to—for   28 I will cheerfully obey those who know and can do better than I . . . —is still an impure one: to be strictly just, it must have the sanction and consent of the governed. It can have no pure right over my person and property but what I concede to it. The progress from an absolute to a limited monarchy, from a limited monarchy to a democracy, is a progress toward a true respect for the individual. Even the Chinese philosopher[11] was wise enough to regard the individual as the basis of the empire. Is a democracy, such as we know it, the last improvement possible in government? Is it not possible to take a step further toward recognizing and organizing the rights of man? There will never

---

10. Orpheus, a poet and singer of Greek mythology who, through his music, changed the nature of those who listened to it.
11. Confucius.

be a really free and enlightened State until the State comes to recognize the individual as a higher and independent power, from which all its own power and authority are derived, and treats him accordingly. I please myself with imagining a State at last which can afford to be just to all men, and to treat the individual with respect as a neighbor; which even would not think it inconsistent with its own repose if a few were to live aloof from it, not meddling with it, nor embraced by it, who fulfilled all the duties of neighbors and fellow-men. A State which bore this kind of fruit, and suffered it to drop off as fast as it ripened, would prepare the way for a still more perfect and glorious State, which also I have imagined, but not yet anywhere seen.

Questions for Critical Thinking

1. Thoreau writes that "any man more right than his neighbors constitutes a majority of one already." In a complex society churning with contradictory opinions and viewpoints, how can such rightness be practically determined?

2. What position or policy of the present administration do you find objectionable to your personal conscience and how do you register your opposition?

3. What implicit definition of freedom does Thoreau seem to propose in his essay on civil disobedience?

4. In a complex society bristling with claims and counterclaims, what restraints on acts of individual conscience do you think are justified?

5. When, in your opinion, is the majority wrong? What instance can you give of a current law expressing the will of the majority that is wrong?

6. If conscience should dictate moral choice to the extent recommended by Thoreau, how can we distinguish between the rightness of competing claims, say, for example, the claim of the racist determined to safeguard "racial purity" by enforcing restrictions on minorities, or the claim of the antiabortionist who adamantly opposes abortion for any reason? What difference can you detect between the two?

7. What, in your opinion, makes moral right? Do you regard moral right as an absolutist principle regardless of application, or do you see moral right as "situational," varying from case to case?

8. A philosopher once opined that no man ever consciously does wrong, since he always internally sees himself and his action as desirable and right. What is your opinion of this view and how would it apply to Thoreau's ideas?

Writing Assignment

What are the moral obligations and duties of a good citizen? Write an essay exploring this question.

Writing Advice

Beware of platitude as you begin to think about writing this essay. Since grammar school, most of us have had drubbed into us various hallowed beliefs about good citizenship, and it is the easiest thing in the world to simply cull some platitudes from that communal bin and work them into this essay. If you take that tack, however, you are sure to find yourself writing in empty generalities.

To overcome this reflex, ask yourself how you really feel about citizenship and what you think constitutes its worthy practice. Try to cite particular and everyday examples to support your idea of the most important precepts of citizenship. Avoid mentioning the most obvious notions about citizenship, or if you must include them, do so with a large brush rather than in fine detail. For example, it is obvious that the practice of good citizenship requires one to vote and to pay taxes. But these are elemental and basic duties that should not evoke a rhetorical shower of extravagant praise. (It is difficult, moreover, to write about John Q. Citizen tromping off to vote without bursting into Constitutional loftiness.) Better to try and particularize your own idea of good citizenship, even if your examples are minute ones such as one neighbor cooking a hot meal for another who is elderly and invalided. Remember that the best and easiest writing is usually the most focused and particularized, and the worst and hardest usually the most elevated and grand.

Alternate Writing Assignment

In an essay define what you think "moral right" is and give several examples of it.

PHILOSOPHY

THE DILEMMA OF DETERMINISM
William James

William James (1842–1910), American philosopher, was born in New York City and educated at Harvard, from which he received an M.D. degree in 1869. James enjoyed a long and fruitful tenure at Harvard, where he taught for some 35 years and gradually became identified with the philosophical school of pragmatism, which stressed that truth should be measured by experimental verification and practical results. The brother

From *A Modern Introduction to Philosophy*, rev. ed. Edited by Paul Edwards and Arthur Pap. (Glencoe: Macmillan, 1965) 25–37. [This selection is reprinted, with omissions, from "The Dilemma of Determinism," an essay which first appeared in 1884.]

of novelist Henry James, William was himself a prolific writer and explainer that made him one of the most influential thinkers of his day. His books include *The Will to Believe* (1897), *The Varieties of Religious Experiences* (1902), and *Pragmatism* (1907).

Reading Advice

Of all the reading matter you are likely to encounter, philosophical explanations and writings are likely to be the most baffling. They are baffling because they are necessarily abstract, dealing as they do with rarefied ideas and concepts. Moreover, they are often made baffling by an academic style and their removal from our everyday preoccupations and concerns. That denseness, however, is hardly the case with James. A skilled explainer, he bases this discussion of determinism on examples drawn from everyday life, using, as an instance, a notorious murder of his day to illustrate a crucial objection.

Whether we do what we do from free choice or because it was all predetermined is the topic of James's essay, which was first presented as a speech. James the pragmatist had little patience with philosophical conundrums, and in this essay he plainly and squarely sets out his position—and the contradiction he sees as implicit in the determinists' viewpoint. In the end, however, as even James admits, the question of whether the world is free or foreordained, is one that can never be truly demonstrated and can be resolved by nothing more complex—if anything can be more complex—than personal belief.

A common opinion prevails that the   1
juice has ages ago been pressed out of the free-will controversy, and that no new champion can do more than warm up stale arguments which everyone has heard. This is a radical mistake. I know of no subject less worn out, or in which inventive genius has a better chance of breaking open new ground—not, perhaps, of forcing a conclusion or of coercing assent, but of deepening our sense of what the issue between the two parties really is, and of what the ideas of fate and of free will imply. At our very side almost, in the past few years, we have seen falling in rapid succession from the press works that present the alternative in entirely novel lights. Not to speak of the English disciples of Hegel, such as Green and Bradley; not to speak of Hinton and Hodgson, nor of Hazard here—we see in the writings of Renouvier, Fouillée, and Delboeuf how completely changed and refreshed is the form of the old disputes. I cannot pretend to vie in originality with any of the masters I have named, and my ambition limits itself to just one little point. If I can make two of the necessarily implied corollaries of determinism clearer to you than they have been made before, I shall have made it possible for you to decide before or against that doctrine with a better understanding of what you are about. And if you prefer not to decide at all, but to remain doubters, you will at least see more plainly what the subject of your hesitation is. I thus declaim openly on the threshold

all pretension to prove to you that the freedom of the will is true. The most I hope is to induce some of you to follow my own example in assuming it true, and acting as if it were true. If it be true, it seems to me that this is involved in the strict logic of the case. Its truth ought not to be forced willy-nilly down our indifferent throats. It ought to be freely espoused by men who can equally well turn their backs upon it. In other words, our first act of freedom, if we are free, ought in all inward propriety to be to affirm that we are free. This should exclude, it seems to me, from the free-will side of the question all hope of a coercive demonstration—a demonstration which I, for one, am perfectly contented to go without.

With thus much understood at the outset, we can advance. But, not without one more point understood as well. The arguments I am about to urge all proceed on two suppositions: first, when we make theories about the world and discuss them with one another, we do so in order to attain a conception of things which shall give us subjective satisfaction; and, second, if there be two conceptions, and the one seems to us, on the whole, more rational than the other, we are entitled to suppose that the more rational one is truer of the two. I hope that you are all willing to make these suppositions with me; for I am afraid that if there be any of you here who are not, they will find little edification in the rest of what I have to say. I cannot stop to argue the point; but I myself believe that all the magnificent achievements of mathematical and physical science—our doctrines of evolution, of uniformity of law, and the rest—proceed from our indomitable desire to cast the world into a more rational shape in our minds than the shape into which it is thrown there by the crude order of our experience. The world has shown itself, to a great extent, plastic to this demand of ours for rationality. How much farther it will show itself plastic no one can say. Our only means of finding out is to try; and I, for one, feel as free to try conceptions of moral as of mechanical or of logical rationality. If a certain formula for expressing the nature of the world violates my moral demand, I shall feel free to throw it overboard, or at least to doubt it, as if it disappointed my demand for uniformity of sequence, for example; the one demand being, so far as I can see, quite as subjective and emotional as the other is. The principle of causality, for example—what is it but a postulate, an empty name covering simply a demand that the sequence of events shall some day manifest a deeper kind of belonging of one thing with another than the mere juxtaposition which now phenomenally appears? It is as much an altar to an unknown god as the one that Saint Paul found at Athens. All our scientific and philosophic ideals are altars to unknown gods. Uniformity is as much so as is free will. If this be admitted, we can debate on even terms. But if any one pretends that while freedom and variety are, in the first instance, subjective demands, necessity and uniformity are something altogether different, I do not see how we can debate at all.

To begin, then, I must suppose you acquainted with all the usual arguments   3
on the subject. I cannot stop to take up the old proofs from causation, from
statistics, from the certainty with which we can foretell one another's conduct,
from the fixity of character, and all the rest. But there are two *words* which
usually encumber these classical arguments, and which we must immediately
dispose of it we are to make any progress. One is the eulogistic word *freedom,*
and the other is the opprobrious word *chance.* The word "chance" I wish to
keep, but I wish to get rid of the word "freedom." Its eulogistic associations
have so far overshadowed all the rest of its meaning that both parties claim the
sole right to use it, and determinists today insist that they alone are freedom's
champions. Old-fashioned determinism was what we may call *hard* determinism.
It did not shrink from such words as fatality, bondage to the will, necessitation,
and the like. Nowadays, we have a *soft* determinism which abhors harsh words,
and, repudiating fatality, necessity, and even predetermination, says that its real
name is freedom; for freedom is only necessity understood, and bondage to the
highest is identical with true freedom. Even a writer as little used to making
capital out of soft words as Mr. Hodgson hesitates not to call himself a "free-
will determinist."

Now, all this is a quagmire of evasion under which the real issue of fact has   4
been entirely smothered. Freedom in all these senses presents simply no problem at all. No matter what the soft determinist mean by it—whether he mean
the acting without external constraint; whether he mean the acting rightly, or
whether he mean the acquiescing in the law of the whole—who cannot answer
him that sometimes we are free and sometimes we are not? But there *is* a
problem, an issue of fact and not of words, an issue of the most momentous
importance, which is often decided without discussion in one sentence—nay,
in one clause of a sentence—by those very writers who spin out whole chapters
in their efforts to show what "true" freedom is; and that is the question of
determinism, about which we are to talk tonight.

Possibilities and Actualities

Fortunately, no ambiguities hang about this word or about its opposite,   5
indeterminism. Both designate an outward way in which things may happen,
and their cold and mathematical sound has no sentimental associations that can
bribe our partiality either way in advance. Now, evidence of an external kind
to decide between determinism and indeterminism is, as I intimated a while
back, strictly impossible to find. Let us look at the difference between them
and see for ourselves. What does determinism profess?

It professes that those parts of the universe already laid down absolutely   6
appoint and decree what the other parts shall be. The future has no ambiguous
possibilities hidden in its womb: the part we call the present is compatible with
only one totality. Any other future complement than the one fixed from eternity

is impossible. The whole is in each and every part, and welds it with the rest into an absolute unity, an iron block, in which there can be no equivocation or shadow of turning.

> *With earth's first clay they did the last man knead,*
> *And there of the last harvest sowed the seed.*
> *And the first morning of creation wrote*
> *What the last dawn of reckoning shall read.*

Indeterminism, on the contrary, says that the parts have a certain amount   7
of loose play on one another, so that the laying down of one of them does not necessarily determine what the others shall be. It admits that possibilities may be in excess of actualities, and that things are not revealed to our knowledge may really in themselves be ambiguous. Of two alternative futures which we conceive, both may now be really possible; and the one become impossible only at the very moment when the other excludes it by becoming real itself. Indeterminism thus denies the world to be one unbending unit of fact. It says there is a certain ultimate pluralism in it; and, so saying, it corroborates our ordinary unsophisticated view of things. To that view, actualities seem to float in a wider sea of possibilities from out of which they are chosen; and, somewhere, indeterminism says, such possibilities exist, and form a part of truth.

Determinism, on the contrary, says they exist *nowhere,* and that necessity on   8
the one hand and impossibility on the other are the sole categories of the real. Possibilities that fail to get realized are, for determinism, pure illusions: they never were possibilities at all. There is nothing inchoate, it says, about this universe of ours, all that was or is or shall be actual in it having been from eternity virtually there. The cloud of alternatives our minds escort this mass of actuality withal is a cloud of sheer deceptions, to which "impossibilities" is the only name which rightfully belongs.

The issue, it will be seen, is a perfectly sharp one, which no eulogistic   9
terminology can smear over or wipe out. The truth *must* lie with one side or the other, and its lying with one side makes the other false.

The question relates solely to the existence of possibilities, in the strict sense   10
of the term, as things that may, but need not, be. Both sides admit that a volition, for instance, has occurred. The indeterminists say another volition might have occurred in its place: the determinists swear that nothing could possibly have occurred in its place. Now, can science be called in to tell us which of these two point-blank contradicters of each other is right? Science professes to draw no conclusions but such as are based on matters of fact, things that have actually happened; but how can any amount of assurance that something actually happened give us the least grain of information as to whether another thing might or might not have happened in its place? Only facts can be proved by other facts. With things that are possibilities and not facts, facts

have no concern. If we have no other evidence than the evidence of existing facts, the possibility-question must remain a mystery never to be cleared up.

And the truth is that facts practically have hardly anything to do with making 11 us either determinists or indeterminists. Sure enough, we make a flourish of quoting facts this way or that; and if we are determinists, we talk about the infallibility with which we can predict one another's conduct; while if we are indeterminists, we lay great stress on the fact that it is just because we cannot foretell one another's conduct, either in war or statecraft or in any of the great and small intrigues and businesses of men, that life is so intensely anxious and hazardous a game. But who does not see the wretched insufficiency of this so-called objective testimony on both sides? What fills up the gaps in our minds is something not objective, not external. What divides us into *possibility* men and *anti-possibility* men is different faiths or postulates—postulates of rationality. To this man the world seems more rational with possibilities in it—to that man more rational with possibilities excluded; and talk as we will about having to yield to evidence, what makes us monists or pluralists, determinists or indeterminists, is at bottom always some sentiment like this.

The Idea of Chance

The stronghold of the deterministic sentiment is the antipathy to the idea 12 of chance. As soon as we begin to talk indeterminism to our friends, we find a number of them shaking their heads. This notion of alternative possibility, they say, this admission that any one of several things may come to pass, is, after all, only a round-about name for chance; and chance is something the notion of which no sane mind can for an instant tolerate in the world. What is it, they ask, but barefaced crazy unreason, the negation of intelligibility and law? And if the slightest particle of it exists anywhere, what is to prevent the whole fabric from falling together, the stars from going out, and chaos from recommencing her topsy-turvy reign?

Remarks of this sort about chance will put an end to discussion as quickly 13 as anything one can find. I have already told you that "chance" was a word I wished to keep and use. Let us then examine exactly what it means, and see whether it ought to be such a terrible bugbear to us. I fancy that squeezing the thistle boldly will rob it of its sting.

The sting of the word "chance" seems to lie in the assumption that it means 14 something positive, and that if anything happens by chance, it must needs be something of an intrinsically irrational and preposterous sort. Now, chance means nothing of the kind. It is a purely negative and relative term, giving us no information about that of which it is predicated, except that it happens to be disconnected with something else—not controlled, secured, or necessitated by other things in advance of its own actual presence. As this point is the most subtle one of the whole lecture, and at the same time the point on which all the rest hinges, I beg you to pay particular attention to it. What I say is that it tells us nothing about what a thing may be in itself to call it "chance." It may be a bad thing, it may be a good thing. It may be lucidity, transparency, fitness incarnate, matching the whole system of other things, when it has once befallen, in an unimaginably perfect way. All you mean by calling it "chance" is that this is not guaranteed, that it may also fall out otherwise. For the system of other things has no positive hold on the chance-thing. Its origin is in a certain fashion negative: it escapes, and says, "Hands off!" coming, when it comes, as a free gift, or not at all.

This negativeness, however, and this opacity of the chance-thing when thus   15
considered *ab extra,*[1] or from the point of view of previous things or distant things, do not preclude its having any amount of positiveness and luminosity from within, and at its own place and moment. All that its chance-character asserts about it is that there is something in it really of its own, something that is not the unconditional property of the whole. If the whole wants this property, the whole must wait till it can get it, if it be a matter of chance. That the universe may actually be a sort of joint-stock society of this sort, in which the sharers have both limited liabilities and limited powers, is of course a simple and conceivable notion.

Nevertheless, many persons talk as if the minutest dose of disconnectedness   16
of one part with another, the smallest modicum of independence, the faintest tremor of ambiguity about the future, for example, would ruin everything, and turn this goodly universe into a sort of insane sand-heap or nulliverse—no universe at all. Since future human volitions are, as a matter of fact, the only ambiguous things we are tempted to believe in, let us stop for a moment to make ourselves sure whether their independent and accidental character need be fraught with such direful consequences to the universe as these.

What is meant by saying that my choice of which way to walk home after   17
the lecture is ambiguous and matter of chance as far as the present moment is concerned? It means that both Divinity Avenue and Oxford Street are called; but that only one, and that one *either* one shall be chosen. Now, I ask you seriously to suppose that this ambiguity of my choice is real; and then to make the impossible hypothesis that the choice is made twice over, and each time falls on a different street. In other words, imagine that I first walk through Divinity Avenue, and then imagine that the powers governing the universe annihilate ten minutes of time with all that it contained, and set me back at the door of this hall just as I was before the choice was made. Imagine then that, everything else being the same, I now make a different choice and traverse Oxford Street. You, as passive spectators, look on and see the two alternative universes—one of them with me walking through Divinity Avenue in it, the

---

1. "from without"

other with the same me walking through Oxford Street. Now, if you are determinists you believe one of these universes to have been from eternity impossible: you believe it to have been impossible because of the intrinsic irrationality or accidentality somewhere involved in it. But looking outwardly at these universes, can you say which is the impossible and accidental one, and which the rational and necessary one? I doubt if the most iron-clad determinist among you could have the slightest glimmer of light at this point. In other words, either universe *after the fact* and once there would, to our means of observation and understanding, appear just as rational as the other. There would be absolutely no criterion by which we might judge one necessary and the other matter of chance. Suppose now we relieve the gods of their hypothetical task and assume my choice, once made, to be made forever. I go through Divinity Avenue for good and all. If, as good determinists, you now begin to affirm, what all good determinists punctually do affirm, that in the nature of things I couldn't have gone through Oxford Street—had I done so it would have been chance, irrationality, insanity, a horrid gap in nature—I simply call your attention to this, that your affirmation is what the Germans call a *Macht-spruch,* a mere conception fulminated as a dogma and based on no insight into details. Before my choice, either street seemed as natural to you as to me. Had I happened to take Oxford Street, Divinity Avenue would have figured in your philosophy as the gap in nature; and you would have so proclaimed it with the best deterministic conscience in the world.

But what a hollow outcry, then, is this against a chance which, if it were   18
present to us, we could by no character whatever distinguish from a rational necessity! I have taken the most trivial of examples, but no possible example could lead to any different result. For what are the alternatives which, in point of fact, offer themselves to human volition? What are those futures that now seem matters of chance? Are they not one and all like the Divinity Avenue and Oxford Street of our example? Are they not all of them *kinds* of things already here and based in the existing frame of nature? Is any one ever tempted to produce an *absolute* accident, something utterly irrelevant to the rest of the world? Do not all the motives that assail us, all the futures that offer themselves to our choice, spring equally from the soil of the past; and would not either one of them, whether realized through chance or through necessity, the moment it was realized, seem to us to fit that past, and in the completest and most continuous manner to interdigitate with the phenomena already there?

A favorite argument against free will is that if it be true, a man's murderer   19
may as probably be his best friend as his worst enemy, a mother be as likely to strangle as to suckle her first-born, and all of us be as ready to jump from fourth-story windows as to go out of front doors, etc. Users of this argument should probably be excluded from debate till they learn what the real question is. "Free-will" does not say that everything that is physically conceivable is also morally possible. It merely says that of alternatives that really *tempt* our will

more than one is really possible. Of course, the alternatives that do thus tempt our will are vastly fewer than the physical possibilities we can coldly fancy. Persons really tempted often do murder their best friends, mothers do strangle their first-born, people do jump out of fourth stories, etc.

The more one thinks of the matter, the more one wonders that so empty   20
and gratuitous a hubbub as this outcry against chance should have found so great an echo in the hearts of men. It is a word which tells us absolutely nothing about what chances, or about the *modus operandi* of the chancing; and the use of it as a war-cry shows only a temper of intellectual absolutism, a demand that the world shall be a solid block, subject to one control—which temper, which demand, the world may not be bound to gratify at all. In every outwardly verifiable and practical respect, a world in which the alternatives that now actually distract *your* choice were decided by pure chance would be by *me* absolutely undistinguished from the world in which I now live. I am, therefore, entirely willing to call it, so far as your choices go, a world of chance for me. To *yourselves,* it is true, those very acts of choice, which to me are so blind, opaque, and external, are the opposites of this, for you are within them and effect them. To you they appear as decisions; and decisions, for him who makes them, are altogether peculiar psychic facts. Self-luminous and self-justifying at the living moment in which they occur, they appeal to no outside moment to put its stamp upon them or make them continuous with the rest of nature. Themselves it is rather who seem to make nature continuous; and in their strange and intense function of granting consent to one possibility and with-holding it from another, to transform an equivocal and double future into an inalterable and simple past.

But with the psychology of the matter we have no concern this evening.   21
The quarrel which determinism has with chance fortunately has nothing to do with this or that psychological detail. It is a quarrel altogether metaphysical. Determinism denies the ambiguity of future volitions, because it affirms that nothing future can be ambiguous. But we have said enough to meet the issue. Indeterminate future volitions *do* mean chance. Let us not fear to shout it from the house-tops if need be; for we now know that the idea of chance is, at bottom, exactly the same thing as the idea of gift—the one simply being a disparaging, and the other a eulogistic, name for anything on which we have no effective *claim.* And whether the world be the better or the worse for having either chances or gifts in it will depend altogether on *what* these uncertain and unclaimable things turn out to be.

The Moral Implications of Determinism

And this at last brings us within sight of our subject. We have seen what   22
determinism means: we have seen that indeterminism is rightly described as

meaning chance; and we have seen that chance, the very name of which we are urged to shrink from as from a metaphysical pestilence, means only the negative fact that no part of the world, however big, can claim to control absolutely the destinies of the whole. But although, in discussing the word "chance," I may at moments have seemed to be arguing for its real existence, I have not meant to do so yet. We have not yet ascertained whether this be a world of chance or no; at most, we have agreed that it seems so. And I now repeat what I said at the outset, that, from any strict theoretical point of view, the question is insoluble. To deepen our theoretic sense of the *difference* between a world with chances in it and a deterministic world is the most I can hope to do; and this I may now at last begin upon, after all our tedious clearing of the way.

I wish first of all to show you just what the notion that this is a deterministic world implies. The implications I call your attention to are all bound up with the fact that it is a world in which we constantly have to make what I shall, with your permission, call judgments of regret. Hardly an hour passes in which we do not wish that something might be otherwise; and happy indeed are those of us whose hearts have never echoed the wish of Omar Khayyam— 23

> *That we might clasp, ere closed, the book of fate,*
>   *And make the writer on a fairer leaf*
> *Inscribe our names, or quite obliterate.*

> *Ah! Love, could you and I with fate conspire*
> *To mend this sorry scheme of things entire,*
>   *Would we not shatter it to bits, and then*
> *Remould it nearer to the heart's desire?*

Now, it is undeniable that most of these regrets are foolish, and quite on a par in point of philosophic value with the criticisms on the universe of that friend of our infancy, the hero of the fable, "The Atheist and the Acorn"— 24

> *Fool! had that bough a pumpkin bore,*
> *Thy whimsies would have worked no more, etc.*

Even from the point of view of our own ends, we should probably make a botch of remodelling the universe. How much more then from the point of view of ends we cannot see! Wise men therefore regret as little as they can. But still some regrets are pretty obstinate and hard to stifle—regrets for acts of wanton cruelty or treachery, for example, whether performed by others or by ourselves. Hardly any one can remain *entirely* optimistic after reading the confession of the murderer at Brockton the other day: how, to get rid of the wife whose continued existence bored him, he inveigled her into a deserted spot, shot her four times, and then, as she lay on the ground and said to him,

"You didn't do it on purpose, did you, dear?" replied, "No, I didn't do it on purpose," as he raised a rock and smashed her skull. Such an occurrence, with the mild sentence and self-satisfaction of the prisoner, is a field for a crop of regrets, which one need not take up in detail. We feel that, although a perfect mechanical fit to the rest of the universe, it is a bad moral fit, and that something else would really have been better in its place.

But for the deterministic philosophy the murder, the sentence, and the   25 prisoner's optimism were all necessary from eternity; and nothing else for a moment had a ghost of a chance of being put in their place. To admit such a chance, the determinists tell us, would be to make a suicide of reason; so we must steel our hearts against the thought. And here our plot thickens, for we see the first of those difficult implications of determinism and monism which it is my purpose to make you feel. If this Brockton murder was called for by the rest of the universe, if it had come at its preappointed hour, and if nothing else would have been consistent with the sense of the whole, what are we to think of the universe? Are we stubbornly to stick to our judgment of regret, and say, though it *couldn't* be, yet it *would* have been a better universe with something different from this Brockton murder in it? That, of course, seems the natural and spontaneous thing for us to do; and yet it is nothing short of deliberately espousing a kind of pessimism. The judgment of regret calls the murder bad. Calling a thing bad means, if it means anything at all, that the thing ought not be, that something else ought to be in its stead. Determinism, in denying that anything else can be in its stead, virtually defines the universe as a place in which what ought to be is impossible—in other words, as an organism whose constitution is afflicted with an incurable taint, and irreme-diable flaw. The pessimism of a Schopenhauer says no more than this—that the murder is a symptom; and that it is a vicious symptom because it belongs to a vicious whole, which can express its nature no otherwise than by bringing forth just such a symptom as that at this particular spot. Regret for the murder must transform itself, if we are determinists and wise, into a larger regret. It is absurd to regret the murder alone. Other things being what they are, *it* could not be different. What we should regret is that whole frame of things of which the murder is one member. I see no escape whatever from this pessimistic conclusion if, being determinists, our judgment of regret is to be allowed to stand at all.

The only deterministic escape from pessimism is everywhere to abandon   26 the judgment of regret. That this can be done, history shows to be not impos-sible. The devil, *quoad existentiam,* may be good. That is, although he be a *principle* of evil, yet the universe, with such a principle in it, may practically be a better universe than it could have been without. On every hand, in a small way, we find that a certain amount of evil is a condition by which a higher form of good is brought. There is nothing to prevent anybody from generalizing this view, and trusting that if we could but see things in the largest of all ways, even such matters as this Brockton murder would appear to be paid for by the uses which follow in their train. An optimism *quand même,*[2] a systematic and infatuated optimism like that ridiculed by Voltaire in his *Candide,* is one of the possible ideal ways in which a man may train himself to look upon life. Bereft of dogmatic hardness and lit up with the expression of a tender and pathetic hope, such an optimism has been the grace of some of the most religious characters that ever lived.

> *Throb thine with Nature's throbbing breast,*
> *And all is clear from east to west.*

Even cruelty and treachery may be among the absolutely blessed fruits of time, and to quarrel with any of their details may be blasphemy. The only real blasphemy, in short, may be that pessimistic temper of the soul which lets it give way to such things as regrets, remorse, and grief.   27

Thus, our deterministic pessimism may become a deterministic optimism at the price of extinguishing our judgments of regret.   28

But does not this immediately bring us into a curious logical predicament? Our determinism leads us to call our judgments of regret wrong, because they are pessimistic in implying that what is impossible yet ought to be. But how then about the judgments of regret themselves? If they are wrong, other judgments, judgments of approval presumably, ought to be in their place. But as they are necessitated, nothing else *can* be in their place; and the universe is just what it was before—namely, a place in which what ought to be appears impossible. We have got one foot out of the pessimistic bog, but the other one sinks all the deeper. We have rescued our actions from the bonds of evil, but our judgments are now held fast. When murders and treacheries cease to be sins, regrets are theoretic absurdities and errors. The theoretic and the active life thus play a kind of see-saw with each other on the ground of evil. The rise of either sends the other down. Murder and treachery cannot be good without regret being bad: regret cannot be good without treachery and murder being bad. Both, however, are supposed to have been foredoomed; so something must be fatally unreasonable, absurd, and wrong in the world. It must be a place of which either sin or error forms a necessary part. From this dilemma there seems at first sight no escape. Are we then so soon to fall back into the pessimism from which we thought we had emerged? And is there no possible way by which we may, with good intellectual consciences, call the cruelties and the treacheries, the reluctances and the regrets, *all* good together?   29

Certainly there is such a way, and you are probably most of you ready to formulate it yourselves. But, before doing so, remark how inevitably the question of determinism and indeterminism slides us into the question of optimism and pessimism, or, as our fathers called it, "The question of evil." The theological   30

---

2. "even though; nevertheless"

form of all these disputes is simplest and the deepest, the form from which there is the least escape—not because, as some have sarcastically said, remorse and regret are clung to with a morbid fondness by the theologians as spiritual luxuries, but because they are existing facts in the world, and as such must be taken into account in the deterministic interpretation of all that is fated to be. If they are fated to be error, does not the bat's wing of irrationality cast its shadow over the world? . . .

Morality and Indeterminism

The only consistent way of representing a pluralism and a world whose parts   31 may affect one another through their conduct being either good or bad is the indeterministic way. What interest, zest, or excitement can there be in achieving the right way, unless we are enabled to feel that the wrong way is also a possible and a natural way—nay, more a menacing and an imminent way? And what sense can there be in condemning ourselves for taking the wrong way, unless we need have done nothing of the sort, unless the right way was open to us as well? I cannot understand the willingness to act, no matter how we feel, without the belief that acts are really good and bad. I cannot understand the belief that an act is bad, without regret at its happening. I cannot understand regret without the admission of real, genuine possibilities in the world. Only then is it other than a mockery to feel, after we have failed to do our best, that an irreparable opportunity is gone from the universe, the loss of which it must forever after mourn.

If you insist that this is all superstition, that possibility is in the eye of science   32 and reason impossibility, and that if I act badly 'tis that the universe was foredoomed to suffer this defect, you fall right back into the dilemma, the labyrinth, of pessimism and subjectivism, from out of whose toils we have just wound our way.

Now, we are of course free to fall back, if we please. For my own part,   33 though, whatever difficulties may beset the philosophy of objective right and wrong, and the indeterminism it seems to imply, determinism, with its alternative pessimism or romanticism, contains difficulties that are greater still. But you will remember that I expressly repudiated awhile ago the pretension to offer any arguments which could be coercive in a so-called scientific fashion in this matter. And I consequently find myself, at the end of this long talk, obliged to state my conclusions in an altogether personal way. This personal method of appeal seems to be among the very conditions of the problem; and the most any one can do is to confess as candidly as he can the grounds for the faith that is in him, and leave his example to work on others as it may.

Let me, then, without circumlocution say just this. The world is enigmatical   34 enough in all conscience, whatever theory we may take up toward it. The indeterminism I defend, the free-will theory of popular sense based on the judgment of regret, represents that world as vulnerable, and liable to be injured by certain of its parts if they act wrong. And it represents their acting wrong as a matter of possibility or accident, neither inevitable nor yet to be infallibly warded off. In all this, it is a theory devoid either of transparency or of stability. It gives us a pluralistic, restless universe, in which no single point of view can ever take in the whole scene; and to a mind possessed of the love of unity at any cost, it will, no doubt, remain forever inacceptable. A friend with such a mind once told me that the thought of my universe made him sick, like the sight of the horrible motion of a mass of maggots in their carrion bed.

But while I freely admit that the pluralism and the restlessness are repugnant   35 and irrational in a certain way, I find that every alternative to them is irrational in a deeper way. The indeterminism with its maggots, if you please to speak so about it, offends only the native absolutism of my intellect—an absolutism which, after all, perhaps, deserves to be snubbed and kept in check. But the determinism with its necessary carrion, to continue the figure of speech, and with no possible maggots to eat the latter up, violates my sense of moral reality through and through. When, for example, I imagine such carrion as the Brockton murder, I cannot conceive it as an act by which the universe, as a whole, logically and necessarily expresses its nature without shrinking from complicity with such a whole. And I deliberately refuse to keep on terms of loyalty with the universe by saying blankly that the murder, since it does flow from the nature of the whole, is not carrion. There are *some* instinctive reactions which I, for one, will not tamper with. The only remaining alternative, the attitude of gnostical romanticism, wrenches my personal instincts in quite as violent a way. It falsifies the simple objectivity of their deliverance. It makes the goose-flesh the murder excites in me a sufficient reason for the perpetration of the crime. It transforms life from a tragic reality into an insincere melodramatic exhibition, as foul or as tawdry as any one's diseased curiosity pleases to carry it out. And with its consecration of the *roman naturaliste* state of mind, and its enthronement of the baser crew of Parisian *littérateurs* among the eternally indispensable organs by which the infinite spirit of things attains to that sub-jective illumination which is the task of its life, it leaves me in presence of a sort of subjective carrion considerably more noisome than the objective carrion I called it in to take away.

No! better a thousand times, than such systematic corruption of our moral   36 sanity, the plainest pessimism, so that it be straightforward; but better far than that, the world of chance. Make as great an uproar about chance as you please, I know that chance means pluralism and nothing more. If some of the members of the pluralism are bad, the philosophy of pluralism, whatever broad views it may deny me, permits me, at least, to turn to the other members with a clean breast of affection and an unsophisticated moral sense. And if I still wish to think of the world as a totality, it lets me feel that a world with a chance in it of being altogether good, even if the chance never come to pass, is better than a world with no such chance at all. That "chance" whose very notion I am exhorted and conjured to banish from my view of the future as the suicide of reason concerning it, that "chance" is—what? Just this—the chance that in moral respects the future may be other and better than the past has been. This is the only chance we have any motive for supposing to exist. Shame, rather, on its repudiation and its denial! For its presence is the vital air which lets the world live, the salt which keeps it sweet. . . .

Questions for Critical Thinking

1. If determinism is true and our acts are all predestined and exempt from free choice, what implications for Thoreau's line of reasoning in "Civil Disobedience" does this doctrine pose?

2. What does subscribing to the concept of determinism do to the religious idea of moral choice and sin?

3. James assumes that if determinism is right indeterminism must be wrong, and that this equation applies equally rigidly the other way around. What is your opinion of this assumption?

4. With which of these competing philosophies—determinism or indeterminism— would Camus and his existentialist way of thinking fit? Why?

5. On which premise of the two competing philosophies—determinism or indeterminism—is the world of social convention and daily life based?

6. What serious objection might be raised to James's argument against determinism?

7. Which concept of the universe—determinism or indeterminism—squares more reasonably with a belief in God? Why?

8. What does the concept of indeterminism necessarily imply about God?

Writing Assignment

James says that some determinists argue that they are the truest advocates of freedom. Write an essay explaining how a determinist might think himself or herself a true advocate of freedom.

Writing Advice

To write this essay you need to be quite clear about what determinists mean by freedom. You also need to have a good grasp of the thinking behind determinism.

James gives us insight into both topics, but you will most likely have to do some additional outside reading.

Basically, what you are asked to do is to give a definition first of determinism, then of freedom, as the determinists interpret the word. Then you are asked to demonstrate how freedom can possibly coexist in a universe whose every action and incident is foreordained. Once you grasp how determinists explain this seeming contradiction, you can construct hypothetical examples to illustrate their argument.

If you think the issue an insoluble one, that freedom cannot possibly exist where the outcome of every choice is already predetermined, you might consider this: a belief in determinism could rid the believer from all sense of responsibility for personal failure, mistakes, or wrong choices. Ask yourself what effect such a belief might have on you. Freed of the responsibility for the outcome of your every decision, might you not be inclined to become carefree, even reckless, in your decision-making and behavior? Could this be what the determinists have in mind when they claim to be the truest advocates of freedom? Can you think of other examples of the consequences of this belief that might support their claim?

Note that an essay of this kind has the natural tendency to become airily abstract and overly generalized. Guard against this impulse, as James does, by inventing everyday anecdotes and incidents to support and highlight your explanations.

Alternate Writing Assignment

Write an essay exploring how a societal belief in determinism would necessarily alter our judicial system of crime and punishment.

HISTORY

THE DECLARATION OF INDEPENDENCE
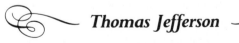 *Thomas Jefferson*

Thomas Jefferson (1743–1826), third president of the United States, was born in Virginia and educated at the College of William and Mary. Jefferson was trained in law and soon developed a reputation as a first-rate writer of resolutions and addresses. A versatile thinker with an avid interest in many projects and disciplines, Jefferson was a scientist, architect, and philosopher, the founder of the University of Virginia, planner of the city of Washington, D.C., and mastermind behind the momentous Louisiana Purchase, which added 800,000 square miles of land to the United States.

Reading Advice

Few secular documents have such a ring of historical inevitability as this one or are likely to seem more scriptural. Part of the reason is the sheer elegance and loftiness of the work itself, the balanced and parallel sentences, the ornate and stylish inversions that adorn the writing. But perhaps another part lies in the success of the American Revolution, which elevated and draped its incipient documents in the clothing of victorious history. Had England won and overthrown the colonists, Jefferson's declaration might have seemed the incendiary and seditious oratory of a failed revolutionary. Instead, it comes down to us with a graven loftiness, ringing with an appealing and almost inevitable wisdom. Jefferson wrote under the watchful eyes of Benjamin Franklin (himself no shabby stylist), John Adams, and members of the Continental Congress, but aside from minor changes suggested by Adams and Franklin, the resulting document was wholly his own.

Because the Declaration of Independence is so widely revered and taught, it is easy for us to overlook its appealing style and rhetorical power. Our suggestion is that you read it anew with fresh eyes. Forget that it is a hallowed document and seminal to the founding of the United States. Read it simply as a statement of grievances and the fighting words of a people struggling to free themselves of a colonial master.

In Congress, July 4, 1776
The Unanimous Declaration of the Thirteen United States of America

*W*hen in the Course of human events, 1 it becomes necessary for one people to dissolve the political bands which have connected them with another, and to assume among the Powers of the earth, the separate and equal station to which the Laws of Nature and of Nature's God entitle them, a decent respect to the opinions of mankind requires that they should declare the causes which impel them to the separation.

We hold these truths to be self-evident, that all men are created equal, that 2 they are endowed by their Creator with certain unalienable Rights, that among these are Life, Liberty and the pursuit of Happiness. That to secure these rights, Governments are instituted among Men, deriving their just powers from the consent of the governed. That whenever any Form of Government becomes destructive of these ends, it is the Right of the People to alter or to abolish it, and to institute a new Government, laying its foundation on such principles and organizing its powers in such form, as to them shall seem most likely to effect their Safety and Happiness. Prudence, indeed, will dictate that Governments long established should not be changed for light and transient causes; and accordingly all experience hath shown, that mankind are more disposed to suffer, while evils are sufferable, than to right themselves by abolishing the forms to which they are accustomed. But when a long train of abuses and usurpations, pursuing invariably the same Object evinces a design to reduce them under absolute Despotism, it is their right, it is their duty, to throw off such Government, and to provide new Guards for their future security.—Such has been the patient sufferance of these Colonies; and such is now the necessity which constrains them to alter their former Systems of Government. The history of the present King of Great Britain is a history of repeated injuries and usurpations, all having in direct object the establishment of an absolute Tyranny over these States. To prove this, let Facts be submitted to a candid world.

He has refused his Assent to Laws, the most wholesome and necessary for the public good.   3

He has forbidden his Governors to pass Laws of immediate and pressing importance, unless suspended in their operation till his Assent should be obtained; and when so suspended, he has utterly neglected to attend to them.   4

He has refused to pass other laws for the accommodation of large districts of people, unless those people would relinquish the right of Representation in the Legislature, a right inestimable to them and formidable to tyrants only.   5

He has called together legislative bodies at places unusual, uncomfortable, and distant from the depository of their Public Records, for the sole purpose of fatiguing them into compliance with his measures.   6

He has dissolved Representative Houses repeatedly, for opposing with manly firmness his invasions on the rights of the people.   7

He has refused for a long time, after such dissolutions, to cause others to be elected; whereby the Legislative Powers, incapable of Annihilation, have returned to the People at large for their exercise; the State remaining in the mean time exposed to all the dangers of invasion from without, and convulsions within.   8

He has endeavoured to prevent the population of these States; for that purpose obstructing the Laws for Naturalization of Foreigners; refusing to pass others to encourage their migration hither, and raising the conditions of new Appropriations of Lands.   9

He has obstructed the Administration of Justice, by refusing his Assent to Laws for establishing Judiciary Powers.   10

He has made Judges dependent on his Will alone, for the tenure of their offices, and the amount and payment of their salaries.   11

He has erected a multitude of New Offices, and sent hither swarms of Officers to harass our People, and eat out their substance.

He has kept among us, in times of peace, Standing Armies without the Consent of our legislature.   13

He has affected to render the Military independent of and superior to the Civil Power.   14

He has combined with others to subject us to a jurisdiction foreign to our constitution, and unacknowledged by our laws; giving his Assent to their acts of pretended Legislation: 15

For quartering large bodies of armed troops among us: 16

For protecting them, by a mock Trial, from Punishment for any Murders   17
which they should commit on the Inhabitants of these States:

For cutting off our Trade with all parts of the world: 18

For imposing taxes on us without our Consent: 19

For depriving us in many cases, of the benefits of Trial by Jury: 20

For transporting us beyond Seas to be tried for pretended offences: 21

For abolishing the free System of English Laws in a neighbouring Province,   22
establishing therein an Arbitrary government, and enlarging its Boundaries so
as to render it at once an example and fit instrument for introducing the same
absolute rule into these Colonies:

For taking away our Charters, abolishing our most valuable Laws, and altering   23
fundamentally the Forms of our Governments:

For suspending our own Legislatures, and declaring themselves invested with   24
Power to legislate for us in all cases whatsoever.

He has abdicated Government here, by declaring us out of his Protection   25
and waging War against us.

He has plundered our seas, ravaged our Coasts, burnt our towns, and destroyed   26
the lives of our people.

He is at this time transporting large armies of foreign mercenaries to com-   27
pleat the works of death, desolation and tyranny, already begun with circumstances of Cruelty & perfidy scarcely paralleled in the most barbarous ages,
and totally unworthy the Head of a civilized nation.

He has constrained our fellow Citizens taken Captive on the High Seas to   28
bear Arms against their Country, to become the executioners of their friends
and Brethren, or to fall themselves by their Hands.

He has excited domestic insurrections amongst us, and has endeavoured to   29
bring on the inhabitants of our frontiers, the merciless Indian Savages, whose
Known rule of warfare, is an undistinguished destruction of all ages, sexes and
conditions.

In every stage of these Oppressions We have Petitioned for Redress in the   30
most humble terms: Our repeated Petitions have been answered only by repeated
injury. A Prince, whose character is thus marked by every act which may define
a Tyrant, is unfit to be the ruler of a free People.

Nor have We been wanting in attention to our British brethren. We have   31
warned them from time to time of attempts by their legislature to extend an
unwarrantable jurisdiction over us. We have reminded them of the circumstances of our emigration and settlement here. We have appealed to their native
justice and magnanimity, and we have conjured them by the ties of our common
kindred to disavow these usurpations, which would inevitably interrupt our
connections and correspondence. They too have been deaf to the voice of
justice and of consanguinity. We must, therefore, acquiesce in the necessity,

which denounces our Separation, and hold them, as we hold the rest of mankind, Enemies in War, in Peace Friends.

We, therefore, the Representatives of the United States of America, in 32 General Congress, Assembled, appealing to the Supreme Judge of the world for the rectitude of our intentions, do, in the Name, and by Authority of the good People of these Colonies, solemnly publish and declare, That these United Colonies are, and of Right ought to be Free and Independent States, that they are Absolved from all Allegiance to the British Crown, and that all political connection between them and the State of Great Britain, is and ought to be totally dissolved; and that as Free and Independent States, they have full Power to levy War, conclude Peace, contract Alliances, establish Commerce, and to do all other Acts and Things which Independent States may of right do. And for the support of this Declaration, with a firm reliance on the Protection of Divine Providence, we mutually pledge to each other our Lives, our Fortunes and our sacred Honor.

Questions for Critical Thinking

1. In what sense can it still be said that "all men are created equal" when we know today from biology and genetics that people are not born with equal intelligence, physical prowess, or talent?

2. What do you think should be the government's course of action if it were ever conclusively demonstrated that any group of citizens were intrinsically less talented or gifted than others?

3. What force or factor in American life today do you see as militating most against the drive for equality among the various ethnic groups?

4. What passage or passages in the Declaration of Independence seem to ring with exaggeration and hyperbole?

5. Looked at from the viewpoint of determinism, how would your interpretation of the Declaration of Independence and the American Revolutionary War likely differ from your present views?

6. What is your opinion of the claim that all people and groups in America today enjoy the same degree of freedom and equality?

7. Aside from its animosity to the king of England and Great Britain, against which people does the declaration seem the most prejudiced and hostile?

8. In cataloguing the grievances the colonists felt against the king of England, what main rhetorical technique does Jefferson employ and to what effect?

Writing Assignment

Write an essay giving your views on the mechanisms and means the government can use to promote equality among all citizens.

Writing Advice

What, in your view, is equality? How can it be achieved, given the fact that everyone is born genetically different as well as under different economic and social circumstances? These are the two core questions you must answer in this essay. The first calls for a definition—an amplified explanation of what you mean by equality. The second requires an explanation of process, meaning a point-by-point detailing of the steps government can take to promote equality.

You could begin by specifying what kind of equality you mean. Since nature's distribution of intelligence and talents among people is inherently unequal, it is obvious that governmental programs must focus on promoting political, legal, or educational equality. A discussion of what the government can do in these respective areas could be the subtopics of your essay. Ask yourself, then, what specific educational programs or steps the government can take to ensure equal opportunity. Read what the experts have to say but formulate your own opinion. You may cite your own experience or the experiences of friends and acquaintances as examples. You might, for example, speculate on an opportunity you think you missed because you could not afford the cost and how a government subsidy might have helped you.

Note that you may also take the opposite tack and argue that nothing more needs to be done, since the government already does as much as is necessary. You would, of course, need to support this particular viewpoint with examples, details, and appropriate testimony.

Alternate Writing Assignment

Write an essay that defines your concept of "freedom" and which details how you think freedom is upheld, or not, within all of American society.

HISTORY

THE LEOPOLD AND LOEB CASE
Clarence Darrow

Clarence Seward Darrow (1857–1938), American lawyer, born in Kinsman, Ohio, was often associated during his long legal career with defense of the "underdog." A staunch opponent of the death penalty, Darrow defended over 100 persons charged with

From Arthur Weinberg, *Attorney for the Damned* (Chicago: University of Chicago Press, 1989). © 1959, 1989 by Arthur Weinberg.

murder, none of whom was ever condemned. Darrow was an agnostic throughout his life and defended John Thomas Scopes, who was charged under a Tennessee law with teaching evolution (*see* "A Witness at the Scopes Trial," Fay-Cooper Cole, Chapter 1.) He was also an author who wrote, among other works, *Farmington* (a novel, 1904), and *Crime: Its Cause and Treatment* (1922). A collection of Darrow's defense summations were edited and published in 1957 under the title *Attorney for the Damned*.

Reading Advice

Some background is necessary before you can understand this speech, which is excerpted from a courtroom plea made by Clarence Darrow in a capital punishment case. Basically, the facts are these: In May 22, 1924, the well-to-do family of 14-year-old Bobbie Franks received a telephone call from someone who claimed to have kidnapped the boy and was holding him for $10,000 ransom. While the family was feverishly negotiating with the kidnappers, maintenance men found the boy's battered body in a culvert by a Chicago railroad. Nearby, an observant workman noticed a pair of horn-rimmed spectacles. Police subsequently traced the spectacles to a 19-year-old University of Chicago student, Nathan Leopold, Jr., who claimed to have lost them weeks earlier while bird-watching. Leopold was linked with a friend and fellow student, Richard Loeb, who broke down under questioning and admitted that he had hatched what he had hoped would be the "perfect crime" and had persuaded Leopold to be his accomplice.

Because both defendants were the children of wealthy families, the case quickly became a *cause célèbre*. The families hired famed 67-year-old trial lawyer Clarence Darrow to handle their sons' defense. Darrow persuaded the boys to plead guilty, and then worked to persuade the trial judge, John R. Caverly, that his clients were "mentally diseased" and should not be executed. His lengthy argument, excerpted here, raised the question of determinism and psychological compulsion, and when he was finished speaking a reporter present at the trial noted that Darrow's eyes "were not the only ones that held tears."

On September 10, 1924, both defendants were sentenced to 99 years in prison at the Joliet penitentiary. Loeb was killed in a prison fight 12 years later, allegedly by an inmate repulsing his homosexual advances. Leopold became a model prisoner, helping to organize the prison library and volunteering for malaria research. He was paroled on March 13, 1958, and moved to Puerto Rico, where he established himself as an ornithologist, writer, and mathematics teacher at the University of Puerto Rico. Upon his death from arteriosclerosis in 1971, he donated his eyes to the eyebank and his body to medical research.

I have tried to study the lives of these   1
two most unfortunate boys. Three months ago, if their friends and the friends of the family had been asked to pick out the most promising lads of their acquaintance, they probably would have picked these two boys. With every opportunity, with plenty of wealth, they would have said that those two would succeed.

In a day, by an act of madness, all this is destroyed, until the best they can   2
hope for now is a life of silence and pain, continuing to the end of their years.

How did it happen?

Let us take Dickie Loeb first.

I do not claim to know how it happened; I have sought to find out. I know   3
that something, or some combinations of things, is responsible for this mad
act. I know that there are no accidents in nature. I know that effect follows
cause. I know that, if I were wise enough, and knew enough about this case, I
could lay my finger on the cause. I will do the best I can, but it is largely
speculation.

The child, of course, is born without knowledge.   4

Impressions are made upon its mind as it goes along. Dickie Loeb was a   5
child of wealth and opportunity. Over and over in this court Your Honor has
been asked, and other courts have been asked, to consider boys who have no
chance; they have been asked to consider the poor, whose home had been the
street, with no education and no opportunity in life, and they have done it,
and done it rightfully.

But, Your Honor, it is just as often a great misfortune to be the child of the   6
rich as it is to be the child of the poor. Wealth has its misfortunes. Too much,
too great opportunity and advantage, given to a child has its misfortunes, and
I am asking Your Honor to consider the rich as well as the poor (and nothing
else). Can I find what was wrong? I think I can. Here was a boy at a tender
age, placed in the hands of a governess, intellectual, vigorous, devoted, with a
strong ambition for the welfare of this boy. He was pushed in his studies, as
plants are forced in hothouses. He had no pleasures, such as a boy should have,
except as they were gained by lying and cheating.

Now, I am not criticizing the nurse. I suggest that some day Your Honor   7
look at her picture. It explains her fully. Forceful, brooking no interference,
she loved the boy, and her ambition was that he should reach the highest
perfection. No time to pause, no time to stop from one book to another, no
time to have those pleasures which a boy ought to have to create a normal life.
And what happened? Your Honor, what would happen? Nothing strange or
unusual. This nurse was with him all the time, except when he stole out at
night, from two to fourteen years of age. He, scheming and planning as healthy
boys would do, to get out from under her restraint; she, putting before him
the best books, which children generally do not want; and he, when she was
not looking, reading detective stories, which he devoured, story after story, in
his young life. Of all this there can be no question.

What is the result? Every story he read was a story of crime. We have a   8
statute in this state, passed only last year, if I recall it, which forbids minors
reading stories of crime. Why? There is only one reason. Because the legislature

in its wisdom felt that it would produce criminal tendencies in the boys who read them. The legislature of this state has given its opinion, and forbidden boys to read these books. He read them day after day. He never stopped. While he was passing through college at Ann Arbor he was still reading them. When he was a senior he read them, and almost nothing else.

Now, these facts are beyond dispute. He early developed the tendency to 9 mix with crime, to be a detective; as a little boy shadowing people on the street; as a little child going out with his fantasy of being the head of a band of criminals and directing them on the street. How did this grow and develop in him? Let us see. It seems to be as natural as the day following the night. Every detective story is a story of a sleuth getting the best of it: trailing some unfortunate individual through devious ways until his victim is finally landed in jail or stands on the gallows. They all show how smart the detective is, and where the criminal himself falls down.

This boy early in his life conceived the idea that there could be a perfect 10 crime, one that nobody could ever detect; that there could be one where the detective did not land his game—a perfect crime. He had been interested in the story of Charley Ross, who was kidnapped. He was interested in these things all his life. He believed in his childish way that a crime could be so carefully planned that there would be no detection, and his idea was to plan and accomplish a perfect crime. It would involve kidnapping and involve murder.

There had been growing in Dickie's brain, dwarfed and twisted—as every 11 act in this case shows it to have been dwarfed and twisted—there had been growing this scheme, not due to any wickedness of Dickie Loeb, for he is a child. It grew as he grew; it grew from those around him; it grew from the lack of the proper training until it possessed him. He believed he could beat the police. He believed he could plan the perfect crime. He had thought of it and talked of it for years—had talked of it as a child, had worked at it as a child—this sorry act of his, utterly irrational and motiveless, a plan to commit a perfect crime which must contain kidnapping, and there must be ransom, or else it could not be perfect, and they must get the money. . . .

The law knows and has recognized childhood for many and many a long 12 year. What do we know about childhood? The brain of the child is the home of dreams, of castles, of visions, of illusions and of delusions. In fact, there could be no childhood without delusions, for delusions are always more alluring than facts. Delusions, dreams and hallucinations are a part of the warp and woof of childhood. You know it and I know it. I remember, when I was a child, the men seemed as tall as the trees, the trees as tall as the mountains. I can remember very well when, as a little boy, I swam the deepest spot in the river for the first time. I swam breathlessly and landed with as much sense of glory and triumph as Julius Caesar felt when he led his army across the Rubicon. I have been back since, and I can almost step across the same place, but it seemed an ocean then. And those men whom I thought so wonderful were dead and left nothing behind. I had lived in a dream. I had never known the real world which I met, to my discomfort and despair, and that dispelled the illusions of my youth.

The whole life of childhood is a dream and an illusion, and whether they take one shape or another shape depends not upon the dreamy boy but on what surrounds him. As well might I have dreamed of burglars and wished to be one as to dream of policemen and wished to be one. Perhaps I was lucky, too, that I had no money. We have grown to think that the misfortune is in not having it. The great misfortune in this terrible case is the money. That has destroyed their lives. That has fostered these illusions. That has promoted this mad act. And, if Your Honor shall doom them to die, it will be because they are the sons of the rich. . . .   13

I know where my life has been molded by books, amongst other things. We all know where our lives have been influenced by books. The nurse, strict and jealous and watchful, gave him one kind of book; by night he would steal off and read the other.   14

Which, think you, shaped the life of Dickie Loeb? Is there any kind of question about it? A child. Was it pure maliciousness? Was a boy of five or six or seven to blame for it? Where did he get it? He got it where we all get our ideas, and these books became a part of his dreams and a part of his life, and as he grew up his visions grew to hallucinations.   15

He went out on the street and fantastically directed his companions, who were not there, in their various moves to complete the perfect crime. Can there be any sort of question about it?   16

Suppose, Your Honor, that instead of this boy being here in this court, under the plea of the State that Your Honor shall pronounce a sentence to hang him by the neck until dead, he had been taken to a pathological hospital to be analyzed, and the physicians had inquired into his case. What would they have said? There is only one thing that they could possibly have said. They would have traced everything back to the gradual growth of the child.   17

That is not all there is about it. Youth is hard enough. The only good thing about youth is that it has no thought and no care; and how blindly we can do things when we were young!   18

Where is the man who has not been guilty of delinquencies in youth? Let us be honest with ourselves. Let us look into our own hearts. How many men are there today—lawyers and congressmen and judges, and even state's attorneys—who have not been guilty of some mad act in youth? And if they did not get caught, or the consequences were trivial, it was their good fortune.   19

We might as well be honest with ourselves, Your Honor. Before I would tie a noose around the neck of a boy I would try to call back into my mind the emotions of youth. I would try to remember what the world looked like to me when I was a child. I would try to remember how strong were these instinctive,   20 persistent emotions that moved my life. I would try to remember how weak and inefficient was youth in the presence of the surging, controlling feelings of the child. One that honestly remembers and asks himself the question and tries to unlock the door that he thinks is closed, and calls back the boy, can understand the boy.

But, Your Honor, that is not all there is to boyhood. Nature is strong and   21
she is pitiless. She works in her own mysterious way, and we are her victims. We have not much to do with it ourselves. Nature takes this job in hand, and we play our parts. In the words of old Omar Khayyam, we are only:

> *But helpless pieces in the game He plays*
> *Upon this checkerboard of nights and days;*
> *Hither and thither moves, and checks, and slays,*
> *And one by one back in the closet lays.*

What had this boy to do with it? He was not his own father; he was not   22
his own mother; he was not his own grandparents. All of this was handed to him. He did not surround himself with governesses and wealth. He did not make himself. And yet he is to be compelled to pay.

There was a time in England, running down as late as the beginning of the   23
last century, when judges used to convene court and call juries to try a horse, a dog, a pig, for crime. I have in my library a story of a judge and jury and lawyers trying and convicting an old sow for lying down on her ten pigs and killing them.

What does it mean? Animals were tried. Do you mean to tell me that Dickie   24
Loeb had any more to do with his making than any other product of heredity that is born upon the earth? . . .

For God's sake, are we crazy? In the face of history, of every line of philos-   25
ophy, against the teaching of every religionist and seer and prophet the world has ever given us, we are still doing what our barbaric ancestors did when they came out of the caves and the woods.

From the age of fifteen to the age of twenty or twenty-one, the child has   26
the burden of adolescence, of puberty and sex thrust upon him. Girls are kept at home and carefully watched. Boys without instruction are left to work the period out for themselves. It may lead to excess. It may lead to disgrace. It may lead to perversion. Who is to blame? Who did it? Did Dickie Loeb do it?

Your Honor, I am almost ashamed to talk about it. I can hardly imagine that   27
we are in the twentieth century. And yet there are men who seriously say that for what nature has done, for what life has done, for what training has done, you should hang these boys.

Now, there is no mystery about this case, Your Honor. I seem to be criticizing   28
their parents. They had parents who were kind and good and wise in their way. But I say to you seriously that the parents are more responsible than these boys. And yet few boys had better parents.

Your Honor, it is the easiest thing in the world to be a parent. We talk of   29
motherhood, and yet every woman can be a mother. We talk of fatherhood,
and yet every man can be a father. Nature takes care of that. It is easy to be a
parent. But to be wise and farseeing enough to understand the boy is another
thing; only a very few are so wise and so farseeing as that. When I think of
the light way nature has of picking our parents and populating the earth, having
them born and die, I cannot hold human beings to the same degree of responsibility that young lawyers hold them when they are enthusiastic in a prosecution. I know what it means.

I know there are no better citizens in Chicago than the fathers of these poor   30
boys. I know there were no better women than their mothers. But I am going
to be honest with this court, if it is at the expense of both. I know that one
of two things happened to Richard Loeb: that this terrible crime was inherent
in his organism, and came from some ancestor; or that it came through his
education and his training after he was born. Do I need to prove it? Judge
Crowe said at one point in this case, when some witness spoke about their
wealth, that "probably that was responsible."

To believe that any boy is responsible for himself or his early training is an   31
absurdity that no lawyer or judge should be guilty of today. Somewhere this
came to the boy. If his failing came from his heredity, I do not know where or
how. None of us are bred perfect and pure; and the color of our hair, the color
of our eyes, our stature, the weight and fineness of our brain, and everything
about us could, with full knowledge, be traced with absolute certainty to
somewhere. If we had the pedigree it could be traced just the same in a boy
as it could in a dog, a horse or a cow.

I do not know what remote ancestors may have sent down the seed that   32
corrupted him, and I do not know through how many ancestors it may have
passed until it reached Dickie Loeb.

All I know is that it is true, and there is not a biologist in the world who   33
will not say that I am right.

If it did not come that way, then I know that if he was normal, if he had   34
been understood, if he had been trained as he should have been it would not
have happened. Not that anybody may not slip, but I know it and Your Honor
knows it, and every schoolhouse and every church in the land is an evidence
of it. Else why build them?

Every effort to protect society is an effort toward training the youth to keep   35
the path. Every bit of training in the world proves it, and it likewise proves
that it sometimes fails. I know that if this boy had been understood and properly
trained—properly for him—and the training that he got might have been the
very best for someone; but if it had been the proper training for him he would
not be in this courtroom today with the noose above his head. If there is
responsibility anywhere, it is back of him; somewhere in the infinite number
of his ancestors, or in his surroundings, or in both. And I submit, Your Honor,

that under every principle of natural justice, under every principle of conscience, of right, and of law, he should not be made responsible for the acts of
someone else. . . .

It is when these dreams of boyhood, these fantasies of youth still linger, and   36
the growing boy is still a child—a child in emotion, a child in feeling, a child
in hallucinations—that you can say that it is the dreams and the hallucinations
of childhood that are responsible for his conduct. There is not an act in all this
horrible tragedy that was not the act of a child, the act of a child wandering
around in the morning of life, moved by the new feelings of a boy, moved by
the uncontrolled impulses which his teaching was not strong enough to take
care of, moved by the dreams and the hallucinations which haunt the brain of
a child. I say, Your Honor, that it would be the height of cruelty, of injustice,
of wrong and barbarism to visit the penalty upon this poor boy.

Questions for Critical Thinking

1. To what extent do you think a criminal responsible for his or her criminal deeds?

2. Darrow characterizes Dickie Loeb's scheme for committing the perfect crime as
   "utterly irrational and motiveless." What is your own stand on the philosophical
   belief in motiveless action?

3. After reading Darrow's speech and about the case in the headnote, how would
   you have voted if you had been on the jury—for the death penalty or for life in
   prison? Why?

4. What is your opinion of Darrow's assertion that the parents were more responsible
   for the murder than were the boys?

5. In the nature versus nurture debate, which side does Darrow seem to favor in
   his summation? Why? Where do you stand on this ancient question?

6. Darrow claims that there are "no accidents in nature." What do you think about
   this claim?

7. To what extent, in your opinion, can free will and character override the influences
   of parental upbringing and background?

8. What is your own stand on the question of evil? Do you regard evil as a phenomenon that exists intrinsically in nature or one that depends entirely on human
   perception and definition?

Writing Assignment

Write an essay on the problem of evil.

Writing Advice

This is the kind of broad assignment that requires a writer to first narrow it to a
smaller topic. You may do so through a variety of prewriting techniques, some of
which we covered in the essay, "Writing Expository Prose," in Chapter 1. Make notes

on the subject of evil. Jot down ideas as they occur to you. Go to the library and browse through books on the subject. Talk to a minister or a philosophy instructor. Scribble and think on paper as you begin the preliminary writing.

In narrowing the subject into a specific topic, you could take one of several tacks. You could, for example, make your essay an extended definition of evil. You could write an essay speculating on evil's causes and motives. Or you could begin this way: "Evil in the abstract is philosophy's nightmare. But I think I have a good grasp of at least one instance of evil." And then you relate your instance and show how it embodies what you mean by evil. This particular approach is known as *development by example* and comes naturally for most writers, professional or amateur, since it is always easier to write about specifics than about generalities.

Taking that tack will lead you to write a rather practical and nuts-and-bolts essay but not one that is particularly philosophical or abstract. A more ambitious approach would be an essay that attempts to define evil. Here, you would begin with a lexical definition of evil and then amplify on it with your own ideas and examples as well as with the opinions of philosophers. The essay you end up with using this approach will naturally be more theoretical and reflective, but it would also be one allowing more scope for the imaginative expression of opinion.

In either case, the secret of writing a good essay on this broad topic is to convert it into a writable topic. Make your topic as specific and concrete as you can. Word it in such a way as to take advantage not only of what you know or have read about evil but also of what you have experienced. Doing so will allow you to add specific and intimate details to your essay that are sure to make it livelier and more engaging.

Alternate Writing Assignment

Are any acts or deeds "utterly irrational and motiveless"? In an essay take a stand one way or another on this question.

HISTORY

THE MAGNA CARTA AND ITS IMPLICATIONS FOR FREEDOM
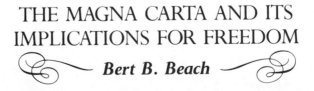
Bert B. Beach

Bert Beverly Beach (b. 1928) was born in Gland, Switzerland, to Seventh-day Adventist missionary parents. He was educated at Pacific Union College, Stanford University, and the Sorbonne, University of Paris (Ph.D. 1958). Beach is an active contributor to many

From *The Magna Carta and Its Implications for Freedom,* by Bert B. Beach, reprinted by permission of the author and Pacific Press Publishing Association, Boise, Idaho © 1989.

journals, a sometime history professor, and director of public affairs for the General Conference of Seventh Day Adventists. He is the author of, among other books, *Vatican II* (1968) and *Ecumenism: Boon or Bane* (1974).

Reading Advice

The Magna Carta, the subject of this chapter excerpted from a book, is perhaps not as popularly known as the Declaration of Independence, but many historians regard its importance as unique in the evolution of human freedom. Basically, the historical background is this: On June 15, 1215, a meeting took place between "bad" King John of England and his barons, who were revolting, in a meadow near the Thames River, some 20 miles from London. At the end of sometimes stormy negotiations that lasted a week, the king reluctantly put his signature to a document demanded by his barons that protected them from what they saw as royal encroachment on their traditional prerogatives.

Thus was the Magna Carta introduced into English law, with consequences and ramifications neither its reluctant signer nor the quarrelsome barons could have anticipated. Beach explains how a subsequent draft of this primal document, along with the accumulated interpretations by many successive generations, led directly to the legal and political principles embodied in our own Constitution.

*I*n June 1215, the English barons forced   1
King John to give his assent to a document—the Magna Carta—constituting a fundamental guarantee of rights and privileges. As the title of this chapter indicates, liberty in Magna Carta is there more by *implication* and extension than by direct proclamation. There is no general statement that all men are to be free or born free, much less equal. There is not even an embryonic articulation of the later American or French natural rights and freedom conception. It is in no way an early manifesto of the rights of the working man; it is not a religious liberty declaration. It is a pragmatic document dealing with feudal rights and taxation, but great principles of law and freedom have been extrapolated from this document over many centuries. In the thinking of many, the Magna Carta is considered to be the progenitor of constitutional government and, in this sense, it has an ancestral relationship to the United States Constitution and its Bill of Rights.

Background

William the Conqueror secured for himself and his early successors on the   2
English throne during the last part of the 11th century a position of unprecedented power over land, barons, and the Church of Rome in England. Later successors had problems establishing their power and there developed in the 12th century a tradition of each new king enlarging his base of support by

bolstering his coronation oath with written promises, called charters, sealed with the king's seal.

Furthermore, there was a trend with agents of the crown growing stronger   3
and the barons growing weaker in regards to two things: 1) financial liability of the barons to the crown, and 2) judicial authority of feudal lords over their own people.

While Henry II (1154–1189) was probably the greatest of England's medi-   4
eval kings, his two sons were really failures as kings. Richard I the Lionhearted gained a tremendous reputation as "the greatest chivalric warrior in Christendom," but he was misguided in government and unconversant in the law. Furthermore, he spent almost all of his decade as king (last decade of the 12th century) in various crusading or other adventures overseas. When he died in 1199, his brother John took over. He was potentially a good administrator, but suffered probably from both paranoia and depression. He suspected all of treachery, was brutally cruel, greedy, self-indulgent, disloyal and at times paralyzed by indecision and inaction. Maybe he was manic-depressive. Unfortunately, in those days they did not have psychiatrists.

Already during Richard's reign taxes had greatly increased, due largely to   5
the crusade costs, his ransom from captivity, and the war with France. Under John the situation got worse. He took as his queen a French girl already betrothed to a French nobleman. The latter appealed to King Philip Augustus of France, who was King John's overlord in regards to Normandy, Anjou and Aquitaine. John simply ignored the summons of the French king and in 1204 was declared a contumacious vassal. John did nothing and lost about half his possessions!

His second defeat came from Pope Innocent III, who happened to be polit-   6
ically one of the strongest popes of history. An investiture quarrel had developed between John and Innocent over the appointment by the pope of Stephen Langton as archbishop of Canterbury. John refused to recognize him. The pope responded by placing England under interdict (suspension of church services) from 1208–13 and in 1209 John was excommunicated. John confiscated a great part of the church's landed wealth. The pope then encouraged the King of France to invade England. Faced by baronial revolt, deposition, and invasion, John collapsed and abnegated himself before the pope. He accepted Langton as archbishop and even agreed to become the pope's vassal by making England the fief of the papacy. The pope now forbade the French king to invade England and, in fact, gave John full support, no matter how tyrannical he behaved, until the king's death. On the other hand, Archbishop Langton became a leader for the baronial rebels!

To make things even worse, as regards the prestige of the crown in England,   7
in 1214 John was again humiliated in a war against his archenemy Philip Augustus of France.

The crown under John had now reached not only rock-bottom but the   8
breaking point. The barons were tired of paying aid, relief, wardship, scutage—
in short paying increasing taxes—to a king who lost it all in disastrous and
expensive ventures, with nothing to show. At least in the days of Richard there
had been some glory!

Baronial Revolt

Finally, the barons revolted. It appears that a majority of the people sided   9
with the majority of the barons against the king. This was the first full-fledged
rebellion against the king since the Norman invasion. It was probably Stephen
Langton who gave the baronial movement identity and conscious aims. Their
grievances were stipulated in the form of a "great charter." John had not issued
a general charter at his coronation. There now developed a demand for such
a solemn charter of liberties modeled on the coronation charter of Henry I.

On June 15, 1215 a dramatic event occurred at Runnymede, a little meadow   10
on the Thames, some 20 miles west from London and a couple of miles from
Windsor Castle. King John rode from the castle while the barons, bishops and
followers came by boat from London. A document of demands was made and
by the end of the week, the Magna Carta emerged with some 63 points.

Magna Carta Itself

The Magna Carta itself is not an interesting document. It is not well-written.   11
It is not systematic or organized. There are no sweeping generalizations regarding freedom of people.

It deals with immediate, specific problems and rights in which the nobility   12
was interested. Most clauses deal with feudal dues (taxation), law courts, and
administrative abuses (behavior of royal officials was to be controlled). There
are some political clauses. The document closes with a form of security or
guarantee that the king will obey the charter to which he has affixed his seal.
Twenty-five noble guardians of the charter were appointed. They knew their
king! Sure enough, John very soon after Runnymede repudiated the Magna
Carta, claiming he had been under duress. He asked the pope, whose vassal he
now was, to relieve him of his oath. The pope, trained at Bologna in Roman
law, could not get excited about such an ephemeral thing as English common
law, and furthermore, this could reflect negatively on papal authority in England,
if the authority of the king were curbed. John was allowed to repudiate his
oath (Cantor, Norman F, *The English,* p. 196).

The Magna Carta seemed dead. However, the barons invoked the security   13
clause and proclaimed feudal rebellion. War began, but John died in 1216, after
losing most of his baggage and treasure in the quicksand while carelessly taking

a shortcut across an arm of the sea without due regard for the tide and in anger overindulging in peaches and new cider (Hall, Walter Phelps and Albion, Robert Greenhalgh, *A History of England and the British Empire,* Volume 1, p. 129).

The regency of Henry III reissued the Magna Carta in 1216, with some   14
omissions and changes. In 1225 at the majority of the king, the Magna Carta was reissued—now about 1/3 shorter. Interestingly enough, it is this "Great Charter of 9 Henry III" that is the Magna Carta of English law and history, and not the prototype of 1215. The Magna Carta expounded by Sir Edward Coke (died 1634), the great champion of English common law, is the 1225 document.

Significance of the Magna Carta

Scholars are divided regarding the exact nature of the Magna Carta. There   15
has been a tendency over the centuries for the Magna Carta to grow in importance, until it reached the height of its prestige in the 19th century. Beginning with 1890 and Edward Jenks of Oxford and other scholars, there has been some revisionism and toning down of the Magna Carta's triumphant musical score. The grand opera has become for some an operetta!

There are really in practice, one might say, two Magna Cartas: 1) the hap   16
hazard expression of baronial grievances—the letter of the 13th century document, and 2) an exalted, though ill-defined symbolic charter of liberties, a timeless guarantee of liberty, as has been said, "to every being who breathes English air," or in the words of William Pitt the elder the "Bible of the Constitution."

The first Magna Carta, emphasized by the historical revisionists, is seen   17
mainly as a dated, selfish feudal document, the barons only looking after their narrow selfish interests. There is of course a lot of truth in this debunking view. True, in the thirteenth century, few people benefitted from the Magna Carta. However, with the passing of time and the invocation of the Magna Carta with each conflict between king and baronage and later between king and parliament, or between the royal prerogative and the common law, the Magna Carta became an ever more exalted theoretical manifesto and symbol of liberty. As the centuries succeeded each other, "The Great charter was becoming a symbol, a battle cry against oppression, not a sober statement of the common law" (*Encyclopedia Britannica,* Vol. 14, 1970 edition, p. 579). It provided memorable phrases to be used in courts of law, in parliament, or in the church. When liberty was in danger, appeal was made to the Great Charter, the principal bulwark of English liberties!

The church was to be free and have the right of free election—freedom of   18
religion. No free man was to be imprisoned or outlawed except by lawful judgment of his peers or the law of the land—due process of law, jury trial. No sheriff or royal officer was to take away any free man's house or carts or wood (to build a royal castle) without the owner's consent—property rights.

During the century of Tudor absolutism, the Magna Carta seemed almost   19
forgotten. Thus in Shakespeare's day, it was not particularly popular or seen to
be relevant. In his play "King John" (ca. 1595), Shakespeare does not even
mention Magna Carta. However, just 30 years later, during the Civil War, when
the Parliamentarians wanted to deal with the Stuart kings and their exalted
divine right concepts, the Magna Carta sprang into real prominence and has
continued to be seen by most as a fundamental palladium of English liberty.

The lasting significance of the Magna Carta does not come from the Victorian   20
view that it was a semi-sacred document, covered with veiled nobility and
romance, and that it somehow accounted for the prosperity and virtue of the
English, the supremacy of the royal navy and for the great empire on which
the sun never set! No, its significance lies rather in the fact that it was a first
step toward constitutional government—a small step at Runnymede, but a
giant step for constitutional rights. Bad King John (no other British king has
ever had this name!) gave his assent to two basic principles: 1) Certain laws
and customs are greater than the king himself. The ruler is responsible to law.
The law is eternal to the king. The king and administrators operate the law,
but the legal system is above them. To change the law, the ruler has to obtain
the consent of the community. 2) If the ruler does not observe the laws, the
people reserve the right to force him to do so (Hall, *op. cit.,* p. 128).

Influence in America

The Magna Carta has had significant fall-out in areas governed or influenced   21
by the Anglo-American legal and political system, not from the language regarding feudal relationships and rights, but from more general clauses in which
future generations have seen their protection. For example, the habeas corpus
clause of the United States Constitution of 1787 goes back to clause 39, and
so do the due process clauses of the 5th and 14th amendments to the Constitution. The fundamental human rights embodied in the U.S. Constitution trace
their ancestry to the Magna Carta of 1215/25. This explains why the American
Bar Association has raised a monument at Runnymede in honor of the Magna
Carta. In 1907, the "Magna Carta Day Association, International, Inc." was
founded in the United States to emphasize the common political and legal
heritage of the English-speaking peoples and their support of civil and religious
liberty. The early colonies in America used words from the Magna Carta in
their fundamental laws. In fact, George Washington called the U.S. Constitution
"the Magna-Carta of our country." The Magna Carta has had its influence in
the fundamental laws of various countries that belong to the (British)
Commonwealth.

The great significance of the Magna Carta is not found in its individual   22
clauses, but in the circumstances and comprehensiveness of the grant, especially
as seen and magnified by later generations. That is why June 15, 1215 and

wicked King John are remembered and the drama of that day has been impressed on the Anglo-Saxon psyche. As one who upholds the principles of liberty, I rank the Magna Carta among the most significant documents of history and man's continual struggle for freedom under law.

Questions for Critical Thinking

1. What was the most important principle extracted from the provisions of the Magna Carta?

2. One encyclopedia says that inferences of liberty drawn from the Magna Carta were based on "bad historical scholarship or false reasoning." How do you account for the popularity of these inferences and the fact that many of them have since become embedded in our political thinking as fundamental rights?

3. What inferences about the source of political power might one draw from the history of the Magna Carta?

4. What is your opinion about the attempts of successive generations to reinterpret the Constitution of the United States?

5. What underlying and implicit definition of the law do democracies subscribe to and how is this definition related to the Magna Carta?

6. According to the author, Pope Innocent III played a significant role in the reign of King John. What do you think is the proper role for any religious leader to play in a democracy?

7. Which in your opinion should prevail in the event of conflict between the two— the demands of religious conscience or the demands of good citizenship? Why?

Writing Assignment

A great deal is sometimes made of the difference between Supreme Court justices who are "strict constructionalists" of the Constitution—meaning those who believe that the document should be read literally without regard to interpretation based on changing times—versus those who believe in reinterpretation based on contemporary knowledge and thinking. Write an essay declaring into which camp you fall and defending your choice.

Writing Advice

Begin by defining your terms. Read up on exactly what constitutes a "strict constructionalist" justice versus one who believes in interpreting the constitution to suit the times. Once you have a clear idea of the differences between the two sides, decide where you stand and why. Make notes on the views of one camp versus the other, and try to understand the rationale behind their respective views on constitutional issues.

Once you know where you stand, you must also be able to say why. Supporting details you can cite will include the views of experts on constitutional matters, the words and opinions of the justices themselves, and your own personal political philosophy. Note that it is not enough to say, in effect, that you believe in justices who are strict constructionalists because you think the constitution is a permanent and unchanging document. This line of argument will quickly mire you in a tautology, since strict constructionalists are loosely defined as justices who believe that the constitution should be an unchanging document from one generation to the next. You must go a step further and demonstrate why it is wrong to reinterpret the constitution to suit the times, or why it is right to do so. You may have to cite examples of constitutional decisions to support your argument.

Alternate Writing Assignment

Write an essay saying which of the political freedoms guaranteed by the Constitution you regard as the most important, which the least, and why.

LITERATURE

THE WALL
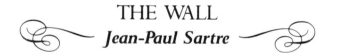
Jean-Paul Sartre

Jean-Paul Sartre (1905–1980), French philosopher, playwright, and writer, was one of the leading exponents of twentieth-century existentialism. During World War II, Sartre served in the French army and was taken prisoner, but he escaped to become a leader in the French resistance. In his writings Sartre often pictured humans as lonely beings terrified with the responsibilities of being free in a meaningless and absurd world. In 1964, Sartre declined the Nobel Prize for Literature, arguing that awards exerted too much influence on a writer's career and thought. His own books and plays were immensely influential and successful during his lifetime and include *Being and Nothingness* (1943), *No Exit* (play, 1944), *The Age of Reason* (1945), and *Troubled Sleep* (1949).

Reading Advice

Existentialist storytellers may believe in a purposeless and arbitrary universe, but seldom do they practice this dogma in constructing their stories. To the contrary, their tales are usually pointed and laden with a weighty freight of philosophical meaning and moral purpose. In this classic example, "The Wall," Sartre shows us a world of arbitrary imprisonment and death—the milieu of the brutal Spanish Civil War—where the innocent as well as the guilty are indiscriminately condemned.

Notice, as you read, the strong code of ethics by which the narrator lives. As the protagonist or chief character of the story, he is the embodiment of the existential worldview and beliefs. Purposelessness reigns and randomness runs rampant over his world, in which there are no believers, even in a foxhole. But this insane universe, this inverted parody of a rational world, is not merely a hypothetical subset of reality but an intensified, representative view of the sick and bizarre universe in which the existentialist narrator lives and suffers.

*T*hey pushed us into a big white room   1
and I began to blink because the light hurt my eyes. Then I saw a table and four men behind the table, civilians, looking over the papers. They had bunched another group of prisoners in the back and we had to cross the whole room to join them. There were several I knew and some others who must have been foreigners. The two in front of me were blond with round skulls; they looked alike. I supposed they were French. The smaller one kept hitching up his pants; nerves.

It lasted about three hours; I was dizzy and my head was empty; but the   2
room was well heated and I found that pleasant enough: for the past 24 hours we hadn't stopped shivering. The guards brought the prisoners up to the table, one after the other. The four men asked each one his name and occupation. Most of the time they didn't go any further—or they would simply ask a question here and there: "Did you have anything to do with the sabotage of munitions?" or "Where were you the morning of the 9th and what were you doing?" They didn't listen to the answers or at least didn't seem to. They were quiet for a moment and then looking straight in front of them began to write. They asked Tom if it were true he was in the International Brigade; Tom couldn't tell them otherwise because of the papers they found in his coat. They didn't ask Juan anything but they wrote for a long time after he told them his name.

"My brother José is the anarchist," Juan said, "you know he isn't here any   3
more. I don't belong to any party, I never had anything to do with politics."

They didn't answer. Juan went on, "I haven't done anything. I don't want to   4
pay for somebody else."

His lips trembled. A guard shut him up and took him away. It was my turn.   5
"Your name is Pablo Ibbieta?"   6
"Yes."   7
The man looked at the papers and asked me, "Where's Ramon Gris?"   8
"I don't know."
"You hid him in your house from the 6th to the 19th."   9
"No."

They wrote for a minute and then the guards took me out. In the corridor   10
Tom and Juan were waiting between two guards. We started walking. Tom
asked one of the guards, "So?"

"So what?" the guard said.   11

"Was that the cross-examination or the sentence?"

"Sentence," the guard said.

"What are they going to do with us?"

The guard answered dryly, "Sentence will be read in your cell."   12

As a matter of fact, our cell was one of the hospital cellars. It was terrifically   13
cold there because of the drafts. We shivered all night and it wasn't much better
during the day. I had spent the previous five days in a cell in a monastery, a
sort of hole in the wall that must have dated from the middle ages: since there
were a lot of prisoners and not much room, they locked us up anywhere. I
didn't miss my cell; I hadn't suffered too much from the cold but I was alone;
after a long time it gets irritating. In the cellar I had company. Juan hardly ever
spoke: he was afraid and he was too young to have anything to say. But Tom
was a good talker and he knew Spanish well.

There was a bench in the cellar and four mats. When they took us back we   14
sat and waited in silence. After a long moment, Tom said, "We're screwed."

"I think so too," I said, "but I don't think they'll do anything to the kid."   15

"They don't have a thing against him," said Tom. "He's the brother of a
militiaman and that's all."

I looked at Juan: he didn't seem to hear. Tom went on, "You know what   16
they do in Saragossa? They lay the men down on the road and run over them
with trucks. A Moroccan deserter told us that. They said it was to save ammunition."

"It doesn't save gas," I said.

I was annoyed at Tom: he shouldn't have said that.

"Then there's officers walking along the road," he went on, "supervising it   17
all. They stick their hands in their pockets and smoke cigarettes. You think they
finish off the guys? Hell no. They let them scream. Sometimes for an hour. The
Moroccan said he damned near puked the first time."

"I don't believe they'll do that here," I said. "Unless they're really short on
ammunition."

Day was coming in through four airholes and a round opening, they had   18
made in the ceiling on the left, and you could see the sky through it. Through
this hole, usually closed by a trap, they unloaded coal into the cellar. Just below
the hole there was a big pile of coal dust; it had been used to heat the hospital
but since the beginning of the war the patients were evacuated and the coal
stayed there, unused; sometimes it even got rained on because they had forgotten
to close the trap.

Tom began to shiver. "Good Jesus Christ I'm cold," he said. "Here it goes   19
again."

He got up and began to do exercises. At each movement his shirt opened   20
on his chest, white and hairy. He lay on his back, raised his legs in the air and
bicycled. I saw his great rump trembling. Tom was husky but he had too much
fat. I thought how rifle bullets or the sharp points of bayonets would soon be
sunk into this mass of tender flesh as in a lump of butter. It wouldn't have
made me feel like that if he'd been thin.

I wasn't exactly cold, but I couldn't feel my arms and shoulders any more.   21
Sometimes I had the impression I was missing something and began to look
around for my coat and then suddenly remembered they hadn't given me a
coat. It was rather uncomfortable. They took our clothes and gave them to
their soldiers leaving us only our shirts—and those canvas pants that hospital
patients wear in the middle of summer. After a while Tom got up and sat next
to me, breathing heavily.

"Warmer?"

"Good Christ, no. But I'm out of wind."

Around eight o'clock in the evening a major came in with two *falangistas*.   22
He had a sheet of paper in his hand. He asked the guard, "What are the names
of those three?"

"Steinbock, Ibbieta and Mirbal," the guard said.   23

The major put on his eyeglasses and scanned the list: "Steinbock . . . Steinbock . . . Oh yes . . . You are sentenced to death. You will be shot tomorrow
morning." He went on looking. "The other two as well."

"That's not possible," Juan said. "Not me."   24

The major looked at him amazed. "What's your name?"

"Juan Mirbal," he said.

"Well, your name is there," said the major. "You're sentenced."   25

"I didn't do anything," Juan said.

The major shrugged his shoulders and turned to Tom and me.   26

"You're Basque?"

"Nobody is Basque."

He looked annoyed. "They told me there were three Basques. I'm not going   27
to waste my time running after them. Then naturally you don't want a priest?"

We didn't even answer.

He said, "A Belgian doctor is coming shortly. He is authorized to spend the   28
night with you." He made a military salute and left.

"What did I tell you," Tom said. "We get it."

"Yes," I said, "it's a rotten deal for the kid."

I said that to be decent but I didn't like the kid. He face was too thin and   29
fear and suffering had disfigured it, twisting all his features. Three days before
he was a smart sort of kid, not too bad; but now he looked like an old fairy
and I thought how he'd never be young again, even if they were to let him go.
It wouldn't have been too hard to have a little pity for him but pity disgusts
me, or rather it horrifies me. He hadn't said anything more but he had turned

grey; his face and hands were both grey. He sat down again and looked at the ground with round eyes. Tom was goodhearted, he wanted to take his arm, but the kid tore himself away violently and made a face.

"Let him alone," I said in a low voice, "you can see he's going to blubber."   30

Tom obeyed regretfully; he would have liked to comfort the kid, it would   31
have passed his time and he wouldn't have been tempted to think about himself. But it annoyed me: I'd never thought about death because I never had any reason to, but now the reason was here and there was nothing to do but think about it.

Tom began to talk. "So you think you've knocked guys off, do you?" he asked   32
me. I didn't answer. He began explaining to me that he had knocked off six since the beginning of August; he didn't realize the situation and I could tell he didn't *want* to realize it. I hadn't quite realized it myself, I wondered if it hurt much, I thought of bullets, I imagined their burning hail through my body. All that was beside the real question; but I was calm: we had all night to understand. After a while Tom stopped talking and I watched him out of the corner of my eye; I saw he too had turned grey and he looked rotten; I told myself "Now it starts." It was almost dark, a dim glow filtered through the airholes and the pile of coal and made a big stain beneath the spot of sky; I could already see a star through the hole in the ceiling: the night would be pure and icy.

The door opened and two guards came in, followed by a blonde man in a   33
tan uniform. He saluted us. "I am the doctor," he said. "I have authorization to help you in these trying hours."

He had an agreeable and distinguished voice. I said, "What do you want   34
here?"

"I am at your disposal. I shall do all I can to make your last moments less difficult."

"What did you come here for? There are others, the hospital's full of them."

"I was sent here," he answered with a vague look. "Ah! Would you like to   35
smoke?" he added hurriedly, "I have cigarettes and even cigars."

He offered us English cigarettes and *puros,* but we refused. I looked him in   36
the eyes and he seemed irritated. I said to him, "You aren't here on an errand of mercy. Besides, I know you. I saw you with the fascists in the barracks yard the day I was arrested."

I was going to continue, but something surprising suddenly happened to   37
me; the presence of this doctor no longer interested me. Generally when I'm on somebody I don't let go. But the desire to talk left me completely; I shrugged and turned my eyes away. A little later I raised my head; he was watching me curiously. The guards were sitting on a mat. Pedro, the tall thin one, was twiddling his thumbs, the other shook his head from time to time to keep from falling asleep.

"Do you want a light?" Pedro suddenly asked the doctor. The other nodded   38

"Yes": I think he was about as smart as a log, but he surely wasn't bad. Looking in his cold blue eyes it seemed to me that his only sin was lack of imagination. Pedro went out and came back with an oil lamp which he set on the corner of the bench. It gave a bad light but it was better than nothing: they had left us in the dark the night before. For a long time I watched the circle of light the lamp made on the ceiling. I was fascinated. Then suddenly I woke up, the circle of light disappeared and I felt myself crushed under an enormous weight. It was not the thought of death, or fear; it was nameless. My cheeks burned and my head ached.

I shook myself and looked at my two friends. Tom had hidden his face in   39
his hands. I could only see the fat white nape of his neck. Little Juan was the worst, his mouth was open and his nostrils trembled. The doctor went to him and put his hand on his shoulder to comfort him: but his eyes stayed cold. Then I saw the Belgian's hand drop stealthily along Juan's arm, down to the wrist. Juan paid no attention. The Belgian took his wrist between three fingers, distractedly, the same time drawing back a little and turning his back to me. But I leaned backward and saw him take a watch from his pocket and look at it for a moment, never letting go of the wrist. After a minute he let the hand fall inert and went and leaned his back against the wall, then, as if he suddenly remembered something very important which had to be jotted down on the spot, he took a notebook from his pocket and wrote a few lines. "Bastard," I thought angrily, "let him come and take my pulse. I'll shove my fist in his rotten face."

He didn't come but I felt him watching me. I raised my head and returned   40
his look. Impersonally, he said to me, "Doesn't it seem cold to you here?" He looked cold, he was blue.

"I'm not cold," I told him.

He never took his hard eyes off me. Suddenly I understood and my hands   41
went to my face: I was drenched in sweat. In this cellar, in the midst of winter, in the midst of drafts, I was sweating. I ran my hands through my hair, gummed together with perspiration; at the same time I saw my shirt was damp and sticking to my skin: I had been dripping for an hour and hadn't felt it. But that swine of a Belgian hadn't missed a thing; he had seen the drops rolling down my cheeks and thought: this is the manifestation of an almost pathological state of terror; and he had felt normal and proud of being alive because he was cold. I wanted to stand up and smash his face but no sooner had I made the slightest gesture than my rage and shame were wiped out; I fell back on the bench with indifference.

I satisfied myself by rubbing my neck with my handkerchief because now I   42
felt the sweat dropping from my hair onto my neck and it was unpleasant. I soon gave up rubbing, it was useless; my handkerchief was already soaked and I was still sweating. My buttocks were sweating too and my damp trousers were glued to the bench.

Suddenly Juan spoke. "You're a doctor?"   43

"Yes," the Belgian said.

"Does it hurt . . . very long?"

"Huh? When . . . ? Oh, no," the Belgian said paternally. "Not at all. It's over   44
quickly." He acted as though he were calming a cash customer.

"But I . . . they told me . . . sometimes they have to fire twice."

"Sometimes," the Belgian said, nodding. "It may happen that the first volley
reaches no vital organs."

"Then they have to reload their rifles and aim all over again?" He thought   45
for a moment and then added hoarsely, "That takes time!"

He had a terrible fear of suffering, it was all he thought about: it was his   46
age. I never thought much about it and it wasn't fear of suffering that made
me sweat.

I got up and walked to the pile of coal dust. Tom jumped up and threw me   47
a hateful look: I had annoyed him because my shoes squeaked. I wondered if
my face looked as frightened as his: I saw he was sweating too. The sky was
superb, no light filtered into the dark corner and I had only to raise my head
to see the Big Dipper. But it wasn't like it had been: the night before I could
see a great piece of sky from my monastery cell and each hour of the day
brought me a different memory. Morning, when the sky was a hard, light blue,
I thought of beaches on the Atlantic; at noon I saw the sun and I remembered
a bar in Seville where I drank *manzanilla* and ate olives and anchovies; afternoons
I was in the shade and I thought of the deep shadow which spreads over half
a bull-ring leaving the other half shimmering in sunlight; it was really hard to
see the whole world reflected in the sky like that. But now I could watch the
sky as much as I pleased, it no longer evoked anything in me. I liked that better.
I came back and sat near Tom. A long moment passed.

Tom began speaking in a low voice. He had to talk, without that he wouldn't   48
have been able to recognize himself in his own mind. I thought he was talking
to me but he wasn't looking at me. He was undoubtedly afraid to see me as I
was, grey and sweating: we were alike and worse than mirrors of each other.
He watched the Belgian, the living.

"Do you understand?" he said. "I don't understand."   49

I began to speak in a low voice too. I watched the Belgian. "Why? What's
the matter?"

"Something is going to happen to us that I can't understand."

There was a strange smell about Tom. It seemed to me I was more sensitive   50
than usual to odors. I grinned. "You'll understand in a while."

"It isn't clear," he said obstinately. "I want to be brave but first I have to   51
know . . . Listen, they're going to take us into the courtyard. Good. They're
going to stand up in front of us. How many?"

"I don't know. Five or eight. Not more."

"All right. There'll be eight. Someone'll holler 'aim!' and I'll see eight rifles   52 looking at me. I'll think how I'd like to get inside the wall, I'll push against it with my back . . . with every ounce of strength I have, but the wall will stay, like in a nightmare. I can imagine all that. If you only knew how well I can imagine it."

"All right, all right!" I said, "I can imagine it too."

"It must hurt like hell. You know, they aim at the eyes and the mouth to   53
disfigure you," he added mechanically. "I can feel the wounds already; I've had pains in my head and in my neck for the past hour. Not real pains. Worse. This is what I'm going to feel tomorrow morning. And then what?"

I well understood what he meant but I didn't want to act as if I did. I had   54
pains too, pains in my body like a crowd of tiny scars. I couldn't get used to it. But I was like him, I attached no importance to it. "After," I said, "you'll be pushing up daisies."

He began to talk to himself: he never stopped watching the Belgian. The   55
Belgian didn't seem to be listening. I knew what he had come to do; he wasn't interested in what we thought; he came to watch our bodies, bodies dying in agony while yet alive.

"It's like a nightmare," Tom was saying. "You want to think something, you   56
always have the impression that it's all right, that you're going to understand and then it slips, it escapes you and fades away. I tell myself there will be nothing afterwards. But I don't understand what it means. Sometimes I almost can . . . and then it fades away and I start thinking about the pains again, bullets, explosions. I'm a materialist, I swear it to you; I'm not going crazy. But something's the matter. I see my corpse; that's not hard but *I'm* the one who sees it, with *my* eyes. I've got to think . . . think that I won't see anything anymore and the world will go on for the others. We aren't made to think that, Pablo. Believe me: I've already stayed up a whole night waiting for something. But this isn't the same: this will creep up behind us, Pablo, and we won't be able to prepare for it."

"Shut up," I said, "Do you want me to call a priest?"   57

He didn't answer. I had already noticed he had the tendency to act like a   58
prophet and call me Pablo, speaking in a toneless voice. I didn't like that: but it seems all the Irish are that way. I had the vague impression he smelled of urine. Fundamentally, I hadn't much sympathy for Tom and I didn't see why, under the pretext of dying together, I should have any more. It would have been different with some others. With Ramon Gris, for example. But I felt alone between Tom and Juan. I liked that better, anyhow: with Ramon I might have been more deeply moved. But I was terribly hard just then and I wanted to stay hard.

He kept on chewing his words, with something like distraction. He certainly   59
talked to keep himself from thinking. He smelled of urine like an old prostate case. Naturally, I agreed with him, I could have said everything he said: it isn't

natural to die. And since I was going to die, nothing seemed natural to me, not this pile of coal dust, or the bench, or Pedro's ugly face. Only it didn't please me to think the same things as Tom. And I knew that, all through the night, every five minutes, we would keep on thinking things at the same time. I looked at him sideways and for the first time he seemed strange to me: he wore death on his face. My pride was wounded: for the past 24 hours I had lived next to Tom, I had listened to him, I had spoken to him and I knew we had nothing in common. And now we looked as much alike as twin brothers, simply because we were going to die together. Tom took my hand without looking at me.

"Pablo, I wonder . . . I wonder if it's really true that everything ends."   60

I took my hand away and said, "Look between your feet, you pig."

There was a big puddle between his feet and drops fell from his pants-leg.   61

"What is it," he asked, frightened.

"You're pissing in your pants," I told him.

"It isn't true," he said furiously. "I'm not pissing. I don't feel anything."   62

The Belgian approached us. He asked with false solicitude, "Do you feel ill?"   63

Tom did not answer. The Belgian looked at the puddle and said nothing.   64

"I don't know what it is," Tom said ferociously. "But I'm not afraid. I swear I'm not afraid."

The Belgian did not answer. Tom got up and went to piss in a corner. He   65
came back buttoning his fly, and sat down without a word. The Belgian was taking notes.

All three of us watched him because he was alive. He had the motions of a   66
living human being, the cares of a living human being; he shivered in the cellar the way the living are supposed to shiver; he had an obedient, well-fed body. The rest of us hardly felt ours—not in the same way anyhow. I wanted to feel my pants between my legs but I didn't dare; I watched the Belgian, balancing on his legs, master of his muscles, someone who could think about tomorrow. There we were, three bloodless shadows; we watched him and we sucked his life like vampires.

Finally he went over to little Juan. Did he want to feel his neck for some   67
professional motive or was he obeying an impulse of charity? If he was acting by charity it was the only time during the whole night.

He caressed Juan's head and neck. The kid let himself be handled, his eyes   68
never leaving him, then suddenly, he seized the hand and looked at it strangely. He held the Belgian's hand between his own two hands and there was nothing pleasant about them, two grey pincers gripping this fat and reddish hand. I suspected what was going to happen and Tom must have suspected it too: but the Belgian didn't see a thing, he smiled paternally. After a moment the kid brought the fat red hand to his mouth and tried to bite it. The Belgian pulled away quickly and stumbled back against the wall. For a second he looked at us with horror; he must have suddenly understood that we were not men like

him. I began to laugh and one of the guards jumped up. The other was asleep, his wide open eyes were blank.

I felt relaxed and over-excited at the same time. I didn't want to think any more about what would happen at dawn, at death. It made no sense. I only found words or emptiness. But as soon as I tried to think of anything else I saw rifle barrels pointing at me. Perhaps I lived through my execution twenty times; once I even thought it was for good: I must have slept a minute. They were dragging me to the wall and I was struggling; I was asking for mercy. I woke up with a start and looked at the Belgian: I was afraid I might have cried out in my sleep. But he was stroking his moustache, he hadn't noticed anything. If I had wanted to, I think I could have slept a while; I had been awake for 48 hours. I was at the end of my rope. But I didn't want to lose two hours of life: they would come to wake me up at dawn, I would follow them, stupefied with sleep and I would have croaked without so much as an "Oof!"; I didn't want that, I didn't want to die like an animal, I wanted to understand. Then I was afraid of having nightmares. I got up, walked back and forth, and, to change my ideas, I began to think about my past life. A crowd of memories came back to me pell-mell. There were good and bad ones—or at least I called them that *before*. There were faces and incidents. I saw the face of a little *novillero* who was gored in Valencia during the *Feria,* the face of one of my uncles, the face of Ramon Gris. I remembered my whole life: how I was out of work for three months in 1926, how I almost starved to death. I remembered a night I spent on a bench in Grenada: I hadn't eaten for three days. I was angry, I didn't want to die. That made me smile. How madly I ran after happiness, after women, after liberty. Why? I wanted to free Spain, I admired Pi y Margall, I joined the anarchist movement, I spoke in public meetings: I took everything as seriously as if I were immortal.

At that moment I felt that I had my whole life in front of me and I thought, "It's a damned lie." It was worth nothing because it was finished. I wondered how I'd been able to walk, to laugh with the girls: I wouldn't have moved so much as my little finger if I had only imagined I would die like this. My life was in front of me, shut, closed, like a bag and yet everything inside of it was unfinished. For an instant I tried to judge it. I wanted to tell myself, this is a beautiful life. But I couldn't pass judgment on it; it was only a sketch; I had spent my time counterfeiting eternity, I had understood nothing. I missed nothing: there were so many things I could have missed, the taste of *manzanilla* or the baths I took in summer in a little creek near Cadiz; but death had disenchanted everything.

The Belgian suddenly had a bright idea. "My friends," he told us, "I will undertake—if the military administration will allow it—to send a message for you, a souvenir to those who love you . . ."

Tom mumbled, "I don't have anybody."

69

70

71

I said nothing. Tom waited an instant then looked at me with curiosity. "You   72
don't have anything to say to Concha?"

"No."

I hated this tender complicity: it was my own fault, I had talked about   73
Concha the night before, I should have controlled myself. I was with her for a
year. Last night I would have given an arm to see her again for five minutes.
That was why I talked about her, it was stronger than I was. Now I had no
more desire to see her, I had nothing more to say to her. I would not even
have wanted to hold her in my arms: my body filled me with horror because
it was grey and sweating—and I wasn't sure that her body didn't fill me with
horror. Concha would cry when she found out I was dead, she would have no
taste for life for months afterward. But I was still the one who was going to
die. I thought of her soft, beautiful eyes. When she looked at me something
passed from her to me. But I knew it was over: if she looked at me *now* the
look would stay in her eyes, it wouldn't reach me. I was alone.

Tom was alone too but not in the same way. Sitting cross-legged, he had   74
begun to stare at the bench with a sort of smile, he looked amazed. He put
out his hand and touched the wood cautiously as if he were afraid of breaking
something, then drew back his hand quickly and shuddered. If I had been Tom
I wouldn't have amused myself by touching the bench; this was some more
Irish nonsense, but I too found that objects had a funny look: they were more
obliterated, less dense than usual. It was enough for me to look at the bench,
the lamp, the pile of coal dust, to feel that I was going to die. Naturally I
couldn't think clearly about my death but I saw it everywhere, on things, in
the way things fell back and kept their distance, discreetly, as people who speak
quietly at the bedside of a dying man. It was *his* death which Tom had just
touched on the bench.

In the state I was in, if someone had come and told me I could go home   75
quietly, that they would leave me my life whole, it would have left me cold:
several hours or several years of waiting is all the same when you have lost the
illusion of being eternal. I clung to nothing, in a way I was calm. But it was a
horrible calm—because of my body; my body, I saw with its eyes, I heard with
its ears, but it was no longer me; it sweated and trembled by itself and I didn't
recognize it any more. I had to touch it and look at it to find out what was
happening, as if it were the body of someone else. At times I could still feel it,
I felt sinkings, and fallings, as when you're in a plane taking a nosedive, or I
felt my heart beating. But that didn't reassure me. Everything that came from
my body was all cockeyed. Most of the time it was quiet and I felt no more
than a sort of weight, a filthy presence against me; I had the impression of
being tied to an enormous vermin. Once I felt my pants and I felt they were
damp; I didn't know whether it was sweat or urine, but I went to piss on the
coal pile as a precaution.

The Belgian took out his watch, looked at it. He said, "It is three-thirty." 76

Bastard! He must have done it on purpose. Tom jumped; we hadn't noticed 77 time was running out; night surrounded us like a shapeless, somber mass, I couldn't even remember that it had begun.

Little Juan began to cry. He wrung his hands, pleaded, "I don't want to die. 78 I don't want to die."

He ran across the whole cellar waving his arms in the air then fell sobbing 79 on one of the mats. Tom watched him with mournful eyes, without the slightest desire to console him. Because it wasn't worth the trouble: the kid made more noise than we did, but he was less touched: he was like a sick man who defends himself against his illness by fever. It's much more serious when there isn't any fever.

He wept: I could clearly see he was pitying himself; he wasn't thinking about 80 death. For one second, one single second, I wanted to weep myself, to weep with pity for myself. But the opposite happened: I glanced at the kid, I saw his thin sobbing shoulders and I felt inhuman: I could pity neither the others nor myself. I said to myself, "I want to die cleanly."

Tom had gotten up, he placed himself just under the round opening and 81 began to watch for daylight. I was determined to die cleanly and I only thought of that. But ever since the doctor told us the time, I felt time flying, flowing away drop by drop.

It was still dark when I heard Tom's voice: "Do you hear them?" 82

Men were marching in the courtyard.

"Yes."

"What the hell are they doing? They can't shoot in the dark."

After a while we heard no more. I said to Tom, "It's day."

Pedro got up, yawning, and came to blow out the lamp. He said to his 83 buddy, "Cold as hell."

The cellar was all grey. We heard shots in the distance. 84

"It's starting," I told Tom. "They must do it in the court in the rear."

Tom asked the doctor for a cigarette. I didn't want one; I didn't want 85 cigarettes or alcohol. From that moment on they didn't stop firing.

"Do you realize what's happening," Tom said.

He wanted to add something but kept quiet, watching the door. The door 86 opened and a lieutenant came in with four soldiers. Tom dropped his cigarette.

"Steinbock?"

Tom didn't answer. Pedro pointed him out. 87

"Juan Mirbal?"

"On the mat."

"Get up," the lieutenant said.

Juan did not move. Two soldiers took him under the arms and set him on 88 his feet. But he fell as soon as they released him.

The soldiers hesitated.

"He's not the first sick one," said the lieutenant. "You two carry him; they'll   89
fix it up down there."

He turned to Tom. "Let's go."

Tom went out between two soldiers. Two others followed, carrying the kid   90
by the armpits. He hadn't fainted; his eyes were wide open and tears ran down
his cheeks. When I wanted to go out the lieutenant stopped me.

"You Ibbieta?"

"Yes."

"You wait here; they'll come for you later."

They left. The Belgian and the two jailers left too, I was alone. I did not   91
understand what was happening to me but I would have liked it better if they
had gotten it over with right away. I heard shots at almost regular intervals; I
shook with each one of them. I wanted to scream and tear out my hair. But I
gritted my teeth and pushed my hands in my pockets because I wanted to stay
clean.

After an hour they came to get me and led me to the first floor, to a small   92
room that smelt of cigars and where the heat was stifling. There were two
officers sitting smoking in the armchairs, papers on their knees.

"You're Ibbieta?"

"Yes."

"Where is Ramon Gris?"

"I don't know."

The one questioning me was short and fat. His eyes were hard behind his   93
glasses. He said to me, "Come here."

I went to him. He got up and took my arms, staring at me with a look that   94
should have pushed me into the earth. At the same time he pinched my biceps
with all his might. It wasn't to hurt me, it was only a game: he wanted to
dominate me. He also thought he had to blow his stinking breath square in my
face. We stayed for a moment like that, and I almost felt like laughing. It takes
a lot to intimidate a man who is going to die; it didn't work. He pushed me
back violently and sat down again. He said, "It's his life against yours. You can
have yours if you tell us where he is."

These men dolled up with their riding crops and boots were still going to   95
die. A little later than I, but not too much. They busied themselves looking for
names in their crumpled papers, they ran after other men to imprison or
suppress them; they had opinions on the future of Spain and on other subjects.
Their little activities seemed shocking and burlesqued to me; I couldn't put
myself in their place, I thought they were insane. The little man was still looking
at me, whipping his boots with the riding crop. All his gestures were calculated
to give him the look of a live and ferocious beast.

"So? You understand?"   96

"I don't know where Gris is," I answered. "I thought he was in Madrid."   97

The other officer raised his pale hand indolently. This indolence was also   98 calculated. I saw through all their little schemes and I was stupefied to find there were men who amused themselves that way.

"You have a quarter of an hour to think it over," he said slowly. "Take him   99
to the laundry, bring him back in fifteen minutes. If he still refuses he will be executed on the spot."

They knew what they were doing: I had passed the night in waiting; then   100
they had made me wait an hour in the cellar while they shot Tom and Juan and now they were locking me up in the laundry; they must have prepared their game the night before. They told themselves that nerves eventually wear out and they hoped to get me that way.

They were badly mistaken. In the laundry I sat on a stool because I felt very   101
weak and I began to think. But not about their proposition. Of course I knew where Gris was; he was hiding with his cousins, four kilometers from the city. I also knew that I would not reveal his hiding place unless they tortured me (but they didn't seem to be thinking about that). All that was perfectly regulated, definite and in no way interested me. Only I would have liked to understand the reasons for my conduct. I would rather die than give up Gris. Why? I didn't like Ramon Gris any more. My friendship for him had died a little while before dawn at the same time as my love for Concha, at the same time as my desire to live. Undoubtedly I thought highly of him: he was tough. But it was not for this reason that I consented to die in his place; his life had no more value than mine; no life had value. They were going to slap a man up against a wall and shoot at him till he died, whether it was I or Gris or somebody else made no difference. I knew he was more useful than I to the cause of Spain but I thought to hell with Spain and anarchy; nothing was important. Yet I was there, I could save my skin and give up Gris and I refused to do it. I found that somehow comic; it was obstinacy. I thought, "I must be stubborn!" And a droll sort of gaiety spread over me.

They came for me and brought me back to the two officers. A rat ran out   102
from under my feet and that amused me. I turned to one of the *falangistas* and said, "Did you see the rat?"

He didn't answer. He was very sober, he took himself seriously. I wanted to   103
laugh but I held myself back because I was afraid that once I got started I wouldn't be able to stop. The *falangista* had a moustache. I said to him again, "You ought to shave off your moustache, idiot." I thought it funny that he would let the hairs of his living being invade his face. He kicked me without great conviction and I kept quiet.

"Well," said the fat officer, "have you thought about it?"   104

I looked at them with curiosity, as insects of a very rare species. I told them,   105
"I know where he is. He is hidden in the cemetery. In a vault or in the gravediggers' shack."

It was a farce. I wanted to see them stand up, buckle their belts and give   106
orders busily.

They jumped to their feet. "Let's go. Molés, go get fifteen men from Lieu-   107
tenant Lopez. You," the fat man said, "I'll let you off if you're telling the truth,
but it'll cost you plenty if you're making monkeys out of us."

They left in a great clatter and I waited peacefully under the guard of   108
falangistas. From time to time I smiled, thinking about the spectacle they would
make. I felt stunned and malicious. I imagined them lifting up tombstones,
opening the doors of the vaults one by one. I represented this situation to
myself as if I had been someone else: this prisoner obstinately playing the hero,
these grim falangistas with their moustaches and their men in uniform running
among the graves; it was irresistibly funny. After half an hour the little fat man
came back alone. I thought he had come to give the orders to execute me. The
others must have stayed in the cemetery.

The officer looked at me. He didn't look at all sheepish. "Take him into the   109
big courtyard with the others," he said. "After the military operations a regular
court will decide what happens to him."

"Then they're not . . . not going to shoot me? . . ."

"Not now, anyway. What happens afterwards is none of my business."   110

I still didn't understand. I asked, "But why . . . ?"

He shrugged his shoulders without answering and the soldiers took me away.   111
In the big courtyard there were about a hundred prisoners, women, children
and a few old men. I began walking around the central grass-plot, I was
stupefied. At noon they let us eat in the mess hall. Two or three people
questioned me. I must have known them, but I didn't answer: I didn't even
know where I was.

Around evening they pushed about ten new prisoners into the court. I   112
recognized Garcia, the baker. He said, "What damned luck you have! I didn't
think I'd see you alive."

"They sentenced me to death," I said, "and then they changed their minds.   113
I don't know why."

"They arrested me at two o'clock," Garcia said.

"Why?" Garcia had nothing to do with politics.

"I don't know," he said. "They arrest everybody who doesn't think the way   114
they do." He lowered his voice. "They got Gris."

I began to tremble. "When?"

"This morning. He messed it up. He left his cousin's on Tuesday because   115
they had an argument. There were plenty of people to hide him but he didn't
want to owe anything to anybody. He said, 'I'd go and hide in Ibbieta's place,
but they got him, so I'll go hide in the cemetery.'"

"In the cemetery?"

"Yes. What a fool. Of course they went by there this morning, that was sure   116
to happen. They found him in the gravediggers' shack. He shot at them and
they got him."

"In the cemetery!"

Everything began to spin and I found myself sitting on the ground: I laughed   117
so hard I cried.

Questions for Critical Thinking

1. How do you explain the title of this story? What does the wall symbolize?

2. The narrator says in paragraph 52 that "it wasn't fear of suffering that made me sweat." What, then?

3. Aside from being under a common sentence of death, what existential quality do the prisoners all share and suffer from?

4. What ironic common quality does the author share with his captors, and how does his recognition of it contribute to his development as a character?

5. How do you think the reactions of a captive who believes in God might have differed from the narrator's under similar circumstances of arbitrary imprisonment and death?

6. Juan, the innocent boy, and Tom, the guilty assassin, are both executed. What point do you infer from this indiscriminate killing?

7. Why is the narrator so convulsed with humor at the denouement of the story?

8. Do you regard the narrator as a hero or a traitor? Why?

Writing Assignment

Although the narrator does not believe in God or in the purposefulness of life, he still seems to live by an internalized moral code. Write an essay in which you infer and interpret the basic principles of this code from his narration.

Writing Advice

Writing this essay will require you to read between the lines, since well-constructed narrators rarely, if ever, characterize their own actions. It is left, instead, for the reader to deduce motive and underlying cause from what the narrator does, says, or thinks. Consider, for example, this passage:

> . . . I would rather die than give up Gris. Why? I didn't like Ramon Gris anymore. My friendship for him had died a little while before dawn at the same time as my love for Concha, at the same time as my desire to live. Undoubtedly I thought highly of him: he was tough. But it was not for this reason that I consented to die in his place; his life had no more value than mine; no life had value. They were going to slap a man up against a wall and shoot at him till he died, whether it was I or Ramon Gris or some-body else made no difference. I knew he was more useful to the cause of Spain but I thought to hell with Spain and anarchy; nothing was important. Yet I was there, I could save my own skin and give up Gris and I refused to do it.

Why? The narrator himself struggles to fathom his reasons. But the passage is an example of the narrator's internal moral code whose outline we can dimly glimpse in this and other incidents throughout the story. Putting that code into words is what you must do to write this essay.

The specific details you must draw on to prove your interpretation will come, naturally enough, from the story itself. And they should be as plentiful as necessary to make your interpretation convincing. If you think that the narrator lives by a code of principled compassion for his fellow beings, you should prove that by citing incidents and scenes that reveal this side of him. Finally, remember that while there may be no absolutely right or wrong answer, some interpretations will simply be more provable than others. It would be difficult, for example, to write a convincing essay demonstrating that the narrator is really a closet Christian who acts out of a benevolent belief in the Golden Rule. There simply is no evidence in the story to support such a reading. You are better off following another line of interpretation, for which evidence can be found.

Alternate Writing Assignment

Write an essay interpreting the prisoner's world of arbitrary captivity and death as the equivalent of the purposeless universe in which the atheist lives.

LITERATURE

THREES

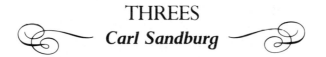 *Carl Sandburg*

Carl Sandburg (1878–1967), American poet and biographer, was born in Illinois, the son of poor Swedish immigrants, and educated at Knox College. Sandburg quit school at 13 to work as a laborer, finishing his education after serving in the Spanish-American War. Moving to Milwaukee and then to Chicago, he became a journalist and eventually an editorial writer for the *Chicago Daily News*. His poetry began attracting attention after its appearance in the magazine *Poetry*. Among his many publications are *Chicago Poems* (1918), *Smoke and Steel* (1920), *Complete Poems* (1950; Pulitzer Prize), and his first novel, *Remembrance Rock* (1948), published when Sandburg was 70. His most ambitious undertaking was a six-volume biography of Abraham Lincoln (1926–29; Pulitzer Prize). Sandburg's poetry was strongly influenced by Walt Whitman and is characterized by simple language, unconventional meter and diction, and a focus on commonplace subjects.

Reading Advice

For what principles are people willing to sacrifice life and limb, and how has the expression of them changed over the generations? That is the question at the heart of this poem. Sandburg, writing with characteristic crispness and vigor, soars over revolutions and wars separated by years and generations, and unearths a surprising pattern in the words that set them ablaze.

> I was a boy when I heard three red words
> a thousand Frenchmen died in the streets
> for: Liberty, Equality, Fraternity—I asked   1
> why men die for words.
>
> I was older; men with mustaches, sideburns,
> lilacs, told me the high golden words are:
> Mother, Home, and Heaven—other older men with
> face decorations said: God, Duty, Immortality   2
> —they sang these threes slow from deep lungs.
>
> Years ticked off their say-so on the great clocks
> of doom and damnation, soup and nuts: meteors flashed
> their say-so: and out of great Russia came three
> dusky syllables workmen took guns and went out to die 3
> for: Bread, Peace, Land.
>
> And I met a marine of the U.S.A., a leatherneck with
> a girl on his knee for a memory in ports circling the
> earth and he said: Tell me how to say three things
> and I always get by—gimme a plate of ham and eggs—   4
> how much?—and, do you love me, kid?

Questions for Critical Thinking

1. The words men are willing to die for are arranged in this poem in a progressive pattern. What is this pattern, and what does it suggest?

2. What concrete and specific equivalents can you give for the word *freedom?*

3. For what word or words would you be prepared to risk your life or freedom?

4. In contrast to the imagery used in prose, the imagery of poetry is often characterized by an economy of words. What example can you point to in this poem as an example of this economy?

5. Vernacular speech is seldom used to express the basic ideals and principles of a revolution. What effect do you think clothing a revolution's ideals and principles in formal language is likely to have on their believability by subsequent generations?

Writing Assignment

Write an analysis of this poem.

Writing Advice

When you analyze a poem you say what you think it means, support your reading with quotations from the work itself, and comment on the techniques of its poetic form. But an analysis should not stop at a simple paraphrase or restatement of meaning. It should also add your own considered opinion to the interpretation. For example, you might comment on the historical characterizations of eras and revolutions implicitly sketched in the poem. You might even venture to contrast the words of one era with another.

Essentially, what you are trying to do is to sum up the meaning of the poem in a theme—a brief statement condensing its principal emphasis. The author has said something in the somewhat stylized language of poetry, and you are trying to unravel and restate its meaning in your own words. Once you have declared the theme of a poem, you then prove it with a discussion that cites passages and words from the work itself.

Alternate Writing Assignment

Write an essay on the three words you think exert the greatest mass political appeal to people today. Explain why you think these words are so popular.

LITERATURE

THE UNKNOWN CITIZEN
W. H. Auden

W. H. Auden (1907–1973), Anglo-American poet, born in York, England, and educated at Oxford, is ranked among the foremost poets of the twentieth century. Auden served as a stretcher-bearer during the Spanish Civil War and lived in Germany during the early days of Nazism. Versatile and wide-ranging in his work, Auden regarded himself primarily as a Christian poet. His publications include *Spain* (1937), *New Year Letter* (1941), *For the Time Being, a Christian Oratorio* (1945), and *The Age of Anxiety* (1947; Pulitzer Prize). Auden became a naturalized United States citizen in 1946 and was a professor of poetry at Oxford from 1956 to 1961. After residing in various countries, including Italy and Austria, he returned to England in 1971.

Reading Advice

Poetry is generally a more abrupt form than fiction. Usually it plunges straightaway into its subject, after cursorily setting the opening context in its title. In this case, the title tells us that the poem is an inscription on a monument dedicated to an unknown citizen. We gather that the speaker of the poem—the person from whose perspective it is written and who "speaks" the lines—is the state. Once we know all that, the rest follows naturally.

"The Unknown Citizen" is one of Auden's most widely anthologized poems. It enjoyed enormous popularity during the 1960s and the early 1970s when the turmoil of Vietnam had raised the perplexing question about the duty of citizens to resist participation in what they regarded as an unjust war. The poem relates the life history of a docile soul who never disturbed the peace, opposed the government, or raised his voice in dissent, and ends by asking whether such a one could be considered either free or happy.

(To JS/07/M/378 This Marble Monument Is Erected by the State)

He was found by the Bureau of Statistics to be
One against whom there was no official complaint,
And all the reports on his conduct agree
That, in the modern sense of an old-fashioned word, he was a saint,
For in everything he did he served the Greater Community.
Except for the War till the day he retired
He worked in a factory and never got fired,
But satisfied his employers, Fudge Motors Inc.
Yet he wasn't a scab or odd in his views,
For his Union reports that he paid his dues,
(Our report on his Union shows it was sound)
And our Social Psychology workers found
That he was popular with his mates and liked a drink.
The Press are convinced that he bought a paper every day
And that his reactions to advertisements were normal in every way.
Policies taken out in his name prove that he was fully insured,
And his Health-card shows he was once in hospital but left it cured.
Both Producers Research and High-Grade Living declare

He was fully sensible to the advantages of the Instalment Plan
And had everything necessary to the Modern Man,
A phonograph, a radio, a car and a frigidaire.
Our researchers into Public Opinion are content
That he held the proper opinions for the time of year;
When there was peace, he was for peace; when there was war, he went.
He was married and added five children to the population,
Which our Eugenist says was the right number for a parent of his generation,
And our teachers report that he never interfered with their education.
Was he free? Was he happy? The question is absurd:
Had anything been wrong, we should certainly have heard.

Questions for Critical Thinking

1. What commonplace public monument does the title of this poem parody?

2. What implicit criticism does this poem make against the lifestyle of the unknown citizen? What is your opinion of this criticism?

3. What freedom can one be said to have if one never does anything contrary to the prevailing popular opinion?

4. How might the unknown citizen regard Thoreau and the lifestyle he advocates?

5. Was the unknown citizen free? Was he happy? What is your answer to these questions raised in the poem?

6. What contradictions do you see existing in a democracy between the individual's desires for conformity and the duties of good citizenship?

Writing Assignment

Write an essay on the price to be paid for, and/or the consolations to be found in, a life of conformity.

Writing Advice

To some extent, all of us conform to society's rules, regulations, and mores. We do so everyday, sometimes consciously, sometimes reflexively. When we drive our cars, we do not ask why we should stay on the right side of the road or why we should stop at red lights. We simply do these things. On the other hand, sometimes we conform, perhaps agaqinst our inner urges, by saying or doing the expected thing, even when we might like to say and do something quite different. You might think your friend's sister a complete fool, while pretending that she is utterly clever and witty. What price do we pay for curbing our inner wishes and urges and doing what we think is expected of us? What comfort do we gain? These are the questions posed by this assignment.

In supporting your opinions you will need examples of your conformities, what they have cost you, and what consolations you have gained by making them. You may use yourself and your own life as the prime source for examples, or you may focus on the life and experience of someone else—your father or mother, perhaps. Note that you may tackle the topic with any emphasis you like. You might, for example, focus on the consolations of comforming—being thought of as a "good sport." Or you may focus on what price you have paid for conforming—in your self-respect or your self-image. Or you may write about a combination of both.

Alternate Writing Assignments

1. Write an essay speculating on the criticism Thoreau might have leveled at the unknown citizen. Be as specific as you can.

2. The poem says that the unknown citizen never interfered in the education of his children. In an essay, explore the effect education is likely to have on the political opinions of citizens.

ART

LIBERTY LEADING THE PEOPLE

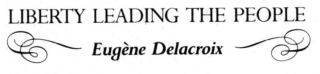

Eugène Delacroix

About the Artist

Eugene Delacroix (1798–1863), French painter, is regarded as the premier painter of the romantic movement in France. Believed by some to have been the illegitimate son of the French statesman and diplomat Talleyrand (1754–1838), Delacroix is noted for his lavish color and bold, exuberant forms. He was a meticulous craftsman and experimenter, leaving behind many notebooks filled with studies and sketches, as well as a journal he kept for 31 years of his life. An intimate of a number of the famous personages of his day, Delacroix painted portraits of several of his contemporaries. But it was from literature and mythology that he derived many of his subjects, rendering them in a style exploding with color, form, and movement. The best collection of his work is preserved at the Louvre in Paris.

About the Art

Liberty Leading the People is regarded as the finest representation of the revolutionary temper of nineteenth-century Europe. It pictures liberty as a majestic half-naked woman spurring a charge of motley revolutionaries, consisting of a Parisian urchin who waves two pistols, a top-hatted dandy armed with a musket, and a member of the proletariat who wields a cutlass. The horde, urged on by the regal woman who brandishes the tricolors of the republic and wears the cap of liberty, is trampling over dead and dying bodies of combatants, street-fighters as well as slain troops. Her exposed breasts suggest a mythic mother figure. A wounded revolutionary on the ground lifts himself up to peer hopefully at her while, in the background of Paris, through the smoke, looms the stately towers of Notre Dame. The work is considered representative of romanticism, an art movement that elevates and mythologizes its subjects, rendering them in a lofty, unrealistic style. In this painting, for example, battle is glorified in the idealized figure of the gallant woman while the grotesqueness and horror of the slaughter are muted.

ART

FORWARD

Jacob Lawrence

About the Artist

Jacob Lawrence (b. 1917) is a black American artist whose work emphasizes social themes usually expressed in angular shapes and forms. His major works include the *Harlem*, *Migration of the Negro*, and *Coast Guard* series. Lawrence, whose work hangs in such notable museums as the Whitney Museum of American Art, New York, has taught at major art schools in the United States.

About the Art

In 1967, Lawrence was approached by Simon and Schuster to do a children's book. Encouraged to choose his own subject matter, he decided on the story of Harriet Tubman, whose "dramatic tale of flight and fugitives" he thought would appeal to children. Titled *Harriet and the Promised Land* (1967), the book included 17 paintings (gouache on paper) illustrating the verse story. *Forward*, the painting included in this book, is typical of Lawrence's style for this series. The painting contains a woman carrying a baby and people in flight. Notice the deep perspective as well as the exaggerated anatomy of the people, especially their knotty hands and feet. Some of the reviewers of the Tubman series considered the paintings too disturbing for children, and one librarian even complained that Lawrence made Harriet look grotesque and ugly. In a letter, Lawrence made this reply:

If you had walked in the fields, stopping for short periods to be replenished by underground stations; if you couldn't feel secure until you reached the Canadian border, you, too, madam, would look grotesque and ugly. Isn't it sad that the oppressed often find themselves grotesque and ugly and find the oppressor refined and beautiful.

—quoted in Barbara Seese, "The Black Experience —Pictures Tell the Story," University of Washington Daily, *October 10, 1978.*

In 1973 the Brooklyn Museum and the Brooklyn Public Library awarded Lawrence the Books for Children Citation for his volume.

3—1   *Eugène Delacroix, Liberty Leading the People, 1830. Approx. 8′6″ x 10′8″. Louvre, Paris, Giraudon/Art Resource, N.Y.*

3–2 *Jacob Lawrence, Forward, 1967, 61 × 90.8 cm. North Carolina Museum of Art. Purchased with funds from the state of North Carolina.*

Chapter Writing Assignment

Read the assigned selections and study the paintings of the chapter. Then write an essay that supports or opposes one of the following assertions:

(a) Freedom is a concept that applies only to humans and not at all to animals.

(b) Humans do not enjoy real freedom but only the illusion of freedom.

(c) All political freedom emanates from the barrel of a gun.

(d) Belief in free will is a necessary precondition to the exercise of moral choice.

(e) Determinism is a more comforting philosophical creed than indeterminism.

(f) Determinism is a philosophical concept that robs humans of their sense of moral dignity.

Be sure to refer to specific pieces in this chapter as well as to the paintings and to cite any other writers not anthologized here whose opinions may bear on your argument.

CHAPTER FOUR

Why Do We Love?
LOVE

Human beings fall in love; geese mate for life. That, in a nutshell, is one of the stranger paradoxes about love.

Claimed as an emotion unique to our species, love is frequently passionate, inconstant, and seldom enduring, with unhappy side effects of revenge, spite, and hatred when it is thwarted. As a lover, you run a far greater statistical risk of being murdered by the beloved you have wronged than by the combination of urban stranger, gunman, terrorist, and robber whose random malice is such a staple of the news media. Yet the hymnist choirs that love is the truest, the purest of human virtues; and the poet and balladeer forever sing over its adventures, misalliances, mistakes, tragedies, and capricious outcomes.

We speak, of course, of love as it applies to a romantic beloved, for it is this love that has spawned a snarled web of conflicting myths and beliefs. Love of country, of father, mother, or sibling, love even of an idea or of work is graspable and easy to understand and likely to occasion no more than a speculative quibble. It is love of the romantic "other" that is ruinously tangled with myth, legend, lore, and notoriously imponderable. And it is about this kind of love that we are likely to find the balladeers and poets moaning, singing, and weeping in a good two-thirds of all literature that has ever been put to pen.

It is probably no exaggeration to say that virtually every reader of this book has experienced love of this kind at one time or another and has an opinion on that universal emotion. Yet for all its popularity and nearly universal appeal, love stubbornly remains a mystery and exists with as much murkiness in the popular understanding as in the laboratory. Poets, songwriters, and pundits tell us that love is blind; that it knows all; that it strikes like a thunderbolt; that it sneaks up like a thief; that it happens only once in a lifetime or twice before tea; and that it conquers and overcomes all in its path, tingles our spines, makes us feel fine, and lasts for eternity or until the end of time.

Indeed, love is as murky a chasm of legend and lore as any human emotion has ever dug, and it is no accident that while we do not fall in envy, ecstasy, adoration, piety, charity, or patriotism, we do fall—breathlessly and madly—in love. And then we are just as likely to defy Newtonian gravity and fall—wrathfully and vindictively— out of love, making love perhaps the only emotion in and out of which humans regularly and metaphorically plunge.

Yet who can deny the exhilaration and newness with which love tingles and gladdens the heart? When we are in love, we know it instantly. We hear symphonies in the wind, glimpse scribbles in the stars. But being felled by the thunderbolt of love does not necessarily help us understand or explain it. Poets, writers, artists, philosophers, and just plain folk have all taken a stab at saying what love is, and their combined imaginations and thoughts have produced as much mythology and legend as truth and clarity.

Something of this enigmatic contrariness is evident throughout the selections of this chapter. We begin with the philosophical contribution of Robert Solomon's "What Love Is," which argues that lovers live in a mutual "loveworld" from which the rest of the world is excluded. John Alan Lee tells us about his sociological research, which revealed that love is not monolithic or uniform but occurs in many variations. Joseph Wood Krutch turns a naturalist's eye on the subject and discovers in nature more bizarre customs and sheer wantonness than ever dreamt of by humans.

The history section provides us with three poignant stories of love: the first, "A Second Birth: George Eliot and George Henry Lewes," by Phyllis Rose, chronicles one of literature's most renowned love affairs, which transformed a dowdy middle-aged spinster into a great novelist; the second, "Dashiell Hammett," by Lillian Hellman, shows us another literary love affair through the eyes of a bereaved lover, herself a gifted playwright; the third, "Love in a Concentration Camp," by Viktor Frankl, paints a touching picture of love's power to sustain a heavy heart during moments of despair.

In the literature section, we are treated to Robert Browning's imaginative recreation of a monologue poor lovelorn Andrea del Sarto might have muttered to his faithless wife, Lucrezia, who cuckolds him while squandering his money on her lover. And we witness the tension and trouble brewing between Colonel Peregrine and his mousy but secretly passionate wife, Evie, in Somerset Maugham's "The Colonel's Lady."

The theme of the mystery and enigma of love is also reflected in the two paintings at the end of the chapter. *The Judgement of Paris*, by Peter Paul Rubens, depicts one of the most calamitous beauty contests of Greek mythology, which resulted in a passionate, adulterous love affair and eventually led to the Trojan war. René Magritte's *The Lovers*, which shows us two hooded figures groping intimately for one another, leaves us speculating on whether it is truly possible for lovers ever to know each other.

So what, after all, is love? It is, declaims the dictionary ponderously, "a deep and tender feeling of affection for or attachment or devotion to a person or persons." Whispers one poet who knows better, "Love is a circle that doth restless move / In the same sweet eternity of love."[1] Murmurs another, the greatest of all these visionary singers, "Love is a spirit all compact of fire."[2] A third cynically observes, "Love has pitched his mansion in / The place of excrement."[3] And all these sage souls, in telling us about love, strain as one for metaphor, while love flits beyond the reach of words to smite its ecstatic victims with an unseen, unmetaphoric club.

Why do we love? And why do we who make so much of love not mate forever as do lowly geese? Perhaps the answer is that we humans do not dance to the tugs of nature's string as do her more obedient subjects. Sometimes, we skip a step or twirl a pirouette entirely our own. And it is this unprompted twitch—which makes us both better and worse than nature with her dutiful flocks of monogamous geese—that we call love.

PHILOSOPHY

WHAT LOVE IS
 Robert C. Solomon

Robert C. Solomon (b. 1942) is an American philosopher and teacher. He was educated at the University of Pennsylvania (B.A. 1963) and the University of Michigan (M.A. 1965; Ph.D., 1967). He is the author of numerous articles and books, among them *The Passions* (1976); *Introducing Philosophy: Problems and Perspectives* (1977); and *Love: Emotion, Myth and Metaphor* (1981). Solomon is also the author of several published and recorded songs.

---

1. Robert Herrick (1591–1674).
2. William Shakespeare (1564–1616), "Venus and Adonis."
3. W. B. Yeats (1865–1939), "Crazy Jane Talks to the Bishop."

Reading Advice

Although this article is from a popular book concerning what is probably the most obsessive subject in our society, nevertheless, it still bears the stamp of the author's academic training. Its diction is lively and brisk but still occasionally technical. The author writes in an energetic style and draws on clever metaphors and even the occasional folksy image to support his point, but it is not a simple one.

Basically, the author argues that love is not so much an emotion, an attitude, or even a feeling, as it is an internalized world mutually constructed and experienced by the lovers. This is the sort of philosophical point that a hardheaded scientist might call a *construct*, meaning a theory designed to explain data. When it comes to love, everyone is potentially a source of both conflicting opinions and data. Explaining what they mean is the great imponderable, but that is exactly what Solomon valiantly tries to do with his theory.

*T*he question, What is love? is neither 1
a request for a confession nor an excuse to start moralizing. It is not an invitation to amuse us with some *bon mot* ("Love is the key that opens up the doors of happiness") or to impress us with an author's sensitivity. And love is much more than a "feeling." When a novelist wants us to appreciate his character's emotions, he does not just describe sweaty palms and a moment of panic; he instead describes *a world,* the world as it is experienced—in anger, or in envy, or in love. Theorizing about emotion, too, is like describing an exotic world. It is a kind of conceptual anthropology—identifying a peculiar list of characters—heroes, villains, knaves or lovers—understanding a special set of rules and roles—rituals, fantasies, myths, slogans and fears. But these are not merely empirical observations on the fate of a feeling; none of this will make any sense to anyone who has not participated also. Love can be understood only "from the inside," as a language can be understood only by someone who speaks it, as a world can be known only by someone who has—even if vicariously— *lived* in it.

To analyze an emotion by looking at the world it defines allows us to cut 2
through the inarticulateness of mere "feelings" and do away once and for all with the idea that emotions in general and love in particular are "ineffable" or beyond description. This might make some sense if describing an emotion were describing something "inside of us." It is not easy, for example, to describe how one feels when nauseous; even describing something so specific as a migraine headache falls back on clumsy metaphors ("as if my head's in a vise," "as if someone were driving a nail through my skull"). But once we see that every emotion defines a world for itself, we can then describe in some detail what the world involves, with its many variations, describe its dimensions and its dynamics. The world defined by love—or what we shall call the *loveworld*—is

a world woven around a single relationship with all else pushed to the periphery. To understand love is to understand the specifics of this relationship and the world woven around it.

Love has been so misunderstood both because so often it has been taken to be *other*-worldly rather than one world of emotion among others, and because it has sometimes been taken to be a "mere emotion"—just a feeling and not a world at all. Because of this, perhaps it would be best to illustrate the theory that every emotion is a world by beginning with a less problematic emotion, namely, *anger*. Anger too defines its world. It is a world in which one defines oneself in the role of "the offended" and defines someone else (or perhaps a group or an institution) as "the offender." The world of anger is very much a courtroom world, a world filled with blame and emotion litigation. It is a world in which everyone else tends to become a co-defendant, a friend of the court, a witness or at least part of the courtroom audience. (But when you're *very* angry, there are no innocent bystanders.) We have already once quoted Lewis Carroll from *Alice in Wonderland*: " 'I'll be judge, I'll be jury,' said cunning old Fury." It is a world in which one does indeed define oneself as judge and jury, complete with a grim righteousness, with "justice"—one's own vengeance—as the only legitimate concern. It is a *magical* world, which can change a lackadaisical unfocused morning into a piercing, all-consuming day, an orgy of vindictive self-righteousness and excitement. At the slightest provocation it can change an awkward and defensive situation into an aggressive confrontation. To describe the world of anger is therefore to describe its fantasies, for example, the urge to kill, though rarely is this taken seriously or to its logical conclusion. It has its illusions too, for instance, the tendency to exaggerate the importance of some petty grievance to the level of cosmic injustice; in anger we sometimes talk as if "man's inhumanity to man" is perfectly manifested in some minor slight at the office yesterday. It is a world with a certain fragility; a single laugh can explode the whole pretense of angry self-righteousness. And it is a world with a purpose—for when do we feel more self-righteous than in anger? Getting angry in an otherwise awkward situation may be a way of saving face or providing a quick ego boost; "having a bad temper" may be not so much a "character trait" as an emotional strategy, a way of *using* emotion as a means of controlling other people. To describe anger, in other words, is to describe the way the world is structured—and why—by a person who is angry.

The world of love—the loveworld—can be similarly described as a theatrical scenario, not as a courtroom but rather as "courtly," a romantic drama defined by its sense of elegance (badly interpreted as "spiritual"), in which we also take up a certain role—"the lover"—and cast another person into a complementary role—"the beloved." But where anger casts two antagonistic characters, romantic love sets up an idea of unity, absolute complementarity and total mutual support and affection. It is the *rest* of the world that may be

3

4

the antagonist. Boris Pasternak describes the loveworld beautifully—the world as Adam and Eve, naked, surrounded by chaos.

It is a world we know well, of course—the world of *Casablanca, Romeo and Juliet* and a thousand stories and novels. It is a world in which we narrow our vision and our cares to that single duality, all else becoming trifles, obstacles or interruptions. It is a magical world, in which an ordinary evening is transformed into the turning point of a lifetime, the metamorphosis of one's self into a curious kind of double being. It may seem like a sense of "discovery"; in fact it is a step in a long search, a process of creation. . . .

Like every emotional world, the loveworld has its essential rules and rituals, its basic structures and internal dynamics. Some of these rules and structures are so obvious that it is embarrassing to have to spell them out; for example, the fact that the loveworld (typically) includes two people, instead of only one (as in shame) or three (as in jealousy) or indeed an entire class of people (as in national mourning or revolutionary resentment). Or the fact that the loveworld involves extremely "positive" feelings about the person loved, perhaps even the uncritical evaluation that he or she is "the most wonderful person in the world." Or the fact that the loveworld is held together by the mutual desire to be together (to touch, be touched, to caress and make love) no less essentially than the world of Newton and Einstein is held together by the forces of electromagnetism and gravity. Such features are so obvious to us that we fail to think of them as the structures of love; we take them for granted and, when asked to talk about love, consider them not even worth mentioning. Having thus ignored the obvious, love becomes a mystery. But other seemingly equally "obvious" features of love may not be part of the structure of the loveworld at all—for example, the comforting equation between love and trust. Here, indeed, there is some room for "mystery" in love, not the emotion itself but its essential lack of predictability, the fascination with the unknown and the attraction that comes not with trust but with vulnerability, sometimes even suspicion and doubt. Similarly, we presume as in a cliché that romantic love presupposes respect ("How can you say that you love me when you don't even respect me?"). But it may be too that the nature of romantic love renders respect irrelevant, so that even when respect begins as a prerequisite for romantic attraction it gets booted out of the loveworld just as assuredly as a pair of fine leather shoes gets doffed as we get into bed. . . . The problem with talking about love is not that there is a mystery to be cleared up or that so much seems so obvious but rather that we take what we are told so uncritically, conflate the loveworld with everything that is good, true and desirable, confuse the structures of love with the conditions for security and happiness, assume without thinking that because suspicion is so painful trust must be essential to love, assume as a matter of wishful thinking that the same person who is in

5

love with us must, if our lives are to be unified, respect us for what we do as well. . . .

The "Object" of Love

Talking about the loveworld is not only a way to avoid the hopeless conception of love as a feeling; it is also a way of rejecting an insidious view of love—and emotions in general—which many philosophers have come to accept as "obvious," particularly in this century. The view simply stated, is that love is an attitude *toward* someone, a feeling directed *at* a person, instead of a shared world. The view is often disguised by a piece of professional jargon—an impressive word, "intentionality." It is said that emotions are "intentional," which is a way of saying that they are "about" something. What an emotion is "about" is called its "intentional object" or, simply, its "object." Thus shame is an emotion which is "about" oneself, while anger is "about" someone else. The language comes from the medieval scholastics, by way of an Austrian philosopher named Franz Brentano, one of whose students in Vienna was the young Sigmund Freud. Thus Freud talks all the time about the "object" of love, not without some discomfort, for though the conception fits his general theories perfectly, he nonetheless sensed correctly that some considerable conceptual damage was being done to the emotion thereby.

The idea—though not the terminology—of "intentionality" and "intentional objects" was introduced into British philosophy by the Scottish philosopher David Hume. He analyzed a number of emotions in terms of the "objects" with which they were "naturally associated," for example pride and humility, which both took as their "objects" oneself, and hatred and love, which both took as their objects another person. But we can already see what is going to be so wrong with this familiar type of analysis. First of all, all such talk about "objects" leaves out the crucial fact that, in love at least, it is the other as a "subject" that is essential. To be in love (even unrequited) is to be looked *at,* not just to look. Thus it is the eyes, not the body (nor the soul), that present the so-called "beloved," not as object but as subject, not first as beautiful or lovable but always as (potentially) loving. It's the eyes that have it, nothing else.

. . . Every lover, I would suppose, has beautiful eyes, for it is only the eyes that look back at you, that refuse to allow even the most beautiful lover to become a mere "object" of love, thus refuting with a glance some of the greatest philosophers in history.

Love is not just an attitude directed toward another person; it is an emotion which, at least hopefully, is *shared with* him or her. . . . Sometimes, perhaps, and in some emotions, "object"-talk makes perfectly good sense; sadness at the loss of one's high school class ring, or the love of one's favorite first edition. But any account of love that begins with the idea of an "object" of love is probably going to miss the main point of the emotion, namely, that it is not an emotion "about" another person so much as, in our terms, a world we share. . . .

One obvious misunderstanding is this: the Christian view of love is not alone   11
in teaching us that love is essentially *selfless.* Proponents of romantic love have argued that too. The idea is that love is thoroughly "about" another person, so that any degree of self-love is incompatible with, or at least a detraction from, "true," that is, selfless love. But this is not only not true; it is impossible. There is no emotion without self-involvement, and no love that is not also "about" oneself. The other side is just as confused, however; La Rochefoucauld, for example, insists that "all love is self-love." But to be self-involved is not yet to be selfish, nor does self-involvement in any way exclude a total concern for the other person as well. The practical consequence of this confusion, in turn, is the readiness with which we can be made to feel guilty at the slightest suggestion that our love is not "pure" but turns on "selfish" motives, and it renders unaskable what is in fact a most intelligible question—namely, "What am I getting out of this?"—to which the answer may well be, "Not enough to make it worthwhile." But then, love is not just what one "gets out of it" either.

Talking about love as a world with two people avoids these problems and   12
misunderstandings. But there is one last set of complications which has been much discussed in the "object" way of talking which deserves special mention. The idea that the "object" of my love is another person suggests too easily that love is "about" a person *simpliciter,* the whole person, nothing but and nothing less than the whole person. This is simply untrue. I love *you,* indeed, but I love you only in so far as you fit into the loveworld. That may be for any number of reasons—because I think you're beautiful, because you love me too, because I admire you in your career, because we cook fine meals together. The list might well seem endless, but it never is. I might love you for just one reason, or I might love you for a hundred and fifty reasons. But those reasons (I might always discover more) circumscribe your place in the loveworld. The person I love is, consequently, not simply *you,* the whole person, but rather you circum-scribed by that set of reasons. I might say, in a moment of enthusiasm, "I love everything about you," but that's just myopia, or poor editing. Sometimes I'm surprised. I find a new virtue that I've never seen before. But sometimes I'm disappointed too. Sometimes I manufacture new and imagined virtues, as Sten-dhal suggests in his theory of "crystallization"—the "discovery" of ever new virtues in one's lover. But love is never unqualified acceptance of a lover, "no matter what," however much one would like to be loved, if not to love, without qualification. But this raises sticky questions about the vicissitudes of love, not least the nature of these reasons and the possibility that, if I love you "for reasons," might I not love someone else, just as much as or instead of you, for precisely those same reasons? Or is it possible that one might not know *whom*

one loves, if it is true, for example, as every teenager soon learns, that one can love "on the rebound," transferring the frustrated love of one lover immediately onto another, who becomes something of a sparring partner to keep us in shape for the more important bout to come, holding a role in a loveworld in which he or she has no real place. The identity of the "beloved," in other words, is by no means so obvious as the "object of love"-talk would make it seem. It is even possible that the "beloved," as Plato argued in a more pious way, is nothing more than a set of ideal properties, indifferent indeed to the particular person who at any given instant happens to exemplify them.

To make matters even more complicated, we might point out that similar 13 questions arise regarding one's own identity in the loveworld. I do not love "with all my heart and all my soul," but rather (if we want to talk about hearts and souls at all) only with half a heart—but not half-heartedly—and with a fraction of a soul. I love you in so far as I am a lover, but I am only rarely *just* a lover. No matter how much I'm in love, I do not live just in the loveworld. You may be the essence of the loveworld, but you don't fit into my career or, for that matter, into the world I enter when I watch Japanese movies. I love you when I feel romantic, perhaps too when I'm just relaxed, but when I'm frustrated about my work, or absorbed in a lawsuit, the self that is so involved is not the same self that loves you. It's not that I don't love you, or that I love you any less; it's just that the loveworld isn't my only world, or yours either, even if we agree that it is, for us, the best of our possible worlds. To say that love is a world of two people, therefore, is not at all to say something simple, much less "obvious." . . .

What Love's About: Self

What love is about—the poles of the loveworld and the goal of its devel-   14 opment—is the creation of self. But this does not mean that love is just about oneself, any more than love is just about another. For the self that is created through love is a *shared* self, a self that is conceived and developed together. It is not only the loveworld that is indeterminate but, as part and parcel of our largely indeterminate culture, our selves are always under-determined too. Jean-Paul Sartre states this as a paradox, that we are always more than we are. Our selves are formed in the cradle of the family, soon to be confused by the welter of different roles into which we are thrown with playmates, peers and even the most rudimentary social rituals and responsibilities. And all along we find ourselves redefining ourselves in terms of other people, people with whom we identify, those whom we admire, those we despise as well as all of those more or less anonymous faces and voices that surround us every day—smiling, abusing, criticizing, congratulating and cajoling. And in that confusion of roles and rituals which in our society (not all others) tends to be without an anchor, without an "essence" according to which we could say, once and for all, "I am x," we look for a context that is small enough, manageable enough, yet powerful enough, for us to define ourselves, our "real" selves—we think wishfully—and what could be smaller or more manageable than the tiniest possible interpersonal world, namely, a world of only two people. And so, in love, we define ourselves and define each other, building on but sometimes fighting against the multitude of identities that are already established, starting with but not always ending with the images, fantasies and roles which drew us together in the first place, made us seem so compatible, even "meant for each other." Romantic love is part of our search for selfhood, and the power of the emotion, our sense of tragedy when it fails as well as its overall importance in our culture, turns largely on the fact that it comes to provide what is most crucial to us—even more than survival and the so-called "necessities" of life—namely, our selves.

. . . In love, what is so peculiar is that the self that is created in the devel- 15 opment of the emotion is a shared self, an *ego à deux,* whereas in most emotions the self is set up in opposition to or in isolation from other people. In romantic love, as opposed to motherly or brotherly love, for example, the self is also created virtually anew, as if "from scratch," no matter how many influences may be behind it and no matter how thoroughly this might be explained by someone outside that tiny yet seemingly all-inclusive loveworld. To understand romantic love, therefore, is to understand this peculiar creation of a shared self, and to explain the importance of this one emotion in our world is to explain, most of all, its singular success in promoting our sense of ourselves and the meaningfulness not of a mere "relationship" but of life itself.

Most if not all emotions have as a motive the enhancement of self, or what 16 I call the *maximization of self-esteem.* Thus in describing the world of anger, . . . I commented that anger is a spectacularly *self-righteous* emotion. Through anger, we feel good about ourselves, morally superior, even in (especially in) circumstances which would otherwise feel extremely awkward. . . .

But of all the emotional strategies for self-enhancement, none succeeds so 17 well as love. For one thing, the inevitable opposition in anger invites a counterattack of equal self-righteousness, and competitive emotions make it highly likely that one of us, at least, will lose. But in love two selves mutually reinforce one another, rather than compete with one another, and so the self-enhancement of love, insulated from the outside by indifference, mutually supported in a reciprocal way on the inside, tends to be an extremely powerful and relatively durable emotional strategy. . . .

Love and Autonomy:
The "Dialectic" of Togetherness

So what is love? It is, in a phrase, an emotion through which we create for 18 ourselves a little world—the loveworld, in which we play the roles of lovers and, quite literally, create our selves as well. Thus love is not, as so many of the great poets and philosophers have taken it to be, any degree of admiration or worship, not appreciation or even desire for beauty, much less, as Erich Fromm was fond of arguing, an "orientation of character" whose "object" is a secondary consideration. Even so-called "unrequited" love is shared love and shared identity, if only from one side and thereby woefully incomplete. Of course, occasionally an imagined identity may be far preferable to the actuality, but even when this is the case unrequited love represents at most a hint toward a process and not the process as such. Unrequited love is still love, but love in the sense that a sprout from an acorn is already an oak, no more. . . .

In love we transform ourselves and one another, but the key to this emotion   19
is the understanding that the transformation of selves is not merely reciprocal, a swap of favors like "I'll cook you dinner if you'll wash the car." The self transformed in love is a shared self, and therefore by its very nature at odds with, even contradictory to, the individual autonomous selves that each of us had before. Sometimes our new shared self may be a transformation of a self that I (perhaps we) shared before. Possibly all love is to some extent the transposition of seemingly "natural" bonds which have somehow been abandoned or destroyed, and therefore the less than novel transformation of a self that has always been shared, in one way or another. But the bonds of love are always, to some extent, "unnatural," and our shared identity is always, in some way, uncomfortable. Aristophanes' delightful allegory about the double creatures cleft in two and seeking their other halves is charming but false. Love is never so neat and tidy, antigen and antibody forming the perfect fit. The Christian concept of a couple sanctified as a "union" before God is reassuring, as if one thereby receives some special guarantee, an outside bond of sorts, which will keep two otherwise aimless souls together. But the warranty doesn't apply. What is so special about romantic love, and what makes it so peculiar to our and similar societies, is the fact that it is entirely based on the idea of individuality and freedom, and this means, first of all, that the presupposition of love is a strong sense of individual identity and autonomy which exactly contradicts the ideal of "union" and "yearning to be one" that some of our literature has celebrated so one-sidedly. And, second, the freedom that is built into the loveworld includes not just the freedom to come together but the freedom to go as well. Thus love and the loveworld are always in a state of tension, always changing, dynamic, tenuous and explosive.

. . . To understand love is to understand this tension, this dialectic between   20
individuality and the shared ideal. To think that love is to be found only at the ends of the spectrum—in the first enthusiastic "discovery" of a shared togetherness or at the end of the road, after a lifetime together—is to miss the loveworld almost entirely, for it is neither an initial flush of feeling nor the retrospective congratulations of old age but a struggle for unity and identity. And it is this struggle—neither the ideal of togetherness nor the contrary

demand for individual autonomy and identity—that defines the dynamics of that convulsive and tenuous world we call romantic love.

Questions for Critical Thinking

1. If, as the author says, *love* is a particular world that can only be understood "from the inside," how is it then possible for anyone but the lover or beloved to understand how a particular lover feels?

2. Given the author's definition of love, how do you think he would feel about marriage counseling by priests or other celibates? How do you feel?

3. The author says in paragraph 9 that the "eyes" of the lover looking back at the beloved refute "at a glance some of the greatest philosophers in history" who analyze love in terms of "intentionality" and the "love object." What exceptions, if any, can you think of that might refute this dogma?

4. What differences do you think exist between the way humans and animals love?

5. If the beloved is nothing more than a set of ideal properties in search of a human match, what ideal properties would characterize your beloved?

6. How would the author's definition of love apply to the bigamist or lover simultaneously in love with more than one beloved?

7. What is a "womanizer" and how does that term fit in with the author's definition of love? How do you account for the fact that the world has no female equivalent such as "manizer?"

8. What differences between the way men and women love does the author's definition allow? In your opinion, do men love differently than women, and if so, how?

Writing Assignment

Assuming that you have been in love at least once or are presently in love, write an essay defining and explaining the "shared self" that the love affair made of you. Be specific in telling how this "shared self" you became differed from your real self.

Writing Advice

You are asked to explain the "shared self" you experienced in a love affair or are presently experiencing, and to say how it differs from your real self. One way to do this assignment is to develop your essay by examples. Note that the best kinds of examples are always the most specific and concrete. For example, if you say that your "shared self" was adventurous and carefree while your usual self was humdrum and boring, you should be as vivid as possible in giving examples that explain the difference. You might have gone mountain climbing with your beloved, a thing you would never have attempted in your own humdrum persona. If so, give us all the gritty details of rocks and rappelling. Show us the shale dust in your mouth and bracing mountain air tugging at your parka. When you tell us about your humdrum self before the love affair, lead us to the tiddlywinks table and show us the heavy air of solitary boredom that used to hang over your Saturday nights.

Implicit in this description of your "before and after" love self is the contrast between the two. You could, in fact, organize this essay as a simple contrast between your "shared self" and your loveless alter ego. Or you could develop an implicit contrast while focusing on giving examples and details of yourself before and after falling in love. Which method of development you choose is a matter of taste, depending on on how you wish to treat the subject and the emphasis you wish to pursue.

Alternate Writing Assignment

Write an essay comparing and contrasting the way men love with the way women love. Give specific examples to support your opinion on the similarity or difference.

PHILOSOPHY

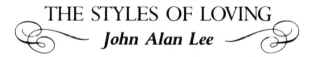

THE STYLES OF LOVING
John Alan Lee

John Alan Lee (b. 1933) is a Canadian sociologist who was born in Ontario and earned his Ph.D. at the University of Sussex. He has researched diverse topics such as faith healing, educational television, and the assimilation of minorities. Among his books are *The Colors of Love* (1976), and *Getting Sex: A New Approach: More Fun, Less Guilt* (1978).

Reading Advice

In contrast to the previous article, which took a philosophical and speculative approach to love, this one is grounded in empirical research. The author distributed questionnaires probing for experiences and attitudes about love and then analyzed their responses for broad themes and similarities. His conclusion is that love is not one feeling but a complex compound of many feelings.

In rhetorical terms, this is a division and classification article, with the author dividing love into its primary terms and then isolating each type for a separate discussion. His language is not especially technical, since the article was adapted for, and originally published in, the semipopular magazine *Psychology Today*. Nevertheless, the classification scheme it proposes is complex. We suggest that you begin by jotting down the major love types and then summarizing the characteristics the author attributes to each.

We will accept variety in almost any-   1
thing, from roses and religions to politics and poetry. But when it comes to love, each of us believes we know the real thing, and we are reluctant to accept other notions. We disparage other people's experiences by calling them infatuations, mere sexual flings, unrealistic affairs.

For thousands of years writers and philosophers have debated the nature of   2
love. Many recognized that there are different kinds of love, but few accepted them all as legitimate. Instead, each writer argues that his own concept of love is the best. C. S. Lewis[1] thought that true love must be unselfish and altruistic, as did sociologist Pitirim Sorokin. Stendhal,[2] by contrast, took the view that love is passionate and ecstatic. Others think that "real" love must be wedded to the Protestant ethic, forging a relationship that is mutually beneficial and productive. Definitions of love range from sexual lust to an excess of friendship.

The ancient Greeks and Romans were more tolerant. They had a variety of   3
words for different and, to them, equally valid types of love. But today the concept has rigidified; most of us believe that there is only one true kind of love. We measure each relationship against this ideal in terms of degree or quantity. Does Tom love me more than Tim does? Do you love me as much as I love you? Do I love you enough? Such comparisons also assume that love comes in fixed amounts—the more I give to you, the less I have for anyone else; if you don't give me everything, you don't love me enough.

"There is hardly any activity, any enterprise, which is started with such   4
tremendous hopes and expectations, and yet which fails so regularly, as love," wrote Erich Fromm. I think that part of the reason for this failure rate is that too often people are speaking different languages when they speak of love. The problem is not *how much* love they feel, but *which kind*. The way to have a mutually satisfying love affair is not to find a partner who loves "in the right amount," but one who shares the same approach to loving, the same definition of love.

---

1. C. S. Lewis, British novelist and critic (1898–1963).
2. Stendhal, pen name of Marie Henri Beyle, French novelist and biographer (1783–1842).

The Structure of Love My research explored the literature of love and the   5
experiences of ordinary lovers in order to distinguish these approaches. Color
served me as a useful analogy in the process. There are three primary colors—
red, yellow and blue—from which all other hues are composed. And empiri-
cally I found three primary types of love, none of which could be reduced to
the others, and a variety of secondary types that proved to be combinations of
the basic three. In love, as in color, "primary" does not mean superior; it simply
refers to basic structure. Orange is no more or less a color than red, and no
less worthy. In love, one can draw as many distinctions as one wishes; I have
stopped, somewhat arbitrarily, with nine types.

EROS Stendhal called love a "sudden sensation of recognition and hope." He   6
was describing the most typical symptom of eros: an immediate, powerful
attraction to the physical appearance of the beloved. "The first time I saw him
was several weeks before we met," a typical erotic lover said in an interview,
"but I can still remember exactly the way he looked, which was just the way I
dreamed my ideal lover would look." Erotic lovers typically feel a chemical or
gut reaction on meeting each other; heightened heartbeat is not just a figment
of fiction, it seems, but the erotic lover's physiological response to meeting the
dream.

Most of my erotic respondents went to bed with their lovers soon after   7
meeting. This was the first test of whether the affair would continue, since
erotic love demands that the partner live up to the lover's concept of bodily
perfection. They may try to overlook what they consider a flaw, only to find
that it undermines the intensity of their attraction. There is no use trying to
persuade such a lover that personal or intellectual qualities are more lasting or
more important. To do so is to argue for another approach to love.

My erotic respondents all spoke with delight of the lover's skin, fragrance,   8
hair, musculature, body proportions, and so on. Of course, the specific body
type that each lover considered ideal varied, but all erotics had such an ideal,
which they could identify easily from a series of photographs. Erotic lovers
actively and imaginatively cultivate many sexual techniques to preserve delight
in the partner's body. Nothing is more deadly for a serious erotic lover than to
fall in love with a prudish partner.

Modern usage tends to define *erotic* as *sexual;* we equate erotic art with   9
pornography. But eros is not mere sexual attraction; it is a demanding search
for the lover's ideal of beauty, a concept that is as old as Pygmalion.[3] Eros
involves mental as well as sexual attraction, which is faithful to the Platonic
concept. Most dictionaries define Platonic love as "devoid of sensual feeling,"

---

3. Pygmalion, a sculptor who made an ivory statue representing his ideal of womanhood, and then fell
in love with his own creation (Greek mythology).

which is certainly not what Plato had in mind. On the contrary, it was sensual feeling for the beautiful body of another person that evoked eros as the Greeks understood it.

The Dream of the Ideal The fascination with beauty that marks eros is the   10
basis for personal and psychological intimacy between the lovers. The erotic lover wants to know everything about the beloved, to become part of him or her. If an erotic relationship surpasses the initial hurdles of expectation and physical ideals, this desire for intimacy can sustain the relationship for years. (And this knowledge must be first-hand. The playful lover may ask a friend what so-and-so is like in bed. No erotic lover would dream of relying on such vicarious evidence.)

An essential component of successful erotic love is self-assurance. It takes   11
confidence to reveal oneself intensely to another. A lover who doubts himself, who falls into self-recriminations if his love is not reciprocated, cannot sustain eros.

The typical erotic lovers in my sample avoided wallowing in extremes of   12
emotion, especially the self-pity and hysteria that characterize mania. They recalled happy and secure childhoods, and reported satisfaction with work, family, and close friends. They were ready for love when it came along, but were not anxiously searching. They consider love to be important, but they do not become obsessive about it; when separated from the beloved, they do not lose their balance, become sick with desire, or turn moody. They prefer exclusive relationships but do not demand them, and they are rarely possessive or afraid of rivals. Erotic lovers seek a deep, pervasive rapport with their partners and share development and control of the relationship.

But because the erotic lover depends on an ideal concept of beauty, he is   13
often disappointed. The failure of eros has littered our fiction with bitter and cynical stories of love, and caused conventional wisdom to be deeply suspicious of ideal beauty as a basis for relationships. Indeed, I found that the purer the erotic qualities of a respondent's love experience, the less his chances of a mutual, lasting relationship.

An erotic lover may eventually settle for less, but he or she never forgets   14
the compromise, and rarely loses hope of realizing the dream. However, I found several cases of "love at first sight" in which initial rapture survived years of married life. The success of a few keeps the dream alive for many more.

LUDUS About the year one A.D. the Roman poet Ovid came up with the term   15
amor ludens, playful love, love as a game. Ovid advised lovers to enjoy love as a pleasant pastime, but not to get too involved. The ludic lover refuses, then, to become dependent on any beloved, or to allow the partner to become overly attached to him or her, or too intimate.

Other types of lovers dismiss ludus as not a kind of love at all; erotic types   16
disdain its lack of commitment, moralists condemn its promiscuity and hedon-
ism. But to make a game of love does not diminish its value. No skilled player
of bridge or tennis would excuse inept playing because "it's only a game," and
ludus too has its rules, strategies, and points for skill. Ludus turns love into a
series of challenges and puzzles to be solved.

Ludic Strategies For example, ludus is most easily and most typically played   17
with several partners at once, a guarantee against someone on either side getting
too involved. "Love several persons," a 17th-century manual advises, for three
lovers are safer than two, and two much safer than one. A ludic lover will often
invent another lover, even a spouse, to keep the partner from becoming too
attached.

But most of my ludic respondents had other tactics. They were careful not   18
to date a partner too often; they never hinted at including the partner in any
long-range plans; they arranged encounters in a casual, even haphazard, way:
"I'll give you a call"; "See you around sometime." Such indefiniteness is designed
to keep the partner from building up expectations or from becoming preoccupied with the affair.

Of course, as in many games, one must be on guard against cheats. Cheats   19
in ludic love are cynical players who don't care how deeply involved the partner
becomes, who may even exploit such intensity. Such players scandalize ludic
lovers who believe in fair play. Insincerity and lies may be part of the game, so
long as both partners understand this.

The ludic lover notices differences between bodies, but thinks it is stupid   20
to specialize. As the ludic man said in *Finian's Rainbow,* when he is not near the
girl he loves, he loves the girl he's near. But ludus is not simply a series of
sexual encounters. A lover could get sex without the rituals of conversation,
candles and wine. In ludus, the pleasure comes from playing the game, not
merely winning the prize.

Actually, sexual gratification is only a minor part of the time and effort   21
involved in ludic love. Of any group, ludic respondents showed the least interest
in the mutual improvement of sex techniques. Their attitude was that it is
easier to find a new sex partner than to work out sexual problems and explore
new sexual pleasures with the current one; this view contrasts sharply with
that of erotic and storgic lovers. Ludic people want sex for fun, not emotional
rapport.

Don Juans Aren't Always Doomed Ludus had enjoyed recurring popularity   22
through history. Montesquieu[4] could write of 18th-century France: "A husband

---

4. Baron de la Brède et de Montesquieu, French political philosopher, jurist, and writer (1689–1755).

who wishes to be the only one to possess his wife would be regarded as a public killjoy." The first Don Juan emerged in Tirso de Molina's *The Trickster of Seville* in 1630, the diametric opposite of the erotic Tristan,[5] the courtly ideal. Tirso's hero conquered only four women, but a century later Mozart's Don Giovanni won a thousand and three in España alone.

Of course the various fates of the legendary ludic lovers reflect society's 23
ambivalence toward them. They usually go to hell, get old and impotent, or meet their match and surrender. Rarely is ludus tolerated, much less rewarded.

But I was struck by the fact that most of my ludic respondents neither 24
suffered nor regretted their ways. Like successful erotics, they play from a base of self-confidence. They believe in their own assets so much that they convince themselves that they do not "need" other people, like most mortals. These ludic lovers prefer to remain in perfect control of their feelings; they do not think that love is as important as work or other activities; they are thus never possessive or jealous (except as a teasing ploy in the game). They typically recall their childhoods as "average," and their current lives as "OK, but occasionally frustrating."

My ludic respondents seemed quite content with their detachment from 25
intense feelings of love, but most failed the acid test of ludus: the ability to break off with a partner with whom they were through. Their intentions were ludic, but they had Victorian hangovers. They tended to prolong the relationship for the sake of the partner, until the inevitable break was painful. Ovid would not have approved. "Extinguish the fire of love gradually," he admonished, "not all at once . . . it is wicked to hate a girl you used to love."

The legendary ludic lovers, like Don Juan and Alfie, were generally men, 26
and only in recent years—with the pill and penicillin—have women won entry into the game. Ludus is also frequently identified with male homosexual love; the term "gay" may have originated from the assumption that homosexuals adopt a noncommittal, playful approach to sex and love, which is not neces- sarily so.

There is a variant of this type of love that I call *manic ludus,* in which the 27
lover alternates between a detached, devil-may-care attitude toward the partner, and a worried, lovesick desire for more attention. People in this conflicting state would like to be purely ludic, but they lack the vanity or self-sufficiency to remain aloof from intimacy. They both need and resent love, and they cannot control their emotions long enough to maintain a cool relationship.

STORGE (pronounced stor-gay) is, as Proudhon described it, "love without 28
fever, tumult or folly, a peaceful and enchanting affection" such as one might have for a close sibling. It is the kind of love that sneaks up unnoticed; storgic

---

5. Tristan, a prince at King Arthur's court who fell in love with the Irish princess Iseult and died with her.

lovers remember no special point when they fell in love. Since storgic lovers consider sex one of the most intimate forms of self-disclosure, sex occurs late in the relationship.

Storge is rarely the stuff of dramatic plays or romantic novels, except perhaps as a backdrop or point of comparison. In *Of Human Bondage,* the hero, Philip, follows a manic love affair with Mildred with a storgic marriage to Sally, whom he has known all along.   29

Storge superficially resembles ludus in its lack of great passion, but the origins of the two types are quite different. The ludic lover avoids intensity of feeling consciously aware of its risks. The storgic lover is unaware of intense feeling. It simply doesn't occur to him that a lover should be dewy-eyed and sentimental about a beloved. Such behavior is as out of place in storgic love as it would be for most of us in relating to a close friend. Storgic love "just comes naturally" with the passage of time and the enjoyment of shared activities. You grow accustomed to her face.   30

In most modern cities people do not live near each other long enough to develop the unself-conscious affection that is typical of storgic love. I found some such cases among people who grew up in rural areas. However, among my urban respondents, who usually had few lasting contacts with their child-hood friends, there were some storgic types who based their love on friendship and companionship. This characteristic distinguishes storge from other types of love, in which the partners may not treat each other at all like friends.   31

When a storgic lover gets involved with another type of lover, serious misunderstandings are likely to occur. The goals of storge, for instance, are marriage, home and children, avoiding all the silly conflicts and entanglements of passion. But to the erotic or ludic lover, storge is a bore. Storge implies a life that is reasonable and predictable; why make it more complicated by engaging in emotionally exhausting types of love? Erotic lovers would never understand that question.   32

The Strengths of Storge Storge is a slow-burning love, rarely hectic or urgent, though of course storgic lovers may disagree and fight. But they build up a reservoir of stability that will see them through difficulties that would kill a ludic relationship and greatly strain an erotic one. The physical absence of the beloved, for instance, is much less distressing to them than to other lovers; they can survive long separations (Ulysses and Penelope are a classic example of that ability).   33

Even if a break-up occurs, storgic lovers are likely to remain good friends. A typical storgic lover would find it inconceivable that two people who had once loved each other could become enemies, simply because they had ceased to be lovers.   34

In a ludic or erotic relationship, something is happening all the time. In eros, there is always some secret to share, a misunderstanding to mend, a   35 separation to survive with letters and poems. In ludus, inactivity quickly leads to boredom, and a search for new amusement. In storge, there are fewer campaigns to fight and fewer wounds to heal. There is a lack of ecstasy, but also a lack of despair.

Eros, ludus and storge are the three primary types of love, but few love   36
affairs and few colors, are pure examples of one type. Most reds have a little yellow or blue in them, and most cases of eros have a little storge or ludus.

The color analogy led me to distinguish mixtures from blends (compounds).   37
You can mix two colors and be aware of both components. But it may happen that two primary colors are so evenly blended that an entirely new color emerges, unclassified as a hue of either, with unique properties. This is the case with mania, a fourth color of love.

MANIA The Greeks called it *theia mania,* the madness from the gods. Both   38
Sappho and Plato, along with legions of sufferers, recorded its symptoms: agitation, sleeplessness, fever, loss of appetite, heartache. The manic lover is consumed by thoughts of the beloved. The slightest lack of enthusiasm from the partner brings anxiety and pain; each tiny sign of warmth brings instant relief, but no lasting satisfaction. The manic lover's need for attention and affection from the beloved is insatiable. Cases of mania abound in literature, for its components—furious jealousy, helpless obsession, and tragic endings— are the stuff of human conflict. Goethe made his own unhappy bout with mania the subject of his novel, *The Sorrows of Young Werther,* and Somerset Maugham did the same in *Of Human Bondage.* The manic lover alternates between peaks of ecstasy when he feels loved in return, and depths of despair when the beloved is absent. He knows his possessiveness and jealousy are self-defeating, but he can't help himself.

From God's Curse to Popular Passion Rational lovers throughout the ages,   39
from Lucretius[6] to Denis de Rougemont, have warned us to avoid mania like the plague. Fashions in love, of course, change. To the ancient Greeks, a person who fell head-over-heels, "madly" in love, had obviously been cursed by the gods. Many parents in the Middle Ages strongly disapproved of love matches, preferring their children to arrange "sensible marriages." But mania has gained popularity in the West since the 13th century; today many young people would consider it wrong to marry unless they loved "romantically."

So popular is mania in literature and love that I originally assumed it would   40
be a primary type. But green, a color that occurs in nature more than any other, is not a primary, but a blend of yellow and blue. Similarly, the data from my interviews refused to reduce mania to one clear type. Instead, mania respondents derive their unique style of love from the primaries of eros and ludus.

---

6. Titus Lucretius Carus, Roman poet and philosopher (96?–55 B.C.).

These yearning, obsessed, often unhappy manic lovers are typical of frus-   41
trated eros. With eros, they share the same intensity of feeling, the same urgency
to find the ideal beloved. But erotic lovers are not crushed by disappointment
as manic lovers are; they keep their self-respect. Manic lovers, by contrast, are
self-effacing, ambivalent, lacking in confidence. They don't have a clear idea of
what they are looking for, as erotic lovers do, and they feel helpless, out of
control of their emotions. "I know it was crazy, but I couldn't help myself,"
was a favorite explanation.

Oddly, manic lovers persist in falling in love with people they say they don't   42
even like. "I hate and I love," wailed the Roman poet Catullus. "And if you ask
me how, I do not know. I only feel it, and I'm torn in two." Aldous Huxley's
hero in *Point Counter-Point* "wanted her against all reason, against all his ideals
and principles, madly, against his wishes . . . for he didn't like Lucy, he really
hated her."

For these reasons, some psychologists consider mania to be neurotic, unheal-   43
thy. Freud was the most critical of obsessive love, and Theodor Reik, in *Of Love
and Lust,* explains the obsessiveness of mania as a search for the qualities in a
partner that the lover feels lacking in himself. The typical manic lover in my
samples seemed to feel, as the song suggests, that he was nobody until somebody
loved him.

Paradoxically, manic lovers also behave in ways similar to ludus. They try to   44
hold back, to manipulate the lover, to play it cool. But unlike successful ludic
types, manic lovers never quite succeed at detachment. Their sense of timing
is off. They try to be noncommittal, only to panic and surrender in ignominious
defeat.

The Telephone Trauma Consider this typical caper. The manic realizes that he   45
has been taking the initiative too often in calling his beloved, so he asks her to
call the next time. This is a consciously ludic ploy, since no erotic or storgic
lover would keep count or care. But it is part of the game in ludus to keep
things in balance.

The hour of the expected call arrives, and the phone sits silent. The true   46
ludic lover would not be terribly bothered; he or she would quickly make a
few calls and get busy with other lovers. The manic lover falls into a frenzy of
anxiety. Either he breaks down and calls the lover, or he is in such a state of
emotional upset that he is incapable of ludic detachment when the lover does
call: "Where were you? I was so *worried*!"

Manic lovers, in short, attempt to play by the rules of ludus with the passion   47
of eros, and fail at both. They need to be loved so much that they do not let
the relationship take its own course. They push things, and thereby tend to
lose; mania rarely ends happily. Few lovers go to such extremes as violence or
suicide, but most remain troubled by the experience for months, even years.

Like malaria, it may return to seize the manic lover with bouts of nostalgia and unrest.

It is theoretically possible for mania to develop into lasting love, but the   48
manic lover must find an unusual partner—who can ride out the storms of emotion, return the intensity of feeling, and ultimately convince the manic lover that he or she is lovable. A ludic partner will never tolerate the emotional extremes, and a storgic lover will be unable to reciprocate the feelings. A strong-willed erotic partner might manage it.

Ludic Eros Mania can be reduced by resolving the underlying conditions that   49
create and sustain the lover's lack of self-esteem and his desperate need to be in love. Then the lover may move toward a more confident eros or, perhaps, a more playful ludus. This is the part of the color chart labeled *ludic eros,* the sector between the two primaries.

What enables one lover to mix ludus and eros in a pleasant compromise,   50
while another finds them compounded into mania? Having previous experience in love and many good relationships is one factor. The manic lovers in my sample were discontented with life, but ludic-erotic lovers were basically con-tent and knew what kind of partners they wanted. Ludic-erotic people resemble ludus in their pluralism, their desire for many relationships, but they resemble eros in their preference for clearly-defined types. They do not easily accept substitutes, as ludic types do.

Ludic-erotic love walks an exacting tightrope between intensity and detach-   51
ment. Most people think this approach is too greedy, and therefore immoral. To the ludic-erotic lover, it is just good sense.

The Art of Passionate Caution The tightrope isn't always easy. The lover may   52
spend an evening in the most intense intimacy with his partner, but will always back off in a ludic direction at critical moments. Just when you, the beloved, are about to react to his passion with a murmur of confirmation, he leaps from the couch to make a cup of coffee. Or just when he is about to blurt out that he loves you; he bites his lips and says something less committal: "You really turn me on."

The successful combination of ludus and eros is rare, but it exists. The   53
journals of Casanova are a classic example of the bittersweet taste of this type of love. Today many attempts at "open marriages" are in fact advocating a ludic-erotic approach to love: the spouses remain primarily involved with each other, yet may have intense involvements with others so long as these remain temporary.

PRAGMA *is love* with a shopping list, a love that seeks compatibility on practical   54
criteria. In traditional societies, marriages were arranged on similarities of race,

social class, income, and so on. In modern society the pragmatic approach to love argues that lovers should choose each other on the basis of compatible personalities, like interests and education, similar backgrounds and religious views, and the like. Computer-match services take a pragmatic view.

The pragmatic lover uses social activities and programs as a means to an end, and will drop them if there is no payoff in partners. By contrast, a storgic lover goes out for the activities he enjoys, and thereby meets someone who shares those interests. The storgic lover never consciously chooses a partner.   55

Pragma is not a primary type of love but a compound of storge and ludus. The pragmatic lover chooses a partner as if she had grown up with him (storge) and will use conscious manipulation to find one (ludus). Pragma is rather like manufactured storge, a faster means of achieving the time-honored version. If a relationship does not work out, the pragmatic lover will move rationally on, ludic-fashion, to search for another.   56

The pragmatic approach is not as cold as it seems. Once a sensible choice is made, more intense feelings may develop; but one must begin with a solid match that is practically based. Oriental matchmakers noted that in romantic love "the kettle is boiling when the young couple first starts out"—and cools with time, bringing disappointment. An arranged marriage, they say, is like a kettle that starts cold and slowly warms up. Pragmatic love grows over the years.   57

As pragma is the compound, so storge and ludus may combine as a mixture. The distinguishing features of a *storgic-ludic* affair are convenience and discretion. A typical example is that of a married boss and his secretary, in which the relationship is carefully managed so as to disrupt neither the boss's marriage nor the office routine. Of course, such affairs don't always stay in neat storgic-ludic boxes. In the firm, *A Touch of Class,* the affair becomes too intense, threatening to interfere with the man's comfortably companionate marriage.   58

AGAPE (pronounced ah-ga-pay) is the classical Christian view of love: altruistic, universalistic love that is always kind and patient, never jealous, never demanding reciprocity. When St. Paul wrote to the Corinthians that love is a duty to care about others, whether the love is deserved or not, and that love must be deeply compassionate and utterly altruistic, he used the Greek word, *agape.* But all the greater religions share this concept of love, a generous, unselfish, giving of oneself.   59

I found no saints in my sample. I have yet to interview an unqualified example of agape, although a few respondents had had brief agapic episodes in relationships that were otherwise tinged with selfishness. For instance, one of my subjects, seeing that his lover was torn between choosing him or another man, resolved to save her the pain of deciding; he bowed out gracefully. His action fell short of pure agape, however, because he continued to be interested in how   60 well his beloved was doing, and was purely and selfishly delighted when she dropped the other man and returned to him.

Yet my initial sample of 112 people did contain eight case histories that came quite close to the sexual restraint, dutiful self-sacrifice, universality and altruism that characterize agape. These respondents mixed storge and eros; they had an almost religious attitude toward loving, but they fell short of the hypothetical ideal in loving the partner more than anyone else. They felt intense emotion, as erotic lovers do, along with the enduring patience and abiding affection of storge. 61

Storgic-erotic respondents felt an initial attraction to their partners, distinguishable from erotic attraction by the absence of physical symptoms of excitement. And unlike eros, these people felt little or no jealousy; they seemed to find enough pleasure in the act of loving another person so that the matter of reciprocity was almost irrelevant. 62

Testing One's Type of Love Why construct a typology of love in the first place? Love is a delicate butterfly, runs a certain sentiment, that can be ruined with clumsy dissection. Who cares how many species it comes in; let it fly. 63

As far as I am concerned, any analysis that helps reduce misunderstandings is worthwhile, and there is no human endeavor more ripe for misunderstandings than love. Consider. A person who has just fallen in love is often tempted to test his sensations to prove it's "really" love. Usually such tests are based on a unidimensional concept of love, and therefore they are usually 180° wrong. 64

For example, the decision to test love by postponing sex would be disastrous for an erotic love affair, the equivalent of depriving a baby of food for a week to see if it is strong enough to live. A budding erotic love thrives on sexual intimacy. But delaying sex would be absolutely natural and right for a storgic lover, and it might be a positive incentive to a manic lover. 65

The advantage of my typology, preliminary as it is, is that it teases apart some very different definitions of love, and suggests which types of love are most compatible. Generally, the farther apart two types are on the color chart, the less likely that the lovers share a common language of love. One of my ludic respondents berated his storgic lover for trying to trap him into a commitment, while she accused him of playing games just to get her body. Different types, different languages. Eros insists on rapid intimacy, storge resents being rushed. Same feelings of "love," but opposite ways to express it. 66

Obviously, two lovers who represent unlike primaries will have trouble getting along unless they both bend toward a mixture or compromise. But it all depends on what each individual wants out of a relationship. Two storgic lovers have the best chance for a lasting relationship, and two ludic lovers have the worst chance—but they will have fun while it lasts. 67

One swallow does not a summer make, and neither does one manic binge confirm you as an obsessive lover. One playful affair in a storgic marriage does 68 not define you as ludus. While some people have enjoyed a variety of love experiences equally, most of us definitely prefer one type. We live with other kinds, as we live with many colors, but we still have our favorites.

Questions for Critical Thinking

1. How does Lee's research confirm or contradict Solomon's theory about the "love-world" that lovers share?

2. Who is more likely to have an erotic approach to love—someone homely or someone beautiful? Why?

3. The author quotes Ovid as counseling, "Extinguish the fire of love gradually, not all at once . . . it is wicked to hate a girl you used to love." What is your opinion of this advice?

4. Which of the three primary types of love is most likely to flourish in an urban environment with its typical barroom haunts for meeting possible lovers? Why?

5. Lee claims that Ludus is frequently linked with male homosexual love—an association, he says, that may explain the origin of the term "gay." Of three primary types of love, which do you think least likely to be associated with male homosexual love. Why?

6. Which of the three primary types of love has been traditionally associated with women, and which with men? How do you explain this association?

7. What effect upon the way male homosexuals love do you think allowing marriage between them would have?

8. Which of the three primary types of love do you generally practice, and how do you account for your preference?

Writing Assignment

Write an essay in which you analyze and describe a love relationship in terms of the type of love its participants seem to practice.

Writing Advice

The essay calls for a fairly complex analysis. First, think of a love relationship you know well—perhaps one that you have read extenstively about—your parent's, or a best friend's—and then try to decide which form of love it seems to best exemplify. You need to be thoroughly familiar with Lee's types and the characteristics associated with each before you can apply his classification to the particular love relationship. Once you have a couple in mind and think you know which of Lee's types applies to their relationship, you are then ready to gather specifics to justify the classification.

If you say, for example, that your particular lovers represent examples of Ludus, you must support this analysis by citing specifics about the playfulness in their relationship. Similarly, if you think your lovers are Storge or Mania, you must also show what elements of their relationship justify this conclusion. You might begin this way: "My mother and father, who have been married for twenty-five years, are a classic example of a Storge love relationship." And then you say what Storge is, what its primary characteristics are, and show how your mother and father fit its pattern. Note that you may decide that none of Lee's categories fit the particular relationship you are writing about, in which case you should say so. Then you should describe the relationship and show where and how it is an oddball that simply does not fit with any of Lee's types.

Alternate Writing Assignment

Dispute the accuracy of Lee's categories in an essay that draws on your general knowledge of human nature, your reading, and your personal experience with love relationships.

PHILOSOPHY

LOVE IN THE DESERT
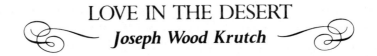
Joseph Wood Krutch

Joseph Wood Krutch (1893–1970) was an American author, editor and teacher, born in Knoxville, Tennessee, and educated at Columbia University (Ph.D. 1923). A prolific and highly regarded social critic and writer, Krutch was drama critic for the *Nation* from 1924 to 1952. He is the author of numerous works of criticism, among them *Comedy and Conscience after the Restoration* (1924), *The Modern Temper* (1929), and *The Measure of Man* (1954). Krutch moved to Arizona in his later years and turned his attention to nature writing, penning such memorable works as *The Twelve Seasons* (1949) and *The Desert Year* (1952).

Reading Advice

The practice of searching nature for parallels to the deepest human emotions and habits is as ancient as the earliest nature writers and writing. Medieval bestiaries openly ascribed human attributes and emotions to the animals, even to the mythical creatures they cataloged. Here Krutch conducts his own search and finds ample evidence to support his contention that humans practice no original variations on sex or love that nature and her creatures have not already repeatedly tried.

Notice how cleverly and seamlessly Krutch incorporates his many examples into the flow of the text. There is no crude disjointedness preceding the appearance of an example, and the entire narrative flows with an uninterrupted smoothness—though it is studded with what, in the hands of a less skilled writer, would have been lumpy specifics and instances.

*T*he ancients called love "the mother of   1 all things," but they didn't know the half of it. They did not know, for instance, that plants as well as animals have their love life and they supposed that even some of the simpler animals were generated by sunlight on mud without the intervention of Venus.

Centuries later when Chaucer and the other medieval poets made "the   2 mystic rose" a euphemism for an anatomical structure not commonly mentioned in polite society, they too were choosing a figure of speech more appropriate than they realized, because every flower really is a group of sex organs which the plants have glorified while the animals—surprisingly enough, as many have observed—usually leave the corresponding items of their own anatomy primitive, unadorned and severely functional. The ape, whose behind blooms in purple and red, represents the most any of the higher animals has achieved along this line and even it is not, by human standards, any great aesthetic success. At least no one would be likely to maintain that it rivals either the poppy or the orchid.

In another respect also plants seem to have been more aesthetically sensitive   3 than animals. They have never tolerated that odd arrangement by which the same organs are used for reproduction and excretion. Men, from St. Bernard to William Butler Yeats, have ridiculed or scorned it and recoiled in distaste from the fact that, as Yeats put it, "love has pitched his mansion in / The place of excrement." As a matter of fact, the reptiles are the only backboned animals who have a special organ used only in mating. Possibly—though improbably, I am afraid—if this fact were better known it might be counted in favor of a generally unpopular group.

All this we now know and, appropriately enough, much of it—especially   4 concerning the sexuality of plants—was first discovered during the eighteenth-century Age of Gallantry. No other age would have been more disposed to hail the facts with delight and it was much inclined to expound the new knowledge in extravagantly gallant terms. One does not usually think of systematizers as given to rhapsody, but Linnaeus, who first popularized the fact that plants can make love, wrote rhapsodically of their nuptials:

The petals serve as bridal beds which the Great Creator has so gloriously arranged, adorned with such noble bed curtains and perfumed with so many sweet scents, that the bridegroom there may celebrate his nuptials with all the greater solemnity. When the bed is thus prepared, it is time for the bridegroom to embrace his beloved bride and surrender his gifts to her: I mean, one can see how testiculi *open and emit* pulverem genitalem, *which falls upon* tubam *and fertilizes* ovarium.

In England, half a century later, Erasmus Darwin, distinguished grandfather   5
of the great Charles, wrote even more exuberantly in his didactic poem, "The
Loves of the Plants," where all sorts of gnomes, sylphs and other mythological
creatures benevolently foster the vegetable *affaires de coeur.* It is said to have
been one of the best-selling poems ever published, no doubt because it combined
the newly fashioned interest in natural history with the long standing obsession
with "the tender passion" as expressible in terms of cupids, darts, flames and
all the other clichés which now survive only in St. Valentine's Day gifts.

Such romantic exuberance is not much favored today when the seamy side   6
is likely to interest us more. We are less likely to abandon ourselves to a
participation in the joys of spring than to be on our guard against "the pathetic
fallacy" even though, as is usually the case, we don't know exactly what the
phrase means or what is "pathetic" about the alleged fallacy. Nevertheless, those
who consent, even for a moment, to glance at that agreeable surface of things
with which the poets used to be chiefly concerned will find in the desert what
they find in every other spring, and they may even be aware that the hare,
which here also runs races with itself, is a good deal fleeter than any Words-
worth was privileged to observe in the Lake Country.

In this warm climate, moreover, love puts in his appearance even before   7
"the yonge sonne hath in the Ram his halfe cours y-ronne" or, in scientific
prose, ahead of the spring equinox. Many species of birds, which for months
have done little more than chirp, begin to remember their songs. In the canyons
where small pools are left from some winter rain, the subaqueous and most
mysterious of all spring births begins and seems to recapitulate the first morning
of creation. Though I have never noticed that either of the two kinds of doves
which spend the whole year with us acquire that "livelier iris" which Tennyson
celebrated, the lizard's belly turns turquoise blue, as though to remind his mate
that even on their ancient level sex has its aesthetic as well as its biological
aspect. Fierce sparrow hawks take to sitting side by side on telegraph wires,
and the Arizona cardinal, who has remained all winter long more brilliantly
red than his eastern cousin ever is, begins to think romantically of his neat but
not gaudy wife. For months before, he had been behaving like an old married
man who couldn't remember what he once saw in her. Though she had followed
him about, he had sometimes driven her rudely away from the feeding station
until he had had his fill. Now gallantry begins to revive and he may even
graciously hand her a seed.

A little later the cactus wren and the curved-bill thrasher will build nests   8
in the wicked heart of the cholla cactus and, blessed with some mysterious
impunity, dive though its treacherous spines. Somewhere among the creosote
bushes, by now yellow with blossoms, the jack rabbit—an unromantic looking
creature if there ever was one—will be demonstrating that she is really a hare,
not a rabbit at all, by giving birth to young furred babies almost ready to go it
alone instead of being naked, helpless creatures like the infant cottontail. The
latter will be born underground, in a cozily lined nest; the more rugged jack
rabbit on the almost bare surface.

My special charge, the Sonoran spadefoot toad, will remain buried no one   9
knows how many feet down for months still to come. He will not celebrate
his spring until mid-July when a soaking rain penetrates deeply enough to
assure him that on the surface a few puddles will form. Some of those puddles
may just possibly last long enough to give his tadpoles the nine or ten days of
submersion necessary, if they are to manage the metamorphosis which will
change them into toadlets capable of repeating that conquest of the land which
their ancestors accomplished so many millions of years ago. But while the
buried spadefoots dally, the buried seeds dropped last year by the little six-
week ephemerals of the desert will spring up and proceed with what looks like
indecent haste to the business of reproduction, as though—as for them is
almost the case—life were not long enough for anything except preparation
for the next generation.

Human beings have been sometimes praised and sometimes scorned because   10
they fall so readily into the habit of pinning upon their posterity all hope for
a good life, of saying, "At least my children will have that better life which I
somehow never managed to achieve." Even plants do that, as I know, because
when I have raised some of the desert annuals under the unsuitable conditions
of a winter living room, they have managed, stunted and sickly though they
seemed, to seed. "At least," they seemed to say, "our species is assured another
chance." And if this tendency is already dominant in a morning glory, human
beings will probably continue to accept it in themselves also, whether, by human
standards, it is wise or not.

As I write this another spring has just come around. With a regularity in   11
which there is something pleasantly comic, all the little romances, dramas and
tragedies are acting themselves out once more, and I seize the opportunity to
pry benevolently.

Yesterday I watched a pair of hooded orioles—he, brilliant in orange and   12
black; she, modestly yellow green—busy about a newly constructed nest hanging from the swordlike leaves of a yucca, where one would have been less
surprised to find the lemon yellow cousin of these birds which builds almost
exclusively in the yucca. From this paradise I drove away the serpent—in this

case a three-foot diamondback rattler who was getting uncomfortably close to the nesting site—and went on to flush out of the grass at least a dozen tiny Gambel's quail whose male parent, hovering close by, bobbed his head plume anxiously as he tried to rally them again. A quarter of a mile away a red and black Gila monster was sunning himself on the fallen trunk of another yucca, and, for all I know, he too may have been feeling some stirring of the spring, though I can hardly say that he showed it.

From birds as brightly colored as the orioles one expects only gay domesticity   13 and lighthearted solicitude. For that reason I have been more interested to follow the home life of the road runner, that unbird-like bird whom we chose at the beginning as a desert dweller par excellence. One does not expect as much of him as one does of an oriole for two good reasons. In the first place, his normal manner is aggressive, ribald and devil-may-care. In the second place, he is a cuckoo, and the shirking of domestic responsibilities by some of the tribe has been notorious for so long that by some confused logic human husbands who are the victims of unfaithfulness not only wear the horns of the deer but are also said to be cuckolded. The fact remains, nevertheless, that though I have watched the developing domestic life of one road runner couple for weeks, I have observed nothing at which the most critical could cavil.

The nest—a rather coarse affair of largish sticks—was built in the crotch   14 of a thorny cholla cactus some ten feet above the ground, which is rather higher than usual. When first found there were already in it two eggs, and both of the parent birds were already brooding them, turn and turn about. All this I had been led to expect because the road runner, unlike most birds, does not wait until all the eggs have been laid before beginning to incubate. Instead she normally lays them one by one a day or two apart and begins to set as soon as the first has arrived. In other words the wife follows the advice of the Planned Parenthood Association and "spaces" her babies—perhaps because lizards and snakes are harder to come by than insects, and it would be too much to try to feed a whole nest full of nearly grown infants at the same time. Moreover, in the case of my couple "self-restraint" or some other method of birth control had been rigorously practiced and two young ones were all there were.

Sixteen days after I first saw the eggs, both had hatched. Presently both   15 parents were bringing in lizards according to a well-worked-out plan. While one sat on the nest to protect the young from the blazing sun, the other went hunting. When the latter returned with a catch, the brooding bird gave up its place, went foraging in its turn and presently came back to deliver a catch, after which it again took its place on the nest. One day, less than a month after the eggs were first discovered, one baby was standing on the edge of the nest itself, the other on a cactus stem a few feet away. By the next day both had disappeared.

Thus, despite the dubious reputation of the family to which he belongs, the   16 road runner, like the other American cuckoos, seems to have conquered both the hereditary taint and whatever temptations his generally rascally disposition may have exposed him to. In this case at least, both husband and wife seemed quite beyond criticism, though they do say that other individuals sometimes reveal a not-too-serious sign of the hereditary weakness when a female will, on occasion, lay her eggs in the nest of another bird of her own species— which is certainly not so reprehensible as victimizing a totally different bird as the European cuckoo does.

Perhaps the superior moral atmosphere of America has reformed the cuc-   17
koo's habit and at least no American representative of the family regularly abandons its eggs to the care of a stranger. Nevertheless, those of us who are inclined to spiritual pride should remember that we do have a native immoralist, abundant in this same desert country and just as reprehensible as any to be found in decadent Europe—namely the cowbird, who is sexually promiscuous, never builds a home of his own and is inveterately given to depositing eggs in the nests of other birds. In his defense it is commonly alleged that his "antisocial conduct" should be excused for the same reason that such conduct is often excused in human beings—because, that is to say, it is actually the result not of original sin but of certain social determinants. It seems that long before he became a cowbird this fellow was a buffalo bird. And because he had to follow the wide ranging herds if he was to profit from the insects they started up from the grass, he could never settle down long enough to raise a family. Like Rousseau and like Walt Whitman, he had to leave his offspring (if any) behind.

However that may be, it still can hardly be denied that love in the desert   18
has its still seamier side. Perhaps the moth, whom we have already seen playing pimp to a flower and profiting shamelessly from the affair, can also be excused on socio-economic grounds. But far more shocking things go on in dry climates as well as in wet, and to excuse them we shall have to dig deeper than the social system right down into the most ancient things-as-they-used to-be. For an example which seems to come straight out of the most unpleasant fancies of the Marquis de Sade, we might contemplate the atrocious behavior of the so-called tarantula spider of the sandy wastes. Here, unfortunately, is a lover whom all the world will find it difficult to love.

This tarantula is a great hairy fellow much like the kind which sometimes   19
comes north in a bunch of bananas and which most people have seen exhibited under a glass in some fruiterer's window. Most visitors to the desert hate and fear him at sight, even though he is disinclined to trouble human beings and is incapable even upon extreme provocation of giving more than a not-too-serious bite. Yet he does look more dangerous than the scorpion and he is, if possible, even less popular.

He has a leg spread of four or sometimes of as much as six inches, and it is   20
said that he can leap for as much as two feet when pouncing upon his insect

prey. Most of the time he spends in rather neat tunnels or burrows excavated in the sand, from which entomologists in search of specimens flush him out with water. And it is chiefly in the hottest months, especially after some rain, that one sees him prowling about, often crossing a road and sometimes waiting at a screen door to be let in. Except for man, his most serious enemy is the "tarantula hawk," a large black-bodied wasp with orange-red wings, who pounces upon his larger antagonist, paralyzes him with a sting and carries his now helpless body to feed the young wasps which will hatch in their own underground burrow.

Just to look at the tarantula's hairy legs and set of gleaming eyes is to suspect   21
him of unconventionality or worse, and the suspicions are justified. He is one of those creatures in whom love seems to bring out the worst. Moreover, because at least one of the several species happens to have been the subject of careful study, the details are public. About the only thing he cannot be accused of is "infantile sexuality," and he can't be accused of that only because the male requires some eleven years to reach sexual maturity or even to develop the special organs necessary for his love making—if you can stretch this euphemistic term far enough to include his activities.

When at last he has come of age, he puts off the necessity of risking contact   22
with a female as long as possible. First he spins a sort of web into which he deposits a few drops of sperm. Then he patiently taps the web for a period of about two hours in order to fill with the sperm the two special palps or mouth parts which he did not acquire until the molt which announced his maturity. Then, and only then, does he go off in search of his "mystic and somber Dolores" who will never exhibit toward him any tender emotions.

If, as is often the case, she shows at first no awareness of his presence, he   23
will give her a few slaps until she rears angrily with her fangs spread for a kill. At this moment he then plays a trick which nature, knowing the disposition of his mate, has taught him and for which nature has provided a special apparatus. He slips two spurs conveniently placed on his forelegs over the fangs of the female, in such a way that the fangs are locked into immobility. Then he transfers the sperm which he has been carrying into an orifice in the female, unlocks her fangs and darts away. If he is successful in making his escape, he may repeat the process with as many as three other females. But by this time he is plainly senile and he slowly dies, presumably satisfied that his life work has been accomplished. Somewhat unfairly, the female may live for a dozen more years and use up several husbands. In general outline the procedure is the same for many spiders, but it seems worse in him, because he is big enough to be conspicuous.

It is said that when indiscreet birdbanders announced their discovery that   24
demure little house wrens commonly swap mates between the first and second

of their summer broods, these wrens lost favor with many old ladies who promptly took down their nesting boxes because they refused to countenance such loose behavior.

In the case of the tarantula we have been contemplating mores which are   25
far worse. But there ought, it seems to me, to be some possible attitude less unreasonable than either that of the old ladies who draw away from nature when she seems not to come up to their very exacting standards of behavior, and the seemingly opposite attitude of inverted romantics who are prone either to find all beasts other than man completely beastly, or to argue that since man is biologically a beast, nothing should or can be expected of him that is not found in all his fellow creatures.

Such a more reasonable attitude will, it seems to me, have to be founded   26
on the realization that sex has had a history almost as long as the history of life, that its manifestations are as multifarious as the forms assumed by living things and that their comeliness varies as much as do the organisms themselves. Man did not invent it and he was not the first to exploit either the techniques of love making or the emotional and aesthetic themes which have become associated with them. Everything either beautiful or ugly of which he has found himself capable is somewhere anticipated in the repertory of plant and animal behavior. In some creatures sex seems a bare and mechanical necessity; in others the opportunity for elaboration has been seized upon and developed in many different directions. Far below the human level, love can be a game on the one hand, or a self-destructive passion on the other. It can inspire tenderness or cruelty; it can achieve fulfillment through either violent domination or pro-longed solicitation. One is almost tempted to say that to primitive creatures, as to man, it can be sacred or profane, love or lust.

The tarantula's copulation is always violent rape and usually ends in death   27
for the aggressor. But over against that may be set not only the romance of many birds but also of other less engaging creatures in whom nevertheless a romantic courtship is succeeded by an epoch of domestic attachment and parental solicitude. There is no justification for assuming, as some romanticists do, that the one is actually more "natural" than the other. In one sense nature is neither for nor against what have come to be human ideals. She includes both what we call good and what we call evil. We are simply among her experiments, though we are, in some respects, the most successful.

Some desert creatures have come quite a long way from the tarantula—and   28
in our direction, too. Even those who have come only a relatively short way are already no longer repulsive. Watching from a blind two parent deer guarding a fawn while he took the first drink at a water hole, it seemed that the deer at least had come a long way.

To be sure many animals are, if this is possible, more "sex obsessed" than   29
we—intermittently at least. Mating is the supreme moment of their lives and for many, as for the male scorpion and the male tarantula, it is also the beginning

of the end. Animals will take more trouble and run more risks than men usually will, and if the Stringbergs are right when they insist that the woman still wants to consume her mate, the biological origin of that grisly impulse is rooted in times which are probably more ancient than the conquest of dry land.

Our currently best-publicized student of human sexual conduct has argued   30
that some of what are called "perversions" in the human being—homosexuality, for example—should be regarded as merely "normal variations" because something analogous is sometimes observed in the animal kingdom. But if that argument is valid then nothing in the textbooks of psychopathology is "abnormal." Once nature had established the fact of maleness and femaleness, she seems to have experimented with every possible variation on the theme. By comparison, Dr. Kinsey's most adventurous subjects were hopelessly handicapped by the anatomical and physiological limitations of the human being.

In the animal kingdom, monogamy, polygamy, polyandry and promiscuity   31
are only trivial variations. Nature makes hermaphrodites, as well as Tiresiases who are alternately of one sex and then the other; also hordes of neuters among the bees and the ants. She causes some males to attach themselves permanently to their females and teaches others how to accomplish impregnation without ever touching them. Some embrace for hours; some, like Onan, scatter their seed. Many males in many different orders—like the seahorse and the ostrich, for example—brood the eggs, while others will eat them, if they get a chance, quite as blandly as many females will eat their mate, once his business is done. Various male spiders wave variously decorated legs before the eyes of a prospective spouse in the hope (often vain) that she will not mistake them for a meal just happening by. But husband-eating is no commoner than child-eating. Both should be classed as mere "normal variants" in human behavior if nothing except a parallel in the animal kingdom is necessary to establish that status. To her children nature seems to have said, "Copulate you must. But beyond that there is no rule. Do it in whatever way and with whatever emotional concomitants you choose. That you should do it somehow or other is all that I ask."

If one confines one's attention too closely to these seamy sides, one begins   32
to understand why, according to Gibbon, some early Fathers of the Church held that sex was the curse pronounced upon Adam and that, had he not sinned, the human race would have been propagated "by some harmless process of vegetation." Or perhaps one begins to repeat with serious emphasis the famous question once asked by the Messrs. Thurber and White, "Is Sex Necessary?" And the answer is that, strictly speaking, it isn't. Presumably the very first organisms were sexless. They reproduced by a "process of vegetation" so harmless that not even vegetable sexuality was involved. What is even more impressive is the patent fact that it is not necessary today. Some of the most successful of all plants and animals—if by successful you mean abundantly

surviving—have given it up either entirely or almost entirely. A virgin birth may require a miracle if the virgin is to belong to the human race, but there is nothing miraculous about it in the case of many of nature's successful children. Parthenogenesis, as the biologist calls it, is a perfectly normal event.

Ask the average man for a serious answer to the question what sex is "for"   33 or why it is "necessary," and he will probably answer without thinking that it is "necessary for reproduction." But the biologist knows that it is not. Actually the function of sex is not to assure reproduction but to prevent it—if you take the word literally and hence to mean "exact duplication." Both animals and plants could "reproduce" or "duplicate" without sex. But without it there would be little or no variation, heredities could not be mixed, unexpected combinations could not arise, and evolution would either never have taken place at all or, at least, taken place so slowly that we might all still be arthropods or worse.

If in both the plant and animal kingdom many organisms are actually aban-   34 doning the whole of the sexual process, that is apparently because they have resigned their interest in change and its possibilities. Everyone knows how the ants and the bees have increased the single-minded efficiency of the worker majority by depriving them of a sexual function and then creating a special class of sexual individuals. But their solution is far less radical than that of many of the small creatures, including many insects, some of whom are making sexless rather than sexual reproduction the rule, and some of whom are apparently dispensing with the sexual entirely so that no male has ever been found.

In the plant world one of the most familiar and successful of all weeds   35 produces its seeds without pollinization, despite the fact that it still retains the flower which was developed long ago as a mechanism for facilitating that very sexual process which it has now given up. That it is highly "successful" by purely biological standards no one who has ever tried to eliminate dandelions from a lawn is likely to doubt. As I have said before, they not only get along very well in the world, they have also been astonishing colonizers here, since the white man unintentionally brought them from Europe, probably in hay. Sexless though the dandelion is, it is inheriting the earth, and the only penalty which it has to pay for its sexlessness is the penalty of abandoning all hope of ever being anything except a dandelion, even of being a better dandelion than it is. It seems to have said at some point, "This is good enough for me. My tribe flourishes. We have found how to get along in the world. Why risk anything?"

But if, from the strict biological standpoint, sex is "nothing but" a mechanism   36 for encouraging variation, that is a long way from saying that there are not other standpoints. It is perfectly legitimate to say that it is also "for" many other things. Few other mechanisms ever invented or stumbled upon opened so many possibilities, entailed so many unforeseen consequences. Even in the face of those who refuse to entertain the possibility that any kind of purpose or foreknowledge guided evolution, we can still find it permissible to maintain that every invention is "for" whatever uses or good results may come from it, that all things, far from being "nothing but" their origins, are whatever they have become. Grant that and one must grant also that the writing of sonnets is one of the things which sex is "for."

Certainly nature herself discovered a very long time ago that sex was—or at least could be used—"for" many things besides the production of offspring not too monotonously like the parent. Certainly also, these discoveries anticipated pretty nearly everything which man himself has ever found it possible to use sex "for." In fact it becomes somewhat humiliating to realize that we seem to have invented nothing absolutely new.   37

Marital attachment? Attachment to the home? Devotion to children? Long before us, members of the animal kingdom had associated them all with sex. Before us they also founded social groups on the family unit and in some few cases even established monogamy as the rule! Even more strikingly, perhaps, many of them abandoned *force majeure* as the decisive factor in the formation of a mating pair and substituted for it courtships, which became a game, a ritual and an aesthetic experience. Every device of courtship known to the human being was exploited by his predecessors: colorful costume display, song, dance and the wafted perfume. And like man himself, certain animals have come to find the preliminary ceremonies so engaging that they prolong them far beyond the point where they have any justification outside themselves. The grasshopper, for instance, continues to sing like a troubadour long after the lady is weary with waiting.   38

Even more humiliating, perhaps, than the fact that we have invented nothing is the further fact that the evolution has not been in a straight line from the lowest animal families up to us. The mammals, who are our immediate ancestors, lost as well as gained in the course of their development. No doubt because they lost the power to see colors (which was not recaptured until the primates emerged), the appeal of the eye plays little part in their courtship. In fact "love" in most of its manifestations tends to play a much lesser part in their lives than in that of many lower creatures—even in some who are distinctly less gifted than the outstandingly emotional and aesthetic birds. On the whole, mammalian sex tends to be direct, unadorned, often brutal, and not even the apes, despite their recovery from color blindness, seem to have got very far beyond the most uncomplicated erotic experiences and practices. Intellectually the mammals may be closer to us than any other order of animals, but emotionally and aesthetically they are more remote than some others—which perhaps explains the odd fact that most comparisons with any of them, and all comparisons with the primates, are derogatory. You may call a woman a "butterfly" or describe her as "birdlike." You may even call a man "leonine." But there is no likening with an ape which is not insulting.   39

How consciously, how poetically or how nobly each particular kind of   40
creature may have learned to love, Venus only knows. But at this very moment
of the desert spring many living creatures, plant as well as animal, are celebrating
her rites in accordance with the tradition which happens to be theirs.

Fortunately, it is still too early for the tarantulas to have begun their amatory   41
black mass, which, for all I know, may represent one of the oldest versions of
the rituals still practiced in the worship of Mr. Swinburne's "mystic and somber
Dolores." But this very evening as twilight falls, hundreds of moths will begin
to stir themselves in the dusk and presently start their mysterious operations
in the heart of those yucca blossoms which are just now beginning to open on
the more precocious plants. Young jack rabbits not yet quite the size of an adult
cottontail are proof that their parents went early about their business, and
many of the brightly colored birds—orioles, cardinals and tanagers—are either
constructing their nests or brooding their eggs. Some creatures seem to be
worshiping only Venus Pandemos; some others have begun to have some inkling
that the goddess manifests herself also as the atavist which the ancients call
Venus Eurania. But it is patent to anyone who will take the trouble to look that
they stand now upon different rungs of that Platonic ladder of love which man
was certainly not the first to make some effort to climb.

Of this I am so sure that I feel it no betrayal of my humanity when I find   42
myself entering with emotional sympathy into a spectacle which is more than
a mere show, absorbing though it would be if it were no more than that.
Modern knowledge gives me, I think, ample justification for the sense that I
am not outside but a part of it, and if it did not give me that assurance, then
I should probably agree that I would rather be "some pagan suckled in a creed
outworn" than compelled to give it up.

Those very same biological sciences which have traced back to their lowly   43
origins the emotional as well as the physiological characteristics of the sentient
human being inevitably furnish grounds for the assumption that if we share
much with the animals, they must at the same time share much with us. To
maintain that all the conscious concomitants of our physical activities are
without analogues in any creatures other than man is to fly in the face of the
very evolutionary principles by which those "hardheaded" scientists set so much
store. It is to assume that desire and joy have no origins in simpler forms of
the same thing, that everything human has "evolved" except the consciousness
which makes us aware of what we do. A Descartes, who held that man was an
animal-machine differing from other animal-machines in that he alone possessed
a gland into which God had inserted a soul, might consistently make between
man and the other animals an absolute distinction. But the evolutionist is the
last man who has a right to do anything of the sort.

He may, if he can consent to take the extreme position of the pure behav-   44
iorist, maintain that in man and the animals alike consciousness neither is nor

can be anything but a phosphorescent illusion on the surface of physiological action and reaction, and without any substantial reality or any real significance whatsoever. But there is no choice between that extreme position and recognition of the fact that animals, even perhaps animals as far down in the scale as any still living or preserved in the ancient rocks, were capable of some awareness and of something which was, potentially at least, an emotion.

Either love as well as sex is something which we share with animals, or it   45 is something which does not really exist in us. Either it is legitimate to feel some involvement in the universal Rites of Spring, or it is not legitimate to take our own emotions seriously. And even if the choice between the two possibilities were no more than an arbitrary one, I know which of the alternatives I should choose to believe in and to live by.

Questions for Critical Thinking

1. In paragraph 6 the author alleges that today we are likely to zealously guard against the "pathetic fallacy." What does he mean by "pathetic fallacy?"

2. What is your opinion of the view that love does not and cannot exist in nature, but is strictly a human feeling?

3. The author describes the tarantula's copulation as "violent rape." What is your definition of rape, and do you think it exists in nature or only in human societies?

4. What important distinction can be made between "rape" among animals and rape as it is committed by humans?

5. What is your opinion of the view attributed by Krutch to Kinsey that homosexuality is merely one among many "normal variations?"

6. What are monogamy, polygamy, and polyandry? Which particular form do you think preferable and why?

7. Do you think Platonic love—that is sexless and unselfish love—possible between unrelated adult men and women of approximately the same age? Why or why not?

Writing Assignment

Some sociologists have proposed that the marital laws be amended to allow for polygyny—a single man with several wives—among the elderly, since that particular group is comprised of a much higher ratio of women to men. Write an essay arguing for or against this proposal.

Writing Advice

This assignment calls for an argument—meaning that you must take a stand on the subject, support it, and expose the weaknesses in the opposition. Freewrite on the subject until you have a strong feeling about it one way or the other. You may have no opinion at the outset or feel only vaguely inclined to one side or the other. But through reading, freewriting, and thinking on paper, you will eventually come to your own bedrock opinion. Ask yourself what harm can come from legally allowing the elderly, among whom there is a severe scarcity of men, to marry in groups. On the other hand, ask yourself why any legalization should be necessary, anyway, since elderly groups are free to informally enter into whatever living arrangements they choose. If you think that the example set would be a bad and corrupting one if polygyny were allowed, reason out this line of argument until you can say why. Once you have formulated your opinion on the issue, then state it in a clear and defensible thesis. Do not forget to express the opposing side's views and to rebut them with your own disarming arguments.

Alternate Writing Assignment

1. Write an essay exploring the difference between "rape" among animals and rape among humans.

2. Write an essay arguing the virtues and advantages of either monogamy, polygamy, or polyandry.

HISTORY

A SECOND BIRTH: GEORGE ELIOT AND GEORGE HENRY LEWES
Phyllis Rose

Phyllis Rose, American author and professor, was born in New York City in 1942 and educated at Radcliffe, Yale, and Harvard (Ph.D., 1970). A professor of English and book reviewer for *The Nation*, *The New York Times Book Review*, and *The Atlantic*, she is also the author of, among other works, *Woman of Letters: A Life of Virginia Woolf* (1978), and *Parallel Lives: Five Victorian Marriages* (1983).

Reading Advice

One of the most enduring and fruitful literary love affairs occurred between Marian Evans (1819–1880) and George Henry Lewes (1817–1878)—she, a late blooming novelist whose work is ranked with the best of her Victorian contemporaries, he, an English critic and author whose work is remembered mainly for its versatility. Literary history credits the love affair between them with creating George Eliot, the pseudonym Lewes chose for Evans when she began writing fiction in her late thirties. During her lifetime with Lewes, Eliot wrote such timeless and acclaimed novels as *Adam Bede* (1859), *Silas Marner* (1861), and her masterpiece, *Middlemarch* (1871–1872). In the excerpt, Rose tells the story from a feminist perspective, showing us Evans in her early years as a sad and desperate spinster withering from lack of love and affection, and tracing the abrupt flowering of talent that followed once Evans and Lewes had settled into comfortable and affectionate domesticity. Although they never married, they lived openly together like any wedded couple—a cohabitation rare for the Victorian era.

Note that this is the sort of article you should read with a biographical dictionary or desk encyclopedia handy since many famous Victorians flit in and out of these pages. While we have provided footnotes for some of them, you might want to look up information about others not covered. The name-dropping is unavoidable because, although the article focuses on a specific literary couple, the author is probing their relationship as a representative Victorian marriage in the context of cultural and social history.

*I*t is so easy, looking backward, knowing   1
the glorious fruits of a life, to assume that the glory was always evident, that the person destined for immortality looked confidently forward to his or her success, that people at the time acted deferentially and helpfully towards the one posterity would consider glorious. Nothing could be further from the truth of the life of George Eliot, who, at the time we begin her story was not George Eliot but Marian Evans, middle-aged, physically unattractive, lonely.

In 1851, after spending the first thirty years of her life in the Midlands, in   2
and around Coventry, she began working in London for the *Westminster Review,* a liberal periodical of some stature which had been particularly distinguished when it was owned by John Stuart Mill and which now belonged to John Chapman, the publisher and bookseller. Chapman and Marian Evans were the entire editorial staff of the *Westminster,* and since Chapman's time was heavily committed to his other businesses, Miss Evans virtually ran the magazine herself. She conceived and commissioned articles, did copy-editing, read proof, and wrote some of the copy—particularly the connective copy in the long surveys of new work abroad and in England. Although the work was unpaid and she had to live on the interest from a legacy of £2,000 left by her father, it provided her with an excellent education in contemporary thought and literature.

Superficially, her life was full. She boarded with the Chapmans, who had a   3
large house in the Strand. She participated in their complicated family life: Chapman's mistress was his children's governess and lived with the family; both wife and mistress recognized Miss Evans's presence as a further complication and watched constantly for signs of her attachment to Chapman evolving beyond

the tolerable. The situation in the Chapman household must have been interesting but could hardly have been satisfying for the woman who was neither wife nor mistress. Still, there were pleasant social evenings. The Chapmans gave evening parties almost every week, and Miss Evans was always invited. Some of the people she met there—for example, Sir James Clark, the queen's physician—liked her so much that they invited her to dine at their homes. Most people were impressed by her intelligence, by her grey eyes, and by her voice, a deep, lovely instrument from which the provincial accent had been trained out when she was at boarding school in her teens. Ralph Waldo Emerson said of her, "That lady has a calm, serious soul."

Through her work for the *Westminster,* Miss Evans met Herbert Spencer,[1]   4
who was about her own age and held a position similar to hers on *The Economist.* His first book, *Social Statics,* had recently been published. It also happened that he lived just across the street from the Chapmans. With so much in common— scientific and philosophical interests, extraordinary intelligence, a taste for music—he and Miss Evans spent a lot of time together. He got reviewer's tickets to the opera, theater, and concerts, and Miss Evans was his favorite companion.

They enjoyed each other's company so much that it became a problem.   5
Spencer, a man not conspicuous for social daring, was afraid that people might assume they were engaged because they appeared together in public so often. Even worse, Miss Evans herself might think that he was in love with her. He knew he was not in love with her and was never likely to be. He found her, with some reason, physically unappealing, and the lack of physical attraction was fatal. As strongly as his judgment prompted him to love her, his instincts would not respond. He took the extraordinary step of warning her that he did not love her and had no intention of doing so. Then, embarrassed by his own lack of tact, he wrote another letter apologizing for having hurt her.

Miss Evans's response was characteristically self-deprecating. "I feel disap-   6
pointed rather than 'hurt' that you should not have sufficiently divined my character to perceive how remote it is from my habitual state of mind to imagine that anyone is falling in love with me." But despite the warning that her love would not be returned, she fell in love with him, or, more precisely, her passionate desire that there should be love in her life came to focus on Spencer. He was available. He was her equal. He was appropriate. He would do.

Aware of the unconventionality of her behavior, she made a declaration of   7
her feelings, asking for his love. He said he could not give it. She asked, then, for merely his companionship and the promise that he would not attach himself to someone else, abandoning her. If that happened, she said, she must die, but short of that she could gather courage from his friendship to carry on with

1. Herbert Spencer (1820–1903), English philosopher.

her work and to make her life useful. "I do not ask you to sacrifice anything—
I would be very good and cheerful and never annoy you. But I find it impossible
to contemplate life under any other conditions."

> Those who have known me best have always said that if I ever loved anyone thor-
> oughly my whole life must turn upon that feeling, and I find they said truly. You
> curse the destiny which has made the feeling concentrate itself on you—but if you
> will only have patience with me you shall not curse it long. You will find that I can
> be satisfied with very little, if I am delivered from the dread of losing it.

I do not want to weaken the impact of this letter, surely one of the saddest
I have ever read, but lest Marian Evans sound entirely like a love-starved
spinster, pathetically abasing herself for a crumb of affection, I must point out
the letter's ending, which sounds another note. "I suppose no woman ever
before wrote such a letter as this—but I am not ashamed of it, for I am
conscious that in light of reason and true refinement I am worthy of your
respect and tenderness, whatever gross men or vulgar-minded women might
think of me." If the need for affection was characteristic of her, so too was
pride in her radical rethinking of how to live, pride in the difference between
her morality and that of most men and women. The strength of her desire to
love and be loved was matched by the energy and daring she was willing to
devote to satisfying that desire.

Still, she had been rejected, and it was a hard thing to take. Her self-esteem   8
could hardly have been lower. When she told a friend in Coventry that she
was being taken to the opera (for Spencer continued to perform that essential
service), she said, "See what a fine thing it is to pick up people who are short-
sighted enough to like one." It seemed that going to the opera would be the
only sensual pleasure she would ever know. "What a wretched lot of old
shrivelled creatures we shall be bye-and-bye."

You would not say of all thirty-three-year-old women that they are middle-   9
aged, but you would certainly have said it of Marian Evans in the summer of
1852. She felt the best was behind her; she looked into the future and saw no
sources of renewal. She feared that old friends would die and that she wouldn't
have the power to make new ones. She feared she had missed out on life. "You
know how sad one feels when a great procession has swept by one, and the
last notes of its music have died away, leaving one alone with the fields and sky.
I feel so about life sometimes." A passage from Margaret Fuller's[2] journal was
achingly appropriate. "I shall always reign through the intellect, but the life!
the life! Oh my God! shall that never be sweet?"

At her advanced age, she could hardly hope for marriage. Even when she   10
had been young, her father and brother had considered her a poor prospect.
She was too ugly. Her only asset on the marriage market was her piety, and
when she lost that her brother was furious, partly with the fury of the outraged

---

2. Margaret Fuller (1810–1850), American writer, feminist, and lecturer.

religious conservative and partly with that of the property-owner whose tenant sublets to a welfare family. By the time of his death, her father must have given up hoping a husband would take over the care of Marian—hence the legacy, to enable her to be independent. Marian must have given up herself.

Yet she had a strongly affectionate nature, supported by a philosophical   11 conviction that people should devote themselves to the happiness of others. In a phrase that she would use to describe some of her heroines, she was ardent, longing to attach herself to other people, other goals. How long can such a person survive as merely a welcome guest at other people's dinner parties? She longed for closer attachments, for an emotional connection which would be central to her life, from which new interests and activities would result as naturally as children result from lovemaking. Although she had accomplished a great deal (her translation of Strauss's *Life of Jesus* was an important contribution to progressive thought), although she had a position of some stature in literary London, although she enjoyed the respect and affection of everyone who met her, although—in sum—her lot was enviable compared to that of most unmarried women in Victorian England, she was lonely. Her powerful imagination could conceive of a life much richer than the one she led. As active as she was, she felt she could be doing more—and events would prove her right. She would look back on these years as a time of inertia and suffering. Her great energy, burning to be put to other uses—nurturing, intimacy, creativity—turned back upon herself for lack of an object. Idle, she brooded; brooding, she despaired.

To avoid feeling sorry for herself, she tried to suppress any awareness of her   12 emotions at all. "If you insist on my writing about 'Emotions,'" she said to one friend, "why, I must get some up expressly for the purpose. But I must own I would rather not, for it is the grand wish and object of my life to get rid of them as far as possible, seeing that they have already had more than their share of my nervous energy. In describing herself, she used the word *plucky* rather than *happy.* She would carry on, with resolute cheerfulness but not with joy, and it seems hardly likely that in this "carried-on" life the writing of fiction would have figured. Those parts of herself she would need in writing novels— passion, sympathy, dramatic power—were too close to the parts of herself she would have had to stifle in order to remain a plucky spinster.

Herbert Spencer was feeling so guilty that he even mentioned marriage to   13 Miss Evans, as a kind of restitution for having engaged her emotions. But she was not interested in the mere form of intimacy. Still, he continued to see her, and one day George Henry Lewes asked if he might join Spencer in his visit to Miss Evans. Another day, to Spencer's vast relief, Lewes decided to stay on alone with Miss Evans after Spencer left.

John Chapman had introduced them in 1851. He and his assistant happened   14 to run into the literary journalist in a bookstore in the Burlington Arcade.

Lewes and Thornton Leigh Hunt had recently begun publishing *The Leader,* a radical weekly for which Hunt wrote the political sections and Lewes covered theater, music, and books. Despite his position in the literary world of the capital, Lewes did not make much of an impression on Miss Evans. Physically, he was unprepossessing—short and scruffy. And although he was the best writer you could get for a certain kind of scientific subject (exactly the right man, for example, for an essay on Lamarck), Miss Evans the editor valued him less as a writer and thinker than many other contributors to the *Westminster.* He had nowhere near the intellectual stature of John Stuart Mill, nor even of Froude, F. W. Newman, or James Martineau. He was a witty man who culti-vated—in the Gallic fashion—a flippant manner, and this, too, did not impress the earnest Miss Evans. And he was, of course, married. Mrs. Lewes had recently given birth to her sixth child.

By the spring of 1853, Miss Evans's opinion of Lewes had changed. She now   15
found him genial and amusing. "Like a few other people in the world, he is much better than he seems, a man of heart and conscience wearing a mask of flippancy." Lewes, like Spencer, was supplied with free tickets to theater, opera, and concerts, and he took Miss Evans along with him. At some point, Lewes must have told her the truth about his marriage, and that more than anything— more than his kindness and attentiveness, more than the free tickets—must have changed her mind about him. Here was a man who needed her.

Lewes had married Agnes Jervis in 1841. She was then a beautiful nineteen-   16
year-old with striking blonde hair, and the two seemed very much in love. Mrs. Carlyle, for one, got pleasure from seeing them together. But by 1849 she noticed a change. "I used to think these Leweses a perfect pair of lovebirds, . . . but the female lovebird appears to have hopped off to some distance and to be now taking a somewhat critical view of her little shaggy mate!" Jane Carlyle saw acutely. Mrs. Lewes had in fact hopped so far from her husband that she was having an affair with his close friend and partner, Thornton Leigh Hunt. (Hunt was married, too.) The child born to Agnes Lewes in the month that her husband was introduced to Miss Evans in the bookstore was fathered not by Lewes (the father of her first three children) but by Hunt. It was her third child by Hunt.

Agnes, her husband, and her lover all had views on sex and love that would   17
have been called at the time "free-thinking" or "advanced" by some, "libertine" by others. They were inheritors of a heady eighteenth-century rationalist tra-dition: what was endorsed by religion and society was not always right. If anything, inherited institutions and traditional authorities were likely to be stupidly tyrannical. One had to be on the lookout. One had to rethink every-thing. One had to beware of authority. One had to rebel. Mr. and Mrs. Lewes believed that only love could bind people together and that neither law nor religion had it in its power to cement a union where feeling no longer existed. And although traditionally, by law, a woman's body belonged to her husband,

they believed it was her own, to give to whomever she chose.

Taking the high rationalist line, Lewes refused to be outraged by his wife's   18
infidelity. He registered no complaint when she gave birth to another man's
child, and even allowed the baby to be given his name, in a spirit, one supposes,
of communal responsibility—a spirited "no" to the pedantry of precise
acknowledgment. He must have thought that Agnes's passion for Hunt would
pass in time, or that a rational, sophisticated man who admired Gallic insou-
ciance ought to be able to live with the fact of his wife's infidelity. In 1850 he
believed in what was much later given the name of "open marriage." But in
October 1851, when Agnes gave birth to another child he had not fathered,
Lewes began to realize that what he had was not an open marriage, or a radical,
free-thinkers' marriage, but no marriage at all. By the start of 1853, when
Agnes was pregnant yet again by Hunt, Lewes had ceased to think of her as his
wife, although he continued to support her and her children.

English law was not adapted to such subtleties of thought and behavior. It   19
understood that a man had the right to exclusive enjoyment, sexually speaking,
of his wife. It was horrified at the possibility that a man might have to pass his
property on to children who were not really his. That, if nothing else, was
sufficient reason for the strong stand the law took against adultery—that is to
say, female adultery. Even before the Matrimonial Causes Act of 1857, English
law allowed a man—albeit with great trouble and at vast expense—to divorce
his wife for adultery. But the law did not allow for quirky, eccentric attempts
to live rationally, for private understandings of what did and did not constitute
adultery. One illegitimate child was quite enough to convince the law that a
man's wife had abandoned his protection, and if a man chose to wait for a
second illegitimate child before he was convinced, then in the eyes of the law
he had condoned his wife's adultery and forfeited his right to divorce her. That
was George Lewes's situation when he began seeing Marian Evans daily and
escorting her to the opera. In law, he had a wife, but in fact he did not. Legally
tied to a woman from whom he could expect no love, no help, no comfort,
he was in as much despair about his emotional life as was, for other reasons,
Miss Evans.

In October 1853, the month that Agnes's third by Hunt was born, Marian   20
Evans moved out of the Chapmans' house, where she had come to feel claustrophobic, and into lodgings of her own in Cambridge Street. Now she had
more freedom. She could receive whatever visitors she chose. When she turned
thirty-four in the following month, she noted that she began her new year
happier than usual. The signs of a closer professional tie with Lewes appear.
When Chapman accepted a negative review by T. H. Huxley of Lewes's book
on Comte, Marian intervened on her friend's behalf, begging Chapman not to
run Huxley's piece. And when, in April, Lewes got sick and was unable to
work, she wrote some of his copy for him. "No opera and no fun for me for
the next month!" Lewes's health did not improve swiftly or completely enough

to suit either of them, and they began to talk about going to the Continent for his health. In July of 1854 they left England for Weimar, travelling together openly and sharing lodgings. From this moment on, until Lewes's death twenty-four years later, they would live together as though they were married.

From the beginning, they were delighted with each other and saw their union as a rebirth. "The day seems too short for our happiness, and we both of us feel that we have begun life afresh—with new ambitions and new powers." They moved from Weimar, which they loved, to Berlin, and with the self-satisfaction of fresh love felt pity for anyone who had to come to such an ugly place alone or with a disagreeable companion. For them, even Berlin was charming. "I am happier every day," wrote Miss Evans to John Chapman, the one person to whom she felt free to describe her illicit happiness (presumably the lecherous publisher was proof against shock), "and find my domesticity more and more delightful and beneficial to me. Affection, respect, and intellectual sympathy deepen, and for the first time in my life I can say to the moments 'Verweilen sie, sie sind so schön.' "[3]

"The literary couple," wrote Elizabeth Hardwick, "is a peculiar English domestic manufacture, useful no doubt in a country with difficult winters. Before the bright fire at tea-time, we can see these high-strung men and women clinging together, their inky fingers touching." One has reason to envy the intellectual compatibility of Miss Evans and Mr. Lewes. They walked together, wrote together, read Homer, and learned languages together. Lewes's scientific interests were a source of new delight to Miss Evans; they even raised tadpoles together. Every night after dinner they read aloud to each other, for as much as three hours. On a typical evening she would begin with an enjoyable book (Boswell's *Life of Johnson*, for example), then subside to a dreary and dry one (Whewell's *History of the Inductive Sciences*), and then wind up with some German poetry, Heine perhaps. They read aloud the third volume of Ruskin's *Modern Painters*, and they read aloud Elizabethan plays.

Their new domestic life centered on work. Lewes was in the midst of writing his excellent *Life of Goethe* and Marian Evans was doing a translation of Spinoza which was destined never to be published. In addition, they wrote articles and reviews because they were constantly in need of money to support Agnes and her children as well as themselves. And what a lot of work they got done! Together they wrote almost half *The Leader*'s supplement for June 16, 1855, Miss Evans contributing a review essay, "Menander and Greek Comedy," and Lewes writing articles on Sydney Smith, Isaac Newton, and Owen Meredith, as well as a review of a French book on longevity.

Although posterity has reversed their positions, in 1855 when they returned from Germany and settled on the south side of the Thames in the London

21

22

23

---

3. "Linger! You are so lovely" (from Goethe's *Faust*).

suburbs, Lewes was by far the more established professionally of the two, and with the self-assurance of the successful, he took more pleasure in Marian's success than in his own. His encouragement and his example of professionalism helped her to develop quickly from an editor into a freelance writer. With money as motivation and with a little praise, he coaxed out her inclination to authorship.

She had long thought of writing fiction and had actually written the first   24
of a novel—a description of a Staffordshire village and the neighboring farm-houses. Gordon Haight estimates the date of composition as 1846. But she laid the fragment aside, never going further. "As the years passed on I lost hope that I should ever be able to write a novel, just as I desponded about everything else in my future life." Some writers, as Freud believed, thrive artistically on misery. They write only when and because life seems to offer no other source of satisfaction. They write to create for themselves, in imagination, the satis-factions that reality seems to deny. But George Eliot was a writer of the other sort, for whom productivity depends upon contentment. In this way, too, she was a realist: she could not create her happiness through fictions, had to proceed to her work from a bedrock of fulfilled life.

When they went to Germany, Miss Evans took along with her the fragmen-   25
tary chapter she had written years before, and one night in Berlin she read it aloud to Lewes. I want to underline that Lewes did not encourage her to bring the manuscript. She says it "happened to be among the papers" she brought with her. Nor did Lewes encourage her to read it aloud. "Something led me to read it to George." Demurely, girlishly, she was blurring the traces of her own activity, and I emphasize the extent to which she took the initiative in this matter because history has so readily perpetuated the fiction that she was the passive party in the birth of George Eliot. But just as she was unafraid to ask for love from Herbert Spencer, she was aggressive enough to raise the possibility of writing novels to Lewes. All she needed in order to continue was the encour-agement she had every human reason to expect he would offer in response.

Lewes's reaction to her reading of the fragmentary chapter could hardly be   26
called overwhelming. On the basis of what he heard, he thought she might be able to write fiction, but he had his doubts. It was wholly descriptive, and everything else she had written was expository. In general, her mind seemed so powerfully analytic that one did not expect her to be creative. He wondered whether she would have the dramatic power necessary for fiction writing—the ability to imagine other people's thoughts and to invent dialogue for them. This was exactly her own doubt. Still she was sufficiently encouraged to continue to think about writing fiction, and as time went by, perhaps sensing her desire for such encouragement, Lewes urged her even more strongly: positively, she must try to write a story. He thought she might be able to pull it off by the sheer force of her intelligence.

One morning her desire to write finally coincided with sufficient self-   27
confidence to form a resolution to do so. "As I was lying in bed, thinking what
should be the subject of my first story, my thoughts merged themselves into a
dreamy doze, and I imagined myself writing a story the title of which was—
'The Sad Fortunes of the Reverend Amos Barton.'" When she told Lewes about
it, he said, "O what a capital title!" And so she set to work. To Lewes's
amazement, the very first chapter of "Amos Barton" convinced him that her
dialogue was excellent. The only other question was whether she could command pathos. Did it follow that a person who was strong in intelligence was
correspondingly feeble in feeling, or that an analytical mind could not also
imagine fiercely? One night in the fall of 1856 Lewes went to town on purpose
to give her quiet to write, and she set out to prove she could evoke emotion,
in treating the death of Milly, Amos Barton's wife. She was determined that
the old dualistic chestnut about intelligence and emotion be laid to rest. She
knew herself to be a deeply feeling woman as well as an intelligent one. When
Lewes returned and read aloud what she had written, both of them were moved
to tears. He went over to her, kissed her, and said, "I think your pathos is even
better than your fun."

Lewes sent "Amos Barton" to John Blackwood in Edinburgh, who, with his   28
characteristic reticence, said the piece "would do." He ran it in *Blackwood's
Magazine* and later published the completed series, *Scenes of Clerical Life*. Although
Blackwood was aware that "George Eliot" was a pseudonym, he believed his
new author was a man, in all probability, a clergyman.

To say that George Eliot was the child of the extraordinarily happy union   29
of Marian Evans and George Henry Lewes is more than wordplay. Literary
parthenogenesis being as impossible for Miss Evans as the biological sort is
generally impossible, George Eliot would almost certainly not have entered the
world without Lewes's participation. But what exactly was his role, the dynamics
of his contribution? The usual explanation—that Marian was "not fitted to
stand alone" and needed someone to lean on—is subtly misleading, making
England's strongest woman novelist seem deficient and dependent.

The myth of George Eliot's dependency—a myth she may have chosen to   30
perpetuate for her own purposes—originates with a phrenological reading of
her character made in her Coventry days. Like many intellectuals of her time
she looked to phrenology as a way of understanding herself, as contemporary
intellectuals look to psychoanalysis. Charles Bray, her Coventry mentor, took
her to London to have a cast made of her head for a phrenological reading.
The reading confirmed that in her brain development Intellect vastly predom-
inated. "Feelings" expressed themselves in another part of the topography of
the skull, and from the bumps in that area, the skilled phrenologist could tell
that Miss Evans's "Animal" and "Moral" instincts were about equal. The moral
feelings were sufficient to keep the animal in order and in proper subservience

but they were not "spontaneously active." In addition, her social feelings were very active, particularly "adhesiveness," a phrenological term for nonsexual love. "She was of a most affectionate disposition," Bray reported, paraphrasing the phrenologist, "always requiring someone to lean upon, preferring what has hitherto been considered the stronger sex, to the other and more impressible. She was not fitted to stand alone."

Phrenologically speaking, Marian Evans had feared for a long time that her moral and animal regions were unfortunately balanced. That is to say, she felt herself to be a sensual person. When her father was alive, she had associated him with the restraining, moral part of herself, and when he died she suffered from a horrid image of herself "becoming earthly sensual and devilish for want of that purifying restraining influence. The phrenological reading confirmed her fears about the sluggishness of her moral region: it was "not spontaneously active." But the part of her phrenological reading that posterity has chosen to emphasize is her dependence, the notion that she required someone to lean on, preferably a man, that she was not fitted to stand alone.   31

In support of this characterization, we are told how Marian Evans threw herself at the feet of the aged Dr. Brabant, the Biblical scholar, offering to devote herself to his work. We are told how she repeatedly mistook intellectual friendships offered by men for offers of sexual love. We are told how, ignoring conventions, she paid men like Dr. Brabant the utmost attention, causing consternation in their families. We hear about the wife and mistress of John Chapman—how jealous they were of Miss Evans's intimacy with Chapman and how threatened they felt when she moved into their household. We are told about her attempt to throw herself on Herbert Spencer and the relief with which she sank onto the proffered arm of the already married George Henry Lewes. And in all this we are supposed to see a "need"—not a desire, mind you, but a neurotic "need"—for affection. In the face of all these terrified wives and families, of men who realize with dismay that this gentle woman who has captivated them wants even more than they thought—we are supposed to see a woman who cannot stand alone. What I see is a woman of passionate nature who struggles, amidst limited opportunity, to find someone to love and to love her; a woman who goes to quite unconventional lengths and is willing to be unusually aggressive—almost predatory—in her efforts to secure for herself what she wants. To want love and sex in one's life is hardly, after all, a sign of neurosis. And is it a sign of dependence for a woman to want love and sex from a man? It is a small matter of emphasis only, but it does seem to me to make some difference whether we think of one of the most powerful female writers ever as neurotically dependent on men or as brave enough to secure for herself what she wanted.   32

"Under the influence of the intense happiness I have enjoyed in my married life from thorough moral and intellectual sympathy, I have at last found out   33 my true vocation after which my nature has always been feeling and striving without finding it." I take seriously this account of how George Eliot seized her identity as a writer. I see the story of George Eliot's "birth" as a moving testimony to the connection there may be between creativity and sexuality. Lewes's editorial help and his encouragement at the start of her writing career were certainly important in George Eliot's birth, but they were responses to gestures Miss Evans made. They were not the motivating force. That came from inside her, welling up along with the joy, the self-esteem, and the sense of fulfillment which followed her belated acquisition of love. It was a second spring in her life, and its warmth released powers inside her which had been held back, powers which might earlier have drowned her meager, virginal equanimity.

Questions for Critical Thinking

1. Applying Lee's categories ("Styles of Loving") to this description of the love affair between George Eliot and George Henry Lewes, what type of love would you say the couple shared?

2. How, in your opinion, does inequality in a relationship or marriage add to or detract from its participants' prospects for happiness?

3. The author asks rhetorically in defending George Eliot's behavior, "Is it a sign of dependence for a woman to want love and sex from a man?" What answer would you give to that question?

4. What is your opinion of Lewes's conduct in supporting both his wife and the three illegitimate children she bore during their marriage? What would likely be your reaction if you found yourself in his shoes?

5. Of the five Victorian love relationships covered in the book from which this was excerpted, the extramarital relationship between George Eliot and George Henry Lewes was judged by the author to have been the happiest. In what way does marriage contribute to, or detract from, a couple's happiness?

6. How does this example of love support or contradict Solomon's theory of the "loveworld?"

7. Elsewhere in the book from which this selection was excerpted, the author declares that women who are "particularly sensitive to power" seem to prefer marrying men who have some "handicap." Why would a man with a "handicap" be an attractive marriage partner to a woman who is sensitive to power?

8. What, in your opinion, is the present status of equality between the sexes?

Writing Assignment

Write an essay on the possible effects of infidelity on a love relationship.

Writing Advice

The analysis of effect is the opposite of an analysis of cause: the second focuses on the antecedents to some happening or event; the first, on the consequences of some action. For example, if you are writing an analysis of cause about a certain automobile accident, you would properly focus on the circumstances and conditions that preceded, and might have contributed to, the accident. You might investigate the conditions of the road, the car, the weather, the driver, weighing what possible part each might have played. On the other hand, if you were analyzing the effects of an automobile accident, your focus would be on its aftermath rather than its antecedents. You might analyze the effects on the driver—whether physical or psychological—on the car, or on the driver's insurance premium. In any case, your focus would be on what happened after, not before, the accident.

In this essay, you are asked to predict the possible effects of infidelity on a relationship. Personal experience might seem one most obvious source of specific details for such an essay. If you have experiences to relate, either because they happened to you or to a relative or friend, you can use them, so long as you provide the proper preamble and context. Beware, however, of generalizing grossly from what might be a unique experience or effect. Nor should you use this essay as a medium for your anger and bile directed against your ex-lover, the rat.

Happily, not all of us have been heartbroken by an unfaithful spouse or lover. Some of us will, therefore, have to dig into library materials for details. Here you are likely to get a clearer-headed view from the experts, in addition to all the anecdotes and stories you could possibly use.

Alternate Writing Assignment

It would be healthier for both sexes if women became as sexually aggressive as men. Attack or defend that statement in an essay.

HISTORY

DASHIELL HAMMETT
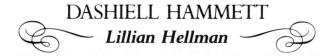
Lillian Hellman

Lillian Hellman (1905–1984), American dramatist and memoirist, was born in New Orleans and attended New York University and Columbia. Hellman worked variously as a manuscript reader, theatrical playreader, and scenario reader before she met Dashiell

Hammett, with whom she began studying writing in 1932. At Hammett's suggestion, she wrote a theatrical adaptation of William Roughhead's *Bad Companions*, which became *The Children's Hour* (produced at Maxine Elliott's Theater, November 20, 1934) and her first critical success. Her subsequent plays included such hits as *The Little Foxes* (first produced at the National Theater in New York, February 15, 1939) and *Watch on the Rhine* (first produced at Martin Beck Theater, in New York, April 1, 1941). Hellman won critical praise for her dramatic technique and her mastery of the theatrical dialogue. She received many theatrical prizes, including two New York Critics Circle Awards and the National Institute of Arts and Letters Gold Medal for drama.

Reading Advice

Lillian Hellman and Dashiell Hammett met in 1929 and enjoyed a romantic relationship on and off over the next 31 or so years which Hellman later movingly described in her memoir *An Unfinished Woman* (1969). Hammett (1894–1961), also a writer, is generally credited with creating the "hard-boiled," "tough-as-nails" persona who has become a fixture in detective stories. Consisting of several novels regarded as classics of the genre, his work includes such all-time detective story favorites as *The Maltese Falcon* (1930), and *The Thin Man* (1932). The relationship between the two lovers, as Hellman describes it, was sometimes serene, often stormy, frequently cantankerous, but also notable for mutual affection, loyalty, and endurance that persisted until 1961 with Hammett's death.

This excerpt from Hellman's autobiography bears the imprint of both reminiscence and excerpting since it tends to weave in and out of incidents, scenes, and tenses, almost like a diary. Hellman is in one breath narrating a recollection, and in another, commenting on it from the perspective of many years later. The backward look of nostalgia, a common vein throughout these pages, is what ties together this slightly scattershot collection of vignettes and scenes. Bear this in mind as you read and you will have an easier time following the author's reminiscences.

*F*or years we made jokes about the day   1
I would write about him. In the early years, I would say, "Tell me more about the girl in San Francisco. The silly one who lived across the hall in Pine Street."

And he would laugh and say, "She lived across the hall in Pine Street and   2
was silly."

"Tell more than that. How much did you like her and how—?"   3

He would yawn. "Finish your drink and go to sleep."

But days later, maybe even that night, if I was on the find-out kick, and I   4
was, most of the years, I would say, "O.K., be stubborn about the girls. So tell me about your grandmother and what you looked like as a baby."

"I was a very fat baby. My grandmother went to the movies every afternoon.   5
She was very fond of a movie star called Wallace Reid and I've told you all this before."

I would say I wanted to get everything straight for the days after his death   6
when I would write his biography and he would say that I was not to bother
writing his biography because it would turn out to be the history of Lillian
Hellman with an occasional reference to a friend called Hammett.

The day of his death came on January 10, 1961. I will never write that   7
biography because I cannot write about my closest, my most beloved friend.
And maybe, too, because all those questions through all the thirty-one on and
off years, and the sometimes answers, got muddled, and life changed for both
of us and the questions and answers became one in the end, flowing together
from the days when I was young to the days when I was middle-aged. And so
this will be no attempt at a biography of Samuel Dashiell Hammett, born in
St. Mary's County, Maryland, on May 27, 1894. Nor will it be a critical appraisal
of his work. In 1966 I edited and published a collection of his stories. There
was a day when I thought all of them very good. But all of them are not good,
though most of them, I think, are very good. It is only right to say immediately
that by publishing them at all I did what Hammett did not want to do: he
turned down all offers to republish the stories, although I never knew the
reason and never asked. I did know, from what he said about "Tulip," the
unfinished novel that I included in the book, that he meant to start a new
literary life and maybe didn't want the old work to get in the way. But sometimes
I think he was just too ill to care, too worn out to listen to plans or read
contracts. The fact of breathing, just breathing, took up all the days and nights.

In the First World War, in camp, influenza led to tuberculosis and Hammett   8
was to spend years after in army hospitals. He came out of the Second World
War with emphysema, but how he ever got into the Second World War at the
age of forty-eight still bewilders me. He telephoned me the day the army
accepted him to say it was the happiest day of his life, and before I could finish
saying it wasn't the happiest day of mine and what about the old scars on his
lungs, he laughed and hung up. His death was caused by cancer of the lungs,
discovered only two months before he died. It was not operable—I doubt that
he would have agreed to an operation even if it had been—and so I decided
not to tell him about the cancer. The doctor said that when the pain came, it
would come in the right chest and arm, but that pain might never come. The
doctor was wrong: only a few hours after he told me, the pain did come.
Hammett had had self-diagnosed rheumatism in the right arm and had always
said that was why he had given up hunting. On the day I heard about the
cancer, he said his gun shoulder hurt him again, would I rub it for him. I
remember sitting behind him, rubbing the shoulder and hoping he would always
think it was rheumatism and remember only the autumn hunting days. But the
pain never came again, or if it did he never mentioned it, or maybe death was
so close that the shoulder pain faded into other pains.

He did not wish to die and I like to think he didn't know he was dying. But   9
I keep from myself even now the possible meaning of a night, very late, a short
time before his death. I came into his room, and for the only time in the years
I knew him there were tears in his eyes and the book was lying unread. I sat
down beside him and waited a long time before I could say, "Do you want to
talk about it?"

He said, almost with anger, "No. My only chance is not to talk about it."

And he never did. He had patience, courage, dignity in those last, awful   10
months. It was as if all that makes a man's life had come together to prove
itself: suffering was a private matter and there was to be no invasion of it. He
would seldom even ask for anything he needed, and so the most we did—my
secretary and Helen, who were devoted to him, as most women always had
been—was to carry up the meals he barely touched, the books he now could
hardly read, the afternoon coffee, and the martini that I insisted upon before
the dinner that wasn't eaten.

One night of that last year, a bad night, I said, "Have another martini. It   11
will make you feel better."

"No," he said, "I don't want it."

I said, "O.K., but I bet you never thought I'd urge you to have another
drink."

He laughed for the first time that day. "Nope. And I never thought I'd turn
it down."

Because on the night we had first met he was getting over a five-day drunk   12
and he was to drink very heavily for the next eighteen years, and then one day,
warned by a doctor, he said he would never have another drink and he kept
his word except for the last year of the one martini, and that was my idea.

We met when I was twenty-four and he was thirty-six in a restaurant in   13
Hollywood. The five-day drunk had left the wonderful face looking rumpled,
and the very tall thin figure was tired and sagged. We talked of T. S. Eliot,
although I no longer remember what we said, and then went and sat in his car
and talked at each other and over each other until it was daylight. We were to
meet again a few weeks later and, after that, on and sometimes off again for
the rest of his life and thirty years of mine.

Thirty years is a long time, I guess, and yet as I come now to write about   14
them the memories skip about and make no pattern and I know only certain
of them are to be trusted. I know about that first meeting and the next, and
there are many other pictures and sounds, but they are out of order and out
of time, and I don't seem to want to put them into place. (I could have done
a research job, I have on other people, but I didn't want to do one on Hammett,
or to be a bookkeeper of my own life.) I don't want modesty for either of us,
but I ask myself now if it can mean much to anybody but me that my second

sharpest memory is of a day when we were living on a small island off the coast of Connecticut. It was six years after we had first met: six full, happy, unhappy years during which I had, with help from Hammett, written *The Children's Hour*, which was a success, and *Days to Come*, which was not. I was returning from the mainland in a catboat filled with marketing and Hammett had come down to the dock to tie me up. He had been sick that summer—the first of the sickness—and he was even thinner than usual. The white hair, the white pants, the white shirt made a straight, flat surface in the late sun. I thought: Maybe that's the handsomest sight I ever saw, that line of a man, the knife for a nose, and the sheet went out of my hand and the wind went out of the sail. Hammett laughed as I struggled to get back the sail. I don't know why, but I yelled angrily, "So you're a Dostoevsky sinner-saint. So you are." The laughter stopped, and when I finally came in to the dock we didn't speak as we carried up the packages and didn't speak through dinner.

Later that night, he said, "What did you say that for? What does it mean?"   15
I said I didn't know why I had said it and I didn't know what it meant.

Years later, when his life had changed, I did know what I had meant that   16
day: I had seen the sinner—whatever is a sinner—and sensed the change before it came. When I told him that, Hammett said he didn't know what I was talking about, it was all too religious for him. But he did know what I was talking about and he was pleased.

But the fat, loose, wild years were over by the time we talked that way.   17
When I first met Dash he had written four of the five novels and was the hottest thing in Hollywood and New York. It is not remarkable to be the hottest thing in either city—the hottest kid changes for each winter season—but in his case it was of extra interest to those who collect people that the ex-detective who had bad cuts on his legs and an indentation in his head from being scrappy with criminals was gentle in manner, well educated, elegant to look at, born of early settlers, was eccentric, witty, and spent so much money on women that they would have liked him even if he had been none of the good things. But as the years passed from 1930 to 1948, he wrote only one novel and a few short stories. By 1945, the drinking was no longer gay, the drinking bouts were longer and the moods darker. I was there off and on for most of those years, but in 1948 I didn't want to see the drinking anymore. I hadn't seen or spoken to Hammett for two months until the day when his devoted cleaning lady called to say she thought I had better come down to his apartment. I said I wouldn't, and then I did. She and I dressed a man who could barely lift an arm or a leg and brought him to my house, and that night I watched delirium tremens, although I didn't know what I was watching until the doctor told me the next day at the hospital. The doctor was an old friend. He said, "I'm going to tell Hammett that if he goes on drinking he'll be dead in a few months. It's

my duty to say it, but it won't do any good." In a few minutes he came out of Dash's room and said, "I told him. Dash said O.K., he'd go on the wagon forever, but he can't and he won't."

But he could and he did. Five or six years later, I told Hammett that the   18
doctor had said he wouldn't stay on the wagon.

Dash looked puzzled. "But I gave my word that day."

I said, "Have you always kept your word?"

"Most of the time," he said, "maybe because I've so seldom given it."

He had made up honor early in his life and stuck with his rules, fierce in   19
the protection of them. In 1951 he went to jail because he and two other trustees of the bail bond fund of the Civil Rights Congress refused to reveal the names of the contributors to the fund. The truth was that Hammett had never been in the office of the Congress, did not know the name of a single contributor.

The night before he was to appear in court, I said, "Why don't you say that you don't know the names?"

"No," he said, "I can't say that."

"Why?"

"I don't know why. I guess it has something to do with keeping my word,   20
but I don't want to talk about that. Nothing much will happen, although I think we'll go to jail for a while, but you're not to worry because"—and then suddenly I couldn't understand him because the voice had dropped and the words were coming in a most untypical nervous rush. I said I couldn't hear him, and he raised his voice and dropped his head. "I hate this damn kind of talk, but maybe I better tell you that if it were more than jail, if it were my life, I would give it for what I think democracy is, and I don't let cops or judges tell me what I think democracy is." Then he went home to bed, and the next day he went to jail.

July 14, 1965

It is a lovely day. Fourteen years ago on another lovely summer day the   21
lawyer Hammett said he didn't need, didn't want, but finally agreed to talk to because it might make me feel better, came back from West Street jail with a message from Hammett that the lawyer had written on the back of an old envelope. "Tell Lilly to go away. Tell her I don't need proof she loves me and don't want it." And so I went to Europe, and wrote a letter almost every day, not knowing that about one letter in ten was given to him, and never getting a letter from him because he wasn't allowed to write to anybody who wasn't related to him. (Hammett had, by this time, been moved to a federal penitentiary in West Virginia.) I had only one message that summer: that his prison job was cleaning bathrooms, and he was cleaning them better than I had ever done.

I came back to New York to meet Hammett the night he came out of jail.   22

Jail had made a thin man thinner, a sick man sicker. The invalid figure was trying to walk proud, but coming down the ramp from the plane he was holding tight to the railing, and before he saw me he stumbled and stopped to rest. I guess that was the first time I knew he would now always be sick. I felt too bad to say hello, and so I ran back into the airport and we lost each other for a few minutes. But in a week, when he had slept and was able to eat small amounts of food, an irritating farce began and was to last for the rest of his life: jail wasn't bad at all. True, the food was awful and sometimes even rotted, but you could always have milk; the moonshiners and car thieves were dopes but their conversation was no sillier than a New York cocktail party; nobody liked cleaning toilets, but in time you came to take a certain pride in the work and an interest in the different cleaning materials; jail homosexuals were nasty-tempered, but no worse than the ones in any bar, and so on. Hammett's form of boasting was always to make fun of trouble or pain. We had once met Howard Fast on the street and he told us about his to-be-served jail sentence. As we moved away, Hammett said, "It will be easier for you, Howard, and you won't catch cold, if you first take off the crown of thorns." So I should have guessed that Hammett would talk about his own time in jail the way many of us talk about college.

I do not wish to avoid the subject of Hammett's political beliefs, but the truth is that I do not know if he was a member of the Communist party and I never asked him. If that seems an odd evasion between two people we did not mean it as an evasion: it was, probably, the product of the time we lived through and a certain unspoken agreement about privacy. Now, in looking back, I think we had rather odd rules about privacy, unlike other peoples' rules. We never, for example, asked each other about money, how much something cost or how much something earned, although each of us gave to the other as, through the years, each of us needed it. It does not matter much to me that I don't know if Hammett was a Communist party member: most certainly he was a Marxist. But he was a very critical Marxist, often contemptuous of the Soviet Union in the same hick sense that many Americans are contemptuous of foreigners. He was often witty and biting sharp about the American Communist party, but he was, in the end, loyal to them. Once, in an argument with me, he said that of course a great deal about Communism worried him and always had and that when he found something better he intended to change his opinions. And then he said, "Now please don't let's ever argue about it again because we're doing each other harm." And so we did not argue again, and I suppose that itself does a kind of harm or leaves a moat too large for crossing, but it was better than the arguments we had been having—they had started in the 1940's—when he knew that I could not go his way. I think that must have pained him, but he never said so. It pained me, too, but I knew that, unlike many radicals, whatever he believed in, whatever he had arrived at,

23

came from reading and thinking. He took time to find out what he thought, and he had an open mind and a tolerant nature.

In 1952 I had to sell the farm. I moved to New York and Dash rented a   24
small house in Katonah. I went once a week to see him, he came once a week to New York, and we talked on the phone every day. But he wanted to be alone—or so I thought then, but am now not so sure because I have learned that proud men who can ask for nothing may be fine characters, but they are difficult to live with or to understand. In any case, as the years went on he became a hermit, and the ugly little country cottage grew uglier with books piled on every chair and no place to sit, the desk a foot high with unanswered mail. The signs of sickness were all around: now the phonograph was unplayed, the typewriter untouched, the beloved, foolish gadgets unopened in their pack-ages. When I went for my weekly visits we didn't talk much and when he came for his weekly visits to me he was worn out from the short journey.

Perhaps it took me too long to realize that he couldn't live alone anymore,   25
and even after I realized it I didn't know how to say it. One day, immediately after he had made me promise to stop reading "L'il Abner," and I was laughing at his vehemence about it, he suddenly looked embarrassed—he always looked embarrassed when he had something emotional to say—and he said, "I can't live alone anymore. I've been falling. I'm going to a Veterans Hospital. It will be O.K., we'll see each other all the time, and I don't want any tears from you." But there were tears from me, two days of tears, and finally he consented to come and live in my apartment. (Even now, as I write this, I am still angry and amused that he always had to have things on his own terms: a few minutes ago I got up from the typewriter and railed against him for it, as if he could still hear me. I know as little about the nature of romantic love as I knew when I was eighteen, but I do know about the deep pleasure of continuing interest, the excitement of wanting to know what somebody else thinks, will do, will not do, the tricks played and unplayed, the short cord that the years make into rope and, in my case, is there, hanging loose, long after death. I am not sure what Hammett would feel about the rest of these notes about him, but I am sure that he would be pleased that I am angry with him today.) And so he lived with me for the last four years of his life. Not all of that time was easy, indeed some of it was very bad, but it was an unspoken pleasure that having come together so many years before, ruined so much, and repaired a little, we had endured. Sometimes I would resent the understated or seldom stated side of us and, guessing death wasn't too far away, I would try for something to have afterwards. One day I said, "We've done fine, haven't we?"

He said, "Fine's too big a word for me. Why don't we just say we've done   26
better than most people?"

On New Year's Eve, 1960, I left Hammett in the care of a pleasant practical   27
nurse and went to spend a few hours with friends. I left their house at twelve-

thirty, not knowing that the nurse began telephoning for me a few minutes later. As I came into Hammett's room, he was sitting at his desk, his face as eager and excited as it had been in the drinking days. In his lap was the heavy book of Japanese prints that he had bought and liked many years before. He was pointing to a print and saying to the nurse, "Look at it, darling, it's wonderful." As I came toward him, the nurse moved away, but he caught her hand and kissed it, in the same charming, flirtatious way of the early days, looking up to wink at me. The book was lying upside down and so the nurse didn't need to mumble the word "irrational." From then on—we took him to the hospital the next morning—I never knew and will now not ever know what irrational means. Hammett refused all medication, all aid from nurses and doctors in some kind of mysterious wariness. Before the night of the upside-down book our plan had been to move to Cambridge because I was to teach a seminar at Harvard. An upside-down book should have told me the end had come, but I didn't want to think that way, and so I flew to Cambridge, found a nursing home for Dash, and flew back that night to tell him about it. He said, "But how are we going to get to Boston?" I said we'd take an ambulance and I guess for the first time in his life he said, "That will cost too much." I said, "If it does, then we'll take a covered wagon." He smiled and said, "Maybe that's the way we should have gone places anyway."

And so I felt better that night, sure of a postponement. I was wrong. Before   28
six o'clock the next morning the hospital called me. Hammett had gone into a coma. As I ran across the room toward his bed there was a last sign of life: his eyes opened in shocked surprise and he tried to raise his head. He was never to think again and he died two days later.

But I do not wish to end this book on an elegiac note. It is true that I miss   29
Hammett, and that is as it should be. He was the most interesting man I've ever met. I laugh at what he did say, amuse myself with what he might say, and even this many years later speak to him, often angry that he still interferes with me, still dictates the rules.

But I am not yet old enough to like the past better than the present, although   30
there are nights when I have a passing sadness for the unnecessary pains, the self-made foolishness that was, is, and will be. I do regret that I have spent too much of my life trying to find what I called "truth," trying to find what I called "sense." I never knew what I meant by truth, never made the sense I hoped for. All I mean is that I left too much of me unfinished because I wasted too much time. However.

Questions for Critical Thinking

1. How was the relationship between Hellman and Hammett similar to, and different from, the one between George Eliot and George Henry Lewes?

2. Under John Alan Lee's classification system ("Styles of Loving"), which love type do you think would most accurately describe the relationship between Hellman and Hammett?

3. George Eliot and Henry Lewes, Lillian Hellman and Dashiell Hammett, were all writers. What positive and negative effects can sharing a common occupation have on the relationship between lovers?

4. Aside from her obvious love of Hammett, Hellman also clearly respected and admired him. What part do you think respect plays in a love relationship?

5. Hellman admits knowing that Hammett was going to die but not telling him. What is your opinion of this decision?

6. Hellman and Hammett held differing political beliefs throughout their lives. How important is agreement on politics in a love relationship?

7. What can you deduce about the balance of power that existed in the relationship between Hellman and Hammett?

8. What balance of power between the participants in a love relationship do you think ideal? What do you think possible?

Writing Assignment

Write an essay that describes the personality of Dashiell Hammett, deducing characteristics and traits from Hellman's portrait of him.

Writing Advice

This is a rather straightforward assignment, requiring skilled literary sleuthing. Hellman does tell us outright some things about Hammett: that he was stubborn; that he had a quixotic, almost chivalrous streak; that he was an alcoholic and a communist. But she leaves much unsaid that can be inferred about Hammett by a sensitive reader. For example, what does this particular exchange tell us about Hammett (and it tells a good deal, we think):

> Sometimes I would resent the understated or seldom stated side of us and, guessing death wasn't too far away, I would try for something to have afterwards. One day I said, "We've done fine, haven't we?"
>
> He said, "Fine's too big a word for me. Why don't we just say we've done better than most people?"

This is where you must bring your interpretative skills to play, in sifting through exchanges and scenes such as this one that implicitly characterize Hammett.

The best way to write this essay is to carefully read Hellman's article, making notes about anything Hammett is reported to have done or said that you think characterizes him. Jot down your rough interpretation of the particular remark or incident and try to discern some underlying pattern. Once you have a basic grasp of Hammett's personality, express your notion of it in a thesis that can be supported by quotations from the text. Note that playing the literary detective requires you to similarly support all your conclusions and inferences about Hammett.

Alternate Writing Assignment

In any relationship it is better for a strong man to be paired with a weak woman, or a weak man to be paired with a strong woman, than for both participants to be equally strong. Write an essay supporting or refuting that view.

HISTORY

LOVE IN A CONCENTRATION CAMP
Victor Frankl

Victor Frankl (b. 1905), psychiatrist and author, was born in Vienna and received an M.D. from the University of Vienna. Frankl is the founder of the therapeutic school of logotherapy which, along with Adler's and Freud's, is sometimes referred to as the "third Viennese school of psychotherapy." The winner of numerous international awards and honors, Frankl is a prolific author and contributor to journals. His books include *The Doctor and the Soul: An Introduction to Logotherapy* (1955); *From Death-Camp to Existentialism: A Psychiatrist's Path to a New Therapy* (1959); and *Man's Search for Meaning: An Introduction to Logotherapy* (1963), which has been translated into 14 languages and has sold well over a million and a half copies.

Reading Advice

This piece should present little if any reading difficulty, since it is a straightforward story written in a crisp narrative style. In a brief vignette, taken from Frankl's book *Man's Search for Meaning*, we get a glimpse into the capacity for love to sustain and uplift the spirit during moments of trial and despair. Frankl writes movingly about how the memory of his wife helped him survive the brutality of Nazi concentration camps, where he was imprisoned as a Jew between 1942 and 1945. His wife perished in a Nazi concentration camp.

*I*n spite of all the enforced physical and   1
mental primitiveness of the life in a concentration camp, it was possible for
spiritual life to deepen. Sensitive people who were used to a rich intellectual
life may have suffered much pain (they were often of a delicate constitution),
but the damage to their inner selves was less. They were able to retreat from
their terrible surroundings to a life of inner riches and spiritual freedom. Only
in this way can one explain the apparent paradox that some prisoners of a less
hardy make-up often seemed to survive camp life better than did those of a
robust nature. In order to make myself clear, I am forced to fall back on personal
experience. Let me tell what happened on those early mornings when we had
to march to our work site.

There were shouted commands: "Detachment, forward march! Left-2-3-4!   2
Left-2-3-4! Left-2-3-4! Left-2-3-4! First man about, left and left and left and
left! Caps off!" These words sound in my ears even now. At the order "Caps
off!" we passed the gate of the camp, and searchlights were trained upon us.
Whoever did not march smartly got a kick. And worse off was the man who,
because of the cold, had pulled his cap back over his ears before permission
was given.

We stumbled on in the darkness, over big stones and through large puddles,   3
along the one road leading from the camp. The accompanying guards kept
shouting at us and driving us with the butts of their rifles. Anyone with very
sore feet supported himself on his neighbor's arm. Hardly a word was spoken;
the icy wind did not encourage talk. Hiding his mouth behind his upturned
collar, the man marching next to me whispered suddenly: "If our wives could
see us now! I do hope they are better off in their camps and don't know what
is happening to us."

That brought thoughts of my own wife to mind. And as we stumbled on   4
for miles, slipping on icy spots, supporting each other time and again, dragging
one another up and onward, nothing was said, but we both knew: each of us
was thinking of his wife. Occasionally I looked at the sky, where the stars were
fading and the pink light of the morning was beginning to spread behind a dark
bank of clouds. But my mind clung to my wife's image, imaging it with an
uncanny acuteness. I heard her answering me, saw her smile, her frank and
encouraging look. Real or not, her look was then more luminous than the sun
which was beginning to rise.

A thought transfixed me: for the first time in my life I saw the truth as it   5
is set into song by so many poets, proclaimed as the final wisdom by so many
thinkers. The truth—that love is the ultimate and the highest goal to which
man can aspire. Then I grasped the meaning of the greatest secret that human
poetry and human thought and belief have to impart: *The salvation of man is
through love and in love.* I understand how a man who has nothing left in this

world still may know bliss, be it only for a brief moment, in the contemplation of his beloved. In a position of utter desolation, when man cannot express himself in positive action, when his only achievement may consist in enduring his sufferings in the right way—an honorable way—in such a position man can, through loving contemplation of the image he carries of his beloved, achieve fulfillment. For the first time in my life I was able to understand the meaning of the words, "The angels are lost in perpetual contemplation of an infinite glory."

In front of me a man stumbled and those following him fell on top of him. 6
The guard rushed over and used his whip on them all. Thus my thoughts were interrupted for a few minutes. But soon my soul found its way back from the prisoner's existence to another world, and I resumed talk with my loved one: I asked her questions, and she answered; she questioned me in return, and I answered.

"Stop!" We had arrived at our work site. Everybody rushed into the dark 7
hut in the hope of getting a fairly decent tool. Each prisoner got a spade or a pickax.

"Can't you hurry up, you pigs?" Soon we had resumed the previous day's 8
positions in the ditch. The frozen ground cracked under the point of the pickaxes, and sparks flew. The men were silent, their brains numb.

My mind still clung to the image of my wife. A thought crossed my mind: 9
I didn't even know if she were still alive. I knew only one thing—which I have learned well by now: Love goes very far beyond the physical person of the beloved. It finds its deepest meaning in his spiritual being, his inner self. Whether or not he is actually present, whether or not he is still alive at all, ceases somehow to be of importance.

I did not know whether my wife was alive, and I had no means of finding 10
out (during all my prison life there was no outgoing or incoming mail); but at that moment it ceased to matter. There was no need for me to know; nothing could touch the strength of my love, my thoughts, and the image of my beloved. Had I known then that my wife was dead, I think that I would still have given myself, undisturbed by that knowledge, to the contemplation of her image, and that my mental conversation with her would have been just as vivid and just as satisfying. "Set me like a seal upon thy heart, love is as strong as death."

Questions for Critical Thinking

1. In paragraph 1 the author attributes the survival of less robust natures in the concentration camp to the "life of inner riches and spiritual freedom." What other explanation do you think might also account for this survival?

2. Using John Alan Lee's typology ("Styles of Loving"), how would you classify the love the author expresses for his wife?

3. Do you agree with the author that love is the highest goal to which humans can aspire? What, in your opinion, should be the ultimate and highest goal for aspiring humans?

4. Suppose the author's wife had really been a nagging and waspish shrew, do you think he would have similarly romanticized her in his concentration camp fantasies? Why or why not?

5. Which of the three philosophical theories about love presented at the beginning of this chapter does Frankl's experience seem to most solidly confirm?

6. Do you think the concentration camp guards experienced a similar romanticized longing for their lovers? Why or why not?

7. The author says that love goes beyond the physical "person of the beloved" and finds deeper meaning "in his spiritual being." Can the same be said of hate? Explain the reasoning behind your answer.

8. The author says it would not have mattered to his fantasies if he had known that his wife was dead. Which in your opinion is better—this kind of idealized, even delusional love, or the real everyday love that is focused on a living nearby person? Why?

Writing Assignment

Write an essay about the wonders and disappointments of romantic love.

Writing Advice

This is another broad assignment that will require narrowing into a manageable topic. See the essay "Writing Expository Prose" in Chapter 1 for some suggestions about how to do this narrowing.

There are numerous approaches you could use in writing this essay, but the one that will probably work best for you is the one that takes advantage of your unique experiences with love. If you have never been in romantic love (unlikely but possible), you are probably better off avoiding any narrational angle and trying, instead, for a more academic treatment such as a definition. If that is the course you choose to take, you should begin by reading extensively about romantic love. Any number of pop psychology articles and essays have been written on the subject of romantic love, and hundreds of attempts—some labored, some insightful—have been made to define it. On the other hand, if you know some romantic lovers well—parents, relatives, or close friends—you could write an observational essay that describes their relationship as representative of this kind of love.

Of course, the easiest and most tempting approach, especially if you have the background for it, is simply to narrate and discuss your own experiences with romantic love. Avoid, however, becoming too mawkish and gushy in your treatment. Being in love is wonderful; writing about lovelorn misadventures can easily seduce one into penning unreadable mush. Remember, also, that your narrative must support a thesis or make a point.

Alternate Writing Assignment

Write an essay comparing and contrasting the kind of delusional love that the author experienced with the real everyday love that husbands and wives or live-in partners might share daily. Say which is better and more satisfying and why.

LITERATURE

ANDREA DEL SARTO
(Called "The Faultless Painter")
Robert Browning

Robert Browning (1812–1889), English poet, received a broad and eclectic education, mainly due to the influence of his father, and published his first poem anonymously in 1833. Browning visited Italy in 1834 and that country soon became his second home. In 1846 he married Elizabeth Barrett and moved with her to Italy, where they lived happily for 15 years. After the death of his wife, Browning returned to England and published *Dramatis Personae* (1864). His masterpiece, *The Ring and the Book* (4 vols., 1868–1869) is considered a brilliant psychological study. Browning's work, with its irregular meters and rhythms, is regarded as highly influential on modern poetry.

Reading Advice

"Andrea del Sarto" is a dramatic monologue—a poem spoken by a persona who is characterized by his or her own utterances—and was intended by Browning to be a word picture of the famous Florentine painter. As you read this poem, you must interpret it as you would a long, theatrical soliloquy in which a character unwittingly reveals much about himself. For example, the fact that Andrea is a uxorious husband is easily inferred from the placating tone he takes towards Lucrezia. He does not wish to quarrel with her; he agrees to paint her friend's picture for "his own price," which we gather Andrea thinks far too little. But he is unwilling to oppose Lucrezia in anything, and craves only a little of her attention. All this a sensitive reader will implicitly gather from Andrea's own words.

The background to this poem, among the best known of Browning's brilliant soliloquies, is this: in the fall of 1862, Browning was asked by John Kenyon, his benefactor, to obtain a self-portrait of Andrea and his wife Lucrezia from the Pitti Palace, in Florence. When he failed to acquire the requested painting, Browning wrote this poem and sent it to Kenyon. For facts about Andrea and his relationship with Lucrezia, Browning drew heavily from *Lives of the Painters*, by Giorgio Vasari (1511–1574), who had been one of del Sarto's students.

The son of a Florentine tailor, Andrea was born in 1486 and soon won fame for his flawless technique which earned him praise as the "painter without error." He married Lucrezia in 1513, and she served as models for several of his paintings, including his famous *Madonna del Sacco*. In 1518, Andrea was summoned by Francis I, king of France, to the French court where he did some of his finest work. Vasari reported that he was lured back to Florence by Lucrezia, who squandered his money on a house and on wasteful pleasures. There is also the suggestion in Vasari that Andrea accepted money from King Francis for works never actually completed, and Browning makes reference to this fraud (which modern scholars doubt) in the poem.

In his portrayal of Andrea as an artist of technical perfection but no soul, Browning closely follows Vasari's estimation of Andrea's work as "entirely free of errors" but lacking in "ardour and animation," which the biographer blamed on the artist's "timidity of mind." So accomplished was the sheer technical skill of Andrea that Michelangelo is quoted by Vasari as having remarked about him to the artist Raphael (1483–1520): "There is a little man in Florence, who if he were employed upon such great works as have been given to you, would make you sweat." Stricken with the plague in 1531, Andrea died of it on January 22, abandoned by his servants and Lucrezia.

> *But do not let us quarrel any more,*
> *No, my Lucrezia; bear with me for once:*
> *Sit down and all shall happen as you wish.*
> *You turn your face, but does it bring your heart?*
> *I'll work then for your friend's friend, never fear,*   5
> *Treat his own subject after his own way,*
> *Fix his own time, accept too his own price,*
> *And shut the money into this small hand*
> *When next it takes mine. Will it? tenderly?*
> *Oh, I'll content him,—but to-morrow, Love!*   10
> *I often am much wearier than you think,*
> *This evening more than usual, and it seems*
> *As if—forgive now—should you let me sit*
> *Here by the window with your hand in mine*
> *And look a half-hour forth on Fiesole,*[1]   15
> *Both of one mind, as married people use,*
> *Quietly, quietly the evening through,*
> *I might get up to-morrow to my work*
> *Cheerful and fresh as ever. Let us try.*

---

1. Small town on a hill three miles from Florence.

To-morrow, how you shall be glad for this!   20
Your soft hand is a woman of itself,
And mine the man's bared breast she curls inside.
Don't count the time lost, neither; you must serve
For each of the five pictures we require:
It saves a model. So! keep looking so—   25
My serpenting beauty, rounds on rounds!
—How could you ever prick those perfect ears,
Even to put the pearl there! oh, so sweet—
My face, my moon, my everybody's moon,
Which everybody looks on and calls his,   30
And, I suppose, is looked on by in turn,
While she looks—no one's: very dear, no less.
You smile? why, there's my picture ready made,
There's what we painters call our harmony!
A common greyness silvers everything,—   35
All in a twilight, you and I alike
—You, at the point of your first pride in me
(That's gone you know),—but I, at every point;
My youth, my hope, my art, being all toned down
To yonder sober pleasant Fiesole.   40
There's the bell clinking from the chapel-top;
That length of convent-wall across the way
Holds the trees safer, huddled more inside;
That last monk leaves the garden; days decrease,
And autumn grows, autumn in everything.   45
Eh? the whole seems to fall into a shape
As if I saw alike my work and self
And all that I was born to be and do,
A twilight-piece. Love, we are in God's hand.
How strange now, looks the life he makes us lead;   50
So free we seem, so fettered fast we are!
I feel he laid the fetter: let it lie!
This chamber for example—turn your head—
All that's behind us! You don't understand
Nor care to understand about my art,   55
But you can hear at least when people speak:
And that cartoon,[2] the second from the door
—It is the thing, Love! so such things should be—
Behold Madonna!—I am bold to say.

---

2. Preparatory drawing for a picture

I can do with my pencil what I know,   60
What I see, what at bottom of my heart
I wish for, if I ever wish so deep—
Do easily, too—when I say, perfectly,
I do not boast, perhaps: yourself are judge,
Who listened to the Legate's[3] talk last week,   65
And just as much they used to say in France.
At any rate 't is easy, all of it!
No sketches first, no studies, that's long past:
I do what many dream of, all their lives,
—Dream? strive to do, and agonize to do,   70
And fail in doing. I could count twenty such
On twice your fingers, and not leave this town,
Who strive—you don't know how the others strive
To paint a little thing like that you smeared
Carelessly passing with your robes afloat,—   75
Yet do much less, so much less, Someone says,
(I know his name, no matter)—so much less!
Well, less is more, Lucrezia: I am judged.
There burns a truer light of God in them,
In their vexed beating stuffed and stopped-up brain,   80
Heart, or whate'er else, than goes on to prompt
This low-pulsed forthright craftsman's hand of mine.
Their works drop groundward, but themselves, I know,
Reach many a time a heaven that's shut to me,
Enter and take their place there sure enough,   85
Though they come back and cannot tell the world.
My works are nearer heaven, but I sit here.
The sudden blood of these men! at a word—
Praise them, it boils, or blame them, it boils too.
I, painting from myself and to myself,   90
Know what I do, am unmoved by men's blame
Or their praise either. Somebody remarks
Morello's[4] outline there is wrongly traced,
His hue mistaken; what of that? or else,
Rightly traced and well ordered; what of that?   95
Speak as they please, what does the mountain care?
Ah, but a man's reach should exceed his grasp,

---

3. Pope's envoy.
4. Mountain in Appennines north of Florence.

Or what's a heaven for? All is silver-grey
Placid and perfect with my art: the worse!
I know both what I want and what might gain,   100
And yet how profitless to know, to sigh
"Had I been two, another and myself,
Our head would have o'erlooked the world!" No doubt.
Yonder's a work now, of that famous youth
The Urbinate[5] who died five years ago.   105
('T is copied, George Vasari sent it me.)
Well, I can fancy how he did it all,
Pouring his soul, with kings and popes to see,
Reaching, that heaven might so replenish him,
Above the through his art—for it gives way;   110
That arm is wrongly put—and there again—
A fault to pardon in the drawing's lines,
Its body, so to speak: its soul is right,
He means right—that, a child may understand.
Still, what an arm! and I could alter it: 115
But all the play, the insight and the stretch—
Out of me, out of me! And wherefore out?
Had you enjoined them on me, given me soul,
We might have risen to Rafael, I and you!
Nay, Love, you did give all I asked, I think—   120
More than I merit, yes, by many times.
But had you—oh, with the same perfect brow,
And perfect eyes, and more than perfect mouth,
And the low voice my soul hears, as a bird
The fowler's pipe, and follows to the snare—   125
Had you, with these the same, but brought a mind!
Some women do so. Had the mouth there urged
"God and the glory! never care for gain.
The present by the future, what is that?
Live for fame, side by side with Agnolo![6]   130
Rafael is waiting: up to God, all three!"
I might have done it for you. So it seems:
Perhaps not. All is as God over-rules.
Beside, incentives come from the soul's self;
The rest avail not. Why do I need you?   135

---

5. Reference to Raphael (Raffaello Sanzio, 1483–1520) born at Urbino.
6. Michaelangelo (Michelagniolo Buonarroti, 1475–1564).

What wife had Rafael, or has Agnolo?
In this world, who can do a thing, will not;
And who would do it, cannot, I perceive:
Yet the will's somewhat—somewhat, too, the power—
And thus we half-men struggle. At the end,   140
God, I conclude, compensates, punishes.
'T is safer for me, if the award be strict,
That I am something underrated here,
Poor this long while, despised, to speak the truth.
I dared not, do you know, leave home all day,   145
For fear of chancing on Paris lords.
The best is when they pass and look aside;
But they speak sometimes; I must bear it all.
Well may they speak! That Francis, that first time,
And that long festal year at Fontainebleau!   150
I surely then could sometimes leave the ground,
Put on the glory, Rafael's daily wear,
In that humane great monarch's golden look,—
One finger in his beard or twisted curl
Over his mouth's good mark that made the smile,   155
One arm about my shoulder, round my neck,
The jingle of his gold chain in my ear,
I painting proudly with his breath on me,
All his court round him, seeing with his eyes,
Such frank French eyes, and such a fire of souls   160
Profuse, my hand kept plying by those hearts,—
And, best of all, this, this, this face beyond,
This in the background, waiting on my work,
To crown the issue with a last reward!
A good time, was it not, my kingly days?   165
And had you not grown restless . . . but I knew—
'T is done and past; 't was right, my instinct said;
Too live the life grew, golden and not grey,
And I'm the weak-eyed bat no sun should tempt
Out of the grange whose four walls make his world.   170
How could it end in any other way?
You called me, and I came home to your heart.
The triumph was—to reach and stay there; since
I reached it ere the triumph, what is lost?
Let my hands frame your face in your hair's gold,   175
You beautiful Lucrezia that are mine!
"Rafael did this, Andrea painted that;

The Roman's[7] is the better when you pray,
But still the other's Virgin was his wife—"
Men will excuse me. I am glad to judge   180
Both pictures in your presence; clearer grows
My better fortune, I resolve to think.
For, do you know, Lucrezia, as God lives,
Said one day Agnolo, his very self,
To Rafael . . . I have known it all these years . . .   185
(When the young man was flaming out his thoughts
Upon a palace-wall for Rome to see,
Too lifted up in heart because of it)
"Friend, there's a certain sorry little scrub
Goes up and down our Florence, none cares how,   190
Who, were he set to plan and execute
As you are, pricked on by your popes and kings,
Would bring the sweat into that brow of yours!"
To Rafael's!—And indeed the arm is wrong.
I hardly dare . . . yet, only you to see,   195
Give the chalk here—quick, thus the line should go!
Ay, but the soul! he's Rafael! rub it out!
Still, all I care for, if he spoke the truth,
(What he? why, who but Michel Agnolo?
Do you forget already words like those?)   200
If really there was such a chance, so lost,—
Is, whether you're—not grateful—but more pleased.
Well, let me think so. And you smile indeed!
This hour has been an hour! Another smile?
If you would sit thus by me every night   205
I should work better, do you comprehend?
I mean that I should earn more, give you more.
See, it is settled dusk now; there's a star;
Morello's gone, the watch-lights show the wall,
The cue-owls speak the name we call them by.   210
Come from the window, love,—come in, at last,
Inside the melancholy little house
We built to be so gay with. God is just.
King Francis may forgive me: oft at nights
When I look up from painting, eyes tired out,   215
The walls become illumined, brick from brick
Distinct, instead of mortar, fierce bright gold,

---

7. Another reference to Raphael, who went to Rome in 1508 to help decorate St. Peter's.

That gold of his I did cement them with!
Let us but love each other. Must you go?
That Cousin[8] here again? he waits outside?   220
Must see you—you, and not with me? Those loans?
More gaming debts to pay? you smiled for that?
Well, let smiles buy me! have you more to spend?
While hand and eye and something of a heart
Are left me, work's my ware, and what's it worth?   225
I'll pay my fancy. Only let me sit
The grey remainder of the evening out,
Idle, you call it, and muse perfectly
How I could paint, were I but back in France,
One picture, just one more—the Virgin's face,   230
Not yours this time! I want you at my side
To hear them—that is, Michel Agnolo—
Judge all I do and tell you of its worth.
Will you? To-morrow, satisfy your friend.
I take the subjects for his corridor,   235
Finish the portrait out of hand—there, there,
And throw him in another thing or two
If he demurs; the whole should prove enough
To pay for this same Cousin's freak. Beside,
What's better and what's all I care about,   240
Get you the thirteen scudi for the ruff!
Love, does that please you? Ah, but what does he,
The Cousin! what does he to please you more?

I am grown peaceful as old age to-night.
I regret little, I would change still less.   245
Since there my past life lies, why alter it?
The very wrong to Francis!—it is true
I took his coin, was tempted and complied,
And built this house and sinned, and all is said.
My father and my mother died of want.   250
Well, had I riches of my own? you see
How one gets rich! Let each one bear his lot.
They were born poor, lived poor, and poor they died;
And I have laboured somewhat in my time
And not been paid profusely. Some good son   255

---

8. Renaissance euphemism for "lover."

Paint my two hundred pictures—let him try!
No doubt, there's something strikes a balance. Yes,
You loved me quite enough, it seems to-night.
This must suffice me here. What would one have?
In heaven, perhaps, new chances, one more chance— 260
Four great walls in the New Jerusalem,[9]
Meted on each side by the angel's reed,
For Leonard,[10] *Rafael, Agnolo and me*
To cover—the three first without a wife,
While I have mine! So—still they overcome 265
Because there's still Lucrezia,—as I choose.

Again the Cousin's whistle! Go, my Love.

Questions for Critical Thinking

1. What is the opening context of this poem? Where are Andrea and Lucrezia, and what is she pressing him to do?

2. Andrea advances three explanations for his lackluster career and personal predicament. What are they, and which of the three do you find most believable?

3. What is your opinion of the implication in the poem that the lack of passion in the art of Andrea is partly due to his excessive doting on Lucrezia?

4. Using John Alan Lee's classification, what kind of love do you think Andrea felt for Lucrezia? What kind of lover does Lucrezia seem to be? Justify your answers.

5. What part does love play in encouraging talent, whether artistic or otherwise?

6. What grounds might a modern reader have for accusing Browning of fostering a sexist stereotype of women?

7. "Ah, but what does he, / The Cousin! what does he to please you more?" What do you think is the answer to this question that Andrea asks Lucrezia?

8. Is compulsive doting love, such as Andrea's, freely chosen or psychological in origin? Justify your answer.

Writing Assignment

Using the poem as your only source of specific details, write an essay contrasting the character of Lucrezia with that of Andrea. Be sure to provide support for your depictions of both characters.

---

9. Heaven; see Revelation 21:10–21.
10. Leonardo da Vinci (1452–1519).

Writing Advice

For a description of the nuts-and-bolts of writing a contrast, see the "Writing Advice" section after *Pensees*, by Blaise Pascal, in Chapter 2. Inferring Andrea's character from the monologue is fairly straightforward, since everything he says characterizes him in some measure. On the other hand, deciphering Lucrezia's character from these lines will require some literary detecting. Yet Andrea tells us volumes about her, even revealing confidences about her that he finds painful.

The poem, in sum, indirectly tells much about both Andrea and Lucrezia, if we read diligently between the lines. For example, we get surprisingly specific answers even to this basic question: what does Lucrezia look like? We gather that she is probably petite, for Andrea calls her hand "small" in line 8, and "soft" in line 21. We gather also that she is very feminine from this line: "Your soft hand is a woman of itself / And mine the man's bared breast she curls inside." It is also reasonable to infer that she is pretty, perhaps even beautiful, since Andrea uses her as a model for his paintings. That she is so popular with men—one keeps whistling for her at the gate—is also additional grounds for thinking her physically attractive, if not beautiful. Note that this is exactly the sort of literary probing you will have to do to reconstruct the characters of Andrea and Lucrezia from this monologue.

You might begin by jotting down three of four primary characteristics to use as the basis for your contrast. These may vary a great deal, depending on how you wish to slant your essay, but you might focus on such basic categories as philosophical outlook, intelligence, or morality. For example, an obvious and clear contrast exists between the morals of Andrea and Lucrezia. She is plainly cheating on him, which tells us something definitive about her sense of morality. Yet although he knows that she is being unfaithful, he does nothing, and that likewise reveals volumes about his moral sense.

Once you have settled on the bases of your contrasts, you should comb through the poem to gather evidence about the respective characters of the two. Jot down your interpretations, along with the supporting evidence from the poem itself, in notebook fashion, using the scheme suggested in the "Writing Advice" section after *Pensées*. After doing this legwork, you will have the details necessary to formulate a thesis and write a rough draft of the essay.

Alternate Writing Assignments

1. Write an essay that interprets and gives examples supporting these famous lines in "Andrea Del Sarto" (lines 97 and 98): "Ah, but a man's reach should exceed his grasp, / Or what's heaven for."

2. Write an essay exploring the dangers, and rewards, if you can imagine any, of the excessive dependence of one lover upon another in a romantic affair.

LITERATURE

THE COLONEL'S LADY

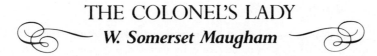

W. Somerset Maugham

W. Somerset Maugham (1874–1965), was an English author born in Paris. From an early age Maugham was afflicted with a self-conscious stammer that made him ill-at-ease with strangers. Orphaned at the age of ten, he was sent to live with an uncle, the Reverend Henry Macdonald Maugham. Although he interned in medicine, Maugham set his sights on a literary career and soon achieved success as a dramatist with the humorous play *Lady Frederick* (1907), followed by other commercially successful plays such as *Our Betters* (1923) and *The Constant Wife* (1927). He had written several novels and short stories before the appearance of his prose masterpiece, *Of Human Bondage* (1915). Despite first making his mark as a dramatist, however, Maugham is today admired primarily as a master of the short story.

Reading Advice

"The Colonel's Lady," a perennial favorite among Maugham readers and a representative showpiece of his storyteller's skills, opens with the stodgy Colonel Peregrine and his mousy lady at breakfast amid portraits of the Colonel's dead ancestors peering down on them from the walls. Maugham has such a telling eye for accurate detail that we are no more than two or three paragraphs into the story before we realize that the colonel is a hearty dimwit and that something is terribly amiss between him and his lady, who is mourning the loss of a passionate love affair—with a younger man.

Although one of the longer fiction pieces in this book, Maugham's story is neither tedious nor long-winded, but unfolds almost briskly. Part of its appeal is due to Maugham's exquisite sense of pacing—his ability to focus the storyline on immediate and important issues while glossing over the trivial—as well as to his deft evocation of character. Consider, for example, this amazingly compressed passage. The colonel takes up his wife's newly published book for the first time and sits down to read it:

> . . . *Interspersed with the pieces that looked so odd, lines of three or four words and then a line of ten or fifteen, there were little poems, quite short, that rhymed, thank God, with the lines all the same length. Several of the pages were just headed with the word* Sonnet, *and out of curiosity he counted the line; there were fourteen of them. He read them. They seemed all right, but he didn't quite know what they were all about. He repeated to himself: "Ruin seize thee, ruthless king."*
>
> *"Poor Evie," he sighed.*

From W. Somerset Maugham, *Creatures of Circumstance* (New York: Doubleday and Co., 1946). Reprinted by permission of A. P. Watt Limited on behalf of The Royal Literary Fund.

At that moment the farmer he was expecting was ushered into the study, and putting the book down he made him welcome. They embarked on their business.

"I read your book, Evie," he said as they sat down to lunch. "Jolly good. Did it cost you a packet to have it printed?"

And there we have it: the colonel at his business of managing a large estate; his rather conventional and obtuse sense of literature; his patronizing encounter with his wife at lunch—all in 146 words. As you read, notice this keen sense of pacing throughout the story, as well as Maugham's ability to cram revealing characterizations into virtually every page.

All this happened two or three years   1
before the outbreak of the war.

The Peregrines were having breakfast. Though they were alone and the table   2
was long they sat at opposite ends of it. From the walls George Peregrine's ancestors, painted by the fashionable painters of the day, looked down upon them. The butler brought in the morning post. There were several letters for the colonel, business letters, *The Times* and a small parcel for his wife Evie. He looked at his letters and then, opening *The Times,* began to read it. They finished breakfast and rose from the table. He noticed that his wife hadn't opened the parcel.

"What's that?" he asked.   3

"Only some books."   4

"Shall I open it for you?"   5

"If you like."   6

He hated to cut string and so with some difficulty untied the knots.   7

"But they're all the same," he said when he had unwrapped the parcel.   8
"What on earth d'you want six copies of the same book for?" He opened one of them. "Poetry." Then he looked at the title page. *When Pyramids Decay,* he read, by E. K. Hamilton. Eva Katherine Hamilton: that was his wife's maiden name. He looked at her with smiling surprise. "Have you written a book, Evie? You are a slyboots."

"I didn't think it would interest you very much. Would you like a copy?"   9

"Well, you know poetry isn't much in my line, but yes, I'd like a copy; I'll   10
read it. I'll take it along to my study. I've got a lot to do this morning."

He gathered up *The Times,* his letters and the book, and went out. His study   11
was a large and comfortable room, with a big desk, leather arm-chairs and what he called "trophies of the chase" on the walls. On the bookshelves were works of reference, books on farming, gardening, fishing and shooting, and books on the last war, in which he had won an M.C. and a D.S.O. For before his marriage he had been in the Welsh Guards. At the end of the war he retired and settled down to the life of a country gentleman in the spacious house,

some twenty miles from Sheffield, which one of his forebears had built in the reign of George III. George Peregrine had an estate of some fifteen hundred acres which he managed with ability; he was a Justice of the Peace and performed his duties conscientiously. During the season he rode to hounds two days a week. He was a good shot, a golfer and though now a little over fifty could still play hard game of tennis. He could describe himself with propriety as an all-around sportsman.

He had been putting on weight lately, but was still a fine figure of a man;   12 tall, with grey curly hair, only just beginning to grow thin on the crown, frank blue eyes, good features and a high colour. He was a public-spirited man, chairman of any number of local organisations and, as became his class and station, a loyal member of the Conservative Party. He looked upon it as his duty to see to the welfare of the people on his estate and it was a satisfaction to him to know that Evie could be trusted to tend the sick and succour the poor. He had built a cottage hospital on the outskirts of the village and paid the wages of a nurse out of his own pocket. All he asked of the recipients of his bounty was that at elections, county or general, they should vote for his candidate. He was a friendly man, affable to his inferiors, considerate with his tenants and popular with the neighbouring gentry. He would have been pleased and at the same time slightly embarrassed if someone had told him he was a jolly good fellow. That was what he wanted to be. He desired no higher praise.

It was hard luck that he had no children. He would have been an excellent   13 father, kindly but strict, and would have brought up his sons as gentlemen's sons should be brought up, sent them to Eton, you know, taught them to fish, shoot and ride. As it was, his heir was a nephew, son of his brother killed in a motor accident, not a bad boy, but not a chip off the old block, no, sir, far from it; and would you believe it, his fool of a mother was sending him to a coeducational school. Evie had been a sad disappointment to him. Of course she was a lady, and she had a bit of money of her own; she managed the house uncommonly well and she was a good hostess. The village people adored her. She had been a pretty little thing when he married her, with a creamy skin, light brown hair and a trim figure, healthy too and not a bad tennis player; he couldn't understand why she'd had no children; of course she was faded now, she must be getting on for five and forty; her skin was drab, her hair had lost its sheen and she was as thin as a rail. She was always neat and suitably dressed, but she didn't seem to bother how she looked, she wore no make-up and didn't even use lipstick; sometimes at night when she dolled herself up for a party you could tell that once she'd been quite attractive, but ordinarily she was— well, the sort of woman you simply didn't notice. A nice woman, of course, a good wife, and it wasn't her fault if she was barren, but it was tough on a fellow who wanted an heir of his own loins; she hadn't any vitality, that's what was the matter with her. He supposed he'd been in love with her when he asked her to marry him, at least sufficiently in love for a man who wanted to marry and settle down, but with time he discovered that they had nothing much in common. She didn't care about hunting, and fishing bored her. Naturally they'd drifted apart. He had to do her the justice to admit that she'd never bothered him. There'd been no scenes. They had no quarrels. She seemed to take it for granted that he should go his own way. When he went up to London now and then she never wanted to come with him. He had a girl there, well, she wasn't exactly a girl, she was thirty-five if she was a day, but she was blonde and luscious and he only had to wire ahead of time and they'd dine, do a show and spend the night together. Well, a man, a healthy normal man had to have some fun in his life. The thought crossed his mind that if Evie hadn't been such a good woman she'd have been a better wife; but it was not the sort of thought that he welcomed and he put it away from him.

George Peregrine finished his *Times* and being a considerate fellow rang the   13
bell and told the butler to take it to Evie. Then he looked at his watch. It was half-past ten and at eleven he had an appointment with one of his tenants. He had half an hour to spare.

"I'd better have a look at Evie's book," he said to himself.   15

He took it up with a smile. Evie had a lot of highbrow books in her sitting-   16
room, not the sort of books that interested him, but if they amused her he had no objection to her reading them. He noticed that the volume he now held in his hand contained no more than ninety pages. That was all to the good. He shared Edgar Allan Poe's opinion that poems should be short. But as he turned the pages he noticed that several of Evie's had long lines of irregular length and didn't rhyme. He didn't like that. At his first school, when he was a little boy, he remembered learning a poem that begun: *The boy stood on the burning deck,* and later, at Eton, one that started: *Ruin seize thee, ruthless king;* and then there was Henry V; they'd had to take that, one half. He stared at Evie's pages with consternation.

"That's not what I call poetry," he said.   17

Fortunately it wasn't all like that. Interspersed with the pieces that looked   18
so odd, lines of three or four words and then a line of ten or fifteen, there were little poems, quite short, that rhymed, thank God, with the lines all the same length. Several of the pages were just headed with the word *Sonnet,* and out of curiosity he counted the lines; there were fourteen of them. He read them. They seemed all right, but he didn't quite know what they were all about. He repeated to himself: *Ruin seize thee, ruthless king.*

"Poor Evie," he sighed.   19

At that moment the farmer he was expecting was ushered into the study,   20
and putting the book down he made him welcome. They embarked on their business.

"I read your book, Evie," he said as they sat down to lunch. "Jolly good.   21
Did it cost you a packet to have it printed?"

"No, I was lucky. I sent it to a publisher and he took it."   22

"Not much money in poetry, my dear," he said in his good-natured,   23
hearty way.

"No, I don't suppose there is. What did Bannock want to see you about this   24
morning?"

Bannock was the tenant who had interrupted his reading of Evie's poems.   25

"He's asked me to advance the money for a pedigree bull he wants to buy.   26
He's a good man and I've half a mind to do it."

George Peregrine saw that Evie didn't want to talk about her book and he   27
was not sorry to change the subject. He was glad she had used her maiden
name on the title page; he didn't suppose anyone would ever hear about the
book, but he was proud of his own unusual name and he wouldn't have liked
it if some damned penny-a-liner had made fun of Evie's effort in one of the
papers.

During the few weeks that followed he thought it tactful not to ask Evie   28
any questions about her venture into verse and she never referred to it. It
might have been a discreditable incident that they had silently agreed not to
mention. But then a strange thing happened. He had to go to London on
business and he took Daphne out to dinner. That was the name of the girl with
whom he was in the habit of passing a few agreeable hours whenever he went
to town.

"Oh, George," she said, "is that your wife who's written a book they're all   29
talking about?"

"What on earth d'you mean?"   30

"Well, there's a fellow I know who's a critic. He took me out to dinner the   31
other night and he had a book with him. 'Got anything for me to read?' I said.
'What's that?' 'Oh, I don't think that's your cup of tea,' he said, 'It's poetry.
I've just been reviewing it.' 'No poetry for me,' I said. 'It's about the hottest
stuff I ever read,' he said. 'Selling like hot cakes. And it's damned good.' "

"Who's the book by?" asked George.   32

"A woman called Hamilton. My friend told me that wasn't her real name.   33
He said her real name was Peregrine. 'Funny,' I said, 'I know a fellow called
Peregrine,' 'Colonel in the army,' he said. 'Lives near Sheffield.' "

"I'd just as soon you didn't talk about me to your friends," said George with   34
a frown of vexation.

"Keep your shirt on, dearie. Who d'you take me for? I just said: 'It's not   35
the same one.' " Daphne giggled. "My friend said: 'They say he's a regular Colonel
Blimp.' "

George had a keen sense of humour.   36

"You could tell them better than that," he laughed. "If my wife had written   37
a book I'd be the first to know about it, wouldn't I?"

"I suppose you would."   38

Anyhow the matter didn't interest her and when the colonel began to talk   39
of other things she forgot about it. He put it out of his mind too. There was
nothing to it, he decided, and that silly fool of a critic had just been pulling
Daphne's leg. He was amused at the thought of her tackling that book because
she had been told it was hot stuff and then finding it just a lot of bosh cut up
into unequal lines.

He was a member of several clubs and next day he thought he'd lunch at   40
one in St. James's Street. He was catching a train back to Sheffield early in the
afternoon. He was sitting in a comfortable armchair having a glass of sherry
before going into the dining-room when an old friend came up to him.

"Well, old boy, how's life?" he said. "How d'you like being the husband of   41
a celebrity?"

George Peregrine looked at his friend. He thought he saw an amused twinkle   42
in his eyes.

"I don't know what you're talking about," he answered.   43

"Come off it, George. Everyone knows E. K. Hamilton is your wife. Not   44
often a book of verse has a success like that. Look here, Henry Dashwood is
lunching with me. He'd like to meet you."

"Who the devil is Henry Dashwood and why should he want to meet me?"   45

"Oh, my dear fellow, what do you do with yourself all the time in the   46
country? Henry's about the best critic we've got. He wrote a wonderful review
of Evie's book. D'you mean to say she didn't show it you?"

Before George could answer his friend had called a man over. A tall, thin   47
man, with a high forehead, a beard, a long nose and a stoop, just the sort of
man whom George was prepared to dislike at first sight. Introductions were
effected. Henry Dashwood sat down.

"Is Mrs. Peregrine in London by any chance? I should very much like to   48
meet her," he said.

"No, my wife doesn't like London. She prefers the country," said George   49
stiffly.

"She wrote me a very nice letter about my review. I was pleased. You know,   50
we critics get more kicks than halfpence. I was simply bowled over by her
book. It's so fresh and original, very modern without being obscure. She seems
to be as much at her ease in free verse as in the classical metres." Then because
he was a critic he thought he should criticise. "Sometimes her ear is a trifle at
fault, but you can say the same of Emily Dickinson. There are several of those
short lyrics of hers that might have been written by Landor."

All this was gibberish to George Peregrine. The man was nothing but a   51 disgusting highbrow. But the colonel had good manners and he answered with proper civility: Henry Dashwood went on as though he hadn't spoken.

"But what makes the book so outstanding is the passion that throbs in every line. So many of these young poets are so anaemic, cold, bloodless, dully intellectual, but here you have real naked, earthy passion; of course deep, sincere emotion like that is tragic—ah, my dear Colonel, how right Heine was when he said that the poet makes little songs out of his great sorrows. You know, now and then, as I read and reread those heart-rending pages I thought of Sappho."   52

This was too much for George Peregrine and he got up.   53

"Well, it's jolly nice of you to say such nice things about my wife's little book. I'm sure she'll be delighted. But I must bolt, I've got to catch a train and I want to get a bite of lunch."   54

"Damned fool," he said irritably to himself as he walked upstairs to the dining-room.   55

He got home in time for dinner and after Evie had gone to bed he went into his study and looked for her book. He thought he'd just glance through it again to see for himself what they were making such a fuss about, but he couldn't find it. Evie must have taken it away.

"Silly," he muttered.   56

He'd told her he thought it jolly good. What more could a fellow be expected to say? Well, it didn't matter. He lit his pipe and read the *Field* till he felt sleepy. But a week or so later it happened that he had to go into Sheffield for the day. He lunched there at his club. He had nearly finished when the Duke of Harverel came in. This was the great local magnate and of course the colonel knew him, but only to say how d'you do to; and he was surprised when the Duke stopped at his table.   57

"We're so sorry your wife couldn't come to us for the weekend," he said, with a sort of shy cordiality. "We're expecting rather a nice lot of people."   58

George was taken aback. He guessed that the Haverels had asked him and Evie over for the week-end and Evie, without saying a word to him about it, had refused. He had the presence of mind to say he was sorry too.   59

"Better luck next time," said the Duke pleasantly and moved on.   60

Colonel Peregrine was very angry and when he got home he said to his wife: 61

"Look here, what's this about our being asked over to Haverel? Why on earth did you say we couldn't go? We've never been asked before and it's the best shooting in the country."   62

"I didn't think of that. I thought it would only bore you."   63

"Damn it all, you might at least have asked me if I wanted to go."   64

"I'm sorry."   65

He looked at her closely. There was something in her expression that he   66
didn't quite understand. He frowned.

"I suppose *I* was asked?" he barked.   67

Evie flushed a little.   68

"Well, in point of face you weren't."   69

"I call it damned rude of them to ask you without asking me."   70

"I suppose they thought it wasn't your sort of party. The Duchess is rather   71
fond of writers and people like that, you know. She's having Henry Dashwood,
the critic, and for some reason he wants to meet me."

"It was damned nice of you to refuse, Evie."   72

"It's the least I could do," she smiled. She hesitated a moment. "George, my   73
publishers want to give a little dinner party for me one day towards the end
of the month and of course they want you to come too."

"Oh, I don't think that's quite my mark. I'll come up to London with you   74
if you like. I'll find someone to dine with."

Daphne.   75

"I expect it'll be very dull, but they're making rather a point of it. And the   76
day after, the American publisher who's taken my book is giving a cocktail
party at Claridge's. I'd like you to come to that if you wouldn't mind."

"Sounds like a crashing bore, but if you really want me to come I'll come."   77

"It would be sweet of you."   78

George Peregrine was dazed by the cocktail party. There were a lot of people.   79
Some of them didn't look so bad, a few of the women were decently turned
out, but the men seemed to him pretty awful. He was introduced to everyone
as Colonel Peregrine, E. K. Hamilton's husband, you know. The men didn't
seem to have anything to say to him, but the women gushed.

"You *must* be proud of your wife. Isn't it *wonderful*? You know, I read it right   80
through at a sitting. I simply couldn't put it down, and when I'd finished I
started again at the beginning and read it right through a second time. I was
simply *thrilled.*"

The English publisher said to him: 81

"We've not had a success like this with a book of verse for twenty years.   82
I've never seen such reviews."

The American publisher said to him: 83

"It's swell. It'll be a smash hit in America. You wait and see."   84

The American publisher had sent Evie a great spray of orchids. Damned   85
ridiculous, thought George. As they came in, people were taken up to Evie,
and it was evident that they said flattering things to her, which she took with
a pleasant smile and a word or two of thanks. She was a trifle flushed with
the excitement, but seemed quite at her ease. Though he thought the whole
thing a lot of stuff and nonsense George noted with approval that his wife was
carrying it off in just the right way.

"Well, there's one thing," he said to himself, "you can see she's a lady and   86
that's a damned sight more than you can say of anyone else here."

He drank a good many cocktails. But there was one thing that bothered   87
him. He had a notion that some of the people he was introduced to looked at
him in rather a funny sort of way, he couldn't quite make out what it meant,
and once when he strolled by two women who were sitting together on a sofa
he had the impression that they were talking about him and after he passed he
was almost certain they tittered. He was very glad when the party came to
an end.

In the taxi on their way back to their hotel Evie said to him: 88

"You were wonderful, dear. You made quite a hit. The girls simply raved   89
about you: they thought you so handsome."

"Girls," he said bitterly. "Old hags."   90

"Were you bored, dear?"   91

"Stiff."   92

She pressed his hand in a gesture of sympathy.   93

"I hope you won't mind if we wait and go down by the afternoon train. I've   94
got some things to do in the morning."

"No, that's all right. Shopping?"   95

"I do want to buy one or two things, but I've got to go and be photographed.   96
I hate the idea, but they think I ought to be. For America, you know."

He said nothing. But he thought. He thought it would be a shock to the   97
American public when they saw the portrait of the homely, desiccated little
woman who was his wife. He'd always been under the impression that they
liked glamour in America.

He went on thinking, and next morning when Evie had gone out he went   98
to his club and up to the library. There he looked up recent numbers of *The
Times Literary Supplement, The New Statesman* and *The Spectator.* Presently he found
reviews of Evie's book. He didn't read them very carefully, but enough to see
that they were extremely favourable. Then he went to the bookseller's in Pic-
cadilly where he occasionally bought books. He'd made up his mind that he
had to read this damned thing of Evie's properly, but he didn't want to ask her
what she'd done with the copy she'd given him. He'd buy one for himself.
Before going in he looked in the window and the first thing he saw was a
display of *When Pyramids Decay.* Damned silly title! He went in. A young man
came forward and asked if he could help him.

"No, I'm just having a look around." It embarrassed him to ask for Evie's   99
book and he thought he'd find it for himself and then take it to the salesman.
But he couldn't see it anywhere and at last, finding the young man near him,
he said in a carefully casual tone: "By the way, have you got a book called *When
Pyramids Decay?*"

"The new edition came in this morning. I'll get a copy."   100

In a moment the young man returned with it. He was a short, rather stout   101
young man, with a shock of untidy carroty hair and spectacles. George Peregrine, tall, upstanding, very military, towered over him.

"Is this a new edition then?" he asked.   102

"Yes, sir. The fifth. It might be a novel the way it's selling."   103

George Peregrine hesitated a moment.   104

"Why d'you suppose it's such a success? I've always been told no one reads   105
poetry."

"Well, it's good, you know. I've read it meself." The young man, though   106
obviously cultured, had a slight Cockney accent, and George quite instinctively
adopted a patronising attitude. "It's the story they like. Sexy, you know, but
tragic."

George frowned a little. He was coming to the conclusion that the young   107
man was rather impertinent. No one had told him anything about there being
a story in the damned book and he had not gathered that from reading the
reviews. The young man went on:

"Of course it's only a flash in the pan, if you know what I mean. The way   108
I look at it, she was sort of inspired like by a personal experience, like Housman
was with *The Shropshire Lad*. She'll never write anything else."

"How much is the book?" said George coldly to stop his chatter. "You needn't   109
wrap it up, I'll just slip it into my pocket."

The November morning was raw and he was wearing a greatcoat.   110

At the station he bought the evening papers and magazines and he and Evie   111
settled themselves comfortably in opposite corners of a first-class carriage and
read. At five o'clock they went along to the restaurant car to have tea and
chatted a little. They arrived. They drove home in the car which was waiting
for them. They bathed, dressed for dinner, and after dinner Evie, saying she
was tired out, went to bed. She kissed him, as was her habit, on the forehead.
Then he went into the hall, took Evie's book out of his greatcoat pocket and
going into the study began to read it. He didn't read verse very easily and
though he read with attention, every word of it, the impression he received
was far from clear. Then he began at the beginning again and read it a second
time. He read with increasing malaise, but he was not a stupid man and when
he had finished he had a distinct understanding of what it was all about. Part
of the book was in free verse, part in conventional metres, but the story it
related was coherent and plain to the meanest intelligence. It was the story of
a passionate love affair between an older woman, married, and a young man.
George Peregrine made out the steps of it as easily as if he had been doing a
sum in simple addition.

Written in the first person, it began with the tremulous surprise of the   112
woman, past her youth, when it dawned upon her that the young man was in
love with her. She hesitated to believe it. She thought she must be deceiving

herself. And she was terrified when on a sudden she discovered that she was passionately in love with him. She told herself it was absurd; with the disparity of age between them nothing but unhappiness could come to her if she yielded to her emotion. She tried to prevent him from speaking but the day came when he told her that he loved her and forced her to tell him that she loved him too. He begged her to run away with him. She couldn't leave her husband, her home; and what life could they look forward to, she an ageing woman, he so young? How could she expect his love to last? She begged him to have mercy on her. But his love was impetuous. He wanted her, he wanted her with all his heart, and at last trembling, afraid, desirous, she yielded to him. Then there was a period of ecstatic happiness. The world, the dull, humdrum world of every day, blazed with glory. Love songs flowed from her pen. The woman worshipped the young, virile body of her lover. George flushed darkly when she praised his broad chest and slim flanks, the beauty on his legs and the flatness of his belly.

Hot stuff, Daphne's friend had said. It was that all right. Disgusting. 113

There were sad little pieces in which she lamented the emptiness of her life 114 when as must happen he left her, but they ended with a cry that all she had to suffer would be worth it for the bliss that for a while had been hers. She wrote of the long, tremulous nights they passed together and the languor that lulled them to sleep in one another's arms. She wrote of the rapture of brief stolen moments when, braving all danger, their passion overwhelmed them and they surrendered to its call.

She thought it would be an affair of a few weeks, but miraculously it lasted. 115 One of the poems referred to three years having gone by without lessening the love that filled their hearts. It looked as though he continued to press her to go away with him, far away, to a hill town in Italy, a Greek island, a walled city in Tunisia, so that they could be together always, for in another of the poems she besought him to let things be as they were. Their happiness was precarious. Perhaps it was owing to the difficulties they had to encounter and the rarity of their meetings that their love had retained for so long its first enchanting ardour. Then on a sudden the young man died. How, when or where George could not discover. There followed a long, heart-broken cry of bitter grief, grief she could not indulge in, grief that had to be hidden. She had to be cheerful, give dinner-parties and go out to dinner, behave as she had always behaved, though the light had gone out of her life and she was bowed down with anguish. The last poem of all was a set of four short stanzas in which the writer, sadly resigned to her loss, thanked the dark powers that rule man's destiny that she had been privileged at least for a while to enjoy the greatest happiness that we poor human beings can ever hope to know.

It was three o'clock in the morning when George Peregrine finally put the 116 book down. It had seemed to him that he heard Evie's voice in every line, over and over again he came upon turns of phrase he had heard her use, there were details that were as familiar to him as to her; there was no doubt about it; it was her own story she had told, and it was as plain as anything could be that she had had a lover and her lover had died. It was not anger so much that he felt, nor horror or dismay, though he was dismayed and he was horrified, but amazement. It was as inconceivable that Evie should have had a love affair, and a wildly passionate one at that, as that the trout in a glass case over the chimney piece in his study, the finest he had ever caught, should suddenly wag its tail. He understood now the meaning of the amused look he had seen in the eyes of that man he had spoken to at the club, he understood why Daphne when she was talking about the book had seemed to be enjoying a private joke, and why those two women at the cocktail party had tittered when he strolled past them.

He broke out into a sweat. Then on a sudden he was seized with fury and he jumped up to go and awake Evie and ask her sternly for an explanation. But he stopped at the door. After all, what proof had he? A book. He remembered that he'd told Evie he thought it jolly good. True, he hadn't read it, but he'd pretended he had. He would look a perfect fool if he had to admit that.   117

"I must watch my step," he muttered.   118

He made up his mind to wait for two or three days and think it all over.   119
Then he'd decide what to do. He went to bed, but he couldn't sleep for a long time.

"Evie," he kept on saying to himself. "Evie, of all people."   120

They met at breakfast next morning as usual. Evie was as she always was,   121
quiet, demure and self-possessed, a middle-aged woman who made no effort to look younger than she was, a woman who had nothing of what he still called It. He looked at her as he hadn't looked at her for years. She had her usual placid serenity. Her pale blue eyes were untroubled. There was no sign of guilt on her candid brow. She made the same little casual remarks she always made.

"It's nice to get back to the country again after those two hectic days in   122
London. What are you going to do this morning?"

It was incomprehensible.   123

Three days later he went to see his solicitor. Henry Blane was an old friend   124
of George's as well as his lawyer. He had a place not far from Peregrine's and for years they had shot over one another's preserves. For two days a week he was a country gentleman and for the other five a busy lawyer in Sheffield. He was a tall, robust fellow, with a boisterous manner and a jovial laugh, which suggested that he liked to be looked upon essentially as a sportsman and a good fellow and only incidentally as a lawyer. But he was shrewd and worldly-wise.

"Well, George, what's brought you here today?" he boomed as the colonel   125
was showed into his office. "Have a good time in London? I'm taking my missus up for a few days next week. How's Evie?"

"It's about Evie I've come to see you," said Peregrine, giving him a suspicious   126
look. "Have you read her book?"

His sensitivity had been sharpened during those last days of troubled thought   127
and he was conscious of a faint change in the lawyer's expression. It was as
though he were suddenly on his guard.

"Yes, I've read it. Great success, isn't it? Fancy Evie breaking out into poetry.   128
Wonders will never cease."

George Peregrine was inclined to lose his temper.   129

"It's made me look a perfect damned fool."   130

"Oh, what nonsense, George! There's no harm in Evie's writing a book. You   131
ought to be jolly proud of her."

"Don't talk such rot. It's her own story. You know it and everyone else   132
knows it. I suppose I'm the only one who doesn't know who her lover was."

"There is such a thing as imagination, old boy. There's no reason to suppose   133
the whole thing isn't made up."

"Look here, Henry, we've know one another all our lives. We've had all   134
sorts of good times together. Be honest with me. Can you look me in the face
and tell me you believe it's a made-up story?"

Harry Blane moved uneasily in his chair. He was disturbed by the distress   135
in old George's voice.

"You've got no right to ask me a question like that. Ask Evie."   136

"I daren't," George answered after an anguished pause. "I'm afraid she'd tell   137
me the truth."

There was an uncomfortable silence.   138

"Who was the chap?"   139

Harry Blane looked at him straight in the eye.   140

"I don't know, and if I did I wouldn't tell you."   141

"You swine. Don't you see what a position I'm in? Do you think it's very   142
pleasant to be made absolutely ridiculous?"

The lawyer lit a cigarette and for some moments silently puffed it.   143

"I don't see what I can do for you," he said at last.   144

"You've got private detectives you employ, I suppose. I want you to put   145
them on the job and let them find everything out."

"It's not very pretty to put detectives on one's wife, old boy; and besides,   146
taking for granted for a moment that Evie had an affair, it was a good many
years ago and I don't suppose it would be possible to find out a thing. They
seem to have covered their tracks pretty carefully."

"I don't care. You put the detectives on. I want to know the truth."   147

"I won't, George. If you're determined to do that you'd better consult   148
someone else. And look here, even if you got evidence that Evie had been
unfaithful to you what would you do with it? You'd look rather silly divorcing
your wife because she'd committed adultery ten years ago."

"At all events I could have it out with her."   149

"You can do that now, but you know just as well as I do that if you do she'll   150
leave you. D'you want her to do that?"

George gave him an unhappy look.   151

"I don't know. I always thought she'd been a damned good wife to me. She   152
runs the house perfectly, we never have any servant trouble; she's done wonders
with the garden and she's splendid with all the village people. But damn it, I
have my self-respect to think of. How can I go on living with her when I know
that she was grossly unfaithful to me?"

"Have you always been faithful to her?"   153

"More or less, you know. After all, we've been married for nearly twenty-   154
four years and Evie was never much for bed."

The solicitor slightly raised his eyebrows, but George was too intent on what   155
he was saying to notice.

"I don't deny that I've had a bit of fun now and then. A man wants it.   156
Women are different."

"We only have men's word for that," said Henry Blane, with a faint smile.   157

"Evie's absolutely the last woman I'd have suspected of kicking over the   158
traces. I mean, she's a very fastidious, reticent woman. What on earth made
her write the damned book?"

"I suppose it was a very poignant experience and perhaps it was a relief to   159
her to get it off her chest like that."

"Well, if she had to write it why the devil didn't she write it under an   160
assumed name?"

"She used her maiden name. I suppose she thought that was enough, and it   161
would have been if the book hadn't had this amazing boom."

George Peregrine and the lawyer were sitting opposite one another with a   162
desk between them. George, his elbow on the desk, his cheek on his hand,
frowned at his thought.

"It's so rotten not to know what sort of a chap he was. One can't even tell   163
if he was by way of being a gentleman. I mean, for all I know he may have
been a farm-hand or a clerk in a lawyer's office."

Harry Blane did not permit himself to smile and when he answered there   164
was in his eyes a kindly, tolerant look.

"Knowing Evie so well I think the probabilities are that he was all right.   165
Anyhow I'm sure he wasn't a clerk in my office."

"It's been a shock to me," the colonel sighed. "I thought she was fond of   166
me. She couldn't have written that book unless she hated me."

"Oh, I don't believe that. I don't think she's capable of hatred."   167

"You're not going to pretend that she loves me."   168

"No."   169

"Well, what does she feel for me?"   170

Harry Blane leaned back in his swivel chair and looked at George reflectively.   171

"Indifference, I should say."   172

The colonel gave a little shudder and reddened.   173

"After all, you're not in love with her, are you?"   174

George Peregrine did not answer directly.   175

"It's been a great blow to me not to have any children, but I've never let   176
her see that I think she's let me down. I've always been kind to her. Within
reasonable limits I've tried to do my duty by her."

The lawyer passed a large hand over his mouth to conceal the smile that   177
trembled on his lips.

"It's been such an awful shock to me," Peregrine went on. "Damn it all, even   178
ten years ago Evie was no chicken and God knows, she wasn't much to look
at. It's so ugly." He sighed deeply. "What would *you* do in my place?"

"Nothing."   179

George Peregrine drew himself bolt upright in his chair and he looked at   180
Harry with the stern set face that he must have worn when he inspected his
regiment.

"I can't overlook a thing like this. I've been made a laughingstock. I can   181
never hold up my head again."

"Nonsense," said the lawyer sharply, and then in a pleasant, kindly manner,   182
"Listen, old boy: the man's dead; it all happened a long while back. Forget it.
Talk to people about Evie's book, rave about it, tell 'em how proud you are of
her. Behave as though you had so much confidence in her, you *knew* she could
never have been unfaithful to you. The world moves so quickly and people's
memories are so short. They'll forget."

"I shan't forget."   183

"You're both middle-aged people. She probably does a great deal more for   184
you than you think and you'd be awfully lonely without her. I don't think it
matters if you don't forget. It'll be all to the good if you can get it into that
thick head of yours that there's a lot more in Evie than you ever had the
gumption to see."

"Damn it all, you talk as if *I* was to blame."   185

"No, I don't think you were to blame, but I'm not so sure that Evie was   186
either. I don't suppose she wanted to fall in love with this boy. D'you remember
those verses right at the end? The impression they gave me was that though
she was shattered by his death, in a strange sort of way she welcomed it. All
through she'd been aware of the fragility of the tie that bound them. He died
in the full flush of his first love and had never known that love so seldom
endures; he'd only known its bliss and beauty. In her own bitter grief she found
solace in the thought that he'd been spared all sorrow."

"All that's a bit above my head, old boy. I see more or less what you mean."   187

George Peregrine stared unhappily at the inkstand on the desk. He was silent   188
and the lawyer looked at him with curious, yet sympathetic, eyes.

"Do you realise what courage she must have had never by a sign to show   189
how dreadfully unhappy she was?" he said gently.

Colonel Peregrine sighed.   190

"I'm broken. I suppose you're right; it's no good crying over spilt milk and   191
it would only make things worse if I made a fuss."

"Well?"   192

George Peregrine gave him a pitiful little smile.   193

"I'll take your advice. I'll do nothing. Let them think me a damned fool and   194
to hell with them. The truth is, I don't know what I'd do without Evie. But
I'll tell you what, there's one thing I shall never understand till my dying day:
What in the name of heaven did the fellow ever see in her?"

Questions for Critical Thinking

1. In paragraph 13, the colonel has a fleeting thought that if "Evie hadn't been such
   a good woman she'd have been a better wife." What do you think he means by
   that? How can being "good" make a woman into a bad wife?

2. Reading between the lines, what do you suppose is the state of sexual relations
   between the colonel and his wife?

3. How would you characterize the colonel as a person?

4. Given the kind of life Evie shared with her husband, what is your opinion of the
   morality of her love affair with the younger man?

5. What is your opinion of the colonel's view that men need extramarital affairs or
   sexual variety more than women?

6. How do you suppose the relationship between the colonel and his wife finally
   ended up?

7. What would be the effect on the story if we came away with the impression that
   Evie's lover had not really existed but was only make-believe?

8. Maugham was a meticulous craftsman and a master of the show-rather-than-tell
   school of storytelling. What, for example, might a sensitive reader deduce about
   the Peregrines from the story's second paragraph?

Writing Assignment

Write an essay speculating on the outcome of the marriage between the Peregrines.
Say how you think the colonel and Evie will end up. Justify your version of events
with reasoned opinions or with citations from the text.

Writing Advice

What do you think will happen to the Peregrines's marriage, now that Evie's unfaithfulness has been revealed? That is the question you must answer in your essay. Naturally, there is no absolutely right or wrong answer, only educated guesses that will vary in their defensibility. If you think, for example, that the colonel will stick with his wife and not divorce her because he is too conscious of his social standing to endure the scandal, then you must not only say so, you must also show us why you believe as you do. Cite passages and scenes from the story that bear out your belief in his conservative nature and your guess as to the story's outcome. On the other hand, if you think that, his sense of male prerogative having been irreparably violated, the colonel will merely wait a while for the literary hubbub to die down and then quietly leave his wife, you must also show what incidents in the story led you to this conclusion.

Note that the persuasiveness of this essay will vary largely with the sophistication of your speculations and reasoning and with the quality of your evidence. If you merely write at length that you think the colonel will eventually abandon his wife and go to live with his mistress, you must also prove that this is a reasonably likely result. To do so, you need to show passages in the text that support your inferences about the colonel's character and your conclusion. In other words, you must firmly anchor your speculations in the story itself, and not simply drift off into some unsupported psychological theory.

Alternate Writing Assignments

1. In an essay that uses the story as your only source, write an extended comparison/contrast of the colonel and his wife.

2. Men and women are entirely different in their sexual attitudes and needs. Support or refute this statement in an essay.

ART

THE JUDGEMENT OF PARIS
Peter Paul Rubens

About the Artist

Peter Paul Rubens (1577–1640), Flemish painter, was born in Siegen, Westphalia, where his family had fled from Antwerp to avoid religious persecution for the father's Calvinist beliefs. After the father's death, the family returned to Antwerp, where Rubens was educated at a Jesuit school, distinguishing himself with a natural flair for languages. Rubens was apprenticed to several minor painters, and spent eight fruitful years of traveling and learning in Italy, where he worked in the service of the Duke of Mantua. He returned to Antwerp in 1608 upon the death of his mother, established an art studio whose productions and works he designed and supervised, and soon achieved distinction as the greatest living painter of his country.

Rubens was an enormously prolific painter, with more than 2,000 paintings being attributed to his studio. After the death of his wife in 1626, Rubens entered the diplomatic service, where he made his mark with his friendly manner and fluency in several languages. He was knighted by the English shortly after performing a diplomatic service to Spain on behalf of the British government in 1628. For the last few years of his life, Rubens was enormously productive. His marriage in 1630 to a woman 37 years his junior represented a period of great personal happiness, during which he painted many of his finest pictures. He died in 1640, at the age of 63, following a severe attack of the gout.

Rubens is noted for his free handling of form and color, and for his lusty and characteristically monumental works. His art is versatile—ranging from religious portraits to mythological themes and animal pictures—and hangs today in virtually every major museum in the United States and Europe.

About the Art

The Judgement of Paris depicts one of Greek mythology's unluckier beauty contests, which led to the protracted and bloody Trojan war and great human slaughter. Basically, the mythological story portrayed in the painting is as follows: Eris, the goddess of strife, had not been invited to a wedding on Mt. Olympus, home of the Greek gods. In a fit of temper, she threw among the partying guests a golden apple on which was inscribed, "to the fairest." Naturally, each goddess present claimed the apple for herself and a dispute broke out among them. They agreed to allow a randomly chosen human to settle their quarrel and, as bad luck would have it, their gaze fell upon Paris, who was tending his flock in the fields below.

The three feuding goddesses—Hera, queen of Mt. Olympus, wife of Zeus, and goddess of matrimony; Athena, goddess of war; and Aphrodite, goddess of love—appeared before the astonished Paris and ordered him to choose who among them was the fairest. The conniving goddesses offered bribes to sway his judgment. Hera promised Paris royal greatness and riches; Athena, success in war; and Aphrodite, the most beautiful woman in the world. Paris chose Aphrodite and awarded her the apple, to the fury of the losers. In return, Aphrodite aided Paris in abducting the most beautiful woman in the world, Helen, wife of Sparta's king Menelaus, and spiriting her off to Troy. Menelaus pursued, and so began the Trojan war, chronicled in Homer's *Iliad*.

In his painting of the scene, Rubens shows the winged-hat Hermes, messenger of the gods, peering out curiously from behind a tree as Paris extends the apple to his ill-fated choice. The goddesses are portrayed as fleshy hausfraus, with Aphrodite shown wearing a string of pearls in her hair. Nor is the scene entirely bereft of humor—witness, for example, the peacock hissing at the dog crouching between Paris's feet.

Rubens's masterful technique is richly displayed in the creamy texture of the goddess's skin and in the wonderful details of their garments and hair.

ART

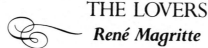

THE LOVERS
René Magritte

About the Artist

René Magritte (1898–1967), Belgian surrealist painter, was strongly influenced by the work of the Italian Giorgio de Chirico (1888–1978). Magritte's work combines a characteristic realism with an attitude of mocking irony. Frequently, his images consist of startling juxtapositions rendered in a static and restrained style.

About the Art

The Lovers shows two veiled dream figures in a rigid, almost stylized posture of closeness and intimacy who are craning as if to kiss but, because of their hooded heads, not actually touching flesh. Some critics speculate that the painting is a reference to Magritte's mother, who drowned with her head wrapped in a gown. Another interpretation is that it depicts an internalized vision of love similar to the one proposed in "What Love Is," by Robert Solomon, who argues that lovers inhabit an imaginary, self-created, and exclusive loveworld.

In Magritte's vision, the lovers are wrapped in a pose of straining intimacy but are blocked from seeing each other's eyes or face by the heavily draped and carefully textured hoods. Yet there is a palpable pull between them, suggesting some joyful sharing, some private internal communing in which both lovers participate and which adds urgency and expectancy to their embrace.

Does a lover ever really know or truly grasp the truth about the beloved? Or is the beloved always an ideal, an icon created and existing only in the hopes and dreams of the lover? These are some of the issues raised by Magritte's mystifying painting.

4—1   *Peter Paul Rubens,* The Judgement of Paris, *1632. Reproduced by courtesy of the Trustees, The National Gallery, London.*

4–2   René Magritte, **The Lovers,** *1928, 21 3/8″ × 28 7/8.″ Richard S. Zeisler Collection, New York.*

Chapter Writing Assignments

After reading the assigned selections and studying the paintings of the chapter, write an essay that debates one of the following assertions:

(a) Even after all these years and numerous studies, love is still an unfathomable mystery.

(b) Love is little more than the peculiar trimmings humans use to adorn and justify sexual urges.

(c) Equality between the sexes is most likely, or least likely, to foster a happy love relationship.

(d) Men and women, because they are congenitally so different, will never be completely able to understand each other.

(e) Love is more likely to succeed between a stronger woman and weaker man than between a stronger man and weaker woman.

(f) Women love; men seek sex; that is the basic difference between the way the two sexes regard romantic affairs.

Be sure to refer to specific pieces anthologized in this chapter as well as to the paintings. If necessary, consult other sources and cite them in support of your views.

CHAPTER FIVE

❧

Why Do We Fight?
WAR

War, declared the Prussian strategist Karl von Clausewitz, is a "continuation of political intercourse by other means." Its unlovely aim is the subjugation of one people to the will and demands of another, and it has been as lamentable a part of human history as painful childbirth and pestilential death. The Sumerians and Greeks viewed military prowess as the path to glory and lethal man-to-man combat as the only test of valor, with no quarter asked, and none given, in the ritualistic killing. The relentless fight between Achilles and Hector on the battlefields of Troy illustrates this ethic in one of literature's most bloody and horrifying scenes. As related in Homer's *Iliad*, the victorious Achilles triumphantly circles the walls of the besieged Troy, his chariot dragging the battered body of the slain Hector in the wake. Over 400 years ago a French knight rhapsodized about war in words that spoke for generations of his bloody kind who had come to love the slaughter:

> How seductive is war! When you know your quarrel to be just and your blood ready
> for combat, tears come to your eyes. The heart feels a sweet loyalty and pity to see
> one's friend expose his body in order to do and accomplish the command of his Creator.
> Alongside him, one prepares to live or die. From that comes a delectable sense which
> no one who has not experienced it will ever know how to explain. Do you think that a
> man who has experienced that can fear death? Never, for he is so comforted, so enrap-
> tured that he knows not where he is and truly fears nothing.
>
> **Barbara W. Tuchman, A Distant Mirror: The Calamitous 14th Century,** *pp.*
> **586—87.**

Baffling though it may seem to us today, war in those ancient days was the normal condition of life that was punctuated with only rare interludes of peace. In story after story, history after history, we see the home folks eagerly awaiting news of their fathers and sons, away fighting on some foreign soil. Watching the spectacle are the gods, who are mostly amused or indifferent, and nature, who is relentless but fickle. This ancient warring world seems to us a vale of tears and bloodshed mired in a perpetual and unrepentant present. One wins, one loses, and finally one dies— nothing more. As W. H. Auden put it: "Joy and suffering are simply what one feels at the moment; they have no meaning beyond that; they pass away as they came; they point in no direction; they change nothing. It is a tragic world but a world without guilt for its tragic flaw is not a flaw in human nature, still less a flaw in an individual character, but a flaw in the nature of existence."[1]

With the advent of Christianity and the spread of the gospel of Jesus that proclaimed moral opposition to the carnage, war gradually lost its glitter of heroic virtue and took on a mask of evil or tragedy. The periodic holy wars between Christians and Muslims known as the Crusades notwithstanding, the admonition to "love your enemy" and the beatitude "Blessed are the peacemakers" began to instill a queasy sense of guilt among the war-lovers. Rather than revel in the glory and spectacle of war as Homer did, writers began to examine its causes and wonder how a handful of schemers—Napoleon, Stalin, Hitler—could acquire the power to terrorize entire generations.

The appetite for war and heroic slaughter has not disappeared from the human bloodstream. It has merely been localized and muted. Even as we write this, scores of local conflicts—regional brushfires that feed on human bodies—rage around the globe. But the catastrophic global war that threatens to engulf the earth and annihilate all its children in an Armageddon of fire and brimstone has so far been blessedly avoided. It has been nearly 50 years since the last true global conflict involving millions of combatants from many nations. Yet the paradox is that this brief lull, this fragile peace has been bequeathed the embattled earth neither by the moralists nor the pacifists but by the war-mongers themselves—the generals and their arms-merchants. Their weapons have simply grown too terrible, too cataclysmic to be unleashed. In the combined arsenals of the United States and the Soviet Union are stockpiled missiles and bombs enough to eradicate a hundred times over all the warm-blooded creatures on the face of the globe. Only reptiles and burrowing insects would be left to eke out a precarious existence on the devastated earth after the unleashing of the terrible bombs. Because of its own self-generated terrors, war has thus paradoxically outstripped the narrow compass of an earthly battlefield. If a global war should ever again be fought, there would be no victor to circle the citadel of Troy, braying with triumph and conquest. There would be only the charred and burnt-out sphere that had once been the blue and lovely earth, a glowing lump of coal adrift in the gloom of space, weighed down by the singed carcasses of those incinerated billions who had once called it home.

This chapter of *Reading, Writing, and the Humanities* offers a sampling of philosophies about war, old as well as new. It opens with Sun Tzu's 2,500-year-old *The Art of War,*

---

1. W. H. Auden. In "Editor's Introduction," *The Portable Greek Reader.* New York: Penguin Books, 1950.

which treats war as if it were a big business whose proper marketing will ensure success in vanquishing and subduing the enemy. It attributes no moral evil to waging war, only to waging it badly. On the other hand, Sigmund Freud's "Why War?" depicts war as a savage vestige of uncontrolled passions. In another philosophic essay, John Keegan discusses why the leaders in a modern war no longer fight beside their troops but hole up in secret hideouts away from the devastation being orchestrated at their commands.

In the history section, an anonymous German soldier and a Japanese housewife give eyewitness accounts of war as it affected them personally, while Jonathan Schell writes a terrifying piece of futuristic history about the catastrophic blight that would follow a nuclear war.

The literature section includes Pirandello's classic short story, "War," about a man who is secretly haunted by the wartime loss of his only son. A chapter from Eric Maria Remarque's novel *All Quiet on the Western Front*, written about World War I, gives us the claustrophobic view of the haplessly slogging foot-soldier. Three poems— "Dulce Et Decorum Est" by Wilfred Owen, "Come Up from the Fields, Father" by Walt Whitman, and "In Goya's greatest scenes we seem to see" by Lawrence Fer- linghetti—portray war as an unromantic inferno that devours youth. A similar theme is echoed in the two paintings, *The Third of May, 1808: The Execution of the Defenders of Madrid*, by Francisco de Goya, and *Guernica*, by Pablo Picasso, which end the chapter.

PHILOSOPHY

THE ART OF WAR
Sun Tzu

Sun Tzu (b. ca. 500 B.C.) was a Chinese general and military theorist during a period of venomous interstate feudal conflicts and growing armies in China. To the massive armies of the day was added the power of the cavalry, and soon the mounted warrior, armed with the Chinese compound bow and the newly invented crossbow, spelled doom for the majestic but clumsy war chariot. At the same time, iron foundries began providing heavier and stronger weapons. With more mobile and better-equipped armies at their disposal, commanders devoted their minds to the science of warfare. It was in this climate that Sun Tzu wrote a treatise carefully outlining the rules for military strategy, tactics, logistics, and espionage. Entitled *The Art of War*, this little book was widely read throughout China and eventually translated into the languages of the West, where it became a required text for students of classical warfare. In the twentieth century *The Art of War* was much admired by Mao Tse-tung and his followers. The excerpt below reveals Tzu's emphasis on brains over brawn.

Reading Advice

Sun Tzu's essay is not written in straightforward prose that develops a main point through logically structured paragraphs. Instead, it presents its arguments in a kind of panel discussion or forum over which Sun Tzu presides while other participants voice their opinions or present additional information, anecdotes, or examples. For instance, the selection begins with a heading titled "Sun Tzu said": This heading is followed by Sun Tzu's statement that "Generally in war the best policy is to take a state intact; to ruin it is inferior to this." But before Sun Tzu moves on to his second point, he is interrupted by Li Ch'uan, who adds, "Do not put a premium on killing." Later on, other voices add to the discussion. In this way, the entire essay becomes a conversation among experienced military leaders on how to conquer with craft and subtlety instead of brute force.

Tzu uses a number of literary devices, such as analogy, paradox, metaphor, and simile to illuminate his strategies. These devices give the work a lofty, poetic tone that belie its underlying purpose, which is to teach warriors how to ruthlessly subdue an enemy. The best way to read the essay is to ponder each idea as it is presented by either Sun Tzu or one of his colleagues. Eventually, you will grasp that all the suggestions advocate a method of warfare that favors mental strategy over spontaneous physical clashes.

Sun Tzu said:

Generally in war the best policy is to take a state intact; to ruin it is inferior   1
to this.

LI CH'ÜAN. Do not put a premium on killing.

To capture the enemy's army is better than to destroy it; to take intact a   2
battalion, a company or a five-man squad is better than to destroy them.

For to win one hundred victories in one hundred battles is not the acme of   3
skill. To subdue the enemy without fighting is the acme of skill.

Thus, what is of supreme importance in war is to attack the enemy's strategy;   4
TU MU. . . . The Grand Duke said: 'He who excels at resolving difficulties does so before they arise. He who excels in conquering his enemies triumphs before threats materialize.'

LI CH'ÜAN. Attack plans at their inception. In the Later Han, K'ou Hsün surrounded Kao Chun. Chun sent his Planning Officer, Huang-fu Wen, to parley. Huang-fu Wen was stubborn and rude and K'ou Hsün beheaded him, and informed Kao Chun: 'Your staff officer was without propriety. I have beheaded him. If you wish to submit, do so immediately. Otherwise defend yourself.' On the same day, Chun threw open his fortifications and surrendered.

All K'ou Hsün's generals said: 'May we ask, you killed his envoy, but yet forced him to surrender his city. How is this?'

K'ou Hsün said: 'Huang-fu Wen was Kao Chun's heart and guts, his intimate counsellor. If I had spared Huang-fu Wen's life, he would have accomplished his schemes, but when I killed him, Kao Chun lost his guts. It is said: "The supreme excellence in war is to attack the enemy's plans." '

All the generals said: 'This is beyond our comprehension.'

Next best is to disrupt his alliances: 5

Tu Yu. Do not allow your enemies to get together.

Wang Hsi. . . . Look into the matter of his alliances and cause them to be severed and dissolved. If an enemy has alliances, the problem is grave and the enemy's position strong; if he has no alliances the problem is minor and the enemy's position weak.

The next best is to attack his army.   6

Chia Lin. . . . The Grand Duke said: 'He who struggles for victory with naked blades is not a good general.'

Wang Hsi. Battles are dangerous affairs.

Chang Yü. If you cannot nip his plans in the bud, or disrupt his alliances when they are about to be consummated, sharpen your weapons to gain the victory.

The worst policy is to attack cities. Attack cities only when there is no   7
alternative.

To prepare the shielded wagons and make ready the necessary arms and   8
equipment requires at least three months; to pile up earthen ramps against the walls an additional three months will be needed.

If the general is unable to control his impatience and orders his troops to   9
swarm up the wall like ants, one-third of them will be killed without taking the city. Such is the calamity of these attacks.

Tu Mu. . . . In the later Wei, the Emperor T'ai Wu led one hundred thousand troops to attack the Sung general Tsang Chih at Yu T'ai. The Emperor first asked Tsang Chih for some wine. Tsang Chih sealed up a pot full of urine and sent it to him. T'ai Wu was transported with rage and immediately attacked the city, ordering his troops to scale the walls and engage in close combat. Corpses piled up to the top of the walls and after thirty days of this the dead exceeded half his force.

Thus, those skilled in war subdue the enemy's army without battle. They   10
capture his cities without assaulting them and overthrow his state without protracted operations.

Li Ch'üan. They conquer by strategy. In the Later Han the Marquis of Tsan, Tsang Kung, surrounded the 'Yao' rebels at Yüan Wu, but during a succession of months was unable to take the city. His officers and men were ill and

covered with ulcers. The King of Tung Hai spoke to Tsang Kung, saying:
'Now you have massed troops and encircled the enemy, who is determined
to fight to the death. This is no strategy! You should lift the siege. Let them
know that an escape route is open and they will flee and disperse. Then any
village constable will be able to capture them!' Tsang Kung followed this
advice and took Yüan Wu.

Your aim must be to take All-under-Heaven intact. Thus your troops are   11
not worn out and your gains will be complete. This is the art of offensive
strategy.

Consequently, the art of using troops is this: When ten to the enemy's one,   12
surround him;

When five times his strength, attack him;   13

CHANG Yü. If my force is five times that of the enemy I alarm him to the
front, surprise him to the rear, create an uproar in the east and strike in
the west.

If double his strength, divide him.   14

Tu Yu. ... If a two-to-one superiority is insufficient to manipulate the
situation, we use a distracting force to divide his army. Therefore the Grand
Duke said: 'If one is unable to influence the enemy to divide his forces, he
cannot discuss unusual tactics.'

If equally matched you may engage him.   15

Ho YEN-HSI. ... In these circumstances only the able general can win.

If weaker numerically, be capable of withdrawing;   16

Tu Mu. If your troops do not equal his, temporarily avoid his initial onrush.
Probably later you can take advantage of a soft spot. Then rouse yourself
and seek victory with determined spirit.

CHANG Yü. If the enemy is strong and I am weak, I temporarily withdraw
and do not engage. This is the case when the abilities and courage of the
generals and the efficiency of troops are equal.

If I am in order and the enemy in disarray, if I am energetic and he
careless, then, even if he be numerically stronger, I can give battle.

And if in all respects unequal, be capable of eluding him, for a small force   17
is but booty for one more powerful.

CHANG Yü. ... Mencius said: 'The small certainly cannot equal the large,
nor can the weak match the strong, nor the few the many.'

Now the general is the protector of the state. If this protection is all-   18
embracing, the state will surely be strong; if defective, the state will certainly
be weak.

CHANG Yü. ... The Grand Duke said: 'A sovereign who obtains the right
person prospers. One who fails to do so will be ruined.'

Now there are three ways in which a ruler can bring misfortune upon   19
his army:

When ignorant that the army should not advance, to order an advance or   20
ignorant that it should not retire, to order a retirement. This is described as
'hobbling the army.'

CHIA LIN. The advance and retirement of the army can be controlled by the
general in accordance with prevailing circumstances. No evil is greater than
commands of the sovereign from the court.

When ignorant of military affairs, to participate in their administration. This   21
causes the officers to be perplexed.

TS'AO TS'AO. . . . An army cannot be run according to rules of etiquette.

TU MU. As far as propriety, laws, and decrees are concerned, the army has
its own code, which it ordinarily follows. If these are made identical with
those used in governing a state the officers will be bewildered.

CHANG YÜ. Benevolence and righteousness may be used to govern a state
but cannot be used to administer an army. Expediency and flexibility are
used in administering an army, but cannot be used in governing a state.

When ignorant of command problems, to share in the exercise of respon-   22
sibilities. This engenders doubts in the minds of the officers.

WANG HSI. . . . If one ignorant of military matters is sent to participate in
the administration of the army, then in every movement there will be
disagreement and mutual frustration and the entire army will be hamstrung.
That is why Pei Tu memorialized the throne to withdraw the Army Supervisor; only then was he able to pacify Ts'ao Chou.

CHANG YÜ. In recent times court officials have been used as Supervisors of
the Army and this is precisely what is wrong.

If the army is confused and suspicious, neighbouring rulers will cause trouble.   23
This is what is meant by the saying: 'A confused army leads to another's victory.'

MENG. . . . The Grand Duke said: 'One who is confused in purpose cannot
respond to his enemy.'

LI CH'ÜAN. . . . The wrong person cannot be appointed to command. . . .
Lin Hsiang-ju, the Prime Minister of Chao, said: 'Chao Kua is merely able
to read his father's books, and is as yet ignorant of correlating changing
circumstances. Now Your Majesty, on account of his name, makes him the
commander-in-chief. This is like glueing the pegs of a lute and then trying
to tune it.'

Now there are five circumstances in which victory may be predicted: 24

He who knows when he can fight and when he cannot will be victorious.   25

He who understands how to use both large and small forces will be victorious.   26

TU YU. There are circumstances in war when many cannot attack few, and
others when the weak can master the strong. One able to manipulate such
circumstances will be victorious.

He whose ranks are united in purpose will be victorious.   27

TU YU. Therefore Mencius said: 'The appropriate season is not as important as the advantages of the ground; these are not as important as harmonious human relations.'

He who is prudent and lies in wait for an enemy who is not, will be   28
victorious.

CH'EN HAO. Create an invincible army and await the enemy's moment of vulnerability.

HO YEN-HSI. . . . A gentleman said: 'To rely on rustics and not prepare is the greatest of crimes; to be prepared beforehand for any contingency is the greatest of virtues.'

He whose generals are able and not interfered with by the sovereign will   29
be victorious.

TU YU. . . . Therefore Master Wang said: 'To make appointments is the province of the sovereign; to decide on battle, that of the general.'

WANG HSI. . . . A sovereign of high character and intelligence must be able to know the right man, should place the responsibility on him, and expect results.

HO YEN-HSI. . . . Now in war there may be one hundred changes in each step. When one sees he can, he advances; when he sees that things are difficult, he retires. To say that a general must await commands of the sovereign in such circumstances is like informing a superior that you wish to put out a fire. Before the order to do so arrives the ashes are cold. And it is said one must consult the Army Supervisor in these matters! This is as if in building a house beside the road one took advice from those who pass by. Of course the work would never be completed!

To put a rein on an able general while at the same time asking him to suppress a cunning enemy is like tying up the Black Hound of Han and then ordering him to catch elusive hares. What is the difference?

It is in these five matters that the way to victory is known.   30

Therefore I say: 'Know the enemy and know yourself; in a hundred battles   31
you will never be in peril.

When you are ignorant of the enemy but know yourself, your chances of   32
winning or losing are equal.

If ignorant both of your enemy and of yourself, you are certain in every   33
battle to be in peril.'

LI CH'ÜAN. Such people are called 'mad bandits.' What can they expect if not defeat?

Dispositions

Sun Tzu said:
Anciently the skilful warriors first made themselves invincible and awaited   1
the enemy's moment of vulnerability.

Invincibility depends on one's self; the enemy's vulnerability on him.   2

It follows that those skilled in war can make themselves invincible but cannot   3
cause an enemy to be certainly vulnerable.

MEI YAO-CH'EN. That which depends on me, I can do; that which depends
on the enemy cannot be certain.

Therefore it is said that one may know how to win, but cannot necessarily   4
do so.

Invincibility lies in the defence; the possibility of victory in the attack.   5

One defends when his strength is inadequate; he attacks when it is abundant.   6

The experts in defence conceal themselves as under the ninefold earth; those   7
skilled in attack move as from above the ninefold heavens. Thus they are capable
both of protecting themselves and of gaining a complete victory.

TU YU. Those expert at preparing defences consider it fundamental to rely
on the strength of such obstacles as mountains, rivers and foothills. They
make it impossible for the enemy to know where to attack. They secretly
conceal themselves as under the nine-layered ground.

Those expert in attack consider it fundamental to rely on the seasons
and the advantages of the ground; they use inundations and fire according
to the situation. They make it impossible for an enemy to know where to
prepare. They release the attack like a lightning bolt from above the nine-
layered heavens.

To foresee a victory which the ordinary man can foresee is not the acme of   8
skill;

LI CH'ÜAN. . . . When Han Hsin destroyed Chao State he marched out of
the Well Gorge before breakfast. He said: 'We will destroy the Chao army
and then meet for a meal.' The generals were despondent and pretended to
agree. Han Hsin drew up his army with the river to its rear. The Chao
troops climbed upon their breastworks and, observing this, roared with
laughter and taunted him: 'The General of Han does not know how to use
troops!' Han Hsin then proceeded to defeat the Chao army and after break-
fasting beheaded Lord Ch'eng An.

This is an example of what the multitude does not comprehend.

To triumph in battle and be universally acclaimed 'Expert' is not the acme   9
of skill, for to lift an autumn down requires no great strength; to distinguish
between the sun and moon is no test of vision; to hear the thunderclap is no
indication of acute hearing.

CHANG YÜ. By 'autumn down' Sun Tzu means rabbits' down, which on the
coming of autumn is extremely light.

Anciently those called skilled in war conquered an enemy easily conquered.   10

And therefore the victories won by a master of war gain him neither rep-   11
utation for wisdom nor merit for valour.

TU MU. A victory gained before the situation has crystallized is one the common man does not comprehend. Thus its author gains no reputation for sagacity. Before he has bloodied his blade the enemy state has already submitted.

HO YEN-HSI. . . . When you subdue your enemy without fighting who will pronounce you valorous?

For he wins his victories without erring. 'Without erring' means that what-   12
ever he does insures his victory; he conquers an enemy already defeated.

CHEN HAO. In planning, never a useless move; in strategy, no step taken in vain.

Therefore the skilful commander takes up a position in which he cannot be   13
defeated and misses no opportunity to master his enemy.

Thus a victorious army wins its victories before seeking battle; an army   14
destined to defeat fights in the hope of winning.

Tu Mu. . . . Duke Li Ching of Wei said: 'Now, the supreme requirements of generalship are a clear perception, the harmony of his host, a profound strategy coupled with far-reaching plans, an understanding of the seasons and an ability to examine the human factors. For a general unable to estimate his capabilities or comprehend the arts of expediency and flexibility when faced with the opportunity to engage the enemy will advance in a stumbling and hesitant manner, looking anxiously first to his right and then to his left, and be unable to produce a plan. Credulous, he will place confidence in unreliable reports, believing at one moment this and at another that. As timorous as a fox in advancing or retiring, his groups will be scattered about. What is the difference between this and driving innocent people into boiling water or fire? Is this not exactly like driving cows and sheep to feed wolves or tigers?'

Those skilled in war cultivate the *Tao* and preserve the laws and are therefore   15
able to formulate victorious policies.

Tu Mu. The *Tao* is the way of humanity and justice; 'laws' are regulations and institutions. Those who excel in war first cultivate their own humanity and justice and maintain their laws and institutions. By these means they make their governments invincible.

Now the elements of the art of war are first, measurement of space; second,   16
estimation of quantities; third, calculations; fourth, comparisons; and fifth, chances of victory.

Measurements of space are derived from the ground.   17

Quantities derive from measurement, figures from quantities, comparisons   18
from figures, and victory from comparisons.

HO YEN-HSI. 'Ground' includes both distances and type of terrain; 'mea-surement' is calculation. Before the army is dispatched, calculations are made respecting the degree of difficulty of the enemy's land; the directness and deviousness of its roads; the number of his troops; the quantity of his war equipment and the state of his morale. Calculations are made to see if the enemy can be attacked and only after this is the population mobilized and troops raised.

Thus a victorious army is as a hundredweight balanced against a grain; a   19
defeated army as a grain balanced against a hundredweight.

It is because of disposition that a victorious general is able to make his people   20
fight with the effect of pent-up waters which, suddenly released, plunge into a bottomless abyss.

CHANG YÜ. The nature of water is that it avoids heights and hastens to the lowlands. When a dam is broken, the water cascades with irresistible force. Now the shape of an army resembles water. Take advantage of the enemy's unpreparedness; attack him when he does not expect it; avoid his strength and strike his emptiness, and like water, none can oppose you.

Energy

Sun Tzu said:

Generally, management of many is the same as management of few. It is a   1
matter of organization.

CHANG YÜ. To manage a host one must first assign responsibilities to the generals and their assistants, and establish the strengths of ranks and files. . . .

One man is a single; two, a pair; three, a trio. A pair and a trio make a five, which is a squad; two squads make a section; five sections, a platoon; two platoons, a company; two companies, a battalion; two battalions, a regiment; two regiments, a group; two groups, a brigade; two brigades, an army. Each is subordinate to the superior and controls the inferior. Each is properly trained. Thus one may manage a host of a million men just as he would a few.

And to control many is the same as to control few. This is a matter of   2
formations and signals.

CHANG YÜ. . . . Now when masses of troops are employed, certainly they are widely separated, and ears are not able to hear acutely nor eyes to see clearly. Therefore officers and men are ordered to advance or retreat by observing the flags and banners and to move or stop by signals of bells and drums. Thus the valiant shall not advance alone, nor shall the coward flee.

That the army is certain to sustain the enemy's attack without suffering   3
defeat is due to operations of the extraordinary and the normal forces.

LI CHUAN. The force which confronts the enemy is the normal; that which goes to his flanks the extraordinary. No commander of an army can wrest the advantage from the enemy without extraordinary forces.

HO YEN-HSI. I make the enemy conceive my normal force to be the extraordinary and my extraordinary to be the normal. Moreover, the normal may become the extraordinary and vice versa.

Troops thrown against the enemy as a grindstone against eggs is an example   4
of a solid acting upon a void.

TS'AO TS'AO. Use the most solid to attack the most empty.

Generally, in battle, use the normal force to engage; use the extraordinary   5
to win.

Now the resources of those skilled in the use of extraordinary forces are as   6
infinite as the heavens and earth; as inexhaustible as the flow of the great rivers.

For they end and recommence; cyclical, as are the movements of the sun   7
and moon. They die away and are reborn; recurrent, as are the passing seasons.

The musical notes are only five in number but their melodies are so numerous   8
that one cannot hear them all.

The primary colours are only five in number but their combinations are so   9
infinite that one cannot visualize them all.

The flavours are only five in number but their blends are so various that   10
one cannot taste them all.

In battle there are only the normal and extraordinary forces, but their   11
combinations are limitless; none can comprehend them all.

For these two forces are mutually reproductive; their interaction as endless   12
as that of interlocked rings. Who can determine where one ends and the other
begins?

When torrential water tosses boulders, it is because of its momentum;   13

When the strike of a hawk breaks the body of its prey, it is because of   14
timing.

TU YU. Strike the enemy as swiftly as a falcon strikes its target. It surely
breaks the back of its prey for the reason that it awaits the right moment
to strike. Its movement is regulated.

Thus the momentum of one skilled in war is overwhelming, and his attack   15
precisely regulated.

His potential is that of a fully drawn crossbow; his timing, the release of the   16
trigger.

In the tumult and uproar the battle seems chaotic, but there is no disorder;   17
the troops appear to be milling about in circles but cannot be defeated.

LI CH'ÜAN. In battle all appears to be turmoil and confusion. But the flags
and banners have prescribed arrangements; the sounds of the cymbals, fixed
rules.

Apparent confusion is a product of order; apparent cowardice, of courage;   18
apparent weakness, of strength.

TU MU. The verse means that if one wishes to feign disorder to entice an
enemy he must himself be well-disciplined. Only then can he feign confusion.

One who wishes to simulate cowardice and lie in wait for his enemy must be courageous, for only then is he able to simulate fear. One who wishes to appear to be weak in order to make his enemy arrogant must be extremely strong. Only then can he feign weakness.

Order or disorder depends on organization; courage or cowardice on cir- 19
cumstances; strength or weakness on dispositions.

LI CH'ÜAN. Now when troops gain a favourable situation the coward is brave; if it be lost, the brave become cowards. In the art of war there are no fixed rules. These can only be worked out according to circumstances.

Thus, those skilled at making the enemy move do so by creating a situation 20
to which he must conform; they entice him with something he is certain to take, and with lures of ostensible profit they await him in strength.

Therefore a skilled commander seeks victory from the situation and does 21
not demand it of his subordinates.

CH'EN HAO. Experts in war depend especially on opportunity and expediency. They do not place the burden of accomplishment on their men alone. He selects his men and they exploit the situation. 22

LI CH'ÜAN. . . . Now, the valiant can fight; the cautious defend, and the wise counsel. Thus there is none whose talent is wasted.

TU MU. . . . Do not demand accomplishment of those who have no talent.

When Ts'ao Ts'ao attacked Chang Lu in Han Chung, he left Generals Chang Liao, Li Tien, and Lo Chin in command of over one thousand men to defend Ho Fei. Ts'ao Ts'ao sent instructions to the Army Commissioner, Hsieh Ti, and wrote on the edge of the envelope: 'Open this only when the rebels arrive.' Soon after, Sun Ch'üan of Wu with one hundred thousand men besieged Ho Fei. The generals opened the instructions and read: 'If Sun Ch'üan arrives, Generals Chang and Li will go out to fight. General Lo will defend the city. The Army Commissioner shall not participate in the battle. All the other generals should engage the enemy.'

Chang Liao said: 'Our Lord is campaigning far away, and if we wait for the arrival of reinforcements the rebels will certainly destroy us. Therefore the instructions say that before the enemy is assembled we should immediately attack him in order to blunt his keen edge and to stabilize the morale of our own troops. Then we can defend the city. The opportunity for victory or defeat lies in this one action.'

Li Tien and Chang Liao went out to attack and actually defeated Sun Ch'üan, and the morale of the Wu army was rubbed out. They returned and put their defences in order and the troops felt secure. Sun Ch'üan assaulted the city for ten days but could not take it and withdrew.

The historian Sun Sheng in discussing this observed: 'Now war is a matter of deception. As to the defence of Ho Fei, it was hanging in the air, weak and without reinforcements. If one trusts solely to brave generals who love fighting, this will cause trouble. If one relies solely on those who are cautious, their frightened hearts will find it difficult to control the situation.'

CHANG YÜ. Now the method of employing men is to use the avaricious and the stupid, the wise and the brave, and to give responsibility to each in situations that suit him. Do not charge people to do what they cannot do. Select them and give them responsibilities commensurate with their abilities.

He who relies on the situation uses his men in fighting as one rolls logs or   24 stones. Now the nature of logs and stones is that on stable ground they are static; on unstable ground, they move. If square, they stop; if round, they roll.

Thus, the potential of troops skilfully commanded in battle may be compared   25 to that of round boulders which roll down from mountain heights.

TU MU. . . . Thus one need use but little strength to achieve much.

CHANG YÜ. . . . Li Ching said: 'In war there are three kinds of situation:

'When the general is contemptuous of his enemy and his officers love to fight, their ambitions soaring as high as the azure clouds and their spirits as fierce as hurricanes, this is situation in respect to morale.

'When one man defends a narrow mountain defile which is like sheep's intestines or the door of a dog-house, he can withstand one thousand. This is situation in respect to terrain.

'When one takes advantage of the enemy's laxity, his weariness, his hunger and thirst, or strikes when his advanced camps are not settled, or his army is only half-way across a river, this is situation in respect to the enemy.'

Therefore when using troops, one must take advantage of the situation exactly as if he were setting a ball in motion on a steep slope. The force applied is minute but the results are enormous.

Questions for Critical Thinking

1. What important requirement runs through most of Sun Tzu's techniques on how a war should be managed? Give an imaginary portrayal of the sort of general who would be best suited to run a war based on Sun's advice.

2. In paragraph 21 of *The Art of War,* Tu Mu states that the military has its own rules of conduct, its own code of ethics, which cannot be used to govern a state. Is Tu Mu correct, or do you believe that such qualities as benevolence and righteousness should be used to administer an army? Give reasons for your answer. Where later on in the essay does Tu Mu seem to contradict himself? How do you explain the contradiction?

3. What, according to Sun, is the relationship between the sovereign and the general? Who has the most authority in war? In your view, is this the correct relationship? Why or why not? What is the relationship in our country between the respective authority of the president and generals?

4. In what way is Sun's idea of troop management similar to our modern idea of business administration? What is the principle behind this type of management?

5. How important, in your opinion, is Sun's requirement of "normal" and "extraordinary" forces? (*See* paragraphs 3–12 of "Energy.") Explain Sun's idea before offering your opinion. What kind of language does the author use to clarify the difference between these two forces? Is the language effective? Why or why not?

6. Ancient Chinese philosophy is filled with paradox, that is, seemingly contradictory statements that nevertheless make sense. Where does the author use paradox in an attempt to demonstrate illusion and reality as applied to war? Do you agree with these ideas? Why or why not?

Writing Assignment

Turning Sun Tzu's ideas upside down, write an essay entitled "The Art of Peace."

Writing Advice

1. Begin with a loosely constructed draft made up of numbered ideas as in Sun's essay. Your ideas, of course, must be based on the premise that peace, rather than war, is the preferred goal. For instance, your list might begin with the following three entries:

   a. When two countries have conflicting ideas, it is more honorable to continue diplomatic discussions than to declare war.

   b. The ability to bargain patiently is one of the most valuable talents in a leader today.

   c. Keeping the world safe from atomic warfare must take precedence over any individual country's false sense of sovereignty or need for power.

2. Once you have completed your list (we suggest six to eight entries), organize them in your order of presentation. You may wish to combine ideas. For instance, entries 1 and 2 above could be organized into one point, as follows: "When the conflicting ideologies or goals of two countries escalate hostilities between them, leaders should be chosen who can bargain patiently with the opposition."

3. Now you should find a thesis to act as the umbrella for all your entries. A good thesis will announce your point of view and limit you to a certain topic. From the incomplete sample list above, the following thesis might be developed: "Because national leaders today cannot afford to involve their countries in a war that could lead to nuclear holocaust, citizens must unite to choose leaders who know how to bargain patiently at the diplomatic conference table."

4. You are now ready to develop the first draft of a structured, thesis-driven essay. All you need now is to find appropriate examples or other details to convince your audience.

Alternate Writing Assignment

1. Write an essay in which you support Sun's approach to war. Focus your essay on a thesis and refer to specific passages in Sun's essay.

2. Write an essay in which you condemn Sun's approach to war. State in your own words what Sun's basic approach is and then refute that approach through valid reasons supported with appropriate details.

PHILOSOPHY

WHY WAR?
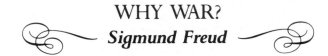
Sigmund Freud

Austrian-born Sigmund Freud (1856–1939), the first researcher to apply scientific detachment to the observation of human behavior and to formulate a comprehensive theory for explaining it, is regarded as the father of modern psychiatry. His most influential contribution was the idea that human behavior is determined not only by conscious rational choices but also by dark and powerful subconscious impulses. Many of the principles he discovered from a study of the disturbed, Freud also applied to normal individuals, as well as to society. He theorized, for example, that all human behavior results from certain instinctual drives, such as the urge for sex or for aggression, and that civilized society can flourish only if these urges are controlled by the superego. In his view, civilization was a thin veneer overlying a turbulent sea of instincts and emotions. As the essay below makes clear, Freud considered war an eruption of the darker human side. After the mass carnage suffered by Europe in World War I, Freud declared himself a pacifist, as did Albert Einstein. In 1931, Einstein suggested to Freud that they openly exchange letters on the subject of how to maintain world peace. Their correspondence was sponsored by the League of Nations, an international organization both supported. The letter below is Freud's reply to Einstein's question "Why War?"

Reading Advice

Freud was on intimate terms with Einstein when he wrote this letter, which he knew would be disseminated to a wider audience. His argument is therefore carefully prepared and eloquently supports his thesis that warfare will end only when humans learn to control their violent impulses inherited from nature. Much of Freud's essay draws on

From *Collected Papers,* Vol. 5, by Sigmund Freud, edited by James Strachey. Published by Basic Books, Inc. by arrangement with Hogarth Press Ltd. and The Institute of Psycho-Analysis, London. Reprinted by permission of Basic Books, Inc., Publishers.

his psychiatric knowledge and background. In the very first paragraph, he admits, "I reflected, moreover, that I was not being asked to make practical proposals but only to set out the problem of avoiding war as it appears to a psychological observer."

The starting point in Freud's argument is that from time out of mind humans have resorted to force to settle their conflicts. Even justice is a form of united might. This central point then allows Freud to theorize at length about the usefulness of a central organization empowered to judge and resolve the conflicts among nations, a proposal he actively advocates with examples from history, as well as current events. He also uses emotional appeal toward the end of his letter (*see* paragraph 16) when he enumerates the horrible effects of modern warfare.

Vienna, September, 1932

Dear Professor Einstein,

When I heard that you intended to invite me to an exchange of views on   1 some subject that interested you and that seemed to deserve the interest of others besides yourself, I readily agreed. I expected you to choose a problem on the frontiers of what is knowable today, a problem to which each of us, a physicist and a psychologist, might have our own particular angle of approach and where we might come together from different directions upon the same ground. You have taken me by surprise, however, by posing the question of what can be done to protect mankind from the curse of war. I was scared at first by the thought of my—I had almost written 'our'—incapacity for dealing with what seemed to be a practical problem, a concern for statesmen. But I then realized that you had raised the question not as a natural scientist and physicist but as a philanthropist: you were following the promptings of the League of Nations[1] just as Fridtjof Nansen,[2] the polar explorer, took on the work of bringing help to the starving and homeless victims of the World War. I reflected, moreover, that I was not being asked to make practical proposals but only to set out the problem of avoiding war as it appears to a psychological observer. Here again you yourself have said almost all there is to say on the subject. But though you have taken the wind out of my sails I shall be glad to follow in your wake and content myself with confirming all you have said by amplifying it to the best of my knowledge—or conjecture.

You begin with the relation between Right[3] and Might.[4] There can be no   2 doubt that that is the correct starting-point for our investigation. But may I replace the word 'might' by the balder and harsher word 'violence'? Today right

---

1. The forerunner of today's United Nations, founded in 1920. Among other functions, the League of Nations—with headquarters in Geneva, Switzerland—was to try to make war obsolete through international cooperation and a system of "collective security."
2. Fridtjof Nansen (1861–1930), Norwegian explorer of the arctic regions, naturalist, and humanitarian.
3. Moral Right, law and justice.
4. Force and power.

and violence appear to us as antitheses.[5] It can easily be shown, however, that the one has developed out of the other; and if we go back to the earliest beginnings and see how that first came about, the problem is easily solved. You must forgive me if in what follows I go over familiar and commonly accepted ground as though it were new, but the thread of my argument requires it.

It is a general principle, then, that conflicts of interest between men are settled by the use of violence. This is true of the whole animal kingdom, from which men have no business to exclude themselves. In the case of men, no doubt, conflicts of *opinion* occur as well which may reach the highest pitch of abstraction and which seem to demand some other technique for their settlement. That, however, is a later complication. To begin with, in a small human horde,[6] it was superior muscular strength which decided who owned things or whose will should prevail. Muscular strength was soon supplemented and replaced by the use of tools: the winner was the one who had the better weapons or who used them the more skillfully. From the moment at which weapons were introduced, intellectual superiority already began to replace brute muscular strength; but the final purpose of the fight remained the same—one side or the other was to be compelled to abandon his claim or his objection by the damage inflicted on him and by the crippling of his strength. That purpose was most completely achieved if the victor's violence eliminated his opponent permanently, that is to say, killed him. This had two advantages: he could not renew his opposition and his fate deterred others from following his example. In addition to this, killing an enemy satisfied an instinctual inclination which I shall have to mention later. The intention to kill might be countered by a reflection that the enemy could be employed in performing useful services if he were left alive in an intimated condition. In that case the victor's violence was content to subjugate him instead of killing him. This was a first beginning of the idea of sparing an enemy's life, but thereafter the victor had to reckon with his defeated opponent's lurking thirst for revenge and sacrificed some of his own security.

Such, then, was the original state of things: domination by whoever had the greater might—domination by brute violence or by violence supported by intellect. As we know, this regime[7] was altered in the course of evolution. There was a path that led from violence to right or law. What was that path? It is my belief that there was only one: the path which led by way of the fact that the superior strength of a single individual could be rivalled by the union of several weak ones. *'L'union fait la force.'*[8] Violence could be broken by union, and the power of those who were united now represented law in contrast to the violence

3

4

---

5. Opposites.
6. Organized group, such as a clan or tribe.
7. System of control.
8. French: union makes strength.

of the single individual. Thus we see that right is the might of a community. It is still violence, ready to be directed against any individual who resists it; it works by the same methods and follows the same purposes. The only real difference lies in the fact that what prevails is no longer the violence of an individual but that of a community. But in order that the transition from violence to this new right or justice may be effected, one psychological condition must be fulfilled. The union of the majority must be a stable and lasting one. If it were only brought about for the purpose of combating a single domineering individual and were dissolved after his defeat, nothing would have been accomplished. The next person who found himself superior in strength would once more seek to set up a dominion by violence and the game would be repeated *ad infinitum.*[9] The community must be maintained permanently, must be organized, must draw up regulations to anticipate the risk of rebellion and must institute authorities to see that those regulations—the laws—are respected and to superintend the execution of legal acts of violence. The recognition of a community of interests such as these leads to the growth of emotional ties between the members of a united group of people—feelings of unity which are the true source of its strength.

Here, I believe, we already have all the essentials: violence overcome by the transference of power to a larger unity, which is held together by emotional ties between its members. What remains to be said is no more than an expansion and a repetition of this.

The situation is simple so long as the community consists only of a number of equally strong individuals. The laws of such an association will determine the extent to which, if the security of communal life is to be guaranteed, each individual must surrender his personal liberty to turn his strength to violent uses. But a state of rest of that kind is only theoretically conceivable. In actuality the position is complicated by the fact that from its very beginning the community comprises elements of unequal strength—men and women, parents and children—and soon, as a result of war and conquest, it also comes to include victors and vanquished, who turn into masters and slaves. The justice of the community then becomes an expression of the unequal degrees of power obtaining within it; the laws are made by and for the ruling members and find little room for the rights of those in subjection. From that time forward there are two factors at work in the community which are sources of unrest over matters of law but tend at the same time to a further growth of law. First, attempts are made by certain of the rulers to set themselves above the prohibitions which apply to everyone—they seek, that is, to go back from a dominion of law to a dominion of violence. Secondly, the oppressed members of the group make constant efforts to obtain more power and to have any

5

6

---

9. Endlessly.

changes that are brought about in that direction recognized in the laws—they press forward, that is, from unequal justice to equal justice for all. This second tendency becomes especially important if a real shift of power occurs within a community, as may happen as a result of a number of historical factors. In that case right may gradually adapt itself to the new distribution of power or, as is more frequent, the ruling class is unwilling to recognize the change, and rebellion and civil war follow, with a temporary suspension of law and new attempts at a solution by violence, ending in the establishment of a fresh rule of law. There is yet another source from which modifications of law may arise, and one of which the expression is invariably peaceful: it lies in the cultural transformation of the members of the community. This, however, belongs properly in another connection and must be considered later.

Thus we see that the violent solution of conflicts of interest is not avoided even inside a community. But the everyday necessities and common concerns that are inevitable where people live together in one place tend to bring such struggles to a swift conclusion and under such conditions there is an increasing probability that a peaceful solution will be found. But a glance at the history of the human race reveals an endless series of conflicts between one community and another or several others, between large and smaller units—between cities, provinces, races, nations, empires—which have almost always been settled by force of arms. Wars of this kind end either in the spoliation or in the complete overthrow and conquest of one of the parties. It is impossible to make any sweeping judgment upon wars of conquest. Some, such as those waged by the Mongols and Turks, have brought nothing but evil. Others, on the contrary, have contributed to the transformation of violence into law by establishing larger units within which the use of violence was made impossible and in which a fresh system of law led to the solution of conflicts. In this way the conquests of the Romans gave the countries round the Mediterranean the priceless *pax Romana,*[10] and the greed of the French kings to extend their dominions created a peacefully united and flourishing France. Paradoxical as it may sound, it must be admitted that war might be a far from inappropriate means of establishing the eagerly desired reign of 'everlasting' peace, since it is in a position to create the large units within which a powerful central government makes further wars impossible. Nevertheless it fails in this purpose, for the results of conquest are as a rule short-lived: the newly created units fall apart once again, usually owing to a lack of cohesion between the portions that have been united by violence. Hitherto, moreover, the unifications created by conquest, though of considerable extent, have only been *partial,* and the conflicts between these have cried out for violent solution. Thus the result of all these warlike efforts has only

7

---

10. Roman Peace. A relatively peaceful period of approximately 200 years between the reigns of the emperors Augustus (27 B.C.–14 A.D.) and Marcus Aurelius (161–180 A.D.).

been that the human race has exchanged numerous, and indeed unending, minor wars for wars on a grand scale that are rare but all the more destructive.

If we turn to our own times, we arrive at the same conclusion which you   8
have reached by a shorter path. Wars will only be prevented with certainty if mankind unites in setting up a central authority to which the right of giving judgment upon all conflicts of interest shall be handed over. There are clearly two separate requirements involved in this: the creation of a supreme authority and its endowment with the necessary power. One without the other would be useless. The League of Nations is designed as an authority of this kind, but the second condition has not been fulfilled: the League of Nations has no power of its own and can only acquire it if the members of the new union, the separate States, are ready to resign it. And at the moment there seems very little prospect of this. The institution of the League of Nations would, however, be wholly unintelligible if one ignored the fact that here was a bold attempt such as has seldom (perhaps, indeed, never on such a scale) been made before. It is an attempt to base upon an appeal to certain idealistic attitudes of mind the authority (that is, the coercive influence) which otherwise rests on the possession of power. We have heard that a community is held together by two things: the compelling force of violence and the emotional ties (identifications is the technical name) between its members. If one of the factors is absent, the community may possibly be held together by the other. The ideas that are appealed to can, of course, only have any significance if they give expression to important concerns that are common to the members, and the question arises of how much strength they can exert. History teaches us that they have been to some extent effective. For instance, the Panhellenic[11] idea, the sense of being superior to the surrounding barbarians—an idea which was so powerfully expressed in the Amphictyonies,[12] the Oracles[13] and the Games[14]—was sufficiently strong to mitigate the customs of war among Greeks, though evidently not sufficiently strong to prevent warlike disputes between different sections of the Greek nation or even to restrain a city or confederation of cities from allying itself with the Persian foe in order to gain an advantage over a rival. In the same way, the community of feeling among Christians, powerful though it was, was equally unable at the time of the Renaissance[15] to deter Christian States, whether large or small, from seeking the Sultan's[16] aid in their

---

11. Embracing or including *all* of the ancient Greeks.
12. Associations of neighboring Greek city-states to protect a religious center or shrine.
13. Religious centers in ancient Greece where the deities—on request—revealed future events through their priests.
14. Periodic athletic competitions considered part of Greek religious observances.
15. The era between the Middle Ages and the modern European world, generally between the 14th and 16th century.
16. The ruler of a Muslim country, usually a ruler of the Ottoman (Turkish) Empire.

wars with one another. Nor does any idea exist today which could be expected to exert a unifying authority of the sort. Indeed it is all too clear that the national ideals by which nations are at present swayed operate in a contrary direction. Some people are inclined to prophesy that it will not be possible to make an end of war until Communist ways of thinking have found universal acceptance. But that aim is in any case a very remote one today, and perhaps it could only be reached after the most fearful civil wars. Thus the attempt to replace actual force by the force of ideas seems at present to be doomed to failure. We shall be making a false calculation if we disregard the fact that law was originally brute violence and that even today it cannot do without the support of violence.

I can now proceed to add a gloss[17] to another of your remarks. You express astonishment at the fact that it is so easy to make men enthusiastic about a war and add your suspicion that there is something at work in them—an instinct for hatred and destruction—which goes halfway to meet the efforts of the warmongers. Once again, I can only express my entire agreement. We believe in the existence of an instinct of that kind and have in fact been occupied during the last few years in studying its manifestations. Will you allow me to take this opportunity of putting before you a portion of the theory of the instincts which, after much tentative groping and many fluctuations of opinion, has been reached by workers in the field of psychoanalysis?

According to our hypothesis human instincts are of only two kinds: those which seek to preserve and unite—which we call 'erotic,' exactly in the sense in which Plato uses the word 'Eros' in his *Symposium,*[18] or 'sexual,' with a deliberate extension of the popular conception of 'sexuality'—and those which seek to destroy and kill and which we class together as the aggressive or destructive instinct. As you see, this is in fact no more than a theoretical clarification of the universally familiar opposition between Love and Hate which may perhaps have some fundamental relation to the polarity of attraction and repulsion that plays a part in your own field of knowledge. We must not be too hasty in introducing ethical judgments of good and evil. Neither of these instincts is any less essential than the other; the phenomena of life arise from the operation of both together, whether acting in concert or in opposition. It seems as though an instinct of the one sort can scarcely ever operate in isolation; it is always accompanied—or, as we say, alloyed[19]—with an element from the other side, which modifies its aim or is, in some cases, what enables it to achieve that aim. Thus, for instance, the instinct of self-preservation is certainly of an erotic kind, but it must nevertheless have aggressiveness at its disposal if it is

9

10

---

17. Commentary.
18. Plato's (427–347 B.C.) book (dialogue) discussing ideal love.
19. Blended, mixed.

to fulfil its purpose. So, too, the instinct of love, when it is directed toward an object, stands in need of some contribution from the instinct of mastery if it is in any way to possess that object. The difficulty of isolating the two classes of instinct in their actual manifestations is indeed what has so long prevented us from recognizing them.

If you will follow me a little further, you will see that human actions are subject to another complication of a different kind. It is very rarely that an action is the work of a *single* instinctual impulse (which must in itself be compounded of Eros and destructiveness). In order to make an action possible there must be as a rule a *combination* of such compounded motives. . . . There is no need to enumerate them all. A lust for aggression and destruction is certainly among them: the countless cruelties in history and in our everyday lives vouch for its existence and its strength. The gratification of these destructive impulses is of course facilitated by their admixture with others of an erotic and idealistic kind. When we read of the atrocities of the past, it sometimes seems as though the idealistic motives served only as an excuse for the destructive appetites; and sometimes—in the case, for instance, of the cruelties of the Inquisition[20]—it seems as though the idealistic motives had pushed themselves forward in consciousness, while the destructive ones lent them an unconscious reinforcement. Both may be true.

I fear I may be abusing your interest, which is after all concerned with the prevention of war and not with our theories. Nevertheless I should like to linger for a moment over our destructive instinct, whose popularity is by no means equal to its importance. As a result of a little speculation, we have come to suppose that this instinct is at work in every living being and is striving to bring it to ruin and to reduce life to its original condition of inanimate matter. Thus it quite seriously deserves to be called a death instinct, while the erotic instincts represent the effort to live. The death instinct turns into the destructive instinct if, with the help of special organs, it is directed outward, on to objects. The living creature preserves its own life, so to say, by destroying an extraneous one. Some portion of the death instinct, however, remains operative *within* the living being, and we have sought to trace quite a number of normal and pathological phenomena to this internalization of the destructive instinct. We have even been guilty of the heresy[21] of attributing the origin of conscience to this diversion inward of aggressiveness. You will notice that it is by no means a trivial matter if this process is carried too far: it is positively unhealthy. On the other hand if these forces are turned to destruction in the external world, the living creature will be relieved and the effect must be beneficial. This would

11

12

---

20. Papal (Roman Catholic) tribunal founded in the 13th century for the purpose of searching out persons holding "false" religious beliefs and punishing those judged guilty.
21. A view contrary to the accepted view of the times.

serve as a biological justification for all the ugly and dangerous impulses against which we are struggling. It must be admitted that they stand nearer to Nature than does our resistance to them, for which an explanation also needs to be found. It may perhaps seem to you as though our theories are a kind of mythology and, in the present case, not even an agreeable one. But does not every science come in the end to a kind of mythology like this? Cannot the same be said today of your own Physics?

For our immediate purpose then, this much follows from what has been said: there is no use in trying to get rid of men's aggressive inclinations. We are told that in certain happy regions of the earth, where nature provides in abundance everything that man requires, there are races whose life is passed in tranquillity and who know neither compulsion nor aggressiveness. I can scarcely believe it and I should be glad to hear more of these fortunate beings. The Russian Communists, too, hope to be able to cause human aggressiveness to disappear by guaranteeing the satisfaction of all material needs and by establishing equality in other respects among all the members of the community. That, in my opinion, is an illusion. They themselves are armed today with the most scrupulous care and not the least important of the methods by which they keep their supporters together is hatred of everyone beyond their frontiers. In any case, as you yourself have remarked, there is no question of getting rid entirely of human aggressive impulses; it is enough to try to divert them to such an extent that they need not find expression in war. 13

Our mythological theory of instincts makes it easy for us to find a formula for *indirect* methods of combating war. If willingness to engage in war is an effect of the destructive instinct, the most obvious plan will be to bring Eros, its antagonist, into play against it. Anything that encourages the growth of emotional ties between men must operate against war. These ties may be of two kinds. In the first place they may be relations resembling those toward a loved object, though without having a sexual aim. There is no need for psychoanalysis to be ashamed to speak of love in this connection, for religion itself uses the same words: 'You shall love your neighbor as yourself.' This, however, is more easily said than done. The second kind of emotional tie is by means of identification. Whatever leads men to share important interests produces this community of feeling, these identifications. And the structure of human society is to a large extent based on them. 14

A complaint which you make about the abuse of authority brings me to another suggestion for the indirect combating of the propensity to war. One instance of the innate and ineradicable inequality of men is their tendency to fall into the two classes of leaders and followers. The latter constitute the vast majority; they stand in need of an authority which will make decisions for them and to which they for the most part offer an unqualified submission. This suggests that more care should be taken than hitherto to educate an upper 15 stratum[22] of men with independent minds, not open to intimidation and eager in the pursuit of truth, whose business it would be to give direction to the dependent masses. It goes without saying that the encroachments made by the executive power of the State and the prohibition laid by the Church upon freedom of thought are far from propitious for the production of a class of this kind. The ideal condition of things would of course be a community of men who had subordinated their instinctual life to the dictatorship of reason. Nothing else could unite men so completely and so tenaciously, even if there were no emotional ties between them. But in all probability that is a Utopian[23] expectation. No doubt the other indirect methods of preventing war are more practicable, though they promise no rapid success. An unpleasant picture comes to one's mind of mills that grind so slowly that people may starve before they get their flour.

The result, as you see, is not very fruitful when an unworldly theoretician 16 is called in to advise on an urgent practical problem. It is a better plan to devote oneself in every particular case to meeting the danger with whatever weapons lie to hand. I should like, however, to discuss one more question, which you do not mention in your letter but which specially interests me. Why do you and I and so many other people rebel so violently against war? Why do we not accept it as another of the many painful calamities of life? After all, it seems quite a natural thing, no doubt it has a good biological basis and in practice it is scarcely avoidable. There is no need to be shocked at my raising this question. For the purpose of an investigation such as this, one may perhaps be allowed to wear a mask of assumed detachment. The answer to my question will be that we react to war in this way because everyone has a right to his own life, because war puts an end to human lives that are full of hope, because it brings individual men into humiliating situations, because it compels them against their will to murder other men, and because it destroys precious material objects which have been produced by the labors of humanity. Other reasons besides might be given, such as that in its present-day form war is no longer an opportunity for achieving the old ideals of heroism and that owing to the perfection of instruments of destruction a future war might involve the extermination of one or perhaps both of the antagonists. All this is true, and so incontestably true that one can only feel astonished that the waging of war has not yet been unanimously repudiated. No doubt debate is possible upon one or two of these points. It may be questioned whether a community ought not to have a right to dispose of individual lives; every war is not open to condemnation to an equal degree; so long as there exist countries and nations that are prepared for the ruthless destruction of others, those others must be armed

---

22. Level, class.
23. An impossible dream of perfection.

for war. But I will not linger over any of these issues; they are not what you want to discuss with me, and I have something different in mind. It is my opinion that the main reason why we rebel against war is that we cannot help doing so. We are pacifists[24] because we are obliged to be for organic reasons. And we then find no difficulty in producing arguments to justify our attitude.

No doubt this requires some explanation. My belief is this. For incalculable   17
ages mankind has been passing through a process of evolution of culture. (Some people, I know, prefer to use the term 'civilization.') We owe to that process the best of what we have become, as well as a good part of what we suffer from. Though its causes and beginnings are obscure and its outcome uncertain, some of its characteristics are easy to perceive. It may perhaps be leading to the extinction of the human race, for in more than one way it impairs the sexual function; uncultivated races and backward strata[25] of the population are already multiplying more rapidly than highly cultivated ones. The process is perhaps comparable to the domestication of certain species of animals and it is undoubtedly accompanied by physical alterations; but we are still unfamiliar with the notion that the evolution of culture is an organic process of this kind. The psychical modifications that go along with the cultural process are striking and unambiguous. They consist in a progressive displacement of instinctual aims and a restriction of instinctual impulses. Sensations which were pleasurable to our ancestors have become indifferent or even intolerable to ourselves; there are organic grounds for the changes in our ethical and aesthetic[26] ideals. Of the psychological characteristics of culture two appear to be the most important: a strengthening of the intellect, which is beginning to govern instinctual life, and an internalization of the aggressive impulses, with all its consequent advantages and perils. Now war is in the crassest opposition to the psychical attitude imposed on us by the cultural process, and for that reason we are bound to rebel against it; we simply cannot any longer put up with it. This is not merely an intellectual and emotional repudiation; we pacifists have a constitutional intolerance of war, an idiosyncracy magnified, as it were, to the highest degree. It seems, indeed, as though the lowering of aesthetic standards in war plays a scarcely smaller part in our rebellion than do its cruelties.

And how long shall we have to wait before the rest of mankind become   18
pacifists too? There is no telling. But it may not be Utopian to hope that these two factors, the cultural attitude and the justified dread of the consequences of a future war, may result within a measurable time in putting an end to the waging of war. By what paths or by what side-tracks this will come about we

---

24. Persons opposed to war and the use of violence to settle disputes.
25. Levels, classes.
26. Relating to the sense of beauty.

cannot guess. But one thing we *can* say: whatever fosters the growth of culture works at the same time against war.

I trust you will forgive me if what I have said has disappointed you, and I remain, with kindest regards,   19

Yours sincerely,

SIGM. FREUD

Questions for Critical Thinking

1. What are the major contrasts of ideas between Freud's essay and that of Sun Tzu? How do the basic assumptions of these two authors differ? Of what would you have to convince Sun Tzu before he could agree with Freud?

2. In a good encyclopedia, look up "League of Nations" (*see also* footnote 1). Then, describe in some detail how and why this organization was conceived. Do you believe such an organization needs to be empowered today? Why or why not?

3. Why does Freud find it necessary to substitute the word "violence" for Einstein's word "might" (*see* paragraph 2)? Could the same ideas be conveyed through the word "might"? Why or why not?

4. Freud believes that for human beings to live in peace, they must be held together by an ideal to which all are emotionally tied. He cites the Panhellenic idea of Greek superiority over the barbarians and the idea of Christian brotherhood as historical examples of ideals that tended, for some time at least, to prevent war (*see* paragraph 8). What ideal, if any, do you think would be powerful enough today to unite the world in a lasting peace? Does this ideal have a chance? If you do not believe that any such ideal exists, then are human beings doomed to war and eventual extinction? Why or why not?

5. What is Freud's view of the possibility that Russian Communism will serve as a springboard for world peace? Do you agree with his view? Why or why not?

6. To what important American constitutional right does the author give tacit support in paragraph 15? In your own view, how important is this right to the pursuit of peace?

7. How optimistic or pessimistic are you about civilization's ability to do away with war? Give reasons for your answer.

Writing Assignment

Following Freud's basic rhetorical approach, write a letter to the current president of the United States, answering the question, "Why Peace?"

Writing Advice

The fact that you are addressing the president of the United States should lend the same kind of formality to your writing evident in Freud's letter to Einstein. The proper way to address the president is simply, "Dear Mr. President": Assume, for this assignment, that you have been asked to give your views on why it is important to maintain peace in the present world. Imagine, moreover, that your letter will be published in a national magazine such as *Time*. Do not, however, try to be journalistic; just use your clearest and most succinct style. The following organization may help you get started:

1. State why the content of your letter has international significance.

2. Give a vivid picture of the results if world peace is not maintained. Freud's letter should give you some ideas.

3. Use the expert testimony of influential pacifists who support your views. For instance, look up the writings of people like Leo Tolstoy, Jane Addams, Albert Gobat, Alfred H. Love, Bertrand Russell, Dr. Benjamin Spock, Martin Luther King, Bertrand Russell, or Pope John Paul.

4. Following Freud's example, appeal to the reader's emotion in closing your letter.

Alternate Writing Assignments

1. Write an essay in which you argue that a truly civilized society is one that has learned to control its instincts toward war.

2. Write an essay in which you argue that the desire for war is an inherent part of human behavior and that pacifism is an impractical ideal.

HISTORY

THE BATTLE OF STALINGRAD, DIARY OF A GERMAN SOLDIER
Anonymous

The entries below come from the diary of an anonymous German soldier who died in the World War II Battle of Stalingrad. His observations are of historical significance because they vividly reveal the early cockiness of the German troops at the start of the

Russian campaign and then their gradual pessimism as the brutal winter set in and Russian resistance stiffened. The battle was fought with ferocity in every part of the city, reducing it to rubble. Patiently waiting for the German army's food and ammunition to be exhausted, the Russians soon surrounded the invaders and on February 2, 1943, forced a humiliating surrender of the German Sixth Army that turned the tide decisively against the Nazis.

Reading Advice

The excerpt consists of separate entries that recount the days the soldier spent with his company, fighting to conquer Stalingrad in 1943. In retrospect, history judges the Nazis to have been a tyrannical regime and merciless foe, and the attack on Russia to rank among Germany's worse treacheries. Notice, however, that the diary writer reflects an entirely different view of events. He begins with a palpable sense of patriotic joy and national pride and gradually progresses, as the brutal war takes its toll, to despair and cynicism. The effectiveness of the piece lies in its heartfelt and honest, if misguided and deluded, account. Ironically, the events and outcome of this diary comprise a kind of a universal chronicle for all soldiers. This particular soldier begins typically with dreams of victory and ambitions of winning a medal; he ends, with grisly typicality, by losing his life on foreign soil hundreds of miles from his home.

*T*oday, after we'd had a bath, the company commander told us that if our future operations are as successful, we'll soon reach the Volga, take Stalingrad and then the war will inevitably soon be over. Perhaps we'll be home by Christmas.   1

July 29. . . . The company commander says the Russian troops are completely broken, and cannot hold out any longer. To reach the Volga and take Stalingrad is not so difficult for us. The Führer knows where the Russians' weak point is. Victory is not far away. . . .   2

August 2. . . . What great spaces the Soviets occupy, what rich fields there are to be had here after the war's over! Only let's get it over with quickly. I believe that the Führer will carry the thing through to a successful end.   3

August 10. . . . The Führer's orders were read out to us. He expects victory of us. We are all convinced that they can't stop us.   4

August 12. We are advancing towards Stalingrad along the railway line. Yesterday Russian "katyushi" and then tanks halted our regiment. "The Russians are throwing in their last forces," Captain Werner explained to me. Large-scale help is coming up for us, and the Russians will be beaten.   5

This morning outstanding soldiers were presented with decorations. . . . Will I really go back to Elsa without a decoration? I believe that for Stalingrad the Führer will decorate even me. . . .   6

August 23. Splendid news—north of Stalingrad our troops have reached the Volga and captured part of the city. The Russians have two alternatives, either to flee across the Volga or give themselves up. Our company's interpreter has   7 interrogated a captured Russian officer. He was wounded, but asserted that the Russians would fight for Stalingrad to the last round. Something incomprehensible is, in fact, going on. In the north our troops capture a part of Stalingrad and reach the Volga, but in the south the doomed divisions are continuing to resist bitterly. Fanaticism. . . .

August 27. A continuous cannonade on all sides. We are slowly advancing. Less than twenty miles to go to Stalingrad. In the daytime we can see the smoke of fires, at night-time the bright glow. They say that the city is on fire; on the Führer's orders our Luftwaffe has sent it up in flames. That's what the Russians need, to stop them from resisting . . .

September 4. We are being sent northward along the front towards Stalingrad. We marched all night and by dawn had reached Voroponovo Station. We can already see the smoking town. It's a happy thought that the end of the war is getting nearer. That's what everyone is saying. If only the days and nights would pass more quickly . . .

September 5. Our regiment has been ordered to attack Sadovaya station— that's nearly in Stalingrad. Are the Russians really thinking of holding out in the city itself? We had no peace all night from the Russian artillery and aeroplanes. Lots of wounded are being brought by. God protect me . . .

September 8. Two days of non-stop fighting. The Russians are defending themselves with insane stubbornness. Our regiment has lost many men from the "katyushi," which belch out terrible fire. I have been sent to work at battalion H.Q. It must be mother's prayers that have taken me away from the company's trenches . . .

September 11. Our battalion is fighting in the suburbs in Stalingrad. We can already see the Volga; firing is going on all the time. Wherever you look is fire and flames. . . . Russian cannon and machine-guns are firing out of the burning city. Fanatics . . .

September 13. An unlucky number. This morning "katyushi" attacks caused the company heavy losses: twenty-seven dead and fifty wounded. The Russians are fighting desperately like wild beasts, don't give themselves up, but come up close and then throw grenades. Lieutenant Kraus was killed yesterday, and there is no company commander.

September 16. Our battalion, plus tanks, is attacking the [grain storage] elevator, from which smoke is pouring—the grain in it is burning, the Russians seem to have set light to it themselves. Barbarism. The battalion is suffering heavy losses. There are not more than sixty men left in each company. The elevator is occupied not by men but by devils that no flames or bullets can destroy.

September 18. Fighting is going on inside the elevator. The Russians inside are condemned men; the battalion commander says: "The commissars have ordered those men to die in the elevator."

If all the buildings of Stalingrad are defended like this then none of our soldiers will get back to Germany. I had a letter from Elsa today. She's expecting me home when victory's won.   16

September 20. The battle for the elevator is still going on. The Russians are firing on all sides. We stay in our cellar; you can't go out into the street. Sergeant-Major Nuschke was killed today running across a street. Poor fellow, he's got three children.   17

September 22. Russian resistance in the elevator has been broken. Our troops are advancing towards the Volga. . . .   18

. . . Our old soldiers have never experienced such bitter fighting before.   19

September 26. Our regiment is involved in constant heavy fighting. After the elevator was taken the Russians continued to defend themselves just as stubbornly. You don't see them at all, they have established themselves in houses and cellars and are firing on all sides, including from our rear—barbarians, they use gangster methods.   20

In the blocks captured two days ago Russian soldiers appeared from somewhere or other and fighting has flared up with fresh vigour. Our men are being killed not only in the firing line, but in the rear, in buildings we have already occupied.   21

The Russians have stopped surrendering at all. If we take any prisoners it's because they are hopelessly wounded, and can't move by themselves. Stalingrad is hell. Those who are merely wounded are lucky; they will doubtless be at home and celebrate victory with their families. . . .   22

September 28. Our regiment, and the whole division, are today celebrating victory. Together with our tank crews we have taken the southern part of the city and reached the Volga. We paid dearly for our victory. In three weeks we have occupied about five and a half square miles. The commander has congratulated us on our victory. . . .   23

October 3. After marching through the night we have established ourselves in a shrub-covered gully. We are apparently going to attack the factories, the chimneys of which we can see clearly. Behind them is the Volga. We have entered a new area. It was night but we saw many crosses with our helmets on top. Have we really lost so many men? Damn this Stalingrad!   24

October 4. Our regiment is attacking the Barrikady settlement. A lot of Russian tommy-gunners have appeared. Where are they bringing them from?   25

October 5. Our battalion has gone into the attack four times, and got stopped each time. Russian snipers hit anyone who shows himself carelessly from behind shelter.   26

October 10. The Russians are so close to us that our planes cannot bomb them. We are preparing for a decisive attack. The Führer has ordered the whole of Stalingrad to be taken as rapidly as possible.   27

October 14. It has been fantastic since morning: our aeroplanes and artillery   28 have been hammering the Russian positions for hours on end; everything in sight is being blotted from the face of the earth. . . .

October 22. Our regiment has failed to break into the factory. We have lost   29
many men; every time you move you have to jump over bodies. You can scarcely breathe in the daytime: there is nowhere and no one to remove the bodies, so they are left there to rot. Who would have thought three months ago that instead of the joy of victory we would have to endure such sacrifice and torture, the end of which is nowhere in sight? . . .

The soldiers are calling Stalingrad the mass grave of the Wehrmacht [German   30
army]. There are very few men left in the companies. We have been told we are soon going to be withdrawn to be brought back up to strength.

October 27. Our troops have captured the whole of the Barrikady factory,   31
but we cannot break through to the Volga. The Russians are not men, but some kind of cast-iron creatures; they never get tired and are not afraid of fire. We are absolutely exhausted; our regiment now has barely the strength of a company. The Russian artillery at the other side of the Volga won't let you lift your head. . . .

October 28. Every soldier sees himself as a condemned man. The only hope   32
is to be wounded and taken back to the rear. . . .

November 3. In the last few days our battalion has several times tried to attack   33
the Russian positions, . . . to no avail. On this sector also the Russians won't let you lift your head. There have been a number of cases of self-inflicted wounds and malingering among the men. Every day I write two or three reports about them.

November 10. A letter from Elsa today. Everyone expects us home for Christ-   34
mas. In Germany everyone believes we already hold Stalingrad. How wrong they are. If they could only see what Stalingrad has done to our army.

November 18. Our attack with tanks yesterday had no success. After our   35
attack the field was littered with dead.

November 21. The Russians have gone over to the offensive along the whole   36
front. Fierce fighting is going on. So, there it is—the Volga, victory and soon home to our families! We shall obviously be seeing them next in the other world.

November 29. We are encircled. It was announced this morning that the   37
Führer has said: "The army can trust me to do everything necessary to ensure supplies and rapidly break the encirclement."

December 3. We are on hunger rations and waiting for the rescue that the   38
Führer promised.

I send letters home, but there is no reply.   39

December 7. Rations have been cut to such an extent that the soldiers are   40
suffering terribly from hunger; they are issuing one loaf of stale bread for five men.

December 11. Three questions are obsessing every soldier and officer: When   41 will the Russians stop firing and let us sleep in peace, if only for one night? How and with what are we going to fill our empty stomachs, which, apart from 3½–7 ozs of bread, receive virtually nothing at all? And when will Hitler take any decisive steps to free our armies from encirclement?

December 14. Everybody is racked with hunger. Frozen potatoes are the best   42 meal, but to get them out of the ice-covered ground under fire from Russian bullets is not so easy.

December 18. The officers today told the soldiers to be prepared for action.   43 General Manstein is approaching Stalingrad from the south with strong forces. This news brought hope to the soldiers' hearts. God, let it be!

December 21. We are waiting for the order, but for some reason or other it   44 has been a long time coming. Can it be that it is not true about Manstein? This is worse than any torture.

December 23. Still no orders. It was all a bluff with Manstein. Or has he been   45 defeated at the approaches to Stalingrad?

December 25. The Russian radio has announced the defeat of Manstein. Ahead   46 of us is either death or captivity.

December 26. The horses have already been eaten. I would eat a cat; they say   47 its meat is also tasty. The soldiers look like corpses or lunatics, looking for something to put in their mouths. They no longer take cover from Russian shells; they haven't the strength to walk, run away and hide. A curse on this war! . . .

Questions for Critical Thinking

1. Thinking back to Sun Tzu's *Art of War*, which principles of warfare did the German military leaders neglect to follow that cost them the Battle of Stalingrad? What, if anything, should the German military leaders have done differently?

2. The many ellipses in the excerpted diary indicate that the editor left out some material. Are you pleased with the editing? Why or why not? What advantage and disadvantage is there in leaving out passages?

3. What view of Hitler is implied throughout the diary? How does this view square with your own knowledge of this Nazi leader?

4. What tactics did the German commanders use to keep the German troops from becoming discouraged? What is your opinion of the ethics of these tactics?

5. How does the Battle for Stalingrad support Freud's view of war? (Reread "Why War?" given previously in this chapter.)

6. At what point in the essay does the author grasp that belief in a quick and decisive victory is only a fantasy? What is your emotional response to his realization? Do you feel pity? Hatred? Disgust? Sadness? Explain your answer.

7. What is the tone of paragraph 36? How do you explain this tone? How does the tone anticipate the final sentence of the diary?

Writing Assignment

Write an essay in which you use the Battle of Stalingrad as an example of how war brutalizes civilized human beings and turns them into bloodthirsty barbarians.

Writing Advice

1. In addition to using the German soldier's diary entries, you will want to supplement your knowledge by reading about this battle in some reliable World War II history. Pay attention to those events of the battle that strike you as particularly brutal and inhuman.

2. An entry from the German soldier's diary, such as the one on August 27, would make an excellent opening to grab the reader's attention and allow you to focus on the fearsome nature of war.

3. You may wish to reread Freud's essay on war to garner support for the view that war appeals to our primitive yearnings.

4. Make sure that your essay develops a single thesis and does not drift into unrelated ideas.

Alternate Writing Assignments

1. Write an essay in which you defend bloody battles, such as the one described by the German soldier, as necessary training grounds for patriotic heroes.

2. Choose a historical battle that you consider justified by history. Then, write an essay in which you state why this particular battle was worth fighting.

HISTORY

THE EFFECTS OF NUCLEAR WAR
Jonathan Schell

Jonathan Schell (b. 1943 in New York City) has been a writer on the staff of the *New Yorker* since 1968. His works include *The Village of Ben Suc* (1967), *The Time of Illusion* (1976), and *The Fate of the Earth* (1982), from which this essay is reprinted.

Reading Advice

We do not know exactly what would happen in a nuclear holocaust since humanity in its entire history has never been cursed with such a global catastrophe. But we do know what devastation was caused by the two atomic bombs dropped on Hiroshima and Nagasaki during World War II, and we can make intelligent projections based on the combination of this knowledge and laboratory research. Scientists and futurists tell us that none would escape the unprecedented horror, that the world would be incinerated in such a baptism of fire and brimstone as to annihilate nearly all life. Such an end is usually regarded as unthinkable.

What this article does is to tackle the unthinkable and make it readable. Its rhetorical organization may be pedantically called analysis of effect. Drawing on research and informed speculation, the author tells us what we can expect if the nuclear arsenals are ever unleashed in a final paroxysm of international folly. Essays that deal with this subject usually set up a comfortable linguistic barrier between the reader and the depicted horror with classic techniques of passive phrasing and stilted diction. This one, however, revels in a gory intimacy with its topic and shows the unadorned and ghastly horror in eminently readable prose. The result is not pleasant bedtime reading but a sobering dose of truth that may restrain us from collectively turning our planet into an orbiting tomb.

*W*hereas most conventional bombs produce only one destructive effect—the shock wave—nuclear weapons produce many destructive effects. At the moment of the explosion, when the temperature of the weapon material, instantly gasified, is at the superstellar level, the pressure is millions of times the normal atmospheric pressure. Immediately, radiation, consisting mainly of gamma rays, which are a very high-energy form of electromagnetic radiation, begins to stream outward into the environment. This is called the "initial nuclear radiation," and is the first of the destructive effects of a nuclear explosion. In an air burst of a one-megaton bomb—a bomb with the explosive yield of a million tons of TNT, which is a medium-sized weapon in present-day nuclear arsenals—the initial nuclear radiation can kill unprotected human beings in an area of some six square miles. Virtually simultaneously with the initial nuclear radiation, in a second destructive effect of the explosion, an electromagnetic pulse is generated by the intense gamma radiation acting on the air. In a high-altitude detonation, the pulse can knock out electrical equipment over a wide area by inducing a powerful surge of voltage through various conductors, such as antennas, overhead power lines, pipes, and railroad tracks. The Defense Department's Civil Preparedness Agency reported in 1977 that a single multi-kiloton nuclear weapon detonated one hundred and twenty-five miles over Omaha, Nebraska, could generate an electromagnetic pulse strong enough to damage solid-state electrical circuits throughout the entire continental United States and in parts of Canada and

Mexico, and thus threaten to bring the economies of these countries to a halt. When the fusion and fission reactions have blown themselves out, a fireball takes shape. As it expands, energy is absorbed in the form of X rays by the surrounding air, and then the air re-radiates a portion of that energy into the environment in the form of the thermal pulse—a wave of blinding light and intense heat—which is the third of the destructive effects of a nuclear explosion. (If the burst is low enough, the fireball touches the ground, vaporizing or incinerating almost everything within it.) The thermal pulse of a one-megaton bomb lasts for about ten seconds and can cause second-degree burns in exposed human beings at a distance of nine and a half miles, or in an area of more than two hundred and eighty square miles, and that of a twenty-megaton bomb (a large weapon by modern standards) lasts for about twenty seconds and can produce the same consequences at a distance of twenty-eight miles, or in an area of two thousand four hundred and sixty square miles. As the fireball expands, it also sends out a blast wave in all directions, and this is the fourth destructive effect of the explosion. The blast wave of an air-burst one-megaton bomb can flatten or severely damage all but the strongest buildings within a radius of four and a half miles, and that of a twenty-megaton bomb can do the same within a radius of twelve miles. As the fireball burns, it rises, condensing water from the surrounding atmosphere to form the characteristic mushroom cloud. If the bomb has been set off on the ground or close enough to it so that the fireball touches the surface, in a so-called ground burst, a crater will be formed, and tons of dust and debris will be fused with the intensely radioactive fission products and sucked up into the mushroom cloud. This mixture will return to earth as radioactive fallout, most of it in the form of fine ash, in the fifth destructive effect of the explosion. Depending upon the composition of the surface, from forty to seventy per cent of this fallout—often called the "early" or "local" fallout—descends to earth within about a day of the explosion, in the vicinity of the blast and downwind from it, exposing human beings to radiation disease, an illness that is fatal when exposure is intense. Air bursts may also produce local fallout, but in much smaller quantities. The lethal range of the local fallout depends on a number of circumstances, including the weather, but under average conditions a one-megaton ground burst would, according to the report by the Office of Technology Assessment, lethally contaminate over a thousand square miles. (A lethal dose, by convention, is considered to be the amount of radiation that, if delivered over a short period of time, would kill half the able-bodied young adult population.)

The initial nuclear radiation, the electromagnetic pulse, the thermal pulse, the blast wave, and the local fallout may be described as the local primary effects of nuclear weapons. Naturally, when many bombs are exploded the scope of these effects is increased accordingly. But in addition these primary

2

effects produce innumerable secondary effects on societies and natural environments, some of which may be even more harmful than the primary ones.
To give just one example, nuclear weapons, by flattening and setting fire to
huge, heavily built-up areas, generate mass fires, and in some cases these may
kill more people than the original thermal pulses and blast waves. Moreover,
there are—quite distinct from both the local primary effects of individual
bombs and their secondary effects—global primary effects, which do not become
significant unless thousands of bombs are detonated all around the earth. And
these global primary effects produce innumerable secondary effects of their
own throughout the ecosystem of the earth as a whole. For a full-scale holocaust
is more than the sum of its local parts; it is also a powerful direct blow to the
ecosphere. In that sense, a holocaust is to the earth what a single bomb is to
a city. Three grave direct global effects have been discovered so far. The first
is the "delayed," or "worldwide," fallout. In detonations greater than one hundred
kilotons, part of the fallout does not fall to the ground in the vicinity of the
explosion but rises high into the troposphere and into the stratosphere, cir-
culates around the earth, and then, over months or years, descends, contami-
nating the whole surface of the globe—although with doses of radiation far
weaker than those delivered by the local fallout. Nuclear-fission products comprise some three hundred radioactive isotopes, and though some of them decay
to relatively harmless levels of radioactivity within a few hours, minutes, or
even seconds, others persist to emit radiation for up to millions of years. The
short-lived isotopes are the ones most responsible for the lethal effects of the
local fallout, and the long-lived ones are responsible for the contamination of
the earth by stratospheric fallout. The energy released by all fallout from a
thermonuclear explosion is about five percent of the total. By convention, this
energy is not calculated in the stated yield of a weapon, yet in a ten-thousand-
megaton attack the equivalent of five hundred megatons of explosive energy,
or forty thousand times the yield of the Hiroshima bomb, would be released
in the form of radioactivity. This release may be considered a protracted after-
burst, which is dispersed into the land, air, and sea, and into the tissues, bones,
roots, stems, and leaves of living things, and goes on detonating there almost
indefinitely after the explosion. The second of the global effects that have been
discovered so far is the lofting, from ground bursts, of millions of tons of dust
into the stratosphere; this is likely to produce general cooling of the earth's
surface. The third of the global effects is a predicted partial destruction of the
layer of ozone that surrounds the entire earth in the stratosphere. A nuclear
fireball, by burning nitrogen in the air, produces large quantities of oxides of
nitrogen. These are carried by the heat of the blast into the stratosphere, where,
through a series of chemical reactions, they bring about a depletion of the
ozone layer. Such a depletion may persist for years. The 1975 N.A.S. report has
estimated that in a holocaust in which ten thousand megatons were detonated

in the Northern Hemisphere the reduction of ozone in this hemisphere could be as high as seventy percent and in the Southern Hemisphere as high as forty percent, and that it could take as long as thirty years for the ozone level to return to normal. The ozone layer is crucial to life on earth, because it shields the surface of the earth from lethal levels of ultraviolet radiation, which is present in sunlight. Glasstone remarks simply, "If it were not for the absorption of much of the solar ultraviolet radiation by the ozone, life as currently known could not exist except possibly in the ocean." Without the ozone shield, sunlight, the life-giver, would become a life-extinguisher. In judging the global effects of a holocaust, therefore, the primary question is not how many people would be irradiated, burned, or crushed to death by the immediate effects of the bombs but how well the ecosphere, regarded as a single living entity, on which all forms of life depend for their continued existence, would hold up. The issue is the habitability of the earth, and it is in this context, not in the context of the direct slaughter of hundreds of millions of people by the local effects, that the question of human survival arises.

Usually, people wait for things to occur before trying to describe them.   3
(Futurology has never been a very respectable field of inquiry.) But since we cannot afford under any circumstances to let a holocaust occur, we are forced in this one case to become the historians of the future—to chronicle and commit to memory an event that we have never experienced and must never experience. This unique endeavor, in which foresight is asked to perform a task usually reserved for hindsight, raises a host of special difficulties. There is a categorical difference, often overlooked, between trying to describe an event that has already happened (whether it is Napoleon's invasion of Russia or the pollution of the environment by acid rain) and trying to describe one that has yet to happen—and one, in addition, for which there is no precedent, or even near-precedent, in history. Lacking experience to guide our thoughts and impress itself on our feelings, we resort to speculation. But speculation, however brilliantly it may be carried out, is at best only a poor substitute for experience. Experience gives us facts, whereas in pure speculation we are thrown back on theory, which has never been a very reliable guide to future events. Moreover, experience engraves its lessons in our hearts through suffering and the other consequences that it has for our lives; but speculation leaves our lives untouched, and so gives us leeway to reject its conclusions, no matter how well argued they may be. (In the world of strategic theory, in particular, where strategists labor to stimulate actual situations on the far side of the nuclear abyss, so that generals and statesmen can prepare to make their decisions in case the worst happens, there is sometimes an unfortunate tendency to mistake pure ratiocination for reality, and to pretend to a knowledge of the future that it is not given to human beings to have.) Our knowledge of the local primary effects of the bombs, which is based both on the physical principles that made their

construction possible and on experience gathered from the bombings of Hiroshima and Nagasaki and from testing, is quite solid. And our knowledge of the extent of the local primary effects of many weapons used together, which is obtained simply by using the multiplication table, is also solid: knowing that the thermal pulse of a twenty-megaton bomb can give people at least second-degree burns in an area of two thousand four hundred and sixty square miles, we can easily figure out that the pulses of a hundred twenty-megaton bombs can give people at least second-degree burns in an area of two hundred and forty-six thousand square miles. Nevertheless, it may be that our knowledge even of the primary effects is still incomplete, for during our test program new ones kept being discovered. One example is the electromagnetic pulse, whose importance was not recognized until around 1960, when, after more than a decade of tests, scientists realized that this effect accounted for unexpected electrical failures that had been occurring all along in equipment around the test sites. And it is only in recent years that the Defense Department has been trying to take account strategically of this startling capacity of just one bomb to put the technical equipment of a whole continent out of action.

When we proceed from the local effects of single explosions to the effects of thousands of them on societies and environments, the picture clouds considerably, because then we go beyond both the certainties of physics and our slender base of experience, and speculatively encounter the full complexity of human affairs and of the biosphere. Looked at in its entirety, a nuclear holocaust can be said to assail human life at three levels: the level of individual life, the level of human society, and the level of the natural environment—including the environment of the earth as a whole. At none of these levels can the destructiveness of nuclear weapons be measured in terms of firepower alone. At each level, life has both considerable recuperative powers, which might restore it even after devastating injury, and points of exceptional vulnerability, which leave it open to sudden, wholesale, and permanent collapse, even when comparatively little violence has been applied. Just as a machine may break down if one small part is removed, and a person may die if a single artery or vein is blocked, a modern technological society may come to a standstill if its fuel supply is cut off, and an ecosystem may collapse if its ozone shield is depleted. Nuclear weapons thus do not only kill directly, with their tremendous violence, but also kill indirectly, by breaking down the man-made and the natural systems on which individual lives collectively depend. Human beings require constant provision and care, supplied both by their societies and by the natural environment, and if these are suddenly removed people will die just are surely as if they had been struck by a bullet. Nuclear weapons are unique in that they attack the support systems of life at every level. And these systems, of course, are not isolated from each other but are parts of a single whole: ecological collapse, if it goes far enough, will bring about social collapse, and social collapse will bring about individual deaths. Furthermore, the destructive consequences of a nuclear attack are immeasurably compounded by the likelihood that all or most of the bombs will be detonated within the space of a few hours, in a single huge concussion. Normally, a locality devastated by a catastrophe, whether natural or man-made, will sooner or later receive help from untouched outside areas, as Hiroshima and Nagasaki did after they were bombed; but a nuclear holocaust would devastate the "outside" areas as well, leaving the victims to fend for themselves in a shattered society and natural environment. And what is true for each city is also true for the earth as a whole: a devastated earth can hardly expect "outside" help. The earth is the largest of the support systems for life, and the impairment of the earth is the largest of the perils posed by nuclear weapons.

The incredible complexity of all these effects, acting, interacting, and interacting again, precludes confident detailed representation of the events in a holocaust. We deal inevitably with approximations, probabilities, even guesses. However, it is important to point out that our uncertainty pertains not to *whether* the effects will interact, multiplying their destructive power as they do so, but only to *how.* It follows that our almost built-in bias, determined by the limitations of the human mind in judging future events, is to underestimate the harm. To fear interactive consequences that we cannot predict, or even imagine, may not be impossible, but it is very difficult. Let us consider, for example, some of the possible ways in which a person in a targeted country might die. He might be incinerated by the fireball or the thermal pulse. He might be lethally irradiated by the initial nuclear radiation. He might be crushed to death or hurled to his death by the blast wave or its debris. He might be lethally irradiated by the local fallout. He might be burned to death in a firestorm. He might be injured by one or another of these effects and then die of his wounds before he was able to make his way out of the devastated zone in which he found himself. He might die of starvation, because the economy had collapsed and no food was being grown or delivered, or because existing local crops had been killed by radiation, or because the local ecosystem had been ruined, or because the ecosystem of the earth as a whole was collapsing. He might die of cold, for lack of heat and clothing, or of exposure, for lack of shelter. He might be killed by people seeking food or shelter that he had obtained. He might die of an illness spread in an epidemic. He might be killed by exposure to the sun if he stayed outside too long following serious ozone depletion. Or he might be killed by any combination of these perils. But while there is almost no end to the ways to die in and after a holocaust, each person has only one life to lose: someone who has been killed by the thermal pulse can't be killed again in an epidemic. Therefore, anyone who wishes to describe a holocaust is always at risk of depicting scenes of devastation that in reality would never take place, because the people in them would already have been

5

killed off in some earlier scene of devastation. The task is made all the more confusing by the fact that causes of death and destruction do not exist side by side in the world but often encompass one another, in widening rings. Thus, if it turned out that a holocaust rendered the earth uninhabitable by human beings, then all the more immediate forms of death would be nothing more than redundant preliminaries, leading up to the extinction of the whole species by a hostile environment. Or if a continental ecosystem was so thoroughly destroyed by a direct attack that it could no longer sustain a significant human population, the more immediate causes of death would again decline in importance. In much the same way, if an airplane is hit by gunfire, and thereby caused to crash, dooming all the passengers, it makes little difference whether the shots also killed a few of the passengers in advance of the crash. On the other hand, if the larger consequences, which are less predictable than the local ones, failed to occur, then the local ones would have their full importance again.

Faced with uncertainties of this kind, some analysts of nuclear destruction have resorted to fiction, assigning to the imagination the work that investigation is unable to do. But then the results are just what one would expect: fiction. An approach more appropriate to our intellectual circumstances would be to acknowledge a high degree of uncertainty as an intrinsic and extremely important part of dealing with a possible holocaust. A nuclear holocaust is an event that is obscure because it is future, and uncertainty, while it has to be recognized in all calculations of future events, has a special place in calculations of a nuclear holocaust, because a holocaust is something that we aspire to keep in the future forever, and never to permit into the present. You might say that uncertainty, like the thermal pulses or the blast waves, is one of the features of a holocaust. Our procedure, then, should be not to insist on a precision that is beyond our grasp but to inquire into the rough probabilities of various results insofar as we can judge them, and then to ask ourselves what our political responsibilities are in the light of these probabilities. This embrace of investigative modesty— this acceptance of our limited ability to predict the consequences of a holocaust—would itself be a token of our reluctance to extinguish ourselves.

There are two further aspects of a holocaust which, though they do not further obscure the factual picture, nevertheless vex our understanding of this event. The first is that although in imagination we can try to survey the whole prospective scene of destruction, inquiring into how many would live and how many would die and how far the collapse of the environment would go under attacks of different sizes, and piling up statistics on how many square miles would be lethally contaminated, or what percentage of the population would receive first-, second-, or third-degree burns, or be trapped in the rubble of its burning houses, or be irradiated to death, no one actually experiencing a holocaust would have any such overview. The news of other parts necessary to put together that picture would be one of the things that were immediately

6

7

lost, and each surviving person, his vision drastically foreshortened by the collapse of his world, and his impressions clouded by his pain, shock, bewilderment, and grief, would see only as far as whatever scene of chaos and agony happened to lie at hand. For it would not be only such abstractions as "industry" and "society" and "the environment" that would be destroyed in a nuclear holocaust; it would also be, over and over again, the small collections of cherished things, known landscapes, and beloved people that made up the immediate contents of individual lives.

The other obstacle to our understanding is that when we strain to picture   8
what the scene would be like after a holocaust we tend to forget that for most people, and perhaps for all, it wouldn't be *like* anything, because they would be dead. To depict the scene as it would appear to the living is to that extent a falsification, and the greater the number killed, the greater the falsification. The right vantage point from which to view a holocaust is that of a corpse, but from that vantage point, of course, there is nothing to report.

Questions for Critical Thinking

1. How does the author keep his readers from becoming utterly confused by the mound of facts in the essay?

2. What is your reaction to the difference between primary and secondary nuclear effects? Is one much worse than the other, or are all effects equally destructive?

3. Why does the author stress the nuclear devastation to our ozone layer? What is so important about ozone?

4. What difficulty is inherent in attempting accurately to describe the effects of another nuclear war? In your opinion, has the author overcome the difficulty? Why or why not?

5. The author states that "experience engraves its lessons in our hearts through suffering and the other consequences that it has for our lives; but speculation leaves our lives untouched, and so gives us leeway to reject its conclusions, no matter how well argued they may be." What example from your own life or that of someone in history can you cite to support the quotation?

6. In paragraph 4, the author alludes to three levels of human life affected by nuclear war. Do you consider these levels separate or do you see them as interacting? Explain your answer.

7. What do you think each of us can do to avoid nuclear war? What principle, if any, is worth defending, even at the risk of a nuclear war?

Writing Assignment

Assuming a reading audience of average people, write an essay convincing your readers of the urgency for nuclear restraint on the part of all world leaders.

Writing Advice

1. You could begin with a descriptive paragraph of a typical home town after nuclear devastation. Focusing on the dominant impression of holocaust, you could use some of the details in Schell's essay to vividly portray the destruction an atom bomb would wreak. Be sure to choose only facts and other details that support the dominant impression and not dilute it with irrelevant and trivial references to nature's beauty or serenity.

2. Once you have set the stage with your dramatic beginning, you can proceed to enumerate reasons why global restraint and international cooperation are essential to prevent a nuclear war that has the ominous possibility of annihilating our world.

3. We suggest that you present three well-developed reasons rather than half a dozen superficial ones.

4. Your conclusion should be a rousing call to action aimed at convincing your reader that peaceful coexistence must be the politics of the future.

Alternate Writing Assignments

1. As an exercise in creating futuristic history, write a description of the city or town in which you live after the detonation of a one-megaton nuclear bomb. Be as accurate as possible, basing your facts on Schell's essay or on any other appropriate source.

2. Write an essay, to be translated and published in a Chinese or Russian college newspaper, in which you plead for universal reduction of nuclear arsenals. Assume an audience of Chinese or Russian students.

HISTORY

I THOUGHT MY LAST HOUR HAD COME
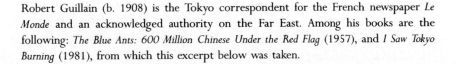
Futaba Kitayama, as told to Robert Guillain

Robert Guillain (b. 1908) is the Tokyo correspondent for the French newspaper *Le Monde* and an acknowledged authority on the Far East. Among his books are the following: *The Blue Ants: 600 Million Chinese Under the Red Flag* (1957), and *I Saw Tokyo Burning* (1981), from which this excerpt below was taken.

Reading Advice

In reporting on the 1945 atomic bombing of Hiroshima, Guillain draws on several eyewitness accounts, including one by Futaba Kitayama, a 36-year-old Japanese housewife who survived the nuclear blast. "Is there any way to describe the horror and the pity of that hell? Let a victim tell of it," writes Guillain in introducing her account. Mrs. Kitayama's harrowing tale then follows. She writes in the straightforward style of a woman recounting what surely must have been the worst experience of her life, with a simplicity that renders her description entirely believable. She seems to be telling a story indelibly impressed on her heart. Nothing seems exaggerated; yet, the picture springs to grisly life because of the telling specific and concrete details that could only have come from an eyewitness.

Monday, August 6, 1945, in Hiro-   1
shima. A few seconds after 8:15 A.M., a flash of light, brighter than a thousand suns, shredded the space over the city's center. A gigantic sphere of fire, a prodigious blast, a formidable pillar of smoke and debris rose into the sky: an entire city annihilated as it was going to work, almost vaporized at the blast's point zero, irradiated to death, crushed and swept away. Its thousands of wooden houses were splintered and soon ablaze, its few stone and brick buildings smashed, its ancient temples destroyed, its schools and barracks incinerated just as classes and drills were beginning, its crowded streetcars upended, their passengers buried under the wreckage of streets and alleys crowded with people going about their daily business. A city of 300,000 inhabitants—more, if its large military population was counted, for Hiroshima was headquarters for the southern Japan command. In a flash, much of its population, especially in the center, was reduced to a mash of burned and bleeding bodies, crawling, writhing on the ground in their death agonies, expiring under the ruins of their houses or, soon, roasted in the fire that was spreading throughout the city—or fleeing, half-mad, with the sudden torrent of nightmare-haunted humanity staggering toward the hills, bodies naked and blackened, flayed alive, with charcoal faces and blind eyes.

Is there any way to describe the horror and the pity of that hell? Let a victim   2
tell of it. Among the thousand accounts was this one by a Hiroshima housewife, Mrs. Futaba Kitayama, then aged thirty-three, who was struck down 1900 yards—just over a mile—from the point of impact. We should bear in mind that the horrors she described could be multiplied a hundredfold in the future.

"I was in Hiroshima, that morning of August 6. I had joined a team of   3
women who, like me, worked as volunteers in cutting firepaths against incendiary raids by demolishing whole rows of houses. My husband, because of a raid alert the previous night, had stayed at the *Chunichi (Central Japan Journal),* where he worked.

"Our group had passed the Tsurumi bridge, Indian-file, when there was an   4
alert; an enemy plane appeared all alone, very high over our heads. Its silver
wings shone brightly in the sun. A woman exclaimed, 'Oh, look—a parachute!'
I turned toward where she was pointing, and just at that moment a shattering
flash filled the whole sky.

"Was it the flash that came first, or the sound of the explosion, tearing up   5
my insides? I don't remember. I was thrown to the ground, pinned to the earth,
and immediately the world began to collapse around me, on my head, my
shoulders. I couldn't see anything. It was completely dark. I thought my last
hour had come. I thought of my three children, who had been evacuated to
the country to be safe from the raids. I couldn't move; debris kept falling,
beams and tiles piled up on top of me.

"Finally I did manage to crawl free. There was a terrible smell in the air.   6
Thinking the bomb that hit us might have been a yellow phosphorus incendiary
like those that had fallen on so many other cities, I rubbed my nose and mouth
hard with a *tenugui* (a kind of towel) I had at my waist. To my horror, I found
that the skin of my face had come off in the towel. Oh! The skin on my hands,
on my arms, came off too. From elbow to fingertips, all the skin on my right
arm had come loose and was hanging grotesquely. The skin of my left hand fell
off too, the five fingers, like a glove.

"I found myself sitting on the ground, prostate. Gradually I registered that   7
all my companions had disappeared. What had happened to them? A frantic
panic gripped me, I wanted to run, but where? Around me was just debris,
wooden framing, beams and roofing tiles; there wasn't a single landmark left.

"And what had happened to the sky, so blue a moment ago? Now it was as   8
black as night. Everything seemed vague and fuzzy. It was as though a cloud
covered my eyes and I wondered if I had lost my senses. I finally saw the
Tsurumi bridge and I ran headlong toward it, jumping over the piles of rubble.
What I saw under the bridge then horrified me.

"People by the hundreds were flailing in the river. I couldn't tell if they were   9
men or women; they were all in the same state: their faces were puffy and
ashen, their hair tangled, they held their hands raised and, groaning with pain,
threw themselves into the water. I had a violent impulse to do so myself,
because of the pain burning through my whole body. But I can't swim and I
held back.

"Past the bridge, I looked back to see that the whole Hachobori district had   10
suddenly caught fire, to my surprise, because I thought only the district I was
in had been bombed. As I ran, I shouted my children's names. Where was I
going? I have no idea, but I can still see the scenes of horror I glimpsed here
and there on my way.

"A mother, her face and shoulders covered with blood, tried frantically to   11
run into a burning house. A man held her back and she screamed, 'Let me go!

Let me go! My son is burning in there!' She was like a mad demon. Under the Kojin bridge, which had half collapsed and had lost its heavy, reinforced-concrete parapets, I saw a lot of bodies floating in the water like dead dogs, almost naked, with their clothes in shreds. At the river's edge, near the bank, a woman lay on her back with her breasts ripped off, bathed in blood. How could such a frightful thing have happened? I thought of the scenes of the Buddhist hell my grandmother had described to me when I was little.

"I must have wandered for at least two hours before finding myself on the Eastern military parade ground. My burns were hurting me, but the pain was different from an ordinary burn. It was a dull pain that seemed somehow to come from outside my body. A kind of yellow pus oozed from my hands, and I thought that my face must also be horrible to see.

"Around me on the parade ground were a number of grade-school and secondary-school children, boys and girls, writhing in spasms of agony. Like me, they were members of the anti–air raid volunteer corps. I heard them crying 'Mama! Mama!' as though they'd gone crazy. They were so burned and bloody that looking at them was insupportable. I forced myself to do so just the same, and I cried out in rage, 'Why? Why these children?' But there was no one to rage at and I could do nothing but watch them die, one after the other, vainly calling for their mothers.

"After lying almost unconscious for a long time on the parade ground, I started walking again. As far as I could see with my failing sight, everything was in flames, as far as the Hiroshima station and the Atago district. It seemed to me that my face was hardening little by little. I cautiously touched my hands to my cheeks. My face felt as though it had doubled in size. I could see less and less clearly. Was I going blind, then? After so much hardship, was I going to die? I kept on walking anyway and I reached a suburban area.

"In that district, farther removed from the center, I found my elder sister alive, with only slight injuries to the head and feet. She didn't recognize me at first, then she burst into tears. In a handcart, she wheeled me nearly three miles to the first-aid center at Yaga. It was night when we arrived. I later learned there was a pile of corpses and countless injured there. I spent two nights there, unconscious; my sister told me that in my delirium I kept repeating, 'My children! Take me to my children!'

"On August 8, I was carried on a stretcher to a train and transported to the home of relatives in the village of Kasumi. The village doctor said my case was hopeless. My children, recalled from their evacuation refuge, rushed to my side. I could no longer see them; I could recognize them only by smelling their good odor. On August 11, my husband joined us. The children wept with joy as they embraced him.

"Our happiness soon ended. My husband, who bore no trace of injury, died suddenly three days later, vomiting blood. We had been married sixteen years and now, because I was at the brink of death myself, I couldn't even rest his head as I should have on the pillow of the dead.

"I said to myself, 'My poor children, because of you I don't have the right   18
to die!' And finally, by a miracle, I survived after I had again and again been given up for lost.

"My sight returned fairly quickly, and after twenty days I could dimly see   19
my children's features. The burns on my face and hands did not heal so rapidly, and the wounds remained pulpy, like rotten tomatoes. It wasn't until December that I would walk again. When my bandages were removed in January, I knew that my face and hands would always be deformed. My left ear was half its original size. A streak of cheloma, a dark brown swelling as wide as my hand, runs from the side of my head across my mouth to my throat. My right hand is striped with a cheloma two inches wide from the wrist to the little finger. The five fingers on my left hand are now fused at the base. . . ."

Questions for Critical Thinking

1. Some people have argued that the United States's bombing of Japan ultimately saved millions of American lives by ending World War II without further losses in a prolonged conventional war. Do you agree with this line of argument? Why or why not? Give reasons for your view.

2. How does Mrs. Kitayama give us a sense of *genius loci* ("genuine location") in the description of her nightmarish adventure? Do you consider her method clarifying or confusing? Give reasons for your answer.

3. How would you describe Mrs. Kitayama's personality to someone who has not read her account? Cite specific passages to support each characteristic you attribute to her.

4. If you were in power, what would you do about the reduction or expansion of nuclear arms? What line of reasoning prompts your answer?

5. In the pursuit of truth, what advantage, if any, do you see in reading a personalized account of the aftereffects of a nuclear blast? Is there a disadvantage? Give reasons for your answer.

6. How does Mrs. Kitayama's account agree with the forecast given by Jonathan Schell in "The Effects of Nuclear War" (in this chapter)? What does he tell the reader that she does not?

7. How do you believe future generations in other countries of the world will judge the United States for having been the first country to drop an atomic bomb on a declared enemy? What is your own present judgment of this act?

8. Under what circumstances, if any, would you suggest that a head of government drop an atomic bomb on another country?

Writing Assignment

Write an essay justifying or condemning the United States for the atomic bombing of Hiroshima.

Writing Advice

Before attempting this assignment, you should be acquainted with the context surrounding this action in World War II. Any reputable encyclopedia, under the heading "World War II," will provide the necessary information, especially the facts concerning campaigns in the Pacific—the Solomon Islands, the Philippines, the Marianas Islands, Okinawa, and Iwo Jima. You also need to have some knowledge of the Yalta Conference (1944) and the Potsdam Conference (1944). An excellent source to consult is *The History of the Atomic Bomb*, by Michael Blow.

Once you are able to understand the tensions that existed between Japan and the Allies in 1945, you can better judge the role of the United States. You need to ask yourself this question: "To avoid the continuance of a war that might have cost many more lives, was it worth unleashing such a devastating weapon as the atomic bomb?" Whether the end justifies the means is the age-old question at the core of this debate. It is an ethical dilemma worth pondering, and writing about it is one way to clarify your own attitudes. We suggest that your opening paragraph contain the thesis in which you clearly state your position.

Alternate Writing Assignments

1. Write an essay analyzing the pros and cons of a strong nuclear arsenal.

2. In an essay, describe the three worst inventions of history, citing reasons for your choices.

LITERATURE

WAR
Luigi Pirandello

Luigi Pirandello (1867–1936), Italian author and playwright, is ranked among the foremost figures of the twentieth-century theater. His earliest writings reflected an intense interest in his birthplace of Sicily. In 1897 he became Professor of Italian

Literature at the Normal College for Women in Rome. Pirandello's fame came slowly after many difficult years of struggle for public recognition, during which his father's mining business failed and his wife fought a 14-year-long battle against mental illness. Pirandello wrote seven novels, among them *The Late Mattia Pascal* (1904), and *The Young and the Old* (1913), and over 300 short stories. But he is best remembered for his plays, which were eventually published and performed to worldwide acclaim. Among his best known plays are *Right You Are If You Think You Are* (1917), *Six Characters in Search of an Author* (1921), and *As You Desire Me* (1930). In 1934, Pirandello won the Nobel Prize for Literature.

Reading Advice

This story about war masks its deadly underlying earnestness under a facile, even funny exterior. Its grim humor stems from its theme—the shattering attempt of a mourning father to ease his bitter personal loss with the hollow illusion of heroic sacrifice and glory that society attributes to its war dead. Each character contributes to this theme by struggling to fathom whether war and its sacrifices are glorious or pointless. What follows is a sort of communal dialogue in which various common attitudes towards war are verbalized and examined. To sort out the various positions, you might consider labeling each passenger and summarizing his or her contribution to the debate. Pay particular attention to the man with the "bulging eyes" and ask yourself whether what he says is really what he feels.

*T*he passengers who had left Rome by 1
the night express had had to stop until dawn at the small station of Fabriano in order to continue their journey by the small old-fashioned local joining the main line with Sulmona.

At dawn, in a stuffy and smoky second-class carriage in which five people 2
had already spent the night, a bulky woman in deep mourning was hoisted in—almost like a shapeless bundle. Behind her—puffing and moaning, fol-lowed her husband—a tiny man, thin and weakly, his face death-white, his eyes small and bright and looking shy and uneasy.

Having at last taken a seat he politely thanked the passengers who had helped 3
his wife and who had made room for her; then he turned round to the woman trying to pull down the dollar of her coat, and politely inquired:

"Are you all right, dear?" 4

The wife, instead of answering, pulled up her collar again to her eyes, so as 5
to hide her face.

"Nasty world," muttered the husband with a sad smile. 6

And he felt it his duty to explain to his traveling companions that the poor 7
woman was to be pitied for the war was taking away from her her only son, a boy of twenty to whom both had devoted their entire life, even breaking up their home at Sulmona to follow him to Rome, where he had to go as a student,

then allowing him to volunteer for war with an assurance, however, that at least for six months he would not be sent to the front and now, all of a sudden, receiving a wire that he was due to leave in three days' time and asking them to go and see him off.

The woman under the big coat was twisting and wriggling, at times growling 8
like a wild animal, feeling certain that all those explanations would not have aroused even a shadow of sympathy from those people who—most likely— were in the same plight as herself. One of them, who had been listening with particular attention, said:

"You should thank God that your son is only leaving now for the front. 9
Mine has been sent there the first day of the war. He has already come back twice wounded and been sent back again to the front."

"What about me? I have two sons and three nephews at the front," said 10
another passenger.

"Maybe, but in our case it is our only son," ventured the husband. 11

"What difference can it make? You may spoil your only son with excessive 12
attentions, but you cannot love him more than you would all your other children if you had any. Paternal love is not like bread that can be broken into pieces and split amongst the children in equal shares. A father gives *all* his love to each one of his children without discrimination, whether it be one or ten, and if I am suffering now for my two sons, I am not suffering half for each of them but double . . ."

"True . . . true . . ." sighed the embarrassed husband, "but suppose (of course 13
we all hope it will never be your case) a father has two sons at the front and he loses one of them, there is still one left to console him . . . while . . ."

"Yes," answered the other, getting cross, "a son left to console him but also 14
a son left for whom he must survive, while in the case of the father of an only son if the son dies the father can die too and put an end to his distress. Which of the two positions is the worse? Don't you see how my case would be worse than yours?"

"Nonsense," interrupted another traveler, a fat, red-faced man with blood- 15
shot eyes of the palest gray.

He was panting. From his bulging eyes seemed to spurt inner violence of an 16
uncontrolled vitality which his weakened body could hardly contain.

"Nonsense," he repeated, trying to cover his mouth with his hand so as to 17
hide the two missing front teeth. "Nonsense. Do we give life to our children for our own benefit?"

The other travelers stared at him in distress. The one who had had his son 18
at the front since the first day of the war sighed: "You are right. Our children do not belong to us, they belong to the Country. . . ."

"Bosh," retorted the fat traveler. "Do we think of the Country when we 19
give life to our children? Our sons are born because . . . well, because they must be born and when they come to life they take our own life with them. This is

the truth. We belong to them but they never belong to us. And when they reach twenty they are exactly what we were at their age. We too had a father and mother, but there were so many other things as well . . . girls, cigarettes, illusions, new ties . . . and the Country, of course, whose call we would have answered—when we were twenty—even if father and mother had said no. Now, at our age, the love of our Country is still great, of course, but stronger than it is the love for our children. Is there any one of us here who wouldn't gladly take his son's place at the front if he could?"

There was a silence all round, everybody nodding as to approve. 20

"Why then," continued the fat man, "shouldn't we consider the feelings of 21 our children when they are twenty? Isn't it natural that at their age they should consider the love for their Country (I am speaking of decent boys, of course) even greater than the love for us? Isn't it natural that it should be so, as after all they must look upon old boys who cannot move any more and must stay at home? If Country exists, if Country is a natural necessity, like bread, of which each of us must eat in order not to die of hunger, somebody must go to defend it. And our sons go, when they are twenty, and they don't want tears, because if they die, they die inflamed and happy (I am speaking, of course, of decent boys). Now, if one dies young and happy, without having the ugly sides of life, the boredom of it, the pettiness, the bitterness of disillusion . . . what more can we ask for him? Everyone should stop crying; everyone should laugh, as I do . . . or at least thank God—as I do—because my son, before dying, sent me a message saying that he was dying satisfied at having ended his life in the best way he could have wished. That is why, as you see, I do not even wear mourning. . . ."

He shook his light fawn coat as to show it; his livid lip over his missing 22 teeth was trembling, his eyes were watery and motionless, and soon after he ended with a shrill laugh which might well have been a sob.

"Quite so . . . quite so . . ." agreed the others. 23

The woman who, bundled in a corner under her coat, had been sitting and 24 listening had—for the last three months—tried to find in the words of her husband and her friends something to console her in her deep sorrow, something that might show her how a mother should resign herself to send her son not even to death but to a probable danger of life. Yet not a word had she found amongst the many which had been said . . . and her grief had been greater in seeing that nobody—as she thought—could share her feelings.

But now the words of the traveler amazed and almost stunned her. She 25 suddenly realized that it wasn't the others who were wrong and could not understand her but herself who could not rise up to the same height of those fathers and mothers willing to resign themselves, without crying, not only to the departure of their sons but even to their death.

She lifted her head, she bent over from her corner trying to listen with 26 great attention to the details which the fat man was giving to his companions about the way his son had fallen as a hero, for his King and his Country, happy and without regrets. It seemed to her that she had stumbled into a world she had never dreamt of, a world so far unknown to her and she was so pleased to hear everyone joining in congratulating that brave father who could so stoically speak of his child's death.

Then suddenly, just as if she had heard nothing of what had been said and   27
almost as if waking up from a dream, she turned to the old man, asking him:

"Then . . . is your son really dead?"   28

Everybody stared at her. The old man, too, turned to look at her, fixing his   29
great, bulging, horribly watery light gray eyes, deep in her face. For some little time he tried to answer, but words failed him. He looked and looked at her, almost as if only then—at that silly incongruous question—he had suddenly realized at last that his son was really dead—gone forever—forever. His face contracted, became horribly distorted; then he snatched in haste a handkerchief from his pocket and, to the amazement of everyone, broke into harrowing, heartrending, uncontrollable sobs.

Questions for Critical Thinking

1. What is the central argument of the story? State it in one sentence.

2. One of the crucial characters in the story is the "fat man." How does he contribute to the central theme of the story?

3. This is not an action-packed story. In fact, very little happens in it. What, then, keeps the story moving toward a climax? When does the climax occur?

4. How would you defend or condemn the view that going to war to defend one's country is a noble and glorious act?

5. How would you view a son who refused, for conscientious reasons, to fight in a war declared by his government?

6. Some proponents of the feminist movement believe that women should be called to war and should bear arms in the same way as men. What is your opinion of this belief? What should be the role of women during war?

7. Pirandello is best known for his plays. Does this story have dramatic possibilities? Why or why not?

8. What does the fat man mean when he says that we belong to our sons, but they never belong to us (*see* paragraph 19)? Do you agree with this statement? Why or why not?

Writing Assignment

Write an essay highlighting the role of parents whose sons have been forced to go to war. State how you feel about this role.

Writing Advice

Pirandello's story can serve as the jumping-off point for this essay. You could, for instance, begin as follows: "Pirandello's 'War' dramatizes the tragic plight of parents forced to sacrifice all hope for the future when they find out that their youthful sons have been killed in war."

The strength of your essay will depend on how clearly you state your own position on the subject and how well you illustrate and support it. If you feel that the loss of a son in combat is an unbearably high price for any parent to pay, no matter what the military goal, then say so forcefully and explain your reasons. Conversely, if you feel that the defense of freedom and country are worth any sacrifice, then present and argue this case. No matter what tack you choose in writing your essay, you should support your opinion with reasons and examples intended to convince an audience. If you personally know a parent who has lost a son in war, describe the family's reaction and beliefs as a supporting example.

Alternate Writing Assignments

1. Write an essay in which you either support or refute one of the two quotations below:

   a. "The inevitableness, the idealism, and the blessing of war, as an indispensable and stimulating law of development, must be repeatedly emphasized."
   —Friedrich A. J. Von Bernhardi (1849–1930), German military writer

   b. "War in fact is becoming contemptible, and ought to be put down by the great nations of Europe, just as we put down a vulgar mob."
   —Mortimer Collins (1827–1876), English poet and novelist

2. Write an essay arguing either for or against forced military service.

LITERATURE

ALL QUIET ON THE WESTERN FRONT
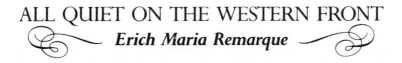
Erich Maria Remarque

Erich Maria Remarque (1897–1970) was a German novelist who, at the age of fifty-two, emigrated to the United States. He became an instant success with his first novel,

All Quiet on the Western Front (1929), from which Chapter 9 is excerpted below. Based on Remarque's own trench-warfare experience during World War I, the story so grimly conveys the horrors of war that the book was ordered burned during the Nazi regime. Other novels by Remarque include *The Way Back* (1931), *Three Comrades* (1937), *Arch of Triumph* (1946), *A Time to Love and a Time to Die* (1954), and *Shadows of Paradise* (1971).

Reading Advice

Remarque's war scenes are written from the first person point of view and presented in such vivid detail as to give the impression of being a diary rather than fiction. The entire piece has such a sense of *verisimilitude*—meaning the appearance and semblance of truth and actuality—as to entirely convince us of the brutalizing effects of war. Remarque himself found it difficult to distinguish between what he literally remembered and what he had wanted to convey dramatically, and the occasional critic noted this defect and labeled his work romanticized journalism. Whatever we choose to call *All Quiet on the Western Front*, its message is clear: War is a cruel game in which the soldiers are tormented pawns used by generals and statesmen as a means of gaining fame, power, and might. The various discussions by the soldiers at camp, on patrol, or in the trenches stress the ironic fact that in war each side thinks it is morally right. If nothing else, Remarque's work tells us that war is not for the tenderhearted but a brutalizing arena where kindness and compassion are replaced by a dogged sense of survival.

*W*e travel for several days. The first   1
aeroplanes appear in the sky. We roll on past transport lines. Guns, guns. The light railway picks us up. I search for my regiment. No one knows exactly where it lies. Somewhere or other I put up for the night, somewhere or other I receive provisions and a few vague instructions. And so with my pack and my rifle I set out again on the way.

By the time I come up they are no longer in the devastated place. I hear we   2
have become one of the flying divisions that are pushed in wherever it is hottest. That does not sound cheerful to me. They tell me of heavy losses that we have been having. I inquire after Kat and Albert. No one knows anything of them.

I search farther and wander about here and there; it is a strange feeling.   3
One night more and then another I camp out like a Red Indian. Then at last I get some definite information, and by the afternoon I am able to report to the Orderly Room.

The sergeant-major detains me there. The company comes back in two days'   4
time. There is no object in sending me up now.

"What was it like on leave?" he asks, "pretty good, eh?"   5

"In parts," I say.   6

"Yes," he sighs, "yes, if a man didn't have to come away again. The second   7
half is always rather messed up by that."

I loaf around until the company comes back in the early morning, grey,   8
dirty, soured, and gloomy. Then I jump up, push in amongst them, my eyes
searching. There is Tjaden, there is Müller blowing his nose, and there are Kat
and Kropp. We arrange our sacks of straw side by side. I have an uneasy
conscience when I look at them, and yet without any good reason. Before we
turn in I bring out the rest of the potato-cakes and jam so that they can have
some too.

The outer cakes are mouldy, still it is possible to eat them. I keep those for   9
myself and give the fresh ones to Kat and Kropp.

Kat chews and says: "These are from your mother?"   10

I nod.   11

"Good," says he, "I can tell by the taste."   12

I could almost weep. I can hardly control myself any longer. But it will soon   13
be all right again back here with Kat and Albert. This is where I belong.

"You've been lucky," whispers Kropp to me before we drop off to sleep,   14
"they say we are going to Russia."

To Russia? It's not much of a war over there.   15

In the distance the front thunders. The walls of the hut rattle.   16

There's a great deal of polishing being done. We are inspected at every turn.   17
Everything that is torn is exchanged for new. I score a spotless new tunic out
of it and Kat, of course, an entire outfit. A rumour is going round that there
may be peace, but the other story is more likely—that we are bound for Russia.
Still, what do we need new things for in Russia? At last it leaks out—the
Kaiser[1] is coming to review us. Hence all the inspections.

For eight whole days one would suppose we were in a base-camp, there is   18
so much drill and fuss. Everyone is peevish and touchy, we do not take kindly
to all this polishing, much less to the full-dress parades. Such things exasperate
a soldier more than the front-line.

At last the moment arrives. We stand to attention and the Kaiser appears.   19
We are curious to see what he looks like. He stalks along the line, and I am
really rather disappointed; judging from his pictures I imagined him to be bigger
and more powerfully built, and above all to have a thundering voice.

He distributes Iron Crosses, speaks to this man and that. Then we   20
march off.

Afterwards we discuss it. Tjaden says with astonishment: 21

"So that is the All-Highest! And everyone, bar nobody, has to stand up stiff   22

---

1. Kaiser Wilhelm II, Emperor of Germany.

in front of him!" He meditates: "Hindenburg[2] too, he has to stand up stiff to him, eh?"

"Sure," says Kat.   23

Tjaden hasn't finished yet. He thinks for a while and then asks: "And would   24
a king have to stand up stiff to an emperor?"

None of us is quite sure about it, but we don't suppose so. They are both   25
so exalted that standing strictly to attention is probably not insisted on.

"What rot you do hatch out," says Kat. "The main point is that you have to   26
stand stiff yourself."

But Tjaden is quite fascinated. His otherwise prosy fancy is blowing bubbles.   27
"But look," he announces, "I simply can't believe that an emperor has to go to
the latrine the same as I have."

"You can bet your boots on it."   28

"Four and a half-wit make seven," says Kat. "You've got a maggot in your   29
brain, Tjaden, just you run along to the latrine quick, and get your head clear,
so that you don't talk like a two-year-old."

Tjaden disappears.   30

"But what I would like to know," says Albert, "is whether there would not   31
have been a war if the Kaiser had said No."

"I'm sure there would," I interject, "he was against it from the first."   32

"Well, if not him alone, then perhaps if twenty or thirty people in the world   33
has said No."

"That's probable," I agree, "but they damned well said Yes."   34

"It's queer, when one thinks about it," goes on Kropp, "we are here to   35
protect our fatherland. And the French are over there to protect their fatherland. Now who's in the right?"

"Perhaps both," say I without believing it.   36

"Yes, well now," pursues Albert, and I see that he means to drive me into a   37
corner, "but our professors and parsons and newspapers say that we are the
only ones that are right, and let's hope so;—but the French professors and
parsons and newspapers say that the right is on their side, now what about
that?"

"That I don't know," I say, "but whichever way it is there's war all the same   38
and every month more countries coming in."

Tjaden reappears. He is still quite excited and again joins the conversation,   39
wondering just how a war gets started.

"Mostly by one country badly offending another," answers Albert with a   40
slight air of superiority.[3]

---

2. Paul von Hindenberg (1874–1934), field marshal and president of Germany.
3. World War I was officially started because a Serbian nationalist assassinated Archduke Ferdinand of Austria-Hungary.

Then Tjaden pretends to be obtuse. "A country? I don't follow. A mountain   41
in Germany cannot offend a mountain in France. Or a river, or a wood, or a
field of wheat."

"Are you really as stupid as that, or are you just pulling my leg?" growls   42
Kropp, "I don't mean that at all. One people offends the other————"

"Then I haven't any business here at all," replies Tjaden, "I don't feel myself   43
offended."

"Well, let me tell you," says Albert sourly, "it doesn't apply to tramps   44
like you."

"Then I can be going home right away," retorts Tjaden, and we all laugh.   45

"Ach, man! he means the people as a whole, the State————" exclaims   46
Müller.

"State, State"—Tjaden snaps his fingers contemptuously. "Gendarmes, police,   47
taxes, that's your State;—if that's what you are talking about, no, thank you."

"That's right," says Kat, "you've said something for once, Tjaden. State and   48
home-country, there's a big difference."

"But they go together," insists Kropp, "without the State there wouldn't be   49
any home-country."

"True, but just you consider, almost all of us are simple folk. And in France,   50
too, the majority of men are labourers, workmen, or poor clerks. Now just
why would a French blacksmith or a French shoemaker want to attack us? No,
it is merely the rulers. I had never seen a Frenchman before I came here, and
it will be just the same with the majority of Frenchmen as regards us. They
weren't asked about it any more than we were."

"Then what exactly is the war for?" asks Tjaden.   51

Kat shrugs his shoulders. "There must be some people to whom the war is   52
useful."

"Well, I'm not one of them," grins Tjaden.   53

"Not you, nor anybody else here."   54

"Who are they then?" persists Tjaden. "It isn't any use to the Kaiser either.   55
He has everything he can want already."

"I'm not so sure about that," contradicts Kat, "he has not had a war up till   56
now. And every full-grown emperor requires at least one war, otherwise he
would not become famous. You look in your school books."

"And generals too," adds Detering, "they become famous through war."   57

"Even more famous than emperors," adds Kat.   58

"There are other people back behind there who profit by the war, that's   59
certain," growls Detering.

"I think it is more of a kind of fever," says Albert. "No one in particular   60
wants it, and then all at once there it is. We didn't want the war, the others
say the same thing—and yet half the world is in it all the same."

"But there are more lies told by the other side than by us," say I; "just think   61 of those pamphlets the prisoners have on them, where it says that we eat Belgian children. The fellows who write those lies ought to go and hang themselves. They are the real culprits."

Müller gets up. "Anyway, it is better that the war is here instead of in Germany. Just you look at the shell-holes." 62

"True," assents Tjaden, "but no war at all would be better still." 63

He is quite proud of himself because he has scored for once over us volunteers. And his opinion is quite typical, here one meets it time and again, and there is nothing with which one can properly counter it, because that is the limit of their comprehension of the factors involved. The national feeling of the tommy resolves itself into this—here he is. But that is the end of it; everything else he criticizes from his own practical point of view. 64

Albert lies down on the grass and growls angrily: "The best thing is not to talk about the rotten business." 65

"It won't make any difference, that's sure," agrees Kat. 66

To make matters worse, we have to return almost all the new things and take back our old rags again. The good ones were merely for the inspection. 67

Instead of going to Russia, we go up the line again. On the way we pass through a devastated wood with the true trunks shattered and the ground ploughed up. 68

At several places there are tremendous craters. "Great guns, something's hit that," I say to Kat. 69

"Trench mortars," he replies, and then points up at one of the trees. 70

In the branches dead men are hanging. A naked soldier is squatting in the fork of a tree, he still has his helmet on, otherwise he is entirely unclad. There is only half of him sitting up there, the top half, the legs are missing. 71

"What can that mean?" I ask. 72

"He's been blown out of his clothes," mutters Tjaden. 73

"It's funny," says Kat, "we have seen that several times now. If a mortar gets you it blows you clean out of your clothes. It's the concussion that does it." 74

I search around. And so it is. Here hang bits of uniform, and somewhere else is plastered a bloody mess that was once a human limb. Over there lies a body with nothing but a piece of the underpants on one leg and the collar of the tunic around its neck. Otherwise it is naked and the clothes are hanging up in the tree. Both arms are missing as though they had been pulled out. I discover one of them twenty yards off in a shrub. 75

The dead man lies on his face. There, where the arm wounds are, the earth is black with blood. Underfoot the leaves are scratched up as though the man had been kicking. 76

"That's no joke, Kat," says I. 77

"No more is a shell splinter in the belly," he replies, shrugging his shoulders. 78

"But don't get tender-hearted," says Tjaden. 79

All this can only have happened a little while ago, the blood is still fresh. 80
As everybody we see there is dead we do not waste any more time, but report
the affair at the next stretcher-bearers' post. After all it is not our business to
take these stretcher-bearers' jobs away from them.

A patrol has to be sent out to discover just how strongly the enemy position 81
is manned. Since my leave I feel a certain strange attachment to the other
fellows, and so I volunteer to go with them. We agree on a plan, slip out
through the wire and then divide and creep forward separately. After a while
I find a shallow shell-hole and crawl into it. From here I peer forward.

There is moderate machine-gun fire. It sweeps across from all directions, 82
not very heavy, but always sufficient to make one keep down.

A parachute star-shell opens out. The ground lies stark in the pale light, 83
and then the darkness shuts down again blacker than ever. In the trenches we
were told there were black troops in front of us. That is nasty, it is hard to see
them; they are very good at patrolling, too. And oddly enough they are often
quite stupid; for instance, both Kat and Kropp were once able to shoot down
a black enemy patrol because the fellows in their enthusiasm for cigarettes
smoked while they were creeping about. Kat and Albert had simply to aim at
the glowing ends of the cigarettes.

A bomb or something lands close beside me. I have not heard it coming and 84
am terrified. At the same moment a senseless fear takes hold of me. Here I am
alone and almost helpless in the dark—perhaps two other eyes have been
watching me for a long while from another shell-hole in front of me, and a
bomb lies ready to blow me to pieces. I try to pull myself together. It is not
my first patrol and not a particularly risky one. But it is the first since my
leave, and besides, the lie of the land is still rather strange to me.

I tell myself that my alarm is absurd, that there is probably nothing at all 85
there in the darkness watching me, otherwise they would not be firing so low.

It is in vain. In whirling confusion my thoughts hum in my brain—I hear 86
the warning voice of my mother, I see the Russians with the flowing beards
leaning against the wire fence, I have a bright picture of a canteen with stools,
of a cinema in Valenciennes; tormented, terrified, in my imagination I see the
grey, implacable muzzle of a rifle which moves noiselessly before me whichever
way I try to turn my head. The sweat breaks out from every pore.

I still continue to lie in the shallow bowl. I look at the time; only a few 87
minutes have passed. My forehead is wet, the sockets of my eyes are damp, my
hands tremble, and I am panting softly. It is nothing but an awful spasm of
fear, a simple animal fear of poking out my head and crawling on farther.

All my efforts subside like froth into the one desire to be able just to stay 88
lying there. My limbs are glued to the earth. I make a vain attempt;—they

refuse to come away. I press myself down on the earth, I cannot go forward, I make up my mind to stay lying there.

But immediately the wave floods over me anew, a mingled sense of shame, of remorse, and yet at the same time of security. I raise myself up a little to take a look round.   89

My eyes burn with staring into the dark. A starshell goes up;—I duck down again.   90

I wage a wild and senseless fight, I want to get out of the hollow and yet slide back into it again; I say "You must, it is your comrades, it is not an idiotic command," and again: "What does it matter to me, I have only one life to lose————"   91

That is the result of all this leave, I plead in extenuation. But I cannot reassure myself; I become terribly faint. I raise myself slowly and reach forward with my arms, dragging my body after me and then lie on the edge of the shellhole, half in and half out.   92

There I hear sounds and drop back. Suspicious sounds can be detected clearly despite the noise of the artillery-fire. I listen; the sound is behind me. They are our people moving along the trench. Now I hear muffled voices. To judge by the tone that might be Kat talking.   93

At once a new warmth flows through me. These voices, these quiet words, these footsteps in the trench behind me recall me at a bound from the terrible loneliness and fear of death by which I had been almost destroyed. They are more to me than life, these voices, they are more than motherliness and more than fear; they are the strongest, most comforting thing there is anywhere: they are the voices of my comrades.   94

I am no longer a shuddering speck of existence, alone in the darkness;—I belong to them and they to me; we all share the same fear and the same life, we are nearer than lovers, in a simpler, a harder way; I could bury my face in them, in these voices, these words that have saved me and will stand by me.   95

Cautiously I glide out over the edge and snake my way forward. I shuffle along on all fours a bit farther, I keep track of my bearings, look around me and observe the distribution of the gunfire so as to be able to find my way back. Then I try to get in touch with the others.   96

I am still afraid, but it is an intelligent fear, an extraordinarily heightened caution. The night is windy and shadows flit hither and thither in the flicker of the gunfire. It reveals too little and too much. Often I pause, stock still, motionless, and always for nothing. Thus I advance a long way and then turn back in a wide curve. I have not established touch with the others. Every yard nearer our trench fills me with confidence—and with haste, too. It would be bad to get hit now.   97

Then a new fear lays hold of me. I can no longer remember the direction.   98
Quiet, I squat in a shellhole and try to locate myself. More than once it has
happened that some fellow has jumped joyfully into a trench, only then to
discover that it was the wrong one.

After a little time I listened again, but still I am not sure. The confusion of   99
shell-holes now seems so bewildering that I can no longer tell in my agitation
which way I should go. Perhaps I am crawling parallel to the lines, and that
might go on forever. So I crawl round once again in a wide curve.

These damned rockets! They seem to burn for an hour, and a man cannot   100
make the least movement without bringing the bullets whistling round.

But there is nothing for it, I must get out. Falteringly I work my way farther,   101
I move off over the ground like a crab and rip my hands sorely on the jagged
splinters, as sharp as razor blades. Often I think that the sky is becoming lighter
on the horizon, but it may be merely my imagination. Then gradually I realize
that to crawl in the right direction is a matter of life or death.

A shell crashes. Almost immediately two others. And then it begins in   102
earnest. A bombardment. Machine-guns rattle. Now there is nothing for it but
to stay lying low. Apparently an attack is coming. Everywhere the rockets shoot
up. Unceasing.

I lie huddled in a large shell-hole, my legs in the water up to the belly.   103
When the attack starts I will let myself fall into the water, with my face as
deep in the mud as I can keep it without suffocating. I must pretend to
be dead.

Suddenly I hear the barrage lift. At once I slip down into the water, my   104
helmet on the nape of my neck and my mouth just clear so that I can get a
breath of air.

I lie motionless;—somewhere something clanks, it stamps and stumbles   105
nearer—all my nerves become taut and icy. It clatters over me and away, the
first wave has passed. I have but this one shattering thought: What will you do
if someone jumps into your shell-hole?—Swiftly I pull out my little dagger,
grasp it fast and bury it in my hand once again under the mud. If anyone jumps
in here I will go for him. It hammers in my forehead; at once, stab him clean
through the throat, so that he cannot call out; that's the only way; he will be
just as frightened as I am; when in terror we fall upon one another, then I must
be first.

Now our batteries are firing. A shell lands near me. That makes me savage   106
with fury, all it needs now is to be killed by our own shells; I curse and grind
my teeth in the mud; it is a raving frenzy; in the end all I can do is groan
and pray.

The crash of the shells bursts in my ears. If our fellows make a counter-raid   107
I will be saved. I press my head against the earth and listen to the muffled

thunder, like the explosions of quarrying—and raise it again to listen for the
sounds on top.

The machine-guns rattle. I know our barbed wire entanglements are strong   108
and almost undamaged;—parts of them are charged with a powerful electric
current. The rifle fire increases. They have not broken through; they have to
retreat.

I sink down again, huddled, strained to the uttermost. The banging, the   109
creeping, the clanging becomes audible. One single cry yelling amongst it all.
They are raked with fire, the attack is repulsed.

Already it has become somewhat lighter. Steps hasten over me. The first.   110
Gone. Again, another. The rattle of machine-guns becomes an unbroken chain.
Just as I am about to turn round a little, something heavy stumbles, and with
a crash a body falls over me into the shell-hole, slips down, and lies
across me—

I do not think at all, I make no decision—I strike madly at him, and feel   111
only how the body suddenly convulses, then becomes limp, and collapses. When
I recover myself, my hand is sticky and wet.

The man gurgles. It sounds to me as though he bellows, every gasping breath   112
is like a cry, a thunder—but it is not only my heart pounding. I want to stop
his mouth, stuff it with earth, stab him again, he must be quiet, he is betraying
me; now at last I regain control of myself, but have suddenly become so feeble
that I cannot any more lift my hand against him.

So I crawl away to the farthest corner and stay there, my eyes glued on him,   113
my hand grasping the knife—ready, if he stirs, to spring at him again. But he
won't do so any more, I can hear that already in his gurgling.

I can see him indistinctly. I have but one desire, to get away. If it is not soon   114
it will be too light; it will be difficult enough now. Then as I try to raise up my
head I see it is impossible already. The machine-gunfire so sweeps the ground
that I should be shot through and through before I could make one jump.

I test it once with my helmet, which I take off and hold up to find out the   115
level of the shots. The next moment it is knocked out of my hand by a bullet.
The fire is sweeping very low to the ground. I am not far enough from the
enemy line to escape being picked off by one of the snipers if I attempt to
get away.

The light increases. Burning I wait for our attack. My hands are white at   116
the knuckles, I clench them so tightly in my longing for the fire to cease so
that my comrades may come.

Minute after minute trickles away. I dare not look again at the dark figure   117
in the shell-hole. With an effort I look past it and wait, wait. The bullets hiss,
they make a steel net, never ceasing, never ceasing.

Then I notice my bloody hand and suddenly feel nauseated. I take some   118
earth and rub the skin with it; now my hand is muddy and the blood cannot
be seen any more.

The fire does not diminish. It is equally heavy from both sides. Our fellows   119
have probably given me up for lost long ago.

It is early morning, clear and grey. The gurgling continues, I stop my ears,   120
but soon take my fingers away again, because then I cannot hear the other
sound.

The figure opposite me moves. I shrink together and involuntarily look at   121
it. Then my eyes remain glued to it. A man with a small pointed beard lies
there; his head is fallen to one side, one arm is halfbent, his head rests helplessly
upon it. The other hand lies on his chest, it is bloody.

He is dead, I say to myself, he must be dead, he doesn't feel anything any   122
more; it is only the body that is gurgling there. Then the head tries to raise
itself, for a moment the groaning becomes louder, his forehead sinks back upon
his arm. The man is not dead, he is dying, but he is not dead. I drag myself
toward him, hesitate, support myself on my hands, creep a bit farther, wait,
again a terrible journey. At last I am beside him.

Then he opens his eyes. He must have heard me, for he gazes at me with a   123
look of utter terror. The body lies still, but in the eyes there is such an
extraordinary expression of fright that for a moment I think they have power
enough to carry the body off with them. Hundreds of miles away with one
bound. The body is still perfectly still, without a sound, the gurgle has ceased,
but the eyes cry out, yell, all the life is gathered together in them for one
tremendous effort to flee, gathered together there in a dreadful terror of death,
of me.

My legs give way and I drop on my elbows. "No, no," I whisper.   124

The eyes follow me. I am powerless to move so long as they are there.   125

Then his hand slips slowly from his breast, only a little bit, it sinks just a   126
few inches, but this movement breaks the power of the eyes. I bend forward,
shake my head and whisper: "No, no, no," I raise one hand, I must show him
that I want to help him, I stroke his forehead.

The eyes shrink back as the hand comes, then they lose their stare, the   127
eyelids droop lower, the tension is past. I open his collar and place his head
more comfortably.

His mouth stands half open, it tries to form words. The lips are dry. My   128
water bottle is not there. I have not brought it with me. But there is water in
the mud, down at the bottom of the crater. I climb down, take out my handkerchief, spread it out, push it under and scoop up the yellow water that strains
through into the hollow of my hand.

He gulps it down. I fetch some more. Then I unbutton his tunic in order   129
to bandage him if it is possible. In any case I must do it, so that if the fellows
over there capture me they will see that I wanted to help him, and so will not
shoot me. He tries to resist, but his hand is too feeble. The shirt is stuck and
will not come away, it is buttoned at the back. So there is nothing for it but
to cut it open.

I look for the knife and find it again. But when I begin to cut the shirt the   130
eyes open once more and the cry is in them again and the demented expression,
so that I must close them, press them shut and whisper: "I want to help you,
Comrade, camerade, camerade, camerade————" eagerly repeating the word,
to make him understand.

There are three stabs. My field dressing covers them, the blood runs out   131
under it, I press it tighter; there; he groans.

That is all I can do. Now we must wait, wait.   132

These hours. . . . The gurgling starts again—but how slowly a man dies! For   133
this I know—he cannot be saved, I have, indeed, tried to tell myself that he
will be, but at noon this pretence breaks down and melts before his groans. If
only I had not lost my revolver crawling about, I would shoot him. Stab him
I cannot.

By noon I am groping on the outer limits of reason. Hunger devours me, I   134
could almost weep for something to eat, I cannot struggle against it. Again and
again I fetch water for the dying man and drink some myself.

This is the first time I have killed with my hands, whom I can see close at   135
hand, whose death is my doing. Kat and Kropp and Müller have experienced
it already, when they have hit someone; it happens to many, in hand-to-hand
fighting especially—

But every gasp lays my heart bare. This dying man has time with him, he   136
has an invisible dagger with which he stabs me: Time and my thoughts.

I would give much if he would but stay alive. It is hard to lie here and to   137
have to see and hear him.

In the afternoon, about three, he is dead.   138

I breathe freely again. But only for a short time. Soon the silence is more   139
unbearable than the groans. I wish the gurgling were there again, gasping hoarse,
now whistling softly and again hoarse and loud.

It is mad, what I do. But I must do something. I prop the dead man up   140
again so that he lies comfortably, although he feels nothing any more. I close
his eyes. They are brown, his hair is black and a bit curly at the sides.

The mouth is full and soft beneath his moustache; the nose is slightly arched,   141
the skin brownish; it is now not so pale as it was before, when he was still
alive. For a moment the face seems almost healthy;—then it collapses suddenly

into the strange face of the dead that I have so often seen, strange faces, all alike.

No doubt his wife still thinks of him; she does not know what has happened. He looks as if he would have often have written to her;—she will still be getting mail from him—To-morrow, in a week's time—perhaps even a stray letter a month hence. She will read it, and in it he will be speaking to her.   142

My state is getting worse, I can no longer control my thoughts. What would his wife look like? Like the little brunette on the other side of the canal? Does she belong to me now? Perhaps by this act she becomes mine. I wish Kantorek were sitting here beside me. If my mother could see me————. The dead man might have had thirty more years of life if only I had impressed the way back to our trench more sharply on my memory. If only he had run two yards farther to the left, he might now be sitting in the trench over there and writing a fresh letter to his wife.   143

But I will get no further that way; for that is the fate of all of us: if Kemmerich's leg had been six inches to the right: if Haie Westhus had bent his back three inches further forward————   144

The silence spreads. I talk and must talk. So I speak to him and to say to him: "Comrade, I did not want to kill you. If you jumped in here again, I would not do it, if you would be sensible too. But you were only an idea to me before, an abstraction that lived in my mind and called forth its appropriate response. It was that abstraction I stabbed. But now, for the first time, I see you are a man like me. I thought of your hand-grenades, of your bayonet, of your rifle; now I see your wife and your face and our fellowship. Forgive me, comrade. We always see it too late. Why do they never tell us that you are poor devils like us, that your mothers are just as anxious as ours, and that we have the same fear of death, and the same dying and the same agony—Forgive me, comrade; how could you be my enemy? If we threw away these rifles and this uniform you could be my brother just like Kat and Albert. Take twenty years of my life, comrade, and stand up—take more, for I do not know what I can even attempt to do with it now."   145

It is quiet, the front is still except for the crackle of rifle fire. The bullets rain over, they are not fired haphazard, but shrewdly aimed from all sides. I cannot get out.   146

"I will write to your wife," I say hastily to the dead man, "I will write to her, she must hear it from me, I will tell her everything I have told you, she shall not suffer, I will help her, and your parents too, and your child————"   147

His tunic is half open. The pocket-book is easy to find. But I hesitate to open it. In it is the book with his name. So long as I do not know his name perhaps I may still forget him, time will obliterate it, this picture. But his name,   148 it is a nail that will be hammered into me and never come out again. It has the power to recall this forever, it will always come back and stand before me.

Irresolutely I take the wallet in my hand. It slips out of my hand and falls 149 open. Some pictures and letters drop out. I gather them up and want to put them back again, but the strain I am under, the uncertainty, the hunger, the danger, these hours with the dead man have made me desperate, I want to hasten the relief, to intensify and to end the torture, as one strikes an unendurably painful hand against the trunk of a tree, regardless of everything.

There are portraits of a woman and a little girl, small amateur photographs 150 taken against an ivy-clad wall. Along with them are letters. I take them out and try to read them. Most of it I do not understand, it is so hard to decipher and I scarcely know any French. But each word I translate pierces me like a shot in the chest;—like a stab in the chest.

My brain is taxed beyond endurance. But I realize this much, that I will 151 never dare to write to these people as I intended. Impossible. I look at the portraits once more; they are clearly not rich people. I might send them money anonymously if I earn anything later on. I seize upon that, it is at least something to hold on to. This dead man is bound up with my life, therefore I must do everything, promise everything in order to save myself; I swear blindly that I mean to live only for his sake and his family, with wet lips I try to placate him—and deep down in me lies the hope that I may buy myself off in this way and perhaps even get out of this; it is a little stratagem: if only I am allowed to escape, then I will see to it. So I open the book and read slowly:—Gérard Duval, compositor.

With the dead man's pencil I write the address on an envelope, then swiftly 152 thrust everything back into his tunic.

I have killed the printer, Gérard Duval. I must be a printer, I think confusedly, 153 be a printer, printer————

By afternoon I am calmer. My fear was groundless. The name troubles me no more. The madness passes. "Comrade," I say to the dead man, but I say it calmly, "to-day you, to-morrow me. But if I come out of it, comrade, I will fight against this, that has struck us both down; from you, taken life—and from me—? Life also. I promise you, comrade. It shall never happen again."

The sun strikes low, I am stupefied with exhaustion and hunger. Yesterday 154 is like a fog to me, there is no hope of ever getting out of this. I fall into a doze and do not at first realize that evening is approaching. The twilight comes. It seems to me to come quickly now. One hour more. If it were summer, it would be three hours more. One hour more.

Now suddenly I begin to tremble; something might happen in the interval. 155 I think no more of the dead man, he is of no consequence to me now. With one bound the lust to live flares up again and everything that has filled my thoughts goes down before it. Now, merely to avert any ill-luck, I babble mechanically: "I will fulfil everything, fulfil everything I have promised you———" but already I know that I shall not do so.

Suddenly it occurs to me that my own comrades may fire on me as I creep 156
up; they do not know I am coming. I will call out as soon as I can so that they will recognize me. I will stay lying in front of the trench until they answer me.

The first star. The front remains quiet. I breathe deeply and talk to myself 157
in my excitement: "No foolishness now, Paul—Quiet, Paul, quiet—then you will be saved, Paul." When I use my Christian name it works as though someone else spoke to me, it has more power.

The darkness grows. My excitement subsides, I wait cautiously until the first 158
rocket goes up. Then I crawl out of the shell-hole. I have forgotten the dead man. Before me lies the oncoming night and the pale gleaming field. I fix my eyes on a shell-hole; the moment the light dies I scurry over into it, grope farther, spring into the next, duck down, scramble onward.

I come nearer. There, by the light of a rocket I see something move in the 159
wire, then it stiffens and I lie still. Next time I see it again, yes, they are men from our trench. But I am suspicious until I recognize our helmets. Then I call. And immediately an answer rings out, my name: "Paul—Paul————"

I call again in answer. It is Kat and Albert who have come out with a 160
stretcher to look for me.

"Are you wounded?" 161

"No, no————" 162

We drop into the trench. I ask for something to eat and wolf it down. 163
Müller gives me a cigarette. In a few words I tell what happened. There is nothing new about it; it happens quite often. The night attack is the only unusual feature of the business. In Russia Kat once lay for two days behind the enemy lines before he could make his way back.

I do not mention the dead printer. 164

But by the next morning I can keep it to myself no longer. I must tell Kat 165
and Albert. They both try to calm me. "You can't do anything about it. What else could you have done? That is what you are here for."

I listen to them and feel comforted, reassured by their presence. It was mere 166
drivelling nonsense that I talked out there in the shell-hole.

"Look there for instance," points Kat. 167

On the fire-step stand some snipers. They rest their rifles with telescopic 168
sights on the parapet and watch the enemy front. Once and again a shot cracks out.

Then we hear the cry:"That's found a billet!" "Did you see how he leapt in 169
the air?" Sergeant Oellrich turns round proudly and scores his point. He heads the shooting list for to-day with three unquestionable hits.

"What do you say to that?" asks Kat. 170

I nod.   171

"If he keeps that up he will get a little coloured bird for his buttonhole by   172
this evening," says Albert.

"Or rather he will soon be made acting sergeant-major," says Kat.   173

We look at one another. "I would not do it," I say.   174

"All the same," says Kat, "It's very good for you to see it just now."   175

Sergeant Oellrich returns to the fire-step. The muzzle of his rifle searches   176
to and fro.

"You don't need to lose any sleep over your affair," nods Albert.   177

And now I hardly understand it myself any more.   178

"It was only because I had to lie there with him so long," I say. "After all,   179
war is war."

Oellrich's rifle cracks out sharply and dry.   180

Questions for Critical Thinking

1. What differences do you perceive between a diary entry and Remarque's fictional account of a battle scene? What similarities are there? You might wish to review the German soldier's diary entries earlier in this chapter to focus on the differences or similarities of each genre.

2. Throughout the narrative, we are allowed intimate glimpses into the narrator's mind and emotions. What seems to comfort and sustain him most during this terrible time of stress—on patrol in the midst of enemy fire? Explain the operating dynamics of this comfort.

3. How is war in this chapter different from war as described by Jonathan Schell in "The Effects of Nuclear War" given previously?

4. Read the following lines from a poem by Thomas Hardy:

   > *Yes; quaint and curious war*
   > *Is! You shoot a fellow down*
   > *You'd treat if met where any*
   > *Bar is Or help to half-a-crown.*

   Where in Remarque's description is a similar sentiment expressed? Do you agree with this idea? Why or why not?

5. Imagine yourself in the position of the narrator, who has been forced to kill a man in a war. You retrieve his wallet containing the picture and address of his wife. Imagine that you write the man's wife a letter. What would you say?

6. Under what circumstance, if any, would you feel justified in killing another human being? Be specific in describing the circumstance and in justifying the killing.

7. How do you think Sun Tzu ("The Art of War," also in this chapter) would react to the narrator's feelings of guilt for having killed an enemy soldier?

8. What does the narrator mean when he says, at the end of the narration, "It was only because I had to lie there with him so long"? Explain the meaning in your own words.

Writing Assignment

Write an essay in which you explain the difference between a romanticized account of war as reflected in fiction and a factual account as given in news reports.

Writing Advice

Remarque's novel is an excellent vehicle to use as a basis for your explanation because it contains elements of both fiction and reality.

1. Begin by dividing a sheet of paper into two columns. On one side list the techniques of romanticizing war and on the other list the techniques of reporting it. Here are possibilities for three sample entries:

Novels	*News*
1. Author can select events and details.	*Events and details must be related as they happened.*
2. Gruesome details can be softened.	*The real details of war are often sordid or even macabre.*
3. Heroic deeds can be exaggerated to inspire the reader.	*Soldiers must be represented as they are— perhaps even stupid, insensitive, or cowardly.*

2. Once you have established your list, you can take a position on the subject. For instance, you could conclude that a novel about war can be more heroic than a news report. Or, you could argue that romanticized stories about war mislead young people into believing that war is glamorous. Or, you could simply state that fiction and news each has its own distinct literary advantages in dealing with war. In any case, your conclusion can serve as a tentative thesis for your paper.

3. Next, you can begin developing paragraphs based on the contrast inherent in your established list. For instance, one paragraph could be based on entry #1. Here your topic sentence could read as follows: "Whereas a novelist has the privilege of selecting events and details to support either a theme or the nature of a certain character, the news reporter must stick to the facts as they occur." Another paragraph could be based on entry #2. Here the topic sentence could read as follows: "Unlike the novelist, who can soften all of the gruesome aspects of war with melodrama or pathos, a news reporter is bound to reflect objectively what happened, even if the facts involve brutal executions, maimed bodies, and foul odors." A third paragraph could develop entry #3 with the following topic sentence: "While the novelist can turn soldiers into modern Agamemnons or

Hectors of myth, the news reporter is professionally bound to report what he observes, even if it includes moments of stupidity, cowardice, or ignominy on the part of the soldiers."

Whether you take a position for or against romanticized accounts of war, or whether you simply explain the difference between romantic and realistic accounts, make your thesis clear and support it thoroughly.

Alternate Writing Assignments

1. Write an imaginary letter to either the wife or the mother of a friend killed in war combat. Use the letter to express your views for or against the necessity of war.

2. Write an essay in which you critically evaluate the genre of romanticized journalism as revealed in Remarque's work. For this assignment, you may wish to read the entire novel *All Quiet on the Western Front.*

LITERATURE

DULCE ET DECORUM EST

 *Wilfred Owen*

Wilfred Owen (1893–1918) was a British poet and among the greatest contributors to the thematic poetry of World War I. He was killed at the age of 25 attempting to lead his men across the Sambre Canal while serving as a platoon leader on the Western Front. A year earlier he had been wounded while serving in the Artist's Rifles. He was awarded the Military Cross for gallantry. Owen's name was completely unknown to the literary world until his friend Siegfried Sassoon discovered the contents of his posthumous volume, *Poems* (1920). The restrained passion as well as pitiful outcries revealed in Owen's war poetry expose the lie behind the hollow and glib patter about honor, glory, and dominion to the ears of soldiers huddled in the dugouts and trenches. Owen's death—ironically a week before the armistice was declared on November 4, 1918—is one of modern poetry's greatest losses.

Reading Advice

On a scrap of paper, which served as an unfinished preface to his volume of poetry, Owen wrote:

Above all, this book is not concerned with Poetry, The subject of it is War, and pity of War. The poetry is in the pity.

Without becoming maudlin, the poem "Dulce et Decorum Est" argues eloquently against the brutal maiming and mangling of young lives in war. What Owen does is evoke the reader's compassion and sympathy for the young men who died like cattle, mowed down by the angry rattle of machine-gun fire or rifle shells on foreign battle-fields. By simply describing a tired, bloodshot, limping battalion under lethal attack by shells filled with poison gas, the poet registers his unmistakable horror and protest. Pay particular attention to the stanza that starts "If in some smothering dreams, you too could pace. . . ." It contains the core of the poem.

> *Bent double, like old beggars under sacks,* 1
> *Knock-kneed, coughing like hags, we cursed through sludge,*
> *Till on the haunting flares we turned our backs,*
> *And towards our distant rest began to trudge.*
> *Men marched asleep. Many had lost their boots,*
> *But limped on, blood-shod. All went lame, all blind;*
> *Drunk with fatigue; deaf even to the hoots*
> *Of gas-shells dropping softly behind.*
>
> *Gas! GAS! Quick, boys!—An ecstasy of fumbling,* 2
> *Fitting the clumsy helmets just in time,*
> *But someone still was yelling out and stumbling*
> *And flound'ring like a man in fire or lime.—*
> *Dim through the misty panes and thick green light,*
> *As under a green sea, I saw him drowning.*
>
> *In all my dreams before my helpless sight* 3
> *He plunges at me, guttering, choking, drowning.*
>
> *If in some smothering dreams, you too could pace* 4
> *Behind the wagon that we flung him in,*
> *And watch the white eyes writhing in his face,*
> *His hanging face, like a devil's sick of sin,*
> *If you could hear, at every jolt, the blood*
> *Come gargling from the froth-corrupted lungs*
> *Bitter as the cud*
> *Of vile, incurable sores on innocent tongues,—*
> *My friend, you would not tell with such high zest*

To children ardent for some desperate glory,
The old lie:
Dulce et decorum est
Pro patria mori.

Questions for Critical Thinking

1. The Latin quotation, from the Roman poet Horace, means "It is sweet and dignified to die for one's country." How do you see this quotation fitting into the theme of Owen's poem?

2. Why does the poet dwell on the gruesome details of the soldier's death by poisonous gas?

3. What connection, if any, do you see between this poem and the eyewitness account of Futaba Kitayama in "I Thought My Last Hour Had Come" (in this chapter)?

4. Do you have an answer to the pacifists who abase or repudiate war because of its horrors? If so, what is your answer? Are you yourself willing to serve in one of the defense forces of our country? Under what circumstances?

Writing Assignment

Write a brief essay comparing and/or contrasting "Dulce et Decorum Est" with "Come Up from the Fields, Father." State which poem you value more and give specific reasons for your choice.

Writing Advice

Before attempting this assignment, read both poems carefully until you fully understand them. Only then ask yourself which poem you prefer. Chances are that the greater appeal of one poem over the other will be based on whether you prefer a poem that touches your emotions or one that challenges your intellect.

Once you are sure *which* poem you prefer, then you can tackle the job of saying *why* you prefer it. Both poems emphasize the irony associated with war, but one is sentimental, whereas the other is dramatic. When you have decided why you prefer one poem over the other, state your preference with clarity in the opening sentence, as in this example: "Wilfred Owen's 'Dulce et Decorum Est' is a more effective poem than Walt Whitman's 'Come Up from the Fields, Father' because the message is not drowned in sentimentality, but revealed through sharply drawn images."

Support your position thereafter with specific passages from the two poems.

Alternate Writing Assignment

Write an essay describing a war hero you profoundly admire. It can be a mythological person such as Achilles or Hector, a hero from ancient history like Alexander the

Great or Mark Antony, or some more contemporary figure like Winston Churchill, General Dwight Eisenhower, or General Charles De Gaulle. If you know of some heroic act by a common soldier, write about him. You may write about any hero of choice, but stick to a wartime personage.

LITERATURE

COME UP FROM THE FIELDS, FATHER

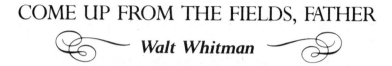
Walt Whitman

Walt Whitman (1819–1892), an American poet whose best-loved poems praise democracy and the brotherhood of man, was known for his vigorous celebration of individual freedom and dignity. Whitman's *Leaves of Grass* (1855), unconventional both in content and poetic technique, has often been praised as one of the most influential collections of poetry in American literature. Whitman started work in 1830 as a printer's devil and later became a compositor. For some time he also taught school and worked as editor of the *Long Islander*, a local newspaper. After publishing *Leaves of Grass* at his own expense, he endured severe negative criticism for his untraditional use of free verse and his exaltation of the human body and sexual love. Despite the intense criticism, Whitman continued to write, his two poems about Lincoln's death, "When Lilacs Last in the Dooryard Bloom'd" and "O Captain! My Captain!" eventually winning him universal praise as a great elegiac writer. Whitman served as a volunteer hospital nurse during the Civil War, writing several war poems, among them the one reprinted below. In 1873, he suffered a paralytic stroke, which caused him to live in a semi-invalid state for the remainder of his life. Whitman had a marked influence on later poets, encouraging them by his example to experiment with poetic form as well as content.

Reading Advice

In this poem Whitman treats the universal tragedy of a mother losing her only son, a common soldier from midwestern farming stock, to war. The poem is written in typical Whitman style—with long rhythmical lines and no rhyme. The movement of the poem arises from the dramatic situation of a mother who receives the heartbreaking news that her son has been mortally wounded during combat. The reader plays the role of silent observer to the dramatic tension.

Come up from the fields, father, here's a letter from our Pete,   1
And come to the front door, mother, here's a letter from thy dear son.

Lo, 'tis autumn,   2
Lo, where the trees, deeper green, yellower and redder,
Cool and sweeten Ohio's villages with leaves fluttering in the moderate
    wind,
Where apples ripe in the orchards hang and grapes on the trellis'd vines,
(Smell you the smell of the grapes on the vines?
Smell you the buckwheat where the bees were lately buzzing?)
Above all, lo, the sky so calm, so transparent after the rain, and with
    wondrous clouds,
Below too, all calm, all vital and beautiful, and the farm prospers well.

Down in the fields all prospers well,   3
But now from the fields come, father, come at the daughter's call,
And come to the entry, mother, to the front door come right away.

Fast as she can she hurries, something ominous, her steps trembling,   4
She does not tarry to smooth her hair nor adjust her cap.

Open the envelope quickly,   5
O this is not our son's writing, yet his name is sign'd,
O a strange hand writes for our dear son, O stricken mother's soul!
All swims before her eyes, flashes with black, she catches the main words
    only,
Sentences broken, gunshot wound in the breast, cavalry skirmish, taken to
    hospital,
At present low, but will soon be better.

Ah, now the single figure to me,   6
Amid all teeming and wealthy Ohio with all its cities and farms,
Sickly white in the face and dull in the head, very faint,
By the jamb of a door leans.

Grieve not so, dear mother (the just-grown daughter speaks through her   7
    sobs,
The little sisters huddle around speechless and dismay'd),
See, dearest mother, the letter says Pete will soon be better.

Alas, poor boy, he will never be better (nor maybe needs to be better, that   8
    brave and simple soul),

While they stand at home at the door he is dead already,
The only son is dead.

But the mother needs to be better,   9
She with thin form presently drest in black,
By day her meals untouch'd, then at night fitfully sleeping, often waking,
In the midnight waking, weeping, longing with one deep longing,
O that she might withdraw unnoticed, silent from life escape and withdraw,
To follow, to seek, to be with her dear dead son.

Questions for Critical Thinking

1. What role does nature play in this poem?

2. In his preface to *Leaves of Grass*, Whitman makes the following statement: "The United States is not best or most in its executives or legislatures, nor in its ambassadors or authors or colleges or churches or parlors, nor even in its newspapers or inventors . . . But always most in the common people." How does the poem "Come Up from the Fields, Father" either support or contradict this statement? Who, in your view, best represents the people of the United States?

3. What is your interpretation of the parenthetical comment in paragraph 8?

4. How does this poem compare or contrast with Pirandelli's "War" given earlier in this chapter? Whom do you pity more, the mother in Whitman's poem or the father in Pirandelli's story? Explain your answer.

Writing Assignment

Write an essay on the importance of the common soldier in time of war.

Writing Advice

Brainstorming as a mode of invention will help you find your main point. On a blank sheet of paper, jot down any thoughts you have on this subject—write down even senseless or incomplete ideas. One student began his list with the following entries:

* Soldiers, soldiers, soldiers—how boring

* I don't want to be one

* But the common soldier is still the backbone of our country's defense

* In a way, the common soldier today is unappreciated

* Tomb of the unknown soldier

* Korea, Vietnam, and Panama are the invasions I know best

* I guess we should give soldiers more credit

* Maybe Veterans Day should be celebrated better

Even this incomplete list reveals some distinct possibilities for use as a topic in an essay. You could suggest, for instance, that even though he is the backbone of our military defense, the common soldier in the United States lacks status and appreciation. Or, you could develop the idea that Veterans Day is filled with fatuous ceremonies when it should be a holiday expressing national gratitude toward those young men who surrendered their lives to defend our homeland. Once you have decided on the point you wish to make, support it with suficient details gathered from your thinking and reading.

Alternate Writing Assignment

Write an essay explaining the importance of the commander of armed forces in time of war. You may choose any war to support your point.

LITERATURE

IN GOYA'S GREATEST SCENES WE SEEM TO SEE
Lawrence Ferlinghetti

Lawrence Ferlinghetti (b. 1919), American poet and publisher, was born in New York. He moved to San Francisco in 1951 to found the City Lights Bookshop, which became a center for writers of the Beat Generation. Although he wrote a novel, *Her* (1960), and numerous essays, Ferlinghetti is still best known for his volumes of verse, among them *A Coney Island of the Mind* (1958), from which the poem below is reprinted; *Starting from San Francisco* (1967); and *Open Eye, Open Heart* (1974). He has been a mentor to numerous Beat writers, including Allen Ginsberg.

Reading Advice

The poet compares Goya's paintings of war (*see* following) with scenes from our modern freeways. What unifies the two images, according to Ferlinghetti, is the unremitting suffering of the people involved. Ferlinghetti's approach is first to draw attention to Goya's canvases, which form the background for blighted landscapes, heaped up cadavers, crying babies, and angry soldiers with bayonets drawn to kill. Then, the poet suddenly shifts to our present-day freeways, which form a background of concrete for alienated, miserable, maimed people driving along in cars. The end result of both scenes is the same—a portrait of humanity in despair.

In Goya's greatest scenes we seem to see
                              the people of the world
          exactly at the moment when
              they first attained the title of
                                  'suffering humanity'   5
          They writhe upon the page
                          in a veritable rage
                                  of adversity
          Heaped up
                  groaning with babies and bayonets   10
                              under cement skies
          in an abstract landscape of blasted trees
              bent statues bats wings and beaks
                  slippery gibbets
              cadavers and carnivorous cocks   15
          and all the final hollering monsters
              of the
                      'imagination of disaster'
          they are so bloody real
                      it is as if they really still existed   20
      And they do
          Only the landscape is changed
      They are still ranged along the roads
          plagued by legionaires
                      false windmills and demented roosters   25

They are the same people
                  only further from home
      on freeways fifty lanes wide
              on a concrete continent
                      spaced by bland billboards   30
                  illustrating imbecile illusions of happiness
      The scene shows fewer tumbrils
                  but more maimed citizens
                          in painted cars
          and they have strange license plates   35
      and engines
              that devour America

Questions for Critical Thinking

1. Go to a library and look up Goya's major paintings in a volume of modern art history. How do these paintings agree with Ferlinghetti's description? What additional comments can you make?

2. Who or what are the "legionnaires," "false windmills," and "demented roosters" of lines 24 and 25? Interpret these symbols to clarify their meanings.

3. Do you agree with the poet's view of the billboards lining our freeways? What are some examples of the illusions to which he refers? Explain all of your answers.

4. Do you support or reject Ferlinghetti's idea that Americans today, living in an era of peace, are as maimed and anguished as the victims of a war? Give reasons for your opinion.

Writing Assignment

Beginning with the line "In (*fill in the blank with a modern painter's name*) greatest scenes we seem to see. . . ," write an essay summarizing the major theme of a painter's work. Of course, you do not need to write in poetic form; lucid prose will do.

Writing Advice

Fulfilling this assignment requires you to carefully study the major paintings of a modern artist. Your college library will have reference books on all major painters. We suggest that you focus on modern painters because they tend to convey familiar themes—society's foibles, human cruelty or indifference, materialism, political and social alienation, hypocrisy, the evils of city life, and so on. Good possibilities, in addition to those represented in this book, are the following artists: Joan Miró, Thomas Hart Benton, José Clemente Orozco, Georgia O'Keefe, Peter Blume, Jacob Lawrence, and Diego Rivera. Be careful to choose an artist whose work particularly interests you and to focus on one painting you think representative of the artist's entire work.

1. Name the painting and describe it—from foreground to background, left to right, or top to bottom—so your reader can visualize the physical representation. Render the colors, as well as shapes, as accurately as possible.

2. After describing the painting, interpret what it means. For instance, if you were to write about Winslow Homer's *The Gulf Stream* (*see* Chapter 6), you would first describe the bare-chested black man, groggy from storm and weak with hunger, lying on the deck of his battered sloop. Mast, rudder, and hatch have washed away, while circling sharks are waiting for him to slip off the sloping deck into the dark blue water highlighted by the foam of rolling whitecaps and red blotches of blood. In the distance looms a menacing twister, while on the horizon sails a shadowy ship. We are left wondering whether the castoff's life will be saved.

3. Now you can draw the meaning from the canvas, perhaps as follows: "Winslow Homer has the ability to portray with apt symbols the human struggle to survive life's difficulties. In his painting *The Gulf Stream*, the central character is no match for the wild and angry ocean that tosses the little sloop about like a cork while mountainous waves filled with ominous-looking sharks rise and fall around the boat. Winslow understood how precarious and overwhelming life can be for frail humanity and how difficult it is to continue the struggle to survive. . . ." and so on. Study your chosen painting carefully and be specific in enumerating its details that support your interpretation.

Alternate Writing Assignment

Write an essay in which you refute Ferlinghetti's poem by arguing that people living in the United States are neither wretched nor maimed but fortunate. Present specific examples of what you consider our blessings.

A R T

THE THIRD OF MAY, 1808: THE EXECUTION OF THE DEFENDERS OF MADRID
Francisco José de Goya y Lucientes

About the Artist

Francisco José de Goya y Lucientes (1746–1824) was a Spanish painter and graphic artist. After studying in Saragossa, Madrid, and Rome, he settled in Madrid and married Josefa Bayeu, sister of Francisco Bayeu, a prominent painter. He attracted royal attention with a series of tapestry designs that realistically reflected the charm of everyday life. Later, the candor of observation in these tapestries blossomed into an attitude of savage satire for which his paintings were known. In 1786, he became court painter for Charles II, and in subsequent years almost all the notables of Madrid sat for him. His portraits of the Duchess of Alba, whom he loved and admired, are considered elegant without being flattering.

In 1781, Goya suffered some kind of poisoning that left him deaf, one consequence of which was an ever-darkening approach to the themes of his paintings. In 1798, Goya created the monumental set of dramatic frescoes in the Church of San Antonio de la Florida, in Madrid. But he is best remembered for the brutal human savagery reflected in his war paintings. For example, *The Third of May, 1808: The Execution of the Defenders of Madrid* is an angry indictment of the inhumanity and atrocity of war. At the age of 70, Goya retired to his villa, whose walls he decorated with a series of nightmarish paintings on macabre subjects, such as *Saturn Devouring His Children* and *Witches' Sabbath*. He died in 1824 after suffering a stroke.

About the Art

In the spring of 1808, while Goya was living in Madrid, Napoleon's Mamelukes, under Murat, marched into the city. While the nobility hid behind doors for fear of their lives, the people, who were practically unarmed, resisted the invaders. The next day, on the third of May, bloody reprisals were made against the populace, many of whom were slaughtered at the city gate. Legend has it that Goya painted the massacre with a spoon, bequeathing us a frightening commentary on the terrible evil of war. We see men with their arms flung into the air, men hiding their faces, men frozen with fear, men clenching their fists, and men lying in pools of blood on the ground, all helpless civilians facing a military firing squad. The impact of the painting is particularly horrifying in its portrayal of war not as an abstract evil but as a scene of nightmarish terror and suffering.

A R T

GUERNICA

Pablo Picasso

About the Artist

Pablo Picasso (1881–1973) was a Spanish painter, sculptor, graphic artist, and ceramist. By general consent, he is the master of the modern school of Paris, the leader of a group of international artists whose pictures transcend the confines of time and place while ignoring the outward appearance of human beings. During his first years in Paris Picasso was dominated by Toulouse Lautrec, who influenced him to paint recognizable harlequins and beggars. But the idea that art in its purest form was, like philosophy, a language of abstraction obsessed Picasso more and more and led him, eventually, to the experiments in cubism that made him famous. By divesting objects of their representational features and reducing them to combinations of geometric planes, Picasso tried to show in a somewhat surrealistic style not how things are but how they are related. In perhaps his most famous surrealistic painting, *Young Girl at the Mirror*, we see a fantastic pattern of silhouettes, colors, and distorted shapes, illustrating the inner turmoils people face.

In his long career Picasso produced thousands of great art works, his technical skills and virtuosity making him master of every instrument known to painting. His works, so free from classical restraints, have inspired artists all over the world to experiment with new forms and structures, and he is honored as the artist who freed art from its bondage to the past and restored it to the principles of invention. He worked with unabated energy until his death at the age of 91.

About the Art

The bombing of the Basque town of Guernica by the German Luftwaffe in April of 1937 led Picasso to create his great mural *Guernica*, a work commissioned by the Republican government of Spain for its pavilion at the Paris Universal Exposition, where, ironically, it hung in close proximity to the German pavilion. Using a geometrical, cubist format, Picasso commemorated the bombing in much the same way the ancient Greeks commemorated their victories or defeats by embellishing the pediments of their temples.

Because it is 25 feet wide, the mural is intended to be viewed slowly from side to side, as well as up and down. Most of the painting is in the form of a triangle, with the apex being a kerosene lamp thrust forward by a woman's arm. Five figures dominate the scene: four women, a child, a fallen warrior, a bull, a horse, and a bird. It is the women who symbolize the horrors of war by running, stumbling, and falling spread eagle on the ground. At the top of the canvas is the surreal image of a watchful eye whose center is an electric light bulb. In the center, a horse braying in agony is juxtaposed to a stolid bull, both perhaps representing the people of Spain.

5–1   *Francisco Goya,* **The Third of May, 1808,** *1814. Approx. 8′8″ × 11′3.″ Museo del Prado, Madrid.*

5–2 *Pablo Picasso, Guernica, 1937. Mural, approx. 11'6" × 25'8." Museo del Prado, Madrid.*

Chapter Writing Assignment

After studying all of the assigned selections about war, including the paintings, write an essay in which you answer one of the following questions:

(a) What is the nature and purpose of war?

(b) Is war an opportunity to display fervent patriotism or is it the vestiges of a barbaric culture?

(c) When is war unavoidable?

(d) What would be the end result for our civilization of a Third World War?

(e) Assuming that all wars are painful to the participants involved, who do you think suffers most during a war?

(f) What kinds of defense mechanisms or self-justifications do participants of war offer?

We encourage you to use ideas, facts, or quotations from the works represented. Be sure that your paper supports a clear thesis.

CHAPTER SIX

❦

Why Do We Suffer?
GOOD AND EVIL

"Why do the wicked prosper and the good suffer?" the Biblical Job asked God, adding his voice to a wail that must have sounded in the unheeding void or the ear of the Almighty since humans first staggered out of the cave and peered at the dawning sun; for all adults eventually and painfully come to see that the world is seldom fair and just. Wicked men and women live to honorable old age and die in their sleep, whereas good hearts and souls perish young, unheralded and unmourned. Disease darts among the mingling throngs of sinner and saint, randomly blighting without regard to meanness or worth. Anyone who has read history, even skimmed it, has come upon grim chronicles such as this one, which tells of the Black Death that swept Europe in 1348, killing a quarter of the population:

> The dreadful pestilence penetrated the sea coast by Southampton and came to Bristol, and there almost the whole population of the town perished, as if it had been seized by sudden death; for few kept their beds more than two or three days, and even half a day. Then the cruel death spread everywhere around, following the course of the sun. And there died at Leicester in the small parish of St. Leonard more than 380 persons, in the parish of Holy Cross, 400; in the parish of St. Margaret's, Leicester, 700; and so in every parish, a great multitude.
> **Henry Knighton,** **The Black Death, 1348. Quoted in** **Eyewitness to History, edited**
> **by John Carey.**

Nor has technology and science, humanity's best hope against the capriciousness of nature with her ghastly train of infirmities and killing diseases, been able to insulate us against such random menace. Today, the AIDS virus slinks through the communal bloodstream, depositing the sickened bodies of the young and hopeful to rot friendless and shunned in hostels of lingering death.

"What cause, what reason, what motive?" we cry out against the monstrous capriciousness of life, where suffering, accident, calamity, and pain strike without regard to guilt or innocence, deserts or worth. We search microscopically through the chronicles of the fallen, anxiously probing for the link between misfortune and wrong. "How old was he?" we ask of the stricken, as if age itself were enough to justify life's malicious blow. "Why did it happen?" we ask, probing for the fatal misstep that would at least make sense of tragedy. Then we wail the everlasting "if-only," the universal cry of the uncomprehending and helpless. Nearly a hundred years after the great ocean liner *Titanic* went down, hundreds still pore with fascination over her final hours and minutes of doom, watching with horror as a noose of happenstance, oversight, and damnation closes in around 1,500 unsuspecting souls. It is not just morbid curiosity: it is the craving we have for a universal principle to justify and explain the wantonly cruel ways of creation.

And so we stumble, in our search for answers, to religion and god.

There have been many gods over the centuries, and many answers have they given to our laments about why we suffer. The Chinese concluded that all vicissitudes originated from the interplay between the opposite forces of yin and yang, which kept life in balance. The ancient Greeks blamed the Fates, three goddesses who wove life's ominous tapestry and assigned human beings their particular lots. For the medieval world, destiny was controlled by a fortune wheel forever and inevitably turning—downward toward bad, and upward toward good. The Elizabethans personified fortune as a fickle and capricious giver and taker, whom their poets and playwrights cursed as a shameless strumpet. The Christian religion proclaimed that in this world undeserved suffering results from the Fall of our original forebears who had once inhabited an idyllic place called Eden. Eternal happiness lay ahead in paradise. There, good will overcome evil, the truth will be known, and all souls will receive their just measures of reward and punishment.

But that far-off place offers scant consolation for most of us. We do not, we cannot see so far ahead as even to glimpse the promised land. We have only this scruffy patch of earth on which we scrabble and suffer, peering hopefully around us for answers. And like the poet who laments, "I am not resigned to the shutting away of loving hearts in the / hard ground," we mourn the passing of friends and loved ones, and wonder how life could be so fastidiously wicked to all—both the good and the evil—without at least pausing to make a distinction.

Why do we suffer? Is it because of a benevolent intelligence, a malevolent one, or an unanswerable emptiness? Is God a hopeful blunder of human imagination? Or are we humans the blunder of God? What part does society play in good and evil?

The essays in this chapter propose different answers to these and other questions thinking men and women commonly ask about suffering. Stephen Jay Gould and David Hume insist that while the operations of pain and pleasure are observable in sensitive beings, nature is neither malevolent nor benevolent, but merely indifferent. Unlike Gould and Hume, Rabbi Harold S. Kushner believes in a benevolent God who, although limited in power, can help human beings come to peaceful terms with suffering.

In the history section, we present two essays about acts of malice and evil that inflicted enormous suffering—one by Bernt Engelmann about a ruthless Nazi official during World War II, and the other by Colin Wilson about Jack the Ripper, that infamous maniacal murderer of London back alleys. We have also included two short stories dealing with suffering dispensed by evil characters. "Barn Burning," by William Faulkner, tells about the suffering of a young boy whose conscience compels him to rebel against his father's unjust ways. "Sonny's Blues," by James Baldwin, reflects the pain and anguish of a black man trying to escape the tawdry life of Harlem to become a great jazz musician. The literature section ends with Robert Frost's "Design," a cynical poem about the dark and terrifying destiny in which all life seems insensibly enmeshed.

The angst of suffering is ably captured in the two paintings that end this chapter—*The Gulf Stream*, by Winslow Homer, and *The Scream*, by Edvard Munch. Homer shows us a sailor abandoned to the ferocity of the maritime elements. Sharks circle the crippled sloop to which he desperately clings, while in the distance sails an unseeing and indifferent ship. Munch depicts the loneliness and isolation of a human being whose inner turmoil and pain are vented in a scream noiselessly depicted on canvas with sharp whorls and colors. We cannot hear the shriek, but we see it horrifyingly graphic on the tormented face of the screamer.

Why do we suffer? "Perform with all your heart your long and heavy task . . . / Then as I do, say naught, but suffer and die," counsels Alfred De Vigny (1797–1863), the French poet, novelist, and dramatist, who walked the earth for 66 years and, before departing, also exclaimed, "I love the majesty of human suffering." There is a grim dignity in his outlook, but bleak consolation. "Whom the Lord loveth he chasteneth," counters the Bible, making of suffering a mark of the Almighty's favor.

These are the extreme positions of the pessimist, whose eyes cannot see beyond the rim of this world, and the devout believer, who would deduce from misfortune a divine plan. Most of us fall somewhere in between. We wonder at the perversity of suffering found everywhere around us; but from it we can grasp no satisfying underlying principle.

PHILOSOPHY

WHY DOES GOD LET PEOPLE SUFFER?
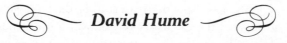
David Hume

David Hume (1711–1776) was a Scottish philosopher and historian. After completing his education in Edinburgh, he travelled to France, where he wrote his first philosophical work, *A Treatise of Human Nature* (1739–1740). His next residence was England, where he published an exhaustive *History of England* (1754–1762) which, despite numerous factual errors, was regarded for many years as the standard history of England. In 1763, Hume returned to France as secretary to the British embassy in Paris.

As a philosopher, Hume is known for his extreme skepticism, believing neither in a soul nor in a substantial world. For him everything boiled down to unreliable human senses whose faulty perceptions, he asserted, were nevertheless irrelevant to the practical concerns of daily life. Other works by Hume include *An Enquiry Concerning Human Understanding* (1748), *An Enquiry Concerning the Principles of Morals* (1751), *The Natural History of Religion* (1755), and *Dialogues Concerning Natural Religion* (1779).

Reading Advice

Reading this essay will require a modern reader to adjust to an eighteenth-century style of erudite writing. Hume is, for his time and the heaviness of his subject, a remarkably clear writer. But he was writing for an audience of sophisticated eighteenth-century readers who would have expected a large dose of heavy scholasticism with their philosophy.

The title of the essay poses a question that you expect to have answered, and Hume does answer with ideas that unfold with logical progression. Notice how first he presents four circumstances that cause creatures to suffer. In each case he argues that an omnipotent and benevolent God could have prevented the circumstance or at least eased it. Next, he suggests that, as a group, created beings are incapable of achieving happiness. Consequently, the only reasonable conclusion possible is that human beings are the abortive products of an amoral, indifferent, blind creative impulse. Hume pursues his argument calmly and without anger or other emotion, gearing his writing to an educated audience familiar with the formality of eighteenth-century philosophical thought.

*T*here seem to be *four* Circumstances, on which depend all, or the greatest Part of the Ills, that molest sensible Creatures; and it is not impossible but all these Circumstances may be necessary and unavoidable. We know so little beyond common Life, or even of common Life, that, with regard to the Oeconomy of a Universe, there is no Conjecture, however wild, which may not be just; nor any one, however plausible, which may not be erroneous. All that belongs to human Understanding, in this deep Ignorance and Obscurity, is to be sceptical, or at least cautious; and not to admit of any Hypothesis, whatever; much less, of any which is supported by no Appearance of Probability. Now this I assert to be the Case with regard to all the Causes of Evil, and the Circumstances, on which it depends. None of them appear to human Reason, in the least degree, necessary or unavoidable; nor can be suppose them such, without the utmost Licence of Imagination.

The *first* Circumstance, which introduces Evil, is that Contrivance or Oeconomy of the animal Creation, by which Pains, as well as Pleasures, are employ'd to excite all Creatures to Action, and make them vigilant in the great Work of Self-preservation. Now Pleasure alone, in its various Degrees, seems to human Understanding sufficient for this Purpose. All Animals might be constantly in a State of Enjoyment; but when urg'd by any of the Necessities of Nature, such as Thirst, Hunger, Weariness; instead of Pain, they might feel a Diminution of Pleasure, by which they might be prompted to seek the Object, which is necessary to their Subsistence. Men pursue Pleasure as eagerly as they avoid Pain; at least, might have been so constituted. It seems, therefore, plainly possible to carry on the Business of Life without any Pain. Why then is any Animal ever render'd susceptible of such a Sensation? If Animals can be free from it an hour, they might enjoy a perpetual Exemption from it; and it requir'd as particular a Contrivance of their Organs to produce that Feeling, as to endow them with Sight, Hearing, or any of the Senses. Shall we conjecture, that such a Contrivance was necessary, without any Appearance of Reason? And shall we build on that Conjecture as on the most certain Truth?

But a Capacity of Pain wou'd not alone produce Pain, were it not for the 3 *second* Circumstance, *viz,* the conducting of the World by general Laws; and this seems no wise necessary to a very perfect Being. It is true; if every thing were conducted by particular Volitions, the Course of Nature wou'd be perpetually broken, and no man cou'd employ his Reason in the Conduct of Life. But might not other particular Volitions remedy this Inconvenience? In short, might not the Deity exterminate all Ill, wherever it were to be found; and produce all Good, without any Preparation or long Progress of Causes and Effects?

Besides, we must consider, that, according to the present Oeconomy of the 4 World, the Course of Nature, tho' suppos'd exactly regular, yet to us appears not so, and many Events are uncertain, and many disappoint our Expectations. Health and Sickness, Calm and Tempest, with an infinite Number of other Accidents, whose Causes are unknown and variable, have a great Influence both on the Fortunes of particular Persons and on the Prosperity of public Societies: And indeed all human Life, in a manner, depends on such Accidents. A Being, therefore, who knows the secret Springs of the Universe, might easily, by particular Volitions, turn all these Accidents to the Good of Mankind, and render the whole World happy, without discovering himself in any Operation. A Fleet, whose Purposes were Salutary to Society, might always meet with a fair Wind: Good Princes enjoy sound Health and long Life: Persons, born to Power and Authority, be fram'd with good Tempers and virtuous Dispositions. A few such Events as these, regularly and wisely conducted, wou'd change the Face of the World; and yet wou'd no more seem to disturb the Course of Nature or confound human Conduct, than the present Oeconomy of things, where the Causes are secret, and variable, and compounded. Some small Touches, given to *Caligula*'s Brain in his Infancy, might have converted him into a *Trajan:*

One Wave, a little higher than the rest, by burying *Caesar* and his Fortune in the bottom of the Ocean, might have restor'd Liberty to a considerable Part of Mankind. There may, for aught we know, be good Reasons, why Providence interposes not in this Manner; but they are unknown to us: And tho' the mere Supposition, that such Reasons exist, may be sufficient to *save* the Conclusion concerning the divine Attributes, yet surely it can never be sufficient to *establish* that Conclusion.

If every thing in the Universe be conducted by general Laws, and if Animals   5 be render'd susceptible of Pain, it scarcely seems possible but some Ill must arise in the various Shocks of Matter, and the various Concurrence and Opposition of general Laws: But this Ill wou'd be very rare, were it not for the *third* Circumstance which I propos'd to mention, *viz,* the great Frugality, with which all Powers and Faculties are distributed to every particular Being. So well adjusted are the Organs and Capacities of all Animals, and so well fitted to their Preservation, that, as far as History or Tradition reaches, there appears not to be any single Species, which has yet been extinguish'd in the Universe. Every Animal has the requisite Endowments; but these Endowments are bestow'd with so scrupulous an Oeconomy, that any considerable Diminution must entirely destroy the Creature. Wherever one Power is encreas'd, there is a proportional Abatement in the others. Animals, which excell in Swiftness, are commonly defective in Force. Those, which possess both, are either imperfect in some of their Senses, or are oppressed with the most craving Wants. The human Species, whose chief Excellency is Reason and Sagacity, is of all others the most necessitous, and the most deficient in bodily Advantages; without Cloaths, without Arms, without Food, without Lodging, without any Convenience of Life, except what they owe to their own Skill and Industry. In short, Nature seems to have form'd an exact Calculation of the Necessities of her Creatures; and like a *rigid Master,* has afforded them little more Powers or Endowments, than what are strictly sufficient to supply those Necessities. An *indulgent Parent* wou'd have bestow'd a large Stock, in order to guard against Accidents, and secure the Happiness and Welfare of the Creature, in the most unfortunate Concurrence of Circumstances. Every Course of Life wou'd not have been so surrounded with Precipices, that the least Departure from the true Path, by Mistake or Necessity, must involve us in Misery and Ruin. Some Reserve, some Fund wou'd have been provided to ensure Happiness; nor wou'd the Powers and the Necessities have been adjusted with so rigid an Oeconomy. The Author of Nature is inconceivably powerful: His Force is suppos'd great, if not altogether inexhaustible: Nor is there any Reason, as far as we can judge, to make him observe this strict Frugality in his Dealings with his Creatures. It wou'd have been better, were his Power extremely limited, to have created fewer Animals, and to have endowed these with more Faculties for their Happiness and Preservation. A Builder is never esteem'd prudent, who undertakes a Plan, beyond what his Stock will enable him to finish.

In order to cure most of the Ills of human Life, I require not that Man   6
should have the Wings of the Eagle, the Swiftness of the Stag, the Force of the
Ox, the Arms of the Lion, the Scales of the Crocodile or Rhinoceros; much
less do I demand the Sagacity of an Angel or Cherubim. I am contented to
take an Encrease in one single Power or Faculty of his Soul. Let him be endow'd
with a greater Propensity to Industry and Labor; a more vigorous Spring and
Activity of Mind; a more constant Bent to Business and Application. Let the
whole Species possess naturally an equal Diligence with that which many
Individuals are able to attain by Habit and Reflection; and the most beneficial
Consequences, without any Allay of Ill, is the most immediate and necessary
Result of this Endowment. Almost all the moral, as well as natural Evils of
human Life arise from Idleness; and were our Species, by the original Constitution of their Frame, exempt from this Vice or Infirmity, the perfect Cultivation of Land, the Improvement of Arts and Manufactures, the exact Execution
of every Office and Duty, immediately follow; and Men at once may fully reach
that State of Society, which is so imperfectly attain'd by the best regulated
Government. But as Industry is a Power, and the most valuable of any, Nature
seems determin'd, suitably to her usual Maxims, to bestow it on men with a
very sparing hand; and rather to punish him severely for his Deficiency in it,
than to reward him for his Attainments. She has so contriv'd his Frame, that
nothing but the most violent Necessity can oblige him to labor, and she employs
all his other Wants to overcome, at least in part, the Want of Diligence, and
to endow him with some Share of a Faculty, of which she has thought fit
naturally to bereave him. Here our Demands may be allow'd very humble, and
therefore the more reasonable. If we requir'd the Endowments of superior
Penetration and Judgment, of a more delicate Taste of Beauty, of a nicer Sen-
sibility to Benevolence and Friendship; we might be told, that we impiously
pretend to break the Order of Nature, that we want to exalt Ourselves into a
higher Rank of Being, that the Presents which we require, not being suitable
to our State and Condition, wou'd only be pernicious to us. But it is hard; I
dare to repeat it, it is hard, that being plac'd in a World so full of Wants and
Necessities; where almost every Being and Element is either our Foe or refuses
us their Assistance; we shou'd also have our own Temper to struggle with, and
shou'd be depriv'd of that Faculty, which can alone fence against these multiply'd Evils.

The *fourth* Circumstance, whence arises the Misery and Ill of the Universe,   7
is the inaccurate Workmanship of all the Springs and Principles of the great
Machine of Nature. It must be acknowledg'd, that there are few Parts of the
Universe, which seem not to serve some Purpose, and whose Removal wou'd
not produce a visible Defect and Disorder in the Whole. The Parts hang all
together; nor can one be touch'd without affecting the rest, in a greater or less
degree. But at the same time, it must be observ'd, that none of these Parts or
Principles, however useful, are so accurately adjusted, as to keep precisely within

those Bounds, in which their Utility consists; but they are, all of them, apt, on every Occasion, to run into the one Extreme or the other. One wou'd imagine, that this grand Production had not receiv'd the last hand of the Maker; so little finish'd is every part, and so coarse are the Strokes, with which it is executed. Thus, the Winds are requisite to convey the Vapours along the Surface of the Globe, and to assist Men in Navigation: But how oft, rising up to Tempests and Hurricanes, do they become pernicious? Rains are necessary to nourish all the Plants and Animals of the Earth: But how often are they defective? how often excessive? Heat is requisite to all Life and Vegetation; but is not always found in the due Proportion. On the Mixture and Secretion of the Humours and Juices of the Body depend the Health and Prosperity of the Animal: But the Parts perform not regularly their proper Function. What more useful than all the Passions of the Mind, Ambition, Vanity, Love, Anger? But how oft do they break their Bounds, and cause the greatest Convulsions in Society? There is nothing so advantageous in the Universe, but what frequently becomes pernicious, by its Excess or Defect; nor has Nature guarded, with the requisite Accuracy, against all Disorder or Confusion. The Irregularity is never, perhaps, so great as to destroy any Species; but is often sufficient to involve the Individuals in Ruin and Misery.

On the Concurrence, then of these *four* Circumstances does all, or the greatest Part of natural Evil depend. Were all living Creatures incapable of Pain, or were the World administer'd by particular Volitions, Evil never cou'd have found Access into the Universe: And were Animals endow'd with a large Stock of Powers and Faculties, beyond what strict Necessity requires; or were the several Springs and Principles of the Universe so accurately fram'd as to preserve always the just Temperament and Medium; there must have been very little Ill in comparison of what we feel at present. What then shall we pronounce on this Occasion? Shall we say, that these Circumstances are not necessary, and that they might easily have been alter'd in the Contrivance of the Universe? This Decision seems too presumptuous for Creatures, so blind and ignorant. Let us be more modest in our Conclusions. Let us allow, that, if the Goodness of the Deity (I mean a Goodness like the human) cou'd be establish'd on any tolerable Reasons *a priori,* these Phaenomena, however untoward, wou'd not be sufficient to subvert that Principle; but might easily, in some unknown manner, be reconcilable to it. But let us still assert, that as this Goodness is not antecedently establish'd, but must be inferr'd from the Phaenomena, there can be no Grounds for such an Inference, while there are so many Ills in the Universe, and while these Ills might so easily have been remedy'd, as far as human Understanding can be allow'd to judge on such a Subject. I am Sceptic enough to allow, that the bad Appearances, notwithstanding all my Reasonings, may be compatible with such Attributes as you suppose: But surely they can never prove these Attributes. Such a Conclusion cannot result from Scepticism;

8

but must arise from the Phaenomena, and from our Confidence in the Reasonings, which we deduce from these Phaenomena.

Look round this Universe. What an immense Profusion of Beings, animated and organiz'd, sensible and active! You admire this prodigious Variety and Fecundity. But inspect a little more narrowly these living Existences, the only Beings worth regarding. How hostile and destructive to each other! How insufficient all of them for their own Happiness! How contemptible or odious to the Spectator! The whole presents nothing but the Idea of a blind Nature, impregnated by a great vivifying Principle, and pouring forth from her Lap, without Discernment or parental Care, her maim'd and abortive Children.   9

Here the Manichaean System occurs as a proper Hypothesis to solve the Difficulty: And no doubt, in some respects, it is very specious, and has more Probability than the common Hypothesis, by giving a plausible Account of the strange Mixture of Good and Ill, which appears in Life. But if we consider, on the other hand, the perfect Uniformity and Agreement of the Parts of the Universe, we shall not discover in it any Marks of the Combat of a malevolent with a benevolent Being. There is indeed an Opposition of Pains and Pleasures in the Feelings of sensible Creatures: But are not all the Operations of Nature carry'd on by an Opposition of Principles, of Hot and Cold, Moist and Dry, Light and Heavy? The true Conclusion is, that the original Source of all things is entirely indifferent to all these Principles, and has no more Regard to Good above Ill than to Heat above Cold, or to Drought above Moisture, or to Light above Heavy.   10

There may *four* Hypotheses be fram'd concerning the first Causes of the Universe; *that* they are endow'd with perfect Goodness, *that* they have perfect Malice, *that* they are opposite and have both Goodness and Malice, *that* they have neither Goodness nor Malice. Mixt Phaenomena can never prove the two former unmixt Principles. And the Uniformity and Steadiness of general Laws seem to oppose the third. The fourth, therefore, seems by far the most probable.   11

Questions for Critical Thinking

1. Do you agree with Hume's idea (*see* paragraph 2) that human beings pursue pleasure as eagerly as they avoid pain? Supply examples to support your answer.

2. What would be your attitude towards a world in which nature always operated for the good of mankind?

3. Hume wishes that human beings had been endowed with a more diligent and industrious nature because, according to him, most evils in life result from idleness. What argument, if any, can you present in favor of having human beings remain as they are presently endowed?

4. What is your opinion of Hume's idea, expressed in paragraph 5, that it would

have been better if God had created fewer living beings but had endowed them with greater ability to be happy and to preserve themselves?

5. What purpose does paragraph 8 serve? How necessary is it?

6. In paragraph 9, Hume suggests that if you inspect the world around you carefully, you will find it hostile, destructive, and odious. What is your reaction to this statement?

7. How does Hume explain the interplay between good and evil in the world? Do you agree with him? Why or why not?

Writing Assignment

Write an essay in which you refute Hume by arguing that nature is purposeful and harmonious.

Writing Advice

This essay is an opportunity for you to play the philosopher. Remember, however, that being philosophical does not necessarily mean abandoning lucidity, brevity, or concreteness.

Your assignment is to argue against Hume's doctrine of pessimism. You must answer the question of why people suffer, but you must have a justifying answer quite different in its tone of optimism from Hume's. Perhaps the safest way to proceed is to divide your essay into the same main points that Hume uses (see "reading advice"). State his position; then argue against it by stating your position, which should be markedly different from his.

Since Hume's thesis is that people suffer because the world is controlled neither by evil nor by benevolent forces but by an indifferent nature, your thesis must propose a different cause for suffering, based on the view that nature is controlled by purposeful, benign forces. Notice that Hume uses specific examples from nature to add vividness and spice to what otherwise might be a deadly boring essay; you must do likewise.

Note also that this is probably the sort of essay best done by the believer in a personal creed of optimism than by the skeptic. It is, of course, possible for a nonbeliever to write a strong essay arguing that nature and the life force are secretly benign, but such an assignment should be far easier for the convinced. Our own view is that when it comes to writing on philosophical topics, the writer is smart to opt for one in which he or she has strong convictions.

Alternate Writing Assignment

1. Reread paragraph 6 of Hume's essay. If you could have an improvement in one human faculty, which one would it be? Write an essay answering this question.

2. Write an essay in which you pinpoint the source of most human suffering. This

essay need not be philosophical but simply practical. For instance, you might suggest laziness as one source, or capricious misfortune, or overpopulation.

PHILOSOPHY

NONMORAL NATURE
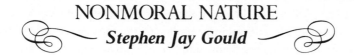
Stephen Jay Gould

Stephen Jay Gould (b. 1941 in N.Y.C.) is a Harvard University professor who teaches geology, biology, and the history of science. He writes a regular column—"This View of Life"—for *Natural History* magazine and is much admired both for his elegant literary style and his ability to render the activities of nature dramatic and fascinating. He is known as a staunch supporter of Darwin's theory of evolutionary biology and insists that it represents "one of the great ideas developed by science." His books include *Ever Since Darwin* (1977) and *Hen's Teeth and Horse's Toes*, from which the essay below is reprinted.

Reading Advice

Gould is the thinking person's columnist. The article below comes from one of his more provocative columns, which tackles the problem of evil and suffering in nature. Gould's aim is not only to discuss this theme philosophically but also to survey the opinions of scientists and theologians of an earlier day as they too searched nature for signs of a beneficent god. Predators, says Gould, are the most philosophically troubling of all creatures to those who would believe that "God's in his heaven, All's right with the world," as the poet Robert Browning (1812–1889) put it.

Especially worrying to thinkers on the subject is the predation of the ichneumon wasp, which first paralyzes then lays its eggs on a caterpillar, leaving its immobile victim to be devoured slowly by the parasitic larvae. In forging his argument supporting a nonmoral nature, Gould focuses on the ichneumon wasp's gruesome parasitism, presenting some typical nineteenth-century interpretations of this predatory act as anthropomorphic rationalizations. For the most part, Gould's explanations are typically lucid and easy to follow, but some of his more technical words will have even the sophisticated reader grabbing for the dictionary.

*W*hen the Right Honorable and   1
Reverend Francis Henry, earl of Bridgewater, died in February, 1829, he left £8,000 to support a series of books "on the power, wisdom and goodness of

God, as manifested in the creation." William Buckland, England's first official academic geologist and later dean of Westminster, was invited to compose one of the nine Bridgewater Treatises. In it he discussed the most pressing problem of natural theology; if God is benevolent and the Creation displays his "power, wisdom and goodness," than why are we surrounded with pain, suffering, and apparently senseless cruelty in the animal world?

Buckland considered the depredation of "carnivorous races" as the primary challenge to an idealized world where the lion might dwell with the lamb. He resolved the issue to his satisfaction by arguing that carnivores actually increase "the aggregate of animal enjoyment" and "diminish that of pain." Death, after all, is swift and relatively painless, victims are spared the ravages of decrepitude and senility, and populations do not outrun their food supply to the greater sorrow of all. God knew what he was doing when he made lions. Buckland concluded in hardly concealed rapture:

> The appointment of death by the agency of carnivora, as the ordinary termination of animal existence, appears therefore in its main results to be a dispensation of benevolence; it deducts much from the aggregate amount of the pain of universal death; it abridges, and almost annihilates, throughout the brute creation, the misery of disease, and accidental injuries, and lingering decay; and imposes such salutary restraint upon excessive increase of numbers, that the supply of food maintains perpetually a due ratio to the demand. The result is, that the surface of the land and depths of the waters are ever crowded with myriads of animated beings, the pleasures of whose life are coextensive with its duration; and which throughout the little day of existence that is allotted to them, fulfill with joy the functions for which they were created.

We may find a certain amusing charm in Buckland's vision today, but such arguments did begin to address "the problem of evil" for many of Buckland's contemporaries—how could a benevolent God create such a world of carnage and bloodshed? Yet this argument could not abolish the problem of evil entirely, for nature includes many phenomena far more horrible in our eyes than simple predation. I suspect that nothing evokes greater disgust in most of us than slow destruction of a host by an internal parasite—gradual ingestion, bit by bit, from the inside. In no other way can I explain why *Alien,* an uninspired, grade-C, formula horror film, should have won such a following. That single scene of Mr. Alien, popping forth as a baby parasite from the body of a human host, was both sickening and stunning. Our nineteenth-century forebears maintained similar feelings. The greatest challenge to their concept of a benevolent deity was not simple predation—but slow death by parasitic ingestion. The classic case, treated at length by all great naturalists, invoked the so-called ichneumon fly. Buckland had sidestepped the major issue.

The "ichneumon fly," which provoked such concern among natural theologians, was actually a composite creature representing the habits of an enormous tribe. The Ichneumonoidea are a group of wasps, not flies, that include more species than all the vertebrates combined (wasps, with ants and bees, constitute the order Hymenoptera; flies, with their two wings—wasps have four—form the order Diptera). In addition, many non-ichneumoid wasps of similar habits were often cited for the same grisly details. Thus, the famous story did not merely implicate a single aberrant species (perhaps a perverse leakage from Satan's realm), but hundreds of thousands—a large chunk of what could only be God's creation.

The ichneumons, like most wasps, generally live freely as adults but pass their larval life as parasites feeding on the bodies of other animals, almost invariably members of their own phylum, the Arthropoda. The most common victims are caterpillars (butterfly and moth larvae), but some ichneumons prefer aphids and others attack spiders. Most hosts are parasitized as larvae, but some adults are attacked, and many tiny ichneumons inject their brood directly into the egg of their host.

The free-flying females locate an appropriate host and then convert it to a food factory for their own young. Parasitologists speak of ectoparasitism when the uninvited guest lives on the surface of its host, and endoparasitism when the parasite dwells within. Among endoparasitic ichneumons, adult females pierce the host with their ovipositor and deposit eggs within. (The ovipositor, a thin tube extending backward from the wasp's rear end, may be many times as long as the body itself.) Usually, the host is not otherwise inconvenienced for the moment, at least until the eggs hatch and the ichneumon larvae begin their grim work of interior excavation.

Among ectoparasites, however, many females lay their eggs directly upon the host's body. Since an active host would easily dislodge the egg, the ichneumon mother often simultaneously injects a toxin that paralyzes the caterpillar or other victim. The paralysis may be permanent, and the caterpillar lies, alive but immobile, with the agent of its future destruction secure on its belly. The egg hatches, the helpless caterpillar twitches, the wasp larva pierces and begins its grisly feast.

Since a dead and decaying caterpillar will do the wasp larva no good, it eats in a pattern that cannot help but recall, in our inappropriate, anthropocentric interpretation, the ancient English penalty for treason—drawing and quartering, with its explicit object of extracting as much torment as possible by keeping the victim alive and sentient. As the king's executioner drew out and burned his client's entrails, so does the ichneumon larva eat fat bodies and digestive organs first, keeping the caterpillar alive by preserving intact the essential heart and central nervous system. Finally, the larva completes its work and kills its victim, leaving behind the caterpillar's empty shell. Is it any wonder that ichneumons, not snakes or lions, stood as the paramount challenge to God's benevolence during the heyday of natural theology?

As I read through the nineteenth- and twentieth-century literature on ich-   9
neumons, nothing amused me more than the tension between an intellectual
knowledge that wasps should not be described in human terms and a literary
or emotional inability to avoid the familiar categories of epic and narrative,
pain and destruction, victim and vanquisher. We seem to be caught in the
mythic structures of our own cultural sagas, quite unable, even in our basic
descriptions, to use any other language than the metaphors of battle and conquest. We cannot render this corner of natural history as anything but story,
combining the themes of grim horror and fascination and usually ending not
so much with pity for the caterpillar as with admiration for the efficiency of
the ichneumon.

I detect two basic themes in most epic descriptions: the struggles of prey   10
and the ruthless efficiency of parasites. Although we acknowledge that we may
be witnessing little more than automatic instinct or physiological reaction, still
we describe the defenses of hosts as though they represented conscious struggles. Thus, aphids kick and caterpillars may wriggle violently as wasps attempt
to insert their ovipositors. The pupa of the tortoiseshell butterfly (usually
considered an inert creature silently awaiting its conversion from duckling to
swan) may contort its abdominal region so sharply that attacking wasps are
thrown into the air. The caterpillars of *Hapalia,* when attacked by the wasp
Apanteles machaeralis, drop suddenly from their leaves and suspend themselves
in air by a silken thread. But the wasp may run down the thread and insert its
eggs nonetheless. Some hosts can encapsulate the injected egg with blood cells
that aggregate and harden, thus suffocating the parasite.

J. H. Fabre, the great nineteenth-century French entomologist, who remains   11
to this day the preeminently literate natural historian of insects, made a special
study of parasitic wasps and wrote with an unabashed anthropocentrism about
the struggles of paralyzed victims (see his books *Insect Life* and *The Wonders of
Instinct*). He describes some imperfectly paralyzed caterpillars that struggle so
violently every time a parasite approaches that the wasp larvae must feed with
unusual caution. They attach themselves to a silken strand from the roof of
their burrow and descend upon a safe and exposed part of the caterpillar:

> The grub is at dinner: head downwards, it is digging into the limp belly of one of
> the caterpillars. . . . At the least sign of danger in the heap of caterpillars, the
> larva retreats . . . and climbs back to the ceiling, where the swarming rabble can-
> not reach it. When peace is restored, it slides down [its silken cord] and returns
> to table, with its head over the viands and its rear upturned and ready to with-
> draw in case of need.

In another chapter, he describes the fate of a paralyzed cricket: 12

> One may see the cricket, bitten to the quick, vainly move its antennae and
> abdominal styles, open and close its empty jaws, and even move a foot, but the
> larva is safe and searches its vitals with impunity. What an awful nightmare for
> the paralyzed cricket!

Fabre even learned to feed paralyzed victims by placing a syrup of sugar and   13
water on their mouthparts—thus showing that they remained alive, sentient,
and (by implication) grateful for any palliation of their inevitable fate. If Jesus,
immobile and thirsting on the cross, received only vinegar from his tormentors,
Fabre at least could make an ending bittersweet.

The second theme, ruthless efficiency of the parasites, leads to the opposite   14
conclusion—grudging admiration for the victors. We learn of their skill in
capturing dangerous hosts often many times larger than themselves. Caterpillars
may be easy game, but psammocharid wasps prefer spiders. They must insert
their ovipositors in a safe and precise spot. Some leave a paralyzed spider in its
own burrow. *Planiceps hirsutus,* for example, parasitizes a California trapdoor
spider. It searches for spider tubes on sand dunes, then digs into nearby sand
to disturb the spider's home and drive it out. When the spider emerges, the
wasp attacks, paralyzes its victim, drags it back into its own tube, shuts and
fastens the trapdoor, and deposits a single egg upon the spider's abdomen.
Other psammocharids will drag a heavy spider back to a previously prepared
cluster of clay or mud cells. Some amputate a spider's legs to make the passage
easier. Others fly back over water, skimming a buoyant spider along the surface.

Some wasps must battle with other parasites over a host's body. *Rhyssella*   15
curvipes can detect the larvae of wood wasps deep within alder wood and drill
down to a potential victim with its sharply ridged ovipositor. *Pseudorhyssa alpestris,*
a related parasite, cannot drill directly into wood since its slender ovipositor
bears only rudimentary cutting ridges. It locates the holes made by *Rhyssella,*
inserts its ovipositor, and lays an egg on the host (already conveniently paralyzed
by *Rhyssella*), right next to the egg deposited by its relative. The two eggs hatch
at about the same time, but the larva of *Pseudorhyssa* has a bigger head bearing
much larger mandibles. *Pseudorhyssa* seizes the smaller *Rhyssella* larva, destroys
it, and proceeds to feast upon a banquet already well prepared.

Other praises for the efficiency of mothers invoke the themes of early, quick,   16
and often. Many ichneumons don't even wait for their hosts to develop into
larvae, but parasitize the egg directly (larval wasps may then either drain the
egg itself or enter the developing host larva). Others simply move fast. *Apanteles*
militaris can deposit up to seventy-two eggs in a single second. Still others are
doggedly persistent. *Aphidius gomezi* females produce up to 1,500 eggs and can
parasitize as many as 600 aphids in a single working day. In a bizarre twist upon
"often," some wasps indulge in polyembryony, a kind of iterated supertwining.
A single egg divides into cells that aggregate into as many as 500 individuals.
Since some polyembryonic wasps parasitize caterpillars much larger than themselves and may lay up to six eggs in each, as many as 3,000 larvae may develop
within, and feed upon a single host. These wasps are endoparasites and do not
paralyze their victims. The caterpillars writhe back and forth, not (one suspects)
from pain, but merely in response to the commotion induced by thousands of
wasp larvae feeding within.

Maternal efficiency is often matched by larval aptitude. I have already men-   17
tioned the pattern of eating less essential parts first, thus keeping the host alive
and fresh to its final and merciful dispatch. After the larva digests every edible
morsel of its victim (if only to prevent later fouling of its abode by decaying
tissue), it may still use the outer shell of its host. One aphid parasite cuts a
hole in the bottom of its victim's shell, glues the skeleton to a leaf by sticky
secretions from its salivary gland, and then spins a cocoon to pupate within
the aphid's shell.

In using inappropriate anthropocentric language for this romp through the   18
natural history of ichneumons, I have tried to emphasize just why these wasps
became a preeminent challenge to natural theology—the antiquated doctrine
that attempted to infer God's essence from the products of his creation. I have
used twentieth-century examples for the most part, but all themes were known
and stressed by the great nineteenth-century natural theologians. How then
did they square the habits of these wasps with the goodness of God? How did
they extract themselves from this dilemma of their own making?

The strategies were as varied as the practitioners; they shared only the theme   19
of special pleading for an a priori doctrine—our naturalists *knew* that God's
benevolence was lurking somewhere behind all these tales of apparent horror.
Charles Lyell, for example, in the first edition of his epochal *Principles of Geology*
(1830–1833), decided that caterpillars posed such a threat to vegetation that
any natural checks upon them could only reflect well upon a creating deity,
for caterpillars would destroy human agriculture "did not Providence put causes
in operation to keep them in due bounds."

The Reverend William Kirby, rector of Barham, and Britain's foremost ento-   20
mologist, chose to ignore the plight of caterpillars and focused instead upon
the virtue of mother love displayed by wasps in provisioning their young with
such care.

> The great object of the female is to discover a proper nidus for her eggs. In
> search of this she is in constant motion. Is the caterpillar of a butterfly or moth
> the appropriate food for her young? You see her alight upon the plants where
> they are most usually to be met with, run quickly over them, carefully examining
> every leaf, and, having found the unfortunate object of her search, insert her
> sting into its flesh, and there deposit an egg. . . . The active Ichneumon braves
> every danger, and does not desist until her courage and address have insured
> subsistence for one of her future progeny.

Kirby found this solicitude all the more remarkable because the female wasp   21
will never see her child and enjoy the pleasures of parenthood. Yet love compels
her to danger nonetheless:

> A very large proportion of them are doomed to die before their young come into
> existence. But in these the passion is not extinguished. . . . When you witness the
> solicitude with which they provide for the security and sustenance of their future

*young, you can scarcely deny to them love for a progeny they are never destined
to behold.*

Kirby also put in a good word for the marauding larvae, praising them for   22
their forbearance in eating selectively to keep their caterpillar alive. Would we
all husband our resources with such care!

> *In this strange and apparently cruel operation one circumstance is truly remark-
> able. The larva of the Ichneumon, though every day, perhaps for months, it
> gnaws the inside of the caterpillar, and though at last it has devoured almost
> every part of it except the skin and intestines, carefully all this time it avoids
> injuring the vital organs, as if aware that its own existence depends on that of the
> insect upon which it preys! . . . What would be the impression which a similar
> instance amongst the race of quadrupeds would make upon us? If, for example,
> an animal . . . should be found to feed upon the inside of a dog, devouring only
> those parts not essential to life, while it cautiously left uninjured the heart, arter-
> ies, lungs, and intestines,—should we not regard such an instance as a perfect
> prodigy, as an example of instinctive forbearance almost miraculous? [The last
> three quotes come from the 1856, and last pre-Darwinian, edition of Kirby and
> Spence's Introduction to Entomology.]*

This tradition of attempting to read moral meaning from nature did not   23
cease with the triumph of evolutionary theory in 1859—for evolution could
be read as God's chosen method of peopling our planet, and ethical messages
might still populate nature. Thus, St. George Mivart, one of Darwin's most
effective evolutionary critics and a devout Catholic, argued that "many amiable
and excellent people" had been misled by the apparent suffering of animals for
two reasons. First, whatever the pain, "physical suffering and moral evil are
simply incommensurable." Since beasts are not moral agents, their feelings
cannot bear any ethical message. But secondly, lest our visceral sensitivities still
be aroused, Mivart assures that animals must feel little, if any, pain. Using
a favorite racist argument of the time—that "primitive" people suffer far less
than advanced and cultured folk—Mivart extrapolated further down the ladder
of life into a realm of very limited pain indeed: Physical suffering, he argued,

> *depends greatly upon the mental condition of the sufferer. Only during con-
> sciousness does it exist, and only in the most highly organized men does it reach
> its acme. The author has been assured that lower races of men appear less keenly
> sensitive to physical suffering than do more cultivated and refined human beings.
> Thus only in man can there really be any intense degree of suffering, because only
> in him is there that intellectual recollection of past moments and that anticipa-
> tion of future ones, which constitute in great part the bitterness of suffering. The
> momentary pang, the present pain, which beasts endure, though real enough, is
> yet, doubtless, not to be compared as to its intensity with the suffering which is
> produced in man through his high prerogative of self-consciousness [from Genesis
> of Species, 1871].*

It took Darwin himself to derail this ancient tradition—and he proceeded   24
in the gentle way to characteristic of his radical intellectual approach to nearly

everything. The ichneumons also troubled Darwin greatly and he wrote of them to Asa Gray in 1860:

> I own that I cannot see as plainly as others do, and as I should wish to do, evidence of design and beneficence on all sides of us. There seems to me too much misery in the world. I cannot persuade myself that a beneficent and omnipotent God would have designedly created the Ichneumonidae with the express intention of their feeding within the living bodies of Caterpillars, or that a cat should play with mice.

Indeed, he had written with more passion to Joseph Hooker in 1856: "What a book a devil's chaplain might write on the clumsy, wasteful, blundering, low, and horribly cruel works of nature!"

This honest admission—that nature is often (by our standards) cruel and 25 that all previous attempts to find a lurking goodness behind everything represent just so much special pleading—can lead in two directions. One might retain the principle that nature holds moral messages, but reverse the usual perspective and claim that morality consists in understanding the ways of nature and doing the opposite. Thomas Henry Huxley advanced this argument in his famous essay on *Evolution and Ethics* (1893):

> The practice of that which is ethically best—what we call goodness or virtue— involves a course of conduct which, in all respects, is opposed to that which leads to success in the cosmic struggle for existence. In place of ruthless self-assertion it demands self-restraint; in place of thrusting aside, or treading down, all competitors, it requires that the individual shall not merely respect, but shall help his fellows. . . . It repudiates the gladiatorial theory of existence. . . . Laws and moral precepts are directed to the end of curbing the cosmic process.

The other argument, radical in Darwin's day but more familiar now, holds 26 that nature simply is as we find it. Our failure to discern a universal good does not record any lack of insight or ingenuity, but merely demonstrates that nature contains no moral messages framed in human terms. Morality is a subject for philosophers, theologians, students of the humanities, indeed for all thinking people. The answers will not be read passively from nature; they do not, and cannot, arise from the data of science. The factual state of the world does not teach us how we, with our powers for good and evil, should alter or preserve it in the most ethical manner.

Darwin himself tended toward this view, although he could not, as a man 27 of his time, thoroughly abandon the idea that laws of nature might reflect some higher purpose. He clearly recognized that specific manifestations of those laws—cats playing with mice, and ichneumon larvae eating caterpillars—could not embody ethical messages, but he somehow hoped that unknown higher laws might exist "with the details, whether good or bad, left to the working out of what we may call chance."

Since ichneumons are a detail, and since natural selection is a law regulating 28 details, the answer to the ancient dilemma of why such cruelty (in our terms) exists in nature can only be that there isn't any answer—and that framing the question "in our terms" is thoroughly inappropriate in a natural world neither made for us nor ruled by us. It just plain happens. It is a strategy that works for ichneumons and that natural selection has programmed into their behavioral repertoire. Caterpillars are not suffering to teach us something; they have simply been outmaneuvered, for now, in the evolutionary game. Perhaps they will evolve a set of adequate defenses sometimes in the future, thus sealing the fate of ichneumons. And perhaps, indeed probably, they will not.

Another Huxley, Thomas's grandson Julian, spoke for this position, using as   29
an example—yes, you guessed it—the ubiquitous ichneumons:

> *Natural selection, in fact, though like the mills of God in grinding slowly and grinding small, has few other attributes that a civilized religion would call divine. . . . Its products are just as likely to be aesthetically, morally, or intellectually repulsive to us as they are to be attractive. We need only think of the ugliness of* Sacculina *or a bladder-worm, the stupidity of a rhinoceros or a stegosaur, the horror of a female mantis devouring its mate or a brood of ichneumon flies slowly eating out a caterpillar.*

If nature is nonmoral, then evolution cannot teach any ethical theory at all.   30
The assumption that it can has abetted a panoply of social evils that ideologues falsely read into nature from their beliefs—eugenics and (misnamed) social Darwinism prominently among them. Not only did Darwin eschew any attempt to discover an antireligious ethic in nature, he also expressly stated his personal bewilderment about such deep issues as the problem of evil. Just a few sentences after invoking the ichneumons, and in words that express both the modesty of this splendid man and the compatibility, through lack of contact, between science and true religion, Darwin wrote to Asa Gray,

> *I feel most deeply that the whole subject is too profound for the human intellect. A dog might as well speculate on the mind of Newton. Let each man hope and believe what he can.*

Questions for Critical Thinking

1. Reread paragraph 20. Why does Gould assert that a truly moral nature would be self-destructive? What is your view of Gould's opinion?

2. Gould believes that a panoply of social evils has resulted from an attempt to extract codes of morality and ethics from the evolutionary theory. To which specific evils do you suppose he is referring? Do you agree with him? Why or why not?

3. What message, moral or otherwise, do you deduce from biological nature?

4. Why do you suppose Gould chose the example of the ichneumon wasp to make his point about the nonmoral aspect of nature? Can you think of another example that might also be appropriate?

5. What were four specific rationalizations used by nineteenth-century thinkers to excuse the suffering caused in nature? Critically analyze each rationalization by pointing out its weaknesses.

6. In reading Gould's account, which reaction hit you strongest—pity for the caterpillar or admiration for the wasp? Explain your answer.

7. How would David Hume explain the actions of the ichneumon wasp? (*See*, "Why Does God Let People Suffer?" in this chapter).

Writing Assignment

In order to clarify your own view of nature, write an essay in which you judge nature as either moral, immoral, or nonmoral.

Writing Advice

This assignment requires that you think not only about the operations of nature but also speculate about its controlling force or forces. In other words, you must import a religious or philosophical perspective into your discussion. For example, if you believe in a benevolent God, then you must deal with his control or lack of control over those aspects of nature that appear cruel. Indeed, you must explain the seeming crush of evil in nature.

Because the problem is painfully complex and often enigmatic, a good way to proceed is to use Gould's technique of focusing on concrete aspects of nature such as animal habits. If you do not believe in God or if you believe God remains aloof from creation, then your views of nature will doubtless be similar to that of Gould's. If, on the other hand, your commitment is to a benevolent God, then you will disagree with Gould and will need to explain the existence of so much carnage in nature.

We suggest the following organization for your essay:

1. Explanation of your belief about how nature is controlled.

2. Appropriate descriptions from nature.

3. Explanation of why so much slaughter, butchery, and bloodshed exist in nature.

4. Thesis statement (to be placed either at the end or at the beginning of the essay).

Alternate Writing Assignments

1. Write an essay in which you contrast two incidents observed in the animal kingdom—one showing selfishness, the other altruism. The conclusion you draw from the contrast can serve as your thesis.

2. Write an essay in which you argue either that one can or that one cannot extract moral meaning from nature.

PHILOSOPHY

THE STORY OF A MAN NAMED JOB

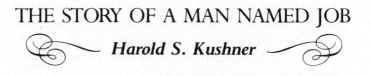
Harold S. Kushner

Harold S. Kushner (b. 1935) is an American rabbi, who was educated at Columbia University and Jewish Theological Seminary. He became widely known in 1981, following the publication of his book *When Bad Things Happen to Good People*, occasioned by the death of his son to progeria, a rare genetic disease. The book, which struck a responsive chord in thousands of hearts troubled by inexplicable suffering and pain, became an instant bestseller.

Reading Advice

This chapter, taken from Rabbi Kushner's book *When Bad Things Happen to Good People* is in the format of a sermon. Following the rules of proper homiletics, the author first summarizes the history of the Biblical story of Job and then relates Job's situation to us, the readers, with the intention of teaching us about universal justice. The author's approach is first to present various propositions about God and the way he rewards or punishes human beings; then, to analyze each proposition in terms of its logic and consequences. Finally, he pinpoints what he considers the best solution and urges that we accept it.

Though his subject is both theological and primal in its philosophical importance, Kushner explains himself simply and well. Even when he covers the three logical propositions about God and Job, he still manages to keep the discussion simple and brisk. Most readers will find this article rather straightforward and easy to grasp.

About twenty-five hundred years ago, 1 a man lived whose name we will never know, but who has enriched the minds and lives of human beings ever since. He was a sensitive man who saw good people getting sick and dying around him while proud and selfish people prospered. He heard all the learned, clever, and pious attempts to explain life, and he was as dissatisfied with them as we are today. Because he was a person of rare literary and intellectual gifts, he wrote a long philosophical poem on the subject of why God lets bad things happen to good people. This poem appears in the Bible as the Book of Job.

Thomas Carlyle called the Book of Job "the most wonderful poem of any   2
age and language; our first, oldest statement of the never-ending problem—
man's destiny and God's way with him here in this earth. . . . There is nothing
written in the Bible or out of it of equal literary merit." I have been fascinated
by the Book of Job ever since I learned of its existence, and have studied it,
reread it, and taught it any number of times. It has been said that just as every
actor yearns to play Hamlet, every Bible student yearns to write a commentary
on the Book of Job. It is a hard book to understand, a profound and beautiful
book on the most profound of subjects, the question of why God lets good
people suffer. Its argument is hard to follow because, through some of the
characters, the author presents views he himself probably did not accept, and
because he wrote in an elegant Hebrew which, thousands of years later, is often
hard to translate. If you compare two English translations of Job, you may
wonder if they are both translations of the same book. One of the key verses
can be taken to mean either "I will fear God" or "I will not fear God," and
there is no way of knowing for sure what the author intended. The familiar
statement of faith "I know that my Redeemer lives" may mean instead "I would
rather be redeemed while I am still alive." But much of the book is clear and
forceful, and we can try our interpretive skills on the rest.

Who was Job, and what is the book that bears his name? A long, long time   3
ago, scholars believe, there must have been a well-known folk story, a kind of
morality fable told to reinforce people's religious sentiments, about a pious man
named Job. Job was so good, so perfect, that you realize at once that you are
not reading about a real-life person. This is a "once-upon-a-time" story about
a good man who suffered.

One day, the story goes, Satan appears before God to tell Him about all the   4
sinful things people were doing on earth. God says to Satan, "Did you notice
My servant Job? There is no one on earth like him, a thoroughly good man
who never sins." Satan answers God, "Of course Job is pious and obedient. You
make it worth his while, showering riches and blessings on him. Take away
those blessings and see how long he remains Your obedient servant."

God accepts Satan's challenge. Without in any way telling Job what is going   5
on, God destroys Job's house and cattle and kills his children. He afflicts Job
with boils all over his body, so that his every moment becomes physical torture.
Job's wife urges him to curse God, even if that means God's striking him dead.
He can't do anything worse to Job than He already has done. Three friends
come to console Job, and they too urge him to give up his piety, if this is the
reward it brings him. But Job remains steadfast in his faith. Nothing that happens
to him can make him give up his devotion to God. At the end, God appears,
scolds the friends for their advice, and rewards Job for his faithfulness. God
gives him a new home, a new fortune, and new children. The moral of the
story is: when hard times befall you, don't be tempted to give up your faith in

God. He has His reasons for what He is doing, and if you hold on to your faith long enough, He will compensate you for your suffering.

Over the generations, many people must have been told that story. Some, no doubt, were comforted by it. Others were shamed into keeping their doubts and complaints to themselves after hearing Job's example. Our anonymous author was bothered by it. What kind of God would that story have us believe in, who would kill innocent children and visit unbearable anguish on His most devoted follower in order to prove a point, in order, we almost feel, to win a bet with Satan? What kind of religion is the story urging on us, which delights in blind obedience and calls it sinful to protest against injustice? He was so upset with this pious old fable that he took it, turned it inside out, and recast it as a philosophical poem in which the characters' positions are reversed. In the poem, Job *does* complain against God, and now it is the friends who uphold the conventional theology, the idea that "no ills befall the righteous." 6

In an effort to comfort Job, whose children have died and who is suffering from the boils, the three friends say all the traditional, pious things. In essence, they preach the point of view contained in the original Job-fable: Don't lose faith, despite these calamities. We have a loving Father in Heaven, and He will see to it that the good prosper and the wicked are punished. 7

Job, who has probably spoken these same words innumerable times to other mourners, realizes for the first time how hollow and offensive they are. What do you mean, He will see to it that the good prosper and the wicked are punished?! Are you implying that my children were wicked and that is why they died? Are you saying that I am wicked, and that is why all this is happening to me? Where was I so terrible? What did I do that was so much worse than anything you did, that I should suffer so much worse a fate? 8

The friends are startled by this outburst. They respond by saying that a person can't expect God to tell him what he is being punished for. (At one point, one of the friends says, in effect, "what do you want from God, an itemized report about every time you told a lie or ignored a beggar? God is too busy running a world to invite you to go over His records with Him.") We can only assume that nobody is perfect, and that God knows what He is doing. If we don't assume that, the world becomes chaotic and unlivable. 9

And so that argument continues. Job doesn't claim to be perfect, but says that he has tried, more than most people, to live a good and decent life. How can God be a loving God if He is constantly spying on people, ready to pounce on any imperfection in an otherwise good record, and use that to justify punishment? And how can God be a just God if so many wicked people are not punished as horribly as Job is? 10

The dialogue becomes heated, even angry. The friends say: Job, you really had us fooled. You gave us the impression that you were as pious and religious as we are. But now we see how you throw religion overboard the first time 11 something unpleasant happens to you. You are proud, arrogant, impatient, and blasphemous. No wonder God is doing this to you. It just proves our point that human beings can be fooled as to who is a saint and who is a sinner, but you can't fool God.

After three cycles of dialogue in which we alternately witness Job voicing   12
his complaints and the friends defending God, the book comes to its thunderous climax. The author brilliantly has Job make use of a principle of biblical criminal law: if a man is accused of wrongdoing without proof, he may take an oath, swearing to his innocence. At that point, the accuser must either come up with evidence against him or drop the charges. In a long and eloquent statement that takes up chapters 29 and 30 of the biblical book, Job swears to his innocence. He claims that he never neglected the poor, never took anything that did not belong to him, never boasted of his wealth or rejoiced in his enemy's misfortune. He challenges God to appear with evidence, or to admit that Job is right and has suffered wrongly.

And God appears.   13

There comes a terrible windstorm, out of the desert, and God answers Job   14
out of the whirlwind. Job's case is so compelling, his challenge so forceful, that God Himself comes down to earth to answer him. But God's answer is hard to understand. He doesn't talk about Job's case at all, neither to detail Job's sins nor to explain his suffering. Instead, He says to Job, in effect, What do you know about how to run a world?

> *Where were you when I planned the earth?*
> *Tell me, if you are wise.*
> *Do you know who took its dimensions,*
> *Measuring its length with a cord? . . .*
> *Were you there when I stopped the sea . . .*
> *And set its boundaries, saying, "Here you may come,*
> *But no further"?*
> *Have you seen where the snow is stored,*
> *Or visited the storehouse of the hail? . . .*
> *Do you tell the antelope when to calve?*
> *Do you give the horse his strength?*
> *Do you show the hawk how to fly?*
>
> (*Job 38, 39*)

And now a very different Job answers, saying, "I put my hand to my mouth.   15
I have said too much already; now I will speak no more."

The Book of Job is probably the greatest, fullest, most profound discussion   16
of the subject of good people suffering ever written. Part of its greatness lies in the fact that the author was scrupulously fair to all points of view, even those he did not accept. Though his sympathies are clearly with Job, he makes sure

that the speeches of the friends are as carefully thought out and as carefully written as are his hero's words. That makes for great literature, but it also makes it hard to understand his message. When God says, "How dare you challenge the way I run my world? What do you know about running a world?", is that supposed to be the last word on the subject, or is that just one more paraphrase of the conventional piety of that time?

To try to understand the book and its answer, let us take note of three   17
statements which everyone in the book, and most of the readers, would like to be able to believe:

> A. God is all-powerful and causes everything that happens in the world. Nothing happens without His willing it.
> B. God is just and fair, and stands for people getting what they deserve, so that the good prosper and the wicked are punished.
> C. Job is a good person.

As long as Job is healthy and wealthy, we can believe all three of those   18
statements at the same time with no difficulty. When Job suffers, when he loses his possessions, his family and his health, we have a problem. We can no longer make sense of all three propositions together. We can now affirm any two only by denying the third.

If God is both just and powerful, then Job must be a sinner who deserves   19
what is happening to him. If Job is good but God causes his suffering anyway, then God is not just. If Job deserved better and God did not send his suffering, then God is not all-powerful. We can see the argument of the Book of Job as an argument over which of the three statements we are prepared to sacrifice, so that we can keep on believing in the other two.

Job's friends are prepared to stop believing in (C), the assertion that Job is   20
a good person. They want to believe in God as they have been taught to. They want to believe that God is good and that God is in control of things. And the only way they can do that is to convince themselves that Job deserves what is happening to him.

They start out truly wanting to comfort Job and make him feel better. They   21
try to reassure him by quoting all the maxims of faith and confidence on which they and Job alike were raised. They want to comfort Job by telling him that the world does in fact make sense, that it is not a chaotic, meaningless place. What they do not realize is that they can only make sense of the world, and of Job's suffering, by deciding that he deserves what he has gone through. To say that everything works out in God's world may be comforting to the casual bystander, but it is an insult to the bereaved and the unfortunate. "Cheer up, Job, nobody ever gets anything he doesn't have coming to him" is not a very cheering message to someone in Job's circumstances.

But it is hard for the friends to say anything else. They believe, and want to   22
continue believing, in God's goodness and power. But if Job is innocent, then

God must be guilty—guilty of making an innocent man suffer. With that at stake, they find it easier to stop believing in *Job's* goodness than to stop believing in God's perfection.

It may also be that Job's comforters could not be objective about what had   23
happened to their friend. Their thinking may have been confused by their own reactions of guilt and relief that these misfortunates had befallen Job and not them. There is a German psychological term, *Schadenfreude,* which refers to the embarrassing reaction of relief we feel when something bad happens to someone else instead of to us. The soldier in combat who sees his friend killed twenty yards away while he himself is unhurt, the pupil who sees another child get into trouble for copying on a test—they don't wish their friends ill, but they can't help feeling an embarrassing spasm of gratitude that it happened to someone else and not to them. Like the friends who tried to comfort Ron or Helen,* they hear a voice inside them saying, "It could just as easily have been me," and they try to silence it by saying, "No, that's not true. There is a reason why it happened to him and not to me."

We see this psychology at work elsewhere, blaming the victim so that evil   24
doesn't seem quite so irrational and threatening. If the Jews had behaved differently, Hitler would not have been driven to murder them. If the young woman had not been so provocatively dressed, the man would not have assaulted her. If people worked harder, they would not be poor. If society did not taunt poor people by advertising things they cannot afford, they would not steal. Blaming the victim is a way of reassuring ourselves that the world is not as bad a place as it may seem, and that there are good reasons for people's suffering. It helps fortunate people believe that their good fortune is deserved, rather than being a matter of luck. It makes everyone feel better—except the victim, who now suffers the double abuse of social condemnation on top of his original misfortune. This is the approach of Job's friends, and while it may solve their problem, it does not solve Job's, or ours.

Job, for his part, is unwilling to hold the world together theologically by   25
admitting that he is a villain. He knows a lot of things intellectually, but he knows one thing more deeply. Job is absolutely sure that he is not a bad person. He may not be perfect, but he is not so much worse than others, by any intelligible moral standard, that he should deserve to lose his home, his children, his wealth and health while other people get to keep all those things. And he is not prepared to lie to save God's reputation.

Job's solution is to reject proposition (B), the affirmation of God's goodness.   26
Job is in fact a good man, but God is so powerful that He is not limited by considerations of fairness and justice.

---

*Ron and Helen had come to the Rabbi for comfort when they lost their child.

A philosopher might put it this way: God may *choose* to be fair and give a   27
person what he deserves, punishing the wicked and rewarding the righteous.
But can we say logically that an all-powerful God *must* be fair? Would He still
be all-powerful if we, by living virtuous lives, could *compel* Him to protect and
reward us? Or would He then be reduced to a kind of cosmic vending machine,
into which we insert the right number of tokens and from which we get what
we want (with the option of kicking and cursing the machine if it doesn't give
us what we paid for)? An ancient sage is said to have rejoiced at the world's
injustice, saying, "Now I can do God's will out of love for Him and not out of
self-interest." That is, he could be a moral, obedient person out of sheer love
for God, without the calculation that moral obedient people will be rewarded
with good fortune. He could love God even if God did not love him in return.
The problem with such an answer is that it tries to promote justice and fairness
and at the same time tries to celebrate God for being so great that He is beyond
the limitations of justice and fairness.

Job sees God as being above notions of fairness, being so powerful that no   28
moral rules apply to Him. God is seen as resembling an Oriental potentate,
with unchallenged power over the life and property of his subjects. And in fact,
the old fable of Job does picture God in just that way, as a deity who afflicts
Job without any moral qualms in order to test his loyalty, and who feels that
He has "made it up" to Job afterward by rewarding him lavishly. The God of
the fable, held up as a figure to be worshiped for so many generations, is very
much like an (insecure) ancient king, rewarding people not for their goodness
but for their loyalty.

So Job constantly wishes that there were an umpire to mediate between   29
himself and God, someone God would have to explain Himself to. But when
it comes to God, he ruefully admits, there are no rules. "Behold He snatches
away and who can hinder Him? Who can say to Him, What are You doing?"
(Job 9:12)

How does Job understand his misery? He says, we live in an unjust world,   30
from which we cannot expect fairness. There is a God, but He is free of the
limitations of justice and righteousness.

What about the anonymous author of the book? What is his answer to the   31
riddle of life's unfairness? As indicated, it is hard to know just what he thought
and what solution he had in mind when he set out to write his book. It seems
clear that he has put his answer into God's mouth in the speech from the
whirlwind, coming as it does at the climax of the book. But what does it mean?
Is it simply that Job is silenced by finding out that there is a God, that there
really is someone in charge up there? But Job never doubted that. It was God's
sympathy, accountability, and fairness that were at issue, not His existence. Is
the answer that God is so powerful that He doesn't have to explain Himself to
Job? But that is precisely what Job has been claiming throughout the book:

There is a God, and He is so powerful that He doesn't have to be fair. What new insight does the author bring by having God appear and speak, if that is all He has to say, and why is Job so apologetic if it turns out that God agrees with him?

Is God saying, as some commentators suggest, that He has other consider-   32
ations to worry about, besides the welfare of one individual human being, when He makes decisions that affect our lives? Is He saying that, from our human vantage point, our sicknesses and business failures are the most important things imaginable, but God has more on His mind than that? To say that is to say that the morality of the Bible, with its stress on human virtue and the sanctity of the individual life, is irrelevant to God, and that charity, justice, and the dignity of the individual human being have some source other than God. If that were true, many of us would be tempted to leave God, and seek out and worship that source of charity, justice, and human dignity instead.

Let me suggest that the author of the Book of Job takes the position which   33
neither Job nor his friends take. He believes in God's goodness and in Job's goodness, and is prepared to give up his belief in proposition (A): that God is all-powerful. Bad things do happen to good people in this world, but it is not God who wills it. God would like people to get what they deserve in life, but He cannot always arrange it. Forced to choose between a good God who is not totally powerful, or a powerful God who is not totally good, the author of the Book of Job chooses to believe in God's goodness.

The most important lines in the entire book may be the ones spoken by   34
God in the second half of the speech from the whirlwind, chapter 40, verses 9–14:

> *Have you an arm like God?*
> *Can you thunder with a voice like His?*
> *You tread down the wicked where they stand,*
> *Bury them in the dust together . . .*
> *Then will I acknowledge that your own right hand*
> *Can give you victory.*

I take these lines to mean "if you think that it is so easy to keep the world   35
straight and true, to keep unfair things from happening to people, *you* try it." God wants the righteous to live peaceful, happy lives, but sometimes even He can't bring that about. It is too difficult even for God to keep cruelty and chaos from claiming their innocent victims. But could man, without God, do it better?

The speech goes on, in chapter 41, to describe God's battle with the sea   36
serpent Leviathan. With great effort, God is able to catch him in a net and pin him with fish hooks, but it is not easy. If the sea serpent is a symbol of chaos and evil, of all the uncontrollable things in the world (as it traditionally is in

ancient mythology), the author may be saying there too that even God has a hard time keeping chaos in check and limiting the damage that evil can do.

Innocent people do suffer misfortunes in this life. Things happen to them far worse than they deserve—they lose their jobs, they get sick, their children suffer or make them suffer. But when it happens, it does not represent God punishing them for something they did wrong. The misfortunes do not come from God at all.   37

There may be a sense of loss at coming to this conclusion. In a way, it was comforting to believe in an all-wise, all-powerful God who guaranteed fair treatment and happy endings, who reassured us that everything happened for a reason, even as life was easier for us when we could believe that our parents were wise enough to know what to do and strong enough to make everything turn out right. But it was comforting the way the religion of Job's friends was comforting: it worked only as long as we did not take the problems of innocent victims seriously. When we have met Job, when we have *been* Job, we cannot believe in that sort of God any longer without giving up our own right to feel angry, to feel that we have been treated badly by life.   38

From that perspective, there ought to be a sense of relief in coming to the conclusion that God is not doing this to us. If God is a God of justice and not of power, then He can still be on our side when bad things happen to us. He can know that we are good and honest people who deserve better. Our misfortunes are none of His doing, and so we can turn to Him for help. Our question will not be Job's question "God, why are You doing this to me?" but rather "God, see what is happening to me. Can You help me?" We will turn to God, not to be judged or forgiven, not to be rewarded or punished, but to be strengthened and comforted.   39

If we have grown up, as Job and his friends did, believing in an all-wise, all-powerful, all-knowing God, it will be hard for us, as it was hard for them, to change our way of thinking about Him (as it was hard for us, when we were children, to realize that our parents were not all-powerful, that a broken toy had to be thrown out because they *could not* fix it, not because they did not want to). But if we can bring ourselves to acknowledge that there are some things God does not control, many good things become possible.   40

We will be able to turn to God for things He can do to help us, instead of holding on to unrealistic expectations of Him which will never come about. The Bible, after all, repeatedly speaks of God as the special protector of the poor, the widow, and the orphan, without raising the question of how it happened that they became poor, widowed, or orphaned in the first place.   41

We can maintain our own self-respect and sense of goodness without having to feel that God has judged us and condemned us. We can be angry at what has happened to us, without feeling that we are angry at God. More than that,   42 we can recognize our anger at life's unfairness, our instinctive compassion at seeing people suffer, as coming from God who teaches us to be angry at injustice and to feel compassion for the afflicted. Instead of feeling that we are opposed to God, we can feel that our indignation is God's anger at unfairness working through us, that when we cry out, we are still on God's side, and He is still on ours.

Questions for Critical Thinking

1. What is at issue in this interpretation of the biblical story about Job? Do you consider the issue important? Why or why not?

2. What is your view of people who insist that we must give blind obedience to God? Can you give a practical reason to explain why so many Christians adopt such a principle?

3. Paragraph 14 alludes to the psychology of blaming victims for their misfortunes. Have there been times when victims were responsible for their own persecutions? If your answer is yes, provide examples from history or your own experience.

4. Are you satisfied with Kushner's resolution to the problem of undeserved pain on the part of good people? Why or why not?

5. What system of rewards and punishment do you think would exist in the best of all possible worlds?

6. What purpose do you see in fables and folk tales, like the story that sparked "Job"? Do you consider these narratives an important part of literature? Why or why not?

7. What is your personal philosophical reaction to unjust suffering? Explain your philosophy fully.

Writing Assignment

Write an essay in which you examine the good that can come from a tragic event in one's life.

Writing Advice

Many of us have been struck by misfortune from which we have belatedly derived consolation. Writing this essay will give you the chance to think out loud about the lessons you have learned or have witnessed others learn from life's worse blows.

1. Begin by thinking of the most painful and unfair event of your own life or that of someone close to you. Jot down the chronology of what happened. (Try not to choose an event that took place recently since you might not be able to view it objectively.)

2. Next, ask yourself what you learned or might have learned from the experience. For instance, a physical ailment may have taught you compassion for others or not to be reckless and take unnecessary risks. An enormous loss, such as the death of a loved one or a broken love relationship, may have taught you patience and endurance.

3. You can now begin developing the actual essay. In the narrative portion, pay attention to details and to the sequence of events. Pace your narrative so that it includes only important events—the way a well-plotted story does. If you fractured your leg in a rock climbing incident, do not report every minute that led up to the accident, just the exciting or suspenseful moments. But do make your narrative vivid by describing the sounds, smells, sights, and emotions of the event.

4. Finally, state exactly what lesson was learned or could have been learned from the tragedy. You do not have to sermonize or preach, but merely state what lesson—however slight—the experience taught.

Alternate Writing Assignments

1. Write an essay in which you give your own answer to the question, "Why do the good suffer and the evil prosper"?

2. Write an essay in which you argue that people must stop having unrealistic expectations of God.

or

Write an essay in which you argue that asking God to protect you is a reasonable request.

HISTORY

TWO GERMANS
Bernt Engelmann

Bernt Engelmann (b. 1921 in Berlin) is a German journalist who was imprisoned by the Nazis because of his resistance activities during World War II. He lived with his family in Duesseldorf until completing his education, and then enlisted in the Luftwaffe as a radio operator until 1942, when he decided to join the anti-Nazi movement. He was consequently imprisoned by the Nazis and sent to Dachau until the liberation by Allied forces in 1945. After the war, he focused on a career as a journalist. He has been both special correspondent and editor of *Der Spiegel*, and, as a freelance writer, has contributed numerous articles to a variety of international periodicals. Among his successful books, widely translated throughout Europe, is *In Hitler's Germany* (1986), from which the excerpts below are reprinted.

Reading Advice

This article is excerpted from a book written about the little-known resistance decent Germans mounted to the terrors of the Nazi regime. Throughout his book, Engelmann interviewed members of the resistance as well as Jewish victims who were rescued and spirited to the safety of neutral countries via an underground railroad. Engelmann is content, for the most part, to let the participants tell their own stories, interrupting only occasionally to provide contextual information or outcomes.

In this particular account, Engelmann serves as a reporter of events involving his own mother, who helped hide one of the Jewish victims of the World War II Nazi hunt. Twenty years after the persecution had taken place, Engelmann interviewed both the female victim and the Gestapo officer in charge of Jewish affairs, who was her persecutor, tying decades together in an ironic cause-effect knot. Whereas this firsthand observance of a historical event may have a biased perspective, it nonetheless provides insight into what actually happened to Jews during the early 1940s as a result of Hitler's purge, euphemistically called "the final solution to the Jewish question." That the Gestapo agent has absolutely no compunction about his past is a source of both horror and dramatic tension.

"*I*, Irene Herz, née Glogauer, was   1
born on June 2, 1902, in Stettin. My parents owned a successful shoe store. Through hard work they had become quite well-to-do. They owned the building the store was in, and lived on the second floor. My father was respected in the town and belonged for years to the board of directors of the Jewish Cultural Community as well as to the Chamber of Commerce. He also served as a National Liberal Party member of the City Council.

"I was the youngest of five children. My eldest brother, who hoped to become   2
a judge, volunteered for military service and was killed in 1914. My second-eldest brother succumbed to severe wounds on the front in 1917. My third brother was drafted in 1918 but was still in flight school when the war ended, after which he studied literature and drama in Berlin. My youngest brother had died as a child of diphtheria. So after the war, in which my father, too, had taken part since 1916, I was the only child at home, and my parents spoiled me terribly. I went to a fancy school for girls, and did not have to help in the shop where my parents worked from morning till night.

"In 1927, when I was twenty-four, I was visiting my brother Heinz in Berlin.   3
Heinz was editor and theater critic for a major newspaper. He had a good
income and a wide circle of friends, to which he introduced me. Among his
friends was Max Herz, who was just opening his medical practice. We liked
each other very much, and when Max proposed to me I accepted gladly. My
parents, too, were happy, though they didn't like the idea of parting with me.
In November 1927 we married in Berlin. It was a very fine wedding, and my
father gave a speech I shall never forget. My husband, eight years older than I,
had lost his left arm in the war, and he still suffered the effects of a bullet
lodged in his lung. My father alluded to these handicaps in his speech. He said
that I, as the daughter of a family that had made so many sacrifices for the
Fatherland, would serve as the left arm for my husband, who had shown no
less patriotism, and would prove a devoted support to him throughout his life.
And that I did, until his early death. He died in 1932 of the delayed effects of
his wounds, and so, ironically, he was spared much misery.

"Our brief marriage was happy. My husband's medical practice flourished,   4
even during the depression. We had two children, a daughter, Hanni, born in
1928, and a son, Klaus, born in 1929. Our only sorrow was that our Hanni
was not progressing in her mental development; this became unmistakable in
my husband's last year. She was physically healthy and pretty as a picture, but
none of the treatment we sought did any good. In 1940, when I was called up
for compulsory service in a factory, I had to put the child in a home. Six weeks
later I was notified she had died. I am certain they killed her, for around that
time the parents of other Jewish children in the home received the same
notification about their boys and girls.

"But 1933 had been the hardest year. Left without a husband, inexperienced   5
in financial matters, with two small children, one of them retarded, I witnessed
the collapse of the world as I had known it. Suddenly, whether we were religious
Jews or only of Jewish origin, we no longer counted as Germans!

"My brother Heinz lost his job at the newspaper in Berlin, and was forbidden   6
to work for any other paper. So he went to Vienna, where he managed to eke
out an existence. He worked as a freelance critic and reviewer, and did some
translating on the side. Upon the annexation of Austria, he was immediately
dismissed, and then things went very badly for him. Every so often I sent him
some money. But then in October 1939 a letter with money from me was
returned, marked 'addressee unknown.' I learned from the Viennese Jewish
Cultural Community that my brother had been 'resettled' in the Government
General [the official name for occupied Poland] and had suffered an 'accident
at work,' from the effects of which he died in December 1939.

"Things went no better with our parents in Stettin. They, who had sacrificed   7
two sons to the Fatherland, had a rude shock in 1933 when they found signs
pasted onto the windows of their shop: 'Germans! Do not buy from these

Jewish traitors to the Volk!' That year my father sold the shoe store, at a price far below its actual value. He hoped they could live on the proceeds and on rents from their building, lie low, and wait for better times. In November 1938, when my parents' apartment was completely smashed up in the Night of Broken Glass, my mother suffered a heart attack, from which she recovered only very slowly. My sixty-three-year-old father was dragged off to Sachsenhausen, where he lost his life. They beat him with dog whips because he had refused to say, 'I am a filthy Jew who has no right to be in Germany.' This I learned from someone who was imprisoned with my father and survived to return to Stettin.

"I wanted to go back to Stettin with my children, to be with my mother. But she herself and all our friends and acquaintances advised me very strongly against it, saying conditions were even worse there than in Berlin.   8

"In February 1940 my poor mother, who had not yet recovered from a bad case of influenza, was deported to Poland along with other Jews from Stettin. They came in the middle of the night and ordered her to get out of her apartment immediately. She was allowed to take only one suitcase with the bare necessities. Everything else had to stay behind. She had to 'voluntarily' renounce any claim on the house in writing, and then she was taken to the freight station for 'shipment.' There she found herself together with all our other relatives who still lived in Stettin. Of the thirteen relatives there, the oldest was Mother's Aunt Selma, who was eighty-six, and the youngest were my father's niece, Hilde Löwenstein, and her two children, three-year-old Katja and six-month-old Michael.   9

"Each of the three hundred Jews was given a piece of cardboard with his or her name and number to wear around the neck. They were all subjected to a thorough body-search, and all money, jewelry, even photos and little mementos, and any provisions they had brought along were taken from them. Before daybreak they had to get onto the train waiting to take them to Poland. I learned later from a lawyer, who had been a good friend of my father's and had been made trustee for the confiscated Jewish property, that my mother died the next day, while marching in bitter cold to a village near Lublin. In the next few weeks all the rest of my family perished there.   10

"At the time I was working in an electronics factory. I had been called up for compulsory work service, and had to wind wire on reels. The overseer, a staunch Nazi, treated me like a leper. When we were given our soup for lunch, all the others, including the Polish forced laborers, were allowed to eat at a table. I had to sit on the cellar steps. In the fall of 1941 I was released, and found a job as a secretary at the Jewish Hospital on Auguststrasse. There I was given a room for myself and my son. I was even allowed to bring along our dog Maxi, whom little Klaus was very fond of. I owed this great improvement in my situation to one of the head physicians, a friend of my husband's.   11

"I lived there until the beginning of June 1942, and Klaus and I felt quite at home. There was a lot of work to do, and I soon learned to do much of it   12 without supervision. My boss was considerate and kind. We got along very well with one another. He asked me one time why I had not emigrated while it was still possible. I told him the thought had never entered my mind. Where would I have gone?

"I had no relatives abroad, and no good friends. I would have been utterly   13 helpless without money, without knowledge of foreign languages, without training in any profession. How would I have managed?

"I would not have wanted to emigrate to Palestine, either. My parents and   14 my husband had always rejected Zionism. Since my marriage I had not participated in the activities of the Jewish community, not even for the High Holy Days. At home, we ate sausage, ham, and pork roast like any other German family, and my husband had office hours on Saturday. We felt only loosely connected with Judaism, and I could not conceive of living in Palestine, surrounded by religious Jews.

"My boss responded that there were nonreligious, socialist Zionists as well.   15 I admitted that I had perhaps even greater prejudices against socialists. I knew, of course, that they were the only ones who had put up any resistance to Hitler and had suffered the direst persecution as a result, but I wanted nothing to do with the reds. My boss laughed and said I probably felt that way because I had been raised to be a patriotic German; perhaps I secretly admired and envied the non-Jewish antifascists. Unlike us Jews, the reds had only to give up their political beliefs, whereas neither baptism nor the most fervent dedication to the German people could help us.

"I have since given much thought to the matter, and have come to the   16 conclusion that my boss was right. If I could have paid lip service to Hitler and thereby escaped all oppression and persecution, I think I would have done it. I daresay my parents and my brother Heinz, who worked for a German nationalist paper until 1933, would have done the same.

"Of course we viewed what had happened since Hitler's seizure of power as   17 a national calamity and shame for Germany. We were affected doubly—as Germans, who were mortified by what was happening, and as Jews, who bore the brunt of it. That double load was actually more than one could bear, yet until June 2, 1942, I still hoped that things would improve for my Klaus and me.

"On that June 2, my fortieth birthday, I was supposed to run an urgent   18 errand for my boss. Before 7:00 A.M. I had to go to an 'Aryan' doctor in Lichterfelde to pick up a medication that we could not obtain otherwise. This former colleague of my boss sometimes helped us out in secret. I set out before 5:00 on my bicycle to get to Lichterfelde on time. We had been forbidden to use all public transportation since April of that year.

"On the way back I stopped in to visit my friend Lilo. I slipped into the   19 building when no one was looking because I did not want to cause trouble for my friends with my Star of David. Lilo came from a Jewish family, but she was 'privileged' because she was married to an 'Aryan.' She did not need to wear a star or mark her door.

"Lilo received me warmly. We celebrated my birthday with real coffee and 20
fresh rolls, which gave me particular pleasure because these things were now forbidden to Jews—along with white bread, cake, wheat flour, eggs, meat, sausage, and whole milk.

"I did not set out for the hospital until 10:30. When I got there, it was 21
almost 11:00. I put my bicycle in the cellar and was about to go upstairs when I remembered that I should go and buy a few cigarettes. At that time Jews still received ration cards for cigarettes; nine days later those too were taken away.

"Across the street was a little shop where I bought something almost every 22
day, especially newspapers. We were forbidden to subscribe to newspapers or to buy them from street vendors or newsstands. But variety stores like Frau Brösicke's were not covered under the ordinance, so every day I bought the *Morning Post* there, but hid it under my coat as I crossed the street.

"When I entered the shop on this particular morning, Frau Brösicke stared 23
at me as though I were a ghost. 'My God, Frau Herz, you're still around!' she exclaimed in horror. Then I heard our little fox terrier Maxi barking. How did he happen to be over here?

"Terror gripped me, but my worst premonitions proved mild when Frau 24
Brösicke told me what happened. Fortunately we were alone in the shop, and she locked the door and took me back into the little room where she lived. She told me that shortly after 6:00 that morning the Gestapo had 'combed through' our hospital. About seventy persons, among them my eleven-year-old son Klaus and my boss and good friend, were driven away in trucks guarded by SS men. Klaus had just had time to give Maxi to Frau Brösicke and leave a message for me: he was already a man, and I shouldn't worry about him.

"My first impulse was to fetch my bicycle and set out to find my boy. I 25
knew where the collection point was for the so-called evacuations. But Frau Brösicke held me back: 'For God's sake, Frau Herz, don't go over there! They're still nosing around! And you can't do anything for the boy—they've gone already. The train left Berlin at 9:30.'

"Everything began to swim before my eyes, and when I came to, I was lying 26
on Frau Brösicke's sofa and she was giving me brandy. We debated what I could do. 'You must get away, Frau Herz,' Frau Brösicke insisted. 'They called out your name several times, I'm positive. By now they must have a search warrant out for you. Isn't there someone who could take you in for a little while?' It was clear to me I could not ask Lilo for help. My only other close friend had moved to Düsseldorf years before. On her last visit to Berlin, about six months before this, she had said, 'You can always come to me, Irene, if things get too hot here. I have room for you and your son.'

"I asked Frau Brösicke to go to the post office to call my friend in Düsseldorf 27 and explain my situation to her. It was my last hope, and I was sure something would go wrong. My friend was often away on trips, and perhaps we would not be able to reach her. But when Frau Brösicke returned, she said, to my great relief, 'Everything's arranged, Frau Herz. Your friend's son is on leave at home. He'll come and fetch you tomorrow. In the meantime, stay here with me, and don't show your nose outdoors!'

"The next evening he appeared. Frau Brösicke let him in, and I was terrified 28 at first when I saw his uniform. He stayed only twenty minutes, but he said, 'Tomorrow this will all be over. I'll come to get you early, and we'll take Maxi along. My uncle will keep him, and he'll be well cared for. We'll take a taxi, first to *Charlottenburg* and then on to the Friedrichstrasse Station. You'll change clothes in the ladies' room of the Central Hotel. You'll be traveling as a nurse.'

"When I protested that I was not allowed to use a taxi or enter a hotel, he 29 waved the objection aside. 'That's over,' he said. 'From tomorrow on you're an Aryan. Don't forget to take off the star! By the way, I need two passport photos of you—would you happen to have any?'

"Fortunately I had two in my pocketbook from several years back, left over 30 from when we were required to get new passports marked with a *J*. I asked him whether I didn't look very Jewish. He just laughed and said, 'You're blond and have gray eyes. You really look more like someone from an old Prussian family. When you're dressed, they'll think you're an aristocratic head nurse. We're giving you a new name, with a 'von' in it. And another thing: you were buried in rubble during an air raid and were injured. You've lost everything, and now you're on your way to visit friends in the country and recuperate. I'll bring gauze along tomorrow. The best thing would be for you to put your arm in a sling.'

"Everything went according to plan, even though I was terribly nervous and 31 probably acted rather strangely. When I opened the suitcase in the ladies' room, I found three brand-new nurse's uniforms, three aprons, three sets of under-wear, stockings, shoes, a cap, and everything else I would need, including a nurse's pin with the red cross on it and an identification card with my own picture glued on and officially stamped. On the front was the official notation, 'Duplicate issued for original lost in terror attack. Air Raid Defense Head-quarters, Berlin.' It was signed and stamped. That made me feel a little more secure, and my new name, Maximiliane von Anders, appealed to me.

"Nevertheless my heart pounded wildly when I went to the ticket counter 32 and had to show my card for the first time. I thought it would be obvious to everyone that there was something fishy about it. But I had no trouble, either then or later on the train, when an SS patrol went from compartment to compartment between Potsdam and Magdeburg, checking everyone. The men in black uniforms just glanced at me in passing, and the patrol leader even wished me a good journey.

"In late afternoon we arrived in Düsseldorf and were greeted on the platform 33
by a gentleman in an elegant summer suit, with an SS badge on his lapel. I was
alarmed, but my friend's son reassured me that this was Herr Desch, a good
friend, and it was a lucky coincidence we had run into him. But in fact it was
no coincidence, as I gathered from a hasty exchange between them. I heard
the words 'Gestapo raid' and 'better not to go through the barricade.' They
must have noticed how frightened I was, because Herr Desch said, 'Please don't
be upset, Sister! You're going on by yourself to Krefeld—I'll see you to your
train. The trip takes half an hour, and in Krefeld a lady will meet you, and all
will be well. Here's your ticket.' The ride to Krefeld passed uneventfully, and a
friendly white-haired lady leaning on a cane greeted me as I got off the train.
She said, 'Welcome, Sister! I'm so glad you got here safely. I'm Frau Ney. Please
let me take your arm—that looks better!' We made our way slowly to the
barrier; from a distance I could see the SS guards, checking everyone carefully.
A man in civilian clothes was standing nearby, keeping a close eye on the process.
He looked to me like a Gestapo agent.

" 'Stay calm, Sister, nothing will happen to us,' Frau Ney murmured. She 34
squeezed my arm slightly, and strangely enough I no longer felt any fear, even
when one of the SS men commanded brusquely, 'Heil Hitler! Identification
check! Show your papers!' 'Make it snappy!' barked the second SS man, who
had a police dog on a leash. Frau Ney paid no attention to the two in their
black uniforms. Without slowing down, she turned to the man in civilian
clothes: 'Good day, Herr Berger! Still on duty so late in the day? Would you
please tell your young men that you know me—otherwise we'll miss our
streetcar.'

"The Gestapo agent nodded to the SS men, and they stepped aside. He 35
wished Frau Ney a good recovery, to which to my amazement, she gave a
friendly reply, 'Thank you, I'm in good hands now. Sister von Anders has me
doing some wonderful exercises.' Then she seemed to remember something
else, and she said, 'Oh, and please tell your dear wife that she can come an
hour later tomorrow, now that I have some help. We can make our own
breakfast, right, Sister?'

"In half an hour we reached the Neys' country cottage in Meerbusch. Frau 36
Ney showed me the pretty room on the second floor that was to be mine and
said, 'This is your home now. I hope you'll feel comfortable with us. At any
rate you're safe here from Herr Berger and his men. He's a dangerous fellow,
ambitious and brutal. I know because his wife has been helping me with the
housework since my hip got so bad. You needn't worry about her—she's a
decent woman, and very unhappy because her husband left the Church. He
thought he would be promoted more rapidly as a "believer in God," as they
call it. He's still at quite a low rank, and they barely make ends meet on his
salary. They have a son who's in university-preparatory school, and a daughter

who's retarded.' I could not help thinking of my own children, and tears came to my eyes. Frau Ney put her arm around me and said gently, 'Go ahead and cry! You have every reason to be sad. But don't despair! God has protected you and will continue to protect you, because he has a task in mind for you.' I asked her, 'What task?' and she replied, 'I don't know—perhaps he rescued you so you could testify to what you've experienced.'

"I have not forgotten that, and never shall, and that is why I have written   37 all of this down."

[Twenty years have passed. The son of Irene's friend in Düsseldorf is report-ing his encounter with Josef Berger, to whom he has revealed Maximiliane von Anders' real identity.]

"How in the world did you pick that name?" he wanted to know, as I was   38 leaving. So I told him how my mother had selected the name Maximiliane von Anders for her friend. Anders meant "different" in German, and Irene was certainly taking on a different identity. The name Maximiliane was a joking reference to her fox terrier Maxi, but it also had an aristocratic ring to it.

For her papers we decided to make Frau Herz three years younger than she   39 really was, but to keep her actual date and place of birth. We made her a head nurse in a lay nursing order, the Handmaidens of the Fatherland League in Berlin-Dahlem, whose records had been destroyed when the headquarters were bombed.

He listened in silence, and from his expression I could not tell whether, in   40 retrospect, he found the story amusing, outrageous, or simply of no consequence.

But I suspected he could not be entirely indifferent to it, even twenty years   41 later. For if he had known Sister Maximiliane's true identity at the time, he would have arrested her immediately and made her a part of the "final solution." He would have received a commendation, and perhaps his promotion would have come sooner. To complicate matters, Sister Maximiliane had helped look after his retarded daughter for almost a year. With great patience she taught the girl to speak a few words. While he greatly appreciated her kindness, he might have found himself in real trouble if the Jewish woman had been unmasked.

But retired Hauptkommissar Berger, whom I visited in 1962, seemed to give   42 little thought either to the loving care his daughter had received at the hands of a Jewish woman in hiding or to the threat that had hung over his career without his knowledge. What troubled him most was his professional slip-up in this case. He muttered, more to himself than to me, "Incredible . . . incredible. And right under my nose."

He received me very cordially when I turned up without calling ahead. It   43 happened to be almost exactly twenty years since our first meeting. When I arrived, he was busy pruning his roses.

"I've been retired for a couple of years now," he told me, "and I devote all   44
my time to gardening. I feel terrific!"

That was clear. He must have been close to seventy, but he looked consid-   45
erably younger, in spite of his white hair. As a Gestapo agent he had been pasty-
faced and nervous but now he looked robust and glowing with health, with a
deep tan and muscled arms.

He showed no reluctance to tell me about events in his life. In the fall of   46
1942 he had finally been promoted to Kommissar and transferred to Düsseldorf.
There he served at headquarters until the beginning of April 1945. Toward the
end of the war he was drafted into the people's militia, where he commanded
a unit of military police in the Ruhr Basin. When the troops in the Rhineland-
Westphalian industrial area capitulated on April 18, 1945, Herr Berger found
himself in British captivity. The British interrogated him and soon realized they
had bagged a fairly high-ranking Gestapo agent. "I was interned for eleven
months," he told me with a sigh. "What an ordeal! At the beginning we suffered
dreadfully from the cold and never had enough to eat, because there were
shortages of everything. And they treated us wretchedly—especially the Poles
who were sent in as guards. Some prisoners were even beaten!"

From the way he sighed, it was clear he viewed this period of imprisonment   47
as a grim and undeserved injustice. As he continued his account, he noticed a
rose that showed signs of powdery mildew, picked up a can of pesticide, and
sprayed the plant thoroughly. "Fortunately the Poles were pulled out, and we
had a much better time of it with the Tommies. That's when I discovered my
talent for gardening. I took care of the gardens at Major Wilkinson's villa, which
had been shamefully neglected. I laid out the beds in perfect squares, trimmed
the hedges till not a twig was out of place, and made the shrubs line up like
soldiers."

I glanced around his own garden, and saw that it was laid out with the same   48
military precision.

"They released me early," he went on, "and for a while I had no job, but   49
then I found a position with the police in Oberhausen, later in Krefeld and
finally with the State Criminal Division as a Hauptkommissar." He spoke with
obvious pride. But he detected dubiousness in my expression. "I always loved
being a policeman," he added, "and it made sense to rehire experts like me. In
fact anyone without blots on his record had a *right* to be employed again. After
all, I had been with the police since 1921."

He had first joined the police after the First World War, in which three of   50
his older brothers had fallen. "I came from a good Catholic family with a
tradition of civil service. My years with the military counted toward my career
in the police, so that by 1925 I had made sergeant and had permanent status.
In 1929 I switched to the detective division and in 1931 became a cub detective
in the fraud department."

Until then Berger had belonged to no political party, but shortly after the   51
seizure of power, in the spring of 1933, he joined the NSDAP, and two years
later the SS. "It was the temper of the times," he commented. "As a civil servant
I didn't want to be on the outside."

Toward the end of 1934 Berger was transferred to the Gestapo, where his   52
first assignment involved combating "communist subversion." "We had our
hands full at that time. Almost every day our informants brought us illegal
pamphlets which had been distributed in the factories, or they reported that
seditious slogans had appeared overnight on walls and bridges. I was constantly
shuttling between Krefeld and Düsseldorf, and my family life was affected by
all the overtime I had to put in—the interrogations tended to drag on
and on."

What Berger neglected to mention was that in the Gestapo he developed   53
into a brutal interrogator, whom all the prisoners feared. Early one morning
in the winter of 1934–35, when Aunt Annie's husband was going to the bakery,
he ran into a worker he knew. The man had blood streaming from his nose
and mouth, and could barely stand on his feet. Graybeard Ney helped the man
home and fetched a doctor. He stayed with the man while he was being
bandaged up, and the sight horrified him so much that he could hardly sleep
the next few nights: the man's back was a bloody pulp from his shoulders to
his buttocks—the work of Berger, who had hauled him in for questioning the
previous day.

"Berger worked him over for hours with a length of rigid rubber tubing,"   54
Herr Ney told us later. "He beat the man with the regularity of a machine, one
blow every five seconds, exactly twelve blows per minute. He wanted to find
out who had painted 'Down with Hitler!' on the factory wall before the early
shift. There were nine suspects, and Berger interrogated them one by one. He
got nothing out of them, but the men were so badly injured it's doubtful any
of them will recover . . ."

When I asked Herr Berger about the methods of interrogation he had used   55
over twenty-five years earlier, he knew exactly what I was referring to. His
reaction, however, surprised me.

"Yes, yes," he said thoughtfully, and without a trace of shame. He even   56
smiled. "All kinds of stories made the rounds, and are still making the rounds,
and much of what people say is exaggerated. But it's true we had to be pretty
tough on the suspects when an 'intensive interrogation' was ordered. I often
had to clench my teeth to make myself go through with it. I got many beatings
as a child, especially from my godfather, who raised me. He tended to get
angry. Anger is a bad thing—I always made a point of maintaining my self-
control. After all, it was just part of our job. By the way, I never struck anyone
unless I had written orders." He paused, as though expecting praise.

By this time Herr Berger had finishing rinsing and oiling his gardening tools   57 and putting them away in the shed. He looked to make sure everything was in its place, straightened a hoe that was hanging a little crooked, then locked up the shed and strolled with me toward the house.

"Order must be maintained," he said. "That was also the original purpose   58
of the concentration camps: to teach those people order and discipline. Later on, of course, excesses did occur, in violation of the guidelines."

I asked him whether he had ever seen a concentration camp.   59

"I went to Esterwegen a couple of times in an official capacity, and later I   60
had a three-week training course at Buchenwald. That was in the winter of 1939–40, soon after the end of the Polish campaign. At the time the camp was overcrowded, but nevertheless everything was in admirable order."

"Really?" I asked.   61

He merely nodded. By this time we had reached the house, and he asked   62
me to take a seat in the living room while he went to wash up and make tea. "I'm alone today," he said. "My wife's gone to visit our daughter. After the war we found a place for her in an institution in the Eifel region."

"Of course that wasn't possible before," I said. He didn't respond. He knew   63
as well as I did that during the Nazi period anyone institutionalized and considered incurable was killed.

While I waited for Herr Berger to return, I looked around the room, which   64
was decorated in "Old German" style. Everything was perfectly in its place, as if no one lived there. Even the books in the bookcase stood lined up like soldiers. Above the sofa hung two plaques, one for the Wartime Cross of Merit 2d Class, conferred on Kommissar Peter Josef Berger in 1943; the other was the Federal Order of Merit conferred on Hauptkommissar Berger on the occasion of his thirty-fifth year of service with the Province Police. On the opposite wall hung various souvenir photographs, one of which particularly caught my attention: it showed about a dozen men in their thirties, some of them quite overweight, all in athletic shorts and shirts. I picked out Herr Berger without difficulty. They were standing on a wide bare space, posing for the picture and obviously enjoying themselves. In the background one could see a long, two-story building in the architectural style characteristic of SS headquarters buildings. When I examined the picture more closely, I saw it bore the caption "Kommissars' Training Course, February 1940, Weimar-Buchenwald."

From the kitchen I could hear the kettle whistling, and I knew that in a   65
moment Herr Berger would return with the tea. I wanted to ask him about his impressions of Buchenwald, but I was sure I would only hear again how clean and orderly he had found the camp.

After he poured the tea, I inquired, "When you were assigned to the Depart-   66
ment for Jewish Affairs of the Gestapo office in Düsseldorf, was that something you had applied for? And how did you feel about what was called in those days the 'Jewish question'?"

For the first time that day Herr Berger seemed unsure of himself. "Yes, well,   67
let me explain," he began. "You probably don't understand . . . You see, I came
from a strict Catholic family. My father was a civil servant loyal to the Kaiser
and active in the Catholic Men's Association. He had nothing in common with
the *völkisch* groups and the anti-Semites, but when I was a child he forbade me
to play with the Jewish children next door. I couldn't even accept a piece of
candy from their mother."

He went on to describe other experiences with Jews: a Jewish cattle dealer   68
frequented his uncle's restaurant, an unpleasant character. In the army Berger
had a Jewish drill sergeant who was such an exemplary soldier that Berger and
his comrades joked that he couldn't really be a Jew—his mother must have
had an affair with an officer.

After dredging up other such memories, he said, "Well, I really can't say I   69
felt hostile toward Jews. In fact—this you won't believe—I almost married
one! Her name was Doris Rosenthal. Her father ran a successful fabric store.
We really liked each other, and Doris said she would convert. I had just become
a tenured civil servant, but old Rosenthal didn't want his daughter to become
a Catholic and marry a policeman. Anyway, it was lucky nothing came of it.
Later on I sometimes thought of that. I really felt sorry for some of the people
when we had to evacuate them . . ."

I was amazed to hear him use the term "evacuate" without the slightest   70
irony, as if he still believed the Gestapo had merely been moving the Jews to
safety!

"I suppose you went through special training before you began work in the   71
Department for Jewish Affairs?"

Herr Berger laughed. "And how! We had racial theory and ideological   72
instruction, and also a special course on the 'Legal Position of the Jews.' Some
of the instructors certainly put us through our paces. But I tell you, after that
training and a few months on the job I could recognize a Jew thirty feet away,
no matter how he tried to blend in or how blond and blue-eyed he was. I had
an unfailing instinct when it came to picking them out!

"Of course," he added hastily, "I often closed one eye when I could do that   73
without running afoul of the guidelines. But I recognized every single one."

His professional pride seemed to have gained the upper hand again, and I   74
couldn't resist asking, "Do you remember Sister von Anders—Sister Maxi?"

Of course he did. After all, she had taken care of his retarded daughter for   75
almost a year. "A splendid woman," he said. "I remember the first time our
Gudrun said 'Papa' to me—without Sister Maxi she might never have done
that."

"Do you remember Major von Elken?" I said quickly.   76

He thought for a moment, then said, "Yes, I know who you're referring to: 77
wasn't he the retired cavalry officer from Potsdam who was determined to go

back on active duty? I met him a few times at Frau Ney's and we chatted a bit. A crusty old gentleman, a soldier of the old school, from the Kaiser's time."

I mentioned several other men and women he had certainly encountered at   78 the Neys' and later also at my mother's, but he shook his head.

"You must remember Monsignor Sprüngli," I said. "I mean the priest who   79 arrived in 1940 from Switzerland to bring presents to the prisoners of war." Aunt Annie had told me that when Herr Berger met Herr Sprüngli, the Gestapo agent had tried to kiss the monsignor's ring.

Herr Berger was beginning to understand why I was inquiring about all   80 these people. "Was the monsignor . . . Certainly he wasn't Jewish, was he?" he asked very hesitantly, and added quickly, "To be quite truthful, I sensed at the time that the priest was not quite what he claimed to be. So he was a Jew? The man must have had damned good nerves!"

"That he did," I replied, "but *he* at least wasn't Jewish. He was a functionary   81 of the Communist Party, serving as a courier for the underground Party leadership. But the others—Sister Maxi, Major von Elken, and the rest—they were Jews on the run, and fortunately your 'infallible instinct' let you down in their case."

It took some time before he regained his composure. Then he said, "Listen   82 here, I was simply doing my duty—no more and no less! I had nothing to be ashamed of, except that I let my superiors talk me into leaving the Church, and right after the war I rejoined. I'm happy to hear that those fine people managed to survive in the face of so many obstacles. I always said: a truly deserving person will come out on top, no matter how hard things are made for him. That goes for me too—or do you think it was easy to rise to the rank of Hauptkommissar with only an eighth-grade education?"

Questions for Critical Thinking

1. What difference in point of view exists between the interview of Irene Herz and that of Peter Josef Berger? How does this difference affect the account?

2. What are some ironies that occur throughout this historical account?

3. What symbolic relationship exists between Mr. Berger and his garden?

4. How would you personally react if our government today required certain groups to be identified the way Hitler identified the Jews by forcing them to display the Star of David on their clothing and houses? Can you envision a circumstance that might allow the repetition of such an order? Explain your answer.

5. What is your view of Jews who hid their identities and gave lip service to Hitler to escape persecution? Do you admire or revile them? Explain your answer.

6. Do you believe in unquestioning obedience on the part of workers employed by

such institutions as the army, the police department, the hospital, the school, or the church? At what point, if any, is disobedience desirable?

7. What answer would David Hume (*see* "Why Does God Let People Suffer?") give to the question of why God allowed six million Jews to be exterminated by Hitler?

Writing Assignment

Write an essay in which you argue the importance of preserving the horror of Nazi concentration camps as part of Europe's history.

Writing Advice

For this writing assignment you have been assigned the position you are to take on an issue—you must argue *for*, not against, remembering the Nazi holocaust.

You might begin by speculating on what could happen if we do *not* remember. For example, you could point out that obliviousness to the grim history of Nazi Germany could lead eventually to the rise of another monstrous dictator in a future age and place who might also set out to systematically slaughter part of the human population.

Having demonstrated what could happen if we do not remember, you might then speculate on the good that can come from always remembering the brutal lessons of history. A brief but excellent book on the subject is *The Lessons of History,* by Will and Ariel Durant. Of course, contemporary examples of entire peoples determined to remember the slaughters and barbarisms of the past are all around us. For instance, today citizens of the Soviet Union and the Warsaw Pact are beginning to cry out against the post–World War II era of Stalin's purges as a warning that all should stand up for individual liberty or risk the return of repression. They remember their own experiences or those of loved ones in Siberian labor camps, who were either tortured or forced to watch their compatriots executed.

Because this assignment is rather a large subject, you need to be especially careful to keep your mind on the primary point—that we must remember the Nazi concentration camps and atrocities or run the risk of their repetition. All your facts and examples must underscore that thesis.

Alternate Writing Assignment

1. Irene Herz's account ends with these words: "I have not forgotten that, and never shall, and that is why I have written all of this down." Write an essay in which you recount an event in your life that you want to preserve as a testimony for posterity. (Posterity could mean your children or family.)

2. Write an essay either attacking or defending Berger's statement that the original purpose of the German concentration camps was to "teach those people order and discipline."

HISTORY

MY SEARCH FOR JACK THE RIPPER
Colin Wilson

Colin Wilson (b. 1931 in Leicester) is an English author who had no formal education after the age of 16. He has worked as a laborer in England and on the Continent. He first received critical acclaim with the publication of *The Outsider* (1956), a novel in which he defined the "outsider" as the individual who sees that life is futile and that society is formed to conceal this terrible truth. Among Wilson's other works are *Beyond the Outsider* (1965), *The Glass Cage* (1966), *Bernard Shaw: A Reassessment* (1969), *Order of Assassins* (1972), and *Hesse, Reich, Borges* (1974). Fascinated with the crimes of the notorious Jack the Ripper, whose brutal murders of prostitutes in London confounded the London police in 1888, Wilson contributed the essay below to a book titled *Unsolved: Classic True Murder Cases* (1987).

Reading Advice

This is the kind of essay whose appreciation would be heightened by the reader's intimate geographical knowledge of London. So specific is the author in mentioning London neighborhoods and street names that the reader would be wise to begin with a map of metropolitan London handy. Appealing to our general fascination with unsolved mysteries, the author, writing almost a century after the last murder was committed by Jack the Ripper, reviews all of the facts available through news reports, court transcripts, and interviews of people now living in the houses where the crimes were committed. In reconstructing each murder, he sets the stage accurately and in detail, describing the dingy and sinister neighborhood of Whitechapel, where most of the brutal murders occurred.

Wilson's approach is to describe each case in chronological order, from beginning to end, including every hideous detail related to the stabbings and beatings of the prostitute victims. The author involves the readers, as if taking them on a geographical tour of the Ripper's territory by addressing them directly with such phrases as "If you take a tube to Aldgate East station. . . ." Or, "If you walk up Commercial Street from Aldgate. . . ." Or, "It is on the right as you go down the Commercial Road toward the East India Dock Road. . . ." Wilson concludes with his own guess as to the murderer's identity as well as a summary of other popular theories, allowing you to draw your own conclusions.

When I was about eight, someone   1
lent my father a great red volume called *The Fifty Most Amazing Crimes of the Last 100 Years*—I'm not sure why, for I've never yet caught my father reading a book. I was strictly forbidden to read it, in case it gave me nightmares. So I seized on it every time I was left alone in the house, and read it from cover to cover.

I have a copy of it beside me as I write. At the top of every article there is   2
a sketch of the criminal. Landru looks villainous and intellectual; Smith, who drowned his wives in the bath, is an unattractive nondescript. But there is no drawing of Jack the Ripper—only a large black question mark. That question mark started me on my search for Jack the Ripper. It is not logical, of course, but the mind of a child is romantic and not logical. Why should the Ripper be more interesting than Landru, just because he was never caught? No-one has yet discovered how Landru destroyed every trace of his victim's bodies, and, in its way, this mystery is far more interesting than guessing at the identity of Jack the Ripper. And yet it is the Ripper who exercises a fascination beyond that of any other mass murderer.

Most of them are boring little men, like Christie and Haigh—shifty, weak   3
and unimpressive. Most of them have had long criminal records—petty theft, swindling, burglary or confidence trickery—like Heath, Kurten and Dr. Marcel Petiot. Murder has not yet produced its Caesar, its Napoleon. Murderers are a dull lot.

Perhaps the Ripper was a sneak-thief, with many prison sentences behind   4
him; perhaps it was only Wormwood Scrubs, and not his death, that put an end to his amazing career. We shall never be certain. And that is enough to make the Ripper almost unique in the annals of mass murder. We know almost nothing about him.

How many murders did he commit? Even that is the subject of debate. All   5
that we do know is that at least five murders of unparalleled brutality were committed in the latter part of the year 1888. Four of them took place in the Whitechapel district of London, at night; the victims were all prostitutes, although none of them was what we would call 'professionals'. All London panicked. There were meetings in the streets; bands of citizens formed themselves into vigilante groups to patrol Whitechapel at night; thousands of men were questioned, and released; men carrying black bags were attacked by mobs; the Commissioner of Police resigned. And finally, after a lull of more than a month, the Ripper committed yet another crime, this time indoors. The pieces

From *Unsolved: Classic True Murder Cases*, by Colin Wilson, 1987. Reprinted by permission of David Bolt Associates.

of the victim—a girl in her early twenties—were left spread around the room like bits of a jigsaw puzzle. The panic reached new proportions; there were so many blue uniforms in Whitechapel that the place resembled a police barracks. And then nothing more happened. The murders stopped.

In the following year, 1889, there were two more murders of prostitutes in the Whitechapel area, but without the same appalling mutilations; we shall never know whether the same man was responsible for these.   6

When I came to London in 1951, Whitechapel exercised a deep and powerful fascination over me, but it was no longer the Whitechapel that Jack the Ripper had wandered around. Whitechapel is still a tough district, but by no means as tough as it had been in 1888. Then, sailors from foreign ships crowded the streets; there were dozens of cheap doss houses where the layabouts could sleep for as little as fourpence a night. And although many 'respectable' married women lived in Whitechapel, a large proportion of the female population was made up of non-professional prostitutes: women without men, women whose men had left them, or simply women whose men had spent their wages on drink.   7

It was a Whitechapel whose narrow, cobbled alleys were lit by gas lamps that stuck out of the walls; a Whitechapel where human derelicts slept out on the pavements or in entries at night; where murder and robbery were so commonplace that the newspapers didn't even bother to report them. This is the reason why the first two crimes attributed to the Ripper were not mentioned in the newspapers until the inquests.   8

All this has changed. In 1888, after the Annie Chapman murder, Bernard Shaw wrote a letter to the press in which he suggested that the murderer was a social reformer who wanted to draw attention to social conditions in the East End. He was probably wrong, but German high-explosives have done what Shaw failed to do, and changed the face of Whitechapel. When I first visited the district, bombs had left great empty spaces, and many of the houses were windowless and filled with rubble. After dark, tramps slept on the floors of these ruins. Huge blocks of council flats had sprung up in Hanbury Street, only a hundred yards from the spot where Annie Chapman was murdered, in a yard behind a barber's shop. The council school at the end of Old Montague Street stood black and empty, with political slogans chalked on its walls; now the school has disappeared, with only the black walls of the playground still standing.   9

The Whitechapel of the Ripper is disappearing day by day. In five years it will be non-existent.   10

Who was the first victim of the Ripper? It might have been Emma Smith, of George Street, Spitalfield, who was stabbed to death in Osborn Street.   11

Osborn Street is a sinister little thoroughfare that runs between Old Montague   12
Street and the Whitechapel Road. Emma Smith lived for twenty-four hours
after the attack, and stated positively that she had been assaulted and robbed
by four men, one of whom had stabbed her with an iron spike in the abdomen.
It was a brutal and stupid murder, and its victim was a pathetic, drunken
prostitute of forty-five, who had never had more than a few shillings in her
purse. She was staggering home drunk at four in the morning when the attack
took place. (There were no licensing hours in those days, and many pubs stayed
open all night.) An hour later, she was admitted to hospital, her head bruised,
her right ear almost torn off. Her death was due to peritonitis.

At the time of the murders, many journalists stated that this was the Ripper's   13
first crime. It seems unlikely, but the murder is worth mentioning for the
insight it gives into the Whitechapel of the 1880's. A man or woman might be
found like this almost any morning, robbed and battered; it was too commonplace to be reported in the daily press.

Many criminologists believe that the murder of Martha Turner was quite   14
definitely the first Ripper crime. This took place on August Bank Holiday, 1888.

Martha Turner was a prostitute who lived in George Yard Buildings, Com-   15
mercial Street. In the early hours of the morning, she was found on one of the
outside landings of the lodging-house; the post mortem revealed that she had
been stabbed thirty-nine times with some weapon like a bayonet, and the
coroner stated that the wounds had been inflicted by a left-handed man. Martha
Turner had been seen talking to a guardsman on the evening before the murder,
and since the injuries resembled bayonet wounds, the police started to look for
a left-handed soldier. All the guards in the Tower of London were paraded, but
no arrest was made. Within a few weeks, the murder had been forgotten. How
could anyone guess that a super-criminal was starting on a series of the most
sensational murders of all time?

No-one knows the precise location of George Yard Buildings where Martha   16
Turner, probably the Ripper's first victim, was stabbed to death, but we know
the district. If you take a tube to Aldgate East station on a Sunday morning,
you will see Whitechapel looking something like the Whitechapel of 1888.
Wander up Middlesex Street—known as 'Petticoat Lane'—and you will find
it hard to breathe among the crowds jammed around the market stalls. To your
right and left there are still cobbled streets that looked exactly the same when
Jack the Ripper walked through them in that 'Autumn of Terror'. Turn off to
your right, walk fifty yards, and you will find yourself in Commercial Street,
the heart and jugular vein of Whitechapel. Late at night, the police still walk
two abreast on these pavements. It is a tough district. And yet if you come
here at five o'clock on a Sunday afternoon, the quiet will surprise you. The
market has closed, and the people of Whitechapel are indoors having their tea,
or sleeping off their lunchtime beer.

In 1888, it would have been very different. To begin with, the pubs would   17
still have been open; drunks would have been snoring in the small alleyways
off Hanbury Street; but you would have been sensible enough not to explore
them, for your chances of being coshed and robbed would have been very high.
Probably in no other part of England was so much of the inhabitants' total
income spent on beer or spirits—and those were the days when pubs were
approximately five times as numerous as they are today. Alcohol was the best
chance of forgetfulness, the best way to escape from the dirt and overcrowding
and near-starvation.

This may be the reason why Jack the Ripper chose Whitechapel as his   18
hunting-ground. In a sink of human misery, the individual life does not count
for much, and the sight of a body prostrate in an alleyway causes no alarm—
and, in fact, this is what happened in the case of Mary Anne Nichols, the
Ripper's second victim.

In the early hours of the morning of August 31st, 1888, a carter named   19
William Cross was walking along Buck's Row, on his way to work. Buck's Row
is another street that has not changed since 1888, although its name is now
Durward Street. On one side of the road are small houses, all absolutely
uniform, and on the other are blocks of warehouses. Cross noticed something
on the other side of the street—a bundle which he took to be a tarpaulin.
Then he saw that it was a woman, apparently drunk. She was sprawled in the
entrance to an old stable-yard, with her head in the gutter. Another man walked
up as he stood there, looking down at her, and the newcomer said: 'Come on,
let's get her on her feet.'

They bent down to turn her over, and Cross jumped back, exclaiming: 20
'Blimey, she's bleeding!'

The other man confirmed this, and commented: 'She's not drunk—she's   21
perishing well dead.'

The two men ran off to find a policeman, and while they were away the   22
body was discovered by another policeman. Within a few minutes, four men
were standing around the body. It was about four o'clock in the morning.

Both the policemen were puzzled; they had beats that took them past where   23
the body was now lying, and both of them had been in the street, at either
end of Bucks Row, for the past quarter of an hour. Neither had seen anyone.
Someone summoned Dr. Ralph Llewellyn, who felt the woman's pulse, commented that she had been dead about half an hour, and told the police to take
her to the mortuary at the Old Montague Street workhouse. The noise of the
discussion attracted several people from the nearby houses. A Mrs Emma Green,
whose bedroom was within ten yards of the spot where the body had been
found remarked that 'whoever had done it' must have been very quiet, since
she had been lying awake for several hours, and had heard no sound.

In the morgue, a young policeman lifted the woman's clothes to gain some   24
idea of the extent of her injuries. What he saw made him vomit. The woman's

body had been ripped open from the throat to the stomach. The policeman rushed off to find Dr Llewellyn, who had to give him first aid before he hurried to the morgue.

The first problem was that of identification. This was quickly solved: the woman's name was Mary Anne Nichols, she was forty-two years old, and was known to her friends and acquaintances as Polly. She had been married to a printer's machinist and had born him five children, but they had been separated for seven years; her love of the gin bottle, and the slovenliness that resulted from it, had made him leave her. But as he stood over her body in the mortuary, he was heard to say: 'I forgive you for everything now that I see you like this.'

Since her marriage had broken up, Polly Nichols had sunk steadily lower. She had lived with several men in quick succession and had taken a job as a servant, but she had to steal from her employers to get money for drink, and had then gone to live in Whitechapel. Here she lived as a prostitute, sleeping in nightly doss houses where a bed could be had for fourpence. The main necessity was drink, however, and she would go with a man for the price of a glass of gin—a few pence. A few hours before her death, Polly had arrived at the doss house in Thrawl Street, completely drunk and without money. The lodging-house keeper turned her away. 'Don't worry,' she told him, 'I'll soon get the money. Look what a fine hat I've got.'

An hour later, an acquaintance saw her at the corner of Osborn Street, where Emma Smith had met her death a few months earlier. Asked if she was having any luck, Polly replied that she wasn't, but staggered off up Osborn Street, singing cheerfully to herself. She probably then turned right into Old Montague Street and wandered towards Vallance Road at the end. And some-where along here, she met a man.

It is still not certain how Jack the Ripper killed Polly Nichols with so little sound. A bruise on her face indicates that he clamped his hand over her mouth as he cut her throat, but they were standing on the three-foot-wide pavement of Bucks Row, and people were sleeping within a few yards. A policeman would have been visible at the end of the street, and there were five others within call. Men were climbing out of bed, getting ready to go to work, and others were returning home from Smithfield meat market or from jobs in the docks.

But the luck was with Jack the Ripper; he murdered Polly Nichols without being heard, and walked off into the dawn. Ultimately, this is one of the most amazing features of the whole business—the extraordinary luck that never deserted the Whitechapel sadist. As far as we know.

The nickname 'Jack the Ripper' was not invented until shortly before the notorious double murder of September 30th, but the police were intrigued to hear the phrase 'Leather Apron' used again and again in connection with the killer. Who was he?

No-one seemed to be sure. Some people described him as a short, villanouslooking cobbler who carried his clicking knife in the pocket of his leather apron. Others said that he led a gang that terrorized prostitutes, and demanded a percentage of their earnings. Yet others were of the opinion that he was a maniac who enjoyed frightening women, but who was probably harmless.

The police traced three men whose nickname was Leather Apron. The most 32 likely suspect was a Polish jew named Pizer, who was arrested on suspicion. His alibi proved to be unshakeable, and he was released.

The enquiries came to nothing, but one journalist who visited a doss house 33 in Dorset Street reported an interesting conversation. An old prostitute had wandered in to drink a glass of gin in the early hours of the morning, and the journalist asked her if she was not afraid of meeting Leather Apron. The woman replied: 'I hope I do meet him. I'm sick of this life. I'd rather be dead.'

It throws some light on the mental state of some of these women, and 34 explains why Jack the Ripper never seemed to have had any difficulty finding a victim, even at the height of the terror.

A week after the murder of Mary Anne Nichols the murderer found his 35 third victim, and the pattern of the crime was curiously similar to that in the previous case. Mary Nichols had been turned away from a doss house in Thrawl Street and went off to seek a 'customer'. Annie Chapman was turned out of a doss house in Dorset Street by the keeper, a man named Donovan, and, like Mary Nichols, her life was sacrificed for fourpence, the cost of a bed.

If you walk up Commercial Street from Aldgate, you will pass Dorset Street 36 on your left-hand side. Since 1888, its name had been changed to Duval Street. An extension of Spitalfields market now stands on the site of the lodging-house from which Annie Chapman was turned away in the early hours of Saturday, September 8th. When she left number 35, Dorset Street, she had only a few hundred yards to walk to her death. Halfway down Hanbury Street stands a barber's shop, number 29, which was still a barber's shop when I came to London; I occasionally went there for a haircut. In front of this shop, she met a man who allowed himself to be accosted. As it happens, 29 Hanbury Street was a convenient meeting-place for a prostitute and a prospective client, for a passage runs by the side of the house, with a door at each end. These doors were never kept closed. And at the far end of the passage was a back-yard— a yard that looked exactly as it did 72 years before, when the Ripper entered it with Annie Chapman.

They tiptoed down the passageway, and crept into a corner of the yard by 37 the fence. The man moved closer; she was not even aware of the knife he held in his left hand. A moment later she was dead; the first thrust had severed her windpipe. The man allowed her to slide down the fence. He slipped out of his dark overcoat, and bent over the woman.

The sight of the blood roused in him a kind of frenzy, and for five minutes 38 he remained there, crouched over her. Then he wiped the knife on her skirt, and cleaned some of the blood off his shoes. It was already getting light. He pulled on the overcoat, and crossed to the tap that projected from the fence three feet to the left of the body. From his overcoat he pulled a bundle, which he soaked in water and used to wipe his hands, then he dropped it under the tap. It was a leather apron.

As he pulled it out of his pocket, an envelope dropped out too. The man   39 picked this up, tore off its corner, which was marked with the crest of the Sussex Regiment, and dropped it into Annie Chapman's blood. It would be another false trail for the police to follow. Before leaving the yard, another idea struck him. He searched the pockets of the dead woman's jacket, and removed two brass rings, a few pennies and some farthings, then arranged these carefully by her feet.

A few pennies! Annie Chapman had actually possessed just enough money   40 to stay in the lodging-house! Did she know this? Or could it be that my reconstruction is wrong, and the Ripper took the pennies from his own pocket, as a sort of ironical payment for the pleasure she had given him?

An hour went by, and one of the inhabitants of the house, John Davies,   41 came downstairs and looked into the yard. The body was huddled against a fence. He rushed to Spitalfields Market, where he worked as a porter, and brought two of his fellow-workmen back with him. A few minutes later the police arrived, and the divisional surgeon, Mr Philips, was summoned. His first act was to remove the handkerchief tied around the woman's throat; immediately, the head rolled sideways—it was only just attached to the body. By now, the windows of all the surrounding houses were crowded with sightseers, and some of the local householders even charged a small fee for access to their windows.

Finally, the body was removed to the mortuary, where Mr Philips discovered   42 that the injuries were even more extensive than they had been in the case of Mary Nichols. In addition to numerous stab wounds, there were incisions in the woman's back and abdomen. Moreover, a careful examination of the body revealed that certain internal organs had been removed and taken away by the murderer. So too had two of her front teeth—a curious touch that repeated a feature of the murder of Mary Nichols.

At the inquest, Dr. Philips expressed the opinion that the murderer must   43 have been a man with some anatomical knowledge and medical skill. And the weapon must have been some kind of long-bladed knife, at least eight inches long, which might have been 'an instrument such as a doctor would use for surgery.'

Of all the Ripper sites, this one is best preserved. When I knocked on the   44 door, it was opened by Mrs Kathleen Manning, who, with her husband and daughter, were the sole occupants of the house; in 1888, sixteen people lived in it! Mrs Manning knew that one of the Ripper murders had been committed there, but she knew no details of the crime. But she told me how, on one occasion, she mentioned casually that Jack the Ripper had committed a murder there. To her surprise, the friend disappeared abruptly into the street, and refused to go back into the house!

Within a hundred yards of this last grim remnant of 1888, blocks of council   45
flats have replaced the insanitary lodging-houses and narrow alleyways through which the Ripper escaped. If the Whitechapel maniac visited his old haunts today, it is doubtful whether he would be able to find his way around!

Children sing and play today on the spot where the Ripper's next victim   46
was killed. It was in the back-yard of the International Working Men's Club at 40, Berners Street, where the Ripper began the most sensational night's work in English criminal history. The yard is now part of the playground of a London council school. No-one I talked to in the area even knew that Jack the Ripper had committed a murder there. But although the club has disappeared, the upper part of Berners Street still looked much as it did when the Ripper walked down it on the night of September 30th, 1888.

The story of that remarkable night begins at 1 a.m., when the steward of   47
the club tried to guide his pony and trap into the back-yard. He had some difficulty, for the pony was obviously unwilling to enter. The cart blocked the gateway, and the man—Louis Delmschutz—dismounted and peered into the darkness, trying to find out what was frightening the pony.

He did not know it, but he was very close to death. A few feet behind him,   48
still holding a knife, was the Whitechapel murderer. But Delmschutz was not aware of this, for he saw the body of a woman lying against the wall, and rushed into the club to raise the alarm.

The man who would soon be known as Jack the Ripper clambered over the   49
wheel of the cart and slipped out into Berners Street. A moment later, he had disappeared into an alleyway.

Delmschutz emerged from the club followed by a crowd of men who babbled   50
in Polish and Russian. Someone struck a light. The body was that of a tall woman, shabbily dressed. Her throat had been cut, and one of her ears was slightly torn. The ripper had been interrupted. The doctor who was called verified that the woman had been killed very recently indeed.

At the moment that the murderer walked out of Berners Street into the   51
Commercial Road, a prostitute named Catherine Eddowes was released from Bishopsgate Police Station, where she had been in charge for drunkenness since 8 o'clock. Five hours in a cell had not sobered her appreciably; she walked down Bishopsgate towards Aldgate, and the man who had just left Berners Street was walking along the commercial road towards his usual haunts. Berners Street was the farthest afield that he had yet ventured; it is on the right as you go down the Commercial Road towards the East India Dock Road—a good half-mile from Commercial Street, the Ripper's usual hunting-ground. Perhaps he was finding the narrow streets of Spitalfields too hot for him; policemen in

rubber-soled boots walked through his alleys, and the tradesmen of Whitechapel also prowled around in bands of 'vigilantes' in the hope of catching the murderer. At all events, the Ripper avoided Spitalfields and walked on towards Bishopsgate.

At the corner of Houndsditch he met Catherine Eddowes. After a brief   52
conversation, the two of them turned off to the right, into Duke Street. Halfway up Duke Street there is a narrow alleyway called St James Passage; in 1888 it had been known as Church Passage. At its far end lies Mitre Square, which looks today almost exactly as it looked in 1888. On its north side stands a warehouse.

The Ripper was standing on the south side of the square, near Church   53
Passage, when PC Watkins walked through the square on his beat; as the policeman walked by, he pressed back into the shadow of a doorway, and, as soon as the steps were out of earshot, he placed a hand over Eddowes' mouth and cut her throat.

Exactly a quarter of an hour later, PC Watkins again walked through Mitre   54
Square, but this time a mutilated body lay in the right-hand corner, near Church Passage. There was no doubt about the identity of the killer, for the body had been stabbed and cut ferociously, and the face had also been mutilated beyond recognition. And two of the woman's internal organs were missing.

The murderer had not given himself much time. The doctor who examined   55
the body agreed that it must have taken at least ten minutes to inflict so many injuries; besides, the removal of the organs revealed some medical skill. And yet the man walked off without fear into Duke Street and right across Whitechapel into Dorset Street, where he found a convenient sink in which to wash his hands. He had torn off a fragment of the woman's apron, and used this to wipe off the blood. Major Smith, of the City Police, actually saw the sink before the bloodstained water had had time to drain away. Possibly some noise frightened the killer there, for he hurried off without finishing the wash, and continued to wipe off the blood as he walked towards Aldgate again. He finally dropped the piece of bloodstained apron in Goulston Street, within a short distance of the scene of the murder.

Although the Ripper did not know it then, Dorset Street was to be the   56
scene of his most horrible murder, six weeks later.

Early the following morning, the Central News Agency received a letter   57
written in red ink, signed 'Jack the Ripper'. It was their second letter bearing this signature. The first had arrived two days before the murder, and promised 'some more work' in the near future. It also promised to clip off the ladies' ears and send them to the police. No-one had taken the first letter seriously— it was assumed to be another practical joke—but this second letter altered the complexion of things. To begin with, it arrived early in the day, before the news of the murders was generally known. Secondly, there *had* been an attempt to

cut off the ear of the first victim in Berners Street, and in his second letter the Ripper apologised for not sending it, saying that he had been interrupted!

The murder of Annie Chapman in Hanbury Street had caused a sensation,   58 but it was nothing to the furore that followed the double murder. Hysteria swept the country. Sir Charles Warren, the unpopular Commissioner of Police, was bombarded with furious telegrams demanding his resignation. (He did, in fact, finally resign.) He was also bombarded with letters full of theories about the identity of the murderer and how to catch him.

It is almost impossible to give an adequate idea of the commotion caused   59 by the murders, but the newspapers of the day devoted more space to them than our own journalists give to a royal wedding.

The police arrested about a dozen men a day, but all of them were released   60 after questioning. Sometimes cranks gave themselves up as Jack the Ripper, for after the two letters had been made public the name had caught the popular imagination.

It took the police some time to identify the two women who had been killed   61 that night. The woman who had been killed in Berners Street was finally identified as Elizabeth Stride, a Swedish woman who had taken to drink and prostitution after some emotional tragedy. (One story has it that she saw her children drowned in an accident on a Thames steamer.) The second victim was less easy to trace, because the mutilations to her face made recognition difficult, and there was one stage when she was identified as an Irishwoman named Mary Anne Kelly—an astounding coincidence in view of what was to come. Eventually, the evidence of her clothes established that she was Catherine Eddowes, aged forty-five, and that she had been in police custody only three-quarters of an hour before she was murdered.

There are very few streets in London whose names have been changed   62 because of some evil notoriety associated with the original name. I know of only one in recent years: Rillington Place, the site of the Christie murders. There seems no doubt that Jack the Ripper holds the record for altering street names: Bucks Row, the scene of the murder of Mary Nichols, is now Dunward Street; Dorset Street, the scene of his last murder, has become Duval Street; and I have never been able to discover what became of George Street, where his first murder took place.

In 1888, Dorset Street was a narrow and shabby thoroughfare running   63 parallel with Spitalfields market, in Brushfield Street. On its north side, extending towards the market, was an entry labelled Millers Court. It was in a house in Millers Court that the Whitechapel murderer killed and dismembered his last victim, a twenty-four-year-old prostitute called Mary Jeanette Kelly.

Five weeks had elapsed since the double murder, and London had begun to   64 hope that the Ripper had left town. The police and vigilante groups began to relax a little. Then, on the morning of November 9th, a man knocked on the door of Mary Kelly to ask for the rent. Getting no reply, he went round to the window and peered through the half-open curtains. What he saw was probably the most appalling sight in London's violent criminal history.

The body that lay on the bed had been taken to pieces like a jigsaw puzzle,   65
and the pieces had been scattered around the room, draped over a picture, or piled upon the sideboard. The heart lay on the pillow, beside the head. The hysteria in London reached new heights.

At some time after two o'clock on the morning of November 9th, the Ripper   66
had been solicited by Mary Kelly outside her room in Millers Court. A man named Hutchinson had actually watched the 'pick-up' and described the man as a 'toff', a short, thickset man with a curling moustache, and carrying a parcel of some sort. A short time later, a neighbour heard Mary Kelly singing 'Sweet Violets'. At 3:10 the same neighbour heard a cry of 'Murder!' And for the next two hours there was silence, as Jack the Ripper dissected the body. Then the Ripper left, and the great mystery begins.

For how did he walk through London in clothes that must have been soaked   67
in blood? Why did he burn a pile of clothes in the grate of Mary Kelly's room? Above all, what happened to the murderer after November 9th? There is no case in history of a maniacal killer who simply stopped of his own accord. Why did he stop?

These questions have puzzled students of crime ever since. There are theories   68
by the dozen, but no shred of evidence. Is it possible, at this late date, that someone will prove the identity of Jack the Ripper? Are there papers somewhere in police files, or in some mental home, that tell the whole story?

We come, then, to the theories of the case. My own conviction is that the   69
Ripper was a sadist—that is, a mentally sick person who found it impossible to gain sexual satisfaction except by inflicting pain, or producing large quantities of blood. It is just conceivable that he might have stopped killing of his own accord, completely satiated by his final crime.

The best-known theory of the Ripper's identity and motives was propounded   70
by Leonard Matters, who declared—without producing a shred of evidence— that the Ripper was a certain Doctor Stanley, a widower who had been pas- sionately fond of his only son. The son had died of syphilis, contracted from Mary Kelly, and Doctor Stanley had then devoted his life to a search for the woman. He questioned all his victims about her, and murdered them to make sure that they kept silent. Finally, after he found Mary Kelly, he ceased to stalk the East End. Matters alleges that Doctor Stanley died in Buenos Aires, and made a circumstantial deathbed confession.

One of the most popular theories in police circles is that George Chapman   71
was Jack the Ripper. Chapman was actually a Pole whose real name was Severin Klossowski and, at the time of the murders, he was working as a barber in Whitechapel. In 1889, Chapman went to America, returning to London in

1892. During the next ten years, Chapman poisoned three women with whom he cohabited. There was no motive for the murders; he gained nothing by them; it is almost certain that they were purely sadistic. Chapman was executed in 1903, and Chief Inspector Abberline, who had been in charge of the Ripper investigations, stated dogmatically that Chapman was the Ripper.

Certainly, the dates correspond closely enough, and Hargrave Adam, who   72 edited *The Trial of George Chapman,* declared that the 'Ripper murders' took place in Jersey City while Chapman was living there in 1890. But it is hard to believe that the man who dismembered Mary Kelly could have changed his method to antimony poisoning.

One of the most plausible theories of the Ripper's identity was recently put   73 forward by Donald McCormick in his book *The Identity of Jack the Ripper.* McCormick points out that among the papers of Rasputin, the Russian 'monk' who was murdered in 1917, there was a document which claimed that Jack the Ripper was an insane Russian who had been sent to England by the Tsarist police, with the sole aim of embarrassing the English police. McCormick unearthed a great deal of evidence to connect the Ripper murders with Russian immigrants in the East End, and particularly with a barber-surgeon named Pedachenko.

He claims to have seen an issue of a Russian secret police gazette which   74 reports the death of Pedachenko in a Russian mental home, and mentions that he had committed five murders of women in the East End in 1888. If this piece of evidence is still in existence, it is probably the most definite lead we have to the Ripper's identity. According to McCormick's theory, Pedachenko lived in Walworth, and was helped in his murders by two accomplices. His description corresponds closely with that given by the witnesses who claimed to have seen the Ripper: a short, broad-shouldered man, with a large moustache, well-dressed and wearing a gold watch-chain. If it is definitely established that the Ripper was Pedachenko, one of the great mysteries of crime will be at an end.

The East End of Jack the Ripper is disappearing fast, but it is still to be   75 found in a few alleyways and narrow entries into old buildings. His murders were a product of these slums and of cheap gin, starving women and fourpence-a-night doss houses. In spite of their 'local colour', it will be as well when they disappear forever.

Afterword

Since Colin Wilson wrote these words in 1960, many of these places have indeed disappeared, although the curious no longer need to hunt for the Ripper murder sites: guided pedestrian tours are regularly held, and they are well attended by Londoners and visitors alike.

But despite much research and many new theories, the identity of the Ripper remains as elusive as ever. In the absence of further evidence,

Pedachenko has fallen from favour as a suspect, but a new candidate was soon afterwards proposed in the person of M. J. Druitt, a young lawyer with a history of mental instability, who may have been in the Whitechapel area at the time of the killings, and who killed himself shortly after the murders ceased. Other potential Rippers include J. K. Stephen, the Duke of Clarence, and— in an extremely complicated theory involving the painter Walter Sickert, freemasonry, more royalty and the Chief of Police—a threefold murderer (for the whole crazy story see Stephen Knight's Jack the Ripper: the Final Solution.*). There is no doubt that the final word on the Whitechapel murderer will not be written for some considerable time yet.*

Questions for Critical Thinking

1. Serial murderers in our era (the Boston Strangler, the Red Light Bandit, the Charlie Manson Family, the Night Stalker) continue to exercise a strong fascination on the public imagination. What do you suppose is the allure of these particular criminals?

2. What is the best way for society to handle serial murderers once they have been caught? Should they be placed behind bars for life without the possibility of parole? Should they be executed? Should they be signed into a mental hospital where they can receive psychotherapy until they no longer have the urge to kill? What other solution do you suggest? Give reasons for your answer.

3. Who deserves legal protection more—mass murderers or their victims? Give reasons for your answer.

4. What comparisons, if any, can you draw between Jack the Ripper and the ichneumon wasp of "Nonmoral Nature"? What differences, if any, are there?

5. Which of the theories presented by the author to explain the Ripper murders seems most logical? Explain your choice. If you have yet another theory to propose, do so.

6. Of all the theories proposed as explanations for the Ripper murders, which one would make the best movie? Give reasons for your choice.

7. How would your views or sympathies be affected if the Ripper had turned out to be a woman rather than a man? Explain your answer.

8. If Jack the Ripper turned out to be your father, what do you think you would do?

Writing Assignment

Write an essay in which you probe the issue of freedom of choice as applied to sadistic murderers like Jack the Ripper. You may approach this general topic from any angle you wish.

Writing Advice

In preparing to write this essay, you may find it helpful to review the following essays from this book: "Why War?" by Sigmund Freud; "The Dilemma of Determinism," by William James; and "The Leopold and Loeb Case," by Clarence Darrow. All of these essays deal with human responsibility and action and can serve as a counterpoint or sounding board for your own ideas.

The basic questions you need to answer are these: How responsible are human beings for their actions? How much freedom of choice do psychopathic murderers have? At what point, if any, is a person no longer responsible? If, at a certain point, responsibility is no longer relevant, then who is to decide when that point has been reached? How should the courts deal with murderers who are found not to be not responsible for their actions?

The challenge of this essay lies in the requirement that you not only take a strong and clear position but that you try to influence your reader to agree with you. Certainly, you will want to use examples of actual culprits who were or were not convicted, but you may also set up a hypothetical situation. The contemporary scene offers numerous examples for you to analyze.

Alternate Writing Assignment

1. Professor Carol Gilligan, a Harvard professor, has begun something of a revolution in ethical theory, pointing out that most of the history of ethics involves a strong male bias and that female ethics may in fact be very different. Write an essay in which you argue either for or against the idea that women are by nature less driven to violent crimes than are men.

2. Write an essay proposing what to do with criminals like Jack the Ripper if they are caught and convicted.

LITERATURE

BARN BURNING
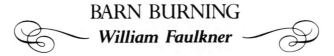
William Faulkner

William Faulkner (1897–1962) was one of America's greatest twentieth-century novelists. Born in the deep South into a family called Falkner, he changed the spelling of his last name to Faulkner when he published his first book, a collection of poems titled *The Marble Faun* (1914). In 1918, he went to Canada to train as a cadet pilot for the Royal Air Force, then attended the University of Mississippi from 1919 to 1920. In

1925, he visited Paris for several months. Six years later he bought "Rowanoak," a prewar mansion near Oxford, Mississippi, where he lived as a semirecluse until his death.

Faulkner became the voice for all of the anguish and disillusionment suffered by the South as it tried to cope with the loss of traditional values and the decay of the land after the Civil War. Most of his novels are set in Yoknapatawpha County, an imaginary area in Mississippi. But, so realistic were Faulkner's descriptions of this fictional county, that visitors from all over the world continually arrive in Oxford to look for certain geographical landmarks found in the novels. Despite their many violent and sordid scenes, Faulkner's novels abound with a sense of profound human compassion. Among his best-known works are *The Sound and the Fury* (1929), *As I Lay Dying* (1930), *Light in August* (1932), *Absalom, Absalom!* (1936), *The Hamlet* (1940), *Requiem for a Nun* (1951), *A Fable* (1954), and *The Reivers* (1962). For his enormous contribution, Faulkner received the 1949 Nobel Prize for Literature. The short story below is reprinted from *Collected Stories of William Faulkner* (1939).

Reading Advice

As you read, keep in mind that the author's purpose is to recreate a slice of ordinary human life as it might have occurred in post–Civil War Mississippi. Specifically, Faulkner dramatizes the theme of how those in authority often abuse weak and innocent people for unethical or immoral ends. In this story, the person in authority is not a powerful governor or even a leader of the community; in fact, he is an ignorant itinerant farm worker who rules his family with the rod of a belligerent despot. You may find the story occasionally puzzling because the author's style is to jumble time sequences and to use unedited internal dialogue as a means of allowing the reader a glimpse into the heart and mind of the main character, Sarty Sartoris. Do not let this mannerism disturb you—simply keep reading, and gradually the meaning of the story will dawn on you.

*T*he store in which the Justice of the   1
Peace's court was sitting smelled of cheese. The boy, crouched on his nail keg at the back of the crowded room, knew he smelled cheese, and more: from where he sat he could see the ranked shelves close-packed with the solid, squat, dynamic shapes of tin cans whose labels his stomach read, not from the lettering which meant nothing to his mind but from the scarlet devils and the silver curve of fish—this, the cheese which he knew he smelled and the hermetic meat which his intestines believed he smelled coming in intermittent gusts momentary and brief between the other constant one, the smell and sense just a little of fear because mostly of despair and grief, the old fierce pull of blood. He could not see the table where the Justice sat and before which his father

and his father's enemy (*our enemy* he thought in that despair; *ourn! mine and hisn both! He's my father!*) stood, but he could hear them, the two of them that is, because his father had said no word yet:

"But what proof have you, Mr. Harris?"   2

"I told you. The hog got into my corn. I caught it up and sent it back to   3
him. He had no fence that would hold it. I told him so, warned him. The next time I put the hog in my pen. When he came to get it I gave him enough wire to patch up his pen. The next time I put the hog up and kept it. I rode down to his house and saw the wire I gave him still rolled on to the spool in his yard. I told him he could have the hog when he paid me a dollar pound fee. That evening a nigger came with the dollar and got the hog. He was a strange nigger. He said, 'He say to tell you wood and hay kin burn.' I said, 'What?' 'That whut he say to tell you,' the nigger said. 'Wood and hay kin burn.' That night my barn burned. I got the stock out but I lost the barn."

"Where is the nigger? Have you got him?"   4

"He was a strange nigger, I tell you. I don't know what became of him."   5

"But that's not proof. Don't you see that's not proof?"   6

"Get that boy up here. He knows." For a moment the boy thought too that   7
the man meant his older brother until Harris said, "Not him. The little one. The boy," and, crouching, small for his age, small and wiry like his father, in patched and faded jeans even too small for him, with straight, uncombed, brown hair and eyes gray and wild as storm scud, he saw the men between himself and the table part and become a lane of grim faces, at the end of which he saw the Justice, a shabby, collarless, graying man in spectacles, beckoning him. He felt no floor under his bare feet; he seemed to walk beneath the palpable weight of the grim turning faces. His father, stiff in his black Sunday coat donned not for the trial but for the moving, did not even look at him. *He aims for me to lie,* he thought, again with that frantic grief and despair. *And I will have to do hit.*

"What's your name, boy?" the Justice said.   8

"Colonel Sartoris Snopes," the boy whispered.   9

"Hey?" the Justice said. "Talk louder. Colonel Sartoris? I reckon anybody   10
named for Colonel Sartoris in this country can't help but tell the truth, can they?" The boy said nothing. *Enemy! Enemy!* he thought; for a moment he could not even see, could not see that the Justice's face was kindly nor discern that his voice was troubled when he spoke to the man named Harris: "Do you want me to question this boy?" But he could hear, and during those subsequent long seconds while there was absolutely no sound in the crowded little room save that of quiet and intent breathing it was as if he had swung outward at the end of a grape vine, over a ravine, and at the top of the swing had been caught in a prolonged instant of mesmerized gravity, weightless in time.

"No!" Harris said violently, explosively. "Damnation! Send him out of here!"   11

Now time, the fluid world, rushed beneath him again, the voices coming to him again through the smell of cheese and sealed meat, the fear and despair and the old grief of blood:

"This case is closed. I can't find against you, Snopes, but I can give you advice. Leave this country and don't come back to it."   12

His father spoke for the first time, his voice cold and harsh, level, without emphasis: "I aim to. I don't figure to stay in a country among people who . . ." he said something unprintable and vile, addressed to no one.   13

"That'll do," the Justice said. "Take your wagon and get out of this country before dark. Case dismissed."   14

His father turned, and he followed the stiff black coat, the wiry figure walking a little stiffly from where a Confederate provost's man's musket ball had taken him in the heel on a stolen horse thirty years ago, followed the two backs now, since his older brother had appeared from somewhere in the crowd, no taller than the father but thicker, chewing tobacco steadily, between the two lines of grim-faced men and out of the store and across the worn gallery and down the sagging steps and among the dogs and half-grown boys in the mild May dust, where as he passed a voice hissed: 15

"Barn burner!"   16

Again he could not see, whirling; there was a face in a red haze, moonlike, bigger than the full moon, the owner of it half again his size, he leaping in the red haze toward the face, feeling no blow, feeling no shock when his head struck the earth, scrabbling up and leaping again, feeling no blow this time either and tasting no blood, scrabbling up to see the other boy in full flight and himself already leaping into pursuit as his father's hand jerked him back, the harsh, cold voice speaking above him: "Go get in the wagon."   17

It stood in a grove of locusts and mulberries across the road. His two hulking sisters in their Sunday dresses and his mother and her sister in calico and sunbonnets were already in it, sitting on and among the sorry residue of the dozen and more movings which even the boy could remember—and battered stove, the broken beds and chairs, the clock inlaid with mother-of-pearl, which would not run, stopped at some fourteen minutes past two o'clock of a dead and forgotten day and time, which had been his mother's dowry. She was crying, though when she saw him she drew her sleeve across her face and began to descend from the wagon. "Get back," the father said.   18

"He's hurt. I got to get some water and wash his . . ."   19

"Get back in the wagon," his father said. He got in too, over the tail-gate. His father mounted to the seat where the older brother already sat and struck the gaunt mules two savage blows with the peeled willow, but without heat. It was not even sadistic; it was exactly that same quality which in later years would cause his descendants to over-run the engine before putting a motor car into motion, striking and reining back in the same movement. The wagon   20 went on, the store with its quiet crowd of grimly watching men dropped behind; a curve in the road hid it. *Forever* he thought. *Maybe he's done satisfied now, now that he has* . . . stopping himself, not to say it aloud even to himself. His mother's hand touched his shoulder.

"Does hit hurt?" she said.   21

"Naw," he said. "Hit don't hurt. Lemme be."   22

"Can't you wipe some of the blood off before hit dries?"   23

"I'll wash to-night," he said. "Lemme be, I tell you."   24

The wagon went on. He did not know where they were going. None of   25
them ever did or ever asked, because it was always somewhere, always a house of sorts waiting for them a day or two days or even three days away. Likely his father had already arranged to make a crop on another farm before he . . . Again he had to stop himself. He (the father) always did. There was something about his wolflike independence and even courage when the advantage was at least neutral which impressed strangers, as if they got from his latent ravening ferocity not so much a sense of dependability as a feeling that his ferocious conviction in the rightness of his own actions would be of advantage to all whose interest lay with his.

That night they camped, in a grove of oaks and beeches where a spring ran.   26
The nights were still cool and they had a fire against it, of a rail lifted from a nearby fence and cut into lengths—a small fire, neat, niggard almost, a shrewd fire; such fires were his father's habit and custom always, even in freezing weather. Older, the boy might have remarked this and wondered why not a big one; why should not a man who had not only seen the waste and extravagance of war, but who had in his blood an inherent voracious prodigality with material not his own, have burned everything in sight? Then he might have gone a step farther and thought that that was the reason: that niggard blaze was the living fruit of nights passed during those four years in the woods hiding from all men, blue or gray, with his strings of horses (captured horses, he called them). And older still, he might have divined the true reason: that the element of fire spoke to some deep mainspring of his father's being, as the element of steel or of powder spoke to other men, as the one weapon for the preservation of integrity, else breath were not worth the breathing, and hence to be regarded with respect and used with discretion.

But he did not think this now and he had seen those same niggard blazes   27
all his life. He merely ate his supper beside it and was already half asleep over his iron plate when his father called him, and once more he followed the stiff back, the stiff and ruthless limp, up the slope and on to the starlit road where, turning, he could see his father against the stars but without face or depth— a shape black, flat, and bloodless as though cut from tin in the iron folds of the frockcoat which had not been made for him, the voice harsh like tin and without heat like tin:

"You were fixing to tell them. You would have told him." He didn't answer.   28

His father struck him with the flat of his hand on the side of the head, hard but without heat, exactly as he had struck the two mules at the store, exactly as he would strike either of them with any stick in order to kill a horse fly, his voice still without heat or anger: "You're getting to be a man. You got to learn. You got to learn to stick to your own blood or you ain't going to have any blood to stick to you. Do you think either of them, any man there this morning, would? Don't you know all they wanted was a chance to get at me because they knew I had them beat? Eh?" Later, twenty years later, he was to tell himself, "If I had said they wanted only truth, justice, he would have hit me again." But now he said nothing. He was not crying. He just stood there. "Answer me," his father said.

"Yes," he whispered. His father turned.   29

"Get on to bed. We'll be there to-morrow."   30

To-morrow they were there. In the early afternoon the wagon stopped before   31
a paintless two-room house identical almost with the dozen others it had stopped before even in the boy's ten years, and again, as on the other dozen occasions, his mother and aunt got down and began to unload the wagon, although his two sisters and his father and brother had not moved.

"Likely hit ain't fitten for hawgs," one of the sisters said.   32

"Nevertheless, fit it will and you'll hog it and like it," his father said. "Get   33
out of them chairs and help your Ma unload."

The two sisters got down, big, bovine, in a flutter of cheap ribbons; one of   34
them drew from the jumbled wagon bed a battered lantern, the other a worn broom. His father handed the reins to the older son and began to climb stiffly over the wheel. "When they get unloaded, take the team to the barn and feed them." Then he said, and at first the boy thought he was still speaking to his brother: "Come with me."

"Me?" he said.   35

"Yes," his father said. "You."   36

"Abner," his mother said. His father paused and looked back—the harsh   37
level stare beneath the shaggy, graying, irascible brows.

"I reckon I'll have a word with the man that aims to begin to-morrow   38
owning me body and soul for the next eight months."

They went back up the road. A week ago—or before last night, that is—   39
he would have asked where they were going, but not now. His father had struck him before last night but never before had he paused afterward to explain why; it was as if the blow and the following calm, outrageous voice still rang, repercussed, divulging nothing to him save the terrible handicap of being young, the light weight of his few years, just heavy enough to prevent his soaring free of the world as it seemed to be ordered but not heavy enough to keep him footed solid in it, to resist it and try to change the course of its events.

Presently he could see the grove of oaks and cedars and the other flowering   40
trees and shrubs where the house would be, though not the house yet. They

walked beside a fence massed with honeysuckle and Cherokee roses and came to a gate swinging open between two brick pillars, and now, beyond a sweep of drive, he saw the house for the first time and at that instant he forgot his father and the terror and despair both, and even when he remembered his father again (who had not stopped) the terror and despair did not return. Because, for all the twelve movings, they had sojourned until now in a poor country, a land of small farms and fields and houses, and he had never seen a house like this before. *Hit's big as a courthouse* he thought quietly, with a surge of peace and joy whose reason he could not have thought into words, being too young for that: *They are safe from him. People whose lives are a part of this peace and dignity are beyond his touch, he no more to them than a buzzing wasp: capable of stinging for a little moment but that's all; the spell of this peace and dignity rendering even the barns and stable and cribs which belong to it impervious to the puny flames he might contrive* . . . this, the peace and joy, ebbing for an instant as he looked again at the stiff black back, the stiff and implacable limp of the figure which was not dwarfed by the house, for the reason that it had never looked big anywhere and which now, against the serene columned backdrop, had more than ever that impervious quality of something cut ruthlessly from tin, depthless, as though, sidewise to the sun, it would cast no shadow. Watching him, the boy remarked the absolutely undeviating course which his father held and saw the stiff foot come squarely down in a pile of fresh droppings where a horse had stood in the drive and which his father could have avoided by a simple change of stride. But it ebbed only for a moment, though he could not have thought this into words either, walking on in the spell of the house, which he could even want but without envy, without sorrow, certainly never with that ravening and jealous rage which unknown to him walked in the ironlike black coat before him: *Maybe he will feel it too. Maybe it will even change him now from what maybe he couldn't help but be.*

They crossed the portico. Now he could hear his father's stiff foot as it came 41 down on the boards with clocklike finality, a sound out of all proportion to the displacement of the body it bore and which was not dwarfed either by the white door before it, as though it had attained to a sort of vicious and ravening minimum not to be dwarfed by anything—the flat, wide, black hat, the formal coat of broadcloth which had once been black but which had now that friction-glazed greenish cast of the bodies of old house flies, the lifted sleeve which was too large, the lifted hand like a curled claw. The door opened so promptly that the boy knew the Negro must have been watching them all the time, an old man with neat grizzled hair, in a linen jacket, who stood barring the door with his body, saying, "Wipe yo foots, white man, fo you come in here. Major ain't home nohow."

"Get out of my way, nigger," his father said, without heat too, flinging the 42 door back and the Negro also and entering, his hat still on his head. And now the boy saw the prints of the stiff foot on the doorjamb and saw them appear on the pale rug behind the machinelike deliberation of the foot which seemed to bear (or transmit) twice the weight which the body compassed. The Negro was shouting "Miss Lula! Miss Lula!" somewhere behind them, then the boy, deluged as though by a warm wave by a suave turn of carpeted stair and a pendant glitter of chandeliers and a mute gleam of gold frames, heard the swift feet and saw her too, a lady—perhaps he had never seen her like before either—in a gray, smooth gown with lace at the throat and an apron tied at the waist and the sleeves turned back, wiping cake or biscuit dough from her hands with a towel as she came up the hall, looking not at his father at all but at the tracks on the blond rug with an expression of incredulous amazement.

"I tried," the Negro cried. "I tole him to . . ."   43

"Will you please go away?" she said in a shaking voice. "Major de Spain is   44
not at home. Will you please go away?"

His father had not spoken again. He did not speak again. He did not even   45
look at her. He just stood stiff in the center of the rug, in his hat, the shaggy iron-gray brows twitching slightly above the pebble-colored eyes as he appeared to examine the house with brief deliberation. Then with the same deliberation he turned; the boy watched him pivot on the good leg and saw the stiff foot drag round the arc of the turning, leaving a final long and fading smear. His father never looked at it, he never once looked down at the rug. The Negro held the door. It closed behind them, upon the hysteric and indistinguishable woman-wail. His father stopped at the top of the steps and scraped his boot clean on the edge of it. At the gate he stopped again. He stood for a moment, planted stiffly on the stiff foot, looking back at the house. "Pretty and white, ain't it?" he said. "That's sweat. Nigger sweat. Maybe it ain't white enough yet to suit him. Maybe he wants to mix some white sweat with it."

Two hours later the boy was chopping wood behind the house within which   46
his mother and aunt and the two sisters (the mother and aunt, not the two girls, he knew that; even at this distance and muffled by walls the flat loud voices of the two girls emanated an incorrigible idle inertia) were setting up the stove to prepare a meal, when he heard the hooves and saw the linen-clad man on a fine sorrel mare, whom he recognized even before he saw the rolled rug in front of the Negro youth following on a fat bay carriage horse—a suffused, angry face vanishing, still at full gallop, beyond the corner of the house where his father and brother were sitting in the two tilted chairs; and a moment later, almost before he could have put the axe down, he heard the hooves again and watched the sorrel mare go back out of the yard, already galloping again. Then his father began to shout one of the sisters' names, who presently emerged backward from the kitchen door dragging the rolled rug along the ground by one end while the other sister walked behind it.

"If you ain't going to tote, go on and set up the wash pot," the first said.   47

"You, Sarty!" the second shouted. "Set up the wash pot!" His father appeared   48
at the door, framed against that shabbiness, as he had been against that other
bland perfection, impervious to either, the mother's anxious face at his shoulder.

"Go on," the father said. "Pick it up." The two sisters stooped, broad,   49
lethargic; stooping, they presented an incredible expanse of pale cloth and a
flutter of tawdry ribbons.

"If I thought enough of a rug to have to git hit all the way from France I   50
wouldn't keep hit where folks coming in would have to tromp on hit," the first
said. They raised the rug.

"Abner," the mother said. "Let me do it."   51

"You go back and git dinner," his father said. "I'll tend to this."   52

From the woodpile through the rest of the afternoon the boy watched them,   53
the rug spread flat in the dust beside the bubbling wash-pot, the two sisters
stooping over it with that profound and lethargic reluctance, while the father
stood over them in turn, implacable and grim, driving them though never
raising his voice again. He could smell the harsh homemade lye they were using;
he saw his mother come to the door once and look toward them with an
expression not anxious now but very like despair; he saw his father turn, and
he fell to with the axe and saw from the corner of his eye his father raise from
the ground a flattish fragment of field stone and examine it and return to the
pot, and this time his mother actually spoke: "Abner. Abner. Please don't. Please,
Abner."

Then he was done too. It was dusk; the whippoorwills had already begun.   54
He could smell coffee from the room where they would presently eat the cold
food remaining from the mid-afternoon meal, though when he entered the
house he realized they were having coffee again probably because there was a
fire on the hearth, before which the rug now lay spread over the backs of the
two chairs. The tracks of his father's foot were gone. Where they had been
were now long, water-cloudy scoriations resembling the sporadic course of a
lilliputian mowing machine.

It still hung there while they ate the cold food and then went to bed, scattered   55
without order or claim up and down the two rooms, his mother in one bed,
where his father would later lie, the older brother in the other, himself, the
aunt, and the two sisters on pallets on the floor. But his father was not in bed
yet. The last thing the boy remembered was the depthless, harsh silhouette of
the hat and coat bending over the rug and it seemed to him that he had not
even closed his eyes when the silhouette was standing over him, the fire almost
dead behind it, the stiff foot prodding him awake. "Catch up the mule," his
father said.

When he returned with the mule his father was standing in the black door,   56
the rolled rug over his shoulder. "Ain't you going to ride?" he said.

"No. Give me your foot."   57

He bent his knee into his father's hand, the wiry, surprising power flowed   58
smoothly, rising, he rising with it, on to the mule's bare back (they had owned
a saddle once; the boy could remember it though not when or where) and with
the same effortlessness his father swung the rug up in front of him. Now in
the starlight they retraced the afternoon's path, up the dusty road rife with
honeysuckle, through the gate and up the black tunnel of the drive to the
lightless house, where he sat on the mule and felt the rough warp of the rug
drag across his thighs and vanish.

"Don't you want me to help?" he whispered. His father did not answer and   59
now he heard again that stiff foot striking the hollow portico with that wooden
and clocklike deliberation, that outrageous overstatement of the weight it carried. The rug, hunched, not flung (the boy could tell that even in the darkness)
from his father's shoulder struck the angle of wall and floor with a sound
unbelievably loud, thunderous, then the foot again, unhurried and enormous;
a light came on in the house and the boy sat, tense, breathing steadily and
quietly and just a little fast, though the foot itself did not increase its beat at
all, descending the steps now; now the boy could see him.

"Don't you want to ride now?" he whispered. "We kin both ride now," the   60
light within the house altering now, flaring up and sinking. *He's coming down the
stairs now,* he thought. He had already ridden the mule up beside the horse
block; presently his father was up behind him and he doubled the reins over
and slashed the mule across the neck, but before the animal could begin to
trot the hard, thin arm came round him, the hard, knotted hand jerking the
mule back to a walk.

In the first red rays of the sun they were in the lot, putting plow gear on   61
the mules. This time the sorrel mare was in the lot before he heard it at all,
the rider collarless and even bareheaded, trembling, speaking in a shaking voice
as the woman in the house had done. His father merely looking up once before
stooping again to the hame he was buckling, so that the man on the mare spoke
to his stooping back:

"You must realize you have ruined that rug. Wasn't there anybody here, any   62
of your women . . ." he ceased, shaking, the boy watching him, the older brother
leaning now in the stable door, chewing, blinking slowly and steadily at nothing
apparently. "It cost a hundred dollars. But you never had a hundred dollars.
You never will. So I'm going to charge you twenty bushels of corn against your
crop. I'll add it in your contract and when you come to the commissary you
can sign it. That won't keep Mrs. de Spain quiet but maybe it will teach you
to wipe your feet off before you enter her house again."

Then he was gone. The boy looked at his father, who still had not spoken   63
or even looked up again, who was now adjusting the loggerhead in the hame.

"Pap," he said. His father looked at him—the inscrutable face, the shaggy   64
brows beneath which the gray eyes glinted coldly. Suddenly the boy went toward
him, fast, stopping as suddenly. "You done the best you could!" he cried. "If
he wanted hit done different why didn't he wait and tell you how? He won't
git no twenty bushels! He won't git none! We'll gether hit and hide hit! I kin
watch . . ."

"Did you put the cutter back in that straight stock like I told you?"   65

"No, sir," he said.   66

"Then go do it."   67

That was Wednesday. During the rest of that week he worked steadily, at   68
what was within his scope and some which was beyond it, with an industry
that did not need to be driven nor even commanded twice; he had this from
his mother, with the difference that some at least of what he did he liked to
do, such as splitting wood with the half-size axe which his mother and aunt
had earned, or saved money somehow, to present him with at Christmas. In
company with the two older women (and on one afternoon, even one of the
sisters), he built pens for the shoat and the cow which were a part of his
father's contract with the landlord, and one afternoon, his father being absent,
gone somewhere on one of the mules, he went to the field.

They were running a middle buster now, his brother holding the plow   69
straight while he handled the reins, and walking beside the straining mule, the
rich black soil shearing cool and damp against his bare ankles, he thought *Maybe*
this is the end of it. Maybe even that twenty bushels that seems hard to have to pay for
just a rug will be a cheap price for him to stop forever and always from being what he
used to be; thinking, dreaming now, so that his brother had to speak sharply to
him to mind the mule: *Maybe he even won't collect the twenty bushels. Maybe it will*
all add up and balance and vanish—corn, rug, fire; the terror and grief, the being pulled
two ways like between two teams of horses—gone, done with for ever and ever.

Then it was Saturday; he looked up from beneath the mule he was harnessing   70
and saw his father in the black coat and hat. "Not that," his father said. "The
wagon gear." And then, two hours later, sitting in the wagon bed behind his
father and brother on the seat, the wagon accomplished a final curve, and he
saw the weathered paintless store with its tattered tobacco- and patent-med-
icine posters and the tethered wagons and saddle animals below the gallery. He
mounted the gnawed steps behind his father and brother, and there again was
the lane of quiet, watching faces for the three of them to walk through. He
saw the man in spectacles sitting at the plank table and he did not need to be
told this was a Justice of the Peace; he sent one-glare of fierce, exultant, partisan
defiance at the man in collar and cravat now, whom he had seen but twice
before in his life, and that on a galloping horse, who now wore on his face an
expression not of rage but of amazed unbelief which the boy could not have
known was at the incredible circumstance of being sued by one of his own

tenants, and came and stood against his father and cried at the Justice: "He ain't done it! He ain't burnt . . ."

"Go back to the wagon," his father said.   71

"Burnt?" the Justice said. "Do I understand this rug was burned too?"   72

"Does anybody here claim it was?" his father said. "Go back to the wagon."   73
But he did not, he merely retreated to the rear of the room, crowded as that other had been, but not to sit down this time, instead, to stand pressing among the motionless bodies, listening to the voices:

"And you claim twenty bushels of corn is too high for the damage you did   74
to the rug?"

"He brought the rug to me and said he wanted the tracks washed out of it.   75
I washed the tracks out and took the rug back to him."

"But you didn't carry the rug back to him in the same condition it was in   76
before you made the tracks on it."

His father did not answer, and now for perhaps half a minute there was no   77
sound at all save that of breathing, the faint, steady suspiration of complete and intent listening.

"You decline to answer that, Mr. Snopes?" Again his father did not answer.   78
"I'm going to find against you, Mr. Snopes. I'm going to find that you were responsible for the injury to Major de Spain's rug and hold you liable for it. But twenty bushels of corn seems a little high for a man in your circumstances to have to pay. Major de Spain claims it cost a hundred dollars. October corn will be worth about fifty cents. I figure that if Major de Spain can stand a ninety-five-dollar loss on something he paid cash for, you can stand a five-dollar loss you haven't earned yet. I hold you in damages to Major de Spain to the amount of ten bushels of corn over and above your contract with him, to be paid to him out of your crop at gathering time. Court adjourned."

It had taken no time hardly, the morning was but half begun. He thought   79
they would return home and perhaps back to the field, since they were late, far behind all other farmers. But instead his father passed on behind the wagon, merely indicating with his hand for the older brother to follow with it, and crossed the road toward the blacksmith shop opposite, pressing on after his father, overtaking him, speaking, whispering up at the harsh, calm face beneath the weathered hat: "He won't git no ten bushels neither. He won't git one. We'll . . ." until his father glanced for an instant down at him, the face absolutely calm, the grizzled eyebrows tangled above the cold eyes, the voice almost pleasant, almost gentle:

"You think so? Well, we'll wait till October anyway."   80

The matter of the wagon—the setting of a spoke or two and the tightening   81
of the tires—did not take long either, the business of the tires accomplished by driving the wagon into the spring branch behind the shop and letting it stand there, the mules nuzzling into the water from time to time, and the boy

on the seat with the idle reins, looking up the slope and through the sooty tunnel of the shed where the slow hammer rang and where his father sat on an upended cypress bolt, easily, either talking or listening, still sitting there when the boy brought the dripping wagon up out of the branch and halted it before the door.

"Take them on the shade and hitch," his father said. He did so and returned. His father and the smith and a third man squatting on his heels inside the door were talking, about crops and animals; the boy, squatting too in the ammoniac dust and hoof-parings and scales of rust, heard his father tell a long and unhurried story out of the time before the birth of the older brother even when he had been a professional horsetrader. And then his father came up beside him where he stood before a tattered last year's circus poster on the other side of the store, gazing rapt and quiet at the scarlet horses, the incredible poisings and convolutions of tulle and tights and the painted leers of comedians, and said, "It's time to eat."

But not at home. Squatting beside his brother against the front wall, he watched his father emerge from the store and produce from a paper sack a segment of cheese and divide it carefully and deliberately into three with his pocket knife and produce crackers from the same sack. They all three squatted on the gallery and ate, slowly, without talking; then in the store again, they drank from a tin dipper of tepid water smelling of the cedar bucket and of living beech trees. And still they did not go home. It was a horse lot this time, a tall rail fence upon and along which men stood and sat and out of which one by one horses were led, to be walked and trotted and then cantered back and forth along the road while the slow swapping and buying went on and the sun began to slant westward, they—the three of them—watching and listening, the older brother with his muddy eyes and his steady, inevitable tobacco, the father commenting now and then on certain of the animals, to no one in particular.

It was after sundown when they reached home. They ate supper by lamplight, then, sitting on the doorstep, the boy watched the night fully accomplish, listening to the whippoorwills and the frogs, when he heard his mother's voice: "Abner! No! No! Oh, God. Oh, God. Abner!" and he rose, whirled, and saw the altered light through the door where a candle stub now burned in a bottle neck on the table and his father, still in the hat and coat, at once formal and burlesque as though dressed carefully for some shabby and ceremonial violence, emptying the reservoir of the lamp back into the five-gallon kerosene can from which it had been filled, while the mother tugged at his arm until he shifted the lamp to the other hand and flung her back, not savagely or viciously, just hard, into the wall, her hands flung out against the wall for balance, her mouth open and in her face the same quality of hopeless despair as had been in her voice. Then his father saw him standing in the door.

"Go to the barn and get that can of oil we were oiling the wagon with," he   85
said. The boy did not move. Then he could speak.

"What . . ." he cried. "What are you . . ."   86

"Go get that oil," his father said. "Go."   87

Then he was moving, running, outside the house, toward the stable: this   88
the old habit, the old blood which he had not been permitted to choose for
himself, which had been bequeathed him willy nilly and which had run for so
long (and who knew where, battening on what of outrage and savagery and
lust) before it came to him. *I could keep on,* he thought. *I could run on and on and
never look back, never need to see his face again. Only I can't. I can't,* the rusted can
in his hand now, the liquid sploshing in it as he ran back to the house and into
it, into the sound of his mother's weeping in the next room, and handed the
can to his father.

"Ain't you going to even send a nigger?" he cried. "At least you sent a nigger   89
before!"

This time his father didn't strike him. The hand came even faster than the   90
blow had, the same hand which had set the can on the table with almost
excruciating care flashing from the can toward him too quick for him to follow
it, gripping him by the back of his shirt and on to tiptoe before he had seen it
quit the can, the face stooping at him in breathless and frozen ferocity, the
cold, dead voice speaking over him to the older brother who leaned against
the table, chewing with that steady, curious, sidewise motion of cows:

"Empty the can into the big one and go on. I'll catch up with you."   91

"Better tie him up to the bedpost," the brother said.   92

"Do like I told you," the father said. Then the boy was moving, his bunched   93
shirt and the hard, bony hand between his shoulderblades, his toes just touching
the floor across the room and into the other one, past the sisters sitting with
spread heavy thighs in the two chairs over the cold hearth, and to where his
mother and aunt sat side by side on the bed, the aunt's arms about his mother's
shoulders.

"Hold him," the father said. The aunt made a startled movement. "Not you,"   94
the father said. "Lennie. Take hold of him. I want to see you do it." His mother
took him by the wrist. "You'll hold him better than that. If he gets loose don't
you know what he is going to do? He will go up yonder." He jerked his head
toward the road. "Maybe I'd better tie him."

"I'll hold him," his mother whispered.   95

"See you do then." Then his father was gone, the stiff foot heavy and   96
measured upon the boards, ceasing at last.

Then he began to struggle. His mother caught him in both arms, he jerking   97
and wrenching at them. He would be stronger in the end, he knew that. But
he had no time to wait for it. "Lemme go!" he cried. "I don't want to have to
hit you!"

"Let him go!" the aunt said. "If he don't go, before God, I am going up   98
there myself!"

"Don't you see I can't?" his mother cried. "Sarty! Sarty! No! No! Help me,   99
Lizzie!"

Then he was free. His aunt grasped at him but it was too late. He whirled,   100
running, his mother stumbled forward on to her knees behind him, crying to
the nearer sister: "Catch him, Net! Catch him!" But that was too late too, the
sister (the sisters were twins, born at the same time, yet either of them now
gave the impression of being, encompassing as much living meat and volume
and weight as any other two of the family) not yet having begun to rise from
the chair, her head, face, alone merely turned, presenting to him in the flying
instant an astonishing expanse of young female features untroubled by any
surprise even, wearing only an expression of bovine interest. Then he was out
of the room, out of the house, in the mild dust of the starlit road and the heavy
rifeness of honeysuckle, the pale ribbon unspooling with terrific slowness under
his running feet, reaching the gate at last and turning in, running, his heart
and lungs drumming, on up the drive toward the lighted house, the lighted
door. He did not knock, he burst in, sobbing for breath, incapable for the
moment of speech; he saw the astonished face of the Negro in the linen jacket
without knowing when the Negro had appeared.

"De Spain!" he cried, panted. "Where's . . ." then he saw the white man too   101
emerging from a white door down the hall. "Barn!" he cried. "Barn!"

"What?" the white man said. "Barn?"   102

"Yes!" the boy cried. "Barn!"   103

"Catch him!" the white man shouted.   104

But it was too late this time too. The Negro grasped his shirt, but the entire   105
sleeve, rotten with washing, carried away, and he was out that door too and in
the drive again, and had actually never ceased to run even while he was
screaming into the white man's face.

Behind him the white man was shouting, "My horse! Fetch my horse!" and   106
he thought for an instant of cutting across the park and climbing the fence
into the road, but he did not know the park nor how high the vine-massed
fence might be and he dared not risk it. So he ran on down the drive, blood
and breath roaring; presently he was in the road again though he could not see
it. He could not hear either: the galloping mare was almost upon him before
he heard her, and even then he held his course, as if the very urgency of his
wild grief and need must in a moment more find him wings, waiting until the
ultimate instant to hurl himself aside and into the weed-choked roadside ditch
as the horse thundered past and on, for an instant in furious silhouette against
the stars, the tranquil early summer night sky which, even before the shape of
the horse and rider vanished, stained abruptly and violently upward: a long,
swirling roar incredible and soundless, blotting the stars, and he springing up
and into the road again, running again, knowing it was too late yet still running

even after he heard the shot and, an instant later, two shots, pausing now without knowing he had ceased to run, crying "Pap! Pap!", running again before he knew he had begun to run, stumbling, tripping over something and scrabbling up again without ceasing to run, looking backward over his shoulder at the glares as he got up, running on among the invisible trees, panting, sobbing, "Father! Father!"

At midnight he was sitting on the crest of a hill. He did not know it was 107 midnight and he did not know how far he had come. But there was no glare behind him now and he sat now, his back toward what he had called home for four days anyhow, his face toward the dark woods which he would enter when breath was strong again, small, shaking steadily in the chill darkness, hugging himself into the remainder of his thin, rotten shirt, the grief and despair now no longer terror and fear but just grief and despair. *Father. My father,* he thought. "He was brave!" He cried suddenly, aloud but not loud, no more than a whisper: "He was! He was in the war! He was in Colonel Sartoris' cav'ry!" not knowing that his father had gone to that war a private in the fine old European sense, wearing no uniform, admitting the authority of and giving fidelity to no man or army or flag, going to war as Malbrouck himself did: for booty—it meant nothing and less than nothing to him if it were enemy booty or his own.

The slow constellations wheeled on. It would be dawn and then sun-up after 108 a while and he would be hungry. But that would be to-morrow and now he was only cold, and walking would cure that. His breathing was easier now and he decided to get up and go on, and then he found that he had been asleep because he knew it was almost dawn, the night almost over. He could tell that from the whippoorwills. They were everywhere now among the dark trees below him, constant and inflectioned and ceaseless, so that, as the instant for giving over to the day birds drew nearer and nearer, there was no interval at all between them. He got up. He was a little stiff, but walking would cure that too as it would the cold, and soon there would be the sun. He went on down the hill, toward the dark woods within which the liquid silver voices of the birds called unceasing—the rapid and urgent beating of the urgent and quiring heart of the late spring night. He did not look back.

Questions for Critical Thinking

1. What levels of suffering can you deduce from the story? Try to organize the levels according to some principle, such as from specific to general or general to specific.

2. The opening courtroom scene establishes the many conflicts in the story. What are the major conflicts discernible?

3. Who seems to suffer most in the story? Give reasons for your choice.

4. What contrast exists between Snopes's definition of justice and that of the community in which he lives? Which definition appeals to you most? Why?

5. What difference in attitude toward suffering do you see between Job (*see* Rabbi Kushner's essay) and Abner Snopes? How do these differing attitudes affect the outcome of the stories about these two men?

6. What character traits does Sarty display? How are they revealed? Do an in-depth character analysis of Sarty by explaining what kind of person he is.

7. What *good* character traits, if any, does Abner Snopes have?

8. What instances of stereotyping does the story reveal? How does the stereotyping strengthen the story's theme?

Writing Assignment

Write an essay analyzing the cause-effect relationship between poverty and crime.

Writing Advice

Since overwhelming evidence from sociology and criminal statistics indicates that crime is more prevalent among the poor than the rich, we shall assume that a causal connection between poverty and crime does exist. Your job is to probe the elements associated with poverty that might make a person vulnerable to the temptations of perjury, robbery, murder, and other crimes. Fairytale stories, such as Charles Dickens's *Oliver Twist* notwithstanding, evidence indicates that the squalor of slums breeds crime and criminals. Why? Is it the despair of poverty? A cultural environment that devalues education? The lack of parental supervision when both parents must work to survive? In preparing to write this essay, you should grapple with these and similar questions. Jot down all of your answers and ideas as they occur to you, not necessarily in logical sequence.

Now you are ready to find your angle. From all of the random ideas you jotted down about the relationship between poverty and crime, choose one (or more) that in your view is the most penetrating in getting to the heart of a person's sense of morality and ethics. This idea (or ideas) can then be worded into a preliminary thesis, as in this example: "Poverty often leads to contempt for the law because people living in squalid and sordid neighborhoods see life as unfair and therefore as a contest between them and those who have what they desire."

Once you have your main point clearly in mind, you can find support for it through facts, examples, experience, expert testimony, and any other valid evidence.

Alternate Writing Assignment

1. Write an essay in which you discuss when it is right to believe in your father and when it is time to doubt him. You will need to ask the question, "What are proper and improper grounds for trust in one's parents?"

2. Write an essay analyzing the role of the women in "Barn Burning" and clarifying your reaction to this role.

LITERATURE

SONNY'S BLUES
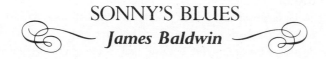
James Baldwin

James Baldwin (1924–1987) was a prominent contemporary novelist and one of the first to establish the black identity. After graduating from high school and holding a number of odd jobs, he moved to Paris in 1948, where he felt that the social environment allowed him the freedom to grow creatively. He remained an expatriate in this city for ten years, writing about his personal struggle to be accepted as a black American writer. The novel *Go Tell It on the Mountain* (1953) and a collection of essays titled *Notes of a Native Son* (1955) were products of this period.

In 1957, Baldwin returned to the United States, where he became deeply involved in the civil rights movement. He wrote flamboyant and emotional essays warning the country that it could no longer treat blacks as second-class citizens without risking violence. Among his essay collections are *Nobody Knows My Name* (1961) and *The Fire Next Time* (1963). From 1963 to the present he continued to be a prolific fiction writer, producing two novels, *Tell Me How Long the Train's Been Gone* (1968) and *If Beale Street Could Talk* (1974), as well as two short-story collections, *Blues for Mister Charlie* (1964) and *The Amen Corner* (1965). His more recent works included *The Devil Finds Work* (1976) and *Just Above My Head* (1979). The story that follows is excerpted from *Going to Meet the Man,* an autobiographical collection, published in 1957.

Reading Advice

When you read this essay, try to see the narrator not merely as Sonny's older and more stable brother but as a perceptive and sensitive spokesman for the black experience that involves grinding poverty and the glittering temptation to drop out. Perhaps the most effective technique used in this story is its tone of nostalgia growing into agony. Allow yourself to be gripped by the tragedy of the situation and to become involved in the deep grief produced by Sonny's life. Sonny's wild and chaotic existence makes the narrator appear highly disciplined and stable and provides a gauge to his personality. Notice the implicit contrasts between the two brothers that emerge from their relationship. It is interesting to note that the narrator emphasizes Sonny's dark skin as well as the dark life into which Sonny plunges in a desperate attempt to find fulfillment by playing jazz.

I read about it in the paper, in the sub- 1
way, on my way to work. I read it, and I couldn't believe it, and I read it again. Then perhaps I just stared at it, at the newsprint spelling out his name, spelling

out the story. I stared at it in the swinging lights of the subway car, and in the faces and bodies of the people, and in my own face, trapped in the darkness which roared outside.

It was not to be believed and I kept telling myself that, as I walked from 2 the subway station to the high school. And at the same time I couldn't doubt it. I was scared, scared for Sonny. He became real to me again. A great block of ice got settled in my belly and kept melting there slowly all day long, while I taught my classes algebra. It was a special kind of ice. It kept melting, sending trickles of ice water all up and down my veins, but it never got less. Sometimes it hardened and seemed to expand until I felt my guts were going to come spilling out or that I was going to choke or scream. This would always be at a moment when I was remembering some specific thing Sonny had once said or done.

When he was about as old as the boys in my class his face had been bright 3 and open, there was a lot of copper in it; and he'd had wonderfully direct brown eyes, and great gentleness and privacy. I wondered what he looked like now. He had been picked up, the evening before, in a raid on an apartment downtown, for peddling and using heroin.

I couldn't believe it: but what I mean by that is that I couldn't find any 4 room for it anywhere inside me. I had kept it outside me for a long time. I hadn't wanted to know. I had had suspicions, but I didn't name them, I kept putting them away. I told myself that Sonny was wild, but he wasn't crazy. And he'd always been a good boy, he hadn't ever turned hard or evil or disrespectful, the way kids can, so quick, so quick, especially in Harlem. I didn't want to believe that I'd ever see my brother going down, coming to nothing, all that light in his face gone out, in the condition I'd already seen so many others. Yet it had happened and here I was, talking about algebra to a lot of boys who might, every one of them for all I knew, be popping off needles every time they went to the head. Maybe it did more for them than algebra could.

I was sure that the first time Sonny had ever had horse, he couldn't have 5 been much older than these boys were now. These boys, now, were living as we'd been living then, they were growing up with a rush and their heads bumped abruptly against the low ceiling of their actual possibilities. They were filled with rage. All they really knew were two darknesses, the darkness of their lives, which was now closing in on them, and the darkness of the movies, which had blinded them to that other darkness, and in which they now, vindictively, dreamed, at once more together than they were at any other time, and more alone.

When the last bell rang, the last class ended, I let out my breath. It seemed 6 I'd been holding it for all that time. My clothes were wet—I may have looked as though I'd been sitting in a steam bath, all dressed up, all afternoon. I sat alone in the classroom a long time. I listened to the boys outside, downstairs, shouting and cursing and laughing. Their laughter struck me for perhaps the first time. It was not the joyous laughter which—God knows why—one associates with children. It was mocking and insular, its intent was to denigrate. It was disenchanted, and in this, also, lay the authority of their curses. Perhaps I was listening to them because I was thinking about my brother and in them I heard my brother. And myself.

One boy was whistling a tune, at once very complicated and very simple, it seemed to be pouring out of him as though he were a bird, and it sounded very cool and moving through all that harsh, bright air, only just holding its own through all those other sounds.

I stood up and walked over to the window and looked down down into the courtyard. It was the beginning of the spring and the sap was rising in the boys. A teacher passed through them every now and again, quickly, as though he or she couldn't wait to get out of that courtyard, to get those boys out of their sight and off their minds. I started collecting my stuff. I thought I'd better get home and talk to Isabel.

The courtyard was almost deserted by the time I got downstairs. I saw this boy standing in the shadow of a doorway, looking just like Sonny. I almost called his name. Then I saw that it wasn't Sonny, but somebody we used to know, a boy from around our block. He'd been Sonny's friend. He'd never been mine, having been too young for me, and, anyway, I'd never liked him. And now, even though he was a grown-up man, he still hung around that block, still spent hours on the street corners, was always high and raggy. I used to run into him from time to time and he'd often work around to asking me for a quarter or fifty cents. He always had some real good excuse, too, and I always gave it to him, I don't know why.

But now, abruptly, I hated him. I couldn't stand the way he looked at me, partly like a dog, partly like a cunning child. I wanted to ask him what the hell he was doing in the school courtyard.

He sort of shuffled over to me, and he said, "I see you got the papers. So you already know about it."

"You mean about Sonny? Yes, I already know about it. How come they didn't get you?"

He grinned. It made him repulsive and it also brought to mind what he'd looked like as a kid. "I wasn't there. I stay away from them people."

"Good for you." I offered him a cigarette and I watched him through the smoke. "You come all the way down here just to tell me about Sonny?"

"That's right." He was sort of shaking his head and his eyes looked strange, as though they were about to cross. The bright sun deadened his damp dark brown skin and it made his eyes look yellow and showed up the dirt in his kinked hair. He smelled funky. I moved a little away from him and I said, "Well, thanks. But I already know about it and I got to get home."

"I'll walk you a little ways," he said. We started walking. There were a couple   16
of kids still loitering in the courtyard and one of them said goodnight to me
and looked strangely at the boy beside me.

"What're you going to do?" he asked me. "I mean, about Sonny?"   17

"Look. I haven't seen Sonny for over a year, I'm not sure I'm going to do   18
anything. Anyway, what the hell *can* I do?"

"That's right," he said quickly, "ain't nothing you can do. Can't much help   19
old Sonny no more, I guess."

It was what I was thinking and so it seemed to me he had no right to   20
say it.

"I'm surprised at Sonny, though," he went on—he had a funny way of   21
talking, he looked straight ahead as though he were talking to himself—"I
thought Sonny was a smart boy, I thought he was too smart to get hung."

"I guess he thought so too," I said sharply, "and that's how he got hung.   22
And how about you? You're pretty goddamn smart, I bet."

Then he looked directly at me, just for a minute. "I ain't smart," he said. "If   23
I was smart, I'd have reached for a pistol a long time ago."

"Look. Don't tell *me* your sad story, if it was up to me, I'd give you one."   24
Then I felt guilty—guilty, probably, for never having supposed that the poor
bastard *had* a story of his own, much less a sad one, and I asked, quickly,
"What's going to happen to him now?"

He didn't answer this. He was off by himself some place. "Funny thing," he   25
said, and from his tone we might have been discussing the quickest way to get
to Brooklyn, "when I saw the papers this morning, the first thing I asked myself
was if I had anything to do with it. I felt sort of responsible."

I began to listen more carefully. The subway station was on the corner, just   26
before us, and I stopped. He stopped, too. We were in front of a bar and he
ducked slightly, peering in, but whoever he was looking for didn't seem to be
there. The juke box was blasting away with something black and bouncy and I
half watched the barmaid as she danced her way from the juke box to her place
behind the bar. And I watched her face as she laughingly responded to something
someone said to her, still keeping time to the music. When she smiled one saw
the little girl, one sensed the doomed, still-struggling woman beneath the
battered face of the semi-whore.

"I never *give* Sonny nothing," the boy said finally, "but a long time ago I   27
come to school high and Sonny asked me how it felt." He paused, I couldn't
bear to watch him, I watched the barmaid, and I listened to the music which
seemed to be causing the pavement to shake. "I told him it felt great." The
music stopped, the barmaid paused and watched the juke box until the music
began again. "It did."

All this was carrying me some place I didn't want to go. I certainly   28
didn't want to know how it felt. It filled everything, the people, the houses,

the music, the dark, quicksilver barmaid, with menace; and this menace was their reality.

"What's going to happen to him now?" I asked again.   29

"They'll send him away some place and they'll try to cure him." He shook   30
his head. "Maybe he'll even think he's kicked the habit. Then they'll let him loose"—he gestured, throwing his cigarette into the gutter. "That's all."

"What do you mean, that's *all*?"   31

But I knew what he meant.   32

"I *mean*, that's *all*." He turned his head and looked at me, pulling down the   33
corners of his mouth. "Don't you know what I mean?" he asked, softly.

"How the hell *would* I know what you mean?" I almost whispered it, I don't   34
know why.

"That's right," he said to the air, "how would *he* know what I mean?" He   35
turned toward me again, patient and calm, and yet I somehow felt him shaking, shaking as though he were going to fall apart. I felt that ice in my guts again, the dread I'd felt all afternoon; and again I watched the barmaid, moving about the bar, washing glasses, and singing. "Listen. They'll let him out and then it'll just start all over again. That's what I mean."

"You mean—they'll let him out. And then he'll just start working his way   36
back in again. You mean he'll never kick the habit. Is that what you mean?"

"That's right," he said, cheerfully. "*You* see what I mean."   37

"Tell me," I said at last, "why does he want to die? He must want to die,   38
he's killing himself, why does he want to die?"

He looked at me in surprise. He licked his lips. "He don't want to die. He   39
wants to live. Don't nobody want to die, ever."

Then I wanted to ask him—too many things. He could not have answered,   40
or if he had, I could not have borne the answers. I started walking. "Well, I guess it's none of my business."

"It's going to be rough on old Sonny," he said. We reached the subway   41
station. "This is your station?" he asked. I nodded. I took one step down. "Damn!" he said, suddenly. I looked up at him. He grinned again. "Damn it if I didn't leave all my money home. You ain't got a dollar on you, have you? Just for a couple of days, is all."

All at once something inside gave and threatened to come pouring out of   42
me. I didn't hate him any more. I felt that in another moment I'd start crying like a child.

"Sure," I said. "Don't swear." I looked in my wallet and didn't have a dollar,   43
I only had a five. "Here," I said. "That hold you?"

He didn't look at it—he didn't want to look at it. A terrible, closed look   44
came over his face, as though he were keeping the number on the bill a secret from him and me. "Thanks," he said, and now he was dying to see me go. "Don't worry about Sonny. Maybe I'll write him or something."

"Sure," I said. "You do that. So long."   45

"Be seeing you," he said. I went down the steps.   46

And I didn't write Sonny or send him anything for a long time. When I   47
finally did, it was just after my little girl died, he wrote me back a letter which
made me feel like a bastard.

Here's what he said: 48

Dear Brother,   49
You don't know how much I needed to hear from you. I wanted to write you
many a time but I dug how much I must have hurt you and so I didn't write. But
now I feel like a man who's been trying to climb up out of some deep, real deep
and funky hole and just saw the sun up there, outside. I got to get outside.

  I can't tell you much about how I got here. I mean I don't know how to tell
you. I guess I was afraid of something or I was trying to escape from something
and you know I have never been very strong in the head (smile). I'm glad Mama
and Daddy are dead and can't see what's happened to their son and I swear if I'd
know what I was doing I would never have hurt you so, you and a lot of other
fine people who were nice to me and who believed in me.

  I don't want you to think it had anything to do with me being a musician. It's
more than that. Or maybe less than that. I can't get anything straight in my head
down here and I try not to think about what's going to happen to me when I get
outside again. Sometime I think I'm going to flip and never get outside and
sometime I think I'll come straight back. I tell you one thing, though, I'd rather
blow my brains out than go through this again. But that's what they all say, so
they tell me. If I tell you when I'm coming to New York and if you could meet
me, I sure would appreciate it. Give my love to Isabel and the kids and I was
sure sorry to hear about little Gracie. I wish I could be like Mama and say the
Lord's will be done, but I don't know it seems to me that trouble is the one thing
that never does get stopped and I don't know what good it does to blame it on
the Lord. But maybe it does some good if you believe it.

Your brother,
Sonny

Then I kept in constant touch with him and I sent him whatever I could   50
and I went to meet him when he came back to New York. When I saw him
many things I thought I had forgotten came flooding back to me. This was
because I had begun, finally, to wonder about Sonny, about the life that Sonny
lived inside. This life, whatever it was, had made him older and thinner and it
had deepened the distant stillness in which he had always moved. He looked
very unlike my baby brother. Yet, when he smiled, when we shook hands, the
baby brother I'd never known looked out from the depths of his private life,
like an animal waiting to be coaxed into the light.

"How you been keeping?" he asked me.   51

"All right. And you?"   52

"Just fine." He was smiling all over his face. "It's good to see you again."   53

"It's good to see you."   54

The seven years' difference in our ages lay between us like a chasm: I   55
wondered if these years would ever operate between us as a bridge. I was
remembering, and it made it hard to catch my breath, that I had been there
when he was born; and I had heard the first words he had ever spoken. When
he started to walk, he walked from our mother straight to me. I caught him
just before he fell when he took the first steps he ever took in this world.

"How's Isabel?"   56

"Just fine. She's dying to see you."   57

"And the boys?"   58

"They're fine, too. They're anxious to see their uncle."   59

"Oh, come on. You know they don't remember me."   60

"Are you kidding? Of course they remember you."   61

He grinned again. We got into a taxi. We had a lot to say to each other, far   62
too much to know how to begin.

As the taxi began to move, I asked, "You still want to go to India?"   63

He laughed. "You still remember that. Hell, no. This place is Indian enough   64
for me."

"It used to belong to them," I said.   65

And he laughed again. "They damn sure knew what they were doing when   66
they got rid of it."

Years ago, when he was around fourteen, he'd been all hipped on the idea   67
of going to India. He read books about people sitting on rocks, naked, in all
kinds of weather, but mostly bad, naturally, and walking barefoot through hot
coals and arriving at wisdom. I used to say that it sounded to me as though
they were getting away from wisdom as fast as they could. I think he sort of
looked down on me for that.

"Do you mind," he asked, "if we have the driver drive alongside the park?   68
On the west side—I haven't seen the city in so long."

"Of course not," I said. I was afraid that I might sound as though I were   69
humoring him, but I hoped he wouldn't take it that way.

So we drove along, between the green of the park and the stony, lifeless   70
elegance of hotels and apartment buildings, toward the vivid, killing streets of
our childhood. These streets hadn't changed, though housing projects jutted
up out of them now like rocks in the middle of a boiling sea. Most of the
houses in which we had grown up had vanished, as had the stores from which
we had stolen, the basements in which we had first tried sex, the rooftops from
which we had hurled tin cans and bricks. But houses exactly like the houses of
our past yet dominated the landscape, boys exactly like the boys we once had
been found themselves smothering in these houses, came down into the streets
for light and air and found themselves encircled by disaster. Some escaped the
trap, most didn't. Those who got out always left something of themselves
behind, as some animals amputate a leg and leave it in the trap. It might be

said, perhaps, that I had escaped, after all, I was a school teacher; or that Sonny had, he hadn't lived in Harlem for years. Yet, as the cab moved uptown through streets which seemed, with a rush, to darken with dark people, and as I covertly studied Sonny's face, it came to me that what we both were seeking through our separate cab windows was that part of ourselves which had been left behind. It's always at the hour of trouble and confrontation that the missing member aches.

We hit 110th Street and started rolling up Lenox Avenue. And I'd know   71
this avenue all my life, but it seemed to me again, as it had seemed on the day I'd first heard about Sonny's trouble, filled with a hidden menace which was its very breath of life.

"We almost there," said Sonny.   72

"Almost." We were both too nervous to say anything more.   73

We lived in a housing project. It hasn't been up long. A few days after it   74
was up it seemed uninhabitably new, now, of course, it's already rundown. It looks like a parody of the good, clean, faceless life—God knows the people who live in it do their best to make it a parody. The beat-looking grass lying around isn't enough to make their lives green, the hedges will never hold out the streets, and they know it. The big windows fool no one, they aren't big enough to make space out of no space. They don't bother with the windows, they watch the TV screen instead. The playground is most popular with the children who don't play at jacks, or skip rope, or roller skate, or swing, and they can be found in it after dark. We moved in partly because it's not too far from where I teach, and partly for the kids; but it's really just like the houses in which Sonny and I grew up. The same things happen, they'll have the same things to remember. The moment Sonny and I started into the house I had the feeling that I was simply bringing him back into the danger he had almost died trying to escape.

Sonny has never been talkative. So I don't know why I was sure he'd be   75
dying to talk to me when supper was over the first night. Everything went fine, the oldest boy remembered him, and the youngest boy liked him, and Sonny had remembered to bring something for each of them; and Isabel, who is really much nicer than I am, more open and giving, had gone to a lot of trouble about dinner and was genuinely glad to see him. And she's always been able to tease Sonny in a way that I haven't. It was nice to see her face so vivid again and to hear her laugh and watch her make Sonny laugh. She wasn't, or, anyway, she didn't seem to be, at all uneasy or embarrassed. She chatted as though there were no subject which had to be avoided and she got Sonny past his first, faint stiffness. And thank God she was there, for I was filled with that icy dread again. Everything I did seemed awkward to me, and everything I said sounded freighted with hidden meaning. I was trying to remember everything I'd heard about dope addiction and I couldn't help watching Sonny for signs.

I wasn't doing it out of malice. I was trying to find out something about my brother. I was dying to hear him tell me he was safe.

"Safe!" my father grunted, whenever Mama suggested trying to move to a   76
neighborhood which might be safer for children. "Safe, hell! Ain't no place safe for kids, nor nobody."

He always went on like this, but he wasn't, ever, really as bad as he sounded,   77
not even on weekends, when he got drunk. As a matter of fact, he was always on the lookout for "something a little better," but he died before he found it. He died suddenly, during a drunken weekend in the middle of the war, when Sonny was fifteen. He and Sonny hadn't ever got on too well. And this was partly because Sonny was the apple of his father's eye. It was because he loved Sonny so much and was frightened for him, that he was always fighting with him. It doesn't do any good to fight with Sonny. Sonny just moves back, inside himself, where he can't be reached. But the principal reason that they never hit it off is that they were so much alike. Daddy was big and rough and loud-talking, just the opposite of Sonny, but they both had—that same privacy.

Mama tried to tell me something about this, just after Daddy died. I was   78
home on leave from the army.

This was the last time I ever saw my mother alive. Just the same, this picture   79
gets all mixed up in my mind with pictures I had of her when she was younger. The way I always see her is the way she used to be on a Sunday afternoon, say, when the old folks were talking after the big Sunday dinner. I always see her wearing pale blue. She'd be sitting on the sofa. And my father would be sitting in the easy chair, not far from her. And the living room would be full of church folks and relatives. There they sit, in chairs all around the living room, and the night is creeping up outside, but nobody knows it yet. You can see the darkness growing against the windowpanes and you hear the street noises every now and again, or maybe the jangling beat of a tambourine from one of the churches close by, but it's real quiet in the room. For a moment nobody's talking, but every face looks darkening, like the sky outside. And my mother rocks a little from the waist, and my father's eyes are closed. Everyone is looking at something a child can't see. For a minute they've forgotten the children. Maybe a kid is lying on the rug, half asleep. Maybe somebody's got a kid in his lap and is absent-mindedly stroking the kid's head. Maybe there's a kid, quiet and big-eyed, curled up in a big chair in the corner. The silence, the darkness coming, and the darkness in the faces frightens the child obscurely. He hopes that the hand which strokes his forehead will never stop—will never die. He hopes that there will never come a time when the old folks won't be sitting around the living room, talking about where they've come from, and what they've seen, and what's happened to them and their kinfolk.

But something deep and watchful in the child knows that this is bound to   80
end, is already ending. In a moment someone will get up and turn on the light.

Then the old folks will remember the children and they won't talk any more that day. And when light fills the room, the child is filled with darkness. He knows that every time this happens he's moved just a little closer to that darkness outside. The darkness outside is what the old folks have been talking about. It's what they've come from. It's what they endure. The child knows that they won't talk any more because if he knows too much about what's happened to *them,* he'll know too much too soon, about what's going to happen to *him.*

The last time I talked to my mother, I remember I was restless. I wanted to 81 get out and see Isabel. We weren't married then and we had a lot to straighten out between us.

There Mama sat, in black, by the window. She was humming an old church 82 song, *Lord, you brought me from a long ways off.* Sonny was out somewhere. Mama kept watching the streets.

"I don't know," she said, "if I'll ever see you again, after you go off from 83 here. But I hope you'll remember the things I tried to teach you."

"Don't talk like that," I said, and smiled. "You'll be here a long time yet." 84

She smiled, too, but she said nothing. She was quiet for a long time. And I 85 said, "Mama, don't you worry about nothing. I'll be writing all the time, and you be getting the checks. . . ."

"I want to talk to you about your brother," she said, suddenly. "If anything 86 happens to me he ain't going to have nobody to look out for him."

"Mama," I said, "ain't nothing going to happen to you *or* Sonny. Sonny's all 87 right. He's a good boy and he's got good sense."

"It ain't a question of his being a good boy," Mama said, "nor of his having 88 good sense. It ain't only the bad ones, nor yet the dumb ones that gets sucked under." She stopped, looking at me. "Your Daddy once had a brother," she said, and she smiled in a way that made me feel she was in pain. "You didn't never know that, did you?"

"No," I said, "I never knew that," and I watched her face. 89

"Oh, yes," she said, "your Daddy had a brother." She looked out of the 90 window again. "I know you never saw your Daddy cry. But *I* did—many a time, through all these years."

I asked her, "What happened to his brother? How come nobody's ever talked 91 about him?"

This was the first time I ever saw my mother look old. 92

"His brother got killed," she said, "when he was just a little younger than 93 you are now. I knew him. He was a fine boy. He was maybe a little full of the devil, but he didn't mean nobody no harm."

Then she stopped and the room was silent, exactly as it had sometimes been 94 on those Sunday afternoons. Mama kept looking out into the streets.

"He used to have a job in the mill," she said, "and, like all young folks, he 95 just liked to perform on Saturday nights. Saturday nights, him and your father would drift around to different places, go to dances and things like that, or just sit around with people they knew, and your father's brother would sing, he had a fine voice, and play along with himself on his guitar. Well, this particular Saturday night, him and your father was coming home from some place, and they were both a little drunk and there was a moon that night, it was bright like day. Your father's brother was feeling kind of good, and he was whistling to himself, and he had his guitar slung over his shoulder. They was coming down a hill and beneath them was a road that turned off from the highway. Well, your father's brother, being always kind of frisky, decided to run down this hill, and he did, with that guitar banging and clanging behind him, and he ran across the road, and he was making water behind a tree. And your father was sort of amused at him and he was still coming down the hill, kind of slow. Then he heard a car motor and that same minute his brother stepped from behind the tree, into the road, in the moonlight. And he started to cross the road. And your father started to run down the hill, he says he don't know why. This car was full of white men. They was all drunk, and when they seen your father's brother they let out a great whoop and holler and they aimed the car straight at him. They was having fun, they just wanted to scare him, the way they do sometimes, you know. But they was drunk. And I guess the boy, being drunk, too, and scared, kind of lost his head. By the time he jumped it was too late. Your father says he heard his brother scream when the car rolled over him, and he heard the wood of that guitar when it give, and he heard them strings go flying, and he heard them white men shouting, and the car kept on a-going and it ain't stopped till this day. And, time your father got down the hill, his brother weren't nothing but blood and pulp."

Tears were gleaming on my mother's face. There wasn't anything I could say. 96

"He never mentioned it," she said, "because I never let him mention it before 97 you children. Your Daddy was like a crazy man that night and for many a night thereafter. He says he never in his life seen anything as dark as that road after the lights of that car had gone away. Weren't nothing; weren't nobody on that road, just your Daddy and his brother and that busted guitar. Oh, yes. Your Daddy never did really get right again. Till the day he died he weren't sure but that every white man he saw was the man that killed his brother."

She stopped and took out her handkerchief and dried her eyes and looked 98 at me.

"I ain't telling you all this," she said, "to make you scared or bitter or to 99 make you hate nobody. I'm telling you this because you got a brother. And the world ain't changed."

I guess I didn't want to believe this. I guess she saw this in my face. She 100 turned away from me, toward the window again, searching those streets.

"But I praise my Redeemer," she said at last, "that He called your Daddy 101 home before me. I ain't saying it to throw no flowers at myself, but, I declare, it keeps me from feeling too cast down to know I helped your father get safely through this world. Your father always acted like he was the roughest, strongest man on earth. And everybody took him to be like that. But if he hadn't had *me* there—to see his tears!"

She was crying again. Still, I couldn't move. I said, "Lord, Lord, Mama, I   102
didn't know it was like that."

"Oh, honey," she said, "There's a lot that you don't know. But you are going   103
to find out." She stood up from the window and came over to me. "You got to hold on to your brother," she said, "and don't let him fall, no matter what it looks like is happening to him and no matter how evil you gets with him. You going to be evil with him many a time. But don't you forget what I told you, you hear?"

"I won't forget," I said. "Don't you worry, I won't forget. I won't let nothing   104
happen to Sonny."

My mother smiled as though she were amused at something she saw in my   105
face. Then, "You may not be able to stop nothing from happening. But you got to let him know you's *there*."

Two days later I was married, and then I was gone. And I had a lot of things   106
on my mind and I pretty well forgot my promise to Mama until I got shipped home on a special furlough for her funeral.

And, after the funeral, with just Sonny and me alone in the empty kitchen,   107
I tried to find out something about him.

"What do you want to do?" I asked him.   108

"I'm going to be a musician," he said.   109

For he had graduated, in the time I had been away, from dancing to the juke   110
box to finding out who was playing what, and what they were doing with it, and he had bought himself a set of drums.

"You mean, you want to be a drummer?" I somehow had the feeling that   111
being a drummer might be all right for other people but not for my brother Sonny.

"I don't think," he said, looking at me very gravely, "that I'll ever be a good   112
drummer. But I think I can play a piano."

I frowned. I'd never played the role of the older brother quite so seriously   113
before, had scarcely ever, in fact, *asked* Sonny a damn thing. I sensed myself in the presence of something I didn't really know how to handle, didn't understand. So I made my frown a little deeper as I asked: "What kind of musician do you want to be?"

He grinned. "How many kinds do you think there are?"   114

"Be *serious*," I said.   115

He laughed, throwing his head back, and then looked at me. "I *am* serious."   116

"Well, then, for Christ's sake, stop kidding around and answer a serious   117
question. I mean, do you want to be a concert pianist, you want to play classical

music and all that, or——or what?" Long before I finished he was laughing again. "For Christ's *sake,* Sonny!"

He sobered, but with difficulty. "I'm sorry. But you sound so——*scared!*" and he was off again.   118

"Well, you may think it's funny now, baby, but it's not going to be so funny when you have to make your living at it, let me tell you *that.*" I was furious because I knew he was laughing at me and I didn't know why.   119

"No," he said, very sober now, and afraid, perhaps, that he'd hurt me. "I don't want to be a classical pianist. That isn't what interests me. I mean"——he paused, looking hard at me, as though his eyes would help me to understand, and then gestured helplessly, as though perhaps his hand would help——"I mean, I'll have a lot of studying to do, and I'll have to study *everything,* but, I mean, I want to play *with*——jazz musicians." He stopped. "I want to play jazz," he said.   120

Well, the word had never before sounded as heavy, as real, as it sounded that afternoon in Sonny's mouth. I just looked at him and I was probably frowning a real frown by this time. I simply couldn't see why on earth he'd want to spend his time hanging around nightclubs, clowning around on bandstands, while people pushed each other around a dance floor. It seemed—— beneath him, somehow. I had never thought about it before, had never been forced to, but I suppose I had always put jazz musicians in a class with what Daddy called "goodtime people."   121

"Are you *serious?*"   122

"Hell, *yes,* I'm serious."   123

He looked more helpless than ever, and annoyed, and deeply hurt.   124

I suggested, helpfully: "You mean——like Louis Armstrong?"   125

His face closed as though I'd struck him. "No. I'm not talking about none of that old-time, down home crap."   126

"Well, look, Sonny, I'm sorry, don't get mad. I just don't altogether get it, that's all. Name somebody——you know, a jazz musician you admire."   127

"Bird."   128

"Who?"   129

"Bird! Charlie Parker! Don't they teach you nothing in the goddamn army?"   130

I lit a cigarette. I was surprised and then a little amused to discover that I was trembling. "I've been out of touch," I said. "You'll have to be patient with me. Now. Who's this Parker character?"   131

"He's just one of the greatest jazz musicians alive," said Sonny, sullenly, his hands in his pockets, his back to me. "Maybe *the* greatest," he added, bitterly, "that's probably why *you* never heard of him."   132

"All right," I said, "I'm ignorant. I'm sorry. I'll go out and buy all the cat's records right away, all right?"   133

"It don't," said Sonny, with dignity, "make any difference to me. I don't care what you listen to. Don't do me no favors."   134

I was beginning to realize that I'd never seen him so upset before. With   135
another part of my mind I was thinking that this would probably turn out to
be one of those things kids go through and that I shouldn't make it seem
important by pushing it too hard. Still, I didn't think it would do any harm to
ask: "Doesn't all this take a lot of time? Can you make a living at it?"

He turned back to me and half leaned, half sat, on the kitchen table.   136
"Everything takes time," he said, "and—well, yes, sure, I can make a living at
it. But what I don't seem to be able to make you understand is that it's the
only thing I want to do."

"Well, Sonny," I said, gently, "you know people can't always do exactly what   137
they *want* to do—"

"*No,* I don't know that," said Sonny, surprising me. "I think people *ought* to   138
do what they want to do, what else are they alive for?"

"You getting to be a big boy," I said desperately, "it's time you started thinking   139
about your future."

"I'm thinking about my future," said Sonny, grimly. "I think about it all the   140
time."

I gave up. I decided, if he didn't change his mind, that we could always talk   141
about it later. "In the meantime," I said, "you got to finish school." We had
already decided that he'd have to move in with Isabel and her folks. I knew
this wasn't the ideal arrangement because Isabel's folks are inclined to be dicty
and they hadn't especially wanted Isabel to marry me. But I didn't know what
else to do. "And we have to get you fixed up at Isabel's."

There was a long silence. He moved from the kitchen table to the window.   142
"That's a terrible idea. You know it yourself."

"Do you have a *better* idea?"   143

He just walked up and down the kitchen for a minute. He was as tall as I   144
was. He had started to shave. I suddenly had the feeling that I didn't know him
at all.

He stopped at the kitchen table and picked up my cigarettes. Looking at   145
me with a kind of mocking, amused defiance, he put one between his lips. "You
mind?"

"You smoking already?"   146

He lit the cigarette and nodded, watching me through the smoke. "I just   147
wanted to see if I'd have the courage to smoke in front of you." He grinned
and blew a great cloud of smoke to the ceiling. "It was easy." He looked at my
face. "Come on, now. I bet you was smoking at my age, tell the truth."

I didn't say anything but the truth was on my face, and he laughed. But now   148
there was something very strained in his laugh. "Sure. And I bet that ain't all
you was doing."

He was frightening me a little. "Cut the crap," I said. "We already decided   149
that you was going to go and live at Isabel's. Now what's got into you all of a
sudden?"

"*You* decided it," he pointed out. "*I* didn't decide nothing." He stopped in   150
front of me, leaning against the stove, arms loosely folded. "Look, brother. I
don't want to stay in Harlem no more, I really don't." He was very earnest. He
looked at me, then over toward the kitchen window. There was something in
his eyes I'd never seen before, some thoughtfulness, some worry all his own.
He rubbed the muscle of one arm. "It's time I was getting out of here."

"Where do you want to *go,* Sonny?"   151

"I want to join the army. Or the navy, I don't care. If I say I'm old enough,   152
they'll believe me."

Then I got mad. It was because I was so scared. "You must be crazy. You   153
goddamn fool, what the hell do you want to go and join the *army* for?"

"I just told you. To get out of Harlem."   154

"Sonny, you haven't even finished *school*. And if you really want to be a   155
musician, how do you expect to study if you're in the *army*?"

He looked at me, trapped, and in anguish. "There's ways. I might be able to   156
work out some kind of deal. Anyway, I'll have the G.I. Bill when I come out."

"*If* you come out." We stared at each other. "Sonny, please. Be reasonable.   157
I know the setup is far from perfect. But we got to do the best we can."

"I ain't learning nothing in school," he said. "Even when I go." He turned   158
away from me and opened the window and threw his cigarette out into the
narrow alley. I watched his back. "At least, I ain't learning nothing you'd want
me to learn." He slammed the window so hard I thought the glass would fly
out, and turned back to me. "And I'm sick of the stink of these garbage cans!"

"Sonny," I said, "I know how you feel. But if you don't finish school now,   159
you're going to be sorry later that you didn't." I grabbed him by the shoulders.
"And you only got another year. It ain't so bad. And I'll come back and I swear
I'll help you do *whatever* you want to do. Just try to put up with it till I come
back. Will you please do that? For me?"

He didn't answer and he wouldn't look at me.   160

"Sonny. You hear me?"   161

He pulled away. "I hear you. But you never hear anything *I* say."   162

I didn't know what to say to that. He looked out of the window and then
back at me. "OK," he said, and sighed. "I'll try."

Then I said, trying to cheer him up a little, "They got a piano at Isabel's.   163
You can practice on it."

And as a matter of fact, it did cheer him up for a minute. "That's right," he   164
said to himself. "I forgot that." His face relaxed a little. But the worry, the
thoughtfulness, played on it still, the way shadows play on a face which is staring
into the fire.

But I thought I'd never hear the end of that piano. At first, Isabel would   165
write me, saying how nice it was that Sonny was so serious about his music
and how, as soon as he came in from school, or wherever he had been when
he was supposed to be at school, he went straight to that piano and stayed

there until suppertime. And, after supper, he went back to that piano and stayed there until everybody went to bed. He was at the piano all day Saturday and all day Sunday. Then he bought a record player and started playing records. He'd play one record over and over again, all day long sometimes, and he'd improvise along with it on the piano. Or he'd play one section of the record, one chord, one change, one progression, then he'd do it on the piano. Then back to the record. Then back to the piano.

Well, I really don't know how they stood it. Isabel finally confessed that it wasn't like living with a person at all, it was like living with sound. And the sound didn't make any sense to her, didn't make sense to any of them— naturally. They began, in a way, to be afflicted by this presence that was living in their home. It was as though Sonny were some sort of god, or monster. He moved in an atmosphere which wasn't like theirs at all. They fed him and he ate, he washed himself, he walked in and out of their door; he certainly wasn't nasty or unpleasant or rude, Sonny isn't any of those things; but it was as though he were all wrapped up in some cloud, some fire, some vision all his own; and there wasn't any way to reach him. 166

At the same time, he wasn't really a man yet, he was still a child, and they had to watch out for him in all kinds of ways. They certainly couldn't throw him out. Neither did they dare to make a great scene about that piano because even they dimly sensed, as I sensed, from so many thousands of miles away, that Sonny was at that piano playing for his life. 167

But he hadn't been going to school. One day a letter came from the school board and Isabel's mother got it—there had, apparently, been other letters but Sonny had torn them up. This day, when Sonny came in, Isabel's mother showed him the letter and asked where he'd been spending his time. And she finally got it out of him that he'd been down in Greenwich Village, with musicians and other characters, in a white girl's apartment. And this scared her and she started to scream at him and what came up, once she began—though she denies it to this day—was what sacrifices they were making to give Sonny a decent home and how little he appreciated it. 168

Sonny didn't play the piano that day. By evening Isabel's mother had calmed down but then there was the old man to deal with, and Isabel herself. Isabel says she did her best to be calm but she broke down and started crying. She says she just watched Sonny's face. She could tell, by watching him, what was happening with him. And what was happening was that they penetrated his cloud, they had reached him. Even if their fingers had been a thousand times more gentle than human fingers ever are, he could hardly help feeling that they had stripped him naked and were spitting on that nakedness. For he also had to see that his presence, that music, which was life or death to him, had been torture for them and that they had endured it, not at all for his sake, but only for mine. And Sonny couldn't take that. He can take it a little better today than 169 he could then but he's still not very good at it and, frankly, I don't know anybody who is.

The silence of the next few days must have been louder than the sound of all the music ever played since time began. One morning, before she went to work, Isabel was in his room for something and she suddenly realized that all of his records were gone. And she knew for certain that he was gone. And he was. He went as far as the navy would carry him. He finally sent me a postcard from some place in Greece and that was the first I knew that Sonny was still alive. I didn't see him any more until we were both back in New York and the war had long been over.   170

He was a man by then, of course, but I wasn't willing to see it. He came by the house from time to time, but we fought almost every time we met. I didn't like the way he carried himself, loose and dreamlike all the time, and I didn't like his friends, and his music seemed to be merely an excuse for the life he led. It sounded just that weird and disordered.   171

Then we had a fight, a pretty awful fight, and I didn't see him for months. By and by I looked him up, where he was living, in a furnished room in the Village, and I tried to make it up. But there were lots of other people in the room and Sonny just lay on his bed, and he wouldn't come downstairs with me, and he treated these other people as though they were his family and I weren't. So I got mad and then he got mad, and then I told him that he might just as well be dead as live the way he was living. Then he stood up and he told me not to worry about him any more in life, that he *was* dead as far as I was concerned. Then he pushed me to the door and the other people looked on as though nothing were happening, and he slammed the door behind me. I stood in the hallway, staring at the door. I heard somebody laugh in the room and then the tears came to my eyes. I started down the steps, whistling to keep from crying, I kept whistling, *You going to need me, baby, one of these cold, rainy days.*   172

I read about Sonny's trouble in the spring. Little Grace died in the fall. She was a beautiful little girl. But she only lived a little over two years. She died of polio and she suffered. She had a slight fever for a couple of days, but it didn't seem like anything and we just kept her in bed. And we would certainly have called the doctor, but the fever dropped, she seemed to be all right. So we thought it had just been a cold. Then, one day, she was up, playing, Isabel was in the kitchen fixing lunch for the two boys when they'd come in from school, and she heard Grace fall down in the living room. When you have a lot of children you don't always start running when one of them falls, unless they start screaming or something. And, this time, Grace was quiet. Yet, Isabel says that when she heard that *thump* and then that silence, something happened in her to make her afraid. And she ran to the living room and there was little Grace on the floor, all twisted up, and the reason she hadn't screamed was that   173 she couldn't get her breath. And when she did scream, it was the worst sound, Isabel says, that she'd ever heard in all her life, and she still hears it sometimes in her dreams. Isabel will sometimes wake me up with a low, moaning, strangled sound and I have to be quick to awaken her and hold her to me and where Isabel is weeping against me seems a mortal wound.

I think I may have written Sonny the very day that little Grace was buried.   174
I was sitting in the living room in the dark, by myself, and I suddenly thought of Sonny. My trouble made his real.

One Saturday afternoon, when Sonny had been living with us, or, anyway,   175
been in our house, for nearly two weeks, I found myself wandering aimlessly about the living room, drinking from a can of beer, and trying to work up the courage to search Sonny's room. He was out, he was usually out whenever I was home, and Isabel had taken the children to see their grandparents. Suddenly I was standing still in front of the living room window, watching Seventh Avenue. The idea of searching Sonny's room made me still. I scarcely dared to admit to myself what I'd be searching for. I didn't know what I'd do if I found it. Or if I didn't.

On the sidewalk across from me, near the entrance to a barbecue joint, some   176
people were holding an old-fashioned revival meeting. The barbecue cook, wearing a dirty white apron, his conked hair reddish and metallic in the pale sun, and a cigarette between his lips, stood in the doorway, watching them. Kids and older people paused in their errands and stood there, along with some older men and a couple of very tough-looking women who watched everything that happened on the avenue, as though they owned it, or were maybe owned by it. Well, they were watching this, too. The revival was being carried on by three sisters in black, and a brother. All they had were their voices and their Bibles and a tambourine. The brother was testifying and while he testified two of the sisters stood together, seeming to say, amen, and the third sister walked around with the tambourine outstretched and a couple of people dropped coins into it. Then the brother's testimony ended and the sister who had been taking up the collection dumped the coins into her palm and transferred them to the pocket of her long black robe. Then she raised both hands, striking the tambourine against the air, and then against one hand, and she started to sing. And the two other sisters and the brother joined in.

It was strange, suddenly, to watch, though I had been seeing these street   177
meetings all my life. So, of course, had everybody else down there. Yet, they paused and watched and listened and I stood still at the window. *"Tis the old ship of Zion,"* they sang, and the sister with the tambourine kept a steady, jangling beat, *"it has rescued many a thousand!"* Not a soul under the sound of their voices was hearing this song for the first time, not one of them had been rescued. Nor had they seen much in the way of rescue work being done around them. Neither did they especially believe in the holiness of the three sisters and the

brother, they knew too much about them, knew where they lived, and how. The woman with the tambourine, whose voice dominated the air, whose face was bright with joy, was divided by very little from the woman who stood watching her, a cigarette between her heavy, chapped lips, her hair a cuckoo's nest, her face scarred and swollen from many beatings, and her black eyes glittering like coal. Perhaps they both knew this, which was why, when, as rarely, they addressed each other, they addressed each other as Sister. As the singing filled the air the watching, listening faces underwent a change, the eyes focusing on something within; the music seemed to soothe a poison out of them; and time seemed, nearly, to fall away from the sullen, belligerent, battered faces, as though they were fleeing back to their first condition, while dreaming of their last. The barbecue cook half shook his head and smiled, and dropped his cigarette and disappeared into his joint. A man fumbled in his pockets for change and stood holding it in his hand impatiently, as though he had just remembered a pressing appointment further up the avenue. He looked furious. Then I saw Sonny, standing on the edge of the crowd. He was carrying a wide, flat notebook with a green cover, and it made him look, from where I was standing, almost like a schoolboy. The coppery sun brought out the copper in his skin, he was very faintly smiling, standing very still. Then the singing stopped, the tambourine turned into a collection plate again. The furious man dropped in his coins and vanished, so did a couple of the women, and Sonny dropped some change in the plate, looking directly at the woman with a little smile. He started across the avenue, toward the house. He has a slow, loping walk, something like the way Harlem hipsters walk, only he's imposed on this his own half-beat. I had never really noticed it before.

I stayed at the window, both relieved and apprehensive. As Sonny disap-   178
peared from my sight, they began singing again. And they were still singing when his key turned in the lock.

"Hey," he said.   179

"Hey, yourself. You want some beer?"   180

"No. Well, maybe." But he came up to the window and stood beside me,   181
looking out. "What a warm voice," he said.

They were singing *If I could only hear my mother pray again!*   182

"Yes," I said, "and she can sure beat that tambourine."   183

"But what a terrible song," he said, and laughed. He dropped his notebook   184
on the sofa and disappeared into the kitchen. "Where's Isabel and the kids?"

"I think they went to see their grandparents. You hungry?"   185

"No." He came back into the living room with his can of beer. "You want   186
to come some place with me tonight?"

I sensed, I don't know how, that I couldn't possibly say no. "Sure. Where?"   187

He sat down on the sofa and picked up his notebook and started leafing   188
through it. "I'm going to sit in with some fellows in a joint in the Village."

"You mean, you're going to play, tonight?"   189

"That's right." He took a swallow of his beer and moved back to the window.   190
He gave me a sidelong look. "If you can stand it."

"I'll try," I said.   191

He smiled to himself and we both watched as the meeting across the way   192
broke up. The three sisters and the brother, heads bowed, were singing *God be
with you till we meet again.* The faces around them were very quiet. Then the
song ended. The small crowd dispersed. We watched the three women and the
lone man walk slowly up the avenue.

"When she was singing before," said Sonny, abruptly, "her voice reminded   193
me for a minute of what heroin feels like sometimes—when it's in your veins.
It makes you feel sort of warm and cool at the same time. And distant. And—
and sure." He sipped his beer, very deliberately not looking at me. I watched
his face. "It makes you feel—in control. Sometimes you've got to have that
feeling."

"Do you?" I sat down slowly in the easy chair.   194

"Sometimes." He went to the sofa and picked up his notebook again. "Some   195
people do."

"In order," I asked, "to play?" And my voice was very ugly, full of contempt   196
and anger.

"Well"—he looked at me with great, troubled eyes, as though, in fact, he   197
hoped his eyes would tell me things he could never otherwise say—"they *think*
so. And *if* they think so—!"

"And what do *you* think?" I asked.   198

He sat on the sofa and put his can of beer on the floor. "I don't know," he   199
said, and I couldn't be sure if he were answering my question or pursuing his
thoughts. His face didn't tell me. "It's not so much to *play.* It's to *stand* it, to be
able to make it at all. On any level." He frowned and smiled: "In order to keep
from shaking to pieces."

"But these friends of yours," I said, "they seem to shake themselves to pieces 200
pretty goddamn fast."

"Maybe." He played with the notebook. And something told me that I should   201
curb my tongue, that Sonny was doing his best to talk, that I should listen.
"But of course you only know the ones that've gone to pieces. Some don't—
or at least they haven't *yet* and that's just about all *any* of us can say." He paused.
"And then there are some who just live, really, in hell, and they know it and
they see what's happening and they go right on. I don't know." He sighed,
dropped the notebook, folded his arms. "Some guys, you can tell from the way
they play, they on something *all* the time. And you can see that, well, it makes
something real for them. But of course," he picked up his beer from the floor
and sipped it and put the can down again, "they *want* to, too, you've got to see
that. Even some of them that say they don't—*some,* not all."

"And what about you?" I asked—I couldn't help it. "What about you? Do 202
you want to?"

He stood up and walked to the window and remained silent for a long time. 203
Then he signed. "Me," he said. Then: "While I was downstairs before, on my
way here, listening to that woman sing, it struck me all of a sudden how much
suffering she must have had to go through—to sing like that. It's *repulsive* to
think you have to suffer that much."

I said: "But there's no way not to suffer—is there, Sonny?" 204

"I believe not," he said and smiled, "but that's never stopped anyone from 205
trying." He looked at me. "Has it?" I realized, with this mocking look, that
there stood between us, forever, beyond the power of time or forgiveness, the
fact that I had held silence—so long!—when he had needed human speech
to help him. He turned back to the window. "No, there's no way not to suffer.
But you try all kinds of ways to keep from drowning in it, to keep on top of
it, and to make it seem—well, like *you.* Like you did something, all right, and
now you're suffering for it. You know?" I said nothing. "Well you know," he
said, impatiently, "Why *do* people suffer? Maybe it's better to do something to
give it a reason, *any* reason."

"But we just agreed," I said, "that there's no way not to suffer. Isn't it better, 206
then, just to—take it?"

"But nobody just takes it," Sonny cried, "that's what I'm telling you! *Everybody* 207
tries not to. You're just hung up on the *way* some people try—it's not
your way!"

The hair on my face began to itch, my face felt wet. "That's not true," I 208
said, "that's not true. I don't give a damn what other people do, I don't even
care how they suffer. I just care how *you* suffer." And he looked at me. "Please
believe me," I said, "I don't want to see you—die—trying not to suffer."

"I won't," he said, flatly, "die trying not to suffer. At least, not any faster 209
than anybody else."

"But there's no need," I said, trying to laugh, "is there? in killing yourself." 210

I wanted to say more, but I couldn't. I wanted to talk about will power and 211
how life could be—well, beautiful. I wanted to say that it was all within; but
was it? or, rather, wasn't that exactly the trouble? And I wanted to promise that
I would never fail him again. But it would all have sounded—empty words
and lies.

So I made the promise to myself and prayed that I would keep it. 212

"It's terrible sometimes, inside," he said, "that's what's the trouble. You walk 213
these streets, black and funky and cold, and there's not really a living ass to
talk to, and there's nothing shaking, and there's no way of getting it out—that
storm inside. You can't talk it and you can't make love with it, and when you
finally try to get with it and play it, you realize *nobody's* listening. So *you've* got
to listen. You got to find a way to listen."

And then he walked away from the window and sat on the sofa again, as   214
though all the wind had suddenly been knocked out of him. "Sometimes you'll
do *anything* to play, even cut your mother's throat." He laughed and looked at
me. "Or your brother's." Then he sobered. "Or your own." Then: "Don't worry.
I'm all right now and I think I'll *be* all right. But I can't forget—where I've
been. I don't mean just the physical place I've been, I mean where I've *been*.
And *what* I've been."

"What have you been, Sonny?" I asked.   215

He smiled—but sat sideways on the sofa, his elbow resting on the back, his   216
fingers playing with his mouth and chin, not looking at me. "I've been something
I didn't recognize, didn't know I could be. Didn't know anybody could be." He
stopped, looking inward, looking helplessly young, looking old. "I'm not talking
about it now because I feel *guilty* or anything like that—maybe it would be
better if I did, I don't know. Anyway, I can't really talk about it. Not to you,
not to anybody," and now he turned and faced me. "Sometimes, you know, and
it was actually when I was most *out* of the world, I felt that I was in it, that I
was *with* it, really, and I could play or I didn't really have to *play,* it just came
out of me, it was there. And I don't know how I played, thinking about it now,
but I know I did awful things, those times, sometimes, to people. Or it wasn't
that I *did* anything to them—it was that they weren't real." He picked up the
beer can; it was empty; he rolled it between his palms: "And other times—
well, I needed a fix, I needed to find a place to lean, I needed to clear a space
to *listen*—and I couldn't find it, and I—went crazy, I did terrible things to *me,*
I was terrible *for* me." He began pressing the beer can between his hands, I
watched the metal begin to give. It glittered, as he played with it, like a knife,
and I was afraid he would cut himself, but I said nothing. "Oh well. I can never
tell you. I was all by myself at the bottom of something, stinking and sweating
and crying and shaking, and I smelled it, you know? *my* stink, and I thought
I'd die if I couldn't get away from it and yet, all the same, I knew that everything
I was doing was just locking me in with it. And I didn't know," he paused, still
flattening the beer can, "I didn't know, I still *don't* know, something kept telling
me that maybe it was good to smell your own stink, but I didn't think that *that*
was what I'd been trying to do—and—who can stand it?" and he abruptly
dropped the ruined beer can, looking at me with a small, still smile, and then
rose, walking to the window as though it were the lodestone rock. I watched
his face, he watched the avenue. "I couldn't tell you when Mama died—but
the reason I wanted to leave Harlem so bad was to get away from drugs. And
then, when I ran away, that's what I was running from—really. When I came
back, nothing had changed, *I* hadn't changed, I was just—older." And he
stopped, drumming with his fingers on the windowpane. The sun had vanished,
soon darkness would fall. I watched his face. "It can come again," he said, almost

as though speaking to himself. Then he turned to me. "It can come again," he repeated. "I just want you to know that."

"All right," I said, at last. "So it can come again. All right."   217

He smiled, but the smile was sorrowful. "I had to try to tell you," he said.   218

"Yes," I said. "I understand that."   219

"You're my brother," he said, looking straight at me, and not smiling at all.   220

"Yes," I repeated, "yes. I understand that."   221

"He turned back to the window, looking out. "All that hatred down there,"   222
he said, "all that hatred and misery and love. It's a wonder it doesn't blow the avenue apart."

We went to the only nightclub on a short, dark street, downtown. We   223
squeezed through the narrow, chattering, jam-packed bar to the entrance of the big room, where the bandstand was. And we stood there for a moment, for the lights were very dim in this room and we couldn't see. Then, "Hello, boy," said a voice and an enormous black man, much older than Sonny or myself, erupted out of all that atmospheric lighting and put an arm around Sonny's shoulder. "I been sitting right here," he said, "waiting for you."

He had a big voice, too, and heads in the darkness turned toward us.   224

Sonny grinned and pulled a little away, and said, "Creole, this is my brother.   225
I told you about him."

Creole shook my hand. "I'm glad to meet you, son," he said, and it was clear   226
that he was glad to meet me *there* for Sonny's sake. And he smiled, "You got a real musician in *your* family," and he took his arm from Sonny's shoulder and slapped him, lightly, affectionately, with the back of his hand.

"Well. Now I've heard it all," said a voice behind us. This was another   227
musician, and a friend of Sonny's, a coal-black, cheerful-looking man, built close to the ground. He immediately began confiding to me, at the top of his lungs, the most terrible things about Sonny, his teeth gleaming like a lighthouse and his laugh coming up out of him like the beginning of an earthquake. And it turned out that everyone at the bar knew Sonny, or almost everyone; some were musicians, working there, or nearby, or not working, some were simply hangers-on, and some were there to hear Sonny play. I was introduced to all of them and they were all very polite to me. Yet, it was clear that, for them, I was only Sonny's brother. Here, I was in Sonny's world. Or, rather: his kingdom. Here, it was not even a question that his veins bore royal blood.

They were going to play soon and Creole installed me, by myself, at a table   228
in a dark corner. Then I watched them, Creole, and the little black man, and Sonny, and the others, while they horsed around, standing just below the bandstand. The light from the bandstand spilled just a little short of them and, watching them laughing and gesturing and moving about, I had the feeling that

they, nevertheless, were being most careful not to step into that circle of light too suddenly: that if they moved into the light too suddenly, without thinking, they would perish in flame. Then, while I watched, one of them, the small, black man, moved into the light and crossed the bandstand and started fooling around with his drums. Then—being funny and being, also, extremely cere-monious—Creole took Sonny by the arm and led him to the piano. A woman's voice called Sonny's name and a few hands started clapping. And Sonny, also being funny and being ceremonious, and so touched, I think, that he could have cried, but neither hiding it nor showing it, riding it like a man, grinned, and put both hands to his heart and bowed from the waist.

Creole then went to the bass fiddle and a lean, very bright-skinned brown   229
man jumped up on the bandstand and picked up his horn. So there they were, and the atmosphere on the bandstand and in the room began to change and tighten. Someone stepped up to the microphone and announced them. Then there were all kinds of murmurs. Some people at the bar shushed others. The waitress ran around, frantically getting in the last orders, guys and chicks got closer to each other, and the lights on the bandstand, on the quartet, turned to a kind of indigo. Then they all looked different there. Creole looked about him for the last time, as though he were making certain that all his chickens were in the coop, and then he—jumped and struck the fiddle. And there they were.

All I know about music is that not many people ever really hear it. And   230
even then, on the rare occasions when something opens within, and the music enters, what we mainly hear, or hear corroborated, are personal, private, van-ishing evocations. But the man who creates the music is hearing something else, is dealing with the roar rising from the void and imposing order on it as it hits the air. What is evoked in him, then, is of another order, more terrible because it has no words, and triumphant, too, for that same reason. And his triumph, when he triumphs, is ours. I just watched Sonny's face. His face was troubled, he was working hard, but he wasn't with it. And I had the feeling that, in a way, everyone on the bandstand was waiting for him, both waiting for him and pushing him along. But as I began to watch Creole, I realized that it was Creole who held them all back. He had them on a short rein. Up there, keeping the beat with his whole body, wailing on the fiddle, with his eyes half closed, he was listening to everything, but he was listening to Sonny. He was having a dialogue with Sonny. He wanted Sonny to leave the shoreline and strike out for the deep water. He was Sonny's witness that deep water and drowning were not the same thing—he had been there, and he knew. And he wanted Sonny to know. He was waiting for Sonny to do the things on the keys which would let Creole know that Sonny was in the water.

And, while Creole listened, Sonny moved, deep within, exactly like someone   231 in torment. I had never before thought of how awful the relationship must be between the musician and his instrument. He has to fill it, this instrument, with the breath of life, his own. He has to make it do what he wants it to do. And a piano is just a piano. It's made out of so much wood and wires and little hammers and big ones, and ivory. While there's only so much you can do with it, the only way to find this out is to try; to try and make it do everything.

And Sonny hadn't been near a piano for over a year. And he wasn't on much better terms with his life, not the life that stretched before him now. He and the piano stammered, started one way, got scared, stopped; started another way, panicked, marked time, started again; then seemed to have found a direction, panicked again, got stuck. And the face I saw on Sonny I'd never seen before. Everything had been burned out of it, and, at the same time, things usually hidden were being burned in, by the fire and fury of the battle which was occurring in him up there.   232

Yet, watching Creole's face as they neared the end of the first set, I had the feeling that something had happened, something I hadn't heard. Then they finished, there was scattered applause, and then, without an instant's warning, Creole started into something else, it was almost sardonic, it was *Am I Blue.* And, as though he commanded, Sonny began to play. Something began to happen. And Creole let out the reins. The dry, low, black man said something awful on the drums, Creole answered, and the drums talked back. Then the horn insisted, sweet and high, slightly detached perhaps, and Creole listened, commenting now and then, dry, and driving, beautiful and calm and old. Then they all came together again, and Sonny was part of the family again. I could tell this from his face. He seemed to have found, right there beneath his fingers, a damn brand-new piano. It seemed that he couldn't get over it. Then, for awhile, just being happy with Sonny, they seemed to be agreeing with him that brand-new pianos certainly were a gas.   233

Then Creole stepped forward to remind them that what they were playing was the blues. He hit something in all of them, he hit something in me, myself, and the music tightened and deepened, apprehension began to beat the air. Creole began to tell us what the blues were all about. They were not about anything very new. He and his boys up there were keeping it new, at the risk of ruin, destruction, madness, and death, in order to find new ways to make us listen. For, while the tale of how we suffer, and how we are delighted, and how we may triumph is never new, it always must be heard. There isn't any other tale to tell, it's the only light we've got in all this darkness.   234

And this tale, according to that face, that body, those strong hands on those strings, has another aspect in every country, and a new depth in every generation. Listen, Creole seemed to be saying, listen. Now these are Sonny's blues. He made the little black man on the drums know it, and the bright, brown   235 man on the horn. Creole wasn't trying any longer to get Sonny in the water. He was wishing him Godspeed. Then he stepped back, very slowly, filling the air with the immense suggestion that Sonny speak for himself.

Then they all gathered around Sonny and Sonny played. Every now and   236 again one of them seemed to say, amen. Sonny's fingers filled the air with life, his life. But that life contained so many others. And Sonny went all the way back, he really began with the spare, flat statement of the opening phrase of the song. Then he began to make it his. It was very beautiful because it wasn't hurried and it was no longer a lament. I seemed to hear with what burning he had made it his, with what burning we had yet to make it ours, how we could cease lamenting. Freedom lurked around us and I understood, at last, that he could help us to be free if we would listen, that he would never be free until we did. Yet, there was no battle in his face now. I heard what he had gone through, and would continue to go through until he came to rest in earth. He had made it his: that long line, of which we knew only Mama and Daddy. And he was giving it back, as everything must be given back, so that, passing through death, it can live forever. I saw my mother's face again, and felt, for the first time, how the stones of the road she had walked on must have bruised her feet. I saw the moonlit road where my father's brother died. And it brought something else back to me, and carried me past it, I saw my little girl again and felt Isabel's tears again, and I felt my own tears begin to rise. And I was yet aware that this was only a moment, that the world waited outside, as hungry as a tiger, and that trouble stretched above us, longer than the sky.

Then it was over. Creole and Sonny let out their breath, both soaking wet,   237 and grinning. There was a lot of applause and some of it was real. In the dark, the girl came by and I asked her to take drinks to the bandstand. There was a long pause, while they talked up there in the indigo light and after awhile I saw the girl put a Scotch and milk on top of the piano for Sonny. He didn't seem to notice it, but just before they started playing again, he sipped from it and looked toward me, and nodded. Then he put it back on top of the piano. For me, then, as they began to play again, it glowed and shook above my brother's head like the very cup of trembling.

Questions for Critical Thinking

1. What major contrasts exist between Sonny and his brother? In what ways are they similar?

2. What elements of Sonny's personality seem to contribute directly to his suffering?

3. What role do drugs play in this story? What is your reaction to the narrator's view of drugs? Do you have a solution to the drug problem of today? If so, what is it?

4. What connection exists between Mama's story about the brothers' uncle and the plot of "Sonny's Blues"?

5. What do the geographical settings of "Barn Burning" and "Sonny's Blues" have in common? How do they both contribute to the main character's situation?

6. How is suffering perceived in this story? How does this perception square with your own view?

7. How does the ambiguity of the ending contribute to the theme of the story? Provide a more obvious ending and speculate on how it changes the story.

Writing Assignment

In his introduction to *Notes of a Native Son* (1955), James Baldwin wrote the following:

> In the context of the Negro problem neither whites nor blacks, for excellent reasons of their own, have the faintest desire to look back; but I think that the past is all that makes the present coherent, and further, that the past will remain horrible for exactly as long as we refuse to assess it honestly.

Write an essay in which you give reasons why neither whites nor blacks have the faintest desire to look at the past. State what you think will happen if both races look back and assess the past honestly.

Writing Advice

Your essay should focus mainly on answering two questions: (1) "When it comes to race relations, why do neither blacks nor whites have the faintest desire to look at the past?" (2) "What will be the result if both blacks and whites look honestly at their checkered past?"

In rhetorical terms, answering the first question will require writing an analysis of cause. Assuming that you agree with the premise of the question, you try to come up with a reasonable explanation of why whites and blacks are loath to examine their mutual past. You will, of course, have to show that Baldwin is right, that such an aversion to assessing the past does exist. Doing so will require a trip to the library to find supporting opinion and testimony from experts.

On the other hand, answering the second question will require writing an analysis of effect predicting the consequences likely to result from such an examination. You ask yourself: If both blacks and whites were able to honestly confront a past characterized by bigotry, victimization, and racial misunderstanding, what benefits do you think are likely to ensue? Would such an honest confronting of history necessarily lead to better understanding between the races? Or is it just as likely to cause renewed recriminations and bitterness? Again, you will have to do some diligent research to find the opinions and testimony of experts you can use as backing for your speculations.

There is, however, another tack that you could take in writing this essay: you could disagree with the premise of the question and argue that Baldwin is wrong in his opinion that blacks and whites are loath to honestly reassess their past. If you choose to follow this particular line of argument, you will, of course, have to demonstrate that just such a sober and searching assessment has repeatedly taken place, and back this opinion with appropriate evidence.

Note that the danger in writing this essay is that such an abstract topic will have a tendency to tempt you to vagueness and unsupported opinion. You can counteract this built-in weakness by citing the concrete opinions and speculations of experts.

Alternate Writing Assignment

1. Using "Sonny's Blues" as a starting point, write an essay in which you demonstrate how one's own suffering makes a person either more or less sympathetic with the suffering of others.

2. Write an essay in which you describe some successful processes to deal with suffering. Use specific examples that prove your point.

LITERATURE

DESIGN
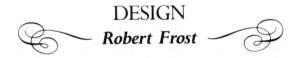
Robert Frost

Robert Frost (1874–1963) was perhaps the most beloved twentieth-century American poet. Born in San Francisco, he moved to the East Coast, where he came to personify the character of New England. His education consisted of some brief studies at Dartmouth and two years at Harvard. In 1912 he traveled to England, where he received his first critical acclaim as a poet with the publication of two collections, *A Boy's Will* (1913) and *North of Boston* (1914). After his success in England, he returned to the United States and settled on a farm near Franconia, New Hampshire.

Much in demand as a teacher of poetry and reader of his own poems, Frost lectured at several universities, including Amherst, Harvard, and the University of Michigan. In later life he made several goodwill trips for the state department of the United States, and in 1961 he recited his poem "The Gift Outright" at the inauguration of John F. Kennedy. Those who watched him in person or on television remember him as a frail, stooped figure with white hair blowing in the freezing winter wind. Among his volumes of poetry are *New Hampshire* (1923), *West-running Brook* (1928), *Collected Poems* (1930), *A Further Range* (1936), *A Witness Tree* (1942), *Steeple Bush* (1947), and *In the Clearing* (1962).

He also wrote two blank verse plays, *A Masque of Reason* (1945) and *A Masque of Mercy* (1947). Frost was awarded the Pulitzer Prize for Poetry in 1924, 1931, 1937, and 1943.

Reading Advice

Like most of Frost's work, this poem is deceptively simple—seemingly a merely naturalistic description of a spider, a flower, and a moth. But after reading the poem two or three times, you will realize that something more profound is actually happening, with the three elements from nature symbolically enacting a larger philosophic question about suffering and its causes. The poem urges us to deal with the complex question of who, if anyone, controls life's haphazard tragedies.

> *I found a dimpled spider, fat and white,*   1
> *On a white heal-all, holding up a moth*
> *Like a white piece of rigid satin cloth—*
> *Assorted characters of death and blight*
> *Mixed ready to begin the morning right,*
> *Like the ingredients of a witches' broth—*
> *A snow-drop spider, a flower like a froth,*
> *And dead wings carried like a paper kite.*

> *What had that flower to do with being white,*   2
> *The wayside blue and innocent heal-all?*
> *What brought the kindred spider to that height,*
> *Then steered the white moth thither in the night?*
> *What but design of darkness to appall?—*
> *If design govern in a thing so small.*

Questions for Critical Thinking

1. Why does the poet label the spider, the flower, and the moth "assorted characters of death and blight"?

2. Does the poet imply an answer to the philosophical question he poses? Explain your answer.

3. Why do you think human beings are often obsessed with wanting to know whether an intelligence governs the universe? Do you think dogs or cats are equally concerned with this question? If not, what is the difference?

4. Would you be satisfied if you knew that a benevolent God governed large matters only and allowed small matters to happen arbitrarily? Explain your answer.

5. Referring back to two of the philosophical essays at the beginning of this chapter, do the arguments by David Hume and Stephen Jay Gould agree with the argument implicit in "Design?" Explain your answer.

Writing Assignment

Using some aspect of nature you have observed in person, write an essay discussing what lesson you learned from the scene.

Writing Advice

What we are asking you to do is to write in prose something similar to what Frost did in poetry. The following steps might be useful:

1. Choose the scene from nature you plan to use as your focal point. The scene can be any random event you have observed: a smart and wiry dog herding cattle home to their barn; a spider devouring its prey; an eagle soaring against the blue sky; a cat tantalizing a mouse; a bee fertilizing a rose; a worm causing the decay of an apple; a mother deer looking after her fawn.

2. Describe the scene in vivid details, paying attention to the sensory connections between the participants—size, color, touch, smell, sound. The goal is to involve your reader in the scene.

3. Without preaching, simply state what you learned from observing this scene, with your conclusion serving as your thesis. Try to make your conclusion as understated as Frost's.

Alternate Writing Assignment

Find another brief nature poem by Robert Frost and explicate it by stating the poem's main argument (its theme) and showing how the poet supports that argument.

ART

THE SCREAM

Edvard Munch

About the Artist

Edvard Munch (1863–1944) was a Norwegian painter and graphic artist who helped give impetus to the modern expressionist movement in painting, especially in Germany.

Munch studied first in Oslo and later in Paris, where he copied the styles of Bonnard, Toulouse-Lautrec, Van Gogh, and Gauguin. In the late 1890s he abandoned impressionism to portray his own sense of isolation in the face of death, fear, and anxiety. In depicting this theme, he developed an exciting, violent, and emotionally charged style. During the 1890s, his most productive period, he created powerful and shocking woodcuts, which were both admired and condemned by critics. Negative reaction to his nightmarish images caused the closing of an important 1892 exhibition in Berlin. In 1899, after suffering severe mental illness, Munch returned from Germany to Norway, where he painted murals for the University of Oslo and for an Oslo chocolate factory. Today his work is represented in leading collections all over the world. Among his best-known pieces are *The Scream* (1893) *The Kiss* (1895), and *The Vampire*.

About the Art

Most of Munch's masterpieces are representations of inner human turmoil and pain. His paintings present an almost unbearable picture of the psychic tensions and anguish people feel. *The Scream*, our choice for this chapter, offers a disturbing vision of suffering caused by panic and anguish. The central figure, stopped on a boardwalk, seems on the verge of cracking up emotionally. Long, swirling lines seem to echo the scream into every corner of the painting, transmogrifying the entire background into a shriek of terror. The central figure remains desperately lonely despite the two persons approaching from a distance. Symbolic of human anguish in a society where people are indifferent or preoccupied, *The Scream* is a painter's equivalent of the suffering the existentialists expressed in their writing.

A R T

THE GULF STREAM
Winslow Homer

About the Artist

Winslow Homer (1836–1910) was an American painter who has earned a place among the greatest painters of the sea. Born in Boston and self-instructed in the rudiments of drawing, he began his artistic career by serving a long apprenticeship in lithography and working as a magazine illustrator during the Civil War. In 1861, he was sent to the battlefront as a correspondent for *Harper's Weekly*. His sketches about the extramilitary life of soldiers drew attention and public praise, as did his studies of everyday American life, such as *Crack the Whip,* now permanently exhibited in the Metropolitan Museum of Art. In 1876, Homer abandoned illustration to devote himself to oil painting. On a holiday among the fishermen of the British seacoast, Homer became fascinated with the ocean and thereafter became an exclusive maritime painter. In 1884, he retired to Maine, built himself a cottage with a clear view of the sea, and save for an occasional visit to the islands of the Gulf Stream, lived alone in his rockbound studio. Awards came in abundance. The French praised him as the only generic American painter; he sold everything he painted. His most famous painting, *The Gulf Stream,* typifies his view of the ocean as nature's most terrifying agent.

About the Art

In the winter of 1889, Homer sailed to the Bahamas, a voyage that inspired *The Gulf Stream.* Like most of Homer's other works, this one has the unity, coherence, and clarity of perfect prose. It reveals accurate observation and detailed interpretation. You are not forced to guess at the meaning of this painting: it is a human being suffering and resigned to his terrible fate. Homer's subject, the sea, is a fit symbol of human life. The water, seductively blue but agitated by a hurricane, has almost completely destroyed the small sloop on which a helpless black sailor is stranded without food or water. Large sharks circling the boat in trails of red blood wait for the besieged sailor to slide overboard. In the far distance looms the silhouette of a large ship, but it is doubtful whether the weary drifter will be spotted and rescued. The painting, in its combination of threatening elements, uses a maritime setting to depict the painful vulnerability of human life.

6—1   *Edvard Munch,* The Scream, *1893. Approx. 36″ × 29.″ Oslo Kommunes Kunstsam-*
linger Munch-Museet.

6–2 *Winslow Homer, The Gulf Stream, 1899. Oil on canvas, 28 1/8" × 49 1/8." The Metropolitan Museum of Art, Wolfe Fund, 1906. Catherine Lorillard Wolfe Collection. (06.1234)*

Chapter Writing Assignments

After carefully reviewing the assigned material, including the paintings, write an essay expanding on one of the following attitudes toward suffering and its causes:

(1.) To prove that a Supreme Being is in charge of the universe and therefore also responsible for suffering is not important. Belief in such a Being is sufficiently important in our lives that questions of proof are secondary.

(2.) One must continue to believe in goodness and beauty despite suffering. In fact, if one maintains the right attitude, suffering can become a step toward moral growth, compassion, and love.

(3.) Evil and suffering are simply part of the human condition. One must learn to adjust and not to expect a painless life.

(4.) "The just man is most free of trouble; the unjust man most full of trouble"— Epicurus (c. 342–270 B.C.)

(5.) In this life, the evil often prosper while the good suffer; therefore, it behooves us to be self-centered and make sure that we do not suffer more than we must.

(6.) Nature is neither benevolent nor malevolent; it simply functions as an evolutionary force.

Be sure to focus your argument on a thesis supported by specific references to the assigned study materials. You may also use examples and details from your own background or from history.

CHAPTER SEVEN

❧

What Divides Us?
CLASS AND CASTE

Nature as a kingdom abounds in unforgiving inequality. Aggressiveness varies among living creatures, as does spunkiness. Members of even the same animal species are often intrinsically unequal in their abilities to run, sense approaching danger, and avoid it. The slower are caught by carnivores and eaten. The improvident starve to death during famine and drought. The weaker are killed and devoured by the stronger, and the sickly seldom survive to nurse and overcome their illness.

There is, however, one stark difference between nature's "class and caste" system and humans'. It is simply this: animals have no choice, no say in the matter, for nature has rigged the game to be played entirely by her own self-imposed rules. The okapi cannot come together and protest against nature for being slower than the gazelle. Lions cannot picket because of the elephant's greater bulk and consequent advantage in an interspecies fight. Class and caste in nature is characterized not by intelligence but by compulsion. Animals can no more change it than can streams run uphill or boulders soar like kites.

With humans, however, it is altogether different. We are a species with remarkable plasticity and have used a variety of class schemes to regiment our numbers. Although we can choose to order ourselves differently, many human societies still hold to cruel and rigid class-typing schemes under which whole races and peoples, perceived as "weaker" and somehow "less worthy," are subdued and dominated. Among many societies, women pay a harsh class penalty for their sex. We do know better than nature. But seldom do we do better.

Here is an example. In 1916 an American, Madison Grant, wrote a book titled *The Passing of the Great Race*. In it he claimed that all the achievements of civilization were due to that branch of the Aryans he called "Nordics"—Scandinavians, Scythians, Baltic Germans, Englishmen, and Anglo-Saxon Americans. His theory was that, cooled to hardness by harsh winters, these northern people were able to dominate the lethargic people of less rigorous climates. That this theory was once accepted as fact by many scholars is proof only of the strain of enthnocentrism—the belief that our society and culture is superior to all others—that tends to permeate our thinking about class and caste.

Of course, students of anthropology today find Grant's thesis loaded with obvious errors. They rejoin that the Chinese created the most enduring civilization in history—with statesmen, inventors, artists, poets, scientists, philosophers, and saints who flourished since 2000 B.C. to the present day. Mexicans can vaunt the splendid monuments of the Mayan, Aztec, and Incan cultures in pre-Columbian America. Hindus can rightfully boast about the black Dravidic peoples of south India who produced great poets and builders, as proved by the *Vedas* and the temples of Madras, Madura, and Trichinopoly, or the beautiful shrine of the Khmers at Angkor Wat.

When or how race or class struggles began is impossible to say, despite the many theories that have been offered. What is clear, however, is that for thousands of years nearly all countries have harbored class distinctions that created artificial barriers and even hatred between people.

Perhaps the oldest and purest form of class distinction is found in the *Rig Vedas* (12th century B.C.) of Hinduism. According to this religious myth, at some period thousands of years back in time, Primeval Man, an archetypal being, was dismembered in a sacrifice to the gods. The result of this cosmic sacrifice was the birth of the various castes of human society: Primeval Man's mouth became the learned caste of *Brahmans* or priests; his arms were made into the *Kshatriyas*, that is the noblemen and warriors; his two thighs became the *Vaisyas* or business class; from his feet came the *Sudras* or lowly servants. The Hindu universe was a closed system that offered no hope of change. Each caste had its appointed duty, which included the performance of certain religious rituals. Extreme upper and lower castes differed so widely in habits of everyday life that it is difficult to imagine how their members managed to live in the same community, but they did and continue to this day.

Various replicas of this rigid caste system emerged at one time or another in most civilizations of our world. Everywhere the learned priests controlled the noblemen, the merchants, and the servants. Nor have matters changed dramatically in our day. We still have what we call the upper class, the middle class, and the lower class, with respect and privilege being accorded the members of the upper class, but only pity reserved for those of the lower class, who sweat and labor to exist. Even in a democracy such as ours, class is a fact of life, though it is palliated by the opportunity for rising in the system that is theoretically available to everyone. With enough talent or ingenuity, a member of the lowest class can ascend the ladder into the top rung, as did John D. Rockefeller, who went from being a poor bookkeeper to becoming one of the world's richest men. Many such stories are still replayed today, with fortunes made and fantastic ascensions achieved by those with grit, energy, and pluck.

When asked, most people in our society say that they deplore caste or class distinctions; yet, according to sociological studies, this claim is hypocritical. Consciously or unconsciously, most of us still hold deeply rooted biases against our fellow human beings if they do not speak our language, share our skin color, worship our god, or revere our cultural traditions. Some of the most sadistic and violent murders are still committed by caste against caste, and class against class.

The essays in this chapter try to give you some historical perspective on the problem of class and caste. We begin the philosophy section with Karl Marx and Frederick Engels's *Communist Manifesto*, a document prophesying that someday the laboring class will control the world. In "The Crowd Phenomenon," José Ortega y Gasset complains bitterly that the masses are making decisions and becoming arbiters of taste when, in his mind, this should be the function of only the elite. The philosophy section ends with Jean-Jacques Rousseau's claim, in "On the Origin of Inequality among Men," that greed and materialism are the root of all class distinctions.

In our history section, Virginia Woolf exhorts women to climb the class ladder by becoming financially and intellectually independent of men. "The Black Slave Driver," an essay by Randall M. Miller, tries to soften the bad reputation of Southern slave drivers by depicting them as competent supervisors rather than cruel monsters. William Worger and John Boykin end the history section with their wide-ranging analysis of South Africa and apartheid.

For the literature section, we have chosen Katherine Mansfield's "The Garden Party," a story about a rich young girl's induction into the tragic life of the poor. We also present Ralph Ellison's "Battle Royal," a story about how a group of white community leaders in the South reveal their lack of humanity when they treat a brilliant young black student as if he were an inferior breed. The literature section ends with a poem by Stephen Spender, which uses vivid imagery to incite our emotions on behalf of children who must attend a school in the slums.

As usual, we end the chapter with two paintings, chosen because they so graphically show the difference between the glamorous life of the privileged rich, as represented by Jean-Honoré Fragonard's *The Swing,* and the mean and scrubby life of the poor, as pictured in Honoré Daumier's *The Third-Class Carriage.*

Nature, declaimed the plucky spinster played by Katherine Hepburn in the movie *The African Queen*, is what we are put on this earth to rise above. If so, when it comes to class and caste, we are still a long way from being virtuous enough to scold nature over the inequalities she has blithely sowed among the innocent throngs of okapis and gazelles, lions and elephants.

PHILOSOPHY

THE COMMUNIST MANIFESTO
Karl Marx and Frederick Engels

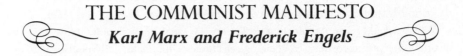

Karl Marx (1818–1883) was a German philosopher credited with formulating the basic theory of socialism and communism. Born into a Jewish family whose patriarch converted from Judaism to Lutheranism when Marx was six years old, Marx revealed a scholarly bent for philosophy and literature early in life. In 1841 he earned a Ph.D. in Philosophy from Bonn University. Because of his radical views about social economics, he was never offered a university position and was forced to earn his living as a journalist. For some time he edited the *Rheinishe Zeitung*, which was eventually suppressed, causing Marx to move to Paris and then to Brussels.

In Paris he began his lifelong association with Friedrick Engels, who helped him solidify his sociopolitical views and also saved him from starvation by providing constant financial aid. As time progressed, Marx was ostracized by the main centers of Continental thought, which thought him too revolutionary. Breaking with the tradition of providing social reform by appeal to natural rights, Marx invoked inevitable laws of history to predict the eventual triumph of the working class.

In 1847 he joined the Communist League and with Engels wrote the famous *Communist Manifesto* (1848). During this time, he earned a bare living by writing for the New York *Tribune* and by accepting money from Engels. His life was further burdened by chronically poor health and the death of several of his children. In 1864 he helped found the International Workingmen's Association, which eventually led to his co-authorship with Engels of *Das Kapital* (1867), a work that offered detailed explanations of socialist theory. While Marx remained little known in his own lifetime, his theories won him renown after his death, causing him to be either admired as a prophet or feared as a tyrant.

Reading Advice

The following excerpt from *The Communist Manifesto* is typical of Marx's polemical style, marked by vituperation and sarcasm. With hard-hitting directness he argues that laborers must unite to abolish all private ownership of property and to ensure the establishment of a common plan for the cultivation of land, the equal distribution of labor, and the free access to education for all. His idea was that nothing must remain in the hands of the rich that has been gained by hard labor of the poor. The section titled "Bourgeois and Proletarians" carefully explains the difference between capitalism and labor. In drawing the contrast, Marx steadily moves forward, point by point, describing all of the evils perpetrated by the rich and arrogant owners of industry on those helpless laborers who produce the goods that are then sold at great profit to the owners. He predicts, however, that inevitably the laboring class, labeled "Proletariat," will rise up against its rulers, labeled "Bourgeoisie," crush the masters and free itself from bondage.

In the section titled "Proletarians and Communists" Marx moves away from comparison/contrast to persuasion—arguing that the Communist cause is also the Proletarian cause. In this section, Marx uses the effective and necessary strategy of establishing the opposition and then arguing it away. He lists every criticism a bourgeois might level against communism and then demonstrates how that criticism is wrong. He ends this section with the words "But let us have done with the bourgeois objection to Communism" (paragraph 126).

Beginning with paragraph 131, he lists his ten-point plan for the establishment of communism. Each point is simple, clear, and to the point. In the last section, titled "Position of the Communists in Relation to the Various Existing Opposition Parties," Marx insists that communism will fight alongside any revolutionary movement against the existing order of things. His rallying cry is, "Working men of all countries, unite!"

A specter is haunting Europe—the 1
specter of Communism. All the Powers of old Europe have entered into a holy alliance to exorcise this specter; Pope and Czar, Metternich and Guizot, French Radicals and German police-spies.

Where is the party in opposition that has not been decried as communistic 2
by its opponents in power? Where the Opposition that has not hurled back the branding reproach of Communism against the more advanced opposition parties, as well as against its reactionary adversaries?

Two things result from this fact. 3

I. Communism is already acknowledged by all European Powers to be itself 4
a Power.

II. It is high time that Communists should openly, in the face of the whole 5
world, publish their views, their aims, their tendencies, and meet this nursery tale of the specter of Communism with a Manifesto of the party itself.

To this end, Communists of various nationalities have assembled in London 6
and sketched the following Manifesto, to be published in the English, French, German, Italian, Flemish and Danish languages.

Bourgeois and Proletarians

The history of all hitherto existing society is the history of class struggles. 7

Freeman and slave, patrician and plebeian, lord and serf, guild-master and 8
journeyman, in a word, oppressor and oppressed, stood in constant opposition to one another, carried on uninterrupted, now hidden, now open fight, a fight that each time ended, either in a revolutionary re-constitution of society at large, or in the common ruin of the contending classes.

In the earlier epochs of history we find almost everywhere a complicated   9
arrangement of society into various orders, a manifold gradation of social rank.
In ancient Rome we have patricians, knights, plebeians, slaves; in the Middle
Ages, feudal lords, vassals, guild-masters, journeymen, apprentices, serfs; in
almost all of these classes, again, subordinate gradations.

The modern bourgeois society that has sprouted from the ruins of feudal   10
society, has not done away with class antagonisms. It has but established new
classes, new conditions of oppression, new forms of struggle in place of the old
ones.

Our epoch, the epoch of the bourgeoisie, possesses, however, this distinctive   11
feature; it has simplified the class antagonisms. Society as a whole is more and
more splitting up into two great hostile camps, into two great classes directly
facing each other: Bourgeoisie and Proletariat.

From the serfs of the Middle Ages sprang the chartered burghers of the   12
earliest towns. From these burgesses the first elements of the bourgeoisie were
developed.

The discovery of America, the rounding of the Cape, opened up fresh ground   13
for the rising bourgeoisie. The East Indian and Chinese markets, the colonization
of America, trade with the colonies, the increase in the means of exchange and
in commodities generally, gave to commerce, to navigation, to industry, an
impulse never before known, and thereby, to the revolutionary element in the
tottering feudal society, a rapid development.

The feudal system of industry, under which industrial production was   14
monopolized by closed guilds, now no longer sufficed for the growing wants
of the new market. The manufacturing system took its place. The guild-masters
were pushed on one side by the manufacturing middle-class: division of labor
between the different corporate guilds vanished in the face of division of labor
in each single workshop.

Meantime the markets kept ever growing, the demand ever rising. Even   15
manufacture no longer sufficed. Thereupon, steam and machinery revolution-
ized industrial production. The place of manufacture was taken by the giant,
Modern Industry, the place of the industrial middle-class, by industrial mil-
lionaires, the leaders of whole industrial armies, the modern bourgeois.

Modern industry has established the world market, for which the discovery   16
of America paved the way. This market has given an immense development to
commerce, to navigation, to communication by land. This development has, in
its turn, reacted on the extension of industry; and in proportion as industry,
commerce, navigation, railways extended, in the same proportion the bourgeoisie developed, increased its capital, and pushed into the background every class
handed down from the Middle Ages.

We see, therefore, how the modern bourgeoisie is itself the product of a   17 long course of development, of a series of revolutions in the modes of production and of exchange.

Each step in the development of the bourgeoisie was accompanied by a corresponding political advance of that class. An oppressed class under the sway of the feudal nobility, an armed and self-governing association in the medieval commune, here independent urban republic (as in Italy and Germany), there taxable "third estate" of the monarchy (as in France), afterwards, in the period of manufacture proper, serving either the semi-feudal or the absolute monarchy as a counterpoise against nobility, and, in fact, corner stone of the great monarchies in general, the bourgeoisie has at last, since the establishment of Modern Industry and of the world-market, conquered for itself, in the modern representative State, exclusive political sway. The executive of the modern State is but a committee for managing the common affairs of the whole bourgeoisie. 18

The bourgeoisie, historically, has played a most revolutionary part. 19

The bourgeoisie, wherever it has got the upper hand, has put an end to all feudal, patriarchal, idyllic relations. It has pitilessly torn asunder the motley feudal ties that bound man to his "natural superiors," and has left no other nexus between man and man than naked self-interest, than callous "cash payment." It has drowned the most heavenly ecstasies of religious fervor, of chivalrous enthusiasm, of Philistine sentimentalism, in the icy water of egotistical calculation. It has resolved personal worth into exchange value, and in place of the numberless indefeasible chartered freedoms, has set up that single, unconscionable freedom—Free Trade. In one word, for exploitation, veiled by religious and political illusions, it has substituted naked, shameless, direct, brutal exploitation. 20

The bourgeoisie has stripped of its halo every occupation hitherto honored and looked up to with reverent awe. It has converted the physician, the lawyer, the priest, the poet, the man of science, into its paid wage laborers. 21

The bourgeoisie has torn away from the family its sentimental veil, and has reduced the family relation to a mere money relation. 22

The bourgeoisie has disclosed how it came to pass that the brutal display of vigor in the Middle Ages, which reactionists so much admire, found its fitting complement in the most slothful indolence. It has been the first to show what man's activity can bring about. It has accomplished wonders far surpassing Egyptian pyramids, Roman aqueducts and Gothic cathedrals; it has conducted expeditions that put in the shade all former Exoduses of nations and crusades. 23

The bourgeoisie cannot exist without constantly revolutionizing the instruments of production, and thereby the relations of production, and with them the whole relations of society. Conservation of the old modes of production in unaltered form was, on the contrary, the first condition of existence for all 24 earlier industrial classes. Constant revolutionizing of production, uninterrupted disturbance of all social conditions, everlasting uncertainty and agitation distinguish the bourgeois epoch from all earlier ones. All fixed, fast frozen relations, with their train of ancient and venerable prejudices and opinions, are swept away, all new formed ones become antiquated before they can ossify. All that is solid melts into the air, all that is holy is profaned, and man is at last compelled to face with sober senses, his real conditions of life, and his relations with his kind.

The need of a constantly expanding market for its products chases the   25
bourgeoisie over the whole surface of the globe. It must nestle everywhere, settle everywhere, establish connections everywhere.

The bourgeoisie has through its exploitation of the world market given a   26
cosmopolitan character to production and consumption in every country. To the great chagrin of reactionists, it has drawn from under the feet of industry the national ground on which it stood. All old established national industries have been destroyed or are daily being destroyed. They are dislodged by new industries, whose introduction becomes a life and death question for all civilized nations, by industries that no longer work up indigenous raw material, but raw material drawn from the remotest zones; industries whose products are consumed not only at home, but in every quarter of the globe. In place of the old wants, satisfied by the productions of the country, we find new wants, requiring for their satisfaction the products of distant lands and climes. In place of the old local and national seclusion and self-sufficiency we have intercourse in every direction, universal interdependence of nations. And as in material, so also in intellectual production. The intellectual creations of individual nations become common property. National one-sidedness and narrow-mindedness become more and more impossible, and from the numerous national and local literatures there arises a world literature.

The bourgeoisie, by the rapid improvement of all instruments of production,   27
by the immensely facilitated means of communication, draws all, even the most barbarian, nations into civilization. The cheap prices of its commodities are the heavy artillery with which it batters down all Chinese walls, with which it forces the barbarians' intensely obstinate hatred of foreigners to capitulate. It compels all nations, on pain of extinction, to adopt the bourgeois mode of production; it compels them to introduce what it calls civilization into their midst, i.e., to become bourgeois themselves. In one word, it creates a world after its own image.

The bourgeoisie has subjected the country to the rule of the towns. It has   28
created enormous cities, has greatly increased the urban population as compared with the rural, and has thus rescued a considerable part of the population from the idiocy of rural life. Just as it has made the country dependent on the towns,

so it has made barbarian and semi-barbarian countries dependent on the civilized ones, nations of peasants on nations of bourgeois, the East on the West.

The bourgeoisie keeps more and more doing away with the scattered state   29
of the population, of the means of production, and of property. It has agglom-
erated population, centralized means of production, and has concentrated property in a few hands. The necessary consequence of this was political centralization. Independent, or but loosely connected provinces, with separate interests,
laws, governments, and systems of taxation, became lumped together in one
nation, with one government, one code of laws, one national class interest, one
frontier and one customs tariff.

The bourgeoisie, during its rule of scarce one hundred years, has created   30
more massive and more colossal productive forces than have all preceding
generations together. Subjection of Nature's forces to man, machinery, application of chemistry to industry and agriculture, steam-navigation, railways,
electric telegraphs, clearing of whole continents for cultivation, canalization of
rivers, whole populations conjured out of the ground—what earlier century
had even a presentiment that such productive forces slumbered in the lap of
social labor?

We see then: the means of production and of exchange on whose foundation   31
the bourgeoisie built itself up, were generated in feudal society. At a certain
stage in the development of these means of production and of exchange, the
conditions under which feudal society produced and exchanged, the feudal
organization of agriculture and manufacturing industry, in one word, the feudal
relations of property became no longer compatible with the already developed
productive forces; they became so many fetters. They had to burst asunder;
they were burst asunder.

Into their place stepped free competition, accompanied by a social and   32
political constitution adapted to it, and by the economical and political sway
of the bourgeois class.

A similar movement is going on before our own eyes. Modern bourgeois   33
society with its relations of production, of exchange and of property, a society
that has conjured up such gigantic means of production and of exchange, is
like the sorcerer, who is no longer able to control the powers of the nether
world whom he has called up by his spells. For many a decade past, the history
of industry and commerce is but the history of the revolt of modern productive
forces against modern conditions of production, against the property relations
that are the conditions for the existence of the bourgeoisie and of its rule. It
is enough to mention the commercial crises that by their periodical return put
on its trial, each time more threateningly, the existence of the entire bourgeois
society. In these crises a great part not only of the existing products, but also
of the previously created productive forces, are periodically destroyed. In these

crises there breaks out an epidemic that, in all earlier epochs, would have seemed an absurdity—the epidemic of overproduction. Society suddenly finds itself put back into a state of momentary barbarism; it appears as if a famine, a universal war of devastation, had cut off the supply of every means of subsistence; industry and commerce seem to be destroyed; and why? Because there is too much civilization, too much means of subsistence, too much industry, too much commerce. The productive forces at the disposal of society no longer tend to further the development of the conditions of the bourgeois property; on the contrary, they have become too powerful for these conditions by which they are fettered, and as soon as they overcome these fetters they bring disorder into the whole of bourgeois society, endanger the existence of bourgeois property. The conditions of bourgeois society are too narrow to comprise the wealth created by them. And how does the bourgeoisie get over these crises? On the one hand by enforced destruction of a mass of productive forces; on the other, by the conquest of new markets, and by the more thorough exploitation of the old ones. That is to say, by paving the way for more extensive and more destructive crises, and by diminishing the means whereby crises are prevented.

The weapons with which the bourgeoisie felled feudalism to the ground are now turned against the bourgeoisie itself. 34

But not only has the bourgeoisie forged the weapons that bring death to itself; it has also called into existence the men who are to wield those weapons— the modern working class—the proletarians. 35

In proportion as the bourgeoisie, i.e., capital, is developed, in the same proportion is the proletariat, the modern working class, developed, a class of laborers who live only so long as they find work, and who find work only so long as their labor increases capital. These laborers, who must sell themselves piecemeal, are a commodity, like every other article of commerce, and are consequently exposed to all the vicissitudes of competition, to all the fluctuations of the market. 36

Owing to the extensive use of machinery and to division of labor, the work of the proletarians has lost all individual character, and, consequently, all charm for the workman. He becomes an appendage of the machine, and it is only the most simple, most monotonous and most easily acquired knack that is required of him. Hence, the cost of production of a workman is restricted almost entirely to the means of subsistence that he requires for his maintenance, and for the propagation of his race. But the price of a commodity, and also of labor, is equal to its cost of production. In proportion, therefore, as the repulsiveness of the work increases the wage decreases. Nay more, in proportion as the use of machinery and division of labor increases, in the same proportion the burden of toil increases, whether by prolongation of the working hours, by increase of the work enacted in a given time, or by increased speed of the machinery, etc. 37

Modern industry has converted the little workshop of the patriarchal master   38
into the great factory of the industrial capitalist. Masses of laborers, crowded
into factories, are organized like soldiers. As privates of the industrial army
they are placed under the command of a perfect hierarchy of officers and
sergeants. Not only are they the slaves of the bourgeois state, they are daily
and hourly enslaved by the machine, by the overlooker, and, above all, by the
individual bourgeois manufacturer himself. The more openly this despotism
proclaims gain to be its end and aim, the more petty, the more hateful and the
more embittering it is.

The less the skill and exertion or strength implied in manual labor, in other   39
words, the more modern industry becomes developed, the more is the labor
of men superseded by that of women. Differences of age and sex have no longer
any distinctive social validity for the working class. All are instruments of labor,
more or less expensive to use, according to their age and sex.

No sooner is the exploitation of the laborer by the manufacturer, so far at   40
an end, that he receives his wages in cash, than he is set upon by the other
portions of the bourgeoisie, the landlord, the shopkeeper, the pawnbroker, etc.

The lower strata of the middle class—the small trades-people, shopkeepers   41
and retired tradesmen generally, the handicraftsmen and peasants—all these
sink gradually into the proletariat, partly because their diminutive capital does
not suffice for the scale on which Modern Industry is carried on, and is
swamped in the competition with the large capitalists, partly because their
specialized skill is rendered worthless by new methods of production. Thus the
proletariat is recruited from all classes of the population.

The proletariat goes through various stages of development. With its birth   42
begins its struggle with the bourgeoisie. At first the contest is carried on by
individual laborers, then by the workpeople of a factory, then by the operatives
of one trade, in one locality, against the individual bourgeois who directly
exploits them. They direct their attacks not against the bourgeois conditions
of production, but against the instruments of production themselves; they
destroy imported wares that compete with their labor, they smash to pieces
machinery, they set factories ablaze, they seek to restore by force the vanished
status of the workman of the Middle Ages.

At this stage the laborers still form an incoherent mass scattered over the   43
whole country, and broken up by their mutual competition. If anywhere they
unite to form more compact bodies, this is not yet the consequence of their
own active union, but of the union of the bourgeoisie, which class, in order to
attain its own political ends, is compelled to set the whole proletariat in motion,
and is moreover yet, for a time, able to do so. At this stage, therefore, the
proletarians do not fight their enemies, but the enemies of their enemies, the
remnants of absolute monarchy, the landowners, the non-industrial bourgeois,

the petty bourgeoisie. Thus the whole historical movement is concentrated in the hands of the bourgeoisie, every victory so obtained is a victory for the bourgeoisie.

But with the development of industry the proletariat not only increases in [44] number; it becomes concentrated in greater masses, its strength grows and it feels that strength more. The various interests and conditions of life within the ranks of the proletariat are more and more equalized, in proportion as machinery obliterates all distinctions of labor, and nearly everywhere reduces wages to the same low level. The growing competition among the bourgeois, and the resulting commercial crisis, make the wages of the workers even more fluctuating. The unceasing improvement of machinery, ever more rapidly developing, makes their livelihood more and more precarious; the collisions between individual workmen and individual bourgeois take more and more the character of collisions between two classes. Thereupon the workers begin to form combinations (Trades' Unions) against the bourgeois; they club together in order to keep up the rate of wages; they found permanent associations in order to make provision beforehand for these occasional revolts. Here and there the contest breaks out into riots.

Now and then the workers are victorious, but only for a time. The real fruit [45] of their battle lies not in the immediate result but in the ever-expanding union of workers. This union is helped on by the improved means of communication that are created by modern industry, and that places the workers of different localities in contact with one another. It was just this contact that was needed to centralize the numerous local struggles, all of the same character, into one national struggle between classes. But every class struggle is a political struggle. And that union, to attain which the burghers of the Middle Ages with their miserable highways, required centuries, the modern proletarians, thanks to railways, achieve in a few years.

This organization of the proletarians into a class, and consequently into a [46] political party, is continually being upset again by the competition between the workers themselves. But it ever rises up again, stronger, firmer, mightier. It compels legislative recognition of particular interests of the workers by taking advantage of the divisions among the bourgeoisie itself. Thus the ten hours' bill in England was carried.

Altogether collisions between the classes of the old society further, in many [47] ways, the course of development of the proletariat. The bourgeoisie finds itself involved in a constant battle. At first with the aristocracy; later on, with those portions of the bourgeoisie itself whose interests have become antagonistic to the progress of industry; at all times, with the bourgeoisie of foreign countries. In all these battles it sees itself compelled to appeal to the proletariat, to ask for its help, and thus, to drag it into the political arena. The bourgeoisie itself, therefore, supplies the proletariat with its own elements of political and general education; in other words, it furnishes the proletariat with weapons for fighting the bourgeoisie.

Further, as we have already seen, entire sections of the ruling classes are, by the advance of industry, precipitated into the proletariat, or are at least threatened in their conditions of existence. These also supply the proletariat with fresh elements of enlightenment and progress.

48

Finally, in times when the class-struggle nears the decisive hour, the process of dissolution going on within the ruling class—in fact, within the whole range of an old society—assumes such a violent, glaring character that a small section of the ruling class cuts itself adrift and joins the revolutionary class, the class that holds the future in its hands. Just as, therefore, at an earlier period, a section of the nobility went over to the bourgeoisie, so now a portion of the bourgeoisie goes over to the proletariat, and in particular, a portion of the bourgeois ideologists, who have raised themselves to the level of comprehending theoretically the historical movements as a whole.

49

Of all the classes that stand face to face with the bourgeoisie today the proletariat alone is a really revolutionary class. The other classes decay and finally disappear in the face of modern industry; the proletariat is its special and essential product.

50

The lower middle class, the small manufacturer, the shopkeeper, the artisan, the peasant, all these fight against the bourgeoisie, to save from extinction their existence as fractions of the middle class. They are therefore not revolutionary, but conservative. Nay, more; they are reactionary, for they try to roll back the wheel of history. If by chance they are revolutionary, they are so only in view of their impending transfer into the proletariat; they thus defend not their present, but their future interests; they desert their own standpoint to place themselves at that of the proletariat.

51

The "dangerous class," the social scum, that passively rotting mass thrown off by the lowest layers of old society, may, here and there, be swept into the movement by a proletarian revolution; its conditions of life, however, prepare it far more for the part of a bribed tool of reactionary intrigue.

52

In the conditions of the proletariat, those of the old society at large are already virtually swamped. The proletarian is without property; his relation to his wife and children has no longer anything in common with the bourgeois family relations; modern industrial labor, modern subjection to capital, the same in England as in France, in America as in Germany, has stripped him of every trace of national character. Law, morality, religion, are to him so many bourgeois prejudices, behind which lurk in ambush just as many bourgeois interests.

53

All the preceding classes that got the upper hand sought to fortify their already acquired status by subjecting society at large to their conditions of appropriation. The proletarians cannot become masters of the productive forces

54

of society, except by abolishing their own previous mode of appropriation, and thereby also every other previous mode of appropriation. They have nothing of their own to secure and to fortify; their mission is to destroy all previous securities for and insurances of individual property.

All previous historical movements were movements of minorities, or in the interest of minorities. The proletarian movements is the self-conscious, independent movement of the immense majority. The proletariat, the lowest stratum of our present society, cannot stir, cannot raise itself up without the whole superincumbent strata of official society being sprung into the air. 55

Though not in substance, yet in form, the struggle of the proletariat with the bourgeoisie is at first a national struggle. The proletariat of each country must, of course, first of all settle matters with its own bourgeoisie. 56

In depicting the most general phases of the development of the proletariat, we traced the more or less veiled civil war, raging within existing society, up to the point where that war breaks out into open revolution, and where the violent overthrow of the bourgeoisie, lays the foundations for the sway of the proletariat. 57

Hitherto every form of society has been based, as we have already seen, on the antagonism of oppressing and oppressed classes. But in order to oppress a class, certain conditions must be assured to it under which it can, at least, continue its slavish existence. The serf, in the period of serfdom, raised himself to membership in the commune, just as the petty bourgeois, under the yoke of feudal absolutism, managed to develop into a bourgeois. The modern laborer, on the contrary, instead of rising with the progress of industry, sinks deeper and deeper below the conditions of existence of his own class. He becomes a pauper, and pauperism develops more rapidly than population and wealth. And here it becomes evident that the bourgeoisie is unfit any longer to be the ruling class in society, and to impose its conditions of existence upon society as an over-riding law. It is unfit to rule, because it is incompetent to assure an existence to its slave within his slavery, because it cannot help letting him sink into such a state that it has to feed him, instead of being fed by him. Society can no longer live under this bourgeoisie; in other words, its existence is no longer compatible with society. 58

The essential condition for the existence, and for the sway of the bourgeois class, is the formation and augmentation of capital; the condition for capital is wage labor. Wage labor rests exclusively on competition between the laborers. The advance of industry, whose involuntary promoter is the bourgeoisie, replaces the isolation of the laborers, due to competition, by their involuntary combination, due to association. The development of Modern Industry, therefore, cuts from under its feet the very foundation on which the bourgeoisie produces and appropriates products. What the bourgeoisie therefore produces, above all, 59 are its own grave diggers. Its fall and the victory of the proletariat are equally inevitable.

Proletarians and Communists

In what relation do the Communists stand to the proletarians as a whole?   60

The Communists do not form a separate party opposed to other working   61
class parties.

They have no interests separate and apart from those of the proletariat as a   62
whole.

They do not set up any sectarian principles of their own, by which to shape   63
and mold the proletarian movement.

The Communists are distinguished from the other working class parties by   64
this only: 1. In the national struggles of the proletarians of the different countries, they point out and bring to the front the common interests of the entire
proletariat, independently of all nationality, 2. In the various stages of development which the struggle of the working class against the bourgeoisie has to
pass through, they always and everywhere represent the interests of the movement as a whole.

The Communists, therefore, are on the one hand practically the most advanced   65
and resolute section of the working class parties of every country, that section
which pushes forward all others; on the other hand, theoretically, they have
over the great mass of the proletariat the advantage of clearly understanding
the line of march, the conditions, and the ultimate general results of the
proletarian movement.

The immediate aim of the Communists is the same as that of all the other   66
proletarian parties: formation of the proletariat into a class, overthrow of the
bourgeois of supremacy, conquest of political power by the proletariat.

The theoretical conclusions of the Communists are in no way based on ideas   67
or principles that have been invented or discovered by this or that would-be
universal reformer.

They merely express, in general terms, actual relations springing from an   68
existing class struggle, from a historical movement going on under our very
eyes. The abolition of existing property relations is not at all a distinctive feature
of Communism.

All property relations in the past have continually been subject to historical   69
change consequent upon the change in historical conditions.

The French Revolution, for example, abolished feudal property in favor of   70
bourgeois property.

The distinguishing feature of Communism is not the abolition of property   71
generally, but the abolition of bourgeois property. But modern bourgeois private

property is the final and most complete expression of the system of producing and appropriating products, that is based on class antagonism, on the exploitation of the many by the few.

In this sense, the theory of the Communists may be summed up in the single sentence: Abolition of private property.   72

We Communists have been reproached with the desire of abolishing the right of personally acquiring property as the fruit of a man's own labor, which property is alleged to be the groundwork of all personal freedom, activity and independence.   73

Hard won, self-acquired, self-earned property! Do you mean the property of the petty artisan and of the small peasant, a form of property that preceded the bourgeois form? There is no need to abolish that; the development of industry has to a great extent already destroyed it, and is still destroying it daily.   74

Or do you mean modern bourgeois private property?   75

But does wage labor create any property for the laborer? Not a bit. It creates capital, i.e., that kind of property which exploits wage labor, and which cannot increase except upon condition of getting a new supply of wage labor for fresh exploitation. Property, in its present form, is based on the antagonism of capital and wage labor. Let us examine both sides of this antagonism.   76

To be a capitalist is to have not only a purely personal, but a social status in production. Capital is a collective product, and only by the united action of many members, nay, in the last resort, only by the united action of all members of society, can it be set in motion.   77

Capital is therefore not a personal, it is a social power.   78

When, therefore, capital is converted into common property, into the property of all members of society, personal property is not thereby transformed into social property. It is only the social character of the property that is changed. It loses its class character.   79

Let us now take wage labor.   80

The average price of wage labor is the minimum wage, i.e., that quantum of the means of subsistence which is absolutely requisite to keep the laborer in bare existence as a laborer. What, therefore, the wage laborer appropriates by means of his labor, merely suffices to prolong and reproduce a bare existence. We by no means intend to abolish this personal appropriation of the products of labor, an appropriation that is made for the maintenance and reproduction of human life, and that leaves no surplus wherewith to command the labor of others. All that we want to do away with is the miserable character of this appropriation, under which the laborer lives merely to increase capital and is allowed to live only in so far as the interests of the ruling class require it.   81

In bourgeois society, living labor is but a means to increase accumulated   82 labor. In Communist society accumulated labor is but a means to widen, to enrich, to promote the existence of the laborer.

In bourgeois society, therefore, the past dominates the present; in Communist society the present dominates the past. In bourgeois society, capital is independent and has individuality, while the living person is dependent and has no individuality.

83

An the abolition of this state of things is called by the bourgeois abolition of individuality and freedom! And rightly so. The abolition of bourgeois individuality, bourgeois independence and bourgeois freedom is undoubtedly aimed at.

84

By freedom is meant, under the present bourgeois conditions of production, free trade, free selling and buying.

85

But if selling and buying disappears, free selling and buying disappears also. This talk about free selling and buying, and all the other "brave words" of our bourgeoisie about freedom in general have a meaning, if any, only in contrast with restricted selling and buying, with the fettered traders of the Middle Ages, but have no meaning when opposed to the Communistic abolition of buying and selling, of the bourgeois conditions of production, and of the bourgeoisie itself.

86

You are horrified at our intending to do away with private property. But in your existing society private is already done away with for nine-tenths of the population; its existence for the few is solely due to its non-existence in the hands of those nine-tenths. You reproach us, therefore, with intending to do away with a form of property, the necessary condition for whose existence is the non-existence of any property for the immense majority of society.

87

In one word, you reproach us with intending to do away with your property. Precisely so: that is just what we intend.

88

From the moment when labor can no longer be converted into capital, money, or rent, into a social power capable of being monopolized, i.e., from the moment when individual property can no longer be transformed into bourgeois property, into capital, from that moment, you say, individuality vanishes.

89

You must, therefore, confess that by "individual" you mean no other person than the bourgeois, than the middle-class owner of property. This person must, indeed, be swept out of the way and made impossible.

90

Communism deprives no man of the power to appropriate the products of society: all that it does is to deprive him of the power to subjugate the labor of others by means of such appropriation.

91

It has been objected that upon the abolition of private property all work will cease and universal laziness will overtake us.

92

According to this, bourgeois society ought long ago to have gone to the dogs through sheer idleness; for those of its members who work acquire noth-

93

ing, and those who acquire anything do not work. The whole of this objection is but another expression of the tautology: that there can no longer be any wage labor when there is no longer any capital.

All objections urged against the Communistic mode of producing and appropriating material products have, in the same way, been urged against the Communistic modes of producing and appropriating intellectual products. Just as, to the bourgeois, the disappearance of class property is the disappearance of production itself, so the disappearance of class culture is to him identical with the disappearance of all culture.   94

That culture, the loss of which he laments, is, for the enormous majority, a mere training to act as a machine.   95

But don't wrangle with us so long as you apply, to our intended abolition of bourgeois property, the standard of your bourgeois notions of freedom, culture, law, etc. Your very ideas are but the outgrowth of the conditions of your bourgeois production and bourgeois property, just as your jurisprudence is but the will of your class made into a law for all, a will whose essential character and direction are determined by the economical conditions of existence of your class.   96

The selfish misconception that induces you to transform into eternal laws of nature and of reason the social forms springing from your present mode of production and form of property—historical relations that arise and disappear in the progress of production—this misconception you share with every ruling class that has preceded you. What you see clearly in the case of ancient property, what you admit in the case of feudal property, you are of course forbidden to admit in the case of your own bourgeois form of property.   97

Abolition of the family! Even the most radical flare up at this infamous proposal of the Communists.   98

On what foundation is the present family, the bourgeois family, based? On capital, on private gain. In its completely developed form this family exists only among the bourgeoisie. But this state of things finds its complement in the practical absence of the family among the proletarians, and in public prostitution.   99

The bourgeois family will vanish as a matter of course when its complement vanishes, and both will vanish with the vanishing of capital.   100

Do you charge us with wanting to stop the exploitation of children by their parents? To this crime we plead guilty.   101

But, you will say, we destroy the most hallowed of relations when we replace home education by social.   102

And your education! Is not that also social, and determined by the social conditions under which you educate; by the intervention, direct or indirect, of society by means of schools, etc.? The Communists have not invented the intervention of society in education; they do but seek to alter the character of   103 that intervention, and to rescue education from the influence of the ruling class.

The bourgeois clap-trap about the family and education, about the hallowed correlation of parent and child, become all the more disgusting, the more, by the action of Modern Industry, all family ties among the proletarians are torn asunder and their children transformed into simple articles of commerce and instruments of labor.

But you Communists would introduce community of women, screams the whole bourgeoisie chorus.

The bourgeois sees in his wife a mere instrument of production. He hears that the instruments of production are to be exploited in common, and, naturally, can come to no other conclusion, than that the lot of being common to all will likewise fall to the woman.

He has not even a suspicion that the real point aimed at is to do away with the status of women as mere instruments of production.

For the rest, nothing is more ridiculous than the virtuous indignation of our bourgeois at the community of women which, they pretend, is to be openly and officially established by the Communists. The Communists have no need to introduce community of women; it has existed almost from time immemorial.

Our bourgeois, not content with having the wives and daughters of their proletarians at their disposal, not to speak of common prostitutes, take the greatest pleasure in seducing each others' wives.

Bourgeois marriage is in reality a system of wives in common, and thus, at the most, what the Communists might possibly be reproached with, is that they desire to introduce, in substitution for a hypocritically concealed, an openly legalized community of women. For the rest, it is self-evident that the abolition of the present system of production must bring with it the abolition of the community of women springing from that system, i.e., of prostitution both public and private.

The Communists are further reproached with desiring to abolish countries and nationalities.

The working men have no country. We cannot take from them what they don't possess. Since the proletariat must first of all acquire political supremacy, must rise to be the leading class of the nation, must constitute itself the nation, it is, so far, itself national, though not in the bourgeois sense of the word.

National differences and antagonisms between peoples are daily more and more vanishing, owing to the development of the bourgeoisie, to freedom of commerce, to the world-market, to uniformity in the mode of production and in the conditions of life corresponding thereto.

The supremacy of the proletariat will cause them to vanish still faster. United action, of the leading civilized countries at least, is one of the first conditions for the emancipation of the proletariat.

In proportion as the exploitation of one individual by another is put an end   115
to, the exploitation of one nation by another will also be put an end to. In
proportion as the antagonism between classes within the nation vanishes, the
hostility of one nation to another will come to an end.

The charges against Communism made from a religious, a philosophical, and   116
generally, from an ideological standpoint, are not deserving of serious examination.

Does it require deep intuition to comprehend that man's ideas, views and   117
conceptions, in one word, man's consciousness, changes with every change in
the conditions of his material existence, in his social relations and in his social
life?

What else does the history of ideas prove than that intellectual production   118
changes in character in proportion as material production is changed? The
ruling ideas of each age have ever been the ideas of its ruling class.

When people speak of ideas that revolutionize society they do but express   119
the fact that within the old society the elements of a new one have been created,
and that the dissolution of the old ideas keeps even pace with the dissolution
of the old conditions of existence.

When the ancient world was in its last throes the ancient religions were   120
overcome by Christianity. When Christian ideas succumbed in the 18th century
to rationalist ideas, feudal society fought its death-battle with the then revolutionary bourgeoisie. The ideas of religious liberty and freedom of conscience
merely gave expression to the sway of free competition within the domain of
knowledge.

"Undoubtedly," it will be said, "religious, moral, philosophical and judicial   121
ideas have been modified in the course of historical development. But religion,
morality, philosophy, political science, and law, constantly survived this change.

"There are, besides, eternal truths, such as Freedom, Justice, etc., that are   122
common to all states of society. But Communism abolishes eternal truths, it
abolishes all religion and all morality, instead of constituting them on a new
basis; it therefore acts in contradiction to all past historical experience."

What does this accusation reduce itself to? The history of all past society   123
has consisted in the development of class antagonisms, antagonisms that assumed
different forms at different epochs.

But whatever form they may have taken, one fact is common to all past   124
ages, viz., the exploitation of one part of society by the other. No wonder, then,
that the social consciousness of past ages, despite all the multiplicity and variety
it displays, moves within certain common forms, or general ideas, which cannot
completely vanish except with the total disappearance of class antagonisms.

The Communist revolution is the most radical rupture with traditional   125
property relations; no wonder that its development involves the most radical
rupture with traditional ideas.

But let us have done with the bourgeois objections to Communism.   126

We have seen above that the first step in the revolution by the working   127
class is to raise the proletariat to the position of ruling class, to win the battle
of democracy.

The proletariat will use its political supremacy to wrest, by degrees, all   128
capital from the bourgeoisie, to centralize all instruments of production in the
hands of the State, i.e., of the proletariat organized as a ruling class; and to
increase the total productive forces as rapidly as possible.

Of course, in the beginning, this cannot be effected except by means of   129
despotic inroads on the rights of property, and on the conditions of bourgeois
production; by means of measures, therefore, which appear economically insufficient and untenable, but which in the course of the movement outstrip
themselves, necessitate further inroads upon the old social order, and are unavoidable as a means of entirely revolutionizing the mode of production.

These measures will of course be different in different countries.   130

Nevertheless in the most advanced countries the following will be pretty   131
generally applicable:

1. Abolition of property in land and application of all rents of land to public   132
   purposes.

2. A heavy progressive or graduated income tax.

3. Abolition of all right of inheritance.

4. Confiscation of the property of all emigrants and rebels.

5. Centralization of credit in the hands of the State, by means of a national
   bank with State capital and an exclusive monopoly.

6. Centralization of the means of communication and transport in the hands
   of the State.

7. Extension of factories and instruments of production owned by the State;
   the bringing into cultivation of waste lands, and the improvement of the
   soil generally in accordance with a common plan.

8. Equal liability of all to labor. Establishment of industrial armies, especially
   for agriculture.

9. Combination of agriculture with manufacturing industries; gradual abolition of the distinction between town and country by a more equable
   distribution of the population over the country.

10. Free education for all children in public schools. Abolition of children's
    factory labor in its present form. Combination of education with industrial
    production, etc., etc.

When, in the course of development, class distinctions have disappeared,   133
and all production has been concentrated in the hands of a vast association of
the whole nation, the public power will lose its political character. Political

power, properly so called, is merely the organized power of one class for oppressing another. If the proletariat during its contest with the bourgeoisie is compelled, by the force of circumstances, to organize itself as a class, if, by means of a revolution, it makes itself the ruling class, and, as such, sweeps away by force the old conditions of production, then it will, along with these conditions, have swept away the conditions for the existence of class antagonism, and of classes generally, and will thereby have abolished its own supremacy as a class.

In place of the old bourgeois society, with its classes and class antagonisms, 134 we shall have an association in which the free development of each is the condition for the free development of all. . . .

Position of the Communists in Relation to the Various Existing Opposition Parties

The Communists fight for the attainment of the immediate aims, for the 135 enforcement of the momentary interests of the working class; but in the movement of the present they also represent and take care of the future of that movement. In France the Communists ally themselves with the Social-Democrats against the conservative and radical bourgeoisie, reserving, however, the right to take up a critical position in regard to phrases and illusions traditionally handed down from the great Revolution.

In Switzerland they support the Radicals, without losing sight of the fact 136 that this party consists of antagonistic elements, partly of Democratic Socialists, in the French sense, partly of radical bourgeois.

In Poland they support the party that insists on an agrarian revolution, as 137 the prime condition for national emancipation, that party which fomented the insurrection of Cracow in 1846.

In Germany they fight with the bourgeoisie whenever it acts in a revolu- 138 tionary way, against the absolute monarchy, the feudal squirearchy, and the petty bourgeoisie.

But they never cease for a single instant to instill into the working class the 139 clearest possible recognition of the hostile antagonism between bourgeoisie and proletariat, in order that the German workers may straightway use, as so many weapons against the bourgeoisie, the social and political conditions that the bourgeoisie must necessarily introduce along with its supremacy, and in order that, after the fall of the reactionary classes in Germany, the fight against the bourgeoisie itself may immediately begin.

The Communists turn their attention chiefly to Germany, because that 140 country is on the eve of a bourgeois revolution, that is bound to be carried out under more advanced conditions of European civilization, and with a more developed proletariat, than that of England was in the seventeenth and of France in the eighteenth century, and because the bourgeois revolution in Germany will be but the prelude to an immediately following proletarian revolution.

In short, the Communists everywhere support every revolutionary move-   141
ment against the existing social and political order of things.

In all these movements they bring to the front, as the leading question in   142
each, the property question, no matter what its degree of development at the time.

Finally, they labor everywhere for the union and agreement of the democratic   143
parties of all countries.

The Communists disdain to conceal their views and aims. They openly   144
declare that their ends can be attained only by the forcible overthrow of all existing social conditions. Let the ruling classes tremble at a Communistic revolution. The proletarians have nothing to lose but their chains. They have a world to win.

Working men of all countries, unite!   145

Questions for Critical Thinking

1. Fundamentally, Marx's entire political theory is based on his view of property ownership. What is his view? Do you agree with it? Explain your answer.

2. Why is Marx so sure that the proletariat will eventually revolt against the capitalistic bourgeoisie and defeat it? Do you agree with his prophecy? Why or why not?

3. Marx laughs at the bourgeois idea that the abolition of all private property will lead to laziness and idleness, insisting that in bourgeois societies, "Those who work acquire nothing, and those who acquire anything, don't work." What is your response to Marx's view?

4. Whom is Marx addressing when he keeps using the pronoun "you" in the section entitled "Proletarians and Communists"? What is his purpose? Is he effective?

5. Marx's official program is summarized in the ten points listed after paragraph 131. Taking each point in turn, analyze the point, indicating its strengths and its weaknesses. Which points do you think would help society? Which points are detrimental? Do you believe a government could make these points work? Explain your answers.

6. In paragraph 87, Marx states: "You are horrified at our intending to do away with private property. But in your existing society private property is already done away with for nine-tenths of the population; its existence for the few is solely due to its non-existence in the hands of those nine-tenths. You reproach us, therefore, with intending to do away with a form of property, the necessary condition for whose existence is the non-existence of any property for the immense majority of society." What is your rejoinder to Marx's attack?

7. Study Marx's statements about women in paragraphs 39, 98, 105, and 110. What is he recommending? How do you view his recommendation?

8. Marx believes that the ruling ideas of each age are simply the ideas of the ruling class. In your view, whose ideas should rule?

Writing Assignment

Write an essay proposing practical ways in which our government can prevent the exploitation of laborers.

Writing Advice

In thinking through this assignment, pay attention to the key terms *ways* and *practical*. Try to make the assignment into a process essay in which each individual step is realistic rather than romantic or fantastic. Here are some suggestions for how to proceed:

1. Begin with your definition of "labor exploitation"; that is, tell your reader what you mean by the term. Then expand your definition by describing what you think are typical cases of labor exploitation. For example, if you live on the West Coast, you may be appalled by what is called "labor pick-ups"—unemployed vagrants who congregate on street corners waiting for a project manager to pick them up to do unskilled work like clearing rubble from an apartment building, stacking bricks in a courtyard, scrubbing graffiti from factory walls, or digging mud out of a flooded garage. Mostly from the ranks of uneducated ethnic minorities or illegal aliens, these laborers work for a pittance of regular market pay. On the East Coast, some industrial capitalists are known to pay the minimum wage for backbreaking work like carrying hod, stacking heavy boxes, or working twelve hours in the farm fields. Often illegal immigrants are hired to do maid service at a fraction of the pay commanded by legal workers. Find similar examples from your own area.

2. Now, answer the question, "What can the government do to prevent this exploitation of labor?" Jot down on a piece of paper some possible answers to the question. Record your ideas unedited, as they occur to you. Once you have exhausted your ideas, go back over the list and choose the three or four most significant and most effective answers, making sure that they are workable. For instance, to suggest that the minimum wage for all work should be $20.00 per hour and that any employer who does not abide by this standard should be placed in jail is an impractical solution because a $20.00 per hour minimum wage floor would bankrupt most businesses. A more practical suggestion would be to require federal and state labor agencies to carefully monitor the labor hiring practices of small businesses and private employers.

3. List in some logical order the steps that can be taken by the government, proceeding from most important to least important or vice versa. A good way to clarify each step is to number it—first, second, third, and so on.

4. To acquire expert testimony for this assignment, you may wish to interview affected individuals, such as your economics or political science instructor, an immigrant laborer, and someone working for an employment agency. Any statistics or facts you can present will add authority to your essay.

If you have followed the suggestions offered above, your ideas should now begin to flow and will develop into a well-reasoned process essay.

Alternate Writing Assignments

1. Write an essay in which you describe a class struggle taking place in the United States today.

2. Write an essay answering the following question: "Is the United States suffering an epidemic of overproduction because we have too much civilization, too much industry, and too much commerce?"

PHILOSOPHY

THE CROWD PHENOMENON
José Ortega y Gasset

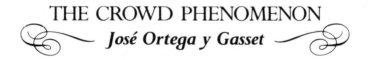

José Ortega y Gasset (1883–1955) was a Spanish essayist and philosopher. Most of his schooling took place in Germany, where he was greatly influenced by neo-Kantian thought and attempted to establish his own philosophy, the "metaphysics of vital reason," in which he sought to explain the "ultimate reality" wherein all else is rooted. In 1910 he accepted a post as professor of metaphysics at the University of Madrid. While teaching, he also wrote several books, among them *Meditaciones del Quijote* (1914) and *España invertebrada* (1921); but it was with *The Revolt of the Masses* (1929), from which the translated excerpt below is reprinted, that he won international fame. In this work, Ortega argued that unless the masses can be directed by an intellectual minority, chaos will result. Although he supported the Republic, he fled at the outbreak of the Spanish Civil War, first to France and then to Argentina. Following World War II he returned to Madrid, where he founded the Institute of Humanities. Among his translated works of that period are the following: *Toward a Philosophy of History* (1941), *The Mission of the University* (1944), *The Dehumanization of Art* (1948), *Man and People* (1957), and *Man and Crisis* (1958).

Reading Advice

The author begins his essay by offering specific examples of how cities are being crowded. He must prove to his reader that this crowding effect exists because his main thesis is derived from it. Once he has proved that "agglomeration" is a fact of life, then he can move to his thesis, which is that we are facing a social crisis due to the fact that the "average" person is taking over. Ortega weaves a subtle warning about this crisis into his essay and leaves it to the reader to contemplate what will eventually happen if the average person is left in charge of society. Writing from an admitted elitist perspective, Ortega does not directly propose any solutions to his imputed "problem" in this excerpt, although he does hint rather broadly that he favors rule in matters of artistic and cultural taste by an intellectual elite. Thoughtful readers will draw their own conclusions about whether Ortega has put his finger on a real problem or is merely reflecting the prejudices of his class.

*T*he most important fact in the public   1
life of the West in modern times, for good or ill, is the appearance of the masses in the seats of highest social power. Since the masses, by definition, neither can nor should direct their own existence, let alone that of society as a whole, this new development means that we are now undergoing the most profound crisis which can afflict peoples, nations, or cultures. Such a crisis has occurred more than once in history. Its physiognomy, its outline and profile, and its consequences are known, and the development can be given a name: the rebellion of the masses.

In order to understand this truly formidable phenomenon we had best avoid   2
the exclusively or primarily political meanings of the words "rebellion," "masses," and "social power." For public life is not only political, but is equally, and even more so, economic, moral, intellectual, and religious. It includes all our collective habits, even our fashions in dress and modes of amusement.

Perhaps the best way of approaching this historical phenomenon is to rely   3
on our visual experience: we can simply look at this aspect of our epoch as it stands plainly before our eyes.

Most simple to enunciate, and not so easy to analyze: I shall call it the   4
phenomenon of agglomeration, of crowding, of the sign which says "Full." The cities are full of people. The houses are full of tenants. The hotels are full of guests. Public transport is full of passengers. The cafes and restaurants are full of customers. The sidewalks are full of pedestrians. The waiting-rooms of famous doctors are full of patients. Public spectacles, unless they be extemporaneous, and public entertainment halls, unless they be minoritarian and experimental, are full of spectators. The beaches are crowded, full. What previously was not

a problem, is now an everyday matter: the search—to find room, to find a place, to find space.

Is there any fact simpler, more obvious, more constant in life today? Let us penetrate beneath this superficial observation. We will then be surprised to see how, unexpectedly, a veritable fountain will spout forth, and in it, in this jet, we will see how, in the white light of day, of this very day, it will break down into its rich spectrum of inner colors.

What do we actually see, and in seeing are surprised? We see the multitude as such in possession of the locales and appurtenances created by civilization. Further reflection will make us surprised at our surprise. Is not this plenitude ideal? A theater's seats are made to be occupied by spectators: it should be full. And the same for public transport and hotel rooms. No doubt about it. But the point is that previously none of these establishments and vehicles were full—and now they are overflowing, with people left outside eager to occupy them all. Though this development is natural and even logical, we know this was not the case before. A change, therefore, has taken place. Something new has been added, and this innovation does, at least initially, justify our surprise.

To be surprised, to wonder, is to begin to understand. It is the sport and special pleasure of intellectual man. The specific trade-mark of his guild is to gaze at the world with the wide-open eyes of wonder. The world is always strange and wonderful for wide-open yes. This faculty of wide-eyed wonder is a delight unavailable to your ordinary football or soccer fan. The man who lives by his intellect goes about the world in the perpetual intoxication of a visionary. His particular attribute: the eyes of wonder, of amazement. Thus the ancients assigned to Minerva an owl, bird of wide open ever-dazzled eyes.

Crowding was not a common feature of the past. Everything was not always full. Why is it now?

The members of this ubiquitous mass have not come from out of the blue. The number of people was constant for a good while; moreover, after any war one would expect the number to decrease. But here we come up against the first important modern factor. The individuals who make up the present mass already existed before—but not as a mass, not as "masses." Scattered about the world in small groups, or even alone, they lived in diverse ways, dissociated and distant from one another. Each group, even each individual, occupied a space, each his own space so to say, in the fields, in a village, a town, or even in some quarter of a big city.

Now, suddenly, they appear on the scene as a mass. Wherever we look we see a concentration, masses. *Wherever?* No; more exactly in the places most in demand, the places created by the relatively sophisticated taste of modern culture, places previously reserved for small groups, for select minorities.

The masses, suddenly, have made themselves visible, and have installed themselves in the preferred places of society. In the past, the mass, where it existed, went unnoticed. It was a background to the social scene, to the stage of society.

Now it has advanced to the footlights, and plays the part of the leading character. There are no longer protagonists as such: there is only the chorus.

The concept of the masses is quantitative—and visual. Let us translate it, without alteration, into sociological terms. We then encounter the concept of the social mass. Society is always a dynamic unity composed of two factors: masses and minorities. The latter are comprised of especially qualified individuals and groups. The masses are made up of persons not especially qualified. By masses, we do not therefore mean, either simply or even principally, the "working class," the working masses as a whole. The mass is the "average man." Thus, the merely quantitative—the multitude, the mass—becomes a qualitative determinant: it is the common quality, the social animal as stray, man in the measure in which he is undifferentiated from other men, man repeating in himself a generic type. What gain is there in this conversion of quantity into quality? Simply this: by means of quality, we can understand the genesis of quantity. It is as obvious as a platitude that the normal formation of a mass, a multitude, is based on a coincidence of desires, of ideas, of manners among the individuals who compose it. It may be pointed out that precisely the same happens in regard to any social group, however select it may claim to be. True enough: but an essential difference exists. 12

In those groups which are neither mass nor multitude, the effective cohesion of the members is based on some desire, idea, or ideal, which in itself alone excludes the majority of people. In order to form a minority—of whatever kind it may be—it is first of all necessary that each member separate himself from the multitude for some *special,* relatively personal, reason. His agreement with the others who form the minority is, therefore, secondary, posterior to having adopted an individual attitude, having made himself *singular,* therefore, there is an agreement not to agree with others, a coincidence in not coinciding. A vivid example of this singularity is to be found in the case of the English Nonconformists: they concurred with each other only on their disconformity with the infinite multitude of others. This formation of a minority precisely in order to separate itself from the majority is a basic impulse. The poet Mallarmé, apropos of the select audience at a recital by a distinguished musician, wittily remarked that by the scarcity of its presence the audience was emphasizing the absence of the multitude. 13

In all truth, the masses, any mass, can make its presence felt as a psychological fact without the need for individuals to appear in agglomeration. We can tell a mass-man when we see one: one person can represent a mass phenomenon. The mass-man is anyone who does not value himself, for good or ill, by any particular criterion, and who says instead that he is "just like everybody else." Despite this ridiculous claim, he will not feel any disquiet, but rather feel reassured, smugly at ease, to be considered identical with all others. A truly humble man who attempts to evaluate his specific worth, and tries to find if 14 he possesses any talent, or excels in any way, may discover in the end that he is endowed with no remarkable qualities, and may conclude that he is ungifted and depressingly ordinary. But he may still consider that he is not part of the mass, not in his own self a mass-man.

In speaking of "select minorities," universal misunderstanding holds sway and manages as usual to distort the meaning, and to ignore the fact that the select individual is not the petulant snob who thinks he is superior to others, but is, rather, the person who demands more from himself than do others, even when these demands are unattainable. For undoubtedly the most radical division to be made of humanity is between two types: those who demand much of themselves and assign themselves great tasks and duties, and those who demand nothing in particular of themselves, for whom living is to be at all times what they already are, without any effort at perfection—buoys floating on the waves.

15

I am here reminded that orthodox Buddhism is composed of two distinct religions: one, more strict and difficult, the other more lax and easy: the Mahayana, the "great vehicle" or "great way," and the Hinayana, the "lesser vehicle," or "lesser way." The decisive difference lies in choosing one or the other vehicle, in making a maximum of demands on oneself or a minimum.

16

The division of society into masses and select minorities is not, then, a division into social classes, but into two kinds of men, and it does not depend on hierarchically superior or inferior classes, on upper classes or lower classes. Of course it is plain enough that among the superior classes, when they genuinely achieve this status and maintain it, there is more likelihood of finding men who choose the "great vehicle," while the inferior are those who normally are not concerned with quality. Strictly speaking, there are "masses" and minorities at all levels of society—within every social class. A characteristic of our times is the predominance, even in those groups who are traditionally selective, of mass and popular vulgarity. Even in intellectual life, which by its very essence assumes and requires certain qualifications, we see the progressive triumph of pseudo-intellectuals—unqualified, unqualifiable, and, in their own context, disqualified. The same holds true for the remnants of the nobility, whether male or female. On the other hand, it is not unusual to find among workers, who formerly might have served as the best example of the "mass," outstandingly disciplined minds and souls.

17

Then there are activities in society which by their very nature call for qualifications: activities and functions of the most diverse order which are special and cannot be carried out without special talent. Thus: artistic and aesthetic enterprises; the functioning of government; political judgment on public matters. Previously these special activities were in the hands of qualified minorities, or those alleged to be qualified. The masses did not try or aspire to intervene: they reckoned that if they did, they must acquire those special

18

graces, and must cease being part of the mass. They knew their role well enough in a dynamic and functioning social order.

If we now revert to the assumptions made at the beginning, the facts will   19
appear as clearly heralding a changed mass attitude. Everything indicates that the "public," that is, the mass, along with wielding power, has decided to occupy the foreground of social life, as well as the front-row seats, and to avail themselves of the pleasures formerly reserved for the few. It is obvious that those seats were never intended for the masses, for they are limited in number; so now there is crowding, making clear to the eye, with visible language, that a new phenomenon exists: the mass, without ceasing to be mass, supplants the minorities.

No one, I believe, begrudges the public's enjoying themselves in greater   20
number and measure than before, since they now have the desire and the means to do so. The only resultant wrong is that the determination of the masses to usurp the place of the minority does not and cannot confine itself to the arena of pleasure alone, but is a generalized practice of the times. And thus (to anticipate what we shall see later), it seems to me that recent political innovations signify nothing less than the political reign of the masses. Western democracy was formerly tempered by a large dash of liberalism and by a ritual trust in the law. In serving these principled ideas the individual bound himself to maintain some discipline in himself. Minorities could take refuge and find support in liberal principles and the judicial norm. Democracy and law (life in common under the law) were synonymous. Today we witness the triumph of hyperdependency in which the mass takes direct action oblivious of the law, imposing its own desires and tastes by material pressure. It is false to say that the masses have grown weary of politics and have handed over its operation to selected people. Exactly the opposite is true.

That is what used to happen: that was liberal democracy. The masses took   21
it for granted that, after all, and despite the defects and faults of the select minorities, these minorities understood something more of political problems than they themselves did. Nowadays the mass believes it has the right to impose and lend force to notions deriving from its own platitudes. I doubt that any previous epoch of history has seen such direct government by the multitude as is current in our time. Thus I speak of hyperdemocracy.

The same happens in other orders of life, particularly in the intellectual   22
order. I may be mistaken, but it seems that the writer nowadays, whenever he assumes the task of saying anything on any subject to which he has given thought, must bear in mind that the average reader, who has never pondered the matter—and always assuming that he reads the writer at all—does not read in order to learn anything, but rather reads him in order to pronounce judgment on whether or not the writer's ideas coincide with the pedestrian and commonplace notions the reader already carries in his head. If the individuals who make up the mass thought of themselves as specially qualified, we

would have on our hands merely a case of personal error, not a matter of sociological subversion. *The characteristic note of our time is the dire truth that the mediocre soul, the commonplace mind, knowing itself to be mediocre, has the gall to assert its right to mediocrity, and goes on to impose itself wherever it can.* In the United States it is considered indecent to be different. The mass crushes everything different, everything outstanding, excellent, individual, select, and choice. Everybody who is not like everybody else, who does not think like everybody else, runs the risk of being eliminated. Of course "everybody else" is not *everybody*. In normal times, "everybody" was the complex union of mass with special, divergent minorities. Today, "everybody" means the mass, the masses—and only the masses.

Questions for Critical Thinking

1. Whom does the author consider the outstanding individual of society? Describe a famous person who might fit the description. Does this person qualify by your criteria as outstanding? Why or why not?

2. What is your opinion of Ortega's assertion that it is dangerous to allow the tastes and thoughts of the masses to dominate society? Explain your answer carefully.

3. What response do you think Karl Marx would give to Ortega's essay? On what ideas would this response be based?

4. What functions of society, if any, do you think should be in the hands of a qualified minority? What happens when these functions are controlled by average persons?

5. What is your reaction to Ortega's attitude about the masses now occupying front-row seats at social and artistic events?

6. What is it that Ortega ultimately fears? Is he justified in his anxiety?

Writing Assignment

Write an essay contrasting city life with rural life in terms of the crowd phenomenon analyzed by Ortega. Your essay should argue for the merits of one over the other.

Writing Advice

The assignment to contrast two items (reveal their differences) is a staple of college writing. You will typically encounter such assignments in biology, where you may be asked to contrast two organisms; in psychology, where you may be asked to contrast two mental abnormalities; in literature, where you may be asked to contrast two characters; or in history, where you may be asked to contrast two political movements.

1. As we have mentioned earlier, the crux of this assignment lies in the prewriting stage, where you should take an organized approach. A simple outline containing

brief entries may be enough. One way for you to proceed is to have two Roman numerals, one for city life and one for rural life, as follows:

I. City life
II. Rural life

2. Now decide on the bases of your contrast. This particular assignment requires that you reread Ortega y Gasset's essay to determine the bases you may wish to use. Because the essay is so packed with ideas, many choices are possible. Choose three or four of your best ideas. Place them as capital letters under your two Roman numerals. We provide the following outline merely as a model for form, not for content. Many other possibilities exist:

I. City life
   A.   Culture
   B.   Conformity
   C.   Excellence

II. Rural life
   A.   Culture
   B.   Conformity
   C.   Excellence

Next, formulate a purposeful outline from which to develop your essay. The outline above requires that the first half of your essay deal with the culture, conformity, and excellence of city life, while the second half will cover these same qualities for rural life. You could then tie the two together in a final paragraph that emphasizes the contrast.

The following outline is another approach possible:

I. Culture
   A.   City life
   B.   Rural life

II. Conformity
   A.   City life
   B.   Rural life

III. Excellence
   A.   City life
   B.   Rural life

This approach requires that you write about culture in the city, immediately contrasting it with culture in the country. Next, you will write about conformity in the city, contrasting it with conformity in the country; and finally, you will write about excellence in the city, contrasting it with excellence in the country— moving back and forth between the two modes of life.

Neither system is automatically better. Simply use the one you find easiest to handle, keeping in mind that your goal is to show where city life differs from country life in three areas—culture, conformity, and excellence.

3. While Ortega y Gasset's essay will provide you with many useful and specific facts, it does not deal with rural life; therefore, you must provide your own details for that part of your essay. Using Ortega y Gasset as a model, support your assertions with specific facts and vivid examples.

4. Finally, remember that your thesis (stated either at the end or beginning of your essay) should take a stand on which is superior, country life or city life. Taking a firm stand on an issue from the outset will help give your essay a tone of authority and definiteness.

Alternate Writing Assignments

1. Write an essay in which you argue that the "average man" contributes something important to the American way of life.

2. Write an essay in which you argue that the "select individual" is the hero of the future.

PHILOSOPHY

ON THE ORIGIN OF INEQUALITY AMONG MEN
Jean-Jacques Rousseau

Jean-Jacques Rousseau (1712–1778) was a Swiss-born philosopher whose ideas about the nature of human beings had an enormous influence on education and on a variety of political theories with disparate goals. For instance, he was hailed as a prophet of modern democracy while at the same time totalitarian movements like communism found inspiration in his theories about the power of collective ideas. In his private life Rousseau was considered a vagabond, a rebel, and a psychologically unstable personality.

Born the son of a Swiss watchmaker, Rousseau lost his mother soon after his birth, an event that triggered a rather haphazard upbringing. At 16, he started wandering all over Europe and met Louise de Warens, who became his patroness and eventually his lover. After serving as a footman in a powerful family in Turin for some time, he moved to Chambery to live with Louise. From there he moved to Paris, where he became an intimate in the circles of the famous French encyclopedist and literary critic, Denis Diderot. At this time Rousseau also began a love affair with Thérèse Le Vasseur, a semiliterate servant girl, who became his common-law wife.

Rousseau argued eloquently that reason and civilization did not lead to a higher order of being; for that, human beings must return to nature and trust their untaught feelings. Nature was good whereas civilization was evil. He wrote down his philosophy in a work titled *Discourse on the Origin of Inequality among Men* (1755), considered his most mature and daring work. Among his other writings are the following: A novel, *Julie, ou La Nouvelle Héloïse* (1761), *Du Contrat Social* (1762), *Émile* (1762), and *Confessions* (1770). Rousseau died in Paris in 1778, lonely and mentally deranged. Few people have equaled his influence on politics, literature, and education. He gave impetus to the French Revolution and to the Romantic Movement of the nineteenth century.

Reading Advice

By focusing on the essential nature of human beings, Rousseau presents some startling ideas for us to ponder. He assumes that in political and social life there is a common good and that cooperation and commitment are advantageous to all. He clearly states that private property leads to human exploitation, which in turn leads to poverty with consequent human suffering. Rousseau's style is highly narrative and often poetic, especially when he describes nature and the more tender feelings that human beings can have for each other. Notice that the organization of his essay follows the simple format of chronicling society's advance from brutes in small geographical areas to complex civilizations spreading all over the globe. Rousseau covers vast spans of time in brief paragraphs by presenting only the major aspects of human existence. In the final paragraph he takes on the role of preacher, sermonizing that human greed is the root of slavery and misery.

*T*he first man who, having enclosed a   1
piece of land, thought of saying 'This is mine' and found people simple enough to believe him, was the true founder of civil society. How many crimes, wars, murders; how much misery and horror the human race would have been spared if someone had pulled up the stakes and filled in the ditch and cried out to his fellow men: 'Beware of listening to this impostor. You are lost if you forget that the fruits of the earth belong to everyone and that the earth itself belongs to no one!' But it is highly probably that by this time things had reached a point beyond which they could not go on as they were; for the idea of property, depending on many prior ideas which could only have arisen in successive stages, was not formed all at once in the human mind. It was necessary for men to make much progress, to acquire much industry and knowledge, to transmit and increase it from age to age, before arriving at this final stage of the state of nature. Let us therefore look farther back, and try to review from

From *A Discourse on Inequality* by Jean-Jacques Rousseau. Translated by Maurice Cranston.

a single perspective the slow succession of events and discoveries in their most natural order.

Man's first feeling was that of his existence, his first concern was that of his preservation. The products of the earth furnished all the necessary aids; instinct prompted him to make use of them. While hunger and other appetites made him experience in turn different modes of existence, there was one appetite which urged him to perpetuate his own species: and this blind impulse, devoid of any sentiment of the heart, produced only a purely animal act. The need satisfied, the two sexes recognized each other no longer, and even the child meant nothing to the mother, as soon as he could do without her.

Such was the condition of nascent man; such was the life of an animal limited at first to mere sensation; and scarcely profiting from the gifts bestowed on him by nature, let alone was he dreaming of wresting anything from her. But difficulties soon presented themselves and man had to learn to overcome them. The height of trees, which prevented him from reaching their fruits; the competition of animals seeking to nourish themselves on the same fruits; the ferocity of animals who threatened his life—all this obliged man to apply himself to bodily exercises; he had to make himself agile, fleet of foot, and vigorous in combat. Natural weapons—branches of trees and stones—were soon found to be at hand. He learned to overcome the obstacles of nature, to fight when necessary against other animals, to struggle for his subsistence even against other men, or to indemnify himself for what he was forced to yield to the stronger.

To the extent that the human race spread, men's difficulties multiplied with their numbers. Differences between soils, climates, and seasons would have forced men to adopt different ways of life. Barren years, long hard winters, scorching summers consuming everything, demanded new industry from men. Along the sea coast and river banks they invented the hook and line to become fishermen and fish eaters. In the forests they made bows and arrows, and became hunters and warriors. In cold countries they covered themselves with the skins of the beasts they killed. Lightning, a volcano, or some happy accident introduced them to fire—a fresh resource against the rigor of winter. They learned to conserve this element, then to reproduce it, and finally to use it to cook the meats they had previously eaten raw.

This repeated employment of entities distinct from himself and distinct from each other must naturally have engendered in men's minds the perception of certain relationships. Those relationships which we express by the words 'large,' 'small,' 'strong,' 'weak,' 'fast,' 'slow,' 'fearful,' 'bold,' and other similar ideas, compared when necessary and almost unthinkingly, finally produced in him some kind of reflection, or rather a mechanical prudence which would indicate to him the precautions most necessary for his safety.

The new knowledge which resulted from this development increased his superiority over other animals by making him conscious of it. He practiced setting snares for them; he outwitted them in a thousand ways, and though many animals might surpass him in strength of combat or in speed of running, he became in time the master of those that might serve him and the scourge of those that might hurt him. Thus the first look he directed into himself provoked his first stirring of pride; and while hardly as yet knowing how to distinguish between ranks, he asserted the priority of his species, and so prepared himself from afar to claim priority for himself as an individual.

Although his fellow men were not to him what they are to us, and although   7
he had hardly any more more dealings with them than he had with other animals, they were not forgotten in his observations. The resemblances which he learned with time to discern between them, his female and himself, led him to think of others which he did not actually perceive; and seeing that they all behaved as he himself would behave in similar circumstances, he concluded that their manner of thinking and feeling entirely matched his own; and this important truth, once well rooted in his mind, made him follow, by an intuition as sure as logic and more prompt, the best rules of conduct it was suitable to observe toward them for the sake of his own advantage and safety.

Instructed by experience that love of one's own wellbeing is the sole motive   8
of human action, he found himself in a position to distinguish the rare occasions when common interest justified his relying on the aid of his fellows, and those even rarer occasions when competition should make him distrust them. In the first case, he united with them in a herd, or at most in a sort of free association that committed no one and which lasted only as long as the passing need which had brought it into being. In the second case, each sought to grasp his own advantage, either by sheer force, if he believed he had the strength, or by cunning and subtlety if he felt himself to be the weaker.

In this way men could have gradually acquired some crude idea of mutual   9
commitments, and of the advantages of fulfilling them; but only so far as present and perceptible interests might demand, for men had no foresight whatever, and far from troubling about a distant future, they did not even think of the next day. If it was a matter of hunting a deer, everyone well realized that he must remain faithfully at his post; but if a hare happened to pass within the reach of one of them, we cannot doubt that he would have gone off in pursuit of it without scruple and, having caught his own prey, he would have cared very little about having caused his companions to lose theirs.

It is easy to understand that such intercourse between them would not   10
demand a language much more sophisticated than that of crows or monkeys, which group together in much the same way. Inarticulate cries, many gestures and some imitative noises must have been for long the universal human language; the addition to this in each country of certain articulated and conventional sounds (the institution of which, I have already said, is none too easy to explain) produced particular languages, crude and imperfect, rather like those we find

today among various savage nations. I pass in a flash over many centuries, pressed by the brevity of time, the abundance of the things I have to say, and by the almost imperceptible progress of the first stages—for the more slowly the events unfolded, the more speedily they can be described.

Those first slow developments finally enabled men to make more rapid ones. 11 The more the mind became enlightened, the more industry improved. Soon, ceasing to doze under the first tree, or to withdraw into caves, men discovered that various sorts of hard sharp stones could serve as hatchets to cut wood, dig the soil, and make huts out of branches, which they learned to cover with clay and mud. This was the epoch of a first revolution, which established and differentiated families, and which introduced property of a sort from which perhaps even then many quarrels and fights were born. However, as the strongest men were probably the first to build themselves huts which they felt themselves able to defend, it is reasonable to believe that the weak found it quicker and safer to imitate them rather than try to dislodge them; and as for those who already possessed huts, no one would readily venture to appropriate his neighbor's, not so much because it did not belong to him as because it would be no use to him and because he could not seize it without exposing himself to a very lively fight with the family which occupied it.

The first movements of the heart were the effect of this new situation, which 12 united in a common dwelling husbands and wives, fathers and children; the habit of living together generated the sweetest sentiments known to man, conjugal love and paternal love. Each family became a little society, all the better united because mutual affection and liberty were its only bonds; at this stage also the first differences were established in the ways of life of the two sexes which had hitherto been identical. Women became more sedentary and accustomed themselves to looking after the hut and the children while men went out to seek their common subsistence. The two sexes began, in living a rather softer life, to lose something of their ferocity and their strength; but if each individual became separately less able to fight wild beasts, all, on the other hand, found it easier to group together to resist them jointly.

This new condition, with its solitary and simple life, very limited in its needs, 13 and very few instruments invented to supply them, left men to enjoy a great deal of leisure, which they used to procure many sorts of commodities unknown to their fathers; and this was the first yoke they imposed on themselves, without thinking about it, and the first source of the evils they prepared for their descendants. For not only did such commodities continue to soften both body and mind, they almost lost through habitual use their power to please, and as they had at the same time degenerated into actual needs, being deprived of them became much more cruel than the possession of them was sweet; and people were unhappy in losing them without being happy in possessing them.

Here one can see a little more clearly how the use of speech became 14 established and improved imperceptibly in the bosom of each family, and one might again speculate as to how particular causes could have extended and accelerated the progress of language by making language more necessary. Great floods or earthquakes surrounded inhabited districts with seas or precipices; revolutions of the globe broke off portions of continents into islands. One imagines that among men thus brought together, and forced to live together, a common tongue must have developed sooner than it would among those who still wandered freely through the forests of the mainland. Thus it is very possible that islanders, after their first attempts at navigation, brought the use of speech to us; and it is at least very probable that society and languages were born on islands and perfected there before they came to the continent.

Everything begins to change its aspects. Men who had previously been 15 wandering around the woods, having once adopted a fixed settlement, come gradually together, unite in different groups, and form in each country a particular nation, united by customs and character—not by rules and laws, but through having a common way of living and eating and through the common influence of the same climate. A permanent proximity cannot fail to engender in the end some relationships between different families. Young people of opposite sexes live in neighboring huts; and the transient intercourse demanded by nature soon leads, through mutual frequentation, to another kind of relationship, no less sweet and more permanent. People became accustomed to judging different objects and to making comparisons; gradually they acquire ideas of merit and of beauty, which in turn produce feelings of preference. As a result of seeing each other, people cannot do without seeing more of each other. A tender and sweet sentiment insinuates itself into the soul, and at the least obstacle becomes an inflamed fury; jealousy awakens with love; discord triumphs, and the gentlest of passions receives the sacrifice of human blood.

To the extent that ideas and feelings succeeded one another, and the heart 16 and mind were exercised, the human race became more sociable, relationships became more extensive and bonds tightened. People grew used to gathering together in front of their huts or around a large tree; singing and dancing, true progeny of love and leisure, became the amusement, or rather the occupation, of idle men and women thus assembled. Each began to look at the others and to want to be looked at himself; and public esteem came to be prized. He who sang or danced the best; he who was the most handsome, the strongest, the most adroit or the most eloquent became the most highly regarded, and this was the first step toward inequality and at the same time toward vice. From those first preferences there arose, on the one side, vanity and scorn, on the other, shame and envy, and the fermentation produced by these new leavens finally produced compounds fatal to happiness and innocence.

As soon as men learned to value one another and the idea of consideration 17 was formed in their minds, everyone claimed a right to it, and it was no longer possible for anyone to be refused consideration without affront. This gave rise to the first duties of civility, even among savages: and henceforth every intentional wrong became an outrage, because together with the hurt which might result from the injury, the offended party saw an insult to his person which was often more unbearable than the hurt itself. Thus, as everyone punished the contempt shown him by another in a manner proportionate to the esteem he accorded himself, revenge became terrible, and men grew bloodthirsty and cruel. This is precisely the stage reached by most of the savage peoples known to us; and it is for lack of having sufficiently distinguished between different ideas and seen how far those people already are from the first state of nature that so many authors have hastened to conclude that man is naturally cruel and needs civil institutions to make them peaceable, whereas in truth nothing is more peaceable than man in his primitive state. Placed by nature at an equal distance from the stupidity of brutes and the fatal enlightenment of civilized man, limited equally by reason and instincts to defending himself against evils which threaten him, he is restrained by natural pity from doing harm to anyone, even after receiving harm himself: for according to the wise Locke: 'Where there is no property, there is no injury.'

But it must be noted that society's having come into existence and relations   18
among individuals having been already established meant that men were required to have qualities different from those they possessed from their primitive constitution. Morality began to be introduced into human actions, and each man, prior to laws, was the sold judge and avenger of the offenses he had received, so that the goodness suitable to the pure state of nature was no longer that which suited nascent society. It was necessary for punishments to be more severe to the extent that opportunities for offense became more frequent; and the terror of revenge had to serve in place of the restraint of laws. Thus although men had come to have less fortitude, and their natural pity had suffered some dilution, this period of the development of human faculties, the golden mean between the indolence of the primitive state and the petulant activity of our own pride, must have been the happiest epoch and the most lasting. The more we reflect on it, the more we realize that this state was the least subject to revolutions, and the best for man; and that man can have left it only as the result of some fatal accident, which, for the common good, ought never to have happened. The example of savages, who have almost always been found at this point of development, appears to confirm that the human race was made to remain there always; to confirm that this state was the true youth of the world, and that all subsequent progress has been so many steps in appearance toward the improvement of the individual, but so many steps in reality toward the decrepitude of the species.

As long as men were content with their rustic huts, as long as they confined   19
themselves to sewing their garments of skin with thorns or fishbones, and

adorning themselves with feathers or shells, to painting their bodies with various colors, to improving or decorating their bows and arrows; and to using sharp stones to make a few fishing canoes or crude musical instruments; in a word, so long as they applied themselves only to work that one person could accomplish alone and to arts that did not require the collaboration of several hands, they lived as free, healthy, good and happy men so far as they could be according to their nature and they continued to enjoy among themselves the sweetness of independent intercourse; but from the instant one man needed the help of another, and it was found to be useful for one man to have provisions enough for two, equality disappeared, property was introduced, work became necessary, and vast forests were transformed into pleasant fields which had to be watered with the sweat of men, and where slavery and misery were soon seen to germinate and flourish with the crops.

Questions for Critical Thinking

1. On what human instinct does Rousseau blame crime, wars, and other historical horrors? Do you agree with his premise? Why or why not?

2. What, according to Rousseau, is the reason human beings cooperate? What strengths or weaknesses do you perceive in his argument about this point?

3. In paragraph 10, the author suggests that "inarticulate cries, many gestures and some imitative noises must have been for long the universal human language." What dangers are inherent in a language that is growing daily more complex and subtle?

4. Rousseau points to competition as a sure path to cruelty and bloodthirstiness. What arguments can you give in support of competition as a characteristic of a healthy society?

5. Using a commonsense approach rather than historical proof, do you agree with Rousseau that human beings in their primitive state were happier and more compassionate than they are now? Give reasons for your answer. To which age in history, if any, would you like to return if you could? Why?

6. How does *The Communist Manifesto* (this chapter) agree or disagree with Rousseau's philosophy? Demonstrate either similarity or contrast in views.

7. In what major way do Rousseau and Ortega y Gasset differ? Describe differences in the societies advocated by each philosopher. Which would you prefer? Explain your answer.

8. Since none of us could argue convincingly that the competition for property has *not* caused some inequality among human beings, what can be done to control the misery resulting from this competition?

Writing Assignment

Write an essay in which you examine three major effects of competition on society and argue why these effects are either good or bad.

Writing Advice

1. To simplify your task, we suggest that you choose either all effects that seem good or all effects that seem bad. If you find it absolutely necessary to deal with both the good and bad effects, then we suggest that you deal entirely first with one and then with the other, rather than mix them up in a single discussion.

2. Choosing the effects—good or bad—will be easier if you focus on a specific segment of society where competition is clearly evident. The more specific the area you choose, the easier it will be for you to write convincingly. Among the many areas from which to choose are the following: academic achievement, athletics, politics, or business.

3. With your general area chosen, you should now narrow the subject further to make it easier to research and write about. If, for example, you were to choose the subject of competition in academic achievement, you could limit yourself to high school students trying to get into high-status colleges like Harvard, Yale, Berkeley, or Stanford. Detailing the negative effects of competition among these students is your next step. Your own experience and that of other students might suggest the following three effects:

   a.   Students study for grades rather than for knowledge.
   b.   Students cheat in order to get high grades.
   c.   Students refuse to help each other in order to keep all knowledge to themselves.

4. Now that you have distinguished three effects, you can tie them together into a thesis statement, as follows:

   The fierce competition for high grades among high school students determined to go to prestigious colleges leads to studying for grades rather than for knowledge, cheating on examinations in order to get high grades, and refusing to help other students in an attempt to keep all knowledge for themselves.

   And there is your beginning.

Alternate Writing Assignments

1. Write an essay in which you compare and contrast the causes of social evils expressed in Karl Marx and Frederick Engels's *Communist Manifesto* with those of Jean-Jacques Rousseau's *On the Origin of Inequality among Men*. Be sure to clarify the bases of your comparison/contrast.

2. Using Rousseau's approach of listing the major stages of human civilization, write an essay in which you praise the advances made by society. Demonstrate the benefits acquired.

HISTORY

A ROOM OF ONE'S OWN
Virginia Woolf

Virginia Woolf (1882–1941) was an English novelist and essayist whose writing style influenced a number of other writers, such as Ernest Hemingway, James Joyce, and William Faulkner. In 1904 she helped found the Bloomsbury Group, a literary clique that included a number of well-known writers and literary critics, among them Lytton Strachey, E. M. Forster, Roger Fry, and Clive Bell.

Born into a financially secure family, Woolf began as a young girl to avidly read books from her father's library. In 1912, she married Leonard Woolf, a writer and editor, with whom she founded Hogarth Press. As a novelist, Woolf was intent on representing not so much plot, setting, or character conflict but the steady flow of thought that welled inside the characters' minds. As a result, she perfected the "stream of consciousness" technique that allowed her to focus on the ordinary experiences in the lives of ordinary people. Throughout her life, Woolf resented the idea that a woman's future was determined by her sex and therefore far more limited than that of a man. This resentment of the social inequality between male and female is revealed in many of her works. Woolf suffered two nervous breakdowns and drowned herself in 1941 because she feared another breakdown from which she might not recover. Among her finest works are *The Voyage Out* (1915), *Night and Day* (1919), *Jacob's Room* (1922), *Mrs. Dalloway* (1925), *To the Lighthouse* (1927), *The Waves* (1931) *The Death of the Moth and Other Essays* (1942), and *A Room of One's Own* (1929), from which the excerpt below is reprinted.

Reading Advice

The selection that follows is taken from the book *A Room of One's Own*, based on a lecture Woolf was asked to give to two women's residential colleges at Cambridge University. However, Woolf took the opportunity to turn the lecture into an expanded work on the lot of women. Still, the effectiveness of this particular essay lies in the fact that Woolf addresses you, the reader, as if you were part of a female lecture audience. This allows her to exhort, scold, and arouse emotion as she sees fit. Infusing her address with a tone of disappointment rising to determination, she demands of women that they free themselves from the shackles that have bound them in the past and made it impossible for them to devote their lives to useful accomplishments.

Early on, in paragraph 2, Woolf points out a strange irony—that in literature women have always appeared to have the highest importance, burning "like beacons in all the works of all the poets"; yet, the shameful historical reality testifies that women were "locked up, beaten, and flung about the room" by males who considered them insignificant. In order to dramatize her point, Woolf imagines what Shakespeare's twin sister might have endured had she existed with the same desires, dreams, and talents Shakespeare himself had. According to Woolf, this female genius would have been forced to smother her vast talents and, frustrated beyond endurance, might have ended her life by committing suicide. Woolf then tells women to take advantage of educational opportunities and also to unite to help other women of talent achieve. She reminds them that today opportunities beyond just breeding offspring are open to women and they should take advantage.

Because of its many references to history and literature, Woolf's essay requires that the reader be well informed about the past. Her prose style is often poetic, as when she creates the "worm winged like an eagle" simile to illumine the difference between the way history and poetry view women (paragraph 4). She also uses symbols, such as the "room" a woman must have, which stands for independence, and the "view" women must not shut out, which stands for freedom of inner vision.

But, you may say, we asked you to speak   1
about women and fiction—what has that got to do with a room of one's own? I will try to explain. When you asked me to speak about women and fiction I sat down on the banks of a river and began to wonder what the words meant. They might mean simply a few remarks about Fanny Burney[1]; a few more about Jane Austen[2]; a tribute to the Brontës[3] and a sketch of Haworth Parsonage[4] under snow; some witticisms if possible about Miss Mitford[5]; a respectful allusion to George Eliot[6]; a reference to Mrs. Gaskell[7] and one would be done. But at second glance the words seemed not so simple. The title women and fiction might mean, and you may have meant it to mean, women and what they are like; or it might mean women and the fiction that they write; or it might mean women and the fiction that is written about them; or it might

1. Frances Burney (1752–1840), English novelist.
2. Jane Austen (1775–1815), English novelist.
3. Charlotte (1816–1855), Emily Jane (1818–1848), and Anne (1820–1849) Brontë. Three sisters and English novelists.
4. The home of the Brontë family.
5. Mary Russell Mitford (1787–1855), English novelist and writer of dramas.
6. George Eliot, pseudonym of Mary Ann Evans (1819–1880), English novelist and poet.
7. Elizabeth Cleghorn Gaskell (1810–1865), English novelist.

mean that somehow all three are inextricably mixed together and you want me to consider them in that light. But when I began to consider the subject in this last way, which seemed the most interesting, I soon saw that it had one fatal drawback. I should never be able to come to a conclusion. I should never be able to fulfil what is, I understand, the first duty of a lecturer—to hand you after an hour's discourse a nugget of pure truth to wrap up between the pages of your notebooks and keep on the mantelpiece forever. All I could do was to offer you an opinion upon one minor point—a woman must have money and a room of her own if she is to write fiction; and that, as you will see, leaves the great problem of the true nature of woman and the true nature of fiction unsolved. I have shirked the duty of coming to a conclusion upon these two questions—women and fiction remain, so far as I am concerned, unsolved problems. But in order to make some amends I am going to do what I can to show you how I arrived at this opinion about the room and the money. I am going to develop in your presence as fully and freely as I can the train of thought which led me to think this. Perhaps if I lay bare the ideas, the prejudices, that lie behind this statement you will find that they have some bearing upon women and some upon fiction. At any rate, when a subject is highly controversial—and any question about sex is that—one cannot hope to tell the truth. One can only show how one came to hold whatever opinion one does hold. One can only give one's audience the chance of drawing their own conclusions as they observe the limitations, the prejudices, the idiosyncrasies[8] of the speaker. Fiction here is likely to contain more truth than fact. Therefore I propose, making use of all the liberties and licenses of a novelist, to tell you the story of the two days that preceded my coming here—how, bowed down by the weight of the subject which you have laid upon my shoulders, I pondered it, and made it work in and out of my daily life. I need not say that what I am about to describe has no existence; Oxbridge[9] is an invention; so is Fernham[10]; "I" is only a convenient term for somebody who has no real being. Lies will flow from my lips, but there may perhaps be some truth mixed up with them; it is for you to seek out this truth and to decide whether any part of it is worth keeping. If not, you will of course throw the whole of it into the wastepaper basket and forget all about it.

I went, therefore, to the shelf where the histories stand and took down one   2
of the latest, Professor Trevelyan's[11] *History of England.* Once more I looked up

---

8. Special traits of character.
9. A composite name derived from Ox(ford) and (Cam)bridge *universities.* Oxbridge also stands for male learning and teaching, male superiority, and the study of a world made by males.
10. Fernham (the name is similar to Newnham) is the invented name of a *college* for females. This institution is poor and without recognition or fame.
11. George Macaulay Trevelyan (1876–1962), English historian. *History of England* was published in 1926.

Women, found "position of," and turned to the pages indicated. "Wife-beating,"
I read, "was a recognized right of man, and was practiced without shame by
high as well as low. . . . Similarly," the historian goes on, "the daughter who
refused to marry the gentleman of her parents' choice was liable to be locked
up, beaten and flung about the room, without any shock being inflicted on
public opinion. Marriage was not an affair of personal affection, but of family
avarice, particularly in the 'chivalrous' upper classes. . . . Betrothal often took
place while one or both of the parties was in the cradle, and marriage when
they were scarcely out of the nurses' charge." That was about 1470, soon after
Chaucer's time.[12] The next reference to the position of women is some two
hundred years later, in the time of the Stuarts.[13] "It was still the exception for
women of the upper and middle class to choose their own husbands, and when
the husband had been assigned, he was lord and master, so far at least as law
and custom could make him. Yet even so," Professor Trevelyan concludes,
"neither Shakespeare's women nor those of authentic seventeenth-century
memoirs, like the Verneys and the Hutchinsons, seem lacking in personality
and character." Certainly, if we consider it, Cleopatra must have had a way with
her; Lady Macbeth, one would suppose, had a will of her own; Rosalind, one
might conclude, was an attractive girl. Professor Trevelyan is speaking no more
than the truth when he remarks that Shakespeare's women do not seem lacking
in personality and character. Not being a historian, one might go even further
and say that women have burned like beacons in all the works of all the poets
from the beginning of time—Clytemnestra, Antigone, Cleopatra, Lady Macbeth, Phaedra, Cressida, Rosalind, Desdemona, the Duchess of Malfi, among
the dramatists; then among the prose writers: Millamant, Clarissa, Becky Sharp,
Anna Karenina, Emma Bovary, Madame de Guermantes—the names flock to
mind, nor do they recall women "lacking in personality and character." Indeed,
if woman had no existence save in the fiction written by men, one would
imagine her a person of the utmost importance; very versatile; heroic and mean;
splendid and sordid; infinitely beautiful and hideous in the extreme; as great
as a man, some think even greater. But this is woman in fiction. In fact, as
Professor Trevelyan points out, she was locked up, beaten and flung about the
room.

A very queer, composite being thus emerges. Imaginatively she is of the
highest importance; practically she is completely insignificant. She pervades
poetry from cover to cover; she is all but absent from history. She dominates
the lives of kings and conquerors in fiction; in fact she was the slave of any
boy whose parents forced a ring upon her finger. Some of the most inspired
words, some of the most profound thoughts in literature fall from her lips; in

3

12. Geoffrey Chaucer (1340–1400), English poet famous for *The Canterbury Tales.*
13. Family of 17th century English monarchs.

real life she could hardly read, could scarcely spell, and was the property of her husband.

It was certainly an odd monster that one made up by reading the historians first and the poets afterward—a worm winged like an eagle; the spirit of life and beauty in a kitchen chopping up suet. But these monsters, however amusing to the imagination, have no existence in fact. What one must do to bring her to life was to think poetically and prosaically at one and the same moment, thus keeping in touch with fact—that she is Mrs. Martin, aged thirty-six, dressed in blue, wearing a black hat and brown shoes; but not losing sight of fiction either—that she is a vessel in which all sorts of spirits and forces are coursing and flashing perpetually. The moment, however, that one tries this method with the Elizabethan woman, one branch of illumination fails; one is held up by the scarcity of facts. One knows nothing detailed, nothing perfectly true and substantial about her. History scarcely mentions her. And I turned to Professor Trevelyan again to see what history meant to him. I found by looking at his chapter headings that it meant—

"The Manor Court and the Methods of Open-field Agriculture . . . The Cistercians and Sheep-farming . . . The Crusades . . . The University . . . The House of Commons . . . The Hundred Years' War . . . The Wars of the Roses . . . The Renaissance Scholars . . . The Dissolution of the Monasteries . . . Agrarian and Religious strife . . . The Origin of English Sea-power . . . The Armada . . ." and so on. Occasionally an individual woman is mentioned, an Elizabeth, or a Mary; a queen or a great lady. But by no possible means could middle-class women with nothing but brains and character at their command have taken part in any one of the great movements which, brought together, constitute the historian's view of the past. Nor shall we find her in any collection of anecdotes. Aubrey[14] hardly mentions her. She never writes her own life and scarcely keeps a diary; there are only a handful of her letters in existence. She left no plays or poems by which we can judge her. What one wants, I thought— and why does not some brilliant student at Newnham or Girton[15] supply it?— is a mass of information; at what age did she marry; how many children had she as a rule; what was her house like; had she a room to herself; did she do the cooking; would she be likely to have a servant? All these facts lie somewhere, presumably, in parish registers and account books; the life of the average Elizabethan woman must be scattered about somewhere, could one collect it and make a book of it. It would be ambitious beyond my daring, I thought, looking about the shelves for books that were not there, to suggest to the students of those famous colleges that they should re-write history, though I acknowledge that it often seems a little queer as it is, unreal, lop-sided; but why should they

4

5

---

14. John Aubrey (1626–1697), English writer who portrayed the lives of famous Englishmen.
15. Two colleges for women in Cambridge University, where Woolf delivered this lecture.

not add a supplement to history? calling it, of course, by some inconspicuous name so that women might figure there without impropriety? For one often catches a glimpse of them in the lives of the great, whisking away into the background, concealing, I sometimes think, a wink, a laugh, perhaps a tear. And, after all, we have lives enough of Jane Austen; it scarcely seems necessary to consider again the influence of the tragedies of Joanna Baillie[16] upon the poetry of Edgar Allan Poe[17]; as for myself, I should not mind if the homes and haunts[18] of Mary Russell Mitford were closed to the public for a century at least. But what I find deplorable, I continued, looking about the book-shelves again, is that nothing is known about women before the eighteenth century. I have no model in my mind to turn about this way and that. Here am I asking why women did not write poetry in the Elizabethan age, and I am not sure how they were educated; whether they were taught to write; whether they had rooms to themselves; how many women had children before they were twenty-one; what, in short, they did from eight in the morning till eight at night. They had no money evidently; according to Professor Trevelyan they were married whether they liked it or not before they were out of the nursery, at fifteen or sixteen very likely. It would have been extremely odd, even upon this showing, had one of them suddenly written the plays of Shakespeare, I concluded, and I thought of that old gentleman, who is dead now, but was a bishop, I think, who declared that it was impossible for any woman, past, present, or to come, to have the genius of Shakespeare. He wrote to the papers about it. He also told a lady who applied to him for information that cats do not as a matter of fact go to heaven, though they have, he added, souls of a sort. How much thinking those old gentlemen used to save one! How the borders of ignorance shrank back at their approach! Cats do not go to heaven. Women cannot write the plays of Shakespeare.

Be that as it may, I could not help thinking, as I looked at the works of   6
Shakespeare on the shelf, that the bishop was right at least in this; it would have been impossible, completely and entirely, for any woman to have written the plays of Shakespeare in the age of Shakespeare. Let me imagine, since facts are so hard to come by, what would have happened had Shakespeare had a wonderfully gifted sister, called Judith, let us say. Shakespeare himself went, very probably—his mother was an heiress—to the grammar school, where he may have learned Latin—Ovid, Virgil and Horace[19]—and the elements of grammar and logic. He was, it is well known, a wild boy who poached rabbits, perhaps shot a deer, and had, rather sooner than he should have done, to marry

---

16. Joanna Baillie (1762–1851), Scottish poetess and writer of dramas.
17. Edgar Allan Poe (1809–1849), American writer of stories and poems.
18. Places frequented by that author.
19. Ancient Roman poets.

a woman in the neighborhood, who bore him a child rather quicker than was right. That escapade sent him to seek his fortune in London. He had, it seemed, a taste for the theater, he began by holding horses at the stage door. Very soon he got work in the theater, became a successful actor, and lived at the hub of the universe, meeting everybody, knowing everybody, practicing his art on the stage, exercising his wits in the streets, and even getting access to the palace of the queen. Meanwhile his extraordinarily gifted sister, let us suppose, remained at home. She was as adventurous, as imaginative, as eager to see the world as he was. But she was not sent to school. She had no chance of learning grammar and logic, let alone of reading Horace and Virgil. She picked up a book now and then, one of her brother's perhaps, and read a few pages. But then her parents came in and told her to mend the stockings or mind the stew and not moon about with books and papers. They would have spoken sharply but kindly, for they were substantial people who knew the conditions of life for a woman and loved their daughter—indeed, more likely than not she was the apple of her father's eye. Perhaps she scribbled some pages up in an apple loft on the sly, but was careful to hide them or set fire to them. Soon, however, before she was out of her teens, she was to be betrothed to the son of a neighboring wool-stapler. She cried out that marriage was hateful to her, and for that she was severely beaten by her father. Then he ceased to scold her. He begged her instead not to hurt him, not to shame him in this matter of her marriage. He would give her a chain of beads or a fine petticoat, he said; and there were tears in his eyes. How could she disobey him? How could she break his heart? The force of her own gift alone drove her to it. She made up a small parcel of her belongings, let herself down by a rope one summer's night and took the road to London. She was not seventeen. The birds that sang in the hedge were not more musical than she was. She had the quickest fancy, a gift like her brother's, for the tune of words. Like him, she had a taste for the theater. She stood at the stage door; she wanted to act, she said. Men laughed in her face. The manager—a fat, loose-lipped man—guffawed. He bellowed something about poodles dancing and women acting—no woman, he said, could possibly be an actress. He hinted—you can imagine what. She could get no training in her craft. Could she even seek her dinner in a tavern or roam the streets at midnight? Yet her genius was for fiction and lusted to feed abundantly upon the lives of men and women and the study of their ways. At last—for she was very young, oddly like Shakespeare the poet in her face, with the same grey eyes and rounded brows—at last Nick Greene the actor-manager took pity on her; she found herself with child by that gentleman and so—who shall measure the heat and violence of the poet's heart when caught and tangled in a woman's body?—killed herself one winter's night and lies buried at some crossroads where the omnibuses now stop outside the Elephant and Castle.[20]

---

20. Elephant and Castle was a pub (tavern) in south London.

That, more or less, is how the story would run, I think, if a woman in 7
Shakespeare's day had had Shakespeare's genius. But for my part, I agree with
the deceased bishop, if such he was—it is unthinkable that any woman in
Shakespeare's day should have had Shakespeare's genius. For genius like Shakespeare's is not born among laboring, uneducated, servile people. It was not
born in England among the Saxons and the Britons. It is not born today among
the working classes. How, then, could it have been born among women whose
work began, according to Professor Trevelyan, almost before they were out of
the nursery, who were forced to it by their parents and held to it by all the
power of law and custom? Yet genius of a sort must have existed among women
as it must have existed among the working classes. Now and again an Emily
Brontë or a Robert Burns[21] blazes out and proves its presence. But certainly
it never got itself on to paper. When, however, one reads of a witch being
dunked, of a woman possessed by devils, of a wise woman selling herbs, or
even of a very remarkable man who had a mother, then I think we are on the
track of a lost novelist, a suppressed poet, of some mute and inglorious Jane
Austen, some Emily Brontë who dashed her brains out on the moor or mopped
and mowed about the highways crazed with the torture that her gift had put
her to. Indeed, I would venture to guess that Anon,[22] who wrote so many
poems without signing them, was often a woman. It was a woman Edward
Fitzgerald,[23] I think, suggested, who made the ballads and the folk songs,
crooning them to her children, beguiling her spinning with them, or the length
of the winter's night.

This may be true or it may be false—who can say?—but what is true in it, 8
so it seemed to me, reviewing the story of Shakespeare's sister as I had made
it, is that any woman born with a great gift in the sixteenth century would
certainly have gone crazed, shot herself, or ended her days in some lonely
cottage outside the village, half witch, half wizard, feared and mocked at. For
it needs little skill in psychology to be sure that a highly gifted girl who had
tried to use her gift for poetry would have been so thwarted and hindered by
other people, so tortured and pulled asunder by her own contrary instincts,
that she must have lost her health and sanity to a certainty. No girl could have
walked to London and stood at a stage door and forced her way into the
presence of actor-managers without doing herself a violence and suffering an
anguish which may have been irrational—for chastity may be a fetish invented
by certain societies for unknown reasons—but were nonetheless inevitable.
Chastity had then, it has even now, a religious importance in a woman's life,
and has wrapped itself round with nerves and instincts that to cut it free and
bring it to the light of day demands courage of the rarest. To have lived a free

---

21. Robert Burns (1759–1796), Scottish farmer whose poetry has become much loved and very popular.
22. Anonymous, that is, an author of unknown identity.
23. Edward Fitzgerald (1809–1883), English poet.

life in London in the sixteenth century would have meant for a woman who was poet and playwright a nervous stress and dilemma which might well have killed her. Had she survived, whatever she had written would have been twisted and deformed, issuing from a strained and morbid imagination. And undoubtedly, I thought, looking at the shelf where there are no plays by women, her work would have gone unsigned. That refuge she would have sought certainly. It was the relic of the sense of chastity that dictated anonymity to women even so late as the nineteenth century. Currer Bell,[24] George Eliot,[25] George Sand,[26] all the victims of inner strife as their writings prove, sought ineffectively to veil themselves by using the name of a man. Thus they did homage to the convention, which if not implanted by the other sex was liberally encouraged by them (the chief glory of a woman is not to be talked of, said Pericles,[27] himself a much-talked-of man), that publicity in women is detestable. Anonymity runs in their blood. The desire to be veiled still possesses them. They are not even now as concerned about the health of their fame as men are, and, speaking generally, will pass a tombstone or a signpost without feeling an irresistible desire to cut their names on it, as Alf, Bert or Chas. must do in obedience to their instinct. . . .

. . . It is fairly evident that even in the nineteenth century a woman was not encouraged to be an artist. On the contrary, she was snubbed, slapped, lectured and exhorted. Her mind must have been strained and her vitality lowered by the need of opposing this, of disproving that. For here again we come within range of that very interesting and obscure masculine complex which has had so much influence upon the woman's movement; that deep-seated desire, not so much that *she* shall be inferior as that *he* shall be superior, which plants him wherever one looks, not only in front of the arts, but barring the way to politics too, even when the risk to himself seems infinitesimal and the suppliant humble and devoted. Even Lady Bessborough, I remembered, with all her passion for politics, must humbly bow herself and write to Lord Granville Leveson-Gower:[28] ". . . notwithstanding all my violence in politics and talking so much on that subject, I perfectly agree with you that no woman has any business to meddle with that or any other serious business, farther than giving her opinion (if she is asked)." And so she goes on to spend her enthusiasm where it meets with no obstacle whatsoever upon that immensely important subject, Lord Granville's maiden speech in the House of Commons.[29] The spectacle is certainly a strange one, I thought. The history of men's opposition to women's emanci-

9

---

24. Pseudonym of Charlotte Brontë (1816–1855), English novelist.
25. Pseudonym of Mary Ann Evans (1819–1880), English novelist and poet.
26. Pseudonym of Amadine Dudevant Dupin (1804–1876), French novelist.
27. Pericles (495–429 B.C.), Athenian general and statesman.
28. Leveson-Gower, Lord Granville (1773–1846), English diplomat and politician.
29. The principal house of the British Parliament.

pation is more interesting perhaps than the story of that emancipation itself. An amusing book might be made of it if some young student at Girton or Newnham would collect examples and deduce a theory—but she would need thick gloves on her hands, and bars to protect her of solid gold.

. . . The pressure of convention decrees that every speech must end with a   10 peroration.[30] And a peroration addressed to women should have something, you will agree, particularly exalting and ennobling about it. I should implore you to remember your responsibilities, to be higher, more spiritual; I should remind you how much depends upon you, and what an influence you can exert upon the future. But those exhortations can safely, I think, be left to the other sex, who will put them, and indeed have put them, with far greater eloquence than I can achieve. When I rummage in my own mind I find no noble sentiments about being companions and equals and influencing the world to higher ends. I find myself saying briefly and prosaically that it is much more important to be oneself than anything else. Do not dream of influencing other people, I would say, if I knew how to make it sound exalted. Think of things in themselves.

And again I am reminded by dipping into newspapers and novels and bio-   11 graphies that when a woman speaks to women she should have something very unpleasant up her sleeve. Women are hard on women. Women dislike women. Women—but are you not sick to death of the word? I can assure you that I am. Let us agree, then, that a paper read by a woman to women should end with something particularly disagreeable.

But how does it go? What can I think of? The truth is, I often like women.   12 I like their unconventionality. I like their subtlety. I like their anonymity. I like—but I must not run on in this way. . . . Let me then adopt a sterner tone. Have I, in the preceding words, conveyed to you sufficiently the warnings and reprobation of mankind? I have told you the very low opinion in which you were held by Mr. Oscar Browning.[31] I have indicated what Napoleon once thought of you and what Mussolini[32] thinks now. Then, in case any of you aspire to fiction, I have copied out for your benefit the advice of the critic about courageously acknowledging the limitations of your sex. I have referred to Professor X and given prominence to his statement that women are intellectually, morally and physically inferior to men. I have handed on all that has come my way without going in search of it, and here is a final warning—from Mr. John Langdon-Davies.[33] Mr. John Langdon-Davies warns women "that

---

30. Summing-up.

31. Oscar Browning (1837–1923), English writer on history and education. He had concluded that among university students "the best woman was intellectually the inferior of the worst man."

32. Benito Mussolini (1883–1945), Italian Fascist dictator. He and Napoleon I (1769–1821) insisted that women were inferior to men.

33. John Langdon-Davies (1897–1971), English journalist and author. He wrote *A Short History of Women*, published in 1927.

when children cease to be altogether desirable, women cease to be altogether necessary." I hope you will make a note of it.

How can I further encourage you to go about the business of life? Young women, I would say, and please listen, for the peroration is beginning, you are, in my opinion, disgracefully ignorant. You have never made a discovery of any sort of importance. You have never shaken an empire or led an army into battle. The plays of Shakespeare are not by you, and you have never introduced a barbarous race to the blessings of civilization. What is your excuse? It is all very well for you to say, pointing to the streets and squares and forests of the globe swarming with black and white and coffee-colored inhabitants, all busily engaged in traffic and enterprise and love-making, we have had other work on our hands. Without our doing, those seas would be unsailed and those fertile lands a desert. We have borne and bred and washed and taught, perhaps to the age of six or seven years, the one thousand six hundred and twenty-three million human beings who are, according to statistics, at present in existence, and that, allowing that some had help, takes time.

There is truth in what you say—I will not deny it. But at the same time may I remind you that there have been at least two colleges for women in existence in England since the year 1866; that after the year 1880 a married woman was allowed by law to possess her own property; and that in 1919— which is a whole nine years ago—she was given a vote? May I also remind you that most of the professions have been open to you for close to ten years now? When you reflect upon these immense privileges and the length of time during which they have been enjoyed, and the fact that there must be at this moment some two thousand women capable of earning over five hundred a year in one way or another, you will agree that the excuse of lack of opportunity, training, encouragement, leisure and money no longer holds true. Moreover, the economists are telling us that Mrs. Seton[34] has had too many children. You must, of course, go on bearing children, but, so they say, in twos and threes, not in tens and twelves.

Thus, with some time on your hands and with some book learning in your brains—you have had enough of the other kind, and are sent to college partly, I suspect, to be un-educated—surely you should embark upon another stage of your very long, very laborious and highly obscure career. A thousand pens are ready to suggest what you should do and what effect you will have. My own suggestion is a little fantastic, I admit; I prefer, therefore, to put it in the form of fiction.

I told you in the course of this paper that Shakespeare had a sister; but do not look for her in Sir Sidney Lee's[35] life of the poet. She died young—alas,

13

14

15

16

---

34. A fictional name, meaning the average English housewife.
35. Sidney Lee (1859–1926), English biographer.

she never wrote a word. She lies buried where the omnibuses now stop, opposite the Elephant and Castle. Now my belief is that this poet who never wrote a word and was buried at the crossroads still lives. She lives in you and in me, and in many other women who are not here tonight, for they are washing up the dishes and putting the children to bed. But she lives; for great poets do not die; they are continuing presences; they need only the opportunity to walk among us in the flesh. This opportunity, as I think, it is now coming within your power to give her. For my belief is that if we live another century or so— I am talking of the common life which is the real life and not of the little separate lives which we live as individuals—and have five hundred[36] a year each of us and rooms of our own; if we have the habit of freedom and the courage to write exactly what we think; if we escape a little from the common living room and see human beings not always in their relation to each other but in relation to reality; and the sky, too, and the trees or whatever it may be in themselves; if we look past Milton's bogey,[37] for no human being should shut out the view; if we face the fact, for it is a fact, that there is no arm to cling to, but that we go alone and that our relation is to the world of reality and not only to the world of men and women, then the opportunity will come and the dead poet who was Shakespeare's sister will put on the body which she has so often laid down. Drawing her life from the lives of the unknown who were her forerunners, as her brother did before her, she will be born. As for her coming without that preparation, without that effort on our part, without that determination that when she is born again she shall find it possible to live and write her poetry, that we cannot expect, for that would be impossible. But I maintain that she would come if we worked for her, and that so to work, even in poverty and obscurity, is worthwhile.

Questions for Critical Thinking

1. What are some advances women have made in their march toward independence and power since Woolf wrote her essay? In your opinion are women better off today than in Shakespeare's time?

2. Woolf points out a vast difference between the way history has treated women and the way fiction considered them. What difference, if any, do you perceive in the way women today are portrayed in fiction versus their actual role in society?

3. Why is it difficult for literary genius to be fostered among servile people? Have any servile people today become famous literary figures? Name such a person if you know one and explain his or her success.

---

36. Pounds sterling.
37. John Milton (1608–1674), English poet and writer, most famous for his long poem, *Paradise Lost.* "Bogey" appears to mean his great reputation as a poet which might overawe and discourage young writers.

4. In paragraph 8, Woolf suggests that anonymity runs in women's blood and that today women are still possessed by the desire to be veiled. Do you agree? Why or why not?

5. In your view, what has been the historical motive for men to keep women in bondage for so long?

6. What was Rousseau's view of women (*see* "On the Origin of Inequality among Men," this chapter)? How do you think Woolf would react to this view?

7. If you were to give a "peroration" (see paragraph 10 of Woolf's essay) to women, what are five points you would deliver? List them in order of their importance.

Writing Assignment

Using Woolf's essay as a springboard or guide, write an essay addressed to young people graduating from high school—either all male, all female, or both. The purpose of your essay is to leave your audience with one nugget of important truth about the future.

Writing Advice

1. Name what you think will be the most precious commodity the future can offer your audience—time, privacy, adventure, independence, money, spiritual values, or something else you consider most important.

2. Choose a symbol for that commodity—a clock for time, an attic for privacy, a mountain for adventure, to name some possibilities. Use your imagination to create the appropriate symbol.

3. Weave your symbol into the title of your essay and formulate a thesis around the symbol. For instance, your title might be, "Respecting the Clock." Your thesis might be, "To know the value of time is to achieve one of life's great wisdoms."

4. Once you have formulated your thesis, you must proceed to prove and support it. Asking some relevant questions is one way to proceed. Using the clock essay as an example, the following questions will be helpful: Why is an understanding of the value of time important? What experiences in my society or in history prove this point? Whom do I admire who has valued time? What happens if one does not value time? You will find that answers to these questions can become part of the proof for your thesis.

5. Try to find some significant thinker who supports your thesis. For instance, Lord Chesterfield, an eighteenth-century statesman and writer, once wrote this to his son: "Know the true value of time; snatch, seize, and enjoy every moment of it. No idleness, no laziness, no procrastination: never put off till tomorrow what you can do today." Or, you may wish to quote a well-known saying, such as "Take care of the minutes, and the hours will take care of themselves." The point is that

quoting appropriate thoughts recorded by others is an excellent way to add depth and wealth to your own writing.

6. Last, make sure that your essay moves with direction. The best way to assure this continuity is to make an outline of some kind and to follow it. You will notice that Woolf's essay consists of the following parts: a) a look at women's role in the past, b) an imaginary sketch of Shakespeare's sister, c) an exhortation for contemporary women to take advantage of opportunities to excel. We suggest that you construct a similar scheme for your essay.

Alternate Writing Assignment

1. Write an essay about one woman who serves as an inspiration to other women because she achieved excellence in some particular field of endeavor despite the disadvantage of being female.

2. Write an essay stating why it is important for a woman to have a college education even if she intends to stay home and nurture her family.

HISTORY

THE BLACK SLAVE DRIVER
Randall M. Miller

Randall M. Miller (b. 1945) is associate professor of history at St. Joseph's College, in Philadelphia. He has written numerous essays about the epoch of slavery in the United States and recently published a volume titled *"Dear Master": Letters of a Slave Family* (1978).

Reading Advice

If you have been used to thinking of the Southern slave driver as a slimy ogre who not only betrayed his own kind but also sabotaged the interests of his employer, then this essay will surprise you. In the unembroidered, straightforward style of most modern historians, the author gives us a nonpartisan portrait of the typical slave driver in the pre–Civil War South. Miller's purpose is to divest the reader of the slave driver myth developed over the years by sources hostile to the Southern economy that depended on slavery for its success. Miller introduces us to the Southern slave driver as a competent black worker who understood farming techniques, business transactions, and the proper psychology required of a supervisor wanting to get top performance levels out of his workers. Here we see a man who was for the most part trustworthy and even kind in a job that required immense diplomacy to survive without causing chaos and rebellion among the plantation slaves.

Wise planters of the ante-bellum South   1
never relaxed their search for talent among their slaves. The ambitious, intelligent, and proficient were winnowed out and recruited for positions of trust and responsibility. These privileged bondsmen—artisans, house servants, foremen—served as intermediaries between the master and the slave community; they exercised considerable power; they learned vital skills of survival in a complex, often hostile world. Knowing, as they did, the master's needs and vulnerabilities, they were the most dangerous of slaves; but they were also the most necessary.

None of these men in the middle has been more misunderstood than the   2
slave driver, policeman of the fields and the quarters. To enforce discipline and guarantee performance in the fields, planters enlisted slave foremen or drivers. On large plantations they worked as assistants to the white overseers; on smaller units they served immediately under the master. Generally, they were of an imposing physical presence capable of commanding respect from the other slaves. Ex-slaves described the drivers as, for example, "a great, big cullud man," "a large tall, black man," "a burly fellow . . . severe in the extreme." Armed with a whip and outfitted in high leather boots and greatcoat, all emblematic of plantation authority, the driver exuded an aura of power.

The English traveler, Basil Hall, thought the driver had power more symbolic   3
than real. The slaves knew better. With hardly repressed anger, ex-slave Adelaine Marshall condemned the black foremen at the Brevard plantation in Texas for "all de time whippin' and stroppin' de niggers to make dem work harder." Many other former slaves echoed this theme of driver brutality; accounts of mutilations, lacerations, burnings, and whippings fill the pages of the slave narratives. But physical coercion alone never moved slaves to industry. The drivers, therefore, were selected as men able to bargain, bribe, cajole, flatter, and only as a last resort, to flog the slaves to perform their tasks and refrain from acts destructive of order in the quarters.

Masters often conferred with their black slave drivers on matters of farming,   4
or on social arrangements in the quarters, and often deferred to their advice. As the driver matured and became more knowledgeable, his relationship with his master became one of mutual regard, in sharp contrast to the master's less settled and more transient relationship with white overseers.

White overseers as well were frequently governed by the driver's counsel, 5
although the relationship between these two species of foreman was sometimes
strained. The overseer's insistence on steady work from the slaves, and the
driver's interest in protecting his people from white abuses, placed the driver
in the agonizing dilemma of torn loyalties and interest. In this conflict the
driver often appealed to the master and won his support. A chorus of complaint
from white Southern overseers alleged that planters trusted the black driver
more than the overseer. The charge seems to have been justified. John Hartwell
Cocke of Virginia regarded his driver as his "humble friend," but held overseers
at arm's length. The astute agricultural reformer and planter, James H. Hammond, unabashedly acknowledged that he disregarded his overseer's testimony
in many instances and instead heeded his driver, whom Hammond considered
a "confidential servant" especially enjoined to guard against "any excesses or
omissions of the overseer." Planters dismissed overseers as an expendable breed,
and, indeed, overseers rarely lasted more than two or three seasons with any
single master. The driver, however, stayed on indefinitely as the master's man,
and some masters came to depend on him to an extraordinary degree.

Through the driver, the planter sought to inculcate the "proper" standards 6
of work and behavior in his slaves. A few carefully enumerated the driver's
duties, leaving him little discretion; but for the most, formal rules were unknown,
and broad policy areas were left to the driver's judgment. Although an overseer
reviewed his work on large farms, the driver made many of the day-to-day
decisions on farming as well as meting out rewards and punishments. By blowing
on a bugle or horn, he woke up the slaves each morning. He determined the
work pace; he directed the marling, plowing, terracing, planting, hoeing, picking, and innumerable other farming operations; he encouraged the slaves in
their religious instruction and sometimes led devotions; he mediated family
disputes. His duties varied from disciplinarian to family counselor or hygienist.
The quick-witted driver who amputated the finger of a woman slave who had
been bitten by a rattlesnake saved her life. More than this, he took over the
function of the master as protector by making slaves instinctively look to him
for aid in times of crisis. So, too, did the driver who held the keys to the
plantation stores and parceled out the weekly rations to the slaves. Whatever
changes might occur in white management, the basic daily functions of the
plantation routine continued unbroken under the driver.

The slave driver had power. For favorites he might sneak extra rations or 7
wink at minor indiscretions; for recalcitrants he might ruthlessly pursue every
violation of the plantation code of conduct. But he wielded power only to a
point, for when the driver's regime became tyrannical or overly dependent on
brute force, he ceased to serve his purpose for the master or the slaves. Planters
wanted stability and profits, not discord. Slaves wanted peace in the quarters
and a minimum of white intrusion into their lives. A factious slave population

sabotaged farming arrangements, ran off, or dissembled in countless ways. To ensure his continued rule, the driver had to curry favor in both camps, black and white. His justice must remain evenhanded, and his discipline rooted in something more enduring than the lash—namely community approbation.

In exchange for the driver's services, the planter compensated him with privileges, even offers of freedom. More immediately, planters tried to encourage the driver in a variety of small ways—with bits of praise, pats on the back, presents. They gave material rewards such as double rations, superior housing, and gifts for the driver's family. Some masters allowed their drivers to marry women "off the plantation," and a few drivers had more than one wife. Planters often set aside extra land for the driver's personal use, and allowed him to draft other slaves to tend his garden and cotton patch. He was usually permitted to sell the produce of his own garden in town for cash. Drivers also went to town to purchase supplies for the master, to do errands, and to transact business for the slaves. They often received cash payments of ten to several hundred dollars a year as gifts, or even wages. During winter months some drivers hired themselves out to earn extra money, and others learned trades with which to build personal estates. Conspicuous consumption heightened the driver's standing and gave sanction to his authority. **8**

Who were these men, and how did they rise in the plantation hierarchy? A collective portrait of the slave driver drawn from slave narratives and planters' accounts yields little support for the generalized charge that drivers were brutish and isolated from their fellow slaves. Although some were kinfolks of other privileged bondsmen, many came from more humble origins. Few slaves were bred to be drivers, and fewer still were purchased for that reason. Most important, no pronounced sense of caste developed in the South to set off drivers from the rest of the slave community. **9**

The awkward attempts of some planters to put distance between slave elites and field hands, by means of special clothes and indulgences, fooled no one. Drivers, after all, took their meals in the quarters, married and raised their families there, worshiped there, and frolicked there. The location of the driver's cabin at the head of the row, midway between the Big House and the quarters, placed the driver closest to the master symbolically, but his place remained in the quarters. Rather than suffer a driver with a puffed-up ego who had little rapport with the slaves, a master might even administer a whipping to him in front of the others. Lashings, demotions, and other humiliations provided ample reminders that the driver was more slave than free. **10**

Drivers were generally in their late-thirties or early forties when appointed, and they usually held long tenures. Yet there were a few in their twenties and at least one in his teens. If the candidate was, as one planter wrote, "honest, industrious, not too talkative (which is a necessary qualification), a man of good **11** sense, a good hand himself, and has been heretofore faithful in the discharge of whatever may have been committed to his care," he would do nicely. Whatever the strictures on verbosity, planters chose articulate men capable of communicating the master's wishes and values to the slaves with a minimum of distortion and at the same time able to relay accurately the messages and impulses of the slaves to the master. Thus one planter sent the driver along with a boatload of slaves divided from the rest by sale so that the driver could "jolly the negroes and give them confidence" and explain the master's side.

In reading black and white accounts of bondage, one is struck by the repeated   12
references to the master's confidence in his black slave driver. He left his family alone with the driver, entrusted his comfort and well-being to his care, and gave the driver free rein in ordering the private affairs of his other slaves. One rice planter, R.F.W. Allston, a shrewd student of slave psychology, confirmed his driver in an impressive, formal ceremony of investiture blessed by a clergyman. William S. Pettigrew of North Carolina often reminded his drivers that their good "credit" depended on their faithful duty during his absence. This call for reciprocity worked in subtle ways to compel the driver to uphold the master's interest. Former driver Archer Alexander described his entrapment. He justified his loyalty to his master, who once sold two of his children away from him, by explaining that the master "trusted me every way, and I couldn't do no other than what was right."

Ambiguities of the driver's relationship with the master and the slaves are   13
best illustrated in the one area he could not readily conceal from the overseer or the master—work. All masters demanded frequent performance reports from their drivers. Masters knew the slaves' minimal capacities, and they could corroborate the driver's testimony with private inspections of the field and with their own crop tallies after harvest. Aware of these facts, slaves conceded the driver's need to keep them moving, and forgave occasional excesses of zeal.

In assigning tasks or setting the work pace, the driver could push the slaves   14
relentlessly to impress the master, apply the slaves' time to his private purposes, or manipulate the system to reward favorites and punish enemies. Those members of the driver's family who toiled in the fields usually drew light chores; as a rule they also escaped the lash. So did lovers. A slave woman who spurned a driver's advances, however, might find herself isolated in a remote section of the field, and thus vulnerable to the driver's amorous assaults, or assigned impossible tasks so that the vengeful driver could punish her under the guise of sound labor management.

In the face of driver abuses, however, no slave was wholly defenseless. If the   15
driver unduly imposed on him, he might run to the master or overseer for relief. Enlightened planters advised against punishing a slave beyond the limits of reasonable service, because hard treatment brought forth scant improvement

and much dissatisfaction. Drivers usually marked out tasks for each slave according to ability, and remained on the ground until everyone finished. Even the cruel driver had little personal interest in overmeasuring tasks, since unfinished work kept him in the fields. Moreover, unrealistic work demands might prompt a general flight to the swamps, sabotage, or worse.

As the lead man in the gang labor system, a thoughtful driver would set a steady pace—singing, shouting, cracking his whip, or working at the head of the gang. In this way the slaves could do their work in a manner that would both satisfy the master and reduce the driver's need to whip or embarrass the weaker, slower slaves. Slave accounts tell of men like Moses Bell, a driver on a wheat farm in Virginia, who helped one woman "cause she wasn't very strong"; or like the driver who countermanded his master's orders and sent a nursing mother back to her cabin because she was "too sick to work." Like any champion of the weak, the driver acquired stature in the eyes of the oppressed. Young slaves appreciated drivers like July Gist, who eased their transition to fieldwork and taught them how to avoid punishment. Gist stressed careful husbandry and never rushed the young slaves as they adapted to the rigors of plowing, hoeing, and picking from sunup to sundown.   16

Unwritten rules governed the driver's conduct. He must not whip with malice or without cause, for example. The driver who exceeded his authority and surpassed whites in viciousness produced bitterness and recalcitrance. Jane Johnson of South Carolina considered the driver "de devil settin' cross-legged for de rest of us on de plantation," and she could not believe that her master intended "for dat nigger to treat us like he did. He took 'vantage of his [the master] bein' 'way and talk soft when he come again." Slaves reserved special enmity for such drivers. After witnessing a driver lash his mother and aunt, Henry Cheatem swore "to kill dat nigger iffen it was de las' thing I eber done." Mary Reynolds despised Solomon for his savage whippings, and even more because he disrupted the slaves' "frolickin'" and religious meetings in the quarters. In her old age she consoled herself with the assurance that the driver was "burnin' in hell today, and it pleasures me to know it."   17

If masters or informal community pressures did not check abusive drivers, the slaves resorted to more direct remedies. For example, a host of Florida slaves plotted a mass escape from the driver Prince's blows. When discovered, several of the conspirators preferred incarceration to further subservience to Prince. Some slaves refused to be whipped or to have their families mistreated in any manner, and a driver who challenged them risked violent resistance. According to an Alabama driver who tried to correct an alleged shirker, the slave "flong down his cradle and made a oath and said that he had as live [lief] die as to live and he then tried to take the whip out of my hand." The slaves could return cruelty with cruelty. One group of Louisiana slaves murdered a driver by placing crushed glass in his food, and another killed their driver and cut him into small pieces to conceal the crime.   18

Many slaves, however, recognized that the driver whipped out of duty rather   19
than desire. Moses Grandy, for example, refused to condemn harsh drivers
because he understood that they must whip with "sufficient severity" to retain
their posts and keep the lash off their own backs. Slaves would grant the driver
that much provided that he showed no taste for it and did not whip when he
was not obligated to do so. Many drivers deluded their masters by putting on
grand exhibitions of zeal in the white men's presence. Some developed the art,
as driver Solomon Northup described it, of "throwing the lash within a hair's
breath of the back, the ear, the nose, without, however, touching either of
them." When his master was out of sight, "Ole" Gabe of Virginia whipped a
post instead of the slaves while the ostensible victims howled for the master's
benefit. He once cracked the post so loudly that his master yelled for him to
desist lest he kill the slave, who then bolted screaming from the barn with
berry juice streaming down his back. This so horrified the master that he
threatened Gabe with a thrashing equal to the one he gave the slave.

The successful driver did not tattle on his people and he kept the white   20
folks out of the slaves' private lives as much as possible. In the letters written
by literate drivers to their masters, the drivers remained remarkably reticent
on life in the quarters: the masters knew little about what went on there from
sundown to sunup because the drivers, their principal agents, did not tell them.
To be sure, severe fighting among the slaves and egregious crimes were impossible to conceal. By and large, however, the drivers successfully contained the
breakdowns of plantation authority, and received sufficient cooperation from
the slaves so that they would not be called upon to explain and to punish.

The conscientious driver widened his circle of friends by doing favors,   21
overlooking faults, never breaking a promise, avoiding confrontations whenever
possible, and working through the informal group structure to resolve disputes
and problems. If clashes occurred—and they were inevitable in the elemental
world of the plantation—the driver gave his opponents an opportunity to save
face rather than shaming them. Sometimes he fattened the slaves' larder by
pilfering for them from the plantation smokehouse, or arranged passes for
them, ostensibly to attend religious meetings or to do chores, but in fact to
visit relatives and friends on other plantations. In the quarters he left the
correction of a wayward child to the child's parents, respected the slaves'
religious leaders, mediated marital squabbles, and protected the weak from
thieves and bullies. Slaves applauded the driver who broke up a boisterous,
quarrelsome couple by placing them in separate cabins, thus restoring quiet to
the quarters and saving the couple from sale at the hands of an irritated master.
In brief, the driver acted the way any responsible community leader would act
to keep his community intact and safe. He earned the slaves' trust. Ex-slave
Billy Stammper summed up the feelings of many slaves toward the driver:
"Cullud folks don' min' bein' bossed by er cullud man if he's smart an' good to
em," which is to say, if he was smart enough to be good to them.

More than any other event, the Civil War tested the driver's loyalty and   22
expanded his opportunities for self-aggrandizement and to help his people.
With the menfolk away during the war, the Southern white lady and the black
slave drivers assumed control of the plantations. Frustrated in their efforts to
engage white overseers, masters ignored the laws and left their plantations in
the hands of house servants, older privileged bondsmen, or drivers of long
service—men they could trust not to ravage their land or their women during
their absence. In their diaries and later in their histories, planters congratulated
themselves that they had not misplaced their trust. However romanticized, the
stories of faithful retainers hiding the family silver and shielding the planter's
family and homestead from Yankee depredations are legion.

But planters who wanted universal, unfeigned loyalty from their drivers   23
asked for too much. In the midst of unraveling planter hegemony, slave foremen
looked to their own interest. Some, like Edmund Ruffin's "faithful and intelligent" Jem Sykes, simply absconded. Some went alone; others inspired a general
stampede. If they remained on the plantations, they sometimes took part in
raids on the master's cellar and storehouse. In the absence of a strong white
power the slaves neglected the upkeep of the farm and equipment and idled
away their days as much as possible. Apparently, drivers could not or would
not push their people under such circumstances. The worst excesses occurred
in the sugar parishes of Louisiana, where drivers had commanded unusually
harsh regimes. The Union advance in 1863 excited many slaves to flee the
plantations, but not before they murdered some of their overseers and masters.
One Rapides Parish planter wrote that the presence of Federal troops "turned
the negroes crazy . . . and everything like subordination and restraint was at an
end." The slaves slaughtered livestock and plundered furiously. In this, the
drivers "everywhere have proved the worst negroes," perhaps in a bid to retain
their leadership through exaggerated displays of violence.

Most drivers, however, remained calm. Conservative men by temperament,   24
they were not about to launch a premature, perhaps suicidal, revolution. On
the Chesnut plantation, for example, the drivers early expressed enthusiasm for
the Confederate side, thus satisfying their master of their loyalty. In 1864,
however, they declined an offer to fight for the Confederacy in exchange for
freedom because, as Mrs. Chesnut sagely observed, "they are pretty sure of
having it anyway."

Many masters found their drivers "much changed" by emancipation. An   25
embittered Mary Jones of Georgia wrote of the metamorphosis of the driver
Cato who headed up a black delegation demanding land: "Cato has been to me
a most insolent, indolent, and dishonest man; I have not a shadow of confidence
in him, and will not wish to retain him on the place." The Edmonstons of South
Carolina found that with freedom their Henry, for fifteen years the master's
"right hand man," dropped his "affection and cheerful simplicity" and became

"grasping" in his "exorbitant demands" for land. Where they remained as foremen over hired gangs of freedmen, they ingratiated themselves with their charges by easing up on work requirements and stealing for the hands. Much of their authority disappeared with emancipation. When Mrs. R.F.W. Allston visited the plantation of her brother-in-law in April, 1865, she confronted a sullen and insolent group of former slaves who had recently completed their plunder of the plantation provision houses. Mrs. Allston called for Jacob, the head man and sole manager of the estate during the war, and ordered him to give the keys to her. A "huge man" then stepped forward to warn Jacob that if he complied, "blood'll flow." Mrs. Allston departed without the keys.

The paternalistic order of the past was rapidly disrupted by impersonal   26 economic forces in the prostrate postwar South. Planters attempted to lock their former slaves into long-term labor contracts, and looked to the drivers to hold the people on the farms. But neither drivers nor slaves would stay under such conditions. Some owners, short of capital, divided their holdings into tenant parcels and installed a black family on each, sharing the crops of each parcel with the tenant after the harvest. There was, however, no room in this arrangement for the driver.

But with the possible exception of the former slave artisans, the former   27 driver was the most qualified freedman to survive on his own. Indeed, for devotees of Horatio Alger, some former drivers provided inspiring, if somewhat scaled-down, models of success. The story of Limus, a former driver on the sea islands of South Carolina, is a case in point. A "black Yankee" in habits and values, the fifty-year-old freedman started with his one-half acre plot and a beaten-down horse, and raised vegetables and poultry for the Hilton Head market nearby. He also hunted and fished to supplement his income and his family's diet. With two wives and two families to support, he could hardly afford to relax. He worked fourteen acres of cotton on abandoned land to the three to six acres of his fellow freedmen. He also purchased a large boat on which he transported passengers and produce to Hilton Head. His prior marketing experience as a driver stood him in good stead as he negotiated contracts with whites and blacks alike, and he established himself as the principal supplier for the Union troops stationed in the area. By practicing ruthless underconsumption and efficient management, he saved almost five hundred dollars in his first year of freedom, money which he plowed back into his enterprises.

Some drivers had received gifts of cash and land during slavery from which   28 they could build their estates in freedom; they were able to exploit old relationships for credit; they had learned marketing skills and how to deal with whites in a cash economy, so that they were not so easily cheated or overawed by whites after the war; they understood every level of farm management and practice; and with the artisans they were the slaves most likely to have imbibed the Protestant work ethic of self-denial and persevering labor. If alert and lucky, they could turn the limited opportunities of freedom to their pecuniary gain, provided they did not alienate their benefactors. Recognizing this continued dependence on white aid, one driver warned his fellow freedmen to ignore carpetbagger blandishments, for the "outsiders" would "start a graveyard" if they persuaded blacks to "sass" whites. Even in freedom the former driver straddled two worlds.

The experience of the slave driver should remind us that slavery affected   29 each slave differently—that to fathom the complexities and subtleties of the peculiar institution and those trapped within it, we must take into account each slave's occupational role, his place in the slave and plantation hierarchy, his manner of interaction with the white and black communities, his self-image, to name the most obvious factors. Slave drivers have not fared well in our histories of American Negro slavery. The prevailing neo-abolitionist historiography has limned a portrait of the driver as an unscrupulous, brutal, even sadistic betrayer of his race. He was nothing of the sort. While the driver's behavior was sometimes extreme, it strikingly exemplified the ambiguities and paradoxes of the slave system. Drivers did not brood in self-pity or guilt over their miserable condition and the heavy demands made on them from above and below. They took their world for granted and made the best out of a bad situation. They had to do so. Both white and black depended on the man in the middle.

Questions for Critical Thinking

1. Why have historians been so slow to revise the portrait of the black plantation driver? Why do you think he was allowed to be misrepresented for so long?

2. The author indicates that the plantation owner often trusted his black driver more than he did his white overseer. Do you consider this understandable? Why or why not?

3. Which portrait of the slave driver do you believe to be more accurate—the traditional view of him as a brutish person, isolated from his fellow slaves, who felt betrayed by him—or the view of Miller's essay, which describes the driver for the most part as well-disposed toward his charges and forming an important liaison between the master and the slaves? Give reasons for your choice.

4. Why was R. F. W. Allston (*see* paragraph 12) considered a shrewd student of slave psychology? Do you agree that he was shrewd? What suggestions might you have given a plantation owner who wished to keep his driver happy and loyal?

5. Paragraph 15 alludes to female slaves who were vulnerable to the driver's sexual advances. What is your assessment of the possibility of sexual harassment in the work place today? Are females adequately protected?

6. Paragraph 22 alludes to "romanticized stories" about the loyal acts performed by slave drivers during the Civil War. What famous stories might the author have in mind? Why would story writers be tempted to romanticize these men?

7. Has our society rid itself of the black slave driver or has he resurfaced in a different form? If he has, give examples of his duties.

8. What advice would *The Communist Manifesto* have given to the slaves of the South? Would this advice have been appropriate? Explain your answer.

Writing Assignment

Write an essay in which you describe a person in the work force today playing a similar role to that of the pre–Civil War slave driver as analyzed by Miller. Pass critical judgment on the value of this person to the welfare of our economy.

Writing Advice

1. Of course, your first task will be to identify a person or role about which you can write. We believe a choice will emerge rather quickly when you think about the various industries in our country—farms, factories, hospitals, prisons, to name only a few. Who are the people typically assigned the job of supervising workers? What are their general characteristics and abilities? Watch out for male stereotyping as you think about this subject.

2. Once you have chosen your particular subject, you will want to offer a general picture of what that person is like. You can avoid stereotyping by letting your reader know that not every person in the position you are describing lives up to your description. For instance, if you were describing a typical head nurse on a hospital surgery ward, you would avoid stating, "She is inevitably a large woman, with her hair tied back in a bun tucked under her nurse's cap. Her voice is strident and she loves to shout orders to the nurses' aides on the floor." Fair-minded persons will find that such a description does not match their own observations of head nurses. It would be safer to write, "Whereas some head nurses are accused of being mean-tempered and imperious by those who work for them, the typical nursing supervisor is a woman dressed in a crisply white uniform that is symbolic of her professional competence in dealing with the medicines and procedures required by various postsurgical patients." You can draw a general portrait without basing it on mythical or prejudiced ideas concerning race or sex.

3. Once you have given a general description of your subject, you can then offer specific examples, as does the author of "The Black Slave Driver." Your examples should be chosen so as to reinforce your general view. For example, if you have described the typical army sergeant as rank conscious, ill-mannered, and abrasive, then supply some examples from military life to support your description.

4. Finally, draw your conclusion about what this person contributes to the welfare of our economy. If you believe this person contributes little or nothing, then say that, but remember that you must prove your opinion with reliable and appropriate evidence.

Alternate Writing Assignment

1. Write an essay in which you describe the paradoxes and ambiguities set in relief by the role of the slave driver in the pre–Civil War South.

2. Write an essay explaining how both the master and the slaves on a plantation depended on the slave driver as an important middleman in the pre-Civil War South.

HISTORY

MAKING SENSE OF SOUTH AFRICA
William Worger and John Boykin

William Worger (b. 1950), formerly of New Zealand, now lives in California, where he is an assistant professor in the Stanford History Department. A specialist in the history of South Africa, he is the author of *South Africa's City of Diamonds 1867–1895* (1987).

John Boykin (b. 1952) is senior editor of *Stanford*, the magazine of the Stanford University Alumni Association, in which this article was originally published. Boykin is a freelance writer whose book, *The Gospel of Coincidence*, is in progress.

Reading Advice

This essay about South Africa effectively explains a complex subject, covering hundreds of years and many different peoples, both African and European. How the two authors divided up their task of writing is not made clear; however, the result is a capsulized version of a stormy period in South African history. The authors have kept their writing simple by being direct and by limiting themselves to essential facts. If you have wondered, "Just what are Afrikaners? How did Apartheid begin? What are Sharpeville and Soweto? Who is Steve Biko?" these questions are answered in the essay. If you were never clear on the difference between the concepts of "homeland" and "township" or between the "African National Congress" and the "United Democratic Front," these differences are clarified. Moreover, if you saw the 1987 film *Cry Freedom*, then this essay will hold additional appeal for you.

In an attempt to be objective, the authors present arguments both for and against sanctions as a way of effecting change in the governance of South Africa. They believe that these economic pressures—as well as military, athletic, and moral pressures—have strongly influenced South Africa's internal political debate, which, they say, "ultimately, is the only thing that can force reform." If you are interested in the problems of South Africa, you can use this essay as an excellent basis for further study.

South Africa's three million mixed-race 1 "Coloureds" and 900,000 Indians, called Asians, have some rights denied Africans—the right to vote for same-race representatives and to own property free and clear. But they, like Africans, must live in townships (i.e., ghettos associated with white communities) officially segregated for them by race.

The five million whites enjoy a practical monopoly of political power, hold 2 the bulk of South Africa's land and wealth, and enjoy unfettered freedom of movement. They amount to 15 percent of the population.

Some expressions of apartheid, such as laws requiring blacks always to carry 3 passes and use separate public bathrooms, have been repealed of late. But things have not necessarily changed: For example, people of different races are now legally permitted to marry—but may not then live together.

While international pressure against apartheid forces the South Africa gov- 4 ernment to assure outsiders that progress is being made, it is under intense and growing right-wing internal pressure not only to hold the line, but to turn back the clock to total separation of races. And the bottom line is that internal politics count far more than external pressure.

In Afrikaans apartheid means apartness; in practice it means inequality. 5

God's Chosen People

While archaeological evidence shows that there has been African residence 6 in what is now South Africa since at least the third century A.D., whites have been there for only about 335 years. Until diamonds and gold were discovered there in the late 1800s, South Africa was a sleepy little backwater. Few Europeans cared to move there. There was no single government, language, culture, or economic common denominator.

Cape Town, the best sheltered deepwater port along the southern African 7 coast, was the only place in the region where ships sailing between India or China and Europe could pick up supplies. In 1652 the Dutch East Indies

Company sent settlers to Cape Town to establish a way station to service its ships. A small number of Khoisan people (pejoratively called bushmen or Hottentots) were already living in the area. The company had hoped to utilize them as its laborers, but had nothing to offer that the Khoisan wanted in return for their labor. So the company imported black slaves from elsewhere, a practice that continued for almost 200 years.

The Dutch East Indies Company—not the Dutch government—owned or   8
controlled the environs of Cape Town from 1652 until 1795, when the British, worried that Napoleon might capture this strategic outpost for his empire, beat him to it. Neither the Dutch nor the British home offices ever had any interest in exploring, colonizing, developing, or expanding beyond the area around Cape Town.

The settlers, however, were not as complacent. All during the 1700s they   9
spread out eastward along the southern coast. As they did, for the first time they began encountering some of the large number of Africans (other than Khoisan) living in what is now South Africa. By this time the Europeans had had a very long time to nurse the belief that they were in an uninhabited land— a myth that would later be invoked by the South African government to justify white domination and to portray blacks as newcomers. Blacks have in fact always outnumbered whites in every major region of the country, though the black majority became numerically overwhelming only in the late 1800s.

When in 1834 the British outlawed slavery throughout the British empire,   10
slave-owning Dutch settlers in the east opposed to British notions of equal rights for blacks and whites began moving into the interior, a migration called the Great Trek.

During the Great Trek, on December 16, 1838, 500 of these Dutch trekkers   11
were confronted by 10,000 Zulu. According to later stories, the Dutch prayed, to the effect that if God gave them victory in this battle, they would proclaim the day a sabbath and interpret the victory as his sign of a covenant that they were his chosen people—just like the Children of Israel, who in their day also conquered a Promised Land and subjugated its people.

The Dutch, armed with guns, defeated the spear-carrying Zulu so soundly   12
that the river flowed the Zulu blood. Today, the Day of the Covenant eclipses Christmas as the most celebrated holiday for Afrikaners and has formed the basis for the Dutch Reformed Church's religious rationalization for apartheid.

Afrikaners

The people who govern South Africa today are the descendants of those   13
early Dutch (as well as German and French) settlers. They called themselves Boers ("farmers") until the early twentieth century, when they decided they

were a distinct people, Afrikaners. Their language, Afrikaans, is a variation on Dutch.

The Anglo-Boer War (1899–1902) drove many of them off the land and   14
left them extremely poor. In their struggle for existence, they tried to improve their competitive position vis-à-vis the other poor segment of society, the blacks, with legislation that put blacks at a disadvantage. They got their chance to carry that agenda to an extreme in 1948 when the Afrikaner Nationalist Party took power. It quickly began instituting its full set of segregationist policies called apartheid.

Origins of Apartheid

The basic forms of racial discrimination we associate with apartheid—pass   15
laws, urban segregation, discriminatory treatment in the courts, and the like— were originally developed to control black laborers in the diamond and gold mining industries in the late 1800s.

Diamonds were discovered in 1867, gold in 1886. In the diamond rush of   16
the 1870s, some white claimholders struck it rich, some didn't: Those who didn't assumed that it was because their black workers were stealing diamonds from the claim. Coming from a long tradition of using slave labor, they also resented having to cut into profits by paying workers. So in the early 1870s diamond mine owners began introducing controls. They pushed through pass laws that made it hard for blacks to change employers (so employers wouldn't be competing for workers, which kept wages low) or to get around in urban areas. They searched workers for secreted diamonds before they left the mines, but even that didn't seem secure enough.

So in 1885 De Beers Consolidated took a new approach: closed compounds.   17
Mine workers were not allowed to leave the premises for the duration of their three-, six-, or nine-month contracts. At the end of the contract periods, workers were kept naked in a retaining room for a week so that any diamonds they might have swallowed would be excreted and recovered. Gold mine owners followed, to a lesser extent, the De Beers pattern, requiring blacks to live in company compounds.

The pattern of racial segregation in cities across South Africa today is mod-   18
eled after nineteenth-century Kimberley, the diamond headquarters, and Johannesburg, the gold headquarters. Both were populated primarily by black workers but run by white authorities. Both required that blacks live only in certain locations. "Servants"—in theory anyone, in practice only blacks—had to carry passes certifying that they were legally employed in the town. If they were found on the street without their passes, they were put in jail. Those without jobs then had to find employers, generally whites, or leave the white areas.

Such pass laws were later adopted by other towns that likewise needed   19 plenty of cheap black labor. Thus, in time, the pattern of treating blacks as temporary sojourners in urban areas, subject to discriminatory laws and practices, spread to society at large.

Homelands

South Africa became politically unified and essentially self-governing when   20
the British pulled out in 1910. Within three years the new government passed the Native Land Act, which specified that 7 percent of the land was to be reserved for Africans. The idea was that these areas were the Africans' authentic ancestral homelands. Only in these reservations would Africans by permitted to own land; outside of them, they would be permitted to work only in a wage labor relationship with whites.

The homelands were expanded in 1936 from 7 percent of the land area to   21
13 percent—still far short of the amount necessary to support the rural African population. By the 1950s, with the new Afrikaner government having instituted apartheid, the idea emerged that Africans should be systematically removed to these areas. Between the '60s and early '80s, as many as five million Africans were taken from white areas, loaded onto trucks, and deposited in the homelands, a process of eradicating "black spots" that continues today. Many of those removed to the homelands now commute hours each day to work in white-owned shops and factories.

Today there are ten homelands: 13 percent of the land area on which 77   22
percent of South Africa's total population is supposed to live. (In practice, only about 40 percent of Africans—most of whom are women, the young, and the old—spend most of their time in the homelands; the rest live in or near white areas.) Not only are the homelands made up of the poorest land in all of South Africa, they are gerrymandered to skirt good land, towns, roads, and coastline. KwaZulu, the most blatant example, consists of dozens of small, unconnected fragments. Run by men controlled by the South African government, the homelands have no freedom of speech, no manufacturing infrastructure, few jobs, and huge debts to the South African government for the very police and military brought in to keep the homelands' population in line.

In the 1950s the government declared that the homelands would become   23
independent nations. Among the implications: Africans would never be citizens of South Africa and therefore never have rights of any consequence. Four of the ten homelands have accepted nominal independence, though no country except South Africa recognizes them as legitimate nations. And in practice, all ten are independent only in the sense that the South African government can ignore their problems most of the time and intervene whenever doing so serves its interests.

Homelands, in effect, then, are South Africa's dumping grounds.   24

Black Resistance

No people accepts subjugation without some degree of resistance. There   25
have been a few headline-grabbing instances of black violence in South Africa,
but generally, black resistance to white domination has been surprisingly peaceful: petitions, boycotts, strikes, civil disobedience. White reaction to black
protests and strikes has been, by contrast, consistently violent.

The forerunner of today's African National Congress (ANC) was formed in   26
1912, just two years after Great Britain pulled out of South Africa. Blacks
continued to send petitions to England in the misplaced hope that it would
still exercise some influence. Throughout the 1920s, '30s, '40s, and '50s, petitions, demonstrations marches, strikes, and other forms of peaceful protest by
blacks were met with indifference, whips, tear gas, and bullets by authorities.

In the late 1940s—about the time the newly elected Afrikaner Nationalist   27
Party was beginning to institute apartheid—a new generation of leaders arose
in the ANC, most notably Oliver Tambo and Nelson Mandela. They argued that
appealing to the good nature of whites was getting them nowhere. More
dramatic and radical—yet still non-violent—action was needed. Blacks burned
passes, boycotted buses, and marched; their leaders were arrested and held
without trial.

South African government leaders have often argued that disruptions and   28
internal calls for reform are the work of communist agents. It's an easy charge
to make, given a law that defines as a communist anyone who "aims at bringing
about any political, industrial, racial, or economic change within the Union by
the promotion of disturbance or disorder."

The ANC has never formulated a radical, revolutionary vision of the future.   29
It has proposed to nationalize certain key monopolistic industries, but only, it
has argued, to break the economic basis of racial discrimination.

Sharpeville and Its Aftermath

In 1960 several hundred blacks were protesting pass laws in the township   30
or ghetto of Sharpeville, south of Johannesburg. As police began to break up
the demonstration, the protesters turned away. The police fired into the fleeing
crowd, shooting many demonstrators in the back, killing 69 and injuring 186.

The incident captured the world's attention. The international community   31
criticized the South Africa government far more forcefully than in the past.
Foreign companies began pulling out of South Africa—not so much because
of moral objections, but because they feared that the government was losing
control and that the business climate was therefore going sour.

In response to the pull-outs, the South African government put on a show   32
of force. One of its first acts was to ban the two main black organizations, the

ANC and the Pan African Congress (PAC). No longer able to operate in the open, both organizations went underground and began programs of violent resistance that targeted government installations such as power plants, communications and transport facilities, and fuel dumps—but not places where people were likely to gather.

Nelson Mandela and other black leaders were arrested in 1963 and charged   33
with sabotage. Mandela stated in his defense that, with the banning of black political organizations and thus "all lawful modes of expressing opposition to [the principle of white supremacy] closed by legislation," blacks had either to "accept a permanent state of inferiority or to defy the government. We chose to defy the law." He was convicted and sentenced to life in prison, where he has been ever since. Only a handful of black leaders has been permitted to operate more or less freely since his arrest.*

Soweto and Steve Biko

Police violence killed far more people in the span of a few months in 1976   34
in the township of Soweto, outside Johannesburg, than have black opponents of white supremacy in more than a century of resistance. High school students in June 1976 protested being forced to use the Afrikaans language, arguing that it was the language of their oppressors and an impractical one at that, since commerce was dominated by English speakers. The students boycotted classes and occupied buildings to prevent others from attending classes.

To force the teenagers back to class, the police used tear gas and then bullets.   35
As they saw their children being gassed and shot, parents joined in. What began as a school protest about language soon escalated into a township-wide uprising protesting the lack of electricity and running water in the township and the high rents people were forced to pay to live in shacks.

By the time police got the situation in Soweto under control in February   36
1977, official (probably conservative) estimates are that some 600 protesters had been killed, 134 of them under the age of 18. There were five white casualties. In the aftermath of the uprising, the government arrested practically all black leaders that it could identify and closed down most black newspapers.

This was the context in which Steve Biko was arrested. Biko had emerged   37
as the leader of a black consciousness movement among university students in the late 1960s. At first dismissed by the government as being of little importance, his influence grew as blacks throughout South Africa—as well as some whites—responded enthusiastically to his denunciations of white supremacy and his affirmation of black pride. A charismatic leader, he became a symbol

---

*Nelson Mandela was freed from prison on February 11, 1990.

of black resistance when he was tortured to death in prison. His story is told in the 1987 film *Cry Freedom.*

The Botha Decade

Jimmy Carter's administration, with its emphasis on human rights, put an   38
unprecedented amount of heat on South Africa. Vice president Walter Mondale visited and called for one man, one vote; U.N. Ambassador Andrew Young visited and condemned white racism. Largely as a result, P.W. Botha, who became president of South Africa in 1978, took pains to insist that his government was in the process of reform—slow and gradual, but reform nonetheless.

Ronald Reagan preferred a carrot-and-stick approach that he called con-   39
structive engagement: America would lighten up its criticisms as long as South Africa proved that it was making real changes, and would reward South Africa for those changes. As it has turned out, however, South Africa has taken the reduction in criticism—ample carrot, not much stick—as an excuse for slowing the pace of reforms.

Botha's greatest reform has been the introduction of a new constitution in   40
1983, whereby South Africa ceased to be a nation for whites only. It set up a tricameral parliament: one house for whites, one for Coloureds, one for Asians. Africans were still excluded. Far from considering this progress, Africans took the new constitution as confirmation that they would *never* be citizens, never be given rights.

For their part, the Coloureds and and Asians regarded the change as tokenism   41
and an attempt to co-opt them. They expressed their contempt by boycotting the polls: Only about 10–15 percent of those eligible have ever actually voted under the new constitution.

United Democratic Front

At the same time the 1983 constitution was instituted, the United Demo-   42
cratic Front (UDF) was founded in the belief that reforms to date had been merely cosmetic. An umbrella organization of church groups, trade unions, welfare organizations, and the like; Africans, Asians, Coloureds, some liberal whites—anyone opposed to the government's policies—it was the first broad-based organization to appear since the banning of the ANC nearly a quarter century before. Strongly influenced by people like ministers Allan Boesak and 1984 Nobel Peace Prize winner Bishop Desmond Tutu, it has consistently advocated peaceful tactics and peaceful solutions.

As the UDF quickly grew and came to be perceived by whites as more and   43
more of a threat, the government cracked down and arrested UDF leaders. In

1988 six were convicted of treason for urging their followers to boycott municipal elections, which they branded a farce. Only Tutu and Boesak, by virtue of
their positions within the church and high international profiles, have been
more or less left alone.

By allowing a tiny handful of moderate black critics like Tutu and Boesak   44
to speak out, the government—despite having arrested the vast majority of
others—can point to them as proof that it allows free speech.

Prospects for a Black Revolution

There seem to be more than enough blacks in South Africa to overwhelm   45
the whites and drive them out. Why haven't they?

Primarily, because all the power of a modern industrial state—ranging from   46
computers to machine guns—rests in the hands of the whites, and the world
has yet to see a successful revolution in a state with so much power at its
disposal. Nor has the government hesitated to use its considerable firepower
to beat down any uprising: Whereas 69 blacks died at Sharpeville and 600 at
Soweto, well over 2,000 blacks have been killed, most by police and soldiers,
since the onset of a new round of protest in 1984.

A very distant second reason is that blacks themselves are far from unified.   47
The South African government's divide-and-conquer strategy has been very
effective. Specifically:

Blacks are prevented from having any forum in which to organize. They are   48
split among homelands, which are themselves fragmented. Many townships,
such as Soweto, have been carefully planned to be easily surrounded and isolated
anytime trouble breaks out.

The government has cultivated an effective network of individual blacks   49
working as infiltrators, informants, and collaborators, (such as mayors, council
members, chiefs, and policemen) to alert it to any brewing trouble.

Any assembly of two or more unrelated people may be considered an illegal   50
gathering. This is why funerals have become the main occasion of political
expression for blacks.

By controlling the press and restricting foreign reporters during its four-   51
year-long state of emergency, the government can keep other blacks, South
African whites, and the rest of the world from knowing about any uprising or
the degree of force used to suppress it. When *Cry Freedom* was shown in South
Africa (before being banned the next day), many of the whites who saw it
reported being unaware that bulldozers, tear gas, and guns had been used on
such a massive scale to suppress dissent in their own country.

As part of the divide-and-conquer approach, certain rights and privileges   52
are given to some and not to others (urban blacks vs. rural blacks, Asians and

Coloureds vs. Africans, domestic servants vs. miners): the haves therefore develop some stake in the system.

South Africa has been involved in more or less undercover wars in Moz-   53
ambique and Angola and in raids into the rest of southern Africa for the past decade, to discourage those countries from supporting and supplying the ANC and to keep conflict beyond its own boundaries. The recent peace treaty nego-tiated between South Africa and Cuba and Angola requires Angola to remove ANC bases from the country.

Would-be leaders are identified and silenced by the government, so they   54
don't operate freely long enough to develop much influence. Boesak, speaking at Stanford in January, said that any black South African mother of a gifted child knows that that child will be killed. There has therefore been no oppor-tunity to formulate or communicate a clear vision of what kind of black nation would replace the white regime, should the opportunity arise.

Sanctions

Short of revolution, sanctions by the international community are often .   55
proposed to pressure the South African government to reform apartheid.

Sanctions of one kind or another have been in place against South Africa   56
for over 25 years, to varying effect. The first serious international condemna-tions of apartheid were heard in the 1950s after the South African government sent bulldozers into certain black areas of Johannesburg and Cape Town, destroyed all the homes, and trucked the residents elsewhere.

In the 1960s, countries began refusing entry to South African passport   57
holders. It became hard for South African sports teams to find foreign teams willing to play with them. South Africa has been barred from the Olympics since 1968. In the '60s, the U.S. and other countries began imposing a series of economic sanctions against South Africa. In 1977, in the aftermath of Steve Biko's death, the U.N. Security Council voted unanimously for a mandatory arms embargo on South Africa.

The South African commodity whose embargo would put the most severe   58
economic pressure on the country is gold, on which its economy is heavily dependent. The nations of the world have not, however, chosen to embargo South African gold. Nor have its diamonds, a more practical target, been embargoed.

Sanctions as a weapon of foreign policy rarely force the intended changes   59
in any target country's conduct, and South Africa has been no exception. There are, however, other reasons why sanctions are imposed. Often they are used simply to make a moral statement. When discussing South Africa, the U.S. has argued that sanctions don't work—but that argument has not stopped America from imposing sanctions on Libya, Poland, Panama, and any number of other

countries. Boesak, speaking at Stanford in January, argued that sanctions can work: that, combined with the country's own problems, they were enough to tip the balance in convincing South Africa that it could no longer afford to continue the war in Angola. Stiffer sanctions could help crack the tougher nut of apartheid in South Africa itself.

Boesak acknowledged that stricter sanctions would indeed temporarily hurt blacks in South Africa, but wondered aloud why the U.S. was suddenly so concerned about their welfare. He would accept that additional suffering as part of the process of relieving greater suffering. He argued not that sanctions alone are sufficient to force the South African government to abolish apartheid, but that they are something the U.S. can do to keep up the pressure and that South Africa's powerful ally has a moral obligation to do so. The key sanctions he specified that could make a difference are embargoing gold, refusing to renegotiate international bank loans, and discontinuing air travel.   60

Though sanctions have not forced serious changes, the cumulative effect of economic, military, athletic, and moral pressure has strongly influenced South Africa's internal political debate—which, ultimately, is the only thing that can force reform.   61

At present, there has been no suggestion that George Bush's policies toward South Africa will differ from Reagan's. If stiffer sanctions such as those Boesak calls for *were* imposed, there is little likelihood that they would quickly force the South African government to abolish apartheid. They would, however, make it significantly more difficult and expensive to operate a system so thoroughly condemned by the rest of the world, and that in turn could erode government resistance to serious reform.   62

Questions for Critical Thinking

1. What do you believe is the major motivating factor for the South African government to maintain apartheid? How do you see the future unraveling in this part of the world?

2. How does religion enter the belief that white domination in South Africa is not only acceptable but morally right? How does this belief square with your own view of religion?

3. What effect did the diamond industry have on apartheid? How could such an effect have been avoided?

4. What is your opinion of the homelands given to the blacks?

5. How do the goals of the ANC compare with those of Marx's *Manifesto* (this chapter)? How do they differ?

6. Is the essay an unbiased report or do you discover a side taken? Explain your answer with specific passages from the essay.

7. Since blacks are the overwhelming majority in South Africa, why have they not simply revolted and driven out the whites? Give your personal opinion on this question.

8. What difference, if any, do you perceive between apartheid in South Africa and segregation in the United States? What attitude toward apartheid in South Africa should our government take?

Writing Assignment

Write an essay comparing the roles of Nelson Mandela in South Africa and Martin Luther King in the United States.

Writing Advice

Comparing means showing how two items are alike; therefore, this assignment requires that you show similarities, not differences, between Mandela and King.

1. As in our suggestions earlier for contrast essays, you will need to decide on the areas for comparison. They will emerge as soon as you ask the following sample questions: (1 What goals did the two leaders establish? (2 What changes did they bring about in their countries? (3 How were they perceived by the opposition? (4 How did their own followers view them? (5 How did their governments treat them? (6 What role, if any, did their wives play? (7 What place will they hold in history? These are merely a few pertinent questions to ask. Thinking in depth about these two men will result in many more.

2. Write the questions on paper and then answer them briefly in writing. After reading your answers, select those that stress similarities between the two men. For instance, an answer to 1 immediately suggests the following similarity: both men sought freedom from white supremacy and were willing to defy the law with consequent punishment to achieve this freedom. As a result of their activities, both men had to spend time in jail. Answers to the other questions will suggest additional similarities.

3. In order to make your essay appealing, choose three or four similarities between the two men and develop them. A little library research on Martin Luther King's speeches will provide memorable material on King (especially excellent quotations), while a perusal of newspapers and major periodicals during the early months of 1990, when the press often focused on Mandela's release from prison, will unearth much useful information on Mandela.

4. Make sure that your essay is controlled by a thesis statement that clarifies the comparison. Here is an example: "Nelson Mandela in South Africa and Martin Luther King in the United States have become revered symbols of freedom from white oppression for the people of their respective countries."

Alternate Writing Assignments

1. Write an essay answering the following question: What implications, if any, are there for us in the United States when any other country of the world is permitted to institutionalize racial discrimination?

2. Write an essay proposing the kinds of pressures you consider appropriate for world leaders to place on the governments of countries that continue to treat segments of their populations as if they were noncitizens.

LITERATURE

THE GARDEN PARTY

Katherine Mansfield

Katherine Mansfield (1888–1923) was a British author and master of the short story. Born in New Zealand as Kathleen Beauchamp, she first studied to be a violincellist. Not until 1908 did she turn to literature as a career. Her first volume of short stories, titled *In a German Pension* (1911) drew little attention from literary critics, but the stories in *Bliss* (1920) and *The Garden Party* (1922) established her as a major writer. Subsequent volumes of stories include *The Dove's Nest* (1923) and *Something Childish* (1924). Her collected short stories appeared in 1937. In 1918, after one unhappy marriage, she married the noted editor and critic John Middleton Murray. During the last five years of her life, Mansfield suffered from tuberculosis, to which she succumbed at the age of 35. She is often compared with Anton Chekhov in the way she creates simple but compelling vignettes of society.

Reading Advice

The story below unfolds with delicate plainness. Laura, a young girl and the central character of the story, experiences an elusive moment of insight during an elegant family garden party. Although she is spoiled and wealthy, Laura is not insensitive. Therefore, when the news arrives that a poor neighboring laborer has been thrown out of his cart and killed when his horse shied at a traction engine, she feels that it would be inappropriate to continue the party in such close proximity to the dead man's home. But her mother and sister find her feelings absurd, considering that the man's family is poor and used to tragic accidents of this kind, and they insist that she continue to help host the party. Nevertheless, after the event is over, Laura takes a basket filled with leftovers to the little cottage where the dead man's family resides. She finds the widow's face swollen with grief, which makes her sad. Then, on her way out, she catches a glimpse of the dead man lying on a bed, looking completely peaceful and detached from his wretched surroundings. At this moment Laura achieves some deep insight into the meaning of life and death, but the exact nature of this insight is left up to the individual reader to interpret. The story's effectiveness lies in the exact details and dialogue associated with each scene.

*A*nd after all the weather was ideal. 1
They could not have had a more perfect day for a garden-party if they had ordered it. Windless, warm, the sky without a cloud. Only the blue was veiled with a haze of light gold, as it is sometimes in early summer. The gardener had been up since dawn, mowing the lawns and sweeping them, until the grass and the dark flat rosettes where the daisy plants had been seemed to shine. As for the roses, you could not help feeling they understood that roses are the only flowers that impress people at garden-parties; the only flowers that everybody is certain of knowing. Hundreds, yes, literally hundreds, had come out in a single night; the green bushes bowed down as though they had been visited by archangels.

Breakfast was not yet over before the men came to put up the marquee. 2

"Where do you want the marquee put, mother?" 3

"My dear child, it's no use asking me. I'm determined to leave everything 4
to you children this year. Forget I am your mother. Treat me as an honoured guest."

But Meg could not possibly go and supervise the men. She had washed her 5
hair before breakfast, and she sat drinking coffee in a green turban, with a dark wet curl stamped on each cheek. Jose, the butterfly, always came down in a silk petticoat and a kimono jacket.

"You'll have to go, Laura; you're the artistic one." 6

Away Laura flew, still holding her piece of bread-and-butter. It's so delicious 7
to have an excuse for eating out of doors, and besides, she loved having to arrange things; she always felt she could do it so much better than anyone else.

Four men in their shirt-sleeves stood grouped together on the garden path. 8
They carried staves covered with rolls of canvas, and they had big tool-bags slung on their backs. They looked impressive. Laura wished now that she had not got the bread-and-butter, but there was nowhere to put it, and she couldn't possibly throw it away. She blushed and tried to look severe and even a little bit short-sighted as she came up to them.

"Good morning," she said, copying her mother's voice. But that sounded so 9
fearfully affected that she was ashamed, and stammered like a little girl, "Oh—er—have you come—is it about the marquee?"

"That's right, miss," said the tallest of the men, a lanky, freckled fellow, and   10
he shifted his tool-bag, knocked back his straw hat and smiled down at her.
"That's about it."

His smile was so easy, so friendly that Laura recovered. What nice eyes he   11
had, small, but such a dark blue! And now she looked at the others, they were
smiling too. "Cheer up, we won't bite," their smiles seemed to say. How very
nice workmen were! And what a beautiful morning! She mustn't mention the
morning; she must be businesslike. The marquee.

"Well, what about the lily-lawn? Would that do?"   12

And she pointed to the lily-lawn with the hand that didn't hold the bread-   13
and-butter. They turned, they stared in the direction. A little fat chap thrust
out his under-lip, and the tall fellow frowned.

"I don't fancy it," said he. "Not conspicuous enough. You see, with a thing   14
like a marquee," and he turned to Laura in his easy way, "you want to put it
somewhere where it'll give you a bang slap in the eye, if you follow me."

Laura's upbringing made her wonder for moment whether it was quite   15
respectful of a workman to talk to her of bangs slap in the eye. But she did
quite follow him.

"A corner of the tennis-court," she suggested. "But the band's going to be   16
in one corner."

"H'm, going to have a band, are you?" said another of the workmen. He   17
was pale. He had a haggard look as his dark eyes scanned the tennis-court.
What was he thinking?

"Only a very small band," said Laura gently. Perhaps he wouldn't mind so   18
much if the band was quite small. But the tall fellow interrupted.

"Look here, miss, that's the place. Against those trees, over there. That'll   19
do fine."

Against the karakas. Then the karakas-trees would be hidden. And they were   20
so lovely, with their broad, gleaming leaves, and their clusters of yellow fruit.
They were like trees you imagined growing on a desert island, proud, solitary,
lifting their leaves and fruits to the sun in a kind of silent splendour. Must they
be hidden by a marquee?

They must. Already the men had shouldered their staves and were making   21
for the place. Only the tall fellow was left. He bent down, pinched a sprig of
lavender, put his thumb and forefinger to his nose and snuffed up the smell.
When Laura saw that gesture she forgot all about the karakas in her wonder
at him caring for things like that—caring for the smell of lavender. How many
men that she knew would have done such a thing? Oh, how extraordinarily
nice workmen were, she thought. Why couldn't she have workmen for friends
rather than the silly boys she danced with and who came to Sunday night
supper? She would get on much better with men like these.

It's all the fault, she decided, as the tall fellow drew something on the back   22 of an envelope, something that was to be looped up or left to hand, of these absurd class distinctions. Well, for her part, she didn't feel them. Not a bit, not an atom. . . . And now there came the chock-chock of wooden hammers. Some one whistled, some one sang out, "Are you right there, matey?" "Matey!" The friendliness of it, the—the—Just to prove how happy she was, just to show the tall fellow how at home she felt, and how she despised stupid conventions, Laura took a big bite of her bread-and-butter as she stared at the little drawing. She felt just like a work-girl.

"Laura, Laura, where are you? Telephone, Laura!" a voice cried from the 23 house.

"Coming!" Away she skimmed, over the lawn, up the path, up the steps, 24 across the veranda, and into the porch. In the hall her father and Laurie were brushing their hats ready to go to the office.

"I say, Laura," said Laurie very fast, "you might just give a squiz at my coat 25 before this afternoon. See if it wants pressing."

"I will," said she. Suddenly she couldn't stop herself. She ran at Laurie and 26 gave him a small, quick squeeze. "Oh, I do love parties, don't you?" gasped Laura.

"Ra-ther," said Laurie's warm, boyish voice, and he squeezed his sister too, 27 and gave her a gentle push. "Dash off to the telephone, old girl."

The telephone. "Yes, yes; oh yes. Kitty? Good morning, dear. Come to lunch? 28 Do, dear. Delighted of course. It will only be a very scratch meal—just the sandwich crusts and broken meringue-shells and what's left over. Yes, isn't it a perfect morning? Your white? Oh, I certainly should. One moment—hold the line. Mother's calling." And Laura sat back. "What mother? Can't hear."

Mrs. Sheridan's voice floated down the stairs. "Tell her to wear that sweet 29 hat she had on last Sunday."

"Mother says you're to wear that *sweet* hat you had on last Sunday. Good. 30 One o'clock. Bye-bye."

Laura put back the receiver, flung her arms over her head, took a deep 31 breath, stretched and let them fall. "Huh," she sighed, and the moment after the sigh sat up quickly. She was still, listening. All the doors in the house seemed to be open. The house was alive with soft, quick steps and running voices. The green baize door that led to the kitchen regions swung open and shut with a muffled thud. And now there came a long, chuckling absurd sound. It was the heavy piano being moved on its stiff castors. But the air! If you stopped to notice, was the air always like this? Little faint winds were playing chase, in at the tops of the windows, out at the doors. And there were two tiny spots of sun, one on the inkpot, one on a silver photograph frame, playing too. Darling little spots. Especially the one on the inkpot lid. It was quite warm. A warm little silver star. She could have kissed it.

The front door bell pealed, and there sounded the rustle of Sadie's print 32 skirt on the stairs. A man's voice murmured; Sadie answered, careless, "I'm sure I don't know. Wait. I'll ask Mrs. Sheridan."

"What is it, Sadie?" Laura came into the hall.   33

"It's the florist, Miss Laura."   34

It was, indeed. There, just inside the door, stood a wide, shallow tray full   35
of pots of pink lilies. No other kind. Nothing but lilies—canna lilies, big pink flowers, wide open, radiant, almost frighteningly alive on bright crimson stems.

"O-oh, Sadie!" said Laura, and the sound was like a little moan. She crouched   36
down as if to warm herself at the blaze of lilies; she felt they were in her fingers, on her lips, growing in her breast.

"It's some mistake," she said faintly. "Nobody ever ordered so many. Sadie,   37
go and find mother."

But at that moment Mrs. Sheridan joined them.   38

"It's quite right," she said calmly. "Yes, I ordered them. Aren't they lovely?"   39
She pressed Laura's arm. "I was passing the shop yesterday, and I saw them in the window. And I suddenly thought for once in my life I shall have enough canna lilies. The garden-party will be a good excuse."

"But I thought you said you didn't mean to interfere," said Laura. Sadie had   40
gone. The florist's man was still outside at his van. She put her arm round her mother's neck and gently, very gently, she bit her mother's ear.

"My darling child, you wouldn't like a logical mother, would you? Don't do   41
that. Here's the man."

He carried more lilies still, another whole tray.   42

"Bank them up, just inside the door, on both sides of the porch, please,"   43
said Mrs. Sheridan. "Don't you agree, Laura?"

"Oh, I *do,* mother."   44

In the drawing-room Meg, Jose and good little Hans had at last succeeded   45
in moving the piano.

"Now, if we put this chesterfield against the wall and move everything out   46
of the room except the chairs, don't you think?"

"Quite."   47

"Hans, move these tables into the smoking-room, and bring a sweeper to   48
take these marks off the carpet and—one moment, Hans—" Jose loved giving orders to the servants, and they loved obeying her. She always made them feel they were taking part in some drama. "Tell mother and Miss Laura to come here at once."

"Very good, Miss Jose."   49

She turned to Meg. "I want to hear what the piano sounds like, just in case   50
I'm asked to sing this afternoon. Let's try over 'This Life is Weary.'"

Pom! Ta-ta-ta *Tee*-ta! The piano burst out so passionately that Jose's face   51
changed. She clasped her hands. She looked mournfully and enigmatically at her mother and Laura as they came in.

> *This Life is* Wee-*ary,*
> *A Tear—A Sigh.*
> *A Love that* Chan-*ges,*
> *This Life is* Wee-*ary,*
> *A Tear—A Sigh.*
> *A Love that* Chan-*ges,*
> *And then . . . Good-bye!*

But at the word "Good-bye," and although the piano sounded more desperate   52
than ever, her face broke into a brilliant, dreadfully unsympathetic smile.

"Aren't I in good voice, mummy?" she beamed.   53

> *This Life is* Wee-*ary,*
> *Hope comes to Die.*
> *A Dream—a* Wa-*kening.*

But now Sadie interrupted them. "What is it, Sadie?"   54

"If you please, m'm, cook says have you got the flags for the sandwiches?"   55

"The flags for the sandwiches, Sadie?" echoed Mrs. Sheridan dreamily. And   56
the children knew by her face that she hadn't got them. "Let me see." And she
said to Sadie firmly, "Tell cook I'll let her have them in ten minutes."

Sadie went.   57

"Now, Laura," said her mother quickly. "Come with me into the smoking-   58
room. I've got the names somewhere on the back of an envelope. You'll have
to write them out for me. Meg, go upstairs this minute and take that wet thing
off your head. Jose, run and finish dressing this instant. Do you hear me,
children, or shall I have to tell your father when he comes to-night? And—
and, Jose, pacify cook if you do go into the kitchen, will you? I'm terrified of
her this morning."

The envelope was found at last behind the dining-room clock, though how   59
it had got there Mrs. Sheridan could not imagine.

"One of you children must have stolen it out of my bag, because I remember   60
vividly—cream cheese and lemon-curd. Have you done that?"

"Yes."   61

"Egg and—" Mrs. Sheridan held the envelope away from her. "It looks like   62
mice. It can't be mice, can it?"

"Olive, pet," said Laura, looking over her shoulder.   63

"Yes, of course, olive. What a horrible combination it sounds. Egg and olive."   64

They were finished at last, and Laura took them off to the kitchen. She   65
found Jose there pacifying the cook, who did not look at all terrifying.

"I have never seen such exquisite sandwiches," said Jose's rapturous voice.   66
"How many kinds did you say there were, cook? Fifteen?"

"Fifteen, Miss Jose."   67

"Well, cook, I congratulate you." 68

Cook swept up crusts with the long sandwich knife, and smiled broadly. 69

"Godber's has come," announced Sadie, issuing out of the pantry. She had 70
seen the man pass the window.

That meant the cream puffs had come. Godber's were famous for their 71
cream puffs. Nobody ever thought of making them at home.

"Bring them in and put them on the table, my girl," ordered cook. 72

Sadie brought them in and went back to the door. Of course Laura and Jose 73
were far too grown-up to really care about such things. All the same, they
couldn't help agreeing that the puffs looked very attractive. Very. Cook began
arranging them, shaking off the extra icing sugar.

"Don't they carry one back to all one's parties?" said Laura. 74

"I suppose they do," said practical Jose, who never liked to be carried back. 75
"They look beautifully light and feathery, I must say."

"Have one each, my dears," said cook in her comfortable voice. "Yer ma 76
won't know."

Oh, impossible. Fancy cream puffs so soon after breakfast. The very idea 77
made one shudder. All the same, two minutes later Jose and Laura were licking
their fingers with that absorbed inward look that only comes from whipped
cream.

"Let's go into the garden, out by the back way," suggested Laura. "I want to 78
see how the men are getting on with the marquee. They're such awfully nice
men."

But the back door was blocked by cook, Sadie, Godber's man and Hans. 79

Something had happened. 80

"Tuk-tuk-tuk," clucked cook like an agitated hen. Sadie had her hand clapped 81
to her cheek as though she had toothache. Hans's face was screwed up in the
effort to understand. Only Godber's man seemed to be enjoying himself; it was
his story.

"What's the matter? What's happened?" 82

"There's been a horrible accident," said cook. "A man killed." 83

"A man killed! Where? How? When?" 84

But Godber's man wasn't going to have his story snatched from under his 85
very nose.

"Know those little cottages just below here, miss?" Know them? Of course, 86
she knew them. "Well, there's a young chap living there, name of Scott, a carter.
His horse shied at a traction-engine, corner of Hawke Street this morning, and
he was thrown out on the back of his head. Killed."

"Dead!" Laura stared at Godber's man. 87

"Dead when they picked him up," said Godber's man with relish. "They 88
were taking the body home as I come up here." And he said to the cook, "He's
left a wife and five little ones."

"Jose, come here." Laura caught hold of her sister's sleeve and dragged her 89 through the kitchen to the other side of the green baize door. There she paused and leaned against it. "Jose!" she said, horrified, "however are we going to stop everything?"

"Stop everything, Laura!" cried Jose in astonishment. "What do you mean?" 90

"Stop the garden-party, of course." Why did Jose pretend? 91

But Jose was still more amazed. "Stop the garden-party? My dear Laura, 92 don't be so absurd. Of course we can't do anything of the kind. Nobody expects us to. Don't be so extravagant."

"But we can't possibly have a garden-party with a man dead just outside the 93 front gate."

That really was extravagant, for the little cottages were in a lane to themselves 94 at the very bottom of a steep rise that led up to the house. A broad road ran between. True, they were far too near. They were the greatest possible eyesore, and they had no right to be in that neighbourhood at all. They were little mean dwellings painted a chocolate brown. In the garden patches there was nothing but cabbage stalks, sick hens and tomato cans. The very smoke coming out of their chimneys was poverty-stricken. Little rags and shreds of smoke, so unlike the great silvery plumes that uncurled from the Sheridans' chimneys. Washer-women lived in the lane and sweeps and a cobbler, and a man whose house-front was studded all over with minute bird-cages. Children swarmed. When the Sheridans were little they were forbidden to set foot there because of the revolting language and of what they might catch. But since they were grown up, Laura and Laurie on their prowls sometimes walked through. It was dis-gusting and sordid. They came out with a shudder. But still one must go everywhere; one must see everything. So through they went.

"And just think of what the band would sound like to that poor woman," 95 said Laura.

"Oh, Laura!" Jose began to be seriously annoyed. "If you're going to stop a 96 band playing every time some one has an accident, you'll lead a very strenuous life. I'm every bit as sorry about it as you. I feel just as sympathetic." Her eyes hardened. She looked at her sister just as she used to when they were little and fighting together. "You won't bring a drunken workman back to life by being sentimental," she said softly.

"Drunk! Who said he was drunk?" Laura turned furiously on Jose. She said, 97 just as they had used to say on those occasions, "I'm going straight up to tell mother."

"Do, dear," cooed Jose. 98

"Mother, can I come into your room?" Laura turned the big glass door- 99 knob.

"Of course, child. Why, what's the matter? What's given you such a colour?" 100 And Mrs. Sheridan turned round from her dressing-table. She was trying on a new hat.

"Mother, a man's been killed," began Laura. 101

"*Not* in the garden?" interrupted her mother. 102

No, no!" 103

"Oh, what a fright you gave me!" Mrs. Sheridan sighed with relief, and took 104
off the big hat and held it on her knees.

"But listen, mother," said Laura. Breathless, half-choking, she told the dread- 105
ful story. "Of course, we can't have our party, can we?" she pleaded. "The band
and everybody arriving. They'd hear us, mother; they're nearly neighbours!"

To Laura's astonishment her mother behaved just like Jose; it was harder to 106
bear because she seemed amused. She refused to take Laura seriously.

"But, my dear child, use your common sense. It's only by accident we've 107
heard of it. If some one had died there normally—and I can't understand how
they keep alive in those poky little holes—we should still be having our party,
shouldn't we?

Laura had to say "yes" to that, but she felt it was all wrong. She sat down 108
on her mother's sofa and pinched the cushion frill.

"Mother, isn't it really terribly heartless of us?" she asked. 109

"Darling!" Mrs. Sheridan got up and came over to her, carrying the hat. 110
Before Laura could stop her she had popped it on. "My child!" said her mother,
"the hat is yours. It's made for you. It's much too young for me. I have never
seen you look such a picture. Look at yourself!" And she held up her hand-
mirror.

"But, mother," Laura began again. She couldn't look at herself; she turned 111
aside.

This time Mrs. Sheridan lost patience just as Jose had done. 112

"You are being very absurd, Laura," she said coldly. "People like that don't 113
expect sacrifices from us. And it's not very sympathetic to spoil everybody's
enjoyment as you're doing now."

"I don't understand," said Laura, and she walked quickly out of the room to 114
her own bedroom. There, quite by chance, the first thing she saw was this
charming girl in the mirror, in her black hat trimmed with gold daisies, and a
long black velvet ribbon. Never had she imagined she could look like that. Is
mother right? she thought. And now she hoped her mother was right. Am I
being extravagant? Perhaps it was extravagant. Just for a moment she had
another glimpse of that poor woman and those little children, and the body
being carried into the house. But it all seemed blurred, unreal, like a picture
in the newspaper. I'll remember it again after the party's over, she decided.
And somehow that seemed quite the best plan. . . .

Lunch was over by half-past one. By half-past two they were all ready for 115
the fray. The green-coated band had arrived and was established in a corner of
the tennis-court.

"My dear!" trilled Kitty Maitland, "aren't they too like frogs for words? You 116
ought to have arranged them round the pond with the conductor in the middle
on a leaf."

Laurie arrived and hailed them on his way to dress. At the sight of him   117
Laura remembered the accident again. She wanted to tell him. If Laurie agreed
with the others, then it was bound to be all right. And she followed him into
the hall.

"Laurie!"   118

"Hallo!" He was half-way upstairs, but when he turned round and saw Laura   119
he suddenly puffed out his cheeks and goggled his eyes at her. "My word,
Laura! You do look stunning," said Laurie. "What an absolutely topping hat!"

Laura said faintly "Is it?" and smiled up at Laurie, and didn't tell him after   120
all.

Soon after that people began coming in streams. The band struck up;   121
the hired waiters ran from the house to the marquee. Wherever you looked
there were couples strolling, bending to the flowers, greeting, moving on over
the lawn. They were like bright birds that had alighted in the Sheridans' garden
for this one afternoon, on their way to—where? Ah, what happiness it is
to be with people who all are happy, to press hands, press cheeks, smile into
eyes.

"Darling Laura, how well you look!"   122

"What a becoming hat, child!"   123

"Laura, you look quite Spanish. I've never seen you look so striking."   124

And Laura, glowing, answered softly, "Have you had tea? Won't you have an   125
ice? The passion-fruit ices really are rather special." She ran to her father and
begged him. "Daddy darling, can't the band have something to drink?"

And the perfect afternoon slowly ripened, slowly faded, slowly its petals   126
closed.

"Never a more delightful garden-party . . ." "The greatest success . . ." "Quite   127
the most . . ."

Laura helped her mother with the good-byes. They stood side by side in the   128
porch till it was all over.

"All over, all over, thank heaven," said Mrs. Sheridan. "Round up the others,   129
Laura. Let's go and have some fresh coffee. I'm exhausted. "Yes, it's been very
successful. But oh, these parties, these parties! Why will you children insist on
giving parties!" And they all of them sat down in the deserted marquee.

"Have a sandwich, daddy dear. I wrote the flag."   130

"Thanks." Mr. Sheridan took a bite and the sandwich was gone. He took   131
another. "I suppose you didn't hear of a beastly accident that happened today?" he said.

"My dear," said Mrs. Sheridan, holding up her hand, "we did. It nearly ruined   132
the party. Laura insisted we should put it off."

"Oh, mother!" Laura didn't want to be teased about it.   133

"It was a horrible affair all the same," said Mr. Sheridan. "The chap was   134
married too. Lived just below in the lane, and leaves a wife and half a dozen
kiddies, so they say."

An awkward little silence fell. Mrs. Sheridan fidgeted with her cup. Really,   135
it was very tactless of father . . .

Suddenly she looked up. There on the table were all those sandwiches, cakes,   136
puffs, all uneaten, all going to be wasted. She had one of her brilliant ideas.

"I know," she said. "Let's make up a basket. Let's send that poor creature   137
some of this perfectly good food. At any rate, it will be the greatest treat for
the children. Don't you agree? And she's sure to have neighbours calling in and
so on. What a point to have it all ready prepared. Laura!" She jumped up. "Get
me the big basket out of the stairs cupboard."

"But, mother, do you really think it's a good idea?" said Laura.   138

Again, how curious, she seemed to be different from them all. To take scraps   139
from their party. Would the poor woman really like that?

"Of course! What's the matter with you to-day? An hour or two ago you   140
were insisting on us being sympathetic, and now——"

Oh, well! Laura ran for the basket. It was filled, it was heaped by her mother.   141

"Take it yourself, darling," said she. "Run down just as you are. No, wait,   142
take the arum lilies too. People of that class are so impressed by arum lilies."

"The stems will ruin her lace frock," said practical Jose.   143

So they would. Just in time. "Only the basket, then. And, Laura!"—her   144
mother followed her out of the marquee—"don't on any account——"

"What, mother?"   145

No, better not put such ideas into the child's head! "Nothing! Run along."   146

It was just growing dusky as Laura shut their garden gates. A big dog ran   147
by like a shadow. The road gleamed white, and down below in the hollow the
little cottages were in deep shade. How quiet it seemed after the afternoon.
Here she was going down the hill to somewhere where a man lay dead, and
she couldn't realize it. Why couldn't she? She stopped a minute. And it seemed
to her that kisses, voices, tinkling spoons, laughter, the smell of crushed grass
were somehow inside her. She had no room for anything else. How strange!
She looked up at the pale sky, and all she thought was, "Yes, it was the most
successful party."

Now the broad road was crossed. The lane began, smoky and dark. Women   148
in shawls and men's tweed caps hurried by. Men hung over the palings; the
children played in the doorways. A low hum came from the mean little cottages.
In some of them there was a flicker of light, and a shadow, crab-like, moved
across the window. Laura bent her head and hurried on. She wished now she
had put on a coat. How her frock shone! And the big hat with the velvet
streamer—if only it was another hat! Were the people looking at her? They
must be. It was a mistake to have come; she knew all along it was a mistake.
Should she go back even now?

No, too late. This was the house. It must be. A dark knot of people stood   149
outside. Beside the gate an old, old woman with a crutch sat in a chair, watching.

She had her feet on a newspaper. The voices stopped as Laura drew near. The group parted. It was as though she was expected, as though they had known she was coming here.

Laura was terribly nervous. Tossing the velvet ribbon over her shoulder, she said to a woman standing by, "Is this Mrs. Scott's house?" and the woman, smiling queerly, said, "It is, my lass." 150

Oh, to be away from this! She actually said, "Help me, God," as she walked up the tiny path and knocked. To be away from those staring eyes, or to be covered up in anything, one of those women's shawls even. I'll just leave the basket and go, she decided. I shan't even wait for it to be emptied. 151

Then the door opened. A little woman in black showed in the gloom. 152

Laura said, "Are you Mrs. Scott?" But to her horror the woman answered, "Walk in please, miss," and she was shut in the passage. 153

"No," said Laura, "I don't want to come in. I only want to leave this basket. Mother sent——" 154

The little woman in the gloomy passage seemed not to have heard her. "Step this way, please, miss," she said in an oily voice, and Laura followed her. 155

She found herself in a wretched little low kitchen, lighted by a smoky lamp. There was a woman sitting before the fire. 156

"Em," said the little creature who had let her in. "Em! It's a young lady." She turned to Laura. She said meaningly, "I'm 'er sister, miss. You'll excuse 'er, won't you?" 157

"Oh, but of course!" said Laura. "Please, please don't disturb her. I——I only want to leave——" 158

But at that moment the woman at the fire turned round. Her face, puffed up, red, with swollen eyes and swollen lips, looked terrible. She seemed as though she couldn't understand why Laura was there. What did it mean? Why was this stranger standing in the kitchen with a basket? What was it all about? And the poor face puckered up again. 159

"All right, my dear," said the other. "I'll thenk the young lady." 160

And again she began, "You'll excuse her, miss, I'm sure," and her face, swollen too, tried an oily smile. 161

Laura only wanted to get out, to get away. She was back in the passage. The door opened. She walked straight through into the bedroom, where the dead man was lying. 162

"You'd like a look at 'im, wouldn't you?" said Em's sister, and she brushed past Laura over to the bed. "Don't be afraid, my lass——" and now her voice sounded fond and sly, and fondly she drew down the sheet——"'e looks a picture. There's nothing to show. Come along, my dear." 163

Laura came. 164

There lay a young man, fast asleep——sleeping so soundly, so deeply, that he was far, far away from them both. Oh, so remote, so peaceful. He was dreaming. 165

Never wake him up again. His head was sunk in the pillow, his eyes were closed; they were blind under the closed eyelids. He was given up to his dream. What did garden-parties and baskets and lace frocks matter to him? He was far from all those things. He was wonderful, beautiful. While they were laughing and while the band was playing, this marvel had come to the lane. Happy . . . happy . . . All is well, said that sleeping face. This is just as it should be. I am content.

But all the same you had to cry, and she couldn't go out of the room without saying something to him. Laura gave a loud childish sob.   166

"Forgive my hat," she said.   167

And this time she didn't wait for Em's sister. She found her way out of the   168
door, down the path, past all those dark people. At the corner of the lane she met Laurie.

He stepped out of the shadow. "Is that you, Laura?"   169

"Yes."   170

"Mother was getting anxious. Was it all right?"   171

"Yes, quite. Oh, Laurie!" She took his arm, she pressed up against him.   172

"I say, you're not crying, are you?" asked her brother.   173

Laura shook her head. She was.   174

Laurie put his arm round her shoulder. "Don't cry," he said in his warm,   175
loving voice. "Was it awful?"

"No," sobbed Laura. "It was simply marvellous. But, Laurie—" She stopped,   176
she looked at her brother. "Isn't life," she stammered, "isn't life—" But what life was she couldn't explain. No matter. He quite understood.

"*Isn't* it, darling?" said Laurie.   177

Questions for Critical Thinking

1. Who is the central consciousness of the narration? What does he or she add to the story?

2. Why does the author go into such detail about the decorations, music, and food of the garden party? How are these details related to the plot and theme of the story?

3. What is Mrs. Sheridan's reaction to the tragedy taking place in the laborer's cottage? How does her reaction compare or contrast with the reactions of people today to similar situations? Use an example to explain your answer.

4. What is your attitude toward expensive parties that are part of the American tradition, such as senior proms? Are they worth the money involved or could students have just as much fun spending less money?

5. Imagine yourself a member of the Sheridan family hearing the news about the young laborer thrown to his death. What behavior or action would you advise? Be specific in your answer.

6. In a sense, Laura is attracted to people who are beneath her in economic class. Where in the story is this attraction indicated? Refer to specific passages.

7. How would Karl Marx view the carter's family in relationship to the Sheridans? How would José Ortega y Gasset view the two? Which view is closest to your own?

8. What comment is made about life in the final paragraphs of the story? How well does the story illumine its theme? Give reasons for your answer.

Writing Assignment

Write an essay listing the disadvantages of being rich.

Writing Advice

Your assignment is clearcut and limited. Do not be tempted to draw a comparison or contrast between being rich and being poor, for doing so would go beyond the boundaries of the assignment, which simply asks you to stick to the disadvantages of being rich.

Your first reaction may be to think of wealth as having no disadvantages. Not so, however, as proved by the suicides of many wealthy people who obviously never attained happiness or inner peace in spite of their riches. What you need is to focus on those aspects of wealth that may shackle personal freedom, limit spiritual growth, or hinder intimacy between people. For example, you might decide that Donald Trump serves as an example of a person whose wealth ruined his ability to remain close to his wife and children. You could speculate that acquiring entities became such an obsession with him that he never had enough but had to keep acquiring more high-rise apartments, more hotels, more yachts, and so forth. As material luxuries became his god, his family somehow took second place, behind the glamorous women who longed for his presence and money—at least that is what newspaper headlines seemed to indicate. Your point could be that money's ability to buy almost everything but inner peace leaves the rich person at the mercy of a multitude of temptations not felt by the poor. What we are emphasizinge here is that this essay lends itself well to the use of examples to prove your major points. Just keep the following in mind about examples:

First, examples must be smaller than the point they prove. Consider this student writing:

Great wealth can be burdensome. For example, acquisitions can be oppressive.

The example is not an example at all but simply a repetition of the main point. Here is an improved version:

Great wealth can be burdensome. For example, servants must be supervised; yachts must be kept in repair; and vacation homes must be secured.

Second, examples must be relevant, proving the point in question. Here is a passage that makes use of an irrelevant example:

> Great wealth is an impediment to spiritual growth, as can be seen in the life of the shah of Iran, who sat on a peacock throne while the poor Iranian peasants starved in the fields.

The fact that Muhammad Reza Pahlevi, shah of Iran, had a ceremonial throne does not mean that he lacked spirituality. From all historical records, the shah was a religious man, who prayed and meditated daily. In 1963, he launched a reform program that included land redistribution to the peasants, the promotion of literacy, and the emancipation of women. To prove that his wealth hindered his spirituality would take more than the peacock throne example.

Last, examples should be vivid, especially if you are choosing an anecdote. Follow Mansfield's style of marshaling details and dialogue to enhance the narration.

Alternate Writing Assignments

1. Write an essay arguing for greater awareness and sensitivity on the part of the rich toward the poor.

2. Write an essay contrasting two present-day nations, one wealthy and one poor. Be sure to clarify the bases of your contrast.

LITERATURE

BATTLE ROYAL
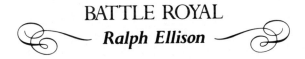
Ralph Ellison

Ralph Ellison (b. 1914) is an American novelist whose reputation is based on one novel, *Invisible Man* (1952), considered a classic because it tells of the author's own harrowing experiences as a black man in the South. Born in Oklahoma City, Ellison studied music for three years at Tuskegee Institute in Alabama, a school founded by Booker T. Washington. In 1936, Ellison went to New York City, where he met two other black writers, Langston Hughes and Richard Wright, who influenced him to work with the Federal Writers Project. In 1942, he became editor of *Negro Quarterly* and also published some short stories and essays in magazines such as *New Challenge,* and *New Masses.* In 1970, Ellison was appointed Albert Schweitzer Professor of Humanities at New York University. He has never published another novel, and his short stories remain uncollected despite the fact that they are frequently anthologized.

Reading Advice

All of us recall hearing or reading about fraternity initiations where novices were forced to perform humiliating acts in order to be accepted into the fraternity. This story is about a much grimmer initiation ritual—that of being initiated into a life of repression by certain dominant social forces. The narrator is a young black man living in the South, where white men treat him as if he were little better than an animal. It is the narrator's mental and emotional progress you observe as he details the racking experience of trying to find a place for himself in a hostile environment controlled by hypocritical, lecherous white males. Notice also that the narrator is closely linked to his grandfather, whose dying words add momentum to the story. As you read, remember that the incident is being recreated 20 years after it happened. You need to ask yourself how these 20 years have changed the narrator's views about the situation. What discoveries has he made during the intervening decades? Ask yourself whether your society is free of the kind of prejudice revealed in this story, or does it simply masque its prejudice more subtly?

*I*t goes a long way back, some twenty   1
years. All my life I had been looking for something, and everywhere I turned someone tried to tell me what it was. I accepted their answers too, though they were often in contradiction and even self-contradictory. I was naïve. I was looking for myself and asking everyone except myself questions which I, and only I, could answer. It took me a long time and much painful boomeranging of my expectations to achieve a realization everyone else appears to have been born with: That I am nobody but myself. But first I had to discover that I am an invisible man!

And yet I am no freak of nature, nor of history. I was in the cards, other   2
things having been equal (or unequal) eighty-five years ago. I am not ashamed of my grandparents for having been slaves. I am only ashamed of myself for having at one time been ashamed. About eighty-five years ago they were told they were free, united with others of our country in everything pertaining to the common good, and, in everything social, separate like the fingers of the hand. And they believed it. They exulted in it. They stayed in their place, worked hard, and brought up my father to do the same. But my grandfather is the one. He was an odd old guy, my grandfather, and I am told I take after him. It was he who caused the trouble. On his deathbed he called my father to him and said, "Son, after I'm gone I want you to keep up the good fight. I never told you, but our life is a war and I have been a traitor all my born days, a spy in the enemy's country ever since I give up my gun back in the Reconstruction. Live with your head in the lion's mouth. I want you to overcome

'em with yeses, undermine 'em with grins, agree 'em to death and destruction, let 'em swoller you till they vomit or bust wide open." They thought the old man had gone out of his mind. He had been the meekest of men. They younger children were rushed from the room, the shades drawn and the flame of the lamp turned so low that it sputtered on the wick like the old man's breathing. "Learn it to the younguns," he whispered fiercely; then he died.

But my folks were more alarmed over his last words than over his dying. It was as though he had not died at all, his words caused so much anxiety. I was warned emphatically to forget what he had said and, indeed, this is the first time it has been mentioned outside the family circle. It had a tremendous effect upon me, however. I could never be sure of what he meant. Grandfather had been a quiet old man who never made any trouble, yet on his deathbed he had called himself a traitor and a spy, and he had spoken of his meekness as a dangerous activity. It became a constant puzzle which lay unanswered in the back of my mind. And whenever things went well for me I remembered my grandfather and felt guilty and uncomfortable. It was as though I was carrying out his advice in spite of myself. And to make it worse, everyone loved me for it. I was praised by the most lily-white men in town. I was considered an example of desirable conduct—just as my grandfather had been. And what puzzled me was that the old man had defined it as *treachery.* When I was praised for my conduct I felt a guilt that in some way I was doing something that was really against the wishes of the white folks, that if they had understood they would have desired me to act just the opposite, that I should have been sulky and mean, and that that really would have been what they wanted, even though they were fooled and thought they wanted me to act as I did. It made me afraid that some day they would look upon me as a traitor and I would be lost. Still I was more afraid to act any other way because they didn't like that at all. The old man's words were like a curse. On my graduation day I delivered an oration in which I showed that humility was the secret, indeed, the very essence of progress. (Not that I believed this—how could I, remembering my grandfather?—I only believed that it worked.) It was a great success. Everyone praised me and I was invited to give the speech at a gathering of the town's leading white citizens. It was a triumph for the whole community.

It was in the main ballroom of the leading hotel. When I got there I discovered that it was on the occasion of a smoker, and I was told that since I was to be there anyway I might as well take part in the battle royal to be fought by some of my schoolmates as part of the entertainment. The battle royal came first.

All of the town's big shots were there in their tuxedoes, wolfing down the buffet foods, drinking beer and whiskey and smoking black cigars. It was a large room with a high ceiling. Chairs were arranged in neat rows around three sides of a portable boxing ring. The fourth side was clear, revealing a gleaming of space of polished floor. I had some misgivings over the battle royal, by the way. Not from a distaste for fighting but because I didn't care too much for the other fellows who were to take part. They were tough guys who seemed to have no grandfather's curse worrying their minds. No could mistake their toughness. And besides, I suspected that fighting a battle royal might detract from the dignity of my speech. In those pre-invisible days I visualized myself as a potential Booker T. Washington. But the other fellows didn't care too much for me either, and there were nine of them. I felt superior to them in my way, and I didn't like the manner in which we were all crowded together in the servants' elevator. Nor did they like my being there. In fact, as the warmly lighted floors flashed past the elevator we had words over the fact that I, by taking part in the fight, had knocked one of their friends out of a night's work.

We were led out of the elevator through a rococo hall into an anteroom   6 and told to get into our fighting togs. Each of us was issued a pair of boxing gloves and ushered out into the big mirrored hall, which we entered looking cautiously about us and whispering, lest we might accidentally be heard above the noise of the room. It was foggy with cigar smoke. And already the whiskey was taking effect. I was shocked to see some of the most important men of the town quite tipsy. They were all there—bankers, lawyers, judges, doctors, fire chiefs, teachers, merchants. Even one of the more fashionable pastors. Something we could not see was going on up front. A clarinet was vibrating sensuously and the men were standing up and moving eagerly forward. We were a small tight group, clustered together, our bare upper bodies touching and shining with anticipatory sweat; while up front the big shots were becoming increasingly excited over something we still could not see. Suddenly I heard the school superintendent, who had told me to come, yell, "Bring up the shines, gentlemen! Bring up the little shines!"

We were rushed up to the front of the ballroom, where it smelled even   7 more strongly of tobacco and whiskey. Then we were pushed into place. I almost wet my pants. A sea of faces, some hostile, some amused, ringed around us, and in the center, facing us, stood a magnificent blonde—stark naked. There was dead silence. I felt a blast of cold air chill me. I tried to back away, but they were behind me and around me. Some of the boys stood with lowered heads, trembling. I felt a wave of irrational guilt and fear. My teeth chattered, my skin turned to goose flesh, my knees knocked. Yet I was strongly attracted and looked in spite of myself. Had the price of looking been blindness, I would have looked. The hair was yellow like that of a circus kewpie doll, the face heavily powdered and rouged, as though to form an abstract mask, the eyes hollow and smeared a cool blue, the color of a baboon's butt. I felt a desire to spit upon her as my eyes brushed slowly over her body. Her breasts were firm and round as the domes of East Indian temples, and I stood so close as to see the fine skin texture and beads of pearly perspiration glistening like dew around the pink and erected buds of her nipples. I wanted at one and the same time to run from the room, to sink through the floor, or go to her and cover her from my eyes and the eyes of the others with my body; to feel the soft thighs, to caress her and destroy her, to love her and to murder her, to hide from her, and yet to stroke where below the small American flag tattooed upon her belly her thighs formed a capital V. I had a notion that of all in the room she saw only me with her impersonal eyes.

And then she began to dance, a slow sensuous movement; the smoke of a   8
hundred cigars clinging to her like the thinnest of veils. She seemed like a fair bird-girl girdled in veils calling to me from the angry surface of some gray and threatening sea. I was transported. Then I became aware of the clarinet playing and the big shots yelling at us. Some threatened us if we looked and others if we did not. On my right I saw one boy faint. And now a man grabbed a silver pitcher from a table and stepped close as he dashed ice water upon him and stood him up and forced two of us to support him as his head hung and moans issued from his thick bluish lips. Another boy began to plead to go home. He was the largest of the group, wearing dark red fighting trunks much too small to conceal the erection which projected from him as though in answer to the insinuating low-registered moaning of the clarinet. He tried to hide himself with his boxing gloves.

And all the while the blonde continued dancing, smiling faintly at the big   9
shots who watched her with fascination, and faintly smiling at our fear. I noticed a certain merchant who followed her hungrily, his lips loose and drooling. He was a large man who wore diamond studs in a shirtfront which swelled with the ample paunch underneath, and each time the blonde swayed her undulating hips he ran his hand through the thin hair of his bald head and, with his arms upheld, his posture clumsy like that of an intoxicated panda, wound his belly in a slow and obscene grind. This creature was completely hypnotized. The music had quickened. As the dancer flung herself about with a detached expression on her face, the men began reaching out to touch her. I could see their beefy fingers sink into her soft flesh. Some of the others tried to stop them and she began to move around the floor in graceful circles, as they gave chase, slipping and sliding over the polished floor. It was mad. Chairs went crashing, drinks were spilt, as they ran laughing and howling after her. They caught her just as she reached a door, raised her from the floor, and tossed her as college boys are tossed at a hazing, and above her red, fixed-smiling lips I saw the terror and disgust in her eyes, almost like my own terror and that which I saw in some of the other boys. As I watched, they tossed her twice and her soft breasts seemed to flatten against the air and her legs flung wildly as she spun. Some of the more sober ones helped her to escape. And I started off the floor, heading for the anteroom with the rest of the boys.

Some were still crying and in hysteria. But as we tried to leave we were   10
stopped and ordered to get into the ring. There was nothing to do but what

we were told. All ten of us climbed under the ropes and allowed ourselves to
be blindfolded with broad bands of white cloth. One of the men seemed to
feel a bit sympathetic and tried to cheer us up as we stood with our backs
against the ropes. Some of us tried to grin. "See that boy over there?" one of
the men said. "I want you to run across at the bell and give it to him right in
the belly. If you don't get him, I'm going to get you. I don't like his looks."
Each of us was told the same. The blindfolds were put on. Yet even then I had
been going over my speech. In my mind each word was as bright as a flame.
I felt the cloth pressed into place, and frowned so that it would be loosened
when I relaxed.

But now I felt a sudden fit of blind terror. I was unused to darkness. It was   11
as though I had suddenly found myself in a dark room filled with poisonous
cottonmouths. I could hear the bleary voices yelling insistently for the battle
royal to begin.

"Get going in there!"   12

"Let me at that big nigger!"   13

I strained to pick up the school superintendent's voice, as though to squeeze   14
some security out of that slightly more familiar sound.

"Let me at those black sonsabitches!" someone yelled.   15

"No, Jackson, no!" another voice yelled. "Here, somebody, help me hold   16
Jack."

"I want to get at that ginger-colored nigger. Tear him limb from limb," the   17
first voice yelled.

I stood against the ropes trembling. For in those days I was what they called   18
ginger-colored, and he sounded as though he might crunch me between his
teeth like a crisp ginger cookie.

Quite a struggle was going on. Chairs were being kicked about and I could   ·19
hear voices grunting as with terrific effort. I wanted to see, to see more
desperately than ever before. But the blindfold was as tight as a thick skin-
puckering scab and when I raised my gloved hands to push the layers of white
aside a voice yelled, "Oh, no you don't, black bastard! Leave that alone!"

"Ring the bell before Jackson kills him a coon!" someone boomed in the   20
sudden silence. And I heard the bell clang and the sound of the feet scuffling
forward.

A glove smacked against my head. I pivoted, striking out stiffly as someone   21
went past, and felt the jar ripple along the length of my arm to my shoulder.
Then it seemed as though all nine of the boys had turned upon me at once.
Blows pounded me from all sides while I struck out as best I could. So many
blows landed upon me that I wondered if I were not the only blindfolded
fighter in the ring, or if the man called Jackson hadn't succeeded in getting me
after all.

Blindfolded, I could not longer control my motions. I had no dignity. I   22
stumbled about like a baby or a drunken man. The smoke had become thicker

and with each new blow it seemed to sear and further restrict my lungs. My saliva became like hot bitter glue. A glove connected with my head, filling my mouth with warm blood. It was everywhere. I could not tell if the moisture I felt upon by body was sweat or blood. A blow landed hard against the nape of my neck. I felt myself going over, my head hitting the floor. Streaks of blue light filled the black world behind the blindfold. I lay prone, pretending that I was knocked out, but felt myself seized by hands and yanked to my feet. "Get going, black boy! Mix it up!" My arms were like lead, my head smarting from blows. I managed to feel my way to the ropes and held on, trying to catch my breath. A glove landed in my midsection and I went over again, feeling as though the smoke had become a knife jabbed into my guts. Pushed this way and that by the legs milling around me, I finally pulled erect and discovered that I could see the black, sweat-washed forms weaving in the smoky-blue atmosphere like drunken dancers weaving to the rapid drum-like thuds of blows.

Everyone fought hysterically. It was complete anarchy. Everybody fought   23
everybody else. No group fought together for long. Two, three, four, fought one, then turned to fight each other, were themselves attacked. Blows landed below the belt and in the kidney, with the gloves open as well as closed, and with my eye partly opened now there was not so much terror. I moved carefully, avoiding blows, although not too many to attract attention, fighting group to group. The boys groped about like blind, cautious crabs crouching to protect their midsections, their heads pulled in short against their shoulders, their arms stretched nervously before them, with their fists testing the smoke-filled air like the knobbed feelers of hypersensitive snails. In one corner I glimpsed a boy violently punching the air and heard him scream in pain as he smashed his hand against a ring post. For a second I saw him bent over holding his hand, then going down as a blow caught his unprotected head. I played one group against the other, slipping in and throwing a punch then stepping out of range while pushing the others into the melee to take the blows blindly aimed at me. The smoke was agonizing and there were no rounds, no bells at three minute intervals to relieve our exhaustion. The room spun round me, a swirl of lights, smoke, sweating bodies surrounded by tense white faces. I bled from both nose and smoke, the blood spattering upon my chest.

The men kept yelling, "Slug him, black boy! Knock his guts out!"   24

"Uppercut him! Kill him! Kill that big boy!"   25

Taking a fake fall, I saw a boy going down heavily beside me as though we   26
were felled by a single blow, saw a sneaker-clad foot shoot into his groin as the two who had knocked him down stumbled upon him. I rolled out of range, feeling a twinge of nausea.

The harder we fought the more threatening the men became. And yet, I   27
had begun to worry about my speech again. How would it go? Would they recognize my ability? What would they give me?

I was fighting automatically when suddenly I noticed that one after another   28
of the boys was leaving the ring. I was surprised, filled with panic, as though
I had been left alone with an unknown danger. Then I understood. The boys
had arranged it among themselves. It was the custom for the two men left in
the ring to slug it out for the winner's prize. I discovered this too late. When
the bell sounded two men in tuxedoes leaped into the ring and removed the
blindfold. I found myself facing Tatlock, the biggest of the gang. I felt sick at
my stomach. Hardly had the bell stopped ringing in my ears than it clanged
again and I saw him moving swiftly toward me. Thinking of nothing else to do
I hit him smash on the nose. He kept coming, bringing the rank sharp violence
of stale sweat. His face was a black blank of a face, only his eyes alive—with
hate of me and aglow with a feverish terror from what had happened to us
all. I became anxious. I wanted to deliver my speech and he came at me as
though he meant to beat it out of me. I smashed him again and again, taking
his blows as they came. Then on a sudden impulse I struck him lightly and we
clinched. I whispered, "Fake like I knocked you out, you can have the prize."

"I'll break your behind," he whispered hoarsely.   29

"For *them*?"   30

"For *me*, sonabitch!"   31

They were yelling for us to break it up and Tatlock spun me half around   32
with a blow, and as a joggled camera sweeps in a reeling scene, I saw the
howling red faces crouching tense beneath the cloud of blue-gray smoke. For
a moment the world wavered, unraveled, flowed, then my head cleared and
Tatlock bounced before me. That fluttering shadow before my eyes was his
jabbing left hand. Then falling forward, my head against his damp shoulder, I
whispered,

"I'll make it five dollars more."   33

"Go to hell!"   34

But his muscles relaxed a trifle beneath my pressure and I breathed, "Seven?"   35

"Give it it to your ma," he said, ripping me beneath the heart.   36

And while I still held him I butted him and moved away. I felt myself   37
bombarded with punches. I fought back with hopeless desperation. I wanted
to deliver my speech more than anything else in the world, because I felt that
only these men could judge truly my ability, and now this stupid clown was
ruining my chances. I began fighting carefully now, moving in to punch him
and out again with my greater speed. A lucky blow to his chin and I had him
going too—until I heard a loud voice yell, "I got my money on the big boy."

Hearing this, I almost dropped my guard. I was confused: Should I try to   38
win against the voice out there? Would not this go against my speech, and was
not this a moment for humility, for nonresistance? A blow to my head as I
danced about sent my right eye popping like a jack-in-the-box and settled my
dilemma. The room went red as I fell. It was a dream fall, my body languid

and fastidious as to where to land, until the floor became impatient and smashed up to meet me. A moment later I came to. An hypnotic voice said FIVE emphatically. And I lay there, hazily watching a dark red spot of my own blood shaping itself into a butterfly, glistening and soaking into the soiled gray world of the canvas.

When the voice drawled TEN I was lifted up and dragged to a chair. I sat   39
dazed. My eye pained and swelled with each throb of my pounding heart and I wondered if now I would be allowed to speak. I was wringing wet, my mouth still bleeding. We were grouped along the wall now. The other boys ignored me as they congratulated Tatlock and speculated as to how much they would be paid. One boy whimpered over his smashed hand. Looking up front, I saw attendants in white jackets rolling the portable ring away and placing a small square rug in the vacant space surrounded by chairs. Perhaps, I thought, I will stand on the rug to deliver my speech.

Then the M.C. called to us, "Come on up here boys and get your money."   40

We ran forward to where the men laughed and talked in their chairs, waiting.   41
Everyone seemed friendly now.

"There it is on the rug," the man said. I saw the rug covered with coins of all dimensions and a few crumpled bills. But what excited me, scattered here and there, were the gold pieces.

"Boys, it's all yours," the man said. "You get all you grab."   42

"That's right, Sambo," a blond man said, winking at me confidentially.   43

I trembled with excitement, forgetting my pain. I would get the gold and   44
the bills, I thought. I would use both hands. I would throw my body against the boys nearest me to block them from the gold.

"Get down around the rug now," the man commanded, "and don't anyone   45
touch it until I give the signal."

"This ought to be good," I heard.   46

As told, we got around the square rug on our knees. Slowly the man raised   47
his freckled hand as we followed it upward with our eyes.

I heard, "These niggers look like they're about to pray!"   48

Then, "Ready," the man said. "Go!"   49

I lunged for a yellow coin lying on the blue design of the carpet, touching   50
it and sending a surprised shriek to join those around me. I tried frantically to remove my hand but could not let go. A hot, violent force tore through my body, shaking me like a wet rat. The rug was electrified. The hair bristled up on my head as I shook myself free. My muscles jumped, my nerves jangled, writhed. But I saw that this was not stopping the other boys. Laughing in fear and embarrassment, some were holding back and scooping up the coins knocked off by the painful contortions of others. The men roared above us as we struggled.

"Pick it up, goddamnit, pick it up!" someone called like a bass-voiced parrot.   51
"Go on, get it!"

I crawled rapidly around the floor, picking up the coins, trying to avoid the   52
coppers and to get greenbacks and the gold. Ignoring the shock by laughing,
as I brushed the coins off quickly, I discovered that I could contain the electricity—a contradiction but it works. Then the men began to push us onto
the rug. Laughing embarrassedly, we struggled out of their hands and kept after
the coins. We were all wet and slippery and hard to hold. Suddenly I saw a
boy lifted into the air, glistening with sweat like a circus seal, and dropped, his
wet back landing flush upon the charged rug, heard him yell and saw him
literally dance upon his back, his elbows beating a frenzied tattoo upon the
floor, his muscles twitching like the flesh of a horse stung by many flies. When
he finally rolled off, his face was gray and no one stopped him when he ran
from the floor amid booming laughter.

"Get the money," the M.C. called. "That's good hard American cash!"   53

And we snatched and grabbed, snatched and grabbed. I was careful not to   54
come too close to the rug now, and when I felt the hot whiskey breath descend
upon me like a cloud of foul air I reached out and grabbed the leg of a chair.
It was occupied and I held on desperately.

"Leggo, nigger! Leggo!"   55

The huge face wavered down to mine as he tried to push me free. But my   56
body was slippery and he was too drunk. It was Mr. Colcord, who owned a
chain of movie houses and "entertainment palaces." Each time he grabbed me
I slipped out of his hands. It became a real struggle. I feared the rug more than
I did the drunk, so I held on, surprising myself for a moment by trying to
topple *him* upon the rug. It was such an enormous idea that I found myself
actually carrying it out. I tried not to be obvious, yet when I grabbed his leg,
trying to tumble him out of the chair, he raised up roaring with laughter, and,
looking at me with soberness dead in the eye, kicked me viciously in the chest.
The chair flew out of my hand and I felt myself going and rolled. It was as
though I had rolled through a bed of hot coals. It seemed a whole century
would pass before I would roll free, a century in which I was seared through
the deepest levels of my body to the fearful breath within me and the breath
seared and heated to the point of explosion. It'll all be over in a flash, I thought
as I rolled clear. It'll all be over in a flash.

But not yet, the men on the other side were waiting, red faces swollen as   57
though from apoplexy as they bent forward in their chairs. Seeing their fingers
coming toward me I rolled away as a fumbled football rolls off the receiver's
fingertips, back into the coals. That time I luckily sent the rug sliding out of
place and heard the coins ringing against the floor and the boys scuffling to
pick them up and the M.C. calling, "All right, boys, that's all. Go get dressed
and get your money."

I was limp as a dish rag. My back felt as though it had been beaten with   58
wires.

When we had dressed the M.C. came in and gave us each five dollars, except   59

Tatlock, who got ten for being the last in the ring. Then he told us to leave. I was not to get a chance to deliver my speech, I thought. I was going out into the dim alley in despair when I was stopped and told to go back. I returned to the ballroom, where the men were pushing back their chairs and gathering in small groups to talk.

The M.C. knocked on a table for quiet. "Gentlemen," he said, "we almost   60 forgot an important part of the program. A most serious part, gentlemen. This boy was brought here to deliver a speech which he made at his graduation yesterday . . ."

"Bravo!"   61

"I'm told that he is the smartest boy we've got out there in Greenwood.   62 I'm told that he knows more big words than a pocket-sized dictionary."

Much applause and laughter.   63

"So now, gentlemen, I want you to give him your attention."   64

There was still laughter as I faced them, my mouth dry, my eyes throbbing.   65 I began slowly, but evidently my throat was tense, because they began shouting, "Louder! Louder!"

"We of the younger generation extol the wisdom of that great leader and   66 educator," I shouted, "who first spoke these flaming words of wisdom: 'A ship lost at sea for many days suddenly sighted a friendly vessel. From the mast of the unfortunate vessel was seen a signal: 'Water, water; we die of thirst!" The answer from the friendly vessel came back: "Cast down your bucket where you are." The captain of the distressed vessel, at last heeding the injunction, cast down his bucket, and it came up full of fresh sparkling water from the mouth of the Amazon River.' And like him I say, and in his words, 'To those of my race who depend upon bettering their condition in a foreign land, or who underestimate the importance of cultivating friendly relations with the Southern white man, who is his next-door neighbor, I would say: "Cast down your bucket where you are"—cast it down in making friends in every manly way of the people of all races by whom we are surrounded . . .' "

I spoke automatically and with such fervor that I did not realize that the   67 men were still talking and laughing until my dry mouth, filling up with blood from the cut, almost strangled me. I coughed, wanting to stop and go to one of the tall brass, sand-filled spittoons to relieve myself, but a few of the men, especially the superintendent, were listening and I was afraid. So I gulped it down, blood, saliva and all, and continued. (What powers of endurance I had during those days! What enthusiasm! What a belief in the rightness of things!) I spoke even louder in spite of the pain. But still they talked and still they laughed, as though deaf with cotton in dirty ears. So I spoke with greater emotional emphasis. I closed my ears and swallowed blood until I was nauseated. The speech seemed a hundred times as long as before, but I could not leave out a single word. All had to be said, each memorized nuance considered, rendered. Nor was that all. Whenever I uttered a word of three or more syllables

a group of voices would yell for me to repeat it. I used the phrase "social
responsibility" and they yelled:

"What's the word you say, boy?"   68

"Social responsibility," I said.   69

"What?"   70

"Social . . ."   71

"Louder."   72

". . . responsibility."   73

"More!"   74

"Respon—"   75

"Repeat!"   76

"—sibility."   77

The room filled with the uproar of laughter until, no doubt, distracted by   78
having to gulp down my blood, I made a mistake and yelled a phrase I had
often seen denounced in newspaper editorials, heard debated in private.

"Social . . ."   79

"What?" they yelled.   80

". . . equality—"   81

The laughter hung smokelike in the sudden stillness. I opened my eyes,   82
puzzled. Sounds of displeasure filled the room. The M.C. rushed forward. They
shouted hostile phrases at me. But I did not understand.

A small dry mustached man in the front row blared out, "Say that slowly,   83
son!"

"What, sir?"   84

"What you just said!"   85

"Social responsibility, sir," I said.   86

"You weren't being smart, were you boy?" he said, not unkindly.   87

"No, sir!"   88

"You sure that about 'equality' was a mistake?"   89

"Oh, yes, sir," I said. "I was swallowing blood."   90

"Well, you had better speak more slowly so we can understand. We mean   91
to do right by you, but you've got to know your place at all times. All right,
now, go on with your speech."

I was afraid. I wanted to leave but I wanted also to speak and I was afraid   92
they'd snatch me down.

"Thank you, sir," I said, beginning where I had left off, and having them   93
ignore me as before.

Yet when I finished there was a thunderous applause. I was surprised to see   94
the superintendent come forth with a package wrapped in white tissue paper,
and, gesturing for quiet, address the men.

"Gentlemen, you see that I did not overpraise the boy. He makes a good   95
speech and some day he'll lead his people in the proper paths. And I don't have
to tell you that this is important in these days and times. This is a good, smart

boy, and so to encourage him in the right direction, in the name of the Board of Education I wish to present him a prize in the form of this . . ."

He paused, removing the tissue paper and revealing a gleaming calfskin   96
briefcase.

". . . in the form of this first-class article from Shad Whitmore's shop."   97

"Boy," he said, addressing me, "take this prize and keep it well. Consider it   98
a badge of office. Prize it. Keep developing as you are and some day it will be filled with important papers that will help shape the destiny of your people."

I was so moved that I could hardly express my thanks. A rope of bloody   99
saliva forming a shape like an undiscovered continent drooled upon the leather and I wiped it quickly away. I felt an importance that I had never dreamed.

"Open it and see what's inside," I was told.   100

My fingers a-tremble, I complied, smelling fresh leather and finding an   101
official-looking document inside. It was a scholarship to the state college for Negroes. My eyes filled with tears and I ran awkwardly off the floor.

I was overjoyed; I did not even mind when I discovered the gold pieces I   102
had scrambled for were brass pocket tokens advertising a certain make of automobile.

When I reached home everyone was excited. Next day the neighbors came   103
to congratulate me. I even felt safe from grandfather, whose deathbed curse usually spoiled my triumphs. I stood beneath his photograph with my briefcase in hand and smiled triumphantly into his stolid black peasant's face. It was a face that fascinated me. The eyes seemed to follow everywhere I went.

That night I dreamed I was at a circus with him and that he refused to laugh   104
at the clowns no matter what they did. Then later he told me to open my briefcase and read what was inside and I did, finding an official envelope stamped with the state seal; and inside the envelope I found another and another, endlessly, and I thought I would fall of weariness. "Them's years," he said. "Now open that one." And I did and in it I found an engraved stamp containing a short message in letters of gold. "Read it," my grandfather said. "Out loud."

"To Whom It May Concern," I intoned. "Keep This Nigger-Boy Running."   105

I awoke with the old man's laughter ringing in my ears.   106

Questions for Critical Thinking

1. What is the function of the grandfather's dying words in this story? How does the narrator's dream about his grandfather tie in with those words?

2. What is your reaction to the behavior of the leading white citizens in the story? How would you expect such people to behave?

3. The narrator tells us that before discovering himself, he had to discover that he was an "invisible man." What is your interpretation of his invisibility?

4. What advice does the grandfather give for dealing with white supremacy? Express your judgment of the grandfather's attitude.

5. In what ways, if any, has the treatment of blacks by whites changed since the story was written?

6. What is the audience's reaction to the narrator's use of big words during his speech? What accounts for their reaction? What particular word immediately caused a hostile reaction? Why?

7. What is your opinion of the gift presented to the narrator in appreciation of his speech? Support your opinion with reasons.

8. In his graduation speech the narrator said that "humility was the secret, indeed, the very essence of progress." If you were asked to name the one quality that is most likely to guarantee progress, which quality would you choose? Give reasons for your choice.

9. What similarities can you find between the conditions described in "Making Sense of South Africa" (this chapter) and this story?

Writing Assignment

Read the following quotation, written in 1835 by Alexis de Tocqueville, a French aristocrat who visited the United States for some 18 months:

> *I see that in a certain portion of the territory of the United States at the present day, the legal barrier which separated the two races is tending to fall away, but not that which exists in the manners of the country. Slavery recedes, but the prejudice to which it has given birth remains stationary.*

—from ***Democracy in America***

Write an essay demonstrating either that few changes have taken place or that many changes have taken place since de Tocqueville made his observation of race relations in our country.

Writing Advice

The key words on which you must focus is *manners* and *prejudice*. Think about your own community and ask yourself this question: Do the manners of the community still reveal prejudices against blacks, or have blacks been fully accepted as equals with whites? Specific areas you may wish to explore are the following: employment opportunities, education, legal actions, medical treatment, interracial marriage, social activities, and church membership.

It is important that you take a definite stand after thinking about the topic assigned. Let us say you have decided that, contrary to de Tocqueville's view, prejudice against blacks in our society has not remained stationary, but has diminished considerably. (Do not dilute your opinion by pointing out certain vestiges of prejudice that manage to reveal themselves now and then.) Your essay will be crisper if you state your opinion candidly and support it with evidence. Without the proper evidence, your observations are bound to be unconvincing and perhaps even fatuous. Let us assume, for instance, that you have chosen to write about the receding prejudice against blacks in employment opportunities. What is your evidence? You might point with confidence to the fact that most large firms, whether private or public, have adopted rules of affirmative action to make sure that blacks are given a fair chance when they compete against whites applying for the same jobs. In fact, you may suggest that some whites are beginning to feel excluded from certain jobs, despite their excellent qualifications, because blacks get first crack at them. Use specific examples to enhance your position. One student, who had considerable experience working for fast-food chains, wrote that she applied for a job at a well-known chain, but was passed up in favor of an inexperienced black. Our point is that regardless of the position you take, evidence is the indispensable ingredient for its defense.

In sum, take a position, find evidence to support your position, and organize the evidence in some comprehensible way.

Alternate Writing Assignments

1. Write an essay describing an act of modern prejudice and analyze why the act occurred and how it could have been avoided.

2. Write an essay in which you show how racial and ethnic variety in a community can be an advantage.

LITERATURE

AN ELEMENTARY SCHOOL CLASSROOM IN A SLUM
Stephen Spender

Stephen Spender (b. 1909) is an English poet and critic. At Oxford University, where he received his education, he was identified with W. H. Auden, C. Day Lewis, and Louis MacNeice, who were considered poets inspired by social protest. His autobiography, *World Within World* (1951), is an accurate reflection of the social and political atmosphere in the 1930s. His poetry is a passionate argument against the evils of the modern world, with its industries and slums. Among the collections of his poetry are the following: *Twenty Poems* (1930), *The Still Centre* (1939), *Poems of Dedication* (1946), *The Edge of Being* (1949), *Collected Poems, 1928–1953* (1955), and *Selected Poems* (1964). His literary and social criticism can be found in *The Destructive Element* (1935), *Forward From Liberalism* (1937), *The Creative Element* (1953), and *The Making of a Poem* (1955). He also wrote one novel, *The Backward Son* (1940). In 1974 he published *Love-Hate Relations: English and American Sensibilities,* a work analyzing the literary relationship between England and the United States.

Reading Advice

Because this poem is compact, you will need to read and ponder it several times before you can extract the full meaning of its four stanzas. By simply presenting some startling images, the poet registers a social protest about the cramped and ugly conditions of a slum school. The tone of the poem is angry because the schoolchildren—frail, hungry, and tattered—must sit in a classroom where they learn about Shakespeare's dramatic worlds and exciting foreign countries while their own lives are spent in the prisons of poverty and despair, from which they will never be freed. By suggesting ironically that it is wrong to tempt these hopeless victims by teaching them about happier, more exciting places they can never hope to experience, the poet tries to gain the reader's sympathies to the cause of improving slum schools.

> *Far far from gusty waves, these children's faces.*
> *Like rootless weeds the torn hair round their paleness.*
> *The tall girl with her weighed-down head. The paper-*
> *seeming boy with rat's eyes. The stunted unlucky heir*
> *Of twisted bones, reciting a father's gnarled disease,*
> *His lesson from his desk. At back of the dim class,*
> *One unnoted, sweet and young: his eyes live in a dream*
> *Of squirrels' game, in tree room, other than this.*
>
> *On sour cream walls, donations. Shakespeare's head*
> *Cloudless at dawn, civilized dome riding all cities.*   10
> *Belled, flowery, Tyrolese valley. Open-handed map*
> *Awarding the world its world. And yet, for these*
> *Children, these windows, not this world, are world,*
> *Where all their future's painted with a fog,*
> *A narrow street sealed in with a lead sky,*
> *Far far from rivers, capes, and stars of words.*
>
> *Surely Shakespeare is wicked, the map a bad example*
> *With ships and sun and love tempting them to steal—*

For lives that slyly turn in their cramped holes
From fog to endless night? On their slag heap, these children   20
Wear skins peeped through by bones and spectacles of steel
With mended glass, like bottle bits in slag.
All of their time and space are foggy slum
So blot their maps with slums as big as doom.

Unless, governor, teacher, inspector, visitor,
This map becomes their window and these windows
That open on their lives like crouching tombs
Break, O break open, till they break the town
And show the children to the fields and all their world
Azure on their sands, to let their tongues   30
Run naked into books, the white and green leaves open
The history theirs whose language is the sun.

Questions for Critical Thinking

1. What images are found in stanza 1? Explain them by paraphrasing the stanza in your own words.

2. How attractive is this classroom?

3. What hope, if any, does the poem offer for the future of these children?

4. How does the poet achieve the angry tone of the poem? Is the tone justified?

Writing Assignment

Using Stephen Spender's ability to use vivid images as a model, write a description of an elementary school classroom as you remember it from childhood.

Writing Advice

All of us remember the elementary school we attended; somehow those memories are imprinted more clearly in our minds than later ones. So, take advantage of these indelible impressions and transfer them to paper. Here are some questions that may help jog your memory:

1. Where was your school located—in the country, in the suburbs, in the inner city? Give a specific location, such as: "The elementary school I attended was called 'Musterschule' (German for 'model school') and was nestled among elm trees at the top of a hill overlooking the center of Bern, the capital of Switzerland."

2. What did the classroom look like? Was it traditional or avant-garde? Was it drab or colorful? What kinds of artifacts, posters, or maps decorated the walls?

3. Think of your classmates and describe three or four of them. Here is an example: "The girl who occupied the desk directly behind me was a chubby, cherublike creature with perennially pink cheeks and black corkscrew curls dancing around her round face. She was always poking my back to ask me silly questions or to offer me peppermint chewing gum. . . ."

4. Who was your teacher? What mood did she or he create?

5. What kind of intellectual foundation did your elementary school provide?

Find some scheme by which to organize your essay. For instance, you might start with the outside of the school building and move inside to the classroom, which you can describe from front to back or from side to side. Then, describe the students and teacher. Finally, end by describing how well this class prepared you for the rigors of college.

Alternate Writing Assignment

Write an essay suggesting how society or the government can make sure that all children—even those in slums—receive a good elementary school education.

A R T

THE SWING

Jean Honoré Fragonard

About the Artist

Jean Honoré Fragonard (1732–1806) was a painter to the rich before, during, and after the French Revolution. No artist was better at representing the pomaded elegance of France in her most sensual moments. With his precocious talent, he became, at the age of 15, a pupil of Jean-Baptiste-Siméon Chardin, but grew to hate the master's repetitious still lives and moved on to become an assistant to Francois Boucher, whose frivolous representations of French life appealed to him. Fragonard's paintings soon won him the prestigious Prix de Rome, and with it King Louis XV's patronage. In 1761, he was elected to the Academy and was given a studio in the Louvre, which he maintained until he was thrown out by Napoleon in 1806, the year Fragonard died. Fragonard became a status symbol for the fashionable French, who used his paintings to decorate their boudoirs and salons. To overcome a reputation for frivolity and sensual pleasures, he got married and had a family; however, his respectability was all pretense, and scandal followed him, especially when he could not resist the attraction of his sister-in-law. During the Revolution, he managed to keep from being guillotined, but his paintings lost their popularity because his hedonistic themes were out of step with Napoleon's Age of Reason.

About the Art

This is an amorous world that Fragonard paints. He portrays romance with a great deal of sex appeal and glamour. In *The Swing,* one in a series of paintings about the course of love in the hearts of young girls, the artist seems to assume that passion or deep commitment are not nearly so important as playing the game of love according to the rules and etiquette of elegance and studied grace. In the painting, a young gallant has managed to get an old bishop to swing the subject of his attraction higher and higher while the gallant places himself in a strategic position to admire his sweetheart. The girl, of course, is perfectly aware of her charms as she coquettishly tosses one of her delicate shoes at the little statue of the god of discretion, who holds his finger to his lips as if to warn, "Now, now; don't go too far." The setting is a luxuriant, perfumed bower—completely appropriate for a secret rendezvous in a rococo world. But do the dark clouds in the background warn of revolution as a result of such frivolity?

A R T

THE THIRD-CLASS CARRIAGE
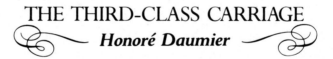
Honoré Daumier

About the Artist

Honoré Daumier (1808–1879) was a French lithographer and painter, who became a spokesman for the poor and their dreary lives, which he represented on canvas. Born in Marseilles, he moved to Paris when he was still a child and decided at the age of 17 to leave home and to choose art as a career. Without means of support, he lived in the gutter and in the Louvre, where he studied all of the great masters, especially Rembrandt and Michelangelo. He also spent hours painting from nature and modeling in clay and wax. At 21, having mastered lithography, he joined the staff of one of Paris's radical newspapers, for which he drew cartoons. He was forced to serve a term in jail for drawing a caricature of Louis-Philippe. Unrepentant, he returned from jail to continue his post on the newspaper. In 1848, the same year he married a seamstress, he took up oil painting, but was criticized as incompetent by the critics of the day. He continued stoically to paint, despite the public's initial lack of appreciation. In the end, his eyes failed him, and in his declining years he could not get 50 francs for a watercolor. He died without a penny to his name in a little house that the artist Jean-Baptiste Corot had anonymously taken for him.

About the Art

To move from Fragonard's *The Swing* to Daumier's *The Third-class Carriage* is to make the leap from the supremely wealthy class to the poverty-stricken class. Daumier could not afford professional models for his paintings, so he chose the working populace of Paris as his subjects. Avoiding heroic or fancy trappings, he trained his eye on the commonest elements of life—lowly travelers, poor laborers, and hungry farmers—all drawn with wonderful compassion. The greatest of his works is *The Third-class Carriage*, represented below. Compared with *The Swing*, it seems unfinished and dully monochromatic; yet, it is extremely moving in its portrayal of the dreary aspect of French life. The figures, crowded into the carriage, all have bulk—reflecting the heaviness of their burdensome lives. The colors in the painting run from the subtlest mixtures of deep reds and greens into a rich monochrome of brown. These are real people with sad faces. They are tired and have no time, save for labor and sighs. In this picture we see the poor as a separate class of suffering humanity.

7–1   *Jean Honoré Fragonard, The Swing, 1766. Approx. 35″ × 32.″ Reproduced by permission of the Trustees of the Wallace Collection, London.*

7–2   *Honoré Daumier,* The Third-Class Carriage, *c. 1862, 25 3/4" × 35 1/2." The Metropolitan Museum of Art, Bequest of Mrs. H. O. Havemeyer, 1929. The H. O. Havemeyer Collection. (29.100.129)*

Chapter Writing Assignments

Drawing on all of the information you have acquired from the readings and paintings in this chapter, choose one of the ideas below and use it as a springboard for an essay on class struggle.

1. Society is divided into two great classes: hosts and guests.

2. The history of society is basically a history of class struggle.

3. To believe in equality for everyone is not necessarily to believe that everyone is equally endowed by nature. The fact of unequal endowments is all the more reason to make sure that everyone has an equal opportunity, since otherwise the more gifted could become the oppressors of the less gifted.

4. The desire for private property has always been the major cause of exploiting and oppressing the most vulnerable elements of human society.

5. The masses must not be allowed to lead society; rather, that privilege should be granted to people of superior talents and brains. Let us not succumb to the egalitarian error.

6. Racial antipathies are generated predominantly by differences of acquired culture—language, dress, habits, morals, or religion. There is no cure for such antipathies except a broadened education. A knowledge of history, for instance, will teach that civilization is a cooperative product to which people of all kinds have contributed.

Be sure to refer to specific pieces anthologized in this chapter as well as to the paintings. Moreover, do not hesitate to consult other sources and to cite them in support of your thesis.

CHAPTER EIGHT

✿

What End Awaits?
DEATH AND IMMORTALITY

Five billion people now walk the face of the earth, surviving stragglers from a horde of some 100 billion estimated to have lived on our planet since the dawn of humanity. Gone forever are the other 95 billion souls—lusty, squabbling, opinionated, pious, and wicked—who once knew the warmth of our sun.

"What will happen to me when I die?" It is the one age-old question fussing parents dread being asked by their children at bedtime. It is a question that most of us have timorously whispered to our own parents during the ritualistic tucking-in, as the evening shadows quietly gather at bedside, reminding us of our inevitable and distant doom. What is death? What happens to us when we die? Do we simply smother under a crushing darkness, the unique self and inner light snuffed out by biological disintegration? Or does an immortal spark fly upward to persist in a different place, time, and context than our material minds can presently imagine? What will happen when we die?

There are two popular but contradictory answers. Accepted by the materialists is the one from biology, which insists that life and consciousness are strictly caused by organic forces. The picture they paint of death as final and irreversible dissolution is grim:

> You do not die all at once. Some tissues live on for minutes, even hours, giving still their cellular shrieks, molecular echoes of the agony of the whole corpus. Here and there a spray of nerves dances on. True, the heart stops; the blood no longer courses; the electricity of the brain sputters, then shuts down. Death is now pronounceable. But there are outposts where clusters of cells yet shine, besieged, little lights blinking in the advancing darkness. Doomed soldiers, they battle on. Until Death has secured the premises all to itself.
>
> **"The Corpse," from Mortal Lessons, Richard Selzer, M.D.**

The other, more hopeful, answer comes from the accounts of those who have suffered a near-death experience. Here is a typical story from one of these survivors:

> I got up and walked into the hall to go get a drink, and it was at that point, as they found out later, that my appendix ruptured. I became very weak, and I fell down. I began to feel a sort of drifting, a movement of my real being in and out of my body, and to hear beautiful music. I floated down the hall and out the door onto the screened-in porch. There, it almost seemed that clouds, a pink mist really, began to gather around me, and then I floated right straight on through the screen, just as though it weren't there, and up into this pure crystal light, an illuminating white light. It was beautiful and so bright, so radiant, but it didn't hurt my eyes. It's not any kind of light you can describe on earth. I didn't actually see a person in this light, and yet it has a special identity, it definitely does. It is a light of perfect understanding and perfect love.
>
> The thought came to my mind, "Lovest thou me?" This was not exactly in the form of a question, but I guess the connotation of what the light said was, "If you do love me, go back and complete what you began in your life." And all during this time, I felt as though I were surrounded by an overwhelming love and compassion.

"The Experience of Dying," quoted in Life After Life, Raymond Moody, M.D.

Many paradoxes, many mysteries attend death. To study philosophy is to learn how to die, insisted one thinker. Another speculated that no man ever faces his own death, since the knowledge of one's personal death presumes both subsequent consciousness and restoration to life. Such philosophical subtleties do not comfort some among us, who remain horrified to the end of their days by the thought of their bodies putrefying beneath the soil, gnawed down to a crust by eyeless worms. Others who have grown world-weary take the stoical view that eternal life on this earth would be futile and pointless. Condemned criminals facing execution have likewise reflected these dual attitudes. "I don't mind dying; I just don't want to know when," calmly muttered Caryl Chessman, a robber and rapist, just before his execution. Leanderess Riley, on the other hand, a half-blind and nearly deaf condemned murderer, fought the prison guards on the way to the gas chamber, shrieking passionately for life. Nearly all of us, except the suicidally depressed or the painfully ill, would prefer death to strike as a thief in the night, as we sleep, in some distant and unexpected instant.

Death seems to us most loathsome when it wantonly plunders young talent and promise. John Keats, the lyric poet, died of consumption at the age of 27, a time when most today have scarcely begun to flourish. John Kennedy was struck down by an assassin's bullet in his 46th year of a bountiful life. Wolfgang Amadeus Mozart died at 35, leaving behind a magnificent but incomplete *Requiem*. Such examples fill us with rage at the senseless waste of hope and youth. But the lamentation for what might have been, the longing for a glimpse of another sunrise is not cherished only by the young. Even the old and the humble wish for a few more days, sometimes for modest hopes and ambitions. "I want to see my magnolia tree blossom this spring," a nonagenarian whispered to us recently.

Perhaps it is humanity's instinctive hatred of death that has lead all cultures to conceive of a hereafter. The ancient Egyptians believed in a Hall of Double Maati in the Underworld, where all creatures appeared after death to have their hearts weighed against a feather before judgment by the God Osiris. The early Chinese and Indians looked forward to Nirvana, a state of supreme liberation and bliss, attained only by souls who had completed an appropriate number of deaths and rebirths in the cycle of samsara. In many Hindu myths, Death is pictured as a woman who represents desire and anger, and Nirvana the cessation of these passions. The early Greeks believed that only extraordinary heroes achieved an afterlife in the "Elysian Fields," a paradise on the very edge of the world in the Far West, where souls transformed into immortals could sport and cavort with the gods, feasting forever on nectar and ambrosia. Later, much later, Christianity introduced the doctrine of Eternal Judgment, preaching that after death all souls must face the judgment bar of God, answering for actions and thoughts recorded beside their names in the Book of Life.

What, then, are we to believe today about death? Various writers and artists, represented in this chapter, share with us their thoughts. In the philosophy section, Loren Eiseley focuses on little creatures from nature to show how all the living desperately cling to life. In his classic, *The Inferno*, Dante pictures a Hell where doomed souls suffer eternal punishment for earthly sins. The section ends with a sermon by John Haynes Holmes, who proposes ten logical reasons for believing in immortality.

In the history section, we offer an excerpt from Barbara Tuchman's historical account of the medieval plague in which millions perished. Next, Emily Carr poetically describes an Indian graveyard, while Anthony Brandt puzzles over the changed and contrasting personalities his grandmother and mother assumed in the face of mental decay and death.

In the literature section, Virginia Woolf narrates the moving account of the death struggles of a dying moth. Richard T. Gill's "The Code" is a short story about a young boy's experience with death and his subsequent religious doubts. The poet Dylan Thomas counsels his father to rage against death, while his counterpart, Edna St. Vincent Millay, defiantly voices her disapproval of consigning loving hearts to the cold ground.

As usual, the chapter ends with two art works. The first, a painting by Hans Baldung, portrays Death as a seductive male who reaches to embrace a young woman; the second, the panel of an altarpiece painted by Hubert and Jan van Eyck, depicts the horrors of hell which the damned must endure, and shows us glimpses of the glories of heaven, to be enjoyed by God's chosen.

What happens to us when we die? It is an old mystery, fleetingly pondered by every creature who has ever felt the warmth of our sun. If the materialists are right and death is the cessation of all personal identity and consciousness, there will be no posthumous triumph or revelation for anyone—not for the materialist, the spiritualist, the scoffer, or the devout believer. Only if there is an afterlife will we know the final truth and be either discomfited or vindicated. Otherwise, there shall only be the indifferent darkness.

PHILOSOPHY

THE BROWN WASPS
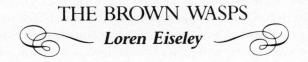
Loren Eiseley

Loren Eiseley (1907–1977) was an American anthropologist, archaeologist, essay writer, and poet. Before graduating from college, Eiseley rode the rails as a hobo, enjoying the freedom of studying nature in a nonacademic setting. After completing his graduate work at the University of Pennsylvania, he began a distinguished career as an anthropologist and archaeologist, publishing the results of his studies in a literary style that attracted readers in large and devoted numbers. He wrote poetically about nature and could make small incidents seem beautiful and philosophically significant. In his essays, such natural events as the mating of birds, the spinning of a spider web, or the activities of a fox become matters of inspiration. The essay below comes from the collection of essays, *Immense Journey* (1957). Among his many other books are *The Unexpected Universe* (1969), *The Invisible Pyramid* (1970), and *The Night Country* (1971).

Reading Advice

Eiseley's style is unabashedly poetic and graceful. An example of his mastery of the language can be found in his imagistic use of adjectives and adverbs that reveal in one word what a more prosaic writer might well take two sentences to tell. Consider these examples: the *painful* awkwardness with which the men's heads rest on the backs of the benches, the *apologetic* lurch of one old man, the dirt kicked *gaily* by the mouse, the *attentive* little eyes of the pigeons, the *shouting* workmen, or the *hard*, *bird* eye of youth. We are first alerted to Eiseley's theme by his rather curious statement: "I have spent the major portion of my life in the shade of a non-existent tree." We then learn that the tree had "taken root" in the author's mind as a familiar place to which he clings as he grows old, and that all of us have a hunger for such familiar places. Beginning with the displaced brown wasps who try to nest in a hive that has been abandoned, the essay tells a touching tale about all life's efforts to come to grips with its own mortality.

*T*here is a corner in the waiting room   1
of one of the great Eastern stations where women never sit. It is always in the shadow and overhung by rows of lockers. It is, however, always frequented— not so much by genuine travelers as by the dying. It is here that a certain element of the abandoned poor seeks a refuge out of the weather, clinging for

a few hours longer to the city that has fathered them. In a precisely similar
manner I have seen, on a sunny day in midwinter, a few old brown wasps creep
slowly over an abandoned wasp nest in a thicket. Numbed and forgetful and
frost-blackened, the hum of the spring hive still resounded faintly in their
sodden tissues. Then the temperature would fall and they would drop away
into the white oblivion of the snow. Here in the station it is in no way different
save that the city is busy in its snows. But the old ones cling to their seats as
though these were symbolic and could not be given up. Now and then they
sleep, their gray old heads resting with painful awkwardness on the backs of
the benches.

Also they are not at rest. For an hour they may sleep in the gasping exhaustion   2
of the ill-nourished and aged who have to walk in the night. Then a policeman
comes by on his round and nudges them upright.

"You can't sleep here," he growls.   3

A strange ritual then begins. An old man is difficult to waken. After a   4
muttered conversation the policeman presses a coin into his hand and passes
fiercely along the benches prodding and gesturing toward the door. In his wake,
like birds rising and settling behind the passage of a farmer through a cornfield,
the men totter up, move a few paces, and subside once more upon the benches.

One man, after a slight, apologetic lurch, does not move at all. Tubercularly   5
thin, he sleeps on steadily. The policeman does not look back. To him, too, this
has become a ritual. He will not have to notice it again officially for
another hour.

Once in a while one of the sleepers will not awake. Like the brown wasps,   6
he will have had his wish to die in the great droning center of the hive rather
than in some lonely room. It is not so bad here with the shuffle of footsteps
and the knowledge that there are others who share the bad luck of the world.
There are also the whistles and the sounds of everyone, everyone in the world,
starting on journeys. Amidst so many journeys somebody is bound to come
out all right. Somebody.

Maybe it was on a like thought that the brown wasps fell away from the old   7
paper nest in the thicket. You hold till the last, even if it is only to a public
seat in a railroad station. You want your place in the hive more than you want
a room or a place where the aged can be eased gently out of the way. It is the
place that matters, the place at the heart of things. It is life that you want, that
bruises your gray old head with the hard chairs; a man has a right to his place.

But sometimes the place is lost in the years behind us. Or sometimes it is   8
a thing of air, a kind of vaporous distortion above a heap of rubble. We cling
to a time and a place because without them man is lost, not only man but life.
This is why the voices, real or unreal, which speak from the floating trumpets
at spiritualist seances are so unnerving. They are voices out of nowhere whose
only reality lies in their ability to stir the memory of a living person with some

fragment of the past. Before the medium's cabinet both the dead and the living revolve endlessly about an episode, a place, an event that has already been engulfed by time.

This feeling runs deep in life; it brings stray cats running over endless miles, 9 and birds homing from the ends of the earth. It is as though all living creatures, and particularly the more intelligent, can survive only by fixing or transforming a bit of time into space or by securing a bit of space with its objects immortalized and made permanent in time. For example, I once saw, on a flower pot in my own living room, the efforts of a field mouse to build a remembered field. I have lived to see this episode repeated in a thousand guises, and since I have spent a large portion of my life in the shade of a nonexistent tree I think I am entitled to speak for the field mouse.

One day as I cut across the field which at that time extended on one side 10 of our suburban shopping center, I found a giant slug feeding from a runnel of pink ice cream in an abandoned Dixie cup. I could see his eyes telescope and protrude in a kind of dim uncertain ecstasy as his dark body bunched and elongated in the curve of the cup. Then, as I stood there at the edge of the concrete, contemplating the slug, I began to realize it was like standing on a shore where a different type of life creeps up and fumbles tentatively among the rocks and sea wrack. It knows its place and will only creep so far until something changes. Little by little as I stood there I began to see more of this shore that surrounds the place of man. I looked with sudden care and attention at things I had been running over thoughtlessly for years. I even waded out a short way into the grass and the wild-rose thickets to see more. A huge black-belted bee went droning by and there were some indistinct scurryings in the underbrush.

Then I came to a sign which informed me that this field was to be the site 11 of a new Wanamaker suburban store. Thousands of obscure lives were about to perish, the spores of puffballs would go smoking off to new fields, and the bodies of little white-footed mice would be crunched under the inexorable wheels of the bulldozers. Life disappears or modifies its appearances so fast that everything takes on an aspect of illusion—a momentary fizzing and boiling with smoke rings, like pouring dissident chemicals into a retort. Here man was advancing, but in a few years his plaster and bricks would be disappearing once more into the insatiable maw of the clover. Being of an archaeological cast of mind, I thought of this fact with an obscure sense of satisfaction and waded back through the rose thickets to the concrete parking lot. As I did so, a mouse scurried ahead of me, frightened of my steps if not of that ominous Wanamaker sign. I saw him vanish in the general direction of my apartment house, his little body quivering with fear in the great open sun on the blazing concrete. Blinded and confused, he was running straight away from his field. In another week scores would follow him.

I forgot the episode then and went home to the quiet of my living room. It   12
was not until a week later, letting myself into the apartment, that I realized I
had a visitor. I am fond of plants and had several ferns standing on the floor
in pots to avoid the noon glare by the south window.

As I snapped on the light and glanced carelessly around the room, I saw a   13
little heap of earth on the carpet and a scrabble of pebbles that had been kicked
merrily over the edge of one of the flower pots. To my astonishment I discovered a full-fledged burrow delving downward among the fern roots. I waited
silently. The creature who had made the burrow did not appear. I remembered
the wild field then, and the flight of the mice. No house mouse, no *Mus
domesticus,* had kicked up this little heap of earth or sought refuge under a fern
root in a flower pot. I thought of the desperate little creature I had seen fleeing
from the wild-rose thicket. Through intricacies of pipes and attics, he, or one
of his fellows, had climbed to this high green solitary room. I could visualize
what had occurred. He had an image in his head, a world of seed pods and
quiet, of green sheltering leaves in the dim light among the weed stems. It was
the only world he knew and it was gone.

Somehow in his flight he had fought his way to this room with drawn shades   14
where no one would come till nightfall. And here he had smelled green leaves
and run quickly up the flower pot to dabble his paws in common earth. He
had even struggled half the afternoon to carry his burrow deeper and had
failed. I examined the hole, but no whiskered twitching face appeared. He was
gone. I gathered up the earth and refilled the burrow. I did not expect to find
traces of him again.

Yet for three nights thereafter I came home to the darkened room and my   15
ferns to find the dirt kicked gaily about the rug and the burrow reopened,
though I was never able to catch the field mouse within it. I dropped a little
food about the mouth of the burrow, but it was never touched. I looked under
beds or sat reading with one ear cocked for rustlings in the ferns. It was all in
vain; I never saw him. Probably he ended in a trap in some other tenant's room.

But before he disappeared I had come to look hopefully for his evening   16
burrow. About my ferns there had begun to linger the insubstantial vapor of
an autumn field, the distilled essence, as it were, of a mouse brain in exile from
its home. It was a small dream, like our dreams, carried a long and weary
journey along pipes and through spider webs, past holes over which loomed
the shadows of waiting cats, and finally, desperately, into this room where he
had played in the shuttered daylight for an hour among the green ferns on the
floor. Every day these invisible dreams pass us on the street, or rise from
beneath our feet, or look out upon us from beneath a bush.

Some years ago the old elevated railway in Philadelphia was torn down and   17
replaced by a subway system. This ancient El with its barnlike stations containing
nut-vending machines and scattered food scraps had, for generations, been the

favorite feeding ground of flocks of pigeons, generally one flock to a station along the route of the El. Hundreds of pigeons were dependent upon the system. They flapped in and out of its stanchions and steel work or gathered in watchful little audiences about the feet of anyone who rattled the peanut-vending machines. They even watched people who jingled change in their hands, and prospected for food under the feet of the crowds who gathered between trains. Probably very few among the waiting people who tossed a crumb to an eager pigeon realized that this El was like a food-bearing river, and that the life which haunted its banks was dependent upon the running of the trains with their human freight.

I saw the river stop.   18

The time came when the underground tubes were ready; the traffic was   19
transferred to a realm unreachable by pigeons. It was like a great river subsiding suddenly into desert sands. For a day, for two days, pigeons continued to circle over the El or stand close to the red vending machines. They were patient birds, and surely this great river which had flowed through the lives of unnumbered generations was merely suffering from some momentary drought.

They listened for the familiar vibrations that had always heralded an approaching   20
train; they flapped hopefully about the head of an occasional workman walking along the steel runways. They passed from one empty station to another, all the while growing hungrier. Finally they flew away.

I thought I had seen the last of them about the El, but there was a revival   21
and it provided a curious instance of the memory of living things for a way of life or a locality that has long been cherished. Some weeks after the El was abandoned workmen began to tear it down. I went to work every morning by one particular station, and the time came when the demolition crews reached this spot. Acetylene torches showered passers-by with sparks, pneumatic drills hammered at the base of the structure, and a blind man who, like the pigeons, had clung with his cup to a stairway leading to the change booth, was forced to give up his place.

It was then, strangely, momentarily, one morning that I witnessed the return   22
of a little band of the familiar pigeons. I even recognized one or two members of the flock that had lived around this particular station before they were dispersed into the streets. They flew bravely in and out among the sparks and the hammers and the shouting workmen. They had returned—and they had returned because the hubbub of the wreckers had convinced them that the river was about to flow once more. For several hours they flapped in and out through the empty windows, nodding their heads and watching the fall of girders with attentive little eyes. By the following morning the station was reduced to some burned-off stanchions in the street. My bird friends had gone. It was plain, however, that they retained a memory for an insubstantial structure now compounded of air and time. Even the blind man clung to it. Someone

had provided him with a chair, and he sat at the same corner staring sightlessly at an invisible stairway where, so far as he was concerned, the crowds were still ascending to the trains.

I have said my life has been passed in the shade of a nonexistent tree, so   23 that such sights do not offend me. Prematurely I am one of the brown wasps and I often sit with them in the great droning hive of the station, dreaming sometimes of a certain tree. It was planted sixty years ago by a boy with a bucket and a toy spade in a little Nebraska town. That boy was myself. It was a cottonwood sapling and the boy remembered it because of some words spoken by his father and because everyone died or moved away who was supposed to wait and grow old under its shade. The boy was passed from hand to hand but the tree for some intangible reason had taken root in his mind. It was under its branches that he sheltered; it was from this tree that his memories, which are my memories, led away into the world.

After sixty years the mood of the brown wasps grows heavier upon one.   24 During a long inward struggle I thought it would do me good to go and look upon that actual tree. I found a rational excuse in which to clothe this madness. I purchased a ticket and at the end of two thousand miles I walked another mile to an address that was still the same. The house had not been altered.

I came close to the white picket fence and reluctantly, with great effort,   25 looked down the long vista of the yard. There was nothing there to see. For sixty years that cottonwood had been growing in my mind. Season by season its seeds had been floating farther on the hot prairie winds. We had planted it lovingly there, my father and I, because he had a great hunger for soil and live things growing, and because none of these things had long been ours to protect. We had planted the little sapling and watered it faithfully, and I remembered that I had run out with my small bucket to drench its roots the day we moved away. And all the years since it had been growing in my mind, a huge tree that somehow stood for my father and the love I bore him. I took a grasp on the picket fence and forced myself to look again.

A boy with the hard bird eye of youth pedaled a tricycle slowly up   26 beside me.

"What'cha lookin' at?" he asked curiously.   27

"A tree," I said.   28

"What for?" he said.   29

"It isn't there," I said to myself mostly, and began to walk away at a pace   30 just slow enough not to seem to be running.

"What isn't there?" the boy asked. I didn't answer. It was obvious I was   31 attached by a thread to a thing that had never been there, or certainly not for long. Something that had to be held in the air, or sustained in the mind, because it was part of my orientation in the universe and I could not survive without it. There was more than an animal's attachment to a place. There was something else, the attachment of the spirit to a grouping of events in time; it was part of our mortality.

So I had come home at last, driven by a memory in the brain as surely as   32
the field mouse who had delved long ago into my flower pot or the pigeons flying forever amidst the rattle of nut-vending machines. These, the burrow under the greenery in my living room and the red-bellied bowls of peanuts now hovering in midair in the minds of pigeons, were all part of an elusive world that existed nowhere and yet everywhere. I looked once at the real world about me while the persistent boy pedaled at my heels.

It was without meaning, though my feet took a remembered path. In sixty   33
years the house and street had rotted out of my mind. But the tree, the tree that no longer was, that had perished in its first season, bloomed on in my individual mind, unblemished as my father's words. "We'll plant a tree here, son, and we're not going to move any more. And when you're an old, old man you can sit under it and think how we planted it here, you and me, together."

I began to outpace the boy on the tricycle.   34

"Do you live here, Mister?" he shouted after me suspiciously. I took a firm   35
grasp on airy nothing—to be precise, on the bole of a great tree. "I do," I said. I spoke for myself, one field mouse, and several pigeons. We were all out of touch but somehow permanent. It was the world that had changed.

Questions for Critical Thinking

1. What emotional impact does the opening paragraph create? How is the impact achieved?

2. Do you agree with the author that, given the circumstances in which the old men live, they are better off dying in a crowded train station than in some lonely room? What does the author mean when he says, "Amid so many journeys somebody is bound to come out all right"? (*See* paragraph 6.)

3. What role do dreams play in this essay? Do you agree with the author on the importance of such dreams? Why or why not?

4. It has been said that "You can't go home again." How does this saying relate to the tree mentioned by the author several times? Explain how you feel about "going home" as meant by the author.

5. What does the author mean by the comment, "After sixty years the mood of the brown wasps grows heavier upon one"? (*See* paragraph 24.)

6. How does the fact that the author is an archaeologist color his interpretation of the field that was turned into a suburban store?

7. What advantage, if any, can be gained from paying scrupulous attention to nature the way the author does?

8. What do Loren Eiseley and Annie Dillard have in common as writers? (Reread "Heaven and Earth in Jest," in Chapter 1.)

Writing Assignment

Describe some aspect of animal life that parallels or illumines the human predicament.

Writing Advice

This assignment asks you to write an essay essentially similar to Eiseley's, where you reflect upon the human condition by describing or discussing some aspect of nature which mirrors it. To write this essay, you will need to develop the keen eye of the naturalist. We suggest you follow these steps:

1. Keep your eyes and ears open to your surroundings, especially the outdoors. If you have a backyard, sit quietly in it and look carefully at the animal and plant life that surrounds you. You may even wish to kneel on the lawn to observe between the blades of grass or peer under bushes. A window can also make an excellent observation post. From there you can bird-watch to great advantage or observe the antics of local cats and other animals. Be patient. You may need to repeat the experiment before you observe something worth noting.

2. Make notes of the details you observe—a dog chasing a cat, a bee buzzing over a flower, tree leaves shivering in the wind, ants dragging bits of food toward an ant hill, dark or white clouds hanging in the sky. Any activity is worth noting, including colors, movements, expressions, or attitudes.

3. Now draw an analogy between what you observed and some aspect of human life. For instance, you might observe how a bee flies over a patch of bright yellow marigolds. He hovers over each flower, lighting briefly on it before buzzing off to the next hostess. But when he encounters a dead blossom, wilted and brown, he flits away from it with seeming disdain. This scene might remind you of how we often ignore the broken, feeble, or old members in society, passing by them without so much as a glance of compassion, preferring the company of the young and glamorous. Or, you might watch a pale green blade of grass growing out of a crack of cement, reminding you of the courage displayed by people devoted to a cause that seems hopeless.

4. Once you have your scene and the lesson about life it exemplifies, work to make the description come to life by choosing vivid details that involve all of the senses—sight, hearing, smell, taste, and touch. You can state the lesson taught either at the beginning of your essay or at the end, but do so in one sentence, such as, "This feeble blade of pale green grass, stretching for the sun through a cement crack, reminded me of my friend Larry, who, despite a diving accident that rendered him paralyzed from the waist down, is courageously attending college in a wheelchair, determined to become a lawyer."

Alternate Writing Assignments

1. Write an essay explaining the role of nostalgic thoughts concerning one's childhood. Indicate how important these thoughts are in most people's lives.

2. Write an essay in which you explain the saying "You can't go home again."

PHILOSOPHY

THE INFERNO, CANTOS III–VI
Dante Alighieri
Translated by John Ciardi

Dante Alighieri (1265–1321), Italian poet, born in Florence to a family of waning nobility, is regarded as among the greatest poets of all time. Dante was allied to the Guelph party, supporters of Otto IV, whose bitter rivals were the Ghibellines, or supporters of Frederick II. He fought in the Florentine cavalry that routed the Ghibellines in 1289, and shortly afterwards suffered bereavement with the death of his childhood sweetheart, believed to be Beatrice Portinari. After marrying Gemma Donati, who bore him several children, Dante became active in the factious political affairs of Florence, eventually aligning himself with the White Guelphs. Following a series of political reversals, he found himself dispossessed and banished from his native Florence. He wandered throughout Italy, serving various princes, and eventually died at the court of Guido da Polenta in Ravenna. His reputation is based largely on the magnificent *Divine Comedy*, which was composed during his exile and which established Tuscan as the literary language of Italy. Dante also wrote *La vita nuova* (c. 1292) [The New Life].

Reading Advice

Classical works usually come down to us accompanied by a thicket of footnotes and endnotes, which most readers have the tendency to ignore. Doing so as you read the *Divine Comedy* would be a mistake. The poem is complexly rich in symbolism and allusion that would try even a Dante scholar. Without the explanations provided by the endnotes, the nuances and richness of the text would be utterly lost to the lay reader. We strongly suggest, then, that you read this as you would a play by Shakespeare, by also reading the clarifications provided by the endnotes.

The *Divine Comedy* tells the story of a soul's passage through the three spheres of the afterlife—hell, purgatory, and heaven. Written in the Tuscan vernacular, the poem consists of 100 cantos made up of 14,000 lines. The poem is written in *terza rima*, a complex stanza form of interlocking pentameter rhymes set in the scheme of aba, bcb, cdc, and so on. It is highly musical and allegorical, and pictures an unchanging universe ruled over by God, who gradually reveals his ways to the pilgrim.

Dante called his work *Commedia*; the sixteenth-century added the adjective *Divina*, which is now a permanent part of its title. In his passage through hell and purgatory, Dante is guided by the Roman poet Virgil (70 B.C.–19 B.C.). In heaven, he is guided by Beatrice, for whom the entire poem is a memorial. Dante used the poem as an occasion to strike back at his political enemies, many of whom he portrayed as groveling in the miseries of hell. In sheer imaginative breadth and vision, the *Divine Comedy* is unequaled in literary history, prompting the American poet T. S. Eliot to proclaim, "Dante and Shakespeare divide the world between them; there is no third."

The poem begins with Canto I (not reproduced here) when Dante suddenly realizes that he has drifted from the True Way and wandered into the Dark Wood of Error. Three beasts of worldliness block his path: the Leopard of Malice and Fraud, the Lion of Violence and Ambition, and the She-Wolf of Incontinence. Just as Dante thinks that there is no escape, the figure of Virgil appears, having been sent by Beatrice to be his guide. Virgil explains that there is no way around the three worldly beasts, and that they must take the longer and harder way through hell and purgatory. They start out on their trek and come soon to the gates of hell, whose description begins with Canto III.

Canto III

THE VESTIBULE OF HELL   *The Opportunists*

The Poets pass the Gate of Hell and are immediately assailed by cries of anguish. Dante sees the first of the souls in torment. They are THE OPPORTUNISTS, those souls who in life were neither for good nor evil but only for themselves. Mixed with them are those outcasts who took no sides in the Rebellion of the Angels. They are neither in Hell nor out of it. Eternally unclassified, they race round and round pursuing a wavering banner that runs forever before them through the dirty air; and as they run they are pursued by swarms of wasps and hornets, who sting them and produce a constant flow of blood and putrid matter which trickles down the bodies of the sinners and is feasted upon by loathsome worms and maggots who coat the ground.

The law of Dante's Hell is the law of symbolic retribution. As they sinned so are they punished. They took no sides, therefore they are given no place. As they pursued

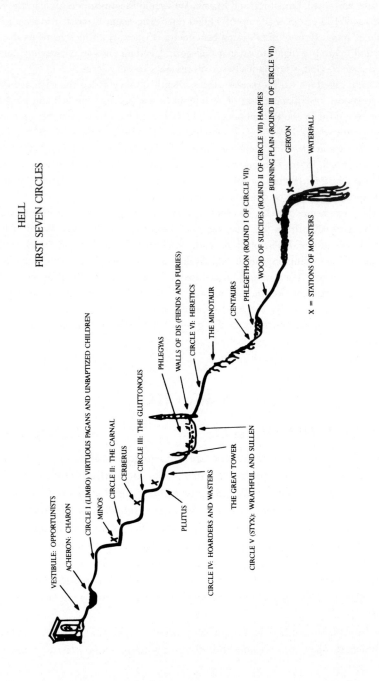

HELL

FIRST SEVEN CIRCLES

VESTIBULE: OPPORTUNISTS

ACHERON: CHARON

CIRCLE I (LIMBO) VIRTUOUS PAGANS AND UNBAPTIZED CHILDREN

MINOS

CIRCLE II: THE CARNAL

CERBERUS

CIRCLE III: THE GLUTTONOUS

PHLEGYAS

WALLS OF DIS (FIENDS AND FURIES)

CIRCLE VI: HERETICS

THE MINOTAUR

CENTAURS

PHLEGETHON (ROUND I OF CIRCLE VII)

WOOD OF SUICIDES (ROUND II OF CIRCLE VII) HARPIES

BURNING PLAIN (ROUND III OF CIRCLE VII)

GERYON

WATERFALL

PLUTUS

CIRCLE IV: HOARDERS AND WASTERS

THE GREAT TOWER

CIRCLE V (STYX): WRATHFUL AND SULLEN

X = STATIONS OF MONSTERS

the ever-shifting illusion of their own advantage, changing their courses with every changing wind, so they pursue eternally an elusive, ever-shifting banner. As their sin was a darkness, so they move in darkness. As their own guilty conscience pursued them, so they are pursued by swarms of wasps and hornets. And as their actions were a moral filth, so they run eternally through the filth of worms and maggots which they themselves feed.

Dante recognizes several, among them POPE CELESTINE V, but without delaying to speak to any of these souls, the Poets move on to ACHERON, the first of the rivers of Hell. Here the newly-arrived souls of the damned gather and wait for monstrous CHARON to ferry them over to punishment. Charon recognizes Dante as a living man and angrily refuses him passage. Virgil forces Charon to serve them, but Dante swoons with terror, and does not reawaken until he is on the other side.

I AM THE WAY INTO THE CITY OF WOE.
I AM THE WAY TO A FORSAKEN PEOPLE.
I AM THE WAY INTO ETERNAL SORROW.

SACRED JUSTICE MOVED MY ARCHITECT.
I WAS RAISED HERE BY DIVINE OMNIPOTENCE,
PRIMORDIAL LOVE AND ULTIMATE INTELLECT.

ONLY THOSE ELEMENTS TIME CANNOT WEAR
WERE MADE BEFORE ME, AND BEYOND TIME I STAND
ABANDON ALL HOPE YE WHO ENTER HERE.

These mysteries I read cut into stone
    above a gate. And turning I said: "Master,
    what is the meaning of this harsh inscription?"

And he then as initiate to novice:
    "Here must you put by all division of spirit
        and gather your soul against all cowardice.   15

This is the place I told you to expect.
    Here you shall pass among the fallen people,
    souls who have lost the good of intellect."

So saying, he put forth his hand to me,
    and with a gentle and encouraging smile
    he led me through the gate of mystery.

Here sighs and cries and wails coiled and recoiled
  on the starless air, spilling my soul to tears.
  A confusion of tongues and monstrous accents toiled

in pain and anger. Voices hoarse and shrill
  and sounds of blows, all intermingled, raised
  tumult and pandemonium that still

whirls on the air forever dirty with it
  as if a whirlwind sucked at sand. And I
  holding my head in horror, cried: "Sweet Spirit,   30

what souls are these who run through this black haze?"
  And he to me: "These are the nearly soulless
  whose lives concluded neither blame nor praise.

They are mixed here with that despicable corps
  of angels who were neither for God nor Satan,
  but only for themselves. The High Creator

scourged them from Heaven for its perfect beauty,
  and Hell will not receive them since the wicked
  might feel some glory over them." And I:

"Master, what gnaws at them so hideously
  their lamentation stuns the very air?"
  "They have no hope of death," he answered me,

"and in their blind and unattaining state
  their miserable lives have sunk so low
  that they must envy every other fate.   45

No word of them survives their living season.
  Mercy and Justice deny them even a name.
  Let us not speak of them: look, and pass on."

I saw a banner there upon the mist.
  Circling and circling, it seems to scorn all pause.
  So it ran on, and still behind it pressed

a never-ending rout of souls in pain.
  I had not thought death had undone so many
  as passed before me in that mournful train.

And some I knew among them; last of all
　　I recognized the shadow of that soul
　　who, in his cowardice, made the Great Denial.

At once I understood for certain: these
　　were of that retrograde and faithless crew
　　hateful to God and to His enemies.   60

These wretches never born and never dead
　　ran naked in a swarm of wasps and hornets
　　that goaded them the more the more they fled,

and made their faces stream with bloody gouts
　　of pus and tears that dribbled to their feet
　　to be swallowed there by loathsome worms and maggots.

Then looking onward I made out a throng
　　assembled on the beach of a wide river,
　　whereupon I turned to him: "Master, I long

to know what souls these are, and what strange usage
　　makes them as eager to cross as they seem to be
　　in this infected light." At which the Sage:

"All this shall be made known to you when we stand
　　on the joyless beach of Acheron." And I
　　cast down my eyes, sensing a reprimand   75

in what he said, and so walked at his side
　　in silence and ashamed until we came
　　through the dead cavern to that sunless tide.

There, steering toward us in an ancient ferry
　　came an old man with a white bush of hair,
　　bellowing: "Woe to you depraved souls! Bury

here and forever all hope of Paradise:
　　I come to lead you to the other shore,
　　into eternal dark, into fire and ice.

And you who are living yet, I say begone
　　from these who are dead." But when he saw me stand
　　against his violence he began again:

"By other windings and by other steerage
  shall you cross to that other shore. Not here! Not here!
  A lighter craft than mine must give you passage."   90

And my Guide to him: "Charon, bite back your spleen:
  this has been willed where what is willed must be,
  and is not yours to ask what it may mean."

The steersman of that marsh of ruined souls,
  who wore a wheel of flame around each eye,
  stifled the rage that shook his woolly jowls.

But those unmanned and naked spirits there
  turned pale with fear and their teeth began to chatter
  at sound of his crude bellow. In despair

they blasphemed God, their parents, their time on earth,
  and race of Adam, and the day and the hour
  and the place and the seed and the womb that gave them birth.

But all together they drew to that grim shore
  where all must come who lose the fear of God.
  Weeping and cursing they come for evermore,   105

and demon Charon with eyes like burning coals
  herds them in, and with a whistling oar
  flails on the stragglers to his wake of souls.

As leaves in autumn loosen and stream down
  until the branch stands bare above its tatters
  spread on the rustling ground, so one by one

the evil seed of Adam in its Fall
  cast themselves, at his signal, from the shore
  and streamed away like birds who hear their call.

So they are gone over that shadowy water,
  and always before they reach the other shore
  a new noise stirs on this, and new throngs gather.

"My son," the courteous Master said to me,
  "all who die in the shadow of God's wrath
  converge to this from every clime and country.   120

> And all pass over eagerly, for here
>   Divine Justice transforms and spurs them so
>   their dread turns wish: they yearn for what they fear.
>
> No soul in Grace comes ever to this crossing;
>   therefore if Charon rages at your presence
>   you will understand the reason for his cursing."
>
> When he had spoken, all the twilight country
>   shook so violently, the terror of it
>   bathes me with sweat even in memory:
>
> the tear-soaked ground gave out a sigh of wind
>   that spewed itself in flame on a red sky,
>   and all my shattered senses left me. Blind,
>
> like one whom sleep comes over in a swoon,
>   I stumbled into darkness and went down.

Notes

7–8. *Only those elements time cannot wear:* The Angels, the Empyrean, and the First Matter are the elements time cannot wear, for they will last to all time. Man, however, in his mortal state, is not eternal. The Gate of Hell, therefore, was created before man. The theological point is worth attention. The doctrine of Original Sin is, of course, one familiar to many creeds. Here, however, it would seem that the preparation for damnation predates Original Sin. True, in one interpretation, Hell was created for the punishment of the Rebellious Angels and not for man. Had man not sinned, he would never have known Hell. But on the other hand, Dante's God was one who knew all, and knew therefore that man would indeed sin. The theological problem is an extremely delicate one.

It is significant, however, that having sinned, man lives out his days on the rind of Hell, and that damnation is forever below his feet. This central concept of man's sinfulness, and, opposed to it, the doctrine of Christ's ever-abounding mercy, are central to all of Dante's theology. Only as man surrenders himself to Divine Love may he hope for salvation, and salvation is open to all who will surrender themselves.

8. *and to all time I stand:* So odious is sin to God that there can be no end to its just punishment.

9. *Abandon all hope ye who enter here:* The admonition, of course, is to the damned and not to those who come on Heaven-sent errands. The Harrowing of Hell (see Canto IV, note to 1. 53) provided the only exemption from this decree, and that only through the direct intercession of Christ.

57. *who, in his cowardice, made the Great Denial:* This is almost certainly intended to be Celestine V, who became Pope in 1294. He was a man of saintly life, but allowed himself to be convinced by a priest named Benedetto that his soul was in danger since no man could live in the world without being damned. In fear for his soul he withdrew from all worldly affairs and renounced the papacy. Benedetto promptly assumed the mantle himself and become Boniface VIII, a Pope who became for Dante a symbol of all the worst corruptions of the church. Dante also blamed Boniface and his intrigues for many of the evils that befell Florence. We shall learn in Canto XIX that the fires of Hell are waiting for Boniface in the pit of the Simoniacs, and we shall be given further evidence of his corruption in Canto XXVII. Celestine's great guilt is that his cowardice (in selfish terror for his own welfare) served as the door through which so much evil entered the church.

80. *an old man:* Charon. He is the ferryman of dead souls across the Acheron in all classical mythology.

88–90. *By other windings:* Charon recognizes Dante not only as a living man but as a soul in grace, and knows, therefore, that the Infernal Ferry was not intended for him. He is probably referring to the fact that souls destined for Purgatory and Heaven assemble not at his ferry point, but on the banks of the Tiber, from which they are transported by an Angel.

100. *they blasphemed God:* The souls of the damned are not permitted to repent, for repentance is a divine grace.

123. *they yearn for what they fear:* Hell (allegorically Sin) is what the souls of the damned really wish for. Hell is their actual and deliberate choice, for divine grace is denied to none who wish for it in their hearts. The damned must, in fact, deliberately harden their hearts to God in order to become damned. Christ's grace is sufficient to save all who wish for it.

133–34 DANTE'S SWOON: This device (repeated at the end of Canto V) serves a double purpose. The first is technical: Dante uses it to cover a transition. We are never told how he crossed Acheron, for that would involve certain narrative matters he can better deal with when he crosses Styx in Canto VII. The second is to provide a point of departure for a theme that is carried through the entire descent: the theme of Dante's emotional reaction to Hell. These two swoons early in the descent show him most susceptible to the grief about him. As he descends, pity leaves him, and he even goes so far as to add to the torments of one sinner. The allegory is clear: we must harden ourselves against every sympathy for sin.

Canto IV

CIRCLE ONE: Limbo   *The Virtuous Pagans*

Dante wakes to find himself across Acheron. The Poets are now on the brink of Hell itself, which Dante conceives as a great funnel-shaped cave lying below the northern hemisphere with its bottom point at the earth's center. Around this great circular depression runs a series of ledges, each of which Dante calls a CIRCLE. Each circle is assigned to the punishment of one category of sin.

As soon as Dante's strength returns, the Poets begin to cross the FIRST CIRCLE. Here they find the VIRTUOUS PAGANS. They were born without the light of Christ's revelation, and, therefore, they cannot come into the light of God, but they are not tormented. Their only pain is that they have no hope.

Ahead of them Dante sights a great dome of light, and a voice trumpets through the darkness welcoming Virgil back, for this is his eternal place in Hell. Immediately the great Poets of all time appear—HOMER, HORACE, OVID, and LUCAN. They greet Virgil, and they make Dante a sixth in their company.

With them Dante enters the Citadel of Human Reason and sees before his eyes the Master Souls of Pagan Antiquity gathered on a green, and illuminated by the radiance of Human Reason. This is the highest state man can achieve without God, and the glory of it dazzles Dante, but he knows also that it is nothing compared to the glory of God.

> A monstrous clap of thunder broke apart
>   the swoon that stuffed my head; like one awakened
>   by violent hands, I leaped up with a start.

And having risen; rested and renewed,
   I studied out the landmarks of the gloom
   to find my bearings there as best I could.

And I found I stood on the very brink of the valley
   called the Dolorous Abyss, the desolate chasm
   where rolls the thunder of Hell's eternal cry,

so depthless-deep and nebulous and dim
   that stare as I might into its frightful pit
   it gave me back no feature and no bottom.

Death-pale, the Poet spoke: "Now let us go
   into the blind world waiting here below us.
   I will lead the way and you shall follow."   15

And I, sick with alarm at his new pallor,
   cried out, "How can I go this way when you
   who are my strength in doubt turn pale with terror?"

And he: "The pain of these below us here,
   drains the color from my face for pity,
   and leaves this pallor you mistake for fear.

Now let us go, for a long road awaits us."
   So he entered and so he led me in
   to the first circle and ledge of the abyss.

No tortured wailing rose to greet us here
   but sounds of sighing rose from every side,
   sending a tremor through the timeless air,

a grief breathed out of untormented sadness,
   the passive state of those who dwelled apart,
   men, women, children—a dim and endless congress.   30

And the Master said to me: "You do not question
   what souls these are that suffer here before you?
   I wish you to know before you travel on

that these were sinless. And still their merits fail,
   for they lacked Baptism's grace, which is the door
   of the true faith you were born to. Their birth fell

before the age of the Christian mysteries,
   and so they did not worship God's Trinity
   in fullest duty. I am one of these.

For such defects are we lost, though spared the fire
   and suffering Hell in one affliction only:
   that without hope we live on in desire."

I thought how many worthy souls there were
   suspended in that Limbo, and a weight
   closed on my heart for what the noblest suffer.   45

"Instruct me, Master and most noble Sir,"
   I prayed him then, "better to understand
   the perfect creed that conquers every error:

has any, by his own or another's merit,
   gone ever from this place to blessedness?"
   He sensed my inner question and answered it:

"I was still new to this estate of tears
   when a Mighty One descended here among us,
   crowned with the sign of His victorious years.

He took from us the shade of our first parent,
   of Abel, his pure son, of ancient Noah,
   of Moses, the bringer of law, the obedient.

Father Abraham, David the King,
   Israel with his father and his children,
   Rachel, the holy vessel of His blessing,   60

and many more He chose for elevation
   among the elect. And before these, you must know,
   no human soul had ever won salvation."

We had not paused as he spoke, but held our road
   and passed meanwhile beyond a press of souls
   crowded about like trees in a thick wood.

And we had not traveled far from where I woke
   when I made out a radiance before us
   that struck away a hemisphere of dark.

We were still some distance back in the long night,
    yet near enough that I half-saw, half-sensed,
    what quality of souls lived in that light.

"O ornament of wisdom and of art,
    what souls are these whose merit lights their way
    even in Hell. What joy sets them apart?"   75

And he to me: "The signature of honor
    they left on earth is recognized in Heaven
    and wins them ease in Hell out of God's favor."

And as he spoke a voice rang on the air:
    "Honor the Prince of Poets; the soul and glory
    that went from us returns. He is here! He is here!"

The cry ceased and the echo passed from hearing;
    I saw four mighty presences come toward us
    with neither joy nor sorrow in their bearing.

"Note well," my Master said as they came on,
    "that soul that leads the rest with sword in hand
    as if he were their captain and champion.

It is Homer, singing master of the earth.
    Next after him is Horace, the satirist,
    Ovid is third, and Lucan is the fourth.   90

Since all of these have part in the high name
    the voice proclaimed, calling me Prince of Poets,
    the honor that they do me honors them."

So I saw gathered at the edge of light
    the masters of that highest school whose song
    outsoars all others like an eagle's flight.

And after they had talked together a while,
    they turned and welcomed me most graciously,
    at which I saw my approving Master smile.

And they honored me far beyond courtesy,
    for they included me in their own number,
    making me sixth in that high company.

So we moved toward the light, and as we passed
    we spoke of things as well omitted here
    as it was sweet to touch on there. At last   105

we reached the base of a great Citadel
    circled by seven towering battlements
    and by a sweet brook flowing round them all.

This we passed over as if it were firm ground.
    Through seven gates I entered with those sages
    and came to a green meadow blooming round.

There with a solemn and majestic poise
    stood many people gathered in the light,
    speaking infrequently and with muted voice.

Past that enameled green we six withdrew
    into a luminous and open height
    from which each soul among them stood in view.

And there directly before me on the green
    the master souls of time were shown to me.
    I glory in the glory I have seen!   120

Electra stood in a great company
    among whom I saw Hector and Aeneas
    and Caesar in armor with his falcon's eye.

I saw Camilla, and the Queen Amazon
    across the field. I saw the Latian King
    seated there with his daughter by his throne.

And the good Brutus who overthrew the Tarquin:
    Lucrezia, Julia, Marcia, and Cornelia;
    and, by himself apart, the Saladin.

And raising my eyes a little I saw on high
    Aristotle, the master of those who know,
    ringed by the great souls of philosophy.

All wait upon him for their honor and his.
    I saw Socrates and Plato at his side
    before all others there. Democritus   135

who ascribes the world to chance, Diogenes,
    and with him there Thales, Anaxagoras,
    Zeno, Heraclitus, Empedocles.

And I saw the wise collector and analyst—
    Dioscorides I mean. I saw Orpheus there,
    Tully, Linus, Seneca the moralist,

Euclid the geometer, and Ptolemy,
    Hippocrates, Galen, Avicenna,
    and Averrhoës of the Great Commentary.

I cannot count so much nobility;
    my longer theme pursues me so that often
    the word falls short of the reality.   150

The company of six is reduced by four.
    My Master leads me by another road
    out of that serenity to the roar

and trembling air of Hell. I pass from light
    into the kingdom of eternal night.

Notes

13 ff. *death-pale:* Virgil is most likely affected here by the return of his own place in Hell. "The pain of these below" then (line 19) would be the pain of his own group in Limbo (the Virtuous Pagans) rather than the total of Hell's suffering.

31 ff. *You do not question:* A master touch of characterization. Virgil's *amour propre* is a bit piqued at Dante's lack of curiosity about the position in Hell of Virgil's own kind. And it may possibly be, by allegorical extension, that Human Reason must urge the soul to question the place of reason. The allegorical point is conjectural, but such conjecture is certainly one of the effects inherent in the use of allegory; when well used, the central symbols of the allegory continue indefinitely to suggest new interpretations and shades of meaning.

53. *a Mighty One:* Christ. His name is never directly uttered in Hell.

53. *descended here:* The legend of the Harrowing of Hell is Apocryphal. It is based on I *Peter* iii, 19: "He went and preached unto the spirits in prison." The legend is that Christ in the glory of His resurrection descended into Limbo and took with Him to Heaven the first human souls to be saved. The event would, accordingly, have occurred in 33 or 34 A.D. Virgil died in 19 B.C.

102. *making me sixth in that high company:* Merit and self-awareness of merit may well be a higher thing than modesty. An additional point Dante may well have had in mind, however, is the fact that he saw himself as one pledged to continue in his own times the classic tradition represented by these poets.

103–105. These lines amount to a stylistic note. It is good style (*'l tacere è bello* where *bello* equals "good style") to omit this discussion, since it would digress from the subject and, moreover, his point is already made. Every great narrator tends to tell his story from climax to climax. There are times on the other hand when Dante delights in digression. (See General Note to Canto XX.)

106. A GREAT CITADEL. The most likely allegory is that the Citadel represents philosophy (that is, human reason without the light of God) surrounded by seven walls which represent the seven liberal arts, or the seven sciences, or the seven virtues. Note that Human Reason makes a light of its own, but that it is a light in darkness and forever separated from the glory of God's light. The *sweet brook flowing* round them all has been interpreted in many ways. Clearly fundamental, however, is the fact that it divides those in the Citadel (those who wish to know) from those in the outer darkness.

109. *as if it were firm ground:* Since Dante still has his body, and since all others in Hell are incorporeal shades, there is a recurring narrative problem in the *Inferno* (and through the rest of the *Commedia*): how does flesh act in contact with spirit? In the *Purgatorio* Dante attempts to embrace the spirit of Casella and his arms pass through him as if he were empty air. In the Third Circle, below (Canto VI, 34 – 36), Dante steps on some of the spirits lying in the slush and his foot passes right through them. (The original lines offer several possible readings of which I have preferred this one.) And at other times Virgil, also a spirit, picks Dante up and carries him bodily.

It is clear, too, that Dante means the spirits of Hell to be weightless. When Virgil steps into Phlegyas' bark (Canto VIII) it does not settle into the water, but it does when Dante's living body steps aboard. There is no narrative reason why Dante should not sink into the waters of this stream and Dante follows no fixed rule in dealing with such phenomena, often suiting the physical action to the allegorical need. Here, the moat probably symbolizes some requirement (The Will to Know) which he and the other poets meet without difficulty.

THE INHABITANTS OF THE CITADEL. They fall into three main groups:

1. *The heroes and heroines:* All of these it must be noted were associated with the Trojans and their Roman descendants. (See note on AENEAS AND THE FOUNDING OF ROME, Canto II.) The Electra Dante mentions here is not the sister of Orestes (see Euripides' *Electra*) but the daughter of Atlas and the mother of Dardanus, the founder of Troy.

2. *The philosophers:* Most of this group is made up of philosophers whose teachings were, at least in part, acceptable to church scholarship. Democritus, however, "who ascribed the world to chance," would clearly be an exception. The group is best interpreted, therefore, as representing the highest achievements of Human Reason unaided by Divine Love. *Plato and Aristotle:* Through a considerable part of the Middle Ages Plato was held to be the fountainhead of all scholarship, but in Dante's time practically all learning was based on Aristotelian theory as interpreted through the many commentaries. *Linus:* the Italian is "Lino" and for it some commentators read "Livio" (Livy).

3. *The naturalists:* They are less well known today. In Dante's time their place in scholarship more or less corresponded to the role of the theoretician and historian of science in our universities. *Avicenna* (his major work was in the eleventh century) and *Avverhoës* (twelfth century) were Arabian philosophers and physicians especially famous in Dante's time for their commentaries on Aristotle. *Great Commentary:* has the force of a title, i.e., The Great Commentary as distinguished from many lesser commentaries.

The Saladin: This is the famous Saladin who was defeated by Richard the Lion-Heart, and whose great qualities as a ruler became a legend in medieval Europe.

Canto V

CIRCLE TWO   *The Carnal*

The Poets leave Limbo and enter the SECOND CIRCLE. Here begin the torments of Hell proper, and here, blocking the way, sits MINOS, the dread and semi-bestial judge of the damned who assigns to each soul its eternal torment. He orders the Poets back; but Virgil silences him as he earlier silenced Charon, and the Poets move on.

They find themselves on a dark ledge swept by a great whirlwind, which spins within it the souls of the CARNAL, those who betrayed reason to their appetites. Their sin was to abandon themselves to the tempest of their passions: so they are swept forever in the tempest of Hell, forever denied the light of reason and of God. Virgil identifies many among them. SEMIRAMIS is there, and DIDO, CLEOPATRA, HELEN, ACHILLES, PARIS, and TRISTAN. Dante sees PAOLO and FRANCESCA swept together, and in the name of love he calls to them to tell their sad story. They pause from their eternal flight to come to him, and Francesca tells their history while Paolo weeps at her side. Dante is so stricken by compassion at their tragic tale that he swoons once again.

So we went down to the second ledge alone;
    a smaller circle of so much greater pain
    the voice of the damned rose in a bestial moan.

There Minos sits, grinning, grotesque, and hale.
    He examines each lost soul as it arrives
    and delivers his verdict with his coiling tail.

That is to say, when the ill-fated soul
    appears before him it confesses all,
    and that grim sorter of the dark and foul

decides which place in Hell shall be its end,
    then wraps his twitching tail about himself
    one coil for each degree it must descend.

The soul descends and others take its place:
    each crowds in its turn to judgment, each confesses
      each hears its doom and falls away through space.   15

"O you who come into this camp of woe,"
    cried Minos when he saw me turn away
    without awaiting his judgment, "watch where you go

once you have entered here, and to whom you turn!
    Do not be misled by that wide and easy passage!"
    And my Guide to him: "That is not your concern;

it is his fate to enter every door.
    This has been willed where what is willed must be,
    and is not yours to question. Say no more."

Now the choir of anguish, like a wound,
    strikes through the tortured air. Now I have come
    to Hell's full lamentation, sound beyond sound.

I came to a place stripped bare of every light
    and roaring on the naked dark like seas
    wracked by a war of winds. Their hellish flight   30

of storm and counterstorm through time foregone,
    sweeps the souls of the damned before its charge.
    Whirling and battering it drives them on,

and when they pass the ruined gap of Hell
    through which we had come, their shrieks begin anew.
    There they blaspheme the power of God eternal.

And this, I learned, was the never ending flight
    of those who sinned in the flesh, the carnal and lusty
    who betrayed reason to their appetite.

As the wings of wintering starlings bear them on
    in their great wheeling flights, just so the blast
    wherries these evil souls through time foregone.

Here, there, up, down, they whirl and, whirling, strain
    with never a hope of hope to comfort them,
    not of release, but even of less pain.   45

As cranes go over sounding their harsh cry,
    leaving the long streak of their flight in air,
    so come these spirits, wailing as they fly.

And watching their shadows lashed by wind, I cried:
    "Master, what souls are these the very air
    lashes with its black whips from side to side?"

"The first of these whose history you would know,"
    he answered me, "was Empress of many tongues.
    Mad sensuality corrupted her so

that to hide the guilt of her debauchery
    she licensed all depravity alike,
    and lust and law were one in her decree.

She is Semiramis of whom the tale is told
   how she married Ninus and succeeded him
   to the throne of that wide land the Sultans hold.   60

The other is Dido; faithless to the ashes
   of Sichaeus, she killed herself for love.
   The next whom the eternal tempest lashes

is sense-drugged Cleopatra. See Helen there,
   from whom such ill arose. And great Achilles,
   who fought at last with love in the house of prayer.

And Paris. And Tristan." As they whirled above
   he pointed out more than a thousand shades
   of those torn from the mortal life by love.

I stood there while my Teacher one by one
   named the great knights and ladies of dim time;
   and I was swept by pity and confusion.

At last I spoke: "Poet, I should be glad
   to speak a word with those two swept together
   so lightly on the wind and still so sad."   75

And he to me: "Watch them. When next they pass,
   call to them in the name of love that drives
   and damns them here. In that name they will pause."

Thus, as soon as the wind in its wild course
   brought them around, I called: "O wearied souls!
   if none forbid it, pause and speak to us."

As mating doves that love calls to their nest
   glide through the air with motionless raised wings,
   borne by the sweet desire that fills each breast—

Just so those spirits turned on the torn sky
   from the band where Dido whirls across the air;
   such was the power of pity in my cry.

"O living creature, gracious, kind, and good,
   going this pilgrimage through the sick night,
   visiting us who stained the earth with blood,   90

were the King of Time our friend, we would pray His peace
on you who have pitied us. As long as the wind
will let us pause, ask of us what you please.

The town where I was born lies by the shore
where the Po descends into its ocean rest
with its attendant streams in one long murmur.

Love, which in gentlest hearts will soonest bloom
seized my lover with passion for that sweet body
from which I was torn unshriven to my doom.

Love, which permits no loved one not to love,
took me so strongly with delight in him
that we are one in Hell, as we were above.

Love led us to one death. In the depths of Hell
Caïna waits for him who took our lives."
This was the piteous tale they stopped to tell.   105

And when I had heard those world-offended lovers
I bowed my head. At last the Poet spoke:
"What painful thoughts are these your lowered brow covers?"

When at length I answered, I began "Alas!
What sweetest thoughts, what green and young desire
led these two lovers to this sorry pass."

Then turning to those spirits once again,
I said: "Francesca, what you suffer here
melts me to tears of pity and of pain.

But tell me: in the time of your sweet sighs
by what appearances found love the way
to lure you to his perilous paradise?"

And she: "The double grief of a lost bliss
is to recall its happy hour in pain.
Your Guide and Teacher knows the truth of this.   120

But if there is indeed a soul in Hell
to ask of the beginning of our love
out of his pity, I will weep and tell:

On a day for dalliance we read the rhyme
*   of Lancelot, how love had mastered him.*
*   We were alone with innocence and dim time.*

Pause after pause that high old story drew
*   our eyes together while we blushed and paled;*
*   but it was one soft passage overthrew*

our caution and our hearts. For when we read
*   how her fond smile was kissed by such a lover,*
*   he who is one with me alive and dead*

breathed on my lips the tremor of his kiss.
*   That book, and he who wrote it, was a pander.*
*   That day we read no further." As she said this,*   135

the other spirit, who stood by her, wept
*   so piteously, I felt my senses reel*
*   and faint away with anguish. I was swept*

by such a swoon as death is, and I fell,
*   as a corpse might fall, to the dead floor of Hell.*

Notes

2. *a smaller circle:* The pit of Hell tapers like a funnel. The circles of ledges accordingly grow smaller as they descend.

4. *Minos:* Like all the monsters Dante assigns to the various offices of Hell, Minos is drawn from classical mythology. He was the son of Europa and of Zeus who descended to her in the form of a bull. Minos became a mythological king of Crete, so famous for his wisdom and justice that after death his soul was made judge of the dead. Virgil presents him fulfilling the same office at Aeneas' descent to the underworld. Dante, however, transforms him into an irate and hideous monster with a tail. The transformation may have been suggested by the form Zeus assumed for the rape of Europa—the monster is certainly bullish enough here—but the obvious purpose of the brutalization is to present a figure symbolic of the guilty conscience of the wretches who come before it to make their confessions. Dante freely reshapes his materials to his own purposes.

8. *it confesses all:* Just as the souls appeared eager to cross Acheron, so they are eager to confess even while they dread. Dante is once again making the point that sinners elect their Hell by an act of their own will.

27. *Hell's full lamentation:* It is with the second circle that the real tortures of Hell begin.

34. *the ruined gap of Hell:* See note to Canto II, 53. At the time of the Harrowing of Hell a great earthquake shook the underworld shattering rocks and cliffs. Ruins resulting from the same shock are noted in Canto XII, 34, and Canto XXI, 112 ff. At the beginning of Canto XXIV, the Poets leave the *bolgia* of the Hypocrites by climbing the ruined slabs of a bridge that was shattered by this earthquake.

THE SINNERS OF THE SECOND CIRCLE (THE CARNAL): Here begin the punishments for the various sins of Incontinence (The sins of the She-Wolf). In the second circle are punished those who sinned by excess of sexual passion. Since this is the most natural sin and the sin most nearly associated with love, its punishment is the lightest of all to be found in Hell proper. The Carnal are whirled and buffeted endlessly through the murky air (symbolic of the beclouding of their reason by passion) by a great gale (symbolic of their lust).

53. *Empress of many tongues:* Semiramis, a legendary queen of Assyria who assumed full power at the death of her husband, Ninus.

61. *Dido:* Queen and founder of Carthage. She had vowed to remain faithful to her husband, Sichaeus, but she fell in love with Aeneas. When Aeneas abandoned her she stabbed herself on a funeral pyre she had had prepared.

　　According to Dante's own system of punishments, she should be in the Seventh Circle (Canto XIII) with the suicides. The only clue Dante gives to the tempering of her punishment is his statement that "she killed herself for love." Dante always seems readiest to forgive in that name.

65. *Achilles:* He is placed among this company because of his passion for Polyxena, the daughter of Priam. For love of her, he agreed to desert the Greeks and to join the Trojans, but when he went to the temple for the wedding (according to the legend Dante has followed) he was killed by Paris.

74. *those two swept together:* Paolo and Francesca (PAH-oe-loe: Frahn-CHAY-ska).

Dante's treatment of these two lovers is certainly the tenderest and most sympathetic accorded any of the sinners in Hell, and legends immediately began to grow about this pair.

The facts are these. In 1275 Giovanni Malatesta (Djoe-VAH-nee Mahl-ah-TEH-stah) of Rimini, called Giovanni the Lame, a somewhat deformed but brave and powerful warrior, made a political marriage with Francesca, daughter of Guido da Polenta of Ravenna. Francesca came to Rimini and there an amour grew between her and Giovanni's younger brother Paolo. Despite the fact that Paolo had married in 1269 and had become the father of two daughters by 1275, his affair with Francesca continued for many years. It was sometime between 1283 and 1286 that Giovanni surprised them in Francesca's bedroom and killed both of them.

Around these facts the legend has grown that Paolo was sent by Giovanni as his proxy to the marriage, that Francesca thought he was her real bridegroom and accordingly gave him her heart irrevocably at first sight. The legend obviously increases the pathos, but nothing in Dante gives it support.

103. *that we are one in Hell, as we were above:* At many points of The Inferno Dante makes clear the principle that the souls of the damned are locked so blindly into their own guilt that none can feel sympathy for another, or find any pleasure in the presence of another. The temptation of many readers is to interpret this line romantically: i.e., that the love of Paolo and Francesca survives Hell itself. The more Dantean interpretation, however, is that they add to one another's anguish (a) as mutual reminders of their sin, and (b) as insubstantial shades of the bodies for which they once felt such great passion.

104. *Caïna waits for him:* Giovanni Malatesta was still alive at the writing. His fate is already decided, however, and upon his death, his soul will fall to Caïna, the first ring of the last circle (Canto XXXII), where lie those who performed acts of treachery against their kin.

124–5. *the rhyme of Lancelot:* The story exists in many forms. The details Dante makes use of are from an Old French version.

126. *dim time:* The original simply reads "We were alone, suspecting nothing." "Dim time" is rhyme-forced, but not wholly outside the legitimate implications of the original, I hope. The old courtly romance may well be thought of as happening in the dim ancient days. The apology, of course, comes after the fact: one does the possible then argues for justification, and there probably is none.

134. *that book, and he who wrote it, was a pander:* "Galeotto," the Italian word for "pander," is also the Italian rendering of the name of Gallehault, who in the French Romance Dante refers to here, urged Lancelot and Guinevere on to love.

Canto VI

CIRCLE THREE   *The Gluttons*

Dante recovers from his swoon and finds himself in the THIRD CIRCLE. A great storm of putrefaction falls incessantly, a mixture of stinking snow and freezing rain, which forms into a vile slush underfoot. Everything about this Circle suggests a gigantic garbage dump. The souls of the damned lie in the icy paste, swollen and obscene, and CERBERUS, the ravenous three-headed dog of Hell, stands guard over them, ripping and tearing them with his claws and teeth.

These are the GLUTTONS. In life they made no higher use of the gifts of God than to wallow in food and drink, producers of nothing but garbage and offal. Here they lie through all eternity, themselves like garbage, half-buried in fetid slush, while Cerberus slavers over them as they in life slavered over their food.

As the Poets pass, one of the speakers sits up and addresses Dante. He is CIACCO, THE HOG, a citizen of Dante's own Florence. He recognizes Dante and asks eagerly for news of what is happening there. With the foreknowledge of the damned, Ciacco then utters the first of the political prophecies that are to become a recurring theme of the Inferno. The Poets then move on toward the next Circle, at the edge of which they encounter the monster Plutus.

My senses had reeled from me out of pity
 for the sorrow of those kinsmen and lost lovers.
 Now they return, and waking gradually,

I see new torments and new souls in pain
 about me everywhere. Wherever I turn
 away from grief I turn to grief again.

I am in the Third Circle of the torments.
 Here to all time with neither pause nor change
 the frozen rain of Hell descends in torrents.

Huge hailstones, dirty water, and black snow
 pour from the dismal air to putrefy
 the putrid slush that waits for them below.

Here monstrous Cerberus, the ravening beast,
 howls through his triple throats like a mad dog
  over the spirits sunk in that foul paste.   15

His eyes are red, his beard is greased with phlegm,
 his belly is swollen, and his hands are claws
 to rip the wretches and flay and mangle them.

And they, too, howl like dogs in the freezing storm,
    turning and turning from it as if they thought
    one naked side could keep the other warm.

When Cerberus discovered us in that swill
    his dragon-jaws yawed wide, his lips drew back
    in a grin of fangs. No limb of him was still.

My Guide bent down and seized in either fist
    a clod of the stinking dirt that festered there
    and flung them down the gullet of the beast.

As a hungry cur will set the echoes raving
    and then fall still when he is thrown a bone,
    all of his clamor being in his craving,   30

so the three ugly heads of Cerberus,
    whose yowling at those wretches deafened them,
    choked on their putrid sops and stopped their fuss.

We made our way across the sodden mess
    of souls the rain beat down, and when our steps
    fell on a body, they sank through emptiness.

All those illusions of being seemed to lie
    drowned in the slush; until one wraith among them
    sat up abruptly and called as I passed by:

"O you who are led this journey through the shade
    of Hell's abyss, do you recall this face?
    You had been made before I was unmade."

And I: "Perhaps the pain you suffer here
    distorts your image from my recollection.
    I do not know you as you now appear."   45

And he to me: "Your own city, so rife
    with hatred that the bitter cup flows over
    was mine too in that other, clearer life.

Your citizens nicknamed me Ciacco, The Hog:
    gluttony was my offense, and for it
    I lie here rotting like a swollen log.

Nor am I lost in this alone; all these
   you see about you in this painful death
   have wallowed in the same indecencies."

I answered him: "Ciacco, your agony
   weighs on my heart and calls my soul to tears;
   but tell me, if you can, what is to be

for the citizens of that divided state,
   and whether there are honest men among them,
   and for what reasons we are torn by hate."   60

And he then: "After many words given and taken
   it shall come to blood; White shall rise over Black
   and rout the dark lord's force, battered and shaken.

Then it shall come to pass within three suns
   that the fallen shall arise, and by the power
   of one now gripped by many hesitations

Black shall ride on White for many years,
   loading it down with burdens and oppressions
   and humbling of proud names and helpless tears.

Two are honest, but none will heed them. There,
   pride, avarice, and envy are the tongues
   men know and heed, a Babel of despair."

Here he broke off his mournful prophecy.
   And I to him: "Still let me urge you on
   to speak a little further and instruct me: 75

Farinata and Tegghiaio, men of good blood,
   Jacopo Rusticucci, Arrigo, Mosca,
   and the others who set their hearts on doing good—

where are they now whose high deeds might be-gem
   the crown of kings? I long to know their fate.
   Does Heaven soothe or Hell envenom them?"

And he: "They lie below in a blacker lair.
   A heavier guilt draws them to greater pain.
   If you descend so far you may see them there.

> But when you move again among the living,
>   oh speak my name to the memory of men!
>   Having answered all, I say no more." And giving
>
> his head a shake, he looked up at my face
>   cross-eyed, then bowed his head and fell away
>   among the other blind souls of that place.   90
>
> And my Guide to me: "He will not wake again
>   until the angel trumpet sounds the day
>   on which the host shall come to judge all men.
>
> Then shall each soul before the seat of Mercy
>   return to its sad grave and flesh and form
>   to hear the edict of Eternity."
>
> So we picked our slow way among the shades
>   and the filthy rain, speaking of life to come.
>   "Master," I said, "when the great clarion fades
>
> into the voice of thundering Omniscience,
>   what of these agonies? Will they be the same,
>   or more, or less, after the final sentence?"
>
> And he to me: "Look to your science again
>   where it is written: the more a thing is perfect
>   the more it feels of pleasure and of pain.   105
>
> As for these souls, though they can never soar
>   to true perfection, still in the new time
>   they will be nearer it than they were before."
>
> And so we walked the rim of the great ledge
>   speaking of pain and joy, and of much more
>   that I will not repeat, and reached the edge
>
> where the descent begins. There, suddenly,
> we came on Plutus, the great enemy.

Notes

13. *Cerberus:* In classical mythology Cerberus appears as a three-headed dog. His master was Pluto, king of the Underworld. Cerberus was placed at the Gate of the Underworld to allow all to enter, but none to escape. His three heads and his ravenous disposition make him an apt symbol of gluttony.

14. *like a mad dog:* Cerberus *is* a dog in classical mythology, but Dante seems clearly to have visualized him as a half-human monster. The beard (line 16) suggests that at least one of his three heads is human, and many illuminated manuscripts so represent him.

38. *until one wraith among them:* As the poets pass, one of the damned sits up and asks if Dante recognizes him. Dante replies that he does not, and the wraith identifies himself as a Florentine nicknamed Ciacco, *i.e.,* The Hog.

Little is known about Ciacco (TCHA-koe). Boccaccio refers to a Florentine named Ciacco (Decameron IX, 8), and several conflicting accounts of him have been offered by various commentators. All that need be known about him, however, is the nature of his sin and the fact that he is a Florentine. Whatever else he may have been does not function in the poem.

42. *You had been made before I was unmade:* That is, "you were born before I died." The further implication is that they must have seen one another in Florence, a city one can still walk across in twenty minutes, and around in a very few hours. Dante certainly would have known everyone in Florence.

61. CIACCO'S PROPHECY: This is the first of the political prophecies that are to become a recurring theme of the *Inferno.* (It is the second if we include the political symbolism of the Greyhound in Canto I.) Dante is, of course, writing after these events have all taken place. At Easter time of 1300, however, the events were in the future.

The Whites and the Blacks of Ciacco's prophecy should not be confused with the Guelphs and the Ghibellines. The internal strife between the Guelphs and the Ghibellines ended with the total defeat of the Ghibellines. By the end of the 13th century that strife had passed. But very shortly a new feud began in Florence between White Guelphs and Black Guelphs. A rather gruesome murder perpetrated by Focaccio de' Cancellieri (Foe-KAH-tchoe day Khan-tchell-YAIR-ee) became the cause of new strife between two branches of the Cancellieri family. On May 1 of 1300 the White Guelphs (Dante's party) drove the Black Guelphs from Florence in bloody fighting. Two years later, however ("within two suns"), the Blacks, aided by Dante's detested Boniface VIII, returned and expelled most of the prominent Whites, among them Dante; for he had been a member of the Priorate (City Council) that issued a decree banishing the leaders of both sides. This was the beginning of Dante's long exile from Florence.

70. *two are honest:* In the nature of prophecies this remains vague. The two are not identified.

76–77. FARINATA will appear in Canto X among the Heretics: TEGGHIAIO and JACOPO RUSTICUCCI, in Canto XVI with the homosexuals, MOSCA in Canto XXVIII with the sowers of discord. ARRIGO does not appear again and he has not been positively identified. Dante probably refers here to Arrigo (or Oderigo) dei Fifanti, one of those who took part in the murder of Buondelmonte (Canto XXVIII, line 106, note).

87. *speak my name:* Excepting those shades in the lowest depths of Hell whose sins are so shameful that they wish only to be forgotten, all of the damned are eager to be remembered on earth. The concept of the family name and of its survival in the memories of men were matters of first importance among Italians of Dante's time, and expressions of essentially the same attitude are common in Italy today.

103. *your science:* "Science" to the man of Dante's time meant specifically "the writings of Aristotle and the commentaries upon them."

Questions for Critical Thinking

1. Before the gates of hell race a slew of souls whom Dante identifies as the opportunists—those who took the side neither of good nor evil but were completely for themselves. What fate is reserved for these souls? Why do you think Dante was so bitter in his condemnation of them? What is your opinion of this punishment?

2. What is your opinion of the justice of hell which punishes sinners in a manner befitting their sin?

3. The *Divine Comedy* is a long poem. What advantages do you think writing it in poetic form gave Dante? What disadvantages?

4. A Homeric simile is a lengthy comparison between two images, often extending between stanzas. Find an example of an Homeric simile in Canto 1, and comment on its effectiveness.

5. What were the sins of those souls committed to limbo? What is your opinion of the justice of their fate?

6. What underlying attitude towards sin and wrong does the *Divine Comedy* implicitly embody which we are less apt to subscribe to today? What is mainly responsible for our changed attitude towards sin and wrong?

7. What is your attitude towards the belief in a hell of eternal damnation and torture? If you do not believe in hell, what punishment, if any, do you think awaits the sinner?

8. If the *Divine Comedy* were written today, what audience do you think would mainly find it appealing? What reception do you think it would likely receive from most ordinary readers?

Writing Assignment

Write an essay exploring the different attitudes of religion and psychology towards wrongdoing. Say what differences you detect in these attitudes and how you account for them.

Writing Advice

One obvious way to write this essay is to do a straightforward comparison/contrast. For an explanation of the method we recommend for writing straight comparison/ contrasts see the *Writing Advice* section after *Pensées* by Blaise Pascal, Chapter 2. But this assignment is slightly more complicated, since it asks you to explore the different attitudes implicit in religion and psychology towards wrongdoing. Better that your contrast emerge naturally from a discussion of the underlying terminologies and values used by religion and psychology respectively to adjudge wrongdoing than that you try to subsume the entire essay under a rigid comparison/contrast pattern.

Begin, therefore, by inquiring into the differing terminologies of religion and psychology in dealing with wrongdoing. Obviously, religion calls wrongdoing "sin." What is the equivalent concept in psychology? What, for that matter, is the religious definition of "sin," and what the definition of its equivalent in psychology? Ask yourself, also, what motivation religion and psychology respectively attribute for wrongdoing. If your answer is that religion assumes sin is prompted by the devil, ask yourself what is the equivalent, if any, of the devil in psychology.

The second part of the essay asks you to account for the differences in the attitudes of religion and psychology towards wrongdoing. We know that religion assumes that sin is freely chosen for reasons of evil by the sinner while psychology argues that some wrongdoing is traceable to underlying compulsions or to mental illness. One broad distinction between the two, then, is that religion accounts for sin as a moral lapse, whereas psychology proposes a more medical or naturalistic explanation. What difference do you think these divergent explanations are likely to make on the way the wrongdoer is viewed by religion and psychology? That is one of the primary questions you must answer in this essay.

Alternate Writing Assignments

1. Write an argument against the possible existence of hell. Specify, as clearly as you can, why you think such a place cannot exist.

2. Write an essay analyzing the characteristics and images Dante associates with the first three circles of hell.

PHILOSOPHY

TEN REASONS FOR BELIEVING IN IMMORTALITY

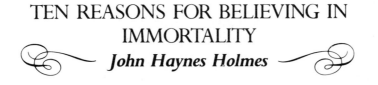

John Haynes Holmes

John Haynes Holmes (1897–1964) was an American minister and social activist, known for fearlessly defending many controversial causes, including pacifism and civil liberties for all. He was a prolific writer. His 20 books include *Religion for Today* (1917), *My Gandhi* (1953), *The Collected Hymns of John Haynes Holmes* (1960), and an autobiography, titled *I Speak for Myself* (1959).

Reading Advice

This essay was first delivered as a sermon in 1929 and only lightly edited when it was published in a collection of sermons titled *The Community Pulpit* later the same year. Sermons, of course, have certain requirements that essays written for the sole purpose of being read do not have. First of all, the content must be so clear as to be understood on first hearing because the speaker cannot constantly repeat his pronouncements in case the audience misunderstood—the way a passage can be restudied or slowly digested when it is being read rather than heard. Second, complex ideas from other literary sources must be delivered in a style that can be understood by the average listener in the audience. For instance, notice how Holmes carefully selected or paraphrased the words of Plato, William James, Waldo Emerson, and Thomas Paine so that his use of these men's thoughts would not cause his audience to become lost in a maze of oversubtle, impalpable abstrusions. This simplifying of complex ideas makes your task of grasping these ideas easy. In this particular essay, immortality, often the subject of impossibly difficult writing, turns out to be pleasantly understandable. All you need to do is follow along patiently, mulling over each numbered point, to come up with your own beliefs.

Nobody can speak on the immortality   1
of the soul at this late date without being acutely conscious of the fact that there is nothing new that can be said. Since the time of Plato, at least, five hundred years before the birth of Jesus, the discussion of immortality has been conducted by the greatest minds upon the highest levels of human thought. Theology, philosophy, psychology and science have all been called upon to make their contributions to the theme. Poetry has offered its voice and religion its faith, with the result that every corner of knowledge has been explored, every depth of truth uncovered and revealed! There is always the possibility, of course, that the veil which hangs over every grave to divide this life from the mystery that lies beyond, may some day be lifted to our gaze. There are those who claim—not without some reason, it seems to me—that they have penetrated this veil, and thus have looked upon the reality of survival after death. But short of some such remarkable discovery as this, there is nothing new to be anticipated in this field. Everything has been said that can be said. The case for immortality is in!

Now it is this case which I want to present to you this morning. Since I   2
cannot hope to say anything that is new, I want to see what I can do in the way of saying something that is old. I cannot say much, to be sure, for no discourse however merciless in length, can compass the range and beauty of the argument for immortality. But since ten is a goodly number, I take ten of the reasons which have brought conviction to the minds of men and offer these as the case for immortality today. I trust that it may be interesting, and also persuasive, especially to the members of our younger generation, to be reminded of what has been thought upon this question for many years.

By way of introduction, may I make mention of some two or three reasons   3
for believing in immortality which do not concern me. I speak of these not because they are important, but because some of you may wonder, if I am silent, why they do not appear in my list of ten.

Thus I do not see any reason for believing in immortality because Jesus is   4
reputed to have risen from the dead. In the first place, I do not believe that he rose from the dead. There is no evidence to substantiate this miracle. In the

For "Ten Reasons for Believing in Immortality," by John Haynes Holmes, from *A Modern Introduction to Philosophy.* Published by The Free Press. Reprinted by permission of Roger W. Holmes.

second place, even if he did break the barriers of the tomb, I fail to see what the resurrection of the body has to do with the immortality of the soul. The two things are irrelevant, the one to the other. What we have here is one of the myths of Christianity which, even if it were true, would have nothing seriously to do with our question.

Again, I find no argument for immortality in the succession of the seasons, the revival of nature of the spring, the blossoming of the flowers after the winter's cold. Poets are fond of this idea, as Shelley, for example, when he wrote his famous line,

> If winter comes, can spring be far behind?

I think we may see in it a pretty parable, a rather beautiful poetic concept. But as an argument for immortality, it is what Ruskin called an instance of the "pathetic fallacy." The flowers that blossom in the spring are not the flowers that died the preceding autumn. The tide of life that flows on through nature, season after season, is the tide that flows on through humanity, generation after generation, and it touches as little in the one case as in the other the survival of the individual. Like most parables, this does not hold when applied rigorously to the issue that is involved.

Again, I must confess that I am not convinced by the argument that men must be immortal because the heart demands it. It is natural that we should cling to those we love. It is inevitable that we should believe that providence, if it be beneficent, must give answer to our plea that we have not permanently separated from our friends and kindred. Whittier was yielding to the deepest impulses of the soul when he suggested in his "Snow Bound" that "Life is ever Lord of Death," because "Love can never lose its own." This is the cry of the human heart, and I personally believe that it is not destined to go unanswered. But a longing is one thing, and a reason is another. I see no evidence, in the scheme of things, that what we want we are therefore going to have. On the contrary, Felix Adler has taught us that frustration is the basic principle of life, that experience is "permeated with the sense of incompleteness," and that this "sense of incompleteness" is a perpetual doom that is laid upon us as "a necessary instrument of spiritual development." Whether this be true or not I do not know, but in either case I still believe that love gives no guarantee of its own survival.

But there are arguments for immortality which seem to suggest that it is true. Surveying all the field, I find myself agreeing with William James that, while we are under no compulsion to believe in immortality, as we are under a compulsion, for example, to believe that "things equal to the same thing are equal to each other," yet we are free to believe, if we so desire, without being guilty of superstition. "You may believe henceforward," said Professor James, "whether you care to profit by the permission or not." There are perfectly good and sufficient reasons, in other words, why an intelligent man may intelligently believe in immortality. Ten of these reasons I propose to submit to you this morning, beginning with those which open up the question, so to speak, and ending with those which close it as a conviction of the soul.

(1) First of all, may I offer the suggestion, not important in itself and yet of real significance to the thinking mind, that we may believe in immortality because there is no reason for *not* believing in it. In discussions of this question we are constantly reminded that immortality has never been proved. To which there is the immediate and inevitable reply that immortality has never been disproved! As there is no positive testimony to prove it true, so is there no negative testimony to prove it untrue. What we have here is an absence of testimony, and such "absence of testimony," says John Fiske, "does not even raise a negative presumption, except in cases where testimony is accessible." In this case, testimony is not accessible. Therefore the question is open "for those general considerations of philosophic analogy and moral probability which are the grounds upon which we can call for help in this arduous inquiry." As the question is open, so must our minds be open. My first reason, therefore, for believing in immortality or for being ready to believe in immortality, is the primarily interesting fact that there is no reason for not believing in immortality. My mind is absolutely at one with that of John Stuart Mill when he said upon his question, "To anyone who feels it conducive either to his satisfaction or to his usefulness to hope for a future state, . . . there is no hindrance to his indulging that hope."

(2) My second reason for believing in immortality is to be found in the universality of the idea. In saying this, I am not seeking to substantiate my position by taking a majority vote upon the question. I am not arguing that a proposition is necessarily true because most persons have believed it. All too many beliefs have clung pertinaciously to the human mind, only in the end to be revealed as superstitions, and it may very well be that this concept of immortality is one of them.

What I have in mind here is the very different consideration that immortality is not merely a belief to be accepted but an idea to be explained. "Here is this wonderful thought," says Emerson, "Wherever man ripens, this audacious belief presently appears. . . . As soon as thought is exercised, this belief is inevitable. . . . Whence came it? Who put it in the mind?" In itself it is remarkable, this idea that the death of the body is not the extinction of personality. Who has ever looked upon a dead body without marveling that man has ever thought of survival beyond the grave? Emerson could not explain the fact, as it has appeared in all ages and among all peoples, except upon the supposition that the thought of immortality is "not sentimental" but "elemental"—elemental in the sense that it is "grounded in the necessities and forces we possess."

That this idea is something more than idle speculation is shown by the whole philosophy of evolution, which has given to us that fundamental interpretation of life as "the continuous adjustment of inner relations to outer relations." An organism lives by successfully adjusting itself to the conditions of its environment, by developing itself inwardly in such a way as to meet the conditions of reality. When we find in plant or animal some inner faculty or attitude which is universally present, and which persists from generation to generation, we may be perfectly sure that it represents some correspondence with reality which has made survival possible. Life, in other words, is so definitely a matter of the successful coordination of inner relations with outer relations, that it is altogether impossible to conceive that in any specific relation the subjective term is real and the objective term is non-existent. What exists within is the sign and symbol, and guarantee, of what exists without.

Now man has never existed without the thought of immortality. From the earliest period of his life upon the earth, he has been profoundly concerned with this idea. He has never been able to live without it; even when he has tried to deny it, he has not been able to get rid of it. The immortal life is part of his being, as a line on the surface of a coin is a part of the pattern of its design. And as the line upon the coin could not have been set there except as the impression of the die which stamped its mark upon the metal, so the idea of immortality could not have appeared within the consciousness of man, except as the impression of the reality which made it what it is. Our faculties, our attributes, our ideas, as we have seen, are the reflection of the environment to which we adapt ourselves as the condition of survival. What we feel within is the reaction upon what exists without. As the eye proves the existence of light, and the ear the existence of sound, so the immortal hope may not unfairly be said to prove the existence of the immortal life. It is this that we mean when we say that the universality of the idea is an argument for the acceptance of the idea. In his great essay on "Immortality," Emerson tells us of two men who early in life spent much of their time together in earnest search for some proof of immortality. An accident separated them, and they did not meet again for a quarter of a century. They said nothing, "but shook hands long and cordially. At last his friend said, 'Any light, Albert?' 'None,' replied Albert. 'Any light, Lewis?' 'None,' he replied." And Emerson comments "that the impulse which drew these two minds to this inquiry through so many years was a better affirmative evidence for immortality than their failure to find a confirmation was a negative."

(3) This universal diffusion of the idea of immortality takes on an added significance when I come to my third reason for believing in immortality. I refer to the fact so memorably stated by Cicero. "There is in the minds of men," he says, "I know not how, a certain presage, as it were, of a future existence; and this takes deepest root in the greatest geniuses and the most exalted souls." The leaders of the race, in other words, have always believed in immortality. They are not separated in this case, as in so many cases, from the masses of ignorant and superstitious men by doctrines of dissent. On the

contrary, in this case the ideas of the highest are at one with the hopes of the humblest among mankind.

In referring thus to the great names that are attached to the idea of immortality, I would not have you believe that I am making any blind appeal to the concept of authority. I have never seen any reason for arbitrarily separating our minds from the companionship of other minds. There is such a thing, even for the independent thinker, as a consensus of best opinion which cannot be defied without the weightiest of reasons. And in this matter of immortality there is a consensus of best opinion which constitutes, to my mind, one of the most remarkable phenomena in the whole history of human thinking. I have no time this morning to list the names of those who have believed in the immortality of the soul. If I did so, I should have to include the names of scientists from Aristotle to Darwin and Eddington, of philosophers from Plato to Kant and Bergson, of poets from Sophocles to Goethe and Robert Browning, of ethical teachers and public leaders from Socrates to Tolstoi and Mahatma Gandhi. There are dissenters from the doctrine, like Epictetus yesterday and Bernard Shaw today, but the consensus of opinion the other way is remarkable. Even the famous heretics stand in awe before this conception of eternity. Thus, Voltaire declared that "reason agrees with revelation . . . that the soul is immortal." Thomas Paine affirmed that he did not "trouble (himself) about the manner of future existence," so sure he was that "the Power which gave existence is able to continue it in any form." Even Robert G. Ingersoll confessed, as he stood by his brother's grave, that love could "hear the rustle of an angel's wing." In the light of such testimony as this, are we not justified in believing that there is reason for believing in immortality? If not, then we know, with James Martineau, "who are those who are mistaken. Not the mean and grovelling souls who never reached to so great a thought. . . . No, the deceived are the great and holy, whom all men revere; the men who have lived for something better than their happiness and spent themselves on the altar of human good. Whom are we to reverence, and what can we believe, if the inspirations of the highest nature are but cunningly-devised fables?"

(4) This conviction of immortality as rooted in the minds of men, and the greatest men, brings us immediately to the consideration of human nature itself as evidence for its own survival. Thus, my fourth reason this morning for believing in immortality is found in what I would call man's over-endowment as a creature of this earth, his surplus equipment for the adventure of his present life. If we want to know what is needed for successful existence upon this planet, we have only to look at any animal. His equipment of physical attributes and powers seems perfectly adapted to the necessities of his natural environment. The outfit of man, on the contrary, seems to constitute something like "a vast over-provision" for his necessities. If this life is all, in other words, what need has man for all these mental faculties, moral aspirations, spiritual ideals, which make him to be distinctly a man as contrasted with the animal?

14

15

If existence upon the earth is his only destiny, why should man not prefer the swiftness of the deer, the strength of the lion, the vision of the eagle, to any endowment of mind and heart, as more adequate provision for the purely physical task of physical survival in a physical world? What we have here is a fundamental discrepancy between the endowment of man and the life he has to live; and this constitutes, if this life be all, an unparalleled violation of the creative economy of the universe. In every other form of life, an organism is equipped to meet the exactions of its immediate environment. Man is equipped for this environment, and also for something more. Why is this not proof that he is destined for something more? As we estimate the length of the voyage of a ship by the character of its equipment, never confusing a little coasting vessel with a transatlantic liner or an arctic exploration steamer, why should we not estimate the length of man's voyage upon the seas of life in exactly the same way? What man bears within himself is evidence that he is destined for some farther port than any upon these shores. What he is in mind and heart and spirit, in the range of his interests and the lift of his soul, can only be explained on the supposition that he is preparing for another and a vaster life. I believe that man is immortal because already the signs of immortality are upon him.

(5) This consideration is basic, and sums up our whole case for immortality as rooted in human nature. But it opens out into other considerations which may well be taken as other reasons for believing in immortality. Thus, I would specify as my fifth reason for believing in immortality the lack of coordination, or proportion, between a man's body and a man's mind. If these two are to be regarded as aspects of a single organism, adapted only to the conditions of this present life, why do they so early begin to pull apart, and the weakness of the one to retard and at last to defeat the other? For a while, to be sure, there seems to be a real coordination between soul and body, between the personality, on the one hand, and the physical frame which it inhabits, on the other. Thus the child is in nothing so delightful as in the fact that it is a perfect animal. Then, as maturity approaches, two exactly opposite processes begin to take place within the life of the human being. On the one hand, the body begins to lose its resiliency and harden, to stop its growth and become static, then to decay and at last to dissolve. There is a definite cycle, in other words, in the physical life of the individual. There is a beginning, then a pause, and then an end. It is from first to last a process of completion. But there is no completion in the life of the soul. "Who dares speak the word 'completed,' " says Professor Munsterberg, the great psychologist. "Do not our purposes grow? Does not every newly-created value give us the desire for further achievement? Is our life ever so completely done that no desire has still a meaning?" The personality of man is an enduring thing. As the body weakens through the years, so the soul only grows the stronger and more wonderful. As the body approaches irrevocably to its end, so the soul only mounts to what seems to be a new beginning. We come to death, in other words, only to discover within ourselves

16

exhaustless possibilities. The aged have testified again and again to this amazing truth that as the body turns to ashes, the spirit mounts as to a flame. Victor Hugo, protesting against the waning of his powers, said, "For half a century I have been writing my thoughts in prose and verse . . . but I feel that I have not said a thousandth part of what is in me." Said James Martineau, on his 80th birthday, "How small a part of my plans have I been able to carry out! Nothing is so plain as that life at its fullest on earth is but a fragment." Robert Browning catches this thought in his poem, "Cleon," where he makes his hero say,

> . . . *Every day my sense of joy*
> *Grows more acute, my soul . . . enlarged, more keen,*
> *While every day my hairs fall more and more,*
> *My hand shakes, and the heavy years increase*
> *The horror quickening still from year to year,*
> *When I shall know most, and yet least enjoy.*

What to do, in such emergency, except what Cleon did,

> . . . *imagine to (our) need*
> *Some future state* . . .

(6) But there is a lack of coordination not only between our personalities   17
and our physical bodies, but also between our personalities and the physical world. This is my sixth reason for believing in immortality—that our souls have potentialities and promises which should not, as indeed they cannot, be subject to the chance vicissitudes of earthly fortune. What are we going to say, for example, when we see some life of eminent utility, of great achievement, of character and beauty and noble dedication to mankind, not merely borne down by the body, but cut off sharply before its time by an automobile accident, a disease germ, a bit of poisoned food? What shall we think when we see a Shelley drowned in his thirtieth year by the heedless sea, a Phillips Brooks stricken in the prime of his manhood by a diphtheric sore-throat, a Captain Scott frozen in mid-career by an accident of weather? Is it possible that these lives of ours are dependent upon a fall of snow, a grain of dust, a passing breeze upon the sea? Is it conceivable that our personalities, with all their potencies of spirit, can be destroyed, as our bodies can be broken, by the material forces of the world? Are we to believe that eternal powers can be annihilated by transient accidents? I cannot think so! Rather must I think, as Professor George Herbert Palmer thought, as he looked upon the dead body of his wife, one of the greatest and most beautiful women of her time, stricken ere her years were ripe. "Though no regrets are proper for the manner of her death," said this noble husband, "yet who can contemplate the fact of it and not call the world irrational if, out of deference to a few particles of disordered matter, it excludes so fair a spirit?"

(7) But this question of the irrationality of a world which would allow death   18
to exercise mastery over a radiant spirit, has application not merely to the
individual but also to the race. This brings me to my seventh reason for believing
in immortality—a reason drawn from the logic of evolution. There is nothing
more familiar, of course, than the fact that this world is the result of a natural
process of development which has been going on for unnumbered millions of
years. If this process is rational, as man's processes are rational, it must have
been working all these eons of time to the achievement of some permanent
and worthy end. What is this end? It is not the physical world itself, for the
day must come when this earth will be swallowed up by the sun, and all the
universe be merged again into the original fire-mist from which it sprang. It is
not the works of man, for these perish even as man lives, and must vanish
utterly in the last cataclysm of ruin. It is not man himself, for man, like the
earth on which he lives, must finally disappear. Is there nothing that will remain
as the evidence and vindication of this cosmic process? Or must we believe
that, from the beginning, it has been like a child's tower of blocks built up only
to be thrown down?

It was the challenge of this contingency, of evolution coming in the end to   19
naught that moved no less a man than Charles Darwin, agnostic though he
was, to proclaim the conviction that "it is an intolerable thought that (man)
and all other sentient beings are doomed to complete annihilation after such
long-continued slow process." Unless the universe is crazy, something must
remain. The process must justify itself by producing something that endures.
And what can this thing be but the spiritual essence of man's nature—the soul
which is immortal? "The more thoroughly we comprehend the process of
evolution," says John Fiske, in an unforgettable statement, "the more we are
likely to feel that to deny the everlasting persistence of the spiritual element
in man is to rob the whole process of its meaning. Its goes far toward putting
us to permanent intellectual confusion." Which led him to his famous verdict
upon all the evidence: "I believe in the immortality of the soul as a supreme
act of faith in the reasonableness of God's work."

(8) This leads us deep into the realm of science—to a fundamental principle   20
that provides my eighth reason for believing in immortality. I refer to the
principle of persistence or conservation. The gist of this doctrine is that nothing
in the universe is ever lost. All energy is conserved. No matter what changes
take place in any particular form of energy, that energy persists, if not in the
old form then in a new, and the sum total of energy in the universe remains
the same. "Whatever is," says Sir Oliver Lodge, speaking of forms of energy in
the physical universe, "whatever is, both was and shall be." And he quotes the
famous statement of Professor Tait, that "persistence, or conservation, is the
test or criterion of real existence."

Now if this principle applies to the "real existence" of the material world,   21 why not to the "real existence" of the spiritual world as well? If it is impossible to think of physical energy as appearing and disappearing, coming into and going out of existence, why is it not equally impossible to think of intellectual or moral or spiritual energy as acting in this same haphazard fashion? We would laugh at a man who contended that the heat in molten metal, which disappears under the cooling action of air or water, had thereby been destroyed. Why should we not similarly laugh at a man who argues that the personality of a human being, which disappears under the chilling influence of death, has thereby been annihilated? What the personality may be, I do not know. Whether it is a form of energy itself, as some scientists assert, or "belongs to a separate order of existence," as Sir Oliver Lodge, for example, argues, I cannot say. But of this thing I am sure—that the soul of man is just as much a force in the world as magnetism or steam, or electricity, and that if the cosmic law of conservation forbids the destruction of the latter, it must as well forbid the destruction of the former. Anything else is inconceivable. The universe cannot be so thrifty of its physical, and so wasteful of its spiritual, resources. It is madness to conceive that the heat of an engine must be preserved, while the love of a heart may be thrown away. What prevails in the great realm of matter can be only an anticipation of what must equally prevail in the greater realm of spirit. For the universe is one. Its laws are everywhere the same. What science has discovered about the conservation of energy is only the physical equivalent of what religion has discovered about the immortality of the soul.

(9) We are coming now to ultimate things—to those first and last questions   22
of origins and meanings. This brings me to my ninth reason for believing in immortality—the fact, namely, that all the values of life exist in man, and in man alone. For the world as we know it and love it is not the world as we receive it, but the world as we make it by the creative genius of the inward spirit. Consider this earthly scene with man eliminated! The sun would be here, and the stars. Mountains would still lift themselves to the skies, and oceans spread afar to vast horizons. Birds would sing, and leaves rustle, and sunsets glow. But what would it all mean without man to see and hear, to interpret? What do the stars mean to the eagle, or the sea to the porpoise, or the mountain to the goat? It is man's ear which has heard the cuckoo as a "wandering voice," his eye which has seen "the floor of heaven thick inlaid with patines of bright gold," his mind which has found "sermons in stone, books in the running brooks, and good in everything." All that is precious in the world—all its beauty, its wonder, its meaning—exists in man, and by man, and for man. The world is what man has done with it in the far reaches of his soul. And we are asked to believe that the being who sees and glorifies shall perish, while the world which he has seen and glorified endures! Such a conclusion is irrational. The being who created the world must himself be greater than the world. The soul which conceives Truth, Goodness and Beauty, must itself be as eternal as the Truth, Goodness, and Beauty which it conceives. Nothing has any value

without man. Man, therefore, is the supreme value. Which is the essence of the Platonic philosophy of eternal life for man!

"Tell me, then," says Socrates in the "Phaedo," "what is that the inherence   23
of which renders the body alive?

"The soul, Cebes replied . . .   24

"Then whatever the soul possesses, to that she comes bearing life?   25

"Yes, certainly.   26

"And is there any opposite to life?   27

"There is . . . Death.   28

"And will the soul . . . ever receive the opposite of what she brings?   29

"Impossible, replied Cebes.   30

"Then, said Socrates, the soul is immortal!"   31

(10) These, now, are my main reasons for believing in immortality. I have   32
but one more, the tenth to add. It is the pragmatic argument that faith in an eternal life beyond the grave justifies itself in terms of the life that we are now living upon this side of the grave. For immortality does not concern the future alone; it concerns, also, the present. We are immortal today, if we are ever going to be immortal tomorrow. And this means that we have the chance to put to the test, even now and here, the belief to which we hold. It is the essence of the pragmatic philosophy that what is true will conduce to life, as food conduces to health, and that what is false will destroy life, as poison the body. Whatever is true enlarges and lifts and strengthens the life of man; whatever is false represses and weakens and disintegrates his life. Now what does immortality do when we put its affirmation to this test? What are the consequences which follow if we live as though we were eternal spirits? Can there be any doubt as to the answer?

We see a universe where spiritual values, not material forces, prevail; where   33
personality, whether in ourselves or in others, is precious, and therefore to be conserved; where principles, not possessions, are the supreme concern of life; where man is equal to his task, and labors not in vain for the high causes of humanity; where sacrifice is not foolish but wise, and love "the greatest thing in the world." The man who lives an immortal life takes on immortal qualities. His character assumes the proportions of his faith, and his work the range of his high destiny. "Immortality makes great living," says Dr. Fosdick. Therefore I believe in immortality.

Ten reasons! Are these all? No, they are not all! They are simply ten of the   34
many reasons for the most persistent faith which has ever beset the heart of man. In choosing these ten, I have sought to gather reasons which were reasons, and not mere superstitions—arguments which appeal to intellect rather than emotion, and which are based upon experience rather than credulity. That these reasons prove the idea of immortality to be true, I cannot claim. But there is many an idea which we accept for good reasons, even though it be not proved, as there is many a verdict in court which is returned for good reasons, even

though it be not proved, and immortality is one of them. What impresses me, as I follow the course of this great argument through the ages, is what impressed the mind of James Martineau when he said, "We do not believe immortality because we have proved it, but we forever try to prove it because we believe it." Hence the judgment of the poet, Tennyson—

> O, yet we trust that somehow good
>> Will be the final goal of ill,
>> To pangs of nature, sins of will,
> Defects of doubt, and taints of blood.
>
> That nothing walks with aimless feet;
>> That not one life shall be destroyed,
>> Or cast as rubbish to the void,
> When God hath made the pile complete. . . .
>
> I stretch lame hands of faith, and grope
>> And gather dust and chaff, and call
>> To what I feel is Lord of all,
> And faintly trust the larger hope.

Questions for Critical Thinking

1. Since the title of the essay is "Ten Reasons for Believing in Immortality," what is the author's purpose in mentioning four reasons that are not convincing?

2. How useful is the author's first point—that the lack of proof about something can serve as a reason to believe in it? Can you provide an example from your personal experience when you have used this argument to reassure yourself about a belief?

3. What difference is there between the author's second reason for believing in immortality and his comment in paragraph 6 that he is not convinced by the argument that "men must be immortal because the heart demands it"? What is your judgment of the author's conclusion?

4. What weakness, if any, do you detect in the author's third reason for believing in immortality? (*See* paragraphs 13 and 14.)

5. What analogy does the author use to prove that human beings must have a different destiny than other lower animals? How effective, in your opinion, is the analogy? (*See* paragraph 15.)

6. As you review in your mind Loren Eiseley's essay about the brown wasps in this chapter, do you find any common link between that essay and the one by Holmes? Be specific in answering this question.

7. Do you agree with the author that while the body grows weaker and less adventuresome with old age, the soul becomes stronger and more daring? Supply examples from history or your own experience to support your view.

8. Choose among the essays you have studied so far one that seems to sharply contradict this one. What central ideas of either essay has convinced you to believe its proposition more than other's?

9. What would an opponent of immortality for the soul consider Holmes's weakest point?

Writing Assignment

Write a critical review of Holmes's essay, paying attention to the following matters: validity of argument (evidence), clarity of organization, and effectiveness of style.

Writing Advice

Since the assignment sets clear parameters for your writing, you need to obey them and not stray beyond these limits. The following steps in tackling the assignment might be useful:

1. Formulate a thesis statement in which you pass judgment on the essay, either praising or denouncing it. Here is an example of each position you might take:

   Pro: In his essay "Ten Reasons for Believing in Immortality," John Haynes Holmes appeals to our sense of logic, our desire for order, and our love of beauty to convince us that souls do not die but continue to exist in the universal hereafter.

   Con: "Ten Reasons for Believing in Immortality," a sermon by John Haynes Holmes, pretends to be a careful philosophical presentation of truth, but in actuality is simply wishful thinking about a problem no human being can solve with any kind of realistic accuracy.

2. Focus on the argument itself, evaluating its strengths or weaknesses. A good argument must be supported by evidence (facts, statistics, examples, and expert testimony) to support the proposition. Study the essay carefully to see if such evidence is there or not. Use examples from the essay to indicate either strength or weakness in this area.

3. Now, deal with the overall organization of the essay. Remember that a well-organized essay is one that helps readers follow the author's train of thought without forcing them to wonder where in the world all these words are leading. We doubt that too many students will want to attack the essay for being disorganized since the ten steps are such clear guidelines for the progression of the

author's ideas. However, one could still render a negative judgment on the essay despite its clear organization.

4. Finally, write about the author's style. Most students will quickly recognize that the author is allusive as well as poetic. For instance, his numerous references to famous people like Plato, Cicero, Kant, Darwin, Browning, Tennyson, Emerson, and others give his arguments a sense of authority. He often uses the emotional language of poetry to tug at the heart strings of his readers, occasionally actually quoting the lines of famous poets. His own thoughts are often expressed in the figurative language of poetry, as when he states, "The immortal life is part of his being, as a line on the surface of a coin is a part of the pattern of its design." This is a poetic analogy. Holmes also uses metaphorical language, as in the following statement: "What man bears within himself is evidence that he is destined for some father port than any upon these shores." We offer these few examples as an incentive for you to find more. You may also wish to note the educational level toward which Holmes's essay is geared.

When you have fully dealt with the three areas required by the assignment, make sure that you use appropriate transitions leading from one area to the next. The goal is to produce an essay that presents your judgment smoothly as well as forcefully.

Alternate Writing Assignments

1. Write an essay in which you explain what role the concept of authority should play in a human being's belief about immortality. You may argue either for or against the importance of authority in shaping one's beliefs.

2. Write an essay in which you explain the difference between body and soul. If you see no difference, then explain that view.

HISTORY

THIS IS THE END OF THE WORLD: THE BLACK DEATH
Barbara Tuchman

Barbara Tuchman (1912–1988) was a prolific writer of historical books and essays on subjects ranging from the Middle Ages to World War II. She combined meticulous research with a lively writing style to produce works fascinating to an audience of professional historians as well as the general reading public. Twice her writing won the

Pulitzer Prize, and she was much sought after as a lecturer on historical events. Among her best-known works are *The Guns of August* (1962); *A Distant Mirror* (1978), from which the essay below is excerpted; and *The First Salute* (1988).

Reading Advice

Tuchman writes history aimed at appealing to the average reader. Notice, for instance, her use of the catchy title, "This Is the End of the World," and the opening paragraph that supplies grisly details of the Black Plague. The entire essay continues in much the same vein, revealing the author's remarkable flair for enlivening her story. She mentions "the sweep of death's scythe," the dead lying "putrid in the streets," "nature's awful energy," and abandoned villages leaving only a "grass-covered ghostly outline" where once people had lived.

Nor does she neglect facts. A careful reading of this essay will teach you a great deal about medieval society and its customs. Tuchman meticulously documents ideas taken from other people's writing, the way college students are required to do in term papers. One feature of Tuchman's style—the tendency to pile fact upon figure or quotation upon quotation—may tempt you to become impatient and to feel that fewer examples or quotations would have made the point just as adequately. But if you read on, assimilating all she has to offer, in the end you will be enriched.

Tuchman insisted on writing history as it actually occurred, which accounts for her unstructured organization. She felt that the usual organization of historical writing according to time or topic was an artificial imposition that could not properly reflect the ironic twists and turns of history's paradoxical flow. Repetition is the chief drawback of her strictly chronological method. Note also that in Tuchman's original work, the footnotes refer to pages in her book, while we have chosen to make them refer to paragraphs. Also, whereas in Tuchman's book the full bibliography is found at the end of the entire book, we have chosen to list a partial bibliography consisting of those works related to the excerpt we have reprinted.

*I*n October 1347, two months after the   1
fall of Calais, Genoese trading ships put into the harbor of Messina in Sicily with dead and dying men at the oars. The ships had come from the Black Sea port of Caffa (now Feodosiya) in the Crimea, where the Genoese maintained a trading post. The diseased sailors showed strange black swellings about the size of an egg or an apple in the armpits and groin. The swellings oozed blood and pus and were followed by spreading boils and black blotches on the skin from internal bleeding. The sick suffered severe pain and died quickly within five days of the first symptoms. As the disease spread, other symptoms of continuous fever and spitting of blood appeared instead of the swellings or

buboes. These victims coughed and sweated heavily and died even more quickly, within three days or less, sometimes in 24 hours. In both types everything that issued from the body—breath, sweat, blood from the buboes and lungs, bloody urine, and blood-blackened excrement—smelled foul. Depression and despair accompanied the physical symptoms, and before the end "death is seen seated on the face."

The disease was bubonic plague, present in two forms: one that infected the bloodstream, causing the buboes and internal bleeding, and was spread by contact; and a second, more virulent pneumonic type that infected the lungs and was spread by respiratory infection. The presence of both at once cause the high mortality and speed of contagion. So lethal was the disease that cases were known of persons going to bed well and dying before they woke, of doctors catching the illness at a bedside and dying before the patient. So rapidly did it spread from one to another that to a French physician, Simon de Covino, it seemed as if one sick person "could infect the whole world." The malignity of the pestilence appeared more terrible because its victims knew no prevention and no remedy.

The physical suffering of the disease and its aspect of evil mystery were expressed in a strange Welsh lament which saw "death coming into our midst like black smoke, a plague which cuts off the young, a rootless phantom which has no mercy for fair countenance. Woe is me of the shilling in the armpit! It is seething, terrible . . . a head that gives pain and causes a loud cry . . . a painful angry knob . . . Great is its seething like a burning cinder . . . a grievous thing of ashy color." Its eruption is ugly like the "seeds of black peas, broken fragments of brittle sea-coal . . . the early ornaments of black death, cinders of the peelings of the cockle weed, a mixed multitude, a black plague like halfpence, like berries. . . ."

Rumors of a terrible plague supposedly arising in China and spreading through Tartary (Central Asia) to India and Persia, Mesopotamia, Syria, Egypt, and all of Asia Minor had reached Europe in 1346. They told of a death toll so devastating that all of India was said to be depopulated, whole territories covered by dead bodies, other areas with no one left alive. As added up by Pope Clement VI at Avignon, the total of reported dead reached 23,840,000. In the absence of a concept of contagion, no serious alarm was felt in Europe until the trading ships brought their black burden of pestilence into Messina while other infected ships from the Levant carried it to Genoa and Venice.

By January 1348 it penetrated France via Marseille, and North Africa via Tunis. Shipborne along coasts and navigable rivers, it spread westward from Marseille through the ports of Languedoc to Spain and northward up the Rhône to Avignon, where it arrived in March. It reached Narbonne, Montpellier, Carcassonne, and Toulouse between February and May, and at the same time in Italy spread to Rome and Florence and their hinterlands. Between June and

August it reached Bordeaux, Lyon, and Paris, spread to Burgundy and Normandy, and crossed the Channel from Normandy into southern England. From Italy during the same summer it crossed the Alps into Switzerland and reached eastward to Hungary.

In a given area the plague accomplished its kill within four to six months   6
and then faded, except in the larger cities, where, rooting into the close-quartered population, it abated during the winter, only to reappear in spring and rage for another six months.

In 1349 it resumed in Paris, spread to Picardy, Flanders, and the Low   7
Countries, and from England to Scotland and Ireland as well as to Norway, where a ghost ship with a cargo of wool and a dead crew drifted offshore until it ran aground near Bergen. From there the plague passed into Sweden, Denmark, Prussia, Iceland, and as far as Greenland. Leaving a strange pocket of immunity in Bohemia, and Russia unattacked until 1351, it had passed from most of Europe by mid-1350. Although the mortality rate was erratic, ranging from one fifth in some places to nine tenths or almost total elimination in others, the overall estimate of modern demographers has settled—for the area extending from India to Iceland—around the same figure expressed in Froissart's casual words: "a third of the world died." His estimate, the common one at the time, was not an inspired guess but a borrowing of St. John's figure for mortality from plague in Revelation, the favorite guide to human affairs of the Middle Ages.

A third of Europe would have meant about 20 million deaths. No one knows   8
in truth how many died. Contemporary reports were an awed impression, not an accurate count. In crowded Avignon, it was said, 400 died daily; 7,000 houses emptied by death were shut up; a single graveyard received 11,000 corpses in six weeks; half the city's inhabitants reportedly died, including 9 cardinals or one third of the total, and 70 lesser prelates. Watching the endlessly passing death carts, chroniclers let normal exaggeration take wings and put the Avignon death toll at 62,000 and even at 120,000, although the city's total population was probably less than 50,000.

When graveyards filled up, bodies at Avignon were thrown into the Rhône   9
until mass burial pits were dug for dumping the corpses. In London in such pits corpses pilled up in layers until they overflowed. Everywhere reports speak of the sick dying too fast for the living to bury. Corpses were dragged out of homes and left in front of doorways. Morning light revealed new piles of bodies. In Florence the dead were gathered up by the Compagnia della Misericordia—founded in 1244 to care for the sick—whose members wore red robes and hoods masking the face except for the eyes. When their efforts failed, the dead lay putrid in the streets for days at a time. When no coffins were to be had, the bodies were laid on boards, two or three at once, to be carried to graveyards or common pits. Families dumped their own relatives into the pits, or buried

them so hastily and thinly "that dogs dragged them forth and devoured their bodies."

Amid accumulating death and fear of contagion, people died without last rites and were buried without prayers, a prospect that terrified the last hours of the stricken. A bishop in England gave permission to laymen to make confession to each other as was done by the Apostles, "or if no man is present than even to a woman," and if no priest could be found to administer extreme unction, "then faith must suffice." Clement VI found it necessary to grant remissions of sin to all who died of the plague because so many were unattended by priests. "And no bells tolled," wrote a chronicler of Siena, "and nobody wept no matter what his loss because almost everyone expected death. . . . And people said and believed, 'This is the end of the world.' "   10

In Paris, where the plague lasted through 1349, the reported death rate was 800 a day, in Pisa 500, in Vienna 500 to 600. The total dead in Paris numbered 50,000 or half the population. Florence, weakened by the famine of 1347, lost three to four fifths of its citizens, Venice two thirds, Hamburg and Bremen, though smaller in size, about the same proportion. Cities, as centers of transportation, were more likely to be affected than villages, although once a village was infected, its death rate was equally high. At Givry, a prosperous village in Burgundy of 1,200 to 1,500 people, the parish register records 615 deaths in the space of fourteen weeks, compared to an average of thirty deaths a year in the previous decade. In three villages of Cambridgeshire, manorial records show a death rate of 47 percent, 57 percent, and in one case 70 percent. When the last survivors, too few to carry on, moved away, a deserted village sank back into the wilderness and disappeared from the map altogether, leaving only a grass-covered ghostly outline to show where mortals once had lived.   11

In enclosed places such as monasteries and prisons, the infection of one person usually meant that of all, as happened in the Franciscan convents of Carcassonne and Marseille, where every inmate without exception died. Of the 140 Dominicans at Montpellier only seven survived. Petrarch's brother Gherardo, member of a Carthusian monastery, buried the prior and 34 fellow monks one by one, sometimes three a day, until he was left alone with his dog and fled to look for a place that would take him in. Watching every comrade die, men in such places could not but wonder whether the strange peril that filled the air had not been sent to exterminate the human race. In Kilkenny, Ireland, Brother John Clyn of the Friars Minor, another monk left alone among dead men, kept a record of what had happened lest "things which should be remembered perish with time and vanish from the memory of those who come after us." Sensing "the whole world, as it were, placed within the grasp of the Evil One," and waiting for death to visit him too, he wrote, "I leave parchment to continue this work, if perchance any man survive and any of the race of Adam escape this pestilence and carry on the work which I have begun." Brother John, as noted by another hand, died of the pestilence, but he foiled oblivion.   12

The largest cities of Europe, with populations of about 100,000, were Paris   13
and Florence, Venice and Genoa. At the next level, with more than 50,000,
were Ghent and Bruges in Flanders, Milan, Bologna, Rome, Naples, and Pal-
ermo, and Cologne. London hovered below 50,000, the only city in England
except York with more than 10,000. At the level of 20,000 to 50,000 were
Bordeaux, Toulouse, Montpellier, Marseille, and Lyon in France, Barcelona,
Seville, and Toledo in Spain, Siena, Pisa, and other secondary cities in Italy, and
the Hanseatic trading cities of the Empire. The plague raged through them all,
killing anywhere from one third to two thirds of their inhabitants. Italy, with
a total population of 10 to 11 million, probably suffered the heaviest toll.
Following the Florentine bankruptcies, the crop failures and workers' riots of
1346–47, the revolt of Cola di Rienzi that plunged Rome into anarchy, the
plague came as the peak of successive calamities. As if the world were indeed
in the grasp of the Evil One, its first appearance on the European mainland in
January 1348 coincided with a fearsome earthquake that carved a path of
wreckage from Naples up to Venice. Houses collapsed, church towers toppled,
villages were crushed, and destruction reached as far as Germany and Greece.
Emotional response, dulled by horrors, underwent a kind of atrophy epitomized
by the chronicler who wrote, "And in these days was burying without sorrowe
and wedding without friendschippe."

In Siena, where more than half the inhabitants died of the plague, work was   14
abandoned on the great cathedral, planned to be the largest in the world, and
never resumed, owing to loss of workers and master masons and "the melancholy and grief" of the survivors. The cathedral's truncated transept still stands
in permanent witness to the sweep of death's scythe. Agnolo di Tura, a chronicler of Siena, recorded the fear of contagion that froze every other instinct.
"Father abandoned child, wife husband, one brother another," he wrote, "for
this plague seemed to strike through the breath and sight. And so they died.
And no one could be found to bury the dead for money or friendship. . . . And
I, Angolo di Tura, called the Fat, buried my five children with my own hands,
and so did many others likewise."

There were many to echo his account of inhumanity and few to balance it,   15
for the plague was not the kind of calamity that inspired mutual help. Its
loathsomeness and deadliness did not herd people together in mutual distress,
but only prompted their desire to escape each other. "Magistrates and notaries
refused to come and make the wills of the dying," reported a Franciscan friar
of Piazza in Sicily; what was worse, "even the priests did not come to hear
their confessions." A clerk of the Archbishop of Canterbury reported the same
of English priests who "turned away from the care of their benefices from fear
of death." Cases of parents deserting children and children their parents were
reported across Europe from Scotland to Russia. The calamity chilled the hearts
of men, wrote Boccaccio in his famous account of the plague in Florence that
serves as introduction to the *Decameron*. "One man shunned another . . . kinsfolk

held aloof, brother was forsaken by brother, oftentimes husband by wife; nay, what is more, and scarcely to be believed, fathers and mothers were found to abandon their own children to their fate, untended, unvisited as if they had been strangers." Exaggeration and literary pessimism were common in the 14th century, but the Pope's physician, Guy de Chauliac, was a sober, careful observer who reported the same phenomenon: "A father did not visit his son, nor the son his father. Charity was dead."

Yet not entirely. In Paris, according to the chronicler Jean de Venette, the   16
nuns of the Hôtel Dieu or municipal hospital, "having no fear of death, tended the sick with all sweetness and humility." New nuns repeatedly took the places of those who died, until the majority "many times renewed by death now rest in peace with Christ as we may piously believe."

When the plague entered northern France in July 1348, it settled first in   17
Normandy and, checked by winter, gave Picardy a deceptive interim until the next summer. Either in mourning or warning, black flags were flown from church towers of the worst-stricken villages of Normandy. "And in that time," wrote a monk of the abbey of Fourcarment, "the mortality was so great among the people of Normandy that those of Picardy mocked them." The same unneighborly reaction was reported of the Scots, separated by a winter's immunity from the English. Delighted to hear of the disease that was scouraging the "southrons," they gathered forces for an invasion, "laughing at their enemies." Before they could move, the savage mortality fell upon them too, scattering some in death and the rest in panic to spread the infection as they fled.

In Picardy in the summer of 1349 the pestilence penetrated the castle of   18
Coucy to kill Enguerrand's mother, Catherine, and her new husband. Whether her nine-year-old son escaped by chance or was perhaps living elsewhere with one of his guardians is unrecorded. In nearby Amiens, tannery workers, responding quickly to losses in the labor force, combined to bargain for higher wages. In another place villagers were seen dancing to drums and trumpets, and on being asked the reason, answered that, seeing their neighbors die day by day while their village remained immune, they believed they could keep the plague from entering "by the jollity that is in us. That is why we dance." Further north in Tournai on the border of Flanders, Gilles li Muisis, Abbot of St. Martin's, kept one of the epidemic's most vivid accounts. The passing bells rang all day and all night, he recorded, because sextons were anxious to obtain their fees while they could. Filled with the sound of mourning, the city became oppressed by fear, so that the authorities forbade the tolling of bells and the wearing of black and restricted funeral services to two mourners. The silencing of funeral bells and of criers' announcements of deaths was ordained by most cities. Siena imposed a fine on the wearing of mourning clothes by all except widows.

Flight was the chief recourse of those who could afford it or arrange it. The   19
rich fled to their country places like Boccaccio's young patricians of Florence,

who settled in a pastoral palace "removed on every side from the roads" with "wells of cool water and vaults of rare wines." The urban poor died in their burrows, "and only the stench of their bodies informed neighbors of their death." That the poor were more heavily afflicted than the rich was clearly remarked at the time, in the north as in the south. A Scottish chronicler, John of Fordun, stated flatly that the pest "attacked especially the meaner sort and common people—seldom the magnates." Simon de Covino of Montpellier made the same observation. He ascribed it to the misery and want and hard lives that made the poor more susceptible, which was half the truth. Close contact and lack of sanitation was the unrecognized other half. It was noticed too that the young died in greater proportion than the old; Simon de Covino compared the disappearance of youth to the withering of flowers in the fields.

In the countryside peasants dropped dead on the roads, in the fields, in their houses. Survivors in growing helplessness fell into apathy, leaving ripe wheat uncut and livestock untended. Oxen and asses, sheep and goats, pigs and chickens ran wild and they too, according to local reports, succumbed to the pest. English sheep, bearers of the precious wool, died throughout the country. The chronicler Henry Knighton, canon of Leicester Abbey, reported 5,000 dead in one field alone, "their bodies so corrupted by the plague that neither beast nor bird would touch them," and spreading an appalling stench. In the Austrian Alps wolves came down to prey upon the sheep and then, "as if alarmed by some invisible warning, turned and fled back into the wilderness." In remote Dalmatia bolder wolves descended upon a plague-stricken city and attacked human survivors. For want of herdsmen, cattle strayed from place to place and died in hedgerows and ditches. Dogs and cats fell like the rest. 20

The dearth of labor held a fearful prospect because the 14th century lived close to the annual harvest both for food and for next year's seed. "So few servants and laborers were left," wrote Knighton, "that no one knew where to turn for help." The sense of a vanishing future created a kind of dementia of despair. A Bavarian chronicler of Neuberg on the Danube recorded that "Men and women . . . wandered around as if mad" and let their cattle stray "because no one had any inclination to concern themselves about the future." Fields went uncultivated, spring seed unsown. Second growth with nature's awful energy crept back over cleared land, dikes crumbled, salt water reinvaded and soured the lowlands. With so few hands remaining to restore the work of centuries, people felt, in Walsingham's words, that "the world could never again regain its former prosperity." 21

Though the death rate was higher among the anonymous poor, the known and the great died too. King Alfonso XI of Castile was the only reigning monarch killed by the pest, but his neighbor King Pedro of Aragon lost his wife, Queen Leonora, his daughter Marie, and a niece in the space of six months. John Cantacuzene, Emperor of Byzantium, lost his son. In France the lame Queen 22

Jeanne and her daughter-in-law Bonne de Luxemburg, wife of the Dauphin, both died in 1349 in the same phase that took the life of Enguerrand's mother. Jeanne, Queen of Navarre, daughter of Louis X, was another victim. Edward III's second daughter, Joanna, who was on her way to marry Pedro, the heir of Castile, died in Bordeaux. Women appear to have been more vulnerable than men, perhaps because, being more housebound, they were more exposed to fleas. Boccaccio's mistress Fiammetta, illegitimate daughter of the King of Naples, died, as did Laura, the beloved—whether real or fictional—of Petrarch. Reaching out to us in the future, Petrarch cried, "Oh happy posterity who will not experience such abysmal woe and will look upon our testimony as a fable."

In Florence Giovanni Villani, the great historian of his time, died at 68 in the midst of an unfinished sentence: "... *e dure questo pistolenza fino a* ... (in the midst of this pestilence there came to an end ...)." Siena's master painters, the brothers Ambrogio and Pietro Lorenzetti, whose names never appear after 1348, presumably perished in the plague, as did Andrea Pisano, architect and sculptor of Florence. William of Ockham and the English mystic Richard Rolle of Hampole both disappear from mention after 1349. Francisco Datini, merchant of Prato, lost both his parents and two siblings. Curious sweeps of mortality afflicted certain bodies of merchants in London. All eight wardens of the Company of Cutters, all six wardens of the Hatters, and four wardens of the Goldsmiths died before July 1350. Sir John Pulteney, master draper and four times Mayor of London, was a victim, likewise Sir John Montgomery, Governor of Calais.

Among the clergy and doctors the mortality was naturally high because of the nature of their professions. Out of 24 physicians in Venice, 20 were said to have lost their lives in the plague, although, according to another account, some were believed to have fled or to have shut themselves up in their houses. At Montpellier, site of the leading medieval medical school, the physician Simon de Covino reported that, despite the great number of doctors, "hardly one of them escaped." In Avignon, Guy de Chauliac confessed that he performed his medical visits only because he dared not stay away for fear of infamy, but "I was in continual fear." He claimed to have contracted the disease but to have cured himself by his own treatment; if so, he was one of the few who recovered.

Clerical mortality varied with rank. Although the one-third toll of cardinals reflects the same proportion as the whole, this was probably due to their concentration in Avignon. In England, in strange and almost sinister procession, the Archbishop of Canterbury, John Stratford, died in August 1348, his appointed successor died in May 1349, and the next appointee three months later, all three within a year. Despite such weird vagaries, prelates in general managed to sustain a higher survival rate than the lesser clergy. Among bishops the deaths have been estimated at about one in twenty. The loss of priests, even if many avoided their fearful duty of attending the dying, was about the same as among the population as a whole.

Government officials, whose loss contributed to the general chaos, found,   26
on the whole, no special shelter. In Siena four of the nine members of the
governing oligarchy died, in France one third of the royal notaries, in Bristol
15 out of the 52 members of the Town Council or almost one third. Tax-
collecting obviously suffered, with the result that Philip VI was unable to collect
more than a fraction of the subsidy granted him by the Estates in the winter
of 1347–48.

Lawlessness and debauchery accompanied the plague as they had during the   27
great plague of Athens of 430 B.C., when according to Thucydides, men grew
bold in the indulgence of pleasure: "For seeing how the rich died in a moment
and those who had nothing immediately inherited their property, they reflected
that life and riches were alike transitory and they resolved to enjoy themselves
while they could." Human behavior is timeless. When St. John had his vision
of plague in Revelation, he knew from some experience or race memory that
those who survived "repented not of the work of their hands. . . . Neither
repented they of their murders, nor of their sorceries, nor of their fornication,
nor of their thefts."

Ignorance of the cause augmented the sense of horror. Of the real carriers,   28
rats and fleas, the 14th century had no suspicion, perhaps because they were
so familiar. Fleas, though a common household nuisance, are not once mentioned in contemporary plague writings, and rats only incidentally, although
folklore commonly associated them with pestilence. The legend of the Pied
Piper arose from an outbreak of 1284. The actual plague bacillus, *Pasturella
pestis,* remained undiscovered for another 500 years. Living alternately in the
stomach of the flea and the bloodstream of the rat who was the flea's host,
the bacillus in its bubonic form was transferred to humans and animals by the
bite of either rat or flea. It traveled by virtue of *Rattus rattus,* the small medieval
black rat that lived on ships, as well as by the heavier brown or sewer rat. What
precipitated the turn of the bacillus from innocuous to virulent form is unknown,
but the occurrence is now believed to have taken place not in China but
somewhere in central Asia and to have spread along the caravan routes. Chinese
origin was a mistaken notion of the 14th century based on real but belated
reports of huge death tolls in China from drought, famine, and pestilence which
have since been traced to the 1330s, too soon to be responsible for the plague
that appeared in India in 1346.

The phantom enemy had no name. Called the Black Death only in later   29
recurrences, it was known during the first epidemic simply as the Pestilence
or Great Mortality. Reports from the East, swollen by fearful imaginings, told
of strange tempests and "sheets of fire" mingled with huge hailstones that "slew
almost all," or a "vast rain of fire" that burned up men, beasts, stones, trees,
villages, and cities. In another version, "foul blasts of wind" from the fires
carried the infection to Europe "and now as some suspect it cometh round the

seacoast." Accurate observation in this case could not make the mental jump to ships and rats because no idea of animal- or insect-borne contagion existed.

The earthquake was blamed for releasing sulfurous and foul fumes from the   30
earth's interior, or as evidence of a titanic struggle of planets and oceans causing waters to rise and vaporize until fish died in masses and corrupted the air. All these explanations had in common a factor of poisoned air, of miasmas and thick, stinking mists traced to every kind of natural or imagined agency from stagnant lakes to malign conjunction of the planets, from the hand of the Evil One to the wrath of God. Medical thinking, trapped in the theory of astral influences, stressed air as the communicator of disease, ignoring sanitation or visible carriers. The existence of two carriers confused the trail, the more so because the flea could live and travel independently of the rat for as long as a month and, if infected by the particularly virulent septicemic form of the bacillus, could infect humans without reinfecting itself from the rat. The simultaneous presence of the pneumonic form of the disease, which was indeed communicated through the air, blurred the problem further.

The mystery of the contagion was "the most terrible of all the terrors," as   31
an anonymous Flemish cleric in Avignon wrote to a correspondent in Bruges. Plagues had been known before, from the plague of Athens (believed to have been typhus) to the prolonged epidemic of the 6th century A.D., to the recurrence of sporadic outbreaks in the 12th and 13th centuries, but they had left no accumulated store of understanding. That the infection came from contact with the sick or with their houses, clothes, or corpses was quickly observed but not comprehended. Gentile da Foligno, renowned physician of Perugia and doctor of medicine at the universities of Bologna and Padua, came close to respiratory infection when he surmised that poisonous material was "communicated by means of air breathed out and in." Having no idea of microscopic carriers, he had to assume that the air was corrupted by planetary influences. Planets, however, could not explain the ongoing contagion. The agonized search for an answer gave rise to such theories as transference by sight. People fell ill, wrote Guy de Chauliac, not only by remaining with the sick but "even by looking at them." Three hundred years later Joshua Barnes, the 17th century biographer of Edward III, could write that the power of infection had entered into beams of light and "darted death from the eyes."

Doctors struggling with the evidence could not break away from the terms   32
of astrology, to which they believed all human physiology was subject. Medicine was the one aspect of medieval life, perhaps because of its links with the Arabs, not shaped by Christian doctrine. Clerics detested astrology, but could not dislodge its influence. Guy de Chauliac, physician to three popes in succession, practiced in obedience to the zodiac. While his *Cirurgia* was the major treatise on surgery of its time, while he understood the use of anesthesia made from the juice of opium, mandrake, or hemlock, he nevertheless prescribed bleeding

and purgatives by the planets and divided chronic from acute diseases on the basis of one being under the rule of the sun and the other of the moon.

In October 1348 Philip VI asked the medical faculty of the University of   33
Paris for a report on the affliction that seemed to threaten human survival. With careful thesis, antithesis, and proofs, the doctors ascribed it to a triple conjunction of Saturn, Jupiter, and Mars in the 40th degree of Aquarius said to have occurred on March 20, 1345. They acknowledged, however, effects "whose cause is hidden from even the most highly trained intellects." The verdict of the masters of Paris became the official version. Borrowed, copied by scribes, carried abroad, translated from Latin into various vernaculars, it was everywhere accepted, even by the Arab physicians of Cordova and Granada, as the scientific if not the popular answer. Because of the terrible interest of the subject, the translations of the plague tracts stimulated use of national languages. In that one respect, life came from death.

Notes

1: "DEATH IS SEEN SEATED": Simon de Covino, q. Campbell, 80.

2: "COULD INFECT THE WORLD": q. Gasquet, 41.

3: WELSH LAMENT: q. Ziegler, 190.

9: "DOGS DRAGGED THEM FORTH": Agnolo di Tura, q. Ziegler, 58. "OR IF NO MAN IS PRESENT": Bishop of Bath and Wells, q. Ziegler, 125.

10: "NO BELLS TOLLED": Agnolo di Tura, q. Schevill, *Siena,* 211. The same observation was made by Gabriel de Muisis, notary of Piacenza, q. Crawford, 113.

11: GIVRY PARISH REGISTER: Renouard, 111. THREE VILLAGES OF CAMBRIDGESHIRE: Saltmarsh. PETRARCH'S BROTHER: Bishop, 273. BROTHER JOHN CLYN: q. Ziegler, 195.

13: APATHY; "AND IN THESE DAYS": q. Deaux, 143, citing only "an old northern chronicle."

14: AGNOLO DI TURA, "FATHER ABANDONED CHILD": q. Ziegler, 58.

15: "MAGISTRATES AND NOTARIES": q. Deaux, 49. ENGLISH PRIESTS TURNED AWAY: Ziegler, 261. PARENTS DESERTING CHILDREN: Hecker, 30. GUY DE CHAULIAC, "A FATHER": q. Gasquet, 50–51.

16: NUNS OF THE HOTEL DIEU: *Chron. Jean de Venette,* 49.

17: PICARDS AND SCOTS MOCK MORTALITY OF NEIGHBORS: Gasquet, 53, and Ziegler, 198.

18: CATHERINE DE COUCY: *L'Art de vérifier,* 237. AMIENS TANNERS: Gasquet, 57. "BY THE JOLLITY THAT IS IN US": *Grandes Chrons.,* VI, 486–87.

19: JOHN OF FORDUN: q. Ziegler, 199. SIMON DE COVINO ON THE POOR: Gasquet, 42. ON YOUTH: Gazelles, *Peste.*

20: KNIGHTON ON SHEEP: q. Ziegler, 175. WOLVES OF AUSTRIA AND DALMATIA: ibid., 84, 111. DOGS AND CATS: Muisis, q. Gasquet, 44, 61.

21: BAVARIAN CHRONICLER OF NEUBERG: q. Ziegler, 84. WALSINGHAM, "THE WORLD COULD NEVER": Denifle, 273.

22: "OH HAPPY POSTERITY": q. Ziegler, 45.

23: GIOVANNI VILLANI, "e dure questo": q. Snell, 334.

24: PHYSICIANS OF VENICE: Campbell, 98. SIMON DE COVINO: ibid., 31. GUY DE CHAULIAC, "I WAS IN FEAR": q. Thompson, *Ec. and Soc.,* 379.

27: THUCYDIDES: q. Crawford, 30–31. CHINESE ORIGIN: Although the idea of Chinese origin is still being repeated (e.g., by William H. McNeill, *Plagues and People,* New York, 1976, 161–63), it is disputed by L. Carrington Goodrich of the Association for Asian Studies, Columbia Univ., in letters to the author of 18 and 26 October 1973. Citing contemporary Chinese and other sources, he also quotes Dr. George A. Perera of the College of Physicians and Surgeons, an authority on communicable diseases, who "agrees with me that the spaces between epidemics in China (1334), Semirechyé (1338–9) and the Mediterranean basin (1347–9) seem too long for the first to be responsible for the last."

28: REPORTS FROM THE EAST: Barnes, 432; Coulton, *Black Death,* 9–11.

30: ANONYMOUS FLEMISH CLERIC, "MOST TERRIBLE": His correspondence was edited in the form of a chronicle by De Smet, in *Recueil des chroniques de Flandres,* III, q. Ziegler, 22. GENTILE DA FOLIGNO, "COMMUNICATED BY AIR": Campbell, 38.

32: REPORT OF THE UNIVERSITY OF PARIS: Hecker, 51–53; Campbell, 15.

Bibliography

L'Art de vérifier les dates des faits historiques, par un Religieux de la Congregation de St.-Maur, vol. XII. Paris, 1818.

Campbell, Anna M., *The Black Death and Men of Learning.* Columbia University Press, 1931.

Chronicle of Jean de Venette. Trans. Jean Birdsall. Ed. Richard A. Newhall. Columbia University Press, 1853.

Crawfurd, Raymond, *Plague and Pestilence in Literature and Art.* Oxford, 1914.

Deaux, George, *The Black Death, 1347.* London, 1969.

Denifle, Henri, *La Désolation des églises, monastères et hopitaux en France pendant la geurre de cent ans,* vol. I. Paris, 1899.

Gasquet, Francis Aidan, Abbot, *The Black Death of 1348 and 1349,* 2nd ed. London, 1908.

Grandes Chroniques de France, vol. VI (to 1380). Ed. Paulin Paris. Paris, 1838.

Hecker, J. F. C. *The Epidemics of the Middle Ages.* London, 1844.

Saltmarsh, John, "Plague and Economic Decline in England in the Later Middle Ages," *Cambridge Historical Journal,* vol. VII, no. 1, 1941.

Schevill, Ferdinand, *History of Florence.* New York, 1961.

Snell, Frederick, *The Fourteenth Century.* Edinburgh, 1899.

Thompson, James Westfall, *Economic and Social History of Europe in the Later Middle Ages.* New York, 1931.

Ziegler, Philip, *The Black Death.* New York, 1969. (The best modern study.)

Questions for Critical Thinking

1. Has modern medicine made illnesses like the bubonic plague obsolete and no longer a threat to our civilization? What modern illness, if any, do you consider to have similar consequences to those of the medieval plague described?

2. What psychological effects on society do disasters such as plagues, earthquakes, and fires have? What traits do they serve to bring out in people?

3. Tuchman points out that the poor were far more susceptible to the plague than were the rich? Would this still hold true today? Why or why not?

4. In your view, what is the duty of priests and physicians during such virulent epidemics as those of the plague? Is it their obligation to assist the dying, or should they care for their own health first?

5. What role did human ignorance play in the tragedy of the plague?

6. Reread "Why Does God Let People Suffer?" by Hume, and "Nonmoral Nature,"

by Gould. How would these two essays explain the medieval plague? What is your own explanation?

7. If John Haynes Holmes had been alive during the plague, how might he have tried to comfort the families of victims who died in the plague? (*See* this chapter.)

8. How would you try to comfort or encourage a loved one afflicted with a mortal illness?

9. Tuchman documents her work heavily. How does she keep from producing a dull and tedious text?

Writing Assignment

Choosing a major disaster of past or recent history, write an essay describing what happened and how it affected society. Add the weight of scholarship to your paper by paraphrasing or quoting appropriate sources drawn from library research. Use two or three sources following the format used in the Tuchman excerpt. While this may not be the format required in a formal research paper, it will give you practice at integrating exterior sources into your writing.

Writing Advice

Your first step is to choose a disaster to use as your topic. Many calamities have struck the world throughout the ages, notable among them the following:

1. The earthquake of Lisbon in 1755

2. The earthquake of Assam, India, in 1897

3. The earthquake of Chile in 1960

4. A California carthquake of the last decade

5. The plague of Athens in 450 B.C.

6. The Roman plague of the third century A.D.

7. The Great Plague of London in 1665

8. The eruption of the volcano Vesuvius in Italy in A.D. 79.

9. The eruption of the Krakatoa volcano near Java in 1883

10. The United States polio epidemic of the 1950s

11. The present AIDS epidemic

12. A notable airplane crash

Once you have chosen your topic, go to the library and read about it. Any major modern disaster will be amply chronicled in the newspapers and periodicals of the era. On the other hand, if you have chosen a disaster of the distant past, such as the

Lisbon earthquake of 1755 or the eruption of Vesuvius in A.D. 79, your best source will be the history books. Using Tuchman's account of the medieval plague as your model, try to illustrate how the disaster affected the daily life of all citizens—poor or wealthy, ignorant or educated, powerless or powerful. We suggest placing each complete idea on a separate note card for organizational flexibility.

After taking notes, you can shuffle your cards until they are in the right order for incorporating into the essay. Write a first draft based on the facts and notes jotted down on the cards, making sure that all ideas are connected with smooth transitions and explanations. Vigorously edit your draft—pruning deadwood, rewriting sentences that sound choppy or confusing, correcting grammatical errors, and choosing the best diction for your particular purpose and audience. Again, using the Tuchman essay as your model, place a list of reference notes at the end of your essay, followed by a brief bibliography.

Alternate Writing Assignments

1. Using Tuchman's notes and bibliography as a base for research, write an essay about some person, place, or event mentioned by Tuchman.

2. Write an essay explaining the value of learning about past catastrophic events in the world. What lessons can one learn from them, and what do they contribute to one's sense of history?

HISTORY

CENTURY TIME
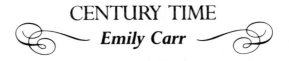
Emily Carr

Emily Carr (1871–1945) was a painter and writer born of English parents in British Columbia. Determined to portray her beloved Northwest in painting, she attended art school in San Francisco at the age of 16, later moving to London and Paris to perfect her skills. She did not win critical acclaim until she was 50 years old, when she found her work suddenly much in demand. Her growing popularity as an artist caused her to work harder than her constitution could stand. At the age of 70, when poor health made strenuous painting of large canvases impossible, she began to write, and published her first book, *Klee Wyck* (1941), from which the sketch below is reprinted. Other books are *The Book of Small* (1942), reminiscences of her childhood, and *Growing Pains: The Autobiography of Emily Carr* (1946).

Reading Advice

Emily Carr had great respect for the Indians she knew in western Canada. She admired their calm acceptance of life and their recognition of the small part each person or event plays in the larger scheme of things. You will detect this respect and admiration as you read Carr's description of an Indian cemetery. The little sketch is as strong and vivid as are Carr's paintings on canvas. She achieves power in writing largely by the use of active, short verbs: *push, creep, spread, call, reverse, hinder, hurry, open, step, exult.* Although she writes in short, simple sentences, her work resonates with a richness and mysticism. The surprise ending of this essay teaches us that the exact year in which a person died was of no importance to the Indians, who thought of time only in centuries.

You would never guess it was a ceme- 1
tery. Death had not spoiled it at all.

It was full of trees and bushes except in one corner where the graves were. 2
Even they were fast being covered with greenery.

Bushes almost hid the raw, split-log fence and the gate of cedar strips with 3
a cross above it, which told you that the enclosed space belonged to the dead. The land about the cemetery might change owners, but the ownership of the cemetery would not change. It belonged to the dead for all time.

Persistent growth pushed up through the earth of it—on and on eternally— 4
growth that was the richer for men's bodies helping to build it.

The Indian settlement was small. Not many new graves were required each 5
year. The Indians only cleared a small bit of ground at a time. When that was full they cleared more. Just as soon as the grave boxes were covered with earth, vines and brambles began to creep over the mounds. Nobody cut them away. It was no time at all before life spread a green blanket over the Indian dead.

It was a quiet place this Indian cemetery, lying a little aloof from the village. 6
A big stump field, swampy and green, separated them. Birds called across the field and flew into the quiet tangle of the cemetery bushes and nested there among foliage so newly created that it did not know anything about time. There was no road into the cemetery to be worn dusty by feet, or stirred into gritty clouds by hearse wheels. The village had no hearse. The dead were carried by friendly hands across the stump field.

The wooded part of the cemetery dropped steeply to a lake. You could not 7
see the water of the lake because of the trees, but you could feel the space between the cemetery and the purple-topped mountain beyond.

In the late afternoon a great shadow-mountain stepped across the lake and   8
brooded over the cemetery. It had done this at the end of every sunny day for
centuries, long, long before that piece of land was a cemetery. Dark came and
held the shadow-mountain there all night, but when morning broke, it was
back again inside its mountain, which pushed its grand purple dome up into
the sky and dared the pines swarming around its base to creep higher than
half-way up its bare rocky sides.

Indians do not hinder the progress of their dead by embalming or tight   9
coffining. When the spirit has gone they give the body back to the earth. The
earth welcomes the body—coaxes new life and beauty from it, hurries over
what men shudder at. Lovely tender herbage bursts from the graves, swiftly,
exulting over corruption.

Opening the gate I entered and walked among the graves. Pushing aside the   10
wild roses, bramble blossoms and scarlet honeysuckle which hugged the crude
wooden crosses, I read the lettering on them—

> SACRED OF KATIE—IPOO
> SAM BOYAN HE DIDE—IPOO
> RIP JULIE YECTON—IPOO
> JOSEPH'S ROSIE DI—IPOO

Even these scant words were an innovation—white men's ways; in the old   11
days totem signs would have told you who lay there. The Indian tongue had
no written words. In place of the crosses the things belonging to the dead
would have been heaped on the grave: all his dear treasures, clothes, pots and
pans, bracelets—so that everyone might see what life had given to him in
things of his own.

"IPOO" was common to almost every grave. I wrote the four-lettered word   12
on a piece of paper and took it to a woman in the village.

"What does this mean? It is on the graves."   13

"Mean die time."   14

"Die time?"   15

"Uh huh. Tell when he die."   16

"But all the graves tell the same."   17

"Uh huh. Four this kind," (she pointed separately to each of the four letters,   18
IPOO) "tell now time."

"But everybody did not die at the same time. Some died long ago and some   19
die now?"

"Uh huh. Maybe some year just one man die—one baby. Maybe influenza   20
come—he come two time—one time long far, one time close. He makes lots,
lots Injun die."

"But, if it means the time people died, why do they put 'IPOO' on the old   21
graves as well as on the new?"

Difficult English thoughts furrowed her still forehead. Hard English words   22
came from her slow tongue in abrupt jerks. Her brown finger touched the I
and the P. "He know," she said, "he tell it. This one and this one" (pointing to
the two O's) "small—he no matter. He change every year. Just this one and
this matter" (pointing again to I and P). "He tell it."

Time was marked by centuries in this cemetery. Years—little years—what   23
are they? As insignificant as the fact that reversing the figure nine turns it into
the letter P.

Questions for Critical Thinking

1. What is your preference in a cemetery—a place of natural, uncluttered beauty
   or a place where impressive monuments commemorate the dead? Give reasons
   for your answer.

2. Why do you suppose the Indian village had no hearse and no road into the
   cemetery, requiring that the dead be carried by friends to the burial ground?

3. What is the difference in meaning between an ancient Indian's burial and a modern
   White Man's burial? Which do you consider more appropriate? Is it important
   that a grave make some statement about the dead person? Why or why not?

4. What belief does John Haynes Holmes share in common with the Indians of Emily
   Carr's essay?

5. What is your judgment of the Indians' idea that time should be measured by
   centuries rather than years? Would such a measurement of time work in our
   society?

Writing Assignment

Write an essay in which you describe an ideal funeral, interpreting the meaning of
each part of the ceremony—as if you were explaining it to a stranger.

Writing Advice

In a sense you will be writing a process essay, dividing the funeral ceremony into
separate steps whose meanings you should explore and interpret. Here are some
questions that may help you find your topic and a suitable scheme for organizing it:

1. Where will the funeral take place—out of doors, in a church, at someone's home,
   on the ocean, or elsewhere?

2. Who will be in charge of the actual events—a friend or loved one, a clergyman,
   a group of people, some special individual?

3. What will the ceremony consist of—music, speeches, testimonies from friends and loved ones, a sermon, or total silence? Be sure to give a clear step-by-step description of what should happen.

Writing down each step and numbering it separately will save your essay from becoming jumbled. Here is an example of what you might write:

> I should like my ideal funeral to take place in a small chapel on the edge of a river, with only the closest and dearest members of the deceased invited to be present. The chapel indicates a belief in God and a place where he can be worshiped in serenity and beauty by believers. The river is symbolic of time flowing onward, never repeating itself and never stopping, but holding the life of each human being in its flow.
>
> The funeral service should begin with the chapel bell tolling, reminding those left behind that it is now time to gather and pay their final respects to the deceased.
>
> The deceased, in a simple closed wooden casket, should be placed on a bed of green maple branches and stationed at the foot of the altar, where the guests stand in a circle around the casket, demonstrating their willingness to remain close to this human being on his final journey.

Remember, the objective is to describe a funeral ritual that will be in harmony with your personal beliefs about life and death.

Alternate Writing Assignments

1. Write an essay criticizing the United States funeral industry for its crass materialism as reflected in its advertising industry.

2. Write an essay explaining the importance of funeral or memorial services in terms of their psychological impact on the bereaved.

Or

Write an essay arguing against funeral or memorial services. Support your claims with appropriate evidence.

HISTORY

RITE OF PASSAGE
Anthony Brandt

Anthony Brandt (b. 1936) is an American free-lance writer, who has published articles and poems in a variety of magazines. He has also written a book titled *Reality Police: the Experience of Insanity in America* (1975). The biographical account below appeared in *The Atlantic* for February, 1981.

Reading Advice

This is an essay about a grim, lingering death. It is enlivened by anecdotes and vignettes that describe various members of the family who play their appointed roles, but the main portion of the essay is taken up with the personalities of the author's mother and grandmother, both of whom eventually succumb to the same fate. While it is not pleasant reading, the essay shines with a grim truth as it gives an amplified account of the horrors of senility and of the suffering endured by those who are its witnesses. What concerns Brandt most, however, is not the fact of senility, dreadful as it is, but the fact that his grandmother became "something truly ugly" while her daughter, his mother, stricken with the same illness, remained abidingly cheerful, "shining with a clear light that must be her soul." The contrast is doubly paradoxical in that the personalities of the two ill women seemed to become antithetical to their earlier, healthy natures. Brandt is led to wonder, as we are, if there is meaning here—some pattern larger than life.

Some things that happen to us can't be   1
borne, with the paradoxical result that we carry them on our backs the rest of our lives. I have been half obsessed for almost thirty years with the death of my grandmother. I should say with her dying: with the long and terrible changes that came at the worst time for a boy of twelve and thirteen, going through his own difficult changes. It felt like and perhaps was the equivalent of a puberty rite: dark, frightening, aboriginal, an obscure emotional exchange between old and young. It has become part of my character.

I grew up in New Jersey in a suburban town where my brother still lives   2
and practices law. One might best describe it as quiet, protected, and green; it was no preparation for death. Tall, graceful elm trees lined both sides of the street where we lived. My father's brother-in-law, a contractor, built our house; we moved into it a year after I was born. My grandmother and grandfather (my mother's parents; they were the only grandparents who mattered) lived up the street "on the hill"; it wasn't much of a hill, the terrain in that part of New Jersey being what it is, but we could ride our sleds down the street after it snowed, and that was hilly enough.

Our family lived, or seemed to a young boy to live, in very stable, very   3
ordinary patterns. My father commuted to New York every day, taking the Jersey Central Railroad, riding in cars that had windows you could open, getting off the train in Jersey City and taking a ferry to Manhattan. He held the same job in the same company for more than thirty years. The son of Swedish immigrants, he was a funny man who could wiggle his ears without raising his eyebrows and made up the most dreadful puns. When he wasn't being funny

"Rite of Passage" by Anthony Brandt from *The Atlantic,* February 1981. Reprinted by permission of the author.

he was quiet, the newspaper his shield and companion, or the *Saturday Evening Post,* which he brought home without fail every Wednesday evening, or *Life,* which he brought home Fridays. It was hard to break through the quiet and the humor, and after he died my mother said, as much puzzled as disturbed, that she hardly knew him at all.

She, the backbone of the family, was fierce, stern, the kind of person who 4 can cow you with a glance. My brother and I, and my cousins, were all a little in awe of her. The ruling passion in her life was to protect her family; she lived in a set of concentric circles, sons and husband the closest, then nieces, nephews, brothers, parents, then more distant relatives, and outside that a few friends, very few. No one and nothing else existed for her; she had no interest in politics, art, history, or even the price of eggs. "Fierce" is the best word for her, or single-minded. In those days (I was born in 1936) polio was every parent's bugbear; she, to keep my brother and me away from places where the disease was supposed to be communicated, particularly swimming pools, took us every summer for the entire summer to the Jersey shore, first to her parents' cottage, later to a little cottage she and my father bought. She did that even though it meant being separated from my father for nearly three months, having nobody to talk to, having to handle my brother and me on her own. She hated it, she told us years later, but she did it: fiercely. Or there's the story of one of my cousins who got pregnant when she was sixteen or seventeen; my mother took her into our house, managed somehow to hide her condition from the neighbors, then, after the birth, arranged privately to have the child adopted by a family the doctor recommended, all this being done without consulting the proper authorities, and for the rest of her life never told a single person how she made these arrangements or where she had placed the child. She was a genuine primitive, like some tough old peasant woman. Yet her name was Grace, her nickname Bunny; if you saw through the fierceness, you understood that it was a version of love.

Her mother, my grandmother, seemed anything but fierce. One of our 5 weekly routines was Sunday dinner at their house on the hill, some five or six houses from ours. When I was very young, before World War II, the house had a mansard roof, a barn in the back, lots of yard space, lots of rooms inside, and a cherry tree. I thought it was a palace. Actually it was rather small, and became smaller when my grandmother insisted on tearing down the mansard roof and replacing it with a conventional peaked roof; the house lost three attic rooms in the process. Sunday dinner was invariably roast beef or chicken or leg of lamb with mashed potatoes and vegetables, standard American fare but cooked by my grandparents' Polish maid, Josephine, not by my grandmother. Josephine made wonderful pies in an old cast-iron coal stove and used to let me tie her with string to the kitchen sink. My grandfather was a gentle man who smoked a pipe, had a bristly reddish moustache, and always seemed to wind up paying everybody else's debts in the family; my mother worshipped him. There were usually lots of uncles at these meals, and they were a playful bunch. I have a very early memory of two of them tossing me back and forth between them, and another of the youngest, whose name was Don, carrying me on his shoulders into the surf. I also remember my grandmother presiding at these meals. She was gray-haired and benign.

Later they sold that house. My benign grandmother, I've been told since, was in fact a restless, unsatisfied woman; changing the roof line, moving from house to house, were her ways of expressing that dissatisfaction. In the next house, I think it was, my grandfather died; my grandmother moved again, then again, and then to a house down the street, at the bottom of the hill this time, and there I got to know her better. I was nine or ten years old. She let me throw a tennis ball against the side of the house for hours at a time: the noise must have been terribly aggravating. She cooked lunch for me and used to make pancakes the size of dinner plates, and corn fritters. She also made me a whole set of yarn figures a few inches long, rolling yarn around her hand, taking the roll and tying off arms, legs, and a head, then sewing a face onto the head with black thread. I played with these and an odd assortment of hand-me-down toy soldiers for long afternoons, setting up wars, football games, contests of all kinds, and designating particular yarn figures as customary heroes. Together we played a spelling game: I'd be on the floor playing with the yarn figures, she'd be writing a letter and ask me how to spell "appreciate" (it was always that word), and I'd spell it for her while she pretended to be impressed with my spelling ability and I pretended that she hadn't asked me to spell that same word a dozen times before. I was good, too, at helping her find her glasses.

One scene at this house stands out. My uncle Bob came home from the war and the whole family, his young wife, other uncles, my mother and father and brother and I, gathered at the house to meet him, and he came in wearing his captain's uniform and looking to me, I swear it, like a handsome young god. In fact he was an ordinary man who spent the rest of his life selling insurance. He had been in New Guinea, a ground officer in the Air Corps, and the story I remember is of the native who came into his tent one day and took a great deal of interest in the scissors my uncle was using. The native asked in pidgin English what my uncle would require for the scissors in trade, and he jokingly said, well, how about a tentful of bananas. Sure enough, several days later two or three hundred natives came out of the jungle, huge bunches of bananas on their shoulders, and filled my uncle's tent.

Things went on this way for I don't know how long, maybe two years, maybe three. I don't want to describe it as idyllic. Youth has its problems. But this old woman who could never find her glasses was wonderful to me, a grandmother in the true likeness of one, and I couldn't understand the changes when they came. She moved again, against all advice, this time to a big, bare apartment on the other side of town. She was gradually becoming irritable and difficult, not much fun to be around. There were no more spelling games; she stopped writing letters. Because she moved I saw her less often, and her home could no longer be a haven for me. She neglected it, too; it grew dirtier and dirtier, until my mother eventually had to do her cleaning for her.

Then she began to see things that weren't there. A branch in the back yard   9
became a woman, I remember, who apparently wasn't fully clothed, and a man was doing something to her, something unspeakable. She developed diabetes and my mother learned to give her insulin shots, but she wouldn't stop eating candy, the worst thing for her, and the diabetes got worse. Her face began to change, to slacken, to lose its shape and character. I didn't understand these things; arteriosclerosis, hardening of the arteries, whatever the explanation, it was only words. What I noticed was that her white hair was getting thinner and harder to control, that she herself seemed to be shrinking even as I grew, that when she looked at me I wasn't sure it was me she was seeing anymore.

After a few months of this, we brought her to live with us. My mother was   10
determined to take care of her, and certain family pressures were brought to bear too. That private man my father didn't like the idea at all, but he said nothing, which was his way. And she was put in my brother's bedroom over the garage, my brother moving in with me. It was a small house, six rooms and a basement, much too small for what we had to face.

What we had to face was a rapid deterioration into senile dementia and the   11
rise from beneath the surface of this smiling, kindly, white-haired old lady of something truly ugly. Whenever she was awake she called for attention, calling, calling a hundred times a day. Restless as always, she picked the bedclothes off, tore holes in sheets and pillows, took off her nightclothes and sat naked talking to herself. She hallucinated more and more frequently, addressing her dead husband, a dead brother, scolding, shouting at their apparitions. She became incontinent and smeared feces on herself, the furniture, the walls. And always calling—"Bunny, where are you? Bunny, I want you!"—scolding, demanding; she could seldom remember what she wanted when my mother came. It became an important event when she fell asleep; to make sure she stayed asleep the radio was kept off, the four of us tiptoed around the house, and when I went out to close the garage door, directly under her window (it was an overhead door and had to be pulled down), I did it so slowly and carefully, half an inch at a time, that it sometimes took me a full fifteen minutes to get it down.

That my mother endured this for six months is a testimony to her strength   12
and determination, but it was really beyond her and almost destroyed her health. My grandmother didn't often sleep through the night: she would wake up, yell, cry, a creature of disorder, a living *memento mori,* and my mother would have to tend to her. The house began to smell in spite of all my mother's efforts to

keep my grandmother's room clean. My father, his peace gone, brooded in his chair behind his newspaper. My brother and I fought for *Lebensraum,* each of us trying to grow up in his own way. People avoided us. My uncles were living elsewhere—Miami, Cleveland, Delaware. My grandmother's two surviving sisters, who lived about ten blocks away, never came to see her. Everybody seemed to sense that something obscene was happening, and stayed away. Terrified, I stayed away, too. I heard my grandmother constantly, but in the six months she lived with us I think I went into her room only once. That was as my mother wished it. She was a nightmare, naked and filthy without warning.

After six months, at my father's insistence, after a night nurse had been   13
hired and left, after my mother had reached her limits and beyond, my parents started looking for a nursing home, anyplace they could put her. It became a family scandal; the two sisters were outraged that my mother would consider putting her own mother in a home, there were telephone calls back and forth between them and my uncles, but of course the sisters had never come to see her themselves, and my mother never forgave them. One of my uncles finally came from Cleveland, saw what was happening, and that day they put my grandmother in a car and drove her off to the nearest state mental hospital. They brought her back the same day; desperate as they were, they couldn't leave her in hell. At last, when it had come time to go to the shore, they found a nursing home in the middle of the Pine Barrens, miles from anywhere, and kept her there for a while. That, too, proving unsatisfactory, they put her in a small nursing home in western New Jersey, about two hours away by car. We made the drive every Sunday for the next six months, until my grandmother finally died. I always waited in the car while my mother visited her. At the funeral I refused to go into the room for one last look at the body. I was afraid of her still. The whole thing had been a subtle act of violence, a violation of the sensibilities, made all the worse by the fact that I knew it wasn't really her fault, that she was a victim of biology, of life itself. Hard knowledge for a boy just turned fourteen. She became the color of all my expectations.

Life is savage, then, and even character is insecure. Call no man happy until   14
he be dead, said the Greek lawgiver Solon. But what would a wise man say to this? In that same town in New Jersey, that town I have long since abandoned as too flat and too good to be true, my mother, thirty years older now, weighing in at ninety-two pounds, incontinent, her white hair wild about her head, sits strapped into a chair in another nursing home talking incoherently to her fellow patients and working her hands at the figures she thinks she sees moving around on the floor. It's enough to make stones weep to see this fierce, strong woman, who paid her dues, surely, ten times over, reduced to this.

Yet she is *cheerful.* This son comes to see her and she quite literally babbles   15
with delight, introduces him (as her father, her husband—the connections are

burnt out) to the aides, tells him endless stories that don't make any sense at all, and *shines,* shines with a clear light that must be her soul. Care and bitterness vanish in her presence. Helpless, the victim of numerous tiny strokes—"shower strokes," the doctors call them—that are gradually destroying her brain, she has somehow achieved a radiant serenity that accepts everything that happens and incorporates and transforms it.

Is there a lesson in this? Is some pattern larger than life working itself out; 16 is this some kind of poetic justice on display, a mother balancing a grandmother, gods demonstrating reasons beyond our comprehension? It was a bitter thing to put her into that place, reeking of disinfectant, full of senile, dying old people, and I used to hate to visit her there, but as she has deteriorated she has also by sheer force of example managed to change my attitude. If she can be reconciled to all this, why can't I? It doesn't last very long, but after I've seen her, talked to her for half an hour, helped feed her, stroked her hair, I walk away amazed, as if I had been witness to a miracle.

Questions for Critical Thinking

1. Is the author justified in making so much out of the death of his grandmother, telling us that it was the equivalent of a "puberty rite"? Explain why the event has become such an influence.

2. What is the purpose of providing such a detailed account of the general family life that formed the backdrop of the author's youth? How is it related to his general questioning of life?

3. Does it seem right on the part of the narrator not to have visited his grandmother during the six months she was in a nursing home and to have refused to pay his respects when she lay in the funeral home? Give reasons for your answer.

4. What connection is there between the title of the sketch and the events related? What is the meaning of the term "aboriginal" as used in paragraph 1?

5. Is it possible that the author's mother was in reality neither "fierce" nor "stern," but warm and loving? Was the mother's change in personality once she became senile her true self? Explain your answers.

6. What aspects of Loren Eiseley's "The Brown Wasps" are remindful of Brandt's "Rite of Passage"?

7. Do you approve or disapprove of the fact that both the narrator's grandmother and mother were placed in nursing homes when they became senile and difficult to handle? Could an alternative plan have worked better?

Writing Assignment

Write an essay discussing how our society might improve the lot of old people afflicted by extreme senility caused by Alzheimer's disease, hardening of the arteries, a stroke, or some other aging syndrome. Focus on the problems of proper medical treatment, a good environment, compassionate nursing care, nutritious food, and attention from loved ones.

Writing Advice

1. Begin with a sketch.

Most of us have unwittingly been witnesses to cases of senility in our own family or that of someone close to us. Perhaps one of your own grandparents became senile and your parents had to suffer the results. Using Brandt's essay as a model, write a vivid sketch of the way the stricken person behaved. Provide examples of how the senility changed the victim and altered the lives of the caretakers. Here is an illustration of what we have in mind:

> At the height of her senility, my grandmother would get up in the middle of the night, shuffle barefoot to the dining room, where she would tremulously take her best porcelain out of the china closet and begin setting the table. When Grandfather, disturbed by the noise, would appear at the door to see what was happening, she would smile blithely and report that "Aunt Gertrude and Lois are arriving for lunch very soon." No amount of reasoning on the part of my grandfather would convince her to go back to bed.

The objective is to render an exact picture of the senile person's condition and how those in attendance tried to respond. Be honest in your appraisal of everyone's role. If the situation was not always rosy, you need not hesitate to say so, as in this account:

> Most of the time my grandfather took care of my grandmother patiently and lovingly. He used to tell me "It is a privilege to take care of her now because she was such a wonderful wife and mother when she was well." But, of course, occasionally, I would hear irritation in his exhausted voice when he would tell her, "Emmy, for God's sake, don't throw the peanuts on the floor!" Or, after answering the same question for the umpteenth time, he would shake his head and mutter, "I've already told you five times, woman."

2. Go from the specific to the general.

Once you have set the stage with your own personal knowledge of a situation involving senility, you are ready to make suggestions for improving the generally sorry life of all beset by it. As indicated earlier, the areas to consider are medicine, nursing, housing, food, and companionship. You might suggest that in many cases the senile person would be better off in a nursing facility than at home, provided that the care is excellent and the facility pleasant. Again, be specific in the suggestions you make. The following is an example of a specific suggestion:

> People who are senile should be dressed nicely—the women in clean and pretty dresses and the men in spotless slacks with crisp shirts. The clothes should be washable and easy to maintain, but they should look attractive. One nursing home in the City of

Detroit checks out all patients before visiting hours, to make sure that they look as appealing as possible. To maintain the senile person's dignity, even in dress, is an essential and moral obligation the younger generation has toward the older.

Since finances are always of crucial importance in any lingering illness, you will need to explain how you propose to finance your scheme for caring for the senile— whether through taxes, retirement plans, family savings, or a combination of them. Again, avoid superficiality and generalization.

3. Use facts and statistics.

To be convincing, your essay must provide statistics on costs of caring for the senile, incidence of senility, and life expectancy of those so stricken. Some research into magazines or books about gerontology will provide this information.

4. Turn your main idea into a clear thesis.

Control your essay with a clear thesis, such as this one: "One obligation each younger generation has to the older generation is to make sure that people who are incurably senile receive tender and expert care as long as they are alive."

Alternate Writing Assignments

1. Write an essay explaining the obligation of children toward parents who have become hopelessly senile and therefore difficult to control or care for.

3. Write a sketch about a strong emotional encounter between you and a grandparent or parent and indicate what light the experience sheds on generational relationships.

LITERATURE

THE DEATH OF THE MOTH
— Virginia Woolf —

Virginia Woolf (1882–1941) was an English novelist and essayist whose writing style influenced a number of other writers, such as Ernest Hemingway, James Joyce, and William Faulkner. In 1904 she helped found the Bloomsbury Group, a literary clique that included a number of well-known writers and literary critics, among them Lytton Strachey, E. M. Forster, Roger Fry, and Clive Bell.

Born into a financially secure family, Woolf began as a young girl to avidly read books from her father's library. In 1912, she married Leonard Woolf, a writer and editor, with whom she founded Hogarth Press. As a novelist, Woolf was intent on representing not so much plot, setting, or character conflict but the steady flow of thought that welled inside the characters' minds. As a result, she perfected the "stream of consciousness" technique that allowed her to focus on the ordinary experiences in the lives of ordinary people. Throughout her life, Woolf resented the idea that a woman's future was determined by her sex and therefore far more limited than that of a man. This resentment of the social inequality between male and female is revealed in many of her works. Woolf suffered two nervous breakdowns and drowned herself in 1941 because she feared another breakdown from which she might not recover. Among her finest works are *The Voyage Out* (1915), *Night and Day* (1919), *Jacob's Room* (1922), *Mrs. Dalloway* (1925), *To the Lighthouse* (1927), *A Room of One's Own* (1929), *The Waves* (1931) and *The Death of the Moth and Other Essays* (1942), from which the excerpt below is reprinted.

Reading Advice

This is the sort of unclassifiable mood-piece writing rarely encountered nowadays except in the odd literary magazine. The Victorians indulged in it more than we do, presumably because their slower pace of life gave them the leisure to read speculative and philosophical works. To savor this piece, you should read it more than once, and slowly.

Basically, the situation it describes is this: the author is reading at a window and periodically glancing out at the splendor of autumnal life, when she notices a small daytime moth darting within the square of a mullioned window pane. Soon the creature's movements become more sluggish as its energy flags. It begins to die. She bends over and watches it struggle vainly against the crush of death until the moth finally succumbs and stiffens. In Woolf's hands, this trivial incident becomes the subject of poetic and philosophical musing. Her descriptions are wonderfully vivid, as when she depicts a flock of fluttering rooks as a net cast over the tops of trees. She sees the moth as infused with a thread of life, a pure bead of energy that struggles mightily against its doom. The result is a lovely philosophical piece that gives a delicate poetic glimpse into life and death.

*M*oths that fly by day are not prop-   1
erly to be called moths; they do not excite that pleasant sense of dark autumn nights and ivy-blossom which the commonest yellow-underwing asleep in the shadow of the curtain never fails to rouse in us. They are hybrid creatures, neither gay like butterflies nor sombre like their own species. Nevertheless the present specimen, with his narrow hay-coloured wings, fringed with a tassel of the same colour, seemed to be content with life. It was a pleasant morning, mid-September, mild, benignant, yet with a keener breath than that of the summer months. The plough was already scoring the field opposite the window,

and where the share had been, the earth was pressed flat and gleamed with moisture. Such vigour came rolling in from the fields and the down beyond that it was difficult to keep the eyes strictly turned upon the book. The rooks too were keeping one of their annual festivities; soaring round the tree tops until it looked as if a vast net with thousands of black knots in it had been cast up into the air; which, after a few moments sank slowly down upon the trees until every twig seemed to have a knot at the end of it. Then, suddenly, the net would be thrown into the air again in a wider circle this time, with the utmost clamour and vociferation, as though to be thrown into the air and settle slowly down upon the tree tops were a tremendously exciting experience.

The same energy which inspired the rooks, the ploughmen, the horses, and 2 even, it seemed, the lean bare-backed downs, sent the moth fluttering from side to side of his square of the window-pane. One could not help watching him. One was, indeed, conscious of a queer feeling of pity for him. The possibilities of pleasure seemed that morning so enormous and so various that to have only a moth's part in life, and a day moth's at that, appeared a hard fate, and his zest in enjoying his meagre opportunities to the full, pathetic. He flew vigorously to one corner of his compartment, and, after waiting there a second, flew across to the other. What remained for him but to fly to a third corner and then to a fourth? That was all he could do, in spite of the size of the downs, the width of the sky, the far-off smoke of houses, and the romantic voice, now and then, of a steamer out at sea. What he could do he did. Watching him, it seemed as if a fibre, very thin but pure, of the enormous energy of the world had been thrust into his frail and diminutive body. As often as he crossed the pane, I could fancy that a thread of vital light became visible. He was little or nothing but life.

Yet, because he was so small, and so simple a form of the energy that was 3 rolling in at the open window and driving its way through so many narrow and intricate corridors in my own brain and in those of other human beings, there was something marvellous as well as pathetic about him. It was as if someone had taken a tiny bead of pure life and decking it as lightly as possible with down and feathers, had set it dancing and zigzagging to show us the true nature of life. Thus displayed one could not get over the strangeness of it. One is apt to forget all about life, seeing it humped and bossed and garnished and cumbered so that it has to move with the greatest circumspection and dignity. Again, the thought of all that life might have been had he been born in any other shape caused one to view his simple activities with a kind of pity.

After a time, tired by his dancing apparently, he settled on the window ledge 4 in the sun, and, the queer spectacle being at an end, I forgot about him. Then, looking up, my eye was caught by him. He was trying to resume his dancing, but seemed either so stiff or so awkward that he could only flutter to the bottom of the window-pane; and when he tried to fly across it he failed. Being intent on other matters I watched these futile attempts for a time without thinking, unconsciously waiting for him to resume his flight, as one waits for a machine, that has stopped momentarily, to start again without considering the reason of its failure. After perhaps a seventh attempt he slipped from the wooden ledge and fell, fluttering his wings, on to his back on the window sill. The helplessness of his attitude roused me. It flashed upon me that he was in difficulties; he could no longer raise himself, his legs struggled vainly. But, as I stretched out a pencil, meaning to help him to right himself, it came over me that the failure and awkwardness were the approach of death. I laid the pencil down again.

The legs agitated themselves once more. I looked as if for the enemy against which he struggled. I looked out of doors. What had happened there? Presumably it was mid-day, and work in the fields had stopped. Stillness and quiet had replaced the previous animation. The birds had taken themselves off to feed in the brooks. The horses stood still. Yet the power was there all the same, massed outside indifferent, impersonal, not attending to anything in particular. Somehow it was opposed to the little hay-coloured moth. It was useless to try to do anything. One could only watch the extraordinary efforts made by those tiny legs against an oncoming doom which could, had it chosen, have submerged an entire city, not merely a city, but masses of human beings; nothing, I knew, had any chance against death. Nevertheless after a pause of exhaustion the legs fluttered again. It was superb this last protest, and so frantic that he succeeded at last in righting himself. One's sympathies, of course, were all on the side of life. Also, when there was nobody to care or to know, this gigantic effort on the part of an insignificant little moth, against a power of such magnitude, to retain what no one else valued or desired to keep, moved one strangely. Again, somehow, one saw life, a pure bead. I lifted the pencil again, useless though I knew it to be. But even as I did so, the unmistakable tokens of death showed themselves. The body relaxed, and instantly grew stiff. The struggle was over. The insignificant little creature now knew death. As I looked at the dead moth, this minute wayside triumph of so great a force over so mean an antagonist filled me with wonder. Just as life had been strange a few minutes before, so death was now as strange. The moth having righted himself now lay most decently and uncomplainingly composed. O yes, he seemed to say, death is stronger than I am.

Questions for Critical Thinking

1. What about the moth makes its death in this essay seem so poignant? Would the effect have been the same if the creature observed had been, say, an elephant? Why or why not?

2. Why is mid-September the appropriate season and setting for the topic of this particular essay?

3. Although this is written in the style of an eyewitness account, the author never refers to herself as "I" but only as "one." What advantage does she gain by the use of "one" that would have been missing had she used "I"?

4. What particular risk of failure do you think the author ran in trying to write about the death struggles of such a lowly creature as a moth?

5. How does the author orchestrate her descriptions of the moth's struggle to match those of the fields? Why does she engage in this orchestration?

6. What do you find to be the least satisfying element of this particular piece?

Writing Assignment

Write an essay describing a death, whether of a human or animal, that you have either personally witnessed or of which you have intimate knowledge.

Writing Advice

Good descriptive writing is always particularly focused on its topic, and possibly no finer example of this focus can be found than in the Woolf essay, "The Death of the Moth." In it, Woolf never wavers even for an instant in aiming specific details directly at her subject. She writes successively about the surrounding fields, the windowpane, the moth's struggles, all with an exacting, meticulous eye. Nothing distracts or blurs her focus. And while few of us can match Woolf with her singular flair for the brilliant image—the comparison between the fluttering rooks and a net flung over the treetops is particularly wonderful—any of us can, with care, emulate her steady focus.

To write this essay, then, you should first select a dominant impression—the theme you will use as the unifying backbone of your description. Woolf, for example, in describing her moth, focuses on the intense energy that burned within the tiny creature. She describes the moth fluttering vigorously from one corner to the other of the windowpane. She compares its energy to a thread of vital light, a bead of pure life. Nor does she ever waver or stray from this impression. Such use of a single overall impression generally adds concreteness and unity to descriptive writing.

To write your own description, begin by asking yourself what single dominant impression characterizes the death you are trying to depict on paper. Write that impression down as if it were a thesis, then try to find appropriate adjectives and images to reinforce and support it. Once you have your impression, do not stray or wander from it or allow yourself to be distracted. If you happen upon a particularly ingenious image that does not fit in with your overall impression, discard it mercilessly. Nothing quite dilutes the effect of a descriptive passage than an image, however brilliant, that does not belong.

Remember, also, that good descriptive writing seldom gushes from the pen in a frenzied rush. Almost always it results from a writer's painstaking effort and laborious rewriting. Woolf's work may read as if the words had spontaneously come tumbling out onto the page. Most likely, however, they dripped out one by one, line by line, sentence by sentence. That is the slow but sure way in which descriptions are usually written.

Alternate Writing Assignment

Write an essay on the ongoing debate about the legal and medical definition of death.

LITERATURE

THE CODE
Richard T. Gill

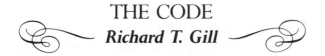

Richard Thomas Gill (b. 1927) has been the principal bass of the New York Metropolitan Opera since 1973 and is an occasional contributor to the *New Yorker* and *Atlantic Monthly*. Gill received his Ph.D. at Harvard, where he also taught as an assistant professor. He is the author of several books including *Economic Development: Past and Present* (1963) and *Economics and the Public Interest* (second edition 1972). Gill has also presented a 15-part series on public television on "Economics and the Public Interest."

Reading Advice

"The Code," told as a first-person narrative, recounts the story of the strange masculine bond that develops between a boy and his father, with troubling and unforeseen consequences for both of them. In some ways, it is a typical *New Yorker* story about mannered and conventional characters who speak a dialogue of crisp standard English as they wrestle with a philosophical, rather than a physical or material, dilemma. Dramatic incident and action are understated, investing the story with an underlying tension, and the conclusion is ambiguous and wistful. As you read, notice how much the narrator unwittingly reveals about himself, his family, and his social class. Notice, also, how the unspoken understanding between the son and the father eventually becomes a wall between them.

I remember, almost to the hour, when I   1
first began to question my religion. I don't mean that my ideas changed radically just at that time. I was only twelve, and I continued to go to church faithfully and to say something that could pass for prayers each night before I went to

sleep. But I never again felt quite the same. For the first time in my life, it had occurred to me that when I grew up I might actually leave the Methodist faith.

It all happened just a few days after my brother died. He was five years old,   2
and his illness was so brief and his death so unexpected that my whole family was almost crazed with grief. My three aunts, each of whom lived within a few blocks of our house, and my mother were all firm believers in religion, and they turned in unison, and without reservation, to this last support. For about a week, a kind of religious frenzy seized our household. We would all sit in the living room—my mother, my aunts, my two sisters, and I, and sometimes Mr. Dodds, the Methodist minister, too—saying prayers in low voices, comforting one another, staying together for hours at a time, until someone remembered that we had not had dinner or that it was time for my sisters and me to be in bed.

I was quite swept up by the mood that had come over the house. When I   3
went to bed, I would say the most elaborate, intricate prayers. In the past, when I had finished my "Now I lay me down to sleep," I would bless individually all the members of my immediate family and then my aunts, and let it go at that. Now, however, I felt that I had to bless everyone in the world whose name I could remember. I would go through all my friends at school, including the teachers, the principal, and the janitor, and then through the names of people I had heard my mother and father mention, some of whom I had never even met. I did not quite know what to do about my brother, whom I wanted to pray for more than for anyone else. I hesitated to take his name out of its regular order, for fear I would be committed to believing that he had really died. But then I *knew* that he had died, so at the end of my prayers, having just barely mentioned his name as I went along, I would start blessing him over and over again, until I finally fell asleep.

The only one of us who was unmoved by this religious fervor was my father.   4
Oddly enough, considering what a close family we were and how strongly my mother and aunts felt about religion, my father had never shown the least interest in it. In fact, I do not think that he had ever gone to church. Partly for this reason, partly because he was a rather brusque, impatient man, I always felt that he was something of a stranger in our home. He spent a great deal of time with us children, but through it all he seemed curiously unapproachable. I think we all felt constrained when he played with us and relieved when, at last, we were left to ourselves.

At the time of my brother's death, he was more of a stranger than ever.   5
Except for one occasion, he took no part in the almost constant gatherings of the family in the living room. He was not going to his office that week—we lived in a small town outside Boston—and he was always around the house, but no one ever seemed to know exactly where. One of my aunts—Sarah, my

mother's eldest sister—felt very definitely that my father should not be left to himself, and she was continually saying to me, "Jack, go upstairs and see if you can find him and talk to him." I remember going timidly along the hallway on the second floor and peeking into the bedrooms, not knowing what I should say if I found him and half afraid that he would scold me for going around looking into other people's rooms. One afternoon, not finding him in any of the bedrooms, I went up into the attic, where we had a sort of playroom. I remember discovering him there by the window. He was sitting absolutely motionless in an old wicker chair, an empty pipe in his hands, staring out fixedly over the treetops. I stood in the doorway for several minutes before he was aware of me. He turned as if to say something, but then, looking at me or just above my head—I was not sure which—he seemed to lose himself in his thoughts. Finally, he gave me a strangely awkward salute with his right hand and turned again to the window.

About the only times my father was with the rest of us were when we had 6 meals or when, in the days immediately following the funeral, we all went out to the cemetery, taking fresh flowers or wreaths. But even at the cemetery he always stood slightly apart—a tall, lonely figure. Once, when we were at the grave and I was nearest him, he reached over and squeezed me around the shoulders. It made me feel almost embarrassed as though he were breaking through some inviolable barrier between us. He must have felt as I did, because he at once removed his arm and looked away, as though he had never actually embraced me at all.

It was the one occasion when my father was sitting in the living room with 7 us that started me to wondering about my religion. We had just returned from the cemetery—two carloads of us. It was three or four days after the funeral and just at the time when, the shock having worn off, we were all experiencing our first clear realization of what had happened. Even I, young as I was, sensed that there was a new air of desolation in our home.

For a long time, we all sat there in silence. Then my aunts, their eyes moist, 8 began talking about my brother, and soon my mother joined in. They started off softly, telling of little things he had done in the days before his illness. Then they fell silent and dried their eyes, and then quickly remembered some other incident and began speaking again. Slowly the emotion mounted, and before long the words were flooding out. "God will take care of him!" my Aunt Sarah cried, almost ecstatically. "Oh, yes, He will! He will!" Presently, they were all talking in chorus—saying that my brother was happy at last and that they would all be with him again one day.

I believed what they were saying and I could barely hold back my tears. But 9 swept up as I was, I had the feeling that they should not be talking that way while my father was there. The feeling was one that I did not understand at all at the moment. It was just that when I looked over to the corner where he was sitting and saw the deep, rigid lines of his face, saw him sitting there silently, all alone, I felt guilty. I wanted everyone to stop for a while—at least until he had gone upstairs. But there was no stopping the torrent once it had started.

"Oh, he was too perfect to live!" Aunt Agnes, my mother's youngest sister, 10 cried. "He was never a bad boy. I've never seen a boy like that. I mean he was never even naughty. He was just too perfect."

"Oh, yes. Oh, yes," my mother sighed.

"It's true," Aunt Sarah said. "Even when he was a baby, he never really cried. There was never a baby like him. He was a saint."

"He *was* a saint!" Aunt Agnes cried. "That's why he was taken from us!"

"He was a perfect baby," my mother said.

"He was taken from us," Aunt Agnes went on, "because he was too perfect to live."

All through this conversation, my father's expression had been growing more 11 and more tense. At last, while Aunt Agnes was speaking, he rose from his chair. His face was very pale, and his eyes flashed almost feverishly. "Don't talk like that, Agnes!" he exclaimed, with a strange violence that was not anger but something much deeper. "I won't have you talking like that any more. I don't want anybody talking like that!" His whole body seemed to tremble. I had never seen him so worked up before. "Of course he was a bad boy at times!" he cried. "Every boy's bad once in a while. What do you have to change him for? Why don't you leave him as he was?"

"But he was such a perfect baby," Aunt Sarah said. 12

"He *wasn't* perfect!" my father almost shouted, clenching his fist. "He was no more perfect than Jack here or Betty or Ellen. He was just an ordinary little boy. He wasn't perfect. And he wasn't a saint. He was just a little boy, and I won't have you making him over into something he wasn't!"

He looked as though he were going to go on talking like this, but just then 13 he closed his eyes and ran his hand up over his forehead and through his hair. When he spoke again, his voice was subdued. "I just wish you wouldn't talk that way," he said. "That's all I mean." And then, after standing there silently for a minute, he left the living room and walked upstairs.

I sat watching the doorway through which he had gone. Suddenly, I had no 14 feeling for what my mother and my aunts had been saying. It was all a mist, a dream. Out of the many words that had been spoken that day, it was those few sentences of my father's that explained to me how I felt about my brother. I wanted to be with my father to tell him so.

I went upstairs and found him once again in the playroom in the attic. As 15 before, he was silent and staring out the window when I entered, and we sat without speaking for what seemed to me like half an hour or more. But I felt that he knew why I was there, and I was not uncomfortable with him.

Finally, he turned to me and shook his head. "I don't know what I can tell   16
you, Jack," he said, raising his hands and letting them drop into his lap. "That's
the worst part of it. There's just nothing I can say that will make it any better."

Though I only half understood him then, I see now that he was telling me   17
of a drawback—that he had no refuge, no comfort, no support. He was telling
me that you were all alone if you took the path that he had taken. Listening
to him, I did not care about the drawback. I had begun to see what a noble
thing it was for a man to bear the full loss of someone he had loved.

II

By the time I was thirteen or fourteen I was so thoroughly committed to   18
my father's way of thinking that I considered it a great weakness in a man to
believe in religion. I wanted to grow up to face life as he did—truthfully,
without comfort, without support.

My attitude was never one of rebellion. Despite the early regimen of Sunday   19
school and church that my mother had encouraged, she was wonderfully gentle
with me, particularly when I began to express my doubts. She would come
into my room each night after the light was out and ask me to say my prayers.
Determined to be honest with her, I would explain that I could not say them
sincerely, and therefore should not say them at all. "Now, Jack," she would
reply, very quietly and calmly, "you mustn't talk like that. You'll really feel much
better if you say them." I could tell from the tone of her voice that she was
hurt, but she never tried to force me in any way. Indeed, it might have been
easier for me if she *had* tried to oppose my decision strenuously. As it was, I
felt so bad at having wounded her that I was continually trying to make things
up—running errands, surprising her by doing the dishes when she went out
shopping—behaving, in short, in the most conscientious, considerate fashion.
But all this never brought me any closer to her religion. On the contrary, it
only served to free me for my decision *not* to believe. And for that decision,
as I say, my father was responsible.

Part of this influence, I suppose, was in his physical quality. Even at that   20
time—when he was in his late forties and in only moderately good health—
he was a most impressive figure. He was tall and heavychested, with leathery,
rough-cast features and with an easy, relaxed rhythm in his walk. He had been
an athlete in his youth, and, needless to say, I was enormously proud of his
various feats and told about them, with due exaggeration, all over our neighborhood. Still, the physical thing had relatively little to do with the matter. My
father, by that time, regarded athletes and athletics with contempt. Now and
again, he would take me into the back yard to fool around with boxing gloves,
but when it came to something serious, such as my going out for football in
high school, he invariably put his foot down. "It takes too much time," he

would tell me. "You ought to be thinking of college and your studies. It's nonsense what they make of sports nowadays!" I always wanted to remind him of *his* school days, but I knew it was no use. He had often told me what an unforgivable waste of time he considered his youth to have been.

Thus, although the physical thing was there, it was very much in the back-   21
ground—little more, really, than the simple assumption that a man ought to know how to take care of himself. The real bond between us was spiritual, in the sense that courage, as opposed to strength, is spiritual. It was this intangible quality of courage that I wanted desperately to possess and that, it seemed to me, captured everything that was essential about my father.

We never talked of this quality directly. The nearest we came to it was on   22
certain occasions during the early part of the Second World War, just before I went off to college. We would sit in the living room listening to a speech by Winston Churchill, and my father would suddenly clap his fist against his palm. "My God!" he would exclaim, fairly beaming with admiration. "That man's got the heart of a tiger!" And I would listen to the rest of the speech, thrilling to every word, and then, thinking of my father, really, I would say aloud that, of all men in the world, the one I would most like to be was Churchill.

Nor did we often talk about religion. Yet our religion—our rejection of   23
religion—was the deepest statement of the bond between us. My father, per-haps out of deference to my mother and my sisters and aunts, always put his own case very mildly. "It's certainly a great philosophy," he would say of Christianity. "No one could question that. But for the rest . . ." Here he would throw up his hands and cock his head to one side, as if to say that he had tried, but simply could not manage the hurdle of divinity. This view, however mildly it may have been expressed, became mine with absolutely clarity and certainty. I concluded that religion was a refuge, without the least foundation in fact. More than that, I positively objected to those—I should say those *men,* for to me it was a peculiarly masculine matter—who turned to religion for support. As I saw it, a man ought to face life as it really is, on his own two feet, without a crutch, as my father did. That was the heart of the matter. By the time I left home for college, I was so deeply committed to this view that I would have considered it a disloyalty to him, to myself, to the code we had lived by, to alter my position in the least.

I did not see much of my father during the next four years or so. I was   24
home during the summer vacation after my freshman year, but then, in the middle of the next year, I went into the Army. I was shipped to the Far East for the tail end of the war, and was in Japan at the start of the Occupation. I saw my father only once or twice during my entire training period, and, naturally, during the time I was overseas I did not see him at all.

While I was away, his health failed badly. In 1940, before I went off to   25
college, he had taken a job at a defense plant. The plant was only forty miles

from our home, but he was working on the night shift, and commuting was extremely complicated and tiresome. And, of course, he was always willing to overexert himself out of a sense of pride. The result was that late in 1942 he had a heart attack. He came through it quite well, but he made no effort to cut down on his work and, as a consequence, suffered a second, and more serious, attack, two years later. From that time on, he was almost completely bedridden.

I was on my way overseas at the time of the second attack, and I learned   26 of it in a letter from my mother. I think she was trying to spare me, or perhaps it was simply that I could not imagine so robust a man as my father being seriously ill. In any event, I had only the haziest notion of what his real condition was, so when, many months later, I finally did realize what had been going on, I was terribly surprised and shaken. One day, some time after my arrival at an American Army post in Japan, I was called to the orderly room and told that my father was critically ill and that I was to be sent home immediately. Within forty-eight hours, I was standing in the early-morning light outside my father's bedroom, with my mother and sisters at my side. They had told me, as gently as they could, that he was not very well, that he had had another attack. But it was impossible to shield me then. I no sooner stepped into the room and saw him than I realized that he would not live more than a day or two longer.

From that moment on, I did not want to leave him for a second. Even that   27 night, during the periods when he was sleeping and I was of no help being there, I could not get myself to go out of the room for more than a few minutes. A practical nurse had come to sit up with him, but since I was at the bedside, she finally spent the night in the hallway. I was really quite tired, and late that night my mother and my aunts begged me to go to my room and rest for a while, but I barely heard them. I was sure he would wake up soon, and when he did, I wanted to be there to talk to him.

We did talk a great deal that first day and night. It was difficult for both of   28 us. Every once in a while, my father would shift position in the bed, and I would catch a glimpse of his wasted body. It was a knife in my heart. Even worse were the times when he would reach out for my hand, his eyes misted, and begin to tell me how he felt about me. I tried to look at him, but in the end I always looked down. And, knowing that he was dying, and feeling desperately guilty, I would keep repeating to myself that he knew how I felt, that he would understand why I looked away.

There was another thing, too. While we talked that day, I had a vague feeling   29 that my father was on the verge of making some sort of confession to me. It was, as I say, only the vaguest impression, and I thought very little about it. The next morning, however, I began to sense what was in the air. Apparently, Mr. Dodds, the minister, whom I barely knew, had been coming to the house lately to talk to my father. My father had not said anything about this, and I learned it only indirectly, from something my mother said to my eldest sister at the breakfast table. At the moment, I brushed the matter aside. I told myself it was natural that Mother would want my father to see the minister at the last. Nevertheless, the very mention of the minister's name caused something to tighten inside me.

Later that day, the matter was further complicated. After lunch, I finally did go to my room for a nap, and when I returned to my father's room, I found him and my mother talking about Mr. Dodds. The conversation ended almost as soon as I entered, but I was left with the distinct impression that they were expecting the minister to pay a visit that day, whether very shortly or at suppertime or later in the evening, I could not tell. I did not ask. In fact, I made a great effort not to think of the matter at all.   30

Then, early that evening, my father spoke to me. I knew before he said a word that the minister *was* coming. My mother had straightened up the bedroom, and fluffed up my father's pillows so that he was half sitting in the bed. No one had told me anything, but I was sure what the preparations meant. "I guess you probably know," my father said to me when we were alone, "we're having a visitor tonight. It's—ah—Mr. Dodds. You know, the minister from your mother's church.   31

I nodded, half shrugging, as if I saw nothing the least unusual in the news. "He's come here before once or twice," my father said. "Have I mentioned that? I can't remember if I've mentioned that."   32

"Yes, I know. I think Mother said something, or perhaps you did. I don't remember."

"I just thought I'd let you know. You see, your mother wanted me to talk to him. I—I've talked to him more for her sake than anything else."

"Sure. I can understand that."

"I think it makes her feel a little better. I think—" Here he broke off, seeming dissatisfied with what he was saying. His eyes turned to the ceiling, and he shook his head slightly, as if to erase the memory of his words. He studied the ceiling for a long time before he spoke again. "I don't mean it was all your mother exactly," he said. "Well, what I mean is he's really quite an interesting man. I think you'd probably like him a good deal."   33

"I know Mother has always liked him," I replied. "From what I gather most people seem to like him very much."

"Well, he's that sort," my father went on, with quickening interest. "I mean, he isn't what you'd imagine at all. To tell the truth, I wish you'd talk to him a little. I wish you'd talk things over with him right from scratch." My father was looking directly at me now, his eyes flashing.

"I'd be happy to talk with him sometime," I said. "As I say, everybody seems to think very well of him."

"Well, I wish you would. You see, when you're lying here day after day, you get to thinking about things. I mean, it's good to have someone to talk to." He   34 paused for a moment. "Tell me," he said, "have ever ever . . . have you ever wondered if there wasn't some truth in it? Have you ever thought about it that way at all?"

I made a faint gesture with my hand. "Of course, it's always possible to wonder." I replied. "I don't suppose you can ever be completely certain one way or the other."

35

"I know, I know," he said, almost impatiently. "But have you ever felt—well, all in a sort of flash—that it *was* true? I mean, have you ever had that feeling?"

He was half raised up from the pillow now, his eyes staring into me with a feverish concentration. Suddenly, I could not look at him any longer. I lowered my head.

36

"I don't mean permanently or anything like that," he went on. "But just for a few seconds. The feeling that you've been wrong all along. Have you had that feeling—ever?"

I could not look up. I could not move. I felt that every muscle in my body had suddenly frozen. Finally, after what seemed an eternity, I heard him sink back into the pillows. When I glanced up a moment later, he was lying there silent, his eyes closed, his lips parted, conveying somehow the image of the death that awaited him.

37

Presently, my mother came to the door. She called me into the hall to tell me that Mr. Dodds had arrived. I said that I thought my father had fallen asleep but that I would go back and see.

38

It was strangely disheartening to me to discover that he was awake. He was sitting there, his eyes open, staring grimly into the gathering shadows of the evening.

"Mr. Dodds is downstairs," I said matter-of-factly. "Mother wanted to know if you felt up to seeing him tonight."

For a moment, I thought he had not heard me; he gave no sign of recognition whatever. I went to the foot of the bed and repeated myself. He nodded, not answering the question but simply indicating that he had heard me. At length, he shook his head. "Tell your mother I'm a little tired tonight," he said. "Per-haps—well, perhaps some other time."

39

"I could ask him to come back later, if you'd like."

"No, no, don't bother. I—I could probably use the rest."

I waited a few seconds. "Are you sure?" I asked. "I'm certain he could come back in an hour or so."

Then, suddenly, my father was looking at me. I shall never forget his face at that moment and the expression burning in his eyes. He was pleading with me to speak. And all I could say was that I would be happy to ask Mr. Dodds to come back later, if he wanted it that way. It was not enough. I knew, instinctively, at that moment that it was not enough. But I could not say anything more.

40

As quickly as it had come, the burning flickered and went out. He sank

41

back into the pillows again. "No, you can tell him I won't be needing him tonight," he said, without interest. "Tell him not to bother waiting around." Then he turned on his side, away from me, and said no more.

So my father did not see Mr. Dodds that night. Nor did he ever seen him   42
again. Shortly after midnight, just after my mother and sisters had gone to bed, he died. I was at his side then, but I could not have said exactly when it occurred. He must have gone off in his sleep, painlessly, while I sat there awake beside him.

In the days that followed, our family was together almost constantly. Curi-   43
ously enough, I did not think much about my father just then. For some reason, I felt the strongest sense of responsibility toward the family. I found myself making the arrangements for the funeral, protecting Mother from the stream of people who came to the house, speaking words of consolation to my sisters and even to my aunts. I was never alone except at night, when a kind of oblivion seized me almost as soon as my head touched the pillow. My sleep was dreamless, numb.

Then, two weeks after the funeral, I left for Fort Devens, where I was to   44
be discharged from the Army. I had been there three days when I was told that my terminal leave would begin immediately and that I was free to return home. I had half expected that when I was at the Fort, separated from the family, something would break inside me. But still no emotion came. I thought of my father often during that time, but, search as I would, I could find no sign of feeling.

Then, when I had boarded the train for home, it happened. Suddenly, for   45
no reason whatever, I was thinking of the expression on my father's face that last night in the bedroom. I saw him as he lay there pleading with me to speak. And I knew then what he had wanted me to say to him—that it was really all right with me, that it wouldn't change anything between us if he gave way. And then I was thinking of myself and what I had said and what I had *not* said. Not a word to help! Not a word!

I wanted to beg his forgiveness. I wanted to cry out aloud to him. But I was   46
in a crowded train, sitting with three elderly women just returning from a shopping tour. I turned my face to the window. There, silent, unnoticed. I thought of what I might have said.

Questions for Critical Thinking

1. The author says in paragraph 3 that after the death of his brother he began to recite intricate bedtime prayers that included blessing even people he had only heard about but never met. What explanation can you give for this sudden compulsion?

2. How did the male bond between the narrator and his father affect the code about religion that developed between them? Do you think a similar code might have emerged had the narrator been a daughter? Why or why not?

3. Which of the two sexes do you think is more likely to be committed to deep religious belief? What explanation can you give to account for the religious difference between them?

4. Before the father became ill, how would you characterize the difference in religious outlook—if any existed—between the narrator and his father? How would you explain this difference?

5. What do you think caused the change of heart in the father's religious views? What is your opinion of the sincerity of such latter-found beliefs?

6. Why does the father not give in to his own spiritual hunger and consult the minister in spite of his son's silent disapproval?

7. What explanation can you give to account for the son's inability or unwillingness to communicate emotionally with his dying father?

8. What do you think the narrator might have said to comfort his father?

Writing Assignment

As an exercise in literary scholarship, write an essay reconstructing the chronology of major events in this story, citing evidence to support your conclusions. Specifically, say in what year the story began and in what year it ended. Make a guess as to the father's age at his death, and the age of the narrator, justifying your conjectures with evidence from the text.

Writing Advice

This is rather a straightforward assignment and will give you an inkling into the kind of tight chronology most good stories implicitly follow. Embedded in the story are clues to the age of the narrator and his father at the occurrence of every major event in the narrative. You must infer the ages of the narrator and his father at the time of every major occurrence in the story. Note that in writing this essay you can make certain safe assumptions. First, most straight-line students enter college at 18 and graduate four years later. Second, you can research the date of historical events mentioned in the narrative and use them as references. For example, the narrator tells us that he was sent to postwar Japan as a soldier and was there when his father had a final and fatal heart attack. This clue should give you some inkling of not only the age of the narrator but also the age of his stricken father. Simply listing ages and dates will not satisfy the assignment. Rather, as a literary scholar would do, you must explain the evidence from the text that supports your inferences.

Alternate Writing Assignments

1. Write an essay on the consolations and comforts offered by religious belief.

2. Why did the narrator not unbend and allow his dying father to see the minister? Write an essay that answers this question.

LITERATURE

DO NOT GO GENTLE INTO THAT GOOD NIGHT
Dylan Thomas

Dylan Thomas (1914–1953), a Welsh poet, is ranked among the greatest lyric poets of the twentieth century. Born in Swansea, Wales, to a teacher, Thomas left school early to work as a journalist. He achieved overnight fame with the publication of his first book of poems, *Eighteen Poems* (1934). Thomas, who was gifted with a beautiful elocutionary voice, made a series of successful reading tours of the United States and also recorded his own work. His other works include *Twenty-Five Poems* (1936), *The Map of Love* (1939), and a posthumously published play, *Under Milk Wood* (1954).

Reading Advice

This particular poem is written as a villanelle, a French poetic form consisting of nineteen lines divided into five tercets (stanzas of three lines) and a final stanza of four lines. It is a form using only two rhymes and two refrain lines which are repeated with thundering emphasis. In spite of the tight compression of the form, or perhaps because of it, Thomas manages to achieve an elevated tone of powerful solemnity. The poem is addressed to the poet's father, who we gather is dying, and begs him not to "go gentle into that good night," cataloguing inspiring images of others who also "rage against the dying of the light."

1

> Do not go gentle into that good night,
> Old age should burn and rave at close of day;
> Rage, rage against the dying of the light.

Though wise men at their end know dark is right,   2
Because their words had forked no lightning they
Do not go gentle into that good night.

Good men, the last wave by, crying how bright   3
Their frail deeds might have danced in a green bay,
Rage, rage against the dying of the light.

Wild men who caught and sang the sun in flight,   4
And learn, too late, they grieved it on its way
Do not go gentle into that good night.

Grave men, near death, who see with blinding sight   5
Blind eyes could blaze like meteors and be gay,
Rage, rage against the dying of the light.

And you, my father, there on the sad height,   6
Curse, bless, me now with your fierce tears, I pray.
Do not go gentle into that good night.
Rage, rage against the dying of the light.

Questions for Critical Thinking

1. The poet does not specifically mention his father until the final stanza. What does he accomplish with this late mention?

2. Many poets will occasionally take poetic license with language in writing a poem. What conspicuous example of poetic license can you cite in this poem?

3. What effect is achieved in the poem by calling the night "good" rather than some more somber adjective?

4. What does the poem say about the attitude of wise men at the end of their lives? How does this attitude contrast with that of wild men?

5. One student who has worked with the dying in hospitals criticized this poem as being grossly untrue to the attitude and frame of mind of the dying. What is your opinion of this criticism?

6. Nowhere in the poem are women mentioned. What is your opinion of this omission?

Writing Assignment

Write an essay that analyzes and discusses the categories of dying men mentioned in the poem. Discuss and justify the poet's choice of men and the characteristics he associates with them at their ending.

Writing Advice

The poem specifically mentions four kinds of men—the wise, the good, the wild, and the grave—and imagistically identifies them with certain characteristics and attitudes. It is your job to unravel the images and explain the characteristics the poet associates with each kind of men. Note that there is no absolutely right or wrong answer in this assignment. Good poems may be interpreted intelligibly many different ways, complexity of meaning being part of poetry's appeal. Moreover, even the plainest poetic image will seem ambiguous when set beside its prose equivalent. Whether your interpretation is right or wrong, therefore, is not the final test. It is, rather, whether or not you adequately prove your interpretation. Doing so means citing specific images from the work and writing at length to explain what you think they mean. Mention also why you think the author chose to categorize all men into these four types, whether his choice is justified by universality, essential appeal, familiarity to readers, or any other reason.

Alternate Writing Assignment

The villanelle is a constricted poetic form that would seem ill-suited to a poem of such passion and gravity. Write an essay analyzing the contribution of this unique poetic form to Thomas's "Do Not Go Gentle into That Good Night."

LITERATURE

DIRGE WITHOUT MUSIC
Edna St. Vincent Millay

Edna St. Vincent Millay (1892–1950), American poet, was born in Rockland, Maine, and educated at Vassar. During the early 1920s she was part of the bohemian art scene of Greenwich Village, New York, where she lived and wrote satiric sketches for *Vanity Fair* under the pen name of Nancy Boyd. Her first book of poetry, *Renascence* (1917), a critical success, was followed by *A Few Figs from Thistles* (1920), *Second April* (1921), and *The Ballad of the Harp Weaver* (1922; Pulitzer Prize). Millay married in 1923 and moved to "Steepletop," a farm near Austerlitz, New York. She continued to write and publish poetry and verse drama, although her later socially conscious work is not as highly regarded as her earlier lyrics. Her later volumes include *Fatal Interview* (1931), *Conversation at Midnight* (1937), and *Make Bright the Arrows* (1940). She outlived her husband, Eugan Jan Boissevain, a Dutch coffee importer, by less than a year. In 1976 "Steepletop," her marital home, was dedicated as an art colony.

Reading Advice

Millay's forte is lyric poetry, a brief and highly personal poetic form notable for the imaginative use of language and imagery and the creation of a unified theme. The lyric poem originated with the Greeks, who identified the form as the personal expression of one singer accompanied by a lyre, distinguishing it from choric poetry, which was recited by a group. Opening with the expression of a personal and poignant view about death, the poem enlarges on this theme with imagery and a mournful refrain.

I am not resigned to the shutting away of loving hearts in the hard ground.
So it is, and so it will be, for so it has been, time out of mind:
Into the darkness they go, the wise and the lovely. Crowned
With lilies and with laurel they go; but I am not resigned.   4

Lovers and thinkers, into the earth with you.
Be one with the dull, the indiscriminate dust.
A fragment of what you felt, of what you knew,
A formula, a phrase remains,—but the best is lost.   8

The answers quick and keen, the honest look, the laughter, the love,—
They are gone. They are gone to feed the roses. Elegant and curled
Is the blossom. Fragrant is the blossom. I know. But I do not approve.
More precious was the light in your eyes than all the roses in the world.   12

Down, down, down into the darkness of the grave
Gently they go, the beautiful, the tender, the kind;
Quietly they go, the intelligent, the witty, the brave.
I know. But I do not approve. And I am not resigned.   16

Questions for Critical Thinking

1. How does the poem characterize the dead for whom it mourns? What do those for whom the poem mourns have in common?

2. What does the line "crowned with lilies and laurel they go" mean? With what are lilies and laurels associated?

3. What rhyme scheme does the poem use? What effect on the poem, read silently or aloud, does this rhyme have?

4. Aside from the meter and muted rhyme, what other common poetic device does the poem rather heavily use? Comment on its effectiveness.

Writing Assignment

Write an essay comparing/contrasting the attitudes towards death expressed in Dylan Thomas's "Do Not Go Gentle into That Good Night" and Edna St. Vincent Millay's "Dirge Without Music."

Writing Advice

Begin by reading both poems successively, noting how they differ in their basic expressed attitudes towards death. To do a systematic contrast, you might use the chart we recommend in Chapter 2 for writing the essay on Pascal's *Pensées*. The bases of your contrast being already specified in the assignment—attitudes towards death— you do not have to find your own, but need only to distill and express what you think are the implicit attitudes towards death in each poem and to show how they are alike or how they differ. In writing your comparison/contrast, you should also cite lines and phrases from both poems to support your interpretation of their underlying attitudes. For example, if you think that the Thomas poem urges defiance, you might quote some lines to illustrate that reading. Likewise, if you think the Millay poem expresses unacceptance of death, you should also support that interpretation with a quotation or two. Focus, in short, on the poems themselves, on the attitudes towards death you think they embody, and then draw a comparison/contrast between them.

Alternate Writing Assignment

What do you think would be the religious answer to the attitude towards death expressed in this poem? Write an essay in which you give the doctrinal reply to Millay's poem of a devout religious believer.

ART

DEATH AND THE WOMAN
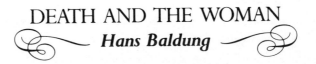
Hans Baldung

About the Artist

Hans Baldung (ca. 1485–1545) was born near Strasbourg and apprenticed to Albrecht Dürer the Elder at Nuremberg. In 1509 Baldung was officially admitted to the Bourgoisie in Strasbourg. Then he spent five years in Fribourg working on a commission to paint the main altarpiece of the cathedral, a task he completed in 1516. The remainder of his career was spent in Strasbourg, where he was frequently involved in religious disputes stemming from his decided Lutheranism. In the artistic realm, he differed profoundly with his master, Düer, over such matters as color, sense of light, and interpretation of subjects and themes.

About the Art

This painting of "Death and the Woman" was done about 1517, and its voluptuous nudity bordered on obscenity at the time. The figure of Death is well-muscled in his arms, shoulders, and legs, while his head remains a skull. The woman's body is the same color as the winding sheet she is removing, seemingly in a sensual anticipation of Death's kiss as he welcomes her into the Underworld. This audacious presentation of death as a male lover seducing a woman is typical of Baldung's jarring juxtaposition of harmony and discord, which paradoxically both shocked and delighted his viewers.

A R T

THE LAST JUDGEMENT

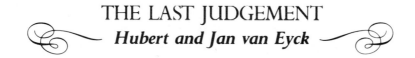

Hubert and Jan van Eyck

About the Artist

Jan van Eyck (ca. 1390–1441) was long credited with the invention of oil painting, and indeed he did make many of the early contributions to the development of the medium. Van Eyck also perfected the technique of "atmospheric perspective," based on the fact that the air between us and what we look at acts as a screen that makes distant shapes appear through a bluish haze. He began his career in Holland, worked for a while in Lille, and then moved to Bruges, where he spent the last 12 years of his life. He was highly regarded by Duke Philip the Good of Burgundy, and was a respected member of the town, with his work much in demand.

About the Art

This painting of "The Last Judgement," and one of "The Crucifixion," make up a pair of small panels (22¼″ by 7¾″) painted between 1420 and 1425 and intended for an altarpiece. Some scholars attribute them to Jan's older brother, Hubert van Eyck. In *The Last Judgement* we see the dead rising from their graves in the earth or at sea on the Day of Judgment in hope and fear. The bowels of the earth open to receive the damned into the underworld, while the saved are elevated into the serenity of heaven, where all is tranquillity, order, and contemplation of the glorified Christ. In hell the bodies of the damned are being torn apart by more hideous monsters than any that had been painted before. Earth is seen as a narrow gateway between these two destinations, presided over by an angel of death standing on the shoulders of a huge skeleton, symbolizing death and destruction.

8–1   Hans Baldung, **Death and the Woman**, *1517. Oeffentliche Kunstsammlung Basel, Kunstmuseum.*

8–2   Jan van Eyck, **The Last Judgement.**
*One of two panels. Tempera and oil on canvas,
transferred from wood. 22¼" x 7¾". The Metropolitan Museum of Art, Fletcher Fund, 1933.*

Chapter Writing Assignments

After reviewing the readings and paintings in this chapter, choose one of the subjects below and develop it into an essay about the meaning of death. Feel free to quote or paraphrase any ideas from the essays studied that might further the development of your thesis.

1. The mysteries of death and afterlife provide room for infinite philosophical speculation.

2. Is it ever reasonable to prefer death over life?

3. Without the promise of a life beyond death, existence on earth is meaningless and without purpose.

4. Can it ever be right to administer a lethal dose of morphine to a terminally ill patient?

5. A connection must exist between ultimate justice and death.

6. "The fear of death is worse than death."

—***Robert Burton,*** "Anatomy of Melancholy"

INDEX

INDEX

A 0
B 1
C 2
D 3
E 4
F 5
G 6
H 7
I 8
J 9